D1308950

Each new text comes with access to the exciting learning environment of a robust eBook containing **hundreds of online links to primary sources, images, web resources, simulations, maps, audio, and more.**

Teaching and Learning Styles

Each new text comes with access to **4ltrpress.cengage.com/world**, where we offer a suite of digital tools—including **interactive quizzing, flashcards, and more**—for the many different learning styles of today's students.

For instructors' different teaching styles, we offer Webtutor on Blackboard® and WebCT®, as well as PowerLecture™– a suite of PowerPoint® presentations, instructor's manual, and ExamView computerized testing.

At fewer than **550 pages each**, Volumes 1 & 2 of *WORLD* present all concepts, definitions, learning objectives, and study tools found in a book twice its size.

Value

WORLD offers full content coverage, review cards, and valuable material at **4ltrpress.cengage.com/world** – all for **$61.95 per split volume** and **$74.95 for the comprehensive edition.**

Comprehensive
978-0-495-80205-0

Volume 1: To 1500
978-1-439-08412-2

Volume 2: Since 1450
978-1-439-08413-0

WADSWORTH
CENGAGE Learning

WORLD: Volume II
Craig A. Lockard

Senior Publisher: Suzanne Jeans

Senior Acquisitions Editor: Nancy Blaine

Development Manager: Jeff Greene

Senior Development Editor: Tonya Lobato

Assistant Editor: Lauren Floyd

Editorial Assistant: Emma Goehring

Senior Media Editor: Lisa Ciccolo

Senior Marketing Manager: Katherine Bates

Marketing Coordinator: Lorreen Pelletier

Marketing Communications Manager:
Christine Dobberpuhl

Senior Content Project Manager:
Carol Newman

Senior Art Director: Cate Rickard Barr

Print Buyer: Becky Cross

Senior Rights Acquisition Account Manager:
Katie Huha

Text Permissions Editor: Tracy Metivier

Senior Photo Editor: Jennifer Meyer Dare

Photo Researcher: Carole Frohlich

Production Service: Lachina Publishing Services

Text Designer: Dutton & Sherman Design

Cover Designer: Studio Montage

Cover Image: Mosque at Touba/Galen
Frysinger

Compositor: Lachina Publishing Services

For product information and technology assistance, contact us at
Cengage Learning Customer & Sales Support, 1-800-354-9706

For permission to use material from this text or product,
submit all requests online at **cengage.com/permissions**.
Further permissions questions can be emailed to
permissionrequest@cengage.com.

Library of Congress Control Number: 2009929342

Student Edition:

ISBN-13: 978-1-4390-8413-7

ISBN-10: 1-4390-8413-0

Wadsworth
20 Channel Center Street
Boston, MA 02210
USA

Cengage Learning is a leading provider of customized learning solutions with office locations around the globe, including Singapore, the United Kingdom, Australia, Mexico, Brazil and Japan. Locate your local office at **international.cengage.com/region**

Cengage Learning products are represented in Canada by Nelson Education, Ltd.

For your course and learning solutions, visit **www.cengage.com**.

Purchase any of our products at your local college store
or at our preferred online store **www.ichapters.com**.

Printed in the United States of America
1 2 3 4 5 6 7 13 12 11 10 09

Brief Contents

Amsterdams Historisch Museum; Visual Connection Archive; Wally McNamee/Corbis

iii

Contents

Courtesy of the Trustees of the Victoria and Albert Museum

Pitt Rivers Museum, Oxford University

PART VI Global Systems: Interdependence and Conflict in the Contemporary World, Since 1945 686

Corbis

Glenn Hunt/AAP

Maps

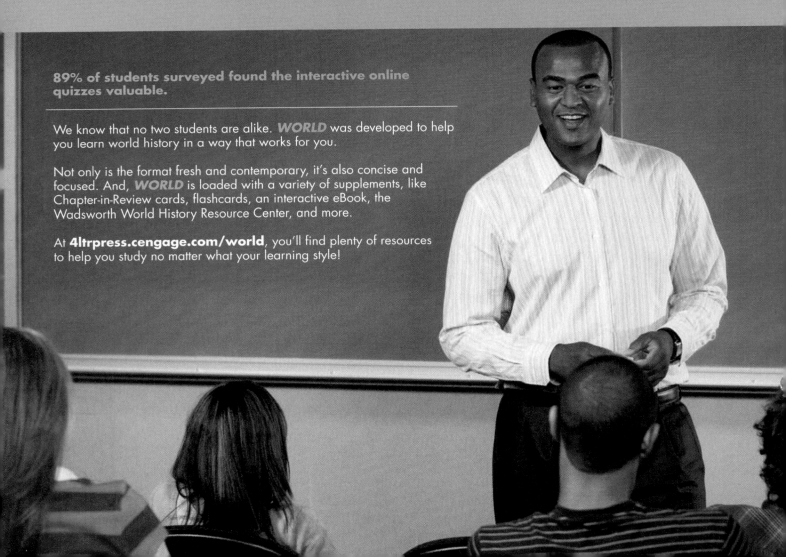

{ Explore It Your Way! }

"What appeals to me is the fully virtual eBook with find/search feature which is absolutely irreplaceable and eternally helpful. I wish I had the eBook for when I was starting college."
William Manning, Student at Florida Atlantic University

We know that no two students read in quite the same way. Some of you do a lot of your reading online.

To help you take your reading **outside the covers** of **WORLD,** each new text comes with access to the exciting learning environment of an interactive eBook containing **tested online links to:**

- **Primary source documents**
- **Interactive maps**
- **Web links for further investigation**
- **Interactive quizzes**
- **Audio resources**
- **Historical simulation activities**
- **Profiles of key historical figures**

Access the eBook at 4ltrpress.cengage.com/world.

PART IV

Connecting the Globe:

Forging New Networks in the Early Modern World, 1450–1750

NORTH AND CENTRAL AMERICA
The bridging of the Atlantic by a Spanish expedition led by Christopher Columbus in 1492 had major consequences. In the century to follow, the Spanish conquered various Caribbean islands, Mesoamerica, and southwestern North America. The English and French established settlements and then colonies along the Atlantic coast and gradually expanded westward, at the expense of Native American societies that were devastated by diseases brought from Eurasia. In the southern colonies and the Caribbean islands, plantations worked by African slaves became the major economic activity.

ARCTIC OCEAN

NORTH AMERICA

BRITISH AMERICA (13 COLONIES)

Mississippi R.

MEXICO

ATLANTIC OCEAN

SPANISH AMERICAN EMPIRE

PACIFIC OCEAN

Amazon

PERU

ANDES

BRAZIL

SOUTH AMERICA

SOUTH AMERICA
The arrival of the Spanish and Portuguese changed the politics, economies, and demographics of the region. The Spanish toppled the Inca Empire and colonized much of South and Central America, while the Portuguese dominated Brazil. The European colonizers established mines, ranches, and plantations. After diseases from Eurasia killed much of the Native American population, the colonizers imported African slaves as workers. As a result, European, Native American, and African peoples and cultures blended to foster unique Latin American societies.

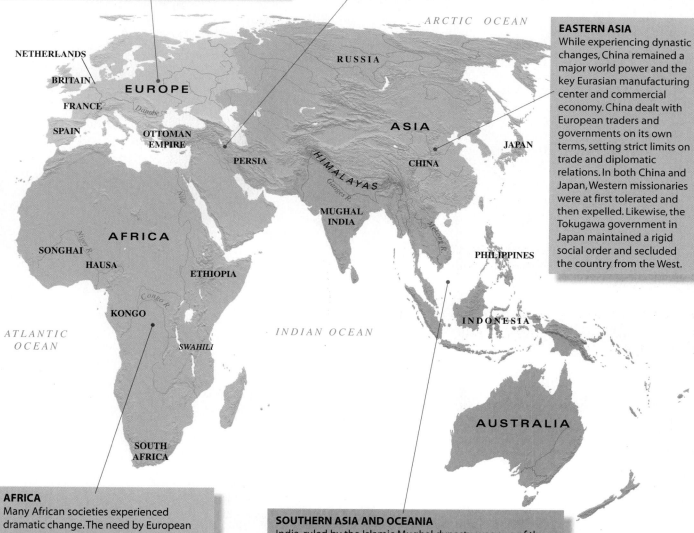

EUROPE

Several European societies emerged as major world powers. The Portuguese and Spanish in the 1500s, followed by the Dutch, English, and French in the 1600s and 1700s, established footholds and colonies in Africa, the Americas, and Asia. The resources obtained abroad, especially the minerals and plantation crops of the Americas and Southeast Asia, brought wealth to Europe. Exposure to a wider world fostered capitalism, science, technology, and a questioning of long-standing religious doctrine, resulting in the Protestant Reformation and the Enlightenment.

WESTERN ASIA

The Ottoman Empire became the world's major Islamic power, controlling not only much of Western Asia but also much of North Africa and southeastern Europe. Rivals of the major European powers, especially the Russians, the Ottoman Turks prospered by fostering learning, accommodating ethnic minorities, and importing military and technical expertise. To their east, the Persians under the Safavid dynasty dominated parts of Central Asia and flourished for several centuries.

EASTERN ASIA

While experiencing dynastic changes, China remained a major world power and the key Eurasian manufacturing center and commercial economy. China dealt with European traders and governments on its own terms, setting strict limits on trade and diplomatic relations. In both China and Japan, Western missionaries were at first tolerated and then expelled. Likewise, the Tokugawa government in Japan maintained a rigid social order and secluded the country from the West.

AFRICA

Many African societies experienced dramatic change. The need by European powers for cheap labor in their American colonies fostered the trans-Atlantic slave trade, which disrupted much of the West and Central African coast as millions of Africans were enslaved and shipped to the Americas. Although some African states, such as Ashante and Benin, flourished from the slave trade and other commerce, warfare between states became more common. The Portuguese conquered the states of Angola and Kongo and destabilized the East African coastal cities, while the Dutch established a foothold in South Africa.

SOUTHERN ASIA AND OCEANIA

India, ruled by the Islamic Mughal dynasty, was one of the world's major powers, with a flourishing economy that attracted merchants from many societies. After obtaining footholds in India, Europeans then sought wealth in nearby Southeast Asia. First the Portuguese and then other European powers gained a modest presence in Southeast Asia, the Spanish colonizing the Philippines and the Dutch parts of Indonesia. While Europeans began exploring the Pacific Basin, their impact on Oceania was slight. Nonetheless, the Spanish trade across the Pacific between the Philippines and Mexico laid a foundation for the global economy.

CHAPTER 15

Global Connections and the Remaking of Europe,

1450–1750

Learning Outcomes

After reading this chapter, you should be able to answer the following questions:

LO¹ How did exploration, colonization, and capitalism increase Western power and wealth?

LO² How did the Renaissance and Reformation mark a crucial cultural and intellectual transition?

LO³ What types of governments emerged in Europe in this era?

LO⁴ How did major intellectual, scientific, and social changes help to reshape the West?

"O, wonder! How many goodly creatures are there here! How beauteous mankind is! O brave new world That hath such people in't!**"**

—Miranda, in *The Tempest* by William Shakespeare, 1611[1]

The European and world economy changed rapidly in the sixteenth century, and few places exemplified change more than the port city of Antwerp (AN-twuhrp), on the River Scheldt (skelt) in what is now Belgium. In 1567 an Italian diplomat and historian, Ludovico Guicciardini (loo-do-VEE-ko GWEE-char-DEE-nee), visited the mostly Flemish-speaking city and its fabulous Bourse (boors), a huge, multistory building that served as a marketplace and stock exchange. Guicciardini observed that "all of these persons being people who are earning money, invest it not only in commerce but also in building, in buying lands and properties, and thus the city flourishes and increases marvelously."[2] From the late 1400s until the late 1500s, Antwerp was the European hub for ever-widening world networks of commerce. Every week, fabulous merchandise arrived from all over the world: as many as 2,500 ships anchored at one time in the harbor, many laden with gold and silver from the Americas, and the Bourse became the clearinghouse for their cargo. Antwerp represented a postmedieval Europe shaped by the fruits of overseas exploration, conquest, and expanding commerce. The new economic thrust was one aspect of the many changes that the English playwright Shakespeare referred to as a "brave new world."

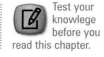 Test your knowlege before you read this chapter.

What do you think?

European exploration and colonization would have been improbable without the technologies and influences of Islamic and Asian societies.

Strongly Disagree   *Strongly Agree*
  1   2   3   4   5   6   7

In 1500, as the Early Modern Era began, western Europeans were still medieval in many respects: they were dominated by the multinational Roman church, their countries had little sense of national identity, they were skeptical of science, and they were minor participants in hemispheric commerce and barely aware of distant lands. By the mid-1700s, however, Europe and parts of the wider world had undergone a profound economic, intellectual, and political transition: Europeans conquered and settled the Americas and established colonies or trading networks in Asia and Africa. As a result, wealth

<<**Amsterdam Stock Exchange** During the seventeenth century, the Dutch port city of Amsterdam was the center of European commerce and played a key role in the world economy. The Amsterdam stock market, shown here in a painting by Dutch artist Job Adriaenz, attracted merchants and financiers from all over Europe.

Amsterdams Historisch Museum

> "For the first time since the Roman Empire and Charlemagne, large centralized states developed in Europe, particularly in England and France."

flowed into Europe, fostering investment in science and technology. New knowledge of, and influences from, non-European cultures reshaped European thinking and cultures. The Catholic Church faced severe challenges as some European thinkers were influenced as much or more by secular ideas. Although such changes often resulted in strains that produced long and bloody wars, they nevertheless remade Europe's political and social systems. By 1750 Europeans had left many of their medieval institutions and beliefs behind and were on the verge of introducing even more profound changes to the world.

LO¹ Transitions: Overseas Expansion and Capitalism

The foundations for the dramatic changes that reshaped many Early Modern European societies were established in late medieval times and embellished by developments after 1500. The European encounter with America, the growth of a trans-Atlantic slave trade, and the opening of direct trade with Asia all increased European wealth and stimulated the development of capitalism, an economic system in which property, exchange, and the means of production are privately owned. Inherently dynamic, capitalism gradually expanded its scale of operation to a global level. The economic revolution fostered stronger European states and reshaped the daily lives of nearly all Europeans.

The Roots of Europe's Transformation

Significant economic changes accelerated during the 1400s. Commerce and merchants flourished, cities grew larger and more numerous, and the feudal social systems and the values that supported them broke down. Commerce, with its widening trade networks, became a part of everyday life. The ability of the middle classes to buy more luxury goods spurred the growth of industries like textile manufacturing. However, most Europeans were still neither urban nor middle class; 80 percent were peasants who worked the soil. Although many peasants were now free or tenant farmers rather than serfs, most were still heavily burdened with taxes and service obligations to lords. They also tithed crops and livestock to the church. Only a few received any formal education.

Yet, despite being rooted in farming, the economy was changing, partly as a result of population growth and climate change. The European population (excluding Russia) increased from 70 to 100 million between 1500 and 1600, and then to 125 million by 1750, making for larger commercial markets. The global cooling that began around 1300 intensified, reached its height in the late 1600s, and then began to thaw around 1715, finally ending in the mid-1800s. This "Little Ice Age" brought winter freezing to canals and rivers, caused poor harvests, and helped motivate overseas explorers to seek better conditions and food sources elsewhere. Importing foods from the Americas, such as corn and potatoes, helped avert mass famine.

The Advent of Capitalism

Political and economic changes were felt more strongly by urban populations, especially merchants. By 1500, cities such as Paris and London had grown to over 200,000 and were unique in the world for their growing political power and autonomy. Unlike Chinese or Ottoman cities, European cities existed in a politically fragmented region rather than a centralized empire. Not having to answer to centralized authorities, city leaders could bargain with kings for advantages and autonomy. More favorable attitudes toward commerce gave some European merchants unusual power. Western European banks also favored economic growth. Blessed with these advantages, late medieval Europeans developed capitalism, a dynamic system that was highly oriented to economic growth. In the 1400s, cities such as Venice and Genoa in Italy, and Bruges (broozh) and Antwerp in what is today Belgium, became centers of capital-

Antwerp Marketplace The marketplace at the center of Antwerp, in what is today Belgium, was the main hub for European trade in the 1500s, the place where goods from all over Europe and from Africa, the Americas, and Asia were bought and sold. Musées Royaux Beaux-Arts de Belgique

istic enterprise. But early capitalism was limited by the Catholic Church's condemnation of usury and by cumbersome business methods. Not until after 1500 did the scope and nature of capitalism, fostered by overseas exploration and conquest, change dramatically.

Large, Centralized States

Political systems of western Europe also began to shift in the 1500s. After the ending of the Roman Empire in the Late Classical Era, western Europe had remained politically fragmented, but in the 1500s, some small states were gradually transformed into integrated monarchies, which became enriched by resources obtained by their merchants and adventurers in Africa, the Americas, and Asia. Both merchants and monarchs resented the independence of the landed aristocracy and cooperated to destroy their influence in a series of bloody wars. For the first time since the Roman Empire and Charlemagne, large cen-

tralized states developed in Europe, particularly in England and France. The growth of these strong but competitive states made the political system dynamic and unstable.

Mapping the Globe

New intellectual currents also emerged that fostered broader horizons, especially improvements in mapmaking. In 1375 Abraham Cresques (kres-kay), a Jewish cartographer on the Spanish island of Majorca (muh-JOR-kuh), used Christian, Muslim, and Jewish traditions and travelers' accounts to produce a map that placed Jerusalem rather than Europe at the center of the world. In the 1400s, Portuguese mapmakers drew innovative maps that influenced Flemish mapmakers of the 1500s, such as Gerardus Mercator (muhr-KAY-tuhr). But these maps were also misleading and, unlike Cresques' effort, did not de-center Europe.

 Explore new encounters in the early modern world in this interactive simulation.

Eastern Inspiration, Western Innovation

Developments in technology and mathematics, many inspired by earlier Arab, Chinese, and Indian innovations, were also important. Between 1450 and 1550, Europe's technology surpassed that of the Arabs and was catching up to China's. The major improvements came in shipbuilding, navigation, weaponry, and printing. European ships took advantage of lateen sails developed by Arabs and sternpost rudders from China, and they also used the Chinese magnetic compass to navigate. Facing much rougher waters than the placid Mediterranean and Indian Ocean, the people along Europe's Atlantic coast also had to build sturdier ships, giving them a naval advantage. Europeans also greatly improved gunpowder weapons and printing processes, both invented in China. The introduction of the European printing press in the mid-1400s made possible the dissemination of both Christian and secular knowledge to an increasingly literate audience. Some 13,000 books were published in Europe by 1500. Europeans also blended imported mathematical concepts, such as the Indian numerical system and Arab algebra, with their own insights to improve quantification.

"Gold, God, and Glory": Explorations and Conquests

During these centuries, the rise of Europe as a world power took place within a context of European overseas expansion and conquest (see Chapters 16–18). Historians use a standard shorthand, "Gold, God, and Glory," to describe European motives. "Gold" was the search for material gain by acquiring and selling Asian spices, African slaves, American metals, and other resources. "God" refers to the militant crusading tradition of Christianity, including the rivalry with Islam and the hatred of non-Christian religions. "Glory" describes the goals of the competing monarchies, who sought to establish their claims to new territories so as to strengthen their position in European politics. Motivated by these three aims, various western European peoples expanded overseas during the Early Modern Era, gaining control over widening segments of the globe.

> **"Between 1450 and 1550, Europe's technology surpassed that of the Arabs and was catching up to China's."**

Portugal and Spain Lead the Way

During the 1400s, the seafaring peoples of the Iberian peninsula, the Spanish and Portuguese, ventured out into the Atlantic and discovered the Azores (A-zorz), Madeira (muh-DEER-uh), and Canary island chains off northwest Africa (see Map 15.1). Several factors pushed Iberians to pioneer in overseas expeditions: a favorable geographic location facing the Atlantic Ocean and North Africa, a maritime tradition of deep-sea fishing, an aggressive Christian crusading tradition, and possession of the best ships and navigation techniques in Europe by the 1400s. The Iberians also had economic motives. Early Iberian exploration sought a way to circumnavigate the Venetian monopoly over the valuable trade from southern Asia through Persia and Egypt. The Iberians also sought gold from West Africa as well as new food sources, because Iberia did not produce enough meat and wheat to feed its growing population.

 Interactive Map

This maritime exploration and conquest required new technologies, such as a new type of ship to sail the rough Atlantic. Building on Chinese and Arab innovations, the Portuguese invented the caravel, an easily maneuverable type of ship designed to travel long distances. Later the Iberians built larger ships such as galleons, which provided much more room for cargo and larger crews. To chart the position of the sun and stars, Iberian sailors used the astrolabe (AS-truh-labe), invented by tenth-century Arabs. Some Europeans also learned how to mount weapons on ships, which enabled them to overwhelm coastal defenses and defeat lightly armed ships. By the late 1500s, the English were building the most maneuverable ships and the best iron cannon, and by the 1700s, European land and sea weapons greatly outclassed those of once militarily powerful China, India, Persia, and Ottoman Turkey.

Driven by Competition

The intense competition between major European powers led to increased exploration, the building of trade networks, and a scramble for colonies, subject territories where Europeans could directly

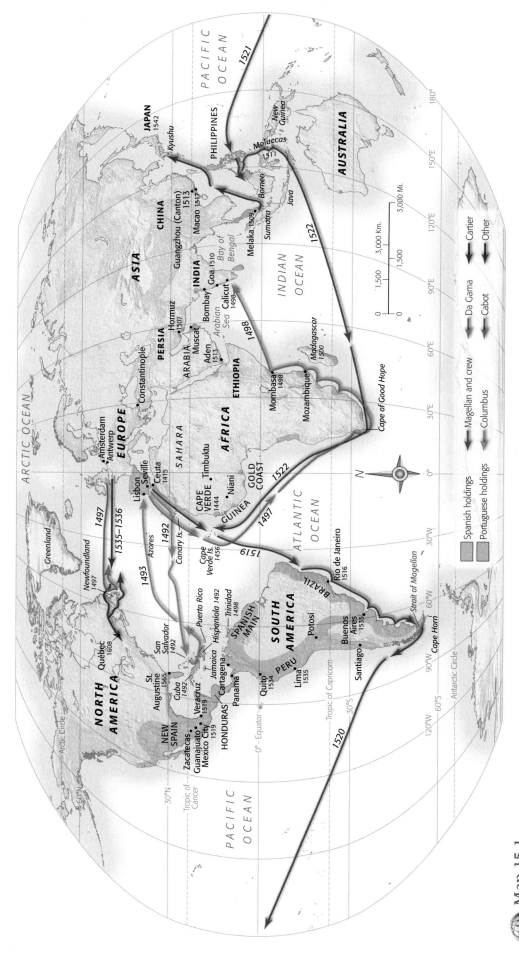

Map 15.1
European Exploration, 1450–1600

Between the early 1400s and mid-1600s, explorers sponsored by Portugal, Spain, France, Holland, and England discovered the sea route around Africa to South and Southeast Asia, crossed the Atlantic to the Americas, and sailed across the Pacific Ocean from the Americas to Asia.

control primary production. In the 1400s, the Portuguese began direct encounters with the peoples of coastal Africa, and by 1500, Portuguese explorers had reached East Africa and then sailed across the Indian Ocean to India. Soon, they seized key Asian ports such as Hormuz on the Persian Gulf, Goa in India, and Melaka in Malaya. Meanwhile, the Spanish discovered that a huge landmass to the west, soon to be named America, lay between Europe and East Asia. By the later 1500s, the Spanish had conquered much of the Americas, including the great Inca and Aztec Empires, making them the most powerful European state for some decades. Portugal, England, France, and Holland had also established American colonies by the early 1600s.

At the same time, Europeans established colonies in Africa and carried increasing numbers of enslaved Africans to the Western Hemisphere to work on plantations growing cash crops for European consumption. In the sixteenth and seventeenth centuries, the Portuguese, Dutch, and Spanish colonized several Asian port cities and various Southeast Asian islands, including the Philippines, Java, and the Spice Islands of Indonesia. American minerals, especially silver, supported a great expansion of the European economy and allowed Europeans to buy into the rich Asian trade. These conquests and economic activities enabled the transfer of vast quantities of resources to Europe.

The Foundations of Colonial Imperialism

During the Early Modern Era, Europeans gradually brought various peoples into their economic and political sphere, laying the foundations for a system of Western dominance in the world after 1750. The Portuguese and Spanish prospered in the 1500s from their overseas activities, while in the 1600s the overseas trade of the Dutch, English, and French enabled them to become the most powerful European countries. But European influence was still limited in many autonomous regions, including China, Siam, Japan, and Morocco. Nonetheless, overseas trade and exploitation provided some European societies with valuable human labor and natural resources and contributed to the growth of capitalism.

The Rise of Capitalism

Arising first in western Europe, capitalism has taken many forms and fostered new values around the world. Under capitalism, the drive for profit from privately owned and privately invested capital has largely determined what goods are produced and how they are distributed. Capitalism was unique when it first arose in Europe because, on a much greater scale than ever before, money in the form of investment capital was used to make profits. The various forms of capitalism that emerged as the economic system spread had certain common features: the need for constant accumulation of additional capital, economic self-interest, the profit motive, a market economy of some sort, and competition. These features shaped both economic and social relations between people. For example, individual carpenters who once shared their services with the community on a barter basis, or who belonged to a guild that operated for the benefit of all local carpenters, began to charge fees instead, competing for customers with other carpenters. By the 1800s, capitalism also included private ownership of the means of production, such as factories, businesses, and farms.

The Economic Center Shifts to Amsterdam

Capitalism was not necessarily inevitable. The profit motive and competition were incompatible with certain traditional cultures that disapproved of individuals accumulating more wealth than their neighbors. In precapitalist societies, governments siphoned off surplus wealth, and the elite spent their resources on conspicuous consumption of luxuries, such as the building of magnificent cathedrals, palaces, and pyramids. In medieval Europe, merchant and craft guilds emphasized ethics, accepting a strict regulation of economic activity for the greater good. By contrast, capitalists invested some profits in further exchange or production, reinvestment that differentiated capitalism from earlier economic systems. During the 1500s, the English and the people of the Low Countries, especially the Flemish and Dutch, developed the most dynamic forms of capitalism, and soon they eclipsed Italy, shifting the economic balance of power in Europe from the Mediterranean to the north. By the 1620s, Amsterdam in Holland had emerged as Europe's capitalist powerhouse, dominating much European and Asian trade. This clean, orderly, and prosperous Dutch city boasted amenities that were rare elsewhere, such as street lamps and watch patrols to prevent crime.

> **❝ Expanding capitalism fostered new economic ideas, social groups, and consumption patterns. ❞**

Emergence of the Bourgeoisie

Expanding capitalism fostered new economic ideas, social groups, and consumption patterns. Spurred by increasing trade, old concepts of investing wealth in land ownership gradually gave way to the view that capital should instead be invested in business and industry to help increase production of ships, armor, arms, and textiles, and thus create more capital. The increase in available capital began to change business methods, especially the use of credit on a large scale, which fostered banking. Capitalism also produced a new social group known as the bourgeoisie, an urban-based, mostly commercial, middle class of merchants, financiers, and other businessmen. The new materialism of the cities encouraged more people of all backgrounds to purchase consumer goods, from tea, coffee, and sugar to clocks, china, and glassware.

CHRONOLOGY

Political, Economic, and Intellectual Developments, 1500–1750

1500–1770	Era of commercial capitalism
1533–1586	Reign of Ivan the Terrible in Muscovy
ca. 1600–1750	Scientific Revolution
ca. 1600–1750	Baroque era
1609	Dutch independence
1618–1648	Thirty Years' War
1641–1645	English Civil War
1648	Congress of Westphalia
1661–1715	Reign of Louis XIV in France
1675–1800	Enlightenment
1682–1725	Reign of Peter the Great in Russia
1688	English Bill of Rights
1688–1689	Glorious Revolution and Declaration of Rights in England
1700–1709	Great Northern War
1701–1714	War of the Spanish Succession
1707	United Kingdom of England, Scotland, and Wales

Economic Secularization

As a new capitalist order emerged, many Christian Europeans changed their attitudes toward charging interest for loans and seeking profit. The medieval church had denounced charging interest as usury, a mortal sin, and had also opposed commercial profit, leaving much commerce and banking to the Jewish minority. By the late 1500s, however, many rejected these church teachings and instead heeded the cynical saying that "he who takes usury goes to hell; he who doesn't goes to the poorhouse." This reflected a gradual shift toward an entirely different type of society in western Europe. Jacob Fugger (FOOG-uhr) (1459–1525) of Augsburg (AUGZ-burg), a southern German city, was one European who prospered from the new economic trends, eventually becoming Europe's richest man. He wrote the epitaph for his own tomb, praising himself as "behind no one in attainment of extraordinary wealth, in generosity, purity of morals and greatness of soul."[3]

Agricultural Backlash

While western Europe became increasingly capitalist, parts of eastern Europe discouraged capitalism. In the 1500s, as the demand for agricultural products increased while cooler climates hindered farming, eastern European nobles faced a labor shortage on their estates. Allied with the landowning aristocracy, kings in Poland, Lithuania, Prussia, and Russia mandated serfdom on the peasantries and imposed new laws forbidding people to leave the land. At the same time, by providing little support to the local merchant classes, these governments thwarted capitalist expansion and diminished the political influence of cities.

Commercial Capitalism and Mercantilism

As a dynamic, flexible economic system, capitalism continually evolved and expanded. Under the form of capitalism that was dominant in western Europe between 1500 and 1770, commercial capitalism, most capital was invested in commercial enterprises such

bourgeoisie
The urban-based, mostly commercial, middle class that arose with capitalism in the Early Modern Era.

commercial capitalism
The economic system in which most capital was invested in commercial enterprises such as trading companies, including the world's first joint-stock companies.

mercantilism
An economic approach that emerged in Early Modern Europe based on a government policy of building a nation's wealth by expanding its reserves of precious metals.

Reformation
The movement to reform Christianity that was begun by Martin Luther in the sixteenth century.

> "Renaissance philosophy, known as humanism, emphasized humanity and its creations rather than God."

as trading companies, including the world's first joint-stock companies. To increase their efficiency and profits, these precursors of today's giant multinational corporations pooled their resources by selling shares, or stocks, to merchants and bankers. Joint-stock companies encouraged investment and mobilized great capital. They employed cashiers, bookkeepers, couriers, and middlemen skilled in various languages, and invested in diversified economic activities such as real estate, mining, and industry. Few Asian or African merchants could compete with this collective power.

Mercantilism

Commercial capitalism was strongly shaped by the cooperation of the state and big business enterprises, which worked together for their mutual benefit. States practiced mercantilism, an economic approach based on a government policy of building a nation's wealth by expanding its reserves of gold and silver bullion. The Atlantic states of England, Holland, France, and Spain particularly pursued mercantilism. Trading was controlled by semi-military, government-backed companies protected from competition. To attract bullion held by other nations, these governments tried to limit imports and increase exports. Spurred by mercantilism, during the 1500s commercial capitalism expanded out of western Europe and into Africa, Asia, and the Americas.

LO² The Renaissance and Reformation

Two major movements, the Renaissance and the Reformation, reshaped European thought and culture in the 1500s. During the Renaissance—a dramatic flowering in arts and learning that began in Italy around 1350 (see Chapter 14)—new philosophical, scientific, artistic, and literary currents paved the way for more creative, secular societies. The movement reached its peak in the 1500s, as economic expansion provided more people with money to purchase art and books. In the same century, the Reformation—the movement to reform Christianity—spawned new Christian churches that provided alternatives to the Roman Catholic Church. Both movements transformed western European cultural and religious life.

Renaissance Philosophy and Science

The Renaissance fostered new ideas in philosophy and science. During this spurt in knowledge, thinkers and artists rediscovered the ideas of the Classical Greeks and Romans while absorbing inventions and ideas from the Islamic world and China. The Renaissance promoted values such as individualism, secularism, tolerance, beauty, and creativity. Renaissance philosophy, known as humanism, emphasized humanity and its creations rather than God.

 Medieval, Renaissance, Reformation: Western Civilization, Act II (http://www.omnibusol.com/medieval.html**)** A treasure trove of links on many aspects of society in these centuries.

Humanism and the Church

Humanism also focused on problems in the church. A growing crisis of confidence in the Roman Catholic Church, with its abuses by leadership and clergy, became more serious after 1400. Some Renaissance thinkers favored gradual church reform and less rigid ideas. The French humanist writer François Rabelais (RAB-uh-lay) (ca. 1494–1553) went so far as to call monks "a rabble of counterfeit saints, hypocrites, pretended zealots, who disguise themselves like masquers to deceive the world."[4] By spurring freedom of thought and offering critical insights, humanists began to topple the authoritarian medieval attitudes that had crippled scientific investigation, but popes rejected any significant changes.

Machiavelli: The Study of Power

In the area of political thought, Niccolò Machiavelli (MAK-ee-uh-VEL-ee) (1469–1527), the Florentine author of a political manual, *The Prince*, was perhaps the first European to study power as something separate from moral doctrine. *The Prince* argued that the ruler must always keep end goals in mind and apply ruthless policies, such as deception and violence, in pursuing vital national interests. But the exercise of power did not necessarily require tyranny, because the ruler must avoid being hated. Rulers ignored popular moral values at their peril. Machiavelli also argued that it was not necessary for a leader to have piety, faith, integrity, and humanity—only the appearance of such values. Machiavelli's writings became very influential as a guide for European leaders.

Leonardo da Vinci

Although Greco-Roman traditions greatly influenced Renaissance thought, some thinkers developed more interest in science, often employing experimentation and observation. For example, the Florentine Leonardo da Vinci (lay-own-AHR-doh dah VIN-chee) (1452–1519) argued that simply repeating classical traditions without verifying them placed emphasis on memory more than intelligence. A painter, sculptor, architect, scientist, mathematician, and engineer, da Vinci exemplified the versatile Renaissance personality and openness to varied influences.

The Copernican Revolution

Another influential scientist, Polish astronomer Nicolaus Copernicus (koh-PUR-nuh-kuhs) (1473–1543), studied the skies and Islamic scholarship on astronomy, especially the influential writings of the Arab mathematician Ibn al-Shatir (1304–1375), whose research suggested that the earth might not be the center of the universe. Copernicus then transformed astronomy and physics when he devised his revolutionary "heliocentric," or sun-centered, theory of the solar system in 1507. Copernicus refuted the traditional European idea that earth was the center of the universe, arguing that earth and the planets revolved around the sun. He did not dare publish his findings until after his death, fearing persecution by the church.

 The Prince: Power Politics During the Italian Renaissance Learn from the man himself what it means to be "Machiavellian."

Late Renaissance Art and Literature

The Renaissance reshaped European art and spread Italian artistic influence. The art of this period was founded on a desire to reflect the deepening knowledge of humanity by more accurately representing human concerns in sculpture, painting, architecture, and literature. Some of the inspiration came from the growing contacts with Islamic, Asian, and African cultures. Italians such as the Venetian painter Giovanni Bellini (ca. 1430–1516) worked in or visited Muslim cities such as Istanbul and Cairo, spreading Italian influences but also returning with new perspectives. In the early 1500s, Rome replaced Florence as the new capital of Italian art. Among those who worked in Rome, the eccentric Florentine Michelangelo Buonarroti (mi-kuhl-AN-juh-loh bwawn-uh-RAW-tee) (1475–1564) became famous for his realistic sculptures, paintings, and frescoes. He paid keen attention to the attitudes and gestures of each figure he painted on the ceiling of the Vatican's Sistine Chapel.

The Renaissance also spread well beyond Italy. In the Low Countries, Pieter Bruegel (BROY-guhl) the Elder (ca. 1525–1569) integrated Renaissance and local traditions, painting realistic landscapes and sympathetic scenes of peasant and town life. El Greco (ell GREK-oh) (1541–1614), a native of Crete who studied in Italy before settling in Spain, blended Venetian, Byzantine, and Spanish traditions.

 Read about how Dutch artist Rembrandt Van Rijn earned his livelihood in the free market as a painter.

The Literary Heritage of the Renaissance

As in art, the Renaissance had literary consequences throughout Europe. In England during the brilliant reign of Queen Elizabeth I (r. 1558–1603), playwright William Shakespeare (1564–1616) wrote histories, comedies, and tragedies that many literary scholars have believed transcend time and place. Some of his plays, such as *Henry V* and *Julius Caesar*, addressed English or ancient history, while others, such as *Othello*, *Hamlet*, and *The Merchant of Venice*, commented on the world beyond England. One of his best-known characters, Hamlet, voiced Renaissance exuberance: "What [a] piece of

> "Growing knowledge about other cultures forced some Europeans to reconsider their assumptions about the world, and their new ideas helped reshape literature and social thought."

work is a man, how noble in reason, how infinite in faculties."[5]

In Spain in 1615, Miguel de Cervantes (suhr-VAN-teez) Saavedra (1547–1616) published one of the era's great novels, *Don Quixote* (kee-HO-tee). His book painted a vast panorama of society at the end of Spain's golden age. The main character, Don Quixote, sets out to battle dragons and evil men, right injustice, and protect the innocent, but he mainly makes a grand nuisance of himself. Cervantes reflected Renaissance attitudes by dignifying the human spirit but also, like some classical Greek playwrights, making fun of its plight.

Growing knowledge about other cultures forced some Europeans to reconsider their assumptions

Bruegel's *Peasant Wedding* Painted around 1567, Pieter Bruegel's *The Peasant Wedding* celebrates the rituals of peasant life, in this case a wedding dinner for a village. The Flemish artist may also have intended the painting of the feasting villagers as a satire on self-indulgence.

Musée de la Ville de Paris, Musée Carnavalet/The Bridgeman Art Library International

about the world, and their new ideas helped reshape literature and social thought. The French writer Michel Eyquem de Montaigne (mon-TANE) (1533–1592) idealized Native American societies, popularizing the notion of a "Noble Savage" uncorrupted by "civilization." Shakespeare took up the theme in his 1611 play *The Tempest*, where he mocked the idea of the Noble Savage. In the play he creates a contrast between the civilized Prospero and the savage Caliban (KAL-uh-ban) (an anagram for *cannibal*). His Caliban is fierce and brutal, a far cry from the Noble Savage.

The Reformation and Religious Change

Changing societies and a questioning of the old order also spawned the Reformation. To critics, the Roman church had become corrupt, often led by incompetent popes and clergy who blatantly violated priestly requirements for celibacy and poverty. In addition, the spread of literacy and printed books inspired some individuals to interpret Christian writings for themselves. Throughout the 1500s, various groups sought church reform. Some, later called Protestants, eventually broke completely with Roman Catholicism and established their own churches. The Reformation

Interactive Map

(1517–1615) transformed the religious makeup of Europe and profoundly reshaped Western thought (see Map 15.2). By 1600 almost 40 percent of non-Orthodox Europeans, mostly in the north, had renounced the Catholic faith and adopted some form of Protestantism, such as Lutheranism, Calvinism, and Anglicanism.

Martin Luther

Martin Luther (1483–1546), a German, launched the movement that ended the unity of Western Christianity. Luther studied law, then became an Augustinian monk, and later earned a doctorate in theology, after which he taught at the University of Wittenberg. Eventually Luther concluded that nothing in scripture justified papal power and elaborate church rituals, and that only faith, not good works, could wipe away a person's sin and ensure salvation. Luther's break with the church was prompted by the lucrative

Table Talk
Read Martin Luther in his own words, speaking out forcefully and candidly—and sometimes with humor—against Catholic institutions.

church practice of selling indulgences, clerical statements that canceled punishment due for sins in exchange for cash contributions to the church. In 1517 Luther distributed a paper containing ninety-five statements in Latin attacking indulgences. Soon his statements caused an uproar, and Pope Leo X excommunicated Luther in 1520. Luther then translated the Bible into German and condemned Rome as "the greatest thief and robber that has ever appeared on earth or ever will."[6] Lutherans formed a church rooted in the Augsburg Confession, a doctrinal statement issued in 1530 that argued for the Bible as the only source of faith, stated that every believer had the freedom to interpret scripture, and attacked the cults of the Virgin Mary and the saints, priestly celibacy, and the monastic orders.

> " Luther's break generated unrest and divided Western Christianity. "

Consequences of Luther's Reforms

Luther's break generated unrest and divided Western Christianity. Lutheranism spread widely in northern Germany, Scandinavia, and the eastern Baltic coast. In the 1520s, many Germans threw their support to Luther and the reform cause. But in 1524, a major conflict split the reform movement when peasants, inspired by Luther's challenge to Catholic Church power, revolted against the lords and church leaders who owned the land. Luther, opposed to mixing religion and social protest, unsuccessfully mediated between the sides and then supported the nobles, who crushed the uprisings. The result was more than 100,000 deaths. Many German princes became Lutheran, while their overlord, the Holy Roman Emperor, remained staunchly Catholic.

John Calvin in Geneva

Non-Germans were also inspired by Luther's example. One Protestant movement, Calvinism, was more radical than Lutheranism in rejecting Catholic doctrine. Its founder, John Calvin (1509–1564), was forced to leave France for supporting Luther's ideas and settled in Geneva (juh-NEE-vuh), Switzerland. Unlike Luther, Calvin believed not in human free will but in predestination, the doctrine that an individual's salvation or damnation was already determined at birth by God. Because good

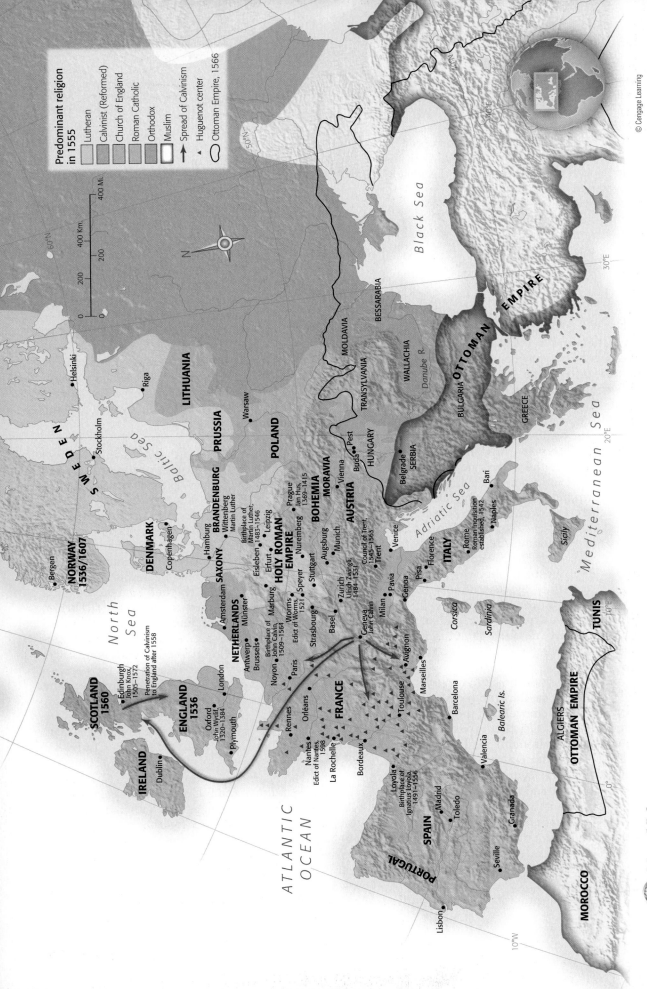

Map 15.2
Reformation Europe

The Protestant Reformation reshaped Europe's religious landscape in the 1500s and early 1600s. By the mid-1550s, some form of Protestantism had become dominant in much of northern Europe, England, and Scotland. Catholicism remained predominant in the southern half of western Europe and parts of eastern Europe.

Predominant religion in 1555

- Lutheran
- Calvinist (Reformed)
- Church of England
- Roman Catholic
- Orthodox
- Muslim

→ Spread of Calvinism
▲ Huguenot center
◯ Ottoman Empire, 1566

400 Mi.
400 Km.
200
200
0
0

N

ATLANTIC OCEAN

IRELAND
Dublin

SCOTLAND 1560
Edinburgh
John Knox, 1505–1572

ENGLAND 1536
Oxford
John Wyclif, 1320–1384
London
Plymouth

Penetration of Calvinism to England after 1558

North Sea

NORWAY 1536/1607
Bergen

SWEDEN
Stockholm
Helsinki

Baltic Sea

DENMARK
Copenhagen

Riga

LITHUANIA

PRUSSIA

Warsaw

POLAND

NETHERLANDS
Amsterdam
Antwerp
Brussels
Münster

Birthplace of John Calvin, 1509–1564
Noyon
Paris

Rennes
Orléans
Nantes
Edict of Nantes, 1598
La Rochelle
Bordeaux

FRANCE

Toulouse

Marseilles
Avignon

Barcelona
Balearic Is.

Valencia

SPAIN
Madrid
Toledo
Granada
Seville

PORTUGAL
Lisbon

MOROCCO

ALGIERS
OTTOMAN EMPIRE

TUNIS

Mediterranean Sea

Corsica
Sardinia

Sicily

ITALY
Genoa
Pisa
Florence
Rome
Roman Inquisition established, 1542
Naples
Bari

Milan
Pavia
Venice

Adriatic Sea

Zurich
Ulrich Zwingli, 1484–1531
Basel
Geneva
John Calvin

Strasbourg

Marburg
Worms
Edict of Worms, 1521
Speyer
Stuttgart
Augsburg
Munich

Council of Trent, 1545–1563
Trent

HOLY ROMAN EMPIRE

SAXONY
Hamburg
Wittenberg
Martin Luther
Eisleben
Birthplace of Martin Luther, 1483–1546
Erfurt
Leipzig

BRANDENBURG

Nuremberg

BOHEMIA
Prague
Jan Hus, 1369–1415

MORAVIA

AUSTRIA
Vienna

HUNGARY
Buda
Pest

Belgrade
SERBIA

BULGARIA

TRANSYLVANIA

WALLACHIA
Danube R.

MOLDAVIA

BESSARABIA

OTTOMAN EMPIRE

GREECE

Black Sea

Loyola
Birthplace of Ignatius Loyola, 1491–1556

60°N
50°N

10°W
0°
10°E
20°E
30°E

© Cengage Learning

behavior and faith could not guarantee reaching Heaven, the authorities must enforce morality to maintain order. Under Calvin, Geneva became a theocratic society, ruled by church leaders who demanded strict morality and attacked worldly pleasures such as swearing, dancing, rolling dice, and playing cards. Calvinism spread rapidly in Switzerland, England, and Holland and also developed centers of strength elsewhere; in Scotland, the Calvinist John Knox founded the Presbyterian Church in 1561.

Henry VIII: A Different Kind of Reformation

In England, unlike Germany and Switzerland, the initiative for religious change came from the king, Henry VIII (r. 1509–1547), who was then a Catholic. Henry had no male heir with his wife, Catherine of Aragon, so he asked the pope to annul his marriage so that he could marry Anne Boleyn (1501–1536). When Rome refused the annulment, Henry chose to break with the church in 1532, rejecting papal supremacy. He announced his divorce, married Anne Boleyn, and arranged to be made head of the Church of England, later known as the Anglican Church. Henry quickly moved to suppress both Calvinism and the Catholic Church. He closed the English monasteries and distributed their lands to his allies among nobles and businessmen. However, the Anglicans largely retained Catholic dogma. Ironically, Henry grew disenchanted with Anne Boleyn, who also bore him no sons, and had her beheaded in 1536. Henry married four more times.

Henry's moves generated religious strife in England. His only male heir, the sickly Edward VI (r. 1547–1553), came to the throne at age ten but died at sixteen of tuberculosis. The Catholic reaction was led by Henry's daughter by Catherine of Aragon, Queen Mary Tudor (TOO-duhr) (r. 1553–1558), who suppressed the Anglican Church. But she was succeeded by Elizabeth I (1533–1603), the daughter of Henry VIII and Anne Boleyn, who restored the Anglican Church. Calvinist influences then began reshaping Anglican dogma. English Calvinists (known as Puritans) were at first tolerated by Anglicans but later persecuted by Elizabeth's successors for opposing moves toward Catholic–Anglican reconciliation. Some Puritans emigrated to Holland. From there one small Puritan group, the Pilgrims, moved to North America in 1620 to seek more religious freedom, helping plant Puritan influence in the New England colonies.

Protestantism and Capitalism

Some scholars believe that Protestant doctrines contributed to, and supplied religious underpinnings for, capitalist values. Some forms of Protestantism were certainly congenial to the thriving new economic attitudes. Like Calvinists and other Protestants, capitalists favored productive labor, frugality, sobriety, and accumulation of wealth as good in themselves. Both Protestantism and capitalism also encouraged individualism, thus undermining the medieval values that the Catholic Church defended. Indeed, capitalism flourished in several Protestant societies, especially Holland, England, and northern Germany. The strongest capitalist societies were also the most Protestant; they were also the most intellectually diverse and gave rise to some secularized free thinkers. Protestantism opened the doors to democracy: once people had freely voiced their opinions on religion, they moved on to seeking a voice in government.

> **Counter Reformation** A movement to confront Protestantism and crush dissidents within the Catholic Church.

The Counter Reformation and Catholic Reform

The Protestant challenge generated a reaction, the Counter Reformation, a movement to confront Protestantism and crush dissidents within the Catholic Church. The church used varied strategies to fight Protestantism, including the Holy Inquisition, the church court formed in medieval times to combat heretical ideas (see Chapter 14). Persecution of dissidents became especially ferocious in Spain, where several thousand people who were believed to hold dissident ideas were burned at the stake. The pope also formed the Congregation of the Index to censor books, and promoted increased missionary activity abroad. The Spanish Basque former soldier, Ignatius of Loyola (loi-OH-luh) (1491–1556), founded the Jesuit order, or Society of Jesus, in 1534, which boasted strict discipline. One prominent Jesuit, the Spanish Basque St. Francis Xavier (ZAY-vee-uhr) (1506–1552), became a pioneering missionary in India, Southeast Asia, and Japan.

The Council of Trent

For all the harsh punitive measures, dissidence within the church persisted, prompting the pope to sponsor a series of conferences, the Council of Trent, to reconsider church doctrines. Although the council (1545–1563) mostly reaffirmed Catholic dogma, it did bring about some reform, imposing more papal supervision of priests and bishops and mandating that all clergy be trained

Witness to the Past

Queen Elizabeth I Rallies Her People

Few women have ever enjoyed the power and respect of England's Renaissance queen, Elizabeth I. Her forty-five years of rule (1558–1603) marked a brilliant period for English culture, especially in literature and theater. On her death, the admiring playwright Ben Jonson wrote her epitaph: "For wit, features, and true passion, Earth, thou hast not such another." The queen may have been, as her detractors claimed, deceptive, devious, and autocratic, but her intelligence and formidable political skills helped her maneuver successfully through the snake pit of both English and European politics. But English–Spanish relations deteriorated, prompting war. In 1588, as the powerful Spanish armada sailed toward the English coast, Elizabeth launched the English ships with a speech to her subjects that ironically played off her gender to reinforce her link with the English people. With the help of foul weather, the English defeated the Spanish, changing the fortunes of both countries.

My loving people. We have been persuaded by some that are careful for our safety, to take heed how we commit ourselves to armed multitudes, for fear of treachery, but I assure you, I do not desire to live to distrust my faithful and loving people. Let tyrants fear; I have always so behaved myself, that, under God, I have placed my chiefest strength and safeguard in the loyal hearts and good will of my subjects, and therefore I am come amongst you, as you see, at this time, not for my recreation and disport, but being resolved in the midst and heat of the battle, to live or die amongst you all, to lay down for my God, and for my kingdoms, and for my people, my honor and my blood, even in the dust.

I know I have the body of a weak and feeble woman; but I have the heart and stomach of a king, and of a king of England too; and I think foul scorn that . . . Spain, or any prince of Europe should dare to invade the borders of my realm; to which rather than any dishonor shall grow by me, I myself will take up arms, I myself will be your general, judge, and rewarder of every one of your virtues in the field.

I know already for your forwardness you have deserved rewards and crowns; and we do assure you in the word of a prince, they shall be duly paid you. In the meantime my lieutenant general shall be in my stead, than whom never prince commanded a more noble or worthy subject; no doubting but by your obedience to my general, by your concord in the camp, and your valor in the field, we shall shortly have a famous victory over those enemies of my God, of my kingdoms, and of my people.

Thinking About the Reading

1. How did Elizabeth justify the forthcoming battle with Spain?
2. What personal qualities did this Renaissance monarch suggest she could offer to her people in their time of peril?

Source: Charles W. Colby, ed., *Selections from the Sources of English History* (Harlow: Longmans, Green, 1899), pp. 158–159. Quotation in introduction from A. L. Rowse, *The Elizabethan Renaissance: The Life of the Society* (New York: Charles Scribner's, 1971), p. 59.

in seminaries. The Trent reforms enabled Catholicism to recover some lost ground, and the Catholic Church endured in a modified form. Catholics gradually turned from confronting Protestants to converting the peoples outside of Europe.

But religious passions continued to foster intolerance. Indeed, in Europe, religious minorities, such as Jews, French Protestants, and English Catholics, faced discrimination and sometimes violence; many emigrated to escape such persecution. Several popes pursued anti-Jewish policies, as did some Protestants: Luther advocated burning synagogues, arresting rabbis, and confiscating Jewish property.

Religious Wars and Conflicts

Religious divisions contributed to a series of European wars and other conflicts from the late sixteenth through early eighteenth centuries. The Spanish Empire, ruled by a branch of the Habsburg family, was particularly troubled by religious tensions. During the 1500s, Spain emerged as a major European power, which, thanks to exploration and conquest, controlled a vast empire in the Americas and Southeast Asia. The Spanish Habsburgs also ruled other Europeans, including Portugal, the Low Countries, and parts of Italy. King Philip II of Spain (r. 1556–1598), known as "the most Catholic of kings," put the resources of the Spanish crown toward defending and spreading the Catholic faith.

The Spanish Armada and the Birth of the Netherlands

Philip faced one of his biggest challenges in the Low Countries, where his suppression of Calvinism antagonized businessmen and the nobility. Inflamed Protestants attacked Catholic churches, and Spain's execution of dissident leaders spurred a general revolt in 1566, in which both Catholics and Protestants rallied behind the Calvinist leader, the Dutchman William of Nassau (NAS-au), Prince of Orange. Philip dispatched an occupation army that executed more than 1,100 Protestants and, in 1576, sacked Antwerp, Europe's wealthiest city. In 1579, hoping to divide his opponents, Philip promised political liberty to the ten largely Catholic Flemish- and French-speaking southern provinces of the Low Countries, thereby forging the foundations of modern Belgium and Luxembourg. Because of English assistance to the Low Country rebels and English attacks on Spanish shipping in the Americas, Philip II tried to invade England by sea in 1588 but faced a determined foe in Queen Elizabeth I (see Witness to the Past: Queen Elizabeth I Rallies Her People). The English ships outmaneuvered Spain's armada of 130 ships and then triumphed when a fierce storm in the English Channel devastated the Spanish fleet. The mostly Protestant, Dutch-speaking northern provinces of the Low Countries broke away from Spain in 1588 and became fully independent in 1609, forming the country that became the Netherlands.

The Edict of Nantes

Between 1562 and 1589, religious conflicts also raged across France. The French Calvinists, known as Huguenots (HYOO-guh-nauts), were led by the powerful Bourbon (BOOR-buhn) family. In 1572, after the assassination of Calvinist leaders on royal orders sparked Huguenot rioting in Paris, Catholic forces massacred 30,000 Huguenots. In 1593 Henry of Bourbon (1553–1610), remarking that "Paris is well worth a mass," renounced Calvinism for Catholicism in order to become King Henry IV. Remaining a Protestant sympathizer, in 1598 he signed the Edict of Nantes (nahnt), which ended the religious conflicts by recognizing Roman Catholicism as the state church of France but giving Huguenots the right to freely practice their religion.

Turkish Expansion, European Resistance

While Protestant–Catholic tensions in Europe were intense, Christian–Muslim conflicts also simmered and often translated into political and military conflict. Many Europeans were concerned about the growing power of the Muslim Ottoman Turks (see Chapter 16), who sought to expand their empire, which already included Greece, much of the Balkans, and Bulgaria. When some people in the Balkans abandoned Christianity for Islam, Christian leaders became alarmed, and the Holy Roman Emperor Charles V marshaled allies to defeat the Turks at Vienna in 1529. Then in 1571 the so-called Holy League of Spain, Rome, and Venice used advanced naval gunnery to destroy the Turkish fleet at the Battle of Lepanto (li-PAN-toh), off Greece, ending Turkish ambitions for a while. In 1683 the Turks besieged Vienna, and Austria was saved only by Polish intervention. Finally, the Austrians pushed the Turks out of Hungary. Ottoman expansion in Europe had ended.

LO³ Changing States and Politics

The encounters with the wider world, capitalism, Renaissance humanism, and the Protestant Reformation reshaped Europe and challenged old beliefs. European politics also changed, as bloody wars drew much of Europe into conflict: kingdoms were torn asunder and reconfigured, old states declined, and new states gained influence. Many of these states used mercantilist policies to strengthen their power, and in some states, some form of royal absolutism flourished. A few other states developed representative governments with elements of democracy.

Regional Wars and National Conflicts

Various wars raged during the Early Modern Era, some prompted by religious divisions, and others spawned by tensions between rival states and empires. Even after religious tensions subsided, warfare remained a constant reality, involving most European societies at one time or another.

> "Even after religious tensions subsided, warfare remained a constant reality, involving most European societies at one time or another."

The Thirty Years' War and the Treaty of Westphalia

The major conflict was the Thirty Years' War (1618–1648), a long series of bloody hostilities that claimed millions of lives and involved many countries. This complex struggle for regional power started in the Holy Roman Empire, as Czech (check) Protestants revolted against oppressive Habsburg Catholic rulers. Eventually the fighting also drew in German princes and two mostly Lutheran countries, Denmark and Sweden. Finally France, although a mostly Catholic country, went to war against its Habsburg rivals who ruled Austria and Spain. In 1648 the conflict ended after a four-year-long European congress in Westphalia (west-FALE-yuh), a German province. The Treaty of Westphalia reaffirmed freedom of religion but did not permanently end Protestant–Catholic conflict. The new balance of power in Europe favored France and curbed the Habsburgs, and France enjoyed unrivaled prestige after 1659. The Holy Roman Emperor lost influence to German princes, Sweden gained territory, and the conference recognized Swiss independence from Habsburg rule. The wars of the later 1600s and early 1700s were fought with well-drilled professional soldiers, large warships, and more deadly gunpowder weapons. Consequently, the human costs of war increased: in the 1709 Battle of Malpaquet, 40,000 French soldiers were killed or wounded.

The War of Spanish Succession

The most widespread conflict, the War of the Spanish Succession (1701–1714), brought together England, Holland, Austria, Denmark, Portugal, and some German states to battle France and Spain over who would inherit the Spanish throne from the last Habsburg king. The Treaty of Utrecht (YOO-trecht), which ended the war, forced Spain to transfer its ter-

Soldiers' Return In the early 1600s, the French artist Jacques Callot made a series of moving etchings about the Thirty Years' War called "Miseries of War." This etching shows a group of discharged soldiers, so impoverished and brutalized by war that they either beg for food or die alongside the road.

ritory in Belgium and Italy to Austria. The once-prosperous Dutch had overextended themselves in the war, damaging their economy, and Venice became a peripheral, declining state. Now a major maritime power, England received most of the spoils of war, including the strategic Gibraltar peninsula at Spain's southern tip. Utrecht resulted in a new balance of power among European states, and most of Europe entered a period of calm.

Absolutist and Despotic Monarchies

States changed during the Early Modern Era, with many governments moving far from medieval forms. New ways of thinking, as well as political, social, and religious strife, set the stage for diverse patterns of government by the seventeenth century. One trend among states was the rise of absolutism, a system of concentrated monarchial authority best represented by the French kings and the Russian czars.

The Sun King

For a time, absolute monarchies dazzled Europe, with King Louis XIV (r. 1661–1715) of France serving as the widely envied model. By the mid-1600s, France, with 18 million people, was western Europe's largest country, was self-sufficient in agriculture, and had some thriving industries. Louis XIV believed that his power derived from God, thus he was a monarch by divine right. Known as the Sun King for the brilliant extravagance of his court, Louis enjoyed great power, demanding obedience from all at the expense of the nobility.

The king tried to control everything. He imposed mercantilism, fostering industries and companies subject to royal domination, and he revoked the Edict of Nantes, forbade Protestant pastors to preach, and closed Protestant schools and churches. His repression of Protestantism led 200,000 Huguenots to emigrate to England, Holland, and North America. Louis also ordered a spectacular palace built at Versailles (vuhr-SIGH), a Paris suburb. Versailles became the center of French life, and French nobles and foreign leaders were compelled to spend time there. The king patronized the arts and literature, and in turn artists celebrated the king, comparing him to classical Greek and Roman leaders.

> 66 New ways of thinking, as well as political, social, and religious strife, set the stage for diverse patterns of government by the seventeenth century. 99

Louis XIV's search for power elsewhere in Europe caused four major wars aimed at preventing Habsburg dominance. Marrying his dreams of personal glory to his goal of state prestige, he built up an effective military force. French power reached its height around 1680, but the wars proved financially ruinous and fell short of their objectives. The War of the Spanish Succession sapped the French treasury and military and enabled Austria, England, and Holland to counterbalance French power. Although France remained a major state after 1715, it had lost some of its glory.

absolutism
A form of government in which sovereignty is vested in a single person, the king or queen; monarchs in the sixteenth and seventeenth centuries based their authority on the theory of the divine right of kings (i.e., that they had received their authority from God and were responsible only to Him).

Ivan IV

Russia also developed a strong and often tyrannical government led by czars. Ivan (ee-VON) IV (r. 1533–1584)—known as Ivan the Terrible because of his paranoia and brutality—built a centralized Russian state while fighting wars with neighboring Poland and Sweden and conquering the Tartar states, founded by Mongols and Turks three centuries earlier, along the lower Volga River. Ivan also ordered the death or torture of many thousands of Russians whom he considered enemies. Muscovite czars after Ivan imposed a rural economy based on serfdom to gain support from the landed nobility. Lords could sell their serfs, making them little better than slaves. The czars imposed tight control over the Russian Orthodox Church after it broke officially from the Greek Orthodox Church in the late 1500s and pursued expansion toward the southeastern Baltic region, where they came into conflict with the Poles and Lithuanians.

Peter the Great

Russia gradually developed an even more powerful state, especially during the reign of Peter I the Great (r. 1682–1725), an enlightened but despotic czar who encouraged Russia's integration with the West. Nearly 7 feet tall and possessed with tremendous energy, Peter saw Russia's only hope as copying Western technology

St. Petersburg This painting, made around 1760, shows the Winter Palace, inhabited by the Russian royal family, occupying the left side of the Neva River in St. Petersburg, a major port that attracted many trading ships. Michael Holford

and administrative techniques. In 1698, the czar launched ambitious political, economic, military, and educational reforms and hired foreign specialists to advise him. Some of Peter's policies to promote western European practices were superficial and unpopular, such as banning beards. He increased royal power at the expense of the church and nobility, and expanded Russia's frontiers, established industries, strengthened autocracy and serfdom, put together a navy to protect his Baltic flank, and developed a more efficient government. Because he hated gloomy Moscow, with its medieval feel, in 1713 Peter began building a new capital on the Baltic, modeled on Amsterdam and Venice, and named it St. Petersburg.

Russian History Index: The World Wide Web Virtual Library (http://vlib.iue.it/hist-russia/Index.html). Contains useful essays and links on Russian history, society, and politics.

Peter also had many foreign achievements. In 1699 he forged a secret alliance with Sweden's rivals, Denmark and Poland, and battled the Swedes in the Great Northern War beginning in 1700. Only in 1709 did an exhausted Sweden abandon the eastern rim of the Baltic to Russia. Russia's growing power unsettled European rivals, as Peter and other Russian czars pursued expansion to the south and east. Anxious to forge permanent access to the warm Mediterranean Sea, because it was open to shipping twelve months a year, Russian forces pushed south toward the Black Sea and the Straits of Bosporus (see Map 15.3). They also began acquiring territory in Siberia and Muslim Central Asia (see Chapter 16). By eventually creating a huge colossus of an empire and exploiting the resources of the newly colonized areas, Russia developed a largely self-sufficient economy. Despite Peter the Great's Westernization policies, most later czars were wary of foreign influence.

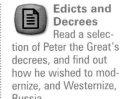

Edicts and Decrees Read a selection of Peter the Great's decrees, and find out how he wished to modernize, and Westernize, Russia.

Interactive Map

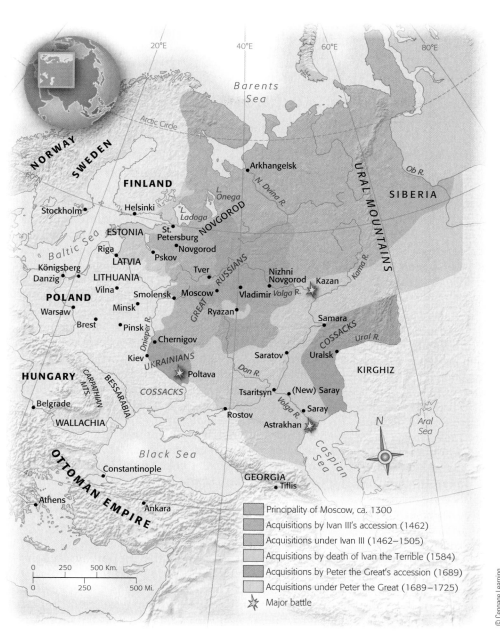

Map 15.3
Russian Expansion, 1300–1750

Beginning in the 1300s, the Russians expanded from a small remote northern state, based in Moscow, into an empire. By the mid-1700s, the Russians had gained political domination over western Siberia, the northern Caucasus, and part of what is today the eastern Baltic region and the Ukraine.

Legend (map key):
- Principality of Moscow, ca. 1300
- Acquisitions by Ivan III's accession (1462)
- Acquisitions under Ivan III (1462–1505)
- Acquisitions by death of Ivan the Terrible (1584)
- Acquisitions by Peter the Great's accession (1689)
- Acquisitions under Peter the Great (1689–1725)
- ✶ Major battle

© Cengage Learning

The Rise of Representative Governments

Some European countries moved toward greater political freedom in this era. Iceland enjoyed self-rule for several centuries, while Switzerland was a multilingual, decentralized, and constitutional confederation of self-governing Catholic and Protestant districts. Among the more powerful states, the Netherlands and England developed the most open and accountable governments: the Netherlands became a republic and England a constitutional monarchy.

The Dutch East India Company

The Netherlands enjoyed a golden age during much of the 1600s. It built a colonial empire, including holdings in the Americas, South Africa, Sri Lanka, and Southeast Asia, and also dominated the Atlantic, Baltic, and Indian Ocean trade. Large Dutch joint-stock companies like the Dutch East India Company controlled the overseas market. The Netherlands became Europe's most prosperous society, with Amsterdam serving as a major hub of world trade. The flow of wealth from overseas activities influenced Dutch political life, fostering an innovative republican system. Holland had long enjoyed a climate of freedom and tolerance, attracting people who sought a more open intellectual atmosphere. After breaking away from Spanish domination, the predominantly Protestant Netherlands became a republic and confederation linked by common institutions such as the assemblies of delegates. But the system was troubled by tensions among elite families, and in 1619 the country entered the Thirty Years' War. Although the peace in 1648 favored business and banking interests, a French invasion of the Netherlands in 1672 shattered the accord.

The Ascendancy of England

Over several centuries, the English forged a colonial empire. England already held Ireland as a colony and sent Protestant settlers to some districts of the mostly Catholic island. Following the 1601 establishment of the English East India Company in Asia, England also founded a colonial empire in North America and the Caribbean. By 1700 it overtook the Dutch as major international traders.

> "Holland had long enjoyed a climate of freedom and tolerance, attracting people who sought a more open intellectual atmosphere."

The English Civil War and Oliver Cromwell

England also experienced profound political changes. In the 1600s, two political upheavals secured first a republic and then a constitutional monarchy. Hostile to absolutism, the English had long struggled to define the relative rights of kings and parliaments. Even one of the most effective European monarchs in history, Queen Elizabeth I, had to tolerate parliamentary influence while using her astute political skills to get her way. However, the Stuarts—the Scottish royal family who became the monarchs of both Scotland and England after Elizabeth I died without an heir—had absolutist ambitions. Stuart king Charles I's decision to make Anglicanism the only recognized faith in both Scotland and England antagonized the Puritans and Presbyterians. In 1641, Parliament condemned despotic Stuart policies, prompting the English Civil War. The parliamentary troops were led by Oliver Cromwell (1599–1658), a member of the rural gentry and a zealous Puritan whose army defeated the royalist forces by 1645. To the great shock of many observers, King Charles I was beheaded.

Parliament abolished the monarchy and proclaimed a republican Commonwealth (1649–1660) dominated by Cromwell. Although the Puritans inclined toward capitalism and protected property rights, their majority in Parliament were fanatics determined to root out what they considered heresy and "godlessness," even expelling the Presbyterians from Parliament. To maintain order, Cromwell became dictator and imposed Puritan morality: he banned newspapers, executed dissidents, and crushed a Catholic rebellion in Ireland by burning crops and massacring thousands. On Cromwell's death, Parliament restored the Stuarts to the throne after they agreed to guarantee individual freedom of religion.

The Glorious Revolution

After the Stuart restoration, the Protestant–Catholic conflicts resumed and eventually led to a broad-based government with a stronger Parliament. Because Stuart king James II (r. 1685–1688) favored absolutist and pro-Catholic policies, Parliament, now dominated by Anglicans, offered the kingship to Dutch leader William of Orange (r. 1689–1702), a champion of the Protestant cause. In 1688 James II was forced to abdicate and flee to France. In what came to be known as the Glorious Revolution (1688–1689), Parliament decreed William and his wife, Mary, sovereigns after they accepted a Bill of Rights recognizing the right of petition and requiring parliamentary approval of taxes. The Toleration Act, establishing freedom of religion, followed.

After the Glorious Revolution, England moved only partway toward a democracy involving all the people. Although royal power was modified, the government represented only the factions that had political influence and wealth: the nobility, wealthy merchants, and property owners. English kings now had far less power than absolutist monarchs, and the great landed aristocratic families, elected from towns and counties, dominated Parliament. Only Parliament could vote the money for the king and his army. In 1707, England, Scotland, and Wales officially combined as the United Kingdom, often known as Great Britain. To control ethnic minorities, the Scottish highlanders were cleared from their lands and forced to move to coastal cities or emigrate, and their Celtic language, Gaelic (GAY-lik), was banned. In colonized Ireland, Protestant English and Scottish settlers acquired land, and Irish Catholics became second-class citizens, denied the right to education, property, and political office.

Rising New States, Declining Old States

The forces unleashed by capitalism, religious change, warfare, and shifting political power caused powerful new states to emerge and longtime powers to decline (see Map 15.4). Among those that emerged was Catholic and German-speaking Austria, which, under the Habsburg monarchs, became a major power after the Thirty Years' War, outshining the German states to the west. The new centralized Austrian empire governed diverse societies: Czechs, Croats, Slovenians, most Hungarians, and some Italians, Romanians, and Serbs.

 Interactive Map

Gustavus Adolphus and the Rise of Sweden

Much of Sweden, another emerging power, became independent of once-mighty Denmark in 1520. Swedish society was distinctive: its peasants had never been serfs, many owned their own land, and peasant representatives served in the national assembly. The Swedish state became a hereditary but not absolutist monarchy, with an efficient administration and Lutheranism as the state religion. Soon Swedes dominated Baltic trade, but eventually lost their economic position to the Dutch. Under King Gustavus Adolphus (r. 1611–1632), a brilliant military strategist and creative administrator, Sweden became one of Europe's most influential states, and by the mid-1600s controlled much of Poland and part of Denmark. By 1721, however, the Swedes had lost all of their possessions in the eastern Baltic except Finland to Russia or Prussia (PRUH-shuh).

The Militarization of Prussia

A third state on the rise in Europe was Prussia, which originated as a small, mostly German-speaking state along the eastern Baltic coast, on the borderlands between the Holy Roman Empire and Poland. Long under Polish rule, the state became independent in 1660. In the mid-1700s, Prussia built one of the most formidable military forces in Europe under an authoritarian but constitutional monarchy. Under King Frederick II the Great (r. 1740–1786), Prussia rapidly expanded its territory at the expense of Poland, Austria, and the Holy Roman Empire. A brilliant leader and strategist, Frederick had many dimensions: he was warlike and ruthless but also a fine musician who enjoyed conversations with philosophers.

A Shifting European Landscape

As new states emerged in Europe, several older states declined. By the 1500s, the Holy Roman Empire had become a political entity without much coherence. The emperors, elected by leading princes, were little more than figureheads presiding symbolically over a collection of some three hundred diverse states. The empire was effectively swept away in 1740, when Austria and Prussia began a 130-year struggle for dominance in the region. Italians also remained divided into small states. Poland and Lithuania, major states in medieval times, also faced change. In 1569 the two predominantly Catholic states combined to form a republican commonwealth, launching a golden age of economic prosperity and tolerance of religious diversity. Jewish communities in Poland and Lithuania, in contrast to the rest of Europe, enjoyed many legal rights and some self-government. Elected kings and noble-dominated national and local assemblies presided

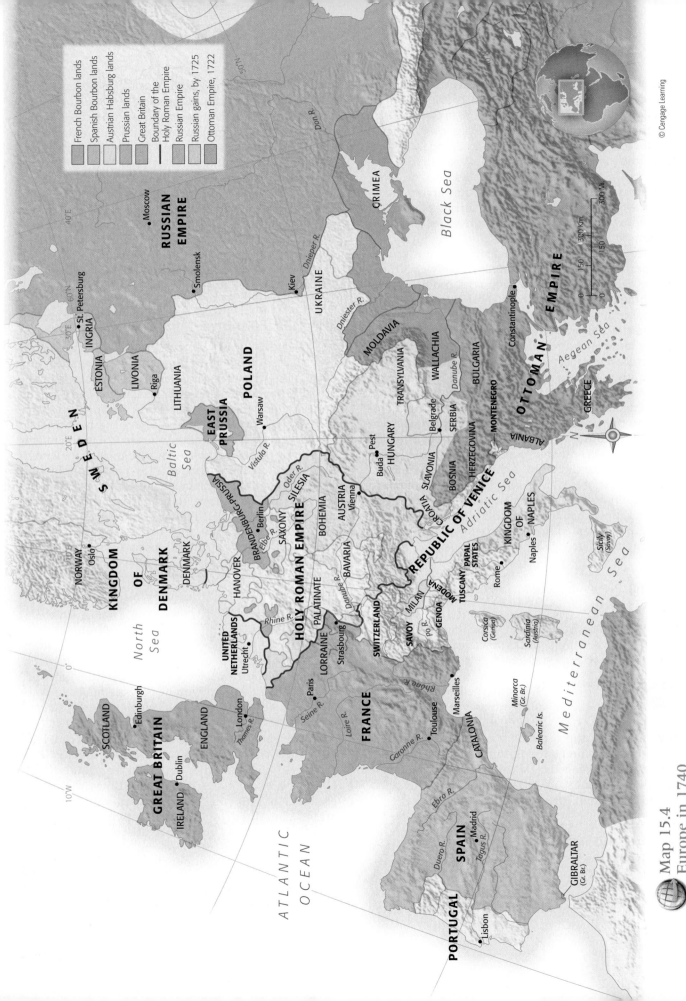

Map 15.4
Europe in 1740

By the mid-1700s, France and Great Britain were the most powerful western European states. While once-powerful Spain and Portugal had lost influence and the Germans and Italians remained divided, Prussia, Sweden, Russia, and Habsburg-ruled Austria were gaining strength.

Legend:
- French Bourbon lands
- Spanish Bourbon lands
- Austrian Habsburg lands
- Prussian lands
- Great Britain
- Boundary of the Holy Roman Empire
- Russian Empire
- Russian gains, by 1725
- Ottoman Empire, 1722

© Cengage Learning

GREAT BRITAIN
- SCOTLAND · Edinburgh
- IRELAND · Dublin
- ENGLAND · London
- Thames R.

ATLANTIC OCEAN

North Sea

NORWAY · Oslo

KINGDOM OF DENMARK
- DENMARK

SWEDEN

Baltic Sea

· St. Petersburg
INGRIA
ESTONIA
LIVONIA · Riga
LITHUANIA

RUSSIAN EMPIRE
- Moscow
- Smolensk
- Kiev
- UKRAINE

POLAND
- Warsaw
- EAST PRUSSIA
- Vistula R.

· Oslo

HANOVER
UNITED NETHERLANDS · Utrecht
BRANDENBURG-PRUSSIA · Berlin
Elbe R.
SAXONY
Oder R.
SILESIA
BOHEMIA
Rhine R.
PALATINATE
LORRAINE · Strasbourg
SWITZERLAND
Danube R.
BAVARIA
AUSTRIA · Vienna

HOLY ROMAN EMPIRE

FRANCE
- Paris
- Seine R.
- Loire R.
- Garonne R. · Toulouse
- Marseilles
- Rhône R.

SAVOY
MILAN
GENOA
MODENA
TUSCANY
PAPAL STATES · Rome
Po R.

Corsica (Genoa)
Sardinia (Austria)

KINGDOM OF NAPLES · Naples

Sicily (Savoy)

REPUBLIC OF VENICE
Adriatic Sea

CROATIA
SLAVONIA
HUNGARY
Buda · Pest
Danube R.
TRANSYLVANIA
BOSNIA
HERZEGOVINA
SERBIA · Belgrade
MONTENEGRO
ALBANIA

MOLDAVIA
Dniester R.
WALLACHIA
Danube R.
BULGARIA

OTTOMAN EMPIRE
· Constantinople
GREECE
Aegean Sea

CRIMEA

Black Sea

Dnieper R.
Don R.

Mediterranean Sea

SPAIN · Madrid
Duero R.
Tagus R.
Ebro R.
CATALONIA
Balearic Is.
Minorca (Gr. Br.)

PORTUGAL · Lisbon

GIBRALTAR (Gr. Br.)

N

0   150   300 Mi.
0   150   300 Km.

10°W   0°   10°E   20°E   30°E   40°E   50°E
50°N   60°N

over a somewhat decentralized semi-democracy. But by the mid-1600s, the commonwealth was struggling amidst rebellion and invasion. After 1717, Poland became little more than an appendage to the expanding Russian empire, and Lithuania became a Russian province.

LO⁴ The Transformation of Cultures and Societies

Europeans' sixteenth- and seventeenth-century voyages of discovery and the colonization that followed altered their view of the world and its peoples, broadened their horizons, and contributed to intellectual change within Europe. In some seventeenth-century societies, a measure of religious tolerance added to the ferment of ideas. New ways of perceiving the natural world fostered an emphasis on reason, while capitalism spurred by overseas expansion reshaped social patterns, creating a transition from a largely rural to an increasingly urban society.

Arts and Philosophy

The expanding horizons of thought opened by the Renaissance and Reformation led to an extravagant artistic movement in the 1600s known as the baroque, a term that originally meant "contorted" or "grotesque." Baroque artists emphasized movement, tension, exaggerated lighting, intense emotions, and decoration. In Italy, baroque art, such as the marble statues and fountains of the Roman architect and sculptor Gianlorenzo Bernini (buhr-NEE-nee) (1598–1680), was expressive and sensuous, rejecting restraint and emphasizing freedom.

A Broader Audience for the Arts

In contrast to Renaissance artists such as Michelangelo, Dutch artists saw their work as a capitalist enterprise and often produced for the wider market rather than for individual patrons. Painters such as Rembrandt van Rijn and Jan Vermeer (1632–1675), influenced by baroque approaches, conveyed an impression of emotion and immediacy in their portraits and other works. Their paintings communicated personality, the thoughts and feelings of individuals, even of ordinary people in Amsterdam. Some music composers also created works to appeal to a wide audience. The German Lutheran composers George Frederick Handel (1685–1750) and Johann Sebastian Bach (1685–1759) produced work of enduring popularity. Handel settled in London, where he wrote his famous choral work, *The Messiah*. Bach wrote pieces for both Protestant and Catholic churches and for many instruments.

> **baroque**
> An extravagant and, to many, shocking European artistic movement of the 1600s that encouraged release from restraints of thought and expression.

66 Baroque artists emphasized movement, tension, exaggerated lighting, intense emotions, and decoration. **99**

The Birth of Modern Science, Philosophy, and Political Science

The rise of baroque art corresponded to the greatest era of philosophical and scientific speculation in Europe since the classical Greeks. The Englishman Francis Bacon (1561–1626) built some of the foundations for this intellectual growth. Bacon sought to eliminate intellectual restraints on science by separating philosophy from theology and advocating the use of reason. He developed a famous maxim: "Knowledge is power." Bacon's scientific method—probably based in part on the ideas of earlier Islamic thinkers—encouraged systematically studying things that need understanding. The scientist should develop an idea, test it experimentally, and then draw conclusions.

Another key thinker and the founding father of modern philosophy, René Descartes (DAY-cart) (1596–1650), promoted pure reason and a rationalist view of the world. Descartes believed that human rationality was founded on a distinction between mind and body. He sought to sweep away traditional learning and establish a new system of knowledge embracing all aspects of reality. The only thing he could not doubt was his own existence: "While I wanted to think everything false, it was absolutely necessary that I, who was thinking thus, must be something. I think, therefore I am."[7] Just as science brought order to the physical world, Descartes intended to bring order to thought.

The English political thinker Thomas Hobbes (1588–1679), a friend of Descartes, believed that society was not perfectible, even with the use of reason or Christian teachings. Hobbes, a pessimist, held that, in the state of nature, with no government to control humanity's anarchic, power-seeking instincts, the life of man was "solitary, poor, nasty, brutish, and short."[8]

Scientific Revolution
An era of rapid European advance in knowledge, particularly in mathematics and astronomy, that occurred between 1600 and 1750.

> "European scientists demolished the medieval view of the earth's position in the cosmos and laid the groundwork for later intellectual and industrial transitions."

His disturbing book, *The Leviathan*, provided a new view of the state and its relationship to the individual. Because war and conflict were inherent to human society, Hobbes believed, people needed despotic power to control them. Values such as truth, reason, or justice, however useful, were just artificial attributes of human society created by social convention and language. People could either give in to violent, selfish human nature or erect a powerful state to ensure harmony.

Science and Technology

The Scientific Revolution (ca. 1600–1750), an era of rapid advance in knowledge, built on the work of thinkers like Bacon and Descartes to gain a new understanding of the natural and physical world and to create several technological innovations. European scientists demolished the medieval view of the earth's position in the cosmos and laid the groundwork for later intellectual and industrial transitions. Although offering new ideas could be dangerous in a continent full of religious conflicts and despotic monarchs, advances occurred in many areas.

The Scientific Revolution derived in part from imported Asian and Islamic ideas and technologies. European scientists were quite familiar with the writings of earlier Muslim thinkers. They also learned from China. The Jesuits who sojourned in China in the sixteenth and seventeenth centuries sent back reports that praised Chinese scientific traditions and inventions. As Europeans assimilated and improved imported models while creating new ones, the general dynamism of science and technology shifted from China and the Middle East to Europe. Between the seventeenth and nineteenth centuries, western Europe caught up with and then surpassed China technologically.

Foundations of Modern Astronomy and Physics

Astronomers made some of the most significant scientific discoveries. The German mystic Johannes Kepler (1571–1630) used mathematics to amplify the discoveries of Copernicus, showing that all of the planets revolved around the sun. The era's greatest astronomer, the Italian Galileo Galilei (gal-uh-LAY-oh gal-uh-LAY-ee) (1564–1642), proved experimentally that Copernicus's theories were correct. Galileo built the first telescope in 1609 and discovered that the moon had mountains, Jupiter had four large moons, and our solar system was but a small part of a Milky Way galaxy containing thousands of stars that could not be seen with the naked eye. These findings were dangerous, however: in 1615 the Catholic Church summoned the scientist to Rome to be tried as a heretic, and he was forced to publicly recant his views in order to leave prison, but he continued publishing his findings. As punishment, Inquisition officials placed him under house arrest for the last decade of his life.

Scientific activity reached its height with Sir Isaac Newton (1642–1727), a mathematics professor at Cambridge University whose development of fundamental laws of physics was the culmination of a century's observations and scientific findings. Newton's importance to the world was proclaimed in a famous epitaph by his contemporary, the poet Alexander Pope: "Nature and Nature's laws lay hidden in night; God said, 'Let Newton be!' and all was light."[9] In 1687, Newton published his *Mathematical Principles of Natural Philosophy*, which accounted for all the motions of the planets, the comets, the moon, and the sea. He found the connection, especially the law of universal gravitation, that tied together varied parts of the physical world into an ordered whole. Newton's ideas dominated Western scientific thinking for the next two hundred years.

 **Letter to the Grand Duchess Christina** Read Galileo's passionate defense of his scientific research against those who would condemn it as un-Christian.

In the wake of scientific discoveries, and sometimes borrowing from advances made in other societies, technology improved. During the 1500s, more advanced gunpowder weapons and such useful items as the watch, lead pencil, thermometer, and concrete became available. In the 1620s, an English mathematician developed the first slide rule, and a German mathematician invented the first mechanical calculator. These devices performed multiplication, division, and much more. The Dutch scientist Christian Huygens (HYE-guhnz) introduced a more accurate clock in 1657. Innovations in industrial machinery led to many advances; by the 1730s, the English textile industry became more efficient with spinning machines, similar to those introduced in China in the 1200s, for making cotton products.

> "The Enlightenment helped replace unquestioning religious faith with observed fact and suggested that objective truth could be established through reason."

The Enlightenment

The Enlightenment, which began in 1675 and continued until 1800, was a philosophical movement based on science and reason that was perhaps the most fertile period in the history of Western philosophy. Without the earlier achievements in the study of science and human reason by scholars like Bacon, Descartes, and Newton, the Enlightenment would have been unthinkable. But the movement also owed something to growing European knowledge of egalitarian Native American societies and of Chinese thought. The Enlightenment helped replace unquestioning religious faith with observed fact and suggested that objective truth could be established through reason. The scientific investigation of the natural world could now be separated from religious doctrines. In England, France, Scotland, and elsewhere, fresh ideas emerged, including new notions of tolerance, individual rights, and the relationship between

Painting of Madame Geoffrin's Salon This mid-eighteenth-century painting by French artist Lemoinnier shows a gathering of Enlightenment thinkers and artists at the elegant Paris salon operated by Madame Geoffrin, seated toward the right.

Reunion des Musées Nationaux/Art Resource, NY

citizens and the state. Overall, the Enlightenment spread a humanistic secularism, promoted critical approaches to knowledge, and aimed at increasing human happiness. It also provided a forum for addressing gender issues.

John Locke and Empiricism

The Englishman John Locke (1632–1704), a physician who lived for a decade in France and Holland, was one of the first major Enlightenment philosophers. Locke made experimental studies of medicine and science that led him to proclaim the value of empiricism, an approach that stressed relying on experience and testing propositions rather than using reason alone to acquire knowledge. Locke became particularly influential as a political theorist, his work providing a foundation for the modern democratic state and notions of human freedom. In contrast to Thomas Hobbes, Locke condemned absolute monarchy and urged people to defend their freedom by uniting in a civil society where people cooperated for common goals but the state enjoyed only limited powers over the individual. The state, he conceded, was needed to protect popular desires but had to preserve self-governance and freedom. If the state transgressed these rights, people had the right to oppose it. He favored individual rights, such as the separation of church and state, but also favored some limits, such as restricting political participation to people with property. Many of Locke's ideas became influential not only in England but also among the founders of the United States, especially Thomas Jefferson.

Voltaire and the Philosophes

The French Enlightenment was fostered by intellectuals known as philosophes (fill-uh-SOHFZ) (philosophers). The best-known philosophe, Voltaire (1694–1778), a poet, dramatist, and historian, believed that science and rational social behavior led people to live happier lives. He was occasionally imprisoned in France for resisting the system, and he spent many years in exile in England, Switzerland, and Prussia. Growing European knowledge of China and Confucianism led him to view China as an admirable political model of a despotic but secular and benevolent state, in contrast to absolutist France. Although he supported tolerance, Voltaire and some other Enlightenment thinkers fiercely attacked established religion and also disliked the Jews for their separation, often involuntary, from mainstream society and their commitment to tradition.

Capitalism's Impact on European Society

Capitalism gradually reshaped rural society. In many places, a changing economy turned many peasants into a displaced labor force. England experienced this change in the 1500s, when King Henry VIII seized the lands of the Catholic Church and distributed them to his cronies, including wealthy businessmen, who began buying land as an investment. The new hard-hearted landowners increased demands on peasants or shifted land use from agriculture to more profitable sheep raising, ejecting peasants from the land. With a policy known as enclosure, landlords, claiming ownership rights, also fenced off common lands once used by the public for grazing livestock and collecting firewood. As their options dwindled, the English peasantry mostly disappeared and were replaced by tenant farmers working for big landlords.

The Dark Side of Capitalism

The transition to capitalism brought poverty to English rural dwellers and other economic consequences. Thousands of English peasants became landless. Some found jobs in towns, creating a labor pool for fledgling industries, and some became rural craftsmen such as weavers, but many could not find steady work and became rural vagabonds. Whereas under feudalism people saw individual well-being as socially controlled, a product of the manor, under capitalism it became individually controlled: people were responsible for their own condition. Capitalism also undermined guilds as businessmen gave crafts production to displaced peasants and paid them for each item they made. In exploiting desperate peasants, businesses destroyed medieval concepts of economic justice. Eventually these trends spread to other western European societies. The great contrast between the few rich and the many poor, amplified by famine and the devastations of war, brought on uprisings in England, especially after the Civil War of the 1640s.

Life was increasingly dangerous and unhealthy for both rural and urban people. Between wars and rebellions, bandits prowled the roads and mercenary soldiers roamed the countryside, attacking merchant convoys and plundering villages. The cities were overcrowded and filled with beggars. Trash-filled streets, polluted water, the stench of human waste, and disease made life deplorable for most people. In the 1600s, one-third of London's children died before the age of one. Reflecting on the difficulties of coping with such misery, an observer in 1751 called gin the principle sustenance of more than 100,000 Londoners.

Redefining the Family

Family life and gender relations also changed in the Early Modern Era. For the growing middle classes of northern Europe, the nuclear family of parents and their children, which was rare in medieval times, increasingly became common. Unlike medieval times, when children were viewed as small adults, societies increasingly recognized childhood as a distinct phase of life, inventing toys and games for children and opening more schools, mostly for boys. However, half or more of children left their families by their early teens, many to become apprentices or servants with other families. The economic roles and status of women also shifted. In contrast to medieval times, when many women never married and also worked in a wide variety of occupations, western European women were now encouraged to look chiefly to marriage and motherhood; their place was in the home.

Women and Sexuality in the Early Modern Era

The experiences of women varied across Europe. For instance, many Dutch women enjoyed liberated lives, some becoming merchants. Elsewhere, some women also engaged in trade. The German Jewish merchant Glukel of Hameln (HAH-muhln) (1646–1724), the mother of eight, traveled widely to trade fairs and wrote memoirs of her experiences. But in most European societies, few women controlled enough financial resources to become major traders. Women's paid work and unpaid housework were increasingly devalued in much of Europe. But some women faced even worse problems as a fear of witchcraft spread throughout Europe and colonial New England in the Early Modern Era. For centuries, people had feared witches, who were thought to be capable of destroying crops and causing personal misfortunes. As wars and religious conflicts raged in the sixteenth and seventeenth centuries, official persecution of alleged witches provided a diversion. Many thousands of women, most of them single, were suspected of being witches and were executed, tortured, or banished from their communities.

Nonconformity to social standards faced increasing hostility. More restrictive views of sexuality led to punishment of women and men who defied convention. Often prompted by churches, governments became more concerned with regulating sexual and moral behavior, partly to encourage family life. Yet, many people ignored such laws, and premarital pregnancy rates ranged from 10 to 30 percent. In addition, Catholic and Protestant churches condemned homosexuality, and men or women engaging in homosexual behavior faced severe sanctions, including execution. Yet, laws were enforced erratically, especially in tolerant England and Scandinavia, and male homosexuals congregated in large cities.

Listen to a synopsis of Chapter 15.

CHAPTER 16

New Challenges for Africa and the Islamic World,
1450–1750

Learning Outcomes

After reading this chapter, you should be able to answer the following questions:

LO¹ How did the larger sub-Saharan African societies and states differ from each other in the sixteenth century?

LO² What were the consequences of African–European encounters in this era, especially the trans-Atlantic slave trade?

LO³ What factors made the Ottoman Empire such a powerful force in the region?

LO⁴ How did the Persian and Central Asian experience differ from that of the Ottomans?

Topkapi Palace Museum

> **❝** Warriors will fight scribes for the control of your institutions; wild bush will conquer your roads; your soil will crack from the drought; your sons will wander in the wilds. Yes, things will fall apart. **❞**
>
> —Igbo ancestral curse[1]

Confirming the Igbo curse, things fell apart for many Africans in the Early Modern Era. Among the many Africans caught up in unprecedented new challenges was Ayuba Suleiman Diallo (ah-YOO-bah SOO-lay-mahn JAH-loh). In 1731 the thirty-year-old educated son of a leading family in the West African kingdom of Bondu was captured by enemies while on a trading mission and sold to the British as a slave. Eventually he was shipped to Maryland, where he was put to work on a plantation growing tobacco. After an attempted escape, he was taken in by Thomas Bluett, an English entrepreneur who recognized both Diallo's talents and his connections to West African commercial life. Diallo's Islamic faith and ability to read and write Arabic reflected the influence of Islam and Arab traditions in parts of West Africa. Bluett emancipated Diallo and then took him to London and presented him at the English court. The British hoped he might help them to increase their commercial and slaving activity in the Senegambia, and he agreed to act as middleman in obtaining more slaves. Finally, after pledging friendship with the British, Diallo was able to return to Bondu and resume his life. Until his death in 1773, Diallo profited from his connection to British merchants as a trading partner. He had been both victim and beneficiary of the new economic forces of his times.

Ayuba Suleiman Diallo's story reflects the changing Atlantic world of the Early Modern Era. African life was transformed, in part because of contact with Europeans, whose presence in Africa gradually increased. The West African trading world that produced Diallo now included English, Portuguese, Dutch, and French companies seeking gold, gum, hides, ivory, and especially slaves. Diallo gained freedom quickly and eventually returned home, but the ancient Igbo

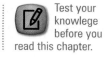

Test your knowlege before you read this chapter.

What do you think?

The overseas expansion of Europe during the Early Modern Era had little impact on Africa and the Middle East.

Strongly Disagree   *Strongly Agree*
1   2   3   4   5   6   7

<<**Glassblowers' Procession** The Ottoman rulers periodically had the members of several hundred occupational guilds in Istanbul parade before them, including storytellers, taxidermists, potters, and even executioners. This painting, from an illuminated manuscript finished around 1582, shows the glassblowers, some of them on a wheeled cart demonstrating their skills.

curse proved prophetic for the many other Africans who were shipped off as slaves.

Not all Africans were affected by European activities: some, like the Fulani, remained untouched by the various slave trades and other disruptive European activities and continued to pursue their ways of life as they always had. Still, Diallo's experience illustrates the expanding influence of Europe in Africa and the Americas during the early modern centuries. Encounters with Europe reshaped parts of Africa and drew them into an emerging Atlantic world, as first the Portuguese and then other Europeans established trading posts along the West African coast. Soon these trading posts, such as Goree Island, became centers for acquiring and shipping slaves. The Portuguese and Dutch also began to conquer and settle several African regions.

Growing European power also gradually affected some of the Islamic lands of the Middle East and Central Asia, though not to the same extent. By the 1500s, Islam had spread from the westernmost fringe of Africa to central Indonesia and the southern Philippines. Islamic political ideas, trade networks, and literary traditions linked many millions of people, and several large and dynamic Islamic states dominated much of the Middle East and South Asia, the successors to the great Islamic empires of earlier centuries. The powerful Ottoman Empire, which included much of western Asia, North Africa, and southeastern Europe, and a new Persian state, the Safavid Empire, had increasing connections of trade and conflict with non-Islamic societies. But while these Islamic societies experienced some changes, they also maintained long-standing traditions and remained largely autonomous.

> "For nearly two centuries, Timbuktu remained the greatest Islamic city in sub-Saharan Africa."

LO¹ Sub-Saharan African Societies

At the beginning of the Early Modern Era, African societies reflected considerable political, economic, and cultural diversity, and many flourished. Some, especially in West and East Africa, formed great empires and states, engaging in extensive long-distance trade, fostering intellectual debate, and connecting with the wider Eastern Hemisphere. Many people in the Sudanic region of West Africa and along the East African coast had adopted Islam. But many other Africans had decentralized political systems based on villages and religions mixing monotheism, polytheism, and animism. Whatever their ways of life and thought, many African societies possessed valuable human and natural resources that attracted Europeans as the era progressed, posing new challenges and changing Africa's relationship to the world.

Early Modern West African States

The last of the great Sudanic empires, Songhai (song-GAH-ee), became the major power in interior West Africa during the 1400s and flourished through much of the 1500s (see Map 16.1). From its capital of Gao (ghow) on the Niger River, Songhai built an empire stretching some 1,500 miles from east Interactive Map to west. The people of Songhai blended Islam with local customs: the women of Songhai and some other Islamic states in the Sudan held a high social position and enjoyed considerable personal liberty, much to the shock of Arab visitors. Many women engaged in small-scale commerce, and in some Sudanic cities, women were free to have lovers as they desired. Some Sudanic societies were matrilineal.

Timbuktu

The Songhai city of Timbuktu became a major terminus for the trans-Saharan trade that shipped to North Africa large supplies of gold and ivory as well as slaves for Arab and European markets. For nearly two centuries, Timbuktu remained the greatest Islamic city in sub-Saharan

Map 16.1
African States and Trade, 1500–1700

Some African states, such as Songhai, Kanem-Bornu, Benin, Lunda, Buganda, and Ethiopia, remained powerful in this era. West African coastal societies were increasingly drawn into world trade, while the East African coastal cities remained significant in Indian Ocean trade.

Map legend:
- Buganda
- Kongo
- Monomotapa
- Kingdom of Songhai, ca. 1500 C.E.
- Kingdom of Kanem-Bornu, ca. 1500 C.E.
- Hausaland
- Kingdom of Ethiopia
- Main coastal trading areas

© Cengage Learning

Africa. An early-sixteenth-century Arab visitor, Leo Africanus, reported that Timbuktu had "numerous judges, doctors of letters, and learned Muslims. The king greatly honors scholarship. Here too, they sell many hand-written books. More profit is had from their sale than from any other merchandise."[2] The Islamic University of Sankore at Timbuktu was modeled after the respected University of Cairo, and its faculty and the student body came from throughout the Islamic realm.

 History and Cultures of Africa (*http://www.columbia.edu/cu/lweb/indiv/africa/index.html*). Provides valuable links to relevant websites on African history.

But Songhai did not remain a dominant state in West Africa. After several strong kings ruled the empire, Songhai's leadership deteriorated and succession struggles emerged. In 1591, when an army from Morocco seized much of the Niger River territory from Songhai, the kingdom collapsed. The end of Songhai marked the end of the era of huge imperial states in the western Sudan.

Other West African States

Besides Songhai, other Sudanic and Guinea Coast societies exercised regional influence and flourished from trade. The Dyula (JOO-lah), a large Mandinka-speaking Muslim mercantile clan, became the most important trading group, with operations throughout West Africa. Dyula merchants moved goods such as gold and salt through the forest with caravans of porters, down the rivers in canoe fleets, and across the grasslands in donkey trains. Women usually dominated the village markets. In fact, many Sudanic and Guinea societies were matrilineal, and some had women chiefs or queens. The Igbo people of southeastern Nigeria worshiped female deities, and some had female leaders. Africans often venerated women elders for their wisdom and closeness to the ancestors.

Idrus Aloma and the Kanem-Bornu Kingdom

Several strong Islamic kingdoms and states arose to the east of the Niger River. Kanem-Bornu (KAH-nuhm-BOR-noo), centered on Lake Chad, had formed in the ninth century and prospered from trans-Saharan trade, especially from trading slaves to North African Arabs for

> "Several strong Islamic kingdoms and states arose to the east of the Niger River."

horses. The kingdom reached its height in the late 1500s and early 1600s under King Idrus Aloma (IH-dris ah-LOW-ma), who extended his territories northward deep into the Sahara and imported guns from the Ottoman Empire. A devout Muslim, Idrus Aloma reformed the easygoing local customs by imposing Islamic law.

The Hausa and the Trans-Saharan Trade

Among other flourishing West African trading states were the city-states of the Hausa (HOUSE-uh) people, of what is now northern Nigeria, eastern Niger, and southern Chad. Headed by kings, these fiercely competitive states dominated some of the trans-Saharan trade into the eighteenth century. Hausa cities were centers for trade and manufacturing cotton cloth and leatherwork, some of which was sold as far away as Europe. Places such as Kano (KAH-no) and Katsina also attracted Muslim scholars in the 1400s and 1500s, and Islam gradually became the dominant faith throughout the Hausa lands. But, in contrast to women in the patriarchal Muslim soci-

CHRONOLOGY

Africa and the Atlantic World, 1482–1750

1482	First Portuguese-Kongo encounter
1487	Portuguese discovery of Cape of Good Hope
1497	Vasco da Gama's first voyage to East African coast
1505	Portuguese pillage of Kilwa
1514	First African slaves to Americas
1507–1543	Rule of Alfonso I in Kongo
1526–1870	Trans-Atlantic slave trade
1652	Dutch settlement of Cape Town
1575	End of Portuguese technical assistance to Kongo
1591	Destruction of Songhai

Sankore Mosque Built in the fourteenth century, the Sankore Mosque in the Sudanic city of Timbuktu, a center of commerce and scholarship in the Songhai Empire, symbolized the spread of Islam in the region but also the adaptation of the faith to West African traditions, reflected in the mosque's unique architecture.

eties in the Middle East, Hausa women continued to play vital political and social roles. For instance, Queen Amina of Zaria (ZAH-ree-uh) extended her city's power while building effective walled defenses against rival states and raiders.

Trade on the Guinea Coast

Important non-Muslim states occupied the Guinea Coast from today's Ghana to eastern Nigeria. The Akan (AH-kahn) peoples of the Volta (VAWL-tuh) River Basin, farmers with a matrilineal social structure, were organized into several small states that prospered from mining and trading gold to the north. In western Nigeria, the Yoruba (YORE-a-bah) peoples developed a series of states, each based on a large city ruled by a king or prince. Yet, women also exercised political influence through the position of *Iyalode* (literally, "mother of the town"), elected by women to the council of chiefs. Many Yoruba towns served as both commercial and political centers and were ruled by elaborate bureaucracies. One great Guinea kingdom, Benin (buh-NEEN), in what is now south-central Nigeria, shared many cultural and political traditions with the Yoruba. European visitors in the 1500s and 1600s admired the prosperous society they encountered, including the capital city of wide streets and large wooden houses with verandas.

Europeans in West Africa

As Arab merchants did before them, the first European explorers and merchants in West Africa could tap into well-established trade networks and markets. At Guinala (gwee-NAH-la)—a Mandinka-governed district in what later became Guinea-Bissau (GIN-ee-bi-SOU)—the Portuguese encountered in 1591 a huge weekly market where more than 12,000 men and women gathered to trade. As one Portuguese merchant wrote, "All that is available in this land and in surrounding lands is offered for sale, that is, slaves, cloth, provisions, cows, and gold."[3] Undoubtedly, some of the merchants at Guinala were Dyula and Hausa.

Bantu Trading Cities and Kingdoms

By the sixteenth century, various Bantu peoples had settled much of eastern, Central, and southern Africa, and some were closely linked to the wider world. The closest ties to hemispheric networks were forged by various city-states along the East African coast, where Bantu settlers and Arab immigrants had created the Swahili (swah-HEE-lee) culture mixing African and Islamic traditions. For nearly two millennia, Indonesians, Indians, Persians, and Arabs had regular contact with East Africa, bringing ideas, products, technologies, and immigrants to enrich the African mosaic. The varied city-states, all thriving centers of trade, achieved considerable grandeur.

Three Traders This bronze plaque, from the sixteenth century, shows three Benin merchants, possibly appointed by the king to negotiate with the Europeans who were then arriving in the region. The merchant in the center holds a staff signifying his royal appointment and royal authority over commerce with non-Benin people.

Trade on the East African Coast

The golden age of the East African coast, with its royal court, mosques, and luxury goods, reached its peak from the twelfth through the fifteenth centuries. Ships from Arabia, Persia, and India regularly visited the coast, and Chinese voyagers explored the area in the early 1400s. East African city-states, such as Kilwa and Malindi, became a significant part of the great trading network around the Indian Ocean, a network generally dominated by seafaring Arabs and Indian Muslims. These Swahili ports functioned as trade centers, collecting goods from the African interior to be exchanged for Asian goods.

The Shona and the Ganda

Other major Bantu states emerged in south-central Africa. On the plateau bordering the great Zambezi (zam-BEE-zee) River, the Shona people flourished from gold mining, exporting gold as well as ivory to the Middle East and India through the coastal city-state of Sofala (so-FALL-a), the southernmost Swahili-speaking city. Swahili boats carried these exports from Sofala to Kilwa, where they were plugged into the international trade networks. By 1500 the once-great Shona kingdom of Zimbabwe (zim-BAH-bway) had collapsed and was replaced by several competing Shona kingdoms. Another Bantu people were the Ganda, who established a small kingdom, Buganda (boo-GON-da), in the 1500s just west of Lake Victoria. By the 1700s, Buganda had a well-developed bureaucracy and a powerful military, as well as an extensive trade network with the East African coastal cities.

The Kingdom of Kongo

In the Congo River Basin as well, several influential Bantu states flourished. The large Kongo kingdom arose in the 1300s along the Congo River in what is today northern Angola and western Congo. Kongo became one of the first great African states to be visited by European explorers. Described by the first Portuguese visitors as powerful and having many vassals, the Kongo kingdom ruled a population of around 2.5 million people by 1500. To the east, the Luba (LOO-buh) and Lunda kingdoms were established around 1350 and 1600, respectively, and built substantial empires in the southern Congo. Their location far inland and their access to trade networks running through Central Africa allowed them to remain independent of European power into the nineteenth century.

The Xhosa and the Zulu

Various Bantu-speaking groups had been migrating into southern Africa for centuries. Most of the Bantu societies formed small states led by chiefs and combined farming with cattle herding. The largest societies, the Xhosa (KHO-sa) and Zulu, mostly lived along or near the Indian Ocean coast of what is today South Africa. Some non-Bantus also lived in the area. Around 50,000 Khoikhoi (koi-koi) pastoralists, also called Hottentots (HOT-n-TOTs), lived in and around the Cape of Good Hope at Africa's southern tip. They were a branch of the Khoisan (KOI-sahn) peoples, long resident in southern Africa, who also included the !Kung (Bushmen) of the Kalahari Desert.

Africa in the Hemispheric System

Africans had long played key roles in the Eastern Hemisphere economic system, but the rapid rise of European power between 1450 and 1600 soon presented them with serious challenges and reshaped their role in the world. Sub-Saharan Africans were vulnerable to European and Arab power, because they did not enjoy the same environmental advantages and interregional connections that had benefited parts of Eurasia and North Africa. By 1500, various Eurasian and North African societies had invented or borrowed from each other cutting-edge technologies such as printing and gunpowder weapons, and they had also created more productive economies. Most sub-Saharan Africans never encountered the Chinese technology and Indian mathematics that spurred Middle Eastern and European development. In addition, much of sub-Saharan Africa had marginally fertile soils, scarce exploitable minerals, and few good harbors.

Africa the Unknown

Although West and East Africans had been major suppliers of gold, ivory, and other commodities to the Middle East and Europe for centuries, only a few Europeans and Africans had made direct contact with each other. During the Intermediate Era, several Italian merchants braved the Sahara Desert to reach the Sudanic trading cities by camel caravan, and the few remaining Christian Nubian kingdoms in the central Nile valley may have maintained a few links with Christian leaders in Europe. But by the 1300s, these kingdoms had been conquered by Muslims, and Christianity died out in Nubia. Only in remote Ethiopia, where the Amharic (ahm-HAHR-ik) people had adopted a form of Christianity related to Eastern Orthodoxy early in the Common Era, did the religion flourish. Ethiopia's state, led by kings who traced their ancestry to the ancient Hebrew king Solomon, had survived 1,500 years in the highlands of Northeast Africa, where it built splendid churches, often on steep mountainsides. But the expansion of Islam cut off the Ethiopians from Europe. Because of these intermittent contacts, Africans and Europeans knew little of each other.

The "Opening" of Africa

Direct contacts between Europe and Africa only began in the early 1400s, when the Portuguese began exploring down the West African coast in search of gold, Christian allies against Islam, and a hoped-for sea route to China and Southeast Asia, the sources of the silk and spices that were so valued in Europe. The Europeans' ignorance of black Africa helped create the myth of Darkest Africa, those areas of the African continent least known to Europeans but, in European eyes, awaiting to be "opened" to the "light of Western civilization." At the same time, Europeans also perplexed Africans. According to the traditions of Niger River Delta peoples in what is today southern Nigeria, the first appearance of white men around 1500 shocked the local fisherman who spotted them: "Panic-stricken, he raced home and told his people what he had seen; whereupon he and the rest of the town set out to purify themselves, [to] rid themselves of the influence of the strange thing that had intruded into their world."[4]

The Beginning of the African Slave Trade

Eventually, after they began establishing control in the Americas, Europeans became particularly interested in

> ❝ Europeans did not invent the African slave trade, but they soon transformed it. ❞

Darkest Africa
Those areas of the African continent least known to Europeans but, in European eyes, awaiting to be "opened" to the "light of Western civilization."

racism
A set of beliefs, practices, and institutions based on devaluing groups that are supposedly biologically different.

> "As they visited more of Africa, the Portuguese shifted from exploration to exploitation."

enslaving Africans. Slavery existed in many African societies, just as it had in other areas of the world, and in East Africa, over the course of twelve centuries, perhaps 10 to 15 million enslaved Africans were taken to the Middle East and beyond by Muslim slave traders. In Europe, societies such as Spain, Portugal, Italy, and France enslaved many of their own people in the 1500s, making them work as domestic servants, plantation laborers, and prostitutes. Thus slavery had no particular "racial" identity yet, but the growing knowledge of Africa combined with the forging of plantation economies in the Americas focused more attention on Africa as a source of slaves. Europeans did not invent the African slave trade, but they soon transformed it.

LO² European Imperialism and the Trans-Atlantic Slave Trade

As Portuguese ships began making ever-longer journeys down the West African coast in search of gold, the encounters that followed fostered trade, conflict, and destruction. By the later 1400s, the Portuguese had made contact with the Kongo, located near the Atlantic coast, which they eventually colonized. Then during the 1500s, the Portuguese became active in East Africa, undermining the coastal trading cities and affecting interior societies. Meanwhile, the Dutch gained a foothold in South Africa. These developments contributed to a new global system of trade and empire that created a wide gulf in wealth, power, and development between Africa and Eurasia by the 1700s.

 Explore new encounters in the early modern world in this interactive simulation.

Racism—a set of beliefs, practices, and institutions based on devaluing groups that are supposedly biologically different—can be traced to early Western relations with sub-Saharan Africa and the exploitation of Africans. The most prominent factor in these relations, the trans-Atlantic slave trade, fostered both commerce and cultural change in West Africa.

The Portuguese and African Encounters

The Portuguese were the first Europeans to have direct encounters with many African societies. Having the world's most advanced and well-armed ships, the Portuguese began exploring the West African coastline in the early 1400s. By 1471 they had reached as far as the modern nation of Ghana on the west coast, where they tapped into the gold trade from the Akan states, calling the region the Gold Coast. As they visited more of Africa, the Portuguese shifted from exploration to exploitation. They colonized the Cape Verde Islands and the nearby coastal region of Guinea-Bissau, and they established various trading forts to obtain gold, ivory, and slaves. In the 1480s, the Portuguese began a long relationship with the prosperous Kongo kingdom of south-central Africa, sending Christian missionaries and skilled craftsmen. Over the next century, they expanded their operations in Africa.

Bartolomeu Dias and Vasco de Gama

Soon Portuguese explorers sailed farther south and then east. In 1487 Bartolomeu Dias (ca. 1450–1500) led an expedition that sailed round the Cape of Good Hope, the southern tip of Africa, into the Indian Ocean, intensifying Portuguese interest in both Africa and Asia. Dias believed that he had discovered the best route to eastern and southern Asia, and his explorations soon intensified contact with South African peoples. More Portuguese exploration followed, eventually reshaping the hemispheric trade system. In 1497 four ships commanded by the zealous Portuguese captain Vasco da Gama (VAS-ko dah GAH-ma) (ca. 1469–1525) left Portugal. Surviving hurricanes and mutinies, da Gama and his remaining crew sailed south around the Cape and then up the East African coast, visiting the Swahili trading cities of Mozambique, Mombasa, and Malindi. Da Gama was disappointed to discover that the merchants in these cities had no interest in his meager trade goods. Shifting his strategy, da Gama engaged a skillful pilot in Malindi and sailed eastward across the Indian Ocean to southwestern India. Even though the Indians told him his merchandise could not compete with better-made products from India, China, Indonesia, and Persia, da Gama had located the sea route to the East. He acquired a small cargo of spices

A Kongolese King Protests the Slave Trade

In the early sixteenth century, the Kongolese king Alfonso I, who had embraced Catholicism and welcomed the Portuguese to his kingdom, wrote more than twenty letters in Portuguese to the king of Portugal, creating the earliest known African commentary on European activities in Africa. Some letters complained of aggressive Portuguese activities and asked that the king halt the slavers from obtaining Kongolese citizens. They also requested educational, medical, and religious assistance from Portugal. The letters, usually polite in tone, revealed gradually diminished hopes as friendly early encounters turned into Portuguese plunder and exploitation. These are excerpts from several letters written in 1526.

Sir, Your Highness should know how our Kingdom is being lost in so many ways that it is convenient to provide the necessary remedy, since this is caused by the excessive freedom given by your factors and officials to the men and merchants who are allowed to come to the Kingdom to set up shop with goods and many things which have been prohibited by us. . . .

And we cannot reckon how great the damage is, since the mentioned merchants are taking every day our natives, sons of the land and the sons of our noblemen and vassals and our relatives, because the thieves and men of bad conscience grab them wishing to have the things and wares of this Kingdom which they are ambitious of; they grab them and get them to be sold; and so great, Sir, is the corruption and licentiousness that our country is being completely depopulated, and Your Highness should not agree with this nor accept it as in your service. And to avoid it we need from . . . [your] Kingdoms no more than some priests and a few people to teach in schools. . . . It is our will that in these Kingdoms there should not be any trade of slaves nor outlet for them. . . . And as soon as they are taken by the white men they are immediately ironed and branded with fire. . . .

It happens that we have continuously many and different diseases which put us very often in such a weakness that we reach almost the last extreme; and the same [thing] happens to our children, relatives and natives owing to the lack in this country of physicians and surgeons who might know how to cure properly such diseases. And as we have got neither dispensaries nor drugs which might help us in this forlornness, many of those who had already been confirmed and instructed in the holy faith of Our Lord Jesus Christ perish and die; and the rest of the people in their majority cure themselves with herbs and breads and other ancient methods, so that they put all their faith in the mentioned herbs and ceremonies if they live. . . . And this is not much in the service of God. . . . We beg of you to be agreeable and kind enough to send us two physicians and two apothecaries and one surgeon, so that they may come with their drug-stores and all the necessary things to stay in our kingdoms, because we are in extreme need of them all.

Thinking About the Reading

1. What do these examples of letters tell us about Portuguese slaving activities and growing power in the Kongo?
2. What did Alfonso believe his kingdom needed from the Portuguese?
3. Why were the Portuguese unlikely to grant Alfonso's requests?

Source: Basil Davidson, ed., *African Civilization Revisited: Chronicles from Antiquity to Modern Times* (Trenton, N.J.: Africa World Press, 1991), pp. 223–226. This excerpt has been reprinted with the permission of Africa World Press in Trenton, NJ.

and precious stones and returned home in triumph. Soon the Portuguese set up trading bases around the Indian Ocean and attempted to limit the maritime commerce of their Arab, Ottoman, Persian, and Indian rivals.

The Portuguese in the Kongo

On the Atlantic coast, the Portuguese had a major impact in the Kongo and the surrounding region. During the early sixteenth century, an enlightened,

Christian king, Alfonso I (r. 1507–1543), ruled the Kongo. He outfought rivals for power after the death of the former king and, the Portuguese claimed, credited his victory to the intercession of a Christian saint, St. James, the brother of Jesus. Initially, the Kongolese were open to foreign influence: the monarch adopted Christianity and clearly wanted to modernize the kingdom along Western lines with Portuguese help. He might have succeeded had the Portuguese not become far more interested in acquiring enslaved Kongolese.

The Portuguese began shipping slaves from Kongo in 1514. Slavery was traditional in Kongo, where owners had a responsibility to treat slaves well. Even Alfonso, who was opposed to slavery in principle, was willing to sell slaves to the Portuguese in exchange for goods and services he regarded as essential to his kingdom's progress. However, in the 1500s, the Portuguese established a colony in Brazil, across the Atlantic from Kongo, and began setting up plantations to grow sugar and other tropical crops, multiplying the need for enslaved labor. Alfonso and his successors permitted only a modest trade in slaves, so the Portuguese resorted to forceful tactics. Alfonso repeatedly asked the Portuguese to halt their armed raids, which were damaging and depopulating his country, but his pleas were unsuccessful (see Witness to the Past: A Kongolese King Protests the Slave Trade). He eventually grew disillusioned with the rapacious Portuguese and wary of their ulterior motives.

> 66 Slavery was traditional in Kongo, where owners had a responsibility to treat slaves well. 99

Queen Nzinga and African Resistance

Halting their cooperation with the Kongo government in 1575, the Portuguese turned to outright conquest. After setting up a base at Luanda (loo-AHN-duh) in 1580, they began a war against a fringe state in the Kongo region, Ndongo (uhn-DONG-go), whose ruler was called the Ngola, hence the Portuguese name for the region, Angola (ahng-GO-luh). Like the Kongolese, the Ndongo warriors were skilled but armed only with arrows, lances, and swords against Portuguese guns, cannons, and steel swords. But the Portuguese encountered a formidable adversary in Queen Nzinga (en-ZING-a) of Ndongo (1624–1663), one of the most remarkable women in African history. A brilliant diplomat, eloquent debater, and skilled warrior who dressed as a man, she shrewdly negotiated with the Portuguese to preserve her kingdom, demanding to be treated as an equal with Europeans. After years of diplomacy alternating with war, the pragmatic Nzinga recognized a lost cause and made peace, a victim of Portugal's superior arms and ruthless quest for gold and slaves. Late in life, she adopted the Christian faith and abandoned her harem of men, many of them slaves. After her death, Ndongo became the foundation for the Portuguese colony of Angola.

In the early seventeenth century, the Portuguese and groups of displaced Africans they had hired and armed began raiding southern Kongo. The Christian Kongolese kings sent a series of moving appeals to the papacy for help, but they were mostly ignored. Kongo soon became engulfed in a long series of civil wars, which only generated more captives to be sold as slaves. During the late 1600s and early 1700s, an unusual Kongolese woman, Dona Beatriz Kimpa Vita, led a spiritual movement combining Catholic and traditional elements in an attempt to reform Kongolese political life. She threatened many powerful government and church interests, however, and in 1706 Catholic missionaries had her burned at the stake. Eventually most of the old Kongolese kingdom was incorporated into Portuguese Angola, and Christianity gradually lost support. The Kongolese kings had cooperated with the Portuguese in good faith, but the Portuguese proved unworthy allies.

Made increasingly vulnerable by occasional warfare and deteriorating economic conditions, Angola and Kongo became deeply enmeshed in the trans-Atlantic slave trade, which, by the later 1600s, had grown much larger than the Arab and Black Sea slave trades. Angola and Kongo were the major suppliers of slaves to Brazil—indeed, the largest single source of enslaved men and women to the Americas, accounting for some 35 to 40 percent of the total. The decline of Kongo allowed its rival, the Lunda kingdom, to expand westward and engage the Portuguese in trade, exchanging slaves and ivory for woolen cloth and guns. These guns gave the Lunda kings control over much of the regional trade.

Portuguese activity extended into the eastern side of Africa after Vasco da Gama's first voyage. In 1502 da Gama led a squadron of twenty ships to supervise an occupation of the trading ports of Mozambique and Sofala. To establish commercial control of the East African coast, Portuguese forces attacked several major Swahili trading cities, plundering them of

Queen Nzinga This drawing by an Italian priest, Father Cavazzi, shows the formidable Queen Nzinga of Ndongo, in Angola, sitting on her throne, wearing a crown topped by a Christian cross while giving an order to attendants.

their riches and burning some of them to the ground. Their East African conquests gave the Portuguese bases from which to extend their power in the Indian Ocean. During the next several decades, the Portuguese conquered or established control of several trading ports in the Persian Gulf, India, Malaya, Indonesia, and China, and they also seized the Spice Islands of eastern Indonesia, the main source for the priceless clove and nutmeg supplies. Using ruthless methods, such as attacking and sinking Arab, Persian, and Indian ships, they were able to gain partial control of the Indian Ocean maritime commerce.

The Decline of Portuguese Influence

The Portuguese became nominal masters of the East African coast, controlling key ports such as Mombasa, but they never really prospered, because the city-states declined into poverty. Merchants quit coming, and many traders fled elsewhere. The fanatically Christian Portuguese suppressed the Islamic Swahili culture and destroyed much of its literary heritage. The Portuguese dominated the coast and what commerce remained for a century, but they gradually lost their ability to control the Indian Ocean maritime trade. By the mid-seventeenth century, their influence was waning all over the coast except in Mozambique. Arabs from Oman, on the northeast Arabian coast, overran the Portuguese settlements in the late 1600s, established a sultanate on Zanzibar (ZAN-zuh-BAHR), and supervised the lucrative slave and ivory trade to the Middle East and India.

New Challenges for the Shona States and Ethiopia

Eventually the Portuguese sought influence inland from the East African coast. In the early 1500s, they

> "The available solution to the labor shortage, African slaves, provided the lowest available cost option and thereby created the racial basis of trans-Atlantic slavery."

built forts at the old coastal trading cities of Sofala and Mozambique as a base for locating and acquiring the rich source of gold on the plateau occupied by the Shona people. Portuguese adventurers seeking wealth began moving up the Zambezi River to the fringes of the largest Shona kingdom, then known as Monomotapa (MO-no-mo-TOP-a). The Portuguese gradually took control of the lower Zambezi valley and its gold trade, establishing a colony later called Mozambique. They dispatched Catholic missionaries upstream, but these had little success in finding converts. In addition, because the Portuguese died in large numbers from tropical diseases such as malaria, the Shona were able to hold out for many years. By 1628, however, a decaying Monomotopa had become a virtual Portuguese puppet state, but in trying to control the gold trade, the Portuguese ended up destroying it. Monomotapa dwindled in size and was eventually overrun by neighboring African states, which forced the Portuguese out of the plateau. Eventually the goldfields became less productive. The Portuguese then began concentrating their efforts on coastal Mozambique. Those Portuguese who settled there, especially in the Zambezi valley, tended to marry African women and adopt many aspects of local culture and customs.

Ethiopian Civil War

The Portuguese also intervened briefly in Ethiopia, where Christians maintained traditions that had been forged many centuries earlier. In the 1520s, the Portuguese sent a small force to help Ethiopians successfully repulse an invasion by Muslim neighbors backed by the rising Ottoman Turkish Empire. In the early 1600s, the Portuguese renewed their contacts with Ethiopia, sending Jesuit missionaries to convert the king, Susenyos (soo-SEN-yos) (r. 1607–1632), from the state church to Catholicism. At Portuguese urging, Susenyos began an effort to reform Ethiopian society and the Ethiopian Church. When both the church and the Amharic population resisted, civil war erupted. In the end, the pro-Portuguese king abdicated, the missionaries and other Portuguese were expelled, and Ethiopia went back to its old ways and faith.

South Africa and Dutch Colonization

European activity also affected the peoples living at the southern tip of Africa, where social, political, and economic developments differed greatly from most of the rest of Early Modern Africa. In 1652 the Dutch established a settlement, Cape Town, on the Cape of Good Hope, to provision the Dutch ships sailing between Europe and Indonesia. After a government was set up, Dutch settlers arrived in Cape Town and took up farming. At first they traded with the local Khoikhoi people for meat, but because they had guns, they soon began seizing what they wanted. In 1659 the Khoikhoi rose against the Dutch. After crushing the poorly armed resistance, the Dutch declared that the Khoikhoi "could not expect to get the land back."5 Eventually the Dutch enslaved or killed all the Khoikhoi living near the Cape and began imposing white supremacy rule over Africans in the lands they controlled. To obtain a labor supply for their farms and households, the Dutch imported slaves from Madagascar, Mozambique, and Indonesia. Soon enslaved Africans and Asians far outnumbered the whites as the agricultural economy developed. Masters and slaves lived close together, but whites always held a politically, legally, and economically superior status.

The Boers and "Trekking"

Continued Dutch immigration led to rapid population growth, and some Dutch, chafing at governmental rules, began looking eastward for new land to settle. The Dutch settlers, later called Boers ("farmers"), began a movement not unlike the Bantu migrations centuries earlier. To survive, many Boers adopted the sheep- and cattle-herding economy of the Bantus. As some Boers expanded east along the coast and into the interior in search of farmland in the 1700s, they encountered the Xhosa and later the Zulu peoples. These encounters—plus Boer attempts to take over the land—produced a series of deadly

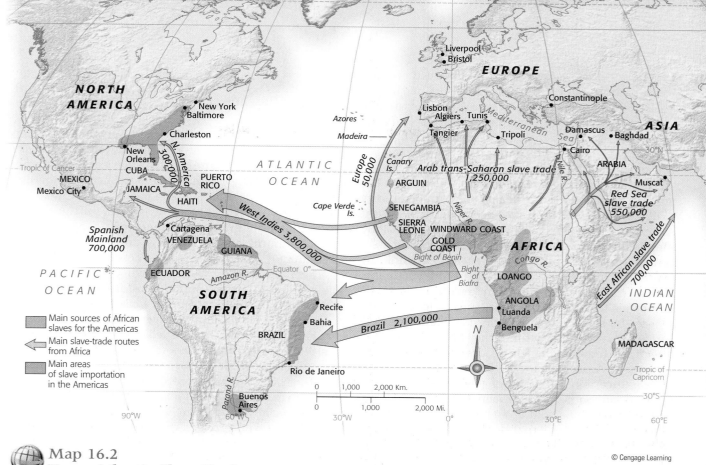

© Cengage Learning

Map 16.2
Trans-Atlantic Slave Trade, 1526–1870

While the Arab-run slave trade from West and East Africa to North Africa and western Asia continued, the trans-Atlantic slave trade was far larger in scope. Millions of Africans were transported across the Atlantic, the greatest number ending up in Brazil and the West Indies. The majority of slaves came from what is today Angola, Congo, and Nigeria.

conflicts that lasted for nearly half a century. The migrations of Boer settlers in cattle-drawn wagons, known as **trekking**, became a tradition, occurring whenever a Boer group wanted to flee government restraints.

The Trans-Atlantic Slave Trade

The economic growth of the American lands colonized by Europeans created a tremendous market for labor that could not be filled by free men and women, coerced Native Americans, or the small number of available European slaves. Newly opened American farms and mines badly needed labor after the massive decline of the Native American population during European conquest and colonization. The available solution to the labor shortage, African slaves, provided the lowest available cost option and thereby created the racial basis of trans-Atlantic slavery. Europeans may have more easily rationalized the ruthless exploitation of Africans because of their different culture and appearance.

trekking
The migrations of Boer settlers in cattle-drawn wagons into the interior of South Africa whenever they wanted to flee government restraints.

The Slave Trade Expands

In the early 1600s, the English, Spanish, French, Dutch, and Danes began following the Portuguese by obtaining enslaved people in West Africa and shipping them across the Atlantic to meet the limitless demands of the new American plantation economies (see Map 16.2). Because the West African coastal region was so fragmented politically, resistance to European slavers

Interactive Map

was difficult. Furthermore, the region contained a population that was highly skilled in both tropical agriculture and mining, the enterprises for which labor was needed in the Americas.

Profits from the slave trade soared along with the volume of transported Africans, and European forts to obtain, store, and ship slaves soon dotted the West African coast from Senegal down to Angola. Many merchants bought slaves at various ports and then transported them all to one West African holding center, such as Accra (ah-CRAW) in today's Ghana, for sale to slave ships, a system known as "bulking." Europeans traded cotton goods, guns, iron, rum, and tobacco for slaves, often with the cooperation of local African chiefs, but sometimes they acquired Africans directly by force, as the Portuguese did in the Kongo. How many Africans were originally enslaved for the trade is uncertain, but they probably added up to some 25 to 30 million people. Between one-third and one-half survived to be sold at auction in the Americas. Most studies conclude that between 9 and 12 million Africans were landed in the Americas over four centuries. Perhaps one-third were women. Millions of slaves died in holding cells in West Africa or on the notorious Middle Passage, the slaves' journey by ship from Africa to the Americas. The trans-Atlantic slave trade reached its peak between 1700 and 1800, with perhaps 100,000 Africans per year being shipped to the Americas.

Horrors of the Middle Passage

Both the Middle Passage and the fate of the enslaved Africans who survived the trip were horrific. Depending on the weather, the trip from Kongo to Brazil took one month and from West Africa to the Caribbean and North America around two months. The slaves on board faced harsh and cruel conditions. Olaudah Equiano (oh-LAU-duh ay-kwee-AHN-oh), an Igbo seized in Nigeria in the 1750s, described the intolerable stench of the hold, which made him ill, and of floggings on the deck for misconduct that sometimes resulted in death, after which the bodies were thrown overboard. Many slaves committed suicide before reaching the Americas. Equiano recounted a case when two other Igbos, in despair, jumped overboard while chained together. Many crews installed nets along the sides of slave ships to catch jumpers. There were also many mutinies, in which slaves attempted (occasionally with success) to gain control of the ship, such as the celebrated 1839 incident aboard a small Spanish ship, the *Amistad,* bound from Sierra Leone to Cuba.

Those who survived the hardships of the Middle Passage faced a bleak future in the Americas. When they arrived, they were sold without regard to personal ties. Equiano wrote of his landing in Barbados: "Without scruple, are relations and friends separated, most of them never to see each other again."[6] The majority of slaves were sold to sugar, cotton, or coffee plantations and endured brutal, exploitative working conditions.

The Middle Passage This painting from the era vividly shows the overcrowded conditions on the ships that carried African slaves, packed like sardines, on the "Middle Passage" across the Atlantic to the Americas. Such brutal conditions resulted in the deaths of many slaves and eventually prompted reformers to demand the end of the slave trade.

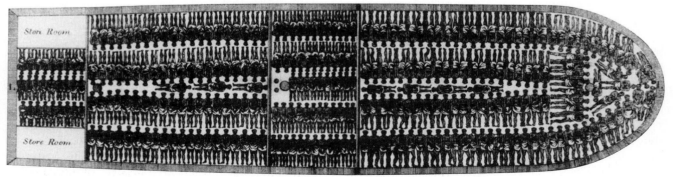

From a Parliamentary Report

Rationalizing the Slave Trade

During the slave trade, Europeans quickly developed feelings of superiority to Africans that resulted in racism. In 1589 the English adventurer Richard Hakluyt described Africans as "a people of beastly living, without a God, law, religion, or common wealth."[7] The English had long seen the color black as signifying "soiled, dirty, foul, malignant, deadly, sinister." Now they contrasted white and black skin color as connoting, as one observer put it, "purity and filthiness, virginity and sin, virtue and baseness, beauty and ugliness, beneficence and evil, God and the devil."[8] Some Westerners thought slavery helped Africans by exposing them to Western values and Christianity.

The Slave Trade and African Societies

The impact of the trans-Atlantic slave trade on Africa varied from region to region. Some coastal regions of West and Central Africa succumbed to chronic raiding and kidnapping as well as occasional warfare, in an "enslave your neighbor or be enslaved" syndrome. European guns traded for slaves made some regions dangerous, leaving plundered villages and broken families. Some peoples, among them Kongolese, Angolans, Yorubas, Igbos, and Akans, were disproportionately transported to the Americas, and their societies were badly disrupted. By linking parts of Africa closely to Europe and the Americas, the slave trade also created an Atlantic System, a large network that spanned western and Central Africa, the east coast and southern region of English North America, the Caribbean Basin, and the northern and eastern coastal zones of South America.

The Impact of the Slave Trade on Africa

The slave trade fostered economic change in Africa. While their major target was slaves, Europeans also coveted gold and cloth, and Western merchants soon monopolized the African coastal trade. But some Africans and people of mixed African and European ancestry also flourished as merchants and slave traders. Others refused to cooperate in slave trading and dealt with Europeans on their own terms. Hence, until the 1700s, the kings of Benin, located inland, prohibited the sale of male slaves and instead obtained the firearms needed to protect the state by trading cotton textiles, pepper, ivory, and beads. Some states prospered by cooperating with the slave trade at the expense of their neighbors, like Dahomey (duh-HO-mee), which formed in the seventeenth century as a dependency of a Yoruba kingdom and grew powerful in the eighteenth century as a major supplier of slaves.

The most far-reaching changes were found in the coastal regions stretching from Senegambia down to Angola, sometimes reaching several hundred miles inland. Some states, such as Kongo, declined, while others, such as Ashante, rose in power. Except in the interior of Angola, most West and Central African societies far from the coast had little direct contact with the European slavers. On the other hand, the Arab slave trade badly disrupted some East African regions, even reaching as far inland as the eastern Congo River Basin. The Sudan region, such as the Hausa states, remained a source of slaves for North Africa.

The activities of Europeans had a long-term impact on Africa. The trans-Atlantic slave trade created economic imbalances that hindered the evolution of local industries and integrated Africa into the world economy as a supplier of resources. The exchange was not entirely one way: American food crops, such as corn and peanuts, became important to African diets, and the slave trade spurred some African states, such as Dahomey, to develop commercially.

 **A Voyage to New Calabar River in the Year 1699** Learn about the slave trade in West Africa, from a Frenchman on an English slave-trading expedition.

Early Imperialism and Colonialism in Africa

One of the main results of European intrusion was imperialism, the control or domination, direct or indirect, of one state or people over another. Often imperialism led to colonialism, government by one society over another society. A few areas, such as Angola, Mozambique, and South Africa, became Western colonies. But the full-blown Western colonial scramble for Africa only began with rapid industrialization in Europe, which contributed to the end of the slave trade in the 1800s but accelerated the need for natural resources for commercial products.

The heritage of racism made Africans and their descendants in the Americas a permanent underclass, treated with contempt by people of European ancestry. Racism became a pervasive ideology supporting bad treatment of particular groups. The first Europeans to encounter great African states like Benin, Kongo, and Kilwa in the late 1400s and early 1500s were awed by their prosperity and marveled at how even the poorest were treated with dignity. By the 1700s, those views had changed profoundly.

> "From their base in central Anatolia, the Ottoman Turks gained power over much of the once-great Byzantine Empire in the 1300s."

LO³ The Ottomans and Islamic Imperial Revival

The Islamic societies of the Middle East, the large region including North Africa and western Asia, did not experience the jarring transitions felt by many Africans during the Early Modern Era. While European nations established supremacy of the seas, Islamic states remained major land powers. The greatest of these, the Turkish Ottoman Empire, began in 1300 and survived until 1923, eventually ruling much of southeastern Europe, the western fringe of Asia, and much of North Africa, including Egypt. By the 1700s, however, the Ottomans and other Middle Eastern states were suffering from chronic warfare, poor leadership, a growing rigidity, and a superiority complex in relationship to the upstart Europeans. Their decline came as Europeans were on the rise.

The Ottoman Empire: Government and Economy

From their base in central Anatolia, the Ottoman Turks gained power over much of the once-great Byzantine Empire in the 1300s. The Ottoman conquest of the Byzantine capital, Constantinople, in 1453 demonstrated conclusively the power of Islamic society, as the capital of Orthodox Christianity was transformed into Muslim-ruled Istanbul. By 1512 the Ottomans controlled all of Anatolia and what is today Bulgaria, Greece, Albania, Serbia, and much of Romania. Between 1514 and 1517, the Ottomans defeated Persian forces and added Syria, Lebanon,

Palestine, and Egypt to their domains. During the sixteenth century, they controlled the Mediterranean, even raiding coastal Spain and Italy.

....

Suleiman the Magnificent

The Ottoman golden age came under the leadership of Sultan Suleiman (SOO-lay-man) the Magnificent (r. 1520–1566), a just, lawful man but also a merciless conqueror to his enemies. Under Suleiman, the Ottomans pushed north of the Danube River and into the eastern Balkans, defeated the Hungarians, and besieged Vienna. They also gained control of Egypt and then the North African coast. Suleiman's empire now stretched from Algeria to the Persian Gulf and from Hungary to Armenia (see Map 16.3). But the Ottomans never controlled much of the Arabian Peninsula, enabling independent sultanates such as Oman to extend their own power to the East African cities. Omani Arabs and other coastal Arabs remained active in the Indian Ocean trade network.

 Interactive Map

CHRONOLOGY

The Middle East, 1500–1750

1501–1736	Safavid dynasty in Persia
1514–1517	Ottoman conquest of Syria, Egypt, and Arabia
1520–1566	Reign of Ottoman sultan Suleiman the Magnificent
1529	First Ottoman siege of Vienna
1554–1659	Sa'dian dynasty in Morocco
1682–1699	Ottoman wars with Habsburg Austria
1715	Beginning of Russian conquest of Turkestan
1722	Afghan invasion of Safavid Persia
1736–1747	Rule of Nadir Shah in Persia

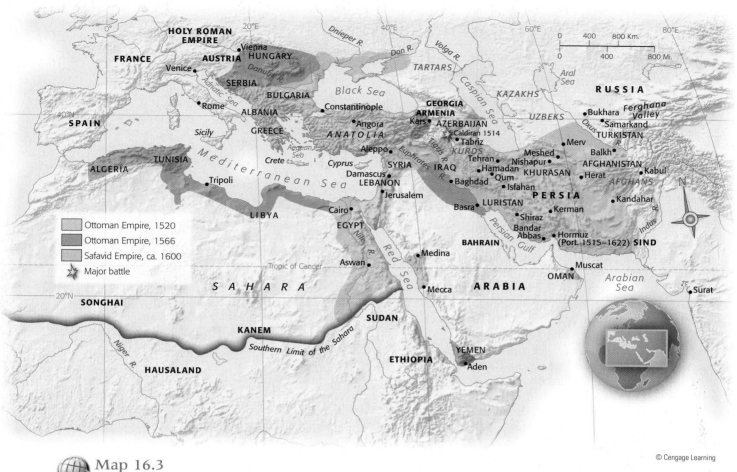

🌐 Map 16.3
The Ottoman and Safavid Empires, 1500–1750

By the later 1500s, the Ottoman Empire included large parts of western Asia, southeastern Europe, southern Russia, and North Africa. Their major rivals, the Safavids, controlled Persia and parts of Iraq, the Caucasus, Afghanistan, and Central Asia.

Suleiman's reign revived the Islamic glory that had faded with the downfall of the Iraq-based Abbasid Empire in the 1200s. Suleiman and other Ottoman sultans claimed to have restored the caliphate, the governing system of early Islamic times that was thought to be ordained by God and that blended political and religious power. In 1538 the Ottoman ruler could boast proudly: "I am God's slave and sultan of this world. I am head of Muhammad's community."9 Suleiman's position at the center of an extensive international political system often involved him in European conflicts, but his broad empire also gave him large commercial benefits. Spices and other products from India, Southeast Asia, and China were shipped to the Ottoman-ruled port of Basra (BAHS-ruh), at the head of the Persian Gulf, and then transported to Ottoman-controlled markets for sale to European merchants. Ottoman ships also controlled the Black Sea trade.

Ottoman Imperialism

Ottoman political success owed much to military power and immigration. The Ottomans adopted gunpowder weapons, especially cannons, which were often built and operated by mercenary Hungarian Christians in Ottoman service. These weapons equaled the best of European gunnery until the late 1600s. The Ottomans also developed an effective navy, often led by Muslim refugees from Spain. These refugees included Jews, who were expelled from Spain in the 1400s and 1500s and who brought valuable expertise and international connections.

> "Istanbul and other major cities served as centers for transregional trade, and artisan and merchant guilds with elected leaders became central to urban life."

Ottoman imperialism supported an effective state led by very able men. The Ottomans chose officials based on merit, allowing Arabs and other non-Turks to serve in the government and military, often in high positions. The sultans governed through an imperial council headed by a prime minister. The ruling elite lived in luxury, residing in beautiful palaces with large harems and many servants. Christian princes remained the major landowners in Ottoman Europe, and the Ottomans especially recruited administrators and soldiers from Christian peoples. At regular intervals, the sultan's agents swept through the provinces selecting Christian youth for training. Essentially becoming slaves, they were required to embrace Islam. The most talented were sent to the palace school to be trained for administration, while the other conscripts joined the elite military corps of infantrymen known as janissaries ("new troops"), who lived in barracks and were not allowed to marry but were well paid.

Under this dynamic state, the Ottoman commercial economy flourished. Istanbul and other major cities served as centers for transregional trade, and artisan and merchant guilds with elected leaders became central to urban life. But the dynamic international trade mostly involved luxuries such as Indian textiles and Chinese porcelain, and the empire was largely self-sufficient in necessities such as food.

Ottoman Society and Culture

The diverse Ottoman society thrived in this era. The empire's multiethnic population, about evenly divided between Christians and Muslims, was large, containing some 50 million people at its peak and dwarfing the largest European country of the time, France, which had less than one-third of the Ottoman total. The size and diversity of the Ottoman population posed administrative challenges, however. Following the pattern in most multicultural Muslim states, the sultans governed the Jewish, Greek Orthodox, and Armenian Christian communities through their own religious leaders. Each religious group had its own laws and courts and enjoyed a toleration rare in the world at that time. The Ottomans attracted many immigrants, among them European merchants and technicians and Christian peasants from the Balkans. Ottoman cities, where varied peoples mixed, were vibrant: urban social life revolved around coffeehouses, public baths, and taverns.

Women in the Ottoman Empire

Women had a higher status in Turkish society than in Arab tradition, and this pattern continued under the Ottomans. Women in the royal family exercised considerable political clout, and upper-class women often owned land, managed businesses, and controlled wealth. Throughout the empire, the courts protected women's rights to inheritance and property. Turkish society was patriarchal, but older women had control of both the young males and females in their families. Yet, women could also be abused by men and more easily divorced, and women who were suspected of illicit sexual activity could be punished or killed.

Ottoman Arts and Sciences

The Ottomans stimulated literary and artistic creativity, often with royal patronage. Istanbul attracted artists and artisans from all over Europe and the Middle East. The Sultan Mehmed II (1432–1481) arranged with the Venetians to have their most famous artist, Giovanni Bellini, spend two years (1479–1480) decorating his palace with paintings. Suleiman the Magnificent welcomed humanist thinkers from Italy to the capital. Ottoman poets wrote ornate verse in Persian or Turkish, and architects, such as the highly innovative Pasha Sinan, designed beautiful domed mosques and other public buildings. Artists also produced beautiful painted tiles and pottery.

 Read about Pasha Sinan, an Ottoman architect, and one of the most innovative in world history.

Although the Ottomans pursued science, by the 1700s they were falling behind some rival states. Ottoman medicine remained vibrant, and scholars published many volumes on astronomy, mathematics, and geography. Muslim geographers also produced world maps more sophisticated than those of

Europe, but the emphasis on law and theology rather than science in Ottoman higher education inhibited technological innovation.

Conservative Islam and the Sufi

The Ottomans drew the religious establishment close to the state, which was headed by a leader who saw himself as anointed by God. Religious leaders emphasized rote learning and memorization rather than analysis of the sacred texts, and some punished deviation from orthodoxy. Furthermore, Islamic leaders were increasingly conservative and hostile to technological innovation. Yet various mystical Sufi sects, seeking a personal experience of God, had large followings. Seyh Bedreddin (SAY beh-DREAD-en), a famous mystic, founded an order of practitioners known as dervishes, who feverishly danced to achieve a trance-like state. Although some Sufi sects operated with official approval and financial support, others were suspected of political disloyalty and of modifying too many Islamic principles.

> 66 Eventually the Ottomans faced new challenges that undermined the state and reduced the size of the empire. 99

Ottoman Challenges and Decline

Eventually the Ottomans faced new challenges that undermined the state and reduced the size of the empire. Well into the 1600s, however, Ottoman armies continued to effectively wage battles against European and Persian rivals. Only in 1683, when Austria and its allies repulsed the last Ottoman attack of Vienna, did European observers begin to perceive the Ottoman decline. In the next few years, the Ottomans were pushed out of many areas in eastern Europe, and by 1699 the Ottomans were forced to cede Hungary to the rival Habsburgs. Although in the early 1700s the Ottomans did reclaim some of these territories, Ottoman power was no longer feared. Some of the decline resulted from failing Ottoman military practices and technology: the discipline among the janissary military forces weakened, and eventually the whole training system for young men was eliminated. The Ottomans' technology also fell behind. The development of Ottoman weaponry, especially artillery, stagnated just as European military technology was rapidly improving.

Internal Conflicts

Problems of governing also stressed the empire. Compared to China or the emerging European states, the Ottoman state was not very centralized, and imperial control was difficult to maintain. In the early 1500s, the Ottomans had conquered the Kurds—a Sunni Muslim ethnic group occupying a large region from what is today eastern Turkey, northern Iraq and Syria, and northwest Iran—and many Kurds increasingly resented Turkish control. At the same time, many Arabs and Balkan Christians who once welcomed Ottoman rule for providing stability and justice began to think of their own peoples as nations repressed by the empire. Ottoman citizens also disliked higher taxes, growing corruption and poverty, and a bloated bureaucracy.

Meanwhile, in Istanbul the ruling elite was able to exercise more power over a weak or incompetent sultan. Potential successors to the throne were often kept locked up in the palace as prisoners until chosen to take the throne. Ottoman sultans had increasing difficulty controlling restless provinces in North Africa and western Asia. Occasional rebellions were met by brute force, but during the 1600s, some areas broke away from the empire. By the mid-1700s, Ottoman influence was deteriorating in large parts of the empire, and the Russians were putting pressure on Ottoman territory north of the Black Sea.

External Challenges

While beginning to deteriorate from within, the Ottomans also faced increasing economic and military challenges from western European nations, the Habsburg realm, and Russia. Increasing European participation in Asian trade weakened Anatolia's historic position as a middleman, undermining economic conditions, and Ottoman rulers did little to support the empire's merchant class, most of whom were Greeks, Armenians, and Jews. With its own industries growing less competitive, the once self-sufficient empire became increasingly dependent on imports from Europe. Western merchants thus gradually bested their Ottoman rivals, reducing the Ottomans to a secondary region in the emerging global trade system. Large Western trading firms, armed with both great capital and better business methods and backed by their own governments, became increasingly influential.

The resurgence of European power led to fierce debates in the empire. Reformers became interested in European products and customs and favored the importing of some European technology. But reformist forces struggled for influence against conservatives, who preferred the status quo, and reformers also found it difficult to overcome an Arab and Turkish superiority complex regarding the once-upstart Europeans.

> "Eventually Persians came to view Shi'ism as central to Persian identity."

caused many Sunni families to emigrate to the Ottoman Empire and elsewhere. Eventually Persians came to view Shi'ism as central to Persian identity.

LO⁴ Persia, Morocco, and Central Asia

Other Islamic societies from Morocco to Central Asia also underwent significant changes during the Early Modern Era. East of the Ottoman Empire, in Persia, a Shi'ite dynasty known as the Safavids became an internationally recognized power. Persian leaders, thinkers, and officials had long played a significant role in Islamic society, and Persian, widely spoken by elites from Istanbul to Delhi, India, was the closest thing to a hemispheric language. The Safavids developed a prosperous economy linked to international trade and fostered a brilliant artistic culture. In northwest Africa, Morocco became notable for its military prowess. Meanwhile, northeast of Persia, various Islamic societies in Central Asia emerged from the ashes of the Mongol Empire but struggled to maintain the ancient Silk Road trade networks.

The Safavid Empire

The Safavid dynasty came to power in Persia at the beginning of the sixteenth century. It was founded by a Turkish group from what is today Azerbaijan (AZ-uhr-bye-ZHAHN) in the Caucasus Mountains. The Safavids belonged to a militant Sufi order that had shifted from the Sunni to the Shi'a branch of Islam. From their base in Azerbaijan, the Safavid movement grew rapidly in alliance with other Shi'ites in the region.

Ismail and the Conquest of Persia

In 1501, the Safavids, led by a charismatic thirteen-year-old boy, Isma'il (1487–1524), invaded and conquered Persia, then a center of Sunni practice and home to a variety of small Sunni Turkish and Persian states. Isma'il, who claimed descent from Mohammad and Sassanian princes, and his dedicated followers wanted to unite the region both politically and religiously. Within ten years, the Turkish Safavids controlled all of Persia. Isma'il thought of himself as an agent of God and mandated the conversion of the Persians to Shi'ism, which took a long time and

The Safavids established a strong political system, but their imperial prospects were limited. Safavid armies rode on horseback and viewed guns as both awkward and unmanly, an attitude that left them vulnerable to the gunpowder weapons possessed by their Portuguese and Ottoman enemies. The Portuguese seized and held the strategic port of Hormuz (hawr-MOOZ), on Persia's southeast coast, for decades in the 1500s. In 1514 the Ottomans drove deep into Safavid territory, acquiring Safavid lands in Armenia and Anatolia. The battle losses to the hated Ottomans demoralized Safavid military leaders and stalled expansion.

The Safavid Zenith under Shah Abbas

Safavid rule reached its peak under Shah (king) Abbas (ah-BAHS) I (r. 1587–1629), who consolidated his power by manipulating or executing his enemies. His capital, Isfahan (is-fah-HAHN), became a beautiful, tree-shaded city of some 1 million people, filled with 160 mosques, 273 public baths, many parks, and a great bazaar that one visitor described as "the surprisingest piece of Greatness in Honor of Commerce that the world can boast of."¹⁰ Shah Abbas planned the city with the help of Shaikh Baha al-Din Muhammad Amili, a famed Persian philosopher, judge, poet, astronomer, and engineer. Abbas maintained good relations with European powers, welcoming ambassadors from a half-dozen European nations and importing English advisers to help train his military forces and manufacture modern cannon and muskets, marking a change in Safavid military strategy. With these weapons, Shah Abbas waged successful wars against the invading Ottomans and Uzbeks and recaptured Hormuz from the Portuguese. For their part, Europeans sought Persia as an ally against their mutual Ottoman enemy. To earn revenue for the government, Abbas and his successors also gradually placed more land under state control. Peasants worked on land owned by the king and received a share of the crop for their labors.

The Safavid Trading Network

The Safavid economy flourished for several centuries. Persia remained a major exporter of silk, a trade increasingly dominated by Armenian settlers from the Caucasus, who also operated the lucrative gold and silver crafts industries. Networks extending all over the Eastern Hemisphere, and long-distance trade by land and sea, had flowed through Persia since ancient times and continued during the Safavid era. Safavid trade with Europe gradually increased: during the 1600s, English, Dutch, and French merchants visited Persian ports to obtain silk, carpets, brocades, cotton, wool, and other products. Foreign merchants from all over were attracted by the great bazaar that developed in Isfahan, where artisans produced fine carpets, textiles, metalwork, and ceramics. Some 25,000 people worked in Isfahan's textile industry.

Armenians, who flourished from Safavid trade, also competed fiercely with Dutch, English, Portuguese, and Indian merchants in parts of Eurasia. The Armenian network radiated outward from New Julfa (JOOL-fa), a mostly Armenian city built by the Safavids near Isfahan. A central council of Armenian merchants in New Julfa coordinated local councils in the Armenian trade diaspora. Armenians shared a common culture and the Christian religion, and their merchants played a key role in the overland trade from India to Central Asia and the Middle East. In the 1660s, New Julfa merchants also negotiated trade agreements with Russia, which allowed them to bypass the Ottoman Empire and reach northern Europe through Russia and the Baltic.

Women in Safavid Society

Safavid society was patriarchal, with men having more rights than women, who were often restricted to the home and expected to veil themselves when they went out of the household. Yet, as in Ottoman Turkey, Persian women often had more influence than was the case among Arabs. Royal women in harems raised royal sons and also at times tried to shape government policies. As in classical Persia two millennia earlier, some women became wealthy and owned land and businesses.

Safavid Culture and Decline

The Safavids patronized art and literature as well as commerce. The major cities, especially Isfahan, became centers for artists, poets, writers, and craftsmen. Safavid artists became especially famous for

> ❝ By the eighteenth century, the Safavid sultans had become weaker, the Shi'ite religious officials had become stronger, and the empire's economy had declined. ❞

miniature paintings, which combined the harmony of color with the rhythm of design, often to illustrate great Persian literature. In 1525 the Safavid sultan commissioned an ambitious project to produce an illustrated version of an old epic poem recounting Persian history. The completed version contained 258 paintings by many artists. This was also a golden age for crafting carpets, textiles, and ceramics, for which Persians became famous. Carpet weaving became both an art form and a national industry, with government-run factories producing a range of silks, brocades, velvets, and other fabrics.

Transformations in Shi'ism

Persian Shi'ism underwent some changes over the years. The Safavids encouraged passion plays and religious processions commemorating the tragic death of the prophet Muhammad's grandson, Husayn, in the Battle of Karbala in 680, the event that split the Islamic community. Sufi influence gradually declined, while religious teachers increasingly emphasized their own authority over that of the Quran and other sacred texts. The result was increasing belief in the infallibility of Islamic leaders, who enjoyed greater power than was common elsewhere in the Islamic world. Even the shahs claimed to represent divine power, giving the state a theocratic cast, but tensions over religious power between the shahs and Shi'ite leaders continued to simmer.

Safavid Decline and the Rise of Nadir Shah

By the eighteenth century, the Safavid sultans had become weaker, the Shi'ite religious officials had become stronger, and the empire's economy had declined. Unable to control the clergy or trust their sons who were plotting for the throne, later Safavid rulers often turned to alcohol for comfort, and corruption grew rampant. In 1722, Afghans seized Isfahan and then repulsed Ottoman forces invading from the west. Isfahan, once one of the world's most beautiful cities, was nearly destroyed. In 1736, a new Persian leader, Nadir Shah (1688–1747), led a force that drove

Letter to Shah Ismail of Persia The Ottoman sultan Selim I, a Sunni Muslim, threatens war against the Persian shah, his Shi'a enemy.

Persian Tiles As Isfahan flourished under Shah Abbas I, wealthy Persians decorated their homes and mosques with tiles featuring scenes, often gardens, painted by local artists. This tile painting shows a woman at leisure in her garden, holding a vase while her servant offers her fruit.

out the Afghan invaders. Casting aside the remaining Safavids, he launched a vigorous new state. His armies went on the offensive, marching into Ottoman lands and north India, where his forces plundered the major city, Delhi. But Nadir Shah's ruthless tactics antagonized many, and economic collapse exposed millions to famine. After ill-advised efforts to reconvert the Persians from Shi'a to Sunni Islam, Nadir Shah was assassinated in 1747. In the decades to follow, Persia was again divided into smaller states, and Western pressure intensified.

Moroccan Resurgence and Expansion

While the Ottomans and Safavids dominated much of the Islamic world, the Moroccans on the far northwestern fringe of Africa forged a strong state, conquered an empire, and linked themselves to various networks of exchange. Moroccan society comprised Berbers, Arabs, and an influential Jewish community, many of whom had been forced out of the Iberian Peninsula. Some Spanish Muslims joined Moroccan military forces, while Jews invigorated commercial life. During the 1400s and 1500s, ships from Europe regularly visited Moroccan ports, exchanging metals, textiles, spices, hardware, and wine for leather, carpets, wool, grain, sugar, and African slaves.

The Sa'dian Dynasty of Morocco

During the later 1400s and early 1500s, Moroccan encounters with the Portuguese eventually brought the Sa'dians to power. Portugal's cultivation of sugar on the Atlantic islands began undermining the Moroccan economy, and the establishment of Portuguese forts along the coast posed a military threat. In response, growing mystical Sufi movements organized tribal coalitions to resist the Portuguese. In 1554 the Sa'dians, a Moroccan family who claimed descent from the prophet Muhammad and had fought against the Portuguese forts, conquered much of Morocco with the support of Sufi and tribal leaders, launching a new era.

The Sa'dians ruled Morocco until 1659, forging a powerful military and a regime quite different from those of the Ottoman territories. The greatest Sa'dian leader, Sultan al-Mansur (man-SOOR) (r. 1578–1603), recruited foreign mercenary soldiers who knew how to use firearms. By 1603 the army of 40,000 included 4,000 Europeans, 4,000 Spanish Muslims, and 1,500 Turks, armed with modern artillery. The Netherlands and England, both rivals of the Portuguese, sold Morocco ships, cannons, and gunpowder. The resulting military power allowed the Moroccans to capture the Portuguese ports along the Atlantic coast, and in 1591 Moroccan forces seized the Songhai city of Timbuktu, gaining control of the trans-Saharan trade linking West and North Africa. In the later 1600s, the Sa'dian system broke down, and a new Moroccan dynasty, the Alawis (uh-LAH-wees), who also claimed descent from the prophet Muhammad, came to power in 1672. This dynasty still rules Morocco today.

Central Asia and Russian Expansion

The most direct and long-lasting confrontations between Muslims and Europeans resulted from Russian imperial expansion into Central Asia and Ottoman territories. Islam had a strong foothold in Central Asia, and many places had large Sufi communities where Sufi masters often gained political power. But as the remnants of the Mongol Empire broke up into various rival societies by the 1400s, Russia capitalized on the political vacuum to extend its own power first into Siberia and then into the Black Sea region and Central Asia. While several western European nations built maritime empires, Russia transformed itself into a great land-based territorial empire. A key role in this Russian expansion was played by the Cossacks (KOS-aks), tough, hard-drinking adventurers and fierce warriors from southern Russia who were descendants of Russians, Poles, and Lithuanians fleeing serfdom, slavery, or jail.

Russian Expansion to the East and South

The expansion east across sparsely populated Siberia began in the 1500s and accelerated during the seventeenth and eighteenth centuries. By 1637 Russian explorers had reached the Pacific Ocean. In 1689, conflict with China forced the Russians to temporarily abandon settlements in the Amur (AH-moor) River Basin north of China (see Chapter 18), but they continued to add other Siberian territory. The Russians also began acquiring territories on their southern fringe, coveting access to the Black Sea and the Straits of Bosporus bisecting Istanbul, through which Russian ships could reach the warm Mediterranean. The southward thrust meant confronting the Tartars (TAHR-tuhrz), Muslim descendants of Mongols and long a threat to the Russians. In the 1400s and 1500s, Tartars, Russians, Ottoman Turks, Poles, and Lithuanians fought for control of today's southern Russia. Between 1552 and 1556, the Russians seized the Tartar state of Kazan (kuh-ZAN), slaughtering many residents in the capital, and then gradually gained more land. Russian commerce benefited from Russia's new domination of the northern Caspian Sea.

Russian Conquests in Central Asia

Soon the Russians turned toward Muslim Central Asia, settled largely by Turkish peoples and often known as Turkestan. By the early 1700s, the Russians had gained territory occupied by the Kazakhs (kah-ZAHKS), a pastoral people who had once ruled a large area, and by 1864 they controlled all of the Kazakh lands to the eastern border with China. They then targeted the Silk Road cities, where the Uzbeks (OOZ-beks)—a people of mixed Turkish, Persian, and Mongol ancestry—proved a formidable threat. But the Sunni Uzbeks, enemies of the Shi'ite Safavics, eventually were weakened. When Safavid hostility closed Persia to Uzbek trade, the prosperity of the Silk Road cities declined, and the roads saw fewer travelers. Eventually the Uzbeks and their neighbors earned smaller revenues and their merchants lost profits. In the early 1700s, the Persians gained control of some Uzbek territory and much of Afghanistan, and by the later 1800s, an expanding Russia was able to conquer all of southern Turkestan.

Listen to a synopsis of Chapter 16.

CHAPTER 17

Americans, Europeans, Africans, and New Societies in the Americas,

1450–1750

Learning Outcomes

After reading this chapter, you should be able to answer the following questions:

LO¹ How did encounters between Europe and the Americas increase in the 1500s?

LO² How did Europeans conquer and begin settling the American societies?

LO³ What were the major consequences of European colonization of the Americas?

LO⁴ What impact did the trans-Atlantic slave trade and emerging Atlantic system have on European and American societies?

> **"**Truly do we live on earth? Not forever on earth; only a little while here. Although it be jade, it will be broken. Although it is gold, it is crushed.**"**
>
> —Aztec poem on the meaning of life, ca. 1500[1]

In the sixteenth century, Spanish colonists in Mexico trained an Aztec historian, Chimalpahin Cuahtlehuanitzin (chee-MAL-pin QUAT-al-WANT-zen), how to read and write in the Western alphabet. Using this alphabet but writing in his native Nahuatl (NAH-waht-ell) language, the Aztec historian created one of the best records of the Mexican world at the moment of contact. He wrote of Aztec military triumphs over neighboring people, and also of the reports that began to reach Tenochtitlan in 1519 of pale-skinned men in huge boats arriving on the eastern coast from the sea, where gods might come from. In fact, Aztec legends claimed that, centuries earlier, a Toltec king driven into exile by rivals had become a god, Quetzalcoatl (kate-zahl-CO-ah-tal), who promised to return some day seeking revenge. These strange men on the coast seemed suspiciously godlike: they dressed in metal, had unfamiliar but lethal metal weapons, rode on large animals as tall as houses—and they arrived around the year some believed that Quetzalcoatl would return.

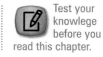

Test your knowlege before you read this chapter.

Cuahtlehuanitzin wrote that, nearly three decades earlier, 13-Flint in the Aztec calendar (1492 in the Gregorian calendar) had been an unusually bad year, bringing an eclipse of the sun, volcanic eruptions, and widespread famine. The Aztec philosophy of life understood such occasional setbacks, but the Aztecs were not prepared for the troubles the Europeans would provoke. The leader of the pale men was the Spanish explorer Hernán Cortés. The invaders arrived in the Aztec lands, Cuahtlehuanitzin remembered, when a terrible and unknown disease, smallpox, began killing off the people. And within two years, these men from afar, with horses, metal armor, and gunpowder weapons, had conquered the Aztec Empire.

The first Europeans to arrive in the Americas claimed to have discovered a "new world," but it was actually an old one, long populated by a mosaic of peoples. The voyages of Christopher Columbus and

Courtesy, Banco de Mexico

<<**A Mestizo Family** The intermarriage of Europeans and Indians was common in Latin America, especially in Mexico. This Mexican painting, by the eighteenth-century artist Las Castas, shows a Spanish man, his Indian wife, and their mixed-descent, or *mestizo*, daughter.

the conquests of such adventurers as Cortés in Mexico often destroyed long-existing American societies and reshaped them, in reality *creating* a "new world." In fact, the whole Western Hemisphere changed. During the 1500s, the Spanish and Portuguese conquered and colonized large areas of what we now call Latin America. A century later, in North America and the Caribbean, the English, French, and Dutch followed, gradually extending their power. As a result of these incursions, few regions experienced more changes than the Americas. Later, European exploration in Southeast Asia also led to the first encounters between Europe and the diverse island societies of the Pacific Ocean.

The transitions that resulted from European encounters with Native Americans affected both sides of the Atlantic. Among the most important consequences was a complex global exchange of crops, animals, peoples, and cultures, while diseases carried from the Eastern Hemisphere set off a demographic disaster for Native American peoples. The societies that emerged from the European colonization of the Americas reflected diverse influences from all over the Atlantic world. Perhaps most important, in some regions of the Americas a plantation economy developed that engaged enslaved Africans and their descendants in agonizing circumstances.

LO¹ Early American–European–Pacific Encounters

American peoples had developed a wide variety of societies, economies, and styles of governing by the fifteenth century, but they faced a great challenge from the coming of the Europeans. Christopher Columbus

> "By 1500 the Aztecs, based in central Mexico, were the most powerful Mesoamerican society, and the Incas, centered in central Peru, controlled most of the Andes region."

began the historic change in 1492. In his wake, various European nations first explored and then conquered, colonized, and settled the entire Western Hemisphere, drawing the Americas into commercial, travel, and religious networks. The exploration of the Americas also spilled over into the Pacific Ocean, though few Pacific islanders encountered the West in this era.

American Societies in 1500

In 1500 the Western Hemisphere contained many societies with distinctive institutions, customs, and survival strategies. Those who lived by hunting, gathering, and fishing could be found in the North American Great Plains, the Pacific Northwest coast, Alaska, northern Canada, and some of the tropical forest regions of Central and South America. Other peoples developed small-scale farming, especially in eastern North America, parts of the North American desert and Amazon Basin, and southeastern Brazil.

The Meso-American Empires

For millennia the most complex Native American societies flourished from intensive farming in Mesoamerica (Mexico and northern Central America) and the Andes region of western South America. By 1500 the Aztecs, based in central Mexico, were the most powerful Mesoamerican society, and the Incas, centered in central Peru, controlled most of the Andes region. The Aztec state, through military conquest by a strong army and well-organized government, completed its empire building in 1428. But the Aztecs only loosely controlled the various peoples in their empire, and by the early 1500s, they faced mounting military confrontations with rivals. Cruel Aztec imperialism, including the widespread use of human sacrifice, had created enemies, some of whom were later willing to cooperate with the Spanish to overthrow Aztec power. The Incas had completed the conquest of their empire in 1440: it was larger than the Roman or Han Chinese Empires of the Classical Era, stretching nearly 2,500 miles north to south, much of it above 8,000 feet in altitude. The Inca state was the most dynamic and integrated of all the American states.

CHRONOLOGY

American Societies and European Discoveries, 1400–1524

1428–1521	Aztec Empire
1440–1532	Inca Empire
1492	Landing in Bahamas by Columbus
1494	Treaty of Tordesillas
1497	John Cabot's landing in North America
1500	Portuguese claim of Brazil
1513	Balboa's sighting of Pacific Ocean
1519–1521	Ferdinand Magellan's circumnavigation of globe
1524	French claim of Canada

Cultures in Decline

Probably in part as a result of climate change, some Native American societies had long passed their peak by 1500. By 1440 the last Maya states of Central America had collapsed, but some 5 to 6 million Maya-speaking people, living mostly in villages, remained as examples of a once-vibrant society, more than 2,000 years old. In North America the mound-building and trade-oriented Mississippian culture had reached its peak in the 1100s, and the major Mississippian town, Cahokia (kuh-HOE-key-uh), had been deserted by 1250. The once-vast Mississippian trading system was in steep decline by the 1400s, by which time the Anasazi (ah-nah-SAH-zee) and other societies of the Southwestern desert had already abandoned their major settlements.

Flourishing Native American societies besides the Aztecs and Incas remained, however, such as the Taino (TIE-no) in the Caribbean islands and the diverse farming peoples along the Atlantic coasts of North America and Brazil. While the first European settlers wrongly considered the Americas to be largely empty land, some

> **Probably in part as a result of climate change, some Native American societies had long passed their peak by 1500.**

regions were densely populated. By 1492 the population of the Western Hemisphere probably numbered between 60 and 75 million people, but because of many millennia of isolation from the Eastern Hemisphere, American peoples had no immunity to the diseases brought by Europeans and later African slaves. Native Americans also had no metal swords or firearms to resist Europeans, rendering them doubly vulnerable.

Bridging the Atlantic Barrier

The Atlantic Ocean was the major barrier between the hemispheres, but Europeans steadily overcame the challenge. In the later tenth century C.E., some Norse Vikings sailed west and established small farming settlements in several glacier-free coastal valleys in southern Greenland. By around 1000, a few of these hardy Norse, perhaps blown off course, reached the Canadian coast and built a small village in Newfoundland, but abandoned it soon thereafter, largely because of conflicts with local Native Americans. The Greenland Norse, however, apparently sent occasional trading and lumbering expeditions to eastern Canada for several hundred years. The Greenland settlements also collapsed by 1450, perhaps as a result of deforestation and colder climates that made the already difficult farming impossible.

The Norse may not have been the only people from the Western Hemisphere to spot the North American coast before 1492. The winters of the Little Ice Age in Europe brought poor harvests and reduced fish catches along Europe's Atlantic coast, pushing some desperate fishermen farther from home. For many years, European and Moroccan fishermen had worked the waters of the North Atlantic in search of cod, whales, and sardines. Perhaps a few of the fishermen saw North America, but if there were any landings, they apparently went unreported in Europe.

Different motives, including the quest for riches, national glory, and Christian converts, encouraged other Europeans to venture out into the Atlantic. While early Portuguese expeditions concentrated on the African route to the East, others, led by Christopher Columbus, hoped to sail westward from Europe to Asia. Contrary to myth, many educated people in Europe accepted that the earth was round and hence could be circumnavigated.

Arawak Women This woodcut, made in the sixteenth century, shows Arawak women on a Caribbean island preparing tortillas and stew.

Courtesy of John Carter Brown Library at Brown University

Columbus's Voyages to the Americas

The first explorers to brave the Atlantic directly from Europe with the purpose of reaching Asia came under the Spanish flag, beginning with Christopher Columbus. Columbus (1451–1506), born in the Italian port of Genoa, had lived for many years in the Portuguese capital, Lisbon, where he married Donha Felipa Moniz. She died soon after giving birth to their son, Diego, but the marriage gave Columbus social status and access to her family's navigational charts and records. Soon Columbus, inspired by the writings of the thirteenth-century Italian adventurer Marco Polo, began planning to sail to China to find the sea route to the silk- and spice-rich lands of China and Southeast Asia, but his inaccurate maps vastly underestimated the size of the earth and the distance to Asia.

Columbus eventually convinced the Spanish monarchs, King Ferdinand and Queen Isabella—fresh from their final triumph over the last Muslim state in southern Spain—to finance his voyages of exploration in hopes of establishing direct ties to Asia. Commanding ships far smaller than the great junks of the Chinese explorer Zheng He in the early 1400s,

Columbus surveyed much of the Caribbean and some of the South American coast in four voyages over the next decade, and believed that he had discovered outlying regions of Asia. When Ferdinand and Isabella realized he was wrong, they were at first disappointed. America was a heartbreaking obstacle on the route to eastern Asia.

On his first voyage in 1492, Columbus encountered the Taino, an Arawak (AR-uh-wahk)-speaking people who lived on Caribbean islands (see Map 17.1). When Columbus and his crew sailed into the Bahamas, they were greeted by curious Taino islanders. The Taino proved friendly, and they may have desired to cultivate a potential ally.  Interactive Map

Even before the arrival of the Spanish, they had often had to resist incursions by the Caribs (KAR-ibs), a more warlike Native American group that had originated in South America.

Taino Society

The Taino had a flourishing society; they smoked cigars, slept in hammocks, possessed a little gold, and some of them lived in

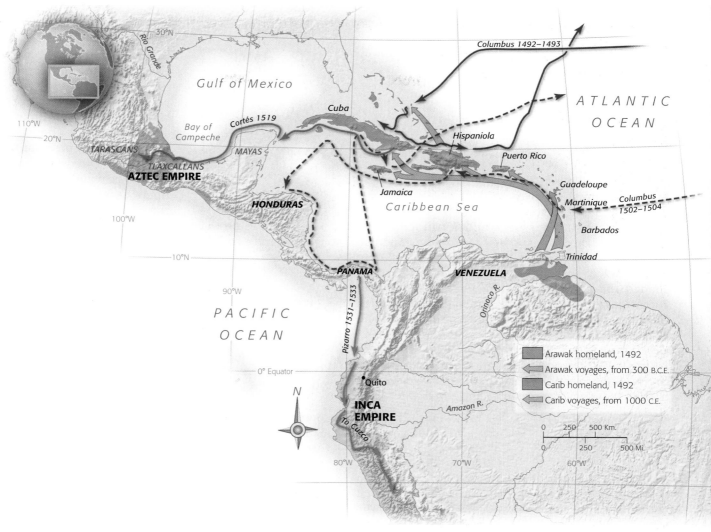

Map 17.1
The Americas and Early European Exploration

The several voyages across the Atlantic led by Columbus explored the Caribbean Basin and set the stage for Spanish conquest of many American societies, most notably of the Aztec and Inca Empires.

sizeable towns built around Mesoamerican-style plazas and ball courts. They combined fishing with highly productive cultivation of corn and manioc, and they carried on extensive interisland trade in large canoes that were not much smaller than Columbus's ships and capable of holding up to 150 people. The women did the farming and often served as community leaders, a status that confounded the Spanish. Columbus developed favorable views of the Taino, seeing them as innocent children of nature: "They are a loving and uncovetous people. They love their neighbors as themselves."[2] Later, however, when Columbus encountered Taino noncooperation or armed resistance to Spanish demands, he modified his views.

Hispaniola

Columbus then moved onto the island he called Hispaniola (HIS-puhn-YO-luh), today the home of Haiti and the Dominican Republic but then dominated by six Taino chiefdoms. Leaving a small colony of Spaniards there, Columbus began his return voyage to Europe by way of Cuba, which Columbus believed might be China. There he dispatched a small party, led by a Jew who spoke Hebrew, Chaldean, and Arabic, to search the interior for, and possibly communicate with, the Chinese ruler. They returned only with some mysterious dried leaves called *tobacos*, which local people smoked. Columbus and his crew sailed back to Spain with six

Taino Indians from the Bahamas to present at court. He was greeted as a hero and promoted to admiral.

The Treaty of Tordesillas

Although he did not find China, Columbus's discovery of the wind patterns that could push ships back and forth across the Atlantic launched a new era of exploration. Spanish authorities quickly planned a second voyage and, to counteract a possible Portuguese challenge, persuaded the pope to issue an order, the Treaty of Tordesillas (tor-duh-SEE-yuhs) in 1494, that divided the newly discovered Atlantic lands into Spanish and Portuguese spheres. Ultimately, the treaty gave Spain the rights to most of the Americas, while the Portuguese received Africa and Brazil. Both Iberian countries promised the pope that they would evangelize the "heathen" peoples they encountered.

Taino Exploitation

During his four voyages, Columbus explored much of the Caribbean region. He brought Spanish colonists with him on his second voyage in 1493 and established on Hispaniola the first permanent European settlement in the Americas. The success of the Spanish colony depended on exploiting the Taino through forced labor. Estimates of the Taino population in the Caribbean in 1492 range from 100,000 to 1 million, but within thirty years all of the Taino on Hispaniola, and many elsewhere, had been wiped out. The Hispaniola colony Columbus governed was a failure economically, and he returned to Spain in 1496. On his third voyage, in 1498, Columbus found Trinidad and the Venezuela coast. Queen Isabella allowed Columbus one final voyage to find a strait that might lead to India. This expedition explored the coast of Central America, from what is today Honduras to Costa Rica. Although Columbus encountered a Maya trading raft he thought might be Chinese, he also began to speak of the Caribbean islands as the "West Indies" as separate from the eagerly sought "East Indies" (India and Southeast Asia). After he and his crew were shipwrecked for a year on Jamaica, he returned to Spain and died in 1506, a broken man.

Eventually some Europeans began referring to the Native Americans as "Indians," a European name

> "Columbus's encounters inspired others, and exploration soon became a multinational effort involving the English, French, Portuguese, and Spanish."

that confuses American peoples with those of India. Because of this, some scholars and activists prefer terms such as "Native American" or "First Nations" to Indian. The term *America* derives from an Italian merchant, Amerigo Vespucci (1454–1512), who claimed to have made several voyages to the Western Hemisphere. His letters to powerful European princes described two separate continents in a "new world" that was soon known as "Amerigo's land."

The Continuing Search for Wealth

Columbus's encounters inspired others, and exploration soon became a multinational effort involving the English, French, Portuguese, and Spanish. By 1525 a series of European expeditions had explored the Atlantic and Caribbean coasts of the Americas from eastern Canada to the southern tip of South America. Some explorers sought to enrich themselves and the European monarchs who sponsored them, while others hoped to gain God's favor through Christian missionary activity.

These exploring expeditions stimulated still further European voyages and claims. Following an expedition led by another Genoese, John Cabot, the English claimed the Atlantic coast of North America in 1497. This action set off a fruitless search for a northwest passage, a sea route that might lead from the Atlantic Ocean through North America to the Pacific, but no practical route existed. In 1500 Portugal established its claim to Brazil, which fell within the longitudes awarded to it by the pope in the Treaty of Tordesillas, and by 1502 Portuguese settlement of Brazil had begun. By 1511 the Spanish controlled Cuba, Puerto Rico, and Jamaica and had a presence on the northern coast of South America. In 1513 a Spanish expedition led by Vasco Nunez de Balboa (bal-BOH-uh) crossed Panama and sighted the Pacific Ocean, which he claimed for Spain. The French claimed eastern Canada in 1524 with a voyage led by an Italian captain from Florence, Giovanni da Verrazano.

The only practical sea route to Asia via the Americas was finally discovered in 1520, in a Spanish expedition led by a Portuguese captain, Ferdinand Magellan (muh-JELL-un) (1480–1521). From Spain his ships sailed down the Atlantic and rounded the southern tip of South America; they then survived a torturous trip through the stormy strait that today bears his name and leads to the Pacific Ocean: the Strait of Magellan. Magellan continued on across the Pacific. It was a long, difficult journey during which no inhabited islands were spotted before Guam, with the crewmen living off rat meat and boiled leather for months. Eventually the expedition landed in the Philippine Islands, where Magellan was killed in a clash with local people. Magellan's one remaining ship continued on westward around Africa, limping into Europe three years after they had left Spain. Europeans now had a better idea of world geography and turned to the conquest and settlement of the Americas.

New Horizons and Exploration in the Pacific

Exploration of the Americas, and the continued search for a sea route to Asia, led to European exploration of the Pacific basin. Long before Europeans arrived, the Pacific islanders, scattered across many island chains, had evolved distinctive traditions and social systems. The Polynesian people living on mountainous islands had varied food sources from farming and fishing that supported denser settlement and states led by kings or powerful chiefs, such as the eight inhabited Hawaiian Islands, divided into four rival chiefdoms, which had a population of perhaps 200,000. By contrast, many peoples living on small atolls only a few feet above sea level relied chiefly on resources from the sea and had smaller populations. Many island societies traded over vast distances, and so were linked into widespread sea networks. Warfare between rival islands and states was also common. Some islanders also faced increasing destruction of their fragile environments. Most Pacific islanders had not been in direct touch with Asia for millennia, making them vulnerable to Eurasian diseases later brought by Europeans.

Although Spanish ships annually sailed across the Pacific Ocean between the Philippines and Mexico beginning in 1565 (see Chapter 18), Europeans made little effort to colonize the vast Pacific region in this era. The first European expedition into the Pacific, led by Magellan in 1521, encountered no island societies before finally chancing on Guam, where they clashed with the local Chamorro (chuh-MOR-oh) people, the first of many unhappy encoun-

ters between Pacific islanders and European visitors. In the 1500s and 1600s, Spanish, Portuguese, English, and Dutch expeditions visited many islands, but they looked unpromising for exploitation.

Spain established the first successful Pacific colony in Guam in 1663, founding a Catholic mission there, but 90 percent of the Chamorros died over the next two decades, mostly from disease brought by the Spanish. In 1671 a demoralized Chamorro chief, though careful not to provoke retaliation, complained to a missionary that "the Spanish would have done better to remain in their own country. We have no need of their help to live happily. They treat us as gross barbarians."[3]

LO² The European Conquest of the Americas

European explorations and the search for riches soon led to colonization in the Americas. Native Americans lacked guns to resist the invaders and were also weakened by division. Thousands of Spanish adventurers roamed the Americas seeking wealth in the 1500s. Many were soldiers engaged in armed conquest, whose leaders were known as conquistadors (kon-KEY-stuh-dorz). The main town established by the Spanish on Hispaniola, Santo Domingo (SAN-toe duh-MING-go), became the early Spanish base for exploration and conquest. The major Spanish conquests came in Mexico and the Andes, while the Portuguese annexed Brazil. Later, the English, French, and Dutch obtained footholds in North America, the Caribbean, and the northeast coast of South America. By 1750 many American societies were under firm colonial control.

 Early America (*http:// earlyamerica .com/earlyamerica/ index.html*). Offers primary sources on the thirteen North American colonies in the eighteenth century.

conquistadors The leaders of Spanish soldiers engaged in armed conquest in the Americas.

> 66 With its gleaming temples and network of canals, the Aztec capital city, Tenochtitlan, astonished the Spanish, and Cortés called it the world's most beautiful city. 99

The Fall of the Aztec and Inca Empires

In 1519 Hernán Cortés (kor-TEZ) (1485–1547) and 550 soldiers from Spanish-controlled Cuba landed on Mexico's east coast, where they founded a settlement that later became the city of Veracruz (VER-uh-KROOZ). Cortés' major target was the rich Aztec Empire. First Cortés defeated and then forged an alliance with the Tlaxcalans, a people who had long resisted the Aztecs. Impressed by Spanish power, the Tlaxcalan nobles adopted Christianity and joined Cortés. Marching inland, Cortés fought and defeated several other peoples on the empire's perimeter, and then marched through the mountains into the Valley of Mexico, the heart of the Aztec Empire. With its gleaming temples and network of canals, the Aztec capital city, Tenochtitlan (teh-noch-tit-lan), astonished the Spanish, and Cortés called it the world's most beautiful city. The Aztec leader, Moctezuma II (mock-teh-ZOO-ma), warmly greeted them. Moctezuma (r. 1502–1520) may initially have identified Cortés with Quetzalcoatl and believed the Spaniards to be gods. Taking advantage of the confusion, the Spanish arrested Moctezuma. With sixty Spanish soldiers supplied with horses and guns, and many Indian allies, Cortés had taken temporary control of the capital of an empire of 25 million subjects. His force was soon joined by a thousand more Spanish soldiers arriving from Cuba.

Cortés and the Aztecs

Soon violence erupted, precipitating war. Spanish thievery and arrogance created hostility, and Aztec mobs killed or captured some Spaniards. Moctezuma, no longer a credible leader, was killed, and the Spanish had to fight their way out of the city, at great cost in Spanish life. Some fleeing Spaniards, loaded down with stolen Aztec gold, fell into the canals and drowned. Forced to return to the coast, Cortés proceeded to make alliances with more Aztec enemies and recruited more Spanish soldiers from Cuba. His enlarged army, numbering around one thousand Spaniards and ten thousand Tlaxcalans and other Indian allies, now laid siege to Tenochtitlan, where thousands of Aztecs resisted fiercely while a smallpox epidemic, inadvertently spread by the Spanish, ravaged their population. In 1521 the Spanish occupied the city and captured the last emperor, Moctezuma's nephew Cuauhtemoc (KWA-the-mock), while Tlaxcalans took revenge on an old enemy by massacring thousands of Aztecs.

Pizarro and the Incas

The Spanish now ruled the Aztec Empire, using the efficient Aztec administration to collect the tribute from the former Aztec subjects. As his people died from disease or faced

demands for harsh labor, one poet lamented that "broken spears lie in the roads; we have torn our hair in our grief. The houses are roofless now, and their walls are red with blood."[4] Spanish conquerors next pushed south to seize Central America, Panama, and, a few years later, the northern part of South America that eventually became Colombia and Venezuela. Later others moved north to what is now Florida, New Mexico, and northern California. From his base in Panama, the Spanish conquistador Francisco Pizarro (ca. 1476–1541) began a long exploration down the west coast of South America. In 1531, as his forces marched into the Andes Mountains, he launched his campaign of conquest. As in Mexico, the first Spaniards arrived after smallpox had already wiped out millions of Incas, including much of the leadership. In 1532, with only 160 Spaniards but with the advantages of artillery and horses, Pizarro ruthlessly defeated the Incas, ignoring pleas from Catholic priests to be more merciful.

The Spanish quickly expanded their territory. By 1534 the conquistadors had seized the Inca capital, Cuzco (KOOZ-ko), and had begun converting it into a Spanish settlement. Pizarro also founded the city of Lima (LEE-muh) along the Pacific coast. Over the next few years, the Spanish gained control over much of what is today Peru, Ecuador, Bolivia, and Chile and brutally crushed Indian uprisings. As Cortés had done

Codex of Aztec Resistance Illustrations in a book published around 1580 revealed a local perspective on the Spanish conquest of the Aztec Empire. This illustration shows Aztec warriors besieging a Spanish force in Tenochtitlan and the difference in weapons technology.

Institut Amatller d'Art Hispanic

in the Aztec lands, Pizarro and his men placed themselves at the top of the efficient Inca administrative system, but Pizarro was later murdered in Lima by rivals.

The Conquest of Brazil and the Caribbean

While the Spanish concentrated on Mexico and the Andes, the Portuguese established small trading posts along the Brazilian coast. The land seemed promising. The Portuguese began obtaining and shipping brazilwood, which made an excellent dye for European textiles, but they remained more focused on exploiting the wealth of Africa and Asia. After a French effort to establish a foothold in Brazil, the Portuguese founded a permanent colony along the southern Brazilian coast in 1532 and began awarding land grants to private entrepreneurs for settlement.

Facing not the large, settled societies of Mexico and the Andes, but rather

> **"While the Spanish concentrated on Mexico and the Andes, the Portuguese established small trading posts along the Brazilian coast. "**

seminomadic food collectors and small farmers, the Portuguese viewed the Indians as potential slaves who had to be compelled to work for Portuguese enterprises. Portuguese slavers from the southern Brazilian settlement at São Paulo (sow PAU-low) pushed deep into the interior raiding for slaves. The colonial government began to combat these activities, and expand its control in the interior, only in 1680. The Dutch also set up plantations that grew huge quantities of sugar for the European market. But the Portuguese eventually expelled their rivals and soon took over the profitable northeast, building a city, Salvador da Bahia, at Bahia (ba-HEE-a).

In the Caribbean, the Spanish competed with the Portuguese, Dutch, English, and French, all of whom founded settlements in the Caribbean from the later 1500s until the late 1600s. The Dutch moved to several small Caribbean islands and also established a foothold in the northwestern South America region known as the Guianas (ghee-AHN-as), founding the colony of Dutch Guiana (now Suriname). The

French seized Haiti, the western half of Hispaniola, which became a center for plantations and a major source of wealth for France, as well as the islands of Guadeloupe (GWAD-eh-loop) and Martinique (mahr-ten-EEK) and a portion of Guiana. Meanwhile, the English made Jamaica, Barbados, British Guiana (now Guyana), and later Trinidad the linchpins for their colonial activity.

> "The English and French focused their colonizing efforts on the eastern seaboard of North America, expanding their settlements at the expense of Native American societies."

In the Caribbean, piracy by Europeans against other Europeans became a major economic activity, much of it directed at prosperous Spanish settlements or at the Spanish galleons hauling rich cargoes of silver, sugar, or imported Asian goods to Europe. In 1670 the English pirate Sir Henry Morgan undertook a particularly brazen attack, leading a force of 1,400 men to sack Panama City, where warehouses stored wealth from Asia and Latin America. The Spanish burned the city rather than allow it to fall to the buccaneers. Some pirates, such as the Englishmen Morgan, John Hawkins, and Sir Francis Drake, became influential and respected figures in their homelands, celebrated for the wealth they captured at the expense of rival countries. As a French buccaneer boasted in 1734, "Fortune is to be found on the sea, where one must go to collect it."[5]

The English, French, and Indians in North America

The English and French focused their colonizing efforts on the eastern seaboard of North America, expanding their settlements at the expense of Native American societies. These societies, which were often matrilineal, were mostly based on farming. Their chiefs held little power in comparison to Eurasian leaders or Inca kings. The Indians soon came to disdain the Europeans as unintelligent, physically weak, and smelly—in contrast to Indians, who valued personal cleanliness, the British and French seldom bathed. Nonetheless, the Indians usually offered hospitality and eagerly traded with and sought allies among the newcomers, but the settlers soon wore out their welcome.

The English

Hoping to outflank rival countries, the English planted a series of settlements up and down the Atlantic coast. In 1587 they founded a small English colony at Roanoke, in what is today North Carolina, but it did not survive. In 1607 the first successful English settlement in North America was established at Jamestown, in today's Virginia, which struggled to survive in the unfamiliar land. The English began sending families from England to farm and establish communities, but in many cases, only the generosity of Native Americans enabled the colonists to survive. By the middle of the seventeenth century, English settlements dotted the coast. The Dutch settlement at New York, founded in 1624, also came under English control once the sponsoring Dutch West India Company concluded it could not compete with English immigration.

The French

Equally ambitious, the French established their first settlement in Acadia in 1604, followed by outposts at Quebec City in 1608 and Montreal in 1642. New France was formally established as a colony in 1627 and covered much of eastern Canada. French Jesuit missionaries (known as "Black Robes") undertook campaigns to convert the Native Americans to Catholicism and traveled widely, as far west as today's Illinois, in their pursuit of conversions. By the 1670s, French explorers and trappers mapped and established trading outposts throughout the Great Lakes and Mississippi River Basin. To counter English and Spanish expansion, in 1699 the French founded New Orleans, which then became the base for French territorial claims in Louisiana and the Mississippi Valley.

The English colonies north of Maryland developed largely as agricultural economies of free white settlers. Although most colonists were farmers, many English and French settlers also came to North America to exploit two valuable commodities, fish and fur. The seas off New England and eastern Canada teamed with cod, which became a major part of the European diet. Later some English and French immigrants moved inland in search of beaver pelts; fur remained the major Canadian export until the rise of wheat farming in the nineteenth century. Although both French and English settlement disrupted the Indian tribes, the French generally maintained better relations with local peoples. Nonetheless, in both French and English colonies, the Native Americans died from either disease or armed conflict or were pushed north and west.

The Iroquois Confederation

Some Indian groups were well organized and proved formidable opponents. The most complex political structure among North American Indians was the Iroquois (EAR-uh-coy) Confederation, a coalition formed in the 1500s to unite five once-warring tribes living in what is today upstate New York. These longhouse-dwelling tribes shared a common enemy in the Huron (HYOOR-uhn) of southern Ontario, who established a rival confederation of allied groups. By the 1630s, the Iroquois numbered some 16,000. Initially the Iroquois alliance was primarily a nonaggression pact among the members. Later, in the 1690s, it became a pantribal government with a council of chiefs and an oral constitution. Some scholars credit Iroquois political ideas, such as a representative congress and freedom of speech, as an influence on the later constitution of the United States. The Iroquois were an effective military alliance, outmaneuvering European arrivals for many years.

LO³ The Consequences of American Colonization

By the late sixteenth century, the Spanish had explored and claimed a massive empire stretching from northern California and the Rocky Mountains southward to southern Chile and Argentina, including parts of the Caribbean. Meanwhile, the English, French, and Dutch established settlements in the Caribbean region and in North America. Despite many similarities in conquest, the American colonies were very different from each other. However, the results almost always came at the expense of the Native American peoples, who suffered especially from the colonists' diseases. Colonization also involved Christian missionary activity and violence.

The Columbian Exchange

One result of European exploration and conquest was the transfer of diseases, animals, and plants from one hemisphere to another, what historians refer to as the Columbian Exchange. A chief consequence was demographic: virulent microbes brought from the Eastern Hemisphere caused massive depopulation and suffering in the Americas. Of course, although often healthier than Eastern Hemisphere peoples, the Native Americans before 1492 did not live in a disease-free paradise. They suffered from such maladies as polio, hepatitis, some varieties of tuberculosis, many intestinal parasites, and syphilis. Only syphilis, a sexually transmitted disease, seems to have made any serious impact when carried to Europe, but it was more an unpleasant nuisance than a mass killer.

The Native Americans had no immunity to diseases brought by Europeans and Africans, such as measles, typhus, influenza, and smallpox; these claimed millions of victims. Within two centuries, the Native American population was reduced by around 90 percent. No group remained untouched, and some were completely eliminated as the diseases spread destruction and havoc. A Maya writer reported that "great was the stench of the dead. The dogs and vultures devoured the bodies. We were born to die!"[6] The American population numbers began recovering as the most resistant individuals survived and as immigrants from Europe and Africa intermarried with Native Americans, producing less susceptible children. Eventually Native American populations grew, particularly in more isolated areas.

The Columbian Exchange affected both sides of the Atlantic. From the one side, Europeans brought their political, cultural, and social institutions, as well as plants such as wheat, orange trees, and grape vines, and domesticated animals. Some imports were useful for American peoples, such as horses brought by the Spanish that enabled some tribes in the North American Great Plains to hunt buffalo more effectively. From the Americas, gold and silver had a major impact on the Eurasian economy. American crops such as tobacco, rubber, American cotton, potatoes, and maize (corn), as well as drugs including quinine and coca, spread across the Atlantic. Some of these crops, such as potatoes, corn, and tomatoes, became diet staples in Europe and Asia. South American chilies became a mainstay of South and Southeast Asian cooking, making the spicy foods even hotter.

The Spanish Empire in the Americas

The conquered Americans were forced to pay the costs of the conquest. In Spanish America and

Columbian Exchange The transportation of diseases, animals, and plants from one hemisphere to another that resulted from European exploration and conquest between 1492 and 1750.

 The Columbian Exchange (*http://nationalhumanitiescenter.org/tserve/nattrans/ntecoindian/essays/columbian.htm*). Links to essays by Alfred Crosby and more.

Portuguese Brazil, some Europeans made great fortunes by exploiting people, land, minerals, animals, and plants. Gold and silver from the Americas financed the building of the Spanish empire. Once in power, the Spanish and Portuguese seized all the riches they could locate, forced or persuaded the Indians to adopt Christianity, destroyed their religious centers, and murdered Indian leaders who refused to cooperate. While many local peoples resisted the occupying powers, these efforts were usually futile in the long run. While taking the local peoples' material wealth, disturbing cultures, and spreading disease, the new settlers also learned survival skills from the people. They also intermarried or had sexual relations with local women, producing people of mixed descent.

In building their American empire, the Spanish appropriated American political structures but also introduced their own institutions. The Spanish colonists established settlements that became large cities, such as Havana, Buenos Aires, Lima, and Mexico City, the last-mentioned built on the site of the Aztec capital, Tenochtitlan. In the 1500s, Spain divided its vast empire into two smaller divisions (viceroyalties): New Spain (governed from Mexico City) and Peru (governed from Lima). The top Spanish official in each was the viceroy, a deputy to the king who was always Spanish-born and held great power. Later two more viceroyalties were created in South America. Given the huge territories, each viceroyalty had to be subdivided into smaller political units known as audiencias, judicial tribunals with administrative functions.

In building their empires, the Spanish and other Europeans sometimes faced considerable resistance. Maya Yucatan fell to the Spanish only in 1545 after a long, bitter military struggle. In the 1530s, many Indians rose up in rebel-

Complaint of the Indians of Tecama Against Their Ecomendero, Juan Ponce De León This summary of Judicial proceedings in Mexico City in 1550 confirms that legislation designed to protect Indians from abuse was often ignored.

66 Within two centuries, the Native American population was reduced by around 90 percent. 99

lion in Peru, and sporadic resistance continued for two centuries. In New Mexico, resentment by some Pueblo peoples against the Spanish and Catholic missionaries, which held little tolerance for Native American customs, led to several revolts. The most serious came in 1680, when a respected shaman, Popé (PO-pay), led a force that pushed the Spanish out of the area. Although the Spanish returned and reestablished authority in 1692, the revolt prompted them to adopt more cooperative policies.

New Latin American Societies

Gradually, distinctive societies and cultures began to emerge in Spanish America and Brazil, a huge area later known as Latin America. A key group in most of these societies were the creoles (KREE-awlz), people of Iberian ancestry who were born in Latin America. Other groups stemmed from the mixing of peoples, creating mestizos, a blend of white and Indian ancestry, and mulattos, a mix of African with white or Indian ancestry or both (see Witness to the Past: Spanish Men and Inca Women). While most creoles enjoyed positions of high status, the two mixed groups held a status between Europeans at the top of the social system and Indians and Africans at the bottom. By the 1700s, the mixed groups also represented a sizeable portion of the population in many colonies. Europeans tended to view the creoles, mestizos, and mulattos with either condescension or contempt: in the 1600s, a creole scholar born in Mexico of Spanish parents complained that people in Europe "are hardly able to discover anything rational in us."[7]

Emergence of Latin American Culture

Many writers and artists were born and educated in the Americas. Perhaps the greatest colonial American poet was the creole Mexican nun Sor (Sister) Juana Inez de la Cruz (1651–1695), who also won renown as a playwright, philosopher, and scientist. As a young woman she mastered Latin and Aztec while studying logic, history, mathematics, and literature. To pursue her intellectual and literary interests, the well-born Sor Juana chose life in a convent over marriage, eventually collecting the largest private library in Mexico, some four thousand volumes.

Latin American culture actually remained more closely connected to the Catholic Church than was the case in western Europe, which was reshaped by the Renaissance and Enlightenment. To screen out what they considered dangerous ideas, the church had to approve all printed matter entering the colonies. Church-controlled universities, which were set up to train creole men for careers as colonial officials and priests, taught largely in Latin and employed clerics as instructors. Spanish officials also brought the ruthless, counter-reform Holy Inquisition to the colonies to root out heresy. People suspected of having secret Jewish or Protestant sympathies were tried. In particular, those of *converso* background—Jews who were forced to convert to Christianity in Spain and their descendants—were subject to investigation, imprisonment, and sometimes gruesome executions.

Latin American societies exhibited dramatic contradictions: while many of the elite looked toward Europe for inspiration, the majority of the population wanted to preserve the languages, beliefs, and ways of life from pre-Columbian times. Latin American writers often examined the conflicted relationship between Spain and Latin America, describing a mix of good and evil or, as one put it, sun and shadow. Such a mix might also describe the experiences of people in the Portuguese, English, and French colonies.

Women in Latin America

Women faced the greatest dilemmas in Latin America, often both accepting and repudiating Spanish rule. They now enjoyed new food sources, but they also clung to their native dress and pride. Despite patriarchal traditions, some Indians and mestizo women engaged in commerce while others worked in domestic service, tended animals, or made clothing, including carding, spinning, and weaving wool from sheep.

Native Americans: Missions and Mistreatment

Both the Spanish and the Portuguese were committed to spreading Catholicism as part of their imperial enterprise. Although they enjoyed only mixed success, missionaries were frequently militant in their faith and often had a profound influence. The mission impact on Latin American Indians came in different forms. Sometimes missionaries altered people's settlement and even economic patterns, requiring seminomadic hunters and gatherers, like the Chumash (CHOO-mash) on the California coast, to live in towns and cultivate crops imported from Europe. In Yucatan, a few missionaries gained control over many Maya people. Although these missionaries sometimes admired Maya culture, such as the ancient writing system, they were also intolerant of non-Christian beliefs and destroyed Maya books and religious symbols, which they considered pagan. In 1562 some priests, who suspected that certain converts continued to secretly worship Maya gods, launched a terrible inquisition and tortured 4,500 Indians, 158 of whom died. The church punished the priest in charge but later made him a bishop.

Christianity in the New World

As the Maya account illustrates, the missionaries often faced resistance. In the former Inca territories, for example, many women openly rejected Catholicism in the 1500s. According to a Spanish observer: "They do not confess, attend catechism classes, or go to mass. Returning to their ancient customs and idolatry, they do not want to serve God or the [Spanish] crown."[8] Native Americans could also put their stamp on Christianity: in 1531 an Aztec peasant supposedly saw a vision of the Virgin Mary at a shrine to the Aztec mother goddess. A church was later built there to honor "Our Lady of Guadalupe," and the image of the virgin as an Indian woman became a symbol of Mexican nationalism.

Spanish actions led to the Black Legend, the Spanish reputation for brutality toward Native Americans, including the repression of native religions, execution of rebels, and forced labor. The Spanish were particularly zealous in persecuting homosexuals. Although the Black Legend exaggerated Spanish atrocities, Spain's enemies in Europe eagerly passed along such stories. Actually, disease killed far more Indians than murder and brutality. Nor were the Spanish the only culprits; the other European settlers could be just as intolerant and forceful in their dealings with local peoples.

> **Black Legend**
> The Spanish reputation for brutality toward Native Americans, including the repression of native religions, execution of rebels, and forced labor.

> 66 Both the Spanish and the Portuguese were committed to spreading Catholicism as part of their imperial enterprise. 99

Spanish Men and Inca Women

In many parts of Latin America, Spaniards married or cohabitated with Native American women, fostering a mixed, or mestizo, population. In Peru, some Spaniards deliberately sought to marry Inca princesses, perhaps to establish local connections in a factionalized colonial society. In this account from the early seventeenth century by the Peruvian historian Garcilaso de la Vega, himself the product of such a match, we learn of an Inca princess who was less than enthusiastic about her Spanish suitor, a captain from a modest background. Her ambivalent response has been viewed by some historians as representing a mixed attitude common in Latin America toward the imposition of European culture: contempt for many European customs and the brutal conquest but also admiration of some European values and Europeans' military power.

. . . a daughter of [Inca leader] Huaina Cápac and herself . . . the owner of the Indians [workers], was married to a very good soldier called Diego Hernández, a very worthy man, who was said in his youth to have been a tailor. . . . [Before the marriage] the princess learned this and refused the match, saying that it was unjust to wed the daughter of Huaina Cápac with a . . . tailor. Although the Bishop of Cuzco as well as . . . other personages who went to attend the ceremony of betrothal, begged and pleaded with her, it was all to no purpose. They then sent to fetch her brother. . . . When he came, he took his sister into a corner of the room and told her privately that it was impolitic for her to refuse the match, for by doing so she would render the whole of the [Inca] royal line odious in the eyes of the Spaniards, who would consider them mortal enemies and never accept their friendship again. She agreed, though reluctantly, to her brother's demands, and so appeared before the bishop, who wished to honor the betrothed by officiating at the ceremony.

When the bride was asked through an Indian interpreter if she consented to become the bride and spouse of the aforesaid, the interpreter said "did she want to be the man's wife?" for the Indian language had no verb for consent or for spouse, and he could therefore not have asked anything else. The bride replied in her own tongue: . . . "Maybe I will, maybe I won't." Whereupon the ceremony continued. . . . They were still alive and living as man and wife when I left Cuzco.

Other marriages of this kind took place throughout the empire, and were arranged so as to give allocations of Indians to [Spanish] claimants and reward them with other people's properties. Many, however, were dissatisfied, some because their income was small and others because their wives were ugly; there is no perfect satisfaction in this world.

Thinking About the Reading

1. What does the reading tell us about social attitudes among Incas and Spaniards in colonial Peru?
2. What do we learn about the treatment of women?
3. How might the princess's attitude be seen as a form of resistance?

Source: Garcilaso de la Vega, *Royal Commentaries of the Incas and General History of Peru*, Part Two. Translated by Harold V. Livermore (Austin: University of Texas Press, 1966), pp. 1229–1230. Copyright © 1966 by the University of Texas Press. Reprinted with permission.

Bartolomé de Las Casas

While many Spaniards saw the Native Americans as savages, some Catholic clerics advocated humane policies and sought to protect them. The Dominican friar Bartolomé de Las Casas (lahs KAH-suhs) (1474–1566), although an ardent missionary for Catholicism, proclaimed that Indians were humans like the Spanish and bemoaned the destruction they experienced. In 1637 the Jesuits, in what is today Uruguay (YOOR-uh-gwye), even armed the Indians to help protect them against slave raiders.

But the battle over how to treat Indians was won by intolerant people, reflecting the values of a Europe

1492: An Ongoing Voyage (*http://metalab .unc.edu/expo/1492 .exhibit/Intro.html*). An electronic exhibit from the Library of Congress on pre- and post-Columbian Europe, Africa, and the Americas.

engulfed in religious conflict between Catholics and Protestants (see Chapter 15). Most Spaniards considered the Indians justly conquered and favored exploitation of people they considered born for servitude, enhancing the Black Legend. These harsh attitudes often affected women even more than men. In 1625, an Indian writer in Peru charged that white men exploited both women's labor and their bodies: "In the mines, Indian women are made into concubines, daughters of Indian men are kidnapped. . . . There is no one who takes these women's side."9 Missionaries gave Indian men and women a superficial Christianity, changing local gods into Christian saints, but many Indians continued to secretly worship old gods and ancestors. After the initial violence, the church treated Indians paternalistically, as children needing guidance. But, as a result of conquest, the Indian quality of life—health, morale, leisure, and joy—mostly declined. Demoralization and disease generated alcoholism and despair.

English and French Colonies in North America

The English and French competed for control in North America while expanding their settlements

 Interactive Map

(see Map 17.2). By the mid-1700s, the territory from New England south to Georgia was divided into thirteen separate English colonies, each administered by an appointed English governor. Immigrants came from England and also from Scotland, Ireland, Germany, and the Netherlands. Some from poor or criminal backgrounds emigrated as indentured laborers, signing contracts to work on farms or in households to repay their passage. Many immigrants took up farming, especially in the northern colonies. By 1730 the thirteen colonies contained around 500,000 European settlers. African slaves or their descendants, constituting 20 percent of the total colonial population, were concentrated in the South but were also found in the northern colonies such as New York.

Intellectual and religious diversity characterized English colonial life. Educated colonists were often influenced by English and French Enlightenment thinkers and espoused democratic ideals and reason. Many early English immigrants were Protestant

religious dissenters seeking freedom of religion. The Puritans had an important influence on the colonial culture, especially in the north, implanting Calvinist attitudes about the value of work and commerce.

The French and English in Canada

North of New York and New England, the English and French clashed for decades over control of Acadia (Nova Scotia) and New France, in what is today eastern Canada. This conflict resulted in part from a larger English–French competition for influence throughout the world. Eventually England triumphed over France in North America. In 1713 the English

© Cengage Learning

Map 17.2
The English and French in North America, ca.1700

While the English colonized much of the Atlantic coast of North America, the French concentrated on what is today eastern Canada and the interior of North America, including the Great Lakes and the Mississippi and Ohio River Basins.

Indian Slavery Spain's enemies publicized cases of Spanish brutality toward Native Americans. This sixteenth-century engraving, by the Dutch observer Theodore de Bry, portrays the misery of Native Americans subjected to slavery and forced labor.

Courtesy of John Carter Brown Library at Brown University

Metis
People in Canada of mixed French and Indian descent.

 A Dominican Voice in the Wilderness: Preaching Against Tyranny in Hispaniola A Dominican friar, and former landholder, expresses his outrage at the injustices committed against the native people of "New Spain."

took control of Acadia, and in 1755 they deported much of the Acadian French population to the French colony of Louisiana, forming the basis for the French-speaking Cajun (KAY-juhn) community there, which today numbers nearly 1 million. In 1759 English forces defeated the French near Quebec City, and in 1760 captured Montreal, gaining control over New France. French cultural influence was eventually confined chiefly to the large area of eastern Canada now known as the province of Quebec. In 1774 the English, recognizing the tenacity of French culture, allowed the French in Quebec to hold public office, speak their language, and freely practice Catholicism. Both the French and English Canadians settled down to farming, like their neighbors in New England.

Europeans and Indian Societies in North America

At the same time, relations between European settlers and Indian societies in North America remained complex. Indians resented and often resisted the foreigners' occupation of their land, and the English and French had to deal carefully with the better-organized tribes and federations. But some Indians, becoming dependent on trading partnerships with Europeans, were inevitably drawn into the often violent English–French competition. Indians such as the Huron allied with the French; some, including the Iroquois, allied with the English; and some opposed both. The fur trade had an additional social impact: as French fur traders set up trading posts far from the cities, they tended to intermarry with Indians, producing the Metis (may-TEES), people of mixed French and Indian

Johnson Hall This grand house, built in the mid-eighteenth century by American fur trader William Johnson in what is now upstate New York, became a meeting place for Native American tribes, such as the Iroquois, allied with the British against the French.

Johnson Hall by Edward Lamson Henry (1841–1919), 1903. Oil on canvas 21-1/4 X 37 inches. Albany Institute of History and Art Purchase 1933.44

descent. In contrast, English colonists tended to immigrate as families, reducing the rates of intermarriage with Indians.

The encounter with Europeans made living much more difficult for North American Indians. In 1705 an English observer, Robert Beverley, noted that "they have on several accounts to lament the arrival of the English [who] have taken away great part of their country, and consequently made everything less plenty among them."[10] The Indians mistrusted colonists, who often broke treaties, but they also desired European trade goods, especially met-

alwork and guns. A few tribes, like the Cherokee in the Carolinas and Georgia, who probably numbered some 30,000 in the mid-1500s, actively adopted European influences, such as new farming methods and patriarchal social traditions. Christian missionaries had less success in North America than in Latin America, although social patterns among Native Americans were irrevocably changed, often forcibly, by European influence.

LO⁴ Slavery and the Atlantic System

Quite different economic and social systems emerged in Latin America and northern English America. In much of Latin America, the Caribbean, and some of the southern colonies of North America, European rule produced an inequitable economic relationship between the colonies and their colonizing countries. In North America, English colonists emphasized commerce and family farming, eventually moving toward economic independence. Perhaps the major impact of American colonization was to link West Africa, the Americas, and Europe into a larger Atlantic System, a vast network that saw the movement of enslaved Africans to the Americas, where they labored on plantations growing sugar, cotton, and tobacco for shipment to Europe. European merchants then used the lucrative proceeds from slave labor to purchase guns, rum, textiles, and other commodities for shipment

haciendas
Vast ranches in Spanish America.

encomienda
("Entrustment") The Crown's grant to a colonial Spaniard in Latin America of a certain number of Indians from whom he extracted tribute.

monoculture
An economy dependent on the production and export of one chief commodity.

development
Growth in a variety of economic areas that benefits the majority of people; the opposite of monoculture.

 Interactive Map

to Africa to obtain more enslaved labor. As a result, African slavery reshaped the economies, social patterns, and cultures of many societies.

Economic Change in Latin America

From the beginning, Latin American colonies were largely geared to export natural resources (see Map 17.3). In the Andes and Mexico, the Spanish developed rich gold and silver mines. The silver mines discovered by the Spanish in 1545 in today's Bolivia became some of the richest in the world. Drafted to labor in the mining economy, Indian mine workers in the main Andean mining center, Potosi (po-tuh-SEE), found life difficult, "working twelve hours a day, going down seven hundred feet, down to where night is perpetual, the air thick and ill smelling. When they arrive at the top out of breath, [they] find a mineowner who scolds them because they did not bring enough load."[11] For much of the eighteenth century, Brazil supplied more than half of the world's gold. While providing few benefits to the Native Americans, mining brought prosperity to colonial cities such as Lima, enriched merchants, filled royal treasuries, and linked the colonies to the world economy. Most of the wealth was exported, ultimately passing through Spain and Portugal to northern Europe as payment for manufactured goods. This transfer enriched first Flanders, then Holland, and later England, helping to finance English industrialization. American silver also bought Europeans access to other world markets, especially in Asia.

Ranching and the *Encomienda*

While mining flourished in only a few mountainous areas, ranching became a major economic activity in many other regions. Cattle and horses brought from Europe enabled many settlers to take up ranching, especially in the grasslands of what is today Argentina and Venezuela. Vast cattle ranches, known in Spanish America as haciendas, were often more than 1 million acres in size. Like the mines, the ranches provided great incomes for monarchs, merchants, and investors.

During the early 1500s, to ensure Indian labor the Spanish imposed some version of the encomienda ("entrustment"), the Crown's grant to a colonial Spaniard of a certain number of Indians from whom he extracted tribute. In exchange for providing labor, such as in the gold and silver mines, the Indians were instructed in Christianity by clergy. While in theory this system protected Indians, in fact it fostered many abuses. A Spanish Franciscan reported that "The Indian slaves who up to the present have died in these [gold] mines cannot be counted."[12] Because of the abuses, by the mid-1500s the institution had been reformed considerably, but the system still allowed temporary conscription of Indian labor.

Economic Stagnation

Despite the early Spanish and Portuguese successes in developing their colonies, Latin America eventually fell behind North America in economic development, a contrast that became dramatic by the 1800s. At the outset, Latin America had many advantages that British North America lacked: rich gold and silver mines, abundant fertile land, and a much larger population. By the 1700s, Latin Americans, unlike North Americans, had built a half-dozen large cities and many fine universities, and the region produced great wealth. But the failure of Latin American and Caribbean societies to match the economic vigor of North America resulted in part from the system of monoculture, an economy dependent on the production and export of one chief commodity. Monocultures were usually based on slave or coerced labor and were completely dependent on the colonizing country to buy the resource, such as sugar, silver, or beef, they produced. In return the colonizing country supplied food and other necessities to the colonized society.

Plantation, mining, or ranching-based economies, however, cannot generate overall development, growth in a variety of economic areas that benefits the majority of people. Monoculture economies generally benefit only one segment of a population, and they prosper or decline depending on world prices for their export commodity. With few alternatives

> 66 From the beginning, Latin American colonies were largely geared to export natural resources. 99

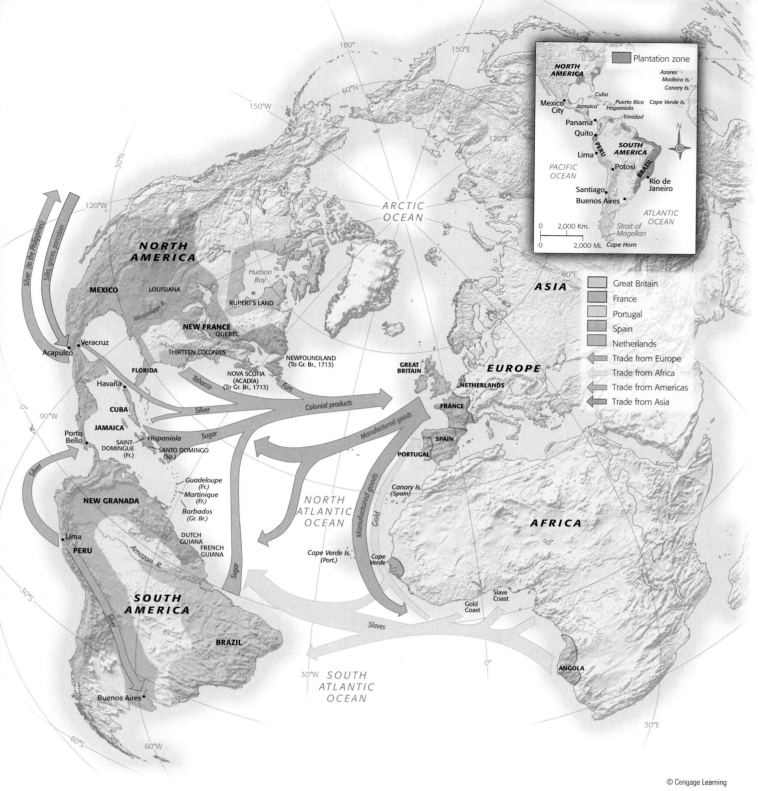

Map 17.3
The Atlantic Economy

The Atlantic economy was based on a triangular trade in which African slaves were shipped to the Americas to produce raw materials that were chiefly exported to Europe, where they were turned into manufactured goods and exported to Africa and the Americas.

Slavery and the Atlantic System **443**

> "The first American plantations emerged in Brazil, where sugar was grown along the coast by the early 1500s."

The Sugar Industry

The growing sugar industry fostered transitions in Europe as well as the Americas. With the rise of the American plantations and cheaper supplies, sugar was transformed from a rare luxury to an everyday necessity, becoming a staple of the European diet. Sugar sweetened bland foods and provided more calories for the often undernourished working classes. In England, the use of sugar in foods allowed people to take their lunches with them and stay at work all day, in this way helping to foster an industrial economy in Britain.

The plantation economies of the Caribbean islands and some coastal districts were essentially sugar "factories," relying on mass production of raw sugar by enslaved workers. A seventeenth-century saying noted that "without sugar, no Brazil; without slaves, no sugar; without Angola, no slaves."[13] The southern English colonies of North America differed from these Caribbean and Latin American economies only in that the crops were more varied: cotton, rice, and tobacco were grown as well as sugar. The populations of all the plantation-based societies were composed chiefly of enslaved people of African ancestry. Slavery as a key institution stretched from the southern half of what became the United States through the Caribbean Basin and down the South American coast to central Brazil in the east and coastal Peru in the west.

to generate wealth, plantation and mining societies remained dangerously specialized, leading to the economic stagnation of Latin America and the Caribbean as the North American economy was on the rise.

The Plantation Zone and African Slavery

At first, mines and ranches dominated the Latin American economy, but the plantation soon became the key economic institution in much of the tropical and subtropical areas of the South American mainland, the Caribbean islands, and southeastern North America. The first American plantations emerged in Brazil, where sugar was grown along the coast by the early 1500s. By the later 1600s, plantations were flourishing in many regions, growing sugar, coffee, cotton, bananas, and sisal (a tough fiber used to make rope) for shipment to North America and Europe. The plantations depended on the labor of African slaves and their descendants.

Plantation Economies

The transition to a plantation economy created the plantation zone, a group of societies with economies relying on enslaved African labor and stretching from Virginia and Kentucky southward through the West Indies and the east coast of Central America to central Brazil and the Pacific coast of Colombia. The changes were particularly striking in the Caribbean islands, where sugar planting transformed whole economies. European settlers were first attracted to Caribbean islands such as Jamaica, Barbados, Hispaniola, Cuba, and Puerto Rico, and in the later 1500s and early 1600s, they set up self-sufficient farms that grew diverse crops. But in the mid-1600s, the growing of sugar, which was much more profitable than the other crops, expanded. Because sugar growing needed plentiful land and cheap labor, white farmers were gradually displaced by plantations using slave labor, while laws that prevented plantation owners from growing anything but sugar protected the profits of the colonial elite.

Africans in America: America's Journey Through Slavery (*http://www.pbs.org/wgbh/aia/home.html*). A useful website offering materials relevant to a documentary series broadcast on Public Television.

Africans in the New World

The needs of the plantation economy, and the high mortality rates of enslaved labor, required the constant importation of slaves from Africa. Between 1500 and 1850, some 9 to 12 million Africans were brought into the Americas as slaves. Most went to the Caribbean islands, where they became the majority population, and to Brazil, which today has the largest population of African descent in the Americas. African slaves were also used outside the plantation zone, in northern English colonies and as far south as Argentina, though on a much smaller scale. By 1850, Brazil received some 40 percent of all

Caribbean Sugar Mill On a West Indian plantation, this windmill crushed sugar cane into juice, which was boiled down in the smoking building on the right to produce sugar granules. Such plantations were the dominant economic activity on the Caribbean islands and in parts of South America, Central America, and southeastern North America.

enslaved Africans, followed by the British Caribbean (21 percent), French Caribbean (15 percent), Spanish America (15 percent), and British North America (5 percent). About one-third of all people of African descent eventually lived in the Western Hemisphere. As the number of transported Africans increased in the later 1600s and early 1700s, many areas were transformed into societies in which slaves constituted a majority. Yet Africans occupied the bottom of the social ladder, where life was extremely harsh. On some sugar plantations, as many as half the slaves died within two or three years of arrival.

> **66** The lives of African slaves and their unfree descendants in the Americas were governed by the imperatives of the marketplace. **99**

In turn, economic conditions contributed to differing administrative policies. In contrast to the Latin American colonial administrations, the British allowed their colonies from New Jersey north through New England considerable freedom to build diversified economies for local and trans-Atlantic markets. Merchants from Boston, Providence, and New York competed with the English in the Caribbean to obtain sugar and molasses, which was converted to rum and shipped to Africa for slaves. Some North Americans, like Europeans, amassed huge profits from the slave trade, profits that were then invested in their own broad-based economies. In sum, those Latin American and Caribbean colonies with the most abundant natural and human resources to exploit enjoyed greater short-term economic growth but less eventual development. By contrast, the northern English colonies, with fewer resources, had the opposite experience.

Read about Caetana, the brave slave rebel who challenged patriarchy.

Economic Growth in English North America

Conditions in the northern English colonies created economies that were strikingly different from the monocultures that were common elsewhere in the Americas. The northern colonies lacked the mineral resources, soil, or climate for profitable mining, plantation farming, or ranching. Slaves in the north mostly worked for farms, businesses, or households. In addition, the immigrant population was largely composed of working farmers, artisans, and merchants, making the northern economies less dependent on slave plantations and the severe social inequality they fostered.

Slave Life and African-American Cultures

The lives of African slaves and their unfree descendants in the Americas were governed by the imperatives of the marketplace. In contrast to the treatment of slaves in many African societies, colonial America gave enslaved people few, if any, rights. Because the markets for sugar and other plantation crops expanded, slave owners sought maximum profit regardless of the human consequences. In Brazil, for example, the majority of enslaved Africans and their unfree descendants worked in agriculture, especially on sugar, coffee, and tobacco estates. The average Brazilian sugar plantation in the seventeenth and eighteenth centuries owned between eighty and one hundred enslaved workers. Most were field hands who were each expected to produce three-quarters of a ton of sugar per year. The slave owner recovered the

cost of purchasing and maintaining slaves after about three years of such production. With two men for every woman, the Brazilian population with African ancestry did not grow very rapidly and required constant replenishment from Africa. Encouraged by the Catholic Church to marry, many Brazilian slaves formed families, even though they could be broken up by sale.

Slave Revolts

Africans and their descendants often resisted the slave system. Slave revolts erupted in Haiti, Mexico, the North American colonies, and elsewhere, but they were brutally crushed and the leaders executed. For example, the 1739 Stono Rebellion in South Carolina, the deadliest of the North American uprisings, largely involved recently imported, frequently Catholic, Kongolese. The captured rebels were beheaded. Some slaves, known as maroons (muh-ROONS) in the English Caribbean, escaped from plantations and set up African-type societies in the interior of several American colonies, including Brazil, Colombia, Jamaica, Haiti, Dutch Guiana, and some of the southern colonies in North America. The largest maroon community was formed in northeast Brazil, where rebellious slaves established a state around 1605, Palmares (paul-MARYS), with a government led by an African-style king and chiefs. With a population of perhaps 30,000, mostly of African ancestry, Palmares flourished, and resisted nearly annual Portuguese assaults, for nearly a century before being crushed by the Portuguese in 1694.

Africans and their descendants, free or unfree, became a part of local societies. Some slaves were eventually freed, a process known as manumission. Manumission was rare in the English colonies and more common in Latin America, especially Brazil, where women, mulattos, and local-born children were most likely to be freed. In both English and Latin America, a few slaves earned enough to buy their own freedom, and some slave owners gave favored slaves an inheritance. As a result, a slowly growing class of free blacks filled niches in American life. Together the enslaved and freed people of color constituted some two-thirds of the population in parts of Brazil and Cuba. While racism—judging people based on observable physical traits such as skin color—remained influential throughout the Americas, Latin Americans tended to rank people according to their occupation and status as well as skin color, making for a flexible social order. In contrast, the English colonies rigidly divided people largely by skin color and whether they had any African ancestry.

Emergence of an African American Culture

The harsh conditions of slave life notwithstanding, unique, new African American cultures emerged. Africans in the Americas and their descendants frequently mixed Western and African customs, and some created hybrid religions based on both African and Christian beliefs. Combining African rhythms with local European and sometimes Native American musical traditions, African Americans also invented musical forms that won wide appeal in the twentieth century, including jazz, blues, salsa, reggae, calypso, and samba. A few African Americans even developed new languages, such as the Gullah (GULL-uh) dialect of the Georgia Sea Islands, which mixed English and African words. African American cultures also influenced other ethnic groups in the Americas. Many non-Africans enjoyed various folktales and traditions of African origin. Africans introduced several crops from their homelands, including watermelons, black-eyed peas, okra, and rice, and contributed their invaluable knowledge of blacksmithing and iron-working to colonial life.

The Atlantic System's Impact

Trans-Atlantic migration, voluntary and forced, and increasingly close economic ties among Europe, Africa, and the Americas created an Atlantic System by which cargoes of plantation crops were shipped east across the Atlantic to Europe, while cargoes of slaves moved west to the Americas. The Atlantic System comprised a large network that spanned western and Central Africa, the east coast and southern region of English North America, the Caribbean Basin, and the northern and eastern coastal zones of South America. Plantations, slavery, and the numerical prominence of Africans and their descendants in the Americas defined this system, which ultimately helped spur major developments in modern world history, including the rise of European capitalism and wealth.

Economic Impact of the Slave Trade

As key economic activities in the Atlantic System, the slave trade and plantation economies provided enormous capital to Europeans and North Americans. Slave trading became a hugely profitable enterprise that was operated on a sophisticated business basis and attracted large amounts of capital, which allowed for rapid expansion of the trade. The prosperity of eighteenth-century European cities such as Bristol and Liverpool in England, and of North American cities such as Boston, Providence, Charleston, and New Orleans, depended heavily on the slave trade. Because the slavers, the cooperating African chiefs and merchants, the plantation owners, the shipbuilders, and the other groups linked directly or indirectly to the trade were all reluctant to abandon a lucrative activity, the trade endured for four hundred years.

The Atlantic System also contributed to European industrialization. Some of the profits from the slave trade and American plantations were invested in enterprises and technology in England, the Netherlands, France, and North America, helping to bring economic development to these societies and later spurring rapid industrialization in England. Some of the investment capital for inventing industrial technologies came from individuals and companies linked to the slave trade and plantations. For example, Glasgow merchants known as the "tobacco lords"—because of their ties to North American tobacco plantations—set up industries in Britain, such as printing companies, tanneries, and ironworks, and also invested in cotton textile plants and coal mines.

Economic Decline of Spain

However, some Europeans made wiser use of American profits than others. However vast the profits earned from overseas commerce, mercantilist economic strategies could not necessarily convert the incoming wealth into a growing domestic economy. Spain, the most powerful European country for most of the 1500s, had reaped vast riches from colonization, but the Spanish did not ultimately use this wealth in ways that promoted their own economic improvement. In fact, much of the exploitation of the Americas hurt Spain. For example, the flood of American bullion into Spain caused severe inflation, resulting in the need to import lower-priced products from other European countries. In addition, the large investments in the colonies were obtained in part by heavily taxing peasants and merchants in Spain. Because most Spanish merchants aspired to be large landowners in Spain, they used their profits to buy land rather than investing in trade or industry. By 1600 Spain was bankrupt, and a Spanish official charged that the country had wasted its wealth on frivolous spending rather than manufacturing. Similarly, the Portuguese squandered their colonial wealth through nonproductive investments, such as building magnificent churches and monasteries rather than financing local industry.

Dutch and British Successes

The Dutch and English did much better investing their profits than the Spanish and Portuguese. Enriched by its strong trade position in northern Europe, the Netherlands became a major banking center and also boasted the world's largest commercial fleet. During the 1600s, Dutch merchants earned vast profits from selling Indonesian coffee and spices to other Europeans, and they invested much of these profits in their domestic economy. The Dutch were the strongest European power for most of the seventeenth century, until they were finally eclipsed by England, which enjoyed the most long-term success. In the 1700s, England held the most powerful position in the Atlantic System, with large amounts of wealth flowing into Britain from the slave, tobacco, and sugar trades. The colonial wealth enriched businessmen and bankers, who could now easily mobilize capital for investment in trade, technology, and manufacturing. These factors gave England unique advantages that it fully exploited in the 1700s and 1800s.

During the Early Modern Era, the Americas were transformed and linked to the rest of the globe, forever reshaping world history. The conquest and exploitation of Native Americans and the acquisition of American resources enriched Europe and shifted economic power in the world. Ultimately, this economic power also added to European political and military strength. By the late 1700s or early 1800s, several European countries, especially Britain, had surpassed a declining China in wealth, living standards, and power.

Listen to a synopsis of Chapter 17.

CHAPTER 18

South Asia, Southeast Asia, and East Asia:
Triumphs and Challenges, 1450–1750

Learning Outcomes

After reading this chapter, you should be able to answer the following questions:

LO¹ What were the major achievements and failures of the Mughal Empire?

LO² How did Southeast Asia become more fully integrated into the world economy?

LO³ What factors enabled China to remain one of the world's strongest societies?

LO⁴ How did Korea and Japan change during this era?

The Namban Bunkakan, Osaka

> **66** The Portuguese saw that Melaka was magnificent, and its port exceedingly crowded. The people gathered around to see what the Portuguese looked like, and they were all surprised by their appearance. [But] these [Portuguese] know nothing of manners. **99**
>
> —Malay Chronicles[1]

Sultan Mahmud Shah (MA-mood Shah) (r. 1488–1511), the Malay ruler of the great trading state of Melaka (muh-LAH-kuh), on the southwest coast of the Malay Peninsula, had a problem. In 1509, five unknown but well-armed ships, each with a banner bearing a cross and full of menacing pale-skinned men, lowered anchor off his capital. Portuguese intentions were unclear to the sultan. They did not act like the peaceful Asian merchants who arrived regularly in trading ships, nor did they bring the customary valuable gifts for the sultan and his officials. Initially, as the Malay chronicles reported, curious Melakans gathered around a Portuguese envoy who came ashore, but the ill-mannered Portuguese violated local customs, antagonized Melaka officials, and alarmed influential local Indian traders. As tensions rose, fighting between Portuguese sailors and Malay visitors to their ship broke out. The Portuguese, unprepared for a full-scale assault on the heavily defended city, sailed away, vowing revenge.

Two years later, in 1511, a Portuguese fleet of some forty ships, mounted with cannon and carrying hundreds of soldiers armed with deadly muskets, sailed back to Melaka to capture the city. The sultan led the defense mounted on his elephant. As the Portuguese gained the upper hand after a bloody month-long assault, they slaughtered much of the population and looted the city. Melaka became the first Southeast Asian society to be severely disrupted by European power.

Many eastern and southern Asians had better success than the Melakans in deflecting the Europeans, who were beginning to arrive in the 1500s seeking markets and resources. The Portuguese in the

 Test your knowlege before you read this chapter.

What do you think?

China was the most powerful nation in the world during the Early Modern Era.

Strongly Disagree						Strongly Agree
I	2	3	4	5	6	7

<< **"Southern Barbarians"** This painting on a sixteenth-century Japanese screen, decorated with gold leaf, depicts a Portuguese sea captain, shaded by a parasol carried by his black servant, being greeted by black-robed Jesuit missionaries in the port of Nagasaki. His porters carry gifts for the Japanese merchants.

> "Babur was a gifted leader whose new dynasty restored the imperial grandeur of India."

1500s, the Dutch in the 1600s, and the English in the 1700s established some degree of control over the Indian Ocean maritime network and colonized a few areas, such as Melaka. But, for all their deadly gunpowder weapons, the Europeans did not yet have a clear military and economic advantage over the stronger Asian states, and as a result their influence was modest. Various Asian leaders manipulated the rival Europeans and sometimes forced them to leave. Asian countries were also protected by distance, because they could be reached only by long and dangerous voyages from Europe. As a result, most Asian societies did not undergo the transitions that were reshaping the Americas and parts of Africa in this era.

Some Asian states also remained politically and economically strong. A Muslim kingdom dominated much of India, many Southeast Asian states flourished from trade, China was still a major power, and the Japanese fiercely defended their interests. As in western Eurasia, connections to networks of exchange stretching around the world helped various Asian states grow commercially. As late as 1750, China and India together still accounted for more than half of world manufacturing, but by the mid-1700s, most of the great Asian states were under stress or collapsing from a combination of internal problems and destabilizing Western activities.

LO¹ Mughal India, South Asia, and New Encounters

During its long history, India's culture was shaped by the Hindu religion. During the Intermediate Era, however, Muslims had become politically influential and had introduced major changes. During the Early Modern Era, a powerful Muslim dynasty, the

Mughals (MOO-guhlz)—Central Asians of mixed Mongol-Turkish descent—ruled much of India and the Hindu majority. At their height in the later 1500s and early 1600s, the Mughals presided over one of the world's most creative societies, and also fashioned a prosperous economy that allowed many Indians, both Muslims and Hindus, to flourish. In the early 1700s, however, the Mughal system rapidly declined and began to collapse, just as pressures came from European societies.

The Mughal Empire

In 1526, Babur (BAH-bur) (1483–1530), a Muslim descendant of Genghis Khan and Tamerlane, led 12,000 troops from Afghanistan and conquered much of north India to form a new ruling dynasty called the Mughal, a corruption of *Mongol* (see Map 18.1). Babur was a gifted leader whose new dynasty restored the imperial grandeur of India. The wealth displayed at the Mughal court prompted a French visitor to wonder whether any other monarch possessed more gold, silver, and jewels. Mughal India had few rivals in military strength, government efficiency, economic power, and royal patronage of the arts.

 Interactive Map

Society and Religion

The Mughals, like earlier Indian governments, managed a highly diverse society. The majority of people shared many traditions and practiced Hinduism, but since the ninth century, a succession of Muslim states had ruled parts of the subcontinent, and perhaps one-quarter of the Indian population embraced Islam. Polytheistic Hinduism and monotheistic Islam offered starkly different visions of the cosmic and social order, and Hindus and Muslims often disagreed and competed for influence in Indian society. Yet at the village level, Hindus and Muslims lived side by side, sharing many customs.

By 1500, Buddhism, which had thrived for centuries, had nearly died out in India, but most people in Tibet and on the island of Sri Lanka (Ceylon) remained Buddhists. Indian society was also fragmented by caste divisions and hundreds of different regional languages. While proud of their Central Asian origins and influenced by Persian culture, the Mughals adapted to Indian conditions. For example, they used Urdu, a mix of Hindi, Arabic, and Persian

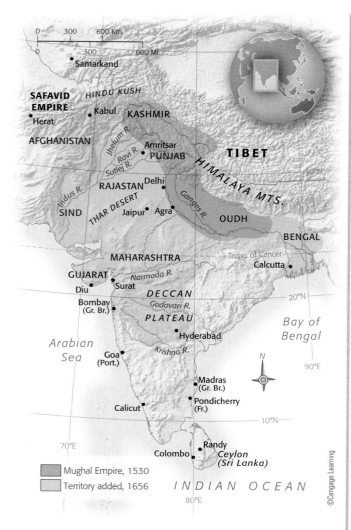

Map 18.1
The Mughal Empire, 1526–1761

By the mid-1600s, the Mughals controlled much of the Indian subcontinent, but some ports fell under European rule. The Portuguese had a colony at Goa and, by the early 1700s, the British had established outposts at Bombay, Calcutta, and Madras, and the French-occupied Pondicherry.

written in the Persian script, as their language of administration. Urdu had developed earlier as a common language among many Indian Muslims.

Akbar the Great

Akbar (AK-bahr) (r. 1556–1605), a grandson of Babur, pursued innovative policies and became the most outstanding Mughal ruler. Akbar, whose name means "Very Great," expanded Babur's

empire over all of north India, including Bengal, and deep into south India. To ensure stability and defuse opposition, Akbar gave Hindus high positions in the government and removed the extra taxes that earlier Muslim rulers in India had imposed, policies that brought him wide popularity. He also reformed the government, cracked down on corruption, and promoted religious toleration and compromise between communities. Akbar tried to abolish what he considered the most pernicious social customs, such as *sati* (burning the wife on the husband's funeral pyre), child marriage, and trial by ordeal, but was unable to curb such practices. Still, Akbar's India enjoyed an enlightened criminal code for the era, and all citizens had the right of appeal to the ruler if they believed themselves wrongly convicted of a crime or mistreated in the courts. Peace and prosperity prevailed during his reign.

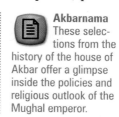

Akbarnama These selections from the history of the house of Akbar offer a glimpse inside the policies and religious outlook of the Mughal emperor.

Jahangir and Shah Jehan

Akbar presided over a golden age, but many of his successors were less tolerant and wise. The Mughals never worked out a stable pattern of succession, and because Muslim rulers in India had many wives and concubines, succession was often wildly contentious. Akbar was poisoned by a rebellious son, who then occupied the throne as Jahangir (ja-HAN-gear) ("World Seizer"). Although Jahangir generally pursued Akbar's public policies, his son, Shah Jahan (r. 1628–1658), promoted Islam relentlessly and destroyed several Hindu temples. He also took extravagant living to new heights, assembling a harem of five thousand concubines. Sitting on his splendid jewel-encrusted Peacock Throne in Delhi, Shah Jahan doubled the tax bills, and launched extensive building projects that virtually bankrupted the state. Unsuccessful military campaigns in Afghanistan and Central Asia added to the problems. Eventually, Shah Jahan was imprisoned by his ambitious, even more intolerant son, Aurangzeb (ow-rang-ZEB) (r. 1658–1707), who greatly expanded the empire in the south, but also set in motion the forces that began to undermine the Mughal state.

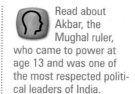

Read about Akbar, the Mughal ruler, who came to power at age 13 and was one of the most respected political leaders of India.

Mughal India, South Asia, and New Encounters **451**

Indian Economy and Society

Under the Mughals, India flourished, as it had for centuries, from industry, farming, and trade. Thanks to manufacturing, especially of textiles and iron, India had long been one of the world's most industrialized societies. By 1750, India still accounted for one-quarter of the world's industrial output, and it remained the largest producer of textiles. Its highly efficient farming, which benefited from investments in reservoirs and irrigation, produced large yields of wheat and rice. Cash crops, including cotton, indigo, pepper, sugar, and opium, found ready markets. The productive Indian economy and agriculture supported a doubling of the population between 1500 and 1750.

Foreign trade spurred the economy, and the bullion it brought to India benefited the Mughal treasury. Indian merchants and bankers maintained and even expanded some of the largest commercial networks in the Early Modern world. By the 1400s, the Indian maritime trade diaspora stretched from Arabia, Persia, northeast Africa, and the Red Sea to Melaka, Sumatra, Siam, and China. In the 1600s, an influx of American silver, used by European merchants to obtain textiles and other products, stimulated a tripling of the money supply. Revenues from commerce and industry allowed the Mughals to build an extensive network of imperial roads, support a luxurious court life, and fund ambitious building projects.

The Indian merchant networks enjoyed vast amounts of capital, as well as sophisticated credit and financing arrangements. Heavily capitalized family- and caste-run firms competed successfully against European and Asian rivals. Some merchants in Surat (SOO-raht), the Gujerat (goo-juh-RAHT) region's main port, were among the world's richest entrepreneurs. Other ports also had successful merchants. A Dutch diplomat wrote that the merchants of Bengal were "exceptionally quick and experienced. They are always sober, modest, thrifty, and cunning in identifying the source for their profit."[2]

Caste and Gender in Mughal India

The Indian traders came from a society divided by caste and gender divisions. Most of the Hindu merchants belonged to various subcastes (*jati*) of the larger caste grouping known as the *vaisya*, who ranked below the priests (*brahmans*) and warriors in a caste system that had been evolving for more than two thousand years. Caste remained dynamic, and subcastes moved up or down in the system. Nor did caste necessarily correspond to wealth, since many traders were affluent.

> "The Indian traders came from a society divided by caste and gender divisions."

Women's influence depended on their caste and family situation. In north India, where both Muslim and Hindu women were often kept in seclusion, they were expected to be chaste and obedient to fathers and husbands in a patriarchal, patrilineal society. Yet some women in the Mughal court exercised influence. For instance, Khanzada Begum (1478–1545), Babur's oldest sister, successfully interceded with rebellious brothers to end a family split and keep Babur's son, Humayun, on the throne. The Mughal women had financial resources, which they often devoted to endow mosques and support religious scholars.

Indian Religion and Arts

The coming of Islam in the centuries before 1500 dramatically changed India's religious and cultural environment. Muslims remained religiously distinct and were often disdainful of Hindus and of the caste system; the two groups never united to form a single people. Nonetheless, Muslim customs, such as veiling and secluding women, influenced upper-class Hindus in north India. The early Mughals, especially Akbar, mostly left the Hindus free to live as they wished, but less-tolerant policies emerged in later years.

Sufism

Mysticism became increasingly popular among both Muslims and Hindus. Sufi influences grew in the Islamic communities beginning in the 1300s, when Muslim rulers welcomed Sufi masters, some of them renowned poets, to their courts. Akbar and Jahangir were particularly sympathetic to Sufism, horrifying Muslim dogmatists, who regarded the mystics as heretics. Sufis argued that a personal bond existed between each believer and God, and they denied that either religious or political institutions could replace that bond. As a result, some Sufi movements, such as the Chishtiya (CHIS-tee-ya), avoided association with secular powers.

Bhakti

Meanwhile, many Hindus, particularly from lower castes, gravitated toward the mystical bhakti (BUK-tee) devotional movement, which had first emerged

in the Intermediate Era. Some bhakti groups challenged accepted wisdom by opposing the caste system, ignoring the high-caste brahmans and their traditional ritual practices, and sympathizing with the poor. Bhakti worship often involved dances, poems, and songs, as in Sufism, and focused on commitment to a particular Hindu god, such as Shiva or Vishnu.

Mysticism helped forge a gradual accommodation between some Muslims and Hindus but appealed more to women than to men. The barriers between the contrasting mystical approaches blurred, and many Muslims and Hindus venerated both Sufi and bhakti saints, making pilgrimages to their tombs. Many bhakti poets were women. The most famous, Mirabai (MEERA-buy) (ca. 1498–ca. 1546), a Rajput who was widowed at a young age, refused the pleas of her in-laws to commit sati and spent the rest of her life writing praises to Vishnu. Some historians view her life as a partly successful struggle against the patriarchal system and the brahmans (Hindu priests).

Sikhs

While many Sufi and bhakti mystics found common ground, other Indians tried to blend or transcend Hinduism and Islam by forming new sects. The largest of these sects, the Sikhs ("Disciples"), adopted elements from both Hinduism and Islam while creating a new religion. Eventually the Sikhs numbered several million people, mostly living in the Punjab region of northwest India. The religion was founded by Guru Nanak (GOO-roo NAN-ak) (1469–1539), born a Hindu, who had been strongly influenced by Hindu bhakti movements. But he argued that devotion was not enough: "God will not ask a man his tribe or sect, but what he has done. There is no Hindu and no Muslim. All are children of God."[3] Nanak was followed by nine spiritual leaders who refined the faith during Mughal times. Akbar respected the faith and granted Sikhs land for a great temple in Amritsar (uhm-RIT-suhr) in the Punjab.

Sikhs shared numerous beliefs and a mystical approach with other faiths but also had distinctive customs. Like Muslims, they worshiped one universal and loving God, rejected the caste system and priests, promoted egalitarianism, forbade alcohol and tobacco, and stressed discipline, hard work, and charity for the needy. Like Hindus, they offered devotional hymns to their god, but Sikhs also differed in significant ways: observant Sikh men adopted a look very different from that of Hindus or Muslims. Prohibited from cutting their hair, many wore turbans. Sikh women enjoyed great freedom compared to Hindus and Muslims, but persistent persecution by Mughal leaders after Akbar led Sikhs, once pacifists, to become militaristic.

Sikhs ("Disciples") Members of an Indian religion founded in the Early Modern Era that adopted elements from both Hinduism and Islam, including mysticism.

Art in the Mughal Empire

Early Modern Indians also made significant achievements in the arts. Based on Persian models, the distinctive Mughal school of miniature painting flourished under royal patronage. The Mughals were also great builders of tombs, mosques, forts, and palaces. Their architectural style, known as Indo-Islamic, blended Indian and Persian influences and made lavish use of mosaics, domes, and gateways. In the audience hall of his spectacular Delhi palace, the ruler Shah Jahan had inscribed: "If on earth be an Eden of bliss, it is this, it is this, it is this!"[4] East of Delhi, at Agra (AH-gruh), Shah Jahan left another legacy, the Taj Mahal (tahzh muh-HAHL). Often considered the world's most beautiful building, the Taj took 22,000 workers twenty-two years to complete. It was the final resting place for Shah Jahan's beloved favorite wife, Mumtaz Mahal (MOOM-taz muh-HAHL).

Mughal Decline and Portuguese Influence

Eventually the Mughals' endless wars of expansion and extravagant royal spending drained state coffers, reducing their ability to maintain power. Before the eighteenth century, the military strength of the Mughal state had been sufficient to keep Europeans and other enemies at bay. Although the state lacked naval power, the Mughal army, numbering some 1 million soldiers, was equipped with gunpowder weapons, such as muskets and field artillery, that rivaled European arms, and it had thousands of elephants to ride into battle and large cavalry units. By the early 1700s, however, the once-vaunted Mughal military machine was faltering, and the Mughals lacked the money to match European military capabilities.

Aurangzeb's Policies

Poor leadership also contributed to the decline. Aurangzeb's ruthless and intolerant policies alienated both Muslims and non-Muslims alike. A man with a more dogmatic view of

Islam and less generous viewpoints than his predecessors toward non-Muslims, Aurangzeb placed higher taxes on non-Muslims and persecuted—sometimes even executed—Hindu and Sikh leaders he saw as a threat to his power. His cruelty toward opponents and toleration of corruption also alienated many pious and tolerant Muslims. Revolt undermined Aurangzeb's later years, eventually leading to the dismantling of the Mughal state as regions broke away. The Marathas (muh-RAH-tuhz), a Hindu group from western India who had long resisted Mughal power, began raiding into the empire in the later 1600s and cutting Mughal supply lines. Some Hindu merchants, disenchanted with Mughal corruption, provided the Marathas with guns. When Safavid Iran conquered much of the Mughal-controlled areas of Afghanistan in the early seventeenth century, Mughal leaders were too busy plotting against each other to respond. They were finally defeated in 1761 by Hindu and Sikh insurgents.

The decline and demise of the powerful Mughal state left India open to penetration by Europeans. The anti-Mughal forces could not unite, leaving India fragmented and vulnerable. The division between Muslims and Hindus, a split intensified by the intolerance of later Mughal rulers, played a critical role in gradual European encroachment. Europeans had long been interested in southern Asia as a source of spices and textiles, and this interest spurred the Portuguese to seek a sea route around Africa and the Spanish to sponsor the Columbian voyages westward across the Atlantic in search of "the Indies." The Portuguese explorers came from a country with superior naval technology, missionary zeal, and a compelling appetite for wealth, but a standard of living little if any higher than that enjoyed by many Indians, Southeast Asians, and Chinese.

Vasco de Gama: The Portuguese in India

The Portuguese were the first Europeans to arrive in India directly from Europe by sea around Africa. Following the Indian Ocean maritime trade route from East Africa, the pioneer Portuguese explorer, Vasco da Gama (ca. 1469–1525), reached the southwestern Indian port of Calicut in 1498 with the help of a pilot hired in East Africa. At Calicut, Da Gama quickly realized the economic potential of Asia and learned that the European goods he carried had little value. Da Gama had one military advantage over the Indians—mounted cannon on his ships—but he was able to obtain a cargo of spices without force, which he sold in Europe at 3,000 percent profit. In 1500 a second Portuguese fleet returned to Calicut,

and, after fighting broke out ashore between the Portuguese and some local people, the Portuguese used their cannon to bombard Calicut, blasting the city to rubble and destroying bigger but less maneuverable Indian and Arab ships that were helping defend the city.

Like all the European powers that followed them to Asia, the Portuguese resorted to violence when they believed it necessary to enforce their power and acquire wealth. Seeking to control the trade from Asia to the West, the Portuguese established fortified settlements at strategic locations around the Indian Ocean in the early 1500s. In 1515 they also occupied Colombo (kuh-LUM-bow) in western Sri Lanka, a source of cinnamon. Soon the Portuguese used their warships to exercise partial control over the maritime trade of the western Indian Ocean, extorting payments from Ottoman, Arab, Indian, and Indonesian merchant ships. Sometimes they used terrorism: in 1502, to take revenge for the Portuguese killed earlier in Calicut, Vasco da Gama attacked, plundered, and burned an Arab passenger ship bound for Calicut carrying more than three hundred people, including several of Calicut's richest merchants and many women and children, killing all of the people aboard. But, despite devoting vast resources, including some eight hundred ships, to the effort, and despite controlling several key ports, the Portuguese never completely dominated the Indian Ocean commerce. Asian merchants often found ways to outmaneuver or evade Portuguese ships, and Asian states resisted Portuguese demands. The Portuguese still had to compete for Asian goods with Asian merchants.

"Christians and Spices"

Although chiefly interested in trade, the Portuguese were also zealous missionary Christians. Da Gama had told Calicut leaders that the Portuguese sought "Christians and spices," a useful shorthand. Hostility to Islam was a cornerstone of Portuguese policy, sometimes leading to persecution of Islamic institutions and repression of believers in Portuguese-held territories. Portuguese men settled in Goa and Colombo, marrying local women and fostering mixed-descent communities, but they also brought rigid gender roles to their Asian colonies, limiting the role of women.

South Asia's New Challenges

Before the mid-1700s, European influence on India and its trade remained relatively modest. Only some 10 percent of the silk and other cloth produced in Bengal in 1750 ended up in Europe. But the Portuguese activity foreshadowed an increasingly active European presence. The Dutch, French, and English followed the Portuguese to Asia, and all attempted to impose their influence on parts of South Asia. The overextended Portuguese were hard-pressed to sustain their power against these European rivals, who had larger populations and were developing better ships and gunpowder weapons.

The Dutch East India Company

The Dutch challenged the Portuguese for domination of the Indian Ocean trade in the early 1600s, eventually destroying their power in South and Southeast Asia and gaining partial control over Indian Ocean commerce. In 1602 Dutch merchants in Amsterdam, with the goal of tapping into the Asian trade, formed the Dutch East India Company, a private company with government backing that had its own armed fleet and operated in conjunction with other Dutch activities. In South Asia the Dutch concentrated their attention on Sri Lanka, gaining control of some of the coastal regions from the Portuguese in the 1640s. They remained in Sri Lanka, often intermarrying with local people, until they were ousted by the British in the early 1800s.

Soon the French joined the competition, forming their own East India Company in 1664. In the later 1600s and early 1700s, the French established a trading presence at Surat and Calcutta, and they built a military and commercial base at the southeast coast town of Pondicherry (pon-dir-CHEH-ree). Vigorous French competition for Indian merchandise generated tensions with the English. The two countries were also bitter rivals in Europe, and the resulting antagonisms sometimes spilled over into conflict in India: in 1746, the English and French fought fierce battles for dominance in southeast India that drew

A Goa Market A Dutch traveler, Jan Huygen Van Linschoten, made this plate while living in the Portuguese-ruled port city of Goa in the 1580s. It shows a street scene, including market stalls and, on the far right, a Portuguese woman walking with two Indian maids. Some Indians, wearing crosses, have become Christians.

Cadbury Collection, Birmingham Central Library and City Archives

in local Indian states and destabilized the region's politics.

The British East India Company

The English became the main threat to the Mughals, Dutch, and French in Asia. In 1600, British investors formed the British East India Company in London. They also built a fort at Madras (muh-DRAS) (today known as Chennai) and established a stable commercial base at Surat in northwest India, with Mughal permission. At Surat the English forged a commercial alliance with the Parsis (PAHR-seez), the Zoroastrian descendants of Persian refugees who were leading traders in India. By the late 1600s, the English were increasing their presence in India and, in 1717, they established bases at Bombay (today called Mumbai) and Calcutta, soon controlling these towns. But outside of Bombay, Calcutta, and Madras, English officials still had to negotiate with the Mughals or local princes for trading privileges. When piracy and banditry grew rapidly as Mughal authority collapsed, the law and order in the three English-run towns, secured by an increasing English military presence, attracted Indian settlers. English and Indian merchants in the three English bases prospered. The growing English presence in India also had consequences in England, where competition from Indian textile imports spurred local textile manufacturers to cut costs, helping stimulate English industrialization.

By the mid-eighteenth century, the English were strong enough to treat local rulers with less deference and expand their control from their three bases into the surrounding regions. When local Indian governments resisted this encroachment, the English resorted to military force. By the 1750s, this had resulted in a war in Bengal, where, from their Calcutta base, the English now began their long period of military conquest in South Asia. Eventually they controlled nearly all of South Asia except for a few small enclaves, such as Portuguese Goa and French Pondicherry. With the English, India faced a major new challenge.

LO² Southeast Asia and Global Connections

Southeast Asia had long been a cosmopolitan center where peoples, religions, ideas, and products

> "Increased trade encouraged political centralization, the growth of cities, and the spread of world religions."

met. Southeast Asians participated in the wider hemispheric trade and most adopted Theravada Buddhism, Confucianism, or Islam. The Portuguese arrival at Melaka inaugurated a new era of transregional contacts during which European adventurers, traders, missionaries, and soldiers were active in the region. Several areas were influenced by the West before 1750, particularly Malaya, the Philippine Islands, and parts of Indonesia. However, in most parts of Southeast Asia, including strong kingdoms such as Siam, Burma, and Vietnam, Western influence remained weak until the nineteenth century.

Southeast Asian Transitions and Trade

In the Early Modern Era, Southeast Asia was undergoing a transition that included commercial growth, political change, increasingly productive agriculture, and expansion of Islam and Buddhism. Partly because of increasing connections with European, Chinese, Arab, and Indian merchants, commerce increased between the 1400s and 1700s, and Southeast Asia remained an essential hub in the maritime trade network linking East Asia with India and the Middle East. Sailing ships still stopped in the region's ports to exchange goods or wait for the monsoon winds to shift.

Increased trade encouraged political centralization, the growth of cities, and the spread of world religions. Larger, more centralized states absorbed neighboring smaller states: on the mainland some twenty states in the fourteenth century had been reduced to less than a dozen by the early eighteenth century, with Siam, Vietnam, and Burma being the most influential. Thanks to the increased amounts of products being obtained and transported, regional ports flourished, and urban merchants became powerful in local politics. Although revenue from trade became more crucial than agricultural taxes in many states, agriculture remained a major activity, and new crops and varieties of rice spurred population growth. At the same time, Theravada Buddhism dug deeper roots on the Southeast Asian mainland, and Islam continued to spread throughout the Malay Peninsula and the islands of Indonesia and the southern Philippines. As a result of increased trade and exposure to new religions, cultures were opened to the outside world.

European Colonialism in Southeast Asia

Southeast Asia's wealth and resources, especially spices such as cloves, nutmeg, and pepper, attracted European merchants and conquerors to the region. The Portuguese who occupied Melaka were the forerunners of a powerful and destabilizing European presence that transformed Southeast Asia between 1500 and 1900. By controlling Melaka, the Portuguese gained an advantage against their European and Malay rivals. A few years later they brutally conquered the Spice Islands, known as Maluku (muh-LOO-ku), in northeast Indonesia, thus gaining control of the valuable spice trade to Europe.

But, as in India, Portuguese power in Southeast Asia proved short-lived. Like the East African ports they occupied earlier, Melaka languished under Portuguese control, since fewer Muslim merchants chose to endure the higher taxes and Portuguese intolerance of Islam. Portuguese policies often involved brute force, and their effort to convert subject peoples to Christianity made them unwelcome. Although the Dutch replaced the Portuguese in Melaka in 1641, for several centuries Portuguese became a language of trade and commerce in some coastal regions of Asia, from Basra in Iraq to ports in Vietnam.

Portuguese activities spurred the Spanish, Dutch, English, and French to compete for markets, resources, Christian converts, and power in Southeast Asia. The Spanish conquered the Philippines, and the Dutch gained some control of the Indian Ocean maritime trade by force and conquered Java and the Spice Islands. Preoccupied with India and the Americas, the English mainly sought only trade relations in this era. The French became involved in Vietnam, beginning in 1615, seeking trade but also dispatching Catholic missionaries, who recruited a small following of Vietnamese. But European power had its limits: Southeast Asian states such as Siam, Vietnam, Burma, and Acheh were strong enough to resist more than three hundred years of persistent effort by Westerners to gain complete political, social, and economic domination, which they achieved only by 1900.

Buddhist and Islamic Societies

Despite such incursions, various Southeast Asian societies remained vigorous in this era, in both the Buddhist and Islamic realms (see Map 18.2). Among the strongest states with a mostly Theravada Buddhist population was Siam, governed from 1350 to 1767 by kings based at Ayuthia. Siam was involved in maritime trade and developed a regional empire, extending its influence into Cambodia and some of the small Lao (laow) states along the Mekong River. Its competition with the Burmese, Vietnamese, and the largest Lao state, Lan Xang (lan chang), for regional dominance occasionally led to war. Indeed, in the 1560s, a Burmese army ravaged Siam and sacked Ayuthia, carrying back to Burma thousands of Siamese prisoners and their families.

Interactive Map

> **Portuguese activities spurred the Spanish, Dutch, English, and French to compete for markets, resources, Christian converts, and power in Southeast Asia.**

Siamese Society

Siam eventually recovered from Burma's conquest and flourished. For example, during the reign of King Narai (na-RY) (r. 1656–1688), the king used some of his revenues to promote literature and art, often with a Buddhist emphasis, thus fostering a cultural renaissance. Because Theravada Buddhist monks sponsored many village schools, Siam had one of the highest literacy rates in the premodern world. Siamese society was hierarchical but tolerant by the world's standards at that time. The royal family and the aristocracy that administered the government were mostly Buddhist, and they remained aloof from the commoners and a large class of slaves. Women enjoyed rights, including that of operating village and town markets. Theravada Buddhism encouraged tolerance toward other faiths

CHRONOLOGY

Southeast Asia, 1450–1750

1350–1767	Ayuthia kingdom in Siam
1511	Portuguese conquest of Melaka
1565	Spanish conquest of Philippines
1619	Dutch base at Batavia
1641	Dutch seizure of Melaka from Portuguese
1668	Siamese expulsion of French

Map 18.2
Southeast Asia in the Early Modern Era

Much of Southeast Asia remained independent, able to deflect European ambitions, but the Portuguese had captured the port of Melaka, Timor, and the Moluccas (Maluku), and the Spanish had colonized the Philippines. In the 1600s, the Dutch displaced the Portuguese from Melaka and the Moluccas, and ruled part of Java from Batavia.

WWW Southeast Asia Guide (*http://www.library.wisc.edu/guides/SEAsia/*). An impressive, easy-to-use site from the University of Wisconsin—Madison.

and cultivated a more liberal society. Ayuthia's openness to merchants and creative people from all over Eurasia made it a vibrant crossroads of exchange and influence.

However, Siam had to contend with increasing European activity. English,

French, and Dutch traders all established operations in Ayuthia. King Narai, who had regularly sent missions to Persia, India, and China, sent three diplomatic missions to the French court of Louis XIV to obtain Western maps and scientific knowledge, and employed several foreigners as officials. One of these, Constantine Phaulkon, was discovered to have plotted with the French to convert Narai to Christianity and station French troops near the capital in 1688.

When the Siamese learned of the plot, they expelled all French diplomats, missionaries, and merchants from Siam and executed Phaulkon. For decades after, the Siamese mistrusted Europeans and refused to grant them any special trading privileges.

> "Trade networks fostered the expansion of Islam and increased its influence throughout the Indonesian islands and the Malay Peninsula."

Hispanization
The process by which, over nearly three centuries of Spanish colonial rule beginning in 1565, the Catholic religion and Spanish culture were imposed on the Philippine people.

Ferdinand Magellan

Islam in Southeast Asia

Some Muslim societies also flourished in Southeast Asia. Trade networks fostered the expansion of Islam and increased its influence throughout the Indonesian islands and the Malay Peninsula. Various societies adapted Islam to their own cultural traditions. Many Javanese superimposed Islam, often with a Sufi flavor, on the existing foundation of Hinduism and mystical animism, producing an eclectic and tolerant mix of faiths. Other peoples embraced a more orthodox version of Islam. As more Muslim merchants called at ports with Muslim rulers, the strengthening of trade ties enriched states. The mixing of Islam and maritime trade encouraged mobility and connections to the wider world.

Islam also changed gender relations. As in most of Southeast Asia, women in Indonesia had often enjoyed independence. However, Islam, rooted in patriarchal Arab traditions, diminished women's rights in some Indonesian societies. For instance, in Acheh (AH-cheh) in northern Sumatra, where four successive women had ruled in the later 1600s, women were eventually prohibited from holding royal power, but elsewhere women often continued to play key roles. Muslim courts on Java and other islands were often filled with hundreds, sometimes thousands, of women. Some were wives and concubines, but most were attendants, guards, or textile workers.

The Philippines Under Spanish Colonization

The greatest Western impact in Southeast Asia before 1800 came in the Philippine Islands, which were conquered by Spain. For nearly three centuries of its colonial rule, beginning in 1565, Spain imposed the Catholic religion and many aspects of Spanish culture with a policy known as Hispanization. However, the Filipinos managed to mix their indigenous customs with the Spanish influences. Under Spanish rule, the Philippines became a key participant in the new world economy.

Spanish interest in the Philippines was a result of their activities in the Americas and their quest for a sea route to Asia. The first Spanish ships to reach the islands in 1521, commanded by Ferdinand Magellan, were part of the first successful effort to circumnavigate the world, though Magellan himself did not complete the voyage. Magellan pressured the Filipinos he encountered to adopt Christianity. He ordered a local chief to burn all his peoples' religious figures and replace them with crosses, which every villager should worship every day on their knees. Magellan's arrogant demands inspired opposition, and he was killed in a skirmish with hostile Filipinos. Today, on the beach on Cebu Island where Magellan died, a memorial honors Lapulapu (LAH-pu-LAH-pu), the chief who led the attack, as the first Filipino to repel European aggression.

Filipino Society

Magellan had chanced upon an island group inhabited by some 1 to 2 million people divided into many distinct ethnic groups and speaking more than one hundred Malay languages. The population was scattered across 7,000 islands, although the majority lived on the two largest islands, Luzon (loo-ZON) and Mindanao (min-duh-NOW). Muslims occupied the southernmost islands, and Islam was slowly spreading northward, but most Filipinos mixed belief in Allah with animism. Remote from the mainland and western Indonesia, the islands had historically received relatively little cultural influence from India or China, but a few hundred Chinese traders lived in the major towns, and some Filipinos traveled as far as Melaka and Burma as maritime traders. Unlike the kingdoms of Java or Siam, the largest Filipino political units were villages led by chiefs.

The Spanish in the Philippines

When, four decades after Magellan's death, the Spaniards returned to conquer and evangelize, they renamed the islands the Philippines after their monarch, Philip II, known as "the most Catholic of kings." Given the ethnic divisions and lack of a dominant Philippine state, the militarily superior Spanish had little trouble conquering the islands and co-opting local chiefs. But the Muslims in the south, called Moros by the Spanish, were never completely pacified, and Spanish authority there remained mostly nominal. The Spanish set up their colonial government and trading base in Manila (muh-NIL-uh), located on a fine natural harbor.

The Catholic Church took a major role in the colonial Philippine enterprise. The church governed various regions outside of Manila and acquired great wealth. In many districts, priests collected taxes and sold the crops, such as sugar, grown by Filipino parishioners. Catholic friars, accompanying the soldiers, began the process of conversion, and several religious orders competed to gain the most converts. Indeed, the Spanish colonial regime gave the missionaries special authority, and the Spanish crown financed the conversion efforts. Missionaries concentrated on the children of village leaders but, to better control and evangelize the Filipinos, they also required people to move into towns. Few schools were opened outside Manila, and what education existed was in church hands. To control competing ideas, the Spanish destroyed nearly all of the pre-Spanish writings, which they considered pagan. Eventually around 85 percent of the Filipinos adopted Roman Catholicism, but many incorporated their own animist traditions into the religion. Friendly spirits became Christian saints, and miracles attributed to Jesus or the Virgin Mary became the new form of magic. Some Filipinos even used religious festivals to subtly express opposition to Spanish rule.

Inequality also showed up in economic and social patterns. The colonial economy forged a rural society based on plantation agriculture and tenant farming, implanting a permanent gap between the extraordinarily rich landowners, who emphasized lucrative cash crops, and the impoverished peasants. Filipinos, once masters of the land, mostly became tenants working for a few powerful landowning families or the church. Priests and landowners told them their religious duty was to labor hard for others—they would get their just rewards later in heaven.

Although the Spanish created a country and expanded the economy, they did not construct a cohesive society. Regional and ethnic loyalties remained dominant. The Spaniards occupied the top spots, controlling the government and church. The great majority of Spanish lived in Manila, often in luxury, and few outside the church ever learned to speak local languages. Below them were mixed-descent people, known as mestizos, and a few Filipino families who descended from chiefs. Below them were Chinese immigrants, who worked as merchants and craftsmen and mostly remained middle class. But while the Spanish needed the Chinese as middlemen, they also despised, persecuted, and sometimes expelled them. On occasion, when their resentment of Chinese wealth or concern with growing Chinese numbers became intense, Spanish forces slaughtered the residents of Manila's large Chinatown.

Chinese Mestizo Couple This painting by a French artist shows two wealthy, well-dressed Chinese mestizos riding in Manila. Chinese mestizos, products of marriages between Chinese immigrants and Filipino or Spanish women, played a key role in colonial life.

From Edgar Wickberg, *The Chinese in Philippine Life 1850-1898* (New Haven, CT and London: Yale University Press, 1965)

The lowest social status was held by the vast majority of Filipinos, whom the Spanish called Indios. They faced many legal restrictions; for example, they were prohibited from dressing like Spaniards. The Filipinos retained their traditionally strong communal orientation, including powerful kinship networks. However, because the Spanish culture and church devalued women, Filipinas lost the high position they had enjoyed in pre-Spanish society and now faced restrictions on their activities. But despite male prejudice and a narrowing of gender roles, Filipinas continued to control family finances and engage in small-scale trade.

Indonesia and the Dutch

In the seventeenth century, the Dutch arrived, displacing the Portuguese from most of their bases and becoming the dominant European power in Southeast Asia. Dutch ships had long carried spices from Portugal to northern Europe. The Dutch gradually expanded their influence from the Spice Islands to other islands, notably Java. Because they built their empire in the Indies over a period of three hundred years, their impact varied widely over time. The Dutch sought wealth but, unlike the Portuguese and Spanish, cared little about spreading their culture and religion. In 1595 a Dutch fleet visited the Spice Islands of Maluku and brought back spices to Holland. Over the next several decades, the Dutch, after bloody battles, dislodged the Portuguese from most of their scattered outposts, capturing the Portuguese-controlled port of Melaka in 1641.

Over the next several centuries, the Dutch gradually gained control of the islands of Indonesia, except for the Portuguese-ruled eastern half of the island of Timor. They quickly became hated for their ruthlessness and slaughtered their Indonesian opponents by the thousands. After Dutch forces attacked and occupied the prosperous trading city of Makassar (muh-KAS-uhr), in southeast Sulawesi (SOO-la-WAY-see), in 1659, the sultan's secretary, Amin, ruefully observed, "Never make friends with the Dutch. No country can call itself safe when they are around."[5] The Dutch were well-organized, resourceful, and shrewd diplomats, allying themselves with one state against a rival state. While exploiting local conflicts, however, they sometimes were drawn into civil wars or were faced with stiff resistance.

The Dutch in Java

With trade as their major goal, for several centuries the Dutch left administration of their Indonesian bases to the Dutch East India Company, which had great capital and large resources for pursuing profit. Holland was ten months away by boat, so there was little guidance and few restraints on the company's power, and it used its goal of gaining a monopoly of trade in Southeast Asia to justify ruthless policies. If the people of a Spice Island grew restless, Dutch forces might exterminate them or carry them off as slaves to Java, Ceylon, or South Africa. For instance, in 1621 the entire population of the spice-producing Banda (BAN-duh) Islands—some 15,000 people—were killed, taken away as slaves, or left to starve.

Eventually the Dutch concentrated on the rich island of Java, which had a flourishing mercantile economy tied to maritime trade and several competing sultanates. In the 1600s, Java boasted at least two cities with more than 100,000 people, and their population was a cosmopolitan mix drawn from throughout Asia. Javan artisans were noted for fine craftsmanship; the island's smiths made perhaps the finest steel swords in the world. Their commercial prowess was renowned in the region, and Javanese women were prominent in business. The Dutch did not come into an underdeveloped society, but one with living standards comparable to those in western Europe.

Capitalizing on Java's political instability and divisions, the Dutch slowly extended their power across the island after establishing a military and commercial base at a village they renamed Batavia, on the northwestern coast, in 1619. Batavia later grew into a city, today known as Jakarta. Most of Java came under direct or indirect Dutch control by the end of the eighteenth century. Soon the Dutch concentrated on making Java a source of wealth. In the highlands of west Java, and later in Sumatra, peasants were forced to grow coffee for export through a system of annual quotas. Coffee—domesticated centuries earlier in Ethiopia and then grown in southern Arabia—had become a popular beverage in both the Middle East and Europe. The huge sums from this process financed much of Holland's industrialization in the nineteenth century. The Dutch co-opted local elites and governed some districts through local rulers. Dutch and Chinese entrepreneurs slowly displaced the Javanese merchant class, once major players in the world economy.

Javanese Social Structure

Through their political and economic activities, the Dutch gradually transformed Javan society and life. As in other colonies, inequality characterized the society. Europeans occupied the top rung, followed by

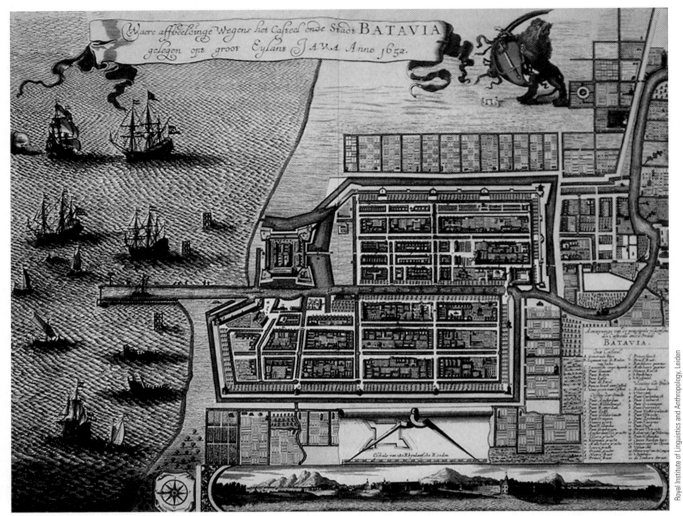

Batavia The Dutch built a port they called Batavia on the northwest coast of Java. Batavia, shown on this map from 1652, grew rapidly as the political and commercial center of the Dutch empire in Southeast Asia.

those of mixed-descent, known as Eurasians, and the co-opted local aristocracy. Javanese now became even more preoccupied with social status, and the peasants were encouraged to treat the aristocratic officials with great awe and respect. The middle class was mostly Chinese. Like the Spanish in the Philippines, the Dutch came to fear the growing Chinese community, a fear that sometimes led to a massacre of Chinese in Batavia. The lower class included not only the peasants but also Javanese merchants.

Denied real power, the Javanese royal courts turned inward to refine the traditional culture. Many Dutch found Javanese culture seductive and took local wives, owned slaves, dressed in Javanese clothes, and indulged in the delicious spicy curries, now enriched by American chilies. Other Dutch, however, criticized this behavior. Whatever their attitude toward local customs, most Dutch lived in Batavia, which was built to resemble a city in the Netherlands. The Dutch, who recognized religious freedom at home, spent little money on Christian missions.

Southeast Asians and the World Economy

During the Early Modern Era, Southeast Asia became even more crucial to the developing world economy. Some historians point to the significance of the Philippine city of Manila in 1571, which became the first hub linking Asia and the Americas across the Pacific. Each year, Philippine crops and other Asian products, including Chinese silk and porcelain, were brought to Manila for export to Mexico. From there, some products were shipped on to Europe on Spanish galleons. These ships symbolized the new global reality. More than half the silver mined in the Americas ended up in China, giving the Asian economy a great push and encouraging increased production of Philippine sugar, Chinese tea, and Indian textiles. The Manila galleon trade was highly speculative, since Spanish businessmen bet their fortunes that the galleons would arrive in Mexico safely. Pirates, storms, and other obstacles made the voyages dangerous. The unpredictable galleon trade fostered a "get-rich-quick" mentality rather than a long-term strategy to bring prosperity to the Philippines.

Despite all the economic changes, Southeast Asians retained considerable continuity with the past. The West was not yet dominant, except in a few widely scattered outposts such as Melaka, the Spice Islands, and the Philippines. European interlopers had to compete with Chinese, Arab, Indian, and Southeast Asian merchants. Nor were Europeans the only growing political power. The Vietnamese, continuing their

long expansion down the Vietnamese coast, had annexed the Mekong Delta by the late 1600s, and the Siamese forced the French to leave. In brief, the European powers had entered a wealthy, open, and dynamic region. Only by the eighteenth century did the Southeast Asian commercial society begin to collapse under the weight of accelerating Western activity and internal strife.

LO³ Early Modern China and New Challenges

Two dynasties, the Ming followed by the Qing (ching), ruled China for more than half a millennium, between the overthrow of the Mongols and the advent of a republic in 1912 (see Map 18.3), marking one of the great eras of orderly

 Interactive Map

Map 18.3
Qing China and East Asia in the Early Modern Era

Qing China remained the colossus of eastern Eurasia, controlling a huge empire that included Tibet, Xinjiang, and Mongolia. Korea and Vietnam remained tributary states of China, but the Russians expanded into eastern Siberia. The Japanese partly secluded themselves from the outside world.

© Cengage Learning

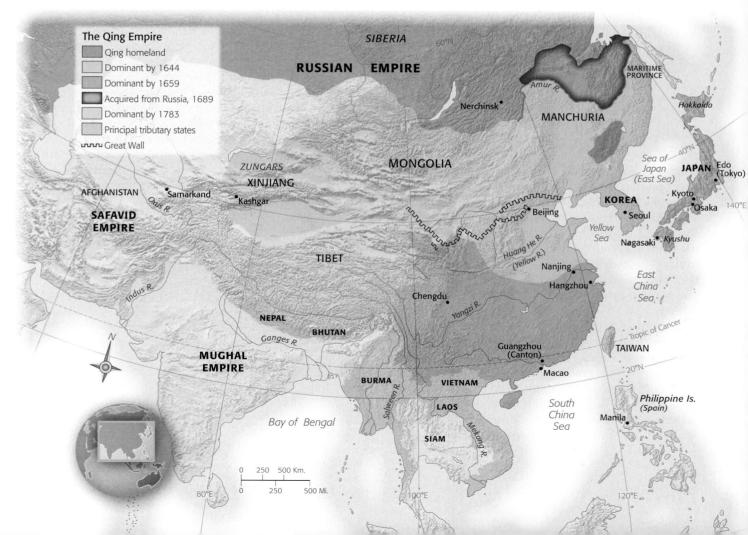

government and social stability in history. Like western Europeans at this time, the Chinese enjoyed widening market networks and more cultivation of cash crops. China still remained one of the strongest, most industrialized societies through the eighteenth century, boasting a vibrant culture and economy. Although encounters with Europeans indicated the challenges ahead just as China began to experience political and technological decay, no other country could match the size, wealth, and power of Early Modern China.

The Later Ming Dynasty

China under the Ming (1368–1644) remained strong and dynamic. The imperial political system administered by the mandarins was supported by a highly productive agriculture and the world's largest, most diversified commercial economy. Although heavily regulated, commercial activity provided the people with numerous products and services, and the Mings' rebuilding of the transportation network centered on the Grand Canal made it easier to ship goods. Cotton, silk, and tea were exported to Japan and Southeast Asia for silver and spices.

> 66 The imperial political system administered by the mandarins was supported by a highly productive agriculture and the world's largest, most diversified commercial economy. 99

Internet Guide for China Studies (*http://www.sino.uni-heidelberg.de/igcs/*). A good collection of links maintained at Germany's Heidelberg University.

For centuries, China had been among the world leaders in scientific thought and technological invention. This inventiveness continued: late Ming and early Qing Chinese developed better cotton gins, spinning wheels, and other technologies for textile and silk production, which fostered growth and the employment of many more workers. Chinese also continued to publish scientific books. At the same time, however, Ming China turned somewhat inward. Always self-sufficient and self-centered, China became increasingly ethnocentric, even anti-foreign; the great maritime voyages of the early fifteenth century had ended, and the Ming court increasingly concentrated on home affairs and the defense of the northern borders. Although some foreign merchants continued to come to China, and Chinese merchants still went to Southeast Asia, the Ming launched a period of increased isolation, in contrast to the cosmopolitanism of the earlier Tang, Song, and Yuan periods. Misrule and other mounting problems helped undercut the Ming and led to dynastic change.

During the later 1500s, crop failures, which caused famine, and a terrible plague killed millions in north China. In the 1590s, the Ming had to dispatch soldiers and ships to defend their Korean vassal from the Japanese, at a huge cost to the treasury. Adding to the pressure, Japanese pirates ravaged the southern coast and peasant revolts broke out. These problems opened the doors to the Manchus (MAN-chooz), a seminomadic pastoral people from Manchuria who were angry at the migration of Chinese settlers into their homeland. United under a strong chief, the Manchus found collaborators among Chinese who were tired of the Ming failures. While peasant rebellions rocked the country, Manchu forces swept into China on horseback, routing the Ming; however, it took several decades to occupy and pacify the country.

The Qing Empire: Society and Culture

The new Manchu rulers installed the Qing dynasty, which ruled from 1644 to 1912. The first Qing rulers were exceptionally competent overseers. Although they retained their ethnic identity, forbidding Manchu intermarriage with Chinese, the Manchus knew that to be successful they would have to adopt Chinese institutions and culture to win the support of the Chinese people. Hence, like most earlier foreign rulers, the Manchus underwent voluntary assimilation to Chinese ways. Chinese served in high offices, and many villagers scarcely knew China had foreign rul-

CHRONOLOGY

China, 1450–1750

1368–1644	Ming dynasty
1557	Portuguese base at Macao
1610	Death of Matteo Ricci in Beijing
1644–1912	Qing dynasty
1689	Treaty of Nerchinsk

ers. Like earlier dynasties, the Qing relied on the mandarins, scholars educated in the Confucian classics, for administration.

Kangzi and Yongzheng

Some Qing emperors were outstanding managers and hard workers, aware of their awesome responsibility and willing to temper arbitrary power. The most admired Qing ruler, the reflective Kangzi (kang-shee) (r. 1661–1722), loved to tour the provinces inspecting public works and joining hunting expeditions. Like other emperors, he was also a noted writer and painter, exemplifying the Confucian ideal of the virtuous ruler. His son and successor, Yongzheng (young-cheng) (r. 1723–1735), tried to improve social conditions. For example, he ordered that anyone held in hereditary servile status anywhere in the empire be freed. The law was aimed at groups in remote regions who still practiced forms of slavery.

The Manchus created the greatest Eurasian land empire since the Mongols, making China one of the world's major political powers. Qing armies reasserted Chinese control of the western and northern frontier, annexing Xinjiang (shin-chang) ("New Dominions"), a desert region largely inhabited by Turkish-speaking Muslims, and Mongolia. For the first time in Chinese history, peace prevailed along the northern and western borderlands. Tibet, long a tributary state to China, was brought into the Manchu fold. The Qing also incorporated Taiwan, off the east coast. This large, fertile island's original inhabitants were Malay peoples, but Chinese began immigrating there in large numbers in the 1600s.

> "The Manchus created the greatest Eurasian land empire since the Mongols, making China one of the world's major political powers."

Qing Social Order

Ming and Qing China owed their political and social stability in part to the Chinese gentry, whose power was based on their combined possession of land and office in an agrarian-based bureaucratic empire. As landlords and moneylenders, the gentry had dominated economic life in villages since the Tang dynasty. Because they owned land and could afford tutors, the gentry men also received a formal education and held scholarly degrees. Under the Ming, a close relationship had developed between the local gentry and the imperial bureaucracy, a relationship that continued under the Qing. Together the Chinese gentry and the Manchu rulers sought to preserve the status quo.

Women had a complex status in the patriarchal society of Qing China. The education of women was frequently debated among the elite and was encouraged by some intellectuals. Some women from

Emperor Kangxi The Qing emperor Kangxi had one of the longest reigns in Chinese history, and his birthdays were given lavish public celebrations. In this print of Beijing, a crowd gathers around the royal dais, while women observe the festivities from courtyards (foreground) and shopkeepers look on from their businesses.

Laurie Platt Winfrey, Inc./The Granger Collection, New York

gentry and merchant families were educated informally, reading and even writing literature. However, elite women also had limited physical mobility because of foot-binding, a custom that was introduced half a millennium earlier but that only became widespread during the Ming. Peasant women were usually illiterate but nonetheless played a key economic role. In the cloth industry, the men planted the cotton, but the women picked the crop, processed it into yarn, and wove the finished product for sale. In many districts, however, peasant women were gradually marginalized as their menfolk or large commercial farmers took over their livelihood.

Neo-Confucianism

Along with social conditions and steady leadership, philosophy also contributed to the stability of the Ming and Qing period. A renaissance of Confucian thought flourished during the Ming and early Qing, when changing times seemed to call for something more than mere memorization of Confucian classics written in the Classical Era. In response to these changes, some scholars developed an interpretation of Confucianism, known as neo-Confucianism, that incorporated elements of Buddhism and Daoism, stressed rational thinking, and reemphasized the natural goodness of people. Some Ming and Qing philosophers offered ideas similar to those of such European philosophers as Sir Francis Bacon, René Descartes, and John Locke. Like Bacon, the neo-Confucian Wang Yang-Ming (1472–1529) pondered the unity of knowledge and conduct, concluding that the first necessarily required the second. Like Descartes, Wang wondered how people know the external world and concluded that "whatever we see, feel, hear, or in any wise conceive or understand is as real as ever."[6] Like Bacon and Locke, many scholars espoused the idea that the mind is reason. A few Chinese scholars, such as the philosopher and poet Tai Chen, studied knowledge from other societies.

A Visual Sourcebook of Chinese Civilization (http://depts.washington.edu/chinaciv/). A wonderful collection of essays, illustrations, and other useful material on Chinese History.

However, as neo-Confucianism became more influential, it turned into a new orthodoxy, limiting Chinese interest in alternative ideas. Some Qing scholars wrote that no more writing was needed, because the truth had been made clear by ancient thinkers: all that was left was to practice their teachings. By the 1700s, fewer Chinese intellectuals showed much interest in practical inquiry or technological development. Neo-Confucianism reinforced a growing social rigidity, including increasing male dominance over women. Thus, although it contributed to the unparalleled continuity of Chinese society, Neo-Confucianism was hostile to originality or ideas from outside.

Art and Literature in Qing China

While intellectual inquiry began to stagnate, China's art and literature, in contrast, remained creative. As they had for centuries, artists painted landscapes featuring misty distances, soaring mountains, and angular pine trees. However, many innovative painters drew on Daoist mysticism to create fanciful scenes at odds with tradition, such as Zhu Da (ca. 1626–1705), who painted bizarre conceptions of nature. Qing authors wrote some of China's greatest fiction. In the early 1700s, the novel *The Scholars,* by Wu Jingzi (woo ching-see), satirized the examination system and revealed the foibles of the pompous and the ignorant. Likewise, *The Story of the Stone* by Cao Xueqin (tsao swee-chin), often considered China's greatest novel, used a large and declining gentry family to discuss, and sometimes satirize, Qing life.

China and the World Economy

China in the later Ming and early Qing had commercial vitality, flourishing industrial production, and extensive foreign trade. Indeed, the Chinese, whose goods often sold hundreds of miles from where they were produced, enjoyed the world's largest and best-integrated commercial economy (see Witness to the Past: A Mandarin's Critique of Chinese Movements). Government taxation policies encouraged both agriculture and industry. A Chinese official wrote in 1637 that there was at least one cotton loom in every ten houses. Gradually, the fertile lower Yangzi (yahng-zeh) Basin, linked by the Yangzi River and Grand Canal to west and north China, became China's industrial heartland, commercial hub, and most prosperous region. Throughout the 1700s, the people of the Yangzi Basin enjoyed living standards comparable to those of the world's other wealthiest regions, England and the Netherlands, both enriched by overseas colonization.

Ming and early Qing China remained a major force in an international economy. China exported such products and resources as porcelain, cotton textiles, silk, tea, quicksilver, and zinc, and was a market for and source of valuable products. As Europeans shipped silver to China to pay for Chinese products, Chinese production increased in response. Chinese population growth was also due to China's link to the international economy, a result of the introduction by Spanish merchants of new crops from the Americas as well as Chinese development of a new fast-growing rice. The thriving economy served a population that reached 250 or 300 million by 1750, one-quarter of the world total. Several major cities had more than 1 million residents, including Nanjing (nahn-JING), Beijing, and Guangzhou (gwong-joe) (known in the West as Canton).

However, despite Ming and Qing China's economic dynamism, full-scale capitalism and industrialization did not develop, a result that has puzzled historians. The commercial revolution and technological advances of the Tang, Song, and Ming failed to bring about in China the revolutionary changes that transformed western European feudalism into capitalism. One reason was that, unlike the English and Dutch, the Chinese lacked an overseas empire that could be exploited to acquire capital for investment. Another basic difference from Europe was the continuity of Chinese traditions. The Han pattern was continued in essentials by the Sui, the Sui by the Tang, and so on in unbroken succession until 1912. In addition, with a fast-growing population,

China had no labor shortage and hence no great spur for technological innovation. Its economy met its basic needs well.

The relations between the imperial government and the merchants may also have been a factor in preventing full-scale capitalism. The imperial system heavily restricted and taxed the merchant class, a major difference from early modern Europe, where big business enterprises and the commercial middle class had a growing influence in politics. During the Song commercial revolution, many mandarins came from merchant backgrounds and tended to protect their family's enterprises as well as business generally, but by the Qing this was no longer true. The government also deprived the merchants of valuable goods, and ultimately inhibited capitalism, by maintaining monopolies over the production and distribution of essential commodities, including arms, textiles, pottery, salt, iron, and wine.

Indeed, few opportunities for unrestricted entrepreneurship existed in Ming and Qing China. Government policies reflected China's priorities as a

Chinese Porcelain Like other peoples around Eurasia, people in southwestern Asia prized Chinese porcelain like the bowl shown above. The Turkish miniature painting below shows several valued pieces of Chinese porcelain, probably part of a bride's dowry, being carried in a decorated cart for display during a wedding procession.

Witness to the Past

A Mandarin's Critique of Chinese Merchants

In the late sixteenth century, a Ming official, Zhang Han (chang han) (1511–1593), wrote an essay criticizing merchants. Because he was from a wealthy merchant family, Zhang had the ambivalent attitude toward merchants that was typical of the Confucian elite of the day. He asserted that merchants were greedy, self-serving, arrogant, and pampered, but he also admired the products provided by commerce and the efficiency with which they were distributed throughout the empire. And he suggested that China could benefit from lower taxes on mercantile activity.

Money and profit are of great importance to men. They seek profit, then suffer by it, yet they cannot forget it. They exhaust their bodies and spirits, run day and night, yet they still regard what they have gained as insufficient. Those who become merchants eat fine food and wear elegant clothes. . . . Opportunistic persons attracted by their wealth offer to serve them. Pretty girls in beautiful long-sleeved dresses and delicate slippers play stringed and wind instruments for them and compete to please them. Merchants boast that their wisdom and ability are such as to give them a free hand in affairs. They believe that they know all the possible transformations in the universe and therefore can calculate all the changes in the human world, and that the rise and fall of prices are under their command. They are confident that they will not make one mistake in a hundred in their calculations. These merchants do not know how insignificant their wisdom and ability really are. As [the *Chuang Tzu,* an ancient Daoist text] says: "Great understanding is broad and unhurried; little understanding is cramped and busy."

Because I have traveled to many places during my career as an official, I am familiar with commercial activities and business conditions in various places. . . . Those who engage in commerce, including the foot peddler, the cart peddler, and the shopkeeper, display not only clothing

and fresh foods from the fields but also numerous luxury items such as priceless jade from [K'un-lun], pearls from the [southern] island of Hainan, gold from Yunnan (in southwest China), and corals from Vietnam. These precious items, coming from the mountains or the sea, are not found in central China. But people in remote areas and in other countries, unafraid of the dangers and difficulties of travel, transport these items step by step to the capital, making it the most prosperous place in the empire. . . . The profits from the tea and salt trades are especially great, but only large-scale merchants can undertake these businesses. Furthermore, there are government regulations on their distribution. . . .

Turning to the taxes levied on Chinese merchants, though these taxes are needed to fill the national treasury, excessive exploitation should be prohibited. . . . But today's merchants are often stopped on the road [at checkpoints] for additional payments and also suffer extortions from the [marketplace] clerks. Such exploitation is hard and bitter enough but, in addition, the merchants are taxed twice. How can they avoid becoming more and more impoverished? . . . Levying taxes on merchants is a bad policy. We should tax people according to their degree of wealth or poverty.

Thinking About the Reading

1. What criticisms does Zhang make of merchants?

2. In Zhang's view, what benefits does China gain from merchant activity?

3. How does Zhang believe merchant activity could be stimulated?

Source: Reprinted with permission of The Free Press, a Division of Simon & Schuster Inc., from *Chinese Civilization and Society,* A Sourcebook, Second Revised & Expanded Edition by Patricia Buckley Ebrey. Copyright © 1993 by Patricia Buckley Ebrey. All rights reserved.

centralized, agriculture-based empire. Those from Fujian (fu-JEN) province, on the southeast coast, remained prominent in Asian trade throughout the Early Modern Era, especially in Southeast Asia.

These fundamental differences from European patterns deflected Chinese energies inward at a fateful turning point in world history, leaving the world's oceans open to Western enterprise.

Confronting Western Challenges

Although it turned inward, China did not cut itself off completely from the outside world. In the 1500s and 1600s, European ships seeking to acquire silk, tea, porcelain, lacquer ware, and other products reached Chinese shores. The Portuguese landed on the China coast in 1514 and began a troubled relationship with China by failing to request permission from imperial officials to trade. They earned reputations as pirates and religious fanatics. With their naval forces spread thinly around Asia and Africa, the Portuguese were no match for Chinese armed junks. In 1557, to stop the piracy, the emperor allowed the Portuguese to establish a trading base at a small unpopulated peninsula, Macao (muh-cow), near Guangzhou on the southeast coast. By the 1580s, Macao had a population of 10,000, including some 500 Portuguese, several hundred African slaves, and Chinese and Japanese merchants.

> "Although it turned inward, China did not cut itself off completely from the outside world."

Matteo Ricci: The Jesuits in China

Christian missionaries from Europe, especially Jesuits, also became active in the late Ming and early Qing. The most influential Jesuit missionary, the Italian Matteo Ricci (ma-TAY-o REE-chee) (1552–1610), was a brilliant scholar and linguist trained in law, mathematics, and geography. In 1583 he entered China from Macao to study Confucianism and foster an interest in Christianity among Confucian scholars. Ricci impressed Chinese officials, and he began training young scholars for the civil service exams. Eventually the emperor allowed Ricci and his Jesuit colleagues to settle in Beijing. Armed with his knowledge of European Renaissance science, Ricci became a scientific adviser to the imperial court, helping improve clocks, calendars, and astronomical observations. On Ricci's death, the Chinese buried him with honors in Beijing. Despite earning Chinese respect, Ricci attracted only a few converts to his faith.

 Journals: Matteo Ricci This story about Jesuit missionaries in China provides an interesting look at the nexus of religion and politics in the early seventeenth century.

For their part, the Jesuits, chiefly well-educated Italians, were much impressed with a China that seemed to have more wealth and a more impressive technology than did Europe. Jesuits wrote letters home describing Chinese ideas and advanced technology, knowledge that circulated widely in Europe. Enjoying their status, the Jesuits lived like mandarins and wore Chinese clothing. Their admiration of Chinese traditions led them to attempt to harmonize Christianity with Chinese philosophy as a way of attracting support from Chinese scholars. The encounter between the Jesuits and the Chinese certainly expanded the horizons of both parties. A few Chinese even visited Europe, including the Christian convert Michael Alphonsus Shen, who demonstrated chopstick techniques for French king Louis XIV and catalogued Chinese books in the Oxford University library.

The efforts of Ricci and his colleagues laid some groundwork for introducing Roman Christianity to China, and by the end of the seventeenth century, some 100,000 Chinese had become Catholics. But this was a tiny percentage of the vast population, and the less-tolerant Catholic missionaries who followed the early Jesuits made even less progress. After the pope prohibited any attempt at mixing Christianity and Confucianism, the faith had less appeal. In the early 1700s, the Qing banned Christianity for undermining such Chinese traditions as ancestor worship, persecuted converts, and expelled missionaries.

China and Russia

China faced other challenges from Western countries in the 1600s. Before 1800, Europeans could be rebuffed because China was militarily and economically strong, but relations with the Dutch and Russians suggested changes to come. The Dutch had established a base on Taiwan in 1624 but were expelled in 1662 by the militarily stronger Ming resistance forces that had moved to the island. In 1683 the Qing took control of Taiwan, but the Dutch remained active in the China trade. In the late 1600s, Russian expeditions crossed Siberia, seeking trade with China as well as sable fur. Over time they consolidated control of the sparsely populated regions north of Xinjiang and Mongolia. In the late 1600s, Russian and Chinese forces fought several battles in Siberia. The Chinese won these conflicts but granted Russians commercial privileges in the Treaty of Nerchinsk of 1689, the first treaty between China and a European power and a symbol of things to come. Russia maintained its ambitions in eastern Siberia, occasionally testing Qing resolve and power.

Needing little from outside, China still had considerable control of the relations with European powers before the 1800s. The Qing minimized contacts by restricting foreign trade to a few border outposts and southern ports, especially Guangzhou (Canton), and politely but firmly refused diplomatic relations on an equal basis with the Western nations. The Chinese were willing to absorb useful technologies to improve mapmaking and astronomy, as reflected in the fruitful relationship between Emperor Kangzi and the early Jesuits, but they were less interested in foreign ideas like Christianity. China's internal problems, such as overpopulation, mounted just as Western economic, industrial, and military power increased and foreign pressures on China intensified in the later 1700s. Having lived under foreign rulers such as the Mongols and Manchus, the Chinese understood political subjugation but could not comprehend that foreign forces might compel them to rethink their cultural traditions. In late imperial China, culture and nation were one, but during the later 1800s, the 2,000-year-old imperial system declined rapidly.

> ❝The Koreans had learned over the centuries how to mix Chinese influences with local traditions, adapting and modifying Chinese political models, Confucian social patterns, and Mahayana Buddhism.❞

power in 1392 and survived until 1910, a longevity of more than five centuries. Strongly Confucian in orientation, the Yi maintained close relations with China. The early Yi era enjoyed progress in science and technology as well as in writing and literature. However, Choson began to decline in the 1500s, damaged by factional disputes and a Japanese invasion that proved most disastrous for Korea.

In 1592 a Japanese army of 160,000 captured the capital, Seoul (soul); however, the Koreans, aided by China and their invention, in 1519, of the first ironclad naval vessels, fought back and soon prevailed. Forced to the peace table, the Japanese agreed to withdraw, but the Japanese invasion destroyed infrastructure, weakened the central government, and generated severe economic problems.

After these invasions, while the Yi maintained their power, Koreans abandoned or modified some customs borrowed from China. In theory the Yi government remained Confucian, but practice varied considerably. The rigid old class system was modified, with class lines becoming more open. The society also enjoyed economic development and change: agriculture became more productive, and population grew, reaching 7 million by 1750. Commerce and the merchant class also expanded. Growing dissension fostered change after the mid-1700s, laying the foundations for a new era.

LO⁴ Continuity and Change in Korea and Japan

For much of the Early Modern Era, Korea and Japan remained more isolated than China from the wider world, although both maintained trade relations with China. Korea faced little Western pressure, local issues and conflicts with Japan being far more important. Japanese history also largely revolved around the country's changing economic and social patterns. For a brief period, Japan encountered a significant European presence, but when the experience proved destabilizing, the Japanese became aloof from the West.

Choson Korea

The Koreans had learned over the centuries how to mix Chinese influences with local traditions, adapting and modifying Chinese political models, Confucian social patterns, and Mahayana Buddhism. The Yi (yee) dynasty, which called its state Choson, came to

---

CHRONOLOGY

Korea and Japan, 1450–1750

1338–1568	Ashikaga Shogunate
1392–1910	Yi (Choson) dynasty in Korea
1549	Beginning of Christian missions in Japan
1592–1598	Japanese invasions of Korea
1603	Founding of Tokugawa Shogunate
1637	Christian rebellion against Tokugawa
1639–1841	Japanese seclusion policy

Ashikaga Japan and the West

Japanese society, with its samurai (SAH-moo-rie) warrior class, distinctive mix of Buddhism, Confucianism, and Shinto, and long history of adapting foreign influences, differed dramatically from those of Korea and China. But by 1500, Japan under the Ashikaga (ah-shee-KAH-gah) Shogunate (1338–1568), was experiencing rapid change that strained the samurai-dominated political and social system. The Kyoto-based Ashikaga shoguns, military leaders who dominated the imperial family in Kyoto and the central government, never had much power beyond the capital. A long civil war, during which Western powers intruded into Japan, unsettled conditions even more.

> "During the Ashikaga years, rapid economic and population growth had major consequences for Japanese society."

Economic Development

During the Ashikaga years, rapid economic and population growth had major consequences for Japanese society. As technological advances improved agriculture, production per acre tripled, and Japan's population doubled from 16 million in 1500 to perhaps 30 million in 1750. The increased productivity in turn stimulated trade and the gradual development of cities and towns. By 1600 the largest city, Kyoto, may have grown to some 800,000 people. In the cities and towns, merchants and craftsmen organized themselves into guilds that protected their interests.

 Nakasendo Highway: A Journey to the Heart of Japan (*http://www.nakasendoway.com/*). This website, hosted at Hong Kong University, uses a famous highway to introduce Tokugawa Japan.

As merchants became more active and assertive, they spurred foreign and domestic trade. Japanese traders and pirates began visiting Korea, China, and Southeast Asia, and Japanese settlers immigrated to Vietnam, Cambodia, Siam, and the Philippines. Several thousand Japanese lived in Manila, and one Japanese even became a governor in Siam. Japan also became a major supplier of silver, copper, swords, lacquer ware, rice wine, rice, and other goods to Asia.

Civil War in Japan

If the Ashikaga economic and military expansion had continued, the Japanese might have been in a position to challenge the Portuguese and other Europeans for influence in Southeast Asia. Instead, political power became increasingly decentralized and unstable, as great territorial landowning magnates, called daimyo, increasingly dominated the regions outside of Kyoto. At the beginning of the 1500s, there were several hundred of these daimyo, each with a supporting samurai force. The most powerful hoped to one day rule Japan. However, the rise of the daimyo precipitated a civil war that raged for more than a century, from the mid-1400s into the late 1500s. The military engagements during the centuries of warrior dominance were mainly matters of hand-to-hand conflict between samurai wielding long, slightly curved, two-handed swords with great efficiency, supported by commoner spearmen.

Ashikaga Decline and Rise of the Tokugawa Shogunate

During the late sixteenth and early seventeenth centuries, three men who successively became shogun gradually restored order. All were brutal warlords but also devotees of the refined tea ceremony and pragmatists willing to challenge powerful institutions. The first, Oda Nobunaga (OH-da no-boo-NAG-ga) (1534–1582), was so wild as a youth that a family servant committed suicide hoping this desperate act might settle the young man down. With the slogan "rule the empire by force," Oda, from a minor daimyo family, became a brilliant military strategist who once defeated an army of 25,000 with his own small force of 2,000 men. Oda deposed the last Ashikaga shogun. Hideyoshi Toyotomi (1536–1598), the second warlord and of peasant origins, had ambitions abroad and dreamed of conquering China. When the Koreans refused his request to use Korea as a staging base for the China invasion, he instead sent a large army into Korea in 1592. The fierce Korean resistance forced the Japanese to abandon the effort on Hideyoshi's death. The last of the three, Tokugawa Ieyasu (ee-yeh-YAH-soo) (1542–1616), one of Hideyoshi's chief generals, ended the warfare and became shogun in 1603.

Europeans in Japan

During the civil war, European traders and missionaries arrived in Japan, and their encounter with the Japanese sparked cultural exchange but also conflict. In 1542 the Portuguese reached Japan, starting an encounter that troubled both sides. The European arrivals caused a sensation among Japanese, and the Europeans were equally astonished at what they found. An Italian

Jesuit in the 1500s put it simply: "Japan is a world the reverse of Europe. Hardly in anything do their ways conform to ours."[7] But for all the mutual astonishment, the Europeans had an economic, religious, and military impact. The Portuguese traded Chinese silk for Japanese gold, and soon Spanish and Dutch merchants arrived to compete in the Japanese market.

Francis Xavier (1506–1552), a Spanish Jesuit missionary, began to preach Christianity in 1549. As a result of energetic Spanish and Portuguese missionary efforts, by 1600 perhaps 300,000 Japanese were Christians, out of a total population of some 18 million. But many Japanese grew increasingly suspicious of the missionaries, resented their intolerance of Japanese faiths and local customs, and could not comprehend the fierce competition between rival Catholic orders. Japanese leaders viewed the armed Christian communities as posing a threat to their power.

The Japanese adopted what was useful to them: Western technologies. Major consequences often followed. They acquired, then quickly improved, muskets from the Portuguese and Spanish, and developed new tactics for using them. European guns sharpened warfare and, because even nonsamurai could obtain them, contributed to the breakdown of social class lines. The increasingly common and deadly violence resulting from guns often prompted peasants to seek solace in religion, and some adopted Christianity.

The Tokugawa Shogunate: Stability and Seclusion

The civil war brought on by the rise of the daimyo, and intensified by gunpowder weapons, ended with the Tokugawa Shogunate, which ruled Japan from 1603 to 1868. Tokugawa Ieyasu was a great warrior and able administrator, but also cruel and treacherous. He subdued his rivals and established a shogunate at Tokyo, then known as Edo (ED-doe), presiding over the most centralized state in premodern Japanese history, in striking contrast to the weak Ashikaga shoguns a century earlier.

The Tokugawa leaders imposed a government mixing authoritarian centralization with the rigidly hierarchical social system that emerged in the later Intermediate Era, which resembled medieval European feudalism in some respects. Japan now had a more powerful shogunate than ever before, while the imperial family in Kyoto remained powerless. To discourage rebellion, some members of each daimyo family were required to live in Edo as hostages. The Tokugawa restored the pre–civil war social structure, with the samurais at the top.

> " The civil war brought on by the rise of the daimyo, and intensified by gunpowder weapons, ended with the Tokugawa Shogunate, which ruled Japan from 1603 to 1868. "

The Closing of Japan

To stop the conflict between the various Europeans and Catholic orders, Tokugawa closed off Japan from the West and ordered home Japanese traders in Southeast Asia. In the process he ejected the feuding Catholic missionaries and merchants, and broke the power of the Christian communities. This led to a rebellion by Japanese Christians in 1637, to which Tokugawa responded by massacring 37,000 Japanese Christians. But trade with China, Korea, and Southeast Asia continued, with Japan paying for silk with its main mineral resource, silver. In addition, after 1639 a few Dutch traders were allowed to remain and set up a base on a small island, Deshima (DEH-shi-ma), in Nagasaki (nah-gah-SAH-kee) Bay. The Dutch were only interested in commerce, not religious conversion, and for the next two centuries the Dutch base served as Japan's only link to the European world.

Tokugawa Rigidity

Tokugawa leaders believed that society could be frozen in a hierarchical pattern, but under the surface of the rigid Tokugawa rule, new social forces simmered. For example, even though the rulers restricted travel between cities or regions, merchants found ways to evade the rules and move their wares. The Japanese population grew rapidly, straining the country's resources. Thousands of local peasant protests, riots, and uprisings reflected more dramatic discontent. Tokugawa Japan also boasted several large cities, with Tokyo and Osaka each more than 1 million in population by 1800. The cities became centers of complex commercial networks, and their demands fostered agricultural productivity and economic prosperity, especially in the Edo region. Merchants and their values became more influential. By the mid-1700s, Japan was a well-organized country, with rising living standards but growing tensions.

The Tokugawa tried to restrict Japanese women. In contrast to some Asian societies, Japanese women had never been secluded and participated in community life. Some women were literate, and a few became noted writers. Nonetheless, like women in most societies, Japanese women had few legal or property rights, faced arranged marriages, and were encouraged to be dependent on men, all patriarchal customs reinforced during the early Tokugawa period. As a result, severe laws against adultery only punished women. Women in samurai families were raised to be courteous, conciliatory, and humble toward their husbands; however, gender expectations and relations among urban merchant and artisan families were less rigid.

Art and Entertainment

In Tokugawa culture, distinctive new forms also emerged in the 1600s. In the major cities, entertainment districts known as the "floating world" were filled with restaurants, theaters, geisha houses, and brothels. The writer Ihara Saikaku (ee-HAR-oo sigh-KOCK-oo), from a merchant family, chronicled the floating world and satirized urban merchant life in often erotic novels. The master artist Moronobu (more-oh-NOH-boo) introduced the colorful woodblock prints known as ukiyo-e (oo-kee-YO-ee), which celebrated the life of the floating world. Later, landscapes, such as views of Mt. Fuji, became popular themes for woodcuts. By the 1800s, many European artists collected and were influenced by these prints. New theater forms included the bunraku puppet theater and the racy kabuki drama. Aimed particularly at the merchant class, kabuki featured gorgeous costumes, beautiful scenery, and scripts filled with violent passion. Men played all the roles. Professional female impersonators were highly honored and spent years mastering the voice, gestures, and other aspects of femininity.

A new literary device, the seventeen-syllable haiku poem, also became popular. Haiku proved an excellent vehicle for discussing the passage of time or briefly summarizing some action or scene through a series of images, such as the famous presentation by the samurai turned wanderer and greatest haiku poet, Matsuo Basho (BAH-show) (1644–1694), of a sudden event on a quiet pond: "An old pond. Frog jumps in. Sound of water."[8]

ukiyo-e Colorful Japanese woodblock prints that celebrated the life of the "floating world," the urban entertainment districts of Tokogawa Japan.

bunraku The puppet theater of Tokugawa Japan.

kabuki The all-male and racy drama that became the favored entertainment of the urban population in Tokugawa Japan.

haiku The seventeen-syllable poem that proved an excellent vehicle for discussing the passage of time and the change of seasons in Early Modern Japan.

Tokugawa Stability and Its Costs

Tokugawa Japan largely enjoyed security and peace for 250 years, but it came at a price. Although commerce thrived, Japan, like China, experienced no political transformation or social rejuvenation, because Tokugawa policies preserved rigid social divisions and shielded Japanese from outside influence. The lack of political and social dynamism left the Tokugawa vulnerable to a later return of Western power, as several Western nations rapidly acquired wealth and resources and improved their technology between 1500 and 1850.

When the West intruded in the mid-nineteenth century, the latent tensions between samurai and merchants and between daimyo and shoguns boiled over, and the Tokugawa lost their grip on power. But Japan, unlike China, was able to respond creatively. Japan's history of borrowing from abroad made it uniquely prepared to make the necessary adjustments, and the Japanese could assimilate Western techniques and customs to Japanese traditions, as they had done with Chinese and Western imports in earlier eras. These differences meant that China and Japan eventually met the challenge from the West in very different ways.

 Listen to a synopsis of Chapter 18.

Kabuki Theater The urban middle classes, especially the merchants and samurais, enjoyed kabuki drama. This eighteenth-century print by one of the most acclaimed artists, Moronobu, shows the audience enjoying a play about a vendetta involving two brothers.

Werner Forman/Art Resource, NY

Societies • Networks • Transitions

Connecting the Early Modern World, 1450–1750

The permanent connecting of the hemispheres that followed Columbus reshaped the world. In the Early Modern Era's new global age, greatly increased communication and mobility resulted in encounters between societies that were once remote from each other. As a result, the exchange among societies of people, diseases, ideas, technologies, resources, and products occurred on a greater scale than ever before. Europeans forged a new world economy, while disrupting, changing, and sometimes destroying the societies they encountered, especially in the Americas and parts of Africa and Southeast Asia. Because of the growing contacts spanning the two hemispheres, for the first time in history an interconnected world became a reality.

But the encounters between Europeans and peoples they could reach only after long sea voyages were only part of the story. The world had many political and economic centers between 1450 and 1750. In the Afro-Eurasian zone, Morocco, the Ottoman Empire, several western European societies, Safavid Persia, Mughal India, China, and a few Southeast Asian societies such as Siam were wealthy, populous, and linked to each other by trade networks and diplomatic ties. They all enjoyed military prowess, had effective states, and fostered creative thinkers. Some African kingdoms, such as Ashante and Buganda, also enjoyed influence and connections to hemispheric trade. No single country or region dominated world politics or the world economy. Yet, the links forged during the Early Modern Era laid a foundation for an even more integrated global system, encompassing even the most remote peoples, in the Modern Era.

 Columbus and the Age of Discovery (http:// muweb.millersville.edu/ columbus/main/html**).** This site, maintained by Millersville University, offers many sources related to the linking of the hemispheres during this era.

New Empires and Military Power

From the dawn of recorded history, some peoples have used military power to impose their will on others and create empires. Increasing wealth and power, as well as more deadly weapons, led some Early Modern Era societies to build large empires. Some, such as Safavid Persia, Mughal India, Qing China, and Russia, ruled land empires.

In contrast to these empires, which annexed nearby and often sparsely populated territories, the Ottoman Turks controlled large areas of southeastern Europe, western Asia, and North Africa, and the Omani Arabs established footholds in East Africa. The Portuguese, Spanish, Dutch, English, and French empires were even more ambitious, incorporating distant peoples in Africa, Asia, and the Americas. These conquests created empires on a geographic scale never imagined before.

Gunpowder Empires

Historians characterize most Early Modern empires as "gunpowder empires" because they depended on bigger and better gunpowder weapons, including cannon mounted on ships, field artillery, and guns. Gunpowder empires dominated Eurasia and the Americas. Various Asian and European societies sought to acquire resources in neighboring societies by building empires rather than relying chiefly on trade. Only a few European countries, however, had the means to dominate very distant societies, and also the incentive: the quest for "gold, god, and glory." The worldwide exploration and conquest that took place during this era resulted from the transformation of European societies by various forces—the rise of capitalism, powerful merchants, and competitive, centralizing states, as well as by rivalry among Christian churches—while improved military and maritime technology provided the means.

Europeans took advantage of their economic growth and military expansion to improve their position in the world and to compete more effectively for resources in the East, where Islamic societies, India, and China had long enjoyed the most political, economic, and cultural power. Advanced naval and military technology, including gunpowder weapons unknown in the Americas and in much of Africa and Southeast Asia, allowed the Portuguese to seize various African and Asian trading ports, and the Spanish to construct a huge empire in the Americas. The Dutch, English, and French soon followed, establishing footholds in North America, the Caribbean, coastal Africa, and southern Asia. Europeans controlled Atlantic shipping and also gained considerable power over Indian Ocean trade, which brought them great wealth. As the English adventurer Sir Walter Raleigh recognized in 1608, "Who so commands the sea commands the trade of the world;

who so commands the trade of the world commands the riches of the world."[1]

A Polycentric World

Despite the growth of empires, the Early Modern world had varied centers of political and economic power, a situation known as polycentrism. Despite their weaponry, Europeans did not become dominant all over the world during this era. European power was limited in Asia, the Middle East, and parts of Africa and South America, and much of North America and the Pacific remained untouched by European exploration. For much of the era, the Ottomans, Mughals, and Chinese were more politically, economically, and culturally influential in Eurasia than European societies. Many Muslims admired Mughal India, which became a destination for merchants, writers, and religious scholars. A Persian poet proclaimed: "Great is India, the Mecca of all in need. A journey to India is of essence to any man made worthy by knowledge and skill."[2] The major Asian states also collected far larger tax revenues than did any European government. Societies in Eurasia, from China to England, and in Africa, from Buganda to Songhai (song-GAH-ee), extended their power into nearby territories, centralized their governments, fostered commerce, and worked to integrate ethnic minorities into the broader society.

The era was dynamic, as encounters fostered compromises and information exchange. Across Eurasia, varied societies experienced economic innovation, free markets, industrialization, and rising living standards, and cities such as Amsterdam in Holland, Isfahan (is-fah-HAHN) in Persia, and Ayuthia (uh-YUT-uh-yuh) in Siam became bustling trade crossroads. Foreign merchants, such as the Dutch and Persians at Ayuthia or Surat, had to adapt to local customs to succeed. Sometimes, as in Siam, Tokugawa Japan, and Morocco, Europeans who disregarded local customs or threatened local governments were expelled. Many Asians and Africans adapted ideas from other cultures to meet their own needs. Among other leaders, the Chinese emperor Kangzi (KANG-see), the Siamese king Narai (na-RY), the Mughal sultan Akbar (AK-bahr), and the Kongo king Alfonso I showed a keen interest in Western ideas and technologies. Narai also borrowed architectural styles and medical knowledge from the Persians and Chinese.

The main European advantage had been in acquiring the resources of the Americas for exploitation, often using enslaved African labor. But the large-scale trans-Atlantic slave trade became possible because the kings or chiefs of some African states, such as Ashante (ah-SHAN-tee) and Dahomey (da-ho-MAY), profited by collaborating with it. Similarly, Spanish rule in the Americas survived only because the conquerors ultimately made compromises with Indian societies. In the Spanish empire, as well as in other empires of the era such as the Ottoman and Mughal, laws recognized local customs, and different groups often maintained their own legal codes.

Innovative thought reflected the vigor of many societies. Science and technology remained creative all over Eurasia. The Chinese and British, for example, published important scientific books and invented new technologies, especially for the textile industry. New astronomical observatories were built in China, India, and the Middle East, although Europeans had by now developed a much keener interest than Asians in clocks and mathematics.

Dutch Diplomats In this print, a Dutch delegation, eager to make an alliance with the Kongolese against the Portuguese, prostrate themselves before the Kongolese king, sitting on his throne under an imported chandelier, in 1642.

From Olfert Dapper, *Beschreibung von Africa*, Amsterdam, 1670

Japan's fostering of schools gave it the world's highest literacy rate, and Siam and Burma also enjoyed high rates of literacy. Leaders of the European Renaissance, Reformation, and Enlightenment, Sufi mystics in the Ottoman and Mughal Empires, the Hindu bhakti (BUK-tee) movement in India, and some Chinese thinkers challenged accepted wisdom. Various European and Chinese philosophers emphasized reason, as did some Latin Americans, such as the Mexican nun and scientist Sor Juana Ines de la Cruz. Indeed, some participants in the European Enlightenment were inspired by their growing knowledge of secular China, which was ruled by emperors who dabbled in philosophy. A French ambassador in 1688 praised Qing China for promoting "virtue, wisdom, prudence, good faith, sincerity, charity, gentleness, honesty [and] civility."[3]

European achievement of global power was not inevitable: in this era China also had a sizeable empire and considerable potential. Early Modern China, boasting the world's largest commercialized economy, remained the engine of the Eurasian economy. China and Europe experienced commercial growth, increases in cash cropping, growing industrial production, and widening marketing networks. The maritime expansion of Europe, however, contrasted sharply with that of the Chinese. Just as western Europeans turned outward, competing with each other for strategic advantage, the Chinese pulled back from their grand maritime expeditions of the early 1400s; their government enjoyed huge budget surpluses until the late 1700s and did not need colonies or foreign trade to prosper. In addition, the Chinese government treated rich merchants warily, viewing commerce as a threat to Confucian values. In contrast, western European merchants had the support of their mercantilist governments, especially in England, the Netherlands, Spain, and France.

Gunpowder and Warfare

Gunpowder weapons were not new. The Chinese invented gunpowder and then made the first true guns in the tenth century C.E., primarily for defensive purposes. The Mongols improved these Chinese weapons into a more effective offensive force, to blow open city gates; by 1241 gunpowder had reached Europe. Early Modern Europeans, Turks, Mughals, and Chinese owed their strength in part to improvements in gunpowder weaponry.

As they spread around Eurasia and North Africa, gunpowder weapons changed warfare. Europeans learned how to make particularly deadly weapons, improving the technology in part because they had easier access to metals. In Europe—full of competitive, often hostile states—no ruler had a monopoly on weapons, so rulers had an incentive to constantly improve their armaments to maintain the balance of power. As a result, warfare among Europeans became far more deadly. The Portuguese, Dutch, and English slaughtered each other in Southeast Asia, and the English and French fought long

wars in North America. A similar increase in battlefield casualties came in Japan in the civil war era of the 1500s, when Japanese sword-smiths learned how to replicate Portuguese and Spanish guns and cannon. Japanese small arms soon proved superior to European rifles. In contrast, the Ottomans did not create a class of Turkish and Arab craftsmen and instead relied heavily on hiring European craftsmen to manufacture their military and naval technology.

But Asians took the development of their gunpowder arsenals only so far. With gunpowder weapons, the Qing greatly expanded China's land frontier deep into Central Asia and Tibet, thereby stabilizing their border regions. After that, secure in their power, the Manchu emperors had little need to increase their offensive capability, while the land-oriented Mughals saw little gain in developing naval armaments. The Chinese, Japanese, and Koreans all had some naval power but no interest in challenging the Europeans in the Indian Ocean. When the Chinese came into contact with foreign firearms in 1500s, they found them superior to their own. Nonetheless, Chinese firearms proved adequate for ejecting the Dutch from Taiwan and the Russians from the Amur Valley in the 1600s. But two centuries later, superior European military technology dramatically changed the hemispheric balance of power.

The Emerging World Economy

With the opening of the Atlantic and Pacific Oceans to regular sea travel, a global network of economic and political relationships emerged that increasingly shaped the destinies of people around the world. Rather than the luxuries of earlier times, such as silks and spices, long-distance trade increasingly moved bulk items: essential natural resources, such as sugar and silver from the Americas, and manufactured goods, such as textiles from Europe and Asia. Traders moved commodities and capital faster and more cheaply over greater distances than ever before. These trends wove together different societies into a world economy. Western Europeans usually benefited the most, and Europeans laid the foundations for a new global system to emerge after 1750.

The New Trading System

The capitalist market economy that gradually developed was increasingly centered on northwestern Europe, especially England and the Netherlands, but a half-dozen other European countries were also enriched by trade (see map). The Spanish conquest of the Americas provided huge quantities of silver from Peru, Bolivia, and Mexico, which financed expansion of the European economy and enabled Europeans to gain access to Asian markets. The Spanish establishment of a base at Manila in 1571

Interactive Map

Early Modern Trade Routes

Between 1500 and 1700, the world economy developed and new trade routes proliferated. Major maritime routes linked Asia and the Americas across the Pacific; Europe, Asia, and the Americas across the Atlantic; and eastern and southern Asia with Africa and Europe across the Indian Ocean.

© Cengage Learning

Map legend:

- Spanish trade routes
- Chinese trade routes
- Arab trade routes
- Portuguese trade routes
- Portuguese trade routes
- British trade routes
- Dutch trade routes

- British control
- Portuguese control
- Spanish control
- Dutch control

0   1,500   3,000 Km.
0   1,500   3,000 Mi.

provided an essential economic link between eastern Eurasia and the Americas. European exploration and settlement in the Americas brought access to resources such as timber, marine mammals, fish, and wildlife.

Growing commercial activity stimulated production for the market, in mining and manufacturing but especially in tropical agriculture. Highly profitable plantations that sprung up around the Caribbean Basin, along the Atlantic coast of North and South America, and on the Atlantic and Indian Ocean islands and the Philippines reflected the expansion of production. A growing trans-Atlantic slave trade provided cheap labor to the American plantations, enabling them to produce inexpensive calories for Europe in the form of sugar and, after 1700, abundant cotton for English mills. Thousands of slaves obtained in eastern Europe, East Africa, Sri Lanka, and Indonesia also labored for European and Muslim enterprises in the Middle East, South Africa, and Southeast Asia.

As a result of the growing commercial activity, by 1750 millions of people worked thousands of miles from their place of birth or otherwise experienced lives very different from those of their ancestors. Chinese merchants lived on Java; Persians served in the Siamese government; Turkish soldiers fought for the sultans of Acheh (AH-cheh) in Sumatra; Portuguese settled in Mozambique; Kongolese labored in Brazil; and French traders explored the Mississippi Basin.

Asia and Europe in the New World Economy

The transition to a European-dominated trading system took place over several centuries. Before the 1800s, Asia boasted the bulk of world economic activity. Asians produced some 80 percent of goods as late as 1775, and this production had probably increased since 1500. The industries of China and India remained the twin pillars of Asian commerce well into the 1700s. Indian textiles such as cashmere and cotton cloth were so popular in Asia, Africa, and Europe that they almost constituted a form of currency. Handicraft industries also flourished in the Ottoman Empire, Persia, Sri Lanka, Burma, Siam, and Java during the sixteenth and seventeenth centuries. These societies imported raw materials from India (including raw cotton), China (especially silk), and Japan (copper) for production into exportable consumer goods. The economies of India and China dwarfed those of any other country. The most economically developed regions within China, Japan, India, and northwestern Europe probably enjoyed comparable standards of living.

Asian merchants, enjoying lower overhead and shrewd business skills, could often outcompete those from Europe. After 1670, Indian merchants even took the Indonesian textile market away from the Dutch. Like Europeans, Asians also traded over long distances. In the 1600s, for example, Arab and Persian traders remained influential at the main Mughal port, Surat, while north Indian merchants were found all over the Persian Gulf.

Many wealthy Asian trading magnates had huge capital resources. A European visitor to Goa in 1510 was amazed at the competition provided by fabulously rich Arab and Indian merchants: "We [Europeans] believe ourselves to be the most astute men that one can encounter, and the people here surpass us in everything. And they can do better calculations by memory than we can do with the pen."[4] European merchants competed best when they were, like the Dutch East Indies Company traders, supported by military force.

European–Asian trade relations often favored Asians. Because Asians had little interest in European manufactured goods such as clothing, which they considered inferior, Europeans bought Asian goods and resources with American silver and gold. For example, Europeans traded with China for products such as tea, so vast amounts of American silver ended up in China, where it served as the basis of the monetary system and promoted economic growth. The Ottoman, Safavid, and Mughal Empires also willingly traded goods for silver, and their goods found a ready market around the world. While European ships carried a growing amount of seaborne trade, European merchants accounted for only a small proportion of trade from India and China. Mughal India traded far more with Central Asians and Ottomans than with the Dutch or English. Asian exports to Europe grew slowly; intra-Asian trade was far larger.

Expanding Trade Networks

The growth of long-distance trade corresponded to the expansion of trade networks operated by different commercial communities. Dutch, English, and French merchants established themselves in India, Southeast Asia, West Africa, eastern Europe, Russia, and the Caribbean Basin. At the same time, Sephardic Jews, originally from Iberia, spread their trading networks throughout western Europe, flourishing particularly in Antwerp, Amsterdam, Seville, and Geneva. Eventually, Jews also became active as merchants in parts of South America, the Caribbean, and the Indian Ocean. The Mendes family, for instance— expelled from Spain in 1492 and eventually based in Istanbul—had business connections in several European cities and helped finance the gem and spice trades across Asia, Europe, and Africa.

Groups specializing in trade were prominent in many lands, and some maintained commercial networks over vast distances. Chinese remained active all over Southeast Asia, establishing permanent settlements in many cities and towns. For example, the Spanish in the Philippines depended on the Chinese merchant class to supply many consumer goods. Traders of French or mixed French and Indian descent traveled deep into the North American continent contacting local peoples. In East Africa, the Omani Arabs had a leading role. In West Africa, Hausa (HOUSE-uh) merchants increasingly dominated the trade networks of the Sudan by the 1600s. The Indian maritime trade network stretched from Arabia, Persia, northeast Africa, and the Red Sea to Melaka, Sumatra, Siam, and China, while their Indian overland trade networks extended across Central Asia, Afghanistan, Tibet, Persia, the Caucasus states, and much of Russia. Armenian merchants based in Safavid Persia flourished in the overland trade from India to Central Asia and the Middle East, and from Persia to Russia, England, and the Baltic. Growing Eurasian trade clearly involved, and often benefited, varied groups.

Environmental Changes

Human activity reshaped the natural world and was influenced by it in turn. As they had for millennia, people tapped the Earth for underground resources, such as coal and iron ore, but large-scale manufacturing, which often pollutes the environment, was found in only a few widely scattered countries, mostly in Eurasia. For farming and light industries, Early Modern economies relied chiefly on traditional power sources, such as people, animals, water, and wind. Nonetheless, natural systems came under more stress as the global population nearly doubled, putting severe pressure on land and resources. Expanding settlements and farming in frontier regions displaced woodlands, grasslands, and wetlands and reduced the variety of plant and animal life. More spectacularly, the exchange of diseases, plants, and animals across the Atlantic altered entire environments and resulted in huge population losses in the Americas.

Climate Change and Population Growth

Between 1300 and 1850, much of the world experienced a fluctuating "Little Ice Age," probably caused by a dimming sun and increased volcanic activity, that had significant consequences for many societies. In North America and Eurasia, this period brought cool temperatures, shorter growing seasons, and famine. The coldest years came between 1570 and 1730, and then through the early 1800s. The lands bordering the North Atlantic saw much colder and wetter conditions, which diminished agricultural production and resulted in widespread starvation in much of Europe. Indeed, harsh weather conditions, combined with occasional outbreaks of bubonic plague, may have been one of the factors that spurred Europeans to seek new lands abroad. Climate change also affected topical regions: West Africa had abundant rain until 1700, when rainfall began diminishing, allowing desert to claim much of the Sahel and pushing savannah farming southward by several hundred miles.

Nonetheless, despite the poor weather, the distribution of new food sources and other resources was widening. For instance, western European societies obtained more food, particularly grain, from eastern Europe, and thus became more linked to that region. Seaborne trade, especially from the Americas, also provided valuable resources, especially to coastal maritime states such as the Netherlands and Britain. Indeed, American crops such as the potato helped Europe stave off even worse climate-related famines. To the east, the Mughals cleared the forests and wetlands of Bengal to create a large area for rice growing, and around the world the expansion of farming came at the expense of shifting cultivators, pastoralists, and food collectors. Some peoples, such as the pastoral Khoikhoi (koi-koi) in South Africa, died off or were enslaved or killed.

Partly because of the spread of food crops, especially from the Americas to Afro-Eurasia, world population increased significantly. In 1500 the earth contained between 400 and 500 million people. Perhaps 60 percent lived in Asia, with China and India each accounting for nearly a quarter of the world total. By 1750 the world population had grown to between 700 and 750 million, probably 80 percent of them peasants living on the land. China and India together, totaling perhaps 400 million, still accounted for over half, while Europe held perhaps 20 percent and Africa 10 percent of the world total.

The Exchange of Diseases, Animals, and Crops

In this era, people, chiefly Europeans and Africans, moved to distant lands, carrying with them species of animals, insects, bacteria, and plants that reshaped local ecosystems. These biological invasions, what historians have termed the Columbian Exchange, particularly accompanied the encounter between Eurasia and the Americas. The European settlers in the Americas brought with them horses and food animals: pigs, chickens, sheep, and cattle. To raise beef cattle, Europeans introduced ranching. Ships returning to Europe carried with them American turkeys, which enriched Eurasian diets.

 The Columbian Exchange (*http://national humanitiescenter.org/ tserve/nattrans/ntecoindian/essays/columbian .htm*). Links to essays by Alfred Crosby and more.

The exchange of diseases between the Eastern and Western Hemispheres was not one-way, but it had a greater impact on the Americas than on Eurasia and Africa. Native Americans had never experienced, and hence had no immunity to, Afro-Eurasian diseases such as smallpox, diphtheria, measles, chicken pox, malaria, bubonic plague, cholera, typhoid fever, and influenza. These diseases devastated the Americas. Smallpox brought the greatest known demographic catastrophe in world history, killing off around 90 percent of the peoples of the Americas. This was a much greater percentage of population than that destroyed by the terrible Black Death, which ravaged much of Eurasia and North Africa in the 1300s. The demographic disaster for the Americas emptied productive land and hence paved the way for Europeans to settle the Americas and to import captive Africans for labor. Only in the highlands, such as the Andes Mountains in South America, did European diseases have a smaller impact. In contrast, only a few American diseases, especially syphilis, brought suffering to people in Europe and Africa.

Crop exchanges also proved momentous. Eurasian and African crops transformed some American regions, and required the introduction of new agricultural practices. Most Native Americans had grown crops such as corn (maize) and potatoes on small plots, but settlers found that Afro-Eurasian crops such as wheat, rice, coffee, barley, and sugar were most successfully grown on large farms or estates. Among these imported crops, sugar had the most impact on the Americas, and vast acreage was devoted to its growth, mostly on plantations. Much of the sugar was exported to Europe for use to sweeten foods such as jam and breads, and beverages such as tea and coffee.

American crops spread widely in the Eastern Hemisphere, where they diversified European diets and habits. Tobacco, for instance, gained popularity in China and Europe, generating both avid devotees and opponents who considered it unhealthy or immoral. Many imports, such as tomatoes, made once-bland European meals more varied. Potatoes became a mainstay of the European diet and the major crop grown in several societies, including Ireland and Scotland. Maize could be grown on marginal land and proved a boon in Africa, southwest Asia, and China, where it was planted on unused hillsides. Corn also fed livestock, and the stalks could be used to make huts and sheds. American chilies, hotter than Asian black peppers, proved hugely popular in South and Southeast Asian cooking, and peanuts became a key crop in West Africa. The new foods offered not only a more varied diet but also a healthier one. By 1750 a diner in many cities in the world could enjoy a fruit salad mixing pieces of Southeast Asian bananas and mangos, Chinese peaches, Southwest Asian pears, African watermelons, Mesoamerican papayas, South American pineapples, and Mediterranean grapes.

European expansion and colonization owed much to the spread of the Eurasian biota, a distinct package of plants, animals, and germs that overwhelmed the rest of the world, especially the Americas and, later, Oceania. Eurasian plants, such as wheat and apple trees, and animals, such as cattle, often replaced indigenous ones in the temperate zones of the Americas and, after 1800, Australia and New Zealand. These changes occurred in part because Europeans viewed animals, plants, and land largely as commodities, to be exploited for their own benefit. The English scientist Sir Francis Bacon expressed these attitudes well: "The world is made for man, not man for the world."[5]

Social and Cultural Change

During the Early Modern Era, the growing networks of trade, information, and technology fostered changes in societies all over the world. Some changes resulted from the increasing migration of peoples, voluntarily or by force. Intermarriage or sexual contact between people from different ethnic groups produced new peoples with mixed cultural backgrounds. Other

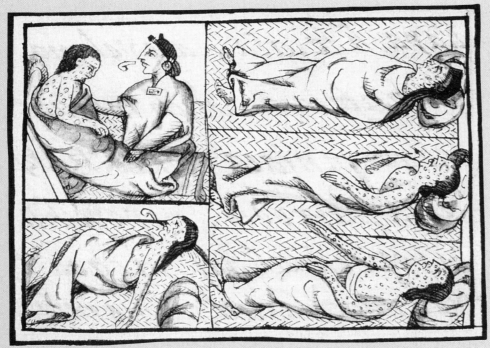

Smallpox Victims in the Americas Eurasian diseases accompanied the Europeans to the Americas, causing a catastrophic loss of life for the Native Americans, who had no immunity. As shown in this print from the 1500s, millions of people sickened and died from smallpox.

Biblioteca Medicea Laurenziana

contributing factors were changing economic systems, the growth of international trade, and the exchange of ideas. Encounters with other ways of living stimulated curiosity and fostered rethinking. Several religions expanded their boundaries and sought converts, challenging ancient, indigenous faiths.

Migration and Hybrid Groups

Improved maritime technology made it possible for people to cross vast oceans, leading to a new system of global migration that brought people with very different customs and values together, not always happily. The largest population movement involved Europeans settling in the Americas and bringing with them enslaved Africans but few European women. Women comprised perhaps only one-fifth of the Spanish and Portuguese who went to the Americas; men thus frequently sought partners among Native American and African women.

Intermarriage and sexual relations across social boundaries led to the creation of American societies that contained many mixed-descent people. By 1750, in Latin America and in French colonies such as Haiti and Louisiana, a large part of the population blended European and Native American backgrounds, creating mestizos, or European and African ancestries, fostering mulattos. For example, many people in Mexico City were mestizo, while in New Orleans blacks and mulattos predominated. In turn, these groups' cultures often mixed the varying social influences, as in northeast Brazil, where people blended African religions and Catholic traditions. Unlike English North America, where any African ancestry usually meant classification as black, in much of Latin America, a complex hierarchy of social categories developed based on gradations of skin color.

Migration and intermarriage also occurred in the Eastern Hemisphere. Dutch and Portuguese adventurers and merchants, most of them men, settled in southern Africa and the port cities of South and Southeast Asia, often taking wives from the local population. Some of the Russians who moved into Siberia and the Black Sea region mixed with local peoples. As had been true for centuries, Arab and Indian traders relocated to distant lands in Africa and Eurasia, often settling permanently. Many Chinese also migrated, usually with their families, and moved into nearby territories such as Taiwan, and male merchants settled in Southeast Asia, in trading centers like the major Siamese city, Ayuthia. Many of the Chinese married Ayuthia women and stayed permanently, their descendants mixing Chinese and Siamese culture. More Chinese also arrived, and by 1735 some 20,000 lived in the kingdom.

Groups of mixed European and Asian ancestry appeared in European colonies in Asia. For instance, the Portuguese men who settled in Goa, Colombo, and Melaka married local women and raised their children as Portuguese-speaking Catholics, but their descendants adopted many local customs. Hence, in Melaka today, while Catholic churches, schools, and festivals remain at the heart of Portuguese community life, the local Portuguese language contains many Malay words, the cuisine has borrowed extensively from Malay and Chinese cooking, and, unlike their merchant, sailor, and soldier ancestors, most men work as fishermen. Throughout the era, Portuguese was the lingua franca of maritime Asia, spoken in many ports, and some of its words were incorporated into local languages such as Malay.

In Africa too—South Africa, Mozambique, Angola, and along the West African coast—the mixing of Europeans and Africans led to hybrid social groups. The offspring of relations between Dutch men and African or Asian women were so common in South Africa that they became a distinct racial group, known as the Coloreds. Prominent slave-trading and merchant families of West Africa often descended from Portuguese men who married women from local chiefly or royal families. Like Brazilian mulattos and many Asian mestizos, African mulattos often spoke a version of Portuguese, the first language with a global reach.

Changing Gender Relations

Although men were much more likely than women to join overseas ventures or cross oceans, women were also affected by the changes of the era. In the Americas, many European men sought Indian women, often by force. One-third of enslaved Africans taken to the Americas were women, some of whom were brought into close contact with slave-owning men, mostly white, who exercised control over their lives. The result was forced sexual activity and mixed-descent children. Christian missionaries working among North American Indians often pursued policies that marginalized women in once-egalitarian cultures, such as the Algonquians of eastern Canada and the Iroquois of New York.

Gender patterns were modified around the world, including in Africa. For instance, in the parts of Africa most affected by slave trading, the absence of men in their productive years encouraged the remaining men to take multiple wives. The traditional role of West African women in local commerce, however, also meant that, along the coast, some became active as slave traders. A few of these, such as Senhora Philippa, who in the 1630s controlled the trading center of Rufisque (ROO-feesk) in today's Senegal, became immensely wealthy. Women also played powerful roles in some of the newer kingdoms fostered by the trans-Atlantic slave trade, such as Dahomey, where queen mothers wielded extraordinary power. A Portuguese missionary to one Senegambia kingdom described a powerful woman, the king's aunt, who was "so respected and obeyed that nothing of importance took place in the kingdom without her knowledge."[6]

In much of Eurasia, women experienced increasing subordination by men, although there were exceptions. Women generally became more restricted in Mughal

India, China, and Japan as patriarchal attitudes strengthened, largely as a result of internal factors. For example, Qing leaders turned more socially conservative, imposing harsher laws against behavior that was considered deviant, such as homosexuality, and stressing the purity of women, which meant less freedom for women to leave home. Indeed, in Southeast Asia, the Spanish and Portuguese were often appalled at the relative freedom of women. Spanish officials criticized Filipinos for tolerating adultery and premarital sex, and they punished those who engaged in these activities. Yet in China, Qing women from elite families published essays and poetry that were widely read and admired. One Chinese poet recalled how her father nurtured her talent: "Understanding that I was quite intelligent, He taught his daughters as he taught his sons, [advising us to] Develop together, support, and do not impede each other."[7]

Missionaries and Religious Change

The encounters between widely differing cultures around the world also had a religious dimension, forcing people to confront different belief systems while widening or sparking divisions in established faiths. Tensions simmering for several centuries in Europe finally fragmented Western Christianity into Catholic and diverse Protestant churches in the 1500s, spurring religious wars, militancy, and hostility toward non-Christians. Scientists such as the Italian astronomer Galileo Galilei were tried by the Holy Inquisition, a Catholic Church institution organized to root out heresy.

Meanwhile, other religious traditions also dealt with tensions and divisions. Mystical Sufi orders became more influential in Islamic societies from Indonesia to West Africa. For example, the early Mughal emperors Babur (BAH-bur) and Akbar were fervent Sufis. Babur wrote in a poem that "I am a king, but yet a slave [follower] of the Dervishes [mystics]."[8] But the Sufis' popularity distressed dogmatists, fostering debate on Sufism's value among Ottoman, Mughal, and Central Asian Muslims. Islamic division hardened in Persia, too. Ordered by their Safavid rulers, Persians shifted from the Sunni to the Shi'a branch of Islam, causing many Sunnis to emigrate. But tensions sometimes led to secular approaches: one such movement, neo-Confucianism, became a strong influence in China, helping secular values to triumph there while Buddhism lost influence among the elites. To comprehend a world charged with diverse and changing ideas, Chinese thinkers, European Enlightenment philosophers, and several Mughal emperors questioned religious dogmas and sought to broaden intellectual horizons.

In contrast, many became religious zealots and engaged in missionary activity. Christians actively sought converts in the Americas, Africa, and Asia. Christian missionaries were often intolerant of local traditions and scornful toward the people they were trying to reach. Catholicism eventually triumphed in Latin America, Kongo, and the Philippines, and it found a few thousand converts in East Asia. Protestant missionaries mostly concentrated on Catholic Europe, Southeast Asia, and North America, where they particularly targeted Native Americans and slaves. But the Christian missionary enterprise faced challenges, including stiff resistance. To gain acceptance, missionaries often had to blend Christianity with local traditions, often against the opposition of church leaders. The intolerance of many Christian missionaries toward other faiths led to their expulsion from Japan and China. East Asians assimilated some useful Western technical and scientific knowledge from the missionaries, such as clockmaking and mapmaking, but most rejected Christianity. Christian missionary efforts had little success among Muslims, Theravada Buddhists, and Hindus.

Christianity was not the only missionary religion: millions of Europeans, Africans, and Asians embraced Islam. Islam spread into the Balkan societies under Ottoman control, and many Serbs, Albanians, and Bulgarians adopted the faith, forging a permanent divide between Christians and Muslims in the region. Islam continued to gain strength in sub-Saharan Africa, Mughal India, and Island Southeast Asia. Unlike Christianity, Islam was not identified with unpopular Western conquest, and it continued to link distant societies. For instance, in the 1600s, Nuruddin al-Raniri, (new-ROOD-in al-RAN-eer-ee) from Gujerat in India, studied in Mecca and then traveled widely, finally settling in Acheh, Sumatra, and becoming an adviser to the king.

Some trends promoted accommodation between divergent faiths. For example, in India the Mughal emperor Akbar preached tolerance and cultural diversity. Akbar's more zealously Islamic successors, however, repressed Hinduism, reviving a long conflict between the two faiths. Theravada Buddhists generally respected all religions. Hence, when the French king, Louis XIV, sent a mission to King Narai of Ayuthia requesting that he and his people adopt Roman Catholicism, the Siamese monarch sent a letter back, arguing that God rejoiced not in religious uniformity but in theological diversities. Meanwhile, Muslims and animists lived side by side without conflict in parts of Africa. Similarly, in some European societies, notably the Netherlands and Poland, Protestants and Catholics learned to live in peace. And growing European knowledge of Chinese society, including Confucianism, led some leaders of the European Enlightenment, such as Voltaire, to view China as an admirable, secular alternative to the religious divisions and orthodoxies of Europe. In this way, Asian ideas influenced some Europeans just as European power expanded, a testament to an increasingly connected world.

Test your understanding of the material covered in Part IV.

Suggested Reading

Adas, Michael, ed. *Islamic and European Expansion: The Forging of a Global Order*. Philadelphia: Temple University Press, 1993. Contains excellent essays by William McNeill, Alfred Crosby, and Philip Curtin on major developments in this era.

Black, Jeremy. *War in the World: Military Power and the Fate of Continents, 1450–2000*. New Haven, CT: Yale University Press, 1998. A global history of land and sea warfare and its contexts.

Brandon, William. *New Worlds for Old: Reports from the New World and Their Effect on the Development of Social Thought in Europe, 1500–1800*. Athens: Ohio University Press, 1986. Examines the impact on Europe of the American discoveries and cultures.

Crosby, Alfred W. *Ecological Imperialism: The Biological Expansion of Europe, 900–1900*. Cambridge: Cambridge University Press, 1993. A pioneering exploration of the environmental changes in the past millennium.

Curtin, Philip D. *The World and the West: The European Challenge and the Overseas Response in the Age of Empire*. Cambridge: Cambridge University Press, 2000. Explores relevant themes in world history since 1500.

Eltis, David. *The Rise of African Slavery in the Americas*. New York: Cambridge University Press, 2000. Overview of slavery and the Atlantic system.

Gunn, Geoffrey C. *First Globalization: The Eurasian Exchange*. Lanham, MD: Rowman and Littlefield, 2003. An idiosyncratic but absorbing study of East–West encounters.

Hobhouse, Henry. *Seeds of Change: Five Plants That Transformed Mankind*. New York: Harper and Row, 1985. A fascinating study of how quinine, sugar, tea, cotton, and the potato changed the world.

Marks, Robert B. *The Origins of the Modern World: A Global and Ecological Narrative*. Lanham, MD: Rowman and Littlefield, 2002. A stimulating, readable, and concise account of how the modern world emerged.

Pacey, Arnold. *Technology in World Civilization*. Cambridge: MIT Press, 1990. Provides a global overview of technological change in this era.

Pilcher, Jeffrey M. *Food in World History*. New York: Routledge, 2006. Examines changing food cultures around the world.

Pomeranz, Kenneth, and Steven Topic. *The World That Trade Created: Society, Culture, and the World Economy, 1400 to the Present*, 2nd ed. Armonk, NY: M. E. Sharpe, 2006. Contains dozens of brief esasys written for the general public.

Richards, John F. *The Unending Frontier: An Environmental History of the Early Modern World*. Berkeley: University of California Press, 2003. A detailed but stimulating study of environmental change, with many case studies.

Smith, Alan K. *Creating a World Economy: Merchant Capital, Colonialism, and World Trade, 1400–1825*. Boulder, CO: Westview Press, 1991. A valuable survey of the world economy in this era.

Wiesner-Hanks, Merry E. *Christianity and Sexuality in the Early Modern World: Regulating Desire, Reforming Practice*. New York: Routledge, 2000. A wide-ranging study of the impact of spreading Christianity on sexual practices.

Wills, John E. *1688: A Global History*. New York: W.W. Norton, 2001. A very readable and informative exploration of various peoples and societies around the world in the late seventeenth century.

PART V

Global Imbalances:

Industry, Empire, and the Making of the Modern World, 1750–1945

NORTH AND CENTRAL AMERICA
In the later 1700s, the thirteen British colonies along the Atlantic coast revolted and established a new democratic nation, the United States, that gradually expanded across the continent. After a civil war ended slavery, the United States rapidly industrialized; as it became the world's major political and economic power in the later 1800s, it attracted immigrants. U.S. military power proved decisive in World Wars I and II. Meanwhile, Canada spread west to the Pacific and achieved self-government. After overthrowing Spanish rule, Mexico was reshaped by liberalism, dictatorship, and revolution.

ARCTIC OCEAN

CANADA

NORTH AMERICA

UNITED STATES

MEXICO

ATLANTIC OCEAN

VENEZUELA

PACIFIC OCEAN

PERU

BRAZIL

SOUTH AMERICA

ANDES

Amazon

ARGENTINA

SOUTH AMERICA
During the early 1800s the Latin American societies overthrew colonialism by force and became independent nations, but they also retained close economic links to Europe, reinforcing their natural resources-based economies and limiting industrialization. The struggles between liberal reformers and conservatives often led to military dictatorship. As European and Asian immigrants reshaped Latin American societies, Latin Americans created distinctive cultures by combining imported and local traditions.

© Cengage Learning

EUROPE

The Industrial Revolution, which began in Britain in the later 1700s, sparked dramatic economic, social, and political change. The French Revolution and the rise of parliamentary democracy in nations such as Britain benefited the middle classes and fostered new national loyalties. Russia conquered Siberia and Central Asia. Britain, France, and Germany renewed imperialism in the later 1800s, forging large empires in Asia and Africa. After 1914 Europe was reshaped by World War I, communist revolution in Russia, economic collapse, the rise of fascism, and World War II.

WESTERN ASIA

Although gradually losing its grip on southeastern Europe and North Africa, the Ottoman Empire maintained control of much of western Asia until after World War I, when Britain and France acquired the Arab territories and the Ottomans collapsed, replaced by a modernizing Turkish state. Persia attempted reforms but still fell under Western domination. Arab nationalism challenged Western power, while secular reformers and pro- and antimodern Muslims struggled for influence throughout the region.

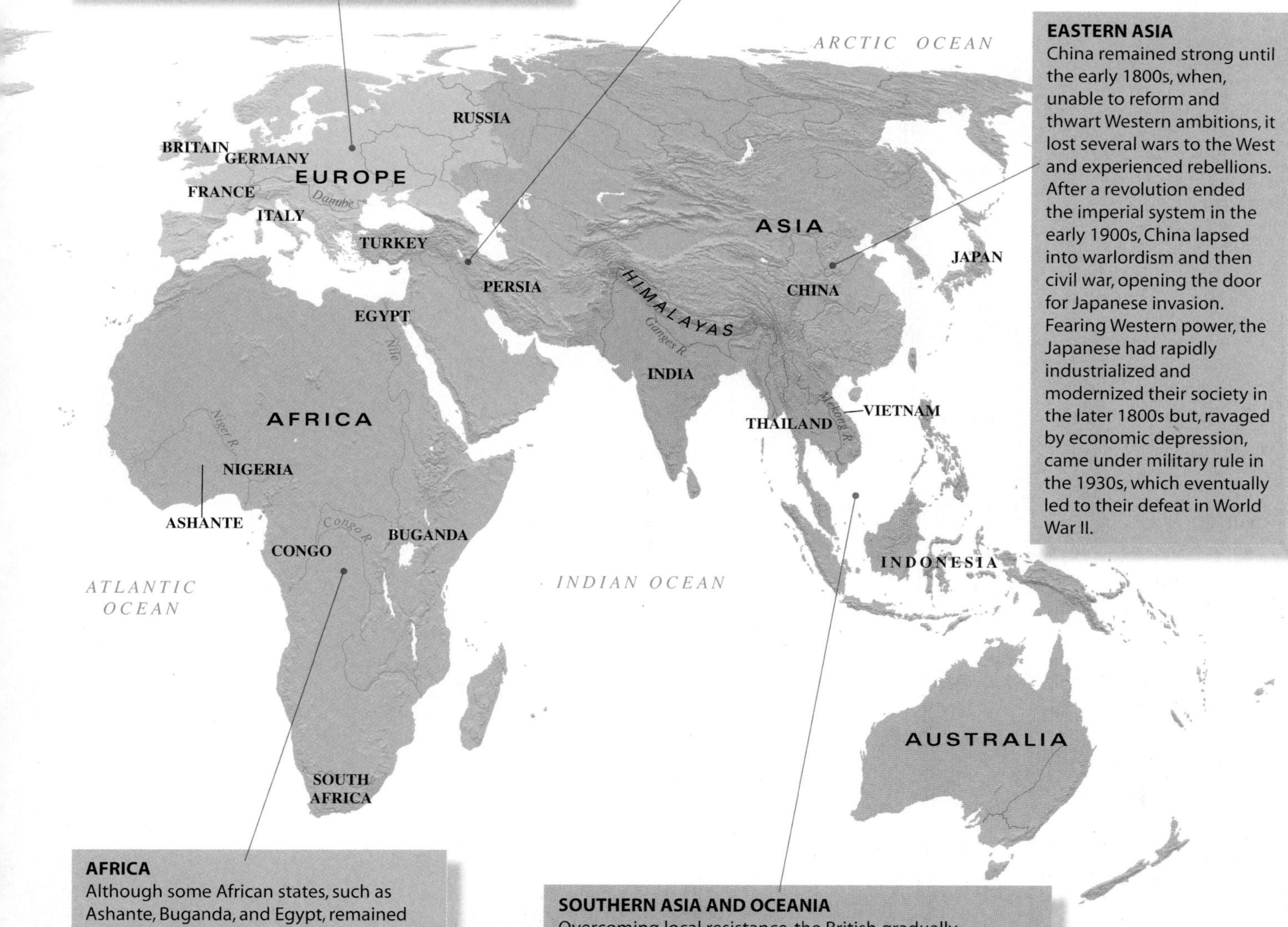

EASTERN ASIA

China remained strong until the early 1800s, when, unable to reform and thwart Western ambitions, it lost several wars to the West and experienced rebellions. After a revolution ended the imperial system in the early 1900s, China lapsed into warlordism and then civil war, opening the door for Japanese invasion. Fearing Western power, the Japanese had rapidly industrialized and modernized their society in the later 1800s but, ravaged by economic depression, came under military rule in the 1930s, which eventually led to their defeat in World War II.

AFRICA

Although some African states, such as Ashante, Buganda, and Egypt, remained strong into the 1800s and instituted reforms, they could not halt increasing Western power. The ending of the trans-Atlantic slave trade by the mid-1800s opened the door to Western colonization of the entire continent. The British and French built large empires in both sub-Saharan Africa and North Africa. Western imperialism created artificial countries, undermined traditional societies, and drained Africa of resources. After World War I African and Arab nationalist movements struggled against Western domination.

SOUTHERN ASIA AND OCEANIA

Overcoming local resistance, the British gradually conquered India, and their rule exploited India's resources, reshaped Indian life, and generated opposition from Indian nationalists seeking independence. Dynamic Southeast Asian states repulsed the West until the mid-1800s, when the British, French, and Dutch colonized all of these resource-rich societies, except Thailand, often against fierce resistance, and the United States replaced Spanish rule in the Philippines, crushing a local independence movement. To the east, Western powers colonized the Pacific islands and Europeans settled in Australia and New Zealand.

Map labels: ARCTIC OCEAN · RUSSIA · BRITAIN · GERMANY · FRANCE · EUROPE · ITALY · Danube · TURKEY · PERSIA · EGYPT · ASIA · HIMALAYAS · Ganges R. · INDIA · JAPAN · CHINA · Nile · Niger R. · AFRICA · NIGERIA · ASHANTE · Congo R. · CONGO · BUGANDA · THAILAND · VIETNAM · Mekong R. · INDONESIA · ATLANTIC OCEAN · INDIAN OCEAN · SOUTH AFRICA · AUSTRALIA

CHAPTER 19

Modern Transitions:
Revolutions, Industries, Ideologies, Empires, 1750–1914

COTTON

LONDON TIME

Learning Outcomes

After reading this chapter, you should be able to answer the following questions:

LO¹ What were the major consequences of the American and French Revolutions?

LO² How did the Caribbean and Latin American revolutions compare with those in Europe and North America?

LO³ How did industrialization reshape economic and social life?

LO⁴ How did nationalism, liberalism, and socialism differ from each other?

LO⁵ What factors spurred the Western imperialism of the later 1800s?

Laurie Platt Winfrey, Inc./The Granger Collection, New York

> **❝**From this foul drain the greatest stream of human industry flows out to fertilize the whole world. From this filthy sewer pure gold flows. Here humanity attains its most complete development and its most brutish.**❞**
>
> —French writer Alexis De Tocqueville on Manchester, England, 1835[1]

On a spring day in 1851, Britons of all social classes headed for the spectacular new Crystal Palace in Hyde Park to see the official opening, led by Queen Victoria herself, of the Great Exhibition. All shared in the excitement of an exhibition designed to celebrate "The Works of Industry of All Nations," with Progress as the organizing theme. The first "world's fair," the Great Exhibition was dazzling. Some 14,000 firms participated in the displays, showcasing British industrial leadership in particular. The hall of machinery contained power textile looms, marine engines, locomotives, and other inventions that had revolutionized British life. Another hall lavishly presented industrial products that British merchants sold all over the world, including fine textiles made from wool, cotton, linen, and silk. Nearly half of the exhibitors represented other countries of Europe and North America.

 Test your knowlege before you read this chapter.

What do you think?

Western industrialization was the primary cause of the resurgence of western imperialism.

Strongly Disagree   Strongly Agree
1   2   3   4   5   6   7

The Great Exhibition of 1851 celebrated the industrialization that had begun three-quarters of a century earlier and was already dramatically transforming the social and physical landscapes in Britain, the United States, and parts of Europe. The age of the machine had arrived: modern industry, a growing economy, and science meant humanity's triumph over the natural world. Industrialization gave Britain and other Western countries the economic and military power to increase their influence around the world.

Along with industrialization, political revolutions and new ideologies were also defining developments in Europe and the Americas between 1750 and 1914. The economic and political changes resulting from industrialization and political revolutions fostered new ideas about politics and government and about the relationship of citizens to the state. Great Britain, France, Germany, and Russia emerged as the main powers in Europe, while the United States became the

≪Crystal Palace Exposition of 1851 Attracting more than 6 million visitors, the Great Exhibition, held at the Crystal Palace in London in 1851, showcased industrial products and the companies that produced them from all over the world, but especially from Europe.

> "Revolutions have been momentous events in modern world history, erupting on every inhabited continent except Australia."

strongest American country. But by the later 1800s, these trends had also yielded mixed blessings, including a renewal of the imperialism, begun in the 1500s, that resulted in various European nations acquiring or expanding empires in Asia and Africa.

LO¹ The Age of Revolution: North America and Europe

Some historians use the phrase "the Age of Revolution" to refer to the period from the 1770s through the 1840s, when revolutions rocked the Atlantic world. During these years, revolutionaries employed armed violence to seize power and forge fundamental changes. Two types of revolutions emerged in modern times. Political revolutions, notably the one resulting in the United States, changed the personnel and structure of government, while social revolutions, such as France's tumultuous upheaval that began in 1789, transformed both the political and social order. For the next two centuries, revolutions transformed states, ideologies, and class structures, especially in Europe, Latin America, and Asia.

Modern Revolutions

Revolutions have been momentous events in modern world history, erupting on every inhabited continent except Australia. In the late 1700s, Europeans and Latin Americans watched fascinated as the disaffected citizens in the thirteen British colonies in North America struggled to overthrow British rule and then established an independent federation that soon became the United States. The American revolutionary leaders proclaimed Enlightenment political theories formulated in Europe, such as democracy and personal freedom, and then sought to apply these theories to their new representative government. The French Revolution electrified Europe by violently replacing the monarchy with a republic and spreading the new values of liberty and social equality. But

the French Revolution also generated terrible violence, the rise of despotic leaders, long years of war, and a transformed nineteenth-century European continent.

Revolutions often shared common features. Revolutionary leaders were frequently well-educated and privileged, but in many cases, they mobilized followers from among disenchanted peasants and urban workers. Many revolutions, including the French, moved from moderate to more extreme actions, such as purging dissidents, rivals, or opponents. And though most revolutions replaced incompetent and oppressive governments, they were also destructive and brutal, and few ultimately satisfied the demands of their people. The majority of these revolutions were sparked by one or more causes, most commonly hunger, poverty, war, overpopulation, the spread of destabilizing capital-

---

CHRONOLOGY

The North American and European Revolutions, 1770–1815

1770s–1840s	Age of Revolution
1773	Boston Tea Party
1776	American Declaration of Independence
1783	Britain's recognition of United States' independence
1787	United States constitutional convention; Northwest Ordinance for forming new states
1789–1815	French Revolution
1791–1792	Constitutional state in Poland-Lithuania
1804	Crowning of Napoleon as emperor of France
1810–1811	Height of Napoleon's empire
1815	Defeat of Napoleon at Battle of Waterloo; Congress of Vienna

---

ism, or, as in British North America, the desire for more personal freedom and self-government.

British Colonialism and the American Revolution

The successful political revolution in British North America resulted from resentments that had festered for decades between British colonists and the imperial government. Britain had forged a foothold on the eastern seaboard of North America in the 1600s, establishing a presence in Canada and in thirteen colonies stretching from New Hampshire south to Georgia. Each colony had unique institutions and economies: the southern colonies depended largely on plantation slavery, whereas the northern colonies combined commerce and manufacturing with farming, a more balanced mix of economic activities. Only 2 million persons lived in the colonies in the 1760s, and the largest town, Boston, had only 20,000 residents. One-fifth of the colonial population was African American, most of who were enslaved.

Given these conditions, the white colonists seemed to have little to rebel against. Except for enslaved African Americans, the American colonists were generally prosperous and enjoyed considerable self-government and religious toleration.

 **The American Revolution (http://revolution.h-net.msu.edu/).** An excellent collection of links, essays, and other resources.

The majority of adult white males, if they owned sufficient property, could vote for local assemblies and mayors. The colonists also faced much lighter taxes than did people in Britain. Most colonists were proud to be British subjects, and by the mid-1700s, the British hold on these colonies seemed strong.

But after the Seven Years' War (1756–1763), tensions increased between the British—who needed American help to pay their war debts—and the colonists. Many colonists felt divorced from Britain and increasingly resented British policies, such as taxation without representation in the British Parliament. Clumsy British attempts to raise taxes, enforce

> "Many colonists felt divorced from Britain and increasingly resented British policies, such as taxation without representation in the British Parliament."

long-ignored laws, and reserve the coveted land west of the Appalachians for Indians angered many colonists, some of whom began tarring and feathering tax collectors. Both men and women also mounted boycotts of British goods. In 1773, to protest a higher tax on tea, outraged colonists, dressed as Indians, raided three British ships in Boston harbor and dumped their cargo of tea overboard, an event known as the Boston Tea Party. Colonists favoring independence, known as Patriots, and those opposed, called Loyalists, increasingly clashed.

Declaration of Independence

The Patriot supporters of independence admired progressive European thought. Deeply influenced by European Enlightenment thinkers such as John Locke in England and Baron de Montesquieu in France, they favored democracy and a republic (see Chapter 15). The Patriots were also stirred by recent English immigrant Tom Paine's (1737–1809) passionate pamphlet *Common Sense*, which urged Americans to oppose tyranny and free themselves by force in order to "begin the world over again." A series of American–British skirmishes escalated in the 1770s, leading to the Second Continental Congress, at which delegates from all thirteen colonies met and declared that the colonies ought to be free and independent states. On July 4, 1776, the delegates approved the Declaration of Independence, written largely by Thomas Jefferson (1743–1826), a Virginia planter, which stated, "We hold these truths to be self-evident, that all men are created equal, that they are endowed by their Creator with certain inalienable Rights, that among these are Life, Liberty and the pursuit of Happiness."[2]

> 66 We hold these truths to be self-evident, that all men are created equal . . . 99
>
> *from the Declaration of Independence*

The United States Declaration of Independence, Thomas Jefferson, (1776) Did you know that Thomas Jefferson was influenced by Enlightenment thinkers? Look for overtones of this philosophy in his United States Declaration of Independence.

Patriots vs. Loyalists

With conflict unavoidable, a revolutionary army organized and commanded by George Washington (1732–1799), a respected Virginia planter and veteran of the Seven Years' War, then fought the British and their Loyalist allies for six bitter years. Although one-third of the colonists remained staunchly loyal to Britain, the revolutionary effort reached to the grassroots as women and men from all quarters raised funds, supported Washington's army, and sabotaged British efforts. Britain's rivals, France and Spain, also aided the Patriot cause. The British were supported by many Indians, who resented the colonists for aggressively occupying Indian lands, and by some black slaves, who were promised their freedom if they helped the Loyalist cause. Some accused the Patriots of hypocrisy, wanting freedom for themselves while maintaining slavery for nonwhites.

The American defeat of British forces at Yorktown, Virginia, in 1781 proved decisive, and, after negotiations, Britain recognized the independence of the thirteen colonies in 1783. Despite their democratic values, the Patriots treated the Loyalists harshly, confiscating their land and jailing them. Ultimately 100,000 Loyalists were expelled or fled to Canada, and many others left for England.

The Legacy of the American Revolution

During the war of independence, the thirteen colonies joined to form an independent federation, the United States of America. The first confederation, which required the unanimous consent of every state for major political changes, proved unworkable. Seeking a stronger central government, delegates from each state met in 1787 at a convention in Philadelphia and approved a constitution for a national government that was mostly written by James Madison (1751–1836), a shy, well-educated Virginian. The constitution called for an elected president and congress presiding over a federal system that granted many powers to the states. The delegates then elected the war hero George Washington as the first president of the republic. Unlike Jefferson and Madison, Washington was not a talented speaker or writer, but Americans admired the general's integrity and suc-

> "The French Revolution was perhaps the world's first true social revolution, traumatic but also inspiring in its message of 'liberty, equality, and fraternity.'"

cess, and they considered him a man who embodied American virtues. The first elected Congress approved ten constitutional amendments, known as the Bill of Rights, which enshrined Enlightenment values such as freedom of speech, assembly, press, and religion.

Despite their rhetoric of liberty and equality, the Patriot founders did not challenge slavery, recognize Native American claims to land, or expand voting rights beyond white men. Most northern states gradually abolished slavery, but the institution was maintained in most of the south. Indians could only watch bitterly as the new national government claimed most of the land east of the Mississippi River and made plans to survey and settle it. Nor did the nation's founders give women equal rights with men, despite their significant contributions to the cause of independence.

American Exceptionalism

Nevertheless, Americans believed they had formed a society unique to history. This idea of a distinctive character and history, known as American "exceptionalism," was intensified after the Revolution. Americans viewed theirs as the most democratic, individualistic, enterprising, and prosperous society on earth. The new country seemed unhindered by the burdens of history that held down other peoples. Americans also argued that their ideas and institutions were relevant for the whole world, echoing the Puritan Massachusetts governor, John Winthrop, who had claimed in 1630 that his new colony constituted a "City upon a Hill, [with] the eyes of all people upon us."[3] Thomas Jefferson, who became the third president of the new republic, declared that America was a standing monument and example for the world.

The French Revolution

The French Revolution was perhaps the world's first true social revolution, traumatic but also inspiring in its message of "liberty, equality, and fraternity." With fair distribution of wealth as a popular principle, the French middle classes took over the government in the name of the common people. But the Revolution also plunged Europe into a prolonged crisis that

Storming the Bastille This painting celebrates the taking of the Bastille, a castle prison in Paris that symbolized hated royal rule, by armed citizens and soldiers. The governor and his officials are led out and will soon be executed.

resulted in a series of wars between France and its European rivals, who feared the spread of radicalism. Ironically, these wars actually helped to spread French revolutionary ideas to other European societies.

Revolutionary Causes

The Revolution had many causes. France's participation in the American War of Independence worsened the government's long-standing financial problems. Included in these problems was an unjust economic system that badly needed reform. For example, the Roman Catholic clergy and the privileged nobility were exempt from most direct taxes, and thus the entire burden was put on artisans and peasants. Several bad harvests increased the common peoples' hunger and misery. To calm rising passions, King Louis XVI (1754–1793), a member of the long-ruling Bourbon family, called the Estates General, a long-dormant consultative body that included the clergy, the nobility, and a Third Estate comprising the middle classes and peasants. Every town debated political issues, drew up lists of complaints, and then elected delegates to the Estates General. High prices, food shortages, and high unemployment spurred resentment of the government and privileged classes; one Third Estate pamphlet called them a malignant disease preying on a sick society.

The leaders of the Third Estate, who represented more than 90 percent of the French population, demanded influence in the Estates General that reflected their numbers. Stalemated in the Estates General, the Third Estate delegates formed a rival national assembly and began writing a new French constitution. In response, the king called in the army to restore order and fired a popular reformist official. These actions provoked anger and violence in 1789 when armed crowds stormed the Bastille, the royal prison and a hated symbol of tyranny, to release the prisoners and seize gunpowder and cannon. The Bastille attack, which resulted in many deaths on both sides, proved so inspirational that the date (July 14) later became France's national holiday.

The Declaration of Rights of Man and Citizen, National Assembly of France (1789) Do you see similarities in France's Declaration of Rights of Man and Citizen and the United States Declaration of Independence? Do you think one was influenced by the other?

As unrest spread through France, the terrified nobility fled. Members of the Third Estate formed a new Constituent Assembly, which voted to destroy the social order and adopted the Declaration of the Rights of Man and of the Citizen, a document strongly influenced by the English Bill of Rights of 1689 and the new United States constitution. The Declaration announced that all people everywhere had a natural right to liberty, property, equality, security, religious toleration, and freedom of expression, press, and association. A new constitution preserved the monarchy but made the king bound by laws and subject to an elected assembly. The leaders also outlawed slavery and targeted corruption in the church.

Counterrevolution and War

Counterrevolution supported by rival countries soon embroiled France in a long series of wars. France's neighbors, fearing the radicalism that the Revolution unleashed, sought a restoration of royal power in France. To preempt an invasion, French leaders declared war in 1792. A national convention, elected by universal male suffrage, now made France a republic, ending the monarchy. In the name of all the world's people, the French began a revolutionary crusade for self-determination and the end of absolute monarchies in Europe. With patriotic enthusiasm, the French public rallied behind the revolutionary government, and in 1793 the revolutionaries executed King Louis XVI for treason. Most European states declared war on France's revolutionary government, but poor leadership on both sides prevented any decisive victory.

Jacobins

As military conflict intensified, so did dissension in France. The country faced not only foreign enemies but also internal dissent and worsening economic problems. Some leaders had emphasized preserving the Revolution's libertarian principles, such as freedom of speech and assembly. However, a more radical faction known as Jacobins (JAK-uh-binz) prioritized order over freedom, imposing a dictatorship to promote internal security. The Jacobins set up the Committee of Public Safety, which used terror against real or imagined opponents by ordering mass executions, often cutting off their victims' heads in public using the gruesome guillotine. Perhaps 40,000 French citizens, mostly rebellious peasants and provincial leaders, were executed, and tens of thousands more were arrested, often on flimsy evidence. Even some Jacobin leaders were executed in factional disputes. The terror abated when the Jacobins lost power in 1795, but their discordant legacy included innovative laws guaranteeing universal public education and public welfare for the poor.

The Legacy of the French Revolution

Although not all of its accomplishments proved long-lasting, the French Revolution showed that an old regime could be destroyed and a new order created by its own people, providing both a model and an inspiration for generations of revolutionaries to come. The Revolution not only installed the middle class in power in France but also ultimately constructed a modern bureaucratic state. The French example also inspired other Europeans to adopt political reform. For example, in 1791, reformers in Poland-Lithuania reshaped the state and expanded voting rights. But a year later, Russia, supported by the Polish nobility, invaded Poland-Lithuania and crushed the reformist government. Ultimately, the terrible violence of the French Revolution dampened its appeal as the Jacobins' terror undermined personal liberty. Indeed, the French trauma and terror turned many westerners against revolutions, which they now feared too often degenerated into anarchy and then despotism.

The declaration of the French "Rights of Man" inspired some to raise the question of women's rights. Olympe de Gouges (1748–1793), a French butcher's daughter, published a manifesto complaining that women were excluded from decision making and tried to organize a female militia to fight for France. For her efforts she was executed. A British campaigner for women's rights, Mary Wollstonecraft (1759–1797), whose outrage was spurred by watching her merchant father abuse her mother, moved to Paris and wrote the *Vindication of the Rights of Women* in 1792, calling for equal opportunities for women in education and society. But despite the efforts of reformers such as de Gouges and Wollstonecraft, women remained excluded from citizenship in France and nearly everywhere else.

The Napoleonic Era and a New European Politics

Although the republican system had inspired many within and outside of France, the end result in France was a military dictatorship. The terror and the shifting fortunes of war led to a resurgence of pro-monarchy feelings in France and prompted antiroyalists to turn to the ambitious General Napoleon Bonaparte (BOW-nuh-pahrt) (1769–1821), a brilliant military strategist from the French-ruled island of Corsica. Bonaparte's ambitions and deeds would shake up the politics of France and Europe.

Bonaparte's Rise to Power

Bonaparte's rise to power was astounding. In 1795 he was a lowly artillery officer just released from prison for alleged Jacobin ties. Through political connections and his forceful personality, he rapidly rose through the ranks to command major military victories in France, Italy, Austria, and Egypt, becoming the most influential French leader of his day. In 1804, responding to growing sentiment that only a dictator could provide stability, Bonaparte crowned himself emperor in a regal coronation and then quickly began to promote reconciliation and economic progress. He also upheld the equality of all citizens before the law, thus making permanent the Revolution's core values. However, the Corsican's general dictatorial tendencies betrayed French liberty, and his militarism led to near-constant warfare with other European nations.

British Coalition

In 1805, Britain, the world's dominant sea power and longtime rival of France, forged a coalition with Austria, Prussia, and Russia to defeat Napoleon. In the following years, France won most of the land battles, enabling it to occupy much of western Europe. By 1810, Bonaparte's family ruled Spain, Naples, and some German states, but their power eventually waned. Armed resistance, a costly French invasion of Russia resulting in humiliating retreat, and an invasion of France by rival powers all sapped Bonaparte's military strength. He was finally overcome by British and Prussian armies at Waterloo, a Belgian village, in 1815. While the Bourbon family reclaimed the French throne, Bonaparte, for a decade the most powerful man in Europe, spent his remaining years in exile on a remote, British-ruled South Atlantic island.

The demise of revolutionary France and the dismantling of Napoleon's empire allowed for a partial return to the political status quo in Europe. The victorious allies met in 1815 at the Congress of Vienna to remold the European state system (see Map 19.1). Dominated by Austria, Britain, Russia, and the revived royalist government of France, the Congress reaffirmed pre-Napoleonic borders and restored most of the former rulers who had been displaced by revolutionaries and reformers. It also led to the confederation of thirty-nine German states, laying the foundation for modern Germany.

Interactive Map

Uprising and Revolt

In the following decades, revolutionary ideas combined with popular discontent continued to unsettle Europe, and various revolutions broke out in 1830–1831 because of discontent with despotic political systems. The French overthrew the increasingly despotic Bourbon king, Charles X, and installed his more progressive cousin and former Jacobin, Louis-Philippe (1773–1850), as a constitutional monarch who recognized democratic liberties. Uprisings in several German and Italian states and in Poland sought voting rights, and a peasant rebellion caused by poverty and unemployment rocked Britain.

Even more turbulent European revolts erupted in 1848, a result of poor harvests, rampant disease, trade slumps, rising unemployment, massive poverty, and a desire for representative government. These upheavals again began in France, forcing the increasingly unpopular King Louis-Philippe to abdicate, and soon spread to Austria, Hungary, and many German and Italian states. But around Europe, conservative regimes crushed the dissident movements within a few months, often causing great bloodshed. A French observer said that "nothing was lacking" in the repression in Paris, "not grapeshot, nor bullets, nor demolished houses, nor martial law, nor the ferocity of the soldiery, nor the insults to the dead."[4] Still, the uprisings helped further spread democratic ideas, and monarchies lost ground as parliamentary power increased in countries such as Denmark and the Netherlands. To prevent revolutionary outbursts, many European governments also began to consider social and economic reforms, such as higher wages, to improve people's lives.

Map 19.1
Europe in 1815

With the Napoleonic wars ended, the Congress of Vienna redrew the map of Europe. France, Austria, Spain, Britain, and a growing Prussia were the dominant states, but the Ottoman Turks still ruled a large area of southeastern Europe.

Legend:
- Kingdom of Prussia
- Austrian Empire
- Boundary of German Confederation

LO² The Age of Revolution: The Caribbean and Latin America

The Age of Revolution was not confined to North America and Europe. Just as in British North America, dissatisfaction with colonialism was common in the Caribbean and Spanish America, and it led to revolutions and wars of independence in these regions in the early 1800s. The first successful movement to overthrow colonialism came in Haiti, where slaves of African ancestry fought their way to power. Many Central and South American countries also eventually won their independence by the 1820s.

Spanish and Portuguese America's Colonial Heritage

The Spanish and Portuguese ruled much larger American empires than did the British. By 1810, some 18 million diverse people lived under Spanish rule from California in the north to the southern tip of South America. This population included Europeans, Indians, Africans, and people of mixed descent. The empire was divided into four administrative units based in Mexico, Colombia, Peru, and Argentina, each supervised by Spanish governors. Corruption ran deep, but the planters, ranchers, mine owners, bureaucrats, and church officials who benefited from Spanish rule or profited from exploiting the economic resources opposed any major change. They preferred a system that sent raw materials, such as silver and beef, to Spain rather than one that developed domestic institutions and markets.

> " By 1810, some 18 million diverse people lived under Spanish rule from California in the north to the southern tip of South America. "

CHRONOLOGY

The Caribbean and Latin American Revolutions, 1750–1840

1791–1804	Haitian Revolution
1808	Move of Portuguese royal family to Brazil
1810–1826	Wars of independence in Spanish America
1810–1811	First Mexican revolution
1816	Argentine independence
1819	Founding of Colombian republic by Bolívar
1822	Mexican independence; Dom Pedro emperor of Brazil
1830	Independence of Colombia, Venezuela, and Ecuador
1839	Division of Central American states

Political Structure

The Spanish ruled their colonies differently than did the British in North America, allowing little self-government, maintaining extractive monocultures, and imposing Roman Catholicism. Only a small minority shared in the wealth produced by the mines, plantations, and ranches. Latin American social conditions did not promote unity or equality. The creoles—whites born in the Americas—resented influential newcomers from Spain, but they also feared that resistance against Spain might get out of control and threaten their privileges. The great majority of the population, a dispossessed underclass of Indians, enslaved Africans, and mixed-descent people, faced growing unemployment and perhaps the world's most inequitable distribution of wealth.

In contrast to British America, Latin America, dominated by a rigid Catholic Church that was wary of dissent, enjoyed little intellectual diversity. The Inquisition denounced as seditious any literature espousing equality and liberty for all people and punished people it considered to be heretics. Local critics accused the government and church of "placing the strongest fetters on Enlightenment and [keeping] thought in chains."[5] Yet one successful dissenter was the Mexican creole Jose Antonio Alzate y Ramirez (1738–1799), who published a magazine that promoted science and Enlightenment rationalism.

Colonial Revolts

Given the political and social inequalities, various revolts punctuated Spanish colonial rule. The largest revolt spread over large parts of Peru in the 1700s and was led by Tupac Amaru II (1740–1781), the wealthy, well-educated mestizo who claimed to be a descendant of an Inca king. Although the better-armed Spanish defeated the rebel bands and executed Tupac and his family, the Tupac Amaru revolt paved the way for larger upheavals across South America several decades later.

Portuguese Brazil also experienced dissent. By the late 1700s, Brazil was the wealthiest part of the Portuguese colonial realm, but only a small, mostly white minority enjoyed the prosperity. Because Brazil was the major importer of slaves, accounting for one-quarter to one-third of all Africans arriving in the Americas, blacks vastly outnumbered Native Americans in Brazil, in contrast to Spanish-ruled Mexico and South America. Disgruntled

Afro-Brazilians demanded a better life, but they faced many setbacks; in 1799, one revolt seeking social equality and political freedom was crushed in the northeastern state of Bahia (buh-HEE-uh).

> "The Afro-Caribbean peoples appropriated European cultural forms and languages, welding them with retained African forms."

Caribbean Societies and the Haitian Revolution

Most of the small Caribbean islands and the Guianas in northeast South America were colonies of Britain, France, or the Netherlands and were inhabited chiefly by African slaves and their descendants, most of whom worked on sugar plantations. The Afro-Caribbean peoples appropriated European cultural forms and languages, welding them with retained African forms. In British-colonized islands such as Jamaica, Barbados, and Antigua, most slaves adopted Christianity and Anglo-Saxon names. The African influences that shaped slave life included musical influences such as drumming, improvisation, and varied rhythms.

Slave Revolts

Slave revolts were common throughout the colonial era, but only one, the Haitian Revolution, overthrew a regime. In 1791, some 100,000 Afro-Haitian slaves, inspired by the French Revolution and its slogans of liberty and equality, rose up against the oppressive society presided over by French planters, thus beginning years of war and bloodshed. Toussaint L'Ouverture (too-SAN loo-ver-CHORE) (1746–1803), a freed slave with a vision of a republic composed of free people, became the insurgent leader.

Haitian Revolution

The Haitian revolution went from triumph to tragedy. For a decade the Afro-Haitians fought the French military, and by 1801, Toussaint's forces had gained control over Haiti and freed the slaves. But Napoleon Bonaparte sent in a larger French force to restore order, and in 1803, French soldiers captured Toussaint, who soon died in a French prison. In 1804, Afro-Haitians defeated Napoleon's army and established the second independent nation in the Western Hemisphere after the United States. Slaves elsewhere in the Americas were cheered by the Haitian Revolution, but horrified planters became more determined to preserve slav-

ery, and the United States, still a slave-owning nation, withheld diplomatic recognition of the black Haitian republic. In Haiti, French planters were either killed or fled, and the ex-slaves took over sugar production, but the promise of a better life for Haiti's people proved short-lived. Toussaint's successor as revolutionary leader, the Africa-born Jean Jacques Dessalines (de-sah-LEEN) (1758–1806), became emperor and ruled despotically, beginning two centuries of tyranny.

South American Independence Wars

As in North America and Haiti, dissatisfaction in Spanish-ruled South America exploded into wars of national independence. In 1800, the Spanish colonial hold on its empire seemed secure, but resentments simmered, especially among creoles, who criticized Spain for its commercial monopoly, its increasing taxes, and the colonial government's favoritism toward those born in Spain. Creoles also often felt more loyalty toward their American region than to distant Spain, and some were influenced by the Enlightenment and the American and French Revolutions. The British, who were pressuring the Spanish and Portuguese to open Latin American markets to British goods, also secretly aided anticolonial groups. At the same time, Spain was experiencing political problems at home, including French occupation during the Napoleonic wars, which weakened the country's ability to suppress unrest in Latin America.

Simón Bolívar

Because Spain refused to make serious political concessions, creole revolutionaries of middle-class backgrounds waged wars of independence between 1810 and 1826, forming new countries. Two separate independence movements began in 1810–1811 in Venezuela and Argentina, and they soon came under the leadership of Simón Bolívar (bow-LEE-vahr) in the north and Jose de San Martin (san mahr-TEEN) in the south. Born into a wealthy Caracas family, Bolívar (1783–1830) had studied law in Spain, admired rationalist Enlightenment thought, and had a magnetic personality that inspired loyalty. He expressed sympathy for

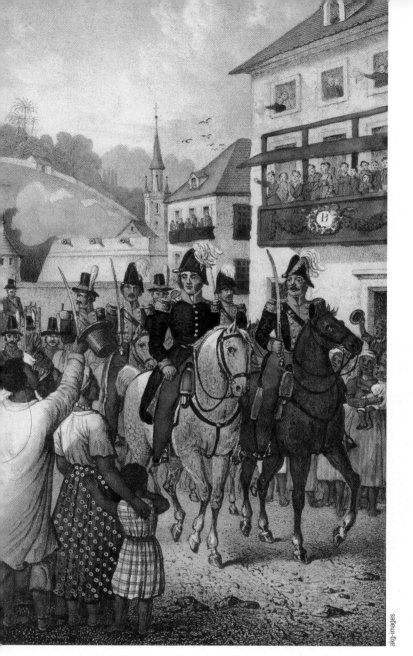

Simón Bolívar The main leader of the anti-Spanish war of independence in northern South America, Bolívar came to be known as "the Liberator," a symbol of Latin American nationalism and the struggle for political freedom.

akg-images

blacks in Haiti and Jamaica and offered an inclusive view of his Latin American people: "We are a microcosm of the human race, a world apart, neither Indian nor Europeans, but a part of each."[6] In 1812, Bolívar formed an army to liberate northern South America, offering freedom to slaves who aided his cause. After many setbacks, Bolívar's forces liberated the north in 1824. San Martin (1778–1850), a former colonel in the Spanish army, led the southern forces against Spain and its royalist allies, helping Argentina gain independence in 1816 and Chile in 1818. In 1824, San

Martin and Bolívar cooperated to liberate Peru, where royalist sympathies were strongest.

Consequences of Victory

But these victories over the colonial regimes did not always meet the expectations of the liberated or the liberators. The wars damaged economies and caused people to flee the fighting. In addition, the creoles who now governed these countries often forgot the promises they had made to the Indians, mestizos, mulattos, and blacks, who had often provided the bulk of the revolutionary armies. And although some slaves were freed, slavery was not abolished. Women also experienced disappointment, especially those who had enthusiastically served the revolution as soldiers and nurses, such as Policarpa Salavarrieta, who was captured by the Spanish. Before she was executed in Bogota's main plaza, she exclaimed: "Although I am a woman and young, I have more than enough courage to suffer this death and a thousand more."[7] Despite such sacrifices, women soon found that they still lived in patriarchal societies that offered them few new legal or political rights. Finally, unlike the founders of the United States, Latin America's new leaders were largely unable to form representative and democratic governments. Simón Bolívar could not hold his own country together, and in 1830 it broke into Colombia, Ecuador, and Venezuela. Meanwhile, Uruguay and Paraguay split off from Argentina, and Bolivia separated from Peru. Disillusioned, Bolívar concluded that Latin America was ungovernable.

The Jamaica Letter, Simón Bolívar Did you know that Simón Bolívar was a pivotal leader of the Latin American independence movement against Spain? Read his thoughts on the prospects of the liberation movement after a major setback against the Spaniards.

Independence Movements in Mexico and Brazil

Political change also came to Mexico and Brazil (see Map 19.2). In 1810, two progressive Mexican Catholic priests, the creole Manuel Hidalgo (ee-DAHL-go) and the mestizo Jose Maria Morelos (hoe-SAY mah-REE-ah moh-RAY-los), mobilized peasants and miners and launched a revolt promoting independence, the abolition of slavery, and social reform to uplift the mestizos and Indians. Conservative royalists

Interactive Map

Map 19.2
Latin American Independence, 1840

By 1840, all of Latin America except for Cuba and Puerto Rico, which were still Spanish colonies, had become independent, with Brazil and Mexico the largest countries. Later the Central American provinces and Gran Colombia would fragment into smaller nations, and Argentina would annex Patagonia.

suppressed the revolt and executed Hidalgo and Morelos. But a compromise between various factions brought Mexico independence in 1822 under a creole general, Agustin de Iturbide (ah-goos-TEEN deh ee-tur-BEE-deh) (1783–1824), who proclaimed himself emperor. However, although initially the anti-Spanish struggle had united creoles, mestizos, and Indians against a common enemy, the alliance unraveled, and a republican revolt soon ousted Iturbide. The Central American peoples split off from Mexico and, after several attempts at unity, by 1839 had splintered into five states.

Brazil escaped many of the bloody conflicts bedeviling Spanish America. In 1808, the Portuguese royal family and government sought refuge in Brazil to escape the Napoleonic wars, and in the following years, Brazilians increasingly viewed themselves as separate from Portugal. When the Portuguese government tried to reclaim the territory, a member of the royal family still in Brazil, Dom Pedro (1798–1834), severed ties with Portugal in 1822 and became emperor of Brazil as Pedro I, Latin America's only constitutional monarch. However, although a parliament was set up and elections were held, most Brazilians had no vote, and Pedro I governed autocratically.

LO³ The Industrial Revolution and Economic Growth

Along with political and social revolutions, the Industrial Revolution, a dramatic transformation in the production and transportation of goods, was a major force reshaping the economic, political, and social patterns of Europe and later of North America and Japan. For the first time in history, people became capable of the rapid, constant, and seemingly limitless increase of goods and services. This revolution was perhaps the greatest transformation in society since settled farming, urbanization, and the first

> "The wars damaged economies and caused people to flee the fighting."

> ❝ We are a microcosm of the human race, a world apart, neither Indian nor Europeans, but a part of each. ❞
>
> *Simón Bolívar*

Industrial Revolution A dramatic transformation in the production and transportation of goods that transformed western Europe from the 1770s to the 1870s.

states arose thousands of years ago. The transition began in Britain and then spread to western Europe and North America, eventually helping transform the West to dominate much of the world by 1914.

The Roots of the Industrial Revolution

The Industrial Revolution and the changes it generated had deep roots in Early Modern Europe. The Renaissance, Reformation, and Enlightenment had generated new ways of thought, including the expanded quest to understand the natural world reflected in the Scientific Revolution (see Chapter 15). The commercial capitalism that arose in the 1500s and 1600s generated trade and conquest overseas, forming political and economic links between the Americas, the African coast, some Asian societies, and western Europe by 1750. These connections allowed Europeans to acquire natural resources and great wealth overseas, which provided capital for investment in new technologies and incentives for producing more commodities for the world market.

British Advantages   Great Britain became the world's leading trading nation in the 1700s. By the 1730s, spinning machines were making the English textile industry more efficient and causing the nation to replace India as the world's leading supplier of cotton textiles. Britain had many advantages over rival countries, including an open intellectual atmosphere, a reasonably democratic political system that included the middle classes in government, a productive economy, favorable terrain on which to build transportation networks, abundant raw materials like coal and iron, and many water sources to run machines. Between the 1780s and 1830s, Britain dominated European industrialization.

Because of its earlier overseas activities in the Americas and Asia, Britain acquired one of the prerequisites for industrialization: adequate capital. Profits from the British-controlled Caribbean islands, North American colonies, and trading posts in India were particularly crucial in funding the Industrial Revolution. Some British companies made vast fortunes from the trans-Atlantic slave trade and the slavery plantations in the Americas. The English region east of Liverpool and northern Wales known as the Midlands, near rich coal and iron ore fields, became the center of British industry. Concentrating production in large factories in or near cities such as Birmingham and Manchester in the Midlands lowered transport costs and tapped a ready labor supply.

Industrial Capitalism

Beginning around 1770, commercial capitalism, dominated by large trading companies, transformed into industrial capitalism, a system centered around manufacturing. During this era, European industrial firms made and exported manufactured goods to other countries and in return imported raw materials, such as iron ore, to make more goods. The Industrial Revolution gave businesses marketable products and a powerful compulsion to market them in ever-increasing quantities. Because of the heavy investments in machines, success depended on a large and steady turnover of goods. Advertising developed to create demand, and banking and financial institutions expanded their operations to better serve business and industry. The industrialists, bankers, and financiers were also supported by political leaders who pursued policies of maximizing private wealth.

Adam Smith

As economic and government efforts were made to support industrial capitalism, some intellectuals felt the need to justify it. Economic philosophers emerged to praise British-style capitalism. The most influential, the Scottish professor Adam Smith (1723–1790), was a friend and supporter of Enlightenment thinkers. In his book *The Wealth of Nations* (1776), Smith helped formulate modern economics theory, known as neoclassical economics. In examining the consequences of economic freedom, Smith concluded that the market should be left alone. He advocated laissez faire, the restriction of government interference in the marketplace, such as laws regulating business and profits. Smith believed in self-interest, arguing that the "invisible hand" of the marketplace would turn the individual greed of the entrepreneur into a rising standard of living for all. Smith also introduced the new idea of a permanently growing economy and ever-increasing wealth as time went on. Smith's free trade ideas helped end the protectionist mercantilism of the Early Modern Era, when several European states worked closely with large commercial enterprises to accumulate wealth.

But Smith saw the potential for both good and evil in industrial capitalism. He championed free trade but also found areas where government regulation might be useful and even essential. Smith acknowledged that free enterprise did not necessarily generate prosperity for all, since the interests of the manufacturers were not necessarily those of society or even of the broader economy. To ensure these larger interests, he encouraged businesses to pay their employees high wages, writing that "no society can surely be flourishing and happy of which the far greater part of its members are poor and miserable. [They should be] well fed, clothed and lodged."[8]

CHRONOLOGY

European Politics and Economy, 1750–1914

1770s	Beginning of Industrial Revolution in England
1774	James Watt's first rotary steam engine
1776	Adam Smith's *The Wealth of Nations*
1800	British Act of Union
1821–1830	Greek war of independence
1830–1831	Wave of revolutions across Europe
1831	Formation of Young Italy movement by Mazzini
1845–1846	Irish potato famine
1848	Wave of revolts across Europe; *The Communist Manifesto* by Marx and Engels
1851	Great Exhibition in London
1859–1870	Unification of Italy
1862–1871	Unification of Germany
1870s–1914	Second Industrial Revolution

The Age of Machines

The Industrial Revolution introduced an era in which machines produced the goods used by people and increasingly performed more human tasks, reshaping peoples' lives. These machines were moved by energy derived from steam and other inanimate sources rather than human or animal sources. As a result, the Industrial Revolution created great material wealth. Between the 1770s and 1914, a Europe of peasant holdings, country estates, and domestic workshops became a Europe of sprawling and polluted industrial cities such as Manchester, with a wide gap between the few rich and the many poor (see Map 19.3). During the Industrial Revolution, the material culture of Europe and North America changed more than it had in the previous 750 years.

 Interactive Map

"Beginning around 1770, commercial capitalism, dominated by large trading companies, transformed into industrial capitalism, a system centered around manufacturing."

Technological Innovation

The Industrial Revolution triggered continual technological innovations as inventions in one industry stimulated inventions in others. The cotton industry mechanized first: new cotton machines created a demand for more plentiful and reliable power than could be provided by traditional water wheels and horses. The steam pump invented by the Englishman Thomas Newcomen in 1712, possibly based on an earlier Chinese model and used mostly for pumping water out of mines, was innovative but inefficient. Seeking more efficiency, James Watt (1736–1819), a Scottish inventor, produced the first successful rotary steam engine in 1774. Steam engines ultimately provided power not only for the textile mills but also for the iron furnaces, flour mills, and mines. When used in railroad engines and steamships, steam power conquered time and space, bringing the world much closer together.

After a while technological and economic growth came to be accepted as

> ❝ The Industrial Revolution introduced an era in which machines produced the goods used by people and increasingly performed more human tasks, reshaping peoples' lives. ❞

Luddites
Anti-industrialization activists in Britain who destroyed machines in a mass protest against the effects of mechanization.

normal, provoking admiration and wonder. The British novelist William Thackeray celebrated the changes in 1860: "It is only yesterday, but what a gulf between now and then! *Then* was the old world. Stagecoaches, riding horses, pack-horses, knights in armor, Norman invaders, Roman legions—all these belong to the old period. But your railroad starts a new era."[9] In others, however, mechanization provoked fear, causing them to turn against industrialization. Between 1815 and 1830, anti-industrialization activists in Britain known as Luddites, mostly skilled textile workers, invaded factories and destroyed machines in a mass protest against the effects of mechanization. The British government sent in 12,000 troops to stop the destruction and made the wrecking of machines a crime punishable by death.

The Spread of Industrialization

For decades Britain was the world's richest, most competitive nation, with a reputation as the workshop of the world. The new factories and machines mass-produced goods of better quality and lower price than traditional handicrafts, helping the British to overcome the old problem of finding commodities to trade to the world. By the mid-1800s, Britain produced two-thirds of the world's coal, half the iron, and half the cotton cloth and other manufactured goods. The British enjoyed political, military, and economic supremacy in Europe and significant power in other regions of the world.

However, the British invested some of their huge profits in western Europe, spreading the Industrial Revolution across the English Channel between the 1830s and 1870s. As iron-smelting technology improved, industrial operations became concentrated in regions rich in coal and iron

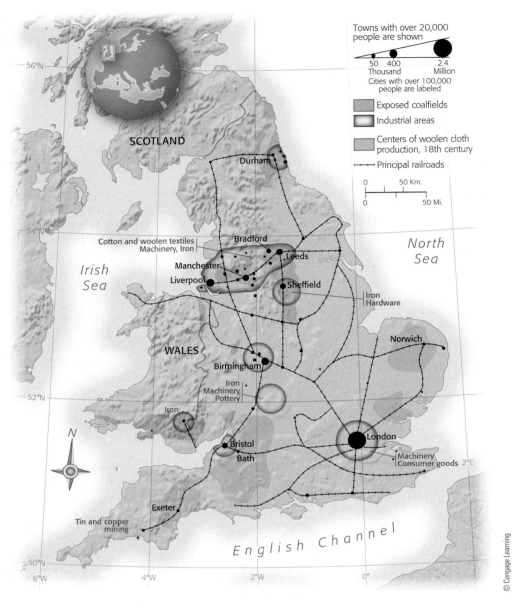

Towns with over 20,000 people are shown

50 Thousand   400   2.4 Million

Cities with over 100,000 people are labeled

Exposed coalfields

Industrial areas

Centers of woolen cloth production, 18th century

Principal railroads

0   50 Km.
0   50 Mi.

SCOTLAND

Durham

54°N

Cotton and woolen textiles
Machinery, Iron

Bradford

Irish Sea

Manchester   Leeds

Liverpool   Sheffield

Iron Hardware

North Sea

WALES

Norwich

Birmingham

Iron
Machinery
Pottery

52°N

Iron

N

Bristol
Bath

London

Machinery
Consumer goods   2°E

Exeter

Tin and copper mining

50°N

English Channel

6°W   4°W   2°W   0°

© Cengage Learning

Map 19.3
Industrial Transformation in England

British industrialization mostly occurred near coalfields and iron ore deposits, spurring the rise of cities such as Birmingham, Leeds, Liverpool, and Manchester.

ore, such as in Belgium. Capitalizing on its reserves of these resources, prosperous trading cities, and a strategic location between France, Holland, and Germany, by 1850 the Belgians had tripled their coal production and increased the number of steam engines from 354 to 2,300. Belgium also capitalized on the transportation revolution, building an ambitious railroad system to transport coal, iron, and manufactured goods and connecting it to neighboring countries.

By the 1830s, France had also begun constructing a national railroad network. In contrast to Britain and Belgium, France had to import coal, and, since it had fewer rich merchants than Britain, the government helped fund industrial activity. In the German states, political fragmentation before 1870 discouraged industrialization, except in several coal-rich regions such as the Ruhr Valley in western Germany and Silesia in Prussia. Some countries, including Portugal,

Industrial Sheffield This painting of one of the key British industrial cities, Sheffield, in 1858 shows the factories, many specializing in producing steel and metal goods, that dominated the landscape.

Spain, and Austria-Hungary, remained largely agricultural. By 1914, however, industrialization was widespread around Europe and had also taken root in North America and Japan, and large numbers of people lived in cities and worked in factories.

Second Industrial Revolution

From about 1870 to 1914, technological change, mass production, and specialization accelerated, causing what some historians call the Second Industrial Revolution. The increasing application of science to industry spurred expansion and improvement in the electrical, chemical, optical, and automotive industries and brought new inventions such as electricity grids, radio, the internal combustion engine, gasoline, and the flush toilet. The United States and Germany led in implementing these changes, and by 1900 Germany was Europe's main producer of electrical goods and chemicals. By the early 1900s, factory production was often done on the assembly line, with work broken down into separate specialized tasks.

 Learn about how songwriter and miner Tommy Armstrong used his song-making talent to address the issue of workers' rights during the Industrial Revolution.

The Second Industrial Revolution promoted a shift to a form of capitalism in which giant monopolies, led by tycoons with unprecedented wealth, replaced the more competitive economy of industrial capitalism. The concentration of capital in what became known as "big business" gave a few businessmen and bankers, such as the Krupp family in Germany and the Rockefellers in the United States, vast economic power and control over many industries. The monopolies emerged because the huge capital investment needed for new factories and important innovations such as electric power eliminated many of the small businesses. A long depression in the late 1800s undermined competition, and spurred a drive to colonize more of the world to ensure access to resources and markets.

ideology
A coherent, widely shared system of ideas about the nature of the social, political, and economic realm.

LO⁴ Nationalism, Liberalism, and Socialism

Besides the political and economic revolutions, the Modern Era also produced three new ideologies—nationalism, liberalism, and socialism—that influenced the European and American political order and that continue to shape our world. An ideology is a secular faith or philosophy: a coherent, widely shared

> "The Second Industrial Revolution promoted a shift to a form of capitalism in which giant monopolies, led by tycoons with unprecedented wealth, replaced the more competitive economy of industrial capitalism."

system of ideas about the nature of the social, political, and economic realm. In the Modern Era, nationalism fostered unified countries, liberalism encouraged democratic parliamentary governments in various nations, and socialism sparked movements to counteract the power and social impact of industrial capitalism.

Nations and Nationalism

Between 1750 and 1914, many societies in Europe and North America sought to form nations, communities of people united by a common culture and organized into independent states. The ideology that sparked this transition was nationalism, a primary loyalty to, and identity with, a nation bound by shared culture, history, government, and territory. Nationalists insisted that support for country transcended loyalty to family, village, church, region, social class, monarch, or ethnic group. Often appealing more to emotion than reason, nationalism particularly interested the rising middle classes and intellectuals struggling to gain more political power. A Swiss newspaper articulated the ideology well in 1848, declaring that the "nation [Switzerland] stands before us as an undeniable reality with her own voice and equipped with extensive powers. The Swiss of different cantons [small self-governing states] will henceforth be perceived and act as members of a single nation."¹⁰ Some historians conceive of the nation as an "imagined community" that grew in the minds of people living in the same society.

Nationalism helped to cause political solidarity, but it also fostered conflicts and wars, becoming an explo-

Extract from *History of Germany in the Nineteenth Century*, Heinrich von Treitschke
Read about influential historical thinker Heinrich von Treitschke's view that militarism, authoritarianism, and war was the path to German greatness. Does his thinking remind you of other influential leaders? Why do you think his views were appealing?

sive force throughout the world. Most historians credit the birth of modern nationalism to France and Great Britain in the late eighteenth and early nineteenth centuries. The French revolutionaries, in "The Declaration of the Rights of Man," proclaimed that all sovereignty emanated from the nation, rather than from individuals or groups, and the Jacobins identified themselves as custodians of French nationhood. The British also began to conceive of themselves as one nation composed of several peoples as the spread of English power led to the deliberate suffocation of Scottish, Welsh, and Irish cultures and languages in the 1800s.

Nationalism transformed Europe's political landscape. In 1750 large parts of Europe were dominated by multinational states that had ethnically diverse populations. For instance, one royal family, the Vienna-based Habsburgs, ruled Austria, Hungary, the Czech lands, Belgium, and parts of Italy. Sweden ruled Finland, and Denmark ruled Norway. But during the 1800s, nationalism fostered the emergence of nation-states, politically centralized countries with defined territorial boundaries, such as Italy, Belgium, and Norway. By 1914 only the Russian and Habsburg-ruled Austro-Hungarian empires remained major multinational states in Europe.

Unified Nations, Frustrated Nations

In the 1800s, some of the most dramatic efforts to create unified nations were made in Greece, Italy, and Germany. The Greeks, long a part of the Turkish-dominated Ottoman Empire, were one of the first modern European peoples to claim nationhood through violence. Many Greeks served in the Ottoman government, and Greek merchants dominated commerce in Ottoman-ruled western Asia. Wealthy Greek merchants sent their sons to western Europe to study, where they picked up nationalist ideas. Some organized a secret society that began an uprising for independence in 1821, killing many Turks. The Ottomans responded by massacring Greek villages, pillaging churches, and hanging the leader of the Greek Orthodox Church in Istanbul, acts that inflamed western Europeans. In 1827 the intervention of Britain, France, and Russia on the Greek side led to the destruction of the Turkish fleet. In 1830 Greece became independent, and in 1843 a rebellion against Greek royal absolutism resulted in a parliamentary government. Inspired by Greek nationalism, Romania also became independent in 1862.

Italian Unification

While the Greeks wanted independence, Italians wanted to realize a long-held dream of unity. For centuries they were divided into many small states, some of them part of the Habsburg and Holy Roman Empires, some ruled by the pope. In 1831 Giuseppi Mazzini (jew-SEP-pay mots-EE-nee) (1805–1872), a fiery Genoese, founded the Young Italy movement as a brotherhood of Italians who believed that Italy was destined to become one nation. Mazzini promoted a republican form of government and women's rights, radical ideas in Italy, and inspired nationalists elsewhere in Europe. In 1859, Italian nationalists began an armed struggle for unity and drove the Habsburg forces out of the north. By 1861, Mazzini had lost influence, but Giuseppi Garibaldi (gar-uh-BOWL-dee) (1807–1882) helped create the kingdom of Italy, which included all of the states except papal-dominated Rome. In 1870, Italian troops entered Rome, reuniting Italy for the first time since the Roman Empire.

German Reunification

German reunification also came in stages. In 1862, Otto von Bismarck (BIZ-mahrk) (1815–1898), the prime minister of Prussia, brought together many northern German states under Prussian domination. Bismarck shared with the Prussian king William I a dislike of business and professional leaders, who favored expanding democratic political rights. Instead Bismarck looked to uniting the Germans through warfare, a policy he characterized as "blood and iron." A series of wars with Denmark, Austria, and France between 1864 and 1870 significantly expanded Prussia's borders. In 1871, King William I of Prussia was declared *kaiser* (emperor) of a united Germany, by now one of Europe's major powers.

Jewish Minorities

Some peoples, such as the Poles and Jewish Europeans, were unable to satisfy their nationalist aspirations. The Jewish minorities faced difficult barriers, scattered as they were around Europe. Many Jews, especially in Russia, Poland, and Lithuania, had been restricted to all-Jewish villages and urban neighborhoods known as ghettoes, and they often maintained conservative cultural and religious traditions. Other Jews, especially in Germany, France, and Britain, often adopted a more secular approach and moved toward assimilation with the dominant culture. Reacting against widespread anti-Semitism, other Jews gravitated to revolutionary groups or to Zionism (ZYE-uh-niz-uhm), a movement founded by Hungarian-born journalist Theodor Herzl (HERT-suhl) (1860–1904) that sought a Jewish homeland.

> **Nationalism helped to cause political solidarity, but it also fostered conflicts and wars, becoming an explosive force throughout the world.**

Irish Struggle for Independence

The Irish were also frustrated in their desire for nationhood. Ireland had been a colony of England for centuries, and Irish opposition to harsh English rule simmered, sometimes erupting in violence. The English attempted to destroy the language, religion, poetry, literature, dress, and music of the Irish people and came to control much of the best farmland in Ireland. Conditions worsened after 1800, when the English mounted even more severe laws to restrict Irish rights, deporting thousands who resisted to Australia. Many Irish men, with few job prospects, were recruited into the British army to fight in England's colonial wars abroad. Then during the 1840s, the potato crop failed for several successive years. One and a half million Irish died from starvation, while English landlords ejected Irish peasants from the land for more profitable sheep raising. Millions of Irish people sought escape from poverty and repression by emigrating to the Americas and Australia.

But the Irish who remained rebelled against British rule every few years. In the mid-1800s, resistance became more organized, led by the Fenians (FEE-ni-ans), a secret society dedicated to Irish independence. By 1905 the Fenians were transformed into Sinn Fein (shin FANE) (Gaelic for "Ourselves Alone"), which first favored peaceful protest and then turned to violence against English targets. Sinn Fein extremists formed the Irish Republican Army, which organized the 1916 Easter Uprising, in which some 1,500 volunteers seized key buildings in Dublin and

liberalism
An ideology of the Modern Era, based on Enlightenment ideas, that favored emancipating the individual from all restraints, whether governmental, economic, or religious.

parliamentary democracy
Government by representatives elected by the people.

proclaimed a republic in Ireland. The English quickly crushed the rising, shot the ringleaders, and jailed 2,000 of the participants, but Sinn Fein and the IRA would continue to bedevil their English colonizers.

Liberalism and Parliamentary Democracy

While nationalism reshaped states, another ideology emerged to offer a vision of democracy, freedom, and representative governance. Influenced by Enlightenment thinkers such as John Locke and Baron de Montesquieu, liberalism favored emancipating the individual from all restraints, whether governmental, economic, or religious. Liberals supported the sovereignty of the people, representative government, the right to vote, and basic civil liberties such as freedom of speech, religion, assembly, and the press. The liberal Scottish philosopher John Stuart Mill (1806–1873) offered the most eloquent defense of individual liberty and free expression, writing that no one should restrict what arguments a legislature or executive should be allowed to hear.

Liberal politicians fought against slavery, advocated religious toleration, and promoted constitutional democracy. Liberalism proved particularly popular in Britain and the United States, and it provided the bedrock for the United States Constitution and Bill of Rights. Many historians argue that democratic decision making is an old and widespread idea. Village democracies that allowed many residents to voice their opinions and shape decisions had long existed in various tribal and other stateless societies of Asia, Africa, and the Americas. But in the nineteenth century, liberalism led to political systems like parliamentary democracy, government by representatives elected by the people. Britain became the most successful parliamentary democracy in Europe

Battle of Langhada The Greek war for independence from the Ottoman Turks gained strong support from liberals and nationalists all over Europe. This painting, by the Greek artist Panagiotis Zographos, uses Byzantine art traditions to show Greek soldiers riding to fight the Turks in the Battle of Langhada.

Gennadeion Library, Athens/Visual Connection Archive

as royal power declined. By the 1800s, the British monarch, even one as popular as Queen Victoria (r. 1837–1901), was no longer very powerful. Instead, prime ministers, elected by the majority of Parliament members, had become the major power holders. The Reform Act of 1832 increased the number of voters to about 650,000, all upper- and middle-class males, but this left out many men and all women.

> "Liberal politicians fought against slavery, advocated religious toleration, and promoted constitutional democracy."

Socialism and Marxist Thought

In contrast to liberalism's promotion of individual liberty, socialism focused on equality and the common ownership of economic institutions such as factories. It grew out of the painful social disruption that accompanied the Industrial Revolution, as utopian socialists in Britain, France, and North America offered visions of perfect societies shaped by the common good. For example, British industrialist Robert Owen (1771–1858) set up a model factory town around his cotton mill and later moved to the United States to found a model socialist community, New Harmony, in Indiana. Some proponents of women's rights, such as Emma Martin (1812–1851) in Britain and Flora Tristan (1801–1844) in France, promoted socialism as the solution to end female oppression. Utopian communities tended to be insular and were viewed with suspicion by many citizens.

Karl Marx

Karl Marx (1818–1883) had the most significant influence on socialist thought, and his ideas, known as Marxism, became one of the major intellectual and political influences around the world. Marx, a German Jew with a passion for justice, came from a wealthy family, studied philosophy at the University of Berlin, and then worked as a journalist in several European cities before settling in London. Marx wrote his classic works in the middle and late 1800s. In England he worked closely with his German friend, Friedrich Engels (1820–1895), who collaborated in writing and editing some of Marx's books and introduced Marx to the degraded condition of English industrial workers.

> ❝ Marx called himself a communist to differentiate himself from earlier socialists, whom he dismissed as naive utopians. ❞

The Communist Manifesto

In *The Communist Manifesto* (1848), Marx developed a vision of social change in which the downtrodden could rise up in a violent socialist revolution, seize power from the capitalists, and create a new society (see Witness to the Past: The Communist View of Past, Present, and Future). Marx argued that, through revolution, workers could change their conditions and alter the inequitable political, social, and economic patterns inherited from the past. He also criticized nationalism, writing that working people had no country, only common interests, and needed to cooperate across borders.

Marx was a product of his scientific age and considered his socialist ideas as laws of history. He argued that historical change resulted from class struggle, in which the confrontation between antagonistic social classes produced change. All social and economic systems, he suggested, contain contradictions that doom them to conflict, which generates a higher stage of development. Eventually, Marx predicted, this process would replace capitalism with socialism, where all would share in owning the means of production and the state would serve the interests of the masses rather than the privileged classes. Finally would come communism, where the state would wither away and all would share the wealth, free to realize their human potential without exploitation by capitalists or governments. Such a vision of change proved attractive to many disgruntled people in Europe and later around the world.

Marx's ideas have been hotly debated by economists and historians ever since. He believed that the nature of the economic system and technology determined all aspects of society, including religious values, social relations, government, and laws. Marx also argued that religion was the "opiate of the

proletariat
The industrial working class.

people," encouraging people to fatalistically accept their lot in this life in hopes of earning a better afterlife rather than protesting or rebelling. He criticized capitalism for creating extremes of wealth and poverty and for separating workers from ownership of the means of production—the farms, mines, factories, and businesses where they labored—to furnish wealth to the owners as well as to the urban-based, mostly commercial, middle class that Marx called the bourgeoisie. Under capitalism, workers had become tenants and employees rather than self-employed farmers and craftsmen. Marx observed that the industrial working class, the proletariat, grew more miserable as wealth became concentrated in giant monopolies in the later 1800s.

With its promise of a more equitable society, Marxism became a major world force. Socialist parties were formed all over Europe in the late 1800s and early 1900s, and, in some cases, more radical socialists soon split off to establish parties that called themselves communist. Marxism also influenced the founding of labor unions in the late nineteenth and early twentieth centuries in Europe and North America. But not all poor people or industrial workers in Europe gravitated to Marxism. While many envied the rich and thought life was unfair, they were also inhibited by family, religion, and social connections from joining radical movements or risking their lives in a rebellion that might fail. Marxism never became as influential in the United States or Great Britain as in parts of Europe. The first successful socialist revolution came, over three decades after Marx had died, in Russia.

Social Democracy and Social Reform

Eventually a more evolutionary version of socialist thought gained influence in many European societies. In contrast to the call by radical Marxists for revolution, some socialists favored a more evolutionary approach of effecting change, establishing a system mixing capitalism and socialism within a parliamentary framework. The first Social Democratic Party was formed in Germany in 1875, and soon others emerged in western and eastern European countries. Criticizing Marxist revolutionaries, a German Social Democratic leader, Eduard Bernstein (1850–1932), argued that socialists should work less for the better future and more for the better present.

Labor Unions

Social Democrats, Marxists, and other socialists actively supported labor unions and strikes to promote worker demands. Although most employers were opposed, unions gradually gained recognition as representatives of the workforce. Between 1870 and 1900, unions gained legal status in many nations, and in Britain, France, Germany, the Netherlands, and Sweden, trade unions and labor parties acquired enough political influence to improve working conditions.

In the later 1800s, governments implemented social reforms to address the ills of the Industrial Revolution, creating the interventionist, bureaucratic state with state-run welfare systems. Many European nations passed laws regulating the length of the working day, laws regarding working conditions, and safety rules. Reformers pushed for nationalizing landed property, state inspections of housing, town planning, and slum clearance. To tackle the problem of poverty, Germany and Britain passed social legislation introducing health and unemployment insurance and creating old-age pensions. Contrary to Marx's expectations, life for many European workers improved considerably by the early 1900s, but many people, including children, still worked in dangerous and unhealthy conditions.

LO⁵ The Resurgence of Western Imperialism

The Industrial Revolution provided economic incentives, and nationalism provided political incentives, for European states to exploit the natural and human resources of other lands. In the nineteenth century, European nations colonized and dominated much of Asia and Africa, an explosion of imperialism that reshaped the global system. As a result, industrial capitalism became a genuine world economy. With the entire world connected by economic and political networks, history from now on transcended regions and became truly world history.

 His Story, Ndansi Kumalo Read a firsthand account of the hardships suffered by the Ndebele, a people of southeastern Africa, in their dealings with European colonists.

Industrialization and Imperialism

The quest for colonies diminished somewhat in the first phase of the Industrial Revolution, even for the strongest European power, Great Britain. From the later 1700s through the mid-1800s, the British feared no competitor in world trade because they had none.

The Communist View of Past, Present, and Future

In 1848, Karl Marx and Friedrich Engels published *The Communist Manifesto* as a statement of beliefs and goals for the Communist League, an organization they had founded. In this excerpt Marx and Engels outlined their view of history as founded on class struggle, stressed the formation of the new world economy, and offered communism as the alternative to an oppressive capitalist system.

A specter is haunting Europe—the specter of communism. All the powers of old Europe have entered into a holy alliance to excise this specter. . . . Where is the party in opposition that has not been decried as communistic by its opponents in power? . . . The history of all hitherto existing society is the history of class struggles. . . . Oppressor and oppressed stood in constant opposition to one another, carried on in an uninterrupted, now hidden, now open fight, a fight that each time ended, either in a revolutionary reconstitution of society at large, or in the common ruin of the contending classes.

In the earlier epochs of history, we find almost everywhere a complicated arrangement of society into various orders, a manifold gradation of social rank. In ancient Rome we have patricians, knights, plebeians, slaves; in the Middle Ages, feudal lords, vassals, guild-masters, journeymen, apprentices, serfs; in almost all these classes, again, subordinate gradations. The modern bourgeois [middle class] society that has sprouted from the ruins of feudal society has not done away with class antagonisms. It has but established new classes, new conditions of oppression, new forms of struggle in place of the old ones.

Our epoch, the epoch of the bourgeoisie, possesses, however, this distinctive feature: it has simplified the class antagonisms. Society as a whole is more and more splitting up into two great hostile camps, into two great classes directly facing each other: bourgeoisie and proletariat (working class). . . . The discovery of America, the rounding of the Cape [of Good Hope], opened up fresh ground for the rising bourgeoisie. The East Indian and Chinese markets, the colonization of America, trade with the colonies, the increase in the means of exchange and in commodities generally, gave to commerce, to navigation, to industry, an impulse never before known, and, thereby, a rapid development to the revolutionary element in the tottering feudal society. . . . Meantime the markets kept ever growing, the demand ever rising. Even manufacture no longer sufficed. Thereupon, steam and machinery revolutionized industrial production. The place of manufacture was taken by the giant, modern industry, the place of the industrial middle class, by industrial millionaires. . . .

Modern industry has established the world market, for which the discovery of America paved the way. . . . The bourgeoisie, by the rapid improvement of all instruments of production, by the immensely facilitated means of communication, draws all, even the most barbarian, nations into civilization. The cheap prices of its commodities are the heavy artillery with which it batters down all Chinese walls. . . . It compels all nations, on pain of extinction, to adopt the bourgeois mode of production. . . . It creates a world after its own image. . . .

[The Communists] have no interests separate from those of the proletariat as a whole. . . . The immediate aim of the Communists is . . . the formation of the proletariat into a class; the overthrow of the bourgeois supremacy; and the conquest of political power by the proletariat. . . . The Communists disdain to conceal their views and aims. They openly declare that their ends can be attained only by the forcible overthrow of all existing social conditions. Let the ruling classes tremble at a Communistic revolution. The proletarians have nothing to lose but their chains. They have a world to win. WORKING MEN OF ALL COUNTRIES, UNITE!

Thinking About the Reading

1. What did Marx and Engels identify as the opposing classes in European history?

2. What developments aided the rise of the bourgeoisie to power?

3. What is the goal of the Communists?

Source: From *The Communist Manifesto,* trans. 1880. http://www.anv.edu.au/polisci/marx/classics/manifesto.html.

Britain already controlled or had gained access to valuable territories in the Americas, Africa, Asia, and the Pacific. While Britain lost its thirteen North American colonies, it took control of French Canada and Australia. Furthermore, the collapse of Spain and Portugal during the Napoleonic wars led to most of their Latin American colonies becoming independent in the 1820s, opening doors for British commercial activity.

> "From the later 1700s through the mid-1800s, the British feared no competitor in world trade because they had none."

the top, followed by Germany and then a fading Britain and France.

As they industrialized, Germany, France, and the United States became more competitive with Britain, and growing economic and political competition renewed the quest for colonies abroad. The shift to domestic economies dominated by large monopolies was a major factor in the new push for colonies in Africa and Asia. The monopolies stimulated empire building by piling up huge profits and hence excess capital that needed investment outlets abroad to keep growing. Furthermore, by the 1880s, some of the wealth generated by the industrial economy began to filter down to the European working classes, stimulating new consumer interests in tropical products such as chocolate, tea, soap, and rubber for bicycle tires. To satisfy the need for resources and markets, Western businessmen looked for new opportunities to exploit in Africa, Asia, and the Pacific, and then pressured their governments to assist their efforts.

New Technologies

British merchants also benefited from new technologies that enabled them to compete all over the world. Steam power meant that British ships could reach distant shores faster. The first exclusively steam-powered ships appeared in 1813 and took 113 days to travel from England around Africa to India, in contrast to eight or nine months by sailing ships. Then in 1869, the completion of the Suez Canal linking the Mediterranean Sea and the Red Sea dramatically cut the travel time between the Indian Ocean and Europe. Britain, the canal's major shareholder, now found it easier to extend its influence to East Africa and Southeast Asia.

> ❝ Western imperialism forged networks of interlinked social, economic, and political relationships spanning the globe. ❞

National rivalries also motivated imperialism. Nations often seized colonies to prevent competitors from gaining opportunities. The result was the greatest land grab in world history: between 1870 and 1914, a handful of European powers divided up the globe among themselves. The national rivalries and intense competition for colonies also planted the roots of conflict in Europe. By the early 1900s, Germany and Austria-Hungary had forged an alliance, and this prompted Britain, France, and Russia to do likewise, setting the stage for World War I.

Shifts in Economic Advantage

Despite a pragmatic preference for peaceful commerce, Britain did obtain some colonies between 1750 and 1870. The British took over territories or fought wars when local governments, such as India, Malaya, and Burma, refused to trade or could not protect British commerce by establishing law and order (see Chapter 22). However, the British economic advantage in world markets gradually diminished as economic leadership in the world changed during the later 1800s. The British invested many of the profits that they earned from India and their Caribbean colonies in other nations, much of it in the United States, Canada, and Australia. Because British investors found it more profitable to invest abroad rather than at home, British industrial plants became increasingly obsolete. In 1860, Britain had been the leading economic power; by 1900, the United States was at

The Scramble for Empire

With the resurgent Western imperialism, millions of people in Africa, Asia, and the Pacific Islands were conquered or impacted by Western nations and thus brought into the Western dominated world economic system. However, many peoples fiercely resisted conquest. The Vietnamese, Burmese, and various Indonesian and African societies held off militarily superior European armies for decades, and even after conquest, guerrilla forces often continued to

; dominated at other countries

attack European colonizers (see Chapters 21 and 22). Countless revolts punctuated colonial rule, from West Africa to the Philippines, and Western ambitions were sometimes frustrated. In Africa, Ethiopians defeated an Italian invasion force bent on conquest. A few Asians maintained their independence by using creative strategies. The Japanese prevented Western political domination by modernizing their own government and economy, and the Siamese (Thai) used skillful diplomacy and selective modernization to deflect Western power.

Imperial Expansion

New technologies permitted and stimulated imperial expansion. The Industrial Revolution gave Europeans better weapons, including the machine gun to enforce their will. A British writer boasted: "Whatever happens we have got the Maxim Gun, and they have not."[11] These weapons gave Europeans a huge advantage against Asians and Africans, and the discovery of quinine to treat malaria enabled European colonists and officials to survive in tropical Africa and Southeast Asia. Later, better communication and transportation networks, such as steamship lines, colonial railroads, and undersea telegraph cables, also helped consolidate Western control.

As the scramble continued, old European empires grew and new ones were founded (see Map 19.4). By 1900, Western colonial powers controlled 90 percent of Africa, 99 percent of Polynesia, and 57 percent of Asia. By 1914, the British Empire, the world's largest, included fifty-five colonies containing 400 million people, ten times Britain's population, inspiring the boast that "the sun never sets on the British Empire." France acquired the next largest empire of twenty-nine colonies. Germany, Spain, Belgium, and Italy joined in the grab for African colonies. Between 1898 and 1902, the United States took over Hawaii, Samoa, Puerto Rico, and the Philippines. Russia also continued its expansion in Eurasia, which began in the Early Modern Era (see Chapter 23).

 Interactive Map

Increasing Globalization

Western imperialism forged networks of interlinked social, economic, and political relationships spanning the globe. Hence, decisions made by a

Lipton Tea European imperial expansion brought many new products to European consumers. Tea, grown in British-ruled India, Sri Lanka (Ceylon), and Malaya, became a popular drink, advertised here in a London weekly magazine.

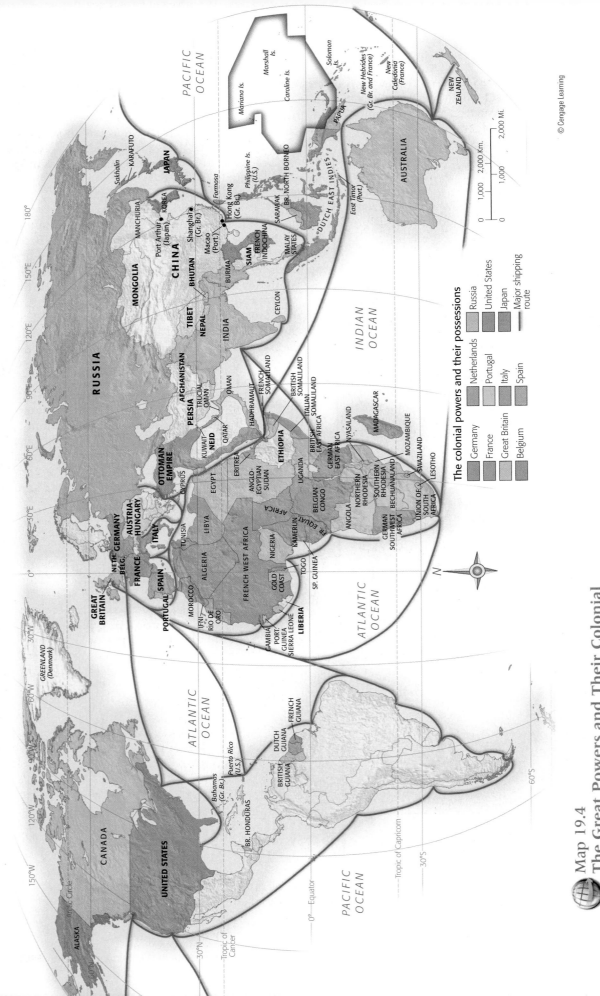

Map 19.4
The Great Powers and Their Colonial Possessions in 1913

By 1913, the British and French controlled huge empires, with colonies in Africa, southern Asia, the Caribbean zone, and the Pacific Basin. Russia ruled much of northern Eurasia, while the United States, Japan, and a half-dozen European nations controlled smaller empires.

The colonial powers and their possessions

- Germany
- France
- Great Britain
- Belgium
- Netherlands
- Portugal
- Italy
- Spain
- Russia
- United States
- Japan
- Major shipping route

© Cengage Learning

government or business in London or Paris soon affected people in faraway Malaya or Madagascar, and silk spun in China was turned into dresses worn by fashionable women in Chicago and Munich. Westerners had the strongest position in this network, ruling many subject peoples and enjoying advantageous trade relations with or strong influence over neocolonies such as China, Siam, Persia, and Argentina. Yet various Asian, African, and Caribbean peoples also challenged the colonial regimes (see Chapters 21, 22, and 25).

The scope of Western imperialism changed world power arrangements. In 1750, China and the Ottoman Empire remained among the world's strongest countries, but by 1914 they could not match Western military and economic power. In 1500, the wealth gap between the more economically developed and the less developed Eurasian and African societies was small, and China and India dominated world trade and manufacturing. By 1914, the gap in total wealth and personal income between industrialized societies, whether in Europe or North America, and most other societies, including China and India, had grown very wide.

Social Darwinism and Imperial Ideology

By the late 1800s, a new ideology known as Social Darwinism supported the revival of imperialism and colonialism. Supporters of imperialism used the ideas about the natural world developed by the British scientist Charles Darwin, who described a struggle for existence among species (see Chapter 20). This idea led other thinkers to conclude that this struggle led to the survival of the fittest, a notion that they then applied to the human world of social classes and nations.

Industrialized peoples considered themselves the most fit and saw exploited peoples as less fit. A German naval officer wrote in 1898 that "the struggle for life exists among individuals, provinces, parties and states. The latter wage it either by the use of arms or in the economic field. Those who don't want to, will perish."[12] Social Darwinists stereotyped Asian and African societies as "backward" and held their own nations up as "superior" peoples who had the right—and obligation—to rule.

Racism

As a result of this ideology, Western racism and arrogance toward other peoples increased. For example, in the 1600s and 1700s, many Western observers had admired the Chinese, and Enlightenment thinkers saw China as a model of secular and efficient government. But by the 1800s, Europeans and North Americans had developed scorn for "John Chinaman" and the "heathen Chinee." Most Western peoples accepted these stereotypes; the British imperialist Cecil Rhodes boasted, "I contend that we British are the finest race in the world, and that the more of the world we inhabit the better it is for the human race."[13]

This perceived superiority legitimized the effort to "improve" other people by bringing them Western culture and religion. The French proclaimed their "civilizing mission" in Africa and Indochina; the British in India claimed that they were "taking up the white man's burden"; and the Americans colonized the Philippines claiming condescendingly to "uplift" their "little brown brothers." Western defenders argued that colonialism, despite much that was shameful, gave non-Western societies better government and drew them out of isolation into the world market. A British newspaper in 1896 claimed that "the advance of the Union Jack means protection for weaker races, justice for the oppressed, liberty for the down-trodden."[14] However, most people in Asia, Africa, and the Pacific opposed colonialism, seeing it only for the terrible toll it took on their lives. The Indian nationalist leader Mohandas Gandhi, educated in Britain, reflected the resentment. When asked what he thought about "Western civilization," he replied that civilizing the West would be a good idea.

> **Industrialized peoples considered themselves the most fit and saw exploited peoples as less fit.**

Speech Before the French National Assembly, July 28, 1883, Jules Ferry Read French imperialist Jules Ferry's reasons for supporting French expansionism.

Listen to a synopsis of Chapter 19.

CHAPTER 20

Changing Societies in Europe, the Americas, and Oceania,
1750–1914

Learning Outcomes

After reading this chapter, you should be able to answer the following questions:

LO^1 How and why did European social, cultural, and intellectual patterns change during this era?

LO^2 How did westward expansion, industrialization, and immigration transform American society?

LO^3 What political, economic, and social patterns shaped Latin America after independence?

LO^4 Why did the foundations for nationhood differ in Canada and Oceania?

" At present, all of the European countries shine with the light of civilization and have an abundance of wealth and power. Their trade is prosperous, their technology is superior, and they greatly enjoy the pleasures and comforts of life. Upon observing such conditions, one is apt to conclude that these countries have always been like this, but such is not the case. The wealth and prosperity one now sees in Europe date to a considerable degree from the period after 1800. It has taken forty years to produce such conditions. "

—**Kume Kunitake**[1]

In 1871, a thirty-three-year-old Japanese samurai and Confucian scholar, Kume Kunitake (1839–1931), boarded an American steamship at Yokohama and began a three-week voyage to San Francisco as a member of an information-gathering delegation sent from Japan to the United States and then Europe. Hoping to avoid conquest, the government had asked Kume's group to assess the factors behind growing Western power in the world. Kume's delegation traveled across America, visiting factories, museums, schools, churches, public parks, and scenic mountains. Kume filtered his perceptive impressions of Western life through the cultural lens of Japan, concluding that "the customs and characteristics of East and West are invariably different." Kume admired U.S. democracy but noted that Americans were "careless about official authority, each person insisting on his own rights." Kume recorded the Americans' friendliness but also their brashness, ambition, and sense of destiny.

After leaving the United States, Kume's delegation traveled to Europe, where Kume was delighted to see how Europeans treasured and even imitated Japanese art. He loved the culture, but as an ardent Confucian rationalist, he disliked Christianity, which he saw as irrational. Kume contrasted the splendor of the churches with the poverty of the people, criticizing what he saw as the "unbounded

 Test your knowlege before you read this chapter.

What do you think?

Unlike European nations, the United States never colonized other regions.

Strongly Disagree   Strongly Agree

1   2   3   4   5   6   7

<<**Australian Gold Rush** The discovery of gold in southeastern Australia set off a gold rush in the 1850s. Hoping to strike it rich, miners, often from other countries, among them Chinese, flocked to the goldfields, and immigration to Australia boomed.

515

greed" of Western rulers and merchants. Finally, returning by ship to Japan, Kume's delegation passed through the colonies of Ceylon, Singapore, and Hong Kong, where he noted ruefully, "Ever since the Europeans began to travel to distant places, the weak countries of the tropics have all been fought over and devoured, and their abundant products taken. They treated the natives with arrogance and cruelty."[2] Kume later became a distinguished professor of history at Tokyo University, and his journals continue to provide insights about the Modern Era's imbalances of wealth and power.

Although Europe, the Americas, and Oceania were geographically and historically distinct, their societies were shaped by similar patterns of capitalism, migration, overseas imperialism, and nation-building between 1750 and 1914. By 1914 the United States, Canada, and Mexico occupied all of North America, while Latin American and the Caribbean societies divided into many countries. In the Pacific Ocean Basin, the Europeans also settled the region known today as Oceania, which comprises Australia and New Zealand, while colonizing other, smaller islands. The United States, Canada, Australia, and New Zealand, and some Latin American countries all became settler societies that were colonized chiefly by European immigrants, who planted European institutions and ideas after indigenous populations were largely wiped out. Europeanization also occurred in societies such as Mexico, Cuba, Venezuela, and Peru, where nonwhite and mixed-descent peoples were a larger percentage of the population. European influence in American and Oceanic settler societies varied by time, circumstances,

> "Expanding economies, better public health, and the introduction of new crops such as potatoes from the Americas lowered Europe's mortality rate and fostered population growth."

and the cultures of ethnic minorities.

In the Americas, the United States and Canada gradually diverged from Latin America in their economic and social patterns and cultures. As Kume observed, many in the United States held vast expectations for their nation's global influence and wealth. By expanding its frontiers and rapidly industrializing in the 1800s, the United States became the colossus of North America and a world power, extending its political and economic influence into Latin America and the Caribbean.

LO[1] The Reshaping of European Societies

Thanks to destabilizing revolutions in political and economic life (see Chapter 19), modern Europeans lived in a world of cities, new forms of work, and temptations to abandon home villages for urban areas or faraway lands in search of work and a better life. Industrialization led to changing social structures and family systems. The world of thought, the arts, and science reflected the new Europe that emerged in the Modern Era, and the resulting innovations influenced peoples around the world.

Population Growth, Emigration, and Urbanization

Expanding economies, better public health, and the introduction of new crops such as potatoes from the Americas lowered Europe's mortality rate and fostered population growth. People married earlier and more frequently, increasing the birthrate. Europe's population (including Russia) grew from 100 million in 1650 to 190 million in 1800 and to 420 million in 1900, one of the world's highest growth rates at that time.

The Threat of Overpopulation

Rapid population growth created new problems, however. Thomas Malthus, an English clergyman and economist, argued in 1798 that population growth was checked by poverty, disease, war, and famine, but if these problems were eliminated, the gains in human security would soon disappear as the world's population outgrew its means of subsistence. Throughout Europe, many were compelled to move overseas or migrate to urban areas. Poles, for example, moved to the mines of northern France and western Germany, and emigration cut Ireland's population by half between 1841 and 1911. Jews, too, migrated as the tensions caused by competition for scarce resources increased. In some areas, they were victims of coordinated mob attacks known as *pogroms* (from the Russian word meaning "round-up"). Some 45 million Europeans emigrated to the Americas, Australia, New Zealand, Algeria, and South Africa to escape poverty (see Map 20.1).

 Interactive Map

Europeans also moved from rural areas to cities, which increased social problems. The larger European cities grew spectacularly between 1800 and 1900: London increased from 900,000 to 4.7 million, Paris from 600,000 to 3.6 million, and Berlin from 170,000 to 2.7 million. Rapidly expanding cities lacked social services such as sanitation, street cleaning, and water distribution. Huge numbers of people lived in poverty, crammed into overcrowded housing with high disease rates. Millions lived in crime-ridden slums. As the English poet William Blake wrote: "Every night and every morn, some to misery are born." The standard of living did not rise much for most Europeans until the 1880s, when incomes began to improve and several countries, including Britain and Germany, developed social welfare programs for their citizens.

Advances in Agriculture

While cities grew dramatically, western European rural life also changed. Agricultural technology and practices developed rapidly, resulting in better yields, more mechanization, and improved animal breeding. Market agriculture largely displaced the subsistence production of earlier times. But even with improved farming methods, peasants often earned low wages, and many small farmers lost their land to more highly capitalized and mechanized operations. Occasional famines also occurred, notably in Ireland and Russia, but by the 1850s, such disasters were rare except as a result of war. In contrast to western Europe, some feudal traditions remained influential in eastern countries like Russia and Poland, where the landed gentry retained authority over peasant lives.

Society and Family Life

Population movement and urbanization were only two manifestations of much broader changes resulting from industrialization. After 1870, the rise of mass-distribution newspapers, organized football (soccer) leagues, more widespread vacation travel, and other activities connected peoples within and between nations. People enjoyed a growing range of options in areas of life that were once fixed by tradition, such as where to live, work, or go to church and whom to marry, but such choices increased moral anxiety and social instability. For example, the middle class increasingly discouraged sexual activity before marriage and limited sexual intercourse within marriage, while the working classes experienced higher rates of illegitimacy, infidelity, and more frequent sexual relations than ever before. Thus, a British factory girl in 1909 complained, "I wanted no one to know that I was a factory girl because I was ashamed at my position. I was always hearing people say that factory girls were loose-living and corrupt."[3]

> 66 Families still provided the framework of social life, but changes occurred. 99

Families still provided the framework of social life, but changes occurred. During the Early Modern Era, some people in northern Europe, especially England and the Low Countries, began to marry later and live in nuclear families, which were

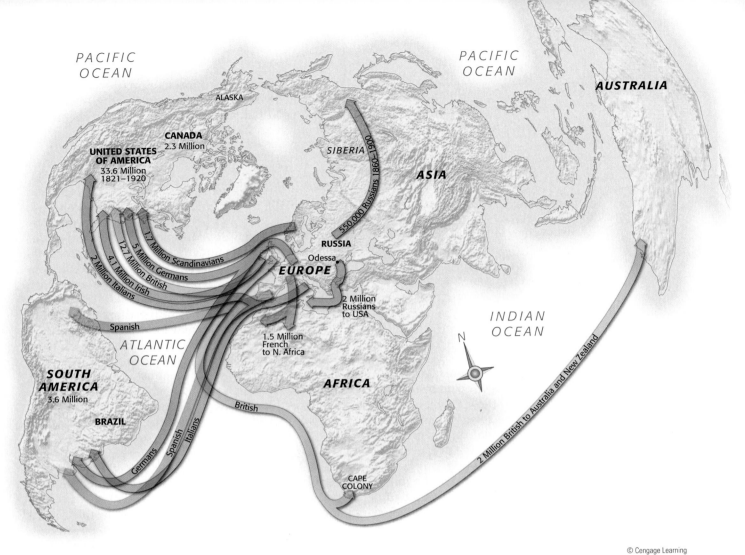

PACIFIC OCEAN

PACIFIC OCEAN

AUSTRALIA

ALASKA

CANADA
2.3 Million

UNITED STATES
OF AMERICA
33.6 Million
1821–1920

SIBERIA

ASIA

550,000 Russians 1860–1900

1.7 Million Scandinavians
5 Million Germans
12.7 Million British
4.1 Million Irish
2 Million Italians

RUSSIA

Odessa

EUROPE

2 Million
Russians
to USA

INDIAN
OCEAN

Spanish

ATLANTIC
OCEAN

1.5 Million
French
to N. Africa

N

SOUTH
AMERICA
3.6 Million

AFRICA

BRAZIL

British

Italians
Germans
Spanish

2 Million British to Australia and New Zealand

CAPE
COLONY

Map 20.1
European Emigration, 1820–1910

Pushed by rapid population growth and poverty, millions of Europeans left their homes to settle in the Americas (especially the United States), North and South Africa, Siberia, Australia, and New Zealand. The British and Irish accounted for the largest numbers of emigrants, nearly 17 million combined. (Reprinted by permission of HarperCollins Publishers, Ltd. © *Times Atlas of World History*, 3rd. ed. Some data from Eric Hobsbawm, *The Age of Empire, 1875–1914* [New York: Pantheon, 1987]).

smaller than extended families of just parents and their children. During the 1800s, the nuclear pattern became common in most of northern Europe, especially among the middle classes, while large extended families remained the norm in southern and eastern Europe. In the 1700s, western Europeans began to adopt the notion that people should have the freedom to choose their partner and marry for love, rather than to meet family demands or economic need. At the same time, middle-class men often assumed that women belonged at home as submissive helpmates and encouraged them to cul-

tivate their beauty and social graces to please their menfolk.

The industrial economy was hard on working families, particularly on women and children. Most Europeans assumed that women were not breadwinners and hence should be paid less than men. Women typically earned only 25 percent of men's wages. Women and children also often did hard manual labor in cotton mills and mines. In 1838, a liberal member of the British parliament reported: "I saw a cotton mill, a sight that froze my blood, full of women, young, all of them, some large with child, and obliged to stand twelve hours each day. The heat was excessive in some of the rooms, the stink pestiferous. I nearly fainted."[4] Increased mechanization and labor reforms, however, meant that fewer women and far fewer children worked full-time in the industrial sector by the early 1900s.

Challenges to Societal Norms

The dynamism of industrializing societies led some to challenge social norms. By the later 1800s, some men and women criticized marriage as stifling and old-fashioned. Prominent people in the artistic and political worlds, such as the popular French actress Sarah Bernhardt and the fiery German socialist Rosa Luxemburg, lived openly with same-sex partners out of wedlock. Homosexuals could be found at all levels of society, but they often faced discrimination and persecution, as did the Irish poet, novelist, and playwright Oscar Wilde (1854–1900), the married father of two, who was tried and imprisoned in 1895 for engaging in homosexual relationships, known as sodomy. The increasing attention to homosexuality and the first scientific studies of it sparked heated and ongoing debates.

Nevertheless, men remained dominant in the political, social, economic, and religious spheres, and women's roles were increasingly restricted to marriage, motherhood, and child rearing. Often women had no legal standing and could not divorce their husbands. Women struggled to adapt to the changing circumstances. Upper- and middle-class women practiced artificial birth control and had fewer children than in earlier eras. In the later 1800s, European women gained more legal rights and economic opportunities. Leading professional women, such as the influential German composer and pianist Clara Schumann (1819–1896) and the British nurse Florence Nightingale (1820–1910), provided role models, and schools for girls grew in number. In 1867 the University of Zurich in Switzerland became the first university to admit women and was soon followed by universities in France, Sweden, and Finland.

The Emergence of Feminism

Some women began movements promoting what later became known as feminism, a philosophy promoting political, social, and economic equality for women with men. One leader of the British movement, Harriett Taylor, wrote bitterly that "all that has been said respecting the social condition of women goes on the assumption of their [innate] inferiority. People do not complain of [women's] state being degraded at all."[5] Inspired by pioneers such as Mary Wollstonecraft in the late 1700s, the first feminist movements emerged in Britain and Scandinavia, with some women, later known as suffragettes, such as the British Emily Pankhurst (1858–1928), pressing for the same voting rights as men. In 1896, Finland became the first European nation to accept female suffrage.

> **feminism**
> A philosophy that became strong in the twentieth century, promoting political, social, and economic equality for women with men.
>
> **suffragettes**
> Women who press for the same voting rights as men.

"Convicts and Lunatics" The movement for women's right to vote, or suffrage, was particularly strong in Britain. This poster, "Convicts and Lunatics," designed by the artist Emily Harding Andrews for the Artist's Suffrage League around 1908, shows a woman graduate, deprived of basic political rights, treated similarly to a convict and a mentally disturbed man.

romanticism
A philosophical, literary, artistic, and musical movement that questioned the Enlightenment's rationalist values and instead glorified emotions, individual imagination, and heroism.

Thought and Religion

The industrial and political revolutions, and the social changes they sparked, fostered new directions in European thought. Philosophers such as the Germans Immanuel Kant (KAHNT) (1724–1804) and Friedrich Nietzsche (NEE-chuh) (1844–1890) contested the values of the Enlightenment, a movement based on reason that began in the 1600s and continued through the 1700s. Kant believed that experience alone was inadequate for understanding, because the perceptions it fosters are ultimately shaped by the mind, which imposes a structure on the sensations we see and converts these sensations into knowledge. He doubted that a perfect society could ever be achieved, arguing that "man wishes concord, but nature, knowing better what is good for his species, wishes discord."[6] To Nietzsche, there was no fundamental truth, including moral and scientific truth, as the Enlightenment philosophers had thought, but rather misconceptions developed by each culture as its members tried to understand the world. With no absolute truth, absolute good and evil cannot exist. In the twentieth century, extreme nationalists and racists distorted Nietzsche's ideas to persecute ethnic minorities.

For many Europeans, religion also changed with the times. Gradually, Protestants and Catholics learned to tolerate each other, but religious passions did not diminish. In the later 1700s and early 1800s, an evangelical revival inspired many English Anglicans and Baptists to seek personal relations with God, as well as social reform and missionary activity. Soon new faiths emerged, such as charismatic British Anglican preacher John Wesley's (1703–1791) Methodist movement, which sought a more emotional faith and appealed particularly to miners and factory workers.

In contrast to evangelical movements, some Europeans embraced secular approaches, as the relevance of religion declined for many. Some middle-class Protestants sought a liberalized faith stressing social tolerance rather than the hellfire and damnation preached by some evangelicals. Thus, by 1851, only half of the English population attended church. The divide between the more liberal and the more devout resulted in public debates across Europe about the role of religion in society. The Roman Catholic and Greek Orthodox Churches also faced challenges. Spurred by the French Revolution, the Catholic clergy in France and Belgium lost the privileged status they had enjoyed for centuries, such as control of education and exemption from taxes. France opened a public school system in the 1890s and mandated state neutrality toward religion in 1905. At the same time, however, the Catholic Church remained important in Austria, southern Germany, Poland, Spain, Portugal, and Italy. The Greek Orthodox world fragmented into national churches in Greece, Serbia, Romania, and Bulgaria.

New Directions in Culture, Science, and Technology

Literature and the arts also reflected the changing times. The growth of a literate public liberated writers, composers, and artists from dependence on wealthy patrons, but they now had to satisfy the new commercial world of a consuming public.

Romanticism Inspired by the political revolutions of the late 1700s and early 1800s, some thinkers and artists adopted romanticism, a philosophical, literary, artistic, and musical movement that questioned the Enlightenment's rationalist values and instead glorified emotions, individual imagination, and heroism. The German Friedrich Schiller (1759–1805), a former soldier, offered intense romantic images with a nationalist tinge, such as a poem that turned the story of William Tell, a legendary hero of Swiss resistance against foreign invasion, into a manifesto for German political freedom. In contrast to romanticism, writers and artists embracing another movement, realism, portrayed a grimy industrial world filled with uncertainty and conflict. For example, the liberal Spanish painter Francisco de Goya (GOI-uh) (1746–1828) produced a moving series on the Napoleonic invasion of Spain that portrayed not warfare's glory and heroism but its horrors: orphans, pain, rape, blood, and despair. The British novelist and former factory worker Charles Dickens (1812–1870) revealed in detail the hardships of industrial life, the injustices of capitalism, and the miseries of the poor.

European classical music enjoyed a golden age during this period. Influenced by the Enlightenment, the Austrian Wolfgang Amadeus Mozart (MOTE-sahrt) (1756–1791) wrote thirty-five symphonies, eight operas, and many concertos. Romanticism inspired many later composers, most famously the German Ludwig van Beethoven (BAY-toe-vuhn) (1770–1827), whose much admired Ninth Symphony set Schiller's poem, "Ode to Joy," to music.

The Influence of Modernism

Between 1880 and 1914, Europe was swept by a quite different movement, modernism, a cultural trend that openly broke with romanticism, realism, and other traditions by welcoming the future and new ideas. Several significant movements influenced by modernism shaped the visual arts in the later 1800s, sparked in part by the increasingly connected world and European exposure to Asian, African, and Pacific art. One such movement was impressionism, whose practitioners such as Claude Monet (moe-NAY) (1840–1926) and Pierre Renoir (ren-WAH) (1841–1919) sought to express the immediate impression aroused in momentary scenes, bathed in changing light and color.

In the 1880s, other French artists experimented with a return to elemental shapes and compositions. The most influential included Paul Cezanne (say-ZAN) (1839–1906), famous for his landscapes and portraits; the prolific Dutch-born Vincent Van Gogh (van GO) (1853–1890), who introduced intense primary colors and thick brushstrokes; and Paul Gauguin (go-GAN) (1848–1903), whose richly colored paintings often featured idyllic scenes of Polynesian life, stimulating European interest in the wider world. By the early 1900s, Pablo Picasso (pi-KAH-so) (1881–1973), a young Spaniard who settled in Paris, was already revolutionizing Western art with his new approaches, such as integrating ideas from African sculpture and masks.

Medicine, Darwin, and Einstein

Europeans also made spectacular achievements in science and technology. Some major breakthroughs came in medicine and public health, such as the development of effective vaccines against deadly diseases such as smallpox that had ravaged the world for centuries. Improved sanitation led to better public health and the prevention of many diseases such as cholera, which was eradicated from Europe's industrial cities by 1874. Scientists also made major contributions to the understanding of nature. British naturalist Charles Darwin (1809–1882)—after years spent traveling around the world studying plants, animals, and fossils in many lands—formulated the theory of evolution emphasizing the natural selection of species. In his book, *On the Origin of Species*, Darwin argued that all existing species of plants and animals, including humans, had either adapted to their environment over millions of years or died out. Eventually evolution became the foundation for the modern biological sciences, but many religious leaders saw it as a degradation of humanity.

The German-born Jewish physicist Albert Einstein (1879–1955) also transformed western science. His papers on the theory of relativity, published in the early 1900s when he worked as a clerk in the Swiss patent office, provided the basis for modern physics, our understanding of the universe, and the atomic age. Einstein offered a new view of space and time, showing that distances and durations are not, as Newton thought, absolute but are affected by one's motion. He also proved that matter can be converted into energy and that everything is composed of atoms, insights that provided the basis for atomic energy. His papers electrified the scientific world and continue to influence modern science.

> 66 New and rapid technological discoveries all over Europe improved people's lives. 99

modernism A cultural trend that openly broke with romanticism and other traditions by embracing progress and welcoming the future.

Radios, Automobiles, and Greenhouse Gases

New and rapid technological discoveries all over Europe improved people's lives. In the early 1800s, electric batteries, motors, and generators emerged as new sources of power. In the 1890s, the Italian Guglielmo Marconi (mahr-KO-nee) (1874–1937) introduced wireless telegraphy: in 1901 he used his invention to communicate between England and Canada, opening another network connecting the world. Various inventors worked on building internal combustion engines, and two Germans, Gottlieb Daimler and Karl Benz, became the "fathers of the automobile," producing the first petroleum-powered vehicle in the 1880s. Meanwhile, some scientists worried about the effects of industrial pollution on the environment. The observation that carbon-dioxide emissions from coal-burning factories heated the atmosphere led the Swedish scientist Svante Arrhenius to speak of a "greenhouse effect" that potentially threatened modern societies, an issue that continues to engage scientists.

LO² The United States: A Rising Global Power

After the American Revolution, in which the thirteen colonies successfully overthrew British control, the newly minted citizens turned to building their nation. The United States became an ongoing experiment as Americans learned how to balance regionalism and national unity, freedom and order, individualism and social obligation, and national autonomy and world leadership.

During the early republic, Americans established new forms of government, reshaped economic patterns, fostered a new culture, and began the movement westward. Later, after the Civil War (1861–1865),

> "During the early republic, Americans established new forms of government, reshaped economic patterns, fostered a new culture, and began the movement westward."

the United States changed dramatically, as slavery ended and the federal government asserted more authority over the states. This centralization, combined with economic protectionism and an abundance of resources, allowed the United States to expand its territory, economy, population, and international influence dramatically.

CHRONOLOGY

The United States and the World, 1750–1914

1787	U.S. Constitution
1803	Louisiana Purchase
1812–1814	U.S.-British War of 1812
1823	Monroe Doctrine
1825	Completion of Erie Canal
1846–1848	U.S.-Mexican War
1848	U.S. acquisition of Texas, California, and New Mexico
1849	California gold rush
1861–1865	Civil War
1862	Lincoln's Emancipation Proclamation
1867	U.S. purchase of Alaska from Russia
1869	Completion of transcontinental railroad
1898	U.S. incorporation of Hawaii
1898–1902	Spanish-American War
1902	U.S. colonization of Philippines
1903	First powered flight by Wright Brothers

Government and Economy

After the War of Independence ended in 1783, its leaders were divided over many issues, including the power of a national government and the comparative autonomy of the separate states. The Constitution and Bill of Rights, approved in 1787, established a relatively powerful central government, elected by voters in each state, within a system, known as federalism, that ensured the sovereignty and recognized the lawmaking powers of each member state. White Americans gained many civil liberties, and white adult males were granted the right to vote, but the government maintained slavery and excluded nonwhites and women from political activity.

The American republic reflected a mix of liberalism and fear of disorder. Inspired by a hatred of despotic government in Europe, the founders made tyranny difficult through the separation of powers into executive and legislative branches and an independent judiciary, with each institution having defined roles. But wary of potential radicalism and shocked by the excesses of the French Revolution, the nation's leaders also discouraged attacks on the interests of the upper classes by limiting voting rights. The indirect election for the presidency through the Electoral College, in which each state chose electors to cast their votes, also reduced popular sovereignty and produced results that did not always reflect the choice of the majority of citizens.

WWW-VL: History: United States (*http://vlib.iue.it/history/USA/*). A virtual library that contains links to hundreds of sites.

American leaders also had to establish a sound economic foundation for the new nation. The southern plantation interests favored free trade to market their crops abroad without obstacles, especially cotton, tobacco, and sugar. Many northerners, meanwhile, hoped to foster an Industrial Revolution like Britain's. The first treasury secretary, the West Indian–born Alexander Hamilton (1757–1804), laid the basis by establishing a national bank, favoring tariffs to exclude competitive foreign goods, and providing government support for industry.

The War of 1812

Hamilton's policies and protectionism encouraged manufacturing but led to another conflict with Great Britain. Tensions over trade, the nebulous U.S.–Canada border, and other issues led to the War of 1812 (1812–1814). The British captured Washington, burning down the White House, and repulsed a U.S. invasion of Canada, but after some U.S. victories, the two sides negotiated peace. Industrialization proceeded in the U.S. Northeast, and in 1813 the first large textile mills to convert raw cotton into finished cloth opened in New England. The northern industrialists who favored protect ionist policies soon prevailed over the southern planters who wanted free trade. Meanwhile, to move resources and products, Americans also built more than 3,300 miles of canals by 1840. The longest of these was the Erie Canal, completed across New York State in 1825, which linked the markets and resources of the Midwest and Mississippi Basin to the port of New York City.

Society and Culture

Gradually Americans forged a society distinct from Britain's. The French writer Alexis de Tocqueville (TOKE-vill) (1805–1859), who visited the United States in the early 1830s, noted the American commitment to democracy and individualism, the "blending of social ranks," and Americans' "unbounded desire for riches."[7] But he also considered slavery and racial prejudice a dark blot on American claims to equality, and he feared that too much individualism and greed for riches undermined community.

Slavery shaped the society of the southern states. Enslaved African Americans endured brutal conditions: beatings were a constant threat, families were frequently torn apart on the auction block, and some white masters felt entitled to use their female slaves as concubines. Slaves' resistance included escape, sabotage, infrequent but potent uprisings, and the sustaining of African traditions and culture. After

> 66 The American republic reflected a mix of liberalism and fear of disorder. 99

> 66 Gradually Americans forged a society distinct from Britain's. 99

1830, an abolitionist movement led by whites and freed African Americans in the North launched relentless critiques of the slave system. Women such as Sarah and Angelina Grimke, two southern sisters who grew to hate the society in which they were raised, were active in the movement and flouted custom by speaking out publicly (see Witness to the Past: Protesting Sexism and Slavery).

While some Americans, especially on the East Coast, still looked to Europe for cultural inspiration, the nation increasingly created its own distinctive literary and intellectual traditions. Later-nineteenth-century writers such as Walt Whitman and Mark Twain helped forge a uniquely American literature that examined society and its problems. Whitman (1819–1892), a journalist influenced by European romanticism, celebrated democracy, the working class, and both heterosexual and homosexual affection while addressing the transformations of the Industrial Revolution. In 1855 Whitman described his ethnically diverse and dynamic nation as "a newer garden of creation, dense, joyous, modern, populous millions, cities and farms. By all the world contributed."[8] Twain (1835–1910), a former printer and riverboat pilot from Missouri turned journalist, was inspired by European realism and sought material for his essays, short stories, and novels all over the country and the world. Unlike the optimistic Whitman, Twain shed light on the underside of American life and character.

American philosophy and religions also went in new directions. Leading American philosophers broke with the European tradition by claiming that ideas had little value unless they enlarged people's concrete knowledge of reality, an approach known as pragmatism developed by William James. While many Americans embraced secular and humanist views, many others were influenced by the religious revivals that periodically swept the country. The Protestant missionary impulse, inherited from the first settlers and augmented by the growth of evangelical churches, fostered religious and moral fervor. As a result, Americans became active as Christian missionaries around the world. At the same time, the nation became more religiously diverse. In 1776, most Americans were Protestant, often Calvinist. By 1914, the United States contained followers of many faiths, including some Buddhist and Muslim immigrants from Asia.

Witness to the Past

Protesting Sexism and Slavery

Sarah Grimke and her younger sister, Angelina, were the daughters of a wealthy slaveholding family in Charleston, South Carolina. Adopting the Quaker faith, which emphasized human dignity, and rejecting their positions as members of the state's elite, they dedicated their lives to advocating women's rights and the abolition of slavery. In 1837 they moved north and began giving lectures before large audiences. Because they spoke out so publicly, they were often criticized by churches for violating gender expectations. Sarah Grimke responded in 1838 by writing letters to her critics that often used Christian arguments to defend women's right and obligation to voice their views. When the letters were published together in one volume, they became the first American feminist treatise on women's rights. The following excerpts convey some of Grimke's arguments:

Here then I plant myself. God created us equal; he created us free agents; he is our Lawgiver, our King and our Judge, and to him alone is woman bound to be in subjection, and to him alone is she accountable for the use of those talents with which her Heavenly Father has entrusted her. . . . As I am unable to learn from sacred writ when woman was deprived by God of her equality with man, I shall touch upon a few points in the Scriptures, which demonstrate that no supremacy was granted to man. . . . [In the Bible] we find the commands of God invariably the same to man and woman; and not the slightest intimation is given in a single passage, that God designed woman to point to man as her instructor. . . .

I hope that the principles I have asserted will claim the attention of some of my sex, who may be able to bring into view, more thoroughly than I have done, the situation and degradation of women. . . . During the early part of my life, my lot was cast among the butterflies of the fashionable world; and of this class of women, I am constrained to say, both from experience and observation, that their education is miserably deficient; that they are taught to regard marriage as the one thing needful, the only notice of distinction; hence to attract the notice and win the attentions of men, by their external charms, is the chief business of fashionable girls. They seldom think that men will be allured by intellectual acquirements, because they find, that where any mental superiority exists, a woman is generally shunned and regarded as stepping out of her "appropriate sphere," which, in their view, is to dress, to dance, to set out to the best possible advantage her person. . . . To be married is too often held up to the view of girls as [necessary for] human happiness and human existence. For this purpose . . . the majority of girls are trained. . . . [In education] the improvement of their intellectual capacities is only a secondary consideration. . . . Our education consists almost exclusively of culinary and other manual operations. . . .

There is another class of women in this country, to whom I cannot refer, without feelings of the deepest shame and sorrow. I allude to our female slaves. . . . The virtue of female slaves is wholly at the mercy of irresponsible tyrants, and women are bought and sold in our slave markets, to gratify the brutal lust of those who bear the name of Christians. . . . If she dares resist her seducer, her life by the laws of some of the slave States may be . . . sacrificed to the fury of disappointed passion. . . . The female slaves suffer every species of degradation and cruelty, which the most wanton barbarity can inflict; they are indecently divested of their clothing, sometimes tied up and severely whipped. . . . Can any American woman look at these scenes of shocking . . . cruelty, and fold her hands in apathy, and say, "I have nothing to do with slavery"? She cannot and be guiltless.

Thinking About the Reading

1. What do the letters tell us about the social expectations and education for white women from affluent families?
2. In what way do Grimke's letters address the issue of slavery?

Source: Sarah M. Grimke, *Letters on the Equality of the Sexes, and the Condition of Woman* (Boston: Issac Knapp, 1838).

ward to his guardian."[10] Over time many Indians were removed from their native lands, even tribes who lived in peace with whites and had adopted aspects of European culture. For example, the Cherokee—farmers who had developed their own written language, published a newspaper, and had a written constitution—had long cultivated good relations with their white neighbors. Yet, after gold was discovered on their land, 15,000 Cherokee from Georgia were forced into concentration camps and then in 1838 sent on a forced march of 1,200 miles, the "Trail of Tears," to Oklahoma. Four thousand Cherokee died from starvation or exposure on the journey.

The Monroe Doctrine

The expansionist impulse also influenced U.S. foreign policy. In 1823 James Monroe (1758–1831), the fifth president of the United States, delivered the Monroe Doctrine, a unilateral statement warning European nations against interfering in the Western Hemisphere and affirming U.S. commitment to shape Latin America's political future after the overthrow of Spanish colonialism. The doctrine claimed that the United States enjoyed a special political and economic status in the Americas, and it effectively marked Latin America as an American sphere of interest, an area in which one great power assumes exclusive responsibility for maintaining peace and attempts to monopolize the resources of that area. Nearly a century after the Monroe Doctrine, Secretary of State Robert Lansing reaffirmed this pattern, claiming that the United States "considers its own interests. The integrity of other American nations is an incident, not an end."[11] As a result, the Monroe Doctrine forged complex links between the United States and the rest of the Americas, often provoking hostility in Latin America, and it set the stage for the rise of the United States as a world power.

War with Mexico and American Military Interventionism

The U.S.-Mexican War of 1846–1848 was a war of expansion that led to a doubling of the U.S. national domain by seizing territory from Mexico. Some 35,000 Americans and their slaves had settled in the Mexican province of Texas. Chafing at Mexican taxes and its antislavery policies, the Americans rebelled and pushed the Mexican forces out, declaring themselves an independent republic in 1836. Soon the Texans sought annexation to the United States, a move favored by the proslavery southern states and opposed by the antislavery northern states. In 1844 the U.S. president and Congress moved to admit Texas to statehood, provoking the ire of Mexicans, who now reasserted their claims.

The war that followed stirred politically divisive and passionate debate among politicians and the media in the United States. After President James Polk (1795–1849) ordered military action, the United States Congress went along, but the war badly divided Americans. A Massachusetts legislative resolution proclaimed "that such a war of conquest, so hateful, unjust and unconstitutional in its origin and character, must be regarded as a war against freedom, against humanity, against justice, against the Union."[12] The war ended when 14,000 U.S. troops invaded Mexico and captured Mexico City. This victory allowed the United States to annex Mexican territories from Texas to California. However, the conflict killed 13,000 Americans and 50,000 Mexicans, and it also fostered an enduring Mexican distrust of the United States.

The war sparked a debate over the political and economic ramifications of extending Manifest Destiny to Latin America and Asia. In 1853 Senator William Seward placed expansion in global perspective, advising Americans: "You are already the great continental power. But does that content you? I trust that it does not. You want the commerce of the world. The nation that draws the most from the earth and fabricates most, and sells the most to foreign nations, must be and will be the great power of the earth."[13] Americans soon engaged in the lucrative China trade, including opium smuggling, while the U.S. Navy led the way in opening up reclusive Japan (see Chapters 22–23).

Many historians argue that during the nineteenth century, the United States began to build a new kind of empire, not a territorial one like the British, French, Spanish, and Russian Empires, but chiefly an informal one based on using financial controls and military operations to extend U.S. power rather than gain formal political control. Hence, American naval forces intervened in Southeast Asia almost annually from the 1830s through the 1860s, often arrogantly. Throughout the nineteenth century, various presidents also sought to obtain nearby Cuba from Spain or helped to finance Cuban revolts to overthrow Spanish rule.

sphere of interest An area in which one great power assumes exclusive responsibility for maintaining peace and attempts to monopolize the area's resources.

The Civil War and Social Change

The Civil War (1861–1865), a major transition for the United States, reshaped U.S. society by ending slavery. Like Sarah Grimke, many Americans had believed that slavery mocked liberal democracy. Slavery had largely disappeared from northern states by the early 1800s, and the U.S. government outlawed the slave trade in 1810, although it continued elsewhere. Economic disparities exacerbated the North-South conflict. By 1860, the North was the home of industry, banks, and great ports such as New York, Boston, and Philadelphia. By contrast, the South was largely a monocultural plantation economy supported by 350,000 white families and 3 million black slaves. The northern leaders mostly favored high customs tariffs to protect their industries, but this policy threatened the South, which depended on exports to survive.

In 1860–1861, eleven southern states seceded from the union, forming the proslavery Confederate States of America. President Abraham Lincoln (1809–1865), a lawyer from Illinois who wanted to end slavery and preserve the union, mobilized the military forces of the remaining states to resist the secession. In 1862 he issued the Emancipation Proclamation, freeing all slaves. After four years of war, the North defeated the South, mainly because of the North's dynamic economy and population advantage of nearly four to one.

The Civil War was in many respects a social and political revolution. Not only did it end slavery, but it also crushed the southern struggle for self-determination, destroyed the South's economic link to Britain, firmly established protectionism as economic policy, and fostered a much stronger federal government. The war resulted in more deaths than all other wars combined that were fought by Americans before or since, killing 360,000 Union and 258,000 Confederate troops, and it devastated the southern countryside. The South began to enjoy balanced economic development only with the growth of industry in the twentieth century, largely paid for by northern investors.

Ethnic Minorities in the Years Following the Civil War

The Civil War emancipated African Americans from slavery but did not eliminate the disadvantages faced by them and other ethnic minorities. Determined to overcome barriers, many former slaves taught themselves to read—usually forbidden under slavery—and some opened schools to expand opportunities for young blacks. Many African Americans left the plantations to find work elsewhere, but their prospects were chiefly limited to sharecropping, such as growing cotton, or physical labor, such as mining or longshoreman work. Long after slavery ended, African Americans faced discrimination reflected in laws restricting their rights and were often prevented from voting. Skin color became the major determinant of social class, and segregation based on this physical feature remained the norm in the South until the 1960s. African Americans attended separate schools, were largely confined to their own neighborhoods, and could not use public facilities, such as parks, restaurants, and drinking fountains, reserved for whites. Those who violated these laws and customs faced jail, beatings, or even executions, known as lynchings (some 235 in 1892 alone), by white vigilantes.

In the aftermath of the Civil War, as peace brought a resumption of westward American expansion into central and western North America, more Native Americans suffered. After 1865, whites subdued the Great Plains and its people and rendered the territory unfit for Indian survival. Settlers, railroad builders, and fur traders massacred 15 million bison, the chief source of subsistence for Indian tribes on the Great Plains, while farmers and ranchers reshaped the environment of the prairies and northern woodlands. In 1886, the Apache of Arizona, under their chief, Geronimo (juh-RON-uh-moe) (1829–1909), finally surrendered after years of fighting. In 1890, the United States Army's massacre of three hundred Lakota Sioux followers of the Ghost Dance, an Indian spiritual revival movement, at Wounded Knee in South Dakota marked the triumph of U.S. colonization of the west. Defeated by the army, decimated by epidemics, and reduced to poverty, Indians were put on reservations controlled by the federal government. They experienced the American dream in reverse, as democracy became tyranny and liberty became confinement.

Industrialization

The northern victory in the Civil War and economic policies of protectionism spurred the great industrial growth in the later 1800s, which fostered a better material life but also generated changes in American class structure and ways of living. The industrial economy in the United States resembled those in Europe but became more productive. In 1860, the United States ranked fourth among industrial nations, but by 1894 it ranked first; in addition, American exports had tripled, and the nation was second only to Britain as a world trader. A surge in technological innovation changed economic life. Electricity as a power source, combined with improved factory production methods, turned out goods faster, more cheaply,

Women Textile Workers In both Europe and North America, women became the largest part of the workforce in the textile industry. These women, working in a New England spinning mill around 1850, endured harsh work conditions and the boring, often dangerous, job of tending machines.

and in greater quantities than ever before, increasing U.S. competitiveness in the world. American and European inventions such as portable steam engines and the internal combustion engine revolutionized industry, leading to a tripling of U.S. factory output between 1877 and 1892.

American life and population patterns were also shaped by an improved transportation and communication network; by 1890 the U.S. railroad network was larger than all European railroad systems combined. Railroad construction owed much to ethnic minorities and immigrants, because many of the workers who drove the spikes and blasted the passages through rocks and mountains were African-Americans, Chinese, or Irish. The transportation revolution continued when Henry Ford (1863–1947) started a motor company in 1903 and began turning out the first affordable cars and refining the mass-production assembly line. In another transportation breakthrough, Orville and Wilbur Wright became the first men to achieve powered flight in 1903, launching the age of aviation.

But industrialization also led to monopoly capitalism, a concentration of industrial and financial resources similar to Europe's that worsened the inequitable distribution of wealth. A few fabulously wealthy tycoons, such as John D. Rockefeller and J. P. Morgan, known to their critics as the Robber Barons, had great influence over politicians, controlled much of the economy, and expected workers to labor at subsistence wages. Using Social Darwinist thinking (see Chapter 19), Rockefeller claimed that "the growth of large business is merely survival of the fittest and a law of God."[14] Although some Americans prospered, industrial workers in cities, factories, and mines often experienced tough conditions and little job security. The work was dangerous, the hours long, and the wages low; children often worked alongside their parents.

Immigration, Urbanization, and Social Movements

This era was also marked by social change, including the influx of millions of immigrants. Some 25 million Europeans immigrated to the United States between 1870 and 1916, and by 1900 more than 1 million Europeans entered the nation each year in search of a better life. At first they came largely from northwestern Europe, especially English, Irish, Germans, and Scandinavians. Later many arrived from southern and eastern Europe, including Italians, Greeks, Serbs, and Poles. The population of European ancestry in the United States increased from 2.5 million in 1770 to 32 million in 1860 and 92 million by 1910. Meanwhile, thousands of Chinese and Japanese immigrants landed on the Pacific Coast in the later 1800s, followed by Filipinos after 1900. Most of these newcomers, both European and Asian, typically faced discrimination and violence, particularly during economic downturns.

The decades between 1865 and 1914 were also marked by movements seeking economic and social change. Economic depression, panics, and bloody labor conflicts fostered working-class radicalism, which threatened the wealthy and the middle class. Farmers and workers resented the wealth of the Robber Barons and the power of large corporations and railroads. Even while increased agricultural output made the United States the world's leading agricultural producer, in the 1890s many farmers went bankrupt, losing their land to banks. Political leaders worried that an inflamed public mood would spark a revolution.

The Emergence of Labor Unions

Although outright revolution did not occur, workers and farmers fought those with power and privilege. Labor unions had first appeared in the 1820s, when women and men campaigned for better conditions and a shorter workday in the textile mills of Lowell, Massachusetts. In 1860 female strikers in the textile mills of nearby Lynn chanted, "American ladies will not be slaves." Eugene Debs (1855–1926), the socialist leader of the railway union, explained in 1893 that "the capitalists refer to you as mill hands, farm hands, factory hands. The trouble is he owns your head and your hands."[15] By the early 1900s, the radical, Marxist-influenced International Workers of the World (better known as the Wobblies) were gaining influence among industrial workers, miners, and longshoremen. Employers and their political allies disparaged union members as communists and fought their demands, eventually destroying the Wobblies as a mass movement.

The Suffrage Movement

Women also struggled for their civil rights. The republic excluded more than half of the population from democracy for the first 150 years. During the 1800s, although large numbers of women worked in factories, shops, and offices, they also managed their homes. Despite their increasing economic roles, women were also urged by religious leaders to be more pious, self-sacrificing, and obedient to men. Women gained basic privileges more on a par with men only after a long effort. The suffrage movement for the vote was born in 1848, when women meeting in Seneca Falls, New York, declared, in a reference to the U.S. Declaration of Independence, that "all men and women are created equal." They opposed a system in which women had no rights to property or even to their own children in case of divorce. After seven decades of marching, publicizing their cause, and lobbying male politicians, suffragettes convinced Congress to give women the right to vote in 1920.

American Capitalism and Empire

As in Europe, industrial capitalism fostered imperialism and warfare. A series of economic depressions from the 1870s through the 1890s spurred public demand for foreign markets and for extending Manifest Destiny to other parts of the world. As a result, by the later 1800s, many American businessmen, farmers, and workers favored acquiring territories overseas to improve national economic prospects. Others hoped to spread American conceptions of freedom, which they increasingly equated with individualism, private property, and a capitalist marketplace economy.

These pressures led to military interventions. The United States sent military forces to at least twenty-seven countries and territories between 1833 and 1898 to protect the economic interests of American businesses during insurrections or civil strife or to suppress the piracy that threatened U.S. shipping. Troops were dispatched at various times to nearly a dozen Latin American nations, China, Indonesia, Korea, and North Africa. U.S. forces also brought the Hawaiian Islands—a Polynesian kingdom where Americans had long settled as traders, whalers, planters, and missionaries—into the U.S. empire. The growing American population in Hawaii, led by sugar planters, resented the Hawaiian monarchy, and in 1893 they overthrew beloved and talented Hawaiian queen Liliuokalani (luh-lee-uh-oh-kuh-LAH-nee) (1838–1917). Aided by

150 U.S. troops, American settlers formed a provisional government and effectively made Hawaii a neocolony. The end of the monarchy transformed the islands not only politically but also socially, as thousands of Japanese, Chinese, Korean, and Filipino immigrants became the main labor force, mostly working on plantations owned by American settlers and companies. By the 1930s, Asians constituted the large majority of Hawaii's population.

The Spanish-American War

The major imperial conflict involving the United States was the Spanish-American War (1898–1902), which pitted American against Spanish colonial forces. The war was a watershed in U.S. foreign affairs that helped make the United States an empire. On the eve of the war, President William McKinley (1843–1901) argued for the necessity for obtaining foreign markets for America's surplus production, linking expanding markets with the maintenance of prosperity. In what Secretary of State John Hay called a "splendid little war," the United States fought with Spain over that country's remaining, restless colonies: Cuba, Puerto Rico, Guam, and the Philippines.

The war unleashed American nationalist fervor as the United States quickly triumphed against the hopelessly outmatched Spanish. A future president, Woodrow Wilson, boasted about America's emergence as a major power in the global system: "No war ever transformed us quite as the war with Spain. No previous years ever ran with so swift a change as the years since 1898. We have witnessed a new revolution, the transformation of America completed."[16] However, to colonize the Philippines, the United States had to brutally suppress a fierce nationalist resistance by Filipinos opposed to U.S. occupation (see Chapter 22). The U.S. struggle against Filipinos, while ultimately successful, resulted in the deaths of thousands of Filipinos and Americans and indicated the challenges and costs of exercising power in the world. The colonization of the Philippines, Puerto Rico, and Guam, and economic and political domination over nominally independent Cuba, also transformed the United States from an informal into a territorial empire much like the Netherlands and Portugal.

> "Creating stable political systems among remote regions proved to be a struggle, and wars and military dictatorships were frequent."

LO³ Latin America and the Caribbean in the Global System

Brazil and most of Spain's Latin American colonies won their independence in the early 1800s, although the Caribbean islands mostly remained colonies (see Chapter 19). But most Latin Americans experienced considerable turmoil, including political instability, economic decline, and regional conflicts. However, by the 1870s, conditions stabilized somewhat. Expanding European markets by then had created a greater demand for Latin American exports and stimulated economic growth. Black slaves gained their freedom, and waves of European immigrants poured into some nations, changing the social and cultural landscape; meanwhile, the United States increasingly exercised power in the region.

Latin American Nations

After winning their independence from Spain and Portugal, Latin Americans faced new challenges. Some countries, such as Argentina, Brazil, and Mexico, were large and unwieldy, while others, such as El Salvador and the Dominican Republic, were small and had limited resources. Except for Brazil, which was governed by an emperor, the new countries were republics.

Creating stable political systems among remote regions proved to be a struggle, and wars and military dictatorships were frequent. Civil wars for dominance continued into the 1860s, often pitting those favoring regionalism against partisans of a strong centralized government. In addition, various frontier disputes fostered occasional wars. For example, Chile fought Peru and Bolivia in 1837 and again in 1879–1884, acquiring territory from those two countries as a result.

Caudillos and Social Structure

Although the Latin Americans achieved political independence, most leaders did not favor dramatic social and economic change. The wealthy upper class largely consisted of creoles who owned

caudillos
Latin American military strongmen who acquired and maintained power through force between the early nineteenth and mid-twentieth centuries.

> "Social and economic inequalities in Latin American countries often led to reforms and sometimes to revolutions."

large businesses, plantations, and haciendas or had seized them from the departing Spaniards. The small middle class of shopkeepers, teachers, and skilled artisans was mainly composed of mestizos and mulattos. More than half of the population, including most Indians and blacks, remained at the bottom of the social structure. Politics usually remained chiefly an affair for the wealthy, and political and economic leaders often restricted the political participation of the poor nonwhite majority. To contain or prevent unrest resulting from the severe gap between rich and poor, military strongmen,

known as caudillos, who acquired and maintained power through force, gained control of many Latin American countries. Some of these, such as the dictator Juan Manuel de Rosas (huan man-WELL deh ROH-sas) (1793–1877) in Argentina, were tyrants who used violence, torture, and murder to maintain power.

Most Latin American nations established some stability by the 1850s, although politics remained highly contentious. Many countries sought both "progress and order," which often led to caudillo rule. But a few fostered multiparty systems in which competing parties sought access to national power in order to reward supporters. The political elite often disagreed on policies. Liberals generally favored federalism, free trade, and the separation of church and state. Conservatives sought centralization, trade protectionism, and maintenance of church power. Conflicts between these groups were sometimes violent.

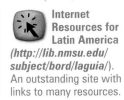
Internet Resources for Latin America *(http://lib.nmsu.edu/subject/bord/laguia/)*. An outstanding site with links to many resources.

Brazil's Quest for Political Order

Brazil was the only Latin American nation to maintain a monarchy rather than a republic. By the 1880s, Brazilians had begun debating both slavery and the legitimacy of the monarchy. As tensions simmered, the army seized power in 1889, exiled Emperor Dom Pedro II, and replaced the monarchy with a republic. However, although a federal system on the U.S. model emerged, suffrage was highly restricted, the majority of Brazilians gained neither property nor civil rights, and many remained desperately poor. In the end, Brazil maintained an authoritarian tradition, but rebellions and regionalism constantly challenged the government.

Revolution in Mexico and Cuba

Social and economic inequalities in Latin American countries often led to reforms and sometimes to revolutions. Revolution was most notable in Mexico; however, the birth of the Mexican republic in 1824 did not bring stability to the vast country. Between 1833 and 1855, a caudillo, General Antonio Lopez de Santa Anna (SAN-tuh AN-uh) (1797–1876), led a series

Experience the Latin American revolutionary era through the eyes of either the Spanish monarchy or the independent movement in this interactive simulation.

Benito Juarez: The Man of Bronze

Santa Anna's misadventures and growing social problems sparked upheaval. In 1861 Mexican liberals led by Benito Juarez (WAHR-ez) (1806–1872), a pragmatic lawyer and Zapotec Indian, defeated the conservatives and suspended repayment of the foreign debt. In 1862 this provoked a short-lived occupation by France, whose ruler, Napoleon III, dreamed of renewed American empire. The French made a member of the Habsburg family, Maximilian of Austria (1832–1867), emperor of Mexico. However, under pressure from Mexican liberals and the United States, France withdrew its troops, and Maximilian's regime collapsed in 1867. Juarez again served as president from 1867 until his death in 1872, seeking social justice, fighting corruption and the privileged classes, freeing peasants, and subordinating the church to the secular state. His reformist policies and his Indian ancestry—his admirers called him the "man of bronze" because of his dark skin—made Juarez Mexico's most honored national leader.

The Dictatorship of Porfirio Diaz

In 1876 Mexico came under the dictatorship of Porfirio Diaz (DEE-ahs) (1830–1915), a caudillo of mestizo ancestry who ruled until 1911. Diaz brought stability and economic progress, allowing the country's population to grow from 9 million in 1874 to 15 million in 1910. But Diaz also allowed foreign business interests and investors to take over much of Mexico's economy, and he did little to help the growing mass of impoverished people, as much of the land became owned by large haciendas and land companies.

Emiliano Zapata and the Mexican Revolution

Eventually, Diaz's economic policies led to civil war and revolution. In 1910

of dictatorships punctuated by civil war. By leading his country into the disastrous U.S.-Mexican War (1846–1848), Santa Anna also lost half of Mexico's territory, including Texas and California, to the United States.

various forces coalesced to fight the unpopular Diaz regime in the Mexican Revolution (1910–1920). One faction was led by political rebels such as the creole Francisco Madero (muh-DER-oh) (1873–1913), a landowner's son who was educated in France and the United States. In the south, the mestizo Emiliano Zapata (zeh-PAH-teh) (1879–1919), a charismatic former peasant, organized a peasant army that seized haciendas and fought the federal army. With the defeat of Diaz, largely by Zapata's forces, the idealistic Madero was elected president but proved a weak leader, and was murdered by a rival. Madero's death caused sporadic violence as all factions used ruthless tactics, and alliances formed and collapsed. Zapata

Women Revolutionaries in Mexico. Hoping for social change and more rights, women joined men in fighting, and sometimes dying, for one or another faction during the Mexican Revolution.

Archivo General de la Nación, Mexico, courtesy of Martha Davidson

The Plan of Ayala Read the accusations leveled by Emiliano Zapata and his followers against Francisco Madero, whom they had just helped come to power in Mexico.

was assassinated by a rival in 1919, but his reputation lived on in death, making him the most celebrated revolutionary hero.

The ongoing violence raised expectations for social change and fostered a yearning for peace. For example, hoping to gain more rights and influence, women played a critical revolutionary role as soldiers, spies, and couriers. Some of their hopes seemed realized in a constitution introduced in 1917, which set forth progressive goals such as an eight-hour workday and paid maternity leave, while ignoring other goals like women's suffrage. In 1920 the revolutionary conflict wound down after claiming 1 million lives. While most Mexicans remained impoverished, a new party led by former revolutionaries formed a government and brought political stability and some progress on women's rights.

José Martí and Cuba

In the Caribbean, Cuba also experienced revolt. The Spanish retained a tight control of Cuba and its valuable sugar plantations, but by the later 1800s, an independence movement had developed. Its major spokesman, the journalist José Martí (mahr-TEE) (1853–1895), was a true citizen of the world who had travelled and lived in Europe, the United States, and various Latin American nations. Martí's writings helped inspire a Cuban revolt in 1895, but he was killed in the fighting, and eventually the revolution was sidetracked by U.S. intervention during the Spanish-American War, which turned Cuba into a U.S. neocolony.

Latin American Economic Patterns

Like North Americans, Latin Americans debated the benefits of free trade as opposed to protectionism, of heavy involvement in the world economy as opposed to self-sufficiency. After the destructive wars of independence, Latin American exports and investments declined. However, in contrast to the protectionist United States, this decline did not prompt Latin American leaders to move toward economic independence. Instead, they largely pursued free trade and maintained the export of raw materials such as Ecuadorian cocoa, Brazilian coffee, Argentine beef, Cuban sugar, and Bolivian and Chilean ores.

> ❝ The decision to concentrate on exporting natural resources left Latin American societies economically vulnerable. ❞

Export-based Economies

The decision to concentrate on exporting natural resources left Latin American societies economically vulnerable. Around the region, earnings from minerals and cash crops like rubber and coffee ebbed and flowed with the fall or rise of world commodity prices. By the twentieth century, the economic fate of Brazil and other Latin American countries became closely tied to fluctuating world prices for those countries' exports, but many countries may have had few viable alternatives to free trade. The impoverished state of most Indians and blacks gave them little purchasing power to support any local industries that might be developed, and attempts to foster industrialization failed in Brazil, Colombia, and Mexico in the 1830s and 1840s because of competition from European imports. Only Argentina made modest progress in manufacturing in the later 1800s.

Foreign Investment and Domination

Investment by North Americans and Europeans in mines and plantations drew Latin America more firmly into the global market, exposing the region's peoples to continued exploitation by outsiders. Independence opened Latin America to U.S., French, and especially British merchants and financiers, who used their economic power to dominate banking and the import trade for industrial goods such as cotton textiles and who also invested in mines and plantations. By the mid-1800s, British businessmen and bankers controlled the imports and exports of both Brazil and Argentina. Argentina was sometimes called an informal member of the British Empire; in 1895, an Argentine nationalist complained that "today our country is tributary to England."[17]

Foreign investment and domination had several consequences for Latin Americans. First, foreign corporations increasingly owned the plantations and mines. Such companies sent their profits to the United States or Europe rather than investing further in Latin America. Second, Latin America became a major contributor to world commodity markets, producing some 62 percent of the world's coffee, 38 percent of the sugar, and 25 percent of the rubber by World War I. Third, by the later 1800s, increased communication and transportation, as well as growing

U.S. demand for markets and raw materials, fostered economic expansion in many countries. Despite this growth, however, inequalities grew between powerful landed families and peasants and workers. Throughout Latin America, powerful families or foreign corporations increasingly owned the usable land, creating imbalances that produced political unrest in the twentieth century.

Social and Cultural Change

The abolition of slavery brought social change in Latin America. Some of the leaders who overthrew Spanish rule, such as Simón Bolívar and Jose de San Martin, had favored emancipation and freed slaves who fought in the wars of independence. Between 1823 and 1854, slavery was legally abolished in most of Latin America and the Caribbean. Most European and American countries outlawed the trans-Atlantic slave trade by 1842, and by the 1880s, only Cuba and Brazil still maintained legal slavery. The Spanish rulers finally granted Cuban slaves their freedom in 1886, and abolitionists became more outspoken in Brazil, where slavery remained common in the sugar and coffee industries until 1889. However, economic conditions for freed slaves did not dramatically improve. Many blacks shifted from being slaves to sharecroppers, tenant farmers, and laborers, experiencing little change in their low social status.

Latin America and Immigration

Meanwhile, the immigration of millions of Europeans and Asians reshaped many Latin American societies. European immigrants, especially Italians, Spaniards, Germans, Russians, and Irish, sought better economic prospects in new lands, particularly in Argentina, Brazil, Chile, Uruguay, and Venezuela. People from overcrowded lands in Asia and the Middle East also immigrated to the Americas in the later 1800s and early 1900s. In Trinidad, British Guiana, and Dutch Guiana, the abolition of slavery prompted the import of workers from India, and Indians eventually accounted for around half of the population in these colonies. Japanese settled in Brazil, Peru, and Paraguay as farmers and traders. Arab immigrants from Lebanon and Syria developed trade diasporas throughout Latin America, and Indonesians moved to Dutch Guiana as plantation workers. Chinese flocked to Peru and Cuba and, in smaller numbers, to

Latin American Resources (*http://www .oberlin.edu/faculty/ svolk/latinam/htm*). An excellent collection of resources and links on history, politics, and culture.

Jamaica, Trinidad, and the Guianas. Latin America's richly diverse population doubled between 1850 and 1900 to more than 60 million.

Despite the newcomers, Latin America remained more conservative than North America in social structure. The creole elite dominated most countries, while European and Asian immigrants and mixed-descent people constituted the middle class. Many mulattos and most blacks and Indians remained in the lower class. Indians in countries such as Mexico, Guatemala, Peru, Bolivia, and Colombia often withdrew into their rural village communities. In 1865 a Mexican described the wide gap between whites and Indians: "The white is the proprietor; the Indian the worker. The white is rich; the Indian poor and miserable."[18]

Brazilian Culture

Because of its large populations of European, African, and mixed-descent people, Brazil developed a society and culture different from those of other Latin Americans countries. Brazilians considered their nation's unique, multiracial society to be less obsessed by skin color than other countries. Unlike in the United States, economic class and skin color did not always coincide, and marriage and cultural mixing between members of different groups was common. Yet blacks were also more likely than whites to experience prejudice and to be poor, a fact reflected in Rio de Janeiro's largely black hillside shantytowns.

Read about respected Brazilian writer, Euclides da Cunha, a spokesman for rising Brazilian nationalism.

Cultural forms reflected the Latin American struggle to reconcile indigenous with imported traditions. Rejecting European models, novelists focused on social themes, such as the Brazilian writer Euclides da Cunha (KOO-nyuh) (1866–1909), who wrote about the country's poor. In contrast, the cosmopolitan, well-traveled Nicaraguan poet Ruben Dario (1867–1916) rejected the expression of ideas in art in favor of escapist and fantastic images and a stress on beauty as an end in itself.

Especially creative cultural innovations came in music and dance. For example, the sensuous dance called the tango emerged in the bars and clubs of poor neighborhoods in Buenos Aires, Argentina, which had more than 1.6 million people by 1914. Its music was based partly on rhythms derived from the drumming of African slaves and featured the accordion-like *bandoneon*, invented in Germany and carried to Argentina by Italian immigrants. The tango became a symbol of lower-class identity and was popular in Europe by the 1900s. Brazil's unique music blended European

samba
A Brazilian popular music and dance that arose in the early twentieth century.

calypso
A song style in Trinidad that often featured lyrics addressing daily life and topical subjects.

melody and African rhythms. The abolition of slavery and the migration of Afro-Brazilians from Bahia State in the northeast to Rio de Janeiro gave rise to samba, a popular music and dance developed by Bahian women that became an integral part of Carnival, the three-day celebration before the long Christian period of penitence known as Lent, which was first organized in Rio de Janeiro in the 1890s. Samba emerged as the soul of Brazil, popular with all classes.

Caribbean Traditions

Like Brazilians, Caribbean peoples also mixed African and European influences to produce distinctive cultures, but often in defiance of colonial restrictions. On Trinidad, British colonial officials who feared the black majority passed laws to prohibit African-based musical forms, but two traditions emerged nevertheless. The first was calypso, a song style that often featured lyrics addressing daily life and topical subjects and that eventually became the major popular music in the English-speaking islands of the eastern Caribbean. The second tradition was the pre-Lent Carnival, which, as in Brazil, assumed great social significance while providing a forum for calypso songs that often questioned colonial policies. A song in the 1880s protested colonial restrictions on music during Carnival: "Can't beat my drum, In my own native land. Can't have Carnival, In my native land."[19]

The United States in Latin America

Latin Americans faced challenges from the increasingly powerful United States, a nation they both envied and feared, whose citizens and military forces occasionally intervened in Central America and the Caribbean. For example, in 1856, William Walker—an American adventurer financed by influential U.S. businessmen who were interested in acquiring natural resources and markets—invaded Nicaragua with a well-armed mercenary force of three hundred Americans and temporarily seized the country. Walker proclaimed himself president, and, despite opposition by Central American leaders, the United States granted his government diplomatic recognition. Walker introduced slavery and tried to make English the official language before being forced out in 1857, becoming a hated symbol in Central America of what Latin Americans often called Yankee imperialism.

The Spanish-American War led to U.S. domination in Cuba, which became a U.S. neocolony. The Platt Amendment to the Cuban constitution, imposed by the United States in 1901, integrated the Cuban and U.S. economies and required that the United States Congress approve any treaties negotiated by Cuban leaders. The American military governor summarized the consequences of the Platt Amendment: "There is little or no real independence left to Cuba. She is absolutely in our hands, a practical dependency of the United States."[20] U.S. businessmen soon owned much of Cuba's economy, including railroads, banks, and mills, and the United States acquired a naval base at Guantanamo (gwahn-TAH-nuh-moe) Bay. Later, Cuban nationalists blamed Cuba's squalid condition not on the often-despotic Cuban governments but on the United States. The Platt Amendment was finally repealed in 1934.

The World of 1898: The Spanish-American War (*http://www.loc.gov/rr/hispanic/1898*). A Library of Congress site that provides excellent documents and resources.

In the early 1900s, the United States became more deeply involved in Central America and the Caribbean. To build a canal across Central America linking the Pacific and Atlantic Oceans, the United States helped Panama secede from Colombia in 1903 and convinced its leaders to lease a 10-mile-wide zone across the isthmus in perpetuity to the United States. Several thousand workers from Panama and elsewhere died in the ten arduous years of construction. In 1914 the Panama Canal, 51 miles long, was completed, one of the great engineering feats of history and a boon to maritime commerce and travel. In 1912 the United States overthrew the president of Nicaragua, who was suspected of inviting the British to build a rival canal across his country. U.S. soldiers also occupied Haiti (1915–1933) and the Dominican Republic (1916–1924) to quell unrest or maintain friendly governments. These interventions set the stage for a more active U.S. imperial policy in Latin America and the Caribbean.

LO⁴ New Societies in Canada and the Pacific Basin

The United States was not the only European-settled colony to build a democratic nation and foster economic strength. To the north of the United States, Canada also expanded across the continent to the Pacific and formed a federation of states. During

this era, Western nations also located and colonized the island societies scattered around the Pacific Basin. Meanwhile, in Australia and New Zealand, British immigrants established settler colonies that helped to transform these South Pacific territories (see Map 20.3).

Making a Canadian Nation

France originally colonized most of what is today eastern Canada, but by 1763, the British had defeated the French forces and gained control of this large region. The victorious British now had to forge a stable relationship with 80,000 French-speaking people who resisted assimilation into British culture. By 1774, the British pragmatically recognized the influential role of the Catholic Church and French civil law in Quebec, while British colonists settled chiefly in the Atlantic coastal region. Although the British governed Quebec and the English-speaking regions separately until 1841, relations between British and French Canadians, with different cultures and languages, remained uneasy, causing a British official in the 1830s to conclude that Canada was "two nations warring in the bosom of a single state."[21]

Relations with the United States

Whatever their ethnic backgrounds, Canada's peoples had to deal with the ambitions of the United States, whose leaders hoped that Canada might eventually join the Union. In a U.S.-British

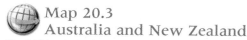

Map 20.3
Australia and New Zealand

The British colonized and gradually settled Australia and New Zealand between the late 1700s and 1914. In 1901 the six Australian colonies became a federation, with a capital eventually built in Canberra.

© Cengage Learning

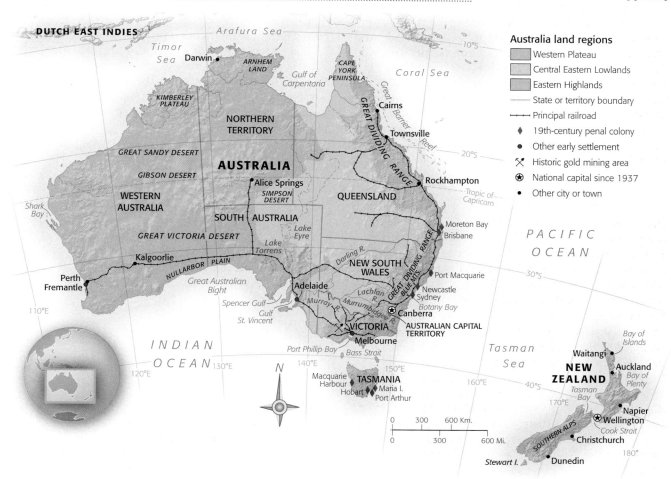

treaty in 1783, the United States recognized British control north of the Great Lakes and the Saint Lawrence River. After the American Revolution, many Loyalists, who had supported continued British rule, moved north to Canada, increasing the English-speaking population substantially and promoting reforms and representative assemblies.

The relations between the United States and British-ruled Canada remained tense for years. Americans suspected that, from their Canada base, the British supported Native Americans, such as the powerful and charismatic Shawnee chief Tecumseh (teh-CUM-sah) (1768–1813), who gathered a large alliance of tribes to drive the white settlers out of Ohio and reinvigorate Indian ways. When conflict between the United States and Britain led to the War of 1812, Tecumseh served with the British. During the war, Americans repeatedly invaded Canada with hopes of annexing the territory but were repulsed. The war ended U.S. attempts to expand north and also laid the seeds for a Canadian identity separate

> "Whatever their ethnic backgrounds, Canada's peoples had to deal with the ambitions of the United States, whose leaders hoped that Canada might eventually join the Union."

from the United States and Britain. In 1846 another treaty fixed the U.S.–Canada boundary in the west.

....

The Dominion of Canada

Canadians could now turn to building a diverse society and democratic nation in peace, welcoming 800,000 British immigrants between 1815 and 1850 while working to modify British control. Growing popular sentiment prompted the British to consider reforms that eventually brought a unified Canada and an elected national parliament. But Canadians rejected complete independence in favor of self-rule within the British Empire as a strategy to help Canada maintain stability, settle the west, foster economic development, and resist U.S. power. In 1858 Canadians built a national capital at Ottawa, and in 1867 leaders negotiated a Canadian Confederation that guaranteed strong provincial rights and preservation of the French language wherever it was spoken. Under this arrangement,

Along the Canadian Pacific Railroad During the late nineteenth century, both native-born Canadians and European immigrants from many lands followed the Canadian Pacific Railroad to settle the newly opened lands of the Midwestern prairies and Western mountains. Some people set up temporary tent villages by railroad stops before taking up farming, mining, logging, trade, or fishing.

Saskatchewan Archives Board #RA 2309

Canada became a dominion, a country having autonomy but owing allegiance to the British crown.

The confederation soon faced new challenges. Expansion of white settlement and political power to the West fired resentment among Indians and people of mixed descent, the French-speaking Metis (may-TEES), which sometimes led to violence. The combative Metis leader, Louis Riel (ree-EL) (1844–1885), who had once studied to be a Catholic priest, led two rebellions before being executed for treason. Eventually, however, Manitoba and British Columbia joined the confederation, and the federal government promised to build a transcontinental railroad. Canada's first prime minister and Riel's chief opponent, Scottish-born John MacDonald (g. 1867–1873, 1878–1891), hoped the railroad would transform the 4 million Canadians into a unified nation; it was completed in 1885. The government negotiated treaties with Native Americans, allocating reservations to many. Although they faced some Indian resistance, white settlers increasingly moved to the western provinces, and towns sprung up along the railroad. By 1905, Canada included all of the present provinces except Newfoundland.

The Canadian economy and ethnic structure were transformed between the 1860s and 1914. Beaver fur and fish had been the major exports of Canada since the 1600s, but now wheat grown in the Great Plains surpassed fur as the major export. Gold strikes in the Yukon and the offering of free land in western Canada attracted immigrants from many lands, including the United States. From 1896 until 1911, more than 2 million British and other European immigrants arrived, often settling in the west, where many built sod houses and grew wheat. Immigrants from eastern and southern Europe as well as China and Japan enriched the ethnic mosaic. Increasingly critical of British imperialism in the world, by 1911 Canadians took control of their own foreign affairs and diplomacy, fostering increased industrialization and warmer relations with the United States, while maintaining the British monarch as symbolic head of state.

Exploration and Colonization of the Pacific Islands

The peoples who lived on the small mountainous islands and flat atolls scattered across thousands of miles in the vast Pacific Ocean Basin were the last to experience European expansion, but when it came, the impact was significant.

By the mid-1700s, the British and French had begun a race to explore what they considered the last frontier, the Pacific Ocean. Eventually these two countries, along with Spain, Germany, Russia, and the United States, had colonized all of the inhabited islands.

dominion
A country that has autonomy but owes allegiance to the British crown; developed in the early twentieth century.

> 66 By the mid-1700s, the British and French had begun a race to explore what they considered the last frontier, the Pacific Ocean. 99

The Explorations of James Cook

The English captain James Cook (1728–1779) led some of the most extensive explorations, greatly aided by the learned Polynesian high priest, Tupaia (ca. 1725–1771). Cook reached the eastern Polynesian island of Tahiti in 1769, where he recruited Tupaia, whose skills as a navigator and speaker of several Polynesian languages greatly aided the expedition. Tupaia drew up the charts that helped Cook map Polynesia, including New Zealand and the coast of Australia, but then died on Java of fever. Cook made two more expeditions to the Pacific in the 1770s; after becoming the first known person to circumnavigate Antarctica, he located the Hawaiian Islands in 1778 and then sailed to Alaska. His early reports created an image of the South Sea islands as paradise, a "Garden of Eden" with amiable people, but Cook was killed in Hawaii after antagonizing local leaders.

Traders and Missionaries in the Pacific

European explorations eventually sparked economic exploitation and Christian missionary activity. In the late 1700s, the Russians established a foothold in Alaska and the Aleutian Islands as a base for hunting seals and sea otters for their fur. By the 1850s, both animals had been hunted to near extinction, and thousands of Aleuts had died from exposure to European diseases. Deep-sea whaling lasted longer, attracting Western and Polynesian sailors. Western traders also sought resources such as sandalwood, greatly valued in Asia for building furniture. It took only ten years to cut and export all of Fiji's sandalwood. Meanwhile, Protestant and Catholic missionaries went to the islands seeking converts, with varied results. The Samoans welcomed the missionaries, often adopting Christianity. Fijians initially rejected missionaries, but later, desiring trade with the West, tolerated them. Fijian converts often pragmatically mixed Christianity with their own traditions. Some peoples, like the inhabitants of New Hebrides, rejected missionaries violently.

Traders and missionaries opened the way for colonization, and between the 1840s and 1900, Western powers colonized all of the Pacific societies. Between the 1840s and 1870s, the French gained domination over many island chains, such as the Society Islands, which included Tahiti, and the Marquesas, while the British colonized various others, among them the Fijian archipelago. By 1898, the Germans and Americans had divided up Samoa, and the British imposed a protectorate over the kingdom of Tonga. By 1900, the Germans had acquired most of Micronesia, and Britain and France controlled much of Melanesia. Hawaii was seized by the United States in 1893.

The Rise of Australia and New Zealand

The British colonized the continent they named Australia and the two large islands they called New Zealand, landmasses in the western Pacific whose human histories long predated the arrival of Europeans. European settlement in Australia began in the 1780s, when the British began transporting convicts, often Irish, from overcrowded British jails to penal colonies they founded at Botany Bay and Sydney Harbor. Agriculture, ranching, and mining became the basis for the Australian economy.

The Aborigines of Australia

British colonization came at the expense of the Aborigines, indigenous peoples who had lived on the continent for thousands of years. Divided into hundreds of scattered tribes and numbering somewhere between 500,000 and 3 million in 1750, Aborigines lived chiefly by fishing and nomadic hunting and gathering and were considered primitive and inferior by European settlers. Many Aborigines resisted encroachments on their land by raiding British settlements; in response, British settlers killed as many as 20,000 Aborigines. As was the case for Native Americans and Pacific

> "Creating a common Australian identity and nationhood took more than a century."

Islanders, diseases brought by Europeans devastated the Aboriginal population, and many were further destabilized by having their land forcibly settled by white newcomers. Eventually, to survive, many Aborigines moved to cities or European cattle and sheep ranches, while others remained on tribal reservations, where they maintained many of their traditions and beliefs.

Creating the Commonwealth of Australia

Creating a common Australian identity and nationhood took more than a century. Throughout the 1800s, Europeans clung to the coastal regions suitable for farming and ranching and avoided the desert interior. The discovery of gold in southeastern Australia in 1851 attracted settlers from Europe, and by the 1860s, more than 1 million whites lived in Australia. Gold mining also prompted Asians to seek their fortunes in Australia, creating resentments among the Europeans. In 1899, one European leader charged that Asians "will soon be eating the heart's blood out of the white population."[22] Violence between Europeans and Asians led to laws restricting Asian immigration, which ended only in the later twentieth century. Another social challenge was the female struggle for influence. By the 1880s, white women's movements were pressing for moral reform and suffrage, and white women gained the right to vote in 1902, but women still enjoyed little political power at the local or national level. Aborigines only gained the right to vote in 1962.

Gradually, Australia became a nation. By 1890, Britain had turned all six of its Australian colonies into self-governing states, which formed the Commonwealth of Australia in 1901, with the British monarch remaining symbolic head of state, like Canada. A transcontinental railroad system, completed in 1917, connected the vast country, but the majority of the 4 million Australians lived in or near five coastal cities. In 1908 Canberra became the nation's capital. Distance from European supplies fostered some local manufacturing, including steel production, and white Australians enjoyed prosperity.

New Zealand and the Maoris

The British also colonized the two large mountainous islands of New Zealand, 1,200 miles east of Australia, at the expense of the Polynesian Maori people, numbering around 100,000 in 1792. The Maori had lived on the islands, which they called Aotearoa, for a millennium, gradually dividing into sometimes warring tribes headed by chiefs and surviving by hunting, fishing, and horticulture. As more British settlers came, territorial disputes with the Maori occurred. The Treaty of Waitangi in 1850 between the British and five hundred Maori chiefs seemingly confirmed the Maori's right to their land while acknowledging British sovereignty. But the British asserted the treaty gave them political and legal power and usurped the chiefs' authority over their lands and people, leading to a series of wars that ended only in the 1870s and resulted in an even sharper decline in the Maori population. Eventually, Maori resistance subsided, and an 1881 peace agreement accorded Maori control over some districts.

Gradually, the European identity in New Zealand grew stronger. Immigrants were attracted by the discovery of gold in 1861, higher living standards than they enjoyed in Europe, a colonial economy based on farming and sheep raising, and a growing government welfare system. New Zealand prospered after 1882, when steamships acquired refrigerated holds to carry lamb and dairy products from the islands to Europe. A parliamentary government including Maori representatives was formed in 1852, and by 1893 both men and women of all communities enjoyed universal suffrage. New Zealand gained self-government as a British dominion in 1907, but it proudly remained an outpost of the British Empire well into the twentieth century.

 Listen to a synopsis of Chapter 20.

CHAPTER 2

Africa, the Middle East, and Imperialism,

1750–1914

Learning Outcomes

After reading this chapter, you should be able to answer the following questions:

LO¹ How did Western nations obtain colonies in sub-Saharan Africa?

LO² How did white supremacy shape South Africa?

LO³ What were some of the major consequences of colonialism in Africa?

LO⁴ What political and economic impact did Europe have on the Middle East?

LO⁵ How did Middle Eastern thought and culture respond to the Western challenge?

> **"**The power of these Europeans has advanced to a shocking degree and has manifested itself in an unparalleled manner. Indeed, we are on the brink of a time of [complete] corruption. As for knowing what tomorrow holds, I am blind.**"**
>
> —Moroccan historian Ahmad Ibn Khalid Al-Nasri, 1860s[1]

Fresh from his victories in Italy and Austria, in 1798 the French general Napoleon Bonaparte vowed to add his name to the list of illustrious European conquerors who had achieved glory and riches before him in the Middle East, the region encompassing North Africa and western Asia. First he planned to invade Egypt, and then he intended to reduce the Ottoman Turks and Persians to French vassals. Eventually he hoped to reach India and found a new religion. With an armada of four hundred ships carrying 50,000 soldiers, Bonaparte quickly established control over northern Egypt. He also took with him some five hundred French scholars to gather valuable information on Egyptian history, society, language, and environment. Near a town in the Nile River Delta, they discovered the Rosetta stone, a tablet made in 196 B.C.E. that contained writings in several languages. One of those languages was Greek, so for the first time, scholars could translate ancient Egyptian hieroglyphics into Western languages.

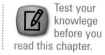 Test your knowlege before you read this chapter.

What do you think?

Europeans typically considered Africans unfit to rule themselves and badly in need of Western leadership.

Strongly Disagree						*Strongly Agree*
1	2	3	4	5	6	7

Bonaparte acted like a Muslim ruler and even hinted that he might embrace Islam. In a bid for popular support, the French general confidently announced: "People of Egypt, I come to restore your rights; I respect God, His Prophet and the Quran. We are friends of all true Muslims. Happiness to the People!"[2] But Bonaparte's policies soon alienated Egyptians, and conquest proved a burden. The French army, small and ill-equipped, withered in the desert heat. An attempt to conquer Syria having failed, Bonaparte left for Paris in 1799, becoming another example of a Western ruler failing to control Muslim peoples.

<< **Tomb of Muhammad Ahmad in Khartoum** Muhammad Ahmad ibn 'Abd Allah, known to history as the Mahdi ("Divinely Guided One"), used Islamic appeals to recruit a large army and lead opposition to the joint British and Egyptian rule in Sudan. He died soon after routing the British forces in 1885, but his tomb remains a symbol of Muslim resistance to Western power.

Although unsuccessful, the French invasion of Egypt provided a harbinger of more invasions of the kind feared by the Moroccan historian Ahmad ibn Khalid al-Nasri, through which Europe would extend its domination in the world. Bonaparte's expedition was a turning point in Western relations with sub-Saharan Africa and the Middle East, the cutting edge of a European thrust that also overwhelmed India, Southeast Asia, and the Pacific islands. The Industrial Revolution, new technology, and capitalism in Europe had greatly accelerated Europe's need for natural resources that could be processed into industrial products, as well as for new markets to consume these goods. These economic factors combined with European political rivalries caused a ruthless policy of incorporating territories in sub-Saharan Africa and the Middle East. While the sub-Saharan and North Africans often resisted European imperialism, their societies' economies, cultures, and political systems were transformed.

LO¹ The Colonization of Sub-Saharan Africa

During the nineteenth century, various Western nations colonized most of sub-Saharan Africa. Although Europeans had established a few small, scattered outposts in West Africa and colonized coastal regions of Angola, Mozambique, and South Africa in the sixteenth and seventeenth centuries, the full-blown quest for colonies began only with the end of the trans-Atlantic slave trade and the spread of the Industrial Revolution in Europe in the mid-1800s. At this time, European imperial ambitions fostered what a British newspaper called the "scramble for Africa," during which the European powers divided up the African continent among themselves, often against fierce resistance, and commenced the full-scale economic penetration of Africa.

> "By 1800 British bankers could make more money investing in manufacturing than in plantations and the slave trade."

The End of the Slave Trade

For more than three centuries, the trans-Atlantic slave trade (1520–1870) dominated relations between Africa, Europe, and the Americas, but growing opposition in all three regions eventually brought it to an end. In the West, especially in Britain, abolitionists were prompted largely by religious and moral outrage at slavery, while others were influenced by the Enlightenment vision of human equality. One sympathizer wrote that people "are not objects. Everyone has his rights, property, dignity. Africa will have its day."[3] Africans and African Americans also struggled against slavery. Slave revolts in the Americas, including the successful revolution in Haiti (see Chapter 19), as well as attempts by slaves to seize control of slave ships conveying them to the Americas, indicated the willingness of many slaves to risk their lives for freedom and also forced many Europeans to rethink their views on slavery.

Another force working against slavery was the Industrial Revolution, which made slavery uneconomical. Overseas markets for factory-made goods became more desirable than cheap labor for plantations. Furthermore, so many colonies produced sugar that the market was flooded and the price fell, making the plantations less profitable at the same time that African states were charging more to provide slaves. By 1800 British bankers could make more money investing in manufacturing than in plantations and the slave trade.

As a result of this combination of moral and economic factors, the slave trade from Africa to the Americas and the slavery era came to an end in the Atlantic world in the nineteenth century. The slave trade was first outlawed in Denmark in 1804, then in Britain in 1807, and then in all British-controlled territories, including their plantation-rich Caribbean colonies, in 1833. Many Latin American nations and Haiti outlawed slavery in the early 1800s, forcing planters to shift to free labor. By 1842 most European and American countries had made it illegal to transport slaves across the Atlantic. The Civil War ended the practice of slavery in the United States in 1865, and in the later 1880s, Brazil and Cuba also finally outlawed slavery.

The East African trade that sent slaves to the Middle East and the Indian Ocean islands—run chiefly

1804	Launching of Fulani jihads by Uthman dan Fodio
1804	Abolition of slave trade by Denmark
1806	British seizure of Cape region from Dutch
1807–1833	Abolition of slave trade in Britain and its territories
1816	Beginning of Shaka's Zulu Empire
1838	Great Trek by South African Boers
1842	Ending of trans-Atlantic slave trade by most European nations
1847	First American freed slave settlement in Liberia
1874–1901	British-Ashante wars
1878	Belgian colonization in Congo
1884–1885	Berlin Conference
1884–1885	Discovery of gold in South Africa
1898	French defeat of Samory Toure
1899–1902	Boer (South African) War
1905	Maji Maji Rebellion in Tanganyika
1912	Founding of African National Congress in South Africa

into the eastern Congo River Basin. In 1873 the British convinced the Zanzibar sultan to close the island's slave market, and as compensation Britain imported vast amounts of ivory, which was used for making piano keys, billiard balls, and cutlery handles. While fewer slaves were now exported, slavers still raided African villages to acquire the labor needed to carry the huge ivory tusks to the coast for export, often in well-armed caravans of up to one thousand people. The British gained control of Zanzibar in 1890, but some slave trading continued in parts of East and Central Africa until the early 1900s.

New Societies and Explorations

Between the later 1700s and later 1800s, the diminishing importance and then ending of the trans-Atlantic slave trade gradually changed the relationship between Africans and Europeans, fostering several new African societies, exploration of Africa by Western adventurers, and increased commerce between Europeans and Africans. As the demand for slaves waned, Europeans became more interested in acquiring African natural resources.

Even before slavery was abolished in the Americas, freed slaves there who returned to Africa from the Americas had established several West African states and port cities. The black founders of these states, and the whites who helped finance them, had both humanitarian aims and commercial goals, wanting to give freed slaves opportunities to run their own lives while also setting up new centers of Western trade. Thousands of freed slaves also settled in coastal towns of the Gold Coast (modern Ghana), Nigeria, and Dahomey, where some became merchants engaged in trade with the Americas.

Africa South of the Sahara (*http://www-sul.stanford.edu/depts/ssrg/africa/*). A valuable site that contains links relevant to African history.

The two largest settlements of freed slaves emerged in Sierra Leone and Liberia. Spurred by abolitionists, in 1787 the British settled four hundred former slaves around the fort at Freetown, which became the core of their colony of Sierra Leone. Over the next few decades, the British shipped more former slaves to Freetown. Freed slaves from the United States were first shipped to Liberia in 1847 and were joined by others after the Civil War. Although Liberia remained an independent state governed by

by Arabs from the eastern Arabian state of Oman—continued longer than the trans-Atlantic trade. In 1835 the Omani leader, Sayyid Sa'id (SIGH-id SIGH-eed) (r. 1806–1856), moved his capital to Zanzibar, an island just off the coast of modern Tanzania, and built a commercial empire of ivory and slaves that flourished for forty years. To obtain slaves and ivory, Omani and Swahili merchants opened or expanded overland trade routes through Tanzania

> **As the demand for slaves waned, Europeans became more interested in acquiring African natural resources.**

the descendants of former slaves, its economy was dominated by U.S.-owned rubber plantations. In both Sierra Leone and Liberia, local Africans often resented the new settlers, who were mostly English-speaking Christians, because they occupied valuable land and often dominated commercial and political power.

The decline of the trans-Atlantic slave trade, which had caused turmoil and made travel dangerous in parts of Africa, also made Africa more accessible to Western explorers. Europeans wanted to discover whether the great African rivers such as the Nile and the Congo were navigable for commercial purposes. Adventurers were obsessed with finding the source of Africa's greatest river, the Nile, and they finally located Lake Victoria in 1860. The most famous explorer, David Livingstone (1813–1873), spent more than two decades traveling in eastern Africa, where he collected information and opened the region to Christian missionary activity and trade with the West.

African Muslim Warrior While Western pressure on coastal societies increased, several Muslim peoples expanded their influence in the West African interior. Some military forces, having acquired Western arms in exchange for slaves and gold, conquered regional empires that flourished for a century or more.

From John H. Hanson, Migration, Jihad, and Muslim Authority in West Africa [Bloomington and Indianapolis: Indiana University Press, 1996]

Livingstone and other European adventurers claimed to have "discovered" inland societies and geographic features, but these European explorers discovered little that Africans and Arabs did not already know, and they usually followed long-established trading routes. The ethnocentric stereotype of intrepid white explorers struggling through virgin territories is a myth, but it shaped Western views. Explorers publicized their findings and spread the notion of "Darkest Africa," which was seen as savage and in need of salvation.

With Africa more open in the 1800s, European traders began to obtain various raw materials needed by the West, such as peanuts, palm oil, gold, timber, and cotton, competing with dynamic West African merchants who, with the end of the slave trade, had set up cash crop plantations. With superior financial resources and governmental support, European companies eventually gained the upper hand over West African merchants. As a result, by 1890 in the trading port of Lagos, once a center of African commerce, only one rich African merchant was still in business.

Islamic Resurgence

Some major developments within Africa in this era derived largely from forces within African societies, such as tensions within Islamic societies of the Sudan that fostered militant expansion. The most notable example, the Fulani jihad (holy war), was part of a larger religious ferment in West Africa that had begun in the Intermediate Era when expanding Islam encountered African traditions. Many West Africans had embraced Islam by blending the religion with their own customs and sometimes animist beliefs. Conflicts broke out sporadically in parts of West Africa in the seventeenth and eighteenth centuries, often involving the Fulani, a pastoral and trading people who lived in communities scattered across the western and central Sudan. By the 1790s, religious conflicts between devout Muslims and those who mixed Muslim and African traditions had spread to the Fulani in the prosperous Hausa states of northern Nigeria.

One of these Fulani, Uthman dan Fodio (AHTH-mun dahn FOH-dee-oh) (1754–1817), a respected Muslim scholar and ardent follower of Sufi mysticism, criticized the tolerant attitude of many Hausa rulers toward religion, called for the conversion of non-Muslim Fulani, and proclaimed the goal of making Islam central to Sudanic life. His magnetic personality and Islamic zeal soon attracted a Fulani and Hausa following. Uthman's attacks on high taxes and social injustice, and his promise to build a government that would spread Islam and purify it of animist beliefs, alarmed Hausa rulers, who tried to restrict his activities. After an attempt was made on his life, Uthman mobilized his followers and launched a jihad in 1804. After conquering the Hausa states and then nearby territories, he created the Sokoto (SOH-kuh-toh) Caliphate, based in the city of Sokoto, and ruled much of what is today northern Nigeria.

Uthman's jihad, and the vision of a purified Islam he offered, sparked others to take up his cause, and during the early 1800s, several other jihadist states, often led by Fulani religious scholars turned state builders, formed in the Sudan. The Islamic revival sparked by the jihads, which continued into the 1880s, allowed a more orthodox Islam to spread widely. As a result, just as Western influence was increasing in some parts of Africa, the Sudan was becoming even more Islamic. But by the later 1800s, as leaders entrenched their powers and forgot Uthman's reformist vision, the Fulani states declined, and Sokoto's power waned in the face of French and British expansion. Nevertheless, Islam remained a vital force in the Sudanic zone.

> "Europeans used deceptive treaties, offered bribes, divided up states, and convinced African leaders that resistance was futile."

and former Confederate soldier who became famous for his travels and published writings on traveling in central Africa. Stanley was familiar with the Congo River Basin, which King Leopold now commissioned Stanley to acquire for Belgium.

Soon other European powers joined the scramble to obtain colonies. In 1884–1885, the colonizing nations held a conference in Berlin to set the ground rules for colonization. For a claim to be recognized, the colonizer had to first give notice to the other Western powers of its intent and then occupy the territory with a military presence. Agents of European governments, such as Stanley working for Belgium, asked African chiefs, most of whom knew no Western languages, to sign treaties of friendship in these languages, but the treaties actually gave the land to European countries. To Africans the Westerners' concept of private ownership was alien, making it easy for European agents to manipulate them. If chiefs refused to sign, they were threatened with war. Fearing a slaughter and hoping to manipulate conditions for their own benefit, many chiefs signed. A Nigerian writer lamented in 1891 that the slavers' forcible possession of Africa's people had only been replaced by the European governments' forcible possession of Africa's land.

European Conquest

Several factors contributed to the acceleration of European conquests in Africa in the late 1800s (see Map 21.1). First, Western companies sought government help to compete with African traders and to pressure states to admit Western merchants. Second, advances in tropical medicine, especially the use of quinine for malaria, freed Europeans from high tropical mortality rates. Third, the invention of more powerful weapons gave Europeans a huge military advantage over African forces. Europeans used deceptive treaties, offered bribes, divided up states, and convinced African leaders that resistance was futile. When faced with resistance, however, Europeans used ruthless force.

Interactive Map

The Belgian Colonization of the Congo

King Leopold of Belgium took the lead in colonization. In 1878, he hired Henry Stanley (1841–1904), a Welsh-born American

The "Pax Britannica" Further weakening the African response, the colonial scramble came at a time when famine, drought, and epidemics of smallpox and cholera were killing millions, especially in eastern Africa. One French missionary reflected the despair: "Why so many calamities in succession? Why?"[4] They also were overwhelmed by the military disparity in weapons and tactics. Using powerful industrialized weapons such as the British Gatling and Maxim machine guns, Westerners willingly slaughtered thousands. In Kenya, British military expeditions attacked villages who resisted. A British officer in Kenya wrote home in 1902 about ordering the destruction of a Gikuyu village because an Englishman had been killed nearby. As a result, every adult villager was either shot or bayoneted, and the British burned all of the huts and then razed the banana farms to the ground. Apparently without irony, the British called their policy of establishing order the "Pax Britannica," or British peace. For most Africans, these were bitter years indeed.

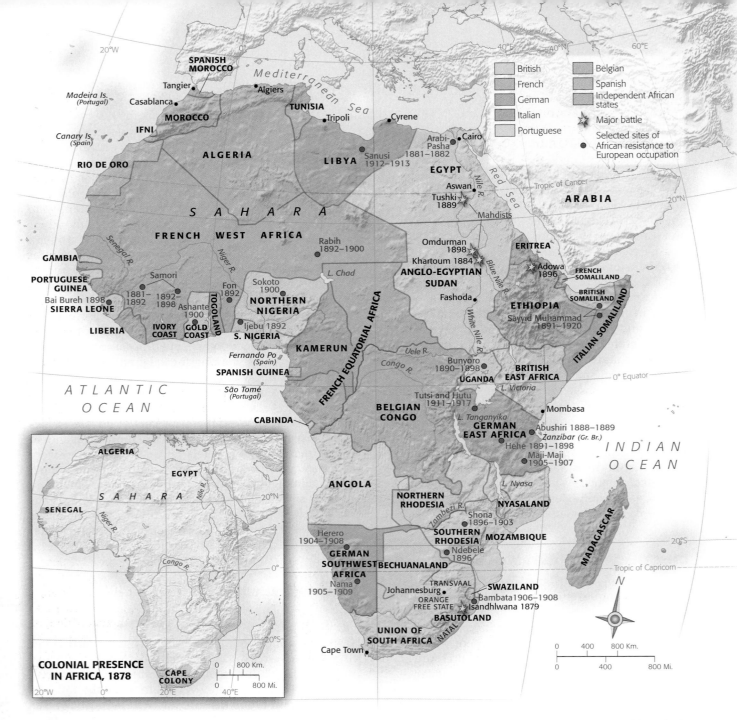

Map 21.1
Africa in 1914

Before 1878, the European powers held only a few coastal territories in Africa, but in that year they turned to expanding their power through colonization. By 1914, the British, French, Belgians, Germans, Italians, Portuguese, and Spanish controlled all of the continent except for Ethiopia and Liberia.

© Cengage Learning

Map labels (main map):

British · French · German · Italian · Portuguese · Belgian · Spanish · Independent African states · Major battle · Selected sites of African resistance to European occupation

SPANISH MOROCCO · Tangier · Algiers · TUNISIA · Tripoli · Cyrene · Mediterranean Sea
Madeira Is. (Portugal) · Casablanca · MOROCCO · IFNI · ALGERIA · LIBYA · Sanusi 1912–1913 · Arabi-Pasha 1881–1882 · Cairo · EGYPT
Canary Is. (Spain) · RIO DE ORO · S A H A R A · Aswan · Tushki 1889 · Mahdists · ARABIA · Tropic of Cancer
FRENCH WEST AFRICA · Rabih 1892–1900 · L. Chad · Omdurman 1898 · ERITREA
GAMBIA · Senegal R. · Niger R. · Samori · Sokoto 1900 · Khartoum 1884 · ANGLO-EGYPTIAN SUDAN · Adowa 1896 · FRENCH SOMALILAND
PORTUGUESE GUINEA · 1881–1892 · 1892–1898 · Fon 1892 · NORTHERN NIGERIA · Fashoda · ETHIOPIA · BRITISH SOMALILAND
Bai Bureh 1898 · SIERRA LEONE · Ashante 1900 · TOGOLAND · Ijebu 1892 · S. NIGERIA · Sayyid Muhammad 1891–1920 · ITALIAN SOMALILAND
LIBERIA · IVORY COAST · GOLD COAST · KAMERUN · Uele R. · Bunyoro 1890–1898
Fernando Po (Spain) · FRENCH EQUATORIAL AFRICA · Congo R. · UGANDA · BRITISH EAST AFRICA
SPANISH GUINEA · São Tomé (Portugal) · Tutsi and Hutu 1911–1917 · L. Victoria · Mombasa
ATLANTIC OCEAN · CABINDA · BELGIAN CONGO · L. Tanganyika · GERMAN EAST AFRICA · Abushiri 1888–1889 · Zanzibar (Gr. Br.) · INDIAN OCEAN
ANGOLA · Hehe 1891–1898 · Maji-Maji 1905–1907 · 0° Equator
NORTHERN RHODESIA · L. Nyasa · NYASALAND · MADAGASCAR
Shona 1896–1903 · MOZAMBIQUE · 20°S
Herero 1904–1908 · Zambezi R. · SOUTHERN RHODESIA · Ndebele 1896 · Tropic of Capricorn
GERMAN SOUTHWEST AFRICA · BECHUANALAND · Johannesburg · TRANSVAAL · SWAZILAND · Bambata 1906–1908
Nama 1905–1909 · ORANGE FREE STATE · Isandhlwana 1879 · BASUTOLAND · NATAL · UNION OF SOUTH AFRICA · Cape Town

Inset map:
COLONIAL PRESENCE IN AFRICA, 1878
ALGERIA · EGYPT · SENEGAL · SAHARA · Niger R. · Nile R. · Congo R. · CAPE COLONY

Finally, after centuries of rivalries and slave wars, Africans could not unite for common defense. Europeans took advantage of the political instability, pitting state against state and ethnic group against ethnic group. For example, the region that became Nigeria had been the home of various independent kingdoms, such as the predominantly animist Yoruba, the Muslim Hausa-Fulani, and village-based stateless societies such as the Igbo. Capitalizing on divisions among them, between 1887 and 1903, the British conquered or otherwise annexed these diverse societies, creating the artificial political unit they called Nigeria, because it occupied both sides of the lower Niger River.

Partition and Resistance

By 1914, European powers had partitioned the entire continent of Africa except for Ethiopia and Liberia. The French empire was concentrated in North, West, and Central Africa and extended across the Sahara from Senegal in the west to Lake Chad in North-Central Africa. The British had four colonies in West Africa, including Nigeria, but they built most of their empire in eastern and southern Africa. The four German colonies were scattered, while Italy concentrated on the Horn region of Northeast Africa, including Somalia and Eritrea, and on Libya in North Africa.

Cecil Rhodes Despite the Berlin Conference, European nations competed fiercely for territories. German colonization of Tanganyika inspired Britain to move into Kenya, Uganda, and Zanzibar, partly to block Germany. In South Africa, the brash British imperialist Cecil Rhodes (1853–1902), a clergyman's son who had made millions in the South African diamond mining industry, wanted to push British power north, outflanking the Portuguese and Germans. Rhodes was largely responsible for extending British influence into the territory he arrogantly named Northern and Southern Rhodesia. British settlers migrated to Southern Rhodesia (today's Zimbabwe) and Kenya, solidifying the British hold on the region.

African Resistance While many Africans had little hope of repulsing the well-armed Europeans, others offered spirited resistance to European conquest and occupation. As a result, it took decades for Europeans to conquer and occupy some territories, such as the western Sudan, where the Mandinka leader Samory Toure resisted for decades. Ethiopia, fortified by high mountains that were difficult to penetrate, was not conquered until the 1930s. In 1896, Emperor Menelik (MEN-uh-lik) II (1844–1914), a reformer, easily defeated an invasion force of 10,000 Italian troops with a French-trained army of 80,000 men.

Read about Samory Toure, the Mandinka king and resistance leader of West Africa.

In the West African region known as the Gold Coast (today's Ghana), the Ashante kingdom offered particularly strong political and military resistance. The Ashante, like many African states, expanded in the early 1800s, clashing with the British, who sought to protect their coastal forts. In 1874, after more British–Ashante conflict over the coastal settlements, the British secured control of the coastal zone but were unable to push very deep into the interior. The British then deliberately fomented a civil war in the remaining Ashante territories to undermine the state, but the Ashante king refused to surrender. In 1896, three thousand well-armed British troops finally occupied the Ashante capital, Kumasi, and exiled the king. However, resistance continued, and the British did not manage to incorporate the Ashante into their Gold Coast colony until 1901.

Sometimes resistance was led by religious leaders. In West Africa, the mystical Sufi brotherhoods sometimes rallied Muslim opposition to the French or British. In Senegal the defiant Wolof people turned to Muslim clerics for leadership, and especially to Amadu Bamba Mbacke (AH-mah-doo BOM-ba um-BACK-ee) (ca. 1853–1927), who had founded a peaceful Sufi order, the *Murids* ("learners seeking God"). Eventually the French realized that they could only rule Senegal with the cooperation of the Murids and reached a compromise: Amadu Bamba acknowledged French administration but was free to expand the Murids, which remain a powerful influence among Senegalese Muslims.

LO² The Making of Settler Societies

While this era saw Europeans advancing in both Asia and Africa, only in Africa did they take over large tracts of land as settlers. The largest settler colony, South Africa, experienced an unusual history: over three centuries of white supremacy introduced by the Dutch colonizers and perpetuated by the British. The first Dutch settlement, Cape Town, was established at the Cape of Good Hope in 1652. Over the next two centuries, Dutch control gradually expanded along the coast and into the interior at the expense of the indigenous Bantu-speaking African peoples, who strongly resisted. European immigrants also settled in British East Africa, the Rhodesias, and the Portuguese colonies. Asian migrants joined them, often as traders.

Europeans and South Africans

From the beginning, South Africa was shaped by conflicts between European settlers and the African peoples whose ancestors had lived in the region for centuries. The Dutch settlers, known as Boers (Dutch for "farmers"), established a system of white supremacy in South Africa based on white rule over non-whites that enforced as much physical separation of the groups as possible. The system became even more rigid among those Boers who boarded wagon trains and migrated east along the coast and into the interior, a journey they called trekking, to find good farming land and to avoid governmental oversight. Trekking led to chronic conflict between the migrating Boers and the Bantu-speaking Xhosa (KHO-sa) people, farmers and pastoralists who already lived in the eastern Cape region. The two groups collided in the late 1700s and fought for nearly half a century. Many thousands died, mostly Xhosa.

The trek became the common way for Boers to flee restraints by any government. In 1806, the British annexed the Cape Colony, giving the Boers even more reason to migrate into the interior. Boers viewed white supremacy as sanctioned by their strict, puritanical Calvinist Christian beliefs, and the slave system also ensured them a cheap labor supply for their farms and ranches. By ending South African slavery, the British harmed the Boer economy. Later, the British granted the right to vote and hold office to Africans and mixed-descent people, known as coloreds, privileges that the Boers considered heresy.

> **Education, Civilization, and "Foreignization" in Buganda** Learn what one African leader thought about the influence of European civilization on the native culture of his people.

Shaka Zulu and Moshoeshoe

In addition to the British, Boers faced conflict with the largest Bantu-speaking South African group, the Zulus. In the early 1800s, some Zulu peo-

> **From the beginning, South Africa was shaped by conflicts between European settlers and the African peoples whose ancestors had lived in the region for centuries.**

ples began a military expansion under an ambitious military genius, Shaka (ca. 1787–1828), whose exploits in war allowed him to become a powerful chief. Planning to gain dominance over the whole region, he united various Zulu clans in Natal (nuh-TALL), the region along South Africa's Indian Ocean coast, into a powerful nation, raising a disciplined army of some 40,000 warriors and developing effective new military tactics. In 1816, he began invading other groups' territories, and the resulting wars killed thousands of Africans, both Zulus and non-Zulus, and wreaked widespread disruption. Eventually Shaka grew more despotic and was assassinated by his brother as the Zulu empire fell. Ironically, by depopulating large areas of the mineral-rich interior plateau, Shaka's wars made it easier for the Boers to move in later.

Some leaders of Bantu-speaking groups found effective ways to avoid conquest by the Zulus and Boers. Perhaps the most successful was Moshoeshoe (MOE-shoo-shoo) (b. ca. 1786), who created a kingdom for his branch of the Sotho (SOO-too) people. With the region in turmoil from warfare because of the Zulu and Boer expansion, Moshoeshoe moved his people to an easily defended flat-top mountain in 1824. There he strengthened his community by taking in African refugees regardless of their ethnic origin and integrating them into his people. The king emphasized not only military defense but also diplomacy, skillfully cultivating friendship with the British as a counterweight to the Boers. While neighboring Africans fell under Boer rule, British support for Moshoeshoe allowed his Sotho kingdom to remain independent until 1871.

 History and Cultures of Africa (http://www.columbia.edu/cu/lweb/indiv/africa/cuvl/cult.html). Provides valuable links to relevant websites on African history.

British–Boer Conflict and White Supremacy

In the decades after British annexation of the Cape, conflict between the Boers and the British intensified, eventually leading to a system of white supremacy in South Africa. In 1838, about one-fifth of all the Boers, alienated by British policies in the Cape Colony, began what they called the Great Trek, boarding their wagons and, with their sheep and cattle, heading in well-armed caravans of several hundred families north into the interior. After many hardships, including fighting with Zulus, they moved into the high plateau of what is now northern South Africa and created two independent Boer republics, Transvaal (TRANS-vahl) and the Orange Free State. Although the Bantu peoples battled the Boers for decades, they were conquered and forced to work on Boer farms. As the Boers consolidated control, their ideas of keeping themselves separate from Africans grew stronger. The evolving Boer ideology considered black Africans an "inferior race" hostile to European values. Devaluing Africans and despising the British, the Boers committed themselves to maintaining their identity and culture whatever the cost.

> "The evolving Boer ideology considered black Africans an 'inferior race' hostile to European values."

The Boer War

However, the discovery in the Boer republics of diamonds in 1867 and gold in the 1880s spurred the British to seek control over Boer territories, and their attempts to annex the Boer republics led to the South African War (1899–1902), often called the Boer War. The war culminated in British victory but also created chronic Boer resentment of the British. During the war, the Boers employed guerrilla tactics, acting as civilians by day and raiding British targets at night. To eradicate local support for the Boer commandos, the British burned Boer farms, destroyed towns, and interned thousands of Boers, including women and children, in concentration camps, where 26,000 died of disease and starvation. These brutalities discredited the war in Britain. Moreover, the British relied on African troops for victory, and thousands of Africans died fighting the Boers in hopes that the British would be less oppressive. But, when the war ended, Africans found they had merely exchanged one set of white masters for another.

Creating South African Society

After the Boer War, British and Boer leaders worked out a compromise in which the South African government became essentially a collaboration between the two groups, restoring Boer rights and strengthening white supremacy policies. To win Boer cooperation, the British extended discriminatory Boer laws; Africans were valued chiefly as cheap unskilled labor for the white-owned economy. Britain's racist policies became a constant source of humiliation and tension for Africans, and continued resistance gradually led the British to build a police state. Furthermore, despite the political compromises they had made, British–Boer tensions simmered as thousands of British settlers arrived, eventually becoming one-third of the white population. Asserting their long-established position in the country, the Boers began to style themselves Afrikaners (people of Africa) and their Dutch-derived language Afrikaans.

Three Peoples Interact

Domination by the Boers and the British reshaped South African life and culture in the later 1800s and early 1900s. Africans were recruited into the white-owned economy and often became Christian. Thousands of Africans moved to cities, especially the Transvaal mining center of Johannesburg, thus becoming removed from their farming villages and transformed into salaried workers. They experienced dreadful work conditions on white-owned factories, farms, and particularly in the mines, where hundreds of miners died each year. The Zulu poet B. W. Vilakezi described the miner's life in the early 1900s: "Roar, without rest, machines of the mines, Roar from dawn till darkness falls. To black men groaning as they labor, Tortured by their aching muscles, Gasping in the fetid air."[5]

> 66 Africans often resisted Western domination by adapting their cultural forms to changing conditions. 99

Africans often resisted Western domination by adapting their cultural forms to changing conditions. For example, Zulu warriors reworked dance tunes and turned them into songs to protest white military incursion. The Sotho people gradually transformed their tradition of poetry praising influential people and ancestors into songs expressing the fears and experiences of male migrants working in the mines and the women left behind in the villages. Educated urban Africans, who formed a middle class of professionals and traders, also found ways to oppose

The Great Trek Many Boers migrated into the South African interior in wagon trains. These migrants, known as Trekkers, endured hardships but also eventually subjugated the local African peoples, taking their land for farming, pasturing, and mining.

WAGGON ASCENDING THE UNCOMMOSS HILL, NATAL.

Mansell/Time & Life Pictures/Getty Images

white supremacy. One of these, the Johannesburg lawyer Pixley ka Isaka Seme, a graduate of Columbia University in New York, helped found the African National Congress in 1912 to promote African rights and spur Africa's cultural regeneration. Some Bantu composers creatively mixed Christian hymns with traditional Xhosa or Zulu choral music. The African National Congress adopted one such hymn, "God Bless Africa," as their official anthem of hope.

Like South Africa, several other colonies restricted African civil and economic rights, particularly Portuguese-ruled Angola and British-ruled Kenya and Southern Rhodesia. These colonial governments reserved for immigrant white farmers not only the best land, such as the fertile Kenyan highlands that were once dominated by the Gikuyu people, but also the most lucrative crops, such as coffee. African farmers also faced barriers in obtaining bank loans to compete with white farmers and were unable to gain any political power. Laws limited contact between whites and Africans except as employers and hired workers.

Asian minorities also became part of colonial societies. Beginning in the 1890s, Indians arrived to build railroads, work on sugar plantations, or become middle-level retail traders. Indians became the commercial middle class of East Africa and occupied a key economic niche in South Africa, the Rhodesias, Mozambique, and Madagascar. Cities such as Nairobi in Kenya, Kampala in Uganda, and Durban in South Africa had substantial Indian populations, and their downtowns were dominated by Indian stores, restaurants, and Hindu temples. In West and Central Africa, Lebanese occupied the middle levels of the economy as shopkeepers in cities and towns. Many black Africans resented the growing influence and wealth of the Asian immigrants, a sentiment that the British exploited to their own advantage.

LO³ The Colonial Reshaping of Sub-Saharan Africa

The experience of living under Western colonial domination from the 1880s to the 1960s reshaped sub-Saharan Africans' politics, society, culture, and economy. Colonialism created artificial states and transformed Africans into subject peoples who enjoyed few political rights. It also allowed Western business interests to penetrate the continent and integrate Africa into the global system as a supplier of valuable raw materials.

Colonial Governments

The colonial policies devised in European cities introduced new kinds of governments in Africa, as each colonizing power sought the best way to achieve maximum control at minimum expense. Two broad types of administration emerged: direct rule and indirect rule. Under direct rule, the administration was largely European, even down to the local level, and chiefs or kings were reduced to symbolic roles. Under indirect rule, the Europeans gave the traditional leaders of a district, the kings or chiefs, considerable local power but kept them subject to colonial officials. In general, indirect rule, which left much of the original society intact, caused less disruption than direct rule, but African leaders were required to consult with the local European adviser on many matters. The advisers enforced colonial law and order, collected taxes, and supervised public works. Because Europeans lacked enough officials to administer a large colony such as Nigeria or Tanganyika, this form of rule was inspired by pragmatism, but it weakened village democracy and did not benefit African societies.

Nigeria, an unwieldy colony that contained some 250 distinct African ethnic groups, provided an example of both kinds of administration. Indirect rule was taken to its fullest extent in largely Muslim northern Nigeria, leaving the traditional Hausa-Fulani courts and social structure largely undisturbed. By contrast, the British governed southern Nigeria chiefly through direct rule, with the result that greater change occurred in the south, including the introduction of Christian missions and cash crop farming. Peoples such as the Igbo and Yoruba successfully adapted to these changes that transformed their regions. The Yoruba successfully blended aspects of their indigenous culture, such as a rich artistic tradition and polytheism, with imported cultural traditions, such as English literature and Christianity, maintaining a high degree of tolerance for divergent views and rejecting helplessness.

> "The colonial policies devised in European cities introduced new kinds of governments in Africa, as each colonizing power sought the best way to achieve maximum control at minimum expense."

> 66 To maintain their privileged position, Europeans also imposed a color bar that kept Africans out of clubs, schools, and jobs reserved for Europeans. 99

Although supporters of colonialism defended Western rule as providing "a school for democracy," the rationale clearly differed from reality. By 1945, fewer than 1 percent of Africans enjoyed political rights or access to democratic institutions. Meanwhile, traditional African leaders enforced European policies if they wanted to keep their positions. Africans often viewed these privileged and wealthy leaders as little better than paid agents of colonialism.

Disrupting African Societies

The boundaries that European colonizers drew up to partition Africa into colonies created artificial countries that often ignored traditional ethnic relationships. Modern countries such as Nigeria, Ghana (the former Gold Coast), Congo, and Mozambique were colonial creations, not nations built on shared culture and identity. Colonizers ignored the interests of local people, sometimes dividing ethnic groups between two or more colonial systems. For example, the Kongolese, once masters of a major African kingdom, were split between Portuguese Angola and the Belgian and French Congos. At the same time, rival societies were sometimes joined, creating a basis for political instability later.

Ethnicity and Ethnocentrism

To maintain their privileged position, Europeans also imposed a color bar that kept Africans out of

direct rule
A method of ruling colonies whereby a largely European colonial administration supervised all activity, even down to the local level, and native chiefs or kings were reduced to symbolic roles

indirect rule
A method of ruling colonies whereby districts were administered by traditional (native) leaders, who had considerable local power but were subject to European officials

clubs, schools, and jobs reserved for Europeans. Europeans typically considered Africans unfit to rule themselves and badly in need of Western leadership. An ethnocentric British scholar argued in 1920 that "the chief distinction between the backward and forward peoples is that the former are of colored skin."[6] Such views ignored several thousand years of African governments, ranging from centralized kingdoms to village democracies, as well as participation in Eastern Hemisphere trade networks from ancient times. Racist ideology spawned the French and Belgian idea of the "civilizing mission," which viewed Africans as children who could attain adulthood only by adopting French language, religion, and culture.

The colonizers often misunderstood African societies and ethnic complexities. The British tended to identify people of similar culture and language as "tribes," such as the Yoruba of Nigeria and Gikuyu of Kenya, even though these peoples were actually collections of subgroups without much historical unity. Despite loose cultural homogeneity, the Yoruba were traditionally divided into several competing states, each with its own king, while the Gikuyu had few political structures higher than the village. In reality, African peoples such as the Yoruba, Gikuyu, Igbo, Xhosa, and Mandinka were ethnic groups, not unlike the politically divided inhabitants of early modern Europe.

Christianity in Africa

Christian missionaries also reshaped African culture and religious life. Christian missions established most of Africa's modern hospitals and schools, institutions that helped Africans but also reflected Western views. Mission doctors practiced Western medicine and denounced African folk medicine. Mission schools taught new agricultural methods, simple mathematics, reading, writing, and Western languages, thus giving a small group of educated Africans the skills they could use in the colonial economy and administration. Critics complained that the mission schools, as an Igbo writer put it, "miseducated" and "de-Africanized" them, perpetuating their status as "hewers of wood and haulers of water"[7] who were unable to challenge their subservience to Europeans. Furthermore, the Africans who attended mission schools and adopted Western ways often became divorced from their traditional African communities.

> "The transformation of African economic life was at least as significant as the political reorganization."

Yet modern education reached only a small minority of Africans. Before 1945, only 5 percent of children attended any government or mission school. The schools typically produced clerks in governments and businesses or cash crop farmers, although a few graduates became teachers, doctors, lawyers, and journalists. The first modern African college was established in Sierra Leone in 1827. But before 1940, the few Africans who could attend a university had to do so usually in Europe or the United States.

Millions of Africans did adopt Christianity, but its impact varied widely. Some Africans became devout Catholics or Protestants, while others only partially embraced Christianity, adopting those beliefs they liked, such as biblical calls for justice and equality, while rejecting others. Some African churches combined Christian doctrines with African practices and beliefs. Hence, in 1901 some Nigerians left the Anglican Church to form their own church, which condoned men having more than one wife. Yorubas, tolerant of diverse religious beliefs, often just added the Christian and Muslim gods to their polytheistic pantheon. Chrstianity also impacted women's lives, reducing women's traditional religious roles and promoting monogamy. Christian leaders sometimes asked men to give up multiple wives, leaving these women without support. Yet, women often welcomed monogamy and favored Christian social values, such as education for girls.

Africans in the World Economy

The transformation of African economic life was at least as significant as the political reorganization. Extracting wealth from a colony required tying its economy more closely to that of the colonizer. Colonial governments imposed economic policies to transform Africans into producers for the world market, hence rejecting the subsistence agriculture that, while having sustained Africans for centuries, now could not produce enough revenues for the government or investors. Requiring taxes to be paid in cash promoted a shift from food cultivation to growing cash crops such as cotton, cocoa, rubber, and palm oil or mining copper, gold, oil, chrome, cobalt, and diamonds. Authorities sometimes resorted to forced labor, most notoriously in the Belgian Congo, where more than half of the Congo's population died from overwork or brutality over a twenty-year period. An American missionary reported in 1895 that the Belgian policies "reduced the people to a state of utter despair. Each town is forced to bring a certain quality [of rubber]. The soldiers drive the people into the bush. If they will not go they are shot down, and their left hands cut off. The soldiers often shoot poor helpless women and harmless children."[8]

Through such measures as these, colonial Africa became linked to the West and the world economy, but often this global economy left Africans vulnerable. Western businesses and planters exercised considerable political influence, while African livelihoods became subject to the fluctuations of global commodities. Colonies also became markets for Western industrial products, displacing village handicrafts, and many Africans lost their economic self-sufficiency. With the growth of an automobile culture in the West, an oil-drilling industry also emerged along the West African coast from southern Nigeria to northern Angola, making these societies dependent on oil exports. Colonies often became economic monocultures dependent on the export of one or two major commodities, such as copper from Northern Rhodesia (now Zambia), cocoa from the Gold Coast, peanuts from Senegal, and cotton from Sudan. Many colonial policies made it difficult for Africans to diversify their economies.

Defining Gender Roles in Colonial Africa

The opportunities and demands of the colonial economy touched nearly everyone in some way, profoundly affecting the lives of both men and women. As men were frequently recruited or forced to migrate to other districts or colonies for mining or industrial labor, a permanent pattern of labor migration became established. This migration disrupted family and village life, helping to further destabilize African society. The male migrants often lived in crowded dormitories or huts that offered little privacy, enjoyed few amenities other than drinking beer in makeshift bars, and were able to visit their families back home for only a few days per year.

African women faced a different combination of hardship and opportunities. In many African societies, women had long enjoyed considerable autonomy, playing a major role as traders and farmers. Now, however, as men migrated for work or took up cash crop farming, women were left with all food production, which was less lucrative than the men's work. The Baule women of Ivory Coast, who had long profited from growing cotton and spinning it into

Punch Cartoon Library & Archive

IN THE RUBBER COILS.
Scene—*The Congo "Free" State.*

Rubber Coils in Belgian Congo The Belgians colonized the Congo hoping to exploit its resources. This critical cartoon, published in the British satirical magazine *Punch* in 1906, shows a Congolese ensnared in the rubber coils of the Belgian king Leopold in the guise of a serpent. Rubber was the major cash crop, introduced by the Belgians to generate profits.

thread, lost their position to Baule men when cotton became a cash crop and textiles an export item. Many women traders who had dominated town markets now faced competition from Indians or Lebanese. But thanks to education, self-help, and ambition, some African women gained skills to support themselves as teachers, nurses, and merchants, but many poor women were overwhelmed by the challenges of trying to preserve their families while fulfilling new responsibilities.

African Resistance and the Colonial Legacy

Africans responded to colonialism in various ways. The Igbos of Nigeria capitalized on change by taking up lucrative cash crop farming or using education to forge careers as professionals or clerks. Other Africans dealt with change by enriching traditional ways. The imaginative Yoruba artist Olowe of Ise (oh-LO-way of ee-SAY) (ca. 1875–1938) emphasized Yoruba themes and ideals in the woodcarvings, elaborately carved doors, and other objects he sculpted for Yoruba kings. Some Africans negotiated change by mixing Western and African ideas, such as the Black Zion movement in South Africa, which maintained that Jesus was African, while also promoting African traditions such as faith healing.

Many Africans, however, chose noncooperation. Tax evasion and other forms of passive protest were rampant, especially in rural areas, while other Africans chose a more activist strategy and formed labor unions. Although unions were usually illegal in colonial systems that protected Western-owned businesses, strikes were common, especially among mine workers, who protested unsafe working conditions or long hours and were often imprisoned for their activism.

Sometimes distress and anger led to more drastic resistance as rebellions punctuated colonial rule. The Maji Maji Rebellion, for example, broke out in German-ruled Tanganyika in 1905 and was suppressed only after a bitter two-year struggle. The disenchanted Maji Maji peasants preferred to be subsistence farmers and grow their own food rather than be exploited commercial farm workers. These feelings led to a rebellion involving thousands. The rebels occupied some towns and sprinkled their bodies with magic water in hopes it would make them immune from bullets, but the Germans, using machine guns against rebels armed only with spears, soon regained the towns. Finally in 1907, the Maji Maji were defeated, at the cost of 26,000 African lives; however, the resistance caused the Germans to end forced labor.

Whether colonialism stimulated modern development or retarded it is one of the central questions of modern African history. Some historians contend that colonialism increased the productive capacity of the land, built cities and transportation networks, brought advances in technology, stimulated Africans to produce more wealth than they ever had before, and created rich opportunities for beneficial trade with the outside world. Other historians, however, point out that colonial rulers stole land, exploited labor, gained profitable access to raw materials, shifted profits back to Europe, limited Africa's eco-nomic growth, and created artificial, unstable countries. Although economic growth occurred, colonial Africa enjoyed little development or balanced growth that benefited the majority of the people. The profits from plantations and mines supported European industrialization and enriched European businesses, leaving sub-Saharan Africa the most impoverished region of the world at the end of the colonial era.

LO⁴ Imperialism, Reform, and the Middle Eastern Societies

Between 1750 and 1914, most Muslim societies suffered repeated challenges from the growing power of western Europe and Russia, even the Ottoman Empire, which fell behind the industrializing West. Expanding European empires ate at the fringes of Persia and the shrinking Ottoman domain, and European economic penetration and cultural influences reshaped Middle Eastern life. The response of Muslims to these changes differed from society to society.

> 66 Perceiving Ottoman decline, the major European powers schemed to outflank each other while building up their influence in the weakening empire. 99

Challenges to the Ottoman Empire

For one thousand years, Islamic influence had spread throughout much of Afro-Eurasia. Muslims dominated the trade routes until the Early Modern Era, and large Islamic states stretched from Morocco to Indonesia. The Ottoman Turks forged a huge empire in southeastern Europe and western Asia, as well as gaining a strong influence across North Africa, while Safavid Persia and Mughal India also exercised regional power. But the rising influence of western Europeans posed a threat to the Islamic states. By 1750, as a result of both Western pressure and internal problems, the Ottoman power had diminished, the Safavids had fallen, the Mughals had lost most of India, and the Dutch ruled much of Indonesia. After 1750, the Islamic world faced new dangers.

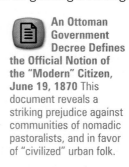 **An Ottoman Government Decree Defines the Official Notion of the "Modern" Citizen, June 19, 1870** This document reveals a striking prejudice against communities of nomadic pastoralists, and in favor of "civilized" urban folk.

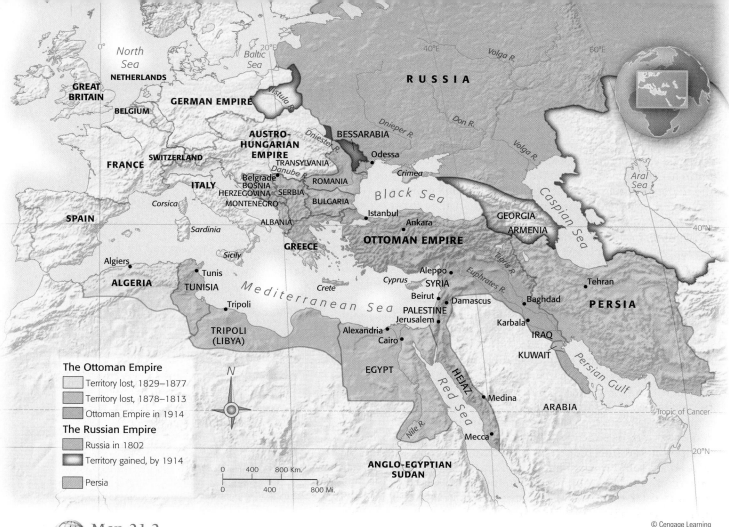

Map 21.2
The Ottoman Empire and Persia, 1914

© Cengage Learning

The Ottoman Empire once included much of southeastern Europe, western Asia, and North Africa. By 1914, it was restricted largely to parts of western Asia.

In the nineteenth century, rising pressure from European nations, especially Russia, undermined the Ottoman Empire and its more than 60 million people (see Map 21.2). Since the 1500s, the Russians had been slowly expanding south toward the Black Sea, and in 1768 they defeated Ottoman forces and gained control over part of the northern Black Sea coast. Between 1792 and 1829, they extended this control to include the Crimean peninsula and the largely Christian Caucasus state of Georgia. In 1853, Czar Nicholas I characterized the weakening Ottoman Empire as "the sick man of Europe," a reputation that would stick.

Interactive Map

Perceiving Ottoman decline, the major European powers schemed to outflank each other while building up their influence in the weakening empire. With European support, the Greeks, Serbs, Romanians, and Bulgarians rebelled and threw off Ottoman power in the 1800s. The Greek revolt, which enjoyed support from Britain, France, and Russia, revealed Ottoman weaknesses (see Chapter 19). A combined Ottoman-Egyptian force had nearly defeated the Greeks when an Anglo-French fleet and the Russian army intervened, shifting the military balance. The 1829 treaty that ended the war recognized Greek independence and gave autonomy to the Ottoman territories of Serbia and Moldavia.

Along with military setbacks, the Ottoman state also had more difficulty satisfying the desires of the empire's multiethnic population. The Turks had long benefited from the empire's ethnic diversity, using the varied peoples to enrich their state. Non-Muslim minorities played major roles in Ottoman commerce, the professions, and government. Moreover, the Ottomans had generally been tolerant of ethnic and religious minorities such as Kurds (mostly Sunni Muslims), Jews, and Arab Christians. To respect minority cultures and keep them from combining politically, the Ottomans allowed each group to basically rule itself through its own religious establishment, such as the Greek Orthodox Church. Christians and Jews felt particularly secure in the major Ottoman cities; Jews in much of the empire enjoyed more security and prosperity than they did in Europe. Multiethnic Istanbul was described in 1873 as "a city not of one nation but of many. Eight or nine languages are constantly spoken in the streets and five or six appear on the shop fronts."[9]

Armenian Nationalism

Despite the accommodation to ethnic diversity, some ethnic minorities became restless. Deteriorating Turkish relations with the Christian Armenians in eastern Turkey and the Caucasus led to a conflict between the two groups. Armenians had generally remained loyal Ottoman subjects, and some held high positions in the government. But during the 1800s, nationalist and socialist ideas percolating in Europe filtered into the Armenian communities and influenced some Armenians to want their own state. Acting on these nationalistic feelings, Armenians founded their own schools, libraries, hospitals, and presses and looked to Europe and North America for financial and moral support, while some extremists made terrorist attacks on Ottoman targets. The conflict intensified, with deadly consequences for the Armenians. In the 1890s and early 1900s, the Ottoman government responded to increasing Armenian assertiveness by seizing Armenian property, killing more than 100,000 Armenians, and exiling thousands more. Many Armenians moved to North America to escape the persecution, but those who remained continued to suffer.

Ottoman Reform and Modernization

Growing internal problems and military setbacks spurred Ottoman efforts to reform and modernize in order to match Western power. To survive, Ottoman sultans tried hard to build a modern, more secular, and more centralized government. However, various groups, including the Islamic religious leaders, the privileged military force known as Janissaries, local officials in Anatolia, and governors of distant Arab provinces benefited from weak central authority, so the process of centralization proved a challenge.

CHRONOLOGY

The Middle East, 1750–1914

1792–1812	Russian control of northern Black Sea lands
1794–1925	Qajar dynasty in Persia
1798–1799	French occupation of Egypt
1805–1848	Rule of Muhammad Ali in Egypt
1829	Greek independence from Ottoman Empire
1840	French colonization of Algeria
1859–1869	Building of Suez Canal
1882	British colonization of Egypt
1890s–1915	Turkish genocide against Armenians
1897	First Zionist conference
1899	British protectorate over Kuwait
1905–1911	Constitutional revolution in Persia
1907–1921	Russian and British spheres of influence in Persia
1908	Young Turk government in Ottoman Turkey
1908	Discovery of oil in Persia
1911–1912	Colonization of Libya and Morocco

Gradually, the system changed as Ottoman leaders and thinkers recognized the need to obtain knowledge and aid from the Christian West. One of the first reformist sultans, Mahmud II (MACH-mood) (r. 1808–1839), asserted central authority over local leaders. Mahmud slowly built a modern state and an army trained by Prussian officers. His successors set up new schools that taught European learning and languages, and by 1900 the University of Istanbul had become the Muslim world's first modern institution of higher education. The Ottomans also replaced many older Islam-based laws with laws based on French codes and increasingly marginalized Islam, demoralizing conservatives.

The growth of a more centralized government and a modern, secular Ottoman nationality continued through the 1800s, aided by the introduction of railroads and telegraphs. To foster a national identity, in 1846 Ottoman rulers declared all citizens equal before the law, announcing that "the differences of religion and sect among the subjects is something not affecting their rights of citizenship. It is wrong to make discriminations among us."[10] In the 1880s, a modernizing group known as the Young Turks emerged in the military and the universities. Their goal was to make Turkey a modern nation with a liberal constitution, and by 1908, when the Young Turks led a military coup that deposed the old sultan, Islam had faded as a political influence. The Young Turks espoused Turkish nationalism and sought to unite all Turkish peoples in western and central Asia, but under the facade of parliamentary government, they ruled as autocrats and military modernizers. During World War I, as an ally of Germany and Austria-Hungary, the Young Turks embraced a Turkish ethnic identity, secularization, and closer ties to the Western world at the expense of Islamic connections. After their defeat in World War I, the Ottoman Empire was dissolved and largely fell under British or French rule.

Egypt: Modernization and Occupation

The most extensive effort to deflect Western pressure through modernization came in Egypt, but only after Ottoman influence waned. The Ottomans, who occupied Egypt in 1517, had governed the province through the Mamluks, a Muslim caste of Turkish origin whose misrule gave French general Napoleon Bonaparte an excuse to invade the country by the later 1700s. While claiming to liberate the Egyptians, Bonaparte hoped to exploit Egypt's agriculture to provide grain for France. When Bonaparte abandoned his Egyptian adventure in 1801, Egypt came under the rule of Muhammad Ali (r. 1805–1848), a Turkish-speaking Albanian who had led the Ottoman forces that helped eject the French.

Muhammad Ali

After being appointed viceroy by the Ottoman sultan, Muhammad Ali moved to centralize his power in what was effectively now an independent country. However, European

> "However, while Muhammad Ali's programs added to Egypt's power and wealth, they did not ultimately protect Egyptian independence and foster development."

Young Turks
A modernizing group in Ottoman Turkey that promoted a national identity and that gained power in the early twentieth century.

powers, who feared his ambitions, required him to officially remain loosely bound to the weakening Ottoman state. The charming sultan impressed Europeans with his talents: "If ever a man had an eye that denoted genius, [he] was the person. Never dead nor quiescent, it was fascinating like that of a gazelle; or, in the hour of storm, fierce as an eagle's."[11]

Muhammad Ali introduced ambitious reforms to transform Egypt into a European-style state with an effective army. He increased trade and moved to foster an industrial revolution by using government revenues from increased agricultural exports to establish factories, foundries, and shipyards. The Egyptian leader established a western-style military and arms industry. He also replaced Islamic with French legal codes, sent Egyptians to study technical subjects in Europe, encouraged the establishment of the first Arab newspapers, and laid the foundation for a Western-influenced state educational system. These changes have led historians to credit Muhammad Ali with founding Egypt as a modern nation-state.

However, while Muhammad Ali's programs added to Egypt's power and wealth, they did not ultimately protect Egyptian independence and foster development. Because Egypt had to import iron and coal, industrialization proved a challenge, and the Egyptian economy became more shackled to European finance. In 1838 the British obtained free trade within Ottoman domains. The resulting influx of cheap British commodities stifled Egypt's textile industry and its cottage handicraft manufacturing. Although the Egyptian cotton industry was stimulated in the 1860s by the American Civil War, which cut exports from the United States to Europe, Europeans were more interested in procuring Egyptian raw cotton for processing in their own mills than they were in buying finished textiles.

The British Seize Europe

Following the European model, Muhammad Ali turned then to seeking resources and markets through the conquest of neighboring societies. Egyptian armies moved south into Nubia and the

Muhammad Ali Meets European Representatives Muhammad Ali, the Egyptian sultan who tried to modernize his state, cultivated ties with Western nations. This painting shows the sultan in 1839 meeting with representatives from several European governments.

eastern Sudanic lands along the Nile River, which they made into an Egyptian colony, and also into the Ottoman territories of Arabia, Palestine, Syria, and Greece. But a northern thrust alarmed the European powers, inspiring them to destroy Egypt as a rival in the region and to gain control of the Suez Canal, which was built as a French–Egyptian collaboration between 1859 and 1869. The 100-mile-long canal—a magnificent technological achievement whose construction had cost the lives of thousands of Egyptian workers—linked the Mediterranean and Red Seas, greatly decreasing the shipping time between Europe and Asia. In 1875, Britain gained control of the canal when Muhammad Ali's grandson, the sultan Ismail, was forced by his country's skyrocketing national debt to sell Egypt's large share in canal ownership.

Eventually, to preempt the ambitions of other European powers, the British decided to seize Egypt using military force. By the 1870s, Egypt was bankrupt and deeply in debt to European financiers and

governments. In addition, some in the country's political and commercial elite, including many Coptic Christians, were oriented toward Western ideas and welcomed the British. But most Egyptians, being chiefly influenced by conservative Islamic ideas and leaders, opposed the growing Western influence. In 1882, increasing local unrest and threats to European residents provided an excuse for the British to bombard Egypt's major port, Alexandria, and then invade the country. Thus, several decades after Muhammad Ali's death, Egypt became part of Britain's growing worldwide empire.

The Mahdi Uprising Soon after gaining control of Egypt, the British had to deal with a challenge coming from the Sudanic region straddling the Nile River to Egypt's south (today the nation of Sudan). In 1881, a militant Arab Muslim in the Sudan, Muhammad Ahmad (1846–1885), the son of a shipbuilder, declared that he was the Mahdi (MAH-dee) ("the Guided One") and pledged to restore Islam's purity and destroy the Egyptian-imposed government, which he accused of corruption, lax morality, and subservience to European advisers. He recruited an army that defeated the Egyptian forces and their British officers, after which he formed an Islamic state. However, in 1898, British and Egyptian forces defeated the Mahdists and formed a new state known as the Anglo-Egyptian Sudan, which was effectively a British colony.

Persia: Challenges and Reforms

Persia, increasingly known as Iran, had long played a central role in the Islamic world, but in the 1700s, it faced new problems under the Qajars (KAH-jars), who took control after the Safavid collapse earlier in the century. The Qajars ruled an impoverished country that had suffered from years of civil war and anarchy, and early Qajar rulers were unable to resolve most of Persia's problems, instead becoming noted for greed, corruption, and lavish living. The majority of Persia's people, including the Qajar rulers, were Shi'ites, but the population also included Christian Armenians, Jews, Zoroastrians, and Sunni Kurds, all of whom sought to increase their autonomy. Shi'ite clerics, however, enjoyed great influence and wealth. Independent of any government, the top Shi'ite clerics engaged in power struggles with the Qajar shahs, arguing that a virtuous and learned Shi'ite scholar should rule Persia and that few Qajar rulers fit that description. Meanwhile, Shi'ites persecuted as heretical the Bahai (buh-HI) religion. Founded in 1867 by the Persian Bahaullah (bah-hah-oo-LAH) (1817–1892) as an offshoot of Persian Shi'ism, Bahai called for universal peace, the unity of all religions, and service to others. Shi'ites killed many Bahais and forced their leaders into exile.

Persia and the West

Persia also faced continuous pressure from Russia and Britain. By the 1870s, Russia had gained territory on both sides of the Caspian Sea, and British power steadily grew in the Persian Gulf and along Arabia's Indian Ocean coast. British entrepreneurs controlled a monopoly on Persian railroad construction, banking, and oil. The Anglo-Iranian Oil Company (later British Petroleum), which struck oil in 1908, became Persia's dominant economic enterprise, but profits went chiefly to Britain. Persians disliked the powerful British economic role, which they considered a humiliation.

> **Bahai**
> An offshoot of Persian Shi'ism that was founded in 1867; Bahai preached universal peace, the unity of all religions, and service to others.

The weakness of the central government, combined with foreign pressure, led to political reforms. Some Qajar shahs provided an opening for change when they attempted to restore central government power. In the later 1800s, they rebuilt an army, set up a Western-style college, introduced a telegraph system, and gave Christian missionaries the right to establish schools and hospitals. However, these reforms threatened the conservative Shi'ite clergy, who hoped to thwart modernization.

> 66 From 1905 to 1911, Persia enjoyed a constitutional revolution that fostered a brief period of democracy. 99

From 1905 to 1911, Persia enjoyed a constitutional revolution that fostered a brief period of democracy. The more liberal Shi'ite clergy, allied with merchants in the capital, Tehran, Armenians, and Western-educated radicals, imposed a democratic constitution that sought to curb royal power by setting up a parliament elected by several major groups and granting freedom of the press. Soon more than four hundred newspapers were published. When a conservative, pro-Russian shah took power in 1907 and attempted to weaken the parliament, liberal newspapers, writers, and musicians lampooned him and his allies.

The progressive direction did not last, however. Britain and Russia formed an alliance and increased pressure on Persia to grant them more influence, straining the progressive leadership. As a result, the constitutionalist forces soon split into pro-Western nationalists seeking separation of religious and civil power, land reform, and universal education, and Shi'ite clerics and nobles who had become alarmed at the secular direction. As violence increased in 1911, the conservative royal government closed down the parliament and ended the democratic experiment. By then, however, Britain and Russia, stationing troops in southern and northern Persia, respectively, had reduced Persia's political and economic independence.

Ottoman Outposts

Declining Ottoman power and growing Western activity eventually had an impact on the Arab provinces of the eastern Ottoman Empire, especially Syria and Lebanon. Despite their diverse ethnic and religious mosaic, which included Arab and Armenian Christians, Sunni and Shi'ite Arabs, and Sunni Kurds, the peoples of these two adjacent territories had mostly lived in autonomous peace under Ottoman rule. A British writer commented on the generally stable conditions and social harmony in the late 1700s, writing that in Lebanon "every man lives in a perfect security of life and property. The peasant is not richer than in other countries, but he is free."[12]

Modernization in Lebanon, Syria, Iraq, and Kuwait

However, in the 1850s, poverty and a stagnant economy began to foster occasional conflicts in Syria and Lebanon, and as a result the densely populated region around Mount Lebanon came under the influence of several Western powers. For example, the French developed a special relationship with the Maronites (MAR-uh-nites), Arab Christians who sought a closer connection with the Roman Catholic Church, and American Protestant missionaries established a college in the main Lebanese city, Beirut, in 1866 that spread modern ideas. By the later 1800s, the weak economy had also encouraged emigration from Syria and Lebanon, especially Lebanese Christians, who often left as families for the United States. By 1914, perhaps 350,000 Arabs from Syria and Lebanon had emigrated to the Americas.

Change also came to Iraq, the heart of ancient Mesopotamia, which lacked political unity and had not prospered under Ottoman rule. The Ottomans divided Iraq into three provinces: (1) a largely Sunni Arab and Kurdish north, (2) a chiefly Sunni Arab center, and (3) a Shi'ite Arab–dominated south. Iraqis suffered from major floods and repeated epidemics of plague and cholera. A British official described Iraq as "a country of extremes, either dying of thirst or of being drowned."[13] Iraq also lacked order, foreign capital, and a transportation system such as railroads or steamships on the rivers, and the literacy rate remained extremely low.

Although the challenges were daunting, Western interest in this Ottoman backwater grew. European travelers were unanimous that Iraq had great economic potential: navigable rivers, fertile land, a strategic location, access to the Persian Gulf, and minerals. To gain a foothold in the region, in 1899 the British established a protectorate over the small neighboring kingdom of Kuwait (koo-WAIT) at the west end of the Persian Gulf. In the early 1900s, the Ottomans and foreign investors poured money into Iraq as they came to believe that it might have considerable oil; however, World War I temporarily halted such efforts.

The French in Northwest Africa

Northwest Africa also experienced European colonization. The Arabic-speaking societies along Africa's Mediterranean coast from Libya to Algeria had never been under firm Ottoman control, and their proximity to Europe made them natural targets for colonization. In 1840 the French embarked on full-scale colonization of Algeria, in part to divert the French public from an unpopular home government. Abd al-Qadir (AB dul-KA-deer), an energetic Algerian Muslim cleric, used Islamic appeals to unite Arab and Berber opposition to the French. His resourceful followers quickly learned how to make guns. The French captured Abd al-Qadir in 1847, but the fighting continued for years. Facing determined resistance, the French attempted to demoralize the Algerians by driving peasants off the best land and selling it to European settlers. To diffuse opposition, they also relocated and broke up tribes. Yet various anti-French revolts, often spurred by appeals to Islamic traditions, erupted until the 1880s. The ruthless French conquest and suppression of rebellions cost tens of thousands of French and hundreds of thousands of Algerian lives.

French policy reshaped Algerian society. The French intended, as an official wrote in 1862, to impose French culture, settlers, and economic priorities on the Arabs. General Bugeaud, the conqueror of Algeria, conceded in 1849 that "the Arabs with great insight understand very well the cruel revolution we have brought them; it is as radical for them as socialism would be for us."[14] Between the 1840s and 1914, more than 1 million immigrants from France, Italy, and Spain poured into Algeria, erecting a racist society similar to that of South Africa. The European settlers eventually elected representatives to the French parliament as Algeria was incorporated into the French state. The mainstay of the settler economy, vineyard cultivation and wine production, displaced food crops and pasture, an economic change that mocked Islamic values prohibiting alcoholic beverages.

Gradually, European power in Northwest Africa increased. In Morocco, a coastal country west of Algeria, Sultan Mawlay Hassan (r. 1873–1895) skillfully worked to preserve the country's independence by playing rival European powers off against each other. However, the French and Spanish, attracted by Morocco's strategic position, by 1912 had divided the country between them. Tunisia, just east of Algeria, had long enjoyed considerable autonomy under

Ottoman rule, and in 1881 France sent in troops to occupy Tunisia. Libya, a sparsely populated, mostly desert land between Tunisia and Egypt, was conquered by the Italians in 1911 and 1912, killing one-third of Libya's people. European colonialism now dominated the whole of North Africa.

> "The revivalists rejected what they considered the corruption of true Islam and embraced what they regarded as God's word in the Quran and the sayings of the Prophet Muhammad."

LO⁵ Middle Eastern Thought and Culture

West Asian and North African societies responded to the challenges facing them in three ways. One response was to form vibrant Islamic revivalist movements that promoted a purer version of Islamic practice rooted in early Muslim tradition. The second response involved reform movements that attempted to combine Islam with modernization and secularization. The early stirrings of Arab nationalism constituted a third response. While governments struggled, revivalist, reform, and nationalist movements pumped fresh vitality into Islamic culture but failed to offer an effective resistance to Western economic and military power.

Islamic Revivalism and the Rise of the Wahhabis

Political crises in the Middle East helped spark influential movements of Islamic revivalism, which sought to purify Islamic practices by reviving what their supporters considered to be a purer vision of Islamic society than the existing one. The revivalists rejected what they considered the corruption of true Islam and embraced what they regarded as God's word in the Quran and the sayings of the Prophet Muhammad. They also reaffirmed the ideal of the theocratic state of the early caliphs in Mecca, which blended religion and government. Muslim revivalists despised Sufism and what they viewed as other corrupting influences. Heeding this criticism, several Sufi brotherhoods eventually moved away from mystical beliefs toward an emphasis on the original teachings of the Prophet Muhammad.

 Middle East Studies Internet Resources (*http://www.columbia.edu/cu/lweb/indiv/mideast/cuvlm/index.html*). A useful collection of links on the Middle East.

While political leaders lost prestige and authority, religious leaders allied to merchant and tribal groups seized the initiative to spread revivalist thought. Carried by scholars, merchants, and missionaries, revivalist Islam spread from the Middle East to societies in every other part of the Islamic world, fostering debates over the role of Islam and how to meet the Western threat. Groups seeking to impose revivalist goals on others sometimes used violence, interpreting the early Muslim idea of jihad, or struggle for the faith, as a call to wage holy war against those Muslims who blended Islamic and local traditions. During the 1800s, revivalist movements stiffened resistance against French colonization in Algeria and West Africa, British colonization in Sudan, and Dutch colonization in Indonesia.

Wahhabism: An Islamic Puritan Movement

Revivalism had its greatest impact in Arabia, where it spurred a militant movement in the 1700s known as Wahhabism (wah-HAH-bi-zuhm). The movement's founder, Muhammad Abd al-Wahhab (al-wah-HAHB) (1703–1792), led a long campaign to purify Arabian Islam. Al-Wahhab had left his home in central Arabia to study Islamic theology in Medina and Iraq, where he adopted a strict interpretation of Islamic law. Returning home, he preached against those who were lax in their religious practice and promoted intolerance toward all alternative views, such as Sufism and Shi'ism. In 1744, his campaign gained a key ally, Muhammad Ibn Saud (sah-OOD), a tribal chief who helped al-Wahhab put together a fighting force to expand their influence.

Wahhabi power ebbed and flowed. During the later 1700s, the Wahhabis took over parts of Arabia and then advanced into Syria and Iraq, where they destroyed the Iraqi city of Karbala (KAHR-buh-luh), the major Shi'ite holy site, to demoralize Shi'ites. By 1805, the Wahhabis controlled Mecca and Medina, Islam's two holiest cities, where they horrified non-Wahhabi Muslims by massacring the residents and trying to destroy all sacred tombs in order to prevent saint worship. Their actions represented a major threat to conventional Islam. In response, Muhammad Ali, the governor of Egypt, used his European-style army and modern weapons to push the Wahhabis back from the holy cities. Despite these setbacks, Wahhabi ideas and zeal spread widely during the 1800s as Western power undermined Middle Eastern governments. Yet many Muslims condemned Wahhabi intolerance, extremism, and such practices as the forced veiling of women.

The History and Doctrines of Wahhabis
Read Abdullah Wahhab's response to critics about the beliefs of the Muwahhidin.

> "Some Muslim thinkers promoted modernization as a strategy for transforming Islamic society in response to the challenges of rising Western power and weakening Muslim governments."

The Founding of Saudi Arabia

In 1902, the still-allied descendants of al-Wahhab and Ibn Saud launched a second great expansion. The head of the Saud family, Abdul Aziz Ibn Saud (1880–1953), sent Wahhabi clergy among the Bedouins to convince them to abandon their nomadic ways and join self-sufficient farming communities. The Wahhabi Bedouin communities adopted extreme asceticism and a literal interpretation of the Islamic legal code, the Shari'a. Wahhabi clergy beat men for arriving late for prayers, and Wahhabi men pledged to die fighting for their beliefs. In 1925, the Saud family established Saudi Arabia, a state based on the Shari'a, and discovery of oil in 1938 gave the Saud family and their Wahhabi allies the wealth to maintain their control.

Modernist Islamic Thought

Islamic revivalism as reflected in the rigid Wahhabi movement was only one of several strands of Islamic thought that emerged during the Modern Era. Some Muslim thinkers promoted modernization as a strategy for transforming Islamic society in response to the challenges of rising Western power and weakening Muslim governments. While Wahhabis rejected modernity, modernist ideas grew stronger among Muslim intellectuals, who argued that Muslims should reject blind faith and reconcile Islam with fresh ideas, social change, and religious moderation.

Modernists detested many conservative Muslim traditions, including the restricted role of women. For example, Qasim Amin (KA-sim AH-mean), a French-educated Egyptian lawyer, argued in 1898 that the liberation of women was essential to the liberation of Egypt, that acquiring their "share of intellectual and moral development, happiness, and authority would prove to be the most significant development in Egyptian history." Women reformers such as Bahithat al-Badiya (buh-TEE-that al-buh-DEE-ya) echoed these sentiments (see Witness to the Past: Egyptian Women and Their Rights). Some radical reformers identified the veil as symbol of female oppression and urged its abolition.

Muslim modernists such as Muhammad Ali in Egypt believed that introducing change would be a straightforward process. They believed that by buying weapons and machines they could strengthen their armies and industries to deflect Western pressure, enrich their countries, and avoid domestic unrest. But their visionary ideas proved impractical and out of step with their largely conservative populations.

By the later 1800s, the challenges increased as Western technical and economic capabilities grew. Like European Enlightenment thinkers they often admired, some Muslim modernists struggled with how to reconcile faith and reason. They worried that the reforms needed to spur modernization required adopting Western philosophical and scientific theories, which were often contrary to Islamic beliefs about society, God, and nature. For example, capitalism undermined the Quranic prohibition against charging interest on loans, and the concept of human rights challenged slavery, which was still widespread in the nineteenth-century Muslim world. Belief in equality contradicted the low status of Muslim women, and the Western notions of popular sovereignty and the nation troubled those who believed that only God could make laws or establish standards, which the state must then administer. Some

Egyptian Women and Their Rights

One of the leading women writers and thinkers in early twentieth-century Egypt, Bahithat al-Badiya (buh-TEE-that al-buh-DEE-ya) (1886–1918), advocated greater economic and educational rights for women in a rapidly changing society. She wrote at a time when Egyptian nationalists were demanding independence from Britain and a modern state, and intellectuals were debating the merits of modernity as opposed to tradition. In 1909, in a lecture to an Egyptian women's club associated with a nationalist organization, Bahithat offered a program for improving women's lives. Struggling against male and Islamic opposition to women's rights, she sought a middle ground between Islamic conservatism and European secular liberalization.

Ladies, I greet you as a sister who feels what you feel, suffers what you suffer, and rejoices in what you rejoice. . . . Complaints about both men and women are rife. . . . This mutual blame which has deepened the antagonism between the sexes is something to be regretted and feared. God did not create man and women to hate each other but to love each other and to live together so the world would be populated. . . . Men say when we become educated we shall push them out of work and abandon the role for which God has created us. But isn't it rather men who have pushed women out of work? Before, women used to spin and to weave cloth for clothes, . . . but men invented machines for spinning and weaving. . . . In the past, women sewed clothes . . . but men invented the sewing machine. . . . Women . . . [made bread] with their own hands. Then men invented bakeries employing men. . . . I do not mean to denigrate these useful inventions which do a lot of our work. . . . Since male inventors and workers have taken away our work should we waste our time in idleness or seek other work to occupy us? Of course, we should do the latter. . . .

Men say to us categorically, "You women have been created for the house and we have been created to be breadwinners." Is this a God-given dictate? . . . No holy book has spelled it out. . . . Women in villages . . . help their men till the land and plant crops. Some women do the fertilizing, haul crops, lead animals, draw water for irrigation, and other chores. . . . Specialized work for each sex is a matter of convention, . . . not mandatory. . . . Women may not have to their credit great inventions but women have excelled in learning and the arts and politics. . . .

Nothing irritates me more than when men claim they do not wish us to work because they wish to spare us the burden. We do not want condescension, we want respect. . . .

If we had been raised from childhood to go unveiled and if our men were ready for it I would approve of unveiling those who want it. But the nation is not ready for it now. . . . The imprisonment in the home of the Egyptian woman of the past is detrimental while the current freedom of the European is excessive. I cannot find a better model [than] today's Turkish woman. She falls between the two extremes and does not violate what Islam prescribes. She is a good example of decorum and modesty. . . . We should get a sound education, not merely acquire the trappings of a foreign language and rudiments of music. Our education should also include home management, health care, and childcare. . . . We shall advance when we give up idleness.

Thinking About the Reading

1. How does Bahithat evaluate women's roles and gender relations in Egypt?
2. What does her moderate advice to Egyptian women suggest about Egyptian society and the power of patriarchy?

Source: Bahithat al-Badiya, "A Lecture in the Club of the Umma Party, 1909," trans. by Ali Badran and Margot Badran, in *Opening the Gate: A Century of Arab Feminist Writing*, ed. by Margot Badran and Miriam Cooke, (Bloomington: Indiana University Press, 1990), pp. 228–238. Copyright © 1990 by Indiana University Press. Reprinted with permission of Indiana University Press.

17 CAIRO. — ʹOpera Square. — LL.

Cairo Opera House Hoping to demonstrate modernization, Egyptian leaders built an opera house in Cairo in the 1860s. One of the first pieces staged was an opera by Italian composer Giuseppe Verdi to celebrate the opening of the Suez Canal in 1869.

reformers doubted whether Islam, with its universalistic idea of a multiethnic community guided by God, was compatible with nationalism, which emphasized the unity of one group of people defined by a common state. The Moroccan historian Ahmad ibn Khalid al-Nasri feared that Western ideas tainted reforms. Writing of military cadets being trained in Western weapons and tactics, he worried that "they want to learn to fight to protect the faith, but they lose the faith in the process of learning how."[15] What role, the modernizers wondered, could clerics and the Shari'a have in a world of machines and nations?

Egypt-based thinkers took the lead in arguing the compatibility of Islam with modernization. The Persia-born activist and teacher Jamal al-Din al-Afghani (1838–1895), for example, preached innovative concepts of Islam. Al-Afghani favored reason and science; in his view, rigid interpretations of Islam combined with local traditions contributed to Arab backwardness. He lamented that, partly because of intolerance to new ideas, "the Arab world still remains

buried in profound darkness."[16] But al-Afghani also promoted resistance to Western power. His strong criticisms of British activity in Egypt and Persia, as well as of Arab leaders he viewed as puppets, led to his exile to Paris, where he published a weekly newspaper that promoted his views.

The Roots of Arab Nationalism

During the 1800s, a pan-Arab national consciousness developed in response to foreign domination by the Ottoman Turks and then by the British and French. But Arab identity was murky, divided by differences in religious and group affiliation. Arabs were predominantly Sunni Muslims, but some, particularly in the Persian Gulf and southern Iraq, were Shi'ites, and others, especially numerous in Egypt, Lebanon, and Syria, were Christians. They did not all have the same agenda or face the same problems. Even within the same society, Arabs were often divided into feuding patriarchal tribes that sometimes disliked rival tribes as much as they disliked Ottoman or European over-lords, while other Arabs remained loyal to Ottoman rule. Furthermore, in 1876, hoping to defuse ethnic nationalism, the Ottomans introduced a new constitution and gave the Arabs seats in the legislature based on their large population in the empire. Thus a pan-Arab or pan-Muslim movement remained unrealistic.

Yet, some thoughtful Arabs began to envision self-governing Arab nations free of Ottoman or Western domination. Arab nationalism emerged from a literary and cultural movement in Syria in the later 1800s. Some of the pioneering writers were Lebanese Christians, one of whom published a poem calling on Arabs to "arise and awake." The writings of modernist Muslim scholars were also influential, although they posed a conflict between a pan-Islamic approach and a stress on Arab identity and language. Arab nationalist groups formed all over the Ottoman Empire in response to Ottoman centralization, but before World War I, they had little public influence.

> **❝ Yet, some thoughtful Arabs began to envision self-governing Arab nations free of Ottoman or Western domination. ❞**

The Zionist Quest

While Middle Eastern societies struggled to respond to the Western challenge, the Zionist movement (see Chapter 19) introduced another. In the Jewish ghettoes of eastern Europe, some thinkers began a quest for a homeland for their long-persecuted people, who had been living in a diaspora scattered around the world since being forced by the Romans to leave Palestine nearly two millennia earlier. Prayers in Jewish synagogues for worshiping "next year in Jerusalem," the ancient Hebrew capital in Palestine, had endured for centuries. While many European Jews rejected Zionism, identifying instead with the country where they lived; for others, Zionism functioned like nationalism, offering promises of a Jewish state. The first Zionist conference, held in Basel, Switzerland, in 1897, identified Palestine, then under Ottoman rule, as the potential Jewish homeland. For centuries, some Jews had visited or settled in Palestine, and perhaps 20,000 lived there in 1870, but the Ottomans refused to give Zionist leaders permission to organize a massive settlement of Jews, because many would likely come from the Ottomans' bitter enemy, Russia.

Soon militant Zionists began promoting Jewish migration to Palestine without Ottoman permission or the support of European governments. By 1914 some 85,000 Jews, most of them newcomers from Russia and Poland, lived in Palestine alongside some 700,000 Arabs. The immigrants established dozens of Jewish collective farms, each known as a kibbutz, whose members shared their wealth and promoted Hebrew as a common language. Immigrants also built the first largely Jewish city, Tel Aviv, purchasing land from absentee Arab and Turkish landowners. The Zionists had a flag, an anthem, an active Jewish press, and the support of international Zionist organizations, but because Jewish aims and institutions had no legal recognition in Palestine, the stage was set for future conflict with Palestinian Arabs, who resented the newcomers and their plans for a Jewish state.

kibbutz
A Jewish collective farm in twentieth-century Palestine that stressed the sharing of wealth.

Listen to a synopsis of Chapter 21.

CHAPTER 22

South Asia, Southeast Asia, and Colonization,

1750–1914

Learning Outcomes

After reading this chapter, you should be able to answer the following questions:

LO¹ How and why did Britain extend its control throughout India?

LO² How did colonialism transform the Indian economy and foster new ideas in India?

LO³ How did the Western nations expand their control of Southeast Asia?

LO⁴ What were the major political, economic, and social consequences of colonialism in Southeast Asia?

Universiteits Bibliothek, Leiden (Snouk Hurgronje Collection), Codex Orientales 7398

"Rice fields are littered with our battle-killed; blood flows or lies in pools, stains hills and streams. [French] Troops bluster on and grab our land, our towns, roaring and stirring dust to dim the skies. A scholar with no talent and no power, could I redress a world turned upside down?**"**

—**Protest by Vietnamese poet Nguyen Dinh Chieu against French conquest, late nineteenth century**[1]

In 1858 the French, seeking to expand their empire in Asia, attacked Vietnam with military force, and over the next three decades, they conquered the country against determined resistance. A blind Vietnamese poet, Nguyen Dinh Chieu (NEW-yin dinh chew) (1822–1888), became a symbol of the Vietnamese resistance to the French when he wrote an oration honoring the fallen Vietnamese soldiers after a heroic defense in a battle in 1862: "You preferred to die fighting the enemy, and return to our ancestors in glory rather than survive in submission to the [Westerners]." The French retaliated by seizing Chieu's land and property. The poet remained unbowed, and in verse spread throughout the land, Chieu rallied opposition. He heaped scorn on his countrymen who collaborated with the French occupiers and advised them to maintain the struggle for independence: "Everyone will rejoice in seeing the West wind [colonialism],Vanish from [Vietnam's] mountains and rivers."[2] Chieu overcame the handicaps of blindness to become a physician, scholar, teacher, and renowned writer and bard, famous for his epic poems sung in the streets. Earning the admiration of his countrymen for his loyalty to family, king, and country, Chieu rejected the French offer of a financial subsidy and the return of his family land if he would rally to their cause.

By providing deadly new weapons and increasing the need for resources and markets, the Industrial Revolution in Europe and North America (see Chapters 19–20) set in motion an intensive Western penetration of other regions, including India and Southeast Asia. With enhanced military, economic, and technological power to assert their will, between 1750 and 1914, a few Western nations brought nearly all

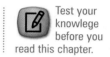

Test your knowlege before you read this chapter.

What do you think?

Europeans typically believed that Western colonialism improved inferior Asian and African societies.

Strongly Disagree   *Strongly Agree*
1   2   3   4   5   6   7

<< **Dipenegara** This painting shows Prince Dipenegara, a Javanese aristocrat who led a revolt against the Dutch colonizers in the 1820s, reading, with several attendants at hand.

of southern and eastern Asia under direct colonial or indirect neocolonial control. Western domination destroyed traditional Asian political systems, reoriented Asian economies, transmitted the ideas and technologies of Western life, and posed challenges for societies and their world-views. In turn, Asian workers produced resources that spurred Western economic growth.

Asians struggled with some success to reshape their relationship with the West. The unyielding resistance to imperialism exemplified by Nguyen Dinh Chieu gave hope to colonized people in Africa and the Middle East. While European power was too great to be overthrown in this period, eventually the Indians, Vietnamese, and Filipinos, among others, used the Western concept of nationalism to assert the rights of their peoples for self-determination.

LO¹ Forming British India

By the early 1700s, the Muslim Mughals who ruled much of India (see Chapter 18) were in steep decline, challenged by both Indians and Europeans. In the sixteenth and seventeenth centuries, the splendor of the Mughal court and India's valuable exports had attracted the Portuguese, Dutch, and British. As the Mughals lost power by the 1800s, the British took advantage of a fragmented India, controlling both India and the island of Sri Lanka. British conquest was in keeping with the history of South Asia, which had often been conquered by outsiders from Western and Central Asia. But unlike the Asian invaders, who often became assimilated into Indian society by adopting Hinduism or Buddhism or spreading Islam, the British maintained their own separate identity and cultural traditions.

Indian Trade, the West, and Mughal Decline

Europeans had long coveted South Asia for its spices and textiles, which had been a part of regional commerce for millennia. The Portuguese were the first

Europeans to trade directly with India. In 1498, they established a base at Goa (GO-uh), and for a century they sought to control the trade from India and Southeast Asia to the West. Soon Dutch traders arrived, eventually destroying Portuguese power in South and Southeast Asia (although Goa remained a Portuguese colony until 1961). The Dutch concentrated on Sri Lanka and, farther east, Indonesia. The British also took action, and by 1696, the British East

CHRONOLOGY

South Asia, 1750–1914

1744–1761	Anglo-French struggle for Coromandel coast
1757	Battle of Plassey
1764	British acquisition of Bengal
1774–1778	Warren Hastings governor of Bengal
1793	New land policy in Bengal
1799	British defeat of Mysore
1802	British colonization of Sri Lanka
1816	British protectorate over Nepal
1819	British occupation of all Maratha lands
1820s	Beginning of British Westernization policy
1839–1842	First Anglo-Afghan War
1849	British defeat of Sikhs in Punjab
1850	Completion of British India
1857–1858	Indian rebellion
1858	Introduction of colonial system in India
1877	Founding of Muslim college at Aligarh
1878–1880	Second Anglo-Afghan War
1885	Formation of Indian National Congress
1903	British invasion of Tibet
1906	Formation of Indian Muslim League

India Company possessed three fortified trading stations in India: at the towns of Calcutta in Bengal, Madras (today known as Chennai) on the southeastern coast, and Bombay (today called Mumbai) on the west coast. Meanwhile, the French formed a small colony in Pondicherry, a town near the British base at Madras.

Europeans encountered a fragmenting India. By 1750, the Mughals were corrupt and weak, because many Indians had already broken away from Mughal control. During the later 1700s, Mughal factions quarreled and different rivals claimed the throne, but the Mughal government controlled little beyond Delhi, and the countryside became increasingly disorderly. Without a powerful imperial state to control it, Indian society—with its diverse cultures, castes, languages, regions, and religions—lacked strong national cohesion and was unable to effectively resist European encroachments.

With the Mughals losing their grip, groups like the Marathas (muh-RAH-tuhs) and the Sikhs built powerful new states. The Marathas were a loosely knit confederacy led by Hindu warriors from west-central India, and the Sikhs were a religious minority in northwest India; both of these groups competed with new Muslim states that were often set up by Mughal governors whose allegiance to the Mughal emperor was nominal. By 1800 the Marathas ruled much of western India, and the Sikhs, under their leader, the dynamic Ranjit Singh (RUN-ji SING) (1780–1839), had conquered the Punjab and Kashmir in the northwest. In southern India, the Mughal collapse left a power vacuum that both Britain and France attempted to fill by supporting their respective Indian allies in the struggle for regional advantage. Ultimately, however, none of the rising Indian states, including the Marathas and Sikhs, gained enough power, acquired enough weapons, or forged enough cooperation to repulse the West.

The Founding and Expansion of British India

The British posed the gravest challenge to India, especially in Bengal, India's richest and most popu-

> "Ultimately, however, none of the rising Indian states, including the Marathas and Sikhs, gained enough power, acquired enough weapons, or forged enough cooperation to repulse the West."

lous region. Bengal was ruled by Muslim governors who mostly ignored the Mughal government in Delhi. When local Indian governments resisted an expansion of the British presence into their lands, the British resorted to military force.

Siraja Dowlah In the mid-1700s, the Bengali ruler, Siraja Dowlah (see-RAH-ja DOW-luh) (ca. 1732–1757), considered the British bothersome leeches on his land's riches. Soon after becoming ruler, Dowlah alienated Western merchants and even his own more cautious officials, and in 1757 he rashly attacked British trading stations. After capturing the main station, Calcutta, Dowlah's forces placed 146 captured British men, women, and children in a crowded jail known as the Black Hole of Calcutta. The next day only 23 of them staggered out, the rest having died from suffocation and dehydration.

Robert Clive Their rage and determination now fired, the British dispatched a force under Robert Clive (1725–1774) to regain Britain's holdings. A former clerk turned into a daring war strategist, the ambitious Clive and his 3,200 soldiers defeated some 50,000 Bengali troops at the Battle of Plassey in 1757 and recaptured Calcutta, marking the dawn of the British epic in India. Clive allied with Hindu bankers and Muslim nobles who were unhappy with Siraja Dowlah, who was executed, and by 1764, Clive controlled Bengal.

The British government, following a policy of mercantilism to acquire wealth for the state, allowed the British East India Company to govern Bengal and other parts of India, as they were acquired, and to exploit the inhabitants while sharing the profits with the British government. The British showed a lust for riches equal to that of the Spanish conquistadors in the 1500s. As governor of Bengal (1758–1760,

sepoys
Mercenary soldiers recruited among the warrior and peasant castes by the British in India.

1764–1767) for the Company, Clive launched an era of organized plunder, allowing British merchants and officials gradually to drain Bengal of its wealth while Company officials, including Clive, lived like kings in Calcutta. After 1760, the cry of "Go East," inspired by Clive's rags-to-riches story, fueled British imperialist ambitions. As they expanded their control of more Indian territory, the British became a new high caste, and, much like the former Mughal rulers, expected the Indians to serve them. Eventually the British Parliament accused Clive of corruption and fraud. Although cleared of the charges, a depressed Clive committed suicide at the age of forty-nine.

Warren Hastings

To transform the economic chaos left by Clive into a more profitable order and to consolidate the British position, the Company appointed Warren Hastings to serve as governor-general (1774–1778) of Bengal. Hastings redesigned the revenue system, made treaty alliances, and also pursued outright annexations to safeguard the British bases. A scholarly man who was influenced by Enlightenment thought, Hastings saw his task as a holding operation of limited ambitions, arguing against full colonization. In contrast to other British officials, Hastings respected the people he governed, advising one of his successors that, like the English, many Indians had a strong intellect, a sound integrity, and honorable feelings and should enjoy the same equal rights as the English colonizers. His successors, however, often disregarded his advice.

Success in Bengal fueled further British expansion in the subcontinent. In 1773, the British government gave the Company authority to administer all British-controlled Indian territories. Nonetheless, the Company still saw its role as mainly commercial. In 1794, the British Parliament forbade further annexation and declared territorial expansion to be repugnant to the honor and the policy of the nation. But despite the ban, governor-generals after Hastings continued to authorize the occupation of more areas of India, often against opposition, to prevent trade

disruption or to counteract rival European nations. Some imperialists talked about Britain's sacred trust to reshape the world, viewing the extension of British authority—and with it British culture, Christianity, and free-trade policies—as a great blessing for Asians.

Administering the British *Raj*

The reality, however, was often something other than a blessing. In acquiring more Indian territory, the British mixed military force, extortion, bribery, and manipulation. Because India was so diverse, British agents and merchants could play off one region against another, Hindu against Muslim, and were aided by Indian collaborators, especially ambitious businessmen. From India's warrior and peasant castes—mostly Hindus but also some Muslims—the British recruited mercenary soldiers, known as sepoys, under the command of British officers. By 1857, there were nearly 200,000 sepoy troops in the Company military force, greatly outnumbering the 10,000 British officers and soldiers.

Virtual Library: South Asia (*http://www .columbia.edu/cu/ libraries/indiv/area/ sarai/*). A major site on India.

During the late 1700s and early 1800s, the British imposed their control over much of western, central, and northern India. They defeated the French on India's southeastern Coromandel coast after a series of imperial conflicts from 1744 to 1761. The Maratha confederacy, which controlled much of western and central India, was divided by rivalries. In 1805, the British occupied the Marathas' northern territories and entered Delhi, and took the remaining Maratha lands in 1819. They then turned their attention to the states of northwest India, where the Rajputs (RAHJ-putz), a Hindu warrior caste, were no longer the feared fighters they had been in earlier centuries and now signed treaties giving Britain claims on their lands. Only the Sikhs remained a threat to the British, but the death of the Sikh leader, Ranjit Singh, in 1839 shattered the Sikhs' unity and undermined their powerful military state. In 1849, after a series of bloody British-Sikh wars, Britain finally triumphed, stationing troops in the many small independent principalities scattered around India. By 1850, the British ruled all Indians

> 66 The British showed a lust for riches equal to that of the Spanish conquistadors in the 1500s. 99

Clive Meets Indian Leaders In this painting, Robert Clive meets the new Bengali official, Mir Jafir, after the British victory in the 1757 Battle of Plassey. Clive supported Mir Jafir's seizure of power from the anti-British leader, Siraja Dowlah.

Interactive Map

directly or through princes who collaborated with them (see Map 22.1).

South Asia Under the East India Tea Company

British expansion in India eventually led to interventions in neighboring societies, including Sri Lanka, the large, fertile island just south of India that the British called Ceylon. Fearing that the French might establish a base there, the British acquired the territory from the Dutch, controlling the entire island by 1815. The British transformed Sri Lanka, seizing rice-growing land from peasants to set up coffee, tea, and rubber plantations and recruiting Tamil-speaking workers from southeast India as laborers. By 1911, the Tamil laborers and their families made up 11 percent of the Sri Lankan population. Largely isolated on plantations, the Tamils maintained their own customs and Hindu religion and had little contact with Sri Lanka's majority population, the Buddhist Sinhalese. By the end of the 1800s, some educated Sinhalese, having turned to nationalism, considered both the British and the Tamils unwanted aliens. Sinhalese–Tamil tensions simmered for generations.

Map 22.1
The Growth of British India, 1750–1860

Gradually expanding control from their bases at Calcutta, Madras, and Bombay, the British completed their military conquest of the final holdout states by the 1850s.

Map legend:
Territory under British control
- Before 1770
- 1770–1800
- 1800–1830
- 1830–1860
- Princely states

© Cengage Learning

Fearing that the Russians, who were conquering Muslim Central Asia, intended to expand into South Asia by land, the British also attempted to secure India's land borders. First they turned to Nepal, a kingdom just north of India in the Himalayan Mountains. Nepal's Hindu ruling caste, the Gurkhas (GORE-kuhz), were fierce fighters who had sometimes invaded north India. British victory over the Gurkhas in 1814–1816 turned Nepal's monarchy into a British protectorate. Soldiers recruited from Nepal, also known as gurkhas, became a special military force for Britain and were employed on battlefields around the world in support of British objectives.

The Afghan Wars

Afghanistan, a mountainous region just west of India, seemed the most vulnerable to Russian expansion. An ethnically diverse region that had enjoyed only short periods of political unity, Afghanistan seemed an unlikely candidate to become a viable independent state. However, Afghans, among them the devoutly Islamic Pashtun tribes in the south, possessed the fighting skills to oppose Europeans who were bent on conquest. In the first Afghan War (1839–1842), Pashtuns massacred most of the 12,000 retreating British and Sepoy troops and the British civilians, including women and children. Undeterred, the British fought the second Afghan War (1878–1880) and replaced a Pashtun leader who favored the Russians with one who gave Britain control of Afghanistan's foreign affairs. With an ally as ruler, the British concluded that Afghanistan could not be annexed by military force.

The Westernization of India

The British East India Company gradually tightened its control of India and began to impose Western values on Indians. After Hastings, the Company shifted from sharing government with local rulers to becoming the sole power and administering India through British officials. In typically arrogant colonial language that ignored centuries of Indian achievements, Sir Thomas Munro, governor of Madras from 1820 to 1827, claimed that the British must maintain their rule until the Indians abandoned their "superstitions" and became "enlightened" enough to govern themselves. Reflecting these views, the Company promoted a policy of Westernization, a deliberate attempt to impose Western culture and ideas.

Westernization began in the 1820s and was strongly influenced by Christian evangelism. British officials, often disregarding Indian religious and cultural sensitivities, encouraged Christian missions and tried to ban customs they disliked. Many Indians rejoiced when they banned *sati*, the northern custom of widows throwing themselves on their husband's funeral pyre. But there was less Indian enthusiasm for British attempts to tinker with Muslim and Hindu law codes that were rooted in religious beliefs. The British also established schools that taught in English rather than an Indian language. This policy was spurred by Lord Macaulay (1800–1859), a reformer and firm believer in Western cultural superiority who considered it pointless to teach Indian languages, declaring in 1832 that "a single shelf of a good European library is worth the whole native literature of India and Arabia."[3] Some Indians considered English education a threat to both Hindu and Muslim customs, while others welcomed the English-medium schools because they opened Indian students to a wider world. The first English institution of higher education, the Hindu College in Calcutta, was founded by Indians in 1818.

Orientalism and William Jones

Not all the British in India found Indian culture to be backward. Some British admirers of Indian culture, reflecting what came to be called Orientalism, showed a scholarly interest in India and its history. Warren Hastings, for example, encouraged the study of Indian culture, languages, and literature, learning Greek, Latin, Persian, and Urdu himself. One of his officials, William Jones (1746–1794), who mastered Arabic, Persian, and Sanskrit, became the most influential Orientalist scholar, but his views often reflected

Westernization
A deliberate attempt to spread Western culture and ideas.

Orientalism
An eighteenth- and nineteenth-century scholarly interest among British officials in India and its history that prompted some to rediscover the Hindu classical age.

British East India Company Court This painted wood model shows an Indian court presided over by an official of the British East India Company.

an attempt to fit India into Western concepts of history and religion. Jones's ideas shaped European scholarly understanding of Indian history for generations, yet by the later 1800s, Orientalist cosmopolitanism and respect had largely been replaced by British nationalism and intolerance.

Ram Mohan Roy

The encounter between India and the West, as well as the British reforms, also fostered a Hindu social reform movement and philosophical renaissance under the brilliant leadership of the Bengali scholar Ram Mohan Roy (1772–1833). After seeing his sister burn to death on a funeral pyre, and concerned about what he saw as the harmful side of customs such as *sati* and caste divisions, Roy began a British-Indian dialogue in hopes of adopting certain Western ways to reform and strengthen Hinduism. To better understand the world by studying non-Hindu religions, Roy mastered their source languages—Hebrew and Greek for Christianity, Arabic and Persian for Islam—and thus became the world's first modern scholar of comparative religion. He founded secondary schools, newspapers, and an organization working for reform of Hindu society and beliefs. Viewing the British positively as promoters of knowledge and liberty, Roy wanted Britain to promote modernization while also seeking Indian advice.

Transforming the Indian Infrastructure

In order to make India more profitable, the British East India Company built roads, railroads, and irrigation systems; most significantly for rural Indians, they revised the land revenue collection, the principal source of public finance. The British viewed Indian rural society as stagnant, unable to provide the tax revenues needed to support British administration. Despite high taxes, bandits, and sometimes warfare, in precolonial times Indian villages generally provided economic security by promoting cooperation among their residents. Land belonged to the royal families, but peasants had the hereditary right to use it. British observers recognized the village system as self-sufficient and stable over time, but they destroyed it anyway when the Company began collecting taxes from farmers in money rather than, as had been common for centuries, a portion of the crop. Under this system, peasant farmers became tenants to landlords and were denied their hereditary rights to use the land. Many landlords sold their land rights at a good profit to businessmen, often city dwellers, who became absentee landlords and grew rich from the crops grown by the peasants. The Company also encouraged a switch from food crops to cash crops such as opium, coffee, rubber, tea, and cotton, often grown on plantations rather than peasant farms. The emphasis on money sacrificed a large measure of the stability and security peasants had once enjoyed.

Resistance: The 1857 Revolt

Despite Indian reform movements such as Roy's, Indians, especially once-prosperous families and peasants alike who lost wealth and stability, usually resented the British East India Company's Westernization and its associated economic policies. Furthermore, Sepoys increasingly resented the aggressive attempts of British officers to convert them to Christianity. Uprisings were recurrent, and in 1857 one revolt, sparked by Sepoy outrage, spread rapidly and offered a serious challenge to British authority.

Indian Railroad Train The railroads built during British rule carried both resources and passengers. This lithograph shows a Sikh signalman at the station and a train conveying Indian women and a European.

Sepoys stationed in Bengal became offended by new army rifle cartridges, which had to be bitten off with the teeth before being rammed down the gun barrel and were rumored to be greased with beef and pork fat, violating the religious dietary prohibitions of both cow-revering Hindus and pork-avoiding Muslims.

> "The British divide-and-rule policy helped maintain British power but also exacerbated hatreds that remain today."

colonial rule. To address the symptoms of deep discontent, the 1858 Government of India Act transferred sovereignty to the British monarch. In 1876, Queen Victoria was proclaimed Empress of India, head of the government known as the British *Raj*, named for the ancient title of Hindu kings. India became the brightest "jewel in the imperial crown," a source of fabulous wealth. The policies pursued by the British Raj reshaped Indian society, sparking new economic, intellectual, and social patterns, and eventually inspiring a new sense of the Indian nation.

The revolt, later called the first War of Independence by Indian Nationalists, began among the sepoys in the army and was soon supported by peasant and Muslim uprisings, along with a few members of Hindu and Muslim princely families. The revolt was confined largely to north and northeast India. Because no rebel leaders envisioned a unified Indian nation, British observers argued that the rebels had limited and selfish goals. But Muslims and Hindus alike felt that their customs and religions were being threatened, and they called for a joint defense of their religions against their common British enemy.

The rebels captured Delhi and besieged several cities, but they could not hold them for long. The desperate struggle involved ruthless tactics; both sides committed massacres. For example, rebels murdered one thousand British residents when they occupied the city of Kanpur. On the other side, when British troops recaptured Delhi, they became berserk and engaged in widespread raping, pillaging, and killing. The Muslim poet Ghalib mourned: "Here is a vast ocean of blood before me. Thousands of my friends are dead. Perhaps none is left even to shed tears upon my death."[4] Anti-British sentiment was not widespread enough, however, to overcome the rebels' problems: inadequate arms, weak communications, and lack of a unified national strategy. When the British captured the last rebel fort, held by the Rani of Jhansi, in 1858, she was killed and the rebellion collapsed, although a few small rebel groups fought skirmishes with the British until 1860.

> 66 India became the brightest 'jewel in the imperial crown,' a source of fabulous wealth. 99

Colonial Government and Education

The British *Raj* bore many similarities to the Mughal system it had replaced. The top British officials, the viceroys, lived in splendor in Delhi. They made efforts to win Indian support by pomp and circumstance, including Mughal-style ceremonies and building a new capital at New Delhi, next to the old Mughal capital of Delhi, with gigantic architecture dwarfing even the monuments of the Mughals. After 1857, British officials mistrusted Indians but, like the Mughals before them, strategically preserved the Indian princes' privileges and palaces in exchange for promoting acceptance of British policies.

Borrowing Mughal practices, the British ruled through a mix of good communications, exploitation of Hindu-Muslim rivalries, and military force. The British connected India with a network of roads, bridges, and railways, and by 1900 India had more than 25,000 miles of track, the fourth largest rail system in the world. The British also deliberately pitted the Hindu majority against the Muslim minority by favoring one or the other group in law, language, and custom. For example, Hindus protested that the main Muslim language, Urdu, was used in many North Indian courts and that Muslim butchers were allowed to kill cows, considered sacred animals by Hindus. The British divide-and-rule policy helped maintain British power but also exacerbated hatreds that remain today. Local revenue supported a huge army of 200,000 men who were needed to keep the peace in India and fight British battles abroad.

LO² The Reshaping of Indian Society

The 1857 revolt prompted the British to replace the British East India Company government with direct

In their efforts to rule, the British also introduced policies of discrimination against Indians and defensive frontier security. The British typically believed that Western colonialism improved inferior Asian and African societies. Indians were excluded from European-only clubs and parks as well as high positions in the bureaucracy, and enjoyed no real power or influence. Colonial Britain also concerned itself with border security and Russian ambitions, invading Tibet in 1903 and compelling Tibetan leaders to agree not to concede territory to Russia or any other foreign power. Lord Curzon (viceroy from 1899 to 1905) remarked that "we do not want their country . . . but it is important that no one else should seize it, and that it should be turned into a sort of buffer state between the Russian and Indian Empires."[5]

The *Raj* also continued the Westernization policy of the British East India Company, promoting British and often Christian values through an expanded English-medium education system. Thanks to these schools, English became the common language for educated Indians. However, only a privileged minority could afford to send their children to the English schools. By 1911, only 11 percent of men and 1 percent of women were literate in any language. Nonetheless, the schools fostered change by introducing new ideas like Christianity, consumerism, and Western philosophy. These Indians sent their sons and a few daughters to British universities, where notions like "freedom" and "self-determination of peoples" stood in sharp contrast to conditions in India. Returning students asked why the British did not practice such ideas in their colony. The growing British-educated professional class organized social, professional, and political bodies concerned with improving Indian life and acquiring more influence in government.

Economic Transformation

The British also transformed the Indian economy. Before 1700, Mughal India had been an economic powerhouse and manufacturing center, and the world leader in producing cotton textiles. India still produced one-quarter of all manufactured goods in 1750. The disparity between urban and rural wealth

> "By turning once self-sufficient peasants into tenants, the British planted the roots of one of contemporary India's greatest dilemmas, inequitable land distribution."

was narrower than in most societies. However, two centuries later, conditions had changed, as British policies, which were designed to drain India of its wealth to benefit Britain, harmed the Indian economy.

The Impact of the British System

The land tax system first introduced by the British East India Company in parts of India exploited the peasantry. By turning once self-sufficient peasants into tenants, the British planted the roots of one of contemporary India's greatest dilemmas, inequitable land distribution. As peasants lost their land rights and came to depend on the whims of landlords, they often fell hopelessly into debt. Furthermore, required now to pay taxes in cash, peasants had to grow cash crops such as cotton, jute, pepper, or opium rather than food. As a result, famine became more common, killing millions as food supplies and distribution became more uncertain.

Other changes also affected rural life. The introduction of steamships freed shipping routes and schedules from the vagaries of monsoon winds, and the opening of the Suez Canal in 1869 made it easier and much faster to ship raw materials from India to Europe, increasing the demand for these resources. The return ships brought to India cheap machine goods, which undermined the role of village craftsmen such as weavers and tinkers. As imported goods displaced artisans and farmers shifted to cash crops, the village economy came to be based on cash transactions. The quest for revenues and the priorities of commerce also ravaged the physical environment.

British trade policies also caused the decline of Indian manufacturing. The British discouraged Indian manufacturing by taxing Indian-made goods passing between Indian states and by prohibiting the import of industrial machinery. Meanwhile, British products flooded the country, destroying the livelihood of many skilled craftsmen, who were left with little choice but to become farm laborers. Yet industrial activity did not disappear from India between 1815 and 1914, and, despite many barriers, a few Indians found ways to prosper. British entrepreneurs established the world's largest jute-manufacturing industry, while Indians continued to compete with British imports by manufacturing cotton textiles and initiating a modern iron and steel sector. Unable to get British funding, some entrepreneurs raised money among Indian investors, and then used their wealth to promote scientific education.

Resistance to British Economics

By the late 1800s, the limits on India's industries became a subject of heated controversy. Indian critics alleged that tariffs protected British industries while strangling Indian industries that might have competed with them. While the British claimed that their rule improved India, the gap between British and Indian wealth grew: by 1895, the per capita income in Britain was fourteen to fifteen times higher than India's. Indian scholars attacked what one called "The Drain" of wealth and argued that British policies gave India "peace but not prosperity; the manufacturers lost their industries; the cultivators were ground down by a heavy and variable taxation; the revenues were to a large extent diverted to England."[6] Defenders of British policies replied that British rule brought investment, imported goods, railroads, and law and order. But critics questioned whether these innovations benefited most Indians or rather resulted in more systematic exploitation by increasingly prosperous British merchants and industrialists.

Population Growth and Indian Emigration

The plight of the Indian peasant was worsened by population growth. Despite the deadly famines, under British rule the Indian population rose from perhaps 100 million in 1700 to 300 million by 1920. The British imposed peace and improved sanitation and health. A similar population increase occurred in Europe at the same time, but growing numbers of Europeans could be absorbed by industrialization or emigration to the Americas and Australia. Unlike Europe, India enjoyed neither an industrial revolution nor an increase in farm productivity. Indian landlords had a stake in the cash crop system and wanted no innovations that might threaten their dominance.

As a result, the number of people far outstripped the amount of available food and land, creating dire poverty and widespread hunger.

As these problems mounted, millions of desperately poor Indians were recruited to emigrate to other lands. Plantations throughout the colonized world wanted Indian labor. Many Indians saw no alternative to leaving, but travel was hazardous. Most Indian emigrants were destined for plantations growing cash crops such as sugar, tea, or rubber and were indentured, meaning they had signed contracts that obligated them to work for a period of years (usually three to five) in order to repay their passage. Between 1880 and 1930, around a quarter million people per year, both men and women, left India. Few returned. The mortality rates for the indentured workers were so high and the indenture terms so unfavorable that critics considered the system another form of slavery.

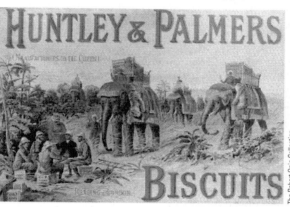

The resulting diaspora made Indians one of the most recognizable global societies. Cities such as Nairobi in Kenya, Rangoon in Burma, and Port of Spain in Trinidad had large Indian neighborhoods. Indians now had key economic roles in many countries. Indian trade networks, usually based on family or caste ties, reached around the Indian Ocean and Pacific Rim. The future leader of the Indian nationalist movement, Mohandas Gandhi (GAHN-dee), then a young law school graduate, experimented with his ideas of nonviolent resistance to illegitimate power while working among Indians in South Africa. Today people of Indian ancestry make up half or more of the populations of Mauritius, Trinidad, Guyana, Suriname, and Fiji and are substantial minorities in Sri Lanka, Malaysia, Singapore, Burma, Kenya, and South Africa.

Indian Thought and Society

In the later 1800s, Indian intellectuals responded to British rule and ideas in several ways. A small group of well-educated Indians wanted to combine the best of East and West. They sought reforms of customs, such as the ban on widow remarriage, that they saw as corruptions of Hinduism, but their influence waned after 1900. Another group, including the nationalist poet Rabindranath Tagore (RAH-bin-drah-NATH ta-GORE) (1861–1941), called attention to the glories of the Hindu past and argued that

Challenging British Imperialism with Spiritual Virtues

On the last day of the nineteenth century, Rabindranath Tagore wrote a poem in Bengali protesting the brutal imperialism of the war Britain was waging against the Boers in South Africa, driven, Tagore believed, by British nationalism. The poem suggested that the patient cultivation of the "spiritual virtues" of India and the East would become a force in the world after the reckless power of Western imperialism, sparked by nationalism, had lost its control over humankind. In this, he echoed the views of many Hindu nationalists and reformers that Hinduism and India had a special devotion to peace and spiritual insights that could benefit the Western world. For this poem and other influential writings, Tagore won the Noble Prize for literature in 1913.

The last sun of the century sets amidst the blood-red clouds of the West and the whirlwind of hatred.
  The naked passion of self-love of Nations, in its drunken delirium of greed, is dancing to the clash of steel and the howling verses of vengeance.
  The hungry self of the Nation shall burst in a violence of fury from its own shameless feeding, for it has made the world its food.
  And licking it, crunching it, and swallowing it in big morsels, It swells and swells,
  Till in the midst of its unholy feast descends the sudden shaft of heaven piercing its heart of grossness.
  The crimson glow of light on the horizon is not the light of thy dawn of peace, my Motherland.
  It is the glimmer of the funeral pyre burning to ashes the vast flesh—the self-love of the Nation—dead under its own excess.
  The morning waits behind the patient dark of the East, Meek and silent.
  Keep watch, India.

Bring your offerings of worship for that sacred sunrise.
  Let the first hymn of its welcome sound in your voice and sing
  "Come, Peace, thou daughter of God's own great suffering.
  Come with thy treasure of contentment, the sword of fortitude, And meekness crowning thy forehead."
  Be not ashamed, my brothers, to stand before the proud and the powerful, With your white robe of simpleness.
  Let your crown be of humility, your freedom the freedom of the soul.
  Build God's throne daily upon the ample barrenness of your poverty.
  And know that what is huge is not great and pride is not everlasting.

Thinking About the Reading

1. How does Tagore perceive nationalism?
2. How does he believe India should respond to Western power?

Source: From *Sources of Indian Tradition, vol. 2*, William Theodore De Bary, ed. Copyright © 1958 Columbia University Press. Reprinted with permission of the publisher.

India needed nothing from the West (see Witness to the Past: Challenging British Imperialism with Spiritual Virtues). One thinker, Swami Vivekananda (SWAH-me VIH-vee-keh-NAHN-da) (1863–1902), was particularly influential in his concern for ending both British cultural and political domination: "O India, this is your terrible danger. The spell of imitating the West is getting such a strong hold upon you. Be proud that thou art an Indian, and proudly proclaim: 'I am an Indian, every Indian is my brother.'"[7] His writings and lectures gave Indians great pride in their own culture.

Sayyid Ahmad Khan and Islamic Modernism

Like Hindus, Muslims were forced to rethink their values and prospects, leading some to embrace Islamic revivalism and others to embrace modernity. To Muslims, India seemed increasingly dominated by European and Hindu values and ideas. In response, some Muslims traveled to the Middle East in pursuit of Islamic knowledge. The most dogmatic and militant form of Islamic revivalism, Wahhabism (see Chapter 21), became popular in the northwest frontier and Bengal. Opposed to modernization, especially progressive ideas such as women's rights, the revivalists clashed with other Muslims, Christians, Sikhs, and Hindus. In contrast to revivalists, Muslim modernists, led by the cosmopolitan Sayyid Ahmad Khan (1817–1898), wanted Muslims to gain strength to achieve power. Khan argued that "the more worldly progress we make, the more glory Islam gains." He wanted to show that Islam was compatible with modern science, and in 1877 he founded a college at Aligarh (AL-ee-GAHR) that offered Western learning within a Muslim context. Aligarh graduates dominated Muslim political activity in India until independence.

Changes in Caste and Gender Roles

India's caste system was also affected by British colonialism. Before the colonial era, Hindus in Bengal, Punjab, and south India generally saw the formal differences among varied castes as of only moderate importance for groups and individuals. From the early 1800s, however—and owing partly to British attempts to win support from high-caste Hindus—British policies sharpened caste identities, classifying people largely through their caste affiliations. In the nineteenth century, much of India became more caste conscious than ever before, with upper castes stressing their uniqueness and lower castes wanting to emulate the upper castes to improve their social status. Hindu thinkers became divided about the caste system. Some social reformers called for abolishing caste, while defenders of Hindu culture praised the ideals of conduct and morality embedded in the caste system.

Gender relations also changed during colonial times. Traditionally, women and men had performed separate but interdependent roles within a household governed by men, but farming families faced a loss of work as land came under the control of absentee landlords who emphasized growing cash crops rather than food. Lower-caste men in north India who sought to emulate the upper castes often placed more restrictions on their women, including forcing some into purdah, or seclusion.

At the same time, however, new opportunities arose for other women. More girls attended school, and many became teachers, nurses, and midwives. The first women doctors graduated in the 1880s. Indian and British reformers sought to improve the lives of Indian women and foster greater equality between the genders. A new marriage act in 1872 provoked controversy by providing for both civil marriage and marriage across caste lines. The British tried incremental reforms, such as banning sati, allowing widow remarriage, and raising the age of female consent from ten to twelve. Both British and Indian reformers tended to support the idea of marriage as based on love but also encouraged wives to show their husbands and children self-sacrificing devotion.

The Rise of Nationalism

British rule under the *Raj* fostered national feelings and bitterness as Indians became more connected to the outside world. By 1900, Indians were publishing six hundred newspapers in various languages, which reported on world events, such as the Irish struggle for independence from England, the Japanese defeat of Russia in war, and the U.S. conquest of the Philippines, all of which inspired Indians to oppose British rule.

In 1885 nationalists formed the Indian National Congress, which worked for peaceful progress toward self-government. But the Congress, as it came to be known, mostly attracted well-educated professionals and merchants of brahman backgrounds and had few working-class or peasant members. British officials were scornful of the Congress, doubting the possibility of Indian unity in such a diverse society. Constitutional reforms in 1909 brought a measure of representative government, but Indians still lacked true legislative and financial power. Growing frustrations led impatient members to form a more aggressive nationalist faction within the Congress. By 1907, this radical group, led by a former journalist of Maratha background, Bal Gangadhar Tilak (1856–1920), transformed the Congress from a gentleman's pressure group into the spearhead of an active independence movement. A fierce opponent of Western influences, Tilak defended Hindu orthodoxy and custom, using religion as a vitalizing force for the nationalist movement. But many politically aware Indians disliked Tilak and remained wary of the Congress. Some feared that democratic values threatened their aristocratic privileges.

cultivation system
An agricultural policy imposed by the Dutch in Java that forced Javanese farmers to grow sugar on rice land.

Muslims perceived the Hindu-dominated Congress, particularly radical leaders like Tilak, as anti-Muslim. In 1906, the All-India Muslim League was founded with the goal of uniting a population scattered in pockets all over the country. Hindus constituted 80 percent of India's population; Muslims were a majority only in eastern Bengal, Sind, north Punjab, and the mountain districts west of the Indus Valley. The Muslim League's first great victory came in 1909, when British reforms guaranteed some seats in representative councils to Muslims, setting a precedence for minority representation and enraging the Congress. Hindu-Muslim rivalries continued to complicate the nationalist movement throughout the twentieth century.

LO³ Southeast Asia and Colonization

Southeast Asian societies had long flourished from trade and had formed strong, often dynamic, states, but by the 1700s, most faced increasing political and economic challenges from Western powers. During the 1800s, the challenges became more threatening, and by 1914, all of the major Southeast Asian societies except the Siamese had come under Western colonial control. The major changes came in Indonesia, Vietnam, and Burma, where the Dutch, French, and British, respectively, increased their power, and in the Philippines, which by the end of the 1800s was controlled by the United States. Thus Southeast Asian societies became tied, more than ever before, to the larger world but lost their political and economic independence.

Dutch Colonialism in Indonesia

Between 1750 and 1914, the Dutch expanded their power in the Indonesian archipelago. They already controlled the Spice Islands (Maluku) of northeast Indonesia and the large island of Java, territories that supplied them with great wealth. In 1799, the Dutch government replaced the Dutch East Indies Company with a formal colonial government that was charged with reenergizing the administration of its scattered territories in Java and Sumatra.

In 1830, Dutch administrators introduced the cultivation system, an agricultural policy that forced farmers on Java to grow sugar on their rice land. The

CHRONOLOGY

Southeast Asia, 1750–1914

1786	British base at Penang Island
1799	Abolition of Dutch East Indies Company
1788–1802	Tayson rule in Vietnam
1802	Nguyen dynasty in Vietnam
1819	British base at Singapore
1823–1826	First Anglo-Burman War
1830–1870	Cultivation system in Java
1851–1852	Second Anglo-Burman War
1858–1884	French conquest of Vietnam
1868–1910	Kingship of Chulalongkorn in Siam
1869	Opening of Suez Canal
1885–1886	Completion of British conquest of Burma
1897	Formation of Federation of Indochina
1898–1902	U.S. conquest of Philippines
1908	Dutch defeat of last Balinese kingdom

government profited by setting a low fixed price to pay peasants for sugar, even when world prices were high. The cultivation system enriched the Dutch but ultimately impoverished many peasants. A Dutch critic of the system described the results: "If anyone should ask whether the man who grows the products receives a reward proportionate to the yields, the answer must be in the negative. The Government compels him to grow on *his* land what pleases *it*; it punishes him when he sells the crop to anyone else but it."[8]

 East and Southeast Asia: An Annotated Directory of Internet Resources (*http://newton.uor.edu/ Departments&Programs/ AsianStudiesDept/ general.html*). This site offers many links on Southeast Asia.

Dutch-owned plantations growing sugar and other cash crops replaced the cultivation system in the 1870s.

In the later 1800s, the Dutch turned their attention to gaining control, and exploiting the resources, of the Indonesian islands they had not already conquered, such as Borneo and Sulawesi (see Map 22.2). The Dutch created Indonesia as a country by uniting the thousands of scattered societies

Interactive Map

and dozens of states of this vast, diverse archipelago into the Dutch East Indies. But the colony, governed from Batavia (now Jakarta) on Java, promoted little common national feeling and remained a collection of peoples with diverse languages and distinctive cultures. Later this diversity made it difficult to build an Indonesian nation with a common identity.

The British in Malaya and Burma

At the same time as the Dutch were expanding their power, the British became more politically and economically active in the southern part of the Malay Peninsula, later known as Malaya, and eventually they subjugated the varied Malay states. British Malaya originated in coastal port cities. Seeking a naval base in the eastern Indian Ocean, the British East India Company purchased Penang (puh-NANG) Island, off Malaya's northwest coast, from a cash-strapped Malay sultan in 1786. This action marked the first stage in creating a regional British sphere of influence. In 1819, a visionary British agent of the British East India Company, Jamaican-born Thomas Stamford Raffles (1781–1826), capitalized on local political unrest to acquire sparsely populated Singapore Island, at the tip of the Malay Peninsula. A fine harbor and strategic location made Singapore the base for Britain's regional thrust and a great source of profits. By the 1860s, the city built on Singapore, with a mostly Chinese population, had become the key China–India trade link and crossroads of Southeast Asian commerce. After obtaining the port city of Melaka from the Dutch in 1824, Britain now governed the three Malayan ports as one colony, known as the Straits Settlements.

"The Dutch created Indonesia as a country by uniting the thousands of scattered societies and dozens of states of this vast, diverse archipelago into the Dutch East Indies."

plural society
A medley of peoples who mix but do not blend, instead maintaining their own cultures, religions, languages, and customs.

British Rule in the Malay States

From their coastal ports, the British extended their influence into the Malay states. British merchants in the Straits Settlements pressured British authorities to intervene in the Malay states to acquire resources and markets. Adding to these challenges for the British was the steady immigration of Chinese to western Malaya, where they contracted with local Malay rulers to mine tin and gold, competing with British merchants. Chinese settlers established towns such as Kuala Lumpur (KWAH-luh loom-POOR), which later grew into major cities.

To facilitate access to these Malayan states, by the 1870s the British used order and security as their rationale for forcing various sultans to accept British domination. Britain soon achieved formal or informal control over nine sultanates, which, together with the Straits Settlements, became British Malaya. These actions eventually resulted in the artificial division of the historical Malay world into two countries, British Malaya (now part of Malaysia) and the Dutch East Indies (now Indonesia). The British also colonized the northern third of Borneo, creating the states of Sabah (British North Borneo) and Sarawak and imposing a protectorate over the old sultanate of Brunei.

British rule changed Malaya. Economic development occurred largely along the west coast, where the British encouraged the planting of pepper, tobacco, oil palm, and especially rubber. As thousands of Chinese and Indian immigrants settled there to work, Malaya developed a mining- and plantation-based economy that produced tin and rubber for Western resource and market needs. Malay villagers, pressured by British taxes to take up rubber planting, became integrated into the world economy and lost their traditional self-sufficiency. At the same time, the British maintained the Malay sultans and aristocracy as symbolic and privileged leaders of the Malay states. Thus a plural society developed, a medley of peoples—Malays, Chinese, and Indians—that mixed but did not blend.

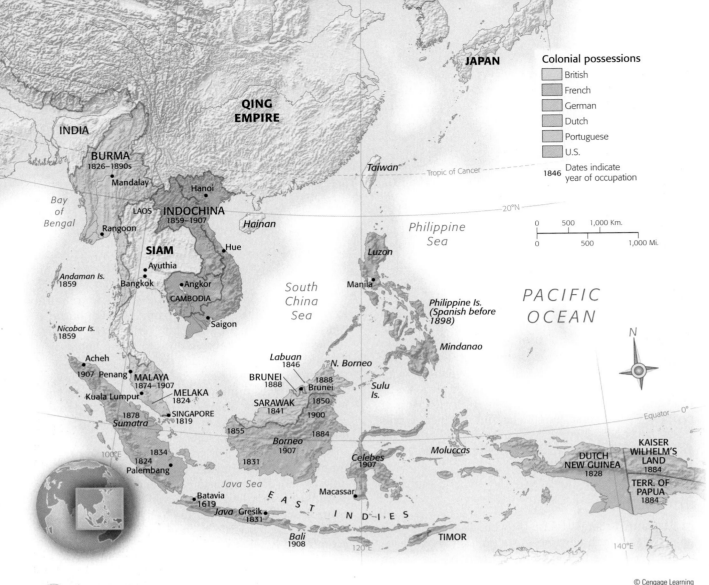

Map 22.2
The Colonization of Southeast Asia

Between 1800 and 1914, the European powers gradually conquered or gained control over the Southeast Asian societies that had not been colonized in the Early Modern Era. Only Siam remained independent.

British Rule in Burma As they expanded their power in India and Malaya, the British coveted Burma's rich lands and worried about Burmese claims to border regions. In three wars between 1824 and 1886, the British conquered Burma (today Myanmar). After the first two brutal wars, the British controlled much of southern Burma, leaving the Burman kings in control of only the north. As with the French in Vietnam, it took decades to colonize the country and overcome resistance. Vastly differing cultures and clashing strategic interests produced violent British-Burmese conflict.

The gradual loss of independence disrupted traditional society and proved devastating to the Burmans, the country's majority ethnic group. As they lost territory in the first two military defeats, Burmans began to feel an impending doom. Fear for the future was expressed in a frenzied cultural activity, including drama, love poetry, and music. For instance, Myawaddy (mee-ya-WAH-dee) (1761–1853), a government minister, soldier, scholar, and musician from a prominent noble family, tried to salvage Burman traditions by writing plays set in villages and collecting folk songs from the Burmans and other ethnic groups in the kingdom. The court, fearing that the Burmese heritage might disappear if the British triumphed, also compiled *The Glass Palace Chronicle*, a history of Burma from earliest times.

Between 1853 and 1878, a new Burmese king, the idealistic Mindon, tried to salvage his country's prospects by pursuing modernization and cultural renewal and seeking good relations with the British. However, worried that he might succeed in strengthening Burma, the British tried to humiliate Mindon and his government; Mindon in turn attempted to break down barriers between the court and the Burmese people. As the Burmans had feared, in 1886 the British completed their conquest, taking control of the government and exiling the royal family. When some Burmese resisted British rule, the British, in what they called "pacification," retaliated by destroying whole villages and executing rebel leaders. The Burman aristocracy and the royal system they had administered were destroyed, and Burma became a province of British India, a humiliating fate for this proud people.

Vietnam: Colonization and Resistance

For centuries a major power in Southeast Asia, Vietnam fell to French colonialism after a bitter struggle. In the 1700s, Vietnam was beset by growing problems, including civil war and rebellion. While a new dynasty reestablished some stability, it was unable to thwart the aggressive actions of the French, who colonized Vietnam against stiff resistance. The unpopular French regime changed Vietnamese society by introducing competitive capitalism into once-cooperative communities, linking the Vietnamese to the uncertainties of the world economy, undermining traditional politics, and otherwise exploiting the Vietnamese people.

The Tayson Rebellion

The Vietnamese state faced many challenges between 1750 and 1850. One challenge emerged with the Tayson Rebellion, launched in 1771 by three brothers from Tayson, a village in southern Vietnam. Social revolutionaries committed to a unified Vietnamese nation and fed up with corruption and misrule, the Tayson brothers and their thousands of armed followers fought for thirty years against the Vietnamese emperors and their French allies. In 1788 the Taysons defeated their foes and reestablished the national unity fractured in the long civil wars. They also sponsored economic expansion and rallied the people against a Chinese invasion.

The Nguyen Dynasty

A little more than a decade later, in 1802, Nguyen Anh (NEW-yin ahn) (1761–1820), the leader of a princely family based in Hue, led a force that defeated the Taysons and established a new imperial dynasty with French assistance, but the Nguyen dynasty he founded was unpopular and unable to address the social and economic inequalities that had inspired the Tayson Rebellion. *The Tale of Kieu*, a 3,300-line poem written by diplomat Nguyen Du (no relation to the dynasty) in the early 1800s, reflected a growing criticism of the greed and hypocrisy of upper-class Vietnamese and articulated the mistreatment of the Vietnamese people. But the internal challenges facing the Nguyen were soon eclipsed when the French conquered Vietnam. In 1858, the militarily powerful French, hoping to gain more commerce by controlling the Mekong and Red River trade routes to China, began what they arrogantly called a "civilizing mission" to spread French culture and Christianity and launched a bloody campaign of conquest against a determined but badly outgunned imperial Vietnamese resistance. In a quarter century of conflict, the French first conquered the south and then moved north, facing Vietnamese opposition the whole way.

Nguyen Quang Bich and the Can Vuong Rebels

By 1884, the French had conquered Vietnam but still had to consolidate their gains before they could impose their goals on the country. Consolidation proved more difficult than expected, as they faced prolonged resistance. It took the French another fifteen years to suppress the heroic efforts of thousands of poorly armed rebel groups known as the can vuong (kan voo-AHN) ("aid-

> **can vuong**
> ("Aid-the-king") Rebel groups who waged guerrilla warfare for fifteen years against the French occupation of Vietnam.

> " In the 1700s, Vietnam was beset by growing problems, including civil war and rebellion. "

the-king"), who resisted fiercely. One of the rebel leaders, the mandarin Nguyen Quang Bich, rejected any compromise with the French: "Please do not mention the word *surrender* any more. You cannot give any good counsel to a man who is determined to die." [9] The can vuong rebels became powerful symbols of resistance for later generations of Vietnamese fighting colonialism and foreign invasion. In suppressing the can vuong struggle, the French massacred thousands.

The French Federation of Indochina

In 1897, the French created the Federation of Indochina, so named because their Southeast Asian colonies were located between India and China. The federation was an artificial unit linking Vietnam, which the French broke into three separate territories, with newly acquired Cambodia and the diverse societies the French combined to create the colony of Laos. Both Cambodia and Laos had very different social, cultural, political, and historical legacies from those of Vietnam and relatively little in common with each other.

The French maintained their rule by force while allowing French commercial interests and settlers to exploit natural resources and markets. Following the pattern of European colonization elsewhere, the colonial regime destroyed the traditional autonomy of the Vietnamese villages by appointing leaders, often from outside, rather than allowing villages to select their own leaders, the traditional system, and by greatly increasing the tax burden to finance colonial administrative costs. Under French rural policies, many peasants lost their land or access to communal lands, and perhaps half of the cultivated land was turned over to private landowners, investors, and rubber planters, mostly French. France also made rice a major export crop, but the expanded production favored large landowners rather than peasants.

Siamese Modernization

The Siamese (today known as the Thai) were the only Southeast Asian country that retained their independence, a success that resulted from certain favorable conditions and wise leadership. In the early 1800s, when the British began pressuring Burma, Siam was a strong, flexible state under the vigorous new Bangkok-based Chakri dynasty, founded in 1767. Seeing Burma's dilemma, able Chakri kings mounted a successful strategy to resist Western pressures. With Britain and France, who both coveted Siam, preoccupied with controlling neighboring societies, Siamese

Bastille Day Parade in Vietnam This painting, by an unknown Vietnamese scholar, subtly criticizes the unpopular French colonization by satirizing the annual French holiday. A French man is shown with his arm around a Vietnamese woman, while unarmed Vietnamese lantern-bearers are being commanded by a French official.

leaders had time to counter a possible Western threat by strengthening government institutions, improving their economic infrastructure, and broadening their popular support in their diverse kingdom.

The farsighted Siamese kings who ruled during the late nineteenth and early twentieth centuries understood the changes in Southeast Asian politics and the rise of Western power, and they promoted a modernization policy designed to ensure political independence and economic growth: they yielded to the West when necessary and consolidated what remained. The price of political independence for Siam was giving up its claims over Laos and transferring northern Malaya to Britain. Siamese leaders also agreed to commercial agreements that opened the country to Western businesses. Nonetheless, the Siamese retained some control over their future. Finally, to minimize conflict with each other, British and French leaders opted to leave Siam as a buffer between British Burma and French Indochina.

WWW
Southeast Asia Guide (*http:// www.library.wisc .edu/guides/SEAsia/*). An easy-to-use site on Southeast Asia.

Two kings and their advisers were most responsible for Siam's success in avoiding colonization and modernizing the kingdom. The first, the scholarly, peace-loving King Mongkut (MAHN-kut) (r. 1851–1868), who had served as a Buddhist monk and teacher for several decades, was probably the most perceptive leader of his time in Southeast Asia. An outspoken man who had studied science and had learned to read Latin, Mongkut signed treaties with various Western powers, often with terms unfavorable for Siam, and invited Western aid to modernize his kingdom. To foster goodwill and provide his heirs with an understanding of the West, Mongkut hired the wives of Christian missionaries to teach English to his wives and sons.

The second king, Mongkut's son, Chulalongkorn (CHOO-lah-LONG-corn) (r. 1868–1910), who had traveled in Asia, built on his father's foundation by emphasizing diplomacy and modernization. Chulalongkorn started a broad reform program that included abolishing slavery, centralizing government services, strengthening the bureaucracy, establishing a Western-style government education system, and stimulating economic growth by encouraging the immigration of Chinese merchants and opening new land for rice production. These measures helped Siam successfully resist the colonizing intentions of the Western powers. When Chulalongkorn died in 1910, Siam (today called Thailand) was still independent.

The Philippines, Spain, and the United States

The Spanish had colonized the Philippines much earlier than the Dutch, French, and British had acquired territory in Southeast Asia (see Chapter 18). However, by the 1870s, Spanish rule had decayed and local resentment had grown. Philippine nationalism sprouted in the struggle against the Spanish, eventually generating an armed revolution that inspired other colonized Asian peoples. But the Filipino nationalists soon faced a more powerful foe, the United States. The military intervention of the United States during the revolution had momentous consequences, as the Americans helped defeat Spain but then crushed the revolutionary movement, replacing Spain as the colonial power.

The Filipino Nationalist Movement

As happened in the Spanish colonies in Latin America (see Chapter 19), hostility toward the corrupt, repressive, and economically stagnant rule of Spain had simmered for decades in the Philippines. Educated, local-born Filipinos of Spanish, indigenous, and mixed-descent (mestizo) background resented colonial power, the privileged immigrants from Spain, and the domination of the Catholic Church.

The Philippine nationalist movement arose to bring together all of the diverse societies of the islands and to oppose continued Spanish domination. Gradually, resentment of Spain turned nationalists toward revolution, which broke out in 1896. One dissident, Emilio Aguinaldo (AH-gee-NAHL-doe) (1870–1964), a small-town mayor of Chinese mestizo background, called on the Filipinos to rebel: "Filipinos! Open your eyes! Lovers of their native land, rise up in arms, to proclaim their liberty and independence." The revolutionaries welcomed women into their movement, even while they maintained conventional gender attitudes, viewing a woman as, in the words of one leader, a "helper and partner in the hardships of life."[10] Despite the revolutionary's heroic efforts, however, by 1897 the Spanish had contained the revolution, though they failed to capture all the leaders or to crush scattered resistance.

George Dewey and American Intervention

The situation changed dramatically in 1898 when the U.S. fleet, commanded by Admiral George Dewey, sailed into Manila Bay and destroyed the Spanish navy, causing thousands of

Spaniards to flee Manila. Americans had engaged in occasional naval skirmishes in Southeast Asia throughout the 1800s, and the American intervention in the Philippines reflected decades of American activity in Southeast Asia as Americans sought resources and markets. But not until the Spanish-American War in 1898 did the United States assert its military power on a large scale in the region. The fighting between U.S. and Spanish forces began in the Caribbean before expanding to the Philippines. The U.S. attack on Manila rejuvenated the revolutionaries led by Aguinaldo, who received initial American support and soon controlled much of the country. The revolutionaries declared independence and established a republican government with a semidemocratic constitution, but U.S. leaders had other plans for the country.

> ❝ Colonial governments varied widely, although Europeans always held ultimate political authority. ❞

The Philippine-American War

Taking up Rudyard Kipling's call to assume world responsibilities and "the white man's burden," U.S. President William McKinley called for colonization of the Philippines, ignoring the deep Filipino desire for independence. McKinley proclaimed: "It is our duty to uplift and civilize and Christianize and by God's Will do our very best by [the Filipinos]."[11] McKinley, who admitted he could not locate the Philippines on a world map, underestimated the Filipino opposition to the U.S. occupation. Some 125,000 American troops fought during the four-year Philippine-American War, and more than 5,000 Americans and some 16,000 Filipinos died in battle. Another 200,000 Filipinos died from famine and disease generated by the conflict.

American soldiers were surprised and demoralized by the ferocity of Filipino resistance. In many districts, Filipino soldiers enjoyed the active support of most of the local population. With peasant help, the elusive revolutionaries lived off the land and practiced a harassing form of guerrilla warfare. Both sides committed atrocities, including torture. Angered by American deaths there, U.S. General Jacob Smith ordered his men to turn Samar Island into a "howling wilderness," to "kill and burn. The more you kill and burn the better you will please me."[12] The reports caused Americans at home to become deeply split on the war. Strong supporters, especially in the business community, coveted Philippine resources and markets, and U.S. newspapers urged the slaughter of all

Filipinos who resisted. The writer Mark Twain excoriated such motives in his 1900 rewriting of "The Battle Hymn of the Republic": "Mine eyes have seen the orgy of the launching of the Sword; He is searching out the hoardings where the strangers' wealth is stored; He hath loosed his fateful lightnings, and with woe and death has scored; His lust is marching on."[13]

By 1902, after the revolutionaries were defeated and many wealthy Filipinos, to protect their interests, had decided to support U.S. rule, the United States declared the Philippines an American colony. The Americans attempted to reshape the society of those they paternalistically called "our little brown brothers," using the United States as the preferred model. They established an elected legislature filled mostly by Filipinos, but its decisions had to be approved by U.S. officials. In contrast to most Western colonies, the American colonial government fostered education, literacy, and modern health care, and the schools produced a large number of Filipinos who were fluent in English. But American rule generally ignored peasant needs while perpetuating the power of the Filipino landowners, who supported U.S. rule.

LO⁴ The Reshaping of Southeast Asia

Colonialism in Southeast Asia had many parallels to that in India and Africa. Although some Southeast Asians benefited, many others experienced worsening living conditions. From a global perspective, colonialism linked Southeast Asia more firmly to a Western-dominated world economy. But colonial policies also affected local political, social, intellectual, and cultural life. Like Indians, Southeast Asians responded to the challenges of colonialism in creative ways.

Colonial Governments

Colonialism destroyed the political autonomy of Southeast Asians. The only colony with much self-government was the U.S.-ruled Philippines, which had an elected legislature. The British did allow Malayans some participation in city or state government and, in 1935, formed a legislature in Burma that included both elected and appointed members. France and the Netherlands, however, although democracies themselves, allowed little democracy in their colonies.

Colonial governments varied widely, although Europeans always held ultimate political authority. As in sub-Saharan Africa (see Chapter 21), Europeans introduced either direct or indirect rule. Direct rule removed traditional leaders, such as the Burmese kings, or made them symbolic only, as with the Vietnamese emperors. Direct rule was used in Burma, the Philippines, Vietnam, and parts of Indonesia. By contrast, in Malaya, Cambodia, Laos, and some parts of Indonesia, Europeans applied indirect rule, governing a district through the traditional leaders, such as Malay sultans, Cambodian kings, or Javanese aristocrats. Whether governing directly or indirectly, the colonial authorities played off one ethnic group or one region against another, in the process creating problems that persisted after independence and made national unity difficult. Colonial boundaries in Southeast Asia ignored traditional ethnic relationships and rivalries, laying a basis for political instability. Countries such as Burma, Indonesia, and Laos were artificial creations of European colonialism rather than organic unities with more or less culturally similar populations.

Southeast Asia in the World Economy

As in India, the transformation of economic life was at least as significant as that of conquest and political reorganization. Southeast Asians had long participated in world trade as exporters of valuable resources, from spices and sugar to tin and gold. Because subsistence food farming could not produce enough revenues for colonial governments or investors, it was supplanted by cash crop farming, replacing the earlier age of commerce. Extracting mineral or agricultural wealth meant that Western businessmen controlled the top level of the economy, including the banks, import-export companies, mines, wells, and plantations. Gradually, as Southeast Asia came to be integrated into the world economy as a producer of raw materials and consumer of Western food and manufactured goods, it became one of the world's most valuable economic areas.

> "Many colonies developed monoculture economies that were dependent on the export of one or two major commodities, such as rubber and tin from Malaya, rice from Burma, or rubber and rice from Vietnam."

Colonial taxation policies encouraged people to grow cash crops, such as rubber, pepper, sugar, coffee, tea, opium, and palm oil; cut timber; mine gold and tin; and drill oil. Many colonies developed monoculture economies that were dependent on the export of one or two major commodities, such as rubber and tin from Malaya, rice from Burma, or rubber and rice from Vietnam. The world price for these exports fluctuated with unstable global demand, fostering a local economy that prospered or floundered depending on decisions made in Europe or North America. These economic activities also had an impact on the natural environment, as forests were cleared for plantations or logged for timber to be shipped out of the region.

For many Southeast Asians, rubber growing became the key factor in shaping their lives. The invention of the first bicycles and then automobiles opened up vast markets for rubber tires. To meet this need, the British introduced rubber cultivation to Malaya, and it then spread to Sumatra, Borneo, southern Thailand, Vietnam, and Cambodia. Thousands of acres of forest were cleared for rubber growing, mostly on European-owned plantations. Malaya became the world's greatest exporter of natural rubber, supplying more than half of the world supply by 1920. To produce rubber, plantation workers suffered long hours, strict discipline, monotonous routine, and poor food. A Vietnamese writer, on witnessing a French-owned rubber estate, said that "every day one was worn down a bit more, cheeks sunken, eyes hollow. Everyone appeared almost dead."[14]

Economic growth had major consequences for everyone but did not benefit all equally. For a small minority, especially the European colonizers and the local officials and merchants who cooperated with them, it brought wealth, but for most Southeast Asians, the results of economic growth were mixed. For instance, the Javanese peasants who grew sugar initially earned new income, and some took advantage of improved irrigation facilities to grow more rice as well as the required sugar. When peasants came to depend on sugar profits for survival, they often became impoverished because of rising costs. By 1900, some Dutch officials admitted that colonial rule had reduced many Javanese to complete poverty.

Java Coffee Plantation This painting from the nineteenth century shows a European manager supervising barefoot laborers who are raking and drying coffee beans, a major Javan cash crop.

tually opened shops in Southeast Asia with their earnings, others remained too poor to return to China and spent their lives as laborers, miners, or plantation workers.

Other Chinese who did prosper as merchants, planters, and mine owners decided to remain in Southeast Asia. Through enterprise, cooperation, and organization, they dominated retail trade, becoming the commercial middle class in every colony except Burma. Some cities, such as Kuala Lumpur and Singapore, were largely Chinese in population; other cities also had substantial Chinese communities. The Chinese who settled permanently married local women or brought families from China. By adjusting to local conditions, the Chinese became a permanent presence in Southeast Asian life.

British Malaya attracted Indian settlers as well as Chinese, creating a more complex ethnic configuration. Indian immigrants had come to the Straits Settlements cities for decades as traders, craftsmen, and workers. Beginning in the 1880s, people from the Tamil-speaking region of southeast India were imported to work on Malayan rubber plantations, where they experienced the harshness of plantation life. The Chinese and Indians together eventually outnumbered the Malays, sparking Malay fears of being overwhelmed by immigrants. The British, to maintain their control, skillfully maintained the political separation of the three groups and discouraged cooperation among them.

Population Trends and Immigration

In addition to exploiting resources and developing economic monocultures, colonial policies also sparked rapid population growth. In 1600, perhaps 20 to 25 million people lived in Southeast Asia. By 1800, this number had grown to 30 or 35 million, and by the late 1930s, it was around 140 or 150 million. The greatest increases came on Java: in 1800, some 10 million people lived on Java, and this figure grew to 30 million by 1900 and 48 million by 1940. Dutch policies contributed to population growth directly or indirectly by fostering better health care and largely maintaining social order. As a result, people lived longer. Economic incentives also encouraged larger families to provide more labor for the fields. Fast-growing populations, especially in Java, Vietnam, and the Philippines, resulted in smaller farm plots and more landless people.

Immigration from other Asian regions also contributed to population growth. Between 1800 and 1941, millions of Chinese and smaller numbers of Indians immigrated to Southeast Asia to work as laborers, miners, planters, and merchants. Chinese immigrants chiefly came from poor, overcrowded coastal provinces in southeast China and typically were males whose goal was to make enough money to return to their native villages wealthy and respected. While some did achieve this goal and many even-

Social and Cultural Changes

Colonial policies altered the lives of men and women, whether rural or urban, immigrant or local-born, in Southeast Asia. Economic changes particularly affected women, who had traditionally played a major economic role in local society as farmers, traders, and weavers and often enjoyed considerable independence from men. Now, as men took up cash crop farming, the responsibility for growing the family's food was often largely left to women, increasing their workload. Economic change also robbed many women of their key role as small traders in the local marketplace, decreasing their status as income earners for the family. The expansion of textile imports also affected women's status. After 1850, when inexpensive industry-made textiles began pouring in from Europe, people began to switch from using local handwoven cloth to imported goods, slowly forcing women out of the business.

> "Colonial policies altered the lives of men and women, whether rural or urban, immigrant or local-born, in Southeast Asia."

Gender Roles and Urbanization

Women did not face their problems passively, however. Some joined movements to assert their rights. Siamese feminists opposed polygamy and supported girls' education. An inspirational Javanese woman, Raden Adjeng Kartini, also founded schools for girls and fostered Indonesian women's awareness of their situation. Today many Indonesians honor Kartini as a heroine whose writings and life influenced the rise of Indonesian feminism and nationalism. Southeast Asia already had large cities, but the coming of Western rule encouraged more rapid urbanization. Cities such as Manila, Jakarta, Rangoon (today known as Yangon), Singapore, Kuala Lumpur, and Saigon (today Ho Chi Minh City) attracted immigrant populations from other societies, such as the Chinese, and migrants from nearby districts. Ethnic variety characterized colonial towns and cities, which offered a diverse assortment of food stalls and restaurants, private schools that catered to different ethnic groups, and buildings erected by different religious sects. Nearly every city contained Muslim mosques, Buddhist, Hindu, and Chinese temples, and Christian churches. Some descendants of Chinese and Indian immigrants assimilated into the surrounding culture; friendships and even marriages crossed ethnic lines. For example, much of Thailand's political and economic leadership today has some mix of Chinese and Siamese ancestry, a result of cultural assimilation or intermarriage.

Read about Kartini, the inspirational social activist and teacher who represented a feminist consciousness new to Indonesia.

Educational and Cultural Transformation

Colonial governments differed in their commitment to education and assimilation. Most colonies left education to the Christian missions. As a result of the influence of mission schools, some Vietnamese, Indonesians, and Chinese became Christian, and hill peoples frequently did so, though few Theravada Buddhists or Muslims abandoned their faiths. A few colonies set up government schools, such as the U.S.-ruled Philippines and independent Siam. At the other extreme was French Vietnam, which spent little public money on schools. In general, in both the mission and government schools, the Western emphasis on individualism conflicted with traditional community values and loosened the social fabric.

Some communities developed alternatives to Western education. Buddhist and Muslim groups, which had sponsored schools for centuries, expanded their schools to enroll more students and teach them from a non-Western perspective. Other schools mixed Eastern and Western ideas. For example, in 1922 a mystical Javanese religious organization established schools that provided an alternative to both Islamic and Christian instruction. These schools emphasized Indonesian arts such as music and dance but also used Western ideas; for example, they encouraged students to express their own ideas and stressed social equality and the psychological development of their students. Many graduates became nationalist leaders.

Southeast Asians also expressed their sentiments in new cultural forms. For instance, on Java, musicians mixed European string instruments with the rhythms of the largely percussion Javanese gamelan orchestra to create a romantic new popular music, *kronchong*, which became widely popular on the island. Later in the early twentieth century, Western composers who observed performances by Javanese and Balinese gamelan orchestras incorporated gamelan influences into their music.

In most colonies, a modern literature developed that reflected both alienation from colonial rule and an awareness of rapid social and cultural change. But its criticism of the colonial regime was suppressed, forcing authors to make their points indirectly. For example, Vietnamese writers used historical themes from precolonial times or critiques of Vietnamese society to discuss contemporary conditions. This evasion was necessary to avoid censorship or even arrest for dissent.

Listen to a synopsis of Chapter 22.

CHAPTER 23

East Asia and the Russian Empire Face New Challenges, 1750–1914

Learning Outcomes

After reading this chapter, you should be able to answer the following questions:

LO¹ What were the causes and consequences of the Opium War?

LO² Why did Chinese efforts at modernization fail?

LO³ What factors aided Japan in the quest for modernization?

LO⁴ How did the Meiji government transform Japan and Korea?

LO⁵ What factors explain the expansion of the Russian Empire?

❝The sacred traditions of our ancestors have fallen into oblivion. Those who watch attentively the march of events feel a dark and wonderful presentiment. We are on the eve of an immense revolution. But will the impulse come from within or without?**❞**

—A Chinese official, 1846[1]

In 1820, Li Ruzhen (LEE Ju-Chen) (1763–1830) published a satiric novel that boldly attacked Chinese social conditions, knowing that it would expose him to criticism from conservatives who favored the status quo. Set in the Tang dynasty a millennium earlier, *Flowers in the Mirror* was a complex novel that explored, among other themes, the relationship between the sexes.

Test your knowlege before you read this chapter.

In one section of *Flowers,* Li describes a trip by three men to a country in which all of the gender roles that had been followed in China for centuries have been reversed. In this country, men suffer the pain of ear piercing and footbinding and endure hours every day putting on makeup, all to please the women who run the country. One of the men, Merchant Lin, is conscripted as a court "lady" by the female "king":

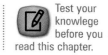

What do you think?

The responses of China and Japan to the Western threat were remarkably similar.

Strongly Disagree						Strongly Agree
1	2	3	4	5	6	7

> In due course, his [bound] feet lost much of their original shape. Blood and flesh were squeezed into a pulp and then little remained of feet but dry bones and skin, shrunk to a dainty size. . . . With blood-red lipstick, and powder adorning his face, and jade and pearl adorning his coiffure and ears, Merchant Lin assumed, at last, a not unappealing appearance.[2]

Li seemed an unlikely man to address so starkly and sympathetically the low social status and daily challenges faced by women. A conventionally educated Confucian scholar who had failed the civil service examinations, Li became a writer on various nonfiction subjects. Growing Western intrusion, unchecked population growth, domestic unrest, political corruption, and growing opium addiction spurred Chinese scholars such as Li to reassess the relevance of Chinese traditions, such as outmoded civil service examinations, the

‹‹Treaty Between Japan and China After an industrializing Japan defeated a declining China in a war over Japanese encroachments in Korea (1894–1895), diplomats from both nations met to negotiate a peace treaty. This painting shows the Chinese and Japanese representatives, easily identified by their different clothing styles, discussing the terms.

Visual Connection Archive

inequality of wealth, and women's footbinding. The growing dissatisfaction with China's practices that Li's provocative book represented, combined with Western intervention in China, set the stage for the immense revolution that would eventually transform this ancient society.

Like the Chinese, the Japanese also faced challenges, even before Western ships forced the nation open in the 1850s. Soon the old system fell, and in the 1870s, Japan's new leaders began an all-out program of modernization in an effort to prevent Western domination. By 1900, the Japanese had heavy industry, a modern military, and a comprehensive educational system. Emulating the Western imperialist countries, they also sought their own resources and markets abroad and soon colonized their neighbor, Korea, which had not modernized.

Although historically linked more closely to Europe than to Asia, Russia also became a factor in Asian politics after it expanded across Siberia to the Pacific. Perched on the borders of Europe, East Asia, and the Islamic Middle East and Central Asia, Russia engaged with societies in each of these regions through trade, warfare, and conquest. After it became dominant in parts of eastern Europe, pushed its borders southward into Ottoman territories, and conquered the Central Asian states, Russia was the largest territorial power in Eurasia.

LO¹ The Zenith and Decline of Qing China

Established by the Manchus, pastoralist invaders from Manchuria, the Qing (ching) (1644–1912) was the last dynasty in China's long history, the final phase

> "In the eighteenth century, Qing China was still one of the world's largest, most insular, most powerful, most prosperous, and most technologically sophisticated societies."

of China's 2,000-year-old imperial system. After reaching its zenith in the eighteenth century, Qing China experienced severe challenges and eventual decay in the nineteenth century. Several catastrophic wars resulted in unequal treaties with the West that increased Western penetration, and dynastic decline fostered major rebellions. Meanwhile, China's economy underwent changes, Christian missionaries posed a challenge to Chinese culture, and increasing poverty prompted millions of Chinese to seek their fortunes abroad. This decline in world standing had as much to do with Europe's rise as with China's failures.

Qing China in an Imperial World

In the eighteenth century, Qing China was still one of the world's largest, most insular, most powerful, most prosperous, and most technologically sophisticated societies, but troubling signs of decay developed. Although the Manchus had followed the political example of earlier Chinese dynasties, they were more despotic. Manchus dominated the top government positions and forbade intermarriage with the Chinese. While the Chinese accepted Manchu rule—as they had tolerated alien rule in the past—they resented the ethnic discrimination. There were other problems as well. Like various earlier dynasties, the Qing had built a great empire by occupying frontier regions and consolidating China's borders, but doing so stretched Qing military power and proved economically costly.

Qing Prosperity Despite the challenges, the Qing generally maintained domestic prosperity for nearly two centuries. Chinese opened new lands for settlement and introduced crops from the Americas that provided additional food sources, such as corn, sweet potatoes, and peanuts. The volume of domestic trade grew in the 1700s, spurred by new textile factories, increased copper mining, and more money in circulation in the world's largest commercial economy. In 1830, China still accounted for one-third of world manufacturing, and in the 1850s, a British observer called the Chinese the world's greatest manufacturing people.

As a result of its prosperity and agricultural growth, China's population doubled from 150 million in 1700 to 300 million by 1800, and then rose to 432 million by 1850. Peasants responded to population pressure by finding additional marginal land to farm and expanding their use of irrigation and fertilizer. But population growth still outstripped the growth of the food supply, straining resources and fostering corruption, which increased Chinese resentment of the Qing government. Although in the 1700s living standards in the more developed regions of China were probably comparable to those of the more affluent parts of western Europe, in the 1800s they deteriorated, partly because of overpopulation.

Chinese culture and society became more conservative under the Manchus. In 1783, the Qing government prohibited books and plays that it considered treasonable to the Manchu state or subversive to traditional Chinese values. The Qing introduced harsher laws against unconventional behavior, such as homosexuality, which Chinese governments had generally tolerated for centuries, and increased social pressures on women to conform to such gender expectations as refusing to remarry after they became widows. The Qing mandated that public meetings be held every month in which an imperial edict be read out. It emphasized Confucian notions of moral virtue, heaping honor on filial sons, loyal officials, philanthropists, and faithful wives. Because increasing numbers of women were literate, the government published instructional books containing historical writings, some of them more than two millennia old, on female obligations. Women were advised not to look around when walking, laugh aloud, talk loudly, or sway their skirts when standing.

> 66 Widespread corruption, increasing poverty, drug trafficking, and local uprisings all added to increasingly severe economic problems. 99

Western Pressure and Qing Decline

China faced problems during the later Qing period and showed clear signs of dynastic decline by 1800. Widespread corruption, increasing poverty, drug trafficking, and local uprisings all added to increasingly severe economic problems. As political, economic, and social conditions deteriorated at home, European nations exerted pressure on the Qing government to grant them more privileges. China had encountered Western adventurers, traders, and missionaries already in the sixteenth and seventeenth centuries. Traders from Portugal, Russian, the Netherlands, and Great Britain had made inroads in the 1700s, and Westerners increasingly wanted more access, including freedom to travel inside China.

Chinese Isolationism

The Chinese debated how much contact with the West to allow. Chinese merchants in coastal cities, who had long traded with Southeast Asia, often supported contact because they could make fortunes by trading with the Europeans. Nevertheless, being largely self-sufficient in food and resources, China did not need foreign trade, and Qing emperors were unwilling to make concessions to the more open trade system desired by the Europeans. Before 1800, the Qing restricted trade to a few ports such as Guangzhou and Siberian outposts, and

CHRONOLOGY

China, 1750–1915

1644–1912	Qing dynasty
1839–1842	Opium War
1842	Treaty of Nanjing
1850–1864	Taiping Rebellion
1856–1860	Arrow War
1894–1895	Sino-Japanese War
1898	100 Days of Reform
1900	Boxer Rebellion
1911	Chinese Revolution
1912	Formation of Chinese Republic
1915	Japan's 21 Demands on China

they refused diplomatic relations on an equal basis with the West. In the 1600s, Catholics and all other missionaries were expelled and prohibited from working in China. The Chinese knew little of the Western world and were confused by the diverse nationalities of the European peoples, whom they disparagingly called "foreign devils." Chinese leaders viewed European merchants as barbarians bearing tribute, and they required visiting diplomats to perform the humiliating custom of *kotow*, in which they prostrated themselves before the emperor.

World-Views of East and West

Chinese and European world-views were also incompatible. The British righteously saw themselves as benefiting China by opening the country to free trade. A British official wrote in 1821 that governments should let the stream of commerce flow as it will. China's attitude toward foreign trade and the outside world was well exemplified in a letter written by the Qing emperor Qianlong (chee-YEN-loong) (r. 1736–1795) to King George III of Britain following a British trade mission in 1793 requesting more access. The emperor denied Britain permission to establish an embassy but commended the king for his respectful spirit of humility in sending tribute: "It behooves you, O king, to display ever greater devotion and loyalty in the future, so that by perpetual submission to our throne, you may secure peace and prosperity for your country hereafter."[3]

> "The opium trade undermined the country's social fiber and impoverished thousands of families."

The Opium Trade and War

Half a century after Emperor Qianlong blithely dismissed the British request with these words, the tables were turned. Their humiliating defeats in two wars in the mid-1800s forcibly jarred the Chinese from their complacency and made clear that the world was changing. These wars forced China to open its doors and to rethink traditional values and institutions.

Guangzhou During the eighteenth century, the Western traders in China were restricted to one riverside district in Guangzhou (Canton), where they built their warehouses, businesses, and homes in European style.

Cultivating an Addiction

In the late 1700s, the British, taking the lead in the China trade, badly wanted more Chinese silk and tea, which had become valued revenue sources for British merchants. But China, desiring little from the West, accepted only precious gold and silver bullion as payment. Between the 1760s and 1780s, the import of silver into China increased more than 500 percent, causing an unfavorable trade disparity for the British. British found a solution in opium, an addictive drug that was grown in India and the Middle East. In the 1720s, the Chinese discovered that they could smoke opium for pleasure by mixing it in a pipe with tobacco. A highly addictive drug, it produced severe withdrawal symptoms such as cramps and nausea.

The British began to grow opium as a cash crop in the Bengal region of India in the 1700s, and soon British and American traders began smuggling opium into China. The Western drug smugglers and the governments that supported them, being concerned only with profits, were indifferent to the terrible moral and social consequences of their enterprise; by 1838, there were 5 to 10 million Chinese addicts. The opium trade undermined the country's social fiber and impoverished thousands of families. One Chinese official concluded that "opium is nothing else but a flowing poison [which] utterly ruins the minds and morals of the people, a dreadful calamity."[4]

Chinese Reaction to Opium Importation

The corrupt opium trade system at Guangzhou fostered conflict. China outlawed the opium trade in 1729, but to continue bringing in their huge profits from this trade, during the 1830s the British doubled opium imports while also pressing for reform of the trading system. Chinese leaders responded by further isolating the Western traders and mounting an attack on the opium trade. The emperor appointed the mandarin Lin Zezu (lin tsay-shoe) (1785–1850) to go to Guangzhou as commissioner and end the opium trade. Lin, an incorruptible Confucian moralist, concluded that if the opium traffic was not stopped, China would become poorer and its people weaker. Lin ordered his officials to raid the Western warehouses, where they seized and destroyed 20,000 chests of opium worth millions of dollars.

The Opium War

Lin's seizure of opium outraged Western traders, and Britain declared war. The following Opium War (1839–1842), as the British called it, proved disastrous for China. The British fleet raided up and down the Chinese coast, blockading and bombarding ports, including Guangzhou. Although China had one of the world's most formidable military forces in 1600, since then Europeans had greatly surpassed China in naval and military technology. The British won most of the battles of the war, and when defeat was certain, dozens of Qing officers committed suicide. The lost battles forced the Chinese to assess the Western threat. While a few were concerned with the inadequacy of Chinese technology, most officials and other educated Chinese remained scornful of all things Western. One official wrote to the emperor that "the English barbarians are a detestable people, trusting entirely to their strong ships and large guns." Average Chinese felt similarly: one placard in Canton in 1841 was addressed to "rebellious barbarian dogs . . . We are definitely going to kill you, cut your heads off, and burn your bodies in the trash."[5]

In 1842, after the British made preparations to blow down the walls of the major city of Nanjing, along the Yangzi River in central China, the Qing were forced to sign the Treaty of Nanjing, which gave Britain permanent possession of Hong Kong, a sparsely populated coastal island downriver from Guangzhou; opened five ports to British trade; abolished Chinese trade monopolies; set fixed tariffs so that China no longer controlled its economic policy; and gave the British extraterritoriality, or freedom from local laws. The Chinese were also forced to pay Britain the war costs. Soon other Western countries signed treaties with China that gave them the same rights as the British. Each successive treaty expanded foreign privileges.

extraterritoriality
Freedom from local laws for foreign subjects.

Letter to Queen Victoria On behalf of the emperor, Lin Zexu implores Queen Victoria to halt the British opium trade in China.

The Treaty System

The Opium War became to the Chinese a permanent symbol of Western imperialism and soon led to other wars and treaties that opened China to the West. After the Opium War, Westerners, especially the British, remained dissatisfied with the amount of trade, and the Chinese sought to evade their obligations. Another conflict, often known as the Arrow War (1856–1860), soon developed over a dispute aboard a Chinese ship, *The Arrow*, registered in Hong Kong. France also entered the war, using the mysterious murder of a French priest as an excuse. Facing two formidable powers, China was again defeated and forced to sign new treaties that favored the West. This treaty opened more ports on the coast and along rivers to Western traders, established foreign embassies in Beijing, and permitted Christian missionaries further access. Again forced to pay the war costs, China fell deeper into debt. The Arrow War also undermined China's position as a regional power, as it was forced to give up its claim to Vietnam, a long-time vassal state being colonized by France, and to acquiesce in the Russian takeover of eastern Siberia.

By restricting China's control of its economy and limiting Chinese power to make rules for Western residents, the treaty system deprived China of some of its autonomy. It also led to the formation of international settlements, zones in major Chinese cities set aside for foreigners in which no Chinese were allowed. They were in effect foreign cities with foreign governments in major ports such as Guangzhou and Shanghai. For example, a small island on the riverfront adjacent to downtown Guangzhou became the home of Western merchants, officials, and missionaries. It boasted mansions, warehouses, clubs, and churches built by and serving Westerners. Chinese were clearly unwelcome except as servants.

The Opium and Arrow Wars and the treaty system they fostered forced the Chinese to debate how best to respond to the new dangers the country faced. Some Chinese officials and other scholars understood the need for China to learn from the West. A few scholars argued that the Chinese should seriously study science, mathematics, and foreign languages. These views influenced the provincial official and reformer Zeng Guofan (zung gwoh-FAN) (1811–1872), who recommended making modern weapons and steamships. But, failing to see the magnitude of the challenges, few mandarins showed interest.

While scholars debated, Western cultural influence increased, and China's problems multiplied. To pay for the wars, the government had to raise taxes, causing many peasants to lose their land. The dispossessed often turned to begging or banditry. Natural disasters further demoralized the country. Between 1800 and 1850, the Yellow River flooded twenty times and then changed course, wiping out hundreds of towns and villages. Christian missionaries opened most of China's Western-type schools and hospitals, providing educational and health benefits to those Chinese who had access to them, but posing a challenge to Chinese religions. The missionaries and other Western residents, often ethnocentric and seeing themselves as agents of what they considered to be a superior Western and Christian civilization, tended to view the Chinese as depraved heathens and mocked their culture. Chinese generally distrusted not only the Christian missionaries but also the several hundred thousand Chinese who became Christian.

The Taiping Rebellion

Deteriorating conditions, government corruption, and the increasing Western presence eventually generated the Taiping Rebellion (1850–1864), the most critical of several midcentury upheavals against the Qing (see Map 23.1). Guangdong (GWAHNG-dong) province, on the southeast coast, experienced particularly severe social and economic dislocations that increased popular unrest. The rebellion began in a remote area and was fueled by economic insecurity, famine, loss of faith in government, and a desire for social change. The leader, Hong Xiuquan (hoong shee-OH-chew-an) (1813–1864), preached a doctrine blending Christianity and Chinese thought advocating for an equal distribution of goods, communal property, and equality between men and women. Hong established a sect, the Taipings (Heavenly Kingdom of Great Peace), that rejected Confucian traditions, and he prohibited opium use, polygamy, footbinding, prostitution, concubinage, and arranged marriages. In 1850, Hong launched a rebellion, invoking Chinese nationalism: "We raise the army of righteousness to liberate the masses for the sake of China."[6] Soon he had attracted millions of supporters from among the poor and disaffected.

 Interactive Map

The Taipings enjoyed early success, but ultimately their efforts failed and weakened China. Taiping armies conquered large parts of central and southern China, but the Taipings suffered from conflicts within their leadership, and their hostility to traditional Chinese culture cost them popular support. Ultimately most of the educated elite rallied to the Qing and organized provincial armies to oppose the Taipings. Westerners often sympathized with the Taipings because of their Christian influences and progressive social message, but they knew that a Qing victory would benefit Western nations. Hence, various Western nations aided the Qing as they defeated the Taipings and aborted the process of dynastic renewal.

The conflict left China in shambles. Many provinces had been devastated, and 20 million Chinese had been killed. An American missionary described the destruction: "Ruined cities, desolate towns and heaps of rubble still mark their path. The hum of busy populations had ceased and weeds and jungle cover the land."[7] The Qing were now deeper in debt to the West and compelled to adopt even more conciliatory attitudes.

Economic Change and Emigration

China's encounters with the West generated several economic changes. The extension of Western businesses into the interior stimulated the growth of the Chinese merchant class and small-scale Chinese-owned industries, such as match factories and flour mills. The Chinese merchants, however, disliked Western economic domination and the Qing government, which offered little resistance to Western imperialism. Gradually, a new working class, including women, labored in mines, factories, railways, and docks. The gulf between peasants in the interior and the merchants and workers in the coastal cities was vast.

China Under Western Control

The unequal treaties enabled Western economic penetration into China, increasing the incorporation of China

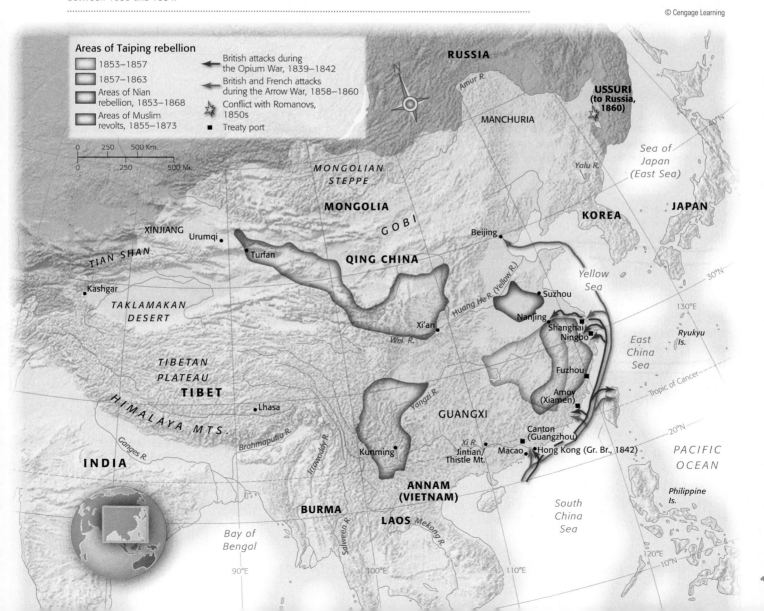

Map 23.1
Conflicts in Qing China, 1839–1870
During the mid-1800s, Qing China experienced repeated unrest, including several major rebellions. The largest and most destructive, the Taiping Rebellion, engulfed a large part of southern and central China between 1850 and 1864.

© Cengage Learning

Rattan Factory in Guangzhou This photo, taken around 1875, shows Chinese men and women workers, mostly of peasant background, in a factory making rattan, along with the factory's European owners.

into a world economy dominated by the West. Westerners often ran Qing government agencies, banks, railroads, factories, and mines and guarded them with Western police. By 1920, foreign companies controlled most of China's iron ore, coal, railroads, and steamships, and Western businessmen became inspired by the notion of the vast China market. As happened in Southeast Asia, imported British textiles frequently displaced Chinese women from textile production, which peasant women had done for centuries to supplement family incomes. The Qing, already deeply in debt to Western governments and banks, had little money left for building China's economic institutions.

The Coolie Trade

Deteriorating economic, social, and political conditions in hard-hit coastal provinces, combined with natural disasters, prompted millions of Chinese to emigrate between the 1840s and 1920s, usually to places where Western colonialism and capitalism were opening new economic opportunities (see Chapters 20 and 22). The Chinese who emigrated formed the basis for local middle-class Chinese business communities. The majority left China as part of the notorious "coolie trade," a labor system known as such because Westerners called the emigrant workers, whether Chinese or Indian, "coolies," a derogatory term. Under this system, desperate Chinese, usually peasants, became indentured workers in faraway places, signing contracts that required them to labor for years on plantations, in mines, or on railroad lines to repay their passage. They endured discrimination and harsh working conditions in alien lands.

Chinese had migrated to Southeast Asia for centuries, but the increased emigration now greatly enlarged the Chinese diaspora to a global scale. The societies where Chinese settled, especially in Southeast Asia, became more closely connected to China through economic and social networks than ever before. Chinese emigrants often returned to their native villages with wealth earned abroad, but others never earned enough money to return to China as they originally hoped. Others established small businesses and settled permanently abroad. The emigrants and their descendants, while often sustaining Chinese culture and language, also mixed Chinese and local customs. Today some 30 million people of Chinese ancestry live outside of China, the large majority of them in Southeast Asia.

LO² From Imperial to Republican China

The rebellions, government stagnation, poverty, and growing Western demands brought about a crisis for the Qing. Some Chinese still concluded that China should reaffirm its traditional ways and reject the West, but others increasingly recognized the need to absorb Western technologies and progress. As challenges mounted and China lost a war with Japan, some organized revolutionary movements. In the early 1900s, revolutionaries successfully overthrew the imperial system to form a republic, but these developments did not solve China's problems.

Pressures on Late Qing China

China's educated elite divided over how much China should modernize its society: conservatives argued against borrowing Western models, whereas liberals wanted moderate reforms. The conservatives, who dominated the bureaucracy, advised that China hold fast to traditions, protecting itself with Confucian moral conduct. Believing China could learn nothing from Westerners, they opposed railroads, underground mines, and other innovations, because these disrupted the harmony between humanity and nature, disturbed the graves of the ancestors, and put boatmen and cart drivers out of work. One conservative wrote that it was "better to

> "Liberals, believing China had to adopt certain Western ideas to survive, sponsored impressive government innovations."

> 66 Foreign pressures also contributed to China's decline as Chinese leaders developed a siege mentality in the face of Western threats. 99

see the nation die than its way of life change."[8] Conservatives were convinced that new technologies undermined social, economic, and even political values.

Liberals, believing China had to adopt certain Western ideas to survive, sponsored impressive government innovations. They streamlined central and regional governments, set up a foreign ministry, formed a college to train diplomats, established industries, and sent some students to schools in the West. Liberals also sought to modernize military forces, building arsenals and shipyards. By 1894, China had a better-trained army and sixty-five warships. Few liberals, however, wanted radical transformation: as one noted, "China should acquire the West's superiority in arms and machinery, but retain China's superiority in Confucian virtue."[9] Perhaps naively, liberals believed they could adopt Western tools while rejecting Western ideas.

The reforms failed to save the Qing, because the technological innovations themselves generated new problems. Newly built warships and railroads then needed coal to make steam to power them, which meant they needed improved coal-mining technology. Technical expertise was in short supply, and the Confucian social order was disrupted. The innovations were also expensive, further complicating the economic problems of a Chinese government that was forced to pay war reparations and to finance a growing debt to Western nations and banks. The problems became worse as China's poorly led, bureaucratic, and overly conservative government failed to make necessary changes. From 1861 to 1908, the imperial government was dominated by the Empress Dowager Ci Xi (zoo shee) (1835–1908), a concubine of the old emperor; on the emperor's death, Ci Xi had become the regent of the child emperor who replaced him. Forceful and intelligent, she was also covetous and irresponsible, squandering military funds to construct the magnificent Summer Palace, just outside Beijing, for her imperial retreat. Some historians identify the ineptitude of Manchu leaders such as Ci Xi as a major factor in China's failure to modernize.

Foreign Pressures on Late Qing China

Foreign pressures also contributed to China's decline as Chinese leaders developed a siege mentality in the face of Western threats. Some foreign powers dominated particular regions as spheres of influence, such as Britain in Guangdong and Germany in Shandong, acquiring resources, establishing enterprises, and manipulating local governments. The United States, Britain, France, and Germany exercised their power over China through gunboat diplomacy, the use of superior firepower to impose a country's will on local populations and governments. The term comes from the use of Western gunboats to patrol some of China's rivers and seacoasts in the late 1800s and early 1900s, interceding to protect Western businessmen, missionaries, and diplomats whose activities generated Chinese hostility. Sovereign Chinese rights and the people's outrage at foreign intrusion counted for little. But gunboats were only part of the story: Americans also promoted free trade, generously funded Christian missionaries, and donated to humanitarian causes such as flood relief and orphanages.

Despite the limits on its autonomy, China never became a full Western colony, such as India or Vietnam, perhaps because too many foreign powers were involved. The United States, which had become one of the most powerful and prosperous Western nations in the late 1800s, discouraged full colonization by promoting what it termed an "open door" policy that allowed equal access by all of the foreign powers to China's vast markets and resources. The open door enabled the Western nations and, eventually, Japan to avoid conflict among themselves and to acquire the economic fruits of empire without the high costs of conquering and governing China.

Chinese Study Maxim Gun After the Taiping Rebellion, the Qing emperor sent two Chinese mandarins to England to examine and purchase new weapons. In this photo, they examine a Maxim gun, one of the first machine guns that gave Western nations a great military advantage.

Late Qing Reforms and Wars

Between 1890 and 1916, the growing foreign challenge now included Japan, which was rapidly industrializing. In search of resources and markets to exploit, in the 1890s, Japan began intervening in Korea, long a vassal state of China. The Koreans asked China for assistance, and the resulting Sino-Japanese War (1894–1895) ended in a humiliating defeat for China. The Qing were forced to pay an indemnity and to recognize Korean independence, and in 1910, Korea became a Japanese colony. Other holdings such as Taiwan were also lost. The defeat by Japan proved a blow to Chinese pride and to the credibility of the Qing rulers.

These crises brought a group of progressive reformers to the attention of the young Manchu emperor, Guangxu, and, in 1898, under their influence, he called for dramatic changes, later known as the 100 Days of Reform, which included a crash program of economic modernization.

The Boxer Rebellion

But the Empress Dowager Xi Ci and her conservative allies blocked the proposals, arrested the reformers, and placed the emperor under house arrest. The ensuing tensions led to the Boxer Rebellion, a popular movement in 1900 that aimed at driving the foreigners out of China, but that resulted in an even stronger Western presence. The Qing gave strong backing to the Boxers ("Righteous Harmony Fists"), an anti-Western, anti-Christian secret society comprising mostly poor peasants. The Boxers attacked foreigners in north China, occupied Beijing, and besieged the foreign embassies. The Qing declared war on all of the foreign powers with which it had been forced to sign unequal treaties. In response, the British, Americans, French, and other powers put aside their differences and organized an international force that routed the Boxers, occupied Beijing, and forced the Qing to pay another huge indemnity and to permit foreign military forces to stay in China. The Russians used the rebellion as an excuse to occupy Manchuria.

The string of defeats generated final frantic efforts at reform and modernization, setting the stage for more dramatic transitions. Fearing China might soon be divided into colonies, the chastened Manchus now began more serious reform efforts,

> "The Boxers attacked foreigners in north China, occupied Beijing, and besieged the foreign embassies."

looking to Japan for models. The Qing abolished the 2,000-year-old Confucian examination system, set up modern, Western-style schools, and sent 10,000 students to Japan. The Qing also formed new government departments, allocated more money to the military, and strengthened provincial and local governments.

Liang Qichao and Liberal Reform

Liberals who had criticized the Qing reformers for going too slowly now became more influential. Many reformers had read and even translated European literature and scholarship, including that of Enlightenment writers, and were deeply impressed by Japan's modernization in the later 1800s. The leading liberal reformer, Liang Qichao (1871–1929), represented change within tradition. A scholar and journalist, Liang promoted a modernization that blended Confucian values and Western learning. He also believed China should industrialize, form a constitutional government, and focus on the idea of nation instead of culture.

Chinese Nationalism and Revolutionary Movements

For some Chinese inspired by nationalism, most importantly Sun Zhong Shan, better known as Sun Yat-Sen (soon yot-SEN), the fiasco of the Boxer Rebellion showed the futility of trying to change China by reform from above and prompted them to organize a revolution from below that could sweep the Manchus from power. Inspired by the Taipings, Meiji Japan (see next section), and the West, Sun Yat-Sen (1866–1925) mixed tradition and modernity; he did not come from an upper-class mandarin background and had no commitment to the traditional system. Convinced that the Qing system was hopeless, Sun decided to devote his life to politics and became the chief architect of the Chinese Revolution.

 Experience nationalism and imperialism through the eyes of either a Chinese citizen or a British official in the early to mid-1800s in this interactive simulation.

In 1895, Sun founded an anti-Manchu secret society that was dedicated to replacing the imperial system with a Western-style republic, and branches were set up in China, Japan, and Hawaii (see Witness to the Past: Planning a Revolutionary New China). Facing arrest in China for treason, Sun traveled extensively, recruiting support among Chinese merchants in Southeast Asia and North America, Chinese businessmen in the treaty ports, Chinese students in Japan, and sympathetic military officers. Sun and his followers thought of themselves as nationalists, more interested in China as a nation than as a culture. The cause of dramatic change also attracted feminists such as Qin Jin (Chin Chin) (1877–1907), who left her arranged marriage for study in Japan and then started a women's magazine and pursued political activity, expressing the hope that one day China would see free women "blooming like fields of flowers."[10] Later she was executed as a revolutionary.

Sun developed his program into what he termed the "Three Principles of the People." The first principle, nationalism, involved overthrowing the Manchus, restoring ethnic Chinese to power, and reclaiming China's historical greatness. For his second principle, he favored republicanism, an elected representative government rather than the constitutional monarchy sought by the liberal reformers. The third principle, people's livelihood, envisioned an equitable economic status for all. Eventually the day would come, he hoped, when the Chinese could look over their shoulder and find the West lagging far behind.

Revolution: Launching the Republican Era

Sun was traveling in the United States raising money for his cause when, on October 10, 1911, some Chinese influenced by Sun's ideas began the uprising. Soldiers in the Yangzi River city of Wuhan (woo-hahn) in central China mutinied against the Qing government and were soon joined by sympathizers in other cities. Within two months, the revolutionary soldiers controlled provinces in central and southern China. As the authority of the Qing government quickly crumbled outside their power base in the north, Sun returned to China for the first time in sixteen years. From their capital in Beijing, the Manchus hesitated, then asked an ambitious general, Yuan Shikai (yoo-AHN shee-KAI) (1859–1916), to deal with the revolutionaries. In control of a large army and in touch with both sides, Yuan decided to replace the dynasty with his own rule, playing the Manchus off against the revolutionaries.

The Guomindang and the End of the Qing Dynasty

The revolution had wide popular support, because many Chinese hated the Manchus. Sun's nationalist message spread rapidly, as he now reorganized his anti-Manchu secret society into a political party, the Guomindang (gwo-min-dong) (Chinese Nationalist Party), which gathered varied nationalists and liberal reformers into the fold. However, although widely respected, Sun was not a forceful leader, and the revolutionaries could agree only on opposing the Manchus.

Two centers of power now existed. General Yuan Shikai held the dominant position in the north and considerable influence over the Qing leaders in Beijing. The revolutionaries controlled the Yangzi Valley and parts of south China, and they made plans to establish a provisional republican government. Sun sought a compromise to save China from civil war, offering to make Yuan president of the republic if Yuan arranged for the abdication of the five-year-old Qing emperor. Yuan agreed, and in February 1912 the Qing dynasty, and with it the 2,000-year-old imperial system, was ended. In March 1912, a republic was established in Nanjing, on the Yangzi River in east-central China. In a move symbolizing a change of direction for China, the new government adopted the Western calendar. But Sun had underestimated Yuan's ambitions. While a modernizer, Yuan hoped to restore an autocratic system with himself at the top. He soon moved the capital back to Beijing in the north.

The new republic began with some signs of liberal accomplishment, including a constitution written by Sun that provided for a two-chamber parliament and a president. In early 1913, a restricted electorate chose a national assembly and provincial assemblies in the first and most open general election in China's long history. Sun's Guomindang, identified with nationalist revolution, won a majority of seats but lacked a consensus about the directions of change. A new women's suffrage movement, influenced by its counterparts in Europe, pressed for equal rights.

Yuan Shikai and the Chinese Civil War

In part because of Yuan Shikai's ambitions, however, the republican system failed to bring stability and liberty, dashing the hopes of Sun and his colleagues. Convinced that China needed a strong leader and government, Yuan considered Sun and the Guomindang formidable obstacles. He had Guomindang leaders assassinated, bought off, or, in the case of Sun, forced into exile. Yuan soon outlawed the Guomindang, suspended parliament, and banned the women's suffrage movement. He enjoyed the support of much of the army, the imperial bureaucracy, and the foreign powers, who preferred a strongman to the democratic uncertainties of Sun. Sun and his closest followers moved to Japan, embittered and

Planning a Revolutionary New China

In 1905, various radical Chinese groups met in Japan and merged into one revolutionary organization, the Tongmen Hui (Chinese Alliance Association), led by Sun Yat-Sen, then based in Tokyo. Most of the members were drawn from among the 10,000 Chinese students enrolled in Japanese universities. Unhappy with the Qing government and impressed by modernizing Japan, they sought to change China through revolution. In their founding proclamation, which was influenced by Western thought, they set out their agenda, visionary but vague, for a three-stage passage from military to constitutional government and a more equitable society.

Since the beginning of China as a nation, we Chinese have governed our own country despite occasional interruptions. When China was occasionally occupied by a foreign race, our ancestors could always . . . drive these foreigners out . . . and preserve China for future generations. . . . There is a difference, however, between our revolution and the revolutions of our ancestors. The purpose of past revolutions . . . was to restore China to the Chinese, and nothing else. We, on the other hand, strive not only to expel the ruling aliens [Manchus] . . . but also to change basically the political and economic structure of our country. . . . The revolutions of yesterday were revolutions by and for the heroes; our revolution, on the other hand, is a revolution by and for the people . . . everyone who believes in the principles of liberty, equality, and fraternity has an obligation to participate in it. . . .

At this juncture we wish to express candidly and fully how to make our revolution today and how to govern the country tomorrow.

1. Expulsion of the Manchus from China. . . . We shall quickly overthrow the Manchu government so as to restore the sovereignty of China to the Chinese.

2. Restoration of China to the Chinese. China belongs to the Chinese who have the right to govern themselves. . . .

3. Establishment of a Republic. Since one of the principles of our revolution is equality, we intend to establish a republic . . . all citizens will have the right to participate in the government, the president of the republic will be elected by the people, and the parliament will have deputies elected by and responsible to their respective constituencies. . . .

4. Equalization of Land Ownership. The social and economic structure of China must be so reconstructed that the fruits of labor will be shared by all Chinese on an equal basis. . . .

To attain the four goals . . ., we propose a procedure of three stages. The first . . . is that of military rule . . . [in which] the Military Government, in cooperation with the people, will eradicate all the abuses of the past; with the arrival of the second stage the Military Government will hand over local administration to the people while reserving for itself the right of jurisdiction over all matters that concern the nation as a whole; during the . . . final stage the Military Government will cease to exist and all governmental power will be invested in organs as prescribed in a national constitution. This orderly procedure is necessary because our people need time to acquaint themselves with the idea of liberty and equality . . ., the basis on which the republic of China rests. . . . On . . . restoring China to her own people, we urge everyone to step forward and to do the best he can. . . . Whatever our station in society is, rich or poor, we are all equal in our determination to safeguard the security of China as a nation and to preserve the Chinese people.

Thinking About the Reading

1. How does the proclamation use Western revolutionary and nationalist ideas?
2. How will revolution build a new China?

Source: Pei-Kai Cheng and Michael Lestz with Jonathan D. Spence, eds., *The Search for Modern China: A Documentary Collection* (New York: W.W. Norton, 1999), pp. 202–206.

demoralized, as Yuan became increasingly autocratic and announced plans to found a new dynasty.

Yuan's plans, however, were put on hold by current problems in China, including constant pressure from foreign powers, the secession of regions occupied largely by non-Chinese, and bankruptcy. Yuan was forced to borrow heavily from foreign governments to keep the country afloat. Tibet and Mongolia expelled their Chinese administrations. World War I also posed a challenge. Although China remained neutral, Japan, allied with Britain, occupied the German sphere of influence in the Shandong peninsula on China's east coast. Japan then presented Yuan with 21 Demands, including control of Shandong, more rights in Manchuria, and the appointment of Japanese advisers to the Chinese government, which infuriated the Chinese people. His imperial restoration plans aborted, a humiliated Yuan died in 1916, and China fell into the abyss of prolonged Civil War. Yuan's years in power had wrecked the republican institutions, and his submission to Japan's 21 Demands suggested that China was even weaker than before.

LO³ Japan and Korea Under Challenge

In the second half of the nineteenth century, Japan met the Western challenge more successfully than China, rapidly transforming itself into a powerful industrialized nation. Although it had serious internal problems, Japan also possessed significant strengths that allowed it to achieve success. The shoguns—military dictators from the Tokugawa family ruling in the name of the emperor—had governed Japan since 1600 and had kept a tight hold on Japanese society. When the first Western ships arrived, the Japanese and Koreans, largely shut off by policies of seclusion from the outside world, were just as far behind the West in military and industrial technology as China, India, and other Asian societies had been. Their choices, however, caused different historical outcomes.

Tokugawa Japan and Qing China

Like China, Japan faced foreign pressures, but Japan successfully met the challenge of the Western

> "Like China, Japan faced foreign pressures, but Japan successfully met the challenge of the Western intrusion, while China gradually lost some of its autonomy."

intrusion, while China gradually lost some of its autonomy. The differences between these two ancient neighbors, historians argue, help explain the different outcomes. Geography played a role. Japan, being compact and linguistically homogeneous, had a strong sense of national unity and of loyalty to the emperor as a national symbol, whereas China's vastness created difficulties in communications and linguistically divided the country. In China, sentiments of loyalty were restricted largely to the family, and the Chinese were slow to assimilate new ideas, whereas Japan had a long tradition of readily borrowing from outside. As a result, Japanese leaders could more easily import and adopt new ideas, technologies, and institutions.

The two neighbors also differed in the influence of their merchants and in their political and military systems. The Japanese merchant class was assertive and was rapidly expanding its scope and power, whereas in China the commercial energies had reached their height centuries earlier, only to be contained and restricted by the government. Furthermore, in contrast to China's centralized empire, the Japanese government was pluralistic; the Tokugawa shogun, based in Edo (today's Tokyo), had to balance the interests of the various daimyo, the influential leaders of regional

CHRONOLOGY

Japan and Korea, 1750–1914

1392–1910	Yi dynasty in Korea
1600–1867	Tokugawa Shogunate
1853	Opening of Japan by Perry
1854	Treaty of Kanagawa
1867–1868	Meiji Restoration
1894–1895	Sino-Japanese War
1904–1905	Russo-Japanese War
1910	Japanese colonization of Korea and Taiwan

landowning families, while keeping the Kyoto-based emperor powerless. The Japanese military leaders, the samurai, still held a respected position in Japanese society. Never having been successfully invaded, the Japanese felt vulnerable when they encountered the well-armed Westerners. They prized political independence far more than cultural purity, while the Chinese were used to foreign rule and prized their Confucian traditions more than political independence. Thus Japanese leaders were far more sensitive to the Western threat than were the Chinese elite.

Late Tokugawa Advantages and Challenges

Japan also benefited from the energy and openness to new ideas of late Tokugawa society. Its many schools resulted in high literacy rates, and several schools specialized in so-called Dutch learning acquired from Dutch traders, including sciences such as medicine, physics, and chemistry. Whatever their status and occupation, the Japanese demonstrated a pattern of hard work, thrift, saving, and cooperation—attributes that lent themselves to modernization.

 The Floating World of Ukiyo-e: Shadow, Dreams, and Substance (*http://www.loc.gov/exhibits/ukiyo-e/*). Japanese prints at the Library of Congress.

Culture in Tokugawa Japan

Tokugawa Japan also enjoyed a thriving urban and artistic life. Cities such as Edo and Osaka, already among the world's largest, offered a flourishing commerce and diverse entertainments. Tokugawa arts produced creations that achieved renown worldwide, such as ceramics, jewelry, furniture, painting, and woodblock prints. Ando Hiroshige (1797–1858) concentrated on Tokyo scenes and landscapes emphasizing nature. The treatment of atmosphere and light in Japanese color prints influenced European impressionist painters of the later 1800s, such as Vincent Van Gogh, who admitted that he strove to emulate Japanese landscape painting.

Despite the richness of their society's culture, by the early 1800s, some Japanese sensed internal decay. The Tokugawa were blamed for the nation's growing domestic problems, including inflation, increasing taxes, and social disorder. In addition, there was the gradual impoverishment of the samurai, whose salaries had been cut over the years, and many ordinary Japanese experienced widespread famine and starvation in the 1830s. The growing social tensions and resentments reached a breaking point, fostering urban riots, peasant revolts, and various plots to depose the Tokugawa shogun.

Addressing the Western Threat

While worried about domestic unrest, Japanese officials were more concerned about the growing Western presence in the region, which they correctly perceived would impact Japan. They knew that Russians had been active in Siberia and the North Pacific since the 1700s and that British ships had sailed along Japan's coast. In 1825, the shogun ordered that whenever a foreign ship was sighted approaching the coast, the samurai should fire on it and drive it away. After China's defeat in the Opium War, Japan's shocked leaders encouraged the samurai to develop new, more effective weapons and contemplated starting a navy. The Japanese considered the Westerners to be money-grasping barbarians who did not understand the proper rules of social behavior and who would contaminate the national spirit. As the samurai vowed to fight to the death to resist Western invasion, this feeling of nationalism grew, putting pressure on the shogun to implement reforms to strengthen the country. At the national level, leaders broke up merchant monopolies, established a bureau to translate Western books, and reduced the number of government officials to save money, but these reforms largely failed to energize the system. Some provincial governments, especially in the southwest, were more aggressive in their efforts to modernize. Samurai in several of these domains learned how to cast better guns and to produce iron suitable for making modern cannon, and one even constructed an electric steam engine in the 1850s.

Read about Ando Hiroshige, the Japanese artist who gained a worldwide reputation for his work that reflected a distinctly Japanese vision of landscape and urban life.

> " Despite the richness of their society's culture, by the early 1800s, some Japanese sensed internal decay. "

The Opening of Japan and Political Crisis

The need for change was made urgent by external forces that arose in the 1850s when the Americans directly challenged Japan's exclusion policy. In 1853, a fleet of eleven U.S. warships commanded by Commodore Matthew Perry sailed into Tokyo Bay and delivered a letter to the shogun from the U.S. president, Millard Fillmore, demanding that the Japanese sign a treaty opening the country or face war when Perry returned the following year. Their three steamships shocked the Japanese with their ability to move against the wind and tide. The shogun, remembering the Opium War, granted Perry's demands in the Treaty of Kanagawa (1854) and then accepted the blame for the nation's humiliation. The treaty opened two ports to U.S. trade and allowed for the stationing of a U.S. consul. By 1856, American diplomats demanded a stronger commercial treaty, the opening of more ports, extraterritoriality, and the admission of Christian missionaries. The shogun reluctantly agreed; he soon signed similar treaties with the Dutch, British, French, and Russians.

> "From ancient times, the peoples of the mountainous Korean peninsula had been shaped by their location between powerful China and Japan."

Western Incursion

Like China, Japan experienced a forcible intrusion from the West that held the seeds of potential colonization. Although the changes still limited the Westerners' movement in Japan, most Japanese leaders saw that Japan was the loser in these dealings. Western merchants soon arrived, flooding the nation with cheap industrial goods to create a market and destroy native industries, as they had done earlier in China and India. International settlements restricted to foreigners were established in Japan's major port cities. Westerners enjoyed ever-increasing economic and legal privileges, and escalating domestic disunity held the potential for enhancing Western power. Western encroachment provoked a crisis for the Tokugawa government and a national debate about whether Japan should accommodate Westerners more or use military force to expel the intruders. One such faction proclaimed, "Revere the Emperor, Expel the Barbarians."

The Failure of the Shogunate

Shaken by the Western presence, the Tokugawa government launched efforts at modernization. It established a shipbuilding industry, promoted manufacturing, and promoted western education

reforms. The Japanese, who had already become interested in Western science and technology, however, saw these government innovations as too little and too late. Across Japan the Tokugawa shogun was now widely perceived as weak. The shogun's strategy of avoiding confrontation led a respected poet to complain angrily: "You, whose ancestors in the mighty days, Roared at the skies and swept the earth, Stand now helpless to drive off wrangling foreigners—How empty your title, 'Queller of the Barbarians.'"[11] Furthermore, the Western powers continually made new demands. By the 1860s, the Japanese seemed to be repeating the experience of China, gradually losing control of their political and economic future.

Challenges to the Korean Kingdom

Although it was faced with growing problems in this era, Korea had chosen relative isolation, similar to Tokugawa Japan. From ancient times, the peoples of the mountainous Korean peninsula had been shaped by their location between powerful China and Japan. Over the centuries, Koreans had mixed China's religions, political structure, and writing system with their own customs but maintained a strong national identity and political independence. Like China, Korea became a unified state presided over by a series of family dynasties ruling with a Confucian ideology.

The last of the Korean dynasties, the Yi (yee) (1392–1910), ruled the state they called Choson (choh-SAN) for more than five centuries, favoring powerful landlord families. By officially closing off Korea from the outside world after the Manchus invaded and pillaged the capital in the early 1600s, the Yi earned Choson the label of "the Hermit Kingdom." However, as in Tokugawa Japan, seclusion from the outside world was not absolute. Korea still traded with China. Better irrigation technologies and new strains of rice from China increased agricultural productivity. Korean scholars also visited China, and on their return some wrote books favorably contrasting Chinese society with what they considered Korea's overly rigid and inequitable social system. A few Koreans met Westerners in China and found their ideas and technologies to be of interest. Several strong kings in the 1700s fostered a renewed culture of learning; some thinkers, to promote justice, examined social conditions by studying the peasants.

However, by the early 1800s, Choson, like Qing China and Tokugawa Japan, began to succumb to stress. As in Japan, the rigid social structure crumbled as the economy grew. Korea's population doubled to some 9 million between 1669 and 1800, increasing pressure on the land. With Buddhism losing influence, some Koreans turned to Christianity. Although officially prohibited, a few French and Chinese Christian missionaries nevertheless illegally entered Korea and spread their message. During the 1800s, Korea also experienced recurrent famines and increased political instability, including peasant uprisings. The Choson government blamed and persecuted Christians and missionaries for causing social turmoil.

The challenges to Korea caused some Koreans to consider their options. As in China and Japan, Korean intellectuals debated the value of Western learning, and some pushed for reforms of the traditional political and social system. With the Yi refusing direct commercial negotiations with the West, Korean military forces drove away French and American ships seeking to open Korea to Western trade, and in 1871, they repulsed a U.S. naval force. The Yi also worried about Russian expansion to the north, in eastern Siberia. By the later 1800s, Korea seemed in need of rejuvenation.

LO⁴ The Remaking of Japan and Korea

The ultimate Japanese response to Western intrusion was radically different from China's, allowing Japan to avoid colonialism and become the only non-Western nation to successfully industrialize and achieve Western standards of living before World War II. This transition owed much to a revolution that ended Tokugawa rule in 1868 and created a new government that fostered dramatic reforms. By the early 1900s, a powerful Japan had increased its influence in the wider world. Meanwhile, Korea was forced to abandon several centuries of isolation and eventually became a Japanese colony.

Tokugawa Defeat and the Meiji Restoration

By the 1860s, the deteriorating situation in Japan led to a revolution against the Tokugawa shogu-nate, known as the Meiji Restoration (1867–1868), because it was carried out in the name of the emperor, whose reign name was Meiji (MAY-gee). The anti-Tokugawa leaders, united mostly by their hatred of the status quo, had varied goals and perspectives. Some were avid Westernizers, others extreme nationalists. Most were ambitious outsiders of samurai background who were alienated from the Tokugawa power structure. Although they came from privileged families, they were unafraid to ally with commoners, especially merchants, and generally were pragmatic men who understood that protecting Japan from foreign domination required radical change.

Meiji Restoration A revolution against the Tokugawa shogunate in Japan in 1867–1868, carried out in the name of the Meiji emperor; led to the successful modernization of Japan.

Demise of the Tokugawa Shogunate

As public respect for the shogun faded, Japanese dissidents turned to the relatively powerless Meiji emperor as an alternative. While the shoguns had exercised power from Edo, the imperial family had lived in Kyoto two hundred miles to the south. In 1868, anti-Tokugawa leaders, backed by military force, seized the imperial palace in Kyoto and convinced the emperor to dismiss the shogun and decree the restoration of his own rule. The decree ousted the Tokugawa family from their land and positions, opened the government to men of talent, appointed the rebels as advisers to the emperor, and announced that "all matters shall be decided by public discussion" and "the evil customs of the past shall be broken off. Knowledge shall be sought throughout the world."[12] The Tokugawa family and their supporters fought back, sparking a bitter one-year civil war that cost many lives. Ultimately, however, the rebel forces prevailed and crushed all armed resistance.

> **66** As public respect for the shogun faded, Japanese dissidents turned to the relatively powerless Meiji emperor as an alternative. **99**

Meiji Reforms

The Meiji regime took shape early, launching a crash program of modernization in just thirty years. Among the major changes introduced by the new leaders, Japan joined the world community and agreed to honor all treaties. The imperial residence was moved from Kyoto to Tokyo

> "The new political system had democratic trappings, but reformers were divided on how much democracy to foster."

(formerly Edo), a much larger and more dynamic city. Perceiving change as a necessary evil, the Meiji leaders pragmatically sought ways to achieve national unity, wealth, defense, and equality with the West. Meiji reformers combined Western models with Japanese traditions to build a distinctive form of industrial society that diffused the threat of colonialism. Despite its flaws, the system introduced by the Meiji proved productive for Japan.

 Explore Japan through the eyes of a young man during the Meiji Restoration in this interactive simulation.

Meiji leaders needed to establish an effective governmental structure and secure the loyalty of the population. One of their first acts was to form a State Council to advise and control the emperor. They then recruited both samurais and commoners into the new bureaucracy while convincing the regional daimyo families to give up control of their land, and the peasants living on it, in exchange for appointment as regional governors with guaranteed salaries. Freeing the peasants made it easier for them to move to cities in search of work, which had been illegal under the Tokugawa. The government employed thousands of Western advisers and workers who gave advice but were required to train Japanese assistants to replace them when their contracts expired. Because it financed these programs through tax revenues, Meiji Japan did not need foreign loans, hence avoiding the debt trap that ensnared most Latin American and Middle Eastern societies as well as China.

The new political system had democratic trappings, but reformers were divided on how much democracy to foster. The Japanese had no tradition of political freedom and had to invent a new word for the concept. In 1889, the Meiji leaders wrote the first constitution in Japanese history and formed a constitutional monarchy symbolically headed by the emperor. The constitution introduced an independent judiciary and a two-house parliament that was elected by the 450,000 men who were tax-paying property holders. Parliament chose members for the cabinet, which made policy and supervised the government apparatus, and the first political parties were formed in the 1880s.

"Rich Country, Strong Army"

Using the slogan "rich country, strong army," the government stressed industrial development and enhanced communications by building railroads and telegraphs. Anxious about Western imperialism in Asia, the Japanese concluded that military power was necessary to assert Japanese interests, so to build up the armed forces, including a modern navy, Meiji leaders drafted commoners as soldiers, once a profession limited to samurai. By breaking down the former distinction between samurai, merchant, and peasant, the military draft promoted social leveling, literacy, and nationalism among the peasants who joined. Compared with China, the Meiji leaders enjoyed more freedom to reshape and strengthen their nation. The various Western powers, largely preoccupied elsewhere, saw Japan mainly as a potential ally against each other.

State Capitalism: A New Economic Model

Meiji policies fostered a modern economy and society. In building an economic foundation, the Japanese created a new model of political economy, state capitalism, an economic system in which the state takes a leading role in supporting business and industrial enterprises and then regulates and closely monitors the economy once it is privatized. An example was Mitsui (MIT-soo-ee), a family-owned company whose business interests dated back to Tokugawa times. The most powerful corporations, the zaibatsu, dominated the national economy and maintained especially close ties to the government. They believed economic independence from the West to be patriotic. State capitalism and the growth of industry often favored city people over the rural peasantry; capital for industrialization was obtained by squeezing the peasants through the land tax. In exchange, however, the government spurred agricultural productivity by providing new seeds, improving land use, and supplying better irrigation.

First Commercial Bank in Edo During the Meiji era, the banking industry grew. This bank, built in Western style in Edo, was owned by the Mitsui family, which also owned large stores, breweries, factories, coal mines, and other enterprises. Mitsui was one of the major business conglomerates in Japan, with branches all over Asia.

The new economic structure perpetuated the traditional group orientation and social controls of Japanese society. Most Japanese identified closely with the company that employed them, and the economy flourished by exploiting Japanese workers. The government kept wages deliberately low so that scarce capital could be devoted to building factories, shipyards, and railroads. Ultimately, the sacrifices paid off by creating new jobs and fostering national wealth, but life in the Meiji era was not easy for most Japanese. For example, as in the United States and Europe, the textile mills mainly employed women, half of them below the age of twenty and 15 percent younger than fourteen, chiefly recruited from rural villages. The young factory women, paid half the salary of male workers, worked twelve-hour shifts, interrupted only by one half-hour meal break.

Mill workers experienced high death, physical abuse, and diseases such as tuberculosis caused by crowded working conditions.

Social Reform in Meiji Japan

Meiji reforms also fostered social change by attacking the rigid Tokugawa class system. New laws allowed people, regardless of background, to change occupations and move freely. They also stripped the samurai of their monopoly on military occupations, leading many to become lawyers, teachers, or journalists—and others to become perennial political dissenters. To involve Japanese of all backgrounds in modernization, the regime constructed a universal school system based on those in European nations such as Germany and paid for by both taxes and tuition. By 1900, Japan was training its own scientists, engineers, and technicians.

Meiji policies stimulated debate about the value of various social patterns. Some reformers blamed the traditional family, ruled firmly by senior men, for discouraging personal independence, but generally the Meiji sought to preserve gender roles. Confucian books popular in Japan claimed that the lifelong duty of women was obedience to men. Meiji policies promoted the idea of "Good Wife, Wise Mother" to strengthen families by having mothers stay at home with their children. But some women, such as activist Fukuda Hideko, rejected such models and argued that "virtually everything [for women] is coercive and oppressive, making it imperative that we women rise up and develop our own social movement."[13]

Westernization and Expansion

During the Meiji era, the Japanese became acquainted with Western philosophy, social theory, economic thought, literature, and fashions, all of which influenced Japanese society. The peak of Westernization came in the 1870s. In these years, the Japanese adopted the Western calendar, added European words to the Japanese language, became familiar with chairs and couches, began eating more meat, raised the Tokugawa ban on Christianity, shook hands rather than bowing, and often married in the Western style. Many Japanese equated all of this with progress.

Observers, foreign and Japanese, debated the impact of the Meiji reforms. Many Westerners were amazed at the dramatic transformation in Japan, but Japanese literature reflected the difficulty of life in a transitional era. In 1911, a Japanese novelist worried about a "nervous collapse" that would devastate the society as a result of the cultural confusion. By the later 1880s, the mania for Western fads had abated, and the Meiji leaders began to foster a synthesis of old and new. By the 1890s, there was a renewed emphasis on traditional values, including the ancient myths about the Japanese people arising from the gods and the divinity of the emperor. The Japanese were never slavish imitators of the West or alienated from their own traditions. In the Meiji view, a new culture combining East and West could be produced and taught to the people, just as had been done in earlier centuries with Korean and Chinese influences. The dramatic changes Japan experienced, however, created tensions within Japanese society and between Japan and other nations that ultimately fostered a more imperialistic foreign policy.

The Sino-Japanese and Russo-Japanese Wars

Eventually, Meiji Japan fought two wars (see Map 23.2). China and Japan battled each other in the Sino-Japanese War (1894–1895) over their competing influence in Korea, which Japan had long coveted for its fertile land but now also viewed as a market for Japanese products. The war resulted in a smashing Japanese military victory and consequent dominance in Korea, as well as in the Chinese island of Taiwan, both of which the Japanese transformed into outright colonies in 1910. Impressed by Japanese military capabilities, Britain forged an alliance with Japan that endured through the Meiji era. Britain's rival, Russia, also had ambitions in Korea. Furthermore, Russia had acquired a foothold in resource-rich Manchuria, a nearby Chinese-controlled region Japan wanted to exploit. The rising tensions led to the Russo-Japanese War (1904–1905), during which the Japanese seized a Russian-held Manchurian port and then destroyed the Russian fleet sent out from Europe.

Interactive Map

The Glory and End of Meiji Japan

The Japanese victory over Russia electrified the world and contributed to the great awakening of Asian nationalism. For the first time, a non-Western nation had defeated a major European power, giving hope to societies under Western domination. The triumph in the war further enhanced the pride of the Japanese people in their nation and confirmed that Japan had, in three decades, become a world power. Among the fruits of victory was the transfer to Japan of some Russian holdings in Manchuria and control of the southern half of Sakhalin island, off the Siberian coast.

The Meiji era, which came to an official end with the death of the Meiji emperor in 1916, had achieved stunning successes. Japan had secured national security and a position as a powerful regional power. The Meiji leaders had negotiated an end to the unequal treaties and had formed an alliance with the powerful British. Japan's wealth and influence were still less than that of the major industrial powers—the United States, Britain, France, and Germany—but Japan was now an industrial nation, on a par with countries such as Russia and Italy. With 50 million people, it prepared to play a bigger role in regional and world affairs. But as the country faced new challenges and setbacks in the next decades, many Japanese wisfully remembered the Meiji as a time of vitality, courage, and hope: "Snow is falling, Meiji recedes in the distance."

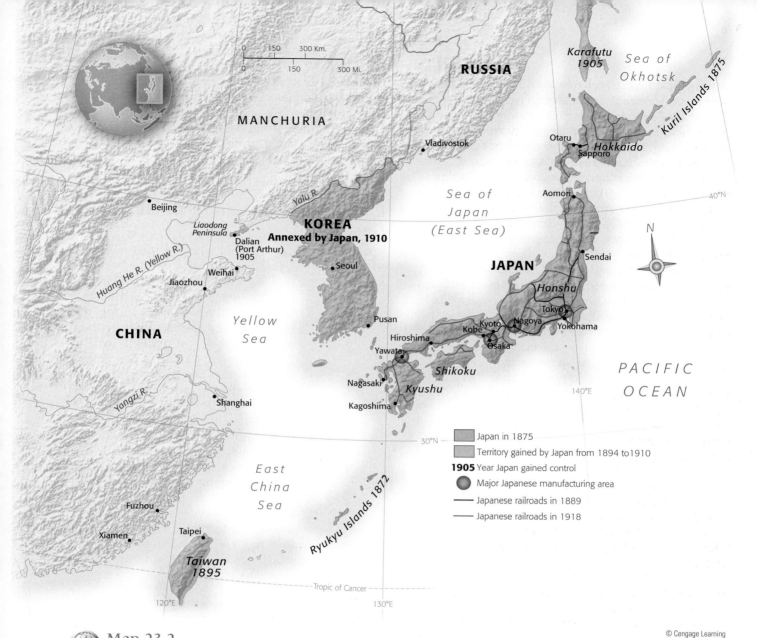

Map 23.2
Japanese Modernization and Expansion, 1868–1913
Japan undertook a crash modernization in the later 1800s. By 1910, its military power had increased, and it had won a war with Russia and colonized Korea, Taiwan, and Sakhalin (then known as Karafutu).

Korean Transitions Under Japan

Rising Japanese power shaped modern Korea. This pattern began in 1876, when Meiji Japan, adopting the model used by the United States to open Japan, sent a naval expedition to Korea that forced the Yi government to open five ports and sign unequal treaties that gave Japan a strong role in Korea's economy. The growing Japanese influence in Korea compelled the Yi government to introduce reforms, such as toleration of Christianity, and sign trade agreements with Western nations. Many Korean peasants, impoverished by Japan's imperialist policies and drought, joined the

Tonghak ("Eastern Learning"), a protest movement with an eclectic ideology not unlike the Taipings in China, that mixed Confucianism, Buddhism, Christianity, and hatred of Japan and the West. Spurred by famine, the movement grew into the nationwide Tonghak Rebellion against the Yi government in 1894. When Korea's longtime ally, China, sent in troops to help the Yi government repress the rebellion, China's rival, Japan, responded by also sending in a force and capturing the Korean capital, Seoul, holding the Yi royal family hostage to gain influence over the Korean government.

The desire of both China and Japan to capitalize on the Tonghak Rebellion led to the Sino-Japanese

War (1894–1895), which resulted in a humiliating Chinese withdrawal and a stronger presence on the part of the Japanese after they stamped out Korean resistance. Some 18,000 Koreans, mostly peasants who rallied to the Yi government, died in fighting the Japanese. Japan forcibly annexed Korea in 1910, transforming it from the "hermit kingdom" into a Japanese colony and ending the decrepit Yi dynasty. One resistance leader expressed the widespread Korean despair: "I was unable to repel our nation's enemies, or hold back our 4000 year long civilization from falling to the ground."[14]

Between 1910 and 1945, Korea was a heavily exploited, harshly ruled Japanese colony. It endured Japanese racism and brutal suppression of Korean nationalism and culture, although the Japanese also increased educational opportunities and built a modern economy. The Japanese seized Korean land for Japanese companies and restricted civil liberties. Nonetheless, Koreans continued to protest and resist. In 1919, the Japanese police brutally crushed peaceful demonstrations by men and women calling for independence, killing or injuring some 24,000 demonstrators and arresting 47,000. Resentment simmered as repressive measures, such as forcing students to speak only Japanese, increased. Koreans often looked for inspiration in Western ideas, including Christianity and Marxism. Many Koreans, however, rejected Western ideas, believing the best strategy was to strengthen Confucianism. There was no dominant nationalist thread.

Japanese relations with Koreans became even more exploitative during World War II. Korean men were conscripted as soldiers and workers, and young Korean women, termed by the Japanese "comfort women," were forced to serve as sex slaves for Japanese soldiers. Even today many Koreans have a deep antipathy for Japan as a result of colonial repression and exploitation.

LO⁵ Russia's Eurasian Empire

Between 1750 and 1914, Russia built a vast Eurasian empire stretching 3,200 miles from the Baltic Sea to the Bering Straits, in the process creating more intensive ties to Asian societies. The expansion continued through the 1800s, making Russia a hemispheric power controlling vast amounts of land. Located on the fringe of Europe, Central Asia, and the Middle East, Russia was influenced by all three regions. Russian society was characterized by autocratic governments, alternating periods of reform and reaction, a feudal-style rural system, and chronic discontent. During this era, Russia played an increasingly critical role in both Asian and European politics.

Europeanization and Czarist Despotism

Russians had long debated whether they belonged to the European tradition or had a unique heritage, and these debates were reflected in Russian politics. Influence from western Europe was particularly strong during the long reign of Catherine the Great (r. 1762–1796). Influenced by the Enlightenment, Catherine denounced slavery, hailed liberty, and patronized the arts and literature. She also presided over a golden age of opulence for the nobility, but Catherine's policies led to worsening social ills and imperialist expansion. Despite her liberal views, she could not encourage freedom among the common people, especially the disgruntled peasantry, because she needed support from the landed aristocracy. Instead, Catherine extended serfdom to Ukraine and denounced the French Revolution as irreligious and immoral. Continuing the expansionism of her predecessors, Catherine's energetic foreign policy added Poland and Finland to Russia's realm and annexed the Crimean peninsula in 1783, where Russia built a major naval base.

> "Located on the fringe of Europe, Central Asia, and the Middle East, Russia was influenced by all three regions."

 Russian History Index: The World Wide Web Virtual Library (*http://vlib.iue.it/ hist-russia/Index.html*). Useful links on Russian history.

To maintain power, the czars who followed Catherine, whether Westernizers or not, often relied on the brutal despotism common in Russian history. Czar Nicholas I (r. 1825–1855) feared alienating the aristocracy, suppressed the restless Poles, and formed a secret police force to harass, imprison, or eliminate opponents. Nicholas also expanded the empire further by invading Hungary and seeking dominance over the Ottomans to secure access for transport of Russia's grain exports through the Black Sea to the Mediterranean. He encouraged Slavic rebellion in the Balkans, which provoked Britain and France and led to the Crimean War of 1854. Some 250,000 soldiers on all sides died in the war. Armies of conscripted

Catherine the Great Resplendent in her royal robes, Catherine the Great triumphantly enters one of the ports of the Crimean peninsula recently captured from the Turks. Catherine presided over an expansion of the Russian Empire and efforts at modernization.

Giraudon/The Bridgeman Art Library International

Russian serfs were no match for modern British and French forces, and Russia was defeated and forced to withdraw from Ottoman territory.

Nicholas's successor, Czar Alexander II (r. 1855–1881), was more oriented to western Europe and followed a reformist domestic policy, emancipating the serfs in 1861 and decentralizing government. But many serfs were unable, as required by the new law, to pay the landowners for the lands they wanted to use, and discontent grew throughout the later 1800s.

Russian Expansion in Asia

During this era, the Russians became more engaged with Asia, expanding their power in Siberia, the Caucasus, and Central Asia to form the largest contiguous land empire in the world (see Map 23.3). By the early 1800s, the Russians were anxious to counter British and French expansion in Asia and the Pacific. With Qing China in decline, Russians occupied the Amur Basin, and in 1860 gained official Chinese recognition of their claims in exchange for helping negotiate the end of the Arrow War pitting China against Britain and France. They also acquired a coastal zone that allowed them to satisfy their long-held goal for an ice-free port on Siberia's Pacific shore, to be used as a base for Russian commercial and military activity in the Pacific Basin. There the Russians built the city of Vladivostok ("Ruler of the East").

Interactive Map

For several centuries, the Russians had also expanded around the Black Sea, seeking an outlet to the Mediterranean Sea and its maritime trade routes. Between 1800 and the 1870s, the Russians extended their control south through the mountainous Caucasus on the east of the Black Sea, absorbing Armenia and Georgia, both largely Christian, as well as Muslim Azerbaijan (az-uhr-bye-JAHN). Sometimes they faced fierce resistance in the Caucasus: they needed four decades to conquer the strongly Islamic Chechens (CHECH-uhnz). The Russians triumphed in 1859 by ravaging Chechen lands, herds, and crops and beheading their captives. These atrocities fostered a Chechen hatred of Russian rule.

The Russians also colonized Muslim Central Asia, the first step in gaining direct access to the Indian Ocean trade and preventing Britain from establishing influence in the region from their base in India. By 1864, the Russians controlled all the lands of the Kazakh (KAH-zahk) people, east of the Caspian Sea, and looked south to the old Silk Road cities of Turkestan. Although they remained vigorous centers of Islamic learning and Sufism, diminished overland trade and warfare with Persians, Russians, and rival states had caused economic decline in most of these Central Asian states. By the 1870s, Russia's military capabilities had enabled it to dominate Turkestan. They also coveted Afghanistan, which eventually became a buffer between British India and Russian Central Asia. Czarist policy in Central Asia and the Caucasus promoted economic changes that chiefly benefited Russians. The czars

CHRONOLOGY

Russia and Central Asia, 1750–1914

1762–1796	Reign of Catherine the Great
1800–1870s	Russian conquest of Caucasus and Turkestan
1861	Emancipation of Russian serfs
1891–1915	Building of Trans-Siberian Railroad
1904–1905	Russo-Japanese War
1905	First Russian Revolution

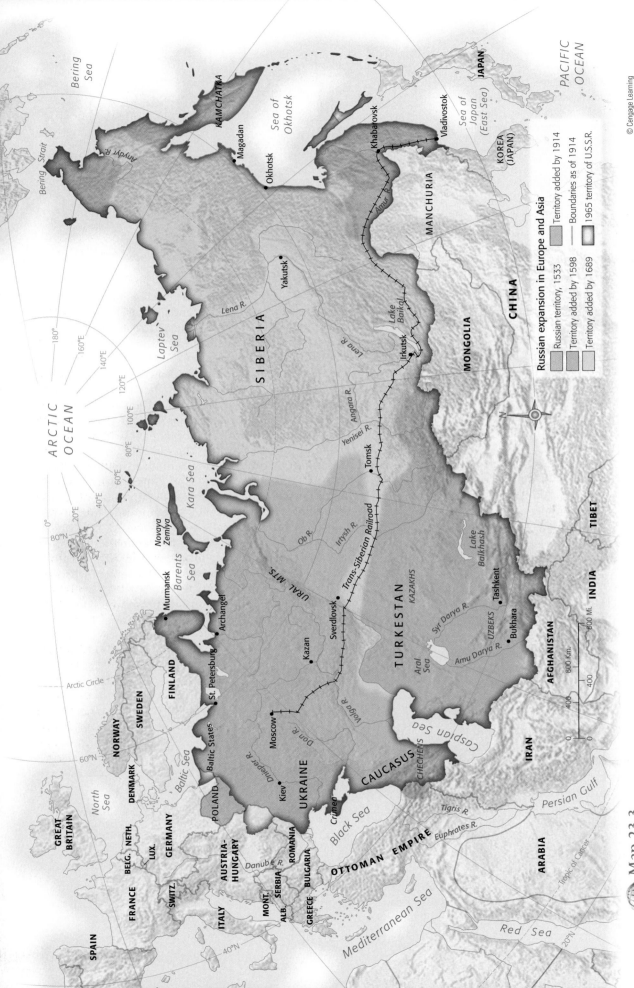

Map 23.3
Expansion of the Russian Empire

Between the 1500s and 1914, Russia gradually gained control of Siberia, Turkestan, the Caucasus, Ukraine, Poland, the Baltic states, and Finland, becoming the world's largest contiguous territorial empire.

Russian expansion in Europe and Asia

Russian territory, 1533	Territory added by 1914
Territory added by 1598	Boundaries as of 1914
Territory added by 1689	1965 territory of U.S.S.R.

© Cengage Learning

also gradually introduced a policy of Russification, the promotion of Russian language and culture for the non-Russian peoples. This policy sparked resentment and spiritual revival among many Muslims.

Weakness in Imperial Russia

Russian expansion brought problems along with the gains: its sheer size hindered governance, fostered corruption, and prevented the ready exploitation of its vast resources. In addition, colonization of non-Russian lands made Russian leaders permanently fear rebellion, and they needed a huge army to maintain security in the colonized territories. The world's longest railroad, the Trans-Siberian, built between 1891 and 1915, fostered Russian settlement of eastern Siberia and helped Russian traders penetrate Manchuria and Korea. But this expansion brought conflict with Japan, generating the Russo-Japanese War (1904–1905). Russia's defeat in that war humiliated the country and its last czar, Nicholas II (r. 1894–1917).

Russian Changes and Revolution

Territorial expansion and political reforms created economic growth and fostered instability. Spurred by the acquisition of the Caucasus and Central Asian markets, Russia enjoyed increased industrialization during the later 1800s and ranked fifth in the world as an industrial power by 1914. With this came discontent among workers, who often resented the exploitation they faced. Women, particularly in the upper classes, also chafed under their traditional roles and sought more education and opportunities. Political and economic reformers were often influenced by western European ideas, but the appeal of these ideas caused Russian thinkers to torment themselves over their national identity and goals. Opposed to the Westernizers were the Slavophiles, who rejected what they saw as decadent Western models and defended Russian culture, such as

Make a decision to join the military or go to university under the rule of the autocratic Russian government in this interactive simulation.

respect for the Russian Orthodox Church. Slavophiles often advocated that Russians unite with other Slavs in eastern Europe and the Balkans to confront the West. One proponent of pan-Slavism wrote in 1871 that Russia was never an integral part of Europe, having different and, in his view, superior traditions.

Whether reformers or conservatives, Westernizers or Slavophiles, Russians were proud of their rich literary and artistic tradition. Novelists such as Fyodor Dostoyevsky (dos-tuh-YEF-skee) (1821–1881) and Leo Tolstoy (tuhl-STOI) (1828–1910) created enduring masterpieces, including Tolstoy's epic novel, *War and Peace* (1869), which profiled two noble families during the Napoleonic Wars. One of Russia's most honored composers, Pyotr Tchaikovsky (chi-KOF-skee) (1840–1893), traveled widely in Europe and wrote popular operas and ballets, including *Swan Lake* and *The Nutcracker*.

Despite such cultural accomplishments, Russian discontent with the autocratic system and the rising costs of empire building increased through the 1800s, resulting in violent resistance. To crush opposition, over the decades the czars sent thousands of dissidents to remote Siberian prison camps, where many died of illness, starvation, overwork, or the harsh climate. Repression fueled resentment of the government. Some anti-czar Russians joined the illegal Socialist Revolutionary Party, founded in 1898, that used terror to strike against the regime. In 1905, the sacrifices imposed on common people by the Russo-Japanese War sparked a major socialist-led revolutionary movement involving widespread violence. The unrest began when 100,000 factory workers in the capital, St. Petersburg, went on strike and then mounted a protest march demanding equality before the law, freedom of speech, and other progressive goals. Russian troops opened fire on the peaceful marchers, killing some 200 and wounding hundreds more. The violence shattered public support for the czar and fueled increasing revolutionary activity, which soon spread to the armed forces. The revolutionaries were split in their goals, a division that enabled the government to crush the uprising, executing thousands of rebels and burning prorebel villages. But the czar bowed to public demands and allowed an elected national assembly with limited powers. In defeat, the socialist movement fractured into hostile factions. However, conflicts among Russians simmered, and in 1917, they produced the greatest upheaval in Russia's history, which ended the czarist system (see Chapter 24).

Listen to a synopsis of Chapter 23.

World Wars, European Revolutions, and Global Depression, 1914–1945

ПРОЛЕТАРИИ ВСЕХ СТРАН СОЕДИНЯЙТЕСЬ!

Learning Outcomes

After reading this chapter, you should be able to answer the following questions:

LO^1 What was the impact of World War I on the Western world?

LO^2 How did communism prevail in Russia and transform that country?

LO^3 How did the Great Depression reshape world politics and economies?

LO^4 What were the main ideas and impacts of fascism?

LO^5 What were the costs and consequences of World War II?

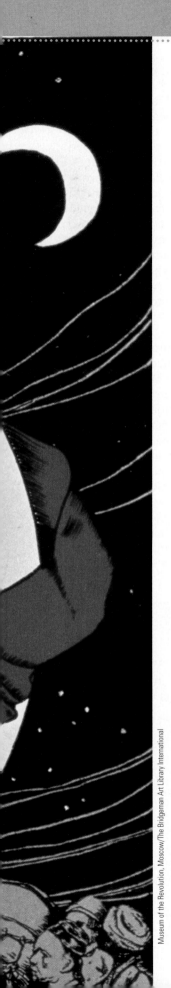

> **"My beautiful, pitiful era. With an insane smile you look back, cruel and weak, like an animal past its prime, at the prints of your own paws."**
>
> —Osip Mandelstam, Russian poet[1]

By April 1917, the French army had been fighting the Germans for more than two and a half years. World War I was creating growing casualty lists and inflicting tremendous hardship on soldiers on both sides. A new French commander, General Philippe Pétain (peh-TANH) (1856–1951), implemented a strategy to minimize French casualties. Pétain regarded his soldiers as more than cannon fodder, a view that made him popular with the fighting men, but he was overruled as the French launched another frontal assault on the well-fortified German lines. The result was a military disaster that caused perhaps 120,000 deaths and broke the fighting spirit of the French troops. Mutinies broke out in the units, ranging from minor infractions of code to violent disturbances. Pétain emerged from World War I a French hero, but he was later excoriated for serving as the nominal head of the Vichy French government under hated Nazi occupation in World War II. Pétain died in prison, a broken man looking back on three tumultuous decades (1914–1945) that had brought so much distress and destruction to the world. Two brutal world wars, a mighty revolution in Russia, a terrible economic depression with worldwide consequences, and the rise of new ideologies all occurred during what Russian Jewish poet Osip Mandelstam aptly described as a "beautiful, pitiful era."

In the years before World War I, some Europeans had believed that the world was poised for a peaceful, prosperous new age of international cooperation in which the horrors of war would be ended forever. The hopes of the idealists were dashed by two world wars that challenged the Western world-view of liberalism and rationalism that had captured the European imagination since the Enlightenment; and the faith in progress was shattered by dictatorship in Russia, economic collapse, and organized slaughter. The disarray in Europe, combined with the spread of new ideologies and technologies, helped undermine Western political influence in the world, except for that of the rising Western power, the United States.

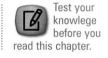
Test your knowlege before you read this chapter.

What do you think?

The world wars weakened Europe's global position while increasing American influence and authority.

Strongly Disagree						*Strongly Agree*
1	2	3	4	5	6	7

---

[1]Quoted in Anne Applebaum, *Gula: A History* (NY: Doubleday, 2003), p. 3.

<<**Global Communism** The communist leaders of the Soviet Union hoped that their revolution in Russia in 1917 would inspire similar revolutions around the world, ending capitalism and imperialism. This poster reflects the dream of a triumphant communism.

LO¹ The Roots and Course of World War I

In August 1914, when war broke out between the major powers of Europe, the British foreign secretary remarked, "The lights are going out all over Europe. We shall not see them again in our lifetime."² The conflict pitted two alliances: Britain, France, and Russia formed the Triple Entente, which later included Serbia, Japan, Italy, Portugal, Romania, Greece, and eventually the United States. These nations, also known as the Allies, faced the Central Powers: Germany, Austria-Hungary, the Ottoman Empire, and Bulgaria. The leaders of the countries involved saw the conflict as nothing short of a struggle to control the global system, with its industrial economies and colonial empires. The Great War, as many Europeans called it, was history's first total war, an armed conflict between industrialized powers that lasted four terrible years. The war brought down empires and dynasties, made the United States a world power, and weakened western Europe's hold over the colonial world. And the end of the conflict made a second major war almost inevitable.

> The Great War (http://www.pitt.edu/~pugachev/greatwar/ww1.html). A useful site on World War I with many essays and links.

> "In the early 1900s, before World War I began, Europeans enjoyed affluence, social stability, and growing democracy; there were few signs of a major war involving the key European powers."

Preludes to War

In the early 1900s, before World War I began, Europeans enjoyed affluence, social stability, and growing democracy; there were few signs of a major war involving the key European powers. The productive European economies benefited from their links to each other and their access to resources and markets in other parts of the world. Whatever their nationality, Europeans looked to the future with confidence, felt superior to the rest of the world, and enjoyed their prosperity. Thanks to imperialism and industrialization, Europeans now consumed new products such as chocolate and rubber tires, and rising populations expanded markets. Between 1880 and 1910, the population grew 43 percent in Germany, 26 percent in Britain, and more than 50 percent in Russia.

European emigration to the Americas and Australia increased markets there for European goods, and improved transportation made it easier to move people, natural resources, and manufactured products over long distances. European capital financed South African gold and diamond mines, Malayan rubber plantations, Australian sheep stations, Russian railways, and Canadian wheat fields, and every sector of the growing U.S. economy.

Economic and Political Competition

But the prosperity, interdependence, and idealism of the era had their limits, and other conditions worked against them to breed tensions and resentments. The quest for imperial glory increased competition between the major European powers for economic and political influence. Britain, France, and Germany were the wealthiest, most powerful nations and fierce rivals with large overseas empires in Africa, Asia, the Pacific, and the Caribbean. Most Europeans still considered wars necessary struggles rather than terrible evils; they also stood by their national interests. The chief of the German General Staff told the German chancellor, "I hold war to be inevitable, and

CHRONOLOGY

World War I, 1914–1919

1908	Austria-Hungarian annexation of Bosnia-Herzegovina
1914	Outbreak of conflict
1916	Battle of Verdun
April 1917	U.S. intervention
March 1917	Fall of czarist government in Russia
March 1918	Brest-Litovsk Treaty
November 1918	End of conflict
1919	Paris Peace Conference

the sooner the better. Everyone is preparing for the great war, which they all expect."[3]

Britain, France, and Germany's fierce economic rivalry, in particular, had stoked the fires of war during the scramble for colonies in the late 1800s. Because they began empire building later than Britain and France, the Germans resented those nations' political control of much of the world and the resources and markets it gave them access to. Germany rapidly industrialized and challenged Britain for economic dominance in overseas markets. Britain, which had commanded the seas for a century, became concerned in 1900, when Germany began building a naval fleet. The growing rivalries led to the manufacture or acquisition of heavier weapons, an increase in the size of armies, and the formation of alliances. France and Russia shared Britain's hostility toward an increasingly aggressive Germany, which in turn felt encircled by these three hostile powers. Austria-Hungary, Germany's most loyal ally, and the Ottoman Empire shared German dislike of Russia. The growing nationalist agitation for self-determination by the many ethnic minorities within these multinational European empires added to the combustible mix.

Tensions in the Balkans

Austria-Hungary faced a particularly difficult challenge in governing the restless Czech, Slovak, and Balkan peoples within its empire. Conflict in the Balkans, the mountainous region in southeastern Europe, was fostered by the rivalries between nations and tensions between Balkan ethnic groups. The Balkans were coveted by the Ottomans (who lost most of their Balkan territory between 1908 and 1913), Russia, and Austria-Hungary. In 1908, Austria-Hungary annexed Bosnia-Herzegovina (boz-nee-uh-HERT-suh-go-vee-nuh), a Balkan territory containing three often-feuding Slavic peoples—Croats, Serbs, and Muslims—and also coveted by the neighboring country of Serbia. If their ally Germany could restrain the major Serbian ally, Russia, the leaders of Austria-Hungary thought war with Serbia over their conflicting Balkan claims might salvage their decaying empire, which once ruled large parts of Europe.

A Preventable Conflict?

Whether World War I could have been prevented is a controversial question for historians. The German monarch, Kaiser Wilhelm II (r. 1888–

> **"Tensions in the Balkans led to war in 1914. "**

1918), who saw himself as a king with divine rights and answerable only to God, deserves some share of blame. He and other political and military leaders underestimated the human costs and long-term consequences of conflict. Although overstating the case, a key British leader later mourned that "the nations slithered over the brink into the boiling cauldron of war without a trace of apprehension or dismay."[4]

The Course of the European War

Tensions in the Balkans led to war in 1914. The pretext was a political dispute between Austria-Hungary and Serbia over the assassination of the Austrian archduke Franz Ferdinand (1863–1914), the heir to the Habsburg throne, and his wife, Sophie, in Sarajevo (sar-uh-YAY-vo), the capital city of Bosnia-Herzegovina, for an official visit. Although he advocated a conciliatory policy toward the Slavic minorities in the empire, the archduke symbolized continuing Austro-Hungarian domination to Serbs. The group behind the assassination, the Black Hand, were Bosnian Serbs who wanted to end Austrian rule in their land and merge Bosnia with Serbia. Pushed by anti-Slav hardliners in the government, Austria-Hungary responded to the assassination by declaring war on Serbia, Russia's ally. Germany followed suit to support Austria-Hungary, its militarily weaker ally, and Britain, France, and Russia declared war against Germany. Several months later, Ottoman Turkey, long a rival of Russia, joined the Central Powers, closing off British and French access to the Black Sea.

 Mud and Khaki, Memoirs of an Incomplete Soldier Read from the memoirs of a British soldier, and imagine the horrors of trench warfare and poison gas in World War I.

A Long, Brutal Conflict

European leaders expected a short war, lasting perhaps six months; instead they got a long, brutal conflict, the most devastating war in history to that point. This was the first fully industrialized war, as whole economies geared for war and modern military technology invented more efficient and indiscriminate ways of killing, including long-range artillery, poison gas, flamethrowers, and aerial bombing. The war massacred a generation of men, doomed youth cut down by shrapnel that tore flesh to pieces, high explosives that pulverized bone, and gas that seared the lungs. The German soldier turned writer Erich Maria

Remarque remembered the "great brotherhood [caused by] the desperate loyalty to one another of men condemned to die." The surviving soldiers were often maimed mentally or physically. Thousands suffered from shellshock, a horrific nervous condition that made normal life difficult or impossible. The war also generated disease and starvation among civilians.

The Western Front

The war on the western front in Belgium and northern France was largely one of soldiers huddling in muddy trenches, gas masks at hand, and using artillery and machine guns to pound the enemy troops in their trenches. In hopes of a breakthrough, one or another general ordered attacks across the barbed wire–filled ground, known as "No Man's Land," between the opposing trenches, which resulted in countless casualties. But for all the sacrifices required of soldiers, the front lines moved little in four years. The cataclysmic Battle of Verdun (vuhr-DUN), a fortress in northeastern France, in February 1916 symbolized the senseless slaughter of the war on the western front. The French stopped a surprise German assault, but more soldiers may have been killed per square yard at Verdun than in any other battle in history, with nearly 1 million French and German casualties. But despite the carnage, and the courage of the soldiers on both sides,

Verdun had little impact on the war itself. By 1917, more effective offensive tactics using large armored tanks put more pressure on the German lines.

The Eastern Front

The war became global in scope (see Map 24.1). In the east, Germany and its allies quickly overran Serbia and Romania and pushed deep into western Russia against poorly organized Russian armies. By 1917, Russian morale was cracking.

Interactive Map

The war had killed or wounded more than 7 million Russians and caused massive dislocations, starvation, and disease. Originally a German ally, Italy switched sides in 1915 but lost heavily in several unsuccessful battles. In the Middle East, fighting took place over a wide area. Initially, the Ottomans took a heavy toll on the Allied troops that were sent to invade Turkey and occupy the Gallipoli Peninsula, the gateway to Istanbul. But an Arab uprising begun in 1916 and a British invasion of Ottoman-controlled Iraq forced the Ottoman forces to fight in western Asia and eventually to retreat from that area. Some fighting also broke out in East Africa, as the British and South Africans invaded the German colony of Tanganyika. On the other side of the world, Japan, a British ally, occupied German-held territory in China and the Pacific.

John Nash, *Over the Top* This painting, by the British artist John Nash, shows the trench warfare common on the western front during World War I. Here Allied soldiers leave their trenches to attack across "No Man's Land" on a snowy day.

Map 24.1
World War I

World War I pitted the Triple Entente of Britain, France, and Russia, and its allies, against the Central Powers: Germany, Austria-Hungary, and the Ottoman Empire. The worst fighting occurred along the western front and in eastern Europe and Russia. The intervention of the United States in 1917 against the Central Powers proved decisive.

© Cengage Learning

Map labels (main map):
Moscow · Petrograd (St. Petersburg) · Helsinki · RUSSIA · Treaty of Brest-Litovsk, March 1918 · Armistice line, December 1917 · Kiev · UKRAINE · FINLAND · ESTONIA · LATVIA · Riga · LITHUANIA · Wilno (Vilnius) · BELARUS · Brest-Litovsk · Masurian Lakes 1914 · Tannenberg 1914 · E. PRUSSIA · Warsaw · KINGDOM OF POLAND (Russia) · Farthest Russian advance, 1914 · GALICIA · MAY 1915 · Berlin · GERMANY · Kiel · Jutland 1916 · DENMARK · British blockade line · NORWAY · SWEDEN · NETHERLANDS · Louvain · BELGIUM · Paris · LUXEMBOURG · ALSACE-LORRAINE · Western front · Rhine R. · Elbe R. · SWITZERLAND · AUSTRIA-HUNGARY · Vienna · Budapest · Caporetto 1917 · AUG. 1917 · MAR. 1918 · Italian front · ITALY · Rome · Sarajevo · MONTENEGRO · SERBIA · Adriatic Sea · ALBANIA · Balkan front · GREECE · BULGARIA · Bucharest · ROMANIA · TRANSYLVANIA · Constantinople · OTTOMAN EMPIRE · Gallipoli 1915 · Dardanelles · Black Sea · Mediterranean Sea · Crete · Cyprus · Malta · Sicily · Sardinia · Corsica · Balearic Is. · SPAIN · Bordeaux · FRANCE · GREAT BRITAIN · London · IRELAND · North Sea · Baltic Sea · ATLANTIC OCEAN · TUNISIA (France) · Tunis · Elba · Po R. · Rhône R. · Seine R. · Loire R. · Garonne R. · Ebro R. · Don R. · Dnieper R. · Dniester R. · Danube R. · Vistula R.

Legend (main map):
Triple Entente and its Allies
Central Powers
Neutral nations
Greatest extent of territory gained by Germany-Austria
Battle line

Scale: 0 200 400 Km. / 0 200 400 Mi.

Inset map labels:
Coblenz · Cologne · Ruhr R. · Rhine R. · GERMANY · Saar R. · Moselle R. · Strasbourg · ALSACE · Epinal · Mulhouse · Basel · LORRAINE · St. Mihiel · Nancy · Verdun · ARGONNE FOREST · Châlons-sur-Marne · Marne R. · Sedan · ARDENNES · LUXEMBOURG · Liège · Meuse R. · BELGIUM · Brussels · Antwerp · Ghent · Ostend · FLANDERS · Scheldte R. · NETHERLANDS · St. Quentin · Aisne R. · Reims · Belleau Wood · Château-Thierry · Marne II · Compiègne · Marne I · Paris · Seine R. · Somme R. · Amiens · Arras · Calais · Dover · English Channel · FRANCE

Legend (inset map):
Germany, 1914
German offensive, 1915
Greatest extent of territory gained by Germany, Sept. 1914
Front at beginning of 1915
German offensive, Summer 1918
Armistice line, November 1918
Major battle

Scale: 0 25 50 Km. / 0 25 50 Mi.

The United States Enters the War

Although the Germans won more battles than they lost, eventually the tide turned against them. Over time, the economic power of the Allies proved decisive. The Allies had superior wealth, better weapons, and more troops. The use of sea power was also crucial in determining the course of the war. Britain and Germany possessed the world's two most powerful navies, and they engaged each other in the North Sea and the eastern Mediterranean. The Germans used their submarines to break Allied supply lines, but their attacks on British and U.S. ships carrying supplies to Britain brought a reluctant United States into the war.

U.S. Intervention: The End of the War

Two fateful developments in 1917—the Russian Revolution, discussed later in this chapter, and the intervention of the United States—altered the conflict. The Russian Revolution overthrew the czarist government and took Russia out of the war in early 1918. Freed from the eastern front, German armies made breakthroughs against the British and French forces in the west. As a German victory seemed more likely, U.S. military leaders, politicians, and businessmen all pressed for intervention. U.S. companies and banks had a big stake in an Allied victory, because Allied defeat might have prevented payment on orders for American products and investments in the British and French economies. Americans were also enraged by German submarine attacks on U.S. merchant ships. After maintaining a perilous neutrality for three years, President Woodrow Wilson committed the United States to war, linking the military commitment to idealistic American values when he told Congress that "the world must be made safe for democracy. We are the champions of the rights of mankind."[5]

The U.S. intervention proved decisive in securing an Allied victory. Beginning on April 17, 1917, some 300,000 American troops poured into Europe and were warmly welcomed in Allied nations. Supported by the United States, the Allies blockaded German ports, creating severe economic problems. As U.S. troops and resources arrived, an Allied offensive pushed the German forces back. Soon Germany's allies began surrendering. The deteriorating conditions demoralized

> "Although powerful Western nations still dominated world politics and the world economy, the war also changed the old global order and began a new one."

Germans. Its overextended army in disarray, and suffering food and fuel shortages at home, Germany was forced to agree to peace in November 1918. Kaiser Wilhelm II and the Austro-Hungarian emperor both abdicated, ending two long-standing European monarchies. The Allies dictated the peace terms.

Consequences of World War I

World War I undermined the power of Germany and shifted more influence to the victors: Britain, France, and the United States. It reshaped Europe politically and rearranged the colonial empires. World War I and its aftermath also affected the societies of Asia and Africa, destroying their hopes for achieving independence or self-rule. Although powerful Western nations still dominated world politics and the world economy, the war also changed the old global order and began a new one.

The Treaty of Versailles

The Paris Peace Conference of 1919, held in the former royal palace in the Paris suburb of Versailles (vuhr-SIGH), reshaped Europe and resulted in the Treaty of Versailles. The U.S. president, Woodrow Wilson, went to Paris hoping to use his nation's growing power to sell an agenda promoting freedom, stability, and conciliatory treatment of Germany, known as the Fourteen Points, to skeptical British and French leaders. Favoring political freedom and stability, however, Wilson had to compromise with the hardline French, who wanted to punish Germany. The final treaty required Germany to partly dismantle its military; abandon its Asian, African, and Pacific colonies; and shift land to its European neighbors, leaving 3 million ethnic Germans outside of Germany in countries such as Czechoslovakia and Poland. The Treaty of Versailles also forced Germany to pay huge annual payments, known as reparations, to the Allies to compensate for their war costs. In short, Germany was left virtually disarmed and bankrupt. The new German leader, Friedrich Ebert, fretted: "The armi-

 Comments of the German Delegation to the Paris Peace Conference on the Conditions of Peace, October 1919 Read Germany's response to the Treaty of Versailles, which deprived it of its colonies, 13 percent of its land, and 10 percent of its population.

stice will not produce a just peace. The sacrifices imposed on us must lead to our people's doom."[6]

The Human Cost of the War

The war had taken an appalling human toll on both sides. Altogether 9 to 10 million soldiers and another 10 million civilians died, leaving a generation of European men decimated. The brutality radicalized many workers and peasants, especially in eastern Europe, and leftist political parties—Socialists and Communists—gained strength. In 1914, Europeans had gone to war with patriotic enthusiasm, but by 1918, some philosophers and writers concluded that the slaughter had destroyed the Western claim to moral leadership in the world. Pacifist, antiwar sentiments grew. The French writer Henri Barbusse, a soldier himself, reflected bitterly: "Shame on military glory, shame on armies, shame on the soldier's calling that changes men by turns into stupid victims and ignoble brutes."[7]

Reconfiguring Europe

The war destroyed several old states and created new ones. Four empires—the Russian, Ottoman, Austro-Hungarian, and German—collapsed. As a result of the Russian Revolution of 1917, Communists gained power in Russia, launching a new political and economic system. President Wilson, believing that ethnically homogeneous nation-states could prevent nationalist rivalries, convinced the Paris Peace Conference to redraw national boundaries to give ethnic minorities their own states. In eastern Europe, Poland, Czechoslovakia, Yugoslavia, and Finland were carved out of the ruins of the German, Austro-Hungarian, and Russian Empires, but most of the new states placed various ethnic groups within arbitrary boundaries, leading to tensions that would contribute to World War II's beginning. The appeal of self-determination also inspired uprisings in Britain's longtime colony, Ireland, and in 1921, Parliament was forced to grant most of the island special status within the British Empire as the self-governing Irish Free State.

However, the victorious powers ignored the principle of self-determination for their farther-flung colonies. Woodrow Wilson advocated democracy and human rights, but in seeking to strengthen Britain and France, he decided to support the preservation of their colonies in Asia, Africa, the Pacific, and the Caribbean. The peace settlement transferred Germany's African colonies to the victors, and Britain and France also gained control of the Middle Eastern societies formerly ruled by Ottoman Turkey. The peace settlements of World War I, by ignoring the political struggles of colonized peoples, thus spurred opposition to the West in Asia and Africa. The deaths of thousands of Asian and African colonial subjects who were conscripted or recruited to fight for Britain, France, or Germany in World War I sparked even deeper resentments. Thus, World War I was one of the key factors in the rise of nationalism, the desire to form politically independent nations, in the colonies between 1918 and 1941 (see Chapter 25).

The global system shaped by colonial empires and Western economic power survived, but European prestige and influence weakened. The war undermined European economies, allowing the United States to leap ahead of Europe. Wilson wanted an open world economy in which American industry could assert its new supremacy. Because European nations had borrowed money from the United States to finance the war, they now owed the United States $7 billion. This war debt allowed the United States, long a debtor nation, to become a creditor nation. By 1919, it was producing 42 percent of all the world's industrial output and had replaced Britain as the banker and workshop of the world.

Wilson also proposed and helped form a League of Nations, the first organization of independent nations to work for peace and humanitarian concerns. But Wilson could not persuade the U.S. Congress, controlled by the largely isolationist Republican opposition, to approve U.S. membership in the league. Hence, the only nation with the power and stature to make the League work stayed outside, leaving Britain and France alone to deal with European and global issues.

> **"**The Russian Revolution had deep roots in Russian history under the czars, the hereditary rulers.**"**

LO[2] The Revolutionary Path to Soviet Communism

The Russian Revolution, a major consequence of World War I, was a formative event of the twentieth century, shaping European and world history, politics, and beliefs. In the wake of the revolution, Russia provided a testing ground for communism, which fostered a powerful state that reshaped Russian society and provided an alternative to the capitalist democracy dominant in North America and western Europe.

The Roots of Revolution

The Russian Revolution had deep roots in Russian history under the czars, the hereditary rulers (see Chapter 23). Controlling a huge Eurasian empire, Russia had enjoyed some limited industrialization, but the powerful and wealthy landed aristocracy opposed further modernization. Socially and economically, Russia was still a somewhat feudalistic country. Although serfdom had been legally abolished in the nineteenth century, peasants often remained subject to the dictates of landowners and enjoyed little social mobility or wealth. Only revolution could forge a decisive change in Russian society.

Growing discontent among intellectuals, the floundering middle class, underpaid industrial workers, and peasants fomented radical movements. All of these groups hated the autocratic czarist system and the privileges enjoyed by the hereditary aristocracy. In 1905 a revolution broke out, only to be brutally crushed by the government, but it left a revolutionary heritage for the Bolsheviks, the most radical of Russia's antigovernment groups, who transformed the revolutionary socialist views promoted by Karl Marx in the mid-1800s into a dogmatic communist ideology. The Bolsheviks started as one faction of a broader socialist movement that split into several rival parties in 1903. The founder and leader of the Bolsheviks, Vladimir Lenin (LEN-in) (1870–1924), was strongly influenced by the works of Karl Marx. Most of the Bolshevik leaders, including Lenin, had spent time as political prisoners in harsh Siberian labor camps for opposing the government, and they were embittered toward the czarist system. They espoused a goal of helping the downtrodden workers and peasants redress the wrongs inflicted upon them by the rich and privileged. A new society, forged by revolutionary violence, could bring about a more equitable distribution of wealth and power for all. Lenin and the Bolsheviks favored a small, disciplined revolutionary organization that would work for workers' interests but abide by the decisions made by the leaders, a system known as the party line.

When World War I broke out, the Russian people rallied around the unpopular czarist government, seeing it as a patriotic war of defense against the

Russian History Index: The World Wide Web Virtual Library (*http://vlib.iue.it/hist-russia/Index.html*). Contains useful essays and links on Russian history, society, and politics.

Lenin The Bolshevik leader Vladimir Lenin stirred crowds with his fiery revolutionary rhetoric, helping to spread the communist message among Russians who were fed up with ineffective government, war, and poverty.

hated Germans, their longtime rivals for dominion in eastern Europe. Only the Bolsheviks opposed the war, which they saw, with some justice, as an imperialistic struggle over markets and colonies. But the war soon lost its allure as Russian military forces collapsed in the face of German armies. Russia lacked the economic power and military and political leadership to compete.

The Bolshevik Seizure of Power

By 1917, the Russian people were sick of war and seeking change, sparking two revolutions. The first revolution erupted in March when riots and strikes caused by food shortages and other problems led to the toppling of the czar and the establishment of a provisional government led by Aleksandr Krenesky (kuh-REN-skee) (1881–1970). But the new provisional government leaders refused to provide the two things most Russians wanted: peace and land. Because of their commitments to the Allies, they vowed to continue fighting the highly unpopular war and declined to redistribute land from the old aristocracy to the peasantry until the war ended.

The political situation became chaotic. While the increasingly discredited provisional government asked for time, radicals organized soviets, local action councils that enlisted workers and soldiers to fight the factory owners and military officers, undermined government authority. The strongest soviet, in the capital, St. Petersburg, had between two thousand and three thousand members and was headed by an executive committee. As the soviets and the government jockeyed for control of St. Petersburg, the Germans, hoping to undermine the Russian provisional government, helped Lenin, in exile in Switzerland, to secretly return to Russia hidden in a railroad boxcar. Using the slogans of "peace, bread, and land" and "all power to the soviets," Lenin rapidly built up Bolshevik influence in the soviets. The provisional government became increasingly discredited and weak.

In October 1917, the Bolsheviks and their 240,000 party members staged an uprising and grabbed power from Kerensky's crumbling provisional government. Aided by the soviets, the Bolsheviks seized key government buildings in St. Petersburg, including the czar's Winter Palace, and pushed other, more moderate parties and soviets aside. Lenin claimed that his goal for Russia was to transfer power from the capitalists to the working class. The Bolsheviks renamed themselves the Communist Party and gained popular support by pulling Russia out of the war. In the Treaty of Brest-Litovsk, negotiated with Germany in March 1918, Russia gave up some of its empire in the west to Germany, abandoning the Ukraine, eastern Poland, the Baltic states, and Finland. They also moved the capital from St. Petersburg, which they renamed Leningrad, to Moscow.

Civil War, Lenin, and a New Society

Once in power, the communist regime had to develop a strategy for dealing with the postwar world. In 1919, Lenin, hoping to protect Russia's revolution by promoting world revolution, organized the Communist International, often known as the Comintern, a collection of communist parties from around the world. It would battle the U.S. vision, articulated by Woodrow Wilson, of promoting capitalism and democracy. Before World War II, however, the United States had the greater success in spreading its influence, partly because it helped stabilize postwar Europe with economic, political, and food assistance to promote pro-capitalist, anticommunist governments. The prospect of world revolution that would foster the spread of communism soon faded.

soviets
Local action councils formed by Russian radicals before the 1917 Russian Revolution that enlisted workers and soldiers to fight the factory owners and military officers.

> **By 1917, the Russian people were sick of war and seeking change, sparking two revolutions.**

The Russian Civil War

The communists were further tested by the Russian Civil War (1918–1921). Conservative, anticommunist forces—who called themselves White Russians in contrast to the communists' military force, the Red Army—included the czarist aristocracy (among them large landowners), generals who were angry at losing their dominance, and a few pro-Western liberals favoring democracy. Heavily funded and armed by Western nations, which were alarmed by the Revolution, the White Russian armies fought the communist forces in the fringe areas of the Russian Empire in the three years following World War I (see Map 24.2). The outside intervention added an international flavor to the Russian Civil War. This intervention had come chiefly from Japan, Britain, France, and the United States. Soon recognizing the whole intervention effort as a quagmire, Wilson lamented that it was harder to get out than it was to go in. U.S. and other Western troops were finally removed in 1920, in some cases after soldiers mutinied. The Western intervention helped to solidify the communist government, which was widely seen by Russians as fighting a nationalist war against foreign powers seeking to restore the old discredited czarist order. Although the communists initially looked vulnerable, they eventually gained the advantage, defeating the White Russians and even reclaiming some of the territory lost in the Brest-Litovsk Treaty, including the Ukraine.

Interactive Map

The USSR Emerges

By 1922, the Communist Party controlled much of the old Russian Empire, but the civil war had left the country in dire straits. Russia's leaders renamed their nation the Union of

Legend:
- Boundary of Russian Empire 1914
- Area controlled by the Bolsheviks, August 1918
- Treaty of Brest-Litovsk, March 1918
- White Russian forces
- Non-Russian anti-Bolshevik forces
- Territory lost to Russia, 1914–1921
- Soviet territory, 1922
- Boundaries, 1922

Map 24.2
Civil War in Revolutionary Russia (1918–1921)

The communist seizure of power in Russia in 1917 sparked a counteroffensive, backed by varied Western nations and Japan, to reverse the Russian Revolution. The communists successfully defended the Russian heartland while pushing back the conservative offensive.

Soviet Socialist Republics (USSR), in theory a federation of all the empire's diverse peoples—such as Kazakhs, Uzbeks, Armenians, and Ukrainians—but in actuality largely controlled by Russians, and hence, to opponents, essentially a continuation of the Russian Empire built by the czars. Soon the USSR turned from world revolution to building what the leaders termed "socialism in one country"—the USSR—using coercion against reluctant citizens if necessary. Yet party leaders did not have a blueprint for transforming Russian society.

Because they had no model of a communist state, the Soviet leaders experimented while using their secret police to eliminate opponents, among them liberals and moderate socialists. The basis for Soviet communism was Marxism-Leninism, a mix of socialism (collective ownership of the economy) and Leninism, a political system in which one party holds a monopoly on power. Lenin initially favored centralization and nationalization of all economic activity, but he was forced by peasant opposition to adopt the New Economic Policy (NEP), a pragmatic approach that mixed capitalism and socialism. The NEP brought economic recovery and included limited capitalism in agriculture, allowing peasants to sell their produce on the open market. But the economy produced few consumer goods, so the peasants had no incentive to sell their produce for profit, because there was little to buy with the money they earned.

Communist Bureaucracy

The long Russian tradition of authoritarian, bureaucratic government under the czars and an obedient population provided a foundation for communist dictatorship. The communists were a small party, and most party leaders were, like Lenin, intellectuals from urban middle-class backgrounds who knew little of Russia's largest social class, the peasants. To regenerate the economy, they eventually adopted not popular control of farms and enterprises by workers and peasants, but a top-down managerial system staffed by officials chiefly of middle-class origin. Peasants and workers became just employees, not partners. Increasingly, the Communist Party and state became bureaucratic. The middle class was now largely composed of state employees, managers, and bureaucrats with salaries and privileges that were denied to the masses and dedicated not to fostering social change but to maintaining their own power. Lenin criticized the bloated bureaucracy and warned, accurately, that his probable successor, Joseph Stalin (STAH-lin) (1879–1953), had dictatorial tendencies. He hoped to reform the party but died in 1924.

Stalinism and a Changed Russia

Lenin's successor, Joseph Stalin (1879–1953), was a master bureaucrat who reshaped Soviet communism and Russia. Born in the Caucasus province of Georgia, the son of a shoemaker, he adopted the name Stalin ("Man of Steel") after joining the Bolsheviks. Stalin outmaneuvered his party rivals to succeed Lenin in 1924, and came to power as the peasants increasingly turned away from the Communist Party. Stalin urged a hard line against those who resisted state policies, eliminated all of his competition in the party, and became a dictator. The system he imposed, known today as Stalinism, included state ownership of all property, such as lands and businesses, a planned economy, and one-man rule.

Stalin: The "Man of Steel"

In 1928, Stalin ended Lenin's NEP and introduced an economic policy based on an annual series of plans for future production, known as Five-Year Plans, formulated by state bureaucrats. The Five-Year Plans produced basic industrial goods, such as steel and coal, but few consumer goods. Stalin also launched a massive crash industrialization program and withdrew the country from the global political and economic system. Under Stalin, the Soviet Union mobilized its own resources, refusing foreign investment. In order to introduce machines to increase farm production, Stalin strengthened the party's grip on the rural sector by collectivizing the land and turning private farms into commonly owned enterprises, in the process destroying the wealthier small farmers, the *kulaks*, as a class. Peasants who refused to join the collective farms were often exiled to Siberia.

The 1930s and 1940s were hard years for the Soviet people, filled with terror. Stalin's rule was marked by purges, or campaigns to eliminate actual or potential opponents; forced-labor camps for

Marxism-Leninism
The basis for Soviet communism, a mix of socialism (collective ownership of the economy) and Leninism.

New Economic Policy (NEP)
Lenin's pragmatic approach to economic development, which mixed capitalism and socialism.

Stalinism
Joseph Stalin's system of government, which included state ownership of all property, such as lands and businesses, a planned economy, and one-man rule.

suspected dissidents; and the widespread use of the secret police (known as the KGB), which spied on and sometimes terrorized the people. Stalin also deported millions of people to the harsh forced-labor camps in Siberia known as gulags (Russian shorthand for State Camp Administration). From 1929 until 1953, some 18 million people passed through the massive gulag system, and about 4.5 million of these never returned home. Gulag inmates toiled, starved, and died building railroads, cutting timber, or digging canals.

Not even beloved artists were spared the repression if they were Jewish, especially given Stalin's embrace of long-standing Russian anti-Semitism. One of Russia's most revered poets, Osip Mandelstam (MAHN-duhl-stuhm) (1891–1938), a Jew whose comment on the era begins this chapter, died in the gulag in 1938. By the early 1950s, the dead and jailed from Stalin's policies numbered around 40 million people, casualties of twenty-five years of repression.

Passive Resistance and Industrialization

The repression also came at a high economic cost. Peasants often destroyed their equipment and livestock as a protest against forced collectivization, and agriculture suffered from these losses for decades. Peasants adopted a stance of passive resistance, doing just the minimum to survive. Russia's annual food production between 1928 and 1980 was less than in 1924. Because agriculture stagnated, the government could not use the surplus to finance industrialization. Instead, it squeezed the urban workers, who became alienated and passively resisted, voicing their feelings in the common expression: "The government pretends they are paying us so we pretend we are working."

Even as the agricultural economy stagnated and the terror continued, however, the communists were reshaping Russian society by introducing modern ideas. Industrialization raised national economic power and the gross national product (GNP), the annual total of all economic activities, to second in the world by 1932. The Five-Year Plans successfully mobilized the population for industrialization, aided by government; as with Meiji Japan, the state, rather than private capital, was the main agent for change. The workforce that was engaged in industrial production nearly tripled between 1928 and 1937. Mass education raised the literacy rate from 28 percent in 1900 to more than 90 percent by the 1980s. Better medical care raised life expectancy from thirty-two in 1914 to seventy in 1960. The transformation in one decade, due in part to the nation's abundant natural resources, was impressive.

The Soviet Model

The USSR was the first society to leave the capitalist world order, industrialize rapidly under direct state control, and establish a new, socialist society. Stalin promoted official atheism and forced artists and writers to glorify Soviet life, a style known as socialist realism. His model held the promise of catching up to the West in a short time and to do so without capitalism, although it came at a high cost in human rights and lives. The USSR's pervasive system of political repression and state control, which was far greater even than that of the czars, limited its appeal to other societies. The USSR can be seen as a combination of Marxist ideology and czarist despotism, driven in turn by the missionary impulse derived from Christianity. The latter gave Soviet leaders the notion of spreading their "true faith" to the world.

> " Europe's very slow and painful recovery from the war fostered political opposition movements that weakened many European governments. "

LO³ The Interwar Years and the Great Depression

In Europe after World War I, peace had brought a great questioning of the old order. By the early 1920s, western Europe had stabilized, and much of the European continent had come under democratically elected governments. Meanwhile, the United States, though suffering severe economic inequalities, enjoyed prosperity. Western affluence, however, was dramatically undermined by the significant event of the 1930s, the Great Depression, a collapse of the world economy that lasted in varying degrees of severity throughout the 1930s. The global extent of the Depression, rooted in developments in Europe and North America after

World War I, illustrated the economic interdependence of the world's societies. The distress caused by the Depression, which affected both industrialized nations and those countries and colonies supplying raw materials, in turn fostered radical political movements.

Europe and Japan in the 1920s

The 1920s was a decade of political, economic, and social change throughout western Europe. Europe's very slow and painful recovery from the war fostered political opposition movements that weakened many European governments. Where these governments were under conservative leaders from the middle and upper classes, the demands of workers for better conditions or unions were usually crushed. The resentment resulting from this repression, however, caused socialist and social democratic parties, such as the British Labor Party, to grow stronger; these parties worked to extend the rights and protections of workers through legislation.

Economic Instability in Europe
For various reasons, some European countries remained politically and economically unstable. For instance, under a new democratic government, the Weimar (VIE-mahr) Republic, Germany struggled with high unemployment, a devastated economy, and the punishing conditions of the Versailles treaty. Costly reparations caused hyperinflation in Germany, which in turn stimulated the growth of extremist political groups. German prosperity was essential to spur the European economy, so the Allies reduced reparations and the United States extended loans, but the Weimar regime continued to face domestic challenges. Meanwhile, certain multiethnic, eastern European countries such as Czechoslovakia, which mixed Czechs and Slovaks with Germans, Poles, Hungarians, and Ukrainians, experienced significant political tensions.

Some western European countries enjoyed a degree of economic recovery that curbed inflation and unemployment. To stimulate their economies, Europeans borrowed U.S. mass production processes, and with growing middle-class prosperity, more Europeans could afford the improved versions of earlier inventions such as cars, radios, and refrigerators. Labor unions also gained strength, helping certain workers achieve an eight-hour day. The center of gravity shifted to the cities and a fast-growing new white-collar class that tended to oppose the socialism that was popular with the working class. Yet Europe's economies were more and more bound up with the world economy, in which they lost ground to

the United States and Japan. Between 1913 and 1928, Europe's share of world exports fell from 53 to 45 percent, a drop that spurred competition for world markets among European nations.

New Social Patterns Emerge
Social change also marked the 1920s, especially in the cities. Europeans developed new patterns

CHRONOLOGY

Europe, North America, and Japan, 1919–1940

1919–1920	First Red Scare in United States
1921	Irish Free State
1921	Formation of Italian fascist movement
1926	Formation of fascist state in Italy
1929–1941	Great Depression
1931	Japanese occupation of Manchuria
1933–1945	Presidency of Franklin D. Roosevelt
1933	Nazi electoral victory in Germany
1933–1938	Anti-Jewish legislation in Germany
1935–1936	Italian conquest of Ethiopia
1936	Start of fascist government in Japan
October 1936	Hitler–Mussolini alliance
1936–1939	Spanish Civil War
1937	Japanese invasion of China
March 1938	Austrian merger with Germany
1938	German annexation of western Czechoslovakia
August 1939	Nazi-Soviet pact
September 1939	German invasion of Poland
1940	Tripartite Pact between Germany, Italy, and Japan

of leisure and consumption. In European cities, affluent people found entertainment at nightclubs, cabarets, and dance halls and shopped at large department stores. Religious observance declined, because many Europeans felt abandoned by God on the battlefields or rejected Christianity as passé.

Gender patterns showed signs of change, too. The new fashion for women emphasized short hair and a boyish figure, while the "new woman," as the popular designation made her, also sought financial independence through paid work. The war had killed millions of young men, leaving fewer men to marry or hire. To fill this gap, women moved into office jobs, and the female secretary replaced the male clerk. More women also became lawyers, physicians, and even members of parliaments. In many countries, women fought for and often achieved legislation guaranteeing women's suffrage and other rights. As gender standards changed, once-shocking attitudes became common, including an openness about sexuality and rejection of traditional marriage. Such freedoms were challenged in the 1930s, when a return to traditional female roles in European nations brought bans on abortion and birth control.

 Read about Yoshiya Nobuko, the popular Japanese writer and gender rebel.

> "In many countries, women fought for and often achieved legislation guaranteeing women's suffrage and other rights."

Japanese Prosperity After the War

Japan was also reshaped by industrialization, democratic politics, and liberalization during the 1920s, generating prosperity and new possibilities for the growing middle class. Powerful business interests dominated the democratic system that had been formed only a few years earlier, and the resulting corruption and volatility disillusioned many Japanese. Internationally, Japan played a visible role in the world. Even before World War I, Japan had acquired imperial holdings in Taiwan and Korea, and as a British ally in World War I, Japan also gained control of the German colonies in the Pacific. Japan's assertive role in the world, however, also created enemies. Tensions with the United States increased, fostered in part by Japanese bitterness toward the blatant racist discrimination against Japanese immigrants in the United States, and by U.S. hostility to Japanese ambitions in Asia and the Pacific.

Shifting Social Morals, Conservative Reaction

Nevertheless, a wave of Western influence permeated the cities. Urban middle-class Japanese were influenced by popular culture from the United States, and baseball became a popular Japanese sport. Young women questioned the Japanese tradition of the submissive female and dominant male. A leading feminist, Kato Shidzue (KAH-to shid-ZOO-ee) (1897–2001), became a strong proponent of family planning after having sojourned in the United States, and later turned to socialism and promotion of equal political rights for women. Conservatives, however, were troubled by shifting social mores. The working classes and rural population were alienated from the Westernized culture of the cities and did not share in the economic prosperity. Perplexed by the divide between traditional and modern values, Japanese thinkers and artists pondered national and cultural identity. For example, the writer Akutagawa Ryunosuke (1892–1927) combined Western and Japanese traditions by adding psychological dimensions to ancient folktales. His influential short story *Rashoman* tells of a rape and murder from several eyewitness perspectives.

The United States in the 1920s

In the postwar United States, Americans became more conservative and isolationist. Anticommunism prompted by the Russian Revolution and growing middle-class prosperity launched the triumph of conservative forces as Americans developed a powerful hostility for socialism of any kind. In 1919–1920, widespread public fear of communism, known as the "Red Scare," generated the first in a series of government crackdowns on dissidents, including suppression of strikes, harassment of labor unions, arrests of political radicals, and deportation of foreigners. The Red Scare froze attitudes toward the Soviet Union and communist movements for generations, as the United States pursued a long-term policy of isolating the USSR from international contact. Not until 1933 would the United States soften its policy of isolation toward the Soviet Union by extending diplomatic recognition.

Domestic government policies often turned a deaf ear to problems affecting the less affluent.

Strikes for better wages by desperate workers, many of whom had joined left-wing unions, proliferated, but federal, state, and local governments all helped employers fight labor unions in the Appalachian coal fields, Detroit auto plants, and South Atlantic textile mills. Another source of tension was the widespread resentment of the United States Congress for passing Prohibition, which outlawed alcohol. Political leaders also ignored terrorism, including lynchings, by white racists against African Americans in the South. Meanwhile, several million African Americans, in what was later called the Great Migration, moved from southern states to the north and west in the 1920s in search of jobs and security. Farmers were devastated by a postwar drop in demand and suffered throughout the decade, but they received little help from the federal government. Finally, the 1920s saw the passage of restrictive immigration policies that sought to exclude undesirable populations.

In contrast to the less affluent, for the top half of the U.S. population, these years were the "Roaring 20s," the hedonistic era when high society let down its inhibitions. Jazz music, rooted in southern black culture, became so popular that the era was often known as "the Jazz Age." Women, who had been active in labor unions, social reform movements, and religious organizations for decades, finally won the vote in 1920, which allowed more of them to enjoy a larger public role.

In contrast to Woodrow Wilson's idealistic globalism, Republican leaders in the 1920s proclaimed an isolationist U.S. foreign policy, ostensibly avoiding interference in other nations' affairs; but despite the rhetoric, interventionism was often practiced. Always pushing outward, restless American citizens sought new Christian converts, commercial markets, and business investments. U.S. presidents justified numerous military interventions to punish opponents and reward allies, especially in Latin America. U.S. Marines remained in Nicaragua for decades (1909–1933), and El Salvador, Haiti, Mexico, and the Dominican Republic all experienced major U.S. military incursions between 1914 and 1940.

Economic Collapse and American Reform

The major spur to change in the interwar years was the Great Depression. The crisis began in the United States in the fall of 1929, when prices on the New York Stock Exchange fell dramatically, ruining many investors. This crash ultimately precipitated a worldwide economic disaster that was unprecedented in intensity, longevity, and spread, affecting industrial and agricultural economies alike. The Depression lasted until 1941.

Causes of the Great Depression

Global factors helped foster the Great Depression. The flow of wealth into the United States intensified existing imbalances in the world economy in trade and investment. Because the United States was generally self-sufficient, it was less dependent on world trade than Britain had been when it was the world's leading economic power. With its growing population and rising standard of living, the United States enjoyed raw materials, thriving industry, and consumer markets within its borders. The nation also maintained protectionist policies and refused to shift to an aggressive free-trade position until well into the 1930s. Furthermore, the world banking and credit structure was very unstable, partly because, unlike Britain in the 1800s, the United States did not use its unmatched economic power to make sure the world economy worked efficiently. Yet U.S. banks, too anxious for profits, became overextended in loans to Britain, France, and Germany.

Conditions within the United States also played a role in generating the Great Depression. A "get-rich-quick" philosophy had led to risky loans and reckless investments. Income was increasingly distributed unevenly: by 1929, the top 20 percent of American families earned 54 percent of the income, whereas the bottom 40 percent earned 12.5 percent. As more wealth gravitated to fewer hands and more people fell into poverty, purchasing power declined, while more consumer products became available, causing a glut. Many manufacturers could not sell enough products at home or abroad to stay in business or avoid layoffs. These problems led to the stock market crash, followed by bank failures. As U.S. banks faced ruin, they called in their debts from western European banks, triggering a chain reaction of bank failures in North America and Europe. In the United States, the GNP fell by one-half in four years; industrial output fell by 50 percent; and unemployment rose from 3 to 25 percent of the labor force by 1932. All areas of the U.S. economy were hurt, and the misery was widespread.

Global Impact of the Great Depression

Global consequences were also severe. Some 30 percent of Germans were out of work by 1932, and German industrial output declined by half. A French politician summed up the disaster in his nation: "The oceans were deserted, the ships laid up in the silent ports, the factory smokestacks dead, long lines of

> "Hungry Americans flocked to breadlines and soup kitchens for food and milk supplied by charitable organizations."

workless in the towns, poverty throughout the countryside. Nations ... shared the common lot of poverty."[8] Societies in Asia, Africa, Latin America, and the Caribbean were devastated as demand for raw materials such as rubber, tin, and sugar plummeted. Only the more insular USSR avoided major pain.

The Great Depression in the United States

The Great Depression brought severe economic distress to the wealthiest industrialized nation, the United States. Home-owners and farmers saw banks foreclose on their property. Migrant workers moved around in a futile search for jobs. Hungry Americans flocked to breadlines and soup kitchens for food and milk that was supplied by charitable organizations. Parts of the Midwest and Southwest became a Dust Bowl, as terrible drought and disappearing topsoil put agriculture badly out of balance. Farm income dropped 50 percent between 1929 and 1933, causing 3 to 4 million people, mostly former farmers, to head to the West Coast, especially California, after selling or losing their land. Panic, despair, and disillusionment seized the country.

Roosevelt's New Deal Reforms

The turmoil caused a turnaround in U.S. government policy and economic theory, as well as a change of leadership. Anger and discontent drove the Republicans from office in 1933 and brought in a new president, Democrat Franklin Delano Roosevelt (1882–1945). Roosevelt expressed optimism, telling the nation that they had nothing to fear but fear itself. He introduced the New Deal, a new government policy of liberal reform within a democratic framework to

Depression Breadline During the Depression, breadlines, such as this one in New York City, were common in the United States as millions of unemployed and desperate people sought food from social service providers, including religious groups.

WORLD'S HIGHEST STANDARD OF LIVING

There's no way like the American Way

alleviate the suffering caused by the Great Depression. His reforms included regulations on banks and stock exchanges to prevent future depressions and public welfare programs, such as public works jobs and social security that guaranteed retirement income for workers. For the first time in U.S. history, the federal government took responsibility for providing pensions and other supportive help to citizens. Roosevelt also legalized strikes and supported the organizing of workers to fight for better working conditions.

The direct involvement of the federal government in helping to alleviate social and economic problems altered the United States. Although it did not end the Depression, the New Deal made government popular and modified the pain enough that radicalism began to wane. By defusing the appeal of socialism and communism, the New Deal reforms, many historians conclude, probably saved U.S. capitalism. In the later 1930s, when the recovery faltered, Roosevelt used the ideas of the British economist John Maynard Keynes (1883–1946), who advocated deficit spending by governments to spur economic growth, a policy known as Keynesian economics. However, it was the mobilization of military forces and manufacturing during World War II that finally ended the Depression.

Global Depression's Impact

By devastating the economies of Europe and Japan, the Depression shattered the illusion of stability and challenged the weaker, less entrenched democratic systems. In most European countries, one-quarter to one-third of people were jobless. Germans often faced malnutrition, and hunger marches became common in Britain. A French observer described Paris as an "abyss of misery, suffering, and disorder, the theaters nearly empty, factories shut, businesses bankrupt; grey faces and bad news everywhere."9 Countries developed public works programs to create jobs and also discouraged imports, further reducing international trade. Weimar Germany, whose democracy was fragile, had an enormous reparations debt and was in no position to launch a New Deal–style recovery.

European and Japanese Responses Some other nations did discover remedies to gradually relieve the distress. Although British heavy industry recovered only modestly, newer industries such as automobiles and electronics showed rapid growth, and increased consumer demand for these products gradually turned around the British economy. The Scandinavian nations of Denmark, Norway, and Sweden had the most success by pursuing what came to be known as "the Middle Way," a combination of undogmatic socialist economics with long-established democratic traditions based on community action. By increasing government intervention in the economy, the social democrats ensured full employment and protected people from hardship.

The Depression hit Japan even harder than Europe and the United States, making clear its near-total dependence on foreign trade. As the world economy collapsed, many foreign markets closed and unemployment skyrocketed. Japan's foreign trade was cut in half in two years, forcing Japan's 100 million people to dramatically reduce consumption not only of luxuries but also of necessities, such as food and fuel. Unlike Britain, France, and the United States, Japan had no access to the resource-rich Western colonies in Southeast Asia. To resolve the nation's problems, Japanese leaders, becoming more authoritarian, turned to radical solutions, including expansion abroad and building a heavy arms industry at home.

The Rise of Mass Culture Tempered by the trauma of war and then by the Depression, Western culture went in new directions during the interwar years. One major trend was the rise of mass culture, popular entertainments attuned to the tastes of a wide segment of the population and disseminated by the new mass media of radio and motion pictures. During the 1920s, radio stations appeared and the recording industry grew. By 1930, 40 percent of U.S. families owned a radio; by 1940, 86 percent did. The number of radios in Britain increased fivefold between 1926 and 1939.

Changing Artistic, Literary, and Scientific Perceptions Western artists and writers responded to the twentieth century in new ways. The innovative and versatile Pablo Picasso (pi-KAH-so) (1881–1973), a Spaniard who settled in Paris, helped invent cubism, a form of painting that rejected visual reality and emphasized instead geometric shapes and forms that often suggested movement. The Irishman James Joyce (1882–1941), who had enjoyed no formal education

cubism
An early-twentieth-century form of painting that rejected visual reality and emphasized instead geometric shapes and forms that often suggested movement.

fascism

A twentieth-century ideology that typically involved extreme nationalism, hatred of ethnic minorities, ruthless repression of opposition groups, violent anticommunism, and authoritarian government.

but became close to many of the nation's leading thinkers and writers, broke traditional rules of grammar, and his books were often banned for using obscenity. In England, Virginia Woolf (1882–1941) converted the novel from a narrative story into a pattern of internal monologues, a succession of images, thoughts, and emotions known as stream of consciousness. Her 1929 novel, *A Room of One's Own*, championed women's growing economic independence.

The social and natural sciences also developed during the first half of the twentieth century, allowing for a greater understanding of human behavior and the physical world. Sigmund Freud (froid) (1856–1939), an Austrian Jewish physician, developed the field of psychoanalysis, a combination of medical science and psychology, and shocked the world by arguing that sex was of great subconscious importance in shaping people's behavior. In physics, Albert Einstein (1879–1955) radically modified the Newtonian vision of physical nature and rejected the absolutes of space and time. Einstein spent the rest of his life seeking a unifying theory to explain every physical process in the universe. He failed to achieve that goal, but some of the ideas he developed contributed to ongoing attempts by physicists to explain the universe.

LO⁴ The Rise of Fascism and the Renewal of Conflict

By devastating the economies of Germany and Japan, the Great Depression helped spread a new ideology in these countries. Although its form varied from country to country, this ideology, fascism, typically involved extreme nationalism, hatred of ethnic minorities, ruthless repression of opposition groups, violent anticommunism, and authoritarian government. Fascist movements began as political parties headed by charismatic leaders who supported military expansion. Fascism was an assault on the liberal values and rational thinking of the Enlightenment. It came to power in Italy, Germany, and Japan and also influenced China and several eastern European and Latin American nations.

Fascism in Italy and Germany

First emerging in Italy in 1921 in the aftermath of World War I, fascism was a response to the inadequacies, corruption, and instability of democratic politics there, as well as to the economic problems caused by World War I. Domestic unrest increased as Italy's peasants sought a more just society, workers demanded the right to form unions, and the economy slumped. Fascism arose from a pragmatic alliance of upper-class conservatives in the military, bureaucracy, and industry with discouraged members of the middle class who faced economic hardships. Both groups feared the possibility of Communist revolution. The middle class chiefly furnished the mass support for fascism. Benito Mussolini (MOO-suh-LEE-nee) (1883–1945), a blacksmith's son, one-time teacher and journalist, and former socialist and World War I veteran, founded the Italian fascist movement, which advocated national unity and strong government (see Witness to the Past: The Doctrine of Fascism).

> 66 Mussolini and his movement soon forged a new Italy. 99

Benito Mussolini

Mussolini and his movement soon forged a new Italy. A spellbinding orator, Mussolini had a talent for arousing mass enthusiasm by promising a vigorous and disciplined Italy. He especially attracted war veterans with his nationalistic rhetoric, accusing socialists of being unpatriotic and using an ancient Roman symbol, the *fasces*, a bundle of sticks wrapped around an ax handle and blade, to symbolize the unity and power he wanted to bring Italy. Mussolini won the support of the Italian king, the Catholic Church, landowners, industrialists, and the lower middle class, from which the fascists organized a uniform-wearing paramilitary group, the Blackshirts, who violently attacked, murdered, and intimidated opponents. In 1922, the king asked Mussolini to form a government. By 1926, Mussolini had killed, arrested, or cowed his opponents, turned Italy into a one-party state with restricted civil liberties, and created a cult of personality around himself. Despite the brutality, many Italians believed Mussolini was restoring social order.

The Rise of Hitler

Fascism became dominant in Germany after the Depression undermined the weak, democratic Weimar Republic that was already straining under the Versailles treaty's terms.

The Doctrine of Fascism

Benito Mussolini gradually developed an ideology for his movement that appealed to the Italian people's nationalistic emotions. The following excerpt comes from an essay under Mussolini's name that was published in an Italian encyclopedia in 1932. In fact, the true author was a Mussolini confidant, the philosopher Giovanni Gentile. The essay reflected Mussolini's vision of fascism as the wave of the future, in which the individual would subordinate her or his desires to the needs of the state.

Fascism, the more it considers and observes the future and the development of humanity quite apart from political considerations of the moment, believes neither in the possibility nor the utility of perpetual peace. It thus repudiates the doctrine of Pacifism—born of the renunciation of the struggle and an act of cowardice in the face of sacrifice. War alone brings up to its highest tension all human energy and puts the stamp of nobility upon the peoples who have the courage to meet it. . . . Fascism [is] the complete opposite of . . . Marxian Socialism, the materialist conception of history. . . . Above all Fascism denies that class-war can be the preponderant force in the transformation of society. . . .

After Socialism, Fascism combats the whole complex system of democratic ideology, and repudiates it, whether in its theoretical premises or in its practical application. Fascism denies that the majority, by the simple fact that it is a majority, can direct human society; it denies that numbers alone can govern by means of periodic consultation. . . . The democratic regime . . . [gives] the illusion of sovereignty, while the real effective sovereignty lies in the hands of other concealed and irresponsible forces. . . .

But the Fascist negation of Socialism, Democracy, and Liberalism must not be taken to mean that Fascism desires to lead the world back to the state of affairs before 1789 [the French Revolution]. . . . Given that the nineteenth century was the century of Socialism, of Liberalism, and of Democracy, it does not . . . follow that the twentieth century must also be the century of Socialism, Liberalism, and Democracy: political doctrines pass, but humanity remains. . . .

The foundation of Fascism is the conception of the State, its character, its duty, and its aim. Fascism conceives of the State as an absolute, in comparison with which all individuals or groups are relative, only to be conceived of in their relation to the State. . . . The Fascist state is itself conscious, and has itself a will and a personality. . . . The Fascist state is an embodied will to power and government, the Roman tradition is here an ideal of force in action. . . . Government is not so much a thing to be expressed in territorial or military terms as in terms of morality and the spirit. It must be thought of as an Empire—. . . a nation which directly or indirectly rules other nations. . . . For Fascism the growth of Empire, . . . the expansion of the nation, is an essential manifestation of vitality, and its opposite a sign of decadence. . . . But Empire demands discipline, the co-ordination of all forces and a deeply felt sense of duty and sacrifice; this fact explains many aspects of the practical working of the regime, the character of many forces in the State, and the necessarily severe measures which must be taken against those who would oppose this spontaneous and inevitable movement of Italy in the twentieth century, and would oppose it by recalling the outworn ideology of the nineteenth century.

Thinking About the Reading

1. Why does fascism reject pacifism, socialism, and liberal democracy?
2. What role does the state play under fascism?

Source: B. Mussolini, "The Political and Social Doctrine of Fascism," *Political Quarterly*, IV (July–September, 1933), pp. 341–356. Copyright © 1993 by Blackwell Publishing. Reprinted with permission by Blackwell Publishing.

The German people, who had an authoritarian political tradition and an economy in shambles, shared a widespread resentment of the World War I reparation payments. The Nazi Party, led by Adolph Hitler (1889–1945), offered a strategy for regaining political and economic strength and efficiency and for keeping workers under control. Hitler was an Austrian-born social misfit and frustrated artist who joined the German army in World War I. Already nurturing a hatred of Jews and labor unions, he became involved in right-wing German politics and, in 1920, helped form the Nazi Party, which promised to halt the unpopular reparations payments imposed by the Treaty of Versailles.

Hitler and the Nazis capitalized on the Great Depression to increase their strength. With economic collapse, the industrial workers moved left toward the communists, while the middle classes moved right toward the growing Nazi movement. Many Germans were willing to believe, as Hitler claimed, that Germany's problems could be blamed on unpopular minorities, especially the Jews, and foreign powers. Hitler understood propaganda and how to use

> "Hitler and the Nazis capitalized on the Great Depression to increase their strength."

a few basic ideas, such as anti-Semitism, and he made up "facts" to gain support. Hitler developed a powerful slogan: "one people, one government, one leader."

Nazism and Its Ideology

The Nazis won the largest number of seats in the 1932 elections, garnering nearly 14 million votes, and after 1933, Hitler tightened his grip on power, imposing ideological conformity, suppressing all dissent, and greatly expanding the army, thus solving the terrible unemployment problem. Massive government work-creation schemes eradicated unemployment by 1936. By 1939, Germany's GNP was 50 percent higher than it had been in 1929, mainly because of the manufacture of heavy machinery and armaments. But Hitler also sought to purify Germany racially, passing a series of anti-Semitic laws between 1933 and 1938. Hitler banned marriage and sexual relations between Jews and so-called Aryan Germans and eventually stripped German Jews of their citizenship.

Hitler's Motorcade In this photo from 1938, Adolph Hitler, standing stiffly in his car, salutes members of a paramilitary Nazi group, the Brownshirts, who parade before him at a Nazi rally in Nuremburg.

Japanese Militarism and Expansion

During the 1930s, Japan and Germany came to resemble each other fairly closely, even if their forms of fascism were very different. Although Japan never developed a mass-based Fascist Party like the Nazis, Japanese politics turned increasingly nationalistic and imperialistic. Japanese leaders often blamed foreign nations, especially the United States and the USSR, for Japan's problems. As in Nazi Germany, big business supported military expansion to gain resources and markets for exploitation.

Soon Japan turned more aggressive and authoritarian. In 1931, it invaded and gained control of the Chinese province of Manchuria. The League of Nations imposed no stiff penalties on Japan, a failure that helped to discredit that organization. The Japanese military, in alliance with big business and bureaucratic interests, now played a key role in the Japanese government. By 1936, the military controlled Japan and, as in Nazi Germany, imposed a fascist government that promoted labor control, censorship, the glorification of war, police repression, and hatred of foreign powers (the West). In 1937, a military skirmish outside of Beijing provided an excuse for Japan to launch a full-scale invasion of China, which prompted the United States to impose an oil embargo on Japan. By 1938, Japan controlled most of eastern China. When Japan signed a pact with Germany and Italy in 1940, the United States and Britain introduced stronger economic sanctions, including an oil embargo. Japan now faced economic collapse or war.

The Road to War

During the later 1930s, international tensions rose and various alliances formed. The United States, Britain, and France, known as the Allies, led a group of western European democracies that wanted to preserve the European state structure, the global economy, and the Western colonial system in Asia and Africa. The fascist countries, led by Germany, Italy, and Japan, known as the Axis Powers, sought to change the political map of Europe and Asia and gain dominance in the world economy. The prelude to another world war was also marked, as it had been for World War I, by diplomatic problems caused in part by a massive arms buildup all over Europe.

> 66 The fascist countries, led by Germany, Italy, and Japan, known as the Axis Powers, sought to change the political map of Europe and Asia and gain dominance in the world economy. 99

Axis Imperialism

The big problem for the Allies was dealing with the imperialism of the Axis nations. Hitler pursued an aggressive foreign policy to dominate eastern Europe and unite the several million ethnic Germans separated by shifting state boundaries. In 1936, Hitler's troops occupied the Rhineland, German territory west of the Rhine River that had been demilitarized after World War I. Demonstrating how fascism had made Italy a strong power, in 1935, Italy invaded and brutally conquered the last independent African kingdom, Ethiopia. The League of Nations voted ineffective sanctions against Italy. Hitler and Mussolini forged a close alliance in 1936, but the later Tripartite Pact of 1940, linking Germany and Italy with Japan for mutual defense, was a marriage of strategic necessity, strained and wary.

The Spanish Civil War

Civil war in Spain heightened European tensions by drawing in foreign intervention and pitting competing ideologies against each other. Liberals and conservatives had struggled for two centuries to shape Spanish politics, and by the 1930s, Spain was polarized between left and right. During the 1936 elections, Spain's Republicans—a left-wing coalition of liberals, socialists, and communists promising reforms—edged out the National Front of conservatives, monarchists, and staunch Catholics. Alarmed, the right rallied around the fascist military forces led by General Francisco Franco (1892–1975), launching the Spanish Civil War (1936–1939). The Loyalist government forces, aided by the USSR, ultimately lost to Franco's fascists at a huge cost in lives on both sides. The war had an international flavor. Germany and Italy helped the Spanish fascists with weapons and advice, and several thousand volunteers from North America and varied European nations fought for the Loyalist cause. But the governments of the Western Allies refused to support the Loyalists, whom they viewed as too radical. The German bombing of Guernica (GWAR-ni-kuh), a village in northern Spain that was inhabited largely by Basque people, caused an international outcry and prompted Pablo Picasso to paint a celebrated testament to the atrocity.

The Failure of Appeasement

In the late 1930s, the Allies led by Britain followed a policy of appeasement toward fascist aggression. They were not yet prepared for war, and the catastrophe of World War I, in which several million young British and French men had died, meant that many saw another war as too terrible to contemplate. Yet war became inevitable. In 1938, Hitler turned his attention to eastern Europe, taking over Austria and then Czechoslovakia. As the war clouds approached, Hitler declared: "We shall not capitulate—no never! We may be destroyed, but if we are, we shall drag a world with us—a world in flames."[10] In August 1939, Hitler and Stalin signed the Nazi-Soviet Pact, a nonaggression agreement, and then Hitler launched an invasion of Poland, forcing France and Britain to declare war against Germany.

LO⁵ World War II: A Global Transition

Historians have sometimes viewed the years from 1914 to 1945 as one continuum, with World War II a continuation and amplification of World War I. Both wars shared some of the same causes, including nationalist rivalries, threats to the European balance of power, and a struggle to control the global economic system. But there were differences, too. For one, World War II also involved a three-way ideological contest between democracy, fascism, and communism. For another, the trench warfare and modest aerial bombing of World War I was superseded by the far more widespread aerial bombing and mobile armies used in World War II, with civilians now fair game.

World War II began as a European conflict, and for the first two years, major battles were confined largely to Europe, the North Atlantic, and North Africa. The firestorm soon became global, however, creating almost a separate war fought in East and Southeast Asia and the western Pacific. The conflict became the most costly war in world history, bringing staggering misery and ultimately killing some 50 million people. The war resulted in some of history's worst genocides and the use of the deadliest weapons ever known. It marked a major transition that reshaped world politics and international relations.

Cataclysmic War and Holocaust

In September 1939, Europe plunged into armed struggle, and in the next year, Germany and its allies

CHRONOLOGY

World War II, 1939–1945

1939	Beginning of war in Europe
June 1941	German invasion of Soviet Union
December 1941	Japanese bombing of Pearl Harbor; invasion of Southeast Asia
1942	Battle of Midway
1944	Allied landing at Normandy
July 1944	Bretton Woods Conference
February 1945	Yalta Conference
April 1945	Allied invasion of Germany
August 1945	U.S. bombing of Hiroshima and Nagasaki

overran nearly all of Europe, except for valiant Britain and neutral Switzerland and Sweden (see Map 24.3). Germany imposed puppet regimes in the conquered territories, including the Vichy (VISH-ee) government in France headed by World War I hero, General Philippe Pétain, described in the chapter-opening vignette. The conquered countries were exploited by Germany, and millions of civilians were enslaved to work on German farms and in factories.

Interactive Map

Churchill and Allied Resistance

But Germany failed to achieve all of its strategic objectives. Led by Prime Minister Winston Churchill (1874–1965), the heroic British withstood a blitz of aerial bombing in 1940 and German submarines in the Atlantic. Italian efforts to carve out a Mediterranean empire faltered, compelling the Germans to divert military resources to North Africa and Greece. Also frustrating Nazi goals were underground movements that emerged all over Europe to fight the Nazis.

In June 1941, the conflict expanded eastward. Germany broke its nonaggression pact and invaded Russia, driving deeply into the country. After misjudging German intentions and reeling from the invasion, the Soviet leader, Joseph Stalin, joined the anti-Axis alliance and received aid from the United

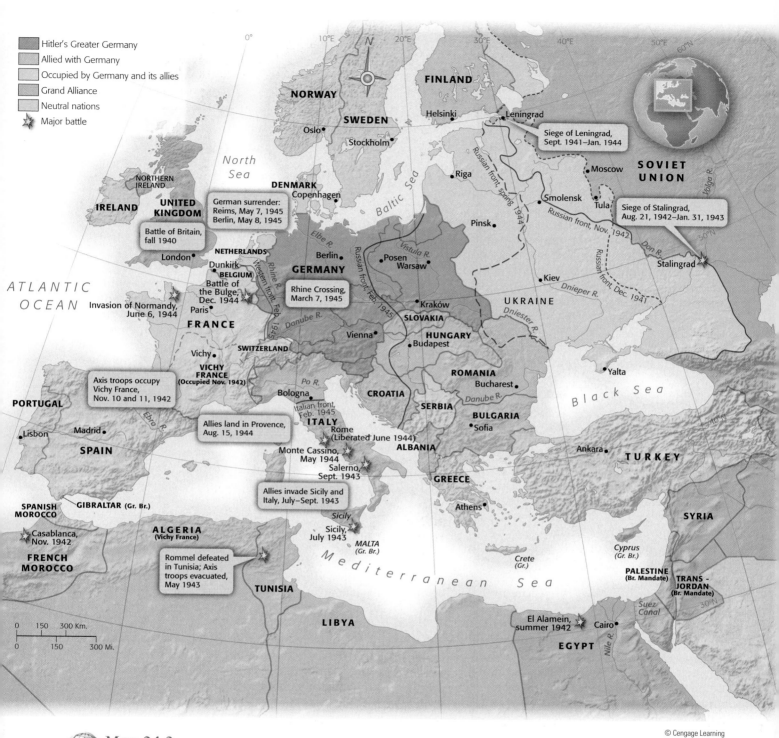

Map 24.3
World War II in Europe and North Africa

The Axis Powers, led by Germany and Italy, initially occupied much of Europe, and in 1941 they invaded the Soviet Union, but they were unable to hold their gains against the counteroffensive of the United States, Britain, the Soviet Union, and the Free French forces.

© Cengage Learning

> "German racist nationalism led to horrific campaigns of extermination against unpopular minorities and conquered peoples."

States and Britain that helped the USSR resist. It was an alliance of convenience, since the Western leaders and Stalin mistrusted each other. By winter 1941, German forces had reached the outskirts of Moscow and encircled another major city, Stalingrad. But although Germany had superior military forces, it ultimately failed to capture the major Russian cities, because the Red Army began an effective counterattack. The turning point came in February 1943, as the Soviet Red Army stopped the Germans at Stalingrad (today Volgograd). By the summer, German forces began a long, humiliating retreat from Russia.

The Holocaust

German racist nationalism led to horrific campaigns of extermination against unpopular minorities and conquered peoples. Hitler ordered what he called the "final solution" of the "Jewish Question." The term Holocaust came to be used for the Nazis' deliberate murder of Jews and Romany (Gypsies), one of the worst genocides, or deliberate mass killings of a target group, in history. Ultimately, some three-quarters of Europe's Jews were killed in the Holocaust. During 1942, the Germans had erected death camps, such as Bergen-Belsen (BUR-guhn-BEL-suhn) in western Germany and Auschwitz (OUSH-vits) in western Poland, targeting especially the large Jewish populations of Germany, Poland, and Ukraine. But Jews everywhere in Nazi-occupied Europe—Vichy France, the Netherlands, Hungary, Russia—were rounded up and put in death camps, where they were killed in gas chambers, starved, or worked to death. In addition to the 6 million Jews and half a million Romany (Gypsies) murdered in the Holocaust, the Nazis were responsible for the deaths of 11 million Slavs (including over 3 million Poles) and half a million other Europeans, including German communists, socialists, anti-Nazi Christians, and homosexuals.

Only a few brave Germans dared to resist or subvert Nazi policies and actions. Those who did, such as the Lutheran theologian Dietrich Bonhoeffer (BON-ho-fuhr) (1906–1945), a strong critic of Nazism and anti-Semitism who supported the underground German resistance, faced retribution. The Nazis sent Bonhoeffer to a concentration camp in 1943 and hanged him in 1945.

> 66 Conflict between Japan and the United States eventually globalized the war. 99

Globalization of the War

Conflict between Japan and the United States eventually globalized the war (see Map 24.4). On December 7, 1941, what President Franklin D. Roosevelt called "a date which will live in infamy," Japanese navy ships and planes attacked the U.S. naval base at Pearl Harbor, Hawaii, destroying a considerable portion of the U.S. Pacific fleet, killing 2,400 Americans, and ending U.S. neutrality. Japanese leaders sought to defeat the Western colonial powers, especially the United States. At the same time they were attacking Pearl Harbor, Japanese military forces launched an invasion of Southeast Asia. Within several months, they controlled most of the region, having forced the United States out of the Philippines and jailed the British and Dutch residents of their respective colonies. For its industrial economy, Japan badly needed the resources of Southeast Asia, especially the oil and rubber of the Dutch East Indies (Indonesia). The Japanese already controlled eastern China after their invasion of 1937. Preoccupied with war in Europe, the Western powers were unable to resist the Japanese advance.

 Interactive Map

The 1941 Pearl Harbor attack outraged Americans who were once reluctant to go to war. A patriotic wave swept the country as America entered the war on both fronts, with early efforts aimed at defeating the Nazis in Europe. The war affected all segments of American society, especially women and ethnic minorities, in various ways. Six million women joined the workforce as the government encouraged women to do their "patriotic duty" in jobs that were once considered unladylike, such as on factory assembly lines. Some 5 million blacks left southern rural areas in the 1930s and 1940s and often found jobs in northern and western cities. After defeating fascism abroad, more white Americans were sympathetic to the demands of black organizations that they now wanted democracy in the United States, especially in the segregated South.

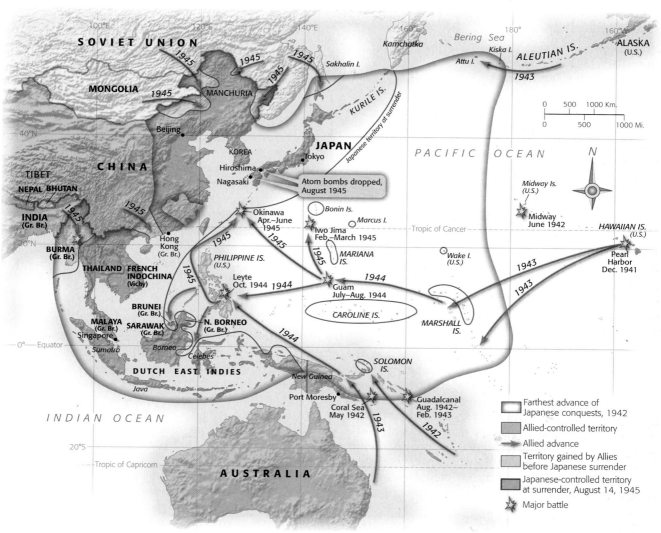

Map 24.4
World War II in Asia and the Pacific

After invading China in 1937, Japan disabled the U.S. fleet at Pearl Harbor in 1941 and in 1941–1942 occupied most of Southeast Asia and the western Pacific. The United States and its Allies pushed back the Japanese forces from their bases in the Pacific and bombed Japan from those bases, but Japan did not surrender until 1945, when the United States dropped atomic bombs on Hiroshima and Nagasaki.

© Cengage Learning

The Decision to Use the Atomic Bomb
Learn why President Truman was advised to drop atomic bombs on Japan, from the chairman of the committee that gave him that advice.

But racism aimed at 110,000 Japanese Americans fueled one of the greatest invasions of civil liberties in U.S. history, as the U.S. government rounded them up, seized their property, and sent them to sparse internment camps in remote areas for the duration of the conflict. Their property was never returned. Many of these Americans were U.S.-born or naturalized citizens living in western states who had faced discrimination for decades. No evi-

dence of espionage by any Japanese American was ever discovered.

The End of the War

The U.S. entry in the war on the Allied side changed the shape of the conflict. The Axis forces had been triumphant through 1942, as Germany dominated much of Europe and North Africa, and Japan controlled most of Asia east of India and large areas of the western Pacific. In 1943, however, the tide began to turn. The Germans were defeated in North Africa, and Allied landings in Italy knocked that country out of the war. In June 1944, British and American forces landed on five beaches at Normandy, on the Atlantic coast of France, and with the help of the anti-Vichy Free French forces under General Charles DeGaulle (duh GAWL) (1890–1970), began pushing the Germans back.

"World War II had heavy costs and large-scale consequences."

The Defeat of Germany

The Axis forces were now on the defensive in Europe, but Germany was defeated only by massive Allied ground offensives and aerial bombardment, which stopped German armed forces and demoralized the civilian German population. The British fire-bombed several German cities and killed thousands of civilians. The Soviet Red Army pushed the Germans back in the east, while U.S. and British forces pushed the battered German army back from the west. Through the winter, the German war economy collapsed. In spring 1945, as British and U.S. armies moved into Germany from the west and the Soviet Red Army from the east, Hitler committed suicide in his underground bunker in Berlin, and Germany surrendered. Soon newsreels of the liberation of the concentration camps revealed to the whole world the full extent of Nazi atrocities.

 Experience the consequences of World War II through the eyes of one of three characters in this interactive simulation.

The Atomic Bomb and the Surrender of Japan

The Japanese defeat was even more dramatic than that of the Nazis in Europe. In June 1942, the United States stopped the Japanese Pacific advance at the battle of Midway Island, west of Hawaii, and began an offensive to isolate the Japanese bases in the Pacific. By mid-1944, it had pushed the Japanese out of most of the western Pacific islands, from which it launched bombing raids on Japan. By early 1945, U.S. forces, aided by the Australians and British, started to retake Southeast Asia and China from Japanese forces. The invasion of the small Japanese island of Okinawa (oh-kee-NAH-wah), in the Ryukyus just south of Japan, cost the lives of 10,000 American troops and 80,000 Japanese civilians, suggesting to U.S. officials what an invasion of the main Japanese islands might entail. Devastating as the war had been, however, Japan resisted American demands for total surrender.

In August 1945, the United States forced the issue by dropping an atomic bomb on the Japanese city of Hiroshima. The bomb demolished most of the city and killed 80,000 people; thousands more were maimed or died later from injuries or radiation. Three days later, an American plane dropped a second bomb on Nagasaki, killing another 60,000 Japanese civilians. The Japanese emperor, Hirohito (HEAR-oh-HEE-toe) (1901–1989), opted for surrender on August 15. He went on the radio to ask his people to "suffer the insufferable, endure the unendurable," and cooperate with the U.S. occupation. For the first time in its long history, Japan had been defeated and successfully invaded. Disgraced, more than five hundred military officers committed suicide. World War II had come to an end.

Historical Reflections

Historians differ on whether it was necessary militarily to drop the atomic bombs on Japan, causing so many civilian deaths and forever changing the nature of war. Many contend that the Japanese would have fiercely resisted an American invasion, and hence the bombs ultimately saved many American and Japanese lives, while others argue that the United States used their terrible new weapon as a warning to the Soviet Union about U.S. capabilities, intended to dissuade Stalin from any expansionist ideas. In any case, Japan lost the war primarily because it overstretched its forces and failed to convert Southeast Asian resources into military and industrial products fast enough to defeat the larger, wealthier United States. Its brutal treatment of the Chinese and Southeast Asians, such as the 1937 "Rape of Nanjing," in which thousands of Chinese were massacred by Japanese troops, caused most Southeast Asians to look on the Japanese as perhaps even worse than the Western colonizers they had replaced.

The Costs and Consequences of Global War

World War II had heavy costs and large-scale consequences. It took a terrible toll in lives: approximately 15 million military and 35 million civilian deaths. Soviet Russia, which lost more than 20 million people, or 10 percent of its population, now had one more bitter memory in a long history of invasions by countries to the west. Poland and Yugoslavia both lost more than 10 percent of their people. Britain lost 375,000 people and France 600,000. Strategic bombing blasted parts of every major German city to rubble. In Asia, more than 2 million Japanese military personnel and probably 1 million Japanese civilians died, and 7 million Chinese were killed or wounded. Fighting on both fronts, some 300,000 American military personnel died. The European and Asian countries involved were economically devastated.

The war cleared the way for new global economic arrangements. In 1944, U.S. president Roosevelt summoned representatives of forty-four countries to a conference held in Bretton Woods, New Hampshire, to establish the postwar world economic order. The Bretton Woods Conference set up the International Monetary Fund and the World Bank, both dominated by the United States, to provide credit to states requiring financial investment for major economic projects. Bretton Woods also fixed currency exchange rates and encouraged trade liberalization, both policies that benefited the United States most.

World War II transformed world politics, removing the twin threats of German Nazism and Japanese militarism. In contrast to World War I, the victorious Allies were more generous toward the vanquished, giving the defeated nations massive aid and guidance to speed economic recovery. U.S. forces occupied Japan for several years, while Germany was temporarily divided into sectors controlled by Russia, Britain, France, and the United States. The war also fostered political changes in Asia. Chinese, Korean, and Vietnamese communists took advantage of Japanese occupation to gain support for their movements, and Western colonial rule was undermined throughout Southeast Asia (see Chapter 25).

Allied leaders also developed new political institutions and links for the postwar world. In February 1945, Roosevelt, Churchill, and Stalin met at a conference at Yalta (YAWL-tuh), in Russia's Crimean peninsula, to determine the postwar political order. The conference agreed to set up a world organization, the United Nations, and also divided Europe into anticommunist and communist spheres of interest. Western leaders, drained by war and seeking postwar stability in Europe, reluctantly agreed to Stalin's demand that the Soviet Union be allowed to dominate eastern Europe by stationing troops there and influencing its governments.

The aftermath of war also fostered a new rivalry between the two emerging superpowers, the United States and the USSR, that complicated the new global political order. The United States, which had not fought on its own soil, emerged from the war politically and economically stronger, becoming the dominant world power. But the USSR emerged from the war as a military power with imperial ambitions.

U.S. Air Force/AP Images

Bombing of Nagasaki This photo shows the awesome power of the atomic bomb dropped by the United States on the Japanese city of Nagasaki in August 1945, three days after the atomic bombing of Hiroshima. Some 60,000 Japanese died in the Nagasaki bombing.

U.S. leaders realized their nation would have to help reconstruct Europe and Japan to restore political stability and thwart Soviet ambitions there.

The political history of the world between 1945 and 1989 would revolve around the conflict between these two competing superpowers. Rapidly rebuilding after the war, the USSR installed communist governments throughout eastern Europe, including one in the eastern part of Germany under Soviet occupation. Indeed, World War II increased the appeal of communism worldwide and led to the establishment of communist regimes in Yugoslavia and North Korea. Both Soviet and U.S. leaders tended to look at the world through the lens of their World War II experience. For the USSR, that meant paranoia about any threat from the West and the need for military power. Americans tended to find a repeat of Hitler's aggression anywhere in the world they experienced a political threat, and they often sought to assert their power proactively. The U.S.–Soviet rivalry created a world very different from that existing before World War II.

Listen to a synopsis of Chapter 24.

CHAPTER 25

Imperialism and Nationalism in Asia, Africa, and Latin America,

1914–1945

Learning Outcomes

After reading this chapter, you should be able to answer the following questions:

LO¹ What circumstances fostered nationalism in Asia, Africa, and Latin America?

LO² How and why did the Communist movement grow in China?

LO³ What were the main contributions of Mohandas Gandhi to the Indian struggle?

LO⁴ How did nationalism differ in Southeast Asia and sub-Saharan Africa?

LO⁵ What factors promoted change in the Middle East and Latin America?

> **"What unhappiness strikes the poor, Who wear a single worn-out, torn cloth. Oh heaven, why are you not just? Some have abundance while others are in want."**
>
> —Peasant folk song protesting colonialism in Vietnam[1]

In 1911, Nguyen Tat Thanh, a young man from an impoverished village in French-ruled Vietnam, signed on as a merchant seaman on a French ship; he would not return to his homeland for another thirty years. Nguyen hated colonialism and was dreaming of an independent nation of Vietnam. While abroad, he worked as a cook in London and photo retoucher in Paris, spending his free time reading books on politics and working with Asian nationalists and French socialists to oppose colonialism, especially in Vietnam. Nguyen became famous among Vietnamese exiles for his efforts to address the delegates at the Paris Peace Conference after World War I about the self-determination of peoples, but the major Western powers, unwilling to consider any change in their colonial domains, refused to permit his entry.

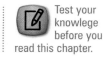 Test your knowlege before you read this chapter.

What do you think?

Nationalism became a strong force for change in Western-dominated societies in Asia, Africa, and Latin America.

Strongly Disagree						Strongly Agree
1	2	3	4	5	6	7

Becoming disillusioned with Western democracy, the Vietnamese exile helped found the French Communist Party and spent time in the Soviet Union, becoming convinced that communism was the most effective strategy for promoting self-determination and nationalism. Later, under a new name, Ho Chi Minh ("He Who Enlightens"), he led the communist forces in Vietnam in their long struggle against French colonialism and then against the Americans. Ho became a worldwide symbol of national assertion, opposition to Western imperialism, and sympathy for the plight of peasants.

Between 1914 and 1945, nationalistic Asians such as Ho Chi Minh challenged the imperialism that had reshaped Asian and African politics and economies in the late nineteenth and early twentieth centuries. Rapid, often destabilizing change sparked nationalism aimed at escaping Western domination or control, especially after World War I weakened the European powers. Nationalist forces were awakened in colonies from Indonesia to Egypt to Senegal, becoming especially strong in India and Vietnam, and the Great Depression

<< Mao Zedong Organizing Communists in China This later artist's rendition shows the young Mao Zedong, the future Chinese Communist leader, organizing a communist group in his native province, Hunan, around 1921. A portrait of Karl Marx decorates the wall.

generated further anger against the imperial system. In some societies in these regions, those seeking to overturn the status quo, such as Ho Chi Minh, mobilized large followings from discontented people. Despite frequent protests, the Western powers were able to retain their empires until after World War II, when nationalist movements became even stronger and made a return to the imperialist era impossible.

> "To cover the costs of managing the colonies, the colonial governments used a variety of methods that increased resentment, including higher taxes and forced labor."

LO¹ Western Imperialism and Its Challengers

The events that rocked the industrialized nations between 1914 and 1945—two world wars, the Russian Revolution, and the Great Depression—also affected the nonindustrialized societies of Asia, Africa, and Latin America, who enjoyed little power in the global system. But developments in nonindustrialized societies also owed much to local dynamics. When social and economic changes resulting from colonialism proved destabilizing, many disenchanted Asians and Africans adopted nationalism and Marxism to strengthen their own societies and resist Western colonizers.

The Impact of Colonialism

The colonialism imposed by Western nations on most Asians, Africans, and West Indians between 1500 and 1914 had a major impact. The slaughter of millions of people during World War I undermined Western credibility and whatever moral authority Western peoples claimed to possess. Thousands of colonial subjects conscripted in Asia and Africa as soldiers and workers died in the war effort. Both France and Germany drafted men, often through harsh and arbitrary methods, while Britain sent Africans and Indians. Some 46,000 Kenyans died fighting for Britain, and at least 25,000 West Africans perished helping France on the front lines. British and French officials had muted African resistance to the draft by promising democratic reforms, special treatment for war veterans,

and compensation for the families of deceased soldiers, but these promises were not carried out.

Colonialism also reshaped societies, often with harmful political, economic, and social results. As discussed in Chapters 21 and 22, colonization had resulted in the creation of artificial states that often ignored the ethnic composition of the territory or the historical configuration and economic bases of states in the region. As a result, colonies such as Dutch-ruled Indonesia, British Nigeria, and the Belgian Congo incorporated diverse and often rival ethnic groups who had little sense of national unity.

To cover the costs of managing the colonies, the colonial governments used a variety of methods that increased resentment, including higher taxes and forced labor. Forced labor was common in the African colonies, such as in Portuguese-ruled Mozambique, where men and women who could not pay the required taxes were sent to plantations and mines to work. Among the worst abuses by colonial regimes in Southeast Asia were their opium and alcohol monopolies, which enriched government coffers by requiring villagers to purchase designated amounts of these products. By 1918, opium sales accounted for one-third of all colonial revenues in Vietnam, and some Vietnamese became addicted to opium. Furthermore, most of the colonies developed economies that locked them into the almost exclusive production and export of one or two primary commodities. These economic limitations hampered later economic diversification.

Colonized peoples also disliked the arrogance of the Western colonizers. Europeans and North Americans assumed that their societies were superior, above those of other peoples of the world. This ethnocentric, often racist attitude was enshrined in the Covenant for the new League of Nations formed after World War I, which considered the colonized peoples not yet able to govern themselves in the modern world. Exploiting their unequal power, the Western officials, businessmen, and planters in the colonies commonly enjoyed mansions, servants, and private clubs, while many local people lived in dire poverty, underfed and malnourished.

At the same time, colonial governments built a modern communications and economic infrastructure that often spurred economic growth. The

Exporting Resources from Indonesia Small boats brought cash crops grown in eastern Java, part of the Dutch East Indies, to the port of Surabaya, from where they were shipped to Europe.

governments of British India, Dutch Indonesia, and British East Africa financed railroads that facilitated the movement of goods and people. Colonialism also fostered the growth of cities like British Kenya's capital, Nairobi, which grew to more than 100,000 people by 1944. Port cities founded by Western colonizers, such as Hong Kong on the China coast and Cape Town in South Africa, became key hubs of world trade. Improved health and sanitation contributed to rapid population growth in colonies such as India, Indonesia, the Philippines, and Vietnam, but this population growth outstripped economic resources, exacerbating poverty and, for Indians and Indonesians, stimulating emigration. In short, while defenders of colonialism boasted of their contributions, critics questioned how much they benefited Asians and Africans.

Competing Ideologies

The capitalism introduced by the West spurred resentment and anticolonial nationalism. Some non-European merchants, such as the Chinese in Southeast Asia and the Lebanese in West Africa, did

> 66 As a result of capitalism's excesses and failures, ideologies of resistance, including nationalism and Marxism, grew in influence in the colonized world. 99

profit from the growing economic opportunities. But colonial social and economic policies that promoted the spread of the capitalist market also destabilized rural villages, fomenting opposition to these policies.

The commercialization of agriculture transformed traditional, often communal, landowning arrangements into private property systems that converted land into a commodity to be exploited on the free market. Lacking the money or connections to compete, many peasants fell into dire poverty.

The Failure of Capitalism

The Great Depression of the 1930s was further reason for colonized peoples to conclude that global capitalism was a failure. The downturn brought economic catastrophe to many nonindustrialized societies as demand for their resources in the industrialized nations plummeted. Collapsing prices for rubber, sugar, and coffee crops harmed Southeast Asians. In Latin America, Argentina saw livestock and wheat prices collapse, and Cuba was staggered by falling sugar prices. As exports declined, colonial revenues also fell. Unequal landowning, growing mass poverty, limited economic opportunities for displaced peasants, and foreign control of the economy produced political unrest and anticapitalist activism.

Nationalism

As a result of capitalism's excesses and failures, ideologies of resistance, including nationalism and Marxism, grew in influence in the colonized world. In time, movements for change became movements for independence. Nationalism became especially popular among the educated middle class—students, lawyers, teachers, merchants, and military officers. Colonial powers set up few universities, but those that existed, such as the University of Rangoon in British Burma (today's Myanmar), offered a venue for nationalist-government conflicts and campus protests. To anticolonial leaders, nationalism promoted a sense of belonging to a nation that transcended parochial differences such as social class and religion. But the "nation" sometimes existed only in people's imagination: in the multiethnic colonies of Africa, Southeast Asia, and the Caribbean, it was difficult to overcome ethnic antagonism and rivalries to create a feeling of nationhood.

Marxism

Some Asians, Africans, and Latin Americans who sought radical change, such as Ho Chi Minh, mixed nationalism with Marxism, the ideas of socialism and revolution advocated by the nineteenth-century German Karl Marx. For them, Marxist ideas provided an alternative vision to colonialism, capitalism, and discredited local traditions and leaders. Young Asians, Africans, and West Indians studying abroad often adopted Marxism after facing bleak employment prospects and political repression back at home. Some of them gravitated to the most dogmatic form of Marxism, the communism practiced in the Soviet Union by the Bolsheviks (see Chapter 24), which required the leadership of a centralized revolutionary party. Radical nationalists, especially in Asia, also adopted revolutionary ideas developed by the Russian communist leader, Vladimir Lenin. Lenin saw the world as divided between imperial countries (the exploiters) and dominated countries (the exploited). Lenin's view appealed to radical nationalists who sought to make sense of their subjugation to the West. Although communist nations, among them the Soviet Union, also proved capable of blatantly imperialistic policies, during the first four decades of the twentieth century, Lenin's theory of capitalism-based imperialism seemed to offer validity.

Lengthening the Imperial Reach

At the same time that anti-imperialist feelings were rising between 1900 and 1945, the Allied victors of World War I were expanding their imperial reach and continuing to intervene in less-powerful nations. After the defeat of Germany and its Ottoman ally, Britain and France took control of the former Ottoman colonies in western Asia and the German colonies in Africa. Some of these societies, such as oil-rich Iraq, had valuable resources. Likewise, Australia and Japan occupied the German-ruled Pacific islands. Supported by colonial governments, Europeans continued to settle in Algeria, Angola, Kenya, South Africa, and Southern Rhodesia and to dispossess local people from their land. Moreover, while the war had ended, Western military conquests in Africa had not. In 1935–1936, Italy invaded and brutally conquered the last independent African state, Ethiopia, killing some 200,000 Ethiopians. The Ethiopian forces faced a fully mechanized and mobile Italian army, and, despite their spirited defense of the mountainous terrain, they succumbed to superior Italian aerial bombing and firepower. Italy's fascist dictator, Benito Mussolini, argued that it was a war to spread "civilization" and "liberate Africans"; in fact, he hoped to settle Italians in Ethiopia.

Meanwhile, the major Western power after World War I, the United States, continued to exercise influence in the Americas. During the Mexican Revolution, President Woodrow Wilson sent thousands of U.S. troops into Mexico to restore order and thereby protect large U.S. investments, particularly in the oil industry. American attitudes favoring the spread of democracy and capitalism in the world also played a role in the interventions, with Wilson

> **"** At the same time that anti-imperialist feelings were rising between 1900 and 1945, the Allied victors of World War I were expanding their imperial reach and continuing to intervene in less-powerful nations. **"**

arguing that he would teach the Latin American republics to elect good leaders. The United States' desire to protect U.S. investments by maintaining stability in Central America meant supporting the governments led by landowners and generals, such as the notoriously corrupt Nicaraguan president, Anastasio Somoza (1896–1956). Repeated U.S. interventions in the region left an aftertaste of local resentment against what Central Americans called "Yankee imperialism."

LO² Nationalism and Communism in China

The Chinese Revolution of 1911–1912, which ended the 2,000-year-old imperial system (see Chapter 23), had led to a republic that Chinese hoped would give the nation renewed strength in the world, but these hopes were dashed when China lapsed into warlordism and civil war, with a central government in name only and subject to pressure from the West and Japan. China's domestic failures and continuing Western imperialism sparked a vigorous nationalism as well as the formation of a communist party and China's eventual reunification.

Warlords, New Cultures, and Nationalism

During the demoralizing Warlord Era (1916–1927), China was divided into territories controlled by rival warlords, local political leaders that had their own armies. The warlords extracted revenue as their armies terrorized the local population. They were a mixed lot. Some called themselves nationalists and reformers and were interested in promoting education and industry; others took bribes to carry out policies favoring merchants or foreign governments. Meanwhile, high taxes, inflation, famine, accelerating social tensions, and banditry made life difficult for most Chinese.

The New Culture Movement Radical new currents arose out of the people's despair. Cities became enclaves of revolutionary ideas for Chinese society and governance. New schools and universities opened, and schools for girls became more common. Thanks to educational opportunities, by the 1920s, many women worked as nurses, teachers, and civil servants, especially in cit-ies. Exposure to Western ideas in universities, especially those run by Christian missionaries, led some Chinese students to question their own cultural traditions, such as footbinding, which largely disappeared except in remote rural areas by 1930.

During this time, Chinese intellectuals supported the New Culture Movement, which sought to erase the discredited past and sprout a literary revival. The movement originated in 1915 at Beijing University, China's intellectual mecca that hired radical professors and encouraged a mixing of Chinese and Western thought. There a group of professors began publishing the literary magazine *New Youth*, which became the chief vehicle for attacking China's traditions, including Confucianism, and advocating for republican government, equality, and scientific progress.

warlords
Local political leaders with their own armies.

New Culture Movement
A movement of Chinese intellectuals started in 1915 that sought to wash away the discredited past and sprout a literary revival.

CHRONOLOGY

China, 1911–1945

1911–1912	Chinese Revolution
1915	Beginning of New Culture Movement
1916–1927	Warlord Era
1919	May Fourth Movement
1926–1928	Northern Expedition to reunify China
1927	Guomindang suppression of communists
1927–1934	Mao Zedong's Jiangxi Soviet
1928–1937	Republic of China in Nanjing
1931	Japanese occupation of Manchuria
1935–1936	Long March by Chinese communists
1937–1945	Japanese invasion of China

The 21 Demands and the May Fourth Movement

Chinese rage against Western and Japanese imperialism increased in the aftermath of World War I. Although China had remained neutral, Japan, allied with Britain, took over the German sphere of influence in the Shandong peninsula of eastern China. In 1919, with the war over, Japan presented China with 21 Demands, including control of Shandong, increased rights in Manchuria, and appointment of Japanese advisers to the Chinese government. The 21 Demands and the decision by the Western allies to allow Japan to take over Shandong provoked a radical nationalist resurgence among students and workers, known as the May Fourth Movement, which opposed imperialism and the ineffective, warlord-controlled Chinese government. Shouting that China's territory could not be given away, the protestors also decried social injustice and government inaction. Capitulating to the protests, the Chinese government refused to sign the Versailles treaty that followed World War I. The new communist government running the Soviet Union openly sided with China, winning admiration among the Chinese.

Some Chinese also began studying communism, finding in it new promise for organizing change. In 1921, professors and students at Beijing University, many of whom had been active in the New Culture and May Fourth Movements, organized the Chinese Communist Party (CCP). Some of the party founders were European- or Japanese-educated reformers who admired Western science and culture, while others were nationalists who despised Western models. The communists recruited support by forming peasant associations, labor unions, women's groups, and youth clubs. Soviet advisers encouraged the party to organize among the urban working class but otherwise largely neglected the Chinese communists.

The Chinese Nationalist Party

The Guomindang (gwo-min-dong), or Nationalist Party, also called for the reunification of China. It was led by Sun Zhongshan, better known as Sun Yat-sen (soon yot-SEN) (1866–1925), who had led the revolutionary movement that overthrew the Qing dynasty but had then been forced into exile (see Chapter 23). Receiving no help from the Western nations, Sun forged closer ties to the Soviet Union, which sent advisers and military aid. In the mid-1920s, Sun's Guomindang and the Chinese communists worked together, in an alliance known as the United Front, to defeat warlordism and prevent foreign encroachment. However, Sun's ideology grew less democratic and more authoritarian, and he came to believe that China's 400 million people were not ready for democracy. Sun died in 1925, and the new Guomindang leader, Sun's brother-in-law, Jiang Jieshi (better known in the West as Chiang Kai-shek) (1887–1975), was more conservative. Chiang was a pro-business soldier and a patriot but indifferent to social change. He began developing a close relationship with the United States while building a modern military force.

> **"** Chinese rage against Western and Japanese imperialism increased in the aftermath of World War I. **"**

The Republic of China

Between 1926 and 1928, the Guomindang forces and their communist allies succeeded in reunifying China with a military drive known as the Northern Expedition, during which they defeated or co-opted the warlords. The foreign powers recognized Chiang's new Republic of China, but the new government was wrought with conflict. Whereas communist and leftist Guomindang leaders sought social change and mobilization of workers, the right wing, led by Chiang, was allied with the antiprogressive Shanghai business community. Chiang expelled the communists from the United Front in 1927 and began a reign of terror against the leftists, killing thousands of them; those who survived went into hiding.

The Modernization of China

From 1928 to 1937, Chiang's Republic of China, based at Nanjing (nahn-JING) along the Yangzi River in east-central China, launched a program to modernize China. The Republic's leaders, many of them Western-educated Christians, fostered economic development and forged a modern state. They built railroads, factories, a banking system, and a modern army, streamlined the government, fostered public health and education, and adopted new legal codes that strengthened women's rights. The regime also negotiated an end to most of the unequal international treaties imposed by the Western nations and Japan in the 1800s. The U.S. government, closely allied with Chiang's regime, provided generous political and financial support for modernization efforts. Spurred by the idealistic desire to help the Chinese by reshaping them along American lines, Americans felt a paternalistic responsibility for China and funded schools, hospitals, orphanages, and churches.

Yet the Republic faced domestic challenges. While the urban elite in big coastal cities prospered, Chiang was unable or unwilling to deal with the growing poverty of the peasantry. Commercialization of agriculture gradually shifted more land to landlords, and by 1930, about one-half of China's peasants lacked enough land to support their families. Adding to the problems, Chiang also tolerated government corruption and rewarded his financial backers in the commercial sector. As unhappiness with the government grew, Chiang, influenced by European fascism, built an authoritarian police state that brutally repressed all dissent.

Our Attitude Toward Modern Civilization of the West A Chinese professor rejects the idea that Eastern civilization is more "spiritual" than the "materialistic" West.

Conflict with Japan

China also faced problems with Japan. In 1931, Japanese forces seized Manchuria, the large northeastern region rich in mineral resources and fertile farmland, and set up a puppet government under the last Manchu emperor, Henry Pu Yi (1906–1967) (see Map 25.1). Japan gradually extended its military and political influence southwest toward the Great Wall that separated Manchuria from northern China. Unable to match Japanese military power, Chiang was forced to follow a policy of appeasement. His attempts to strengthen the Chinese military diverted scarce resources from economic development, and his reluctance to fight Japan left him open to charges that he was unpatriotic.

Interactive Map

Ding Ling and Chinese Radicalism

During the years of warlordism and then the Republic, the challenges facing China were reflected in cultural life. Disillusioned by China's weakness in the world and continued political despotism, many intellectuals lost faith in both Chiang's regime and Chinese traditions. Din Ling (1904–1985), one of China's first feminist writers and a participant in the May Fourth Movement, became alienated from the Republic when the Guomindang killed her political activist husband. After this, Ding dedicated her writing to the revolutionary cause, but she was later persecuted by the communists for the radicalism in her writing.

Chinese Communism and Mao Zedong

As the communists who survived Chiang's terror worked to rebuild their movement, one of the younger party leaders, Mao Zedong (maow dzuh-dong) (1893–1976), pursued his own strategy to mount the revolution he now saw as necessary to replace the Chiang regime and reshape China. From a peasant family led by a domineering father who badly abused Mao's mother, Mao had run away from home to attend high school. In 1918, he moved to Beijing, where he came to embrace communism. In 1927, as Chiang attempted to eliminate communists, Mao fled to the rugged mountains of Jiangxi (kee-ON-see) province in south-central China, where he set up a revolutionary base, known as the Jiangxi Soviet after the political action groups of early-twentieth-century Russia (see Chapter 24). There he organized a guerrilla force to fight the Guomindang. Rejecting the advice of Soviet advisers to depend on support from the urban working class—as the communists had done in Russia in 1917—Mao opted instead to rely on China's huge peasantry, arguing that without the peasants, no revolution could succeed.

Mao Assembles His Red Army

In Jiangxi, Mao built an army out of peasants, bandits, and former Guomindang soldiers and mobilized the local population to provision and feed the army. Mao believed that violence was necessary to oppose Chiang, having earlier written that "a revolution is not a dinner party.... A revolution is an act

> "In Jiangxi, Mao built an army out of peasants, bandits, and former Guomindang soldiers and mobilized the local population to provision and feed the army."

Jiangxi Soviet A revolutionary base, established in 1927 in south-central China, where Mao Zedong organized a guerrilla force to fight the Guomindang.

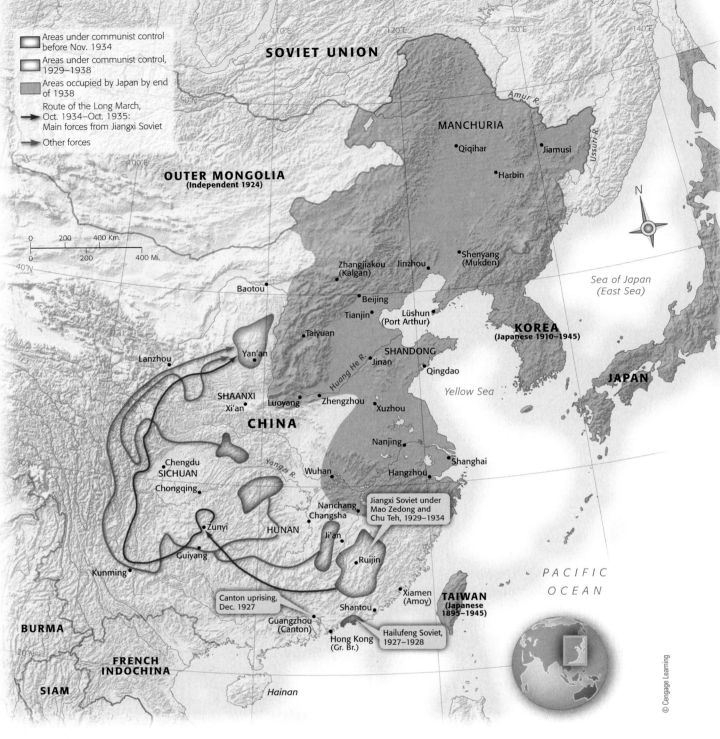

Legend:
- Areas under communist control before Nov. 1934
- Areas under communist control, 1929–1938
- Areas occupied by Japan by end of 1938
- → Route of the Long March, Oct. 1934–Oct. 1935: Main forces from Jiangxi Soviet
- → Other forces

SOVIET UNION

MANCHURIA

Qiqihar • Jiamusi •

Harbin •

OUTER MONGOLIA
(Independent 1924)

Baotou •

Shenyang
(Mukden) •

Zhangjiakou
(Kalgan) • Jinzhou •

Beijing •

Tianjin •

Lüshun
(Port Arthur) •

Taiyuan •

KOREA
(Japanese 1910–1945)

Sea of Japan
(East Sea)

Lanzhou •

Yan'an

SHANDONG

Jinan •

Qingdao •

JAPAN

SHAANXI
Xi'an •

Luoyang • Zhengzhou •

CHINA

Xuzhou •

Yellow Sea

Chengdu •
SICHUAN

Chongqing •

Wuhan •

Nanjing •

Shanghai •

Hangzhou •

Jiangxi Soviet under
Mao Zedong and
Chu Teh, 1929–1934

Nanchang •
Changsha •

Zunyi •

HUNAN

Ji'an •

Guiyang •

Ruijin •

Kunming •

PACIFIC
OCEAN

Canton uprising,
Dec. 1927

Xiamen
(Amoy) •

TAIWAN
(Japanese
1895–1945)

Shantou •

Guangzhou
(Canton) •

Hailufeng Soviet,
1927–1928

BURMA

Hong Kong
(Gr. Br.) •

FRENCH
INDOCHINA

SIAM

Hainan

© Cengage Learning

Map 25.1
Chinese Communist Movement and Chinese-Japanese War

Japan occupied much of northern and eastern China by 1939. In 1935–1936, the Chinese communists made the famous 6,000-mile Long March from their base in Jiangxi in southern China to Yan'an in north-west China.

of violence by which one class overthrows another."[2] Between 1928 and 1934, Mao expanded the Jiangxi Soviet by setting up communist-led local governments and redistributing land from the rich to the poor. As Chiang's repression intensified, top Chinese Communist Party leaders, who had once scorned Mao, moved to the Jiangxi Soviet. Increasingly alarmed by Mao's growing base and communist inroads in other parts of China, Chiang had his army blockade the Jiangxi Soviet to keep out essential supplies. This move forced Mao to reluctantly abandon his base.

The Long March

In 1935, Mao and 100,000 soldiers and followers broke through the blockade and, in search of a safer base, began the Long March, an epic journey in which Mao's Red Army fought their way 6,000 miles on foot and horseback through eleven provinces. During the one-year venture, the communists crossed eighteen mountain ranges, forded twenty-four rivers, and slogged through swamps, averaging seventeen miles per day; they lost 90 percent of their people to death or desertion. Finally, in late 1936, the ragtag survivors arrived in a poor northwestern province, where they moved into cavelike homes carved into the hills around the dusty city of Yan'an (YEH-nan). The Long March saved the communists from elimination by Chiang, making Mao the unchallenged party leader. Mao celebrated the achievement: "The Long March is the first of its kind in the annals of history [and has] proclaimed that the Red Army is an army of heroes."[3] Although the communists were still vulnerable to Chiang's larger, better-equipped forces, Chiang would be forced to shift his military priorities when the Japanese invaded China in 1937.

Japanese Invasion and Communist Revolution

The Japanese invasion of China in 1937 and the disastrous Chinese-Japanese war that followed altered China's politics, as Chiang had to divert money from modernization to the military. Mao captured the patriotic mood of the country by proposing a united front against Japan, and Chiang had little choice but to agree, relieving pressure on Mao's Yan'an base. But by the end of 1938, Japanese forces had swept over most of the eastern seaboard and controlled the best farmland and the industrial cities. War and occupation undermined Chiang's government and allowed the communists to strengthen, thus setting the stage for major changes in Chinese politics in the later 1940s.

Long March An epic journey, full of hardship, in which Mao Zedong's Red Army fought their way 6,000 miles on foot and horseback through eleven Chinese provinces in the mid-1930s to establish a safe base of operation.

The Long March This painting glorifies the crossing, over an old iron-chain bridge, of the Dadu River in western Sichuan province by the communist Red Army during the Long March. This successful crossing, against fierce attacks by Guomindang forces, was a key event in the communists' successful journey to northwest China.

Private Collection

people's war
An unconventional struggle that combined military action and political recruitment, formulated by Mao Zedong in China.

Maoism
An ideology promoted by Mao Zedong that mixed ideas from Chinese tradition with Marxist-Leninist ideas from the Soviet Union.

The Impact of the Second World War on China

The challenges of World War II caused many Chinese to lose faith in the Republic. Chiang's government was forced to relocate inland to Chongqing (CHUNG-king), a city protected by high mountains on the Yangzi River in west-central China. A mass migration of Chinese fleeing the Japanese followed. Unlike the modern, cosmopolitan coastal cities, Chongqing was a city with no bright lights or French restaurants and a depressing climate of fog and humidity. Fatigue, cynicism, and inflation discouraged the Guomindang and its followers. Virtually broke, Chiang's government had to squeeze the peasants in the areas it still controlled for tax revenues to support an army of 4 to 5 million men. Militarily ineffective, politically repressive, and economically corrupt, Chiang's government offered limited resistance to the Japanese, killed and imprisoned opponents of Guomindang rule, and put the personal gain of its leaders above the economic well-being of China's people.

Under such conditions, the communists at Yan'an were able to improve their prospects. Used to poverty, they had a more disciplined army than Chiang's with a higher morale. While Chiang's much larger forces had the main responsibility to fight the Japanese, the communists mounted guerrilla bands, mostly peasants, to harass the occupiers. These guerrillas engaged in an unconventional struggle, which Mao called "people's war," that combined military action and political recruitment. Communist activists set up village governments and peasant associations and encouraged women's rights. The communist message of social revolution, now blended with nationalism, offered hope for a better life to the downtrodden. Thousands of Chinese, including students, intellectuals, writers such as Ding Ling, and workers, flocked to Yan'an to join the communist cause. By 1945, the party had 1.2 million members.

The Victory of Maoism

The experiences of the communist leaders at Yan'an, marked by war and popular mobilization to support revolution, fostered the development of what later came to be known as Maoism, an ideology promoted by Mao that mixed ideas from Chinese tradition with Marxist-Leninist ideas from the Soviet Union. Mao emphasized the subordination of the individual to the needs of the group (a traditional Chinese notion), the superiority of political values over technical and artistic ones, and belief in the human will as a social force. Mao also contended that political power grows out of the barrel of a gun and that the Communist Party must command the military. To combat elitism, Mao introduced mass campaigns in which everyone engaged in physical labor that benefited villages, such as building dams and roads. Mao expressed faith that the Chinese people had the collective power and creativity to build a new society.

During World War II, Mao's communists built the foundation for revolution by gaining domination over much of rural north China. Hence, when the war ended, the Chinese communists were able to succeed in their revolutionary efforts: in the late 1940s, they won a bitter civil war, and in 1949, they established a communist government.

> 66 Nationalist opposition to the British *Raj*, which had been building for decades, was spurred by the severe dislocations caused by World War I. 99

LO³ British Colonialism and the Indian Response

In India, as in China, resentment of Western imperialism, despotic government, and an inequitable social order sparked a powerful nationalist movement. Those who hoped that the end of World War I would bring them self-determination could see that British rhetoric about democracy and freedom did not apply to India. Growing organized opposition to British colonialism led to unrest that forced the British to modify some of their colonial policies. At the same time, growing nationalism eventually led to separate Hindu and Muslim nations after World War II.

British Policies, Ghandi, and Mass Resistance

Nationalist opposition to the British *Raj*, which had been building for decades, was spurred by the severe dislocations caused by World War I. To pay for the war, the British raised taxes and customs duties on

Indians, policies that sparked several armed uprisings. In addition, more than 1 million Indian soldiers fought for Britain in France and the Middle East, and 60,000 of these were killed. Many Indians expected a better future because of the sacrifices they had made, but the British dashed all hopes of major political change by declaring in 1917 that they would maintain India as an integral part of the British Empire. However, British prestige suffered irreparable damage from the losses incurred by war and was no longer the imperial giant it had formerly seemed.

The Amritsar Massacre

Growing problems, including a severe economic slump after the war, heightened Indian discontent and alarmed the British, causing them to clamp down on dissent and political activity and to maintain the laws that had been imposed during the war. In 1919, in the Punjab city of Amritsar, British officers suppressed a demonstration by massacring four hundred protesters and wounding one thousand others, including women and children. Throughout India, the Amritsar massacre was greeted with outrage, which intensified when the British hailed the officer in command as a national hero. Prominent Indians, many once pro-British, were appalled at the cruelty, which shook their faith in British rule. The Nobel Prize–winning writer Rabindranath Tagore (tuh-GAWR) (1861–1941) wrote, "The enormity of the measures taken up for quelling some local disturbances had, with a rude shock, revealed to our minds the helplessness of our position as British subjects in India."[4]

The Emergence of Gandhi

The unrest brought to the fore new Indian nationalist leaders, most importantly Mohandas K. Gandhi (GAHN-dee) (1869–1948). After getting his law

degree in Britain, Gandhi lived for twenty-two years in South Africa, where the British colonial regime practiced racial segregation and white supremacy (see Chapter 21). To assert the rights of the Indian immigrants in South Africa, Gandhi developed tactics of nonviolent resistance, noncooperation with unjust laws and peaceful confrontation with illegitimate authority. After returning to India in 1920, he became the president of the main nationalist organization, the Indian National Congress. Gandhi's message of resisting the colonial regime nonviolently led him to mount mass campaigns against British political and economic institutions. Inspired by his example, huge numbers of ordinary people joined his movement, shaking the foundations of British colonial rule.

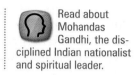

Read about Mohandas Gandhi, the disciplined Indian nationalist and spiritual leader.

Gandhi's doctrine of nonviolence was derived from ideas that had been introduced 2,500 years earlier by the Jains and Buddhists, two of India's religious groups, and also from Quakerism, a pacifist Christian movement Gandhi had encountered in England. Nonviolence—Gandhi often called it passive resistance—was, he wrote, "a method of securing rights by personal suffering; it is the reverse of resistance by arms."[5] Gandhi believed that violence, embodying hate and irrationality, was never justified. The enemy was to be met with reason, and if he responded with violence, this had to be endured in good spirit, requiring severe self-discipline. Gandhi made mass civil disobedience, involving such tactics as marches, sit-ins, and boycotts, the most effective expression of nonviolence. Disobedience also involved hunger strikes, peaceful violation of law, and refusal to pay taxes. Gandhi's Congress colleague, Jawaharlal Nehru (JAH-wa-HAR-lahl NAY-roo), placed Gandhi's strategy in perspective: "Gandhi was like a powerful current of fresh air that made us stretch ourselves and take deep breaths, like a Whirlwind that upset many things but most of all the working of people's minds."[6]

Thanks to Gandhi's efforts, during the 1920s, the Congress developed a mass base that was supported by people from all of India's cultures, religions, regions, and social backgrounds. His tactics bewildered the British, who, while claiming to uphold law, order, and Christian values, clubbed hunger strikers, used horses to trample nonviolent protesters, and arrested Gandhi and other leaders. Still, they

nonviolent resistance Noncooperation with unjust laws and peaceful confrontation with illegitimate authority, pursued by Mohandas Gandhi in India.

CHRONOLOGY

South Asia, 1914–1945

1919	Amritsar massacre
1930	Gandhi's Great Salt March
1931	London Conference
1935	Government of India Act
1937	Provincial elections
1942	Gandhi's Quit India campaign

were forced to make concessions. One of Gandhi's Indian critics told British officials in 1930 that the Congress "has undoubtedly acquired a great hold on the popular imagination."[7]

> "While resistance against British rule continued, a growing Hindu–Muslim division posed a problem for Indian nationalism."

1964), who succeeded Gandhi as Congress leader in 1929, was the strongest advocate of a secular state. Born into a wealthy brahman family, educated in the West, and endowed with unusual charisma, Nehru had a passion for the welfare of the common people and demanded complete freedom from British domination. But while Gandhi wanted to reshape colonial society, Nehru and other Congress leaders focused more on political independence. Few Indian nationalists, whether Hindu or Muslim, shared the Chinese Communist goal of radical social transformation as a necessary part of economic development.

The Great Salt March

The suffering caused by the Great Depression that began in 1929 led to a new Gandhi-led campaign in 1930, beginning with what Gandhi called the Great Salt March. During this event, Gandhi and several dozen followers marched to the west coast, where they produced salt from the Indian Ocean seawater in violation of British laws. Gandhi's action and arrest captured the popular imagination, setting off a wave of demonstrations, strikes, and boycotts against British interests. In quelling the unrest, the British killed 103, injured 420, and imprisoned 60,000 resisters. They released Gandhi a few months later, and he agreed to halt civil disobedience campaigns if the British would promote Indian-made goods and hold a conference to discuss India's political future.

Hindu–Muslim Division

While resistance against British rule continued, a growing Hindu–Muslim division posed a problem for Indian nationalism. Although some Muslims supported the largely Hindu Indian National Congress, others questioned their role in India. While Gandhi respected all religions and welcomed Muslim support, Muslim leaders mounted their own nationalist organizations to work for a potential Muslim country. In 1930, student activists in Britain called their proposed Muslim nation Pakistan, meaning "Land of the Pure" in the Urdu language spoken by many Indian Muslims. Accounting for some 20 percent of British India's population and largely concentrated in the northwest and Bengal, Muslims occupied all niches of society but were divided by social status, ancestry, language, and sect. The great majority were Sunni, but some were Shi'a.

Nehru and Indian Independence

While Muslim leaders often focused on the need for a state that enshrined their religious values, Congress leaders were chiefly Western-oriented Hindu intellectuals who wanted a secular, modern India. The forty-year-old Jawaharlal Nehru (1889–

Muhammed Ali Jinnah and the Muslim League

By the 1930s, the main rival to the Congress was the Muslim League, led by the Western-educated Bombay lawyer Muhammed Ali Jinnah (jee-NAH) (1876–1948), a dapper figure who always spoke English. Jinnah promoted a Two Nations Theory, arguing that Islam and Hinduism were different social orders and that it was a naive Congress dream that the two groups could ever forge a common nationality. Jinnah developed the Muslim League into a mass political movement in competition with the Congress. He cultivated good relations with the British and convinced regional Muslim leaders, some once pro-Congress, to support the Muslim League. The Congress tried to marginalize the Muslim League and refused to form a coalition with it, which proved to be a mistake in the long run. The competing visions of the Congress and the Muslim League complicated British efforts to introduce representative government institutions. The two rival organizations clashed in 1931, when, as a result of Gandhi's agreement to suspend civil disobedience, Indian leaders and British officials met in London to discuss expanded elections. Although Congress objected, Muslims and other minorities did win electoral rights in India's many provinces.

The electoral agreement also did not end anticolonial unrest and counterviolence by the British. However, in 1935, their power in retreat, the British introduced a new constitution that allowed some 35 million Indians who owned property, including 6 million women, to vote for newly formed provincial legislatures. In the first provincial elections, in 1937, the Congress won 70 percent of the popular vote and the majority of seats, defeating the Muslim League even for seats reserved for Muslims. More Indians also rose to leadership positions in the army, police, and civil service. However, British officials argued that the communal divisions necessitated the continuation of British rule to maintain order, and Jinnah, battered but not broken by the disappointing Muslim League electoral performance, redoubled his efforts to unite Muslims against the Congress.

The "Quit India" Campaign

World War II was the deciding event in the path to Indian independence, but it also reshaped the nationalist dialogue by increasing the Hindu–Muslim divide. The British committed Indian troops to the war without consulting Congress leaders, who protested that cooperation must be between equal partners and by mutual consent. In 1942, fearing that the British had no intention of ending their colonial rule, Gandhi mounted a campaign calling on the British to "Quit India." In response, the British arrested Ghandi, Nehru, and the entire Congress leadership and 60,000 party activists, jailing many of them for the duration of the war. World War II harmed the rural poor and urban workers, as prices for essential goods soared. At the same time, famine in Bengal killed 3 million to 4 million people. In response to these hardships, Nehru's main rival for Congress leadership, the militant Bengali Marxist Subhas Chandra Bose (1895–1945), allied with imperial Japan and organized an Indian National Army, recruited largely from among Indian soldiers and Indian emigrants in Southeast Asia. His army invaded India from Japan-held Burma to attack the British. The invasion failed, but many Indians saw Bose and other Indian National Army leaders as national heroes.

The Partitioning of India

Meanwhile, the arrest of Congress leaders meant that Jinnah could consolidate the power of the Muslim League. Jinnah demanded the creation of a separate Muslim state, Pakistan, based on the provinces where Muslims were the majority. Rejecting Muslim separatism, the jailed Gandhi urged Muslims to resist what he termed the suicide of partition. But Gandhi's plea was futile, and British efforts to bring the factions together also failed. After World War II, the struggle between Indian nationalists and the British, and between Hindus and Muslims, resumed, leading to the end of British rule and the creation of two separate independent nations, predominantly Hindu India and a chiefly Muslim Pakistan carved out of the Muslim-majority areas of British India.

Social Change: Caste and Gender Relations

Nationalist politics, economic dislocations, and the stresses posed by rapid population growth had an enduring effect on India's social structure. India's population grew from 255 million in 1871 to 390 million in 1940. The trends that had reshaped the caste system beginning in the 1800s continued, particularly affecting the untouchables, the most powerless group in Hindu society and perhaps one-fifth of India's population. Although Gandhi, a high-caste Hindu, advocated for more dignity for untouchables, increasing attention to caste identities often resulted, tragically, in more discrimination. Untouchable leaders such as Dr. Bhimrao Ramji Ambedkar (BIM-rao RAM-jee am-BED-car) (1893–1956) subsequently launched movements to assert rights for their people. Ambedkar rose from one of the lowest groups, the sweepers who cleaned village streets, to earn a Ph.D. and a law degree from major U.S. and British universities. On his return to India, he started schools, newspapers, and political parties. Ambedkar successfully lobbied the government to promote upward mobility and benefits for the untouchables.

Attitudes toward women were also changing. Hindus increasingly favored widow remarriage, once forbidden, to help offset what they believed to be the higher Muslim birthrate. But while the feminist movement remained weak and had little support among Muslim and peasant women, many women joined the Congress and some demanded a vote equal to men for representative institutions, such as provincial legislatures. With British assent, all of the legislatures granted women the franchise between 1923 and 1930. Gandhi himself, unable to escape patriarchal attitudes, promoted women's traditional roles as wives, mothers, and supporters of men. Impressed by his wife Kasturbai's advocacy of

> " Nationalist politics, economic dislocations, and the stresses posed by rapid population growth had an enduring effect on India's social structure. "

nonviolence, Gandhi believed women were especially suited to passive resistance. He wrote paternalistically that women were the embodiment of humility, sacrifice, and silent suffering. But some women with a more militant vision of change joined men in terrorist organizations aimed at undermining colonialism, like Pritilata Waddedar (1911–1932), a brilliant Bengali university graduate, who led and died in an armed raid on a British club that reportedly boasted a sign: "Dogs and Indians not allowed."

LO⁴ Nationalist Stirrings in Southeast Asia and Sub-Saharan Africa

As in India, the challenges posed by European colonialism were also being addressed by nationalist movements and protests in Southeast Asia and sub-Saharan Africa. In 1930, the Indonesian Nationalist Party, struggling against Dutch colonialism, urged Indonesians to join the cause of national freedom and build a new nation. The plea symbolized the nationalist response in several other Southeast Asian colonies, especially French-ruled Vietnam. Although in sub-Saharan Africa organized nationalist movements, often based on ethnicity, were comparatively weaker politically, they did have meaningful cultural impact.

Changing Southeast Asia

The first stirrings of Southeast Asian nationalism came in the Philippines in the late 1800s, but the revolution was thwarted by Spain first and then the United States. In the Philippines, the U.S. promise of eventual independence tended to reduce radical sentiments. By 1941, nationalism also had a large following in Vietnam, British Burma, and parts of Indonesia, all places that had suffered particularly oppressive colonial rule and where independence would come only through force. Compared to these colonies, nationalism was weaker in French-ruled Cambodia and Laos and in British Malaya, all colonies that had experienced less social, economic, and political disruption.

One of the stronger nationalist movements arose in Burma (today's Myanmar). Despite having limited self-government by the 1930s, including an elected legislature, the colony's majority ethnic group, the Burmans, viewed British rule as oppressive. They also resented Christian converts and the large, often wealthy Indian community, which had immigrated

> ### CHRONOLOGY
> #### Southeast Asia and Africa, 1912–1945
>
> | | |
> |---|---|
> | 1912 | Formation of African National Congress in South Africa |
> | 1912 | Formation of Islamic Union in Indonesia |
> | 1920 | Formation of Indonesian Communist Party |
> | 1920–1922 | Nationalist unrest in Kenya |
> | 1926–1927 | Communist uprising in Indonesia |
> | 1927 | Formation of Indonesian Nationalist Party |
> | 1928–1931 | Peasant rebellions in the Congo region |
> | 1930 | Founding of Indochinese Communist Party |
> | 1932 | Nationalist coup in Thailand |
> | 1935–1936 | Conquest of Ethiopia by Italy |
> | 1941 | Formation of Viet Minh in Vietnam by Ho Chi Minh |
> | 1941–1945 | Japanese occupation of Southeast Asia |

to Burma and dominated the economy. These resentments fostered the rise of nationalism among university students. The nationalists used Theravada Buddhism, the faith of most Burmese, as a rallying cry to press for reform, and some favored women's rights. When the Japanese invaded Burma in 1941, many Burmans welcomed them as liberators.

Although Siam (today's Thailand) was not a colony, nationalism grew there out of tensions between the aristocratic elite and the rising middle class that were exacerbated by the Great Depression. In 1932, military officers of middle-class background, who called themselves nationalists, took power in a coup against the royal government. The Siamese king, whose family had ruled the country since the late 1700s, agreed under pressure to become a constitutional, mostly symbolic monarch. Military leaders then ran the government throughout the 1930s, pursuing nationalist policies, renaming the country Thailand ("Land of Free People"), and urging the Thai people to live modern lives. During the late 1930s,

Thailand forged an alliance with rising imperial Japan, and introduced features of a fascist regime, militarizing the schools and suppressing dissent.

Nationalism in Vietnam and Indonesia

The most powerful nationalist movement in Southeast Asia emerged in Vietnam as a result of its destabilization during French colonial rule, when peasant lands were seized. The earliest nationalists seeking an end to French rule were led by the passionately revolutionary Phan Boi Chau (FAN boy chow) (1867–1940). Phan was born into a family of mandarins who had served the Vietnamese emperors as officials for generations, and he was educated in Confucian learning. By the time of his death in a French prison, Phan had inspired Vietnamese patriotism and resistance. But a younger generation of urban, French-educated intellectuals took a more radical approach—terrorism—assassinating colonial officials and bombing French buildings. One such uprising in 1930 brought about a French reign of terror against all dissidents, which destroyed the major nationalist groups except for the Vietnamese communists.

> "The most powerful nationalist movement in Southeast Asia emerged in Vietnam as a result of its destabilization during French colonial rule, when peasant lands were seized."

Ho Chi Minh and the Indochinese Communist Party

The rise of Vietnamese communism during the repression owed much to Ho Chi Minh, a mandarin's son and former sailor turned left-wing political activist, as described at the start of the chapter. Ho had spent many years organizing the communist movement among Vietnamese exiles in Thailand and China. Ho came to believe that nothing less than Marxist revolution would provide an alternative to the discredited imperial system, an unjust society, and French rule. In 1930, Ho and his colleagues established the Indochinese Communist Party, which united anticolonial radicals from Vietnam, Cambodia, and Laos. They linked themselves to the patriotic traditions of the earlier Vietnamese rebels, who for 2,000 years had led resistance first to Chinese conquerors and then to the French.

One Vietnamese Marxist, writing in 1943, exemplified the links with the past: "And, so it seems we are not lost after all. Behind us we have the immense history of our people. There [are] still spiritual cords attaching us."[8] Remembering Vietnam's long history of resistance to foreign occupation, Vietnamese communism took on a strongly nationalist flavor. In 1941, Ho established the Viet Minh, or Vietnamese Independence League, a coalition of anti-French groups that waged war against both the French colonizers and the Japanese, who occupied Vietnam during World War II.

Indonesian Nationalism

Nationalist activity also emerged in the Dutch East Indies. Diverse organizations sought freedom from Dutch control while calling for the unity of the Indonesian populace, which included hundreds of ethnic groups. One strategy was to adopt a unifying language, a lingua franca widely used as a common tongue among diverse groups that also had their own languages. Nationalist intellectuals began using Malay, which gradually became the language of the press and educational institutions.

Nationalist ideas competed with and sometimes reshaped Indonesian religious traditions. For example, some Muslims, impressed with but also resenting Western economic and military power, sought to reform and purify their faith. Reformers stressed the five pillars of Islam, devalued the writings of religious scholars after

> 66 Nationalist ideas competed with and sometimes reshaped Indonesian religious traditions. 99

Muhammad, and favored the segregation of men and women in public, a custom long ignored by most Indonesians. In 1912, Javanese batik merchants who mixed these reformist religious ideas with nationalism established the colony's first true political movement, the Islamic Union, which by 1919 had recruited 2 million members.

After 1917, the Russian Revolution inspired radical Marxists in the Dutch East Indies. They formed the Indonesian Communist Party in 1920, which grew rapidly by attracting support chiefly from nondevout Muslim peasants and labor union members in Java. Overestimating their strength, the communists sparked a poorly planned uprising in 1926, which was crushed by the government and led to the execution of its leaders.

The destruction of the communists left an opening for other nationalists. The Indonesian Nationalist Party, led mostly by Javanese aristocrats who rejected Islamic reform ideas, was established in 1927 to promote a new national identity. Sukarno (soo-KAHR-no) (1902–1970), the key founder, designed a flag, wrote an anthem, and created a slogan for an independent Indonesia: "one nation—Indonesia, one people—Indonesian, one language—Indonesian." The Dutch authorities arrested Sukarno in 1929 and exiled him to a remote island prison for the next decade, making him a nationalist symbol and increasing his popularity (see Witness to the Past: Sukarno Indicts Dutch Colonialism). However, without his leadership, the Indonesian Nationalist Party grew more slowly throughout the 1930s.

Japanese Occupation: The Remaking of Southeast Asia

The occupation of Southeast Asia by Japanese forces during World War II from 1941 to 1945 boosted nationalism and weakened colonialism. Before 1941, colonial authority had remained strong. Then, in a few weeks in late 1941 and early 1942, everything changed. Japan had already bullied Thailand and the French colonial regime in Vietnam, which now took orders from the pro-Nazi Vichy government in France (see Chapter 24), to allow the stationing of Japanese troops. Then the bombing of Pearl Harbor in 1941 was quickly followed by a rapid Japanese invasion of Southeast Asia. With superior naval and air strength, the Japanese easily overwhelmed the colonial forces. Within four months, they controlled major cities and heavily populated regions, shattering the mystique of Western invincibility and expelling European and American officials. As an Indonesian writer later

remembered, the Japanese occupation "destroyed a whole set of illusions and left man as naked as when he was created."[9] The Japanese talked of "Asia for the Asians," but this rhetoric also masked the Japanese wartime exploitation of natural resources such as rubber and oil.

Indonesia Under the Japanese

Japanese domination was brief, less than four years, yet it led to significant changes. For example, in many places, conflicts between ethnic groups increased because of selective repression. In Malaya, Japanese policy that favored the majority Malays allowed Malay government officials to keep their jobs, while members of the Chinese minority often faced property seizures and arrest, creating antagonism between Malays and Chinese that persisted long after the war. By destroying the link to the world economy, the occupation also caused economic hardship. Western companies closed, causing unemployment, while Japanese forces seized natural resources and food. By 1944, living standards, crippled by severe shortages of essential goods such as food and clothing, were in steep decline. Southeast Asians suffered also from harassment by the Japanese police as well as forced labor: Javanese men became slave laborers and Filipinas, called "comfort women" by the Japanese, served the sexual needs of Japanese soldiers. As their war effort against the United States faltered, the desperate Japanese resorted to even more repressive policies to keep order and acquire resources.

Although often harsh, Japanese rule also offered some political benefits for Southeast Asians, such as promotion into government positions that were once reserved for Westerners. In addition, the Japanese—seeking to purge the area of Western cultural influences—closed Christian mission schools, encouraged Islamic or Buddhist leaders, and fostered a renaissance of indigenous culture and an outpouring of literature. The Japanese also promoted Southeast Asian nationalism, at least indirectly, because of their recruitment of Southeast Asian leaders to lend legitimacy to their rule. The Japanese freed nationalist leaders such as Sukarno from jail and gave them official positions, if little actual power. The nationalists enjoyed a new role in public life and used the Japanese-controlled radio and newspapers to foster nationalist beliefs. The Japanese also recruited young people into armed paramilitary forces, which became the basis for later nationalist armies in Indonesia and Burma that resisted the return of Western colonialism after World War II.

Sukarno Indicts Dutch Colonialism

Sukarno, the fiery Indonesian nationalist, was skilled at articulating his criticisms of colonialism. A splendid orator, he attracted a large following through his use of Indonesian, especially Javanese, religious and cultural symbols and frequent historical references in his speeches. Arrested by the Dutch in 1930, Sukarno delivered a passionate defense speech, known as "Indonesia Accuses," at his trial that became one of the most inspiring documents of Indonesian nationalism. Sukarno stressed the greatness of Indonesia's past as a building block for the future.

The word "imperialism" . . . designates a . . . tendency . . . to dominate or influence the affairs of another nation, . . . a system . . . of economic control. . . . As long as a nation does not wield political power in its own country, part of its potential, economic, social or political, will be used for interests which are not its interests, but contrary to them. . . . A colonial nation is a nation that cannot be itself, a nation that in almost all its branches, in all of its life, bears the mark of imperialism. There is no community of interests between the subject and the object of imperialism. Between the two there is only a contrast of interests and a conflict of needs. All interests of imperialism, social, economic, political, or cultural, are opposed to the interests of the Indonesian people. The imperialists desire the continuation of imperialism, the Indonesians desire its abolition. . . .

What are the roads to promote Indonesian nationalism? . . . First: we point out to the people that they have had a great past. Second: we reinforce the consciousness of the people that the present is dark. Third: we show the people the pure and brightly shining light of the future and the roads which lead to this future so full of promises. . . . The P.N.I. [Indonesian Nationalist Party] awakens and reinforces the people's consciousness of its "grandiose past," its "dark present" and the promises of a shining, beckoning future.

Our grandiose past? Oh, what Indonesian does not feel his heart shrink with sorrow when he hears the stories about the beautiful past, does not regret the disappearance of that departed glory! What Indonesian does not feel his national heart beat with joy when he hears about the greatness of the [Intermediate Era] empires of Melayu and Srivijaya, about the greatness of the empire of Mataram and Madjapahit. . . . A nation with such a grandiose past must surely have sufficient natural aptitude to have a beautiful future. . . . Among the people . . . again conscious of their great past, national feeling is revived, and the fire of hope blazes in their hearts.

Thinking About the Reading

1. What is Sukarno's evaluation of imperialism?
2. How does he think Indonesians should capitalize on their past?

Source: Harry J. Benda and John A. Larkin, eds., *The World of Southeast Asia: Selected Historical Readings* (New York: Harper and Row, 1967), pp. 190–193. Copyright © 1967 Harper and Row. Reprinted with permission of John A. Larkin.

Organizing an Opposition

Some Southeast Asians dared to actively oppose Japanese rule, especially in Vietnam. Vietnamese communism might never have achieved power so quickly had it not been for the Japanese occupation, which discredited the French administration and imposed great hardship on most of the population, a fact that the communists used to their advantage. The Viet Minh, led by Ho Chi Minh, were now armed and trained by American advisers, who, after the United States entered the war and needed local allies, had been sent to help anti-Japanese forces. In 1944, the Viet Minh moved out of their bases along the Chinese border and expanded their influence in northern Vietnam, attracting thousands of poor peasants to the anti-French nationalist cause while attacking the Japanese occupiers with guerrilla tactics. The Viet Minh rapidly gained popular support and recruits, thanks partly to a 1945 Japanese policy that exported scarce food to Japan while a famine killed 2 million Vietnamese.

Post-War Indonesia

Japanese fortunes waned as the United States gained the upper hand in the war, opening the way for political change in Southeast Asia. U.S. bombing of Japanese installations in Southeast Asia alerted local people that the regional balance of power was changing. Tired of economic deprivation and repression, few Southeast Asians regretted Japan's defeat, and some, especially in Malaya, British Bomeo, and the Philippines, even welcomed the return of Western forces. Before World War II, the United States had promised to grant independence to the Philippines and did so in 1946, turning the country over to pro-U.S. leaders, but often the returning Westerners faced growing political volatility. The end of war set the stage for dramatic political change in Vietnam, Indonesia, and Burma, as nationalist forces resisted any return to the prewar status quo and successfully struggled for independence in the late 1940s and early 1950s.

Nationalism and Resistance in Africa

The roots of the African nationalist struggle had been planted in the decades before World War II, but lacking the mass base of Vietnamese or Indian nationalists, protests were less disruptive in Africa than in Southeast Asia and India. One obstacle was that imperial regimes in Africa did not permit enough African participation in government or education to produce a large educated class that could assume the responsibilities and burdens of nationhood.

The Question of National Identity

The artificial division of Africa was the most significant hindrance to nationalist organizing. All over Africa, the colonial regimes, by using divide-and-rule strategies to govern diverse ethnic groups, had made it difficult to create viable national identities. For example, Nigeria, in West Africa, was an artificial creation, the result of the late-nineteenth-century British colonization of diverse and often rival ethnic groups. While some Pan-Nigerian nationalists sought unity, most of the Nigerian nationalist organizations found their greatest support only among particular regions or ethnic groups within Nigeria. In the 1940s, a prominent leader of one of the major ethnic groups,

> "The artificial division of Africa was the most significant hindrance to nationalist organizing."

the Yoruba, complained that "Nigeria is not a nation [but] a mere geographical expression."[10]

West African nationalist currents were strongest in the growing, usually multiethnic cities, such as Lagos in Nigeria, Accra in the Gold Coast, and Dakar in Senegal. These became the breeding grounds of new ideas. City life, which offered a wide range of economic activities, also encouraged the growth of trade union movements, which sponsored occasional strikes to protest colonial policies or economic exploitation. However, rural people, especially farmers, also asserted their rights. For example, during the 1930s, cocoa growers in the British-ruled Gold Coast held back their crops from the government to protest low prices.

Henry Thuku and the African Nationalist Movements

African nationalism was sparked by World War I and the unfulfilled expectations for better lives in its aftermath. During the war, the British, French, and Germans had all drafted or recruited men from their African colonies to fight on European battlefields, where thousands died. When the survivors returned home, the promises the colonial powers had made to them about land or jobs proved empty. For example, Kenyan soldiers came back from the war to find that British settlers had seized their land. In response, Harry Thuku (THOO-koo) (ca. 1895–1970), a middle-class Kenyan and member of Kenya's largest ethnic group, the Gikuyu, created an alliance of diverse Kenyan ethnic groups in 1920 to confront the British. When the British arrested Thuku in 1922, rioting led by Gikuyu women broke out, and the British fired on the rioters, killing more than twenty of them.

Inspired in part by Harry Thuku's movement, nationalist organizations developed in various colonies in the 1920s and met with occasional success, especially in West Africa. These urban-based organizations, led mainly by Western-educated Africans, were formed in part to press for more African participation in local government. Among these was J. E. Casely Hayford (1866–1930), a lawyer and journalist in the British Gold Coast (today's Ghana) who was influenced by Gandhi. Some Africans, including Casely Hayford, favored a Pan-African approach and sought support across colonial borders; they did not view colonial boundaries as the basis for nations. But both nationalists and Pan-Africanists were unable to overcome the divide among rival ethnic groups within each colony and the gap between the cities and the villages. Furthermore, some African merchants, chiefs, and kings profited from their links to the colonizers and discouraged protests. Because of all these challenges, the urban nationalists had little influence before World War II.

Emergence of the African National Congress

In South Africa, the racial inequality and white supremacy established by the Dutch in South Africa and largely maintained by the British remained in place during most of the twentieth century, sparking nationalism that led some to resist oppression. The early South African nationalists, such as the founders of the African National Congress (usually known as the ANC, established in 1912), came from the urban middle class. The ANC encouraged education and preached African independence from white rule but did not directly confront the government until the 1950s. More militant African resistance also flourished, though, especially in the mining industry, where strikes were endemic throughout the twentieth century despite severe government repression.

Music and Protest

Colonial rule did, however, generate new cultural trends that allowed people to express their views, which were often critical, about colonial African life. For instance, during the 1930s, a musical style, highlife, arose in the Gold Coast and soon spread into other British West African colonies. It was carried chiefly by guitar-playing sailors and was an urban-based mix of Christian hymns, West Indian calypso songs, and African dance rhythms. Although the music was closely tied to dance bands and parties, some highlife musicians began addressing social and political issues, and this trend grew with nationalism. The very term *highlife* signified both an envy and disapproval of the Western colonizers and rich Africans, who lived in luxury in mansions staffed by servants. Many highlife songs were sung in pidgin English, a mixture of African and English words and grammar that spread throughout British West Africa as a marketplace lingua franca among ethnically diverse urban populations.

Given a white supremacist government that was anxious to suppress dissent, South African protest was often expressed in music, although usually veiled to avoid arrest. Even hymns in African churches had a protest element, because they were sung using African rather than Western vocal traditions. Knowing that few whites understood lyrics sung in African languages, African workers filled the mining camps and labor movements with political music, offering

highlife
An urban-based West African musical style mixing Christian hymns, West Indian calypso, and African dance rhythms.

pidgin English
The form of broken English that developed in Africa during the colonial era.

African Jazz Band Jazz from the United States had a wide following in the world in the 1920s, 1930s, and 1940s. Jazz especially influenced the music of black South Africans, some of whom formed jazz groups, such as the Harmony Kings.

Courtesy, National Library of South Africa

messages such as "we demand freedom" and "workers unite." In the cities, jazz, which was developed originally by African American musicians across the Atlantic, became a form of resistance to the culture of the white racist Afrikaners. The preferred music of the small, educated black professional and business class, jazz ultimately became a symbol of black nationalism in South Africa.

LO⁵ Remaking the Middle East and Latin America

The peoples of both the Middle East and Latin America were also influenced by nationalism between 1914 and 1945. While North Africans, like sub-Saharan Africans and Southeast Asians, experienced Western colonial rule, Arabs in much of western Asia had been controlled for five hundred years by the Ottoman Turks, and under their rule the region was stagnating economically by the 1800s. European influence intensified after World War I, when the Ottoman colonies in western Asia were transferred to Britain and France, sparking nationalist resentment among the western Asian Arabs. Latin Americans, mostly Christians, achieved their independence in the nineteenth century and shared few recent experiences with colonized Arabs, Africans, and Southeast Asians, but two world wars and the Great Depression in the twentieth century caused turmoil, fostered dictatorships, and, as in other regions, spurred feelings of nationalism.

Estado Novo History of the Middle East Database (*http://www.nmhschool.org/tthornton/mehistorydatabase/mideastindex.php*). A useful site on history, politics, and culture.

The Ottoman Aftermath

World War I was a watershed for Middle Eastern societies, because it dismantled the region's major state, the Turkish-dominated Ottoman Empire, and reshaped Arab politics. In the war, the Turks favored their longtime ally Germany because it shared their hatred of Russia, but the Ottomans and their European allies lost the war. The resulting breakup of the Ottoman Empire led to the emergence of a new, very different Turkish nation.

···················

Syrian and Arab Nationalism

The hardships during World War I spurred Arab nationalism against Ottoman rule. Unrest in Syria brought on fierce Ottoman repression, as the Ottomans sent nationalist dissidents into exile and hanged others for treason. The most serious challenge to Ottoman rule came in Arabia, where Sharif Hussein ibn Ali (1856–1931), the Arab ruler of the Hejaz—the western Arabia region that included the Muslim holy cities of Mecca and Medina—shifted his loyalties in the war from the Ottomans to the British, who promised to support independence for the Arabs in Ottoman territory. In 1916, with British assistance, Sharif Hussein launched an Arab revolt against the Turks, attacking Ottoman bases and communications. The British invaded and occupied southern Iraq, an Ottoman province, which had a strategic position between Arabia, Syria, and Iran and was thought to have oil.

The end of World War I brought crushed dreams and turmoil to the Middle East. Arab nationalists such as Sharif Hussein did not know that during the war the eventually victorious European Allies—Britain, France, and Russia—had made secret agreements to dismantle the Ottoman Empire that ignored Arab interests. When the war ended, British troops occupied much of Iraq and Palestine, and French troops controlled the Syrian coast.

World War I caused great suffering to diverse Ottoman societies. The Caucasus peoples, especially the Christian Armenians, desired independence. Suspecting them of aiding Russia, the Turks turned on the Armenians living in eastern Anatolia. More than 1 million Armenians were deported, chiefly to Syria and Iraq, while perhaps another 1 million died of thirst, starvation, or systematic slaughter by the Ottoman army; some historians consider it a genocide. The violent assault created a permanent Turkish-Armenian hostility. After the war, the Russians regained control of the Caucasus, including Armenia. In a different context, hunger and disease also affected millions of Arabs in the Ottoman Empire, with 200,000 dying in Syria alone during the war.

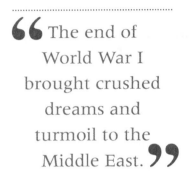

66 The end of World War I brought crushed dreams and turmoil to the Middle East. 99

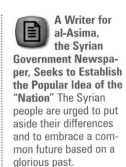

A Writer for al-Asima, the Syrian Government Newspaper, Seeks to Establish the Popular Idea of the "Nation" The Syrian people are urged to put aside their differences and to embrace a common future based on a glorious past.

The Dismemberment of the Ottoman Empire

The Versailles treaty that ended World War I brought major political change, including dismemberment of the Ottoman Empire (see Map 25.2). Turkey's neighbors— the Greeks, Italians, and Armenians—made claims on Anatolia and adjacent islands, and European Zionists asked for a Jewish national home in Palestine (see Chapter 21). The Allies ended Ottoman control of Arab territories and suggested eventual independence to the Kurds, a Sunni Muslim people, distinct from both Arabs and Turks, who inhabited a large, mountainous region of Western Asia and were also the dominant ethnic group in southeast Turkey. Both Syria and Iraq declared their independence from the Ottoman Empire, but the League of Nations, dominated by Western countries, awarded France control over Syria

Interactive Map

and Lebanon, and Britain control over Iraq, Palestine, and Transjordan (today Jordan), under what the League called mandates.

In theory, mandates were less onerous for local people than colonies because they allowed for administrative assistance for a limited time, but Arabs often wanted to build their own governments and shape new social systems. Arab nationalists in Syria proposed a democratic government, but French forces quickly occupied the country and exiled nationalist leaders. The Allies also ignored the desire of the Kurdish people for their own nation. Despite British proposals for such a change, the Kurds remained divided between Turkey, Persia (Iran), Iraq, and Syria, thus becoming the world's largest ethnic group without their own state.

Kemal Ataturk and Turkish Reform

While all of the former Ottoman territories experienced change after World War I, the heart of the empire, Turkey, saw the most revolutionary changes. The disastrous defeat in the war and the humiliating agreements that followed left the Turks helpless and bitter. But under the leadership of the daring war hero and ardent nationalist later known as Kemal Ataturk (kuh-MAHL AT-uh-turk) (1881–1938), the Turks enjoyed a spectacular postwar resurgence. In 1919, Ataturk began mobilizing military forces in eastern Anatolia into a revolutionary organization to oppose the Ottoman sultan, who was discredited by defeats, and to restore dignity to the Turks. Ataturk accepted the loss of Arab lands but wanted to preserve the Turkish majority areas and the eastern Anatolia districts inhabited chiefly by Kurds.

After establishing a rival Turkish government in the central Anatolia city of Ankara, Ataturk led his forces in fighting both the sultan's government in Istanbul and the foreign occupiers, especially the Greek forces that had moved deep into Anatolia. He finally pushed the Greeks back to the Aegean Sea, and eventually Turkey and Greece agreed to a population transfer in which many Greeks living in Turkish territory moved to Greece and the Turks dwelling in Greek lands moved to Turkey. In 1922, Ataturk deposed the Ottoman sultan and set up a republic with himself as president. He was a controversial figure among Turks, particularly devout Muslims, because Ataturk dismissed Islamic culture as an inferior mix of age-old mentalities. He favored modernization, announcing that "our eyes are turned westward. We shall transplant Western institutions to Asiatic soil. We wish to be a modern nation with our mind open, and yet

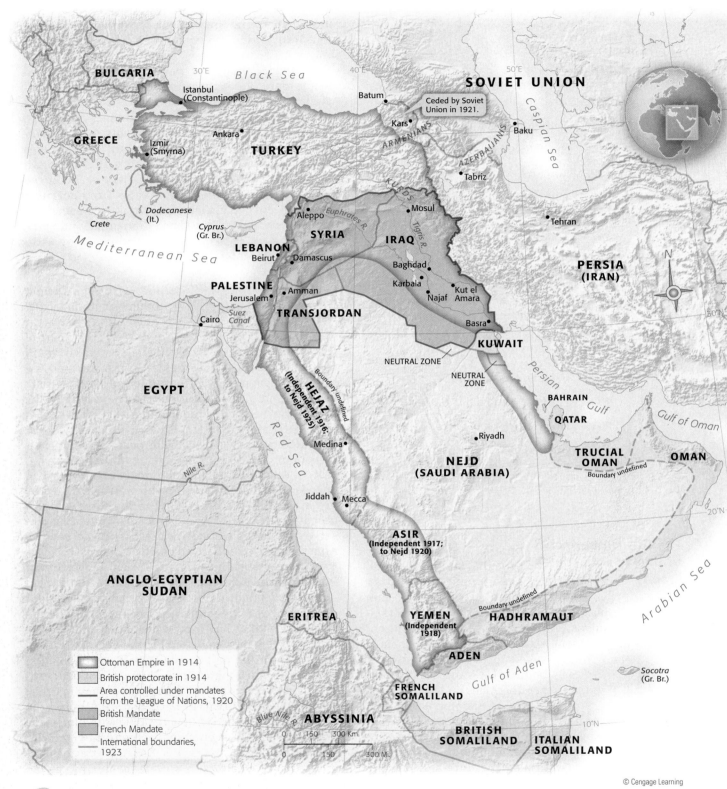

Map 25.2
Partition of the Ottoman Empire

Before 1914, the Ottoman Turks controlled much of western Asia, including western Arabia. After World War II, the League of Nations awarded Iraq, Transjordan, and Palestine to Britain. Syria and Lebanon were given to France, and western Arabia was ruled by Arabs. Eventually, the Saudi family, rulers of the Najd, expanded their rule into western Arabia and created Saudi Arabia.

to remain ourselves."[11] Ataturk claimed that secularization and the emancipation of women were in keeping with the pre-Islamic Turkish tradition.

In the 1920s, these ideas were put into action through a dazzling series of reforms that challenged Muslim traditions and promoted modern Western practices. Ataturk abolished Islamic religious schools and courts, and he removed reference to Islam as the state religion from the constitution. His government resembled a parliamentary democracy and earned the popularity of many urban dwellers, but he exercised near-dictatorial power and alienated the Kurdish minority by suppressing their language and culture. Ataturk left a deeply changed nation, but many of the reforms he introduced were never adopted in the villages, where Islam remained a strong influence.

> "Ataturk abolished Islamic religious schools and courts, and he removed reference to Islam as the state religion from the constitution."

Modern Iran, Egypt, and Iraq

During this era, major changes also occurred in the other major Middle Eastern countries. Like Turkey, Persia, later known as Iran, moved toward modernization, though with fewer permanent changes, and Egyptians and Iraqis turned toward nationalism in response to British attempts to maintain power in those countries.

The Pahlavi Dynasty in Iran

After World War I, Britain was given the power to impose a protectorate over Persia under which the Persian government was maintained but was forced to accept British loans, financial controls, advisers, and military forces. However, Persian opposition prompted the British to withdraw their troops in 1919 and seek a new approach. Britain supported General Reza Khan (REE-za kahn) (1877–1944), a soldier from a modest background who wanted to end the corrupt, ineffective royal dynasty, establish a secular republic, and address economic underdevelopment. In 1921, Reza Khan took control of the government with British backing, ending the monarchy. He was supported by secular Shi'ites, who had long struggled for a more democratic and open society. In 1924, an influential local magazine praised Reza Khan for freeing the country from having a king and expressed the hope that soon it would escape the domination of the powerful Shi'ite clergy. But in 1925, at the urging of Shi'ite clerics, Reza Khan abandoned the republican government and formed the Pahlavi (PAH-lah-vee) dynasty, with himself as shah, or king.

Although restoring a royal government, Reza Khan, like Ataturk in Turkey, set his country on a path toward modernization and, in 1935, renamed his nation Iran, a symbolic break with the past. The shah created a large national army through conscription, introduced a Western law code, and built infrastructure and government

Hulton Archive/Getty Images

Ataturk Wedding Dance The Turkish leader Kemal Ataturk promoted and adopted Western fashions while defying Muslim customs. In this photo from around 1925, Ataturk dances with his daughter at her Western-style wedding.

factories. He further strengthened the economy and Iran's political reputation by taking control over the oil industry. The regime also made social changes that outraged Muslim conservatives, such as outlawing the veiling of women in public and encouraging men to wear Western hats and clothes.

But while merchants and the middle class supported Reza Khan's policies, there was little improvement for poor Iranians, who mostly despised the government. Ultimately, the shah had less success in transforming Iran than Ataturk did in Turkey. Reza Khan's support for Germany during World War II prompted an Anglo-Russian occupation of Iran, which the Allies needed as a supply route. Humiliated, the shah abdicated in favor of his twenty-two-year-old son, Muhammad Reza Pahlavi (REH-zah PAH-lah-vee) (1919–1980), and went into exile. The son ruled until 1979.

Wafd and Egyptian Nationalism

In Egypt and Iraq, British control fostered nationalist Arab resistance. In Egypt during World War I, the British had imposed martial law and drafted peasants to build roads and railroads and dig trenches in war zones. Egyptians resented these policies and the thousands of British soldiers stationed in their country during the war. After the war, nationalists unsuccessfully sought an end to British domination. The leading nationalist party, the Wafd, was a secular movement seeking independence, representative government, civil liberties, and curtailed powers for the pro-British monarchy.

British missteps led to political change. In 1919, the British arrested the Wafd's leader, Saad Zaghlul (sod ZOG-lool) (ca. 1857-1927), and other Wafd leaders. Enraged Egyptians responded with strikes, student demonstrations, sabotage of railroads, and the murder of British soldiers. The anti-British movement united rich and poor, Muslims and Coptic Christians, men and women, and forced the British to release Zaghlul, who then went to the Paris Peace Conference to plead for national self-determination. Like Vietnam's Ho Chi Minh, he was ignored. Postwar unrest forced Britain to grant Egypt limited independence in 1922, controlling Egypt's defense and foreign affairs until 1936, the official end of its occupation. But Britain still kept thousands of troops along the Suez Canal, and it also shared with Egypt the administration of Sudan, the territory bordering Egypt on the south. Resentment of the continuing British presence increased during World War II.

Faisal and the British Administration of Iraq

The British also struggled to control Iraq, an artificial creation that united three Ottoman provinces, each dominated by a different group: Sunni Kurds, Sunni Arabs, and Shi'ite Arabs. Describing their occupation as a "liberation," the British promised to bestow on the Iraqis an efficient administration, honest finance, impartial justice, and security; in reality they discouraged self-government, and British occupation soon embittered many Iraqis. In 1920, Shi'ite clerics seeking an Islamic state proclaimed a holy war against the British, prompting various Shi'a and Sunni tribes to rise in rebellion. The British suppressed the rebellion, but at a great cost in money and lives: some ten thousand Iraqi and four hundred British died in the fighting. The British kept their own casualty lists low by relying heavily on aerial bombing, which flattened whole villages.

Shaken by the fierce resistance, the British changed direction in Iraq. They introduced limited self-government that allowed Iraqi participation in an appointed Council of State. The skilled diplomacy of a pro-Arab British archaeologist, writer, and diplomat, Lady Gertrude Bell (1868–1926), defused tensions. Seeking a king for Iraq who would be content to "reign but not govern," as Bell put it, in 1921 Britain installed a member of the Hashemite (HASH-uh-mite) royal family of Mecca, Sharif Hussein's son Faisal (1885–1935). In 1930, Faisal convinced Britain to grant Iraq independence, but only after he agreed to accept continued British military bases and government advisers. By then the British had found oil in Iraq, making them unwilling to cut their ties. Many Arabs considered Faisal and his Hashemite successors to be British clients serving British interests, but Iraqi politics after 1930 was shaped by a series of Sunni Arab military strongmen who dominated the kings and strongly influenced government policies.

Islam and Zionism

The stranglehold of European power and Western culture remained concerns of most Middle Eastern societies during the era. Although various colonized peoples struggled to free themselves, nationalist success came slowly. In the absence of political success, religion became a focus of attention. Arabs debated the merits of Westernization, the role of Islam in their societies, and the challenge posed by Zionism, an encounter that fostered long-term hostility between Muslims and Jews.

Middle Eastern leaders and intellectuals envied Western economic development, such as industrialization and a wealth of consumer goods, but disagreed about how many Western cultural, political, and social patterns should be adopted. Some sought wholesale transformation; some favored Islamic tradition; and still others sought a middle path between the two, such as mixing Western and Islamic laws. Between 1923 and 1930, Western-style constitutions, which provided for civil liberties and an elected parliament, were adopted in Egypt, Iraq, Lebanon, Transjordan, and Syria. But these parliaments were limited in their duties and unrepresentative. Real power usually remained in the hands of European officials or powerful kings, and most Arab politicians had little respect for civil liberties. Arabs did make progress in education, public health, industrialization, and communications, but change came slowly. The Egyptian literacy rate rose from 9 percent in 1917 to only 15 percent in 1937.

Social Changes in Egypt

Some women also asserted their rights and sought social change. One of these was the Egyptian Huda Shaarawi (HOO-da sha-RAH-we) (1879–1947). From a wealthy Cairo family, Huda had been married off at age thirteen to a much older cousin. Finding the marriage confining, Huda organized nonviolent anti-British demonstrations by women after World War I and then publicly removed her veil in 1923, shocking Egyptians. She founded and led the Egyptian feminist movement, which succeeded in raising the minimum marriage age for girls to sixteen and increasing educational opportunities for women.

The debates over Westernization fostered new intellectual currents in the Islamic world, some pro-Western, others anti-Western. Representing the former approach, a blind Egyptian author, Taha Husayn (1889–1973), educated in traditional Islamic schools but also at the Sorbonne in Paris, became the key figure of Egyptian literature in the era. In his writings, he challenged orthodox Islam and, in 1938, proclaimed that Westernizing Arab culture, which he favored, would fit with Egypt's traditions, which he described as a mix of Pharaonic, Arab, and Western cultures. "I want," he wrote, "our new life to harmonize with our ancient glory."

The Growing Influence of Wahhabism

In contrast, the popular reaction against Westernization came with a new Egyptian religious movement, the Muslim Brotherhood, and the strengthening influence of Wahhabi Islam. The Muslim Brotherhood was founded in 1928 by schoolteacher Hasan al-Banna (1906–1949). Al-Banna despised Western values, arguing that it "would be inexcusable for us to turn aside from the path of truth—Islam—and so follow the path of fleshly desires and vanities—the path of Europe."[12] Expressing a widespread resentment against Western influence, such as films, bars, and modern, figure-revealing women's fashions, the Brotherhood soon developed a following in Sudan and western Asia.

The puritanical Wahhabi movement came to dominate Arabia when tribal chief Abdul Aziz Ibn Saud (sah-OOD) (1902–1969) expanded the power of the Saudi family (see Chapter 21). By 1932, his forces had taken western Arabia and the Islamic holy cities of Mecca and Medina from the Hashemites and formed the country of Saudi Arabia. As king, Abdul Aziz began strictly enforcing Islamic law by establishing Committees for the Commendation of Virtue and the Condemnation of Vice to police personal behavior. At the same time, the Saudis welcomed material innovations from the West, such as automobiles, medicine, and telephones. In 1935 oil was discovered in Saudi Arabia, which contained the world's richest oil reserves. The resulting wealth chiefly benefited the royal family and their allies, the Wahhabi clergy.

Zionism: Jewish Nationalism

The roots of a long-term problem for Arab nationalists were planted in Palestine as the Zionist movement, which sought a Jewish homeland for the Jewish people, compelled many in the Jewish ghettoes of Europe to move there (see Chapters 19 and 21). The Zionist slogan—"a land without a people for a people without a land"—was supported by the British government in 1917 with the issuance of the Balfour Declaration, a letter approving the establishment of Palestine as a national home for the Jewish people. But the Zionist slogan had a flaw: Palestine was not a land without a people. Palestinian Arabs had lived there for many centuries, building cities, cultivating orchards, and herding livestock. A Zionist

Muslim Brotherhood An Egyptian religious movement founded in 1928 that expressed popular Arab reaction to Westernization.

Balfour Declaration A letter from the British foreign minister to Zionist leaders in 1917 that gave British support for the establishment of Palestine as a national home for the Jewish people.

leader later conceded that Jewish settlers were surprised to find people there. In Arab eyes, Jewish immigrants were European colonizers planning to dispossess them.

In the 1920s and 1930s, thousands of European Jews migrated to Palestine with British support, some of them fleeing Nazi Germany. By 1939, the Palestine population of 1.5 million was one-third Jewish. Although Jewish settlers established businesses, industries, and productive farms that contributed greatly to Palestine's economic development, Arabs feared becoming a vulnerable numerical minority in what they considered their own land. Zionist organizations began buying up the best land from absentee Arab landlords who disregarded the customary rights of villagers to use it, uprooting thousands of Arab peasants. As tensions increased, violence spread; sometimes hundreds of Arabs and Jews were killed in armed clashes.

In 1936, a major Arab rebellion fostered a three-year civil war. All Arab factions united to oppose plans for establishing an independent Palestine. Concluding that the Arab–Jewish divide was unbridgeable, Britain proposed a partition into two states and the removal of thousands of Arabs from the Jewish side. Both groups rejected the proposal. In 1939, Britain placed a limit on Jewish immigration and banned land transfers, but the Holocaust during World War II reinforced the Jewish desire for a homeland where they could govern themselves.

The Balfour Declaration Learn which questions were considered—and which were ignored—as Britain prepared to support the Zionist movement.

Politics and Modernization in Latin America

While Islamic societies grappled with colonialism and the encounter with the West, Latin America, with economies reliant on a few natural resource exports such as beef, copper, coffee, and sugar, became more vulnerable to global political and economic crises. Latin Americans paid a price for their openness to the

Latin American Resources (*http://www .oberlin.edu/faculty/ svolk/latinam.htm*). An excellent collection of resources and links on history, politics, and culture.

> "Economic downturns led to political instability, which paved the way for governments led by military dictators, known as caudillos."

world economy as foreign investment fell and foreign markets closed during the Great Depression in the 1930s, cutting the foreign trade of some countries by 90 percent. Economic downturns led to political instability, which paved the way for governments led by military dictators, known as caudillos.

A Continent of Dictators

During the Great Depression, dictators came to power all over the region (see Map 25.3). In 1930–1931, armed forces overthrew governments, among them elected ones, in a dozen Latin American nations, including large countries such as Peru, Argentina, and Brazil. Some of the new governments, such as those in Argentina and Brazil, were influenced by European fascism. Dictators often increased their governments' role in the economy, such as by beginning industries to provide products that were normally imported. They also used their power to amass huge fortunes for themselves and to repress dissent. In El Salvador, for example, President Maximiliano Hernandez Martinez massacred 30,000 protesting Indian peasants. Cubans suffered under brutal dictatorships for most of the era. In 1934, the United States encouraged a coup by Sgt. Fulgencio Batista (fool-HEN-see-oh bah-TEES-ta) (1901–1973), who dominated Cuba for the next twenty-five years as a right-wing dictator.

The challenges of the era also affected Chile, one of the most stable and open Latin American nations. Although the military had occasionally seized power for short periods, Chile had generally enjoyed elected democratic governments and highly competitive elections involving several parties. The dislocations of the Great Depression led to unity for the squabbling leftist and centrist parties, which formed the Popular Front and came to power in the 1939 elections. Their reformist government, supported by labor unions, sponsored industrialization.

A growing women's movement allied with the left also brought some change. Chilean feminists won some basic legal rights and benefits for mothers, but they could not get most of their social agenda, including abortion rights, approved, in part because of opposition by conservative Chilean women.

Interactive Map

![Globe icon] Map 25.3
South and Central America in 1930

By 1930, Latin America had achieved its present political configuration, except that Britain, France, and Holland still had colonies in the Guianas region of South America, and Britain controlled British Honduras (today's Belize) in Central America.

© Cengage Learning

Latin America and the Caribbean,
1909–1945

1909–1933	U.S. military force in Nicaragua
1930–1931	Military governments throughout Latin America
1930–1945	Estado Novo in Brazil
1934	Fulgencio Batista Cuban dictator
1934–1940	Presidency of Lazaro Cardenas in Mexico

Vargas and the Brazilian New State Movement

As elsewhere in Latin America, Brazil experienced political change that was often tinged with nationalism. In the 1920s middle-class reformers challenged domination by a corrupt ruling class that they felt did not listen to the common people or assert Brazil's national interests in the world. Their proposals for a more liberal society included official recognition of labor unions, a minimum wage, restraints in child labor, land reform, universal suffrage, and expansion of education to poor children. Eventually, the Great Depression reshaped Brazilian politics, prompting a civilian-military coup by Getulio Vargas (jay-TOO-lee-oh VAR-gus) (1883–1954) in 1930. A former soldier, lawyer, and government minister, Vargas launched the Estado Novo ("New State"), a fascist-influenced, modernizing dictatorship that ruled until 1945 and practiced torture and censorship to repress opponents. But the Estado Novo also sponsored modernizing reforms that made Vargas widely popular with the lower classes. Gradually, the dictator became more populist and nationalist. He was deposed by the army in 1945 after he had begun moving to the left, leaving behind acute tensions between right-wing and left-wing Brazilians.

Mexican Reforms Under Cardenas

As in Chile and Brazil, strongly progressive and nationalist ideas emerged in Mexico. After the turmoil of the decade-long Mexican Revolution (see Chapter 20), which ended only in 1920, Mexico badly needed funds for reconstruction but faced sharply reduced export earnings and a deepening economic slump. President Plutarcho Elias Calles (KAH-yays)

(r. 1924–1928) put the political system on a solid footing by creating a new party that brought together various factions, yet most Mexicans saw little improvement in their lives. In 1934, Mexicans launched a new era by electing Lázaro Cárdenas (car-DAYN-es) (r. 1934–1940), an army officer with socialist leanings, as president. Peasants had grown cynical about the promises by leaders during the Mexican Revolution to supply them with land. Cardenas fulfilled this promise by assigning land ownership to the *ejidos* (eh-HEE-dos), the traditional agricultural cooperatives, who now apportioned land to their members. As a result, some 800,000 people realized their dream, but economic turmoil caused the payments and services the government had promised to evaporate.

Cárdenas did introduce reforms that made him wildly popular with other Mexicans. He encouraged the formation of a large labor confederation that led to a higher standard of living and more dignity for urban workers. Cárdenas also nationalized the oil industry, spurring celebrations in Mexico and outraging U.S. leaders. Workers gained a role in managing both the oil industry and the railroads. The president supported women's rights, arguing that working women had the same right as men to participate in electoral struggles. Although he was popular among the working classes, wealthy Mexican landowners and merchants, as well as U.S. political and business leaders, hated Cárdenas. He was followed by more moderate leaders who reversed support for the ejidos, favoring instead individual farmers, and ignored women's rights (Mexican women could not vote until 1953). These leaders also cooperated with the United States on immigration issues. During World War II, Mexico and the United States signed an agreement to send more Mexican workers north to fill the job positions in industry, agriculture, and the service sector left vacant by drafted American men. The flow northward of poor Mexicans, legal and illegal, became a floodtide after the war.

Cultural Nationalism in Latin America and the Caribbean

Cultural nationalism influenced Latin American and Caribbean societies. A Brazilian literary trend known as Modernism sought to define a distinct national expression by exploring the country's rich cultural heritage. Rather than emulating European literary trends, modernist writers used forms and ideas reflecting Brazil's uniqueness. For instance, the poet,

Speech to the Nation In this excerpt from a radio address given in 1938, President Lázaro Cárdenas announces his decision to nationalize the Mexican oil industry.

novelist, and critic Mario de Andrade (1893–1945) mixed words from various regional dialects and Native American, African, and Portuguese folklore into his work. Brazilian musicians also incorporated folk music: the composer Heitor Villa-Lobos's music (vee-luh-LO-bose) (1890–1959) expressed the national character that was inspired by Afro-Brazilian and Indian religious rites and urban music. The popular music and dance known as *samba* became not only a world symbol of Brazilian society but also a way for the Afro-Brazilian lower classes to express themselves.

The progressive spirit of the times also spurred literary and artistic movements throughout Latin America. In Chile, writers combined radical politics with cultural renaissance. The work of Marxist-influenced Chilean poet Pablo Neruda (ne-ROO-duh) (1904–1973) bristled with anger over economic inequalities. Sometimes governments retaliated against dissident artists; Neruda wrote some of his greatest poetry while in hiding or exile. Mexico produced several great painters, including Diego Rivera (rih-VEER-a) (1885–1957), a Marxist who became one of the most famous artists in the Western Hemisphere. His huge, realistic murals depicted the common people, especially peasants and workers, struggling for dignity. His wife, Frida Kahlo (KAH-lo) (1907–1954), the daughter of a German Jewish immigrant, specialized in vivid, even shocking paintings that were created mostly from her own experience and often expressed the physical and psychological pain suffered by women.

A cultural renaissance also occurred in the Caribbean, where intellectuals sought to create an authentic West Indian identity. In part this involved overcoming negative attitudes toward acknowledging Africa, as the ancestral home of most West Indians. Afro-Caribbean intellectuals, such as the Trinidadian Marxist C. L. R. James (1901–1989), sought to rebuild Afro-Caribbean pride by celebrating African roots, which he argued were a major contributor to the distinctive West Indian culture. James was a well-traveled historian, prolific writer, and activist who was equally at home in the Caribbean, Europe, Africa, and North America. His ability to combine Afro-Caribbean nationalism with an internationalist perspective inspired intellectuals around the world.

Listen to a synopsis of Chapter 25.

Candido Portinari, *Coffee* Portinari, one of the finest Brazilian painters of the 1930s and 1940s, often portrayed urban and rural labor, reflecting his leftwing political views. He had grown up the son of Italian immigrants on a coffee plantation near Sao Paulo. This painting from 1935 shows plantation workers carrying heavy bags of coffee, much of which will be exported.

Museo Nacional Bellas Artes, Rio de Janeiro/Art Resource, NY

Societies • Networks • Transitions

Global Imbalances in the Modern World, 1750–1945

A world traveler in the nineteenth century could not help but notice the imbalances in wealth and power between the world's societies, imbalances that became even wider in the early twentieth century. The modern world was shaped in part by revolutions and innovations in western Europe and North America. In these societies, capitalism and industrialization fostered wealth and inspired new technologies, such as the steamships and railroads that conveyed travelers, resources, and products over great distances. But the new technologies also included deadly new weapons, such as repeating rifles and machine guns, that enabled the Western conquest of Asian and African societies, reshaping the world's political and economic configuration. Just as Spain and Portugal controlled Latin America until the early 1800s, a half-dozen Western nations ruled, or influenced the governments of, most Asian, African, and Caribbean peoples by 1914. Western domination of the global economy fostered investment but also facilitated a transfer of vast wealth to the West.

While several Western societies exercised disproportionate power in this era, other societies were not passive actors. Societies borrowed ideas, institutions, and technologies from each other, though redefining them to meet their own needs. Societies such as Siam (later Thailand), Persia (later Iran), Turkey, and, most spectacularly, Japan successfully resisted colonialism and, borrowing Western models, introduced some modernization. In fact, resistance to Western power was endemic in the global system, even in colonized societies such as Vietnam, Indonesia, India, and South Africa, where local peoples actively asserted their own interests. The movement of products, thought, and people, on a larger scale than ever before, transcended political boundaries, connecting distant societies. Europeans avidly imported Asian arts, Africans embraced Christianity, and peasants from India settled in the South Pacific and the West Indies. By the 1930s, people around the world, often using borrowed Western ideas such as nationalism and Marxism, were challenging Western political and economic power.

Imperialism, States, and the Global System

The world's governments changed greatly during the Modern Era, fostering new types of empires and states. A more integrated international order, dominated by a few Western nations and, eventually, also by Japan, was built on the foundation of the varied Western and Asian empires that had been the main power centers during the Early Modern Era. Societies worldwide grappled with the global political trends that affected people's well-being and livelihoods.

Global Empires

Powerful societies had formed empires since ancient times, but over the centuries, successive empires grew larger and more complex. In the mid-1700s, more than two-thirds of the world's people lived in one of several large, multiethnic empires whose economies were based largely on peasant agriculture. These empires stretched across the Eastern Hemisphere from Qing China and the Western colonies in Southeast Asia, such as Dutch Java and the Spanish Philippines, to the Ottoman, Russian, and Habsburg Empires. In the Americas, the huge Spanish Empire, Portuguese Brazil, and British North America all resembled the Eurasian empires in their multiethnic populations and agrarian base, although much of the agriculture was done by unfree labor. In addition to empires, there were strong states such as Tokugawa Japan, Siam, and the Ashante kingdom in West Africa. All empires and states depended on a command of military power, especially gunpowder weapons, and on world trade.

Many of the empires of the mid-1700s had crumbled by the early twentieth century. The Spanish, Portuguese, and British lost most of their territories in the Americas, and the Habsburg and Ottoman Empires were dismantled after World War I. In their place,

Queen Victoria as Seen by a Nigerian Carver
This wood effigy of the British monarch was made by a Yoruba artist in just-colonized Nigeria in the late nineteenth century.

Pitt Rivers Museum, Oxford University

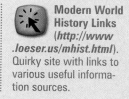
modern empires had emerged. Between 1870 and 1914, a huge portion of the globe, divided up into colonies or spheres of influence by the West, was incorporated into a Western-dominated world economic system. The influential British imperialist and author Rudyard Kipling summarized the rationale for exercising imperial power: "That they should take who have the power, And they should keep who can."[1]

Like empires throughout history, modern imperial states, whatever their democratic forms at home, punished dissent in their colonies. Sometimes protests, such as those led by Mohandas Gandhi in India, forced Western colonizers to modify their policies; more commonly, protest leaders, such as Gandhi, Harry Thuku in Kenya, and Sukarno in Indonesia, were jailed or exiled. Some observers recognized the failure of democratic countries to encourage democracy in their own colonies, as a nineteenth-century English wit charged about his nation's treatment of Ireland: "the moment the very name of Ireland is mentioned, the English seem to bid adieu to common feelings, common prudence and common sense, and to act with the barbarity of tyrants and the fatuity of idiots."[2]

Nationalism and Revolutions

Whether parts of empires or not, societies all over the world struggled to become nations with self-government and common identities. But Western peoples formed the most powerful nations. Many European nations were formidable forces because of their strong government structures and democratic practices that fostered debate; they also enjoyed economic dynamism, possessed advanced weapons, and engaged in fierce rivalries with each other. Across the Atlantic, most Latin American nations struggled to achieve prosperity and internal unity, but the United States matched European capabilities and shared similar imperial ambitions by the later 1800s. By contrast, few people in colonized areas shared any sense of common identity, let alone a national mission; colonial governments were unpopular and usually viewed by the colonized as illegitimate. By drawing up arbitrary colonial borders, often without regard to ethnic connections or economic networks, colonies like Nigeria, Indonesia, and the Congo lacked any national cohesion. The ethnic diversity of most colonies inhibited the formation of nationalist movements.

Still, despite the barriers, nationalism spread, often encouraged by travel, exile, or education. The Venezuelan Símon Bolívar, the Filipino Jose Rizal (rih-ZALL) (1861–1896), and the Vietnamese Ho Chi Minh (1890–1969), all disenchanted with colonial restrictions, embraced a nationalist agenda while living in Europe. Yan Fu, a Chinese student living in England in the 1870s, recalled spending "whole days and nights discussing differences and similarities in Chinese and Western thought and political institutions."[3] Back in China, Yan Fu translated the work of liberal British thinkers and used it to spread nationalism and other Western ideas in China. But nationalists seeking to confront Western power did not all look to the West for inspiration. By 1900, rapidly modernizing Japan was a model nation for many Asians.

But nationalism was not always an imported sentiment. Many Asians had a sense of identity similar to nationalism long before the nineteenth century. People in Korea, Japan, and Vietnam, for example, had long enjoyed some national feeling based on shared religion, a common language, bureaucratic government, and the perception of one or more common enemies. African kingdoms such as Ashante (ah-SHAN-tee), Oyo (OH-yo), and Buganda (boo-GONE-da) enjoyed some attributes of nationhood.

Reflecting such national feeling, in 1898, Hawaii's last monarch, Queen Liliuokalani (luh-lee-uh-oh-kuh-LAH-nee), pleaded with the United States not to colonize the islands, since her people's "form of government is as dear to them as yours is precious to you. Quite as warmly as you love your country, so they love theirs."[4] U.S. leaders ignored her pleas and annexed Hawaii. To protect their power, colonizers labored hard to crush local traditions and to counter nationalism through the use of divide-and-rule strategies, such as the British encouragement of the Hindu–Muslim divide in India. Formerly well-defined states lost their traditional cohesion as they now became parts of empires.

Some societies needed major rebellions and revolutions to reject discredited orders and create new nations. The American and French Revolutions of the later 1700s began an Age of Revolution and inspired people elsewhere to take up arms against unjust or outdated governments. In the U.S. case, disgruntled colonists overthrew British rule and became known around the world as exponents of political freedom. During the mid-nineteenth century, the Taiping (TIE-ping) Rebellion against China's Qing dynasty and the Indian Rebellion against the British East India Company provided fierce challenges to established governments in the world's two most populous societies before ultimately failing. Early in the twentieth century, other revolutions overturned old governments and built nations in Mexico, Turkey, and China; the Chinese revolution ended 2,000 years of imperial control and established the foundation for a modern republic. The Russian Revolution of 1917 installed the world's first communist government, inspiring communist movements and revolutionary nationalists around the world.

The aftermath of World War I brought new revolutionary upheavals and ideologies. Old states collapsed in eastern Europe, fascism spread in Germany and Japan in the economic shambles caused by the Great Depression, and Spain erupted in civil war. In 1914, Marxism—the revolutionary socialist vision developed by Karl Marx (1818–1883)—had relatively little influence outside of Germany and Russia, but by 1945, the ideology had mass support in many places, including China, Korea, Indonesia, and Vietnam. Karl Marx had supplied the critique of class struggle and capitalism and offered Communism as a better way.

Now the Russian leader, Vladimir Lenin (1870–1924), fomented a revolution in 1917, and the Chinese communist leader Mao Zedong (maow dzuh-dong) (1893–1976) contributed a vision of a new, unselfish socialist society, writing that "the people are the sea, we [communists] are the fish, so long as we can swim in that sea, we will survive."[5] By combining communism with nationalism, the Vietnamese revolutionary Ho Chi Minh provided a workable model to overthrow colonialism. The ideas of Lenin, Mao, and Ho made Marxism a major vehicle for change after World War II.

Change in the Global System

During the Modern Era, the global system expanded and changed as Western political and military influence increased. Networks of trade and communication linking distant societies grew, but Western nations benefited more from their exchanges. Aided by this power, Western culture dominated local traditions, especially in Western colonies. For example, children in the U.S.-ruled Philippines, a tropical and predominantly Catholic land, learned English from books showing American youngsters throwing snowballs, playing baseball, and attending Protestant church services. In some cases, this deliberate Westernization reshaped beliefs and ways of life, as occurred among the Filipinos and the Igbos of southern Nigeria. However, Western cultural influence was weak in other colonized societies, especially Muslim ones such as Egypt or the Hausa of northern Nigeria.

There were winners and losers in the new global system. In 1750, Western overseas expansion, including military conquests, had already reshaped the Americas and some regions of Africa and southern Asia. Chinese, Indians, and western Europeans were the richest peoples at this time: collectively they accounted for 70 percent of all the world's economic activity and 80 percent of its manufacturing. China remained the greatest engine of the world economy. Britain was the rising European power, but it faced challenges from France, Russia, Spain, and the Ottoman Empire. The more economically developed districts and the major cities within the two wealthiest countries, Britain and China, apparently enjoyed similar living standards, such as abundant food and long life spans, until at least 1800.

By 1914, however, after a century and a half of Western industrialization, imperial expansion, and colonization, the global system had become more divided than ever before into rich and poor societies. India was now among the poorer countries, and China had succumbed to Western military and economic influence, falling well behind the West. Meanwhile, a few Western nation-states—especially Great Britain, the United States, Germany, and France—had grown rich and influential. Because of their unparalleled military power, all four of these nations ruled colonial empires, from which they extracted valuable resources; played a leading role in world trade; and spread their cultures and ideas. Also among the richest nations, but having less international power, were a few other western European countries, including the Netherlands, Belgium, and Switzerland.

A middle category of countries—Canada, Japan, Russia, Italy, Portugal, and Spain—had a weaker economic base and less military power than those of the richest nations, but they still enjoyed economic and political autonomy. A third category of countries were those that were economically poor and militarily weak, either ruled directly as Western colonies, such as India, Indonesia, Nigeria, or Jamaica, or under strong political and economic influence as neocolonies, such as China, Thailand, and Iran. Economically, Latin American countries, relative to the rich North American and western European nations, were also poor.

Living conditions and governments in the rich countries differed dramatically in 1914 from those in the poor societies. Capitalism fostered growth in Europe and North America, although it took many decades for the benefits to reach the common people. The rich countries, such as Britain and the United States, were highly industrialized and enjoyed well-diversified economies and large middle classes. Many of their people lived in cities and, owing to mass education systems, became literate. These countries also boasted efficient, well-financed, constitutional governments. Rich countries were typically democratic and fostered public discourse of diverse political opinions, such as socialism and feminism. These patterns were also common in the less powerful Western nations and in Japan.

By contrast, the poor societies, especially Western colonies in Asia and Africa, where many people worked the lands owned by foreign landlords or planters, were not industrialized and people earned meager wages. Economic growth was often determined by foreign investment and markets rather than by local needs. For example, rather than growing food for the local community, farmers in Honduras, in Central America, grew bananas for the U.S. market while farmers in French-ruled Senegal, in West Africa, raised peanuts for export. Politically, a small upper class—African chiefs, Indian princes, Javanese aristocrats—played a political role by cooperating with Western rulers. Only a small minority of people had access to formal education, economic opportunity, and political decision making.

Their general poverty and lack of economic and political options did not mean that people in poor societies were always miserable. Celebrating their survival skills in the early 1900s, the Indian writer and thinker

Rabindranath Tagore (rah-BIN-dra-NATH TUH-gore) (1861–1941) found both triumphs and tragedies in Indian peasant life, which "with its everyday contentment and misery, has always been there in the peasants' fields and village festivals, manifesting their very simple and abiding humanity across all of history—sometimes under Mughal rule, sometimes under British rule."[6]

In the colonies, heavy Western cultural influence, such as the policies the French called their "civilizing mission" in Vietnam and West Africa—by which they tried to impose French ways on people they regarded as culturally inferior—was combined with psychological trauma as once-proud peoples succumbed to foreign rule and its racist restrictions. An anti-imperialist African organization complained in 1927 that colonialism had abruptly cut short "the development of the African people. These nations were later declared pagan and savage, an inferior race."[7] Although Western Christian missionaries often found eager converts, nationalists frequently accused them of undermining traditional beliefs. Western domination, however, did not preclude cultural and scientific achievements by colonized people. For example, although their country was a British colony, various Indian mathematicians and scientists won international renown, including Nobel Prize–winning physicist Sir Chandrasekhara Raman (CHAHN-dra-SEE-ker-ah RAH-man) (1888–1970) of Calcutta.

Between 1914 and 1945, the global system underwent further changes. Conflicts became world wars, fought on a greater scale than ever before and on battlefields thousands of miles apart. The United States became the world's richest, most powerful nation. Because of its defeat in World War I, Germany temporarily lost wealth and power. Germany, Italy, and Japan—all middle-ranking nations by the 1930s—challenged the rich nations—Britain, France, and the United States—during World War II. Several Latin American nations and Turkey enjoyed enough economic growth and stability of government to move into the middle-ranking category by the 1940s. Yet most of the societies of Asia, Africa, Latin America, and the Caribbean remained poor colonies or neocolonies.

The World Economy

Even before the Western overseas expansion that occurred between 1500 and 1914, trade had taken place over vast distances. Chinese, Indian, Arab, and Armenian merchants had long dominated the vigorous Asian trade, and for centuries Chinese silks and porcelains and Southeast Asian and Indian spices had reached Europe, the Middle East, and parts of sub-Saharan Africa. European explorers wished to locate the source of these riches, and after 1500, the Portuguese, Dutch, and British played key roles in this trade, beginning the rise of the world economy. European influence on the world economy increased in the 1700s and 1800s when Western traders, supported by their governments, sought new natural resources and

markets in the tropical world, thereby creating a truly global economic exchange. By 1914, the entire world was enmeshed in a vast economic exchange. People often produced resources or manufactured goods—Middle Eastern oil, Indonesian coffee, British textiles—for markets thousands of miles away. Europe's Industrial Revolution, which provided manufactured goods to trade for resources, dramatically reshaped the Western economies in the 1800s but only slowly spread to other regions.

The Inequality of Global Economic Exchange

Economic exchange between societies within the world economy did not proceed on an even playing field. As had been the case for empires throughout history—Assyrian, Roman, Chinese, Inca, Spanish, Dutch—imperialism and colonialism remained the means for transferring wealth to the imperial nations, which used that wealth to finance their own development. The imperial powers, seeking to enhance the value of their colonial economies, also used their control of world trade to shift cash crops like coffee that were indigenous to one part of the world to another.

Gearing economic growth chiefly to the needs of the imperial powers impeded economic development that might have benefited everyone. Many colonies developed economies that produced and exported only one or two primary resources, such as rice and rubber from French Vietnam or sugar from Spanish Cuba. Most of these resource exports were transformed into consumer goods, such as rubber tires and chocolate candies, and sold in stores in Western nations, to the profit of their merchants. For instance, chocolate, whose use for over two millennia was confined to elites in Mexico, gained an eager market among all classes throughout the Western world by the nineteenth century. Meanwhile, the Western manufactured goods exchanged for these resources, especially textiles, found markets in Africa, Asia, and Latin America. Although much of this exchange was largely exploitative, some colonized men and women managed to capitalize on it. For example, Omu Okwei (OH-moo AWK-way) (1872–1943), an Igbo, made a fortune trading palm oil for European imported goods, which she distributed widely in Nigeria through a vast network of women traders.

Societies specializing in producing one or two natural resources were especially vulnerable to a changing world economy. To take one case, British Malaya was a major rubber exporter, but most of its rubber plantations were British-owned, and Malayans had little influence over the world price of rubber, which was determined largely by Western consumers and corporations. The rise and fall of rubber prices affected not only the rubber tappers and their families but also the shops, often owned by Chinese immigrants, who sold them goods. Thus the livelihoods of people all over the world increasingly became subject to chronic fluctuations in the world markets.

The world economy widened the wealth gap between societies. In 1500, the differences in per capita income and living standards between people in the richer regions—China, Japan, Southeast Asia, India, Ottoman Turkey, and western Europe—had probably been minor. And these peoples were roughly only two to three times better off materially than the farmers and city folk of the world's poorest farming societies. By 1750, however, while China, western Europe, and British North America enjoyed similar levels of economic production, the wealth gap between them and others was increasing. By 1900, the wealth gap between the richest and poorest societies had grown to about 10 to 1. This trend accelerated throughout the twentieth century, in part because the wealth produced in Western colonies seldom contributed to local development.

Unequal economic exchange also fostered conflict. Wars erupted as one country threatened another's access to markets and resources. For example, British free-trade policies caused the Opium War with China in the mid-1800s. The Qing government worked to end both the legal and illegal opium trade, but, as the leading opium supplier, Britain needed to protect the opium exports to China from British India, and its defeat of China hastened Chinese decline. In addition, World War I was at least partly caused by the bitter imperial competition among European nations.

The Spread of Industrialization

The Industrial Revolution, which began in Britain in the late 1700s, was not just a Western development. China and India had once been the world's leading manufacturing countries, and knowledge of Chinese mechanical devices probably stimulated several British inventions. Between 1750 and 1850, however, Britain took the lead in modern industrialization, and by the mid-1800s, it produced about half of the world's manufactured goods, while China and India fell behind. Various other European nations, the United States, and Japan industrialized in the later 1800s. Only these few nations increased their resources and weapons as a result of industrialization, and hence only a few became world powers. Some of the profits from colonialism and other overseas activities stimulated European industrialization. For instance, the Dutch based some of their industrial and transportation growth on profits earned from selling coffee and sugar grown by peasants in their Indonesian colony. But even in Europe, agriculture and other nonindustrial activities, such as trade, remained economically important. By 1881, only 44 percent of the British, 36 percent of the German, and 20 percent of the American labor force were employed in industrial or industry-related occupations.

Industrialization gradually spread beyond Europe and North America, but it was highly uneven in its impact and pace. Western policies commonly discouraged colonists from maintaining or opening industries that might compete with Western manufacturers. For instance, India had been the world's greatest textile manufacturer for centuries, but British colonization gradually diminished the indus-

try through tax and tariff policies, opening the way for British-made textiles to dominate the Indian market. The British saw India not only as a market for their goods but also as a source of cash crops. Hence, in 1840, a British official boasted that his nation had "succeeded in converting India from a manufacturing country into a country exporting raw materials."[8] The once-flourishing Indian textile center of Calcutta lost two-thirds of its population between 1750 and 1850 as its manufacturing declined.

Several nations sought to foster development by setting up manufacturing operations. China, Persia, Egypt, the Ottoman Empire, and Mexico introduced textile industries in the nineteenth century. However, the British used tariffs, or stiff duties on imports to Britain, to stifle many of these industries, thereby opening doors for the export of British fabrics and clothing to these countries. Between 1900 and 1945, there was a resurgence of efforts at industrialization in various nations—China, Argentina, Brazil, and Australia—but agriculture remained the economic foundation for most of their population.

Before 1880, few industrial cities had emerged outside of northwestern Europe and North America, but, in a global economy, other urban places had grown dependent on the Industrial Revolution for their livelihood. Shanghai thrived as the commercial gateway to central China's interior; Singapore served as the economic hub for much of Southeast Asia; and Alexandria was the import-export center for Egypt and the upper Nile basin.

Frontiers and Migrations

The rise of a modern world economy, and its constant quest for resources, markets, and labor, accelerated migration. Modern transportation networks and rapid population growth propelled the movement of peoples. Between 1800 and 1900, the world population grew from 900 million to 1,500 million, with two-thirds of these people living in Asia. While some people escaped poverty and overcrowding by moving into frontier regions, many others, more than 100 million between 1830 and 1914, left for distant lands. Some, such as enslaved Africans who were transported to the Americas, were taken from their homes unwillingly. In contrast, millions of Europeans and Asians sought, and often found, better opportunities in other countries.

Settling Frontiers

From ancient times, people left overcrowded lands to move into sparsely settled frontiers, such as Bantu-speaking Africans, who had taken their ironworking and farming technologies from West Africa into the sparsely populated lands of central, eastern, and southern Africa long ago. Similar movements continued in modern times. White Americans moved westward across the North American continent, subduing and killing off the Native American peoples and seizing their land. In Australia, New

Zealand, and South Africa, European colonists also disrupted local peoples. In South America, Brazilians moved from the Atlantic coast westward into the rain forests and grasslands, setting up farms after pushing out local Indians.

Remote from central government controls and traditional social structures, the frontier fostered innovations. Frontier social conditions were often more flexible and offered new opportunities. Cultures met and mixed, and people of different groups intermarried. Cultural blending produced hybrid social groups such as the Russian Cossacks, western American cowboys, and Argentine gauchos. The cowboys and gauchos, who chiefly herded cattle for ranchers, combined European and self-sufficient Native American customs. Eventually, however, the frontier pioneers were absorbed into formal states.

African and European Population Movements

The largest population movements of the era involved the involuntary transport of African slaves across the Atlantic to the Americas and the chiefly voluntary migration of European emigrants to the Americas, southern Africa, Australia, and New Zealand. The Africans, shipped in chains and filth, typically faced brutal lives shortened by harsh conditions. In contrast, most of the Europeans chose to leave their homelands to seek a better life, and often succeeded.

The trans-Atlantic slave trade reached its height between 1760 and 1800. During these years, more than 70,000 people per year were herded onto crowded slave ships and shipped from Africa. The great majority of Africans were landed in Brazil and the Caribbean islands, where people of African ancestry today account for a large part of the population. The gradual abolition of slavery in the Americas eventually ended the trans-Atlantic trade, but the longtime slave trade from East and Central Africa to the Middle East continued until the end of the nineteenth century. By the early 1900s, slavery had declined significantly or been abolished in Africa, the Middle East, and Southeast Asia, largely as a result of the efforts of humanitarian organizations, churches, and both Western and local abolitionists.

During the Modern Era, the European migration across oceans to the Americas and the South Pacific

 Interactive Map

dwarfed other population movements (see map). Unlike the African slaves, many European emigrants were escaping poverty or political repression and expected to improve their lives abroad. While the ships carrying the emigrants were often crowded and unhealthy, Europeans did not arrive in chains, with no possibility of freedom. The emigrants represented Europe's ethnic diversity but came largely from the British Isles, Germany, Italy, Spain, Poland, and Russia. Between 1500 and 1940, some 68 million people left Europe, creating new societies in the Americas, Australia, New Zealand, and southern Africa. The result of this large population movement was a Europeanization of societies, as European cultures were implanted far from their ancestral homes. The tendency to look toward Europe for inspiration was especially strong in Argentina, Chile, Canada, Australia, and New Zealand. In these societies, many immigrants and their descendants tended to maintain their native languages, churches, and social customs and to identify with their homelands. As a result, the numerous Italians in Argentina's capital, Buenos Aires, often spoke Italian, while Anglo-Argentines sent their children to private English-medium schools.

Modern World History Resources (*http://www.historesearch.com/modworld.html*). Has links to sites on many topics and regions.

Immigrants contributed much to their new lands. For example, in the United States, the Scottish-born Andrew Carnegie (1835–1919) helped build the iron and steel industry and with his philanthropy sponsored libraries. Others found different ways to improve their new societies, such as Lithuanian-born left-wing activist Emma Goldman (1869–1940), who emigrated to the United States in 1885. She was later arrested and deported for being an advocate for slum-dwellers and for opposing U.S. entry into World War I.

Asian Migrations

During this era, peoples from eastern and southern Asia also emigrated in large numbers, usually by ship to distant shores. They went in response to the demand among Western colonies and American nations for a labor force for the mines and plantations that supplied their wealth. As a result, Chinese mined tin in Southeast Asia and gold in California and Australia, while Indians worked on rubber plantations in British Malaya and sugar plantations in South Africa. Immigrants often died from overwork or ill health and, as happened with Chinese in California, sometimes suffered from violent discrimination. Yet, many Asians prevailed to raise families in their new nations. Today approximately 40 to 45 million Asians live outside of their ancestral homelands. Chinese and Indians constituted the great majority of Asian migrants, and their descendants became a vital presence in the world economy as merchants, miners, and plantation workers. Today the majority of Chinese in Southeast Asia, the South Pacific and Indian Ocean islands, the Caribbean, and Latin America are engaged in commerce.

Pushed by poverty, overpopulation, or war, people also emigrated from Northeast and Southeast Asia, forming cohesive communities in new lands. Numerous Japanese and Koreans left their homelands between 1850 and 1940. Some settled in Hawaii to work on pineapple plantations or in the canning industry. Many Japanese migrated to the Pacific Coast of the United States and Canada, some taking up farming. When the United States and Canada restricted Japanese immigration in the early 1900s, the Japanese emigrant flow turned to

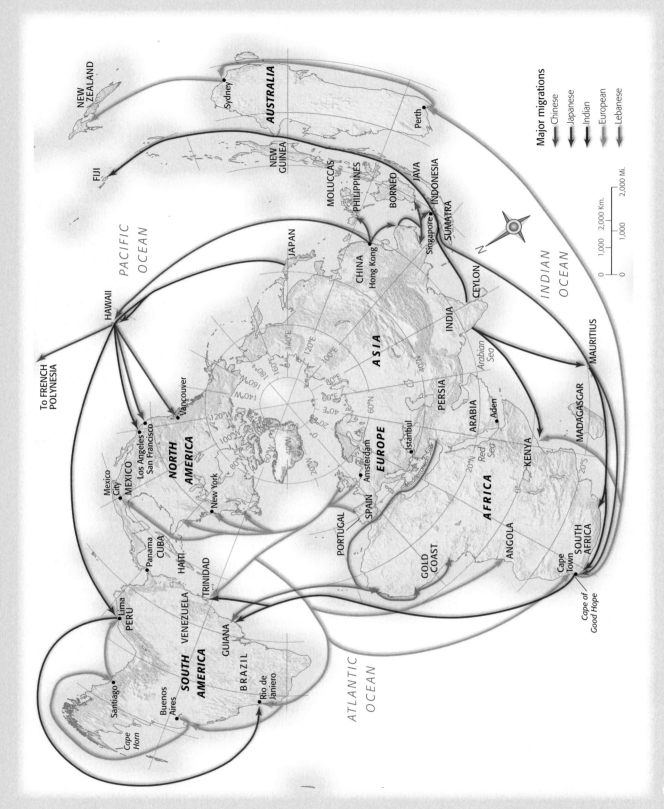

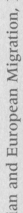

© Cengage Learning

Major migrations

Chinese
Japanese
Indian
European
Lebanese

Asian and European Migration, 1750–1940

During this era, millions of Europeans emigrated to the Americas, South Africa, Australia, and New Zealand. Millions of Asians, especially Chinese and Indians, left their homes to work or settle in Southeast Asia, Africa, the Pacific islands, and the Americas.

Singapore's Chinatown By the early 1900s, Singapore, a major Southeast Asian port and commercial crossroads, was predominantly Chinese in population. The bustling streets were lined by shops, workers' quarters, theaters, and brothels.

Latin America, especially Peru and Brazil. Between 1875 and 1940, Indonesians, mostly Javanese, were recruited to work on plantations in Malaya and British North Borneo but also in Dutch Guiana (today's Suriname), in South America, and on the French-ruled South Pacific island of New Caledonia. Some 50,000 Javanese today live in Suriname. After the United States colonized the Philippines, Filipinos began migrating to Hawaii and the U.S. Pacific coast as factory workers or farm laborers. Today 1.5 million Filipinos live in the United States.

The Spread of Technology and Mass Culture

The modern global system owed much to innovations in technology. Improved methods of communication and transportation allowed people, ideas, and products to travel farther and faster than ever before, enhancing networks of power and exchange. More effective military technologies enabled a few societies to gain control of others and combat rival powers. Finally, the increasing connections around the world enabled ideas and products to spread across borders.

Communication and Transportation

For much of history, communication over long distances had been slow, depending largely on beasts of burden carrying riders or pulling wagons, and later on sailing ships. In 500 B.C.E., a message carried by successive riders on horses could travel the 1,800-mile length of the Persian Empire in nine days. Two millennia later, in the 1600s, it took Dutch ships some nine months to sail from Amsterdam to Dutch-ruled Java to deliver news and orders. Then in the nineteenth century, thanks to the Industrial Revolution, communications changed dramatically. In 1844, the first telegraph messages were exchanged between Washington and Baltimore. By 1870, the cables had reached from Britain to India. The invention of the telephone in 1876 and radio in 1895 further increased the potential for communications. As the possibilities and advantages of broadcasting over great distances became apparent, the New Zealand premier proposed in 1911 that Britain build an empirewide radio network because of "the great importance of radio for social, commercial, and defensive purposes."[9] By the 1920s, radio transmissions had become commonplace in industrial nations, and British broadcasts could reach Canada, South Africa, India, and Australia.

Some technologies conveyed people and commodities as well as messages, transforming peoples' lives around the world. Railroads were built all over the world to carry goods and passengers, and as trains reached stations, telegraph messages smoothed their journeys by passing on traffic and weather information. By 1869, railroads connected the Pacific and Atlantic coasts of North America, and by 1903, anyone determined to make the long journey could ride the 9,000 miles between Paris and Siberia's Pacific coast. While railroads extended land networks, shipping lines that employed steamships linked the world. The opening of the 105-mile-long Suez Canal in 1869 and the 51-mile-long Panama Canal in 1914, both of which cost the lives of thousands of workers during their construction, greatly reduced travel times for many sea journeys and also made it easier and cheaper to ship resources from Asia and Latin America to Europe and North America. Now it only took a few weeks to sail from China or Singapore to New York or London.

In the early 1900s, motor cars and buses continued the revolution in land transportation begun by railroads, allowing people to more easily commute to city jobs and downtown stores or to travel between cities. After World War I, thousands of middle-class Europeans and North Americans owned their own cars, and in the 1930s, the first commercial air flights began, making long-distance journeys even faster. Transportation depended increasingly on fossil fuels, first coal and then oil. The use of vehicles fueled by oil increased the strategic importance of oil-rich regions, such as the Middle East, Indonesia, Mexico, and the Gulf Coast of the United States.

Technologies of Warfare

New technologies included those devoted to warfare that made it easier to kill more people and from a greater distance. Most of these weapons remained largely a monopoly of Western nations and Japan during this era, and thus contributed to the imbalances in global power. White adventurers and settlers used the rifle invented by the American Philo Remington (1816–1889), which was effective at 1,500 yards, to defeat, and seize the lands of, the Native Americans and the Australian Aborigines. Effective rifles also proved devastating in Africa against warriors armed only with spears and arrows. The British-born American explorer Henry Morton Stanley boasted of his use of repeating rifles and terrorism to destroy a hostile Congo village that had greeted him with spears and arrows: "I skirmish in their streets, drive them pell-mell into the woods beyond; with frantic haste I fire the huts, and end the scene by towing their canoes into midstream and setting them adrift."[10]

Military weaponry quickly improved, including more powerful repeating guns. In 1861, an American doctor, Richard Gatling (1818–1903), invented what quickly came to be known as the Gatling gun, which could fire up to three thousand rounds of ammunition per minute. The first totally automatic machine gun, spitting out eleven bullets per second, was invented in 1884 by Hiram Maxim (1840–1916), an American working in Britain, and gave the British an unparalleled military advantage. As a result of such innovations, during World War I the Allied and Central powers inflicted terrible casualties on each other. The Western nations had also by this time developed the first armored tanks and increasingly relied on battleships at sea. Air power became central to combat in the Spanish Civil War and World War II. The methods of warfare were now more indiscriminate in their targets and lethal than ever before in history. In 1945, the United States used the most deadly weapon in history, the atomic bomb, to force Japanese surrender and end World War II.

The Spread of Mass Cultures

The revolution in communications and transportation technologies contributed to the creation and spread of mass cultures, popular entertainments appealing to a large audience that often crossed class divisions and national borders. People were increasingly exposed to cultural products and activities that were common in other regions of their countries or imported from abroad. The emerging mass media, such as newspapers and radio, were centered in rapidly growing cities like New York, Paris, Istanbul, Buenos Aries, and Tokyo. These media disseminated mass culture, reporting on film stars and sports events or playing popular music. As literacy rates rose, the print media gained particular influence. India alone supported six hundred different newspapers in several dozen languages in 1900. Popular books competed with classic works of philosophy and religion for the hearts and minds of readers.

By spreading cultural influences into other societies, mass communications and increased travel sometimes fostered Westernization. Orchestras playing Western classical music appeared in various Asian societies, including India, China, and Japan, by the early 1900s. Films and popular music from the United States had an even larger international audience. American film stars such as Charlie Chaplin, born in Britain, became known throughout the world, and U.S.-born jazz musicians often made a living playing the nightclubs of Europe and Asia, where they inspired local musicians to take up jazz. Many societies adopted and excelled in Western sports. For example, Indians became skilled in British cricket; India's Prince Ranjitsinhji (RAHN-jeet-SING-jee) (1872–1933) became one of the world's best players. European football, also known as soccer, became an international sport that was played all over the world.

Influences from non-Western cultures also spread widely, contributing to creative cultural mixing. In the eighteenth and nineteenth centuries, growing Western interest in Chinese painting, Japanese prints, Indonesian gamelan music, and African woodcarvings influenced Western arts. Later, in the 1930s, Indian films and Indian popular music became popular in Southeast Asia and the Middle East, and Cuban music, a mix of African and Western traditions, developed a large following in West and Central Africa, where it blended with local styles. People found ways to combine imported ideas, whatever their source, with their own traditions. For instance, in his lyrical suite, *Bachianas Brasileiras*, of 1930, the Brazilian composer Heitor Villa-Lobos (HAY-tore VEE-ya LOW-bos) (1887–1959) adapted the Baroque influences of German composer Johann Sebastian Bach (1685–1750) to Brazilian folk and popular music.

The reach of organizations and social movements expanded, as did awareness of the world. Some organizations developed a global focus. For example, the Red Cross, a Christian organization formed in nineteenth-century Switzerland to alleviate human suffering by helping war victims, eventually became an international movement devoted to humanitarian aid around the globe (in the Islamic world it became the Red Crescent). Social movements also crossed borders. For instance, women in China, Japan, Indonesia, Egypt, and Chile, inspired in part by feminist movements in Europe and North America, sought to adapt the notions of women's rights and education to their own societies. The winning of women's suffrage resulted from the efforts of women worldwide. In the United States, Susan B. Anthony (1820–1906) cofounded the key national and international organizations working for women's suffrage, while across the Pacific in 1924, Ichikawa Fusae (ITCH-ee-KAH-wa foo-SIGH) (1893–1918) formed the major women's suffrage group in Japan, which won the right to vote in 1945.

Global crises now became more widely known, and people followed world events in newspapers and radio newscasts. An avid news follower, the Trinidad calypso singer who humorously called himself Atilla the Hun, appraised the devastation in the world of the later 1930s:

> All we can hear is of unrest, riots, revolutions; There is war in Spain and China. Man using all his skill and ingenuity making weapons to destroy humanity. In the [Italian invasion of Ethiopia] it is said, over six hundred thousand maimed and dead. The grim reaper has taken a gigantic toll. Why all the bloodshed and devastation, Decimating the earth's population? Why can't this warfare cease? All that the tortured world needs is peace.[11]

Soon after Atilla's plea, World War II raised the level of violence even further, providing a fitting end to a turbulent, violent era during which the world's people had become more closely linked into a common global system.

 Test your understanding of the material covered in Part V.

Suggested Reading

Bayly, C. A. *The Birth of the Modern World, 1780–1914*. Malden, MA: Blackwell, 2004. A brilliant, detailed study.

Cohen, Robin. *Global Diasporas: An Introduction*. Seattle: University of Washington Press, 1997. A brief, valuable survey.

Cook, Scott B. *Colonial Encounters in the Age of High Imperialism*. New York: Longman, 1996. Examines Western imperialism.

Curtin, Philip D. *The World and the West: The European Challenge and the Overseas Response in the Age of Empire*. New York: Cambridge University Press, 2000. An interesting study of reactions to European imperialism.

Hobsbawm, Eric. *The Age of Extremes: A History of the World, 1914–1991*. New York: Pantheon, 1994. A masterful overview, especially strong on social and cultural history.

Hoerder, Dirk. *Cultures in Contact: World Migrations in the Second Millennium*. Durham, NC: Duke University Press, 2003. A comprehensive, detailed summary of migrations and diasporas.

Marks, Robert B. *The Origins of the Modern World: A Global and Ecological Narrative*. Lanham, MD: Rowman and Littlefield, 2002. A concise, readable examination of some major themes.

Neiberg, Michael S. *Warfare in World History*. New York: Routledge, 2001. Good coverage of this era.

Ponting, Clive. *The Twentieth Century: A World History*. New York: Henry Holt and Company, 1998. Thematic study.

Stavrianos, Leften S. *Global Rift: The Third World Comes of Age*. New York: William Morrow, 1971. A provocative, innovative study.

Wesseling, H. L. *The European Colonial Empires, 1815–1919*. Harlow, United Kingdom: Pearson, 2004. A useful overview of the entire colonial enterprise by a Dutch scholar.

Wolf, Eric R. *Europe and the People Without History*. Berkeley: University of California Press, 1982. A thought-provoking analysis of the Western impact on the wider world from 1400 to 1914.

PART VI

Global Systems:

Interdependence and Conflict in the Contemporary World, Since 1945

NORTH AND CENTRAL AMERICA
The United States became the world's richest nation and greatest political, economic, and military power. It led the Western alliance against the Soviet Union, fighting major wars in Korea and Vietnam and intervening in other nations. After 1990 the United States had no major rival but confronted international terrorism, which prompted it to send military forces into Afghanistan and Iraq. Mexico's economic growth lagged, fostering emigration to the United States, while the Cuban Revolution brought communists to power, provoking U.S. hostility.

ARCTIC OCEAN

CANADA

NORTH AMERICA

UNITED STATES

Mississippi R.

MEXICO

CUBA

ATLANTIC OCEAN

VENEZUELA

PACIFIC OCEAN

Amazon

BRAZIL

SOUTH AMERICA

ANDES

CHILE

ARGENTINA

SOUTH AMERICA
The South American nations, often troubled by tensions between the political left and right, struggled to achieve political stability and economic growth. Some nations, such as Brazil, Argentina, and Chile, alternated between democratic, reformist regimes and brutal military dictatorships. U.S. intervention helped overthrow several leftist governments. After 1990 Argentina faced economic collapse; Brazil and Chile, mixing capitalism and socialism, enjoyed growth; and Venezuela turned to the left.

© Cengage Learning

EUROPE
Although western Europe recovered quickly from World War II, the imperial Western states were unable to maintain control of their colonies. The western European nations forged stable welfare states, providing a social safety net, and moved toward close cooperation and economic unity among themselves. The Soviet Union became a global superpower, controlling eastern Europe, but at the end of the 1980s it and its communist satellites collapsed. Germany, divided after World War II, was reunified, and Russia sought a new role in the world.

WESTERN ASIA
Nationalists gained control of the western Asian nations but faced new challenges. Israel, a new Jewish state in Palestine, won wars against Arab neighbors, and Arab-Israeli hostilities have remained a source of tension. Some nations, such as Turkey, pursued modernization. An Islamic revolution reshaped oil-rich Iran, which fought oil-rich Iraq in the 1980s. Saudi Arabia and several Persian Gulf states flourished from oil wealth. After 2001 U.S.-led forces invaded and occupied Afghanistan and Iraq but, while removing despotic governments, struggled to restore stability.

EASTERN ASIA
Coming to power through revolution in 1949, communists transformed China, creating a socialist society and fighting the United States during the Korean War. After 1978 new communist leaders mixed free markets with socialism and fostered modernization, turning China into an economic powerhouse. Japan recovered rapidly from World War II, embracing democracy and becoming an economic giant. Borrowing Japanese models, South Korea and Taiwan industrialized. North Korea remained a repressive communist state.

AFRICA
As Arab and African nationalism grew stronger, colonies became independent nations, sometimes, as in Algeria and Angola, through revolution. In North Africa, Egypt promoted Arab nationalism and became a regional power but faced economic problems. Most of the new sub-Saharan African nations, which were artificial creations of colonialism, struggled to maintain political stability and foster economic development, but South Africans finally achieved black majority rule.

SOUTHERN ASIA AND OCEANIA
Britain granted independence to predominantly Hindu India but also to largely Muslim Pakistan, which eventually split when Bangladesh seceded. India enjoyed democracy and economic progress, but Pakistan and Bangladesh often fell under military rule. In Southeast Asia, the U.S. and British colonies gained independence peacefully while Indonesians triumphed through revolution. Vietnamese communists first defeated the French and then the United States. Malaysia, Singapore, and Thailand developed economically. Australia and New Zealand established closer links to Asia, and most of the Pacific islands gained independence from Western colonialism.

The Remaking of the Global System,

Since 1945

Learning Outcomes

After reading this chapter, you should be able to answer the following questions:

LO¹ How did decolonization change the global system?

LO² What roles did the Cold War and superpower rivalry play in world politics?

LO³ What were some of the main consequences of a globalizing world economy?

LO⁴ How did growing networks linking societies influence social, political, and economic life?

AP Images/Rajesh Nirgude

66One heart, one destiny. Peace and love for all mankind. And Africa for Africans.**99**

—Bob Marley, reggae superstar[1]

In April 1980, when the new African nation of Zimbabwe (zim-BAHB-way) (formerly Southern Rhodesia) celebrated its independence from British rule, Bob Marley, a reggae music star from Jamaica and a symbol of black empowerment, performed at Zimbabwe's national stadium. Marley's experience there reflected many of the political and cultural trends of the later-twentieth-century world. Marley had been invited to appear in part because his songs, such as "Stir it Up" and "Get Up Stand Up," often dealt with issues such as poverty, racial prejudice, and human rights that resonated with thousands of Zimbabweans in the audience, who had endured decades of uncaring British colonial and then white minority government.

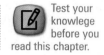 Test your knowlege before you read this chapter.

But Marley's concert was disrupted by the local police, who used tear gas to disperse thousands of black Zimbabweans who gathered outside the overcrowded stadium. The next night, Marley ignored threats of violence against him by local white racists and gave a free concert for 40,000 Zimbabweans, many of them unemployed. Although the free concert encountered no major problems, the violence of the previous night and the threats to his life had shown Marley that the social ills and ethnic hatreds he knew in Jamaica occurred elsewhere in the world as well. In Zimbabwe, where these ills ran particularly deep, they would not be solved by the nation's newly won independence under a black majority government.

An eloquent advocate of political and cultural freedom whose music was enjoyed by millions of fans around the world, Marley and his music touched hearts and minds across racial, political, religious, class, and cultural barriers. Reggae was a truly world music, an intoxicating mix of African, Caribbean, and North American traditions. To the world, Marley personified reggae's progressive politics and spiritual quest. His career reflected a world that was interconnected as never before and in great flux. Since World War II, the pace of change quickened and the global economy grew dramatically. Economic and

What do you think?

The global community has largely been successful in its efforts to deal with growing economic and environmental problems.

Strongly Disagree						Strongly Agree
1	2	3	4	5	6	7

<<**"Our World Is Not for Sale"** In 2004, tens of thousands of activists from all over the world, under the banner of "Our World Is Not for Sale," marched on the streets of Mumbai (formerly Bombay), India's largest city, to protest economic globalization, racial and caste oppression, and the U.S.-led war in Iraq.

cultural networks linked societies ever more closely, while people, ideas, technologies, and products flowed across porous borders. World politics were turbulent, reflecting the conflict between the United States and the Soviet Union (USSR), the world's two most powerful nations, and the struggle of African, Asian, and Latin American countries for decolonization and development. Since 1989, when the Soviet bloc collapsed, the world has groped toward a new political configuration while dealing with mounting challenges.

LO¹ Decolonization, New States, and the Global System

The contemporary world was affected by Western imperialism's aftermath. After World War II, Asia, Africa, and Latin America became the major battlegrounds between the United States and the Soviet Union; these two nations had so much military, political, and economic might in comparison to other countries that they were known as superpowers. The struggle of Asian, African, and Latin American societies to end Western domination and to develop economically also shaped the postwar era. Nationalist movements proliferated, some seeking deep changes through social revolution. The former colonies also became part of a dynamic global system marked by continued imbalances in wealth and power.

Nationalism and Decolonization

The nationalism that spread through Europe and the Americas in the 1800s became a powerful force in the colonized world in the 1900s. Three basic types of nationalist movements developed between the early 1900s and the 1960s. In the first type, which occurred in most colonized societies, the nationalist goal was the end of colonial rule but not necessarily major social and economic change. The second type of nationalist movement, mounted by social revolutionaries inspired by Marxism, wanted not only

> "The nationalism that spread through Europe and the Americas in the 1800s became a powerful force in the colonized world in the 1900s."

political independence but also a new social order free of Western economic domination. In China, for example, the communist movement led by Mao Zedong sought to reorganize Chinese society while limiting contact with the world economy and the United States. Making up a third type were the nationalist movements by long-repressed nonwhite majorities in white settler colonies such as Algeria and Zimbabwe. Whatever the type of nationalist movement, the dislocations caused by the Great Depression and World War II intensified anti-Western and anticolonial feelings.

Colonialism Succumbs to Nationalism

Colonialism gradually crumbled, often after confronting nationalist resistance led by charismatic figures such as Mohandas Gandhi in India, in the three decades after World War II. By the 1950s, most of the Western colonizers realized that the increased military force required to maintain their political control was too expensive. In 1946, the United States began the decolonization trend by granting independence to the Philippines. In the later 1940s, the British gave up their rule in India and Burma, and the Dutch abandoned Indonesia. Between 1946 and 1975, most of the Western colonies in Asia, Africa, and the Caribbean achieved independence (see Map 26.1).

Interactive Map

Some colonizers accepted decolonization only after attempts to quell nationalist uprisings had failed. The Dutch intended to regain their control of Indonesia, a source of immense wealth, after World War II but faced violent, nationalist resistance. In 1950, after losing many soldiers, the Dutch granted Indonesia independence. Similarly, the French had no plans to abandon their profitable colonies in Vietnam and Algeria, but uprisings by revolutionaries in these

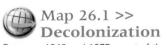
Map 26.1 >> Decolonization

Between 1946 and 1975, most of the Western colonies in Asia, Africa, and the Caribbean won their independence, with the greatest number achieving independence in the 1960s. Decolonization reshaped the global political map.

Former ruler

- Great Britain
- France
- Netherlands
- Italy
- Belgium
- Portugal
- United States
- Other

1960 Year independence achieved

Oceans / Seas

- ATLANTIC OCEAN
- PACIFIC OCEAN
- INDIAN OCEAN
- Mediterranean Sea
- Black Sea
- Caspian Sea
- Arabian Sea
- Bay of Bengal
- Tropic of Cancer
- Tropic of Capricorn
- Equator 0°

Former colonial powers (labels)

- GREAT BRITAIN
- FRANCE
- SPAIN
- PORTUGAL
- BELGIUM
- NETHERLANDS
- ITALY
- JAPAN

Country labels with independence years

- MOROCCO 1956
- WESTERN SAHARA 1975 (Morocco) (From Spain)
- ALGERIA 1962
- TUNISIA 1957
- LIBYA 1951
- MALTA 1964 (From Gr. Br.)
- CYPRUS 1960
- EGYPT 1922
- MAURITANIA 1960
- MALI 1960
- NIGER 1960
- CHAD 1960
- SUDAN 1956
- ERITREA 1993 (From Ethiopia)
- SENEGAL 1960
- CAPE VERDE 1975 (From Port.)
- GAMBIA 1965
- GUINEA-BISSAU 1974
- GUINEA 1958
- SIERRA LEONE 1961
- LIBERIA 1820s
- CÔTE D'IVOIRE 1960
- BURKINA FASO 1960
- GHANA 1957
- TOGO 1960
- BENIN 1960
- NIGERIA 1960
- CAMEROON 1960
- CENTRAL AFRICAN REPUBLIC 1960
- EQUATORIAL GUINEA 1968 (From Spain)
- SÃO TOMÉ AND PRÍNCIPE 1975 (From Port.)
- GABON 1960
- REPUBLIC OF CONGO 1960
- DEM. REP. OF CONGO 1960
- ETHIOPIA
- DJIBOUTI 1977
- SOMALIA 1960
- UGANDA 1962
- KENYA 1963
- RWANDA 1962
- BURUNDI 1962
- TANZANIA 1964
- ANGOLA 1975
- ZAMBIA 1964
- MALAWI 1964
- MOZAMBIQUE 1974
- ZIMBABWE 1980
- NAMIBIA 1990 (From South Africa)
- BOTSWANA 1966
- SWAZILAND 1968
- LESOTHO 1966
- SOUTH AFRICA (Republic 1961)
- MADAGASCAR 1960
- MAURITIUS 1968 (From Gr. Br.)
- SEYCHELLES 1976 (From Gr. Br.)
- COMOROS 1975 (From France)

Middle East / Asia

- SYRIA 1944
- LEBANON 1944
- ISRAEL 1948
- JORDAN 1946
- IRAQ 1932
- KUWAIT 1961
- BAHRAIN 1971
- QATAR 1971
- UNITED ARAB EMIRATES 1971
- OMAN 1971
- YEMEN
- P.D.R. OF YEMEN 1967 (Unified 1990)
- PAKISTAN 1947
- INDIA 1947
- BANGLADESH 1973
- MALDIVES 1975 (From Gr. Br.)
- SRI LANKA (CEYLON) 1948
- MYANMAR (BURMA) 1947
- LAOS 1949
- NORTH VIETNAM 1954 (Unified 1975)
- SOUTH VIETNAM 1954
- CAMBODIA 1953
- MALAYSIA 1963
- BRUNEI 1984 (From Gr. Br.)
- SINGAPORE 1965 (From Malaysia)
- PHILIPPINES 1946
- INDONESIA 1949
- TIMOR-LESTE 1999 (From Indonesia)
- PAPUA NEW GUINEA 1975 (From Australia)
- NORTH KOREA 1948
- SOUTH KOREA 1948 (From Japan)
- JAPAN

Scale

- 0   1,000   2,000 Km.
- 0   1,000   2,000 Mi.

N

colonies forced them to leave. In Vietnam, the communist forces led by Ho Chi Minh fiercely resisted French power, and heavy U.S. aid to the French could not prevent a humiliating French defeat in 1954. The ultimately successful anticolonial struggles by the Indonesian, Vietnamese, and Algerian nationalists had electrifying global effects, giving hope to colonized peoples elsewhere.

The Superpowers

Both superpowers sought to capitalize on the nationalist surge. The Soviet Union generally supported nationalist movements, sometimes supplying arms to revolutionaries. The Soviets also offered economic aid and diplomatic support to Asian and African countries that achieved independence and had strategic value, such as India and Egypt, or valuable resources, such as oil-rich Iran and Indonesia. The United States followed a mixed policy on decolonization. Wanting access to trade and outlets for investment in Asia and Africa, the United States encouraged the Dutch to leave Indonesia and urged independence for some British colonies in Africa, but Americans also opposed communism and the spread of Soviet influence. Consequently, where nationalism was led by communists or had a leftist orientation, as in French-ruled Vietnam, the United

UPI/Bettmann/Corbis

African Independence In 1961, the British monarch, Queen Elizabeth II, made an official visit to newly independent Ghana, the former British colony of the Gold Coast. Here she walks under a ceremonial umbrella with the Ghanaian president, Kwame Nkrumah.

CHRONOLOGY

Global Politics, 1945–1989

1945	Formation of United Nations
1946–1975	Decolonization in Asia, Africa, Caribbean
1946–1989	Cold War
1949	Communist victory in China
1950–1953	Korean War
1954	Vietnamese defeat of French
1955	Bandung Conference
1959–1975	U.S.–Vietnam War
1959	Communist victory in Cuba
1962	Cuban Missile Crisis
1968	Widespread political protests
1975	End of Portuguese Empire

States supported continued colonial power, no matter how unpopular among the colonized people.

Colonialism did not completely disappear. By the 1980s, one major territorial empire, the USSR, remained, and it strained to repress the nationalist demands of the Baltic, Caucasus, and Central Asian peoples it ruled. The Soviet Empire was largely dismantled between 1989 and 1991, when the Soviet Union's communist system collapsed, although Russians still controlled some unwilling subjects, such as the Chechens, a Muslim people in southern Russia. At the beginning of the twenty-first century, Britain, France, and the United States still controlled small empires. Britain and France retained direct control of a few islands and some outposts, notably British Gibraltar, a strategically valuable naval base at the entrance to the Mediterranean Sea, and French Guiana, on the northeast coast of South America. The territories, mostly self-governing, linked to the United States included Puerto Rico, the Virgin Islands, American Samoa, and Guam.

Neo-Colonialism

Decolonization often resulted in neocolonialism, a continuing strong political and economic influence by the former colonizers. This happened in the Philippines, where Americans maintained a major role in the economy and influenced Philippine governments and popular culture. Similarly, the French controlled much of the economy and advised the government in the African nation of Cote d'Ivoire (COAT dee-VWAHR), and many Ivoirians favored French cuisine, literature, and language. Disenchantment with the continuing strong Western presence prompted some Asian and African intellectuals to advocate "decolonizing the mind," to escape what Bob Marley called a "mental slavery" that kept formerly colonized people in awe of Western power, wealth, and culture. "Decolonizing the mind" sometimes meant building a nationalist culture reflecting local traditions or abandoning the use of Western languages in people's writing.

Social Revolutionary States

During the twentieth century, revolutionary activity erupted in Asia, Africa, and Latin America, intensified by the drive to end colonialism and other forms of Western domination. In most cases, this revolutionary activity engaged peasants, who were often impoverished by the loss of their lands or the declining prices for the cash crops they grew. Revolutionary intellectuals, often Marxist, capitalized on this unhappiness to mobilize support, although those who joined their movements did not always embrace the more radical ideas. Understanding this, Amilcar Cabral (AM-ill-car ka-BRAWL) (1924–1973), the revolutionary leader in Portugal's West African colony of Guinea Bissau (GIN-ee bi-SOU), advised his Marxist colleagues to "always bear in mind that the people are not fighting for ideas, for the things in anyone's head. They are fighting to win material benefits, to live better, and in peace, to see their lives go forward, to guarantee the future of their children."[2] Between 1949 and 1980, social revolutionary regimes came to power through force of arms in Algeria Vietnam, China, Cuba, and many other countries. Opposed by the United States and often mistrusted by western European regimes, these states necessarily looked to the USSR for political, economic, and military support.

> "Decolonization often resulted in neocolonialism, a continuing strong political and economic influence by the former colonizers."

Planned Economies

Social revolutionary states had uneven relations with the world economy and the capitalist nations. Influenced by Stalinism, which fostered state-directed economic growth in the USSR in the 1930s, these states usually chose to withdraw from the world economy in order to limit outside interference, renounce foreign debts, and assume control of their economic direction. They created planned economies in which economic decisions were made centrally, by governments, rather than through free markets, as in capitalist societies.

Social revolutionary approaches brought mixed results. Some countries saw their goals sidetracked by civil wars or by rebellions supported by Western powers. For example, in Angola, a country in southwest Africa, South Africa and the United States provided financial and military support to rebels who fought the Marxist-dominated government for more than two decades. The civil war cost more than 200,000 lives, ruined much of the country, and forced the Angolan government to devote most of its resources to the military rather than to supporting its people. After the fighting ended in the late 1990s, the Marxists still held power, but Angolans were poorer than ever: half of the nation's children suffered from malnutrition. In contrast, between 1949 and 1978, communist-run China was able to increase its economic potential and reduce social problems, but at a heavy cost in repressing dissent and limiting personal freedom.

After 1978, China dramatically modified its socialist economy with market forces, such as by allowing foreign investment and free enterprise, which sparked even more rapid growth. The shift of China, followed by Vietnam, toward market economies and greater participation in the world economy in the 1980s suggested that revolution may have helped nations to gain control of their resources but was ultimately insufficient to raise living standards. Yet, China and Vietnam also found that capitalism and free markets could create more wealth than socialism but did not necessarily lead to an equitable distribution of wealth, fostering explosive social tensions.

A New Global System

During the later twentieth century, observers often divided the world into three categories of countries,

"During the later twentieth century, observers often divided the world into three categories of countries, each one having a different level of economic development."

each one having a different level of economic development. One category, the First World, comprised the industrialized democracies of western Europe, North America, Australia–New Zealand, and Japan. The Second World referred to the communist nations, led by the USSR and China. The Third World was made up of most societies in Asia, Africa, Latin America, and the Caribbean that were marked by mass poverty and a legacy of Western colonization or neocolonialism. Some experts added a fourth category, the Fourth World, or the poorest societies, which had very small economies and few exploitable resources, such as Laos, Bangladesh, Haiti, and Mali.

Economies in Transition

The notion of different worlds of economic development helped bring to light the roles played by different countries in global politics and economics between 1945 and the late 1980s, when the Western nations and the communist bloc, both wealthy and powerful compared to other societies, competed for influence in the rest of the world. However, critics argued that lumping the world's societies into a few categories was highly misleading. Furthermore, during the 1980s and 1990s, the global system was changing, complicating attempts to categorize nations. Countries such as Malaysia, South Korea, Dubai, and Chile, once grouped with the Third World, achieved rapid economic growth, and the communist systems that had defined the Second World often collapsed.

Post-War Japan

At the economically developed end of the global system, most Western nations and Japan enjoyed new heights of prosperity from the 1960s through the 1980s. After World War II, the United States offered generous aid to Europe and Japan, helping them to recover from the destruction created by the war; this aid promoted further economic growth in industrialized countries that already had literate, skilled, and mostly urban populations, well-funded governments, and diversified economies. Japan's economy increased fivefold between 1953 and 1973, the fastest economic growth in world history. As Western and Japanese businesses invested heavily around the world, international trade soared. Japan and West Germany became the second and third largest capitalist economies. By the 1970s, several Western nations, including West Germany, Sweden, Canada, and Australia, had standards of living similar to those in the United States, and most had far less inequality in the distribution of wealth and income than did the United States.

Prosperity in the West

Although economic growth rates often slowed after 1990, Western prosperity relative to the rest of the world continued. By 2004, the Human Development Report—an annual study by the United Nations that rates the quality of life of the world's 177 nations—ranked, in order, Norway, Sweden, Australia, Canada, and the Netherlands as the most livable nations; following these were Belgium, Iceland, the United States, Japan, and Ireland. The report ranked thirty-six nations, mostly in sub-Saharan Africa, as having a low quality of life, with massive poverty, inadequate health care, and low rates of literacy. Tanzanian president Julius Nyerere (nye-RE-re) put the gap between rich and poor nations in perspective: "While the United States is trying to reach the moon, Tanzania is trying to reach its villages."[3]

Some nations had more resources and political stability to secure their citizens' lives, while poorer nations faced greater challenges in building stable nation-states. Richer nations usually benefited from democracy and allowed voters to freely choose their leaders. Democratic governments controlled social tensions, and generous welfare systems prevented mass poverty. Many western European states, Canada, and New Zealand adopted ambitious welfare systems, including comprehensive national health insurance. The European welfare states promoted a high degree of social justice and equality, while violence occurred in nations that had abandoned communism and its safety net of free or low-cost education, health care, and housing. The fighting between ethnic groups in Yugoslavia in the 1990s sometimes resulted in brutal atrocities and the forced expulsion of minorities. Only a few non-European nations, such as Sri Lanka and oil-rich Brunei, tried to mount welfare states with free education and health care, but they struggled to pay for them.

LO² Cold War, Hot Wars, and World Politics

A new global political configuration emerged after World War II: two major superpowers, the United States and the Soviet Union, each developed a system of allies in their competition for international influence. The confrontation between the two superpowers fostered the Cold War, a conflict lasting from 1946 to 1989, in which the United States and the USSR competed for allies and engaged in occasional warfare against their rival's allies rather than with each other directly. The United States enjoyed much greater influence than the USSR in the global system and boasted more allies. While the Cold War did not lead to a military conflict in which U.S. and Soviet military forces fought each other, it produced chronic mutual tension and led to covert and military interventions around the world.

> **"** After World War II, U.S. concern shifted from opposing Nazi Germany and imperial Japan to countering the USSR. **"**

The Cold War: Division and Conflict

During the Cold War, the world took on a bipolar political character. Nations practicing capitalism and democracy, led by the United States, called themselves the Free World; those marked by socialist authoritarianism, led by the USSR and known as the Soviet bloc, were on the other side. For more than four decades, U.S.–USSR relations, and the struggle of each superpower to gain an advantage over its rival, dominated international affairs. While seeking to contain the spread of communism, the United States enhanced its own influence, while the USSR worked to spread communism and undercut American influence. Various other countries, in Asia, Africa, and Latin

America, sought to forge a third bloc, asserting their interests while navigating the dangerous shoals of superpower demands. In 1955, leaders from twenty-nine nonaligned Asian and African countries held a conference in Bandung, Indonesia, to oppose colonialism and gain recognition for what they called a Third World bloc, but they had trouble maintaining unity in the decades to follow.

Cold War
A conflict lasting from 1946 to 1989 in which the United States and the USSR competed for allies and engaged in occasional warfare against their rivals' allies rather than against each other directly.

The Ascendancy of the United States

Although Britain had been the world's leading economic, political, and military power in the nineteenth century, the United States became the world's most powerful nation in the twentieth, enjoying far greater wealth, military power, and cultural influence than any other nation, including the USSR. In 1945, the United States already had 1,200 warships, 3,000 bombers, and the atomic bomb; produced half of the world's industrial output; and held two-thirds of the gold. Americans seemed willing to bear a heavy financial and military burden to sustain their leading role in world affairs and to promote U.S. economic growth. U.S. President Dwight D. Eisenhower (g. 1953–1961) defended his nation's foreign policy, which included interventions against unfriendly governments, as necessary to obtain raw materials and preserve profitable markets.

Spread of Communism

After World War II, U.S. concern shifted from opposing Nazi Germany and imperial Japan to countering the USSR. Americans now perceived their wartime ally as a rival for influence. By 1948, the Soviets controlled all of eastern Europe and were allied with communist governments in Mongolia and North Korea. The U.S. policy of preventing the emergence of communist regimes became globalized: first, Americans tried unsuccessfully to prevent communists from coming to power in China in the late 1940s; then they became involved in the Korean War (1950–1953) to fight successfully the North Korean effort to forcibly reunify the Korean peninsula. Yet, despite

"Insurgencies became common as unconventional warfare, such as sniping, sabotaging power plants, and planting roadside bombs, proliferated."

U.S. efforts, communist regimes came to power in China in 1949, North Vietnam in 1954, and Cuba in 1959. Furthermore, waging the Cold War and seeking to contain communism with military force, including a long war in Vietnam, financially burdened the United States, costing it between $4 trillion to $5 trillion and some 113,000 American lives between 1946 and 1989.

The Cold War fostered misunderstandings and tensions between the superpowers. Remembering centuries of invasions from the West, Soviet leaders occupied eastern Europe as a buffer zone and considered the United States and its western European allies a lethal danger; their combined military power greatly exceeded that of the USSR. American leaders mistrusted the USSR and despised communism, which challenged two of America's most treasured values, democracy and market economies. Americans viewed themselves as protecting freedom, while the Soviets claimed that they were helping the world's exploited and impoverished masses and acting as the beacon of anti-imperialism.

The Long Telegram This critique of the Soviet Union's ideology, authored by an American diplomat in 1946, profoundly influenced the foreign policy of the United States.

Interpreting the Cold War

Some historians believe the Cold War brought a long period of peace and stability, while others point to some eighty wars, often related to superpower rivalry, between 1945 and 1989 that resulted in 20 million deaths and perhaps 20 million refugees. The Cold War rivalries also transformed world politics by dragging emerging nations, already damaged by their long, humiliating subservience to Western colonialism, into upheavals that bankrupted economies and devastated entire peoples. In place of a USSR–U.S. war, a series of smaller conflicts occurred involving surrogates, governments, or movements allied to one superpower and fighting the troops from the other superpower. During two of the major conflicts, in Korea and Vietnam, U.S. troops battled not Soviet armies but allied communist forces that were Soviet surrogates. In Vietnam, the Soviets sent military supplies and advisers to help the Vietnamese communists, led by Ho Chi Minh, fight first the French and then the United States, which had helped install a pro-Western government in South Vietnam after the French defeat. The communists gained control of the entire country in 1975. Americans also used surrogates, such as when they supplied Islamic groups fighting the Soviets in Afghanistan in the 1980s.

In this warfare, rebels often used low-technology weapons and military strategies if those methods provided the most practical options available. Insurgencies became common as unconventional warfare, such as sniping, sabotaging power plants, and planting roadside bombs, proliferated. Insurgents fighting superpower forces often resorted to guerrilla warfare, an unconventional military strategy of avoiding full-scale direct confrontations in favor of small-scale skirmishes. In Vietnam, for example, communist guerrillas staged hit-and-run attacks on American patrols and field bases and planted land mines, explosives that detonated when stepped on, on trails used by American troops.

The Cold War fostered interventions—both covert and military—by both superpowers to protect their interests. The USSR sent military forces into Poland, Hungary, and Czechoslovakia to crush anti-Soviet movements and into Afghanistan to support a pro-Soviet government. The Afghanistan intervention was a disaster for the Soviet Union: heavy losses and humiliating withdrawal in 1989 contributed to its collapse. The Soviets, Chinese, and Cubans also gave aid to communist movements around the world, establishing a strong presence in nations such as Indonesia, India, and Chile, where they participated openly in politics. They also launched insurgencies against governments in several countries, such as Peru, Malaysia, and the Philippines, that ultimately failed to mobilize enough local support and were crushed.

For its part, the United States actively sought to shape the political and economic direction of Asian, African, and Latin American societies through generous aid and promoting human rights. Americans donated food, disaster and medical assistance, technical advice, and support to democratic organizations. But other efforts destabilized or helped overthrow governments that were deemed unfriendly to U.S. business and political interests, including regimes in Brazil, Chile, and Guatemala.

Intervention in Iran and Vietnam

The earliest U.S. intervention came in 1953 in oil-rich Iran, which was governed by a nationalist but noncommunist regime that nationalized British- and U.S.-owned oil companies operating in Iran, companies that sent most of their huge profits abroad, paid their Iranian workers less than fifty cents per day, and offered them no health care or paid vacations. In response to the nationalization, Britain and the United States imposed an economic boycott on Iran, making it hard for Iran to sell its oil. American agents recruited disaffected military officers and paid Iranians to spark riots that paralyzed the capital, forcing the nationalists from power and leading to a pro-U.S. but despotic government. The deposed Iranian leader, Mohammad Mossadeq, argued that he faced U.S. wrath for trying to remove "the network of colonialism, and the political and economic influence of the greatest empire on earth [the U.S.] from this land."[4] For the first time ever, the United States had organized the overthrow of a foreign government outside the Western Hemisphere.

To critics, the U.S. actions and other superpower interventions constituted a new form of imperialism. The interventions often proved costly as well. In Vietnam, for example, the communist-led forces achieved a military stalemate that cost the United States vast sums of money, killed some 58,000 Americans, and forced it to negotiate for peace and withdraw, harming U.S. prestige in the world. The war also had spillover effects: it created economic problems in the United States, cost the lives of several million Vietnamese, and required the USSR and China to spend scarce resources to supply their communist allies.

The Nuclear Arms Race and Global Militarization

The arms race between the superpowers and increasing militarization around the world became major components of the Cold War. Both superpowers developed nuclear weapons, explosive devices that owe their destructive power to the energy released by either splitting or fusing atoms. These weapons were the most deadly result of the technological surge that can be traced back to Albert Einstein, Sir Isaac Newton, and the scientific discoveries of the seventeenth and eighteenth centuries. A nuclear explosion produces a powerful blast, intense heat, and deadly radiation over a wide area. The nuclear weapons era began when the United States built the first atomic bombs and dropped two of these bombs on the Japanese cities of Hiroshima and Nagasaki to end World War II. In the following decades, both the United States and the USSR developed even more deadly nuclear warheads. The growth of nuclear arsenals was only the most dangerous part of a larger trend toward increased militarization. Both superpowers and the rest of the world feared the devastating power of nuclear weapons of mass destruction.

> **nuclear weapons** Explosive devices that owe their destructive power to the energy released by either splitting or fusing atoms.

 Global Problems and the Culture of Capitalism (*http://faculty.plattsburgh.edu/richard.robbins/legacy/*). An outstanding site, aimed at undergraduates, with a wealth of resources.

> 66 The growth of nuclear arsenals was only the most dangerous part of a larger trend toward increased militarization. 99

The Nuclear Threat

Fortunately, these weapons were never used after 1945, although the world was close to a nuclear confrontation on several occasions. For example, in the early 1950s, as French colonial forces were losing the fight against communist-led insurgents in Vietnam, the Eisenhower administration in the United States offered atomic bombs to the French, who wisely declined the offer. In 1962, after discovering that the USSR had secretly placed nuclear missiles in Cuba, just 90 miles from Florida, President John F. Kennedy (1917–1963) demanded they be removed but vetoed a U.S. invasion that might have sparked all-out nuclear war. Some of Kennedy's advisers recommended that he attack Cuba with nuclear weapons. He rejected this advice, but his firm stance against missiles in Cuba created a tense crisis. Ultimately, the Soviets withdrew them, averting disaster. In response to a U.S. attack on his boat during the crisis, a Soviet submarine commander armed a missile carrying a nuclear weapon and aimed it at the United States, but he was talked out of firing it by other Soviet officers.

A Balance of Terror

Nuclear weapons shaped global politics. The Cold War fostered a balance of terror, with both superpowers unwilling to use the awesome power at their command for fear the other would retaliate. Historians debate whether the nuclear arms race helped preserve the peace by discouraging an all-out U.S.–USSR military confrontation or instead unsettled international politics and wasted trillions of dollars. Various other countries, including Britain, France, China, India, and Pakistan, also constructed or acquired nuclear bombs, while countries like Iran and North Korea began programs to do the same. In the 1970s, the two superpowers negotiated two treaties to limit further arms proliferation, and in 1987, they signed a treaty to reduce existing nuclear weapons. Nevertheless, more nations sought nuclear capability, provoking concerns about proliferation. But some outside the West argued that the monopoly on such weapons by a few powerful nations was unfair, and Middle Eastern leaders worried about Israeli nuclear efforts.

The Cost of the Cold War

The proportion of total world production and spending devoted to militaries grew dramatically during the Cold War. By 1985, the world was spending some $1.2 trillion annually on military forces and weapons, more than the combined income of the poorest 50 percent of world countries. The two superpowers together, with 11 percent of the world population, accounted for 60 percent of military spending, 25 percent of the world's armed forces, and 97 percent of its nuclear weapons; both the United States and USSR had stockpiles of thousands of nuclear weapons. They both also sold conventional weapons to other countries with which they had friendly relations.

Conflict in the Post-War World

Whether or not related to Cold War rivalries, the varied wars caused enormous casualties, with civilians accounting for some three-fourths of the dead. Two million people died during the Chinese civil war (1945–1949), 800,000 during the violent partition of India (1948), 2 million during the American-Vietnamese War, 1 million during the Nigerian civil war (1967), and more than 2 million in the Cambodian violence from 1970 to 1978. Millions of these deaths resulted from genocide, the deliberate killing of whole groups because of their ethnic or religious origin. Genocide, which had been practiced for centuries, reached its most organized campaign with the Nazi holocaust against the Jews during World War II (see Chapter 24). In the later twentieth century, genocides continued: in the 1990s, members of the Hutu majority slaughtered people belonging to the Tutsi minority in Rwanda (roo-AHN-duh), a Central African country, while extremist Serb Christians, seeking to maintain their political power, killed Bosnian and Albanian Muslims in Yugoslavia, in a policy they called "ethnic cleansing." The Yugoslav killings were finally stopped when the United States and western European nations sent in troops to restore order and punished the worst violators of human rights.

Global Organizations and Activism

During the Cold War, more than ever before in history, public and private organizations emerged with a global reach and mission to promote political cooperation and address various causes. The largest attempt by most of the world's sovereign nations to cooperate for the common good, the United Nations, was founded in 1945 with fifty-one members and became a key forum for global debate and diplomacy. The founding members agreed that the United Nations came about to "save succeeding generations from the scourge of war, reaffirm faith in fundamental rights, and respect international law."[5] As colonies gained independence and joined, the organization grew to more than one hundred members by the mid-1960s and to nearly two hundred by 2000. Pursuing cooperation on humanitarian aims, it developed agencies, such as the World Health Organization, that monitored diseases, funded and fostered medical research, and promoted public health, as well as the United Nations Children Fund, or UNICEF, which promoted children's welfare and education around the world. U.N.-sponsored health and nutrition programs helped increase average life expectancy from 45 in 1900 to 75 in 2000, and greatly reduced the risk of mothers dying in childbirth.

Role of the United Nations

The United Nations influenced international relations by discouraging, although not preventing, states from using force whenever they desired. To gain support for military actions, nations often felt it necessary to make their case before the policy-making Security Council; sometimes they received support, but nations determined to go to war often ignored widespread disapproval by the U.N., as the United States did when it invaded Iraq in 2003. The Security Council sometimes voted to send peacekeeping troops into troubled countries. Each of the five major powers of 1945—the United States, China, Britain, France, and the USSR—received permanent seats with veto power in the Security Council. Both superpowers vetoed decisions that challenged their national interests. For instance, the United States often vetoed resolutions aimed at penalizing its ally, Israel, and also blocked, for more than two decades, the Chinese Communist government from occupying China's seat in the United Nations. But western nations found it more difficult to shape policies after Afro-Asian nations became the majority in the United Nations.

U.N. Peacekeepers in Congo The United Nations has regularly sent peacekeepers into troubled countries such as the Congo. This photo, from 2003, shows U.N. troops from Uruguay guarding a U.N. office while a Congolese woman and her four children, displaced from her village by factional fighting, seek U.N. help.

Toward a Global World-View

Since World War II, groupings of nations also cooperated to improve global conditions by forging international agreements and treaties. For example, most nations ratified an agreement banning biological weapons, such as deadly diseases like anthrax, in 1972. In 1997, most nations signed the Kyoto Protocol, pledging to begin reducing the harmful gases that contribute to global warming. But the United States and several other industrial nations impeded international cooperation by refusing to approve the modest efforts made by these agreements to reduce weapons, promote environmental stability, and establish accountability for international crimes.

Human Rights Watch (http://www.hrw.org/wr2k3/introduction.html). The website of a major human rights organization that reports on the entire world.

Private organizations and activists, chiefly based in western Europe, also worked for issues of peace, social justice, health, refugees, famine, conflict resolution, and environmental protection. Organizations such as Doctors Without Borders, which sent medical personnel to societies facing famine or epidemics, and Amnesty International, which worked to free political prisoners, were supported chiefly by private donations. In addition, leaders from different religious faiths worked for world peace, justice, and humanitarian concerns. For example, the Dalai Lama (DAH-lie LAH-ma) (b. 1935), the highest Tibetan Buddhist spiritual leader, won the Nobel Peace Prize in 1989 for his efforts—through speeches, writings, and conferences—to promote human rights and nonviolent conflict resolution.

World Politics Since 1989

Between 1989 and 1991, the Soviet bloc disintegrated and the communist regimes in eastern Europe and the former USSR collapsed, ending the Cold War and the bipolar world it had defined. Both U.S. and Soviet leaders deescalated tensions between the two superpowers in the later 1980s. When the Cold War ended, the United States became the sole superpower. Yet many scholars concur with George Kennan (1904–2004), the architect of the U.S. policy to contain communism in the 1940s, who concluded that no country "won" the Cold War, because it was fueled by misconceptions and nearly bankrupted both sides. Other nations, especially Japan and West Germany, protected from potential enemies by U.S. military bases, benefited from the conflict by investing heavily in economic growth rather than their own defense. By 2001, the United States had a larger annual military budget than the ten next-largest military spenders combined and was the major supplier of arms to the rest of the world.

War in the Persian Gulf

The first major post–Cold War challenge for the United States came in 1991 when Iraq's brutal dictator, Saddam Hussein (1937–2006), ordered his army to invade and occupy Iraq's small, oil-rich neighbor, Kuwait. The United States had supported Saddam and provided his military with weapons in the 1980s, when Iraq was fighting a war against Iran, whose Islamic government the United States opposed. Now the United States organized an international coalition, funded chiefly by Arab nations, and, in the Gulf War of 1991, rapidly defeated the Iraqis and pushed them out of Kuwait. In the aftermath of the quick victory over Iraq, U.S. president George H. W. Bush proclaimed a "new world order"—a new global system, led by the United States, that was based on American values.

Regional and Religious Conflicts

The end of the long, costly rivalry between capitalist countries and communist societies, however, did not result in universal peace or the triumph of American political values. Instead, the 1990s saw what some observers called a new world disorder. Ethnic and nationalist conflicts exploded in massive violence in Yugoslavia, eastern Europe, and Rwanda. States with weak or dysfunctional governments, such as Haiti in

> "Globalization has increased the interconnectedness between societies; events occurring or decisions taken in one part of the world affect societies far away."

the Caribbean and Somalia in Northeast Africa, also experienced chronic fighting and civil war. Rising tides of religious conflict complicated politics in countries such as India, Indonesia, Algeria, and Nigeria. Militant Islam demonstrated its potency in Iran, Sudan, and Afghanistan and led some extremists to form terrorist groups to fight moderate Islamic regimes, Israel, and Western nations. By the early 2000s, Islamic radicals posed a greater challenge in Southeast Asia and the Middle East than the declining communist movements. The ambitions of aggressive dictators, such as Iraq's Saddam Hussein and the communist regime in North Korea, fostered regional tensions. The promise of a peaceful new world order foundered on the shoals of proliferating regional, nationalist, religious, economic, and ethnic conflicts.

LO³ Globalizing Economies, Underdevelopment, and Environmental Change

In the decades after 1945, the world economy was increasingly characterized by globalization, a pattern in which economic, political, and cultural processes reach beyond nation-state boundaries. This trend reduced barriers between countries and turned the world into a more closely integrated whole. However, it came with some major problems, including the widening inequality of nations, ever-increasing pollution, and a warming climate.

The Transnational Economy and Economic Institutions

Globalization has increased the interconnectedness between societies; events occurring or decisions taken in one part of the world affect societies far away. For example, rising or falling prices on the Tokyo or New York stock exchanges quickly influence stock markets elsewhere. Similarly, the decision by U.S. or British governments to sell supplies of stockpiled rubber, hence depressing world prices, affects the livelihood of rubber growers in Malaysia, Sri

CHRONOLOGY

Global Politics Since 1989

1989–1991	Dismantling of Soviet bloc and empire
1997	Kyoto Protocol on climate change
2001	Al Qaeda attack on United States
2003	U.S. invasion of Iraq

The Globalization Website (*http://www .emory.edu/SOC/ globalization/*). A useful site with many resources and essays on globalization.

Lanka, Brazil, and the Congo. Not all of the transnational economic activity has been legal: heroin and cocaine sold in North America and Europe originates largely in Asia and Latin America and is smuggled by transnational criminal syndicates. Whatever the problems, economic globalization became a fact of contemporary life and had numerous impacts on the world's societies.

After World War II, economic globalization involved the spread of market capitalism as well as flows of capital, goods, services, and people. The United States, now the axis of the world economy, has been the major proponent of globalization, with its leaders arguing that open markets and conditions favorable to investment and trade foster prosperity. By 2000, the United States produced nearly one-third of the world's goods and services; Japan, with the next largest economy, accounted for around one-sixth. International observers described the impact of U.S. leadership metaphorically: when the United States sneezes, the rest of the world catches cold.

The Uneven Impact of Globalization

Despite the growth of the world economy, some argue that globalization promises riches it does not always deliver, distributing the benefits unequally. Economic growth in a country does not, by itself, improve the living conditions of the majority of people; better conditions also require well-functioning governments, secure rights, and social services. Globalization brought more advantages to some nations, and some people within nations, than to others. By the 1990s, two nations, the United States and China, were gaining the most from the trend toward removing trade barriers and fostering competitive markets worldwide. Both absorbed investment capital, aggressively acquired natural resources from around the globe, and supplied diverse products to growing foreign markets. China became the world's third largest economy as its factories turned out clothing, housewares, and other consumer goods. However, not all Chinese have benefited equally: workers have struggled to win rights, economic security, and safe working conditions.

Globalization's impact has been uneven. By the early twenty-first century, a few other nations, such as India, Ireland, Singapore, and South Korea, had, like

the United States and China, also capitalized on globalization, becoming centers of high technology. But not all countries enjoyed such success. By the 1990s, even Japan and some European nations struggled to compete in the globalizing economy, while many Asian and African nations fell deeper into poverty. As United Nations Secretary General Kofi Annan (KO-fee AN-uhn), a Ghanaian, put it in 2002: "Our challenge today is to make globalization an engine that lifts people out of hardship and misery, not a force that holds them down."[6]

Although experiencing occasional setbacks, the Western industrial nations and Japan have generally maintained a favorable position in the global economy. They control most of the capital, markets, and institutions of international finance, such as banks, and their corporations also own assets in other nations. The capitalist systems in the industrialized nations have ranged from the laissez-faire approach, featuring limited government interference, common in the United States, to the mix of free markets and welfare states in western Europe, to the closely linked government–business relationship in Japan and South Korea. These contrast with the economies in many former colonies, especially in Africa, where power holders, who are often closely linked to foreign or domestic business interests, preside over largely poor populations.

Globalization and the Third World

Some once-poor countries have exploited the transnational economy to their advantage, achieving spectacular growth. If revenues are not stolen by corrupt leaders, as has happened in places like Iraq and Nigeria, possession of oil provides an economic foundation for national wealth. A few oil-rich nations, such as the Persian Gulf states of Kuwait and the United Arab Emirates, use oil revenues to improve the material lives of their citizens. Various Asian countries, much like Japan in the late 1800s, have combined capitalist market economies, cheap labor, and powerful governments to orchestrate industrialization. At the same time, they have ensured political stability and attracted foreign investment by repressing political opposition. These countries have favored export-oriented growth, producing consumer goods— clothing, toys, housewares—for sale abroad, especially in the richer, consuming nations of Europe and North America.

Asian countries using this development strategy improved their position in the global system. In the 1980s and 1990s, China, South Korea, Taiwan,

Corbis

Malaysia, Thailand, and Singapore fostered the fastest-growing economies in the world and considerable prosperity. Often the growing middle class and labor leaders have demanded a larger voice in government and political liberalization. By the 1990s, Indonesians, South Koreans, Taiwanese, and Thais had replaced dictatorships with democratic governments that were chosen in free elections. The Asian systems became models for successful development by mixing capitalism, which is useful for creating wealth, with socialism, which can distribute wealth equitably.

International Lending and Trade Agreements

Various institutions shaped the transnational economy. The international lending agencies formed by the World War II Allies in 1944 to aid postwar reconstruction played crucial roles, especially the World Bank, which funded development projects such as dams and agricultural schemes, and the International Monetary Fund (IMF), which regulated currency dealings and helped alleviate severe financial problems. The IMF, which had the right to dictate economic policies to countries borrowing from it, favored Western investment and free markets, often at the expense of government funding for social services such as schools and health clinics. Borrowers failing to make these changes risked loss of IMF loans. Especially in Latin America and Africa, countries fell deeply into debt, often having to devote 40 to 50 percent of their foreign income just to pay the interest on their loans.

Trade agreements and trading blocs also shaped the world economy, reflecting an economic connectedness among nations that was unprecedented in world history. In 1947, twenty-three nations established the General Agreements on Trade and Tariffs (GATT), which set general guidelines for the conduct of world trade and rules for establishing tariffs and trade regulations. The inauguration of the World Trade Organization (WTO) by 124 nations in 1995 marked a new phase in the evolution of the postwar economic system, replacing GATT. By the early twenty-first century, several communist nations with market economies, including China and Vietnam, had joined the WTO. The WTO had stronger dispute-resolution capabilities than GATT, and a member country could not veto a WTO decision that declared one of its regulations, such as environmental protection, to be an unfair restriction on trade. Various regional trading blocs also formed, such as the European Union.

Multinational Corporations

Giant business enterprises, known as multinational corporations because they operate all over the world, gained a leading role in the global marketplace. Some three hundred to four hundred companies, two-thirds of them U.S.-owned, dominated world production and trade. By the early 1980s, the multinationals had together become the third largest economic force in the world, exercising great influence over governments. By 2000, half of the world's one hundred largest economic entities were countries and half were multinational corporations.

The multinational corporations set the world price for various commodities, such as coffee, copper, or oil, and could play off one country against another to get the best deal. They also could easily switch manufacturing and hence jobs from one country to another. Multinationals have created millions of jobs in poor countries. Supporters argue that moving jobs from high-wage to low-wage countries, a pattern known as outsourcing, fosters a middle class of managers and technicians and offers work to people with few other job prospects. Critics reply that most of these jobs pay low wages, require long hours, and often offer little future. For example, the U.S.-based Nike Corporation, praised for creating needed jobs by making shoes in

> 66 Increasing competition from Asia and Latin America challenged Western and Japanese dominance in industrial activity. 99

CHRONOLOGY

The Global Economy and New Technologies

1947	Formation of GATT
1947	Invention of transistor
1958	Invention of silicon microchips
1995	Formation of World Trade Organization

The Global Economy Cambodian Buddhist monks, following ancient traditions, collect their food from the devout in the capital city, Phnom Penh, while advertising for American cigarettes entices Cambodians into the global economy, despite government concerns about the health danger posed by tobacco products.

Vietnam, is also criticized because the Vietnamese employees, mainly women, work in unhealthy conditions, face sexual harassment from their male supervisors, and are fired if they complain.

The Spread of Industrialization

The industrialization that had transformed Europe and North America in the nineteenth century spread to other parts of the world, especially to Asia and Latin America, during the later twentieth century. Increasing competition from Asia and Latin America challenged Western and Japanese dominance in industrial activity. For example, the U.S. share of world industrial production fell from 50 percent in 1950 to below 30 percent in the late 1980s. Americans built more than 75 percent of all cars in 1950 but less than 20 percent by the early 1990s. Consumers worldwide now had more choice.

The Third Industrial Revolution

Technological innovations since 1945 spurred economic growth. The so-called Third Industrial Revolution came about through the creation of unprecedented scientific knowledge of new technologies that were more powerful than any invented before. These new technologies made the creations of the first Industrial Revolution, which began in the late 1700s, and the second Industrial Revolution of the later 1800s seem obsolete. With the new innovations, traditional smokestack industries such as steel mills in industrialized nations were displaced by nuclear power, computers, automation, and robotry. The technological surge also brought rocketry, genetic

Third Industrial Revolution The creation since 1945 of unprecedented scientific knowledge of new technologies more powerful than any invented before.

> "Uneven economic growth contributed to a growing gap between rich nations and poor nations, often described as developing."

engineering, silicon chips, and lasers. Space technology produced the first manned trips to the moon and unmanned crafts exploring the solar system. The British poet Archibald MacLeish observed: "To see the Earth as we now see it, small and blue and beautiful in that eternal silence [of space] where it floats, is to see ourselves as rulers on the Earth together."[7]

The Green Revolution

The Third Industrial Revolution has had potentially dramatic consequences for people around the world. For example, the Green Revolution has fostered increased agricultural output through the use of new high-yield seeds and mechanized farming, such as gasoline-powered tractors and harvesters. Farmers with the money to take advantage of these innovations can shorten the growing season, thus raising two or three crops per year. But not all farmers benefited from the Green Revolution. In countries such as India, the Philippines, and Mexico, the Green Revolution, which requires more capital for seeds and machines but fewer people to work the land, has often harmed poor peasants whose labor was no longer needed or who could not afford the investment.

United Nations Environment Program (*http://www.unep.org/geo2000/ov-e/index.htm*). Provides access to United Nations reports on the world's environmental problems.

The Internet and Globalization

Industry and other economic activities have also become globalized. By the 1990s, more than two hundred export processing zones—industrial parks occupied largely by foreign-owned factories paying low taxes and wages—had been established around the world. For example, factories in northern Mexico, usually U.S.-owned, made goods, such as clothing, largely for the U.S. market and employed nearly half a million workers, mainly women. But not all of the new jobs were in factories. During the later twentieth century, the service and information exchange industries also grew. More people worked in service enterprises, such as fast-food restaurants, while others established transnational computer networks, such as AOL and Google, to help people use the Internet for communication and knowledge acquisition. By the 1990s, India, responding to these trends, was graduating thousands of people each year who were fluent in English and skilled in computer technology, becoming a world center for offshore information and technical services.

Outsourcing

Yet, the opportunities of industrialization and its globalization have come with risks. Hoping to better compete in the world economy, businesses have moved factories to countries with low wages and costs. As North American and western European companies have sought more profits, they have outsourced, or relocated, the jobs once held by several million workers to foreign countries with cheap labor costs and eager workers, such as India and Mexico. For example, in 1990, the U.S. clothing maker Levi Strauss closed its plant in San Antonio, Texas; laid off 1,150 workers, most of them Mexican American women; and relocated the operation to Costa Rica. Viola Casares, one of the fired workers, expressed the despair: "As long as I live I'll never forget how the white man in the suit said they had to shut us down to stay competitive."[8] Between 1981 and 1990, Levi Strauss, losing markets to lower-priced competitors, closed fifty-eight U.S. plants with more than 10,000 workers while shifting half of its production overseas.

Underdevelopment

Uneven economic growth contributed to a growing gap between rich nations and poor nations, often described as developing. The gap was already wide in 1945, since colonialism often did little to raise colonial people's general living standards. A Guyanese historian concluded that "the vast majority of Africans went into colonialism with a hoe and came out with a hoe."[9] Many Asian, African, and Latin American economies grew rapidly in the 1950s and 1960s, when the world economy boomed. In the 1970s and 1980s, however, as the world economy soured and the world prices for many exports collapsed, the growth rates of these economies declined. Then the world economy revived for a few years, only to experience a dramatic downturn in the later 1990s and early 2000s.

Western Investment

Economic growth has not always fostered development, growth that benefited the majority of the population. With economic globalization growing, rich countries pressure or encourage other nations to open their economies to foreign corporations and investment. Some nations, especially in East and Southeast Asia, have prospered from this investment, earning money to build schools, hospitals, and highways, but elsewhere Western investment often has done little to foster locally owned businesses. In Nigeria, for example, as in colonial times, British-owned enterprises have controlled banking, importing, and exporting, and foreign investment has gone mainly into cash crops and oil production, controlled largely by Western companies, such as Royal Dutch Shell. Furthermore, foreign investment and aid has often been misused to support projects favored by influential politicians or siphoned off to corrupt leaders, bureaucrats, and military officers.

Obstacles to Development

While some nations have become richer, others have become poorer. Most poor nations have suffered from some combination of rapid population growth, high unemployment, illiteracy, hunger, disease, corrupt or ineffective governments, and reliance on only a few exports, chiefly natural resources. A United Nations conference on the Environment and Development in 1997 bluntly concluded: "Too many countries have seen economic conditions worsen, public services deteriorate, and the total number of people in the world living in poverty has increased."[10] By the 1990s, the richest one-fifth of the world's people received 80 percent of the total income, while the poorest one-fifth earned less than 2 percent. Furthermore, the policies of rich countries often penalized poor countries (see Witness to the Past: An Agenda for a New Millennium). Despite preaching the benefits of free trade, rich nations have often blocked or restricted exports from poor nations into their own markets while heavily subsidizing their own farmers. Hence, wheat farmers in the West African country of Mali, however industrious, cannot compete with French or U.S. wheat farmers, who can sell their crops at much lower prices because of the financial support from their governments.

Rich and Poor in Brazil The stark contrast between the wealthy and the poor in many nations can be seen in the Brazilian city of Rio de Janeiro. Seeking jobs in expanding industries, millions of migrants flock to the city, building shantytown slums and squatter settlements in view of luxury high-rise apartment and office buildings.

Local Economic Strategies in the Third World

Despite the challenges they have faced since World War II, the nations outside of Europe and North America can boast of achievements. Between 1960 and 2000, they reduced infant mortality by half and doubled adult literacy rates. China, Sri Lanka, Malaysia, and Tanzania have been particularly successful in providing social services, such as schools and clinics, to rural areas. Various countries have developed their own locally based development strategies, such as local cooperative banks that provide credit to farmers and store grain for later consumption by villagers. However, such food supplies did not last long when

An Agenda for the New Millennium

In 2000, the United Nations called together the 188 member states for a summit at its headquarters in New York City to discuss the issues facing the world during the new millennium. In the following document, distributed before the summit, the United Nations secretary general, Kofi Annan of Ghana (GAH-nuh), laid out his vision for the organization and the challenges it faced in a world that had changed dramatically since the organization's formation more than five decades earlier.

If one word encapsulates the changes we are living through, it is "globalization." We live in a world that is interconnected as never before—one in which groups and individuals interact more and more directly across State frontiers. . . . This has its dangers, of course. Crime, narcotics, terrorism, disease, weapons—all these move back and forth faster, and in greater numbers, than in the past. People feel threatened by events far away. But the benefits of globalization are obvious too: faster growth, higher living standards, and new opportunities—not only for individuals but also for better understanding between nations, and for common action.

One problem is that, at present, these opportunities are far from equally distributed. How can we say that the half of the human race which has yet to make or receive a phone call, let alone use a computer, is taking part in globalization? We cannot, without insulting their poverty. A second problem is that, even where the global market does reach, it is not yet underpinned by rules based on shared social objectives. In the absence of such rules, globalization makes many people feel they are at the mercy of unpredictable forces. So, . . . the overarching challenge of our times is to make globalization mean more than bigger markets. To make a success of this great upheaval we must learn how to govern better, and . . . how to govern together. . . . We need to get [our nations] working together on global issues—all pulling their weight and all having their say.

What are these global issues? . . . First, freedom from want. How can we call human beings free and equal in dignity when over a billion of them are struggling to survive on less than one dollar a day, without safe drinking water, and when half of all humanity lacks adequate sanitation? Some of us are worrying about whether the stock market will crash, or struggling to master our latest computer, while more than half our fellow men and women have much more basic worries, such as where their children's next meal is coming from. . . . I believe we can halve the population of people living in extreme poverty; ensure that all children—girls and boys alike, particularly the girls—receive a full primary education; and . . . transform the lives of one hundred million slum dwellers around the world.

The second main [issue] is freedom from fear. Wars between States are mercifully less frequent than they used to be. But in the last decade internal wars have claimed more than five million lives, and driven many times that number of people from their homes. . . . We must do more to prevent conflicts from happening. Most conflicts happen in poor countries, especially those which are badly governed or where power and wealth are very unfairly distributed between ethnic or religious groups. So the best way to prevent conflict is to promote [fair representation of all groups in government], human rights, and broad-based economic development.

The third [issue] is . . . the freedom of future generations to sustain their lives on this planet. Even now, many of us have not understood how seriously that freedom is threatened. We are plundering our children's heritage to pay for our present unsustainable practices. We must stop. We must reduce emissions of . . . "greenhouse gases," to put a stop to global warming. . . . We must face the implications of a steadily shrinking surface of cultivable land, at a time when every year brings many millions of new mouths to feed. . . . We must preserve our forests, fisheries, and the diversity of living species, all of which are close to collapsing under the pressure of human consumption and destruction. . . . We need a new ethic of stewardship to encourage environment-friendly practices. . . . Above all we need to remember the old African wisdom which I learned as a child—that the earth is not ours. It is a treasure we hold in trust for our descendants.

Thinking About the Reading

1. What does Annan see as the major global issues of the new millennium?
2. How are the problems he outlined connected to each other?

Source: United Nations, *The Millennium Report* (*http://www.un.org/millennium/sg/report/state.htm*). Reprinted with permission of the United Nations.

severe drought caused major famine, as occurred in 2005, bringing widespread starvation.

Women, Children, and Economic Innovation

Women and their children have faced the harshest problems as modern economic growth has destroyed the traditional cycles of peasant life and undermined the handicrafts that once provided incomes for women. It has also fragmented families: men sometimes have to find work in other districts or countries, leaving their wives to support and raise the children. For example, in Africa, men migrate each year from Burkina Faso to the cocoa plantations and logging camps of the Ivory Coast, and from Mozambique to the mines of South Africa. Meanwhile, migrant work is becoming more feminized. Women leave India, Sri Lanka, and the Philippines to work as domestic servants for rich Arabs in the Persian Gulf states and Saudi Arabia, some facing sexual harassment or cruel employers. Asian and Latin American women are also recruited to work in homes and businesses in North America and Europe, some of them ending up in sweatshops or brothels.

Experts once assumed that schemes to foster economic development would benefit both genders, but women have generally been left behind because of their inferior social and political status. According to United Nations studies, women do 60 percent of the world's work and produce 50 to 75 percent of the world's food, yet they own only 1 percent of the world's property and earn 10 percent of the world's income. While many poor women earn money from growing food, engaging in small-scale trade, or working as domestic servants, most of women's labor—food preparation, cleaning, child rearing—is unpaid and done at home.

 **Internet Discussion of Marriage and Education for Saudi Women, 1996** Read a range of views on the challenges faced by Saudi women in matters of education, employment, and married life.

Some nations have fostered economic development that helps women and children through bottom-up policies relying on grassroots action: the efforts of common people. The founder of the Grameen Bank in Bangladesh, the economist Muhammad Yunus (b. 1940), felt that the conventional economics taught in universities ignored the poverty and struggles occurring in his nation's villages. Learning that conventional banks did not make loans to the poor, in 1983 Yunus opened the Grameen Bank, which makes credit available on cheap terms to peasants, especially women, for small-scale projects such as buying the tools they needed to earn a living. For example, a borrower might buy a cell phone that villagers could use to make business or personal calls, paying the borrower for each call, or purchase bamboo to make chairs. His bank eventually made loans of less than $100 to more than 2 million people. Only less than 2 percent of borrowers defaulted. The newly empowered women, earning an income for their families, now enjoyed higher social status.

Population, Urbanization, and Environmental Change

Rapid population growth and overcrowded cities became manifestations of global imbalance. With too many farmers competing for too little land, rural folk often had to abandon farming and often ended up in crowded cities—Jakarta in Indonesia, Calcutta in India, Cairo in Egypt, Mexico City—where they survived any way they could, often living in shantytowns or worse. Population growth and the resulting expansion of settlement into marginal lands posed unprecedented environmental challenges and increased competition for limited resources. These trends and the enormous surge of economic activity fueled by the use of fossil fuels have changed the world's environment.

The "Population Bomb"

During the past fifty years, the world's population has grown faster than ever before in history (see Map 26.2). Two thousand years ago, the earth had between 125 and 250 million people. At the end of World War II, the population had risen to 2.5 billion, and by 2006, it had more than doubled to 6.5 billion people. Interactive Map

But fertility rates began dropping in much of the world during the late twentieth century, with the biggest declines occurring in industrialized nations. The reasons for the decline were the introduction and widespread use of artificial birth control, better health care, and larger numbers of women entering the paid workforce. By 1990, more than half of the world's couples with women of reproductive age practiced some form of contraception. Nonetheless, in the 1990s, nearly 100 million people were born each year. Demographers now envision a world population of some 9 to 9.5 billion by 2050, and some experts fear such major population growth could lead to increasingly severe social, economic, and environmental problems for the world.

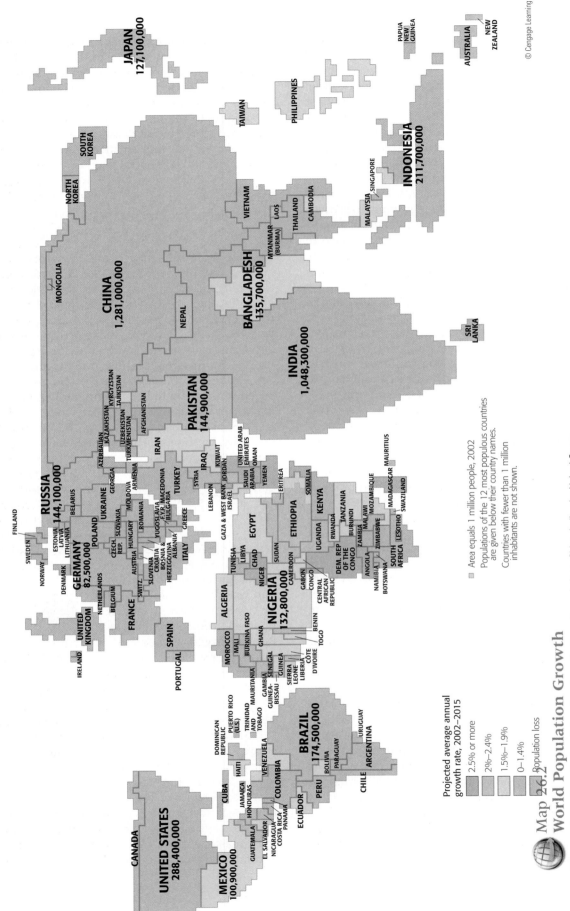

CANADA

UNITED STATES
288,400,000

MEXICO
100,900,000

GUATEMALA
EL SALVADOR
NICARAGUA
COSTA RICA
PANAMA

CUBA
JAMAICA
HONDURAS

HAITI
DOMINICAN REPUBLIC
PUERTO RICO (US)

VENEZUELA
COLOMBIA
ECUADOR
PERU

BOLIVIA

BRAZIL
174,500,000

PARAGUAY

CHILE
ARGENTINA
URUGUAY

TRINIDAD AND TOBAGO

IRELAND
UNITED KINGDOM
NETHERLANDS
BELGIUM
FRANCE
SWITZ.
SPAIN
PORTUGAL

NORWAY
SWEDEN
FINLAND
DENMARK
GERMANY
82,500,000
POLAND
CZECH. REP.
AUSTRIA
SLOVENIA
CROATIA
BOSNIA & HERZEGOVINA
ITALY
ALBANIA

ESTONIA
LATVIA
LITHUANIA
BELARUS
UKRAINE
SLOVAKIA
HUNGARY
ROMANIA
MOLDOVA
YUGOSLAVIA
F.Y.R. MACEDONIA
BULGARIA
GREECE

RUSSIA
144,100,000

MOROCCO
ALGERIA
TUNISIA
LIBYA

MALI
BURKINA FASO
GHANA
MAURITANIA
SENEGAL
GAMBIA
GUINEA-BISSAU
GUINEA
SIERRA LEONE
LIBERIA
CÔTE D'IVOIRE
TOGO
BENIN

NIGERIA
132,800,000

NIGER
CHAD
CAMEROON
CONGO
GABON
CENTRAL AFRICAN REPUBLIC

SUDAN
EGYPT

ETHIOPIA

UGANDA
RWANDA
BURUNDI
DEM. REP. OF THE CONGO

KENYA
TANZANIA

ANGOLA
ZAMBIA
MALAWI
ZIMBABWE
MOZAMBIQUE
NAMIBIA
BOTSWANA
SOUTH AFRICA
LESOTHO
SWAZILAND
MADAGASCAR
MAURITIUS

SOMALIA
ERITREA

TURKEY
SYRIA
LEBANON
GAZA & WEST BANK
ISRAEL
JORDAN
IRAQ
KUWAIT
SAUDI ARABIA
UNITED ARAB EMIRATES
OMAN
YEMEN

ARMENIA
AZERBAIJAN
GEORGIA

IRAN

AFGHANISTAN
TURKMENISTAN
UZBEKISTAN
TAJIKISTAN
KYRGYZSTAN
KAZAKHSTAN

PAKISTAN
144,900,000

INDIA
1,048,300,000

SRI LANKA

NEPAL

BANGLADESH
135,700,000

CHINA
1,281,000,000

MONGOLIA

MYANMAR (BURMA)
LAOS
THAILAND
CAMBODIA
VIETNAM

MALAYSIA
SINGAPORE

INDONESIA
211,700,000

PAPUA NEW GUINEA

AUSTRALIA

NEW ZEALAND

PHILIPPINES

TAIWAN

NORTH KOREA
SOUTH KOREA

JAPAN
127,100,000

© Cengage Learning

Projected average annual growth rate, 2002–2015

2.5% or more
2%–2.4%
1.5%–1.9%
0–1.4%
Population loss

Area equals 1 million people, 2002

Populations of the 12 most populous countries are given below their country names.

Countries with fewer than 1 million inhabitants are not shown.

Map 26.2
World Population Growth

This map shows dramatically which nations have the largest populations: China, India, the United States, Indonesia, and Brazil. It also shows which regions experience the most rapid population growth: Africa, South Asia, and Central America.

jobs, local people have often felt threatened by the newcomers and resent their continuing attachment to their own languages and cultural traditions. While the globalization of trade and jobs dissolves economic boundaries, governments increasingly impose tighter border controls in an effort to discourage illegal immigration. For example, the United States has devoted more resources to patrolling the long border with Mexico but has been unable to stop the flow of Latin Americans flocking north.

By the late twentieth century, the world contained some 100 million voluntary migrants to foreign countries, and the great majority moved for economic rather than political reasons. Many migrants—some from impoverished regions such as Central America and South Asia, others from more prosperous nations such as South Korea and Taiwan—have sought better economic opportunities in the industrialized West. Filipinos are an especially mobile people, migrating for short periods to other Southeast Asian nations and the Middle East and more permanently to North America. Some 8 million Filipinos lived abroad by 2002. Moving to a faraway, alien society is often traumatic, for both the migrant and the family members left behind.

Political turbulence, wars, genocides, and government repression have created some 20 million refugees. Desperate people have fled nations engulfed in political violence, such as Sudan, Guatemala, Afghanistan, and Cambodia, and drought-plagued states such as Ethiopia and Mali. Cubans, Chinese, Laotians (lao-OH-shuhnz), and Vietnamese, among others, have fled communist-run states that restricted their freedoms. Others, such as Haitians, Chileans, and Congolese, have escaped brutal right-wing dictatorships or corrupt despotisms. Millions of refugees have remained for decades, even generations, in squalid refugee camps: for example, many Palestinians who fled conflict in Israel have lived in refugee camps in neighboring Egypt, Jordan, and Lebanon (LEB-uh-nuhn) for more than five decades. Facing increasing numbers of people seeking refugee status, by the 1990s many nations, especially in Europe, became more cautious in granting political asylum.

The Global Spread of Disease

Diseases, whether confined chiefly to a local area or traveling the routes of trade and migration, have produced major pandemics, or massive disease outbreaks, throughout history. Today, although modern medicine has eliminated diseases that had long plagued humanity, some, such as cholera and malaria, still bedevil people who have little access to health care. Cholera still kills several thousand peo-

ple per year in poor countries, and malaria, spread by mosquitoes, debilitates millions of people in tropical regions. Both U.N. agencies and private organizations, such as Doctors Without Borders, have worked hard to reduce health threats and treat victims, but the travel of migrants, tourists, businesspeople, armies, truck drivers, sailors, and others continues to spread diseases.

The AIDS Epidemic The most deadly contemporary scourge affecting nations rich and poor, autoimmune deficiency syndrome (AIDS), is caused by a virus known as human immunodeficiency virus (HIV). AIDS spreads through sexual contact, needle sharing by drug addicts, and blood transfusions. Poverty, which forces many women into prostitution, is also a factor in the spread of AIDS. By 2005, some 42 million people around the world were infected with either HIV or AIDS, and 3.1 million died annually from AIDS, about one-third adult women, who were often infected by their husbands. In some African districts, parental deaths left some 30 percent of children orphans, and as much as 30 percent of the adult population of some African nations was HIV-positive.

By contrast, the disease is less catastrophic in countries with less poverty and better health care and communications. Only 0.2 percent of Americans were infected, and the rate was even lower in Europe. The pandemic has presented an obstacle to economic development and has proved to be a particular disaster in India, Southeast Asia, and east, central, and southern Africa. Because most AIDS victims are in their twenties and thirties, in the worst-affected countries the disease has killed or incapacitated the most highly trained and economically active section of the population. Treating AIDS patients also puts an added stress on the limited resources available for health care. AIDS victims are often rejected by their families and communities, dying alone and neglected by society.

Cultures and Religions Across Borders

The spread of cultural products and religions across national borders and the creative mixing of these with local traditions have been hallmarks of the modern world. These trends have developed within the context of a global system in which people and ideas meet. In societies around the world, popular culture—commonly produced for commercial purposes and spread by the mass media, such as radio, television, and films—has become a part of everyday life for billions of people. Spurred by globalization, religions have struggled for relevance but have also found new believers and adapted to new environments (see Map 26.3).

 Interactive Map

Cultural Synthesis

Societies have long exchanged cultural influences that have enriched local traditions. In the modern era, Western influences have been pervasive; yet, some of the modernization around the world that seems to reflect Westernization has remained superficial. The Internet, movies, pop music, and shopping malls that encourage consumption have attracted some youth in Asia, Africa, and Latin America, but their influence on the broader society, especially in the rural areas, is often more limited. No common world culture has emerged in this era. At the same time, Western technologies sometimes have served local needs. India, for instance, developed the world's largest film industry, producing some 1,000 films per year by 2002, three times more films than the United States or Japan. Modern media have reshaped people's lives, especially in cities, giving many societies a certain common denominator of experience.

The mixing of cultures and the increasing role of the mass media have been reflected in popular music. Anglo-American pop music styles, such as rock, jazz, and rap, all African American forms though having African roots, have found audiences all over the world. Vaclav Havel (vah-SLAV hah-VEL), the leader of the movement that overthrew Czech communism, credited the U.S. rock musician Frank Zappa with inspiring him to become an activist. Using the power of their celebrity and the mass media, Western pop stars have also raised awareness on issues such as racism, political prisoners, famine, and African poverty. Bono, the lead singer for the Irish rock band U2, campaigns tirelessly among political leaders for causes such as debt relief for poor nations. Many forms of music have mixed indigenous and imported influences, often from outside the West. For example, Congolese popular music, which borrowed Latin American dance rhythms, gained audiences throughout Africa and Europe in the 1980s. Indian film music and Arab folk music have influenced the popular

"The spread of cultural products and religions across national borders and the creative mixing of these with local traditions have been hallmarks of the modern world."

music of Southeast Asia and East Africa.

Religion and Globalization

Although in the modern era, secular thought has become more popular than ever before in history, more than three-quarters of the world's people identify with one or another universal religion with roots deep in the past. By 2000, the world contained almost 2 billion Christians, 1.3 billion Muslims, 800 million Hindus, and 350 million Buddhists. Nearly 900 million practiced a local faith, such as animism or Daoism, or professed no religion (see Map 26.3). Religion sometimes has become the basis for national identity, as in chiefly Roman Catholic Poland and Ireland and in Muslim Bangladesh and Pakistan.

Religious leaders have debated how much, if at all, their faiths need to change to better engage the contemporary world. Serious efforts at reform came, for instance, in the Catholic Church in the 1960s when Pope John XXIII (pope 1958–1963) liberalized church practices, such as having the mass in a vernacular language rather than Latin, and encouraged a more active dialogue with other churches and religions. Meanwhile, a movement arose among Catholic clergy and laypeople in Latin America, called liberation theology, that cooperated with socialist and communist groups to improve the lives of the poor. Muslim liberals and militants also confronted each other over which directions Islam should take, arguing over such issues as the role of women, relations with non-Muslims, and whether states with Muslim majorities should make Islamic law the basis of their legal systems.

The easy spread of ideas in the globalized world has worked to the advantage of portable creeds that are not dependent on one culture or setting. In many places, notably Africa, religions tied to local culture, usually some form of polytheism or animism, have faded, while two universal religions, Christianity and Islam, fortified by missionary impulses, have gained wider followings in developing nations. At the same time, organized religion and its influence have declined in East Asia and much of the West. Communists discouraged religious observance in China, while increasing numbers of Japanese found neither their traditional faiths nor imported religions as relevant. Meanwhile, Christian churches in

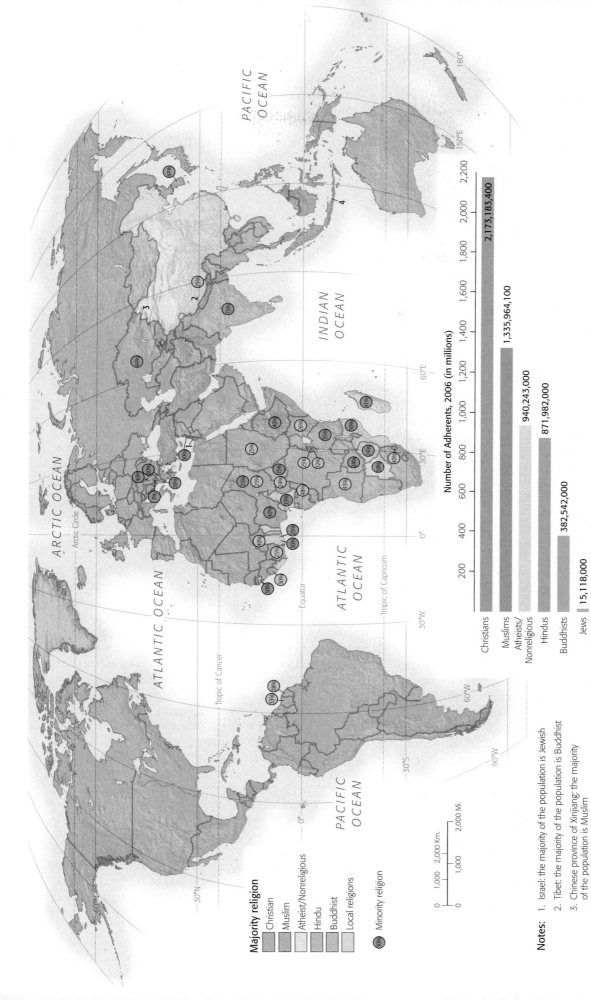

Map 26.3
World Religions

Majority religion
- Christian
- Muslim
- Atheist/Nonreligious
- Hindu
- Buddhist
- Local religions
- 60% Minority religion

Number of Adherents, 2006 (in millions)

Christians — 2,173,183,400
Muslims — 1,335,964,100
Atheists/Nonreligious — 940,243,000
Hindus — 871,982,000
Buddhists — 382,542,000
Jews — 15,118,000
Other religions — 821,244,500

Notes: 1. Israel: the majority of the population is Jewish
2. Tibet: the majority of the population is Buddhist
3. Chinese province of Xinjiang: the majority of the population is Muslim
4. Indonesian island of Bali: the majority of the population is Hindu

Christianity has the most believers and is the dominant faith in the Americas, Oceania, Europe, Russia, and central and southern Africa. Most people in the northern half of Africa, western Asia, and Central Asia embrace Islam. Hindus are concentrated in India, and Buddhists in East and Southeast Asia.

Europe, Canada, and Australia experienced dramatic drops in attendance and membership between 1960 and the early twenty-first century. Traditional church attitudes have also competed with changing social attitudes. Even predominantly Catholic nations in Europe have legalized abortion and moved toward equal rights for homosexuals, policies opposed by the Catholic Church. Both the Netherlands, once a center for a puritanical form of Protestantism, and Spain, before the 1970s one of the staunchest Catholic nations, have approved same-sex marriage.

Religion and Oppression

Long a source of conflict, religion continues to sow tensions between members of different faiths. Hundreds of people were killed or wounded in Nigeria when rival Christians and Muslims sporadically battled for control of several cities. Meanwhile, tensions between Muslims and Hindus sparked sporadic violence in India. Catholics and Protestants opposed each other in Northern Ireland and Uganda, while Sunni and Shi'a Muslims occasionally fought in Pakistan and western Asia. In Iraq, where some 60 percent of the population is Shi'a, the Sunni dictator, Saddam Hussein, restricted Shi'ite religious holidays, executed Shi'ites who opposed his regime, and allowed few Shi'ites into the government. After his regime was toppled by the 2003 U.S. invasion, conflicts between Shi'ites and Sunnis erupted, complicating U.S. efforts to restore political stability.

The Fundamentalist Backlash

Religious militancy has grown among some believers. Some Muslim militants have turned the old notion of *jihad*, or struggle within believers to strengthen their faith, into a campaign for holy war against unbelievers and countries or groups they consider anti-Muslim. The militants, often known as Islamists or jihadis, appeal especially to the young and poor, who are often unemployed and embittered toward their governments and the West. The more puritanical Muslims despise the sexuality and rebellion portrayed in Western television programs and movies.

Some Christians, especially in the United States, Latin America, and Africa, have turned to literal interpretations of the Bible, an approach labeled as fundamentalist, and formed proselytizing churches. These churches have often opposed secular culture, rejected scientific findings they deemed incompatible with biblical accounts, and condemned left-wing political and social movements. Christian and Islamic militancy has sparked similar movements in Buddhism, Hinduism, and Judaism, pitting the zealous believers against those with moderate, tolerant views.

Global Communications

A worldwide communications network has been a chief engine of globalization. The introduction of radio in the early 1900s and then tape recording and television in mid-century laid the basis for this network. These were followed by the invention of the transistor by three American physicists in 1947, which allowed for the miniaturization of electronics. In 1953, portable transistor radios became available and soon reached even remote villages, opening them to the news and culture of the wider world. Even villages without electricity could use transistor radios and cassette players.

Technological breakthroughs provided the foundation for more rapid and widespread communications. For decades, U.S., British, and German engineers gradually built a foundation for computer technology. The first general-purpose computers were built in 1948. In 1958, the first silicon microchips began a computer revolution that led several decades later to the first personal computers. By 2000, the world had more than 150 million personal computers with Internet access, 330 million Internet users, and 1.6 billion web pages, all part of a vast network often termed the information superhighway. Every minute, 10 million electronically transmitted messages, or e-mail, are dispatched via computer. E-mail allows people in different countries, however distant, to communicate instantly with each other. An interested reader in Hong Kong, Ghana, or Finland can access online newspapers such as the *New York Times* or the *Deccan Herald* in India. Along with computers, the rise of 24-hour cable news networks able to reach worldwide audiences, such as U.S.-based CNN (Cable News Network) and the Arab-language Al Jazeera, based in the Persian Gulf state of Qatar, widened access to diverse views.

The rapid evolution of media and information technology has had many consequences. For one, the development of cellular phones, e-mail, and the Internet means that information can be transmitted around the globe beyond the reach of governments, undermining their power to shape their citizens' thinking. In 2006, some U.S.-based Internet providers faced criticism for helping repressive governments such as China control the information flow and identify dissidents. Another major consequence is that technologies have enhanced the value of education and of English, which has gradually become a world language. By 2004, some three-quarters of all websites were in English. Perhaps one-quarter of the world's people know some English, and Asian countries with educated people fluent in English, such as India and Singapore, have an advantage in competing for high-technology industries. These major trends have also enhanced the global exchange of scientific ideas, but in the poorest nations, only a lucky few have satellite dishes, fax machines, and networked computers, and these promising technologies have not changed the lives of peasants and low-wage workers.

Global Movements

Increasing links between far-flung peoples have allowed for social and political movements to transcend borders. A wide variety of transnational organizations has emerged to promote issues such as the treatment of political prisoners, women's rights, and antiracism. As an example, Amnesty International, based in Britain, publicizes the plight of people who have been imprisoned solely for their political views and activities, such as the Burmese opposition leader Aung San Suu Kyi (AWNG sahn soo CHEE), organizing letter-writing and pressure campaigns to seek their release. Other movements have addressed globalization. For instance, the World Social Forum was formed in 2001 and has met annually in Brazil to oppose globalizing free-market capitalism and call for workers' rights and environmental protection.

Global Protest Movements

As the world became more closely linked, social or political movements or upheavals in one nation or region sometimes spread widely. For example, during the 1960s, students, workers, and political radicals in various nations organized protests against the U.S. war in Vietnam, racism, unresponsive governments, capitalism, and other concerns. In 1968, demonstrations, marches, and strikes intensified around the world. These movements were not coordinated

Internet Cafe in Thailand In this photo, a waiter at a cyberspace café, operated by the Swiss multinational ice cream company, Häagen Dazs, in Bangkok, Thailand, helps a young Thai woman navigate one of the café's computers.

> "As the world became more closely linked, social or political movements or upheavals in one nation or region sometimes spread widely."

and addressed largely local grievances, but young protesters were often influenced by the same writers, music, and ideas. To varying degrees, the turbulence affected more than a dozen countries, from the United States and Mexico to France, Czechoslovakia, and Japan. When thousands of demonstrators shouting "Mexico, Freedom" took to the streets of Mexico City to demand democracy and protest police brutality, the police opened fire, killing dozens of protesters and shocking the world. In the wake of the 1968 activism, movements focused on environmental awareness, peace, workers' rights, homosexual rights, and feminism grew in popularity.

Women in a Global Age

Women have been particularly active in seeking to expand their rights. Although most women's organizations work within national boundaries, some activists have placed women's issues on the international agenda, but do not always agree on solutions. In the United Nation's fourth World Conference on Women, held in China in 1995, the 40,000 delegates disagreed sharply on priorities. Delegates from rich nations wanted to expand women's employment options, social freedom, and control over their bodies, while Asian, African, and Latin American delegates were often chiefly interested in making their families more healthy and economically secure. Yet, despite disagreements, women have worked across borders on issues affecting all societies, such as preventing violence against women.

In 2005, Mukhtaran Bibi (MOOK-tahr-an BIH-bee), an illiterate woman from an impoverished Pakistani village, gained worldwide sympathy for her resistance to male brutality. As part of a village dispute, the tribal council had ruled that she be gang-raped to punish her family. Instead of following custom by ending the "disgrace" through suicide, however, she bravely pursued the rapists in court. They were convicted, and she used the money awarded to her by the court to start two village schools, one for boys and one for girls. When a higher court then overturned the men's convictions, her courageous refusal to accept the verdict caused an international outcry. While the Pakistan government tried to suppress the controversy, men and women around the world rallied to her cause. Mukhtaran Bibi inspired millions everywhere with her courage and faith in education and justice.

Global Terrorism

Terrorism, small-scale but violent attacks aimed at undermining a government or demoralizing a population, intensified in the late twentieth and early twenty-first centuries, expanding to global dimensions and reshaping world politics. For centuries, various groups and states used terrorism to support their goals. After 1945, Palestinians under Israeli control, Basque nationalists in Spain, and Irish nationalists in Britain, among others, engaged in terrorism for their causes. Some states also carried out or sponsored terrorism against unfriendly governments or political movements. The United States sponsored terrorism against leftist-ruled Nicaragua in the 1980s, helping form a military force, known as the Contras, that often attacked civilian targets, such as rural schools, daycare centers, and clinics operated by the government.

While terrorism has often remained local in scope, an increasingly interconnected world has spurred some terrorist organizations to operate on a global level, forming networks that have branches in many countries. The most active of these networks, formed by militant Islamists, have exploited communication and transportation networks to operate across national borders, capitalizing on widespread Muslim anger at Israel and U.S. foreign policies. Muslim terrorist groups became increasingly active during the 1970s and 1980s in Egypt, Algeria, and Lebanon, attacking politicians, police, Western residents and tourists, and Israeli and U.S. targets.

As a result, terrorism became a growing threat to life in the Middle East. To oppose Israeli occupation of Arab lands and demoralize Israelis, Palestinian militants strapped explosives to their bodies and detonated them in Israeli buses and businesses. Outraged by the killing and wounding of hundreds of Israeli civilians—both Jewish and Arab—the Israelis responded with force, killing or arresting Palestinians and expelling families of suspected militants from their homes, often bulldozing the houses into rubble. The poet Hanan Ashrawi (HA-non uh-SHRAH-wee), a

Christian Palestinian nationalist, condemned the suicide bombings but also lamented the earlier Israeli destruction of her family's property: "Have you seen a stone house die? It sighs, then wraps itself around its gutted heart and lays itself to rest."[11] Divided by politics, Israelis and Palestinians have shared the bitter experience of grieving for those lost in the chronic violence.

Osama Bin Laden and Al Qaeda

The Soviet military intervention in 1979 to support a pro-Soviet government in mostly Muslim Afghanistan provided the spark for forming a global network of Islamist terrorists. Islamic militants from the Middle East and Pakistan flocked to Afghanistan to assist the Muslim Afghan insurgents resisting the Soviets. In 1988, the most militant of the foreign fighters began to come together in a jihadi organization known as Al Qaeda ("The Base"). Al Qaeda's main leader was the Saudi Osama bin Laden (b. 1957), who came from an extremely wealthy family—his Yemen-born father had made billions in the Saudi construction industry—and had been trained as an engineer. Bin Laden used his wealth to support the Afghan rebels, mostly devout Muslims, who were also funded and armed by the United States. After the Soviets abandoned Afghanistan in 1989, bin Laden used his supporters to set up Al Qaeda cells in Saudi Arabia, whose government he viewed as corrupt, and to target Egypt and Iraq, whose secular regimes suppressed Islamic militants. To recruit, support, and communicate with members, Al Qaeda used modern technology, publicizing their cause by setting up websites, using e-mail and satellite phones, and releasing videotapes to cable news networks of bin Laden's messages.

Declaration of Jihad Against Americans Occupying the Land of the Two Holy Mosques Read a speech given by Osama bin Laden to his followers in Afghanistan, and soon published worldwide.

Eventually, Al Qaeda looked beyond the Middle East for targets. In the mid-1990s, the Afghanistan-based bin Laden began to plot terrorist efforts against his former ally in the Afghan resistance, the United States, whose military bases in Saudi Arabia, support for repressive Arab governments, and close alliance with Israel enraged many Arabs. Bin Laden argued that "to kill the Americans and their allies is an individual duty for every Muslim who can do it in any country in which it is possible to do so."[12] Most Muslims rejected such violent views, but Al Qaeda or related groups sponsored attacks on U.S. targets, such as the embassies in Kenya and Tanzania, causing hundreds of casualties.

September 11, 2001

On September 11, 2001, Al Qaeda members hijacked four U.S. commercial airliners and crashed them into New York's World Trade Center and the Pentagon near Washington, D.C., killing more than three thousand people, mostly civilians. The attacks shocked Americans, who were unused to terrorism at home, as well as people everywhere who opposed indiscriminate killing. U.S. president George W. Bush responded by declaring a war on terrorism. U.S. forces attacked Al Qaeda bases in Afghanistan, and then occupied the country, whose government, controlled by Islamists who had fought the Soviets, shielded bin Laden, but the United States failed to capture bin Laden and still faced resistance from Islamic militants.

In 2003, the United States, claiming that Saddam Hussein's Iraq was closely linked to Al Qaeda and possessed weapons of mass destruction, invaded Iraq, removed Saddam's brutal, despotic government, and imposed a U.S. military occupation. Britain provided the chief support for the U.S. effort. The U.S. troops, however, found no evidence of any ties between Saddam and Al Qaeda or any weapons of mass destruction. The occupation sparked an insurgency, including suicide bombings, and unleashed sectarian divisions that hindered U.S. efforts—supported by many Iraqis—to stabilize and rebuild Iraq. While most of the insurgents were Iraqis, mostly Sunni Muslims fearing domination by the Shi'ite majority, Islamists from other countries flocked to Iraq to attack Americans and help destabilize the country. The U.S. invasion and occupation, and the resistance to it, killed tens of thousands of Iraqi civilians, resulted in more than 25,000 U.S. casualties, alienated many U.S. allies and, like the earlier U.S. conflict in Vietnam, was unpopular around the world. Meanwhile, capitalizing on anti-U.S. sentiment among Muslims, Al Qaeda spawned loosely affiliated terrorist groups, often operating without direct Al Qaeda guidance.

Terrorism by militant Muslims had direct and indirect consequences for societies around the world. Al Qaeda or related groups launched terrorist attacks on several continents, from Spain and Britain to Indonesia, Kenya, and Morocco. Nations with despotic governments, such as China, Egypt, and Uzbekistan, used the threat of terrorism as a reason to restrict civil liberties. Human rights concerns faded amid the Western obsession with terrorism.

Listen to a synopsis of Chapter 26.

CHAPTER 27

East Asian Resurgence,
Since 1945

Learning Outcomes

After reading this chapter, you should be able to answer the following questions:

LO¹ How did Maoism transform Chinese society?

LO² What factors explain the dramatic rise of Chinese economic power in the world since 1978?

LO³ How did Japan rise from the ashes of defeat in World War II to become a global economic powerhouse?

LO⁴ What policies led to the rise of the "Little Dragon" nations and their dynamic economies?

"Once China's destiny is in the hands of the people, China, like the sun rising in the east, will illuminate every corner with a brilliant flame, and build a new, powerful and prosperous [society].**"**

—**Mao Zedong, Chinese communist leader**[1]

On October 1, 1949, the Chinese Communist leader Mao Zedong (maow dzuh-dong) (1893–1976) was driven into downtown Beijing, China's capital, accompanied by a dusty band of the People's Liberation Army. Mao, fifty-five years old, the son of a peasant family, had spent the previous twenty-two years living in remote rural areas. The Republic of China, the government headed by Jiang Jieshi (better known in the West as Chiang Kai-shek) (1887–1975), had lost to Mao's troops, and the president had fled to the large offshore island of Taiwan. Wearing a new suit, Mao climbed to the top of the Gate of Heavenly Peace, the entrance to the Forbidden City of the Qing emperors overlooking Beijing's spacious Tiananmen Square. Millions of Chinese jammed the square to hear their new ruler announce the founding of a new communist government, called the People's Republic of China. Referring to a century of corrupt governments, humiliation, and domination by Western nations and Japan, Mao thanked his allies and firmly proclaimed: "The Chinese people have stood up. Nobody will insult us again."[2]

The formation of the People's Republic marked a watershed in the history of China, the rest of East Asia, and the world. The new government brought to an end a century of severe instability. Its communist leaders were committed to the revolutionary transformation of the society, while making China respected abroad once again. Given China's size and population—1.3 billion by 2005—any major transition there had global significance. By the early twenty-first century, China, with a booming economy, had reclaimed some of the political and economic status it had lost two centuries earlier.

Chinese were not the only East Asians to enjoy a resurgence with a global impact. In the 1980s, observers referred to the Pacific Rim, the economically dynamic Asian countries on the edge of the Pacific

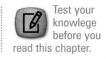 Test your knowlege before you read this chapter.

Pacific Rim
The economically dynamic Asian countries on the western edge of the Pacific Basin: China, Japan, South Korea, Taiwan, and several Southeast Asian nations.

〈〈**The China Stock Exchange** The East Asian nations enjoyed an economic resurgence in this era. Since the 1980s, China has boasted the world's fastest growing economy and a booming stock exchange.

Wally McNamee/Corbis

> "The key question confronting the Chinese communists after 1949 was how to achieve rapid economic development in an overpopulated, battered country."

Basin: China, Japan, South Korea, Taiwan, and several Southeast Asian nations. These observers also predicted that the twenty-first century would be the Pacific Century, marked by a shift of global economic power to the Pacific Rim, whose export-driven nations seemed poised to dominate a post–Cold War era where economic power outweighed military might. Although economic crises and changing world politics have challenged the Pacific Century concept, China, Japan, and their neighbors have remained major players in the global system.

LO¹ Mao's Revolutionary China

The Chinese Revolution that brought the Chinese communists to power in 1949 was one of the three greatest upheavals in modern world history, on line with the French Revolution of 1789 and the Russian Revolution of 1917. China's revolution remade a major world society while restoring China's international status. The communists built a strong government that made China the most experimental nation on earth, veering from one innovative policy to another in an attempt to renovate Chinese life. The People's Republic of China created a new model of economic development different from both Western-dominated capitalism and the highly centralized Soviet communism, but the path was littered with conflict and repression. Furthermore, the Chinese, like all societies, were products of their history. Even under communist rule, China remained partly an ancient empire and partly a modern nation, and its leaders often behaved much like the emperors of old in their autocratic exercise of power.

Communist Triumph, Economy, and Government

The U.S. defeat of Japan in 1945 removed the common enemy of both of China's major political factions, Mao's communists and Chiang Kai-shek's nationalist government, sparking a fierce civil war between them. Chiang disdained Mao as an unpolished peasant, while Mao despised Chiang for favoring the rich, yet both men shared patriotism, an autocratic style, and hunger for power. Chiang's 3.7-million-man army vastly outnumbered the 900,000 communist troops and enjoyed lavish military aid from the United States. The communists, aided by the Soviet Union (USSR), concentrated on north China and Manchuria. In trying to block Mao's forces, Chiang overstretched his supply lines; meanwhile, a rapid decline in the value of Chinese currency demoralized the population. The Chinese sought change, and many of them came to view the communist movement as a more honest alternative to Chiang's Nationalist Party. In the villages that they controlled, the communists promoted a social revolution, known as the "turning over," by encouraging villagers to denounce local landlords, transferring land from richer to poorer peasants, replacing government-appointed leaders with elected village councils, and protecting battered wives.

The military and political tide turned against the Republic. In 1948, Chiang's troops in Manchuria surrendered to the communists. To revive Chiang's prospects, and recognizing the growing unpopularity of his regime, the United States pressured him unsuccessfully to broaden his political base with democratic reforms. Through 1949, the communists took the major cities of north China and pushed Chiang's army south. Finally, Chiang fled to the island of Taiwan, along with thousands of troops and 2 million supporters. On Taiwan, with massive U.S. aid, the leaders of the relocated Republic of China developed a successful capitalist strategy for economic growth. Meanwhile, mainland China moved in a different direction.

Rebuilding China's Economy

The key question confronting the Chinese communists after 1949 was how to achieve rapid economic development in an overpopulated, battered country. Two decades of war had ruined the economy, leaving little capital for industrialization. Unlike Britain and France in the nineteenth century, China had no overseas empire to exploit. The new leaders did not want loans and foreign investment that might reduce their independence and lead to a debt trap. Furthermore, they faced a powerful enemy: propelled by alarm at Mao's policies and anticommunist Cold War concerns, the United

> "By the late 1950s, Mao, growing disenchanted with Stalinism, introduced a second model of development, known as Maoism, that synthesized Marxist and Chinese thought."

communes Large agricultural units introduced by Mao Zedong that combined many families and villages into a common system for pooling resources and labor.

States launched an economic boycott to shut China off from international trade, refused diplomatic recognition, and surrounded China with military bases. Isolated, China created its own models of economic and political development.

Between 1949 and 1957, China followed the Soviet model of central planning known as Stalinism: heavy industry, a powerful bureaucracy, and a managerial system. China received some Soviet aid in the 1950s, but otherwise the Chinese communists financed development through self-reliance and withdrew from the global system. The state emphasized

Internet Guide to Chinese Studies (*http://www.sino.uni-heidelberg.de/igcs/*). An excellent collection of links, maintained at a German university.

austerity and acquired capital from the people by making them work hard for low wages, in hopes that future generations would live better. In the Stalinist years, the communists abolished private ownership of business and industry and transferred land to poor peasants. Soon they began collectivizing the rural economy into cooperatives, in which peasants helped each other and shared tools. As in the Soviet Union, the emphasis on state directive fostered the rise of a new privileged elite in the government and in the ruling Communist Party, which cracked down on dissent.

CHRONOLOGY

China Since 1945

1945–1949	Chinese civil war
1949	Chinese communist triumph
1949–1957	Stalinist model
1950	Occupation of Tibet; new marriage law
1950–1953	Korean War
1957–1961	First use of Maoist model
1958–1961	Great Leap Forward
1960	Sino–Soviet split
1966–1976	Great Proletarian Cultural Revolution
1972	Nixon's trip to Beijing
1976	Death of Mao Zedong; arrest of Gang of Four
1978	Four Modernizations policy; normalization of U.S.–China diplomatic relations
1978–1989	Market socialism
1978–1997	Deng Xiaoping era
1989	Beijing Massacre; introduction of market Leninism
1997	Return of Hong Kong to China

The Emergence of Maoism

By the late 1950s, Mao, growing disenchanted with Stalinism, introduced a second model of development, known as Maoism, that synthesized Marxist and Chinese thought. Under Maoism, which was China's guiding ideology from 1957 to 1961 and then again from 1966 to 1976, the Chinese people were mobilized for development projects, such as building dams, pest elimination, and massive tree-planting campaigns. Mao reorganized the rural economy into communes, large agricultural units that combined many families and villages into a common administrative system for pooling resources and labor. The communes raised agricultural productivity, eliminated landlords, and promoted social and economic equality. Mao located industry in rural areas, thus keeping the peasants at home rather than fostering movement to cities, as happened in other countries.

The Great Leap Forward

The most radical Maoist policy was the Great Leap Forward (1958–1961), an ambitious attempt to industrialize China rapidly and end poverty through collective efforts. Farmers and workers were ordered to build small iron furnaces in their backyards, courtyards, and gardens and to spend their free time turning everything from cutlery to old bicycles into steel. The slogan "Achieve More, Better, Faster" swept through the nation. But the poorly conceived campaign, pushing the people too hard, nearly wrecked the economy and, along with disastrous weather, caused 30 million people to starve. These failures undermined Mao's influence, bringing more moderate policies in the early 1960s.

As in the USSR, the Communist Party, led by Mao as chairman, dominated the political system; party members occupied all key positions in the government and military down to village leaders. Using the slogan "Politics Takes Command," the communists made political values pervasive. All Chinese were required to become members of political discussion groups, but party activists monitored the discussions and reported dissenters. Political education was integrated into the schools, work units, and even leisure activities. The party also sought to eradicate inequalities and emphasized the interests of the group over those of the individual.

Explore life as a Chinese villager during the Mao period of the Great Leap Forward and decide whether to work in government or agriculture in this interactive simulation.

Honoring Chairman Mao Since the beginning of communist rule in China in 1949, this giant portrait of Mao Zedong, the chairman of the Chinese Communist Party, has hung on the Gate of Heavenly Peace, the entrance to the Forbidden City of the Qing dynasty emperors, in the heart of Beijing.

Peter Guttman/Corbis

Officials and intellectuals had to perform physical labor, such as spreading manure to fertilize farm fields, so that they would understand the experience of the workers and peasants.

Five Guarantees

Mao's system required massive social control, enabled by a vast police apparatus; millions suspected of opposing the communists were harassed, jailed, exiled, or killed. Even communist sympathizers, such as the outspoken feminist writer Ding Ling (1902–1986), were purged after falling out of official favor. In exchange for accepting its policies, the state promised everyone the "five guarantees" of food, clothes, fuel, education, and a decent burial. But thousands of people, wanting more personal happiness than the system allowed, fled to British-ruled Hong Kong over the years.

Maoist China in the World

The communists restored China's status as a major world power (see Map 27.1), with only some setbacks, and pursued a foreign policy that maximized stability at home. Mao reasserted Chinese sovereignty in outlying areas of China, and in 1950 sent armies to occupy Tibet, whose people, although conquered and incorporated into China by the Qing dynasty in the 1600s, had broken away from China in 1912. Most Tibetans opposed Chinese rule, sparking periodic unrest. The Chinese suppression of a Tibetan revolt led the highest Tibetan Buddhist leader, the Dalai Lama (DAH-lie LAH-mah) (b. 1935), to flee to India in 1958. In exile, the Dalai Lama became a defiant symbol of Tibetan resistance to Chinese rule, traveling the world to rally support for the Tibetan cause while promoting Buddhist ethics and world peace, for which he won the Nobel Peace Prize in 1989.

Interactive Map

The Korean War

In 1950, China, which supported the communist North Korean government installed in 1948, was drawn into the Korean War between the USSR-backed North Korea and United Nations forces sent to defend pro-U.S. South Korea. When the United Nations forces pushed the North Korean army toward China's border, and the U.S. commander, General Douglas MacArthur, talked reck-

> " Political education was integrated into the schools, work units, and even leisure activities. "

lessly of occupying North Korea and carrying the offensive into China, the Chinese, feeling endangered, entered the conflict. Mao caught U.S. leaders by surprise by dispatching 300,000 troops into Korea, and the Chinese forces pushed United Nations troops back south. The war produced huge casualties on both sides, including several hundred thousand Chinese, and reinforced the hostility and mutual fear between China and the United States.

When the Korean War ended in a stalemate in 1953, the United States, seeking to halt communist expansion, signed a mutual defense treaty with Chiang Kai-shek's regime on Taiwan. The substantial U.S. forces stationed in Taiwan and South Korea joined the thousands of U.S. troops that had remained in Japan, Okinawa, and the Philippines after World War II, while the U.S. Navy patrolled the waters off China, making for a formidable U.S. military presence in East Asia. But the ability to achieve a stalemate in Korea with the powerful United States improved China's international position. In the 1950s, China, allied with the USSR, basically withdrew from the global system, maintaining limited trade with only a handful of Western nations.

The Sino–Soviet Split

China adapted to changing global politics. In the late 1950s, tensions between China and the USSR grew. Chinese leaders did not share the Soviet view that what was good for the USSR was necessarily good for international communism. The Soviet policy of "peaceful coexistence" with the West enraged Mao, who labeled the United States "a paper tiger." Mao also opposed the 1956 decision of the Soviet leader, Nikita Khrushchev (KROOSH-chef), to reveal the excesses of Stalinist police-state rule in Russia, raising the issue of abuse of power by communist dictators. By 1960, the Sino–Soviet split was official; the USSR withdrew advisors and technicians, even the spare parts for the industries they had helped build. The Chinese built up their military strength, tested their first atomic bomb, and occasionally clashed with Soviet forces on their border. To counterbalance the power of the United States and the USSR, China sought allies and influence in Asia and Africa. Yet, despite fierce rhetoric, Chinese leaders generally followed a cautious foreign policy.

PACIFIC OCEAN

JAPAN

Sea of Japan (East Sea)

NORTH KOREA

SOUTH KOREA

East China Sea

Yellow Sea

RUSSIA

KAZAKHSTAN

KYRGYZSTAN

TAJIKISTAN

UZBEKISTAN

TURKMENISTAN

AFGHANISTAN

PAKISTAN

INDIA

MONGOLIA

HEILONGJIANG
Harbin

JILIN

LIAONING
Dalian

INNER MONGOLIA

BEIJING Beijing
Tianjin
TIANJIN
HEBEI

SHANDONG

JIANGSU

SHANGHAI

Nanjing

ANHUI

ZHEJIANG

Hangzhou

FUJIAN

Taipei
TAIWAN

PHILIPPINES

South China Sea

GUANGDONG
Guangzhou
Shenzhen
HONG KONG
MACAO
Xiamen

Dazhai
SHANXI

Huang He R.
(Yellow R.)

HENAN

HUBEI

Wuhan

Yangzi R.

Changsha
HUNAN

JIANGXI

Yanan

Xian
SHAANXI

NINGXIA

GANSU

QINGHAI

CHONGQING

SICHUAN

Chengdu

GUIZHOU

YUNNAN

GUANGXI

Xi R.

HAINAN

VIETNAM

LAOS

THAILAND

BURMA (MYANMAR)

Yangzi R.

XINJIANG

TIBET

Lhasa

NEPAL

BHUTAN

BANGLADESH

(INDIA)

Bay of Bengal

Indian claim

Chinese line of control

Nationalist retreat 1948–1949

Boundary uncertain

N

Tropic of Cancer

20°N

40°N

140°E

120°E

100°E

80°E

60°E

0 150 300 Km.
0 150 300 Mi.

© Cengage Learning

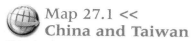

Map 27.1 <<
China and Taiwan

China is a huge country, divided into many provinces, and occupies a large part of eastern Eurasia. In 1949, the government of the Republic of China, defeated by the Chinese communists, moved to the island of Taiwan, off China's Pacific coast.

Nixon and Normalization

During the 1970s, Chinese foreign policy changed dramatically. The change was symbolized by U.S. president Richard Nixon's trip to Beijing in 1972, the first official contact between the two nations since 1949. The two nations shared a hostility toward the USSR; moreover, the bitter U.S. experience fighting communist forces in Vietnam and the gradual withdrawal of U.S. forces from that country had opened the door to foreign policy rethinking in both the United States and China. Chinese leaders perceived the United States as stepping back from Asian military and political commitments, and hence as a diminishing threat. The United States now agreed to quit blocking Chinese membership in the United Nations and, in 1978, normalized diplomatic relations with China. The Chinese also developed better relations with noncommunist nations in Southeast Asia and Africa.

Mao's Cultural Revolution: A New Society

Mao was a complex figure. He was, for example, a self-proclaimed feminist who promoted women's rights, but he was also a sexually promiscuous man who married several times. A poor public speaker with few close friends, he could nevertheless inspire millions to follow his lead. Power-hungry and ruthless, he made many enemies. Although many of his initiatives ultimately failed or resulted in misery for millions of people, he played a powerful role in modern world history, leading the communists to victory, reunifying China, focusing public attention on rural people, and placing his stamp on the world's most populous nation. That impact was particularly strong when Maoism was China's guiding ideology.

Dissatisfied with China's development by the early 1960s, in the mid-1960s Mao sought to regain his dominant status by resurrecting Maoism and offering a vision of a new society that harnessed the collective power of the people. In Mao's vision, individuals, inspired by the slogan "Serve the People," subordinated their own needs to the broader social order. His allies emphasized the cult of Mao and his revolutionary thoughts. This campaign laid the foundation for a major social movement inspired by Mao's thoughts.

The Cultural Revolution

For a decade, between 1966 and 1976, massive turmoil generated by Mao convulsed and reshaped China like a whirlwind. The Great Proletarian Cultural Revolution, as it was called, was a radical movement that represented Mao's attempt to implant his vision, destroy his enemies, crush the stifling bureaucracy, and renew the revolution's vigor. The movement's major supporters—young workers and students known as Red Guards—roamed around cities and the countryside in groups, smashing temples and churches and attacking and arresting anti-Mao leaders. Mao told them to destroy the party and government headquarters and that rebellion was justified. A Mao personality cult spread. The students carried copies of a little red book containing short quotations from Mao's writings, and one observer noted that "giant portraits of [Mao] now hung in the streets, busts were in every chamber, his books and photographs were everywhere on display."[3]

After the Revolution: Reform in Maoist China

The turmoil affected everyone. The chaos of these years caused serious economic problems, disrupting industrial and agricultural production and closing most schools for two years. The upheaval also resulted in thousands being killed, jailed, or removed from official positions, and millions of others were sent to remote rural areas. Anti-Mao officials, intellectuals, and people with upper-class backgrounds faced public criticism, followed by punishment if they failed to admit their political crimes. Soon even Mao was dampening down the radical fervor.

Great Proletarian Cultural Revolution A radical movement in China between 1966 and 1976 that represented Mao Zedong's attempt to implant his vision, destroy his enemies, crush the stifling bureaucracy, and renew the revolution's vigor.

Red Guards Young workers and students who were the major supporters of the Great Proletarian Cultural Revolution in Mao's China.

 One Hundred Items for Destroying the Old and Establishing the New Read this document of support for Mao's socialist ideology and commitment to destroy the old ways of Chinese thinking by a student group of Red Guards.

Despite such extremism, the communist movement to reshape Chinese society largely succeeded. Mao promoted a model of social equality, known as the Iron Rice Bowl, in which the people shared resources—food, draft animals, farm equipment—and the peasants enjoyed status and dignity. Maoism generally improved life for the poorer Chinese, especially in the thousands of villages. An emphasis on preventive medicine included the training of villagers, known as barefoot doctors, as paramedics. As a result, most Chinese now enjoyed decent health care, where once famine and disease were dominant. Mass education raised literacy rates to the levels of those in industrialized nations. Peasants often appreciated the changes.

Women and the Family under Maoism

The communists also tried to overturn centuries-old, Confucian-influenced hierarchical relationships, including patriarchy, by raising the status of women. Two changes profoundly affected women's lives. First, a new marriage law in 1950 abolished arranged marriages, forbade men from taking concubines, and made divorce easier. Second, a land reform empowered women economically by expanding their property rights. Women now enjoyed legal equality with men and greater access to education. Consequently, women played a stronger public role, and more women worked for wages. Yet few held high national positions, and rural areas remained more conservative than the cities in social matters. In general, however, communism changed the family system, often to the

Chinese Political Art This woodcut, carved during the Chinese civil war of the late 1940s, was typical of the political art made during Mao's era. Entitled "Support Our Common People's Own Army," the woodcut shows Chinese peasants working together with the communist military forces.

Woodcut by Ku Yuan, from Mei-shu, 1944

advantage of both women and men. An emphasis on love matches rather than arranged marriages fostered closer emotional ties, and fathers spent more time with their families than had been common a generation earlier.

Religion and the Arts in the New China

As with social patterns, the communists often undermined traditional beliefs and culture. Calling religion a bond enslaving people, Mao moved to control religious behavior and marginalize religious institutions such as Christian churches, Buddhist monasteries, and Islamic mosques. By the 1970s, only a small minority of Chinese openly practiced religion. Only Buddhist, Christian, and Muslim leaders who cooperated with the state maintained their positions. Determined to use the arts as a weapon in the class struggle, Mao sought to foster a "people's art" created by and for the common people. Government policies broadened popular participation in creating art, literature, and music. For example, during the Great Leap Forward, party activists went out to collect literature written by common people. In Shanghai alone, 200,000 people produced 5 million poems. Everyone was urged to work hard for a better future and a new society. The politicization of the arts reached its peak during the Cultural Revolution, and opera and ballet became central for the new revolutionary art.

The End of the Maoist Era

After Mao died in 1976, the Chinese took stock of Mao's legacy. The communists could claim many achievements. They had restored China to great power status and renewed the confidence of the people after thirteen decades of exploitation and invasion by Western nations and Japan. China was no longer a doormat; it even had nuclear weapons. The communists also took much of the sting out of poverty. Most Chinese, though enjoying little material surplus, could satisfy their basic food, housing, and clothing needs. The economy in 1976 was healthier and more broadly based than in 1949, and food was more evenly distributed. Public health and literacy rates had risen substantially.

Tension Under the Surface

Mao's policies, however, had also resulted in failures and political repression. China may have gained control of its economic destiny, but it was still poor by world standards. Mao had discouraged free enterprise and individual initiative. On city streets, few private cars interfered with the bicycles that most Chinese used to get to work or go shopping. Chinese wanted greater material benefits, such as better housing and more consumer goods. In addition, the fierce punishment of dissenters and the turmoil of the Great Leap Forward and Cultural Revolution had ruined numerous lives, and government coercion and corruption were resented. The unfulfilled promises, and the chaos of the Cultural Revolution, disillusioned young Chinese. Bitter disagreements had ripped the Communist Party leadership apart. Mao and his radicalism were often blamed for the problems; many were ready for change.

LO² Chinese Modernization

With Mao gone, Deng Xiaoping (dung shee-yao-ping) (1904–1997), a longtime Communist Party leader who had often clashed with Mao, came to power in 1978 and rejected Mao's view of a self-sufficient, ideologically pure China outside the world economy. Deng believed China needed to modernize its economy and embrace new technology in order to become a major power. In 1978, Deng announced the policy of Four Modernizations: the development of agriculture,

> "From 1978 to 1989, Chinese leaders pursued market socialism, a mix of free enterprise, economic liberalization, and state controls that produced economic dynamism."

market socialism A Chinese economic program used between 1978 and 1989 that mixed free enterprise, economic liberalization, and state controls and that produced economic dynamism in China.

industry, military, and science and technology to turn China into a powerful nation by 2000. His pragmatic policies eventually transformed China into an economic powerhouse.

Economic Reform and Political Repression

From 1978 to 1989, Chinese leaders pursued market socialism, a mix of free enterprise, economic liberalization, and state controls that produced economic dynamism. This pragmatic approach was more concerned with economic results than socialist values. Twice purged for opposing Mao, Deng was fond of a Chinese proverb: "It doesn't matter whether a cat is black or white, only if it catches mice." China began to import technology, foreign expertise, and capitalist ideas to spur manufacturing for the global market and stimulate productivity. Deng improved ties with the United States, Japan, western Europe, and noncommunist Southeast Asia. Dazzled by China's huge potential market for their own products, Western companies were delighted to do business with the Chinese.

Capitalist Ideas in China

Introducing capitalist ideas, the government gradually allowed private enterprises, and ultimately both private and state-owned enterprises were competing with each other. In agriculture, Deng replaced Mao's communes with the contract system in which peasants could bid on and lease (but could not buy) land to work it privately. In many districts, this free market led to soaring productivity and prosperity, with per capita income in rural areas rising fourfold in the first decade. Tapping a skilled, industrious, but cheap labor force, hundreds of Western and Asian companies set up manufacturing operations, producing goods such as clothing and toys. China became a consumer society in the 1980s; even in small cities, shops stocked Japanese televisions and Western soft drinks. Over the next twenty-five years, the economy quadrupled in size, and foreign trade increased ten times over.

A Reawakening of Culture

Deng also loosened political and cultural controls, arguing that liberation of thought and open-mindedness were essential for progress. Western popular culture, especially films, rock music, and discos, won a huge audience; books and magazines from around the world became available; and foreign travelers backpacked in remote areas. Intellectuals, journalists, and artists enjoyed greater freedom; people who had been long silenced or imprisoned were heard from again. Deng also increasingly tolerated religion, allowing Buddhist temples, Muslim mosques, and Christian churches to reopen.

Cultural figures, cowed during Mao's time, began to test the limits of free expression. Novels and short stories revealed the depth of suffering during the Cultural Revolution. Writers reflected a widespread public cynicism about politics; Chinese-made films won international acclaim, even as they contended with wary government censors. Rock musicians, especially Cui Jian (sway jen), a former trumpeter with the Beijing Symphony, became a major voice for alienated urban youth. One fan commented that "Cui Jian says things we all feel, but cannot say."[4]

East and Southeast Asia: An Annotated Directory of Internet Resources (*http://newton.uor.edu/Departments&Programs/AsianStudiesDept/*). A superb set of links, maintained at the University of Redlands.

Problems with Market Socialism

But although most Chinese applauded the ideological loosening and the growing economic options, the dramatic changes under Deng Xiaoping showed a dark underside in the later 1980s. Many districts had seen few benefits from the reorganization of rural life. Chinese authorities imposed one policy for the vast nation rather than allowing districts and villages to find a policy that worked for them. Under Deng's market socialism, some villagers benefited more than others, opening a gap between newly rich and poor. Prices rose rapidly. Corruption increased as bureaucrats and Communist Party officials lined their own pockets. Divisions among political leaders also deepened: Stalinists and Maoists viewed economic liberalization as undermining one-party rule, and the fall of communism in eastern Europe and the USSR in 1989 alarmed hardliners. But reformers, seeing strong controls as inhibiting initiative, pushed democracy as "the fifth modernization." In response, party leaders opposed to liberalization called for cracking down, arresting dissidents. The most famous dissident, a former Red Guard named Wei Jingsheng (way ching-sheng) (b. 1950), spent years in jail.

Tiananmen Square and the Beijing Massacre

In 1989, the tensions in Deng's China reached a boiling point, generating massive protests and subsequent government repression. Thousands of protesters, led by university students and workers, took over Tiananmen Square in Beijing, calling for the resignation of the most unpopular hardline leaders, an end to corruption, and a transition to a democratic system. The party hardliners, in alliance with Deng, purged the moderate party leaders and ordered the army to clear out the demonstrators in what became known as the Beijing Massacre. Sending in tanks, the army killed hundreds and arrested thousands, while millions around the world watched the violence on television. But many Chinese outside the cities, valuing stability more than vague promises of a better world, applauded the government crackdown. The protesters had miscalculated the prospects of democracy in a country with an authoritarian political tradition.

> 66 Cultural figures, cowed during Mao's time, began to test the limits of free expression. 99

Economic Change and Political Challenge

After the Beijing Massacre, the communists modified market socialism into market Leninism, a policy whereby the Chinese state asserted more power over society, while also fostering an even stronger market orientation in the economy. The communist leadership reestablished control in political, social, and cultural spheres, tolerating less dissent than they had in the 1980s, but the economy became further privatized. China now did not fit either the communist or the capitalist model; the party eventually labeled it a socialist market economy.

Dissent and Suppression

However, the control of the Leninist, or one-party, state was not absolute. In some local elections, communist officials did permit competition between candidates, allowing nonparty members to run for office. Many dissenters were able to spread their message. For example, opponents of the environmentally damaging Three Gorges Dam project, constructed to control the Yangzi (yahng-zeh) River and provide electrical power, publicized their views, although they had little success in halting the expensive project, which forced several million people to relocate. However, the Chinese state, often arbitrary in its actions, did use the military and police to intimidate dissidents. China may execute more than 100,000 people per year, mostly criminals but including some accused of economic misbehavior or political opposition. Anxious to preserve national unity, China's leaders also suppressed dissent in Tibet and among Muslim Turkish groups in Xinjiang (shin-jee-yahng), in far western China.

China's Economic Rebirth

After 1980, despite the ebb and flow of party domination, China enjoyed the fastest economic growth in the world, often 10 percent per year, abetted by a get-rich-quick mentality among many Chinese. China's exports increased fifteenfold between 1980 and 2000. After 1989, the communist leadership sought popular support by offering consumer goods and wealth rather than political reform, providing shops with ample consumer goods and households with spending money. In the early days of reform, people aspired to the "three bigs": bicycle, wristwatch, and sewing machine. By 2000, they wanted televisions, washing machines, and video recorders. As a result of the economic growth, the urban middle class grew rapidly. By 2005, China had already moved ahead of Germany as the third largest economy in the world. Some experts have argued that the United States and China are the two countries that have most benefited from economic globalization.

Problems in Prosperity

Although the economic reforms beginning in 1990 have improved living standards for many Chinese, they have also produced numerous downsides. Economic dynamism has occurred largely in a few coastal provinces and special economic zones, where towering skyscrapers and huge, upscale shopping malls dot the landscape of cities such as Shanghai and Shenzen. Elsewhere, however, conditions have often deteriorated. Unemployment grows dramatically as state enterprises close and inflation skyrockets. Although laws make it illegal to migrate to another district without government permission, millions of peasants seeking jobs have nonetheless moved to cities, where they struggle. Another problem is that China has become the number-two producer of greenhouse gases that cause global warming, although its output, about one-eighth of the world total, is only half that of the United States. Water supplies have become badly overstretched, and, with private cars clogging the city streets where bicycles once dominated, smog blankets the cities.

Wealth and Resentment

Political and economic changes have influenced other areas of Chinese life. In the cities, the newly rich entrepreneurs—enjoying luxury cars, access to golf courses, and vacations abroad—have lives that are alien to most Chinese. By 2004, some 236,000 Chinese were millionaires. Even the middle class, chiefly working in business, can aspire to some of these benefits; even teachers, professors, and doctors leave their low-paying state jobs to open businesses or join foreign corporations. The wealthy flaunt their affluence, and the poor resent it. By 2005, peasant protests against seizure of village land to build polluting factories, luxury housing, and golf courses had become frequent. Meanwhile, the shift to market forces leaves millions unable to afford medical care and schooling for their children. Thanks to the decline in health care, especially in rural areas, experts estimate that between half a million and 1.5 million Chinese have HIV or AIDS. Yet, despite reduced job security and social services, people are now freer than before to travel, change jobs, enjoy leisure, and even complain.

As the Chinese society and economy have rapidly changed, the Communist Party has faced problems

> "The communist leadership reestablished control in political, social, and cultural spheres, tolerating less dissent than they had in the 1980s, but the economy became further privatized."

Mao could never have anticipated. A Communist Party that once viewed itself as the protector of workers and peasants now welcomes wealthy businessmen into its ranks. Yet, after Deng's death in 1997, the party split between hardliners and younger reform-minded leaders lost legitimacy; powerful provincial leaders whose first priority is economic growth increasingly ignore Beijing. The rapid economic growth raises questions as to whether Chinese leaders can resolve the increasing inequalities and spread wealth more equitably to check the growth of social tensions.

Social Change, Gender, and Culture

Chinese usually define human rights in terms of the right to property, food, and housing rather than the freedom of individuals to do as they like. Popular participation in government and unfettered free speech are lower priorities than order for average Chinese, but economic growth and the quest for wealth have led to a rapid increase in crime and links between criminal groups and government officials. The close connection between government and business corruption, underworld activity, and financial success has led to Chinese talking about the "Five Colors," or surest roads to riches: (1) Communist Party connections, (2) prostitution, (3) smuggling, (4) illegal drug dealing, and (5) criminal gangs. Mao's China had been one of the world's safest countries, but after 1978, desperate people turned increasingly to crime as the way to get ahead; drug dealing became rampant once again, serving the growing number of people who used narcotics for escape. Maintaining Confucian and Maoist attitudes, Chinese often view wealth as corrupting and mistrust rich business interests.

The New Woman in China

The recent economic and social changes offered women opportunities but also posed problems. Women's economic status has often improved, but many still face restricted gender expectations. The feminist journalist Xue Xinran (shoe shin-rahn) wrote that "Chinese women had always thought that their lives should be full of misery. Many had no idea what happiness was, other than having a son for the family."[5] Rather than remaining in their villages, millions of rural women prefer to migrate to the cities, providing much of the labor force for the new factories that have helped turn China into

China-Profile: Facts, Figures, and Analyses (*http://www.china-profile.com*). Offers useful information on China today.

an economic giant. Women commonly work long hours, and few occupy high positions in the national government, Communist Party, large businesses, or rural communities.

Women have also faced other new hardships. Since by the 1980s China already had 1 billion people, one-fifth of humankind, Deng Xiaoping introduced a one-child-per-family policy to try to stabilize the population and limit growth toward a maximum population of 1.4 billion. But the policy encouraged and sometimes mandated abortion, and, since traditional attitudes favoring sons remained, also resulted in widespread killing of female babies. With more boys than girls being born and raised, an imbalance in numbers between the sexes developed, resulting in a growing trade in the abduction and sale of women to desperate men who were unable to find wives.

Western Influence

Because of China's growing contacts with the larger world economy, Chinese society is affected by global entertainment and consumer culture. Western popular culture, which spread to China in the 1980s, has become a powerful force among youth. Every city has discos and clubs offering Western music, and Chinese imitators of Anglo-American bands have found a vast teen audience. Chinese consumers in many places are served by numerous McDonald's outlets, Hard Rock Cafes, Wal-Marts, and some 85,000 Avon agents selling American cosmetics and beauty products. Partly because of greater contact with the outside world, homosexuals, who faced discrimination under Mao, have been slowly coming out, especially in the cities, where gay bars are common. But Western culture is not the only outside influence. South Korean popular culture and consumer products—music, clothing, television dramas, movies, cosmetics—became very fashionable among young Chinese in the early 2000s, and much of the conversion of millions of Chinese to evangelical Christianity is a result of the thousands of South Korean Protestant missionaries in the country.

Read about Xue Xinran, one of China's most successful and innovative journalists, who explored the lives of Chinese women.

Those Chinese with enough money to afford satellite dishes and personal computers linked to the Internet have gained access to ideas around the world. To restrict the free flow of information and exposure to dissident writings, state officials have tried to crack down on cyberspace, passing laws restricting Internet use, but websites and blogs—

some 14 million are available to Chinese—proliferate rapidly, making monitoring difficult. The government sometimes shuts down newspapers and magazines whose reporting is too daring, but brave journalists and officials have risked punishment by openly criticizing censorship. Another source of knowledge about Western ideas comes from the several hundred thousand Chinese, including the children of high officials, who have studied in Western universities.

Falun Gong

Policies toward religion have been inconsistent. After temples and churches reopened in the 1980s, the government tolerated millions of Chinese turning to the faith of their ancestors: Buddhism, Christianity, Daoism, or Islam. But the government has cracked down on movements that are deemed a threat or that refuse to accept official restrictions. For instance, it has arrested leaders and members of the assertive, missionary *Falun Gong* meditation sect, a mix of Daoist, Buddhist, and Christian influences, and has tried to close down rapidly proliferating Christian churches that have remained independent of government approval. While the Chinese remain a largely secular people, both Falun Gong and the independent churches have millions of followers who seek a deeper spiritual existence and sense of community.

China in the Global System

China's relations with the wider world have been colored by its historical experiences, but in recent years, Chinese have seen their nation stand tall, strong, and increasingly rich. In 1997, they celebrated the peaceful return of Hong Kong from British colonial control. Hong Kong, a prosperous enclave whose towering skyscrapers, bustling shopping malls, and dynamic film industry made it a symbol of East Asian capitalism, was incorporated under the policy of "one nation, two systems." Despite China's occasional interference in Hong Kong politics, a vocal pro-democracy movement in Hong Kong helps to maintain the territory's freedoms. In 1999, Portugal also returned its small coastal colony of Macao, which it had first occupied in the 1500s, to Chinese control.

Since 1976, China has pursued a pragmatic foreign policy designed to win friends and trading partners but to also avoid entangling alliances. China has exercised regional influence by trading extensively with neighbors. It gradually improved relations with the United States and USSR, and cultivated diplomatic relations with other nations, while avoiding close ties that might limit its options. It also became increasingly active in the world community, joining international organizations such as the World Trade Organization. Some 200 million Chinese children study English.

The post-Mao foreign policy enhanced national power while accepting the constraints imposed by the global system. By the twenty-first century, China enjoyed tremendous influence in the world economy. Taking advantage of a cheap but resourceful labor force, thousands of foreign investors have come from the West, Japan, Southeast Asia, South Korea, and even Taiwan, opening factories and negotiating joint ventures with Chinese firms. Meanwhile, China has supported the U.S. economy, becoming the major buyer of the treasury bonds that financed the growing U.S. national debt in the early 2000s. Chinese enterprises have begun buying up companies based on manufacturing and natural resources in other nations. Thus China has become the world's most successful newly industrializing economy, buttressed by a vast resource base and a huge domestic market.

Yet China has met roadblocks in enhancing its global power, among them uncertain relations with its neighbors. The Chinese government, still claiming Taiwan as an integral part of China, continues to threaten that island with forced unification. Although economic and social links between China and Taiwan developed unofficially beginning in the 1980s, few in the island nation, which enjoys democracy and a much higher standard of living, want a merger with the mainland in the near future. Meanwhile, Chinese relations with Japan fluctuate: the two nations need each other economically but are also natural rivals, the Chinese remaining resentful of Japanese brutality during World War II. In contrast to sporadic Chinese–Japanese tensions, China has improved relations with once-bitter enemies such as South Korea and anticommunist countries such as Malaysia, the Philippines, and Australia. In many of these and other countries, large numbers of people are learning Chinese, and some 90,000 foreign students study in China. Nonetheless, historical resentment of Japan and the West provides a strong foundation of Chinese nationalism, which sometimes provokes anti-Japan or anti-U.S. protest demonstrations.

China's tremendous size, population, natural resources, military strength, national confidence, and sense of history have made it a major global power but with a much lower overall standard of living than that of North America, western Europe, Japan, and several industrializing Asian nations. Using such factors as literacy, life expectancy, and per capita income, the 2004 United Nations Human Development Report placed China only 94th out of 177 nations in overall quality of life. Nonetheless, China has been returning to its historical leadership as the Asian dragon and a major engine of the global economy. As during the long period of Chinese power and prosperity between 600 and 1800 C.E., China is once again a major force in world affairs.

LO³ The Remaking of Japan

Japan rose from the shambles of World War II to economic dynamism (see Map 27.2). In August 1945,

 Interactive Map

Japan's major cities were largely destroyed by U.S. bombing and its economy ruined. The Japanese people were psychologically devastated. Yet, within a decade, the country had recovered, and after several decades of the highest economic growth rates in world history, Japan became the world's second largest economy. A system stressing cooperation rather than individualism provided the basis for economic and social stability in an overcrowded land. But by the 1990s, Japan was experiencing political and economic uncertainty.

Occupation, Recovery, and One-Party Democracy

The post–World War II occupation by the United States aided Japan's recovery. In the wake of defeat, the Japanese people felt disoriented. The emperor, Hirohito (here-o-HEE-to) (1901–1989), still a revered figure, asked them to cooperate with the Allied occupation forces, and they did. Japan was placed under a U.S.-dominated military administration, the Supreme Command of Allied Powers (SCAP), which was tasked with rebuilding rather than punishing Japan. The victorious World War II Allies also broke up Japan's empire. Japan lost Korea, Taiwan, and Manchuria, while the United States took control of the Ryukyu Islands, which were returned to Japan in the 1970s, and Micronesia. SCAP's mission was to demilitarize and democratize Japan, using the United States as the model, and to aid economic recovery. SCAP dismantled the Japanese military, removed some civilian politicians, and tried and hanged seven wartime leaders as war criminals. Fearing that punishing the emperor—a member of an imperial family that was more than 1,500 years old—would destabilize Japan, U.S. officials did not charge Emperor Hirohito with war crimes, but he was forced to renounce his godlike aura and become a more public figure.

Post-War Japan SCAP fostered political and social changes; soon, a thriving political democracy took root. A new constitution guaranteed civil liberties and weakened the central government. It also had a unique feature: the document stated that the Japanese people forever renounced war as the nation's sovereign right. The first democratic elections, held in 1946, involved various competing political parties. For the first time in Japanese history, all adult citizens, including women, could vote. Women won other rights as well but were only partly freed from traditional expectations. U.S. officials hoped to foster further democratization, but, after the communist victory in China and the outbreak of the Korean War, the United States shifted its emphasis to integrating Japan into the anticommunist Western alliance, symbolized by the signing in 1951 of a formal U.S.–Japan peace treaty. U.S. military bases have remained in Japan ever since.

Economic Recovery Under SCAP the economy gradually recovered, using the same sort of quasi-capitalist system—a mix of government intervention and free markets—that Japan had had between the 1870s and the early 1930s. Land reform heavily subsidized the peasantry, making them strong government supporters and bringing unprecedented prosperity to the rural areas. SCAP also attempted to break up entrenched economic power, but these efforts were less successful; as before World War II, large industrial-commercial-banking combinations, or conglomerates, still dominated business, making Japan more competitive in the world economy, but workers gained the right to unionize.

Democracy Returns The policies implemented during the SCAP occupation, which officially ended in 1952, were most successful where U.S. and Japanese desires coincided or when the policies fit with the nation's traditions. Democratic government fit both criteria: the Japanese had enjoyed several decades of democracy before the Great Depression,

> "The post–World War II occupation by the United States aided Japan's recovery."

© Cengage Learning

Map 27.2
Japan and the Little Dragons
Japan fostered the strongest Asian economy through the second half of the twentieth century, but in recent decades the Little Dragons—South Korea, Taiwan, Hong Kong, and Singapore—also have had rapid economic growth.

and many Japanese longed for a return to it. Borrowing from abroad also fit with Japanese tradition. For several millennia, the Japanese had been open to acquiring ideas from outside and adapting them to their own traditions. In the late 1940s, with conditions stabilized, Japanese leaders embarked on a strategy of capitalizing on peace to strengthen the nation.

Politics in a One-Party Democracy

Despite stresses, Japan's democratic political system flourished. As in many western European countries, a variety of political parties, including communists, Buddhists, and right-wing nationalists, competed for parliamentary seats. But since the early 1950s, one major party, the center-right Liberal Democratic Party (LDP), has dominated Japanese politics, applying generally conservative, pro-business, and pro-U.S. policies. The electoral system imposed by SCAP gave greater weight to rural voters, the conservative backbone of LDP support, rather than the more liberal urban voters. Prime ministers learned to negotiate with varied opposition parties as well as with diverse factions within the LDP. Nonetheless, critics believe that a political system dominated by one party and a few wealthy kingpins is at best a partial democracy.

However, the need to finance political careers and raise money for elections fostered political corruption. Powerful corporations and criminal gangs

> 66 Despite stresses, Japan's democratic political system flourished. 99

were leading financial contributors. Bribery scandals sometimes forced political leaders to resign. In 1993, the LDP fragmented in factional disputes, and various opposition parties gained support for several years. But in 2001, the LDP returned to power under a reform leader.

To protect its shores, Japanese leaders forged a military alliance with the United States, but the alliance brought Japan problems as well as benefits. Thanks to this alliance, which allowed U.S. bases in Japan, Japan's military spending remained meager compared with that of the United States and the USSR. This ability to devote more resources to the civilian economy and industrial development was a major reason for Japan's rapid economic growth. Despite these benefits of the military alliance with the United States, some leftist parties, labor unions, and militant student groups long opposed the U.S. presence, which they viewed as neocolonialism. Japanese also feared that U.S. military interventions made Japan a potential target for U.S. enemies. Remembering the horrors of World War II, especially the atomic bombings of Hiroshima and Nagasaki that killed some 200,000 Japanese, many Japanese favored pacifism and believed that Japan's economic strength protected them from attack. Yet, with U.S. support, Japan began increasing its military spending in the 1980s, and by 2001 it had the fourth largest military budget in the world, ahead of China. The decision of Japanese leaders in 2004 to send soldiers to support, in noncombat activities, the U.S. war effort in Iraq was widely unpopular in Japan and, to critics, violated the constitutional ban against engaging in war.

The Japanese Economy

Adapting capitalism to its own traditions, Japan has achieved phenomenal economic growth. Wartime destruction had required the rebuilding of basic industries using the latest innovations. Investing in new industries and high-tech fields, the Japanese became the world leaders in manufacturing products such as oil tankers, automobiles, watches, and televisions. From the 1960s through the 1980s, Japan's annual growth rate was three times higher than that of other industrialized nations; by 2000, Japan produced some 16 percent of the world's goods and services, twice that of third-place Germany. What some called Japan's economic miracle was particularly impressive considering the country's lack of natural

CHRONOLOGY

Japan Since 1945

1946–1952	SCAP occupation of Japan
1946	First postwar Japanese elections
1951	U.S.-Japan peace treaty
1960s–1989	Era of rapid Japanese economic growth
1989	Beginning of Japanese economic downturn
1993	Fragmentation of Liberal Democratic Party
1997	Asian financial collapse

Japanese Protest Political demonstrations are common in Japanese cities. During this protest in 2001, liberals and leftists criticized new middle-school textbooks, approved by the Education Ministry, that, the critics claimed, distorted history by emphasizing nationalist viewpoints and downplaying Japanese atrocities in World War II.

resources. Japan has limited productive farmland and no major rivers to produce hydroelectric power, so the Japanese must import minerals needed for industry, such as iron ore, tin, and copper. Oil obtained from Alaska, Southeast Asia, and the Middle East powers Japan's transportation.

The Japanese became known for innovative technologies and high-quality products. Among those technologies was its magnificent mass-transit system, including the state-of-the-art bullet trains that whisked passengers around the country at 125 to 150 miles per hour and were always on time. Electronics manufacturers such as Sony, Atari, and Nintendo invented entertainment-oriented products that became part of life on every continent. In addition, millions of people, from Boston to Bogotá to Bombay, drove Toyotas, Hondas, and other Japanese-made cars.

By the 1980s, the Japanese enjoyed living standards equal to those of most western Europeans. With unprecedented affluence, the Japanese became Western-style consumers; everyone now sought to own cars, televisions, washing machines, and air conditioners. The Japanese also enjoyed the world's highest average life expectancy: seventy-nine or eighty years. A more varied diet, including more meat and dairy products than their ancestors had, produced taller, healthier children. Western foods and beverages became popular, and coffeehouses and bars dotted most streets in commercial and entertainment districts. The rural areas also shared in the prosperity, although life there remained harder. But there was an underside to Japanese economic success: many workers had to make do with part-time jobs offering few benefits, and a small but growing underclass of people had no permanent jobs or homes.

Japan's capitalist economy has differed in fundamental ways from those of other industrial nations. It was a form of mercantilism, a cooperative relationship between government and big business that became known as Japan, Inc. (Japan Incorporated). Under this system, the national government and big business worked together to manage the economy. The government regulated business, setting overall guidelines, sponsoring research and development, and leasing the resulting products or technologies to private enterprise. Most Japanese businesses accepted the government guidelines because they took a longer-term view of profitability than was common in the West. But government–business cooperation occurred chiefly in international trade, the country's lifeblood, and it was made easier by the economic dominance of large Japanese conglomerates. As in many other countries, the government aided Japanese businesses by erecting protectionist barriers and bureaucratic hurdles that impeded foreign businesses in the Japanese market.

Economic growth has generated new problems. As in the West, industrialization fosters wealth but also harms the environment. As cities grew,

Japan, Inc. The cooperative relationship between government and big business that has existed in Japan after 1945.

> "Despite the popular, contemporary image of the timid Japanese female, women have become more assertive."

developers cleared farmland and forests. Pollution of rivers and bays wiped out coastal fishing. Smoggy air, produced by automobile exhaust mixing with pollutants from smokestacks, is rampant; thousands of people have died or been made ill by toxic waste dumped by factories. In addition to declining environmental health, many younger people resent the long hours and sacrifices expected of employees in Japanese companies.

But Japan's business and factory life has played a role in Japanese success. The system takes advantage of Japanese cultural values, such as conformity, hard work, thrift, and foresight, while adding new innovations. The 30 percent of workers employed in larger Japanese companies have often enjoyed lifetime job security and generous welfare benefits such as health insurance, recreation, housing, and car loans. When a corporation has faced financial trouble, top managers usually accept responsibility for the problems, cutting their own pay rather than firing workers.

Japanese Society, Culture, and Thought

Urbanization and affluence have contributed to social change. Sixty percent of Japanese now live in cities of more than 100,000 people. With nearly 30 million people, Tokyo is the world's largest city. With car ownership so popular, some of Tokyo's legendary traffic jams take police several days to untangle. Rush hour on the subways has evolved into "crush hour," with city employees equipped with padded poles pushing commuters into overflowing cars to enable subway train doors to close. Yet, despite Mafia-like organized crime syndicates, Japan's cities are the safest in the world; experts attribute low rates of violent crime in part to strict gun control.

Life in Japan, Inc.

The economy has changed men's lives, especially in the growing middle class. University-educated men typically want to become salaried white-collar office workers for major corporations. Japanese observers describe the salaryman, an urban middle-class male business employee who commits his energies and soul to the company, accepts assignments without complaint, and takes few vacations. Many men working in white-collar jobs are also known as "7-11 husbands" because they leave for work at 7 A.M. and do not return until 11 P.M. After work they and their office mates socialize in restaurants, bars, and nightclubs while their wives take care of the home.

Women and Family Life

Meanwhile, while earning more money, gaining legal protections, and enjoying greater freedom, women still struggle for full equality in a hierarchical society obsessed with patriarchy and seniority. Most women are expected to marry and then retire from the workforce in their early twenties to raise children. According to one young woman, when she and other women graduated from a top Japanese university, "our bright appearance [for the graduation ceremonies] in vividly colored kimonos [traditional robes] was deceiving. Deep in our hearts we knew that our opportunities to use our professional education would be few."[6] As single women began to support themselves, the average age of marriage for women rose from twenty-two in the 1950s to twenty-seven in the 1990s. Accordingly, marriage rates have declined, alarming politicians.

Despite the popular, contemporary image of the timid Japanese female, women have become more assertive. Working against the patriarchal grain of society, feminist organizations and several prominent women's leaders have publicized women's issues, and working women have lobbied companies for equal treatment and pay. Some women have moved into middle management or prestige occupations, such as law, journalism, college teaching, and diplomacy. Yet, women also largely remain outside political and economic power, and only a few attain positions of political leadership.

Family life has gradually changed. Although the traditional arranged marriage remains common, increasing numbers of men and women select their own spouse. Also reflecting a rise in personal freedom, more Japanese get married late or opt to end unhappy marriages in divorce, a rare decision before World War II. Studies have suggested that, while

Japanese Women Commuters A female passenger boards a train compartment reserved for women in a subway station in Tokyo. Tokyo's subways are usually jammed with passengers, and special cars allow women to travel without fear of possible sexual harassment.

many wives are lonely and resentful with their husbands seldom home, the majority prefer spending their growing leisure time away from their husbands. The decline of marriage has also had an impact on homosexuals, making it easier for them to find social acceptance.

Urbanization, Population, and Immigration

Urban housing remains cramped, and the elderly complain of neglect by their children, who have no room for them in their small homes. Birth control and abortion had been widely practiced in overcrowded Japan for centuries; the renewal of these practices after World War II, along with lower marriage rates, has enabled Japan to stabilize its population at 120 million for several decades. Yet declining birthrates also pose an economic dilemma. By 2000, Japan had a birthrate well below replacement standards but did not promote immigration to provide new workers. By 2005, foreigners, mostly Chinese and Koreans, numbered some 2 million in Japan, less than 2 percent of the total population. By contrast, foreigners accounted for 5 percent in Britain, 10 percent in Germany, 12 percent in the United States, and 22 percent in Australia. Paying for benefits and services for the retired has imposed an increasing strain on those working. Despite laws banning discrimination, Japanese leaders have largely failed to elevate the status of the *Burakumin*, a despised underclass for centuries, who number some 1 to 3 million people and traditionally did jobs that were considered unclean.

Education

Youth face their own kinds of pressures. The rigorous education system, which produces a well-trained workforce, is based on stiff examinations. The entrance exam for

Witness to the Past

A Japanese Generation Gap

The rapid pace of change since World War II has fostered growing generation gaps in many nations. In 1993, the Japanese essayist Yoshioka Shinobu (born in 1948) discussed the differences in perceptions between his "baby boomer" cohort born in the decade after 1945 and those Japanese of the next generation. Yoshioka's experiences reflected the exciting era of social experimentation during his teenage years in the 1960s. By contrast, young people in the 1970s faced a tighter economy and less official tolerance of radical ideas and organized political protests.

Whenever I hear someone mention Japan's baby boomers, . . . I think back to a conversation I had . . . [in] 1976 at a rock concert. . . . The band had the latest sound equipment, but its talent was no match for its technology. Bored, . . . I struck up a conversation with two young girls. . . . They had run away from home . . . because they were sick of school, and had come to Tokyo in search of adventure. . . . They had lied about their ages to get part-time jobs, were sharing a tiny apartment, and from time to time went out to concerts. . . . I told them I thought they must be having the time of their lives.

"Your generation had it good," one of the girls answered. "When you ran away from home, there was rock music, underground theater, demonstrations, all kinds of things—you could do whatever you wanted. Our generation has to walk a tightrope, . . . and there's nothing to catch us if we fall. We lose our balance, we die. You guys might have walked a tightrope too, but you had a safety net below. If you didn't like it up on the rope, you could always dive down and let yourself be caught in midair. You could do whatever you wanted to."

She had hit home. So that's how we look in the eyes of someone ten years younger, I thought. My generation . . . had an entirely different understanding of itself. [We] . . . had many names . . .: the baby boomers, the Beatles generation, the anti-Vietnam [War] generation. . . . [Our radical student movements] did much to discredit the established political system, but our generation was more than just a new political force. We began new trends in music, theater, art, and social customs . . . that defied the existing structure of authority and social conventions. In those days, nothing was worse than a willingness to capitulate to the "system" and adopt its narrow conventions.

Consequently, we tried our hands at everything. Singers of traditional [music], who had put in years of hard work climbing the rigid, hierarchical ladder before they were allowed to perform publicly, suddenly found themselves displaced by our barely rehearsed bands and spontaneous concerts. Some put on plays in . . . tents set up in vacant lots, ridiculing the empty and imitative formalism of Japan's commercial theater. Others . . . took off nearly penniless to wander about in foreign countries—their adventureousness helped make travel abroad commonplace.

The two girls were saying that these experiences . . . were only possible because we had a safety net underneath us. . . . The girls had a point. When [my] generation was growing up, the . . . confusion of the early postwar years had given way to spectacular economic growth. . . . This . . . engendered confidence in liberal politics and democratic government, and it also created a willingness to forgive the unruliness of the younger generation. . . . If we were arrested [in antiwar demonstrations] it did not worry us much. . . . The runaway girls told me that the age of such optimism was over. . . . Between my generation and the next, attitudes toward change took a 180-degree turn. For us, changes in society and the individual were exciting and intrinsically valuable. For the younger generation, however, change is frightening and the source of insecurity.

Thinking About the Reading

1. How did Yoshioka's generation contribute to change?
2. What does the essay tell us about Japan's connection to the wider world?

Source: Shinobu Yoshioka, "Talkin' 'bout My Generation," in Merry L. White and Sylvan Barnet, eds., *Comparing Cultures: Readings on Contemporary Japan for American Writers* (Boston: Bedford Books of St. Martin's Press, 1995), pp. 119–122. Reprinted with permission by Yoshioka Shinobu.

the top universities is so rigorous that it is known as "exam hell." The Japanese school year is also longer than that in most other nations. These varied pressures, and the expectations of conforming to the values of mainstream society, have encouraged youth rebellion. University students have often supported left-wing political organizations that protest issues such as U.S. military bases or the destruction of farmland to development. Eventually, however, most young people return to the mainstream upon graduation from university and take jobs in the corporate world. Some who cannot conform emigrate elsewhere in search of a more free-spirited life (see Witness to the Past: A Japanese Generation Gap) .

Defining Japanese Identity

As they have done over the past two centuries, the Japanese have continued to blend traditional and modern cultures and beliefs, East and West. With old values and traditions under stress, Japanese artists and writers now ponder whether the historical process of synthesizing foreign and local ideas has been the nation's salvation or its bane. In 1993, a prominent writer observed: "We are up to our necks in Western culture. But we have planted a little seed. We are beginning to re-create ourselves."[7] Others contend that Japanese needed to become less inward and more global-minded.

The questions about Japanese identity are often analyzed in films and literature that have achieved worldwide recognition. While the Japanese film industry, the world's third largest, produces escapist, action films that gain a large audience at home and abroad, it also makes thought-provoking masterpieces that force audiences to reflect on Japanese life. One of the most skillful directors, Kurosawa Akira (kur-o-SAH-wa a-KEER-a) (1910–1998), was celebrated for films mixing a distinctive Japanese style and setting with universal themes. *Rashomon* (1950), for example, deals with the relativity of truth by examining one event, the killing of a feudal lord and the violation of his wife by a bandit, through varied eyes, including the murdered lord, the wife, the bandit, and a woodcutter who witnessed the act. The Japanese have the world's highest literacy rate (99.9 percent) and the largest numbers of newspaper readers, magazine subscribers, and bookstores per capita. Japan boasts several world-famous novelists, Kawabata Ysunori (ka-wa-BAH-ta yoo-suh-NOOR-ee) (1899–1972) being the first Japanese, in 1968, to receive the Nobel Prize for literature.

Continuity has long characterized Japanese popular culture. Every sport, art form, and religion that has appeared in the past 1,500 years still attracts followers. For example, Japanese remain passionate about sumo wrestling, a sport going back centuries, in which two large Japanese men attempt to push each other out of a small ring. At the same time, change is also characteristically Japanese. While performances of kabuki or bunraku, theatrical forms that appeared in the 1600s, still attract devoted audiences, and young Japanese women often master the even older tea ceremony, many more Japanese follow professional baseball teams consume Japanese comics, or *manga* (MAHN-gah), and animated films, or anime (AN-ih-may), that are popular worldwide. Modern Japanese, especially young people, have avidly adopted cultural forms from around the world.

A Secular Society

Industrialization and urbanization have accelerated the declining influence of organized religion. Some Japanese remain deeply religious: militant Buddhist groups claim several million followers, and various new religions based on Buddhist or Shinto traditions, or a mix of the two, have flourished by addressing material prosperity and family problems. Nonetheless, the contemporary Japanese are a largely secular people. In census questionnaires in 2000, while most Japanese described themselves as Buddhists, Shintoists, or both, less than 15 percent reported any formal religious affiliation. The weak influence of organized religions and their moral systems has not resulted in social breakdown, however. Japanese remain among the world's most law-abiding, peaceful citizens, but morality now is mostly derived from the fear of bringing shame on the family or group rather than fear of retribution by gods or ancestors. The reluctance to disgrace the family suggests that Confucianism, the Chinese ethical system that was imported into Japan 1,400 years ago, remains influential.

Japan in the Global System

The Japanese have had to readjust their views of the economy and international relations over the past several decades. Like their North American and European counterparts, Japanese companies have sought cheaper labor overseas, a practice that has cost Japan jobs. In 1989, the Japanese economy went into a severe downturn, due in part to overvalued stocks that caused a crisis on the Tokyo Stock Exchange, but also to global recession and competition from newly industrializing nations in Southeast Asia. Many Japanese investors went bankrupt, confidence was shaken, and more than 1 million workers were laid off. Only in the early 2000s did Japanese leaders, beginning to overcome political and bureaucratic inertia, introduce policies that fostered higher growth rates and renewed business confidence, but the recovery remained incomplete.

While comfortable as an economic powerhouse, the Japanese remain reluctant to assert their political and military power in the world, remembering how the attempt to dominate eastern Asia brought them disaster during World War II. Japan's main concerns are the continued health of the world economy and access to overseas resources and markets, the two pillars on which its prosperity has depended. Japan maintains a strategic alliance with its major trading partner, the United States, but the two nations have also remained keen economic rivals and engage in occasional trade disputes. Japanese leaders have also worked to promote peaceful exchange with China and South Korea, two countries with long memories of Japanese imperialism. Relations with China have been particularly strained, as the Chinese have demanded that Japan accept responsibility for World War II atrocities in China, such as the murder and injury of thousands of civilians known as the Rape of Nanjing, a Chinese city. Resurgent Japanese and Chinese nationalisms clash. As China and several other Asian nations rise economically, Japan faces more competition.

LO⁴ The Little Dragons in the Asian Resurgence

While China and Japan were rising to regional and global power, a few of their East Asian neighbors also achieved economic development. Known as the Little Dragons because their societies were strongly influenced by the region's dominant Chinese culture, these neighbors—South Korea, Taiwan, Singapore, and Hong Kong—built rapidly growing, industrializing economies. Except for Hong Kong, a British colony until 1997 and a bastion of free enterprise, these societies largely followed the Meiji Japan model of state-directed capitalism, which involved government intervention into otherwise free-market economies. They were also inspired by Japan's resurgence

after World War II. All the Little Dragons shared a Confucian cultural heritage that emphasized hard work, discipline, cooperation, and tolerance for authoritarian governments. They all achieved an export-oriented industrialization that dramatically raised incomes, reduced poverty, and forged high standards in health and education. For South Korea, however, this development came only after a brutal war that left a hostile, rigidly communist North Korea on the border, and Taiwan had to find its own path in the shadow of China.

The Korean War

The Korean War (1950–1953) was rooted in the Korean nationalism that, despite fierce repression, simmered during a half-century of harsh Japanese colonial rule, which was imposed in 1910 (see Chapters 23 and 24). While introducing some economic modernization, the Japanese arrested or executed Korean nationalists, conscripted Korean women to serve Japanese soldiers, and relocated thousands of Korean workers to Japan. To maintain their rule, the Japanese manipulated divisions within Korean society. Christians constituted one influential group that grew in number

> ❝ To maintain their rule, the Japanese manipulated divisions within Korean society. ❞

CHRONOLOGY

The Little Dragons Since 1945

1948–1994	Kim Il-Sung's leadership of North Korea
1950–1953	Korean War
1954	U.S.–Taiwan mutual defense treaty
1980s	South Korean democratization movement
1989	First democratic elections in Taiwan
1989–1991	Collapse of Soviet bloc and Soviet Union
1997	Asian financial collapse
1998	Beginning of South Korean "sunshine policy"

during the twentieth century. By the 1940s, one-fifth of Koreans had become Catholics or Protestants. Inspired by Soviet modernization, another group of Koreans had gravitated toward communism during colonial times. In contrast to these who imported ideas, a majority of Koreans maintained their adherence to Buddhism and Confucianism, regarding these traditional beliefs as central to Korean identity. Although Christians, communists, and traditionalists commonly hated Japanese rule, and members of all groups worked underground to oppose it, they could not cooperate, and no unified nationalist movement emerged.

Kim Il-Sung and Syngman Rhee

Japan's crushing defeat by the United States in 1945 meant political liberation for Korea and a chance to reestablish the nation free of foreign interference. But the United States quickly occupied the southern half of the peninsula and the Soviet Union the north, bisecting Korea and making it a hostage to the Cold War. As the USSR and the United States imposed rival governments, unification quickly became impossible, alarming nationalists of all stripes. With Soviet help, in 1948, communists led by the ruthless Kim Il-Sung (KIM ill-soon) (1912–1994) formed a government in North Korea. A clever strategist who had lived for years in the USSR, Kim quickly built a brutal communist system, eliminated his opponents, and reorganized rural society. But the impatient Kim disastrously overestimated the revolutionary potential of the south, and he also misjudged the Americans, who were determined to stop the spread of Soviet influence.

The United States helped create and then supported a South Korean state headed by Rhee Syngman (REE SING-man) (1865–1965), better known in the West as Syngman Rhee. A longtime nationalist and politically conservative Christian from a powerful landlord family, the autocratic, inflexible Rhee imprisoned or eliminated his opponents and sparked a rebellion by leftist movements, which United States troops helped crush. Although less repressive than Kim's North Korean regime, Rhee's South Korea held some 30,000 political prisoners.

The Korean War and the Superpowers

These developments set the stage for the Korean War (see Map 27.3), a conflict that shaped East Asian politics for half a century. Both Korean states, threatening to reunify Korea with military force, had initiated border skirmishes. In this highly charged context, North Korea, probably with

 Interactive Map

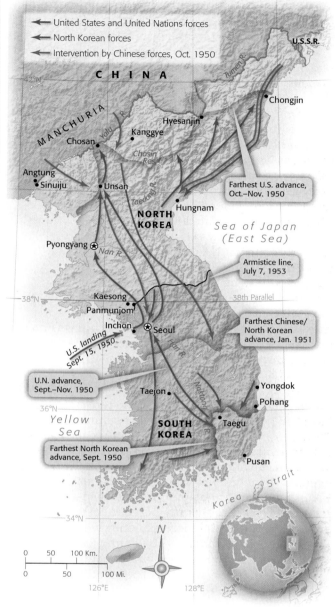

Map 27.3
The Korean War

© Cengage Learning

In 1950, North Korean forces crossed the 38th parallel and invaded South Korea, but they were then pushed back north by United Nations forces led by the United States. The intervention of China in support of North Korea pushed the United Nations forces south and produced a military stalemate, preserving the border between North and South Korea at the 38th parallel.

tacit Soviet and perhaps Chinese approval, invaded the South in 1950. The United Nations, then dominated by Western nations, approved a request by the United States to lead a military intervention to support South Korea, thus turning a Korea crisis into a

Cold War confrontation. U.S. President Harry Truman secretly planned a strike on North Korea with atomic weapons if North Korea's ally, the USSR, entered the war. But while the Soviets gave military supplies and advice to the North Koreans, they sent no combat troops.

The initiative shifted back and forth. United Nations troops, aided by U.S. air power, quickly pushed the North Koreans back across the north-south border. But U.S. general Douglas MacArthur's (1880–1964) decision to invade North Korea and push toward the Chinese border sparked a massive intervention by Chinese troops that drove back United Nations troops and turned a likely U.N. victory into a bitter stalemate. U.S. leaders had misjudged the Chinese willingness and capacity to fight. When the war ended in 1953 with peace talks, the boundary between the Koreas remained in the same place it was before the war but was now a heavily fortified zone. The war was a stalemate, but both sides claimed victory.

The Cost of the Conflict

The war proved costly in human terms, involving perhaps 1 million military dead and 1 or 2 million civilian Korean deaths. The U.N. forces suffered some 43,000 killed and more than 100,000 wounded, 90 percent of them Americans. South Korean military casualties numbered more than 100,000 dead and 160,000 wounded, and the North Koreans lost more than 300,000 soldiers. Chinese casualties were also high, more than 400,000 dead. The fighting also generated millions of Korean refugees who wandered the countryside during the war, and both North and South Korea were left in economic shambles.

The Remaking of South and North Korea

The postwar rise of South Korea was nearly as dramatic as that of Japan. Closely allied to the United States, the South Korean governments evolved from highly repressive military dictatorships in the 1950s to liberal democracies with free elections after the early 1990s. All regimes aimed at economic development. The United States protected the South Korean regimes from any North Korean threats by permanently stationing troops and supplying generous economic and military aid. Five decades after the war, some 40,000 U.S. troops and more than one

> 66 The postwar rise of South Korea was nearly as dramatic as that of Japan. 99

hundred U.S.-owned nuclear weapons remained in South Korea.

Mixing government intervention and free markets, South Korea has enjoyed enormous economic growth. The nation invested heavily in the Middle East, Southeast Asia, and Russia, often to secure oil supplies, while exporting automobiles and electronic products. By the mid-1990s, South Korea had joined the ranks of advanced industrial nations, the first non-Western nation to make that transition since Japan in the late nineteenth century. Having acquired a standard of living South Koreans could only have dreamed of two decades earlier, with nearly full employment and universal literacy, the country became a high-technology model. Prosperity reshaped society. Both boys and girls received free education through age twelve. South Korean women benefited from new job options, often in the professions and business; marriage rates declined and average births per woman fell dramatically from 6 in 1990 to 1.6 in 2005.

Economic growth has also fostered political change. Democracy movements had begun in the 1960s, but they often faced government repression. In 1980, the dictatorship brutally crushed an uprising in a southern province that began when some five hundred people demonstrated, demanding an end to martial law; in response, paratroopers landed and began slaughtering the protesters and local people who got in their way. Hundreds of thousands of enraged Koreans then drove the troops out of the city, only to face a much larger force, which shot their way into the city, killing more than two thousand people. Eventually, political tensions diminished. During the later 1980s, governments fostered more liberalization, tolerated a freer press, and made overtures

Little Dragons Asian Studies (http://coombs.anu.edu.au/WWWVL-AsianStudies.html). A vast online resource maintained at Australian National University, with links to hundreds of sites.

toward former enemies in the USSR and China. By the early 1990s, four decades after the Korean War ended, the South Korean people had forced a change in direction. With the growth of the middle class and organized labor, democracy flowered, though it was sometimes sullied by political corruption.

But while the country fostered economic dynamism, political participation, and personal freedom, problems arose. Many rural people and unskilled workers did not share in the prosperity, and factories expected long hours from poorly paid workers. Thousands of Koreans, many of them middle class, emigrated to the United States. Furthermore, while South Koreans often welcomed the security provided by U.S. bases, others viewed the bases as an affront to Korean nationalism. Koreans on both sides of the demilitarized zone yearned for reunification. After years of hostility, North and South Korea finally achieved a wary peaceful coexistence. A dialogue begun in the later 1990s resulted in limited cross-border trade and allowed a few South Koreans to visit family members in North Korea they had not seen since the early 1950s. Televised images of South Koreans tearfully embracing aging parents

or siblings mesmerized the nation. In 2000, South Korean president Kim Dae-jung (kin day-chung) (b. 1925), a liberal reformer, visited North Korea, an event that would have been unthinkable a decade earlier. Yet national reconciliation remains a distant dream.

South Korean Economic Growth One of South Korea's major, most diverse enterprises, the Hyundai Corporation, formed in 1976, engages in shipping, manufacturing, and trade, producing, among other products, chemicals, machinery, and information and telecommunications equipment. The ships in this company dry dock are being readied to carry Hyundai-made cars to distant markets around the world.

Stalinism in North Korea

North Korea's leaders chose a completely different path from that taken by South Korea. The communist leader Kim Il-Sung's decision to reunite Korea with force, which led to the Korean War, proved a mistake that devastated the country, though North Korea quickly recovered with aid from China and the USSR. From 1948 until his death in 1994, Kim was the nation's president, head of the Communist Party, and commander of the armed forces. He also created a personality cult around himself as the "Great Leader." To ensure loyalty and deflect blame for failures, Kim purged 70 percent of communist cadres and jailed or executed thousands of dissidents.

North Korea adopted a mix of Stalinism and Maoism to shape the economy and society. Soviet-style economic planning and central direction emphasized heavy industry and weapons at the expense of consumer goods. As a result, North Koreans did not enjoy the rising living standards of South Koreans. To inspire the population to work hard, Kim invented a political philosophy of self-reliance that was heavily influenced by Mao Zedong's policy of relying on a country's own strength and limiting contact with the

world economy. North Korea benefited from a favorable industrial base built during Japanese colonial times, since it contained more than three-quarters of Korea's factories and mines. For several decades, the North Korean economy outshined its South Korean rivals. The huge military establishment, however, drained these resources.

Politically, North Korea stressed group loyalty, ultranationalism, and independence from foreign influence, following the model of Korea's hereditary Yi dynasty and Confucian bureaucracy of the early nineteenth century. A small government and military elite, isolated from the bleak existence of the peasantry and workers, enjoyed special privileges and controlled the people by using regimentation and restricting information. The government required each citizen to register at a public security office and urged people to spy on their families and neighbors. To prevent people from hearing contrary views or unapproved culture, the only radios allowed were fixed to receive only the government station. Political prisoners and people caught trying to flee to China or South Korea faced long terms in harsh concentration camps or even execution.

By the 1990s, the regime faced stresses that resulted in increasing international isolation. The economy declined rapidly, thanks to poor management, commodity shortages, and rigid policies. Satellite photos of the Korean peninsula at night revealed the stark differences in electrical power between a brilliantly lit South Korea and a completely dark North Korea. U.S. diplomatic pressure isolated the regime, while efforts to strike back, such as assassination attempts on South Korean leaders, earned North Korea a reputation as an unpredictable terrorist state. When the Soviet bloc collapsed in 1989, Russia and China demanded that North Korea pay cash for oil and other imports.

North Korea's problems increased after Kim Jong-Il (chong-ill) (b. 1942), known as the "Dear Leader" as well as for his reputation as a playboy, succeeded his deceased father in 1995. When the nation soon faced mass starvation, Kim requested and received food aid from South Korea and Japan, and as the food shortages continued, the United Nations also sent food, much of it supplied from the United States. Even with the aid, many people died or were malnourished. Thousands of North Koreans fled to China to find food and work. Observers predicted the regime would collapse, but it avoided that fate. Thanks to isolation and tight information control, most North Koreans believed the state's propaganda.

North Korea became a concern in both regional and world politics. By the late 1990s, its military force was twice as large as South Korea's and apparently had a capability for building nuclear weapons. But with both Koreas possessing lethal military forces, war became less likely. This perception encouraged the search for common ground in pursuing national unification. The economic disasters of the 1990s, especially food shortages, softened the North Korean position, and after 1998, South Korea actively sought better relations to reduce the threat from its dangerous northern neighbor and its unpredictable leader.

Taiwan and China

The triumph of the Chinese communists on the mainland in 1949 led to the relocation of Chiang Kai-shek and his Nationalist government to the mountainous, subtropical Taiwan island, where he reestablished the Republic of China. Two governments claiming to represent China created a long-term diplomatic problem for the world community. Both the governments of the People's Republic on the mainland and of the Republic on Taiwan regarded the island as an integral part of China rather than a separate nation; this "one China policy" was endorsed by most of the world. Taiwan's people built a prosperous society but remained divided about the nation's future and its long-term relationship to China.

Taiwan's Place in Asia Taiwan had only become a part of Chinese territory in the seventeenth and eighteenth centuries, when the Qing dynasty claimed the island and Chinese began settling the island in large numbers, relegating the small Malay-speaking native population to mountain districts. In 1910, Taiwan became a Japanese colony. Japan ruled Taiwan less harshly than it did Korea, financing industrialization that produced a higher standard of living. After World War II, China reclaimed the island, but in 1947, local resentment of Chiang's heavy-handed regime led to an island-wide uprising. Chiang dispatched 100,000 troops from the mainland, who killed 30,000 to 40,000 Taiwanese in quelling the unrest.

As Chiang's Republic of China collapsed in 1948–1949, the president and 2 million mainlanders moved to Taiwan, taking with them their government, the Nationalist Party, the remaining military forces, the priceless art collections of the national museum, and China's national treasury. These mainlanders and their descendants eventually constituted some 15 to 20 percent of the total island population, which numbered 23 million by 2005. The minority mainlanders dominated politics, the economy, and the military. The majority Taiwanese, although Chinese in culture and language, often considered the mainlanders colonizers. Chiang viewed Taiwan as a temporary refuge, because he hoped to reconquer the mainland and then return there. But after his death in 1972, mainlanders cultivated better relations with the Taiwanese.

Taiwan's Economic Boom Learning from their defeat in China, and using we generous U.S. aid, the Republic's leaders promoted rapid industrial and agricultural growth and a more equitable distribution of wealth. As a result, the peasantry prospered. As in South Korea and Meiji Japan, the economy mixed capitalism and foreign investment with a strong government role. Light industry and manufacturing eventually accounted for half of Taiwan's economic production and the bulk of exports. Taiwan became the world's third largest producer of computer hardware. Between the early 1970s and the late 1990s, it enjoyed more years of double-digit growth than any other nation. By the 1980s, the economic indicators far surpassed those on the mainland, including a per capita annual income of $8,000, approximately 99 percent of households owning a color television, 92 percent literacy, and a life expectancy of seventy-five years. Rapid development, however, also brought problems, including environmental destruction, traffic congestion, political corruption, and a severe economic slowdown in 1997.

> "Many of the East and Southeast Asian nations forged closer economic cooperation, with Japan and China forming the hubs."

Modernization in Taiwan

Modernization has challenged Chinese values and traditions. The small roadside cafés selling noodle soup and meat dumplings, a beloved mainstay of local life for generations, are often unable to compete with U.S. fast-food restaurants and convenience stores. While Confucian values, such as the emphasis on hard work, have fostered the material success of the Little Dragons, some Taiwanese have worried that Confucian ethics, including respect for parents and concern for the community rather than the individual, are threatened. In response, the Taiwan government has supported traditional Chinese culture by mandating the teaching of Confucian ethics in the schools. Despite the modernization, traditional Chinese culture remains stronger in Taiwan than in the mainland. More than 90 percent of the people describe themselves as, like their ancestors, Buddhists, Daoists, Confucianists, or a mix of the three ancient traditions.

Like South Korea, Taiwan until the later 1980s followed the authoritarian Little Dragon political model. For several decades, Chiang Kai-shek and his family controlled the island with a police state and made it illegal to advocate making Taiwan permanently independent of China. For four decades, Chiang's political party, the Nationalists, ruled as the sole legal party, but in 1989, nudged by a growing middle class seeking liberalization, they permitted opposition candidates to run in elections. Gradually, the regime recognized civil liberties, including the freedom of speech and press. The 2000 elections swept into office the Democratic Progressive Party (DPP), largely supported by the native Taiwanese; many party leaders, reflecting widespread Taiwanese opinion, advocated that Taiwan become a separate nation, a stance that angered both the Nationalist leaders on Taiwan and the communist leaders on the mainland. However, by 2005, elections showed reduced support for the DPP.

Taiwan and the Mainland

China has remained Taiwan's permanent challenge. Fearing an invasion to forcibly annex the island, Taiwan lavishly funded its military, kept a large standing army, and bought the latest fighter jets and gunboats, at the same time maintaining a defense alliance with the United States and allowing U.S. bases. But in 1978, the United States recognized the People's Republic as China's only government, embraced the one-China policy, and withdrew diplomatic recognition from its longtime ally, the Republic of China on Taiwan. However, the United States remains diplomatically and economically tied to Taiwan. In the later 1980s, Taiwan and China began to improve relations; trade has grown substantially, and many people from Taiwan have visited the mainland. However, doubts about whether China will move toward political liberalization, as well as alarm at occasional Chinese military exercises being conducted near Taiwan, have precluded any serious negotiations on reunification. Thus Taiwan's political future remains an open question.

The Little Dragons in the Global System

The rise of the Pacific Rim, including China, Japan, and the Little Dragons, in the late twentieth century reshaped the global system. The one-quarter of the world's population living along the western edge of the Pacific Basin established policies that allowed them to outpace the West and the rest of the world in economic growth while maintaining political stability. By the 1990s, the Little Dragons had diversified into high technology, thereby posing an economic challenge to Japan and the West.

Some economic trends suggested that the Pacific Rim nations were becoming an Asian counterpart to the European Community. Many of the East and Southeast Asian nations forged closer economic cooperation, with Japan and China forming the hubs. But in 1997, an economic meltdown hit South Korea, Taiwan, Japan, and the industrializing economies of Southeast Asia. As businesses closed, unemployment soared. By the early 2000s, South Korea and Taiwan had regained some of their dynamism but still faced challenges. But on the global stage, China and Japan will undoubtedly play major roles in the years to come, and in many respects, East Asia has returned to its historical role as a key engine of the world economy.

 Listen to a synopsis of Chapter 27.

CHAPTER 28

Rebuilding Europe and Russia,
Since 1945

Learning Outcomes

After reading this chapter, you should be able to answer the following questions:

LO¹ What factors fostered the movement toward unity in western Europe?

LO² How did the rise of welfare states transform western European societies?

LO³ What factors contributed to political crises in the Soviet Union and eastern Europe?

LO⁴ How did the demise of the communist system contribute to a new Europe?

" This [united] Europe must be born. And she will, when Spaniards say "our Chartres," Englishmen "our Cracow," Italians "our Copenhagen," and Germans "our Bruges." Then Europe will live. **"**

—**Spanish writer Salvador de Madariaga, 1948**[1]

Jacques Delors (deh-LOW-er) faced a challenge. Born in 1925, this French banker's son turned socialist politician had lived through a tumultuous time. Now, after holding high economic positions in the French government, he had dedicated himself to building a united Europe. In 1985, he became president of the European Commission, established to further European political cooperation. His goal was to reconcile national loyalties with support for a united Europe. In December 1991, Delors convened the leaders of twelve European nations, already closely linked through a common economic market, in the Dutch city of Maastricht. Communicating his sense of mission, he prodded them to transform the economic and political alliance begun in the late 1940s, and expanded in the 1950s, into a more comprehensive union.

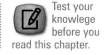

Test your knowlege before you read this chapter.

This meeting on Europe's future took place in the same month that the Soviet Union (USSR) dissolved. With their biggest communist rival no longer a threat, European leaders created a new European Union that would stretch from the Atlantic to the western frontier of Russia, allowing people to cross borders without passports and permitting trade goods to pass freely from country to country. A single currency, the *euro*, would also unite these states. Persuaded by Delors, conference leaders signed the Maastricht Treaty, and it was later ratified by voters in all member nations. While facing bumps in the road, the European Union, given the centuries of European strife that preceded it, was nonetheless a huge achievement.

From 1945 until 1990, three themes dominated European history: (1) the Cold War shaped by the United States and the USSR, the world's rival superpowers; (2) the rebirth of western European wealth and power; and (3) the movement toward European unity represented

<<**Fall of the Berlin Wall** In 1989, as communist governments collapsed in eastern Europe, peaceful protesters climbed on top of the Berlin Wall, which had already been decorated with graffiti. The wall, which divided communist East and democratic West Berlin, was soon torn down.

AP Images/STF

747

> "Emotionally traumatized by the war and its atrocities, Europeans also saw their prestige in tatters around the world."

rious Allies in Nuremberg, Germany, in 1946 condemned Nazi leaders to death and declared crimes against humanity, especially genocide, to be indefensible. A Dutch thinker wrote that the old Europe was dead and beyond redemption.

by the Maastricht Treaty. The trauma of two world wars had fostered a drive for unity by consensus of the nation-states involved rather than through military might. This movement accelerated after 1989, when the governments allied to the USSR collapsed and communism was largely abandoned, opening the way for a new, interconnected Europe in a post–Cold War world in which the United States held dominant power.

LO¹ Western Europe: Revival and Unity

Western Europe emerged from the ashes of World War II economically and morally bankrupt, yet made a rapid recovery with aid from the United States. Most western European societies reestablished working multiparty democracies that accorded personal freedom to their citizens. Beginning in 1947, however, Europe was split into two mutually hostile camps, western and eastern Europe, each with a different model of postwar reconstruction and rival military forces. Gradually, West Germany, France, and Britain served as the core of a rebuilt, increasingly unified European community and were able to regain influence in the world.

Recovery and the Remaking of Nations

World War II had devastated Europe in the 1940s. Some 50 million lives were lost; major cities were reduced to rubble; and Europe's economic potential was cut by some 50 percent. Transportation, food, housing, and fuel were in short supply. The chaos of war and the redrawing of political boundaries after the war caused massive displacement, including 10 million Germans who were forced to leave eastern Europe. Emotionally traumatized by the war and its atrocities, Europeans also saw their prestige in tatters around the world. War crimes trials held by the victo-

The Marshall Plan

Economic growth provided the foundation for a new Europe. In 1947, the U.S. secretary of state, former general George Marshall (1880–1959), who had directed the U.S. army through World War II, proposed that the United States assist in restoring the economic health of Europe. This initiative, the Marshall Plan, created a recovery program aimed at preventing communist expansion and spreading liberal economic principles, such as free markets. Between 1948 and 1952, the United States offered $13 billion in aid, about half going to Britain, France, and West Germany. In exchange, American business enjoyed greater access to European markets. The Marshall Plan restored agricultural and industrial production while bolstering international trade. The rapid economic resurgence from 1948 to 1965 was unmatched in world history except for Japan's recovery in the same years (see Chapter 27).

The European Movement

The British leader Winston Churchill (1874–1965), who served twice as prime minister (1940–1945, 1951–1955), predicted the coming Cold War in 1946, warning "an iron curtain" had descended, dividing capitalist western Europe from communist eastern Europe. This Cold War division, however, as Churchill also predicted, helped stimulate a western European movement for cooperation. Eight hundred delegates met at the Hague, in Holland, in 1948, where they called for a democratic European economic union and the renunciation of national rivalry, generating what soon became the "European Movement."

After the war, western Europeans made a commitment to sustain parliamentary democracy. This was true for both the republics and the surviving constitutional monarchies, including Belgium, Britain, the Netherlands, and the Scandinavian nations, where kings and queens remained symbols of their people but held little power. Four major states—France, Italy, West Germany, and Britain—were the most influential in postwar western Europe. Longtime dictators

CHRONOLOGY

Western Europe, 1945–1989

1946–1949	Greek civil war
1947–1989	Cold War
1947–1969	De Gaulle era in France
1948	Hague Congress on European unity
1948–1949	Berlin crisis
1948–1952	Marshall Plan
1949	Formation of NATO
1951	Formation of European Coal and Steel Community
1957	Formation of European Common Market
1969	West German ostpolitik policy

opposed to change were overthrown and replaced by democrats in Spain, Portugal, and Greece in the 1970s. The end of colonial empires, and the loss of revenues from them, also reshaped European politics.

New political alignments emerged. Given the frequent conflicts between France and Germany in the past, political stability in western Europe depended on improved relations between these two nations, as well as on German recovery from war. Charles De Gaulle (1890–1970), the French Resistance general who largely dominated French politics between 1947 and 1969, overcame centuries of hatred by making French–German reconciliation the cornerstone of French policy. Similarly, the West German leader, Konrad Adenauer (ODD-en-HOUR) (1876–1967), sought a more cooperative relationship with France. This reconciliation was furthered in the 1960s by West German chancellor Willy Brandt (1913–1992), a fervent anti-Nazi who accepted German responsibilities for the war and the new borders imposed after the war, which awarded a large chunk of German territory to Poland. The improved French–German relationship owed much to economic growth. West Germany's economy rapidly expanded in the 1950s and 1960s, benefiting from a collaborative relationship with France.

Politics in Post-War Europe

New political parties and movements took shape. On the right, parties calling themselves Christian Democrats, which had been closely tied to the Catholic Church before World War II, freed themselves from

Basque Terrorism The extremist Basque nationalist movement, the ETA, has waged a terrorist campaign against the Spanish government for decades. They have assassinated dozens of people and exploded bombs at government targets in cities and towns, resulting in the sort of destruction shown here after one attack.

AP Images/EFE/Javier Belver

Greens
A twentieth-century political movement in western Europe that rejected militarism and heavy industry and favored environmental protection over economic growth.

British Commonwealth of Nations
A forum, established by Britain in 1931, for discussing issues of mutual interest with its former colonies.

> "In the thirty years after World War II, most European colonizers abandoned their efforts to quell nationalist movements in Asia and Africa and started to leave their colonial territories."

clerical patronage. Still emphasizing Christian values and protecting the traditional family, these conservative parties were influential in a half-dozen countries, including West Germany and Italy. But because of corruption, these parties had lost considerable support by the 1990s. At the same time, parties on the left competed for support. The social democratic parties, which favored generous welfare programs to provide a safety net for all citizens, came to power in several countries soon after the war and moved toward state ownership of large industries such as steel and railroads. Eventually most of these parties, such as the British Labor Party, abandoned state ownership and economic planning for free markets. Meanwhile, the western European communist parties, with whom the social democrats had largely avoided cooperation, declined rapidly, maintaining a substantial following only in France, Italy, Portugal, and Spain. By the 1980s, a new political movement had had an impact: the Greens favored environmental protection over economic growth and militarism.

Western Europe was not immune to civil unrest. The desire of ethnic minorities for their own nations spurred unrest and terrorism in Spain and Northern Ireland. A chronic ethnic conflict embroiled Spain, where the Basque people, who live mostly in the north and speak a distinct language, sought either autonomy within, or independence from, Spain. An underground Basque independence movement, known as ETA (for "Basque Homeland and Freedom"), has carried out assassinations, bombings, and other terrorist acts against people linked to the Spanish government. Similarly, for decades in Northern Ireland, Catholics and Protestants fought for self-determination, causing a state of civil war as thousands died in terrorist violence. A power-sharing agreement resolved the conflict in the early twentieth century, but tensions remained.

Nationalism and the End of Colonialism

In the thirty years after World War II, most European colonizers abandoned their efforts to quell nationalist movements in Asia and Africa and started to leave their colonial territories. The British, whose empire had occupied an area 125 times larger than Great Britain, realized that imperial glory was past. In 1947, they bowed to the demands of Indian nationalists and recognized the independence of India. The Dutch, facing a determined nationalist resistance, reluctantly abandoned their lucrative colony, Indonesia, in 1950. By the mid-1960s, the British had turned over most of their colonies in Africa, Asia, and the Caribbean to local leaders, retaining control of only a few tiny outposts. Postimperial Britain continued financial assistance and capital investment to many former colonies and maintained a more formal connection with them through the British Commonwealth of Nations, which the British established in 1931 and which comprised fifty-three states by 2000.

By contrast, the French and Portuguese only grudgingly recognized the inevitable. In the mid-1940s, nationalist rebellions broke out in French-controlled Algeria and Vietnam, which France attempted to quell at the cost of much bloodshed. In his criticism of France's use of torture against rebels in Algeria, the French philosopher Jean-Paul Sartre asserted that "France is struggling in the grip of a nightmare it is unable either to flee or to decipher."[2] In 1954, unable to defeat communist-led rebels, the French withdrew from Vietnam, and in 1962, they left Algeria. Eventually, France established close relations with most of its former colonies, including an enduring economic connection that critics considered a form of neocolonialism, or indirect domination. Portugal wasted lives and wealth violently resisting decolonization, but after democrats overthrew the longstanding fascist dictatorship, it granted its African colonies independence in 1975.

Europe and NATO in the Cold War

Beginning in 1946, the Cold War—shaped by rivalry between the two superpowers, the United States and the USSR—influenced the various European nations' roles in the world. The USSR helped install communist governments in eastern Europe and East Germany, while the United States assumed the burden for protecting western Europe. In 1947, the U.S. president, Harry Truman (president 1945–1953), formed a policy, known as the Truman Doctrine, that asserted that the United States was the leader of the free world and was charged with defending countries threatened by Soviet pressure.

A World Divided

Strong European and U.S. fears of possible Soviet attack led to the formation in 1949 of the North Atlantic Treaty Organization, commonly known as NATO, a military alliance that linked nine western European countries with the United States and Canada. NATO allowed coordination of defense policies against the USSR and its communist allies, known as the Soviet bloc, in case of attack. Permanent U.S. military bases were set up in NATO countries, especially West Germany. The Soviets responded in 1955 by forming the Warsaw Pact, a defense alliance that linked the communist-ruled eastern European countries with the USSR (see Map 28.1). By the 1980s, senior officers in NATO and the Warsaw Pact had spent their careers preparing for a war that never came.

 Interactive Map

The Cold War and NATO were partly a response to the postwar division of Germany. Each of the four World War II allies—the United States, Britain, France, and the USSR—had an occupation zone in Germany and had also divided up the pre-1945 German capital, Berlin. In 1948, the three Western powers united their occupation zones. Angered by this move, the USSR blockaded Berlin to prevent supplies from reaching the city's Western-administered zone by land through Soviet-controlled East Germany. For a year, the allies supplied the city by airlift to the Berlin airport. In 1949, the USSR stopped the blockade and allowed the creation of the Federal Republic of Germany, or West Germany, while forming its own allied government, the German Democratic Republic, or East Germany. By 1954, West Germany was fully sovereign and soon joined NATO.

Reassessing Alliances

In the 1960s, Cold War fears slackened in Europe as the danger of actual war faded, leading western Europeans to reappraise their foreign policies. Some Europeans, especially in Britain, promoted the U.S. alliance, while others grew to resent U.S. power. Most Europeans opposed the American war in Vietnam, which American leaders justified as an effort to stop the spread of communism in Asia, as well as U.S. interventions to overthrow left-leaning governments in Latin America. The West German chancellor Willy Brandt, a Social Democrat, began rethinking Cold War attitudes in 1969. Although Brandt was strongly anticommunist, his policy of ostpolitik ("eastern politics") sought a reconciliation between West and East Germany and an expanded western European dialogue with the USSR. This policy led to a thaw in West Germany's relations with the Soviet bloc and gave hope to eastern Europeans who wanted more freedom. Gradually, western Europeans, by building their own military forces, became less reliant on U.S. power and played a larger role in NATO. Despite such differences, however, the alliance and NATO remained strong.

From Cooperation to European Community

As a result of wartime economic destruction, increasing U.S. political and economic power, and the costs of decolonization, during the 1940s, Europeans lost influence to the United

> 66 In the 1960s, Cold War fears slackened in Europe as the danger of actual war faded, leading western Europeans to reappraise their foreign policies. 99

Truman Doctrine A policy formed in 1947 that asserted that the United States was the leader of the free world and was charged with protecting countries like Greece and Turkey from communism.

NATO (North Atlantic Treaty Organization) A military alliance, formed in 1949, that linked nine western European countries with the United States and Canada.

Soviet bloc In the twentieth century, the Soviet Union and the communist states allied with it.

Warsaw Pact A defense alliance formed in 1955 that linked the communist-ruled eastern European countries with the USSR.

ostpolitik ("Eastern politics") A West German policy, promoted by Chancellor Willy Brandt, that sought a reconciliation between West and East Germany and an expanded dialogue with the USSR.

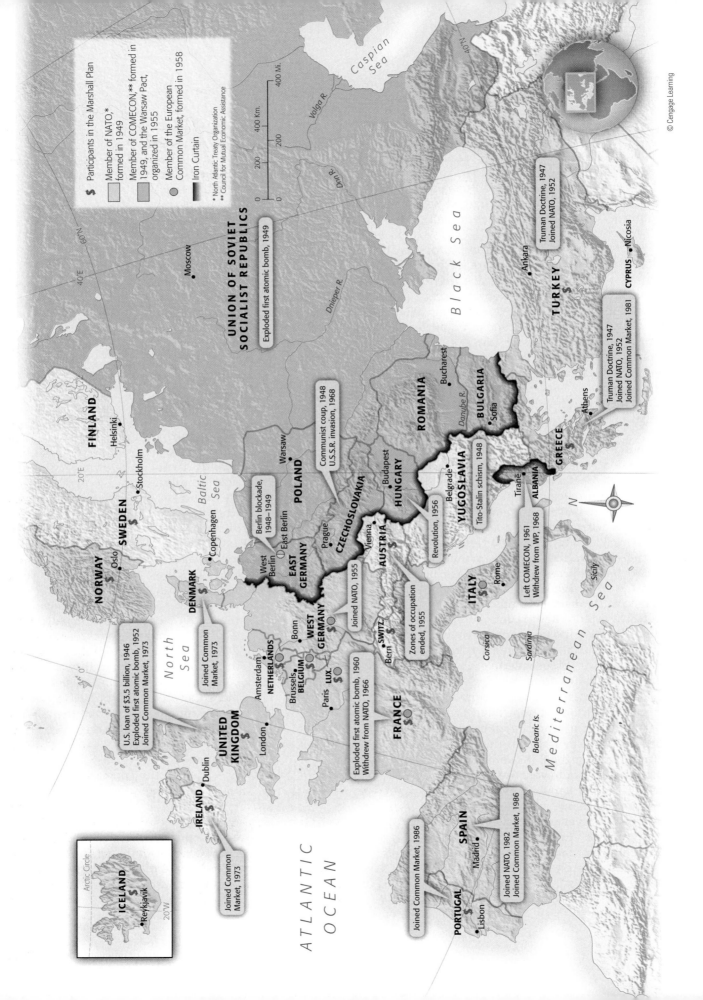

Participants in the Marshall Plan

$ Participants in the Marshall Plan

☐ Member of NATO,* formed in 1949

☐ Member of COMECON,** formed in 1949, and the Warsaw Pact, organized in 1955

● Member of the European Common Market, formed in 1958

▬ Iron Curtain

* North Atlantic Treaty Organization
** Council for Mutual Economic Assistance

400 Mi.

400 Km.

ARCTIC OCEAN

ATLANTIC OCEAN

North Sea

Baltic Sea

Mediterranean Sea

Black Sea

Caspian Sea

Volga R.

Don R.

Dnieper R.

Danube R.

UNION OF SOVIET SOCIALIST REPUBLICS
- Exploded first atomic bomb, 1949
- Moscow

FINLAND
- Helsinki

NORWAY
- Oslo

SWEDEN
- Stockholm

DENMARK
- Copenhagen
- Joined Common Market, 1973

ICELAND
- Reykjavik
- Joined Common Market, 1973

Arctic Circle

IRELAND
- Dublin
- Joined Common Market, 1973

UNITED KINGDOM
- London
- U.S. loan of $3.5 billion, 1946
- Exploded first atomic bomb, 1952
- Joined Common Market, 1973

NETHERLANDS
- Amsterdam

BELGIUM
- Brussels

LUX.

WEST GERMANY
- Bonn

EAST GERMANY
- East Berlin
- West Berlin
- Berlin blockade, 1948–1949

POLAND
- Warsaw

CZECHOSLOVAKIA
- Prague
- Communist coup, 1948
- U.S.S.R. invasion, 1968

FRANCE
- Paris
- Exploded first atomic bomb, 1960
- Withdrew from NATO, 1966

SWITZ.
- Bern

AUSTRIA
- Vienna
- Joined NATO, 1955
- Zones of occupation ended, 1955

HUNGARY
- Budapest
- Revolution, 1956

ITALY
- Rome

YUGOSLAVIA
- Belgrade
- Tito-Stalin schism, 1948

ROMANIA
- Bucharest

BULGARIA
- Sofia

ALBANIA
- Tiranë
- Left COMECON, 1961
- Withdrew from WP, 1968

GREECE
- Athens
- Truman Doctrine, 1947
- Joined NATO, 1952
- Joined Common Market, 1981

TURKEY
- Ankara
- Truman Doctrine, 1947
- Joined NATO, 1952

CYPRUS
- Nicosia

SPAIN
- Madrid
- Joined NATO, 1982
- Joined Common Market, 1986

PORTUGAL
- Lisbon
- Joined Common Market, 1986

Corsica

Sardinia

Sicily

Balearic Is.

© Cengage Learning

Map 28.1 <<
Military Alliances and Multinational Economic Groupings, 1949–1989

Post–World War II Europe was divided by Cold War politics into communist and non-communist blocs. Most western European nations joined the NATO defense alliance. Western Europeans also cooperated in economic matters. By 1989, the Common Market had expanded from six to eleven members. The Soviet bloc counterpart, COMECON, had eight members.

States. The Bretton Woods agreement on international monetary cooperation, negotiated by representatives of forty-four countries in 1944, reshaped the world economy by making the U.S. dollar, pegged to the price of gold, the staple currency for Western nations. Faced with declining economic influence in the world, Europeans concluded they had no choice but to cooperate with each other.

In 1949, ten western European nations formed the Council of Europe, which sought to operate on the basis of a shared cultural heritage and democratic principles. In 1950, the Council produced the European Convention on Human Rights, the root of a Europe-wide justice system and court. But some leaders wanted more, especially Jean Monnet (MOAN-ay) (1888–1979), a French economist and former League of Nations official who was often called the "Father of United Europe," and French prime minister Robert Schuman (1886–1963), a strong proponent of French–German reconciliation. The two men wanted to make further war in Europe not only unthinkable but impossible. To encourage better economic coordination, they devised a plan for a European Coal and Steel Community (ECSC), which was finally formed with the signing of the Treaty of Paris in 1951. The ECSC promoted European economic stabilization and became the beginning of a framework for unity and peace. But some European nations, including Britain, feared loss of economic independence and declined to join.

The Common Market

Building on the foundation of the ECSC, the Common Market, later known as the European Community (EC), was formed in 1957 with six members: France, Italy, West Germany, the Netherlands, Belgium, and Luxembourg. The new organization included a customs union to remove tariff barriers between members, thus opening frontiers to the free movement of capital and labor. The members also set a plan for preserving peace and liberty by pooling economic resources, and they called upon other Europeans to join in their efforts. Soon others did: the EC added Britain, Ireland, and Denmark in 1973.

The EC created unprecedented economic unity in the world's largest free-trade zone, but it only slowly generated political unity. The founders dreamed of a united Europe: societies that depend on one another, they reasoned, will not go to war. But the EC weathered many disagreements as member nations squabbled to get the best deal for their own farmers or businesses, and the British periodically threatened to quit the grouping. Every member economy had to adapt to the laws of the marketplace, dumping uncompetitive industries. Despite such challenges, the EC greatly reduced old national tensions. The members eventually established an elected European Parliament, based in Brussels, Belgium, to devise policies that encouraged cooperation and standardization.

The European Community fostered unprecedented economic growth in the 1960s (see Map 28.2). With higher wages and greater purchasing power, families bought automobiles, washing machines, refrigerators, and televisions. More people worked in the service sector and fewer in agriculture. The middle classes grew rapidly, while blue-collar workers shared middle-class aspirations. Consumer markets reached from Europe's sprawling cities into remote villages, transforming them. Europeans invested in railroads and mass transit—subways and commuter trains—to make transportation more convenient. Yet prosperity did not eliminate all poverty or regional disparities. For example, industrialized northern Italy remained much wealthier than largely agricultural southern Italy.

 Interactive Map

Economic Breakdown

Despite the growing cooperation and the successes it fostered, western Europe still faced mounting economic problems. Europeans were hurt by American decisions that led to the dismantling of the Bretton Woods international monetary system. In 1971, with the U.S. economy undermined by the war in Vietnam, President Richard Nixon devalued the U.S. dollar, the staple currency of the Western nations, and ended its parity with gold. These moves destabilized world trade, triggering soaring prices and trade deficits. Then in 1973, European economies were brought to a standstill by a quadrupling of oil prices, followed by a short embargo on oil exports by the major oil-producing nations, which were angered by Western support of Israel. Frustrated motorists waiting in long lines at gas stations showed how vulnerable prosperity could be in the global system—and that noxious

© Cengage Learning

Map 28.2
Europe's Gross Domestic Product

The gross domestic product, or the official measure of the output of goods and services in a national economy, provides a good summary of a nation's economic production. In the early twenty-first century, Norway, Ireland, and Switzerland were the most productive European countries on a per capita basis, while former Soviet bloc nations had the weakest performance.

GDP per capita
- Over $40,000
- $30,000–40,000
- $25,000–29,999
- $20,000–24,999
- $15,000–19,999
- $10,000–14,999
- Under $10,000

air, toxic waste, and other environmental concerns were the apparent price of industrialization.

Cooperation also could not avert other economic problems deriving from global economic patterns. The end of cheap energy and growing competition from industrializing Asian nations and Japan hurt local European industries and workers. Aging fac-tories, often decaying and inefficient, scaled back operations or closed, causing high unemployment in industrial cities such as Birmingham and Manchester in England. Jobless young people, living in bleak rowhouses or apartments and surviving on welfare payments, sometimes turned to drugs or crime. By 1983, unemployment rates in western Europe had risen to 10 percent. Some Europeans, blaming their problems on immigrant workers, gave a boost to right-wing, anti-immigrant parties. Capitalizing on the economic problems, free-market conservatives often regained political power, and once in power, they penalized striking workers and weakened labor unions.

> "By the 1990s, both white-collar and blue-collar Europeans worked fewer hours each year than their counterparts in the United States and Japan."

LO² Western European Societies and Cultures

In the ashes of World War II, the wartime British prime minister, Winston Churchill, wrote, "What is Europe? A rubble heap, a charnel house, a breeding ground for pestilence and hate."³ Seeing the need for change, western European nations embarked on various experiments to improve the quality of life for all of their citizens. The main experiment was the blending of capitalism and socialism. The economic boom from the late 1940s to the 1970s allowed most western European states to construct social welfare programs that fostered political stability, ensured public health, and eliminated poverty for most citizens. Gender relations, family life, and sexual attitudes were also reshaped, while musicians, philosophers, and churches addressed the changing times.

Social Democracy

The rise of western European welfare states—government systems that offer their citizens a range of state-subsidized health, education, and social service benefits—and the high quality of life they fostered, owed much to an influential political philosophy called social democracy. Social democracy derived from socialists in the early 1900s, who eventually promoted a mixing of liberal democracy, market economies, and a safety net for workers. Since 1945, social democratic parties have governed or been the dominant opposition in many Western countries.

Since the 1940s, social democracy has meant a mixed capitalist-socialist economy, a commitment to parliamentary democracy and civil liberties, support for labor unions, and the goal of moderating the extremes of wealth and poverty. As a result, workers in northern and central Europe gained more rights and protections than workers anywhere else in the world. In West Germany, for example, they received generous pensions and gained seats on the boards of directors of the enterprises that employ them. Whatever their occupation, Europeans have often valued leisure at the expense of work. By the 1990s, both white-collar and blue-collar Europeans worked fewer hours each year than their counterparts in the United States and Japan.

Advantages and Disadvantages

Citizens in nations influenced by social democracy have received generous taxpayer-funded benefits from the state. Europeans tend to define welfare not just as assistance to the poor, as Americans do, but as protections to ensure that everyone enjoys better living standards and opportunities. Free education through the university level (but with stiff university entrance exams) has helped people from working-class and farming backgrounds to move into the middle and upper classes. Governments also subsidize housing for the elderly, child care and support, and unemployment insurance. Extensive mass transit makes travel and commuting affordable for all. Meanwhile, socialized medicine, such as the British National Health Service, which opened in 1948, removed the fear of serious illness and greatly improved public health. Northern European nations now have the most equitable distributions of income in the world and have nearly eliminated slums and real poverty.

These successes have come at some cost. Although the welfare states help create social stability, when economic growth rates level off, the states cannot meet all of the fresh demands placed on them. Funding the welfare programs has required high taxes, often half of a citizen's annual income, and worker protections inhibit companies' flexibility. Furthermore, many people with modest incomes, especially immigrants, live in drab apartment blocks or houses, often far from potential jobs and schools. Still, the Scandinavian nations, which were poor a century ago, have claimed both the strongest social

Swedish Father and Child Swedes have been the most innovative Europeans in social policy, including adopting in 1975 a law requiring employers to grant parental leave. While women mainly take advantage of the law, some men, including this man with his child, take off the full allotted time.

democratic governments and the world's most prosperous societies. The annual Human Development Report, issued by the United Nations, ranked Norway and Sweden as having the highest quality of life in the world in 2004.

Conservative Reaction

Beginning in the 1980s, the welfare states experienced more problems related to a downturn of the world economy. For decades, governments had paid for social services by borrowing against future exports, a strategy known as deficit spending. But falling export profits placed the welfare systems under strain, forcing cutbacks in benefits, and also prompted nations to cut spending for military defense. To enhance their competitiveness, companies began downsizing, thus putting pressure on generous unemployment programs. In some countries, conservative parties gained power and began to modify the welfare systems, as did the British government led by Prime Minister

Margaret Thatcher (governed 1979–1990), a free-market enthusiast.

But the conservative regimes did not dismantle welfare state institutions such as national health insurance, which remained hugely popular. Furthermore, the economic problems, unlike those caused by the Great Depression of the 1930s, did not bring violence or political instability. While occasionally a political party with an anti-immigrant or anti–European Union platform has gained a following, the welfare state provides stability. Even most free-market conservatives have accepted its broad framework, although they seek to make it more efficient and cost effective.

> 66 Beginning in the 1980s, the welfare states experienced more problems related to a downturn of the world economy. 99

EUROPA— Gateway to the European Union (*http://europa.eu/ index_en.htm*). Provides information on many topics.

Social Activism, Reform, and Gender Relations

Western European societies changed dramatically in the decades since 1945. A serious challenge to mainstream society came in 1968, when youth protests broke out in France that were aimed at the aging, autocratic president Charles De Gaulle, an antiquated university education system, and the unpopular U.S. war in Vietnam, France's former colony. University students took to the streets, fighting pitched battles with police, who responded with teargas. Inspired by the student protesters, industrial workers called a general strike, bringing some 10 million workers into the streets. Although De Gaulle outmaneuvered the protesters by rallying conservatives, raising workers' wages, and calling for a new national election, the protests begun in Paris soon spread to Italy and West Germany. Lacking strong public support, Europe's student protests soon fizzled. Still, De Gaulle resigned a year later after the public rejected, in a referendum, his proposals to reorganize the French government.

> "The lives of both men and women were affected by the changes in work, politics, and family life that the women's movements helped foster."

Crime and Punishment in Post-War Europe

Europeans also dealt with social problems common to all industrialized nations, such as drug and alcohol abuse and high divorce rates. But European attitudes and responses to the problems were often different from those in other countries. In contrast to the United States, for example, which has harshly punished drug use and trafficking, by the 1980s, western European legal systems generally treated drug use and minor drug sales as social and medical issues rather than criminal ones. Other laws in Europe also differed from those elsewhere in the world. Europeans generally opposed and abolished capital punishment, and most European nations enacted strict gun-control laws, which fostered low rates of violent crime.

The Sexual Revolution

Read about Simone de Beauvoir, the French feminist and philosopher who had a profound influence on the contemporary women's movement.

Attitudes toward marriage and gender relations also shifted in Europe. After World War II, governments tried to revitalize traditional cultural attitudes, such as the view that women were chiefly homemakers and that families should have many children. But in the 1960s and 1970s, changing attitudes toward sexual activity, often known as the sexual revolution, began to undermine conventional practices. The contraceptive pill, which remained illegal in some Catholic countries until much later, gave women control over their reproduction and sexuality. Changing social attitudes moderated the social shame of divorce, extramarital sex, and unmarried cohabitation, and pornography and obscenity laws were relaxed.

Inspired by feminist thinkers such as the French philosopher Simone de Beauvoir (day bow-VWAR), women's movements grew in strength across Europe and, by the 1970s, pressed their agendas more effectively. Feminists in general wanted legal divorce, easier access to birth control, the right to abortion, and reform of family laws to give wives more influence; they first found success in Protestant countries but later made headway in Catholic nations. In 1973, Denmark, which had legalized some limited abortions in the 1930s, became the first nation to allow abortion on request. Although Pope John Paul II (pope 1978–2005) reiterated the long-standing church ban on contraception, abortion, and divorce, many Catholics ignored their church on these matters. During the 1970s and 1980s, most Catholic nations, including Italy and Spain, followed the earlier examples of France, Britain, and Germany and legalized both divorce and abortion.

Changing Attitudes toward Women, Marriage, and Homosexuality

The lives of both men and women were affected by the changes in work, politics, and family life that the women's movements helped foster. Women increased their political power in part because they had won the right to vote and constituted a majority of the electorate. Men and women now shared the responsibility for financially supporting their families: by the 1980s, women were half the workforce in Sweden, one-third in France and Italy, and one-quarter in conservative Ireland. Women moved into the professions, business, and even politics, at various times heading governments in Britain, Germany, Iceland, and Norway. Even Ireland, where patriarchy remained strong, in 1991 elected its first woman president, social democrat Mary Robinson (b. 1944), who was an outspoken law professor, feminist, single parent, and supporter of homosexual rights. As they became wage earners, women became less dependent on men. Yet, so few women had been able to achieve high corporate positions even in egalitarian Norway that, in 2006, Norway's social democratic government outraged business leaders by requiring that 40 percent of the board members of large private companies must be women.

As a result of less rigid gender roles, marriage patterns and attitudes about homosexuality also gradually changed. In the 1970s, the popular culture still held up the model of the married heterosexual couple, but by the 1980s, more men and women than before remained single. In 1998, 15 percent of women and men between twenty-five and twenty-nine years old in western Europe lived on their own. Increasing personal independence and mobility fostered small nuclear families instead of the large extended families of old, especially in northern Europe. Homosexuals also began to enjoy equal rights. Organizing to change discriminatory laws and attitudes, reform movements began in Switzerland in the 1930s and, after World War II, in several other countries. Nonetheless, in the 1950s, many governments continued to prosecute homosexuals: for example, in West Germany between 1953 and 1965, some 99,000 men were convicted under still-existing Nazi-era laws prohibiting homosexual activity. Laws opposing homosexual behavior began to be reformed or eliminated during the 1960s and 1970s, and most societies developed more tolerant attitudes. By 2001, most of northern Europe had passed laws recognizing domestic partnerships, and discrimination against homosexuals had ebbed. Several nations, including the Netherlands, Belgium, and Spain, legalized homosexual marriage in the early twenty-first century.

Immigration: Reshaping European Cultures

Population movements had been a feature of western European history for centuries, but in the later twentieth century, this pattern took a new turn as several million immigrants settled in various European countries. In response to economic growth that created labor shortages in northern Europe in the 1950s and 1960s, people from poorer southern Europe migrated north in search of better jobs and pay. They were soon joined by Turks, Algerians, Moroccans, and people from West Africa and the Caribbean, who were fleeing even harsher poverty. Meanwhile, many Indians, Pakistanis, and Bangladeshis sought a better life in their former imperial power, Britain, while emigrants left the former Dutch colonies for the Netherlands. By 1974, 10 percent of the working population of France and West Germany were foreign-born.

The Impact of Immigration

The immigration reshaped European societies. By the early twenty-first century, immigrants constituted 10 percent of the population of Germany, 6 percent in France, and 5 percent in Britain. Major European cities such as Paris, London, and Berlin took on an international flavor. Islamic culture flourished in cities such as Hamburg (Germany) and Marseilles (France), where Arab- and Turkish-language radio stations had large audiences. Indian and Pakistani sundry goods and grocery shops and restaurants became features of English city life. People of Asian and African descent were elected to parliaments in countries such as Britain and the Netherlands.

The immigration also posed problems of absorption into European society, especially fostering tensions between whites and the nonwhite immigrants. Over the years, as Turks, Arabs, Africans, and Pakistanis arrived to do the low-paying jobs nobody else wanted and then settled down, they and their local-born children faced discrimination and sometimes violent attack by right-wing youth gangs. Neo-Nazis in Germany sometimes set fire to immigrant apartment buildings, and young toughs in England boasted of "Paki-bashing," or beating up people from the Indian subcontinent. While older immigrants often clung to the cultures and attitudes they brought from their Asian or Middle Eastern villages, such as a husband's authority over his wife and the preference for arranged marriages, their children struggled to reconcile the contrast between their conservative traditions with the materialistic, individualistic, secular societies of Europe.

After 1989, vanishing jobs put both immigrants and local people on the unemployment rolls or in competition for scarce work. Despite the economic problems, illegal immigration also increased. In 2001, perhaps 700,000 people fleeing extreme poverty or harsh repression illegally entered the European Union. Since the mid-1990s, anti-immigrant (especially anti-Muslim) movements have emerged even in famously tolerant countries like Denmark and the Netherlands, especially after the terrorist attacks against the United States in 2001, which shocked Europeans. Facing particular hostility since 2001, some Muslims, rejecting Western culture as immoral and

 European Union in the US (*http://www.eurunion.org/eu/*). Provides a wealth of data on the European Union.

criticizing the Islam brought by their parents from North African, Turkish, or South Asian villages as corrupted by Sufi mysticism, have become more devout than their parents. The most alienated Muslim youth, seeking a purpose in life, have turned to militant Islamic groups for direction.

Importing American Culture

Despite such social challenges, western Europeans enjoyed a resilient cultural life that was enriched by immigrants and imports. The influence of mass culture from the United States became more widespread than before the war. American cigarettes, Coca-Cola, and chewing gum symbolized postwar fashions, while African American jazz musicians often settled in Europe in the 1950s and 1960s to escape racism at home. Young people also enjoyed popular entertainments from outside of North America, such as Caribbean reggae music, Latin American dances, and Japanese animated films. Yet Europeans often treasured entertainers who reflected local culture, such as the waiflike French singer Edith Piaf (1915–1963), who was known for her sad, nostalgic songs.

Rock music helped define youth cultures, allowing young people to embrace an exciting, edgy music that their parents often disliked. After rock emerged in the United States in the mid-1950s, it rapidly gained a huge following in Europe, where American rock stars such as Buddy Holly, Elvis Presley, and Chuck Berry enjoyed massive popularity. By the 1960s, European musicians inspired by U.S. rock and blues had reshaped popular culture. The Beatles, young working-class men from Liverpool, England, matured as musicians and became the symbols of the younger generation for a decade. Beatlemania, as their impact was called, reached around the world.

Eventually, rock music introduced more personal reflection and social commentary. By the mid-1970s, a new style of rock, called punk, appeared that expressed social protest. Punk became especially influential in Britain, where working-class youth faced limited job options. The provocative songs of a leading British punk group, the Sex Pistols, deliberately insulted the monarchy and offended the deeper values of British society, much to the delight of their fans. As punk's energy dissipated, it was replaced in the 1980s by escapist dance music, but influenced later musicians significantly.

African and Asian Cultures in Europe

Cultural forms from Asia and Africa also influenced European culture. For example, in Britain the popular bhangra music emerged from a blending of Indian folk songs with Caribbean reggae and Anglo-American styles, such as rock, hip-hop, and disco. Using a mix of Indian and Western instruments, bhangra became popular with both white and Indian youth in Britain. By the 1980s, bhangra had spread to the Indian diaspora communities in continental Europe, North America, and the Caribbean, sustaining Indian identity. By the early 2000s, bhangra's appeal had widened, becoming a truly world music.

Cultural life was influenced not only by the wave of cultural imports but also by local developments. The creative cinema of France, Italy, and Sweden developed a global audience by depicting psychological and social dilemmas common to all people in a rapidly changing world. Literature also reflected political change. Writers known as postcolonialists sought to escape the world-view shaped by Western colonialism and dominance. For example, the India-born British writer Salman Rushdie (b. 1947), a Cambridge University–educated former actor from a Muslim family, criticized Western society, especially the Western treatment of Asian peoples. At the same time, however, he challenged what he considered the antimodern sensibilities of Islamic culture. His books, especially *The Satanic Verses* (1988), a critical look at Islamic history, created an uproar among conservative Muslims, even inspiring the rulers of Iran to issue death threats, forcing Rushdie to go into hiding.

Thought and Religion

Philosophy flourished in postwar Europe, continuing a secularizing trend that had been strong for more than a century. For several decades after the two world wars, Europeans struggled to understand their horrors, which seemed to contradict the emphasis on rational thought and tolerance that had been building in Europe since the Enlightenment. In seeking answers, some turned to new philosophies, while others struggled to reconcile religious faith and modern life.

Jean Paul Sartre

Existentialism, a philosophy whose speculation on the nature of reality

bhangra
A popular music that emerged in Britain from a blending of traditional folk songs brought by Indian immigrants with Caribbean reggae and Anglo-American styles, such as rock, hip-hop, and disco.

existentialism
A European intellectual approach contending that truth is not absolute but constructed by people according to their society's beliefs.

reflects disillusionment with Europe's violent history, became an influential school of secular thought. The French philosopher Jean Paul Sartre (sahrt) (1905–1980) and the French feminist thinker Simone de Beauvoir (1908–1986), his longtime partner, transformed existentialism into a philosophy with wide appeal. Sartre argued that individuals are defined by a reality that they tend to view as the work of fate or imposed by others. He advised people to find their own meaning and not let others determine their lives. In his view, people must accept responsibility for their actions, and this should lead to political engagement to create a better society. Sartre became active in left-wing political movements, such as those promoting world peace and banning nuclear weapons. Sartre provided a philosophy that every individual could act upon and that reached across political boundaries. During his life, Sartre achieved a level of fame unusual for a philosopher; when he died in 1980, thousands of people attended his funeral.

Deconstruction and Postmodernism

Meanwhile, like existentialism, other influential philosophies debated the nature of reality. Marxism fostered an understanding of social class and gender inequality, but as a political philosophy it lost many followers after the 1960s. In contrast to Marxism, which offers a certitude about truth and the workings of society, an approach called deconstruction, pursued by the Algeria-born Frenchman Jacques Derrida (DER-i-dah) (b. 1930), claimed that all rational thought could be taken apart and shown to be meaningless. Derrida questioned the entire Western philosophical tradition and the notion, still popular in Europe and North America, that Western civilization was superior to other cultures. Inspired by Derrida's questioning of accepted wisdom, by the 1990s, literature and scholarship were influenced by the intellectual approach known as postmodernism, which contends that truth is not absolute but constructed by people according to their society's beliefs. Even scholars, postmodernists argue, cannot completely escape the prejudices of their gender, social class, ethnicity, and culture. Other thinkers, among them many Marxists, rejected the postmodernist notion that truth is relative and objectivity impossible.

Rethinking Religion

While philosophy flourished, organized religious life declined. The horrors of World War II and postwar materialism had destroyed many people's faith. Churchgoing declined precipitously, leaving churches in many cities semideserted. Polls in the 1990s showed that, whereas some two-thirds of Americans had a moderate or strong religious faith, less than half of western Europeans did. Meanwhile, conflicts between rival Christian churches, once a source of tension, lost their intensity. Formed in 1948, the World Council of Churches, based in Switzerland, brought together the main Protestant and Eastern Orthodox churches. Appalled by the Holocaust that had been perpetrated by the Nazis against the Jews, Christian thinkers began acknowledging their faiths' relationship to Judaism by referring, for the first time in history, to Europe's *Judeo-Christian* heritage. Although the Jewish population in Europe decreased sharply because of the Holocaust and post–World War II emigration to Israel and the Americas, Jews remained a key religious minority. Christians had also to deal with another faith: by 2000, immigration and conversions had made Islam the second largest religion in France, Belgium, and Spain after Roman Catholicism.

The Roman Catholic Church, which remained largely conservative but still politically influential, had to address the changes in European societies. Pope John XXIII (pope 1958–1963) began a comprehensive reform with the convocations of church leaders known as the Second Vatican Council (1962–1965), or Vatican II. Vatican II launched the most radical church changes since the Council of Trent in the mid-1500s had responded to the Protestant Reformation. It no longer required Latin in the liturgy, and it removed blame from the Jews for the death of Jesus. Even after

Vatican II: The Catholic Church Engages the Modern World Read how Pope John XXIII opened the Second Vatican Council, at which the Catholic Church reformed itself in significant ways.

Vatican II, however, many Catholics followed only the church teachings that suited them, widely ignoring, for example, the ban on artificial birth control, while some conservative Catholics turned to more traditionalist movements opposing Vatican II.

LO³ Communism in the Soviet Union and Eastern Europe

Like western European countries, the Soviet Union changed after World War II. For several generations during the Cold War, the USSR was the major political, military, and ideological rival to the North American and western European nations. The USSR was the last great territorial empire and enjoyed substantial natural resources while maintaining a powerful state and a planned economy. But by the 1980s, the Soviet system was showing signs of decay.

> "The lives of both men and women were affected by the changes in work, politics, and family life that the women's movements helped foster."

The Soviet State and Economy

The USSR emerged from World War II as the world's number-two military and economic power, no mean achievement given the ravages of war in that land: 20 million killed, millions left homeless, cities blasted into rubble, the countryside laid waste. The trauma of that war helps explain the hostility toward the West:

CHRONOLOGY

The Soviet Union and Eastern Europe, 1945–1989

1945–1948	Formation of communist governments in eastern Europe
1948	Yugoslavia split from Soviet bloc
1953	Death of Stalin
1955	Formation of Warsaw Pact
1956	Khrushchev de-Stalinization policy
1956	Uprising in Hungary
1957	Launch of *Sputnik*
1960	Sino–Soviet split
1961	Building of Berlin Wall
1962	Cuban Missile Crisis
1968	Prague Spring in Czechoslovakia
1979–1989	Soviet war in Afghanistan
1980	Formation of Solidarity Trade Union in Poland
1985	Gorbachev new Soviet leader

Russians resented the sacrifices they had been forced to make because of Germany's conflict with Britain and France. These experiences reinforced traditional Russian paranoia, fostered by two centuries of invasions by Germany or France, and led Russians to maintain a huge defense establishment and their power in eastern Europe, keeping the region as a buffer zone between them and western Europe.

Stalin and the Soviet Bloc

The USSR in the early postwar years reflected the policies of its leader, Josef Stalin (STAH-lin) (1879–1953). Stalin believed that, because of their key role in the victory over Nazism and the Russian occupation of eastern Europe, the Soviets could deal as equals with the West. He therefore left Soviet armies in eastern Europe and helped establish communist governments there. Stalin also kept control of the Baltic states of Estonia, Latvia, and Lithuania, formerly independent nations that the Soviets occupied in World War II. Thus was created the Soviet bloc of nations, divided from the West by an "iron curtain" of heavily fortified borders. In 1949, the USSR gained a key ally with the communist victory in China (see Chapter 27). By 1949, Soviet scientists, helped by information collected by spies in the United States, had built and tested an atomic bomb, enabling the USSR to keep pace with the United States in the emerging arms race.

 Russian History Index: The World Wide Web Virtual Library (*http://vlib.iue.it/hist-russia/Index.html*). Contains useful essays and links on Russian history, society, and politics.

Stalin's years in power had been brutal for the Soviet people. The paranoid dictator, imagining potential enemies everywhere, maintained an iron grip on power. From the late 1920s through the early 1950s, millions of Soviet citizens were exiled to Siberia, and hundreds of others, including top Communist Party officials and military officers Stalin suspected of disloyalty, were convicted of treason in show trials and then executed. After World War II, the Communist Party maintained its tight rein on the arts, education, and science. For instance, party officials banned the poetry of Anna Akhmatova (uhk-MAH-tuh-vuh) (1888–1966), who had courageously recorded the agonies of Stalin's purge victims, and detained her in a filthy hospital. Stalin's government also stepped up Russification, the effort to spread Russian language and culture in the non-Russian parts of the empire, especially Muslim Central Asia.

> "Kruschchev sought to cleanse communism of the brutal Stalinist stain in order to legitimize the system among his people and around the world."

Khrushchev and De-Stalinization

The death of Stalin, who had achieved god-like status in the USSR, in 1953 sparked dissidence and rethinking, which led to modest political change. Stalin's successor, Nikita Khrushchev (KROOSH-chef) (1894–1971), was critical of Stalin's dictatorial ruling style and crimes and courageously began a process of de-Stalinization in 1956. Khrushchev sought to cleanse communism of the brutal Stalinist stain in order to legitimize the system among his people and around the world. Some of his criticism of Stalin circulated underground throughout the Soviet bloc, stirring up dissent in eastern Europe. In Poland, workers went on strike, and hundreds died or were wounded when the government suppressed it with force.

While it began a political thaw at home, de-Stalinization opened a split in the communist world that led eventually to China breaking its alliance with the USSR in 1960 and perhaps planted the seed for the unraveling of the Soviet Empire and system three decades later. Khrushchev promised that, under his leadership, the Soviet standard of living would eventually equal that of the United States. It never happened, but Khrushchev produced some achievements, especially in technology. In 1957, the USSR shocked the United States and the world by launching Sputnik, the first artificial satellite to orbit earth, and in 1961, cosmonaut Yuri Gagaran (guh-GAHR-un) (1934–1968) became the first man to fly aboard a rocket ship into earth orbit. Along with these achievements, however, came some old-style Soviet repressiveness: in 1957, Khrushchev prevented novelist Boris Pasternak (PAS-ter-NAK) (1890–1960) from publishing the novel *Dr. Zhivago*, a critical look at

> 66 Russians, having a long tradition of tolerating authoritarianism, learned how to survive its constraints, cooperating just enough with unpopular policies to avoid trouble. 99

the Bolsheviks during the Russian Civil War (1918–1921), which won a Nobel Prize in 1959 after being smuggled to the West.

The Brezhnev Era

In 1964, Khrushchev was deposed, and a much more staunch repression returned under Leonid Brezhnev (1906–1982), a cautious bureaucrat who imposed a Stalinist system in which the state had a hand in everything. Brezhnev led the country for the next two decades (1964–1982), and under him the Soviet state, run mostly in secret by a group of elderly, bureaucratic men, was intolerant of dissent, although less brutal than in Stalin's time. The secret police (KGB) monitored thought and behavior. Russians, having a long tradition of tolerating authoritarianism, learned how to survive its constraints, cooperating just enough with unpopular policies to avoid trouble. Active dissidence came from a few marginalized intellectuals and artists, some of whom found themselves in the remote prison camps, known as the Gulags, of Siberia. Many died there, but some persecuted intellectuals made notable achievements.

In 1970, the writer Alexander Solzhenitsyn (SOL-zhuh-NEET-sin) (b. 1918), a Red Army veteran imprisoned by Stalin in the Gulags for nine years, was forbidden to receive the Nobel Prize for literature. His novel, *One Day in the Life of Ivan Denisovich*, had exposed the harsh life in the labor camps. Another well-known dissident, Andrei Sakharov (SAH-kuh-rawf) (1921–1989), a physicist who had helped develop the first Soviet atomic bomb but became disillusioned with the government, won the Nobel Peace Prize in 1975 after advocating for an end to the arms race, but he was not allowed to attend the ceremonies.

Crisis in Communism

The Soviets had achieved notable successes, but they had also experienced severe economic problems. The Five-Year Plans introduced by Stalin beginning in 1928 had rapidly transformed the USSR into a fairly modern society. To encourage more economic progress in the postwar years, Soviet leaders had three tools: the Communist Party, the bureaucracy, and the military. By the 1980s, however, all three had proved inadequate to the task. The authoritarian party tolerated little dissent and fostered rigidity. The overcentralized bureaucracy often bungled planning and management. The military, large but inefficient, was held together by brutal discipline, promoted incompetent officers, and wasted resources. In 1987, a West German college student deliberately exposed the flaws by piloting his small, single-engine plane unnoticed right through Soviet air security to land in Red Square, where he was arrested by astonished police.

Increasingly, the economy struggled. The Soviets spent vast sums to achieve nuclear and military parity with the United States, devoting much of their budget to a massive defense establishment, sucking investment from other scientific and technological projects. Some of the retail economy was carried out through the black market, where people often bought food and clothes from illegal vendors operating out of backrooms or on street corners. Worker absenteeism and indifference, caused by the practice of paying workers regardless of effort, made for inefficiency. The economy also took a blow from failure to innovate high technology. The Soviets completely missed the personal computer revolution sweeping

the West beginning in the 1980s. And although they were better off than many Asians, Africans, and Latin Americans, most Soviet citizens lived well below North American and western European standards.

The environment also suffered. Industrial pollution led to dying forests and lakes, toxic farmland, and poisoned air. Diverting rivers for farming and power caused the Aral Sea, once nearly as large as North America's Lake Michigan, to practically dry up, and it also diminished the world's largest inland body of water, the Caspian Sea. In 1986, the nuclear power station at Chernobyl in the Ukraine exploded, causing numerous deaths and injuries, releasing radiation over a wide area of Europe, and revealing the Soviet Union's inadequate environmental protections.

As disillusionment set in, by the 1970s fewer Soviet citizens believed in the communist future. The Soviet people joked cynically: "Under capitalism man exploits man; under communism it's the other way around." In a society that Soviet leaders claimed was classless, the contrast between the wealth of the party, government, and military elite and that of everyone else was striking. Communism had fostered a favored elite, and social decay was evident everywhere: drab working-class lives, rampant corruption and bribery, the shortage of goods, high rates of alcoholism, and demoralized youth abounded.

Aral Sea As water from the rivers that supplied it was diverted for agriculture and industry, the Aral Sea in Soviet Central Asia lost more than half its water between 1960 and 2000. This photo shows a stranded boat where rich lake fisheries once existed.

The Soviet Union in the Cold War

The Cold War ebbed and flowed. The tensions between the United States and the USSR reached a height in the late 1940s through late 1950s. During the Korean War (1950–1953), the Soviets sent supplies to communist North Koreans who were fighting the South Koreans and the United States. Stalin's successors promoted a less aggressive policy, known as "peaceful coexistence," toward the West. From the late 1950s through late 1970s, the tensions between the superpowers eased somewhat, even though Soviet-backed forces took control of North Vietnam in 1954, and Cuba joined the communist camp in 1959.

However, there were also stumbling blocks to better relations. In 1961, the Soviet ally, East Germany, built a high, 27-mile-long wall around the part of Berlin administered by West Germany to prevent disenchanted East Germans from fleeing to the West. The wall became a potent symbol of the Cold War's divisiveness. In 1962, a crisis caused by the secret placing of Soviet nuclear missiles in Cuba, ninety miles from Florida, and by the demand by the United States that the missiles be removed brought the two superpowers to the brink of nuclear war. The Soviets withdrew the missiles, easing tensions. The Soviets also challenged the United States by helping arm the communist forces fighting U.S.-supported governments in South Vietnam, Laos, and the Philippines in the 1950s and 1960s.

The Soviet role in the world reflected national interest rather than communist ideology alone. The Soviets generally subordinated the global crusade for communism to the normal pursuit of allies, security, and political influence. To gain allies, they supported nationalist and revolutionary movements in Asia, Africa, and Latin America. On the whole, however, the Soviets followed pragmatic policies, usually sending military force only when their direct interests were threatened. They could do nothing when China broke with the USSR in 1960 and became a rival for influence in international communism. In contrast, they tolerated no opposition to Soviet power in the east European satellites, moving quickly to suppress revolts in Poland and Hungary in the 1950s, liberalizing tendencies in Czechoslovakia in 1968, and dissident movements in Poland in the 1970s and 1980s. The Brezhnev Doctrine asserted Moscow's right to interfere in the satellites to protect communist governments and maintain the Soviet bloc.

Eventually, however, military interventions proved costly. In 1979, Soviet armies invaded Afghanistan, on the southern border of the USSR, to prop up a pro-Soviet government. But in the 1980s, the United States, along with Arab nations and Pakistan, actively aided the Afghan rebels, mostly militant Muslims, who were fighting the secular Afghan regime and the Soviet occupation. Ultimately, Afghanistan, where the mountain and desert terrain made fighting difficult, proved a disaster for the USSR, costing 13,000 Russian lives and billions of dollars. Unable to subdue the opposition, the Soviets withdrew their forces in 1989. These difficulties of maintaining their hegemony contributed to a major reassessment of the Soviet system in the second half of the 1980s.

Soviet Society and Culture

Soviet society changed over the decades. After World War II, population growth surged, from 180 million in 1950 to 275 million by the late 1980s. The Soviet people were far healthier, better paid, and more educated than their predecessors had been in 1917. Citizens enjoyed social services that were unimaginable fifty years earlier, such as free medical care, old-age pensions, maternity leaves, guaranteed jobs, paid vacations, and day-care centers. In exchange for security, however, people knew they had to accept state power and the subordination of individual rights. These conditions reshaped gender relations, religion, and ethnic relations while also fostering resistance that was expressed through new forms of literature and music.

Women and the Family

The experiences of Soviet women reflected the provision of education and social services. While few women served in the Soviet hierarchy, most women were in the paid workforce, in both low-end and highly skilled jobs; for example, some three-quarters of doctors were women. Young women in rural areas, where people made less money than city workers, often migrated to the cities in search of a better life. Worried that the floodtide of female migrants to cities would diminish the next generation of farmers, the state tried, with limited success, to discourage the migration. While rural women faced an especially hard life, those in cities also faced demoralizing challenges: every day women of modest means stood in long lines in shops to buy food and necessities, washed clothes and dishes in the bathroom sink, and often prepared meals in communal kitchens. Meanwhile, women increasingly divorced abusive husbands, and the state legalized abortion. As a result, the average family became smaller. By the 1980s, both the birthrate and life expectancy were falling rapidly. While officially promoting gender equality, the state also used the schools to perpetuate the Russian stereotype that women were weak and passionate while men were strong and rational. Sometimes feminist activists were harassed, arrested, or even deported.

Religion and the Soviet State

In religious life, the state marginalized faith but did not eliminate it. Successive Soviet leaders promoted atheism and denounced Christianity as superstition, and the Russian Orthodox Church, for centuries a key focus of Russian life, became an informal agent of the state; the clergy, closely watched by the secret police, carefully avoided any suggestion of dissent. Still, Russians often attended church and nurtured their faith. In the 1980s, when the state became more tolerant, millions returned to the church, which performed mass baptisms and countless weddings. Yet Russia remained a largely secular society.

Ethnic Tensions

Soviet social conditions and state policies also affected ethnic relations. Relations between ethnic Russians and the diverse ethnic minorities, ranging from Christian Armenians to Muslim Uzbeks, deteriorated, provoking discontent. Restless ethnic minorities chafed at political, economic, and cultural domination by Russians, who constituted only about half of the Soviet population by the 1980s. In Central Asian Soviet republics such as Kazakhstan and Uzbekistan, newly built industrial cities attracted millions of ethnic Russian migrants, who monopolized most of the managerial and professional positions. Compared to neighboring regions of Asia, communism did bring relatively high living standards to Soviet Central Asia, but many Muslim peoples, such as the Uzbeks and Tajiks, resented the Russification of their cultures. The Baltic peoples (Lithuanians, Latvians, Estonians), forcibly annexed into the USSR during World War II, also hated Russian domination and the policy that replaced local languages with Russian. Some Jews, who were scattered around the country, sought the freedom to openly practice their religion or to emigrate to Israel or North America.

The Cultural Underground

Soviet state policies forced cultural creativity largely underground. Intellectuals duplicated and exchanged

RIA-Novosti

Soviet Rock Band For Soviet youth, rock music became a way of escaping the restrictions of Soviet life. This long-haired rocker from the 1980s wears a shirt with the communist symbol, the hammer and sickle, but the lyrics of rock bands often addressed the problems of Soviet life.

copies of forbidden books and magazines in secret; anti-Stalinist poets explored the breathing space between the official line and prison. Both imported and local versions of rock music became a major vehicle for presenting alternative ideas about life or criticizing the communist system. By the mid-1960s, some young Russians were modeling themselves on the Anglo-American youth counterculture symbolized by "hippies," wearing jeans and miniskirts and listening to the Beatles or their Soviet clones. For Soviet youth, rock music remained virtually the only escape from an oppressive society. Some 160,000 underground rock and jazz bands existed in the Soviet Union by the 1980s. Few musicians dared to challenge the system directly, but they explored the fringes, mocking the bureaucracy or the absurdity of Soviet life. Considering Western rock music to be degenerate and immoral, the authorities subjected innovative musicians to restrictions, although few faced arrest.

Eastern Europe in the Soviet System

Imposition of communist rule sealed the fate of eastern Europe for forty years. Soviet forces stayed in the region after World War II, installing communist governments and incorporating them into the Soviet bloc. Political parties were abolished, churches persecuted, and nationalistic leaders purged. In 1949, the communist nations formed COMECON (Council for Mutual Economic Assistance), which more closely integrated the Soviet and eastern European economies. Communism fostered economic development, especially in Romania and Bulgaria, which had little industrialization before World War II. But many eastern Europeans, especially in the more industrialized Czechoslovakia, Poland, and East Germany, aspired to living standards closer to those in western Europe. To supply consumer goods and finance industrialization, the governments took out loans and built up huge debts. As in the USSR, increased industrial activity created dirty air and toxic waste. Meanwhile, while the Soviets treated the satellite countries as neocolonies and exploited their resources, they also had to give them generous subsidies to maintain control.

Soviet Satellites Of all the eastern European communist nations, Yugoslavia followed the most independent path, breaking with the USSR entirely in 1948. In 1945, the Yugoslav Communist Party, led by Marshal Josip Broz Tito (TEE-toe) (1892–1980), who had been the widely popular leader of the local anti-Nazi resistance, won national elections. Tito wanted to avoid Soviet domination, so his government cooperated with them while also maintaining friendly relations with the West. For several decades, Tito's unique form of communism, which experimented with worker rather than manager control of factories, created enough prosperity and popular support to neutralize his nation's powerful ethnic divisions.

The refusal of eastern European populations to support Soviet domination fostered unrest. Poland, with its strong Catholic allegiances, was the most restless satellite, with its workers demanding more public input into the government. In 1956, Hungarian leaders tried to break with rigid communism by reinstating private property, inviting noncommunists into the government, and declaring the country neutral. When

> "By the 1970s, few Asian, African, or Latin American revolutionaries looked toward Moscow for inspiration."

a worker's council called for socialism that was adapted to Hungary's more liberal conditions, a Soviet bloc force occupied Hungary and executed the anti-Soviet leaders. Nonetheless, Hungary remained open to the West and was more tolerant of dissent than other Soviet satellites. Hungary's blend of state influence and free markets, known as market socialism, created the most prosperous Soviet bloc economy.

Dubcek and Walesa Other disgruntled eastern Europeans also defied Soviet power. In Czechoslovakia in 1968, the reform-minded leader Alexander Dubcek (DOOB-check) (1927–1993), during what was called the "Prague Spring," sought to shift to a more liberal "communism with a human face." Alarmed that the Czechs might start a dangerous trend, the Soviets sent Warsaw Pact troops into the country and replaced Dubcek and his supporters with repressive Soviet puppets. In Poland, the independent Solidarity trade union openly challenged the communist system. The union was formed in 1980 when, in response to high food prices and growing economic inequality, shipyard workers led by Lech Walesa (leck wa-LEN-za) (b. 1943), an electrical engineer, went on strike. As food prices continued to increase, thousands of women also took to the streets, and the dissidents then formed Solidarity, which aimed at economic liberalization. The movement was banned after the government declared martial law. Nonetheless, even though it was illegal, Solidarity had 9.5 million members by 1981 and worked for political as well as economic goals.

With political avenues closed off, young east Europeans used rock music as a protest vehicle. The result was often further repression. Government leaders prohibited performances by the more daring rock bands. Some East German musicians, among them the leading singer-songwriter Wolf Biermann (b. 1936), also a poet and novelist, were forced into exile; he wrote, "The German darkness descends over my spirit. It darkens overpowering in my song. It comes because I see my Germany so deeply torn."[4] These attitudes set the stage for later change.

Soviet Decline and Reform

Soviet problems mounted, forcing a reappraisal of the political and economic system and the nation's place in the world. The USSR had steadily lost ground in world affairs to the United States and economic ground to Japan and West Germany. Communist China went its own way in 1960 and became a bitter rival. The war in Afghanistan and the economic subsidizing of the east European satellites drained Soviet wealth. By the mid-1980s, the USSR had few close remaining allies outside of the Soviet bloc, which was restless. Soviet power in the world had always been mostly military, whereas the United States and its Western allies also had cultural, economic, technological, and even linguistic influence. All over the world, people studied English or French, not Russian. Some observers found more power in rock music, videos, fast food, youth fashions, and news networks than in the Soviet Red Army. By the 1970s, few Asian, African, or Latin American revolutionaries looked toward Moscow for inspiration.

 Letter to Comrades Brezhnev, Kosygin, and Podgorny Read a letter sent by prominent intellectuals to the Soviet leadership, urging a gradual democratization of the country as the only cure for its ills.

This declining international influence, combined with spiraling social and economic problems and a stifling bureaucracy, ultimately led to the rise of younger, reform-minded Soviet leaders who introduced dramatic change. The thaw of the 1970s had given Soviet leaders more contact with the outside world and an appreciation of the growing technological gap between them and the West. The planned economy that had powered a largely peasant society into a superpower now seemed a severe drag. In 1985, Mikhail Gorbachev (GORE-beh-CHOF) (b. 1931) became Soviet leader. While hoping to preserve the basics of the Soviet system, he understood the need to liberalize the economy, decentralize decision making, and relax ideological controls. However, Gorbachev inherited a Communist Party that allowed no political competition and managed a planned economy, run from the top with little room for individual initiative. With such a rigid system, the Soviet leader concluded, the USSR could never match the United States as a superpower.

Gorbachev introduced a dazzling series of reforms to reenergize the Soviet Union. He developed closer relations with the West, abandoning their decades-long ideological struggle. In 1987, the Treaty of Washington between the United States and the USSR lessened the threat of nuclear war by having both countries destroy their short- and long-range missiles. With his glasnost ("openness") policy, Gorbachev democratized the political system, including free elections, a real parliament that included noncommunist parties, the release of most political prisoners, and deemphasis of the role of the Communist Party. Gorbachev also loosened state control of the media, the arts, and scholarship, and let it be known that he would not maintain the unpopular communist governments in eastern Europe. They toppled or collapsed in 1989.

Admitting the faults of Soviet communism, Gorbachev also liberalized the economy, using market mechanisms in a policy known as perestroika ("restructuring") (see Witness to the Past: Restructuring Soviet Society). But the economic changes failed to take off. The intelligentsia wanted democratization, while the working classes preferred consumer goods, which did not come. Top bureaucrats proved resistant to changes that might threaten their role. Conservatives in the Communist Party and the secret police also opposed reforms that might undermine their power. Soon the Soviet system collapsed.

glasnost ("openness") The policy introduced in the Soviet Union by Mikhail Gorbachev in the 1980s to democratize the political system.

perestroika ("Restructuring") Mikhail Gorbachev's policy to liberalize the Soviet economy using market mechanisms.

 The Last Heir of Lenin Explains His Reform Plans: Perestroika and Glasnost Read President Gorbachev's analysis of the Soviet Union's decline, and his prescriptions for reform.

CHRONOLOGY

Europe, 1989–Present

1989	End of communist regimes in eastern Europe
1990	Reunification of Germany
1991	Breakup of Soviet Union
1991–2000	Yeltsin era in Russia
1991–2000	Crises in Yugoslavia
1991	Signing of Maastricht Treaty
2004	Expansion of European Union into eastern Europe

In 1987, Mikhail Gorbachev, the head of the Soviet Communist Party and government, published a book, *Perestroika*, outlining his policy of economic restructuring. His goal was to transform the inefficient, stagnant Soviet economy into one based on a decentralized market orientation similar to the market socialism of Hungary and China. The new policy gave greater autonomy to local government officials and factory managers and attempted to democratize the Communist Party. Causing a sensation, the book was ranked by some observers as the most important publication of the late twentieth century. By the early 1990s, with Gorbachev removed from office, the policy was eclipsed, but the book remained a testimony to the problems that led to the Soviet system's collapse. In this excerpt, Gorbachev defines *perestroika*.

Perestroika means overcoming the stagnation process, breaking down the braking mechanism, creating a dependable and effective mechanism for acceleration of social and economic progress and giving it dynamism.

Perestroika means initiative. It is the comprehensive development of democracy, socialist self-government, encouragement of initiative and creative endeavor, improved order and discipline, more glasnost (openness), criticism and selfcriticism in all spheres of our society. It is utmost respect for the individual and consideration for personal dignity.

Perestroika is the all-round intensification of the Soviet economy, the revival and development of the principles of democratic centralism in running the national economy, the universal introduction of economic methods, the renunciation of management by injunction and by administration methods, and the overall encouragement of innovation and socialist enterprise.

Perestroika means a resolute shift to scientific methods, an ability to provide a solid scientific basis for every new initiative. It means the combination of the achievements of the scientific and technological revolution with a planned economy.

Perestroika means priority development of the social sphere aimed at ever better satisfaction of the Soviet people's requirements for good living and working conditions, for good rest and recreation, education and health care. It means unceasing concern for cultural and spiritual wealth, for the culture of every individual and society as a whole.

Perestroika means the elimination from society of the distortions of social ethics, the consistent implementation of the principles of social justice. It means the unity of words and deeds, rights and duties. It is the elevation of honest, highly-qualified labor, the overcoming of leveling tendencies in pay and consumerism.

This is how we see perestroika today. This is how we see our tasks, and the substance and content of our work for the forthcoming period. It is difficult now to say how long that period will take. Of course, it will be much more than two or three years. We are ready for serious, strenuous and tedious work to ensure that our country reaches new heights by the end of the twentieth century.

Thinking About the Reading

1. What did Gorbachev mean by *perestroika*?
2. What problems did the policy aim to solve?

Source: Mikhail Gorbachev, *Perestroika* (New York: HarperCollins, 1987), pp. 34–35. Copyright © 1987 by Mikhail Gorbachev. Reprinted by permission of HarperCollins Publishers.

LO⁴ Communist Collapse: A New Russia and Europe

For four decades, the Cold War had provided the context for European politics. With the breakup of the communist bloc of nations in 1989 and the USSR in 1991, the political and economic face of Russia and Europe was reshaped. The collapse of these communist regions created hope but also uncertainties. Russia struggled to rebuild and to revive its power, but the capitalism introduced proved destabilizing. While Yugoslavia was torn apart by wars and Germany was reunited, Europeans had to redefine their identity. Western Europe pushed toward unification, but it still had to resolve the conflicting forces of nationalism and cooperation. Most Europeans now chose governments through multiparty elections and pursued individual freedom. By the beginning of the twenty-first century, Europe helped shape the age of globalization.

A New Russia and New Nations

A major development of twentieth-century history was the sudden collapse of the Soviet empire and communism in Europe. In 1985, there had been 5 million Soviet soldiers stationed from East Germany to Siberia's Pacific coast; six years later, the Soviet Union and its satellite nations had unraveled, without a shot being fired. Although the collapse was not a complete surprise, its pace was astonishing. While outside factors played a role in fostering the collapse, Soviet economic decline was probably the decisive cause. The result was a blending of new ideas from the capitalist, democratic West with Soviet-era traditions.

. . . .

Boris Yeltsin

The collapse revealed the failure of the Soviet system, which was founded on one-party rule and strongly shaped by the political repression and centralized economy of Stalinism. Democratic governments and decentralized capitalism—dominant in North America, western Europe, and Japan—had adjusted better to global changes than the planned economies of communist states, and nationalist yearnings among non-Russians within the empire had sapped the foundation of empire. Mikhail Gorbachev's greatest contribution was to face up to the fact of failure. But by 1991, unable to control the forces unleashed, he resigned as the Communist Party leader and was replaced by Boris Yeltsin (YELT-sin) (b. 1931), a communist bureaucrat turned reformer who had strong U.S. support. Yeltsin ended seven decades of communist rule, and in response, Russians toppled statues of Lenin and restored czarist names to cities that had been renamed during the Soviet era.

Yeltsin acquiesced in the breakup of the USSR, a symbol of the nation's demise as a superpower, while maintaining the unity of the largest Soviet republic, Russia, which stretched from the Baltic Sea through ten time zones to the eastern tip of Siberia (see Map 28.3). Glasnost had opened a Pandora's Box. Ethnic hatreds,

Interactive Map

> "In 1985, there had been 5 million Soviet soldiers stationed from East Germany to Siberia's Pacific coast; six years later, the Soviet Union and its satellite nations had unraveled, without a shot being fired."

oligarchs Well-placed former communists who amassed enough wealth to gain control of major segments of the post-Soviet Russian economy.

long suppressed by military force or alleviated by the government-provided safety net, soon exploded to the surface. In 1991, all of the fourteen Soviet republics outside of Russia declared their independence. However, many of the former Soviet republics were now led by former communist officials, whose autocratic ruling style resembled the old Soviet system.

Most of the new states have struggled to achieve economic self-sufficiency and political stability. Some states have been engulfed in conflict between rival ethnic or nationalist groups or have fought each other over territorial claims, as did Christian Armenia and Muslim Azerbaijan. But the results of revolutions are usually unpredictable. In Central Asia, inhabited largely by Muslims, some nominal and others devout in their faith, militant Muslims have launched insurgencies against the secular post-Soviet governments, seeking to replace them with Islamic states. Indeed, Islam gained support among the disenchanted and marginalized, especially jobless young men, in Central Asia. Islamic fervor has forced or prompted many women to don the headscarf and behave modestly. Meanwhile, millions of ethnic Russians in the former Soviet republics faced resentment for their relative affluence and ties to the former colonizer.

. . . .

Difficulties for Yeltsin

Yeltsin had difficulty solving Russia's problems in the 1990s. Hoping to end economic stagnation, he took the advice of Russian free-market enthusiasts and of U.S. advisers, who often knew little of Russian culture, and introduced a strategy known as "shock therapy": rapid conversion of the planned economy to market capitalism. This produced more consumer goods and a growing middle class, but organized crime groups and a few well-placed former communists, known as oligarchs, gained control of major segments of the Russian economy. At the same time, Yeltsin faced secession movements within the Russian federation, especially in Chechnya, a largely

© Cengage Learning

Map 28.3
The Dissolution of the Soviet Union

In 1991, the leaders of Russia, who had abandoned communism, allowed the other fourteen republics to leave the Soviet Union, bringing an end to a vast federation that had endured for more than seven decades. Still, Russia remained the world's largest nation in geographic size, stretching across ten time zones.

Muslim Caucasus territory that Russia had annexed in the 1870s. In 1994, this oil-rich region declared independence. Fearing that recognizing Chechnya's independence would encourage other secession movements, Yeltsin tried to crush the Chechen separatists, drawing the Red Army into a quagmire with thousands of casualties on both sides.

The economic pain of the Russian people was widespread. Millions of workers—and more women than men—lost their jobs as inefficient, obsolete Soviet industries closed. Arguing that the communists had destroyed the family by encouraging women to work, conservatives advocated that women stay at home and tend to family obligations. With the end of free higher education, families preferred to devote their limited money for schooling on their sons. Some desperate women turned to prostitution for survival. Even when their enterprises did not close, factory workers, miners, and state employees, such as teachers, were often not paid for years. Yeltsin dismantled parts of the welfare state; as a result, public health deteriorated. By 1992, inflation was 2,500 percent, devastating people who lived on pensions and fixed incomes.

Stabilization under Vladimir Putin

In 2000, with the Russian economy near collapse and free markets discredited, Yeltsin resigned in disgrace and was replaced by Vladimir Putin (b. 1952), who ended shock therapy and changed the nation's direction. A former secret police colonel who kept a portrait of the modernizing eighteenth-century czar Peter the Great in his office, Putin supported capitalism and democratic reforms, but also pursued policies that were more authoritarian and nationalist than Yeltsin's. Political liberalism faded as Putin took control of much of the media, muffling opposition media outlets, and prosecuting some oligarchs for corruption. The state has also taken over many large private companies, turning the economy into a form of state capitalism not unlike Meiji Japan. Company managers profit while the public pays for losses. The economy made a modest recovery because of improved tax collection and higher prices for two leading Russian exports, oil and natural gas.

Putin brought back stability after fifteen years of turbulence, marrying the old autocratic government with a new, more outward-looking attitude. The Russian Orthodox Church—for centuries closely connected to Russian national identity and political power—regained some of the influence it had lost under communism. In many parts of Russia, Muslims—some 15 percent of the nation's population—and Christians have peacefully adapted to each other. Putin also sought good relations with Germany, France, the United States, and China. In Putin's Russia, however, the contrasts between rich and poor became stark. While Moscow's wealthiest cavorted in fine restaurants and glitzy casinos, towns often went without heat and power. Corruption, poverty, unaccountability, weak legal institutions, and the festering war in Chechnya stifled development. Polls showed that a majority of Russians preferred the communist years. A respected Russian historian harked back to Peter the Great and Catherine the Great, advising Russians, "Our future lies in openness to the entire world and in enlightenment."[5] It remained unclear whether Russia would follow that path.

The New Eastern Europe

The changes in the USSR resonated throughout eastern Europe. In the late 1980s, the Soviet leader, Mikhail Gorbachev, who admired the Hungarian market socialism model, was no longer willing to protect the corrupt, largely unpopular eastern European communist governments. These governments began to fail as democratic movements that were once underground surfaced. Hungary adopted a demo-

> " Political liberalism faded as Putin took control of much of the media, muffling opposition media outlets, and prosecuting some oligarchs for corruption. "

cratic system; Solidarity came to power in Poland; and East Germans streamed across the border into West Germany, an exodus that led to the dismantling of the Berlin Wall. People around the world watched on television as Berliners gleefully knocked down the Berlin Wall, the symbol of Cold War division. Soon the East German regime and the other east European communist governments had collapsed or been overthrown. In Czechoslovakia, the playwright Vaclav Havel (vax-LAV hah-VEL) (b. 1936), who had been frequently arrested for his pro-democracy activities, was elected president after massive demonstrations forced the communist leaders to resign in a largely peaceful transfer of power known as the "Velvet Revolution." Havel announced, "Your government, my people, has been returned to you."[6]

Poland and the Czech Republic

Democratic or semidemocratic governments were installed, seeking to replace centralized planned economies with market forces, but the rapid move to capitalism proved destabilizing. East Europeans took up voting enthusiastically, yet they also experienced the challenges of change. As in the former Soviet Union, the end of communism uncorked ethnic hatreds and rivalries going back centuries: Slovaks seceded from the Czechs, forming their own country, while Romanians repressed the large Hungarian minority. Millions were thrown out of work as obsolete factories closed; shops were full of attractive goods, but few people had the money to buy them. Only Poland and the Czech Republic enjoyed robust economic growth. In addition, certain protections of the communist welfare system, such as free education, health care, and subsidized housing, were removed, causing misery. Finally, by 2000, salaries caught up with prices in some places, but pockets of high unemployment remained, and the gap between rich and poor widened.

The political environment changed as diverse political parties competed for power. Capitalizing on widespread interest in rebuilding the social safety net, former Communist Party members who now called themselves reform communists won some national elections, especially in Poland and Hungary. They competed for power with free-market advocates, pro-Western liberals, and right-wing nationalists.

In a striking repudiation of the Soviet legacy, reform communists often supported joining the European Union and even the NATO military alliance. Anticommunists had few regrets of the changes since 1989: Adam Michnik, a leader of Polish Solidarity, concluded that "without the slightest hesitation it is much better to live in a country that is democratic, prosperous and thus boring"[7] than under the communist regime.

> "Democratic or semidemocratic governments were installed, seeking to replace centralized planned economies with market forces, but the rapid move to capitalism proved destabilizing."

responded with ferocity, prompting another NATO imposed settlement in 2000. Thousands of NATO troops remained in Bosnia and Kosovo, a symbol of eastern Europe's unresolved challenges.

Toward European Unity

Two themes have dominated western Europe in the years after 1989. One was the reunification of Germany. With the fall of communism and the Berlin Wall, the East German state collapsed, and Germany was quickly reunified in 1990, but challenges endured. Europeans also have

Yugoslavia

Interactive Map

The greatest instability came to Yugoslavia, a federation of states that self-destructed in bloody civil wars between ethnic groups (see Map 28.4). Created artificially for political convenience by diplomats after World War I, Yugoslavia contained antagonistic ethnic and religious groups. The largest, the nationalistic Orthodox Serbs, wanted to dominate the federation, while the Catholic Croats and Slovenians and the Bosnian and Albanian Muslims wanted independence for the regions they dominated. After the long-term federal leader, Tito—the product of a mixed Croat–Serb marriage whose autocratic policies limited dissent and kept the lid on ethnic hatreds—died in 1980, Yugoslavia became a seething cauldron of ethnic conflict.

The violence began in 1991, when the Serb-dominated Yugoslav army tried to stop two states, Slovenia and Croatia, from breaking away from the federation. In response, the United Nations sent in peacekeeping troops to secure their independence. In 1992, the Muslim majority in another Yugoslav state, Bosnia, declared independence, a move opposed by the minority Serbs and Croats there. Bosnian Serb militias, aided covertly by the largest Yugoslav state, Serbia, massacred thousands of Muslims, introducing a new term for genocide, "ethnic cleansing," and leading the United Nations to send more peacemakers. As the violence continued, U.S. air strikes under NATO auspices forced the Serbs to accept a peace treaty in 1995. The Bosnia conflict had killed 200,000 people and generated 4 million refugees. In 1999, violence returned when the Albanian majority in Kosovo, the southern region of Serbia, revolted and the Serbs

The Velvet Revolution Protesters took to the streets in Prague, Czechoslovakia, to protest communist government and demand democracy. These protests, known as the Velvet Revolution for their peaceful nature, were led by Vaclav Havel, pictured on the poster carried by a protester.

Peter Turnley/Corbis

continued moving toward continental unity, a second theme, but this movement also faced setbacks.

German Reunification

The hasty German reunification disappointed its proponents. For many East Germans, merging with the prosperous West Germany promised access to a materially comfortable life they could only dream of before. But reunification cost billions and threw the German economy into a tailspin. Before reunification, West Germany had enjoyed a long boom. A decade later, however, the reunified nation of 80 million people, suffering from Europe's slowest economic growth, was stuck in deep recession. Many workers in the former East Germany lost jobs as obsolete factories closed. By 2004, the unemployment rate in the east was twice as high as in the west. Some disillusioned youth turned to right-wing, often neo-Nazi, groups to express their anger against foreigners and immigrants.

The European Union

Worried by Germany's problems, western European leaders believed that hastening unification was the best strategy to

Map 28.4
Ethnic Conflicts in Eastern Europe

Many of the nations in central and eastern Europe contain substantial ethnic minorities, and tensions between various groups have often led to conflict. In Yugoslavia, the conflicts between the major ethnic groups—Serbs, Croats, Bosnian Muslims, and Albanians—led to violence and civil war at the end of the twentieth century.

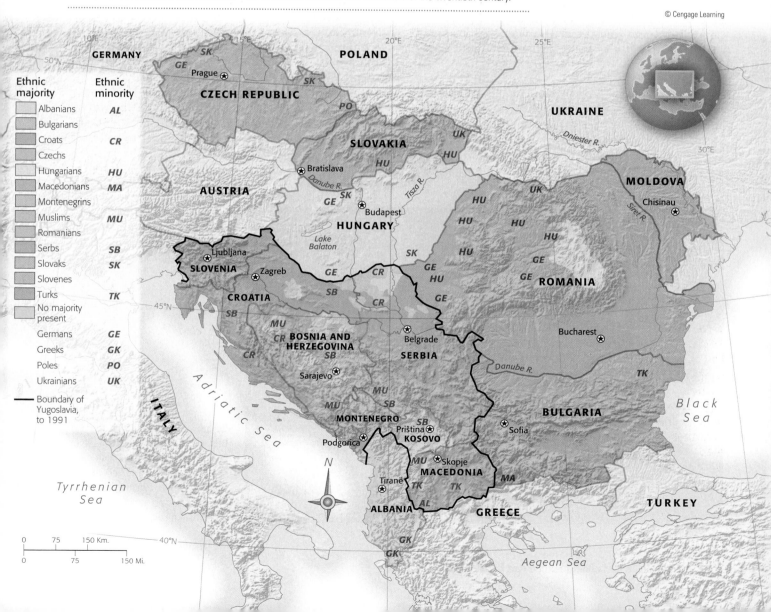

Ethnic majority / Ethnic minority

- Albanians — AL
- Bulgarians
- Croats — CR
- Czechs
- Hungarians — HU
- Macedonians — MA
- Montenegrins
- Muslims — MU
- Romanians
- Serbs — SB
- Slovaks — SK
- Slovenes
- Turks — TK
- No majority present
- Germans — GE
- Greeks — GK
- Poles — PO
- Ukrainians — UK
- —— Boundary of Yugoslavia, to 1991

stabilize post-communist Europe. The Maastricht Treaty, which recognized a single currency, the euro, and a central bank, set a goal of achieving economic and monetary union by 2000. It required budgetary and wage restraint as a prelude to monetary union. The treaty pledged to promote balanced and sustainable economic progress by strengthening economic and social cohesion. By 2002, eleven of fifteen signers of the treaty had adopted the euro as their currency, an index of unity. Millions of Europeans were multilingual, moving easily between cultures, and young Europeans often studied in other European countries, factors that aided unity.

The European Union (EU) doubled its membership from twelve nations in 1993 to twenty-five in 2004, when various eastern European nations joined, including the Czech Republic, Poland, and Hungary. The EU became a bloc of nearly 400 million people, encompassing most of Europe and enjoying a combined economic power equal to that of the United States. Some of the members, such as Sweden, have continued to show steady economic growth. Conducting one-quarter of the world's commerce, the EU became one of the dominant economic forces in the world.

Challenges of Assimilation

However, the European Union hit several major road bumps. Critics had long called the EU a faceless bureaucracy with innumerable rules that compromised national independence and threatened national traditions. Indeed, two of Europe's most prosperous nations, Norway and Switzerland, declined membership, fearing the loss of national identity and the cost of subsidizing poorer members. The EU leaders have been cautious in admitting those former Soviet bloc states that have weak economies and autocratic leaders. Turkey, a largely Muslim nation, has long sought membership, fostering a EU debate about how to define Europe and whether non-Christian nations have a role in it. This debate spilled over into the effort by European diplomats to prepare a constitution for the Union. Amid much controversy, the constitution proposed in 2004 rejected any mention of Europe's Christian heritage. But in 2005, voters in two of the most pro-unity countries, France and the Netherlands, fearing loss of control to the EU bureaucracy, shocked EU leaders by rejecting the constitution. This rejection, along with the accelerating global recession in 2008–2009, raised questions about the EU's future.

Increasing unity did not resolve, and may have contributed to, political, economic, and social problems caused by a changing global economy. The economic austerity policies of the 1990s unsettled welfare states and provoked government changes. Social democrats, who had governed eleven of the sixteen western European nations in the early 1990s, now jockeyed with centrists, free-market conservatives, Greens, anti-immigrant nationalists, and the fading communists for power. Attempts to roll back social benefits sometimes set off massive protests and long strikes. While many Europeans preferred to

European Economic Power
Business and political leaders from India and the European Union met in a summit in 2005 to increase trade relations, reflecting the growing economic power of both India and western Europe.

AP Images/Saurabh Das

maintain the welfare state even at the cost of slower economic growth, both the German and French governments replaced the thirty-five-hour workweek with the forty-hour workweek to increase their economic competitiveness. Yet, some large companies continued to downsize and cut or export jobs. In 2006, thousands in France rioted against loosening job protections.

Europeans also faced other challenges. By 2000, Europe, which a century earlier had been overcrowded and the world's greatest exporter of people, had a declining population, due mainly to the world's lowest birthrate: 1.2 children per woman. Yet, concerned about a much higher birth rate among Muslims, Europeans became increasingly hostile to immigration from the Middle East. Tensions simmered, and in 2005, rioting and vandalism by young Arab and African residents in France, many of them unemployed, caused much damage and heightened awareness of the challenges of assimilation. The European population decline also posed a long-term economic problem, because with more people retiring from than entering the workforce, younger workers had more responsibility for financing government services, such as pensions and health care, for the growing population of elderly. Thus Europeans still struggled to define their place in a changing world.

Europe and Russia in the Global System

With the end of the Cold War, Russia, western Europe, and the former Soviet bloc states searched for new roles in the world. Russia sought to maintain good relations with the EU, the United States, China, and the nearby Islamic nations, such as Iran, but also continued to act in its own self-interest. By 2004, NATO had added many of the former Warsaw Pact nations, discomforting Russia. Western Europeans seemed more reluctant than Americans to devote vast sums to the military or to send their armed forces into combat. The crises in Yugoslavia showed European weakness, with the United States pressing NATO for intervention and then leading the effort to restore order.

European relations with the United States became complicated. Various European nations, as part of a NATO commitment, sent troops to Afghanistan after the 2001 terrorist attacks on the United States and shared the goal of combating international terrorism. But most Europeans mistrusted the U.S. desire to invade oil-rich Iraq in 2003, believing it had little to

do with fighting terrorism and fearing it would destabilize the Middle East. As a result, major European nations such as France and Germany criticized the U.S. invasion and occupation. Although their people strongly opposed the war, some close U.S. allies, such as Italy, Poland, and Spain, sent small token forces, but only Britain had a sizeable military presence in Iraq. This participation ultimately cost British prime minister Tony Blair his popular support, and he resigned in 2007. In 2008, the election of U.S. president Barack Obama, a critic of the war, harkened a new era of U.S.–European relations.

Europeans also disagreed on how best to respond to international terrorism, especially the threat posed by militant Islamic groups. The substantial Muslim immigrant populations in Europe complicated European nations' policies on the Middle East. By 2000, 19 million immigrants, including 13 million Muslims, made up 6 percent of the total EU population. Islamic militancy spread among some people of Arab or South Asian ancestry in Europe, and the major terrorist network, Al Qaeda, had a presence in several nations. Deadly terrorist attacks on commuter trains in Madrid in 2004 and the London subway in 2005, which killed several hundred people, convinced many Europeans that Western military interventions in the Middle East might increase rather than diminish the terrorist threat. In 2006, shocked Europeans found how tense Muslim–Western relations had become when offensive cartoons satirizing the Islamic prophet Muhammad, published by a right-wing, anti-immigrant Danish newspaper, caused massive riots and demonstrations around the Muslim world, resulting in hundreds of deaths and attacks on Danish embassies and business interests.

With the move toward closer political and economic integration, Europe became much more than a collection of separate countries sharing certain cultural traditions and history. Europeans still played key roles in resolving world problems. European nations took the lead in developing international treaties on issues such as climate change, biological and chemical weapons, international criminal courts, and genocide. Some European workers also led movements against the economic globalization they saw as costing jobs and livelihoods. Though their region is no longer the powerful colossus it had been in the nineteenth century, Europeans are carving out a new place in the world.

Listen to a synopsis of Chapter 28.

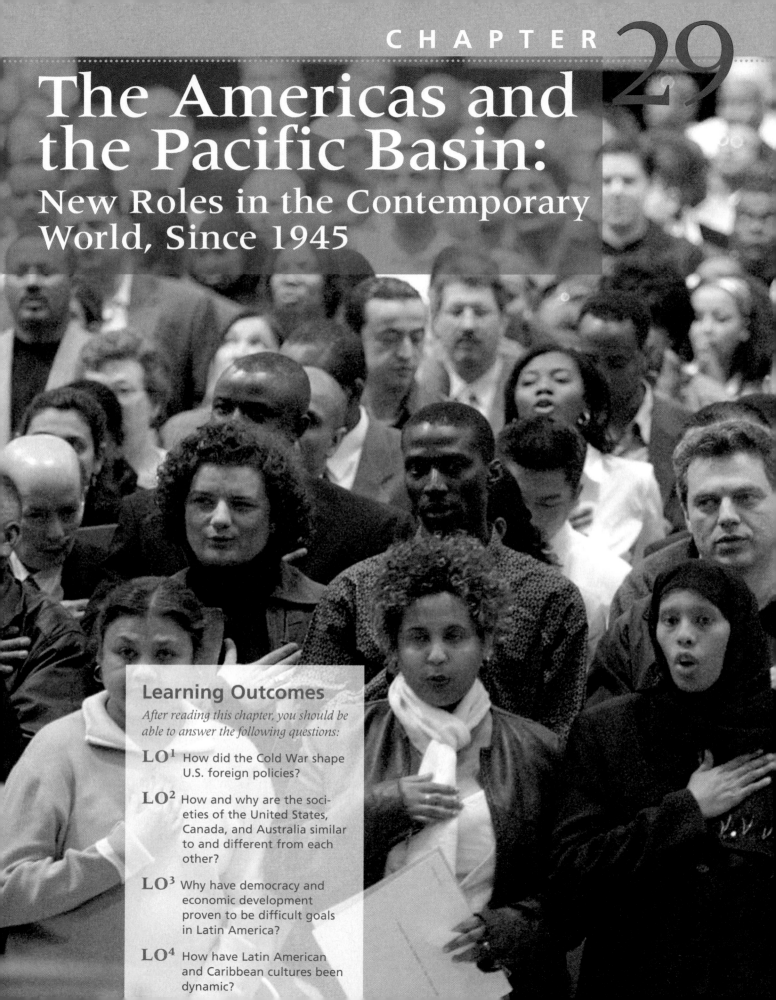

CHAPTER 29

The Americas and the Pacific Basin:
New Roles in the Contemporary World, Since 1945

Learning Outcomes

After reading this chapter, you should be able to answer the following questions:

LO¹ How did the Cold War shape U.S. foreign policies?

LO² How and why are the societies of the United States, Canada, and Australia similar to and different from each other?

LO³ Why have democracy and economic development proven to be difficult goals in Latin America?

LO⁴ How have Latin American and Caribbean cultures been dynamic?

“It's curious. Our generals listen to the [U.S.] Pentagon. They learn the ideology of National Security and commit all these crimes [against the Argentine people]. Then the same [American] people who gave us this gift come and ask, "How did these terrible things happen?”

—**President Raul Alfonsin of Argentina, 1984**[1]

The women appeared one day in 1977 at the historic Plaza de Mayo, adjacent to the presidential palace in Buenos Aires, Argentina. For several years, Argentina's military regime had been waging a bloody campaign to eliminate dissidents, killing or abducting some thirty thousand people and arresting and torturing thousands more. Some of those targeted may have belonged to outlawed leftist groups, but many simply held progressive political ideas. Soon the women's ranks swelled to more than one hundred at each weekly vigil, making their silent protest impossible to ignore. A year later, they numbered more than one thousand. These mothers and grandmothers pinned photographs of missing family members to their chests, silently demanding answers: where were their children, husbands, pregnant daughters, and grandchildren, some of them newborn infants?

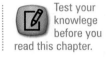

Test your knowlege before you read this chapter.

What do you think?

During the Cold War, the United States did not interfere in Latin American affairs.

Strongly Disagree					Strongly Agree	
1	2	3	4	5	6	7

The "Mothers and Grandmothers of the Plaza de Mayo," as they came to be known, dared to challenge one of Latin America's most brutal tyrannies. Their courageous protest inspired others in Argentina and around the world with hope and moral outrage at repression by military forces. The protest illustrates how some Latin Americans addressed the authoritarian governments under which they lived, as Latin American countries often shifted back and forth between dictatorship and democracy in the decades following World War II. Many Latin Americans came to resent the United States, which often supported despotic governments that repressed their people while welcoming U.S. investment. The gatherings in Buenos Aires continued weekly until 1983, when the regime fell and a civilian government began to investigate the disappearances, but most

<< **A Naturalization Ceremony** Seeking political freedom or economic opportunities, immigrants flock to the United States and many become citizens. At this ceremony, eight hundred residents, representing eighty-eight countries, took the oath of citizenship in Columbus, Ohio, in April 2005.

AP Images/Kichiro Sato

777

Argentineans never learned the fates of their loved ones.

The United States remained the hemisphere's dominant power during this period while gradually expanding its global influence. Wars in Korea and Vietnam were part of the U.S. effort to shape the global system while also opposing the expansion of communism. After World War II, the United States became the global workshop, banker, preacher, and police officer. It enjoyed unrivaled supremacy, a combination of military might, economic power, and political-ideological leadership that was contested only by the Soviet Union between 1946 and 1989. After 1989, the United States became the world's only remaining superpower. U.S. society increasingly differed from those of Canada and the Pacific Basin countries of Australia and New Zealand.

LO¹ The United States as a Superpower

By virtue of its size, power, and wealth, the United States has played a major role in the world after World War II, promoting human rights and freedom, lavishing aid on various allies, and providing leadership in a politically fragmented world. During the Cold War (1946–1989), U.S. policies were shaped by competition with the Soviet bloc for allies and strategic advantage. While people around the world admired American democratic ideals, prosperity, and technological ingenuity, the U.S.-led wars, interventions, support for authoritarian allies, frequent neglect of human rights, and the globalization of capitalism fostered widespread hostility toward the United States. After the Cold War, the United States and its allies faced new challenges, especially the rise of international terrorism.

> "World War II was a watershed for the United States, accelerating political centralization and economic growth."

❝ The Cold War produced an expectation of permanent conflict between two competing ideologies: communism and capitalist democracy. ❞

The Postwar United States and the Cold War

World War II was a watershed for the United States, accelerating political centralization and economic growth. At the same time, it compelled Americans to accept international involvements and thus promoted an activist foreign policy. By the later 1940s, observers began referring to both the United States and the USSR as superpowers because of their unrivaled political, economic, and military might. As U.S.–Soviet rivalry increased, the two superpowers sought to block each other from gaining influence in other countries.

The American Century

The victory over Nazism and Japanese militarism reinforced Americans' confidence and sense of mission. In 1941, Henry Luce, the publisher of one of the most influential news magazines in the United States, *Time*, declared that the twentieth century would be the American Century, and that Americans must accept their duty and opportunity to exercise influence in the world. After the war, the U.S. government pursued a strategy for expanding its economic influence, rebuilding defeated Germany and Japan, establishing global financial networks, lavishing aid on western Europe, and using U.S. military forces to protect U.S. allies in Asia. The United States also opposed radical nationalist movements, especially communist-led revolutionary groups, in Asia, Africa, and Latin America.

For several decades, as the U.S. economy soared, the notion of an American Century seemed realistic. Among the great powers, only the United States had not been bombed or financially drained, and therefore it was able to keep intact a modern industrial system. The United States alone could produce, on a large scale, the consumer goods needed by others. In 1950, it accounted for 27 percent of total world economic output. By becoming the engine of the world economy, Americans experienced an economic boom that lasted until the late 1960s and helped finance an activist U.S. foreign policy. Americans forged close trade links with Canada, western Europe, and Japan while sponsoring large-scale foreign aid programs and investment, especially in Asian and Latin American countries.

Such aid and investment often supported cash-crop agriculture and mining, reinforcing the economic dependence of developing nations by promoting unbalanced economic growth. Later, U.S. investment developed light industry, especially textile factories, that utilized cheap labor in countries such as Mexico and Thailand. Asian, African, and Latin America countries became key U.S. markets, acquiring more than one-third of American exports by the 1990s, while American consumption of ever-more foreign imports, from Japanese cars to Middle Eastern oil, contributed to a chronic trade imbalance. By 2005, imports were 57 percent larger than exports as Americans lived beyond their means, and globalization led to outsourcing of manufacturing and jobs.

The Cold War

The Cold War with the USSR shaped U.S. foreign relations. American leaders saw the Soviet Union as pursuing global aggression and fostering political unrest. Although they had good reason to worry about the Soviet state, which was headed by a ruthless dictator, Joseph Stalin, and possessed formidable military might, U.S. leaders and intelligence analysts often overestimated the Soviet threat. The Cold War produced an expectation of permanent conflict between two competing ideologies: communism and capitalist democracy. Given this assumption, the U.S. government became obsessed with secrecy and control. Two key U.S. institutions carrying out the anti-Soviet strategy, the Central Intelligence Agency (CIA) and the National Security Council, both established in 1947, operated in top secrecy, with little congressional oversight and ever-larger budgets, reaching a total of $40 billion per year for all intelligence agencies by the 1980s. By the early 1950s, the domino theory, which envisioned countries falling one by one to communism, became a mainstay of U.S. policy.

> **domino theory**
> A theory that envisioned countries falling one by one to communism and that became a mainstay of U.S. policy during the Cold War.

 WWW-VL: History: United States (*http://vlib.iue.it/history/USA/*). A virtual library, maintained at the University of Kansas, that contains links to hundreds of sites.

McCarthyism

Anticommunism intensified within the United States when U.S. senator Joseph McCarthy (1909–1957), a hard-drinking former judge, capitalized on Cold War fears and began to identify suspected communists in the government, the military, education, and the entertainment industry. His campaign, which became known as McCarthyism, led to the firing or blacklisting of not only a handful of secret communists but also thousands of Americans who held left-wing political views, which were condemned as "un-American" in the early 1950s. McCarthy called hundreds of people,

multilateralism
In the twentieth and twenty-first centuries, a foreign policy in which the United States sought a common front and a coordination of foreign policies with allies in western Europe, Japan, and Canada, avoiding activities that might enflame world opinion against the United States.

unilateralism
In the twentieth and twenty-first centuries, a foreign policy in which the United States acted alone in its own perceived national interest even if key allies disapproved.

containment
The main U.S. strategy aimed at preventing communists from gaining power, and the USSR from getting political influence, in other nations during the Cold War.

Mutually Assured Destruction
A policy, known as MAD, in which the United States and the USSR used the fear of nuclear weapons to deter each other during the Cold War.

> "Between 1945 and 1975, U.S. power was unmatched in the world, and the United States maintained military bases on every inhabited continent and in dozens of countries around the world."

from movie actors to State Department officials, before his Senate committee, ruining the lives of many innocent people before his popularity waned in 1954. That same year, the U.S. Senate finally censured McCarthy for recklessly charging top military leaders with treason.

Multilateralism vs. Unilateralism

For much of the Cold War era, a broad consensus emerged around opposing the spread of communism and Soviet power, though strategies differed. Some leaders pursued multilateralism, an approach in which the United States sought a coordination of foreign policies with allies in western Europe, Japan, and Canada, avoiding activities that might enflame world opinion against the United States. In contrast, most policymakers, and the presidents they served, favored unilateralism, a foreign policy in which the United States acted alone in its own perceived national interest even if key allies disapproved. The Cold War–driven consensus stifled those who questioned the rationale, tactics, and cost of an activist policy. But by the later 1960s, debates raged over controversial decisions such as military action in Vietnam, undermining the consensus and provoking increasing dissent.

Containing Communism

The main U.S. strategy, known as containment, was aimed at preventing communists from gaining power, and the USSR from getting political influence, in other nations. An influential, top-secret government report, known as NSC-68, prepared by the National Security Council in 1950, provided the rationale for activist policies: "The issues that face us are momentous, involving the fulfillment or destruction not only of this [U.S.] Republic but of civilization itself."[2] NSC-68 sanctioned any tactics, including assassination, in the anticommunism struggle, and inspired a massive, expensive military buildup. The Soviets matched the U.S. military buildup, creating a constant escalation of military spending and ever-more-sophisticated weapons. Under a policy known in the United States as Mutually Assured Destruction, or MAD, the United States and the USSR used the fear of nuclear weapons to deter each other. Some historians believe that MAD prevented a direct military confrontation between the two rivals that might have sparked World War III.

Defense spending reshaped the U.S. economy. Despite the warning of U.S. president Dwight Eisenhower (g. 1953–1961), a chief commander during World War II, to guard against the growing influence of what he termed the military-industrial complex, an alliance of military leaders and weapons producers, defense became an enormous business. It employed one-fifth of the U.S. industrial workforce and one-third of scientists and engineers by the 1960s, while costing U.S. taxpayers hundreds of billions per year. The United States also sold weapons to allied nations, among them despotic regimes, some of which used the weapons against their own people. The United States also trained these regimes' military officers and police forces, who often used the tactics they learned to eliminate dissidents.

Three Decades of U.S. Supremacy

Between 1945 and 1975, U.S. power was unmatched in the world, and the United States maintained military bases on every inhabited continent and in dozens of countries around the world (see Map 29.1). The United States employed military force and covertly aided governments to suppress opposition or, as in Chile in 1973, helped over-

Interactive Map

Map 29.1
U.S. Military Presence in the World, Since 1945

As the major superpower, the United States maintained several dozen military bases outside of North America, while engaging in military operations in Latin America, Africa, Asia, the Middle East, and Europe.

throw governments that were considered unfriendly to U.S. interests, even if, as in Chile, these governments were democratic and had been freely elected. Some foreign observers applauded U.S. efforts to suppress left-wing governments and movements that might have favored the USSR or Communist China, whereas others were hostile to U.S. power and criticized the United States for practicing superpower imperialism.

Yet U.S. power, especially its economic leadership, became less dominant between the mid-1970s and the early 1990s. Reasons for this change included the rise of a rebuilt western Europe and Japan to eco-

nomic power, the military strength of the USSR, the economic challenge from industrializing nations such as South Korea and China, and the damage done to the U.S. economy and prestige by the unsuccessful, widely unpopular war in Vietnam. Also a factor was the economic price Americans paid for global power. Over four decades the Cold War cost the U.S. government around $4 trillion, and while growing U.S. defense budgets of the 1980s did help undermine the Soviet Union, it also transformed the United States from a creditor nation into the world's largest debtor nation, leaving Americans with ballooning federal budget deficits. Only in the 1990s, under President Bill Clinton (g. 1993–2001), did the U.S. government temporarily eliminate the budget deficits that had accelerated between the 1960s and the 1980s.

Wars in Korea and Vietnam

In 1949, the Chinese communist victory in China, a country whose longtime government had been allied with and armed by the United States (see Chapter 27), alarmed Americans. Communist expansion, and the U.S. determination to halt it, led to the Korean War (1950–1953), which was followed a decade later by a more massive U.S. intervention in another Asian society, Vietnam. The conflict in Vietnam was the longest war the United States had ever waged (1963–1975).

The Korean War was sparked when North Korea, ruled by a brutal communist regime allied to the USSR, invaded South Korea, a U.S. ally, with the goal of forcibly reunifying the Korean peninsula (see Chapter 27). The anticommunist mood in the United States, already inflamed by the communist victory in China, made it politically unthinkable for President Harry S Truman not to oppose the North Korean thrust. But Truman never consulted the U.S. Congress, which had the constitutional responsibility to declare war; officially, Korea was a police action under U.N. sponsorship rather than a war, a precedent that allowed future presidents to commit U.S. military forces without congressional approval.

Furthermore, the Soviet support of North Korea with arms and advice, and the intervention of the communist Chinese on the North Korean side, deepened American fear of communist expansion. However, despite the 38,000 Americans killed and over 100,000 wounded, the war ended in stalemate. For the first time since the War of 1812, the United States had failed to decisively win a major military conflict. North Korea remained a rigid communist state, and South Korea did not become a democracy until the 1980s, more than three decades after the war.

The domino theory, which predicted a communist sweep throughout Southeast Asia, and the desire to keep valuable Southeast Asian resources in friendly hands, provided the rationale for financing the French effort to maintain colonial control (1946–1954) in Vietnam. When that effort failed, U.S. involvement increased, leading eventually to the U.S. military fighting Vietnamese communist forces armed by the USSR and China (see Chapter 31). Few U.S. leaders comprehended the depth of Vietnamese anti-Western nationalism and the country's long history of resistance to foreign invaders. As a growing communist-led insurgency, backed by North Vietnam,

challenged a widely unpopular, U.S.-supported South Vietnamese government, the U.S. president, Lyndon B. Johnson (g. 1963–1969), committed military forces and launched an intensive air war against targets in North and South Vietnam and later in neighboring Cambodia and Laos. U.S. troop totals topped off at 550,000 by 1967. Between 1963 and 1975, 2.5 million Americans served in Vietnam; 58,000 died and 300,000 were wounded there.

As support within the United States for the war ebbed with military stalemate and increasing casualties in what seemed a quagmire, Johnson's successor, President Richard Nixon (g. 1969–1973), gradually withdrew U.S. forces and negotiated a political settlement with North Vietnam. But a policy throughout the war of spending lavishly on both "guns and butter"— military and domestic needs—generated huge budget deficits and other economic problems with which the United States struggled from the later 1960s into the 1990s. The war in Vietnam ultimately cost U.S. taxpayers around $1 trillion, as well as the nation's diplomatic prestige and credibility around the globe.

The United States and the Developing Nations

Decolonization, nationalism, the U.S.–Soviet struggle, and persistent poverty combined to make the Asian, African, and Latin American societies prone to crises, sometimes drawing in the United States. The United States often favored decolonization that presented opportunities to U.S. business; for example, it successfully pressured the Dutch to abandon Indonesia. However, the United States opposed independence for colonies, such as French-ruled Vietnam, where communists or other leftists dominated the nationalist movements. After decolonization, Americans offered generous aid to friendly nations and to victims of famine or natural catastrophes. U.S. assistance also sparked the Green Revolution in agriculture, which led to improved food production in countries such as India, Mexico, and the Philippines. However, Cold War challenges often involved the United States in long-term confrontations with communist-led revolutions, and U.S. leaders also staged interventions to help their allies oppose left-leaning governments in Iran, Chile, and Guatemala.

In some U.S. interventions, presidents dispatched troops to overturn a government or to support one side in a civil war or revolutionary situation. U.S. leaders used the threat of communism as the rationale for these actions, but some interventions removed democratic governments, as in Guatemala and Chile, or suppressed democratic movements. For example, President

On Patrol in Vietnam U.S. soldiers sought out National Liberation Front fighters and supporters in the villages, rice fields, and jungles of South Vietnam. They could not easily tell friend from foe and warily dealt with local people.

Lyndon Johnson, claiming that Americans would not permit another communist government alongside Fidel Castro's Cuba in the Western Hemisphere, dispatched twenty thousand U.S. Marines into the Dominican Republic in 1965 to support a military government that was under attack by the democratically elected leaders they had recently overthrown. The elected leaders, while left-leaning, were noncommunist reformers who had wide popular support.

Former Dominican president and the leader of the antimilitary movement, Juan Bosch (1909–2001), declared that "this was a democratic revolution smashed by the leading democracy in the world."[3] In addition to military interventions, the United States also provided friendly governments or anti-leftist groups with weapons, military advisers, intelligence agents, and funding. For example, in Laos from 1960 to 1975, during what was known as the CIA's "secret war" because the U.S. role was kept hidden from Congress and the U.S. public, Americans recruited an army from the Hmong hill peoples to fight communist Laotian and North Vietnamese forces (see Chapter 31).

A final type of intervention involved covert destabilization, which involved American agents working underground to help undermine or spark the overthrow of governments seen as hostile to U.S. interests. Covert actions even included arranging for assassinations of government leaders. U.S. clandestine activity, which undermined elected left-leaning democratic governments in Iran in the 1950s and Thailand and Chile in the 1970s, brought brutal dictatorships to all three countries. U.S. Secretary of State Henry Kissinger defended the U.S. encouragement of a military coup against the democratically elected, leftist Chilean government—a government that respected civil liberties—by explaining, "I don't see why we need to stand by and watch a country go communist due to the irresponsibility of its own people."[4] This attitude that the United States knows best has often infuriated people in other nations. Only in the mid-1970s, with congressional hearings on covert activities, did Americans learn of the U.S. role in Chile and other interventions.

The United States in the Global System after 1989

The demise of the Soviet bloc in 1989 and the dissolution of the USSR in 1991 left the United States the dominant world power, although the European Union and the rising East Asian nations also enjoyed growing influence in the global system. But the lack of a rival superpower did not mean the end of challengers, among them international terrorists. The United States used its unsurpassed military and economic power to maintain a global presence and intervene in several countries, but Americans also paid a price in blood and treasure for activist foreign policies and global leadership.

American Foreign Policy after the Cold War

The United States now struggled to find a new role in a world characterized by what observers called a "New World Disorder" because of an outbreak of small, deadly conflicts. During the early 1990s, for example, President Bill Clinton (g. 1993–2001) sent a small number of U.S. troops, under United Nations auspices, to stabilize Somalia, a famine-racked northeast African state involved in a civil war. The intervention turned out badly, however, when the forces of a local warlord paraded the mutilated bodies of dead U.S. soldiers through the streets, forcing a U.S. withdrawal. In the aftermath, Americans were reluctant to assert power in other places where civilians were being slaughtered by the thousands, such as Rwanda and Liberia. However, working with European allies, Clinton did send U.S. forces to help end the deadly civil wars in the former Yugoslavia, and sought to resolve other foreign policy problems through diplomacy. In the 1990s, the Clinton administration reestablished diplomatic ties with Vietnam and lifted the trade embargo, which it viewed as punitive and counterproductive for U.S. business.

Radical Islam: The Taliban and Al Qaeda

Cold War policies sometimes came back to haunt the United States. In the 1980s, it had given military and financial aid to the Islamic rebels fighting Soviet troops and the pro-Soviet government in Afghanistan (see Chapter 30). Some of this aid went to Arab volunteers, among them the Saudi militant Osama bin Laden (b. 1957), who were fighting alongside the rebels. After the Soviets left Afghanistan in defeat in 1989, Muslim militants, the Taliban, defeated the other factions and imposed a rigid Islamic state, offering refuge for bin Laden's global terrorist network that became Al Qaeda ("the Base"). Al Qaeda now plotted terrorist attacks against the United States and its allies, sometimes using leftover U.S. weapons.

Farther west, Iraq's ruthless dictator, Saddam Hussein, used weapons acquired from the United States, his ally against Iran in the 1980s, to threaten Iraq's neighbors and repress dissident groups. In 1991, the United States led a coalition of nations that pushed invading Iraqi forces out of Kuwait during the Gulf War and then later protected the Kurds in northern Iraq from Saddam's reprisals. The intervention in oil-rich Kuwait was part of a consistent U.S. policy over the decades to protect the flow of oil from the Middle East to the West.

September 11, 2001

The terrorist attack launched by Al Qaeda on the World Trade Center in New York and the Pentagon in Washington, D.C., in September 2001, which killed nearly three thousand Americans, shocked the nation and led to a reshaping of both domestic and foreign policies. The new U.S. president, George W. Bush (b. 1946), introduced policies, such as preventive detention and monitoring of libraries, designed to prevent possible domestic terrorism. By attacking buildings that symbolized U.S. economic and military power to people around the world, the terrorists—young Muslim fanatics mostly from two close U.S. allies, Egypt and Saudi Arabia— hoped to capitalize on widespread anti-U.S. feelings. However, people in most countries, even if they disliked the United States and its power, deplored the bombings and the loss of innocent life.

The Bush Doctrine

The attacks prompted President Bush to declare a war on international terrorism using military force, but terrorist networks had no clear command structure or military resources and could not be influenced by diplomacy. With international support, the United States invaded Afghanistan to destroy Al Qaeda terrorist bases and displace the militant Islamic government that tolerated their presence. Bush announced a new doctrine of preemptive war that sanctioned unilateral military action against potential threats, and he named Iraq, Iran, and North Korea as comprising an "axis of evil" that threatened world peace (see Witness to the Past: Justifying Preemptive Strikes). The Bush doctrine advocated that the United States maintain overwhelming military superiority over all challengers. Critics perceived the Bush doctrine as a recipe for acquiring an American empire through military action, a violation, they charged, of international law.

The concern with international terrorism led to a resumption of unilateralist U.S. foreign policies, in which the United States acted without widespread international support. Rejecting opposition from the United Nations and key U.S. allies, in 2003 the Bush administration used faulty or manipulated intelligence to claim that Iraq possessed weapons of mass destruction and aided Al Qaeda. American forces invaded and occupied Iraq, ending Saddam Hussein's brutal regime, but the U.S. forces found no weapons of mass destruction or evidence of a Saddam–Al Qaeda link; furthermore, the Bush administration had planned poorly for restoring stability in Iraq, a nation rich in oil but troubled by ethnic and religious divisions that exploded into civil war. A mounting insurgency by Iraqis and suicide bombings largely linked to foreign terrorists, who now flocked to Iraq to fight Americans, caused thousands of U.S. casualties, and complicated political and economic reconstruction.

By 2006, basic services, such as electricity, and oil production had still not been restored to prewar levels, and violence continued to plague Iraqi society. The spiraling costs of the Iraq occupation and other expenses, combined with large tax cuts, ballooned U.S. budget deficits that could not be sustained long term without serious damage to the U.S. economy. The unpopular Iraq war, charges that the United States tortured suspected terrorists, and the U.S. rejection of several international treaties, such as that on global warming, further alienated Western allies and divided the American people.

Wars in Iraq and Afghanistan

Flexing its military might rather than diplomatic influence, the United States had assumed heavy burdens, sending troops to Afghanistan, Iraq, and elsewhere while maintaining military bases in several dozen countries and islands around the world. By 2004, the United States accounted for half of all military spending worldwide, spending as much on its military and weapons as all other nations combined, and it also accounted for about half of all arms sales to the world's nations.

The United States plays a vital role in world governance through its diplomatic engagements, vast military deployments, and buttressing of the global economy, a fact appreciated by many nations because the cost is largely borne by U.S. taxpayers. Yet the global recession that began in the United States in 2007 revealed systemic weaknesses in the American economy. Although anti-U.S. sentiment grew in the early twenty-first century, President Barack Obama was elected in 2008 on the promise of a new direction in American diplomacy. In his inaugural address, President Obama pledged a more principled course: "Our security emanates from the justness of our cause; the force of our example; the tempering qualities of humility and restraint."[5] Nevertheless, since the Romans two millennia ago, no other nation has been as dominant in military, economic, political, and social realms as the United States has been after 1990.

LO² The Changing Societies of North America and the Pacific Basin

In the years following World War II, the United States and Canada in North America and Australia and New Zealand in the southwestern corner of the Pacific Basin—all originally settled by people from the British Isles—shared a general prosperity, similar social patterns, and many cultural traditions, but they also played different roles in the world. Besides exercising more political, economic, and military power than these other nations, the United States had a stable democracy and a rapidly changing society. The United States, Canada, and Australia all attracted millions of immigrants from around the world, linking their cultures more closely to other nations.

Prosperity, Technology, and Inequality in the United States

Living in the world's richest nation, many Americans benefited from a growing economy and widespread affluence. During the nation's most prosperous

> **❝ Living in the world's richest nation, many Americans benefited from a growing economy and widespread affluence. ❞**

Witness to the Past

Justifying Preemptive Strikes

In the wake of the shocking terrorist attacks on the United States in September 2001, the administration of President George W. Bush produced a document, the National Security Strategy of the United States, that restated the U.S. desire to spread democracy and capitalism while announcing that the United States would act preemptively, striking first, unilaterally if necessary, against any hostile states that the Bush administration believed might be planning to attack U.S. targets. Depending on the observer, the document either reflected or exploited Americans' fear of terrorist attacks. In 2003, Bush used the preemptive strike rationale to order a military invasion and occupation of Iraq, which he claimed had weapons of mass destruction. After Saddam's fall, Bush offered a new mission: fostering democracy in Iraq as an example for the Middle East. To critics, however, the failure to find such weapons, the faulty intelligence about them, and the huge financial and human costs of the resulting occupation for both Americans and Iraqis all suggested the dangers of a preemptive strategy. Furthermore, they argued, many presidents before Bush had claimed to promote democracy abroad but had rarely done so, especially when they used military force to install a pro-U.S. government in another country.

The great struggles of the twentieth century between liberty and totalitarianism ended with a decisive victory for the forces of freedom—and a single sustainable model for national success: freedom democracy and free enterprise.... Only nations that share a commitment to protecting basic human rights and guaranteeing political and economic freedom will be able to unleash the potential of their people and assure their future prosperity.... Today the United States enjoys a position of unparalleled military strength and great economic and political influence. In keeping with our heritage and principles we do not use our strength to press for unilateral advantage. We seek instead to create a balance of power that favors human freedom.... We will extend the peace by encouraging free and open societies on every continent.

Defending our Nation against its enemies is the first and fundamental commitment of the Federal Government. Today, that task has changed dramatically. Enemies in the past needed great armies and great industrial capabilities

to endanger America. Now, shadowy networks of individuals can bring great chaos and suffering to our shores for less than it costs to purchase a single tank. Terrorists are organized to penetrate open societies and to turn the power of modern technologies against us. To defeat this threat we must make use of every tool in our arsenal.... The war against terrorists of global reach is a global enterprise of uncertain duration.... America will hold to account nations that are compromised by terror, including those who harbor terrorists—because the allies of terror are the enemies of civilization.... Our enemies have openly declared that they are seeking weapons of mass destruction.... The United States will not allow these efforts to succeed.... And, as a matter of common sense and self-defense, America will act against such emerging threats before they are fully formed.... We must be prepared to defeat our enemies' plans. History will judge harshly those who saw this coming danger but failed to act. In the new world we have entered, the only path to peace and security is the path of action....

The struggle against global terrorism is different from any other war in our history. It will be fought on many fronts against a particularly elusive enemy over an extended period of time.... New deadly challenges have emerged from rogue states and terrorists.... Rogue regimes seek nuclear, biological, and chemical weapons.... We must be prepared to stop rogue states and their terrorist clients before they are able to threaten or use weapons of mass destruction against the United States and our allies.... The United States can no longer solely rely on a reactive posture as we have in the past.... We cannot let our enemies strike first.... We must adapt the concept of imminent threat to the capabilities and objectives of today's adversaries.... The greater the threat, the greater the risk of inaction—and the more compelling the case for taking anticipatory action to defend ourselves, even if uncertainty remains as to the time and place of the enemy's attack. To forestall or prevent such hostile acts by our adversaries, the United States will, if necessary, act preemptively.

Thinking About the Reading

1. How does the document reflect the tendency of U.S. leaders to claim a national goal of spreading U.S. political and economic models in the world?
2. What does the document offer as the rationale for preemptive actions?

Source: The National Security Strategy of the United States (http://www.whitehouse.gov/nsc/print/nssall.html).

decade, the 1960s, the production of goods and services doubled, and per capita income rose by half. Many Americans moved into new automobile, aerospace, service, and information technology industries. By 2000, the United States accounted for one-third of the world's total production of goods and services, more than twice as much as second-place Japan, and enjoyed a median annual family income of more than $40,000.

Americans also owned the majority of, and profited from, the giant multinational corporations, such as General Motors and Wal-Mart, that played ever-larger roles in the globalizing world economy. However, there were downsides to this growth. With 6 percent of the world population, Americans also consumed around 40 percent of all the world's resources and produced a large share of the chemicals, gases, and toxic wastes that pollute the atmosphere, alter the climate, and destroy the land. A major world study in 2005 ranked the United States twenty-eighth in meeting sustainable environmental goals, well behind most developed and developing nations.

A Winner-Takes-All Economy

Beginning in the 1970s, a growing economy improved the lot of some people, but it hurt millions of others. Americans celebrated innovations in medicine, space research, transportation, and particularly electronics. Space satellites greatly improved weather forecasting, communications, and intelligence gathering. Computers and handheld devices revolutionized life with their convenience and versatility. But as computers and robots increased efficiency, they also replaced many workers. In the 1980s, one-third of industrial jobs disappeared. Industrialists won corporate bonuses for relocating factories and exporting jobs to Latin America or Asia, devastating factory-dependent American communities. By the early 2000s, although life for the majority of Americans remained comfortable compared to that in most other nations, unemployment for men was the highest it had been in five decades. Some economists referred to a winner-takes-all economy that produced ever-more millionaires but also a struggling middle class and, at the bottom of the social ladder, more

"Except for the richest 1 percent of Americans, whose earnings skyrocketed, average incomes fell between 2001 and 2006."

indigent and homeless people. Except for the richest 1 percent of Americans, whose earnings skyrocketed, average incomes fell between 2001 and 2006.

In contrast to western Europe, Canada, Australia, and New Zealand, the United States never developed a comprehensive welfare state. As a result, despite federal government efforts at abolishing poverty, a widening gap separated the richest one-third and the poorest one-third of Americans. The inequality of wealth in the United States grew dramatically after 1980, and by 1997, the top 1 percent of the population owned 20 percent of all the wealth. By 2004, 12.5 percent of Americans lived below the poverty line. In 2005, the devastating hurricane, Katrina, caused massive damage and flooding in the Gulf Coast, ruining New Orleans, rendering millions homeless, and killing several thousand people. It also starkly revealed America's poverty gap: most of the people who died or were only rescued days later were black and poor, unable to afford transportation out of the area. Partly because of the inequalities in wealth and health care, the United States ranked eighth—behind several European nations, Canada, and Australia—in overall quality of life in the 2004 United Nations Human Development Report.

Suburbia

Changes in the economy went hand in hand with the suburbanization of American life. In the decades following World War II, millions of people sought a better life in suburbia, the bedroom communities on the edges of major cities. Suburbs, occupied typically by white Americans, featured shopping malls and well-funded schools. Suburban developer William Levitt argued that no person who owned his or her own house and yard could be a communist, because he or she was too busy keeping up, and working to pay for, his or her property. The automobile, increasingly affordable for the middle class, combined with government-funded freeway and highway construction, made long commutes from the suburbs to jobs in the central city possible. City cores were increasingly dominated by the local-born poor, often nonwhite, or immigrants, while increasing use of fossil fuels and clearing land for housing and business development harmed the environment.

American Political Life: Conservatism and Liberalism

In the decades after World War II, fiscal conservatives, commonly big business groups favoring low taxes and opposing social welfare, allied with religious groups who disliked social and cultural liberalization, dominated the presidency and often the United States Congress and the judiciary. Liberals played a key role in U.S. political life chiefly in the 1960s and, to a lesser extent, the 1990s; they were generally supported by labor unions and groups that sought social change and a stronger government safety net.

American Society in the 1950s

The widespread desire for stability after the great Depression and a calamitous world war encouraged both a political and social conservatism throughout the 1950s. Americans who questioned the government or prevailing social norms faced harassment, expulsion from job or school, arrest, or accusations of being "un-American." Whatever their social class, more Americans than ever before married, producing a "baby boom" of children born in the years following the war. The mass media portrayed happy women in a world defined by kitchen, bedroom, babies, and home. Society expected homosexuals to remain deep in the closet, and those who did not faced taunting, beatings, or arrest.

The 1960s: A Decade of Change

American politics and society were reshaped again during the 1960s, becoming open to new ideas and lifestyles as liberalism became influential. The era saw many achievements, including the first people to walk on the moon and the idealism that created the Peace Corps, an agency that sent young Americans to help communities in developing nations, chiefly as teachers, health workers, and agricultural specialists. Presidents John F. Kennedy (g. 1961–1963) and Lyndon B. Johnson (g. 1963–1969) launched government programs to address poverty and racism. But the 1960s was also a decade of doubts, anger, and violence. Three national leaders were assassinated, including Kennedy, who was shot in the head while riding in a motorcade in 1963. The war in Vietnam, the civil rights movement for African Americans, and issues of environmental protection and women's empowerment divided the nation. The country's social fabric fragmented as pro-war "hawks" and antiwar "doves" competed for support. Riots and demonstrations punctuated the decade.

During the 1960s, a large segment of young people, chiefly middle class, rebelled against the values of their parents and established society. Some youth, especially high school and university students, worked to change society and politics, registering voters, holding "teach-ins" to discuss national issues, and going door to door to spread their cause. Other youth forged what they called a counterculture that often involved using illegal drugs and engaging in casual sex. The Summer of Love in 1967, during which young people from North America and elsewhere gathered in San Francisco to hear rock music and share camaraderie, and the Woodstock rock music festival of 1969, which attracted more than 300,000 young people, marked the zenith of both the youth counterculture and political activism.

The Conservative Era

In the 1970s, with the winding down of the war in Vietnam and widespread concern at the social excesses of the previous decade, the nation returned to more conservative values and politics. With the exception of the 1990s, when the moderate Bill Clinton (g. 1993–2001) held the presidency, conservatives maintained their dominance of American politics, the economy, and the social agenda until 2008. Religion remained a powerful force, with Americans being more likely to attend churches and profess strong Christian beliefs than most Europeans. By the 1980s, Christian conservatives, mainly evangelical Protestants but also many Catholics, became influential in public life, helping elect political conservatives to office. Some experts attributed the rise of Christian conservatism to a rejection of reason and tolerance. While Americans avidly consumed new technologies, polls showed that, because of religious conservatism, substantial numbers also mistrusted science.

Observers found much to deplore and much to praise in U.S. politics. Money from big corporations and other special interests increasingly played a major role, fostering corruption and

> **"** The widespread desire for stability after the great Depression and a calamitous world war encouraged both a political and social conservatism throughout the 1950s. **"**

widespread political apathy. However, on the positive side, a free media exposed government corruption, including abuse of power by presidents. President Richard Nixon, facing impeachment, resigned in 1973 for sanctioning and then covering up illegal activities by his subordinates. The presidencies of both Ronald Reagan (g. 1983–1989) and Clinton were marred by congressional hearings examining their misdeeds. After the controversial, bitter 2000 and 2004 elections, Americans were sharply divided between the two major political parties and the divergent policies they supported.

Barack Obama: New Possibilities

In 2008, with two wars continuing in Afghanistan and Iraq and a severe recession threatening American prosperity, the Democratic Party won the White House and increased its majorities in the Senate and House of Representatives. President Obama's campaign inspired more Americans than ever before to get involved and vote, causing many observers to note that 2008 represented the beginning of a new political era. In the early months of his presidency, President Obama charted a pragmatic course, sidestepping the bitter partisanship of his predecessors, yet the challenges to Americans loomed ever larger.

American Society and Popular Culture

American society was changed by shifting patterns after World War II, especially suburbanization. Most suburbs lacked ethnic and cultural diversity and isolated residents from the stimulation, as well as the problems, of big-city life. Suburban living also intensified the trend, begun before World War II, toward two-parent, single-breadwinner nuclear families that lived apart from other relatives. Critics lambasted the conformity of life in the standardized suburban tract houses, while changing city life affected both ethnic and gender relations.

The Civil Rights Movement

The most significant social change came with the Civil Rights movement, which was organized by African Americans in the 1950s. Southern states maintained strict racial segregation, forcing blacks to attend separate schools and to even use different public drinking fountains than whites. Racism and poverty often encouraged African Americans in northern industrial cities to concentrate in run-down inner-city neighborhoods, known as ghettos. In 1954, the Supreme Court outlawed segregated schools, and one year later, in Montgomery, Alabama, Rosa Parks (1913–2005), a seamstress and community activist, bravely refused to give up her front seat on a bus to a white man, sparking a mass movement for change.

A black minister, Reverend Martin Luther King, Jr. (1929–1968), led a bus boycott to protest Parks' arrest and fine. Using the strategy of nonviolent resistance pioneered by Mohandas Gandhi in South Africa and India in the early twentieth century, King led a protest movement all over the South. While leading the 1963 March on Washington to demand equal rights for nonwhites, he presented his vision: "I have a dream. When we let freedom ring, all of God's children will be able to join hands and sing in the words of that old spiritual, 'Thank God almighty, we are free at last!'"[6] King's assassination by a white racist in 1968 shocked the nation, but by then the African American struggle for equal rights had inspired similar struggles by nonwhites elsewhere in the world.

Thanks to the efforts of King, Parks, and many others, African Americans gradually gained legal equality, and many became able to move into the middle and upper classes. The 2008 election of President Obama, the first African American to hold the nation's highest office, was a momentous and inspirational achievement. However, in the early twenty-first century, African Americans were still far more likely than whites to live in poverty, face unemployment, and be imprisoned.

A Multicultural America

In the later twentieth century, Americans became an increasingly multiracial, multicultural society. By 2006, the U.S. population of 300 million, the third largest total in the world after China and India, was more diverse than ever, and more than 10 percent were foreign-born. American life took on a cosmopolitan flavor as Latin American grocery stores, Asian restaurants, and African art galleries opened in communities throughout the country, and Spanish was widely spoken.

Ethnic groups grew through legal and illegal immigration. Millions of Latin Americans moved to the United States. By 2000, the Mexican American population alone numbered around 20 million and seemed poised to soon outnumber the 25 million African Americans. Several million Asians also relocated to the United States, especially from China, South Korea, India, and Southeast Asia. Immigrants also arrived from Europe, the Middle East, the Caribbean, and South Pacific islands. Many labored for meager wages

 XinHua/Xinhua Press/Corbis

President Obama Inaugurated on January 20, 2009, President Barack Obama is the son of an American mother and Kenyan father. In the village of Kogelo, Kenya, the birthplace of Obama's father, revellers celebrated the historic occasion.

in crowded sweatshops in big cities, where bosses often ignored safety regulations. Immigration marginalized Native Americans even more than before. While many lived in cities, others remained isolated on reservations. Some of them joined movements to assert their rights, often seeking a return of lands seized by white settlers generations earlier, and a few tribes achieved prosperity by operating gambling casinos; however, most Native Americans remained poor.

The Feminist Revolution

Women's issues became more prominent in U.S. history. In the 1950s, few women worked for high pay, married women could not borrow money in their own names, there was no legal concept of sexual harassment, and men often joked of keeping women "barefoot and pregnant." Beginning in the 1960s, women led a feminist movement demanding equal legal rights with men and improved economic status. In 1963, Betty Friedan's (1921–2006) passionate book, *The Feminine Mystique*, identified women's core prob-

lem as a stunting of their growth by a patriarchal society. With slogans such as "Sisterhood Is Powerful," women came together in groups, such as the National Organization for Women (NOW), to fight against sexism. Thanks in part to feminists' efforts, the median income of women workers climbed from 62 to 70 percent of that of men, and the number of women with paid work more than doubled between 1960 and 2000. Women held governorships, served in Congress, and sat on the Supreme Court. By the twenty-first century, more women than men attended universities, some joining highly paid, traditionally male occupations such as law, university teaching, engineering, and medicine. However, most women with paid jobs struggled to juggle work with family and housekeeping responsibilities, and sexual harassment, domestic violence, and rape remained serious problems.

> **Feminist Manifestoes From the Late 1960s**
> Learn why feminists in the United States opposed all forms of patriarchy, and protested institutions like the Miss America Pageant.

Social and legal changes affected both women and men. Divorce became easier and more common; by the 1990s, more than half of all marriages ended in divorce, and single-parent households grew more frequent. Increasingly, men and women never married. Whatever their gender, Americans remained deeply divided on some women's issues, especially abortion, which was long common but illegal before being declared legal by the Supreme Court in 1973. Americans also disagreed about homosexuality. By the 1960s, gay men and lesbians actively struggled to end harassment and legal discrimination, gaining greater acceptance in society. Yet homosexuals still faced hostility and sometimes violence. During the early twenty-first century, Americans quarreled over allowing homosexuals to marry or establish legal partnerships, a pattern of acceptance that was common in Europe and Canada but opposed by many conservative Americans.

From Rock to Rap

Once importers of culture from Europe, Americans became the world's greatest exporters of popular culture products. U.S.-made films, television programs, books, magazines, and sports reached a global audience, and popular music, especially rock, helped spark a cultural revolution in the 1950s and 1960s. The first exhilarating blasts of rock 'n' roll, notably from the white singer Elvis Presley (1935–1977) and the inventive black guitarist Chuck Berry (b. 1926), delighted youth while often alarming adults. Rock was inspired by black music, chiefly rhythm-and-blues, but also by the country music of white southerners, and it became the heart of the youth movement of the 1960s. Albums by key rock musicians, such as the American folk singer-songwriter Bob Dylan and the British group The Beatles, conveyed messages that shaped political awareness. After the 1960s, rock lost its political edge but, evolving into forms such as punk, grunge, and heavy metal, remained at the heart of U.S. popular music. In the 1980s and 1990s, rap music, or hip-hop, emerged out of black ghettos. An eclectic mix of rock, soul, rhythm-and-blues, and Caribbean music, hip-hop expressed the tensions of urban black youth yearning for independence, dignity, sex, and fun.

The Canadian Experience

Canadians have remained proudly independent of their powerful southern neighbor while nurturing their political and social differences, such as by maintaining two official languages—English and French. Two parties, one liberal and one conservative, have dominated national elections, but smaller left-wing and right-wing parties also play key roles, often governing Canadian provinces. The Party Québécois (KAY-be-KWAH), for example, which supports French Canadian nationalism, is influential in French-speaking Quebec, a province that contains one-quarter of Canada's population, and periodically seeks the separation of Quebec from Canada (see Map 29.2).

 Interactive Map

In 1985, the federal parliament, hoping to preserve a united Canada, responded to French Canadians' resentments against Canada's English-speaking majority by recognizing Quebec as a distinct society within Canada and granting more autonomy to all the provinces.

Canadians, 33 million strong by 2005, cannot ignore their proximity to the United States, which has almost ten times Canada's population and vastly more power in the world. Most of Canada's people live within 100 miles of the U.S. border, and thus have easy access to the U.S. mass media and other cultural influences. Canada has also formed a major trading partnership with its southern neighbor. Americans own some 20 percent of the Canadian economy, prompting some Canadians to welcome U.S. investment as a spur to economic growth and others to resent U.S. domination.

 Free Trade and the Decline of Democracy
Read a cogent critique by Ralph Nader, a consumer advocate and political activist, of international free-trade agreements.

In 1994, the North American Free Trade Agreement (NAFTA) further bound the Canadian, Mexican, and U.S. economies. Yet, despite usually friendly U.S.–Canada relations, Canadians have often opposed U.S. foreign policies, including the wars in Vietnam and Iraq.

Despite occasional economic downturns, Canadians have enjoyed industrialization and prosperity, which in turn have fostered social stability. Agricultural, industrial, and natural resource exports have helped finance rising living standards; vast oil reserves have enriched western provinces. Canada has consistently ranked among the top five nations in the annual United Nations Human Development Index of quality of life, and has built a strong social safety net for its citizens, including national health insurance. Also, Canadians have generally been more liberal on social and economic issues than Americans, approving same-sex marriage, banning the death penalty, and, in some provinces, decriminalizing marijuana use. As the society has become more secular, organized religion has

Map 29.2
Canada

The Canadian federation includes eleven provinces stretching from Newfoundland in the east to British Columbia and the Yukon in the west. In 1999, a large part of northern Canada, inhabited chiefly by the Inuit, became the self-governing region of Nunavut.

had a declining influence in public life, a trend especially notable in Quebec, where the Catholic Church once enjoyed great influence.

Canadian society has become increasingly diverse. The nation has welcomed several million immigrants from all over the world, many from Asia and the Caribbean. In 2005, one of those Caribbean immigrants, Haitian-born Michaelle Jean, a television journalist in Quebec, became Canada's governor general, the nation's official head of state. Unlike Americans, Canadians have adopted laws, especially the Multiculturalism Act of 1988, to allow ethnic minorities to maintain their cultures. Canadians have also recognized the rights of the indigenous Native Americans, known in Canada as the "First Nations," who have pressed land claims. To address the desire for autonomy of the Inuit people of the Arctic region, in 1999 the federal government transformed much of

northern Canada into the self-governing territory of Nunavut (NOO-nuh-voot), whose 27,000 people are mostly Inuit.

The Pacific Basin Societies

The diverse societies scattered around the Pacific Basin experienced major changes during this era as they adjusted to a new world. In the two largest, most populous countries, Australia and New Zealand, the majority population, descended from mainly British and Irish, settlers, had long identified with western European society, building economies that closely resembled those of the industrial West. But the rise of Asian economies prompted Australia and New Zealand to cultivate closer ties with East and Southeast Asian nations. Meanwhile, many Pacific islands that were once ruled by Britain, France, or

New Zealand became independent nations navigating in a globalizing world.

Australia

During this era, Australia became one of the world's most affluent nations, known to its people as the "lucky country" because of its abundant resources and high living standards. Thanks in part to a comprehensive system of social welfare, health care, and education, Australians have forged a quality of life that placed the nation third after Norway and Sweden in the United Nations Human Development Report for 2004. However, the nation has also faced economic and social problems, including a chronic high unemployment rate, enduring sexism, and areas of persisting poverty.

With 20 million people by 2005, Australia has become an increasingly diverse nation. In 1973, the federal government abandoned restrictions on nonwhite, especially Asian, immigration—known as the "white Australia" policy—that had been in place since 1901. The shift to a policy based on skills rather than ethnicity stimulated immigration from Asia and the Middle East, and predominantly Asian neighborhoods developed in major cities. Newcomers from Europe also continued to arrive, and by 2001, nearly one-quarter of Australia's people had been born abroad. Race relations improved as Aborigines, often poor and facing discrimination, gained some self-determination and land rights for their tribal territories. As a result, one group was able to block a dam project in the 1990s that threatened tribal land. Yet, those Aborigines living in cities, often in run-down neighborhoods, have struggled to find their place in the largely white-owned urban economy.

Changing global conditions have forced new economic thinking. With an economy based primarily on the export of natural and animal resources, such as minerals, wheat, beef, and wool, Australia needed secure outside markets. But the formation of the European Community and NAFTA threatened traditional markets in Europe and North America, raising questions about the nation's traditional link to Britain. Subsequently, Australians established closer trade links to nations in Southeast Asia, East Asia, and

Lion's Dance In recent decades, many Asians have settled in Australia. This Chinese lion's dance, in Melbourne's large Chinatown, celebrates the Chinese New Year.

Glenn Hunt/AAP

the Pacific islands. By 2000, Asian nations accounted for some 60 percent of Australia's export market.

New Zealand

Like Australians, New Zealanders had long depended on British patronage, but they now had to adjust to changing global conditions. The nation's economy relied heavily on tourism and the export of agricultural products, mostly to Britain. When Britain joined the European Community, New Zealand's access to British markets was diminished, so New Zealand cultivated closer relations with the United States. However, these relations cooled after New Zealand refused to allow nuclear-armed U.S. ships to make visits to its ports. New Zealand then fostered economic cooperation with nearby Asian and Pacific countries, and by 2000, these countries accounted for one-third of the nation's trade.

New economic directions affected New Zealand's society. While experiencing rising unemployment, New Zealanders were supported by an elaborate social welfare system. Owing in part to expanded educational opportunities, women gained new economic roles and served in politics. In 1999, Helen Clark (b. 1950), a former university professor, became the nation's first female prime minister. Increased immigration from Asia and the Pacific islands and new recognition and rights for the native Maori minority reflected the fact that New Zealanders became more comfortable with ethnic diversity.

The Islanders

While Australians and New Zealanders had long enjoyed independence, the decolonization of the Pacific islands, spurred by the United Nations, had to wait until the 1960s. Between 1962 and 1980, nine independent Pacific nations were formed in Polynesia and Melanesia, and in 1990, the United States gave up control of some of its Micronesian territories. But even most independent islands retained close ties to their former colonizers. Some French-ruled islands, such as Tahiti and New Caledonia, became overseas departments of France, with representation in the French parliament, but many islanders still resented what they considered to be a disguised French colonialism. Whether nation or colony, islanders usually remained dependent on fishing, tourism, and the export of mineral and agricultural products.

Islanders have cooperated on common issues, collectively adapting to change while retaining some indigenous traditions. For example, Western Samoa, first ruled by Germany and then by New Zealand, has an elected parliament, adopted from the West, but clan chiefs still govern the villages, as they have for centuries. But certain forces have undermined traditional village life. Poverty has fostered migration to island cities, such as Suva in Fiji and Pago Pago in American Samoa, and emigration to Australia, New Zealand, Hawaii, and the mainland United States. Some islands have also experienced ethnic or regional conflict as groups compete for political power and scarce land. Together the islanders fought high-technology fishing fleets from industrialized nations, especially Japan, that threatened their own low-technology fishing, and joined with Australia and New Zealand to declare the Pacific a nuclear-free zone. However, some problems affecting islands have defied solution. Because of rising sea levels, which threaten low-lying atolls and coastal plains, many islanders, such as the eleven thousand people on the Tuvalo islands in the central Pacific, will have to relocate over the next century.

LO³ Political Change in Latin America and the Caribbean

The Latin American and Caribbean peoples (see Map 29.3) had a different experience than North Americans and the Pacific Basin societies. Social inequality, economic underdevelopment, and the demands for change often generated revolutionary and progressive political movements in impoverished villages and shantytowns. Sometimes leftists gained power, launching reforms, though only in Cuba did they remain in power for decades. A few Latin American countries and most small Caribbean islands enjoyed a consistent democratic tradition; elsewhere, however, military leaders or autocratic civilians often dominated governments.

Interactive Map

Despotisms and Democracies

Latin American governments struggled to find the right mix of policies to raise living standards and expand political participation. Early in the century, the Mexican Revolution, for example, challenged the inequities in society and wealth but later lost most of its revolution-

Internet Resources for Latin America (*http://lib.nmsu.edu/ subject/bord/laguia/*). This outstanding site, from New Mexico State University, provides information and links.

Map 29.3
Modern Latin America and the Caribbean
Latin America includes the nations of Central and South America and those Caribbean societies that are Spanish-speaking, including Cuba and the Dominican Republic. Brazil, Argentina, and Mexico are the largest Latin American nations. The peoples of the small Caribbean islands also formed independent states.

ary vigor and ultimately failed to resolve Mexico's problems. At other times, paternalistic but authoritarian reformers mobilized workers and peasants for change, but they also failed to empower the mass of the population or significantly improve their lives.

Juan Perón and Argentina

The charismatic Juan Perón (puh-RONE) (1895–1974), a former army officer and hypnotic public speaker who was elected Argentina's president in

1946, was one of the major autocratic reformers. Perón soon marginalized the legislature and crushed his opposition. With help from his hugely popular wife, Evita Perón (1919–1952), an actress and proponent of social justice, the nationalistic Perón won the support of workers and the middle class by emphasizing industrialization and by having his government buy up banks, companies, and railroads that were often owned by unpopular foreign interests. Meanwhile, Evita promoted women's issues, but after she died in 1952, Perón's popular support waned. Corruption, growing unemployment, inflation, strikes, and human rights abuses led to his overthrow in 1955. Perón returned to power briefly in 1973–1974, but otherwise the military ruled Argentina for most of the 1950s through early 1980s, often killing opponents. Yet Perón's followers helped to achieve the restoration of democracy in 1983.

An Era of Turmoil

Right-wing and left-wing forces jockeyed for power in Latin America for decades. In the majority of countries from the 1950s through the late 1980s, right-wing military governments and despots ruled, suppressing labor unions, student protesters, and democracy activists to maintain stability. Some right-wing governments, especially in Central American countries such as El Salvador and Guatemala, organized informal armed units, known as death squads, to assassinate dissidents who were deemed threats to the regime. However, despite the repression, left-wing movements increased their strength. For example, by 1979, the Sandinistas, a revolutionary movement led by Marxists, had mobilized enough popular support to defeat the dictatorship, in power since the 1920s, and gain control of Nicaragua.

During the later 1980s, with right-wing authoritarian rule largely discredited because it was unable or unwilling to address mass poverty, many nations turned to democracy under centrist or moderate leftist leaders. But in most cases, the free markets these democratic governments introduced struggled to resolve severe challenges, allowing both right-wing and extreme leftist forces to increase in strength. Some nations also faced racial and ethnic tensions. In particular, the large Indian communities in Bolivia, Peru, Colombia, Mexico, and Guatemala, often allied with the left, increasingly sought equal rights, a fairer share of the wealth, and recognition of their cultures,

> "Right-wing and left-wing forces jockeyed for power in Latin America for decades."

aspirations often opposed by whites.

Hugo Chavez and Venezuela

By the later 1990s, as disillusionment with capitalism increased, the left was regaining the political initiative. Mobilizing workers and peasants, who had benefited little from the country's oil wealth, the former general Hugo Chavez was elected president of oil-rich Venezuela and introduced socialist policies that alienated the wealthy and middle class but cheered poor Venezuelans, who supported his mar-

CHRONOLOGY

Latin America and the Caribbean, Since 1945

1946–1955	Government of Juan Perón in Argentina
1954	CIA overthrow of Guatemalan government
1959	Triumph of Fidel Castro in Cuba
1962	Cuban missile crisis
1964–1985	Military government in Brazil
1973	Overthrow of Chilean government
1973–1989	Military government in Chile
1979–1989	Sandinista government in Nicaragua
1983	Restoration of Argentina's democracy
1990	U.S. invasion of Panama
1994	Formation of NAFTA
1998	Economic collapse in many nations
2000	Election of President Vicente Fox in Mexico
2002	Election of President Lula da Silva in Brazil

ginalization of the congress and control of the courts. Chavez called his policies the Bolivaran Revolution, linking them to the nineteenth-century, Venezuelan-born liberator, Simón Bolívar. But the United States moved to isolate the dictatorial, pro-Cuba Chavez regime and support the opposition. During the early twenty-first century, voters who were desperate for more equitable economic and social policies also elected pragmatic leftist leaders in countries such as Argentina, Brazil, Chile, and Uruguay. These leaders often began the process—neglected by their cautious predecessors—of prosecuting the human-rights violations that occurred years earlier under military rule. But whether imported economic ideas will work for Latin Americans remains to be seen.

The United States in Latin America

The United States has had a powerful economic and political presence in Latin America since the nineteenth century, and, as the world's major superpower, it had even more of an impact in the second half of the twentieth century. The U.S. role in the region was complex, with the country serving not only as the neighborhood bully at times but also as a leading trading partner, a major source of investment capital, a supplier of military and economic assistance, and an inspiration to the region's democrats and free-market enthusiasts. As a result, many Latin American leaders maintained close relations with various U.S. administrations. U.S. popular culture, particularly films and music, influenced local cultures, while several million Latin Americans have moved to the United States legally or illegally. The United States gained favor in the region by transferring control of the Panama Canal—built by the United States in the early 1900s—to Panama in 1999, yet the agreement also allowed U.S. military bases to remain along the canal.

The United States intervened in Latin American and Caribbean countries under the banner of anti-communism. These interventions aroused much local resentment, as was illustrated by the earliest intervention, in Guatemala in 1954. A force led by exiled Guatemalan military officers, covertly organized, armed, and trained by the U.S. Central Intelligence Agency (CIA), overthrew a democratically elected reformist government that American

> "By the later 1990s, as disillusionment with capitalism increased, the left was regaining the political initiative."

leaders accused of being communist, an unsupported claim. The government had angered U.S. business interests, especially the powerful United Fruit Company, by implementing land reform and encouraging labor unions. The United Fruit Company controlled much of the Guatemalan economy, especially the banana plantations, and had close ties to officials in the Eisenhower administration. The removal of the democratic regime was welcomed by wealthy Guatemalans and U.S. corporations with investments in Guatemala, but the new leaders proved to be murderous tyrants. Forming death squads, they killed more than 200,000 Guatemalans, especially poor Indian peasants and workers, over the next three decades. By 1990, 90 percent of Guatemalans still lived in poverty, and one-third of them lacked adequate food.

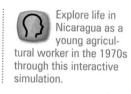 Explore life in Nicaragua as a young agricultural worker in the 1970s through this interactive simulation.

The successful ousting of the Guatemalan government encouraged U.S. leaders to use their power elsewhere to further Cold War foreign policy objectives. Americans offered military assistance and advice to maintain friendly governments in power against the challenge of revolutionary movements in El Salvador, Honduras, and Colombia. As in Guatemala, the United States also used covert operations to help undermine or overthrow governments deemed too left-leaning, for example, in Brazil (1964), Chile (1973), and Nicaragua (1989). The American public was often unaware of the covert U.S. activities until years later. In 1990, U.S. troops invaded Panama to remove and arrest the dictator, Manuel Noriega (b. 1940), a longtime U.S. ally and well-paid CIA informant who was also

 Latin American Network Information Center (*http://lanic.utexas .edu/*). Very useful site on contemporary Latin America, maintained at the University of Texas.

implicated in human-rights abuses and in smuggling narcotics into the United States. In 1994, U.S. troops were sent to Haiti, the Western Hemisphere's poorest country, in support of a reform government that had replaced a brutal dictatorship. U.S. troops have remained in Haiti promoting stability as political rivalries continue, leaving Haitians poorer and more desperate.

Mexico and Brazil: Models of Development?

The Mexican Revolution in the early twentieth century had led to hopes of reducing social inequality, but the nation's leaders soon turned to emphasizing economic growth over uplifting the poor majority. Mexico's limited democracy offered regular elections and some civil liberties, but one party, the Party of Revolutionary Institutions (PRI), controlled the elections and hence the government, often resorting to voter fraud. The PRI was led by businessmen and bureaucrats who fostered stability while deflecting challenges to their power monopoly for decades. In 1968, it shocked the nation by ordering police to open fire on a large demonstration, killing hundreds of university students and other protesters.

> "The Mexican Revolution in the early twentieth century had led to hopes of reducing social inequality, but the nation's leaders soon turned to emphasizing economic growth over uplifting the poor majority."

Vicente Fox and Mexican Reform

By the 1980s, the PRI began to falter. In the early 1990s, a peasant revolt in a poor southern state, Chiapas, revealed starkly the PRI's failure to redress rural poverty. The election of a reformist, non-PRI president, Vicente Fox, a pro-U.S. free-market conservative, in 2000 ended the seven-decades-long PRI monopoly on federal power. However, Fox proved unable to foster much economic or social change, and the PRI still held power in many states. By 2005, a more open and pluralistic political system had emerged, with stronger leftist and right-wing parties contending with the PRI for support. Whether the democratic processes fostered by Fox can be consolidated and endure remained to be seen.

NAFTA

Mexico's economic system also gradually opened, but without diminishing poverty. For decades, the PRI had mixed capitalism with a strong government role. However, the collapse of world oil prices in the 1980s damaged Mexico's development prospects, so PRI leaders replaced protectionist policies with open markets. In 1994, the North American Free Trade Agreement (NAFTA) helped integrate the U.S. and Mexican economies, and many U.S.-owned factories that employed thousands of workers opened on the Mexican side of the border. The majority of these workers, however, have been poorly paid young women. Elsewhere, peasant farmers, unable to compete with highly subsidized U.S. farmers, have often been ruined. Even the urban middle class feels the economic pain as wages stagnate. In 1980, Mexico's economy was nearly four times larger than South Korea's; by 2005, a dynamic South Korea had pushed ahead of Mexico. In addition, Mexico's population quadrupled between 1940 and 2000, pressuring the nation's resources. Because of poverty and overpopulation, thousands of desperate Mexicans continue to cross the border to the United States each year, legally or illegally, in search of a better life.

Brazil

Few Latin American nations have had as much promise and experienced as many problems as Brazil. Occupying half of the South American continent, and with a population in 2005 of some 186 million, Brazil is Latin America's colossus and has its largest economy. From the mid-1940s to the mid-1960s, the nation had a democratic government, which persisted for two decades despite increasing political tensions and periodic economic crises. In 1961, Joao Goulart (jao joo-LART) (1918–1976), a populist reformer supported by leftist groups, assumed the presidency. Under his rule, the economy stumbled, and efforts to organize the impoverished peasants and rural workers antagonized powerful landlords. Seeking to halt change and impose order, the military overthrew Goulart in 1964 and ruled Brazil for the next two decades under a harsh military dictatorship, which arrested some 40,000 citizens. Viewing Brazil as ripe for a communist takeover, the United States had encouraged the military coup. Businessmen and other wealthy Brazilians, fearing disorder, welcomed the change.

Between 1964 and 1985, authoritarian governments, headed by generals and supported by the United States, gave priority to economic growth and national security at the expense of social programs. Relying on brutal repression, the regimes imposed comprehensive censorship, outlawed political parties, and weakened workers' rights. Right-wing vigilante groups and death squads instilled terror, killing or torturing dissidents; one police squad assassinated more than one thousand people. The generals imposed a capitalist economic model recommended by American advisers encouraging free markets, industrialization, and foreign investment.

For a decade, the economy boomed, eliciting foreign praise of the "Brazilian miracle" as annual growth rates averaged 10 percent between 1968 and 1974 and exports soared. The United States and international lending agencies poured in $8 billion in aid. But the "miracle" depended on low wages and redistributing income upward to the rich and middle class: the top 10 percent of people enjoyed 75 percent of the income gain, while half of all households lived below the poverty line. Beginning in the 1960s, Brazilian governments encouraged land speculators and foreign corporations to open up the vast Amazon basin, the world's largest tropical rain forest and river system. The virgin forest was rapidly stripped for logging, farming, mining, and ranching, displacing many of the 200,000 Indians who lived off its resources.

By 1980, the "miracle" was fading as Brazil experienced an inflation rate of more than 100 percent, a massive foreign debt, and sagging industrial production. Meanwhile, numerous sectors of society demanded democracy, and the Catholic Church criticized human-rights violations. In 1985, the growing political liberalization climaxed with a return to democracy and the election of a civilian president. Under the successive democratic governments led by moderate reformers, however, many problems remained unresolved, because leaders feared that policies hurting big business might provoke a military coup. As economic problems increased, inflation soared to 2,500 percent by 1994. Responding to the gross inequality in rural land ownership, landless peasants seized land, but landowners hired gunmen to harass the militants. Social inequities, such as school dropout rates, malnutrition, bankrupt public health services, homelessness, and debt slavery, grew.

Although the economy revived in the later 1990s, Brazilians, wanting further reform, turned to the political left. In 2002, they gave leftist candidates 80 percent of the vote and elected as president socialist labor leader Luis Ignacio da Silva (b. 1944), known as Lula, a former metalworker and longtime dissident. While Lula has fostered faster economic growth, peasant and worker groups believe Lula's economic policies go too far in pleasing financial interests and international lenders. Despite the booming economy, by 2006, corruption scandals threatened the regime.

Revolutionary Cuba

In contrast to Mexico and Brazil, Cuba, led by Fidel Castro (b. 1927), built a society dominated by a powerful communist government. A one-time amateur baseball star who was nearly signed by a U.S. professional team but instead became a lawyer, Castro came to power in 1959, the victor of a revolution against a repressive, corrupt dictator who was long supported by the United States. Castro allied with the Cuban Communist Party and promised radical change, prompting thousands of upper- and middle-class Cubans to flee to the nearby United States. In 1961, the United States moved to isolate and then overthrow his regime by organizing a military force composed of Cuban exiles that landed on a Cuban beach, known as the Bay of Pigs. But the invasion had been poorly planned and enjoyed little popular support in Cuba. Castro's forces routed the invading exiles, a humiliation for the United States.

Needing a protector, Castro became a firm Soviet ally, thereby alarming the United States further. The Cuba–USSR alliance soon precipitated a major crisis. In 1962, U.S. air surveillance of the island revealed Soviet ballistic missiles with a 2,000-mile range and capable of carrying nuclear warheads. The U.S. demand that the missiles be removed sparked what became known as the Cuban missile crisis, during which the United States imposed a naval blockade on Cuba and considered an invasion of the island. With the threat of nuclear confrontation looming, the Soviets backed down and removed the missiles, but afterwards the United States, hoping to bring down Castro's regime, imposed an economic boycott that endured into the twenty-first century, cutting off Cuba from sources of trade and investment.

In the 1960s and 1970s, Castro tried innovative socialist policies, often known as Castroism, to stimulate economic development in Cuba while also tightly controlling its population. Castro called capitalism "repugnant, filthy, gross, alienating because it causes war, hypocrisy and competition"[7]; yet his own policies generated little surplus food and few consumer goods. Nonetheless, Castroism improved the material and social life of the working classes; the regime built schools and clinics, mounted literacy campaigns, and promoted equality for long-marginalized Afro-Cubans and women. In quality-of-life statistics, by the mid-1980s, Cuba, with the lowest infant mortality and

Castroism Innovative socialist policies introduced by Fidel Castro to stimulate economic development in Cuba while tightly controlling its population.

highest literacy rates and life expectancy, ranked well ahead of other Latin American nations. In contrast to some Latin American dictatorships, the Cuban government did not form death squads or sponsor murders of dissidents, but Castro placed limits on free expression, jailing those who defied the ban. The jailed included brave writers, homosexuals, and those advocating free speech and elections. Seeking political freedom, better-paying jobs, or higher living standards, several hundred thousand Cubans have fled over the years, chiefly to the United States.

The Cuban Revolution had international repercussions. Castro exchanged dependence on the United States for dependence on the USSR, which, to maintain the alliance, poured billions of dollars of aid into the country. With the collapse of the USSR in 1991, however, Castro lost his patron and benefactor. Since then Cuba has struggled: the social welfare system has cracked, and the economy has crumbled despite efforts to introduce some market forces. Critics of U.S. policy, including most U.S. allies, have argued that the U.S. embargo helps Castro's regime by reinforcing strong anti-U.S. feelings and discrediting pro-U.S. dissidents. Many Cubans, while desiring a freer, more productive system, do not necessarily want the United States to determine their fate.

Chile: Reform and Repression

While Cubans sought to escape underdevelopment through revolution, Chileans, like Brazilians, tried a succession of strategies, from reform to dictatorship to democracy. Chileans enjoyed a long tradition of elected democratic governments sustained by a large middle class, high rates of literacy and urbanization, and mass-based political parties. Nonetheless, a wealthy elite of businessmen, military officers, and landowners held political power and suppressed labor unrest. Despite a growing manufacturing sector, Chile depended on the export of minerals, especially copper. By the 1960s, a stagnant economy widened the gap between rich and poor.

Salvador Allende

Chile shifted direction with the 1970 elections. Six liberal, socialist, and communist parties united in a left-leaning coalition, the Popular Unity, that was supported largely by small businessmen, the urban working class, and peasants. Their winning presidential candidate, Salvador Allende (ah-YEN-dee) (1908–1973), who had developed compassion for the poor while working as a medical doctor, promised a "Chilean road" to socialism, through constitutional means in a parliamen-

Castro Addressing Crowd A spellbinding orator, the Cuban leader, Fidel Castro, often recruits support for his government and policies by speaking at large rallies.

tary democracy. His regime took over, and paid compensation to, banks and a copper industry that had been dominated by powerful U.S. corporations. Land reform broke up underutilized ranches and divided the land among the peasant residents. Allende's government supported the labor unions and provided urban shantytowns with health clinics and better schools. Both employment and economic production reached the highest levels in Chilean history. The Popular Unity was also committed to the creation of a Chilean cultural renaissance. Democracy flourished and Allende enjoyed growing popularity.

However, the Popular Unity government also generated opposition. The rapid reforms produced shortages of luxury goods, fostering middle-class resentment. Allende's opponents controlled the mass media and judiciary and dominated the congress. At the same time, the U.S. president, Richard Nixon, worried about Allende's friendship with Cuba's Fidel Castro and feared that Allende's socialism without revolution could become a model for Latin America, threatening U.S. interests. The United States mounted an international economic embargo on Chilean exports, while the CIA undertook a disinformation campaign to discredit Allende and organized strikes to paralyze the economy.

American Intervention

In 1973, a military coup supported by the United States overthrew Allende, who died while defending the presidential palace from an assault. The military imposed a brutal military dictatorship led by General Augusto Pinochet (ah-GOOS-toh pin-oh-CHET) (b. 1915). Pinochet launched a reign of terror, suppressing rights and arresting some 150,000 Allende supporters and detaining and routinely torturing hundreds of political prisoners for years. The regime murdered thousands of dissidents, sometimes in front of other prisoners held in the national stadium, and buried the victims in unmarked mass graves. Thousands of Chileans fled the country. Advised by U.S. economists, Pinochet shifted to a free enterprise economy, similar to military-ruled Brazil's, that generated growth and moderate middle-class prosperity purchased at the cost of a monumental foreign debt and environmental degradation. But little of this wealth trickled down to the poor, whose living standards deteriorated.

Chilean Recovery

However, a severe economic crisis that undermined the regime's legitimacy led to a return to a civilian-led liberal democracy. Escalating social tensions and political protests prompted the junta to hold an election and restore democracy in 1989. The resulting center-left governments struggled to maintain middle-class prosperity while promoting a more equitable distribution of wealth. They retained free enterprise while making additions to health, housing, education, and social spending. These policies chipped away at poverty, and unemployment has plummeted. Tax increases and increased welfare have not stifled the annual economic growth of about 10 percent. Chile has become the most prosperous Latin American economy, enjoying a stable democratic system. Yet, many Chileans remain bitter toward the United States for having once helped install and perpetuate a brutal military regime.

LO⁴ Changing Latin American and Caribbean Societies

The societies of Latin America and the Caribbean, while facing daunting economic problems, have experienced distinctive social and cultural patterns. Rather than balanced economic growth, Latin American and Caribbean nations have often emphasized export of traditional natural resources such as oil, sugar, coffee, bananas, wool, and copper. Varied mixes of peoples and traditions speaking different languages often have little in common with each other. But the regions' peoples have fostered dynamic cultural forms that have found international popularity.

Latin American Economies

Although often enjoying economic growth, no Latin American nations have achieved the level of prosperity found in the industrialized West. Latin Americans forged rising literacy rates, lowered infant mortality rates, and more people than ever now own televisions, even in poor neighborhoods. Nonetheless, the world price for most of their natural resource exports usually has declined every year, leaving less money for economic development. To pay the bills, governments have taken out loans, eventually owing billions to international lenders. Rapidly expanding populations, growing at 3 percent per year, add to the social burden and cause environmental problems. Governments have treated indigenous peoples and the rain forests they inhabit as expendable resources.

Latin America has also suffered severe income inequality: by 2000, the top 10 percent of the population earned half of all income, and 70 percent of

neoliberalism
An economic model encouraged by the United States in the developing world that promoted free markets, privatization, and Western investment.

the people lived in poverty. In Brazil, half of the people have had no access to doctors, even while Rio de Janeiro has become the world's plastic surgery capital, with hundreds of cosmetic surgeons catering to wealthy Brazilians and foreigners. To survive, poor peasants in some nations have often turned to growing coca and opium for making cocaine and heroin. But the drug trade, largely sold to the U.S. market, fosters political turbulence and government corruption and profits only a few drug kingpins.

Agriculture has remained a mainstay of most Latin American economies. Landholding is usually concentrated in a small group of aristocratic families and multinational corporations, such as the U.S.-based United Fruit Company. By the 1990s, 60 percent of all agricultural land was held in large estates and farmed inefficiently, contributing to food shortages and malnutrition. Modern agriculture requires large investments for machinery, fertilizers, pesticides, and fuel, but growing beans and corn to feed hungry peasants supplies inadequate revenue.

> 66 Agriculture has remained a mainstay of most Latin American economies. 99

As a result, vast tracts of rain forests and land that once grew food crops have been transformed into beef cattle ranches. In Mexico, beef cattle consume more food than the poorest one-quarter of people.

Hardships in rural areas have generated migration to cities; by 2000, Latin America had become the world's most urbanized, with 75 percent of people living in cities and towns. The migrants live in festering shantytowns and can often find only poorly paid work. Half the urban population lack adequate water, housing, sanitation, and social services. But economic growth has also fostered growing middle classes, which have become one-third of the population in Argentina, Chile, and Uruguay and one-fifth in Brazil and Mexico.

Beginning in the 1980s, many Latin American nations, hoping to emulate the success of the United States, adopted neoliberalism, an economic model that promoted free markets, privatization, and Western investment. The model, encouraged by the United States, generated growth for a decade, but it failed to curb government corruption, install honest judicial systems, foster labor-intensive industries, or reduce the power of rich elites or dependence on foreign

U.S. Factory in Mexico Since the 1980s, growing numbers of U.S. companies have relocated industrial operations to Mexico, building many factories along the Rio Grande River that separates Mexico from Texas. In this factory, in Matamoros, Mexico, the mostly female labor force makes toys for the U.S. market.

loans and investment. Free markets have often meant that a few people enjoyed fabulous wealth while most people remained poor. The nation that most ardently adopted neoliberalism, Argentina, saw its economy collapse in 1998; unemployment soared and, by 2001, half of the people lived in poverty. But although neoliberalism lost credibility, no other economic model, such as Cuban communism or Allende's socialism with democracy, had widespread support or a record of success in Latin America.

> "Beginning in the 1980s, many Latin American nations, hoping to emulate the success of the United States, adopted neoliberalism, an economic model that promoted free markets, privatization, and Western investment."

Latin America: Society and Religion

Political and economic change has modified social arrangements, especially in gender relations and family life. Although men dominate the governments, militaries, businesses, and the Catholic Church, women's struggles have managed to reduce gender inequality, and many women now work outside of the home. Factories relocating from North America attract young women, who are preferred to men because they accept lower wages and have been raised to obey. As women have entered the workforce, family life has undergone strains. By the 1990s, far fewer people married, especially among the poor. But divorce, banned by the Catholic Church, has remained difficult or impossible to get in some nations, and men still enjoy a double standard in sexual behavior. Although abortion is illegal everywhere in the region, Latin America has one of the world's highest abortion rates. Gay men and lesbians also struggle for acceptance, as homosexuality remains illegal in many nations, including Castro's Cuba.

As gender expectations have changed, women have become more active in politics. Between 1945 and 1961, women gained the right to vote. In 1990, Violeta Chamorro (vee-oh-LET-ah cha-MOR-roe) (b. 1919), a newspaper publisher, was elected president of Nicaragua, and she served until 1996. In 2006, Chileans showed a willingness to expand their politi-

> ❝ As gender expectations have changed, women have become more active in politics. ❞

cal horizons by electing as president the pediatrician turned socialist politician Michelle Bachelet (BAH-she-let), a divorced mother of three whose father was murdered while she and her mother were jailed and tortured during the Pinochet years. Leading the victorious center-left coalition, Bachelet struck a blow for gender equity by filling half of her cabinet positions with women, including the key defense and economy ministries.

During military rule in Argentina, Brazil, and Chile, women political prisoners were kept naked and often raped. For instance, Doris Tijereno Haslam (b. 1943), an early member of the leftist Sandinista movement in Nicaragua who fought as a guerrilla commander, was twice arrested and badly tortured by the corrupt dictatorship of General Anastasio Somoza Debayle (1923–1967). After the Sandinista victory in 1979, she headed the national police and served in the congress. Women fought back against discrimination and violence, as in Mexico, where the feminist movement challenged inequitable laws and social practices. A 1974 law guaranteed women equal rights for jobs, salaries, and legal standing.

Another traditional foundation for Latin American society, religion, also was subject to change. In the 1960s, progressive Latin American Roman Catholics developed liberation theology, a movement to make Catholicism more relevant to contemporary society and address the plight of the poor. Priests favoring liberation theology, especially in Brazil, cooperated with Marxist and liberal groups in working for social justice until the Vatican prohibited the movement in the 1980s. On the whole, the Roman Catholic hierarchy remained conservative. Protestantism, chiefly evangelical or pentecostal, grew rapidly with increased missionary efforts, attracting converts with its participatory, emotional services. By the 1990s, Protestants numbered nearly 20 percent of the population in Guatemala and 8 percent in Brazil and Chile. The religious landscape of Latin America looked very different in 2000 than it had a century earlier.

Latin American and Caribbean Cultures

Latin America has fostered creative cultural forms that have reached a global audience. The mass media have both shaped and reflected the prevailing cultures. Inexpensive transistor radios became widely available, and by the 1980s, thousands of radio stations had sprouted all over the region. While most stations were privately owned, governments frequently sought to control their content. In 1950, television came to the main cities, eventually spreading widely. Immensely popular local television soap operas dominated prime-time viewing and gained a large market around the world.

Literature in Latin America

Literature has also flourished, with writers often criticizing or describing social conditions and government failures. Former journalist Gabriel García Márquez (MAHR-kez) (b. 1928), a Nobel Prize–winning Colombian novelist, developed an international audience for imaginative books full of what literary scholars called "magic realism," the representation of possible events as if they were wonders and impossible events as commonplace. His most famous work, *One Hundred Years of Solitude* (1970), charts the history of a Colombian house, the family who live in it, and the town where it was located, through wars, changing politics, and economic crises.

Some writers were critical of those holding power. For example, in Chile, the greatest epic poem of the leftist writer and former diplomat Pablo Neruda (neh-ROO-da) (1904–1973), *General Song*, published in 1950, portrays the history of the entire hemisphere, showing an innocent pre-Columbian America cruelly awakened by Spanish conquest. In 1971, Neruda won the Nobel Prize for literature, distressing those who viewed his radical views as a threat to Latin American society.

Music, Cinema, and Cultural Diversity

Like other peoples, Latin Americans have mixed local cultural traditions with imported influences. The Brazilian New Cinema movement, launched in 1955, tried to replace the influence of Hollywood films with films that reflected Brazilian life. One of the movement's finest films, *Black Orpheus* (1959), which gained an international following, employed a soundtrack of local popular music to examine the annual pre-Lenten Carnival in Rio de Janeiro's shantytowns and the extremes of wealth and poverty revealed in the different ways rich and poor celebrated Carnival. In the 1960s and 1970s, a musical style known as New Song, based chiefly on local folk music and closely tied to progressive politics and protest, gained popularity in a half-dozen countries, becoming especially influential in Chile. Seeking an alternative to the Anglo-American popular culture favored by elite Chileans, Chilean musicians have used indigenous Andean instruments and tunes. During the later 1960s, Chilean New Song pioneers such as Violeta Parra and Victor Jara (HAR-a) wrote or collected songs that addressed problems of Chilean society such as poverty and inequality. Parra (1918–1967) served as the bridge between the older generation of folk musicians and the younger generation of singer-songwriters.

Because of its left-wing connections, New Song was vulnerable to changing political conditions. In 1970, Chilean New Song musicians had joined the electoral campaign of Salvador Allende's leftist Popular Unity coalition, which sought to unseat a centrist administration. After Allende won the presidency, he encouraged the media to pay more attention to New Song and less to popular music from the United States. But in 1973, the Chilean military seized power and arrested, executed, or deported most of the New Song musicians. Before thousands of other detainees held in the national stadium, soldiers publicly cut off Victor Jara's fingers, which he had used to play his guitar, and then executed him, symbolizing the death of free expression in Chile and the government's fear of the power of popular culture.

Cultural diversity characterizes most Latin American nations, especially Brazil, where race remains a central social category. Like the United States, Brazil has never become a true racial melting pot. Race has often correlated with social status: whites dominate the top brackets, blacks the bottom, and mixed-descent Brazilians fall in between. The flexible Brazilian concept of race, however, differs from the biological concept that North Americans have. Dark-skinned people can aspire to social mobility by earning a good income since, as a popular local saying claimed, "money lightens." Furthermore, Afro-Brazilian culture has had a growing influence, and many whites have embraced aspects of black culture.

For Brazil, as for most Latin American nations, professional sports have become a popular enter-

Read about Violeta Parra, the Chilean New Song pioneer who came from a poor working-class background.

tainment and diversion from social problems. European football, or soccer, has been hugely popular for decades, uniting fans of all social backgrounds. Brazilians are proud of the international success of their national team, which won the World Cup championships five times between 1958 and 2002 by employing a creative, teamwork-oriented strategy, known as "samba football," that Brazilians have identified with the national spirit.

Rastafarianism and Reggae

With diverse populations of blacks, whites, and Asians, the Caribbean islands, like Latin America, offered an environment for creative cultural development, especially in religion and music. Jamaica's legacy of slavery and colonialism fostered the development of Rastafarianism, a religion mixing Christian, African, and local influences. The believers revered the emperor Ras Tafari of Ethiopia, the sole unconquered, uncolonized African state in 1930. Its followers, known as Rastas, adopted distinctive practices, including smoking ganja (marijuana), an illegal drug, and sporting dreadlocked hair, that outraged Jamaica's social and economic elite. As a movement of the black poor, Rastafarianism became identified in Jamaica and other Caribbean islands with radical groups seeking to redistribute wealth.

The most influential popular music to come out of the Caribbean had similar mixed origins. In the 1960s, Jamaican musicians created reggae, a style blending North American rhythm-and-blues with Afro-Jamaican traditions and marked by a distinctive beat maintained by the bass guitar. The songs of reggae musicians, who were often Rastas, promoted social justice, economic equality, and the freedom of people, especially Rastas, to live as they liked without interference by the police. The international popularity of reggae owed much to Bob Marley (1945–1981), a Rasta, and his group, the Wailers. Marley became the first international superstar to hail from a developing nation. His explosive performances and provocative lyrics offered clear messages: "Slave driver, the table is turned; Catch a fire, you gonna get burned."[8] After Marley's death from cancer in 1981, many reggae musicians watered down their message.

Latin America and the Caribbean in the Global System

Over the years, various Caribbean and Latin American leaders sought to increase regional economic coop-

eration. Commerce among Latin American nations more than doubled between 1988 and 1994. For example, the Southern Cone Common Market, formed in 1996, included six South American nations with more than 200 million people. Similarly, Caribbean countries cooperated in the Caribbean Community and Common Market, formed in 1973. Some U.S.–Latin American issues remain contested. For instance, while people in the United States have blamed Latin American drug cartels for smuggling illegal drugs into the United States, Latin Americans have often resented the U.S. interventions and economic impositions they consider Yankee imperialism. Latin American and Caribbean leaders have also feared being pushed aside in a world economy dominated by North American, European, and, increasingly, Asian nations.

Globalization influenced Latin Americans and their economies. Asian nations, especially China, Japan, Taiwan, and South Korea, captured a growing share of Latin America's traditional overseas markets while also investing in Latin America and the Caribbean. In a globalized economy, a hiccup in Tokyo or New York caused a stomach ache in Ecuador or El Salvador. Because most Latin American and Caribbean economies followed the track of the U.S. economy, they were particularly vulnerable to change in the United States.

When the 2001 terrorist attacks in the United States diverted U.S. attention to the Middle East, the sudden U.S. disinterest in Latin America and its problems sparked a regional economic downturn that reduced demand for Latin American exports. The economic gains made in the mid-1990s slipped away, and the one-fifth of Latin America's 500 million people who lived in extreme poverty by 2000 faced an even grimmer future. Only a few nations, such as Brazil and Chile, had much hope of improving their status in the global system.

Listen to a synopsis of Chapter 29.

Buffeted by political changes and economic crises, Latin Americans search for their identity and role in a world dominated by other societies.

Rastafarianism A religion from Jamaica that arose in 1930 and that mixed Christian, African, and local influences; Rastafarianism attracted urban slum dwellers and the rural poor by preaching a return of black people to Africa.

reggae A popular music style that began in Jamaica in the 1960s and that blended North American rhythm and blues with Afro-Jamaican traditions; reggae is marked by a distinctive beat maintained by the bass guitar.

CHAPTER 30

The Middle East, Sub-Saharan Africa, and New Conflicts in the Contemporary World, Since 1945

Learning Outcomes

After reading this chapter, you should be able to answer the following questions:

LO¹ How have Arab–Israeli tensions and oil shaped contemporary Middle Eastern politics?

LO² What roles has Islam played in the contemporary Middle East?

LO³ What were the main political consequences of decolonization in sub-Saharan Africa?

LO⁴ What new economic, social, and cultural patterns have emerged in Africa?

❝I saw the Berlin Wall fall, [Nelson] Mandela walk free. I saw a dream whose time has come change my history—so keep on dreaming. In the best of times and in the worst of times gotta keep looking at the skyline, not at the hole in the road.**❞**

—"Your Time Will Come" by South African pop group Savuka, 1993[1]

The writer Chinua Achebe (ah-CHAY-bay) (b. 1930) dissected the underside of African politics in a controversial 1987 blockbuster novel, *Anthills of the Savannah*. *Anthills* mercilessly depicts the immorality, vanity, and destructiveness of a military dictatorship much like the one Achebe had experienced in Nigeria. Nigerian military leaders overthrew a civilian government in 1983 and began arresting people whose corruption was well known, but then proceeded to jail anyone, including journalists, who questioned the regime's economic mismanagement and human-rights abuses. Just as the black and white musicians in the South African pop group, Savuka, could sing of dreams changing history and a new era beginning with the end of white minority rule, Achebe also offered a powerful message about the need for people to protest unaccountable, repressive power. The political and economic realities of contemporary Africa and the Middle East are reflected in these regions' cultures, as writers, musicians, and artists have used their art to spur political and social change.

The problems vividly described by Achebe for Nigeria—corruption, economic stagnation, combustible social tensions, and failed promises of democracy—have applied to most other nations in sub-Saharan Africa and the Middle East. The triumph of nationalism and decolonization reshaped Africa and the Middle East: between 1945 and 1975, country after country became independent or escaped from Western political domination. In contrast to various East Asian, Southeast Asian, and Latin American nations, however, African and Middle Eastern nations have often struggled to survive. While culturally innovative, few of the nations have successfully resolved their social and economic problems. For some nations, Islam has become

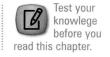

Test your knowlege before you read this chapter.

What do you think?

The Middle East held little strategic importance during the Cold War.

Strongly Disagree						Strongly Agree
1	2	3	4	5	6	7

[1]Written by Johnny Clegg. Publisher: HRBV Music/Thythm Safari

<< Modern vs. Traditional Wearing traditional clothing, including veils and head scarves, Egyptian women walk through downtown Cairo in 1998 in front of billboards promoting popular entertainers. The scene illustrates the encounter between Islamic customs and modern ideas in many Middle Eastern nations.

a rallying cry to assert political interests and preserve cultures. Global superpowers have manipulated governments and intervened to serve their own ends.

> "In the decade after World War II, nationalist governments in the Middle East replaced most of the remaining colonial regimes."

LO¹ The Middle East: New Nations and Old Societies

Few world regions have witnessed more turbulence in the past half-century than the Middle East, the predominantly Muslim nations stretching from Morocco eastward across North Africa and western Asia to Turkey, Iran, and Afghanistan. The major ethnic group, the Arabs, have dominated most of these nations, but Turks, Iranians, Kurds, and Israeli Jews also influence the region. After World War II, Middle Eastern societies ended Western colonization and asserted their own political interests, often under modernizing leaders. But within these societies, dictatorial governments have proliferated, and chronic political instability has been common. Centuries-old hostilities between Sunni and Shi'a Muslims simmer. Meanwhile, the Persian Gulf area, which contains much of the world's oil reserves, has become crucial to the global system.

The Reshaping of the Middle East

In the decade after World War II, nationalist governments in the Middle East replaced most of the remaining colonial regimes. The French abandoned control of Morocco, Tunisia, Lebanon, and Syria, while the Italians left Libya. However, Muslim guerrillas fought 500,000 French troops for eight years to bring independence to Algeria, which had a large European settler population. Some 250,000 Algerians died in the conflict before the French granted independence in 1962. Some Middle Eastern nations, such as Egypt and Morocco, had a long history of national identity, but many were fragile states. For example, after World War I, the British had formed the new states of Iraq, Jordan, and Palestine with arbitrary boundaries, while Afghanistan, Turkey, Lebanon, and Syria included contentious ethnic and religious groups.

Iran and Turkey, which had never been colonized, sought influential roles in the region and built formidable military forces. Both also abused their citizens' human rights, arresting dissidents and restricting ethnic minorities. Turkey, led largely by secular leaders, looked increasingly westward, joining NATO (the North Atlantic Treaty Organization), hosting U.S. military bases, developing democratic institutions, and applying for membership in the European Union. But Turkey's governments, while generally promoting a modern version of women's rights, have also suppressed the largest ethnic minority, the Kurds, who chiefly live in southeastern Turkey. Although the nation's 70 million people are largely Muslim, the government has also limited political activity by groups that favor an Islamic state.

After decolonization, hopes for development throughout the Middle East were soon dashed as vested economic interests and most of the Muslim clergy opposed significant social and economic changes. Many people remained mired in illiteracy, poverty, and disease. Turkey shifted from military-dominated to democratically elected governments by the 1980s, but the military remained powerful, and strict internal security laws resulted in the imprisonment of several thousand people for political offenses.

Lebanese could choose between many competing warlord or religious-based parties, and a new constitution in 2002 allowed both men and women in the small Persian Gulf kingdom of Bahrain (BAH-rain) to elect a parliament. But in most countries, elections were rigged, parliaments were weak, or governments made it difficult for opposition candidates to run. Furthermore, the United States and the Soviet Union, attracted by the region's oil and strategic location along vital waterways, soon filled the power vacuum created by decolonization. Arabs talked about uniting across political borders, but pan-Arab nationalism was never able to overcome political and sectional rivalries and meddling by the superpowers. In addition, many post-1945 challenges have made the Middle East a highly combustible region subject to strains.

Arab Nationalism and Egypt

Confrontation between Arab nationalism and the world's superpowers was acute in Egypt, a former British protectorate and the most populous Arab and to implement land reform, ideas that made him a hero in the Arab world. To generate power and improve flood control, Nasser's regime used Soviet aid to build the massive Aswan High Dam along the Nile, completed in 1970. But his nonaligned foreign policy antagonized a United States that was obsessed with Cold War rivalry. Accusing the West of "imperialist methods, habits of blood-sucking and usurping rights, and interference in other countries,"[2] in 1956 Nasser's government took over ownership of the British-operated Suez Canal, a key passage that was built through Egypt in the nineteenth century. To Egyptians, foreign ownership of the canal had symbolized their subjugation; to Europeans, the canal was the lifeline that moved oil and resources to the West from Asia. To protect that link, Britain, France, and Israel sent in military forces to reclaim the canal, but diplomatic opposition by the pro-Egypt Soviet Union and the United States, which disliked Nasser but feared regional instability, forced their withdrawal. By standing up to the West, Nasser became an even greater Arab hero and a champion of nonalignment, or neutrality, between the two rival superpowers. However, the Israeli defeat of Egypt and its allies in a brief 1967 war humiliated Nasser. Furthermore, although Nasser had introduced social and economic reforms, they fostered little economic or military strength for Egypt.

Arab Human Development Reports (http://www.un.org/english). The general United Nations site contains links to the reports, issued annually beginning in 2002 and available online, that assess the successes and challenges facing the Arab nations.

Nasser's successors followed pragmatic, pro-U.S. policies, and in 1978 signed a peace treaty with Israel brokered by the U.S. president, Jimmy Carter. But a shift to capitalism and heavy U.S. aid largely has not improved living conditions. Egypt's leaders reversed Nasser's land reform and dismantled the socialist economy, allowing a few well-connected capitalists to acquire state property and become fabulously rich while the poorest became even poorer. With little oil and few resources other than the fertile lands along the Nile, Egypt suffers from high malnutrition and unemployment, low rates of literacy and public health, and a huge national debt. Islamic militants, feeding on these frustrations, challenge the secular but corrupt government.

Israel in Middle Eastern Politics

The conflict between Israel and the Arabs, especially the Palestinians, was the Middle East's most

country. In 1952, a charismatic Egyptian leader, General Gamal Abdul Nasser (NAS-uhr) (1918–1970), led a military coup that ended the corrupt pro-British monarchy. Like many Egyptians, Nasser despised the British and the Egyptian leaders who collaborated with them. As an army officer with a commanding personality, he developed a vision of a new Egypt, free of Western domination and social inequality.

As Egypt's president, Nasser, a modernizer, promised to improve the lives of the impoverished masses insurmountable problem for more than half a century. Under the influence of Zionism and its dream of a Jewish homeland, Jews had been emigrating from Europe to Palestine since the late 1800s, building cities and forming productive socialist farming settlements. The growing Jewish presence, however, triggered occasional conflicts with the Palestinian Arab majority. Then the Nazis' murder of 6 million Jews during World War II, and Jewish desire for a safe haven, set the stage for the birth of Israel. But the new nation never established a secure position or fostered allies within the region.

The Birth of Israel

When Jewish refugees, traumatized by the Holocaust, poured into Palestine from post–World War II Europe, moderate Jewish leaders negotiated with the British for a peaceful transfer of power to them in Palestine. Meanwhile, Zionist extremists, impatient with negotiations, used terrorism, such as bombings and assassinations, against the British, Arabs, and moderate Jews. At the same time, Arabs resorted to violent attacks on Jews. Unable to maintain order, Britain abandoned the territory in 1948, referring the Palestine question to the new United Nations as Jewish leaders proclaimed the establishment of the state of Israel. By establishing a multiparty parliamentary democracy and seeking to

rebuild shattered Jewish lives, the Israelis gained the strong support of Western nations and especially the United States, which pumped in several billion dollars in aid annually for the next five decades.

Arab Reaction to the Jewish State

The establishment of a Jewish state in Palestine led to full-scale war in 1948–1949 between Israel and its Arab neighbors, to whom Israel was a white settler state and a symbol of Western colonialism (see Map 30.1). As Palestinian Arabs fled the fighting and the continued terrorism against them by Jewish extremists, Israelis occupied their farms and houses. The Israelis won the war and expelled 85 percent of the Palestinian Arabs from Israel. While some Palestinian exiles became a prosperous middle class throughout the Middle East, most unhappily settled in squalid refugee camps in Egypt, Lebanon, Jordan, and Syria. They supported the Palestine Liberation Organization (PLO), a coalition of Arab nationalist, Muslim, and Christian groups led by Yasser Arafat (YA-sir AR-uh-fat) (1929–2004), an engineer from a wealthy Jerusalem family.

Arafat's pragmatic style united Arab factions, but neither the Western nations nor Israel officially recognized the PLO until the 1990s, prompting it to resort

Interactive Map

Dismantling Israeli Settlements Palestinians have viewed the settlements built by ardent Zionists in the West Bank and Gaza as a provocation. Israeli troops have sometimes been ordered to dismantle settlements and remove the enraged settlers by force. In 2005, all of the Israeli settlements were closed down in Gaza.

AP Images/Oded Balilty

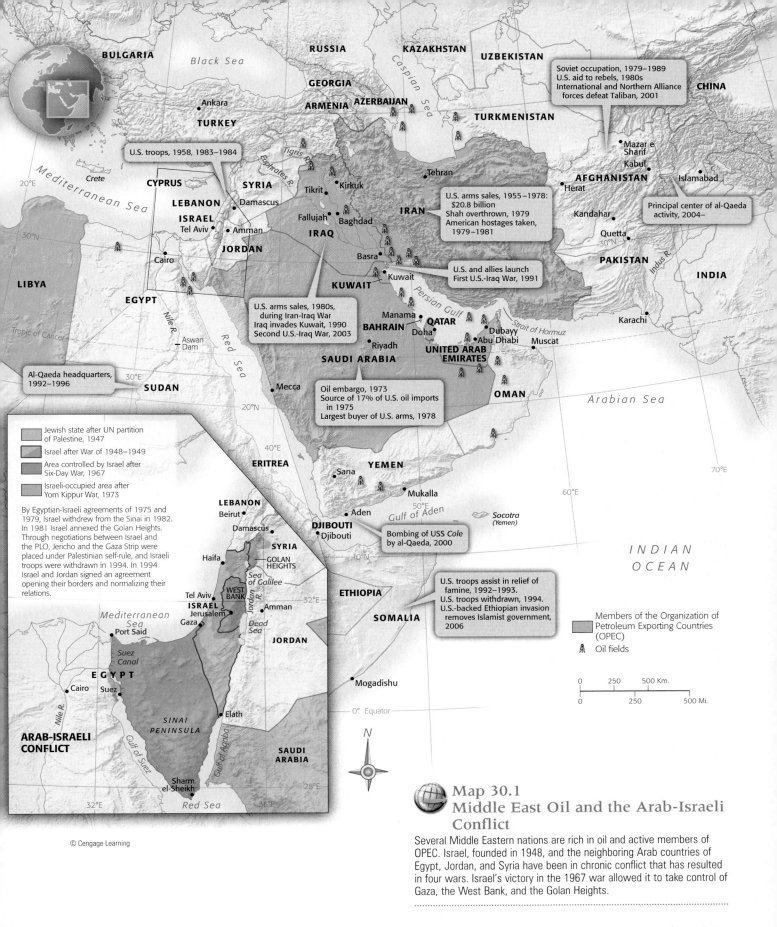

U.S. troops, 1958, 1983–1984

Soviet occupation, 1979–1989
U.S. aid to rebels, 1980s
International and Northern Alliance
forces defeat Taliban, 2001

U.S. arms sales, 1955–1978:
$20.8 billion
Shah overthrown, 1979
American hostages taken,
1979–1981

Principal center of al-Qaeda
activity, 2004–

U.S. and allies launch
First U.S.-Iraq War, 1991

U.S. arms sales, 1980s,
during Iran-Iraq War
Iraq invades Kuwait, 1990
Second U.S.-Iraq War, 2003

Al-Qaeda headquarters,
1992–1996

Oil embargo, 1973
Source of 17% of U.S. oil imports
in 1975
Largest buyer of U.S. arms, 1978

Bombing of USS *Cole*
by al-Qaeda, 2000

U.S. troops assist in relief of
famine, 1992–1993.
U.S. troops withdrawn, 1994.
U.S.-backed Ethiopian invasion
removes Islamist government,
2006

Members of the Organization of
Petroleum Exporting Countries
(OPEC)

Oil fields

Legend (Arab-Israeli Conflict inset):

Jewish state after UN partition
of Palestine, 1947

Israel after War of 1948–1949

Area controlled by Israel after
Six-Day War, 1967

Israeli-occupied area after
Yom Kippur War, 1973

By Egyptian-Israeli agreements of 1975 and
1979, Israel withdrew from the Sinai in 1982.
In 1981 Israel annexed the Golan Heights.
Through negotiations between Israel and
the PLO, Jericho and the Gaza Strip were
placed under Palestinian self-rule, and Israeli
troops were withdrawn in 1994. In 1994
Israel and Jordan signed an agreement
opening their borders and normalizing their
relations.

**ARAB-ISRAELI
CONFLICT**

© Cengage Learning

Map 30.1
Middle East Oil and the Arab-Israeli Conflict

Several Middle Eastern nations are rich in oil and active members of
OPEC. Israel, founded in 1948, and the neighboring Arab countries of
Egypt, Jordan, and Syria have been in chronic conflict that has resulted
in four wars. Israel's victory in the 1967 war allowed it to take control of
Gaza, the West Bank, and the Golan Heights.

> "An Arab-Israeli War in 1967 further complicated regional politics, heightening conflict and reshaping Israeli society."

to terrorism against Israel. The Palestinians remaining in Israel participated in democratic politics but were disproportionally poor and often saw themselves as second-class citizens. Meanwhile, thousands more Jewish immigrants arrived, intensifying divisions in Israeli society between secular and devout Jews. Israelis, obsessed now with military security, devoted half of their total national budget to the military. A cycle of violence followed for years, with a PLO attack on Israeli civilians followed by Israeli reprisals. Mutual distrust and violence increased.

The 1967 War

An Arab-Israeli War in 1967 further complicated regional politics, heightening conflict and reshaping Israeli society. Responding successfully to an ill-advised attack led by Egypt and Jordan, Israel gained control of new territories that had once been part of Palestine: the West Bank, that part of Jordan on the western side of the Jordan River; the eastern half of Jerusalem; the Gaza Strip, a small coastal enclave of Egypt; and the Golan Heights, a Syrian plateau overlooking northeast Israel. The Israeli victory doubled the amount of land controlled by Israel, but the nation now contained 3 million Jews and 2 million Arabs, a combustible situation. Israel treated the Palestinians in the occupied territories as a colonized people, allowing them no political rights. In 1973, another Israeli war with Egypt and Syria proved costly to all sides.

Palestinian Resistance

Increasing Israeli control over the Palestinians in the occupied territories exacerbated the conflict. Although many Israelis wanted to trade occupied land for a permanent peace settlement, ultranationalist Israelis, with government support, began claiming and settling on Arab land, creating another problem: thousands of Jewish settlers, largely militant Zionists and religious conservatives, living amid hostile Arabs. Because

Arab and Israeli Soccer Players Discuss Ethnic Relations in Israel, 2000 Learn how Arabs and Jews get along in the world of professional soccer in Israel.

Israel has remained a democracy with a vibrant free press, Israelis have heatedly debated these policies and the general treatment of Arabs. In 1987, desperate Palestinians began a resistance known as the Intifada ("Uprising") against the Israeli occupation. Negotiations led in 1993 to limited self-government under the PLO in parts of the occupied territories, the basis for a possible Palestinian state, and a peace agreement between Israel and Jordan.

But after a series of political blunders, violence erupted again in 2000, returning the Israel–Palestine problem to center stage. Moderate Israelis and Palestinians lost hope as demoralizing Palestinian suicide bombings of civilian targets, such as restaurants and public buses, and Israeli reprisal attacks on Palestinian neighborhoods renewed fifty years of violence. Israel built a high-security fence separating it from the West Bank that also incorporated some occupied territory, enraging Palestinians. Yet, in 2005, tensions eased. After Yasser Arafat's death, his moderate party chose a less controversial leader, and the Israeli government closed the Israeli settlements in Gaza and disbanded several illegal settlements in the West Bank.

However, in 2006, the Palestinians gave the militant Islamic Hamas movement a majority of seats in the Palestinian parliament, alarming Israelis, because Hamas refused to recognize Israel's right to exist. Hamas owed its victory in part to its longtime social welfare activities and to hundreds of conservative Muslim women who campaigned door to door for the party; six of them won seats. The future of Israeli-Palestinian relations remained uncertain, as no basis for ensuring long-term peace has yet emerged.

Iran, Iraq, and Regional Conflicts

Rich in oil and strategically located along the Persian Gulf, Iran, once known as Persia, had been buffeted between rival European nations for a century. Outside interference in Iranian affairs continued after World War II, when a conflict developed between the young king, Shah Mohammed Pahlavi (pah-LAH-vee) (1919–1980), and nationalist reformers who were opposed to foreign domination. In 1951, nationalists came to power, reducing the shah to a ceremonial role; because Iran had been receiving little revenue from the British-dominated oil industry, the nationalists also took ownership of it. In response, Britain and its ally, the United States—considering the nationalists to be sympathetic to the USSR—cut off aid and launched a boycott, bringing Iran to near bankruptcy and fostering unrest. In 1953, American CIA agents secretly organized opposition among military leaders and paid disgruntled Iranians to riot against the nationalist government. In the turmoil, royalists overthrew the nationalist government and restored the unpopular shah to power, embittering many Iranians. Shah Pahlavi, a ruthless, pleasure-loving man who dreamed of restoring Persia as a great power, allied himself with the strongest superpower, the United States, and allowed U.S. companies to control the oil industry.

> 66 Rich in oil and strategically located along the Persian Gulf, Iran, once known as Persia, had been buffeted between rival European nations for a century. 99

Iran Under the Shah

Along with modernization, the shah's 35 years of rule also brought a huge military force built with oil revenues and political repression. The shah's promotion of a market economy and women's rights was admired in the West but failed to improve living standards for most Iranians. While corrupt elites siphoned off most of the money earmarked for development, including generous U.S. aid, 60 percent of peasants remained landless. Cities became overcrowded as Iranians abandoned destitute rural villages; the shah's policies and persistent inequalities fostered unrest. The shah's secret police eliminated opposition forcibly, imprisoning thousands of political prisoners. Conservative Shi'ite leaders opposed the modernization, such as the unveiled women and crowded bars, which they viewed as a threat to Muslim religion and culture. Then in 1979, the economy slumped. Strikes and protests forced the shah into exile and turned the United States and Iran into bitter foes.

 Get a glimpse into Iranian life in late 1970s Iran by choosing whether or not to support the Shah in this interactive simulation.

Khomeini and Revolution

With the shah's departure, an Islamic revolution began to reshape Iran. While some Shi'ite thinkers discouraged the clergy from political activism, others promoted clerical involvement in governing an Islamic state. The latter's views prevailed when militant Shi'ite clerics, led by the long-exiled Ayatollah Ruhollah Khomeini (roo-HOLE-ah KOH-may-nee)

(1902–1989), took power, eliminated leftists and moderates, and replaced the shah's secular policies with the Islamic Shari'a, which devout Muslims considered the law of God. As Iran became an Islamic state, thousands of Iranians fled abroad. Among the new restrictions, women were forced to wear veils and prohibited from socializing with men from outside their families. Like the shah, the clerics ruled by terror, suppressed ethnic minorities, such as the Kurds in the northwest, and executed opponents.

The Iranian Revolution fostered opposition from outside. The United States became bitterly opposed after Islamic militants seized the U.S. Embassy in Tehran in 1979 and held it and the U.S. diplomats for one year. Iran's Arab neighbors, who had always feared Iran's territorial size, large population, military strength, and regional ambitions, were also worried about Islamic militancy aimed at their more secular governments. Tensions were fueled by centuries of animosity between the mostly Sunni Arabs and the mostly Shi'ite Iranians. An Iranian program to develop nuclear power and, possibly, weapons, also concerned the international community.

 **The Revolution That Failed Women** Read a critical analysis of the status of Iranian women before and after the Revolution.

Reform and Repression

Eventually, Iranian politics changed as the nation mixed theocracy with the trappings of democracy. A more open electoral process allowed opposition parties to win seats in parliament. Beginning in 1997, reformers gained a share of power. This, however, fostered a power struggle between moderate reformers, many of them clerics, and the hard-line clerics who controlled the judicial and electoral systems. With the economy floundering, the reformers sought closer ties to the outside world, democratization, and a loosening of harsh laws but found the United States unwilling to improve relations. Young people, resenting clerical leadership and Islamic laws, often supported reform and increasingly challenged restrictions on personal behavior. But the hard-liners maintained overall political power, banning reformist newspapers and disqualifying reformist political candidates. Shirin Ebadi (shih-RIN ee-BOD-ee) (b. 1947), a feminist Iranian lawyer and human-rights activist, won the Nobel Peace Prize in 2003 for bravely challenging the clerical leadership and favoring a reformist Islam. But in 2005, Iranians lost faith in the ineffective reformist leaders and elected a hardline, anti-reform president who pledged to increase the nation's nuclear capabilities and restore conservative values.

Iraq proved another major source of regional instability. In 1958, the Iraqi army overthrew an unpopular monarchy and began more than four decades of ruthless military dictatorships. These governments, usually led by the Ba'ath ("Renaissance") Party—which favored socialism and Arab nationalism and strongly opposed Israel—fostered secular policies and some economic development, making Iraq one of the most prosperous Arab societies by the 1980s. Representing the Sunni minority of 20 percent, the Ba'ath ruled a nation with a restless Arab Shi'ite majority, located mostly in the south, and a disaffected Kurdish minority in the north. In 1979, army officer Saddam Hussein (1937–2006) took power in Iraq and proved even more brutal than his predecessors.

Saddam Hussein and the Iran-Iraq War

Alarmed by the Iranian Revolution, and hated by Ayatollah Khomeini, who considered Saddam's secular regime godless, Saddam launched a war against Iran in 1980, using poison gas against Iranian soldiers, but he was unable to achieve victory. The United States, with its vested interest in Iraq's oil—the world's second largest proven reserves—and hostility toward Iran, provided arms to Saddam's military. As the casualties mounted, both Iran and Iraq drafted teenagers to fight. The costs of war were staggering: more than 260,000 Iranian and 100,000 Iraqi dead and grave damage to the Iraqi economy, including major destruction in Iraq's main port, Basra.

The Persian Gulf War

When the war ended in 1988 with no victor, Saddam's actions fostered regional tension. The U.S. government continued to support his regime, but in 1991, Iraq invaded prosperous Kuwait, a former British protectorate ruled by an Arab royal family. The United States, worried that oil-rich Saudi Arabia might be next, formed a coalition and launched the Persian Gulf War (1991), which drove Iraqis from Kuwait and killed perhaps 30,000 Iraqi soldiers. But Saddam remained in power, persecuting dissidents and slaughtering Shi'ites and Kurds who rebelled after the Gulf War defeat. At least 30,000 Shi'ites and many thousands of Kurds died from the fighting. Still, Saddam's war-making capabilities were badly damaged, and the United States and United Nations eventually gave the Kurds in the north some protection and greater self-governance, while sanctions imposed by the United Nations restricted Iraq's power. Because of these sanctions and Saddam's economic mismanagement, the Iraqi people struggled to acquire food and medical supplies, and thousands died from the resulting shortages.

Saudi Arabia, Oil, and the World

The Persian Gulf War revealed the close connection between Saudi Arabia, a kingdom built on conservative Islam and oil, and the outside world, especially the United States, which had military bases and a strong economic stake in the kingdom. Comprising mostly bleak desert, Saudi Arabia possesses the world's largest known oil reserves. Beginning in the 1940s, the nation's leaders used oil revenues to fund modernization projects, building highways, hospitals, and universities. By the 1980s, the Saudis had achieved health and literacy rates that were high for the Middle East. Glittering shopping malls served affluent urbanites, yet outside the cities, poor Saudis often still traveled by camel and slept in tents.

Despite the modernization, Saudi political and social life has remained conservative, with the royal family exercising power and living extravagantly while tolerating corruption and quashing dissent. With the acquiescence of the Saudi royal family, the Wahhabis, followers of the most rigid form of Islam, maintain a stranglehold on Islamic thought, practice, and education. Wahhabis believe that women should stay at home and be controlled by men. A special police force patrols the streets and markets to punish women for violating the strict dress codes, which require them to be covered head to foot. In the 1990s, the religious police prevented unveiled female students from fleeing a school dormitory fire, causing dozens of the girls to burn to death. The Shi'ite minority, despised by the Wahhabis, have enjoyed few rights. Saudi and Western critics believe that the narrow Islam taught in Saudi schools promotes extremism and anti-Western sentiment.

Saudi Arabia's policies have strongly influenced world oil prices and availability. The kingdom was the major player in the formation in 1960 of OPEC

Oil Wealth Saudi Arabia contains the world's largest oil operations, mostly located on or near the Persian Gulf. A Saudi worker overlooks one of the nation's many refineries, which produces the oil exports that have brought the nation wealth.

(Organization of Petroleum Exporting Countries), a cartel designed to give the producers more power over the price of oil and leverage over consuming nations. OPEC's members range from Middle Eastern nations such as Algeria, Iran, and the United Arab Emirates to more distant countries such as Mexico, Nigeria, and Indonesia. In 1973, OPEC members, angry at Western support of Israel, reduced the world oil supply to raise prices, badly discomforting industrialized nations. After the embargo ended, the world price remained high, enriching OPEC members and forcing the United States and western Europe to conserve fuel. But in the 1980s, reduced oil consumption broke OPEC's power and prices plummeted, damaging the economies of most OPEC members.

Saudi Arabia remained the world's largest exporter of oil, but by the 1990s, the Saudi economy had soured. Between 1980 and 2000, income levels fell by two-thirds, while members of the royal family spent money lavishly and often violated Wahhabi restrictions with their high living abroad. Resentment of the royal family increased, as did dislike of the royal family's U.S. allies. Some Saudis have embraced militant Islam, a few joining terrorist groups such as Al Qaeda. Most of the young men who hijacked four U.S. airliners and crashed them into the Pentagon and World Trade Center in 2001 were Saudis, and their Al Qaeda leader, Osama bin Laden (b. 1957), became a militant Wahhabi after growing up in a wealthy Saudi family. Yet, thanks to oil, Saudi Arabia and the industrialized nations, especially the United States, have remained close allies despite vast differences.

LO² Change and Conflict in the Middle East

In 1979, the Islamic world celebrated thirteen centuries of Islamic history. For most of those centuries, Muslims had made brilliant contributions to the world, fostering extensive trade networks, spreading scientific knowledge, and founding powerful empires. By the nineteenth century, however, Western powers increasingly meddled with these societies, though the longer history and older traditions of Islam remained relevant into the present. Islamic societies also experienced social and cultural change, as new conflicts resulting from foreign interventions, Islamic militancy, and international terrorism reshaped the region's role in the global system.

Religion, Ethnicity, and Conflict

In parts of the Middle East, ethnic and religious hostilities have fostered long-term conflict. In Lebanon, for example, a long civil war resulted from rivalry between a dozen rival factions, Christian and Muslim, for control of the small state and its resources. In this deeply fragmented land, a national government existed largely only in name during the 1970s and 1980s. Lebanon's main city, Beirut, once a prosperous mecca for trade and tourism, was devastated by factional fighting. Israel, Syria, and the United States were all sucked into the chronic conflict. Syria stationed troops in the north and east, and Israel did the same in the south. In the 1980s, the United States intervened on behalf of a weak national government led by the largest, most pro-Western Christian faction. U.S. warships shelled areas around Beirut dominated by opposition, especially Shi'ite, factions while U.S. Marines secured the Beirut airport. The disastrous U.S. mission made the United States a focus of Arab rage and resulted in some five hundred U.S. deaths from suicide bombers. In the 1990s, the fighting ebbed, and Lebanon regained some stability but little unity.

Elsewhere, in the Sudan, a huge country linking the Middle East and sub-Saharan Africa, the Arab Muslim-dominated government used military force to control the rebellious African Christians and animists in the south, causing 2 million deaths. In 2005, the two sides agreed to end the conflict, but by then the Arab-controlled Sudan government faced a rebellion in Darfur, an impoverished western region where

> "Although deeply divided by clan and factional rivalries, Kurds had long sought either their own nation or self-government within their countries of residence."

African Muslim farmers competed for scarce land with Arab pastoralists. To regain control, the government launched a genocide against the Africans. Thousands of people died from military assaults on their villages or from disease and starvation after they fled, many into neighboring Chad.

Another longtime ethnic conflict concerned Kurds, a large ethnic group—over 20 million strong—inhabiting mountain districts in Iran, Iraq, Syria, and Turkey. Although deeply divided by clan and factional rivalries, Kurds had long sought either their own nation or self-government within their countries of residence. This desire brought them into constant conflict with central governments. Kurdish rebel groups were especially active in eastern Turkey, where the Turkish government, hoping to build a national Turkish identity, repressed Kurdish culture and language. Kurds were also restless in oil-rich northern Iraq, where the dictator, Saddam Hussein, made Kurds a special target of his repression, launching air raids and poison gas attacks against Kurdish villages.

Gender, Religion, and Culture

Gender relations and family life have changed relatively little in the Middle Eastern societies. In a few nations, notably Turkey, Iraq, and Lebanon, urban women expanded their economic opportunities by running businesses and entering the professions. But compared with the rest of the world, most Middle Eastern women remained in the home, often secluded from the outside world, with their lives controlled by the men of their families.

> ❝ Muslim liberals advocated improving women's lives through education, and some women activists argued that the Quran supported women's rights. ❞

Feminism in the Middle East

Male and female reformers have challenged women's subservient status for centuries, and a full-fledged feminist movement emerged in Egypt in the 1920s. Muslim liberals advocated improving women's lives through education, and some women activists argued that the Quran supported women's rights. Turkey, Tunisia, and Iraq adopted Western-influenced family laws allowing civil marriages and divorce, but conservative Muslims prevented their enactment in other Middle Eastern societies. Devout women often opposed secular feminism, arguing that women were best protected by strict Islamic law, but they also became activists when compelled to do so. For instance, Zainab Al-Ghazali (1917–2005) in Egypt founded an organization that built mosques, trained female preachers, and promoted an active women's role in public life; her staunch support of Islamic values upset not only liberal feminists but also Egypt's modernizing President Nasser, who had her jailed and tortured.

Liberal and conservative Muslims disagree on women's dress. Liberals often see the veil as a symbol of female subjugation, and many women have adopted Western dress. But since the 1960s, in secular nations such as Turkey and Egypt, women influenced by revivalist Islam have lobbied to wear the veil or head scarf as a symbol of piety. In Turkey, where the secular government has been wary of Islamic militancy, head scarves have been banned from schools. At the same time, attitudes toward homosexuality have generally become more repressive. In many countries, homosexual behavior, when discovered, frequently results in jail terms or even more severe punishments.

Tradition vs. Modernity

The clash between tradition and modernity in the Middle East has provided a fertile environment for creativity in religion, music, and literature. Islam has remained at the heart of Middle Eastern life, but, despite its message of peace, social justice, and community, it has often proved more divisive than unifying (see Map 30.2). Age-old divisions such as those between Sunni and Shi'a, liberal and conservative, secular and devout, Sufi and anti-Sufi, remain powerful, especially in western Asia.

 Interactive Map

Islamists and *Jihad*

Antimodern, usually puritanical militants known

> "In a troubled world, the Islamic revival satisfies for millions a need for personal solace, a yearning for tradition, and a dream of a just political system as propounded by the earliest Muslims."

as Islamists, who seek an Islamic state and are bitter rivals of secular Muslims, became increasingly influential, especially in Egypt, Algeria, Turkey, and Iran. The writings of the Iranian Ali Shariati (SHAR-ee-AH-tee) (1933–1977), educated in France but a critic of the West, influenced Shi'ites. He castigated Western democracy as subverted by greed but also blamed Islamic tradition for reducing women to, as he put it, the level of a washing machine. Egyptian writer Sayyid Qutb (SIGH-eed ka-TOOB) (1906–1966) sparked political Sunni Islam and redefined *jihad* ("struggle") as violent opposition to the West rather than, as most Muslim thinkers had taught for centuries, personal struggle to maintain faith. Inspired by thinkers like Qutb, the most extreme Islamists, known as *jihadists*, formed organizations such as the Muslim Brotherhood that plotted violence against their modernizing opponents.

History of the Middle East Database (*http://www.nmhschool.org/tthornton/mehistorydatabase/mideastindex.php*). A useful site on history, politics, and culture.

In a troubled world, the Islamic revival satisfies for millions a need for personal solace, a yearning for tradition, and a dream of a just political system as propounded by the earliest Muslims. While most people have rejected extremist groups, disillusionment with governments and resentment of Western power have prompted a growing turn to Islam for moral support. When elections are allowed, Islamic groups with their large followings tend to triumph over secular parties, as happened in Iraq, Egypt, and Palestine in 2005, a reason why pro-Western modernists often fear democracy. During the past several decades, Islamic influence has grown. Shi'ite activists in Iraq have closed bars and harassed unveiled women, while Sunni militants attack followers of Sufi mysticism, which they view as heresy. Islamists in Algeria, Egypt, and Saudi Arabia have mounted movements aimed initially at challenging their governments; some have become involved with international terrorist groups.

![Map 30.2] **Map 30.2**
The Islamic World

© Cengage Learning

The Islamic world includes not only the Middle East—Western Asia and North Africa—but also countries with Muslim majorities in sub-Saharan Africa, Central Asia, and South and Southeast Asia. In addition, Muslims live in most other Eastern Hemisphere nations and in the Americas.

---

rai

("opinion") A twentieth-century pop music of Algeria based on local Bedouin chants, Spanish flamenco, French cafe songs, Egyptian pop, and other influences and featuring improvised lyrics that often deal with forbidden themes of sex and alcohol.

Music and Literature in the Contemporary Middle East

While Islamic militants have condemned music, dance, and other pleasures, many people have been fans of popular culture, especially music. Musicians often hope to encourage national unity or shape society, usually in a more liberal direction. The songs of peace and coexistence sung by hugely popular Lebanese singer Fairuz (fie-ROOZ) were sometimes credited with being the major symbol of hope in that turbulent, civil war–plagued land. Similarly, Israelis revered Yemen-born Shoshana

Damari (1923–2006), whose optimistic songs encouraged Israeli unity by extolling the nation and its military forces. But in religiously dogmatic or ethnically divided states, popular music has sometimes stirred controversy. The Islamic government of Iran, which is opposed to women performing in public, tried to silence all female singers, including the vocalist and film star Googoosh (GOO-goosh), whose melancholic Westernized pop music had a huge audience in Iran during the 1960s and 1970s.

The rai ("opinion") pop music of Algeria is based on local Bedouin chants, Spanish flamenco, French café songs, Egyptian pop, and other influences, and its improvised lyrics often deal with forbidden themes of sex and alcohol. Rai holds great appeal to urban working-class youth in North Africa and to the offspring of Arab immigrants in France, but it is anathema to puritanical Islamic militants in Algeria.

Middle Eastern writers have used their literature to express ideas forbidden in politics and religion. For instance, the novels of the Egyptian Naguib Mahfuz (nah-GEEB mah-FOOZ) (b. 1911) have addressed social problems and questioned conservative religious values. Many of his writings have been banned in Egypt and other Islamic nations, but Mahfuz has achieved worldwide renown and in 1988 became the first Arab writer to win a Nobel Prize for literature. Iranian writers have often risked punishment by satirizing the failings of governments and business.

Turmoil in Afghanistan

Violence and extreme Islamic movements emerged in Afghanistan, fostering instability there for three decades. Afghanistan's diverse Muslim ethnic groups have little sense of national unity in this landlocked land of harsh deserts and rugged mountains. From the early 1800s until 1978, kings from the largest ethnic group, the Pashtuns, loosely governed the territory. In 1978, pro-communist generals seized power, forged close ties with the Soviet Union, and introduced radical social and economic reforms that challenged Islamic traditions. They implemented land reform, promoted women's education, and replaced

> "Afghanistan's diverse Muslim ethnic groups have little sense of national unity in this landlocked land of harsh deserts and rugged mountains."

Islamic law with a secular family law giving women more rights.

When conservative Islamic rebels, known as mujahidin ("holy warriors"), rebelled against the pro-Soviet regime, the Soviet Union invaded in 1979, launching decades of turbulence. The mujahidin, while poorly armed and divided, won small victories against the 150,000 Soviet troops. Both sides resorted to ruthless brutality; indiscriminate Soviet air attacks on the rebels created 5 million refugees and turned the population against the Soviet occupation. The United States, Pakistan, and Arab nations sent military and financial aid to the rebels, including the wealthy Saudi Osama bin Laden (b. 1957), a trained engineer turned Islamic militant. By the mid-1980s, Afghanistan had become an unwinnable quagmire for the Soviet forces, which withdrew in 1989. The pro-Soviet government collapsed, and rival mujahidin groups fought for control. With the USSR gone and the civil war over, the West offered little help to reconstruct the ruined country.

Afghanistan soon returned to global attention. As conflict between rival militias continued, a group of

Arab Art The large monument of Revolution, in Baghdad, sculpted by a major modern Iraqi artist, Jawad Salim (1920–1961), occupies a central place in the city. Commissioned in 1958 after the overthrow of the monarchy, it celebrates the Iraqi struggle for justice and freedom and often provided a motif for Iraqi poets.

Pashtun religious students known as the Taliban ("students") organized a military force to impose order and stamp out what they considered immoral behavior, such as rape and drinking, among the tribal factions fighting for control of the post-Soviet government. The Taliban conquered much of the Pashtun south and then seized the capital, Kabul, in 1996. Eventually they extended their influence north, where ethnic factions continued to resist them. The puritanical Taliban reversed the modernization of the pro-Soviet regime and introduced an especially harsh form of Islamic rule. Women in the capital, Kabul, who once wore jeans and T-shirts and attended universities, were now required to wear long black robes and stay at home. Education for women was banned, and alcohol disappeared from stores. Reflecting their intolerance and disdain for Afghanistan's pre-Islamic past, the Taliban also destroyed spectacular monumental Buddhas carved into a mountainside over a millennium ago, outraging the world.

International terrorist groups with a jihadist agenda began to form around Arab volunteers who had come originally to fight for the mujahidin cause. The Saudi Osama bin Laden became the leader and chief financial backer of the largest international terrorist group, Al Qaeda. Bin Laden called on Muslims to take up arms against the United States and other Western regimes, whom he called "crusaders" after the Christians who invaded the Middle East during the Intermediate Era: "Tell the Muslims everywhere that the vanguards of the warriors who are fighting the enemies of Islam belong to them."[3] In the late 1990s, these Islamic terrorist groups made Taliban-controlled Afghanistan their base, building camps to train more terrorists.

Islamic Militancy, Terrorism, and Western Interventions

The rise of international terrorism linked to Islamist groups and chiefly targeting Americans and Europeans soon resulted in a renewal of superpower intervention. After the Al Qaeda attacks on the United States in September 2001, the United States, with widespread world support, sent military forces into Taliban-ruled Afghanistan. Soon the United States and its allies had displaced the Taliban, destroyed the Al Qaeda bases, and installed a fragile pro-Western government. Many Afghans and most Muslims out-

side of Afghanistan applauded the demise of the Taliban, but instability ensued: tribal warlords controlled large territories; the major Taliban and Al Qaeda leaders, including bin Laden, evaded the U.S. troops and went into hiding; and the United States and western Europe struggled to support the fledgling democracy. By 2005, a Taliban-led insurgency was growing in strength.

The Afghan war was followed by a larger conflict in Iraq. Charging that Iraq's dictator, Saddam Hussein, had weapons of mass destruction and was linked to Al Qaeda, the U.S. president George W. Bush, supported chiefly by Britain, ordered an invasion and occupation of Iraq in 2003 without support from the United Nations, many Western allies, and regional allies such as Turkey and Egypt. Massive looting followed the quick U.S. victory, as museums, ancient historical sites, power plants, armories, and communications networks were plundered. U.S. credibility suffered after the Americans found no nuclear, biological, or chemical weapons or any Saddam–Al Qaeda links. Nor had the Americans adequately planned for the problems of the postwar reconstruction. U.S. forces struggled to contain factional divisions and restore basic services, such as electricity and clean water, to Saddam-era levels. They also struggled to maintain order against a persistent resistance movement, and to defend against terrifying suicide bombings by newly arrived foreign jihadis linked to Al Qaeda. Many Iraqis, especially Shi'ites and Kurds, had hated Saddam's bloody regime and welcomed his demise, but Iraqis also often resented yet another Western occupation. While Arab liberals often hoped democracy would flower in Iraq and throughout the region, the occupation of an oil-rich Arab country, at a high cost in U.S. and Iraqi casualties, tied down the U.S. military and intensified anti-U.S. feeling around the world.

The Middle East in the Global System

The Middle East has been subject to explosive internal forces as well as changes in the global system. By the late twentieth century, observers argued that much of the Middle East had adjusted poorly to a rapidly changing world, lagging behind much of Asia and Latin America in development. In 2002, various Arab thinkers issued an Arab Human Development Report that outlined the economic and social failures of the Arab world, including the marginalization of women and the limited development in health and education (see Witness to the Past: Assessing Arab Development). Debate is also fostered by regional

Assessing Arab Development

Under the auspices of the United Nations Development Programme, a group of Arab scholars and opinion makers from the twenty-two member states of the Arab League, a regional organization, met to consider the Arab condition. In 2002, they issued the first of four planned reports that offered both a description of the Arab condition and a prescription for change. Hailed by Arab and non-Arab observers as a path-breaking effort by Arabs to foster a debate on the inadequacies of Arab development and local barriers to progress, the first document reported great strides in many areas but also unsolved problems. This excerpt is from the Executive Summary.

The Arab Human Development Report 2002 . . . places people squarely at the [center] of development in all its dimensions: economic, social, civil, political, and cultural. It provides a neutral forum to measure progress and deficits, propose strategies to policymakers, and draw attention to country problems that can benefit from regional solutions. It is guided by the conviction that solid analysis can contribute to the many efforts underway to mobilize the region's rich human potential. There has been considerable progress in laying the foundations for health, habitat, and education. Two notable achievements are the enormous quantitative expansion in educating the young and a conspicuous improvement in fighting death. For example, life expectancy has increased by 15 years over the last three decades, and infant mortality rates have dropped by two-thirds. Moreover, the region's growth has been "pro-poor": there is much less dire poverty (defined as an income of less than a dollar a day) than in any other developing region.

But there have been warning signs as well. Over the past twenty years, growth in per capita income was the lowest in the world except in sub-Saharan Africa. . . . If such trends continue [into] the future, it will take the average Arab citizen 140 years to double his or her income. . . . The decline in productivity has been accompanied by deterioration in real wages, which has accentuated poverty. It is evident that . . . Arab countries have not developed as quickly or as fully as other comparable regions. . . . The Arab region is richer than it is developed, . . . hobbled by a . . . poverty of capabilities and . . . opportunities. These have their roots in three deficits: freedom, women's empowerment, and knowledge. Growth alone will neither bridge these gaps nor set the region on the road to sustainable development.

The way forward involves tackling human capabilities and knowledge. It also involves promoting systems of good governance, those that promote, support and sustain human well-being, based on expanding human capabilities, choices, opportunities and freedoms, . . . especially for the poorest and most marginalized members of society. The empowerment of women must be addressed throughout. . . .

[The Report concludes that] People in most Arab countries live longer than the world average life expectancy of 67. However, disease and disability reduce life expectancy by between five and 11 years. Arab women have lower life expectancy than the world average. . . . Arab countries have made tangible progress in improving literacy: . . . female literacy rates tripled since 1970. Yet 65 million adults are illiterate, almost two-thirds of them women. . . . One out of every five Arabs lives on less than $2 per day . . . Arab countries had the lowest freedom score [in the world] in the late 1990s. . . . [Utilization] of Arab women's capabilities through political and economic participation remains the lowest in the world. . . . Serious knowledge deficits include weak systems of scientific research and development.

The Arab world is at a crossroads. The fundamental choice is whether its trajectory will remain marked by inertia, as reflected in much of the present institutional context, and by ineffective policies that have produced the substantial development challenges facing the region; or whether prospects for an Arab renaissance, anchored in human development will be actively pursued.

Thinking About the Reading

1. How have Arabs done in promoting freedom, women's empowerment, and knowledge?
2. What does the report consider the major improvements and the major failures and challenges of the Arab nations?

Source: Arab Human Development Report 2002: Creating Opportunities for Future Generations (UNDP, 2002), available online at http://www.rbas.undp.org/ahdr/press_kits2002/PRExec Summary.pdf. Reprinted with permission of the United Nations Development Programme (UNDP).

cable networks, such as Qatar-based Al Jazeera, as well as websites and blogs that spread awareness of political and social developments.

The region's economic record has been checkered. By 2005, the Middle East had the world's highest unemployment rate, 13.2 percent and, except for sub-Saharan Africa, the slowest economic growth and lowest productivity. Only Turkey has fostered much industrialization and high economic growth rates. Nations with oil, such as Algeria, Iran, and Libya, have remained dangerously dependent on oil revenues, and oil wealth has often led to political corruption. But some small Persian Gulf states like Dubai (doo-BUY) have used their oil wealth to become centers of global commerce. The growing need of industrializing nations such as China and India for oil ensures that the profits will flow to oil-rich nations for years to come. However, Middle Eastern nations that are without oil have struggled to build modern economies with limited resources.

Middle Easterners increasingly have hoped to preserve revered traditional patterns while finding ways to harmonize them with the realities of the modern world. The recent history of the Middle East, like that of India and sub-Saharan Africa, has challenged the widespread notion that contact with the modern world automatically erodes all traditional cultures and steers people inevitably toward Western models. Older patterns of life and thought, including Islam, have persisted in much of the region, and Islamic militancy has tapped a strand of unease with Western ideas. Many Muslims reject what they see as the materialistic, hedonistic values of Western culture. Iranians and Arabs have often agreed with the Indian Muslim poet Muhammad Iqbal (ik-BALL) (1873–1938), who wrote in 1927: "Against Europe I protest, And the attraction of the West: Woe for Europe and her charm, Swift to capture and disarm! Earth awaits rebuilding; rise! Out of slumber deep, Arise!"[4] Other Muslims, however, are wary of Islamic militancy, which has not delivered a better material life in the main country controlled by Islamists, Iran. Middle Eastern reformists such as the Iranian Reza Aslan have sought greater economic development, political freedom, and rights for women. Aslan criticized what he termed the "false idols" of bigotry and fanaticism and argued for a return to Islam's egalitarian roots.

> 66 Middle Easterners increasingly have hoped to preserve revered traditional patterns while finding ways to harmonize them with the realities of the modern world. 99

Interventions by outside powers, such as the United States, reflect the global importance of the Middle East, especially its oil wealth and strategic location among key waterways of world trade. Until cost-effective alternative power sources become common, all industrial economies need access to oil. While U.S. leaders hope democracy will spread, many experts worry that instability in Iraq might unsettle the entire region. Furthermore, few problems, including the Arab–Israel conflict, seem resolvable anytime soon. These challenges make the Middle East a focus of world attention and, some fear, a potential tinderbox.

LO³ Political Change in Sub-Saharan Africa

As in the Middle East, the rise of nationalism and the consequent wave of decolonization in Africa reduced Western political influence, reshaping societies and politics. Between 1957 and 1975, the colonial era ended in sub-Saharan Africa as countries became politically independent. In the early 1960s, as optimistic Africans celebrated their freedom and formed governments, the times were electric with change, and hopes for a better future were high. But with the end of colonial domination, institutions had to be built anew. The years since 1960 have been, in many respects, the most momentous in all of Africa's history. Africans still struggle to find the right mix of policies to resolve their problems.

Nationalism and Decolonization

Rising nationalism sparked decolonization. Between the late nineteenth century and the 1950s, the European colonial powers often maintained control through divide and rule of the different ethnic groups. For example, each of the major Nigerian ethnic groups—the Hausa, Yoruba, and Igbo (Ibo)—had little in common with each other and formed their own nationalist organizations, challenging those Nigerians who sought a united front. Independence sometimes came peacefully after negotiations between nationalist leaders and European rulers, but sometimes only after bitter struggles and violence.

The increasing problems posed for Western colonizers often encouraged them to transfer power peacefully. World War II had undermined Western credibility in the European colonies: many Africans felt revulsion against the Western powers and their pretensions of superiority. The British and French claimed to be fighting for freedom and democracy, but Africans noticed that these values seldom applied in the colonies. With Western vulnerability obvious, nationalist leaders negotiated for reforms in the 1940s. After the war, the British introduced local government in some African colonies, yet most colonial governments did little to prepare their societies for true independence.

> "Between the late nineteenth century and the 1950s, the European colonial powers often maintained control through divide and rule of the different ethnic groups."

pan-Africanism
The dream, originating in the early twentieth century, that all Africans would cooperate to eventually form some sort of united states of the continent.

Nkrumah's Pan-African Dream

The first change came in the British Gold Coast. In 1948, small farmers boycotted European businesses that were suspected of profiteering at their expense. The growing tensions led to riots in the towns. A rising leader in the Gold Coast, Kwame Nkrumah (KWAH-mee nn-KROO-muh) (1909–1972), who had been educated in the West, became convinced that only socialism could save Africa. In 1949, Nkrumah organized a political party, the first real mass organization in Africa, but he was soon arrested by the British, who viewed him as dangerous. Because of the continued unrest, however, the British allowed an election in 1951 for a legislative council, and Nkrumah's party won a huge majority. After negotiations, in 1957 the Gold Coast became independent and was renamed Ghana, after the first great West African kingdom over a millennium earlier. Nkrumah became the nation's first prime minister and the hero of Africa, preaching pan-Africanism, the dream that all Africans would cooperate to eventually form a united continent.

The anticolonial dam had now burst. By 1963, all of the British colonies in West Africa had become independent, largely through a combination of peaceful negotiations and strikes by workers. By contrast, the French at first failed to recognize change: they fought brutal but unsuccessful wars in the 1950s to keep Vietnam and Algeria from leaving the colonial fold. But France eventually gave its colonies the option of voting for a complete break or for autonomy within a French community of closely connected nations. Initially, only the West African colony of Guinea opted to expel the French completely, prompting the French to withdraw all economic aid. Later the French colonies became independent, though they usually maintained close ties to France.

 Comments on Algeria, April 11, 1961 Read excerpts of a press conference held by Charles de Gaulle, in which he declares France's willingness to accept Algerian independence.

CHRONOLOGY

Sub-Saharan Africa, 1945–Present

1948	Introduction of apartheid in South Africa
1949	First mass-based political party in Gold Coast
1952–1960	Mau Mau uprising in Kenya
1957	Independence for Ghana
1957–1975	African decolonization
1967	Assassination of Patrice Lumumba in Congo
1965–1980	White government in Southern Rhodesia
1967–1970	Nigerian Civil War
1975	Independence for Portuguese colonies
1991–1994	Civil war in Somalia
1994	Genocide in Rwanda
1994	Nelson Mandela first black president of South Africa
1998	End of Mobuto era in Congo

Mau Mau During the 1950s, Africans in Kenya, especially the Gikuyu, rebelled against British colonial rule. The British responded by detaining some 90,000 suspected rebels and sympathizers in concentration camps such as this, where many died.

Mau Mau Rebellion
An eight-year uprising in the 1950s by the Gikuyu people in Kenya against British rule.

Violence in Kenya and the Congo

Whereas peaceful power transfers worked in some colonies, widespread violence preceded or accompanied independence in others. For example, many British settlers had migrated to Kenya after both World War I and World War II, taking land from the Africans to establish farms. In 1952, many Gikuyu, Kenya's largest ethnic group, which had suffered the most land losses, began an eight-year uprising against British rule, known as the Mau Mau Rebellion. The British sent thousands of troops to Kenya and committed atrocities against pro–Mau Mau villages, ultimately killing 10,000 Gikuyu and detaining 90,000 others in harsh prison camps. Finally, the British released the nationalist leader, Jomo Kenyatta (ken-YAH-tuh) (ca. 1889–1978), a former herd boy who had studied anthropology in Britain. Negotiations resulted in Kenyan independence in 1963, and Kenyatta became the first freely elected prime minister. Britain also granted independence to Uganda and Tanzania. In Kenya, white settlers who had strongly opposed political rights for the African majority often remained, sometimes serving in the Kenyan government.

Violence also engulfed the Belgian Congo, a vast, natural resource–rich territory containing some two hundred ethnic groups that had been brutally subjugated during the colonial era. At independence, the Congo had only a few university graduates. The only Congolese leader with any national following, the widely admired and left-leaning visionary Patrice Lumumba (loo-MOOM-buh) (1925–1961), opposed the economic domination of Belgian business and mining interests. In 1959, riots broke out in Congolese cities, forcing the Belgians to announce the colony's first free elections, which were won by Lumumba's party. As the Lumumba took power, some Congolese troops mutinied and attacked whites.

Taking advantage of the chaos, Belgian-supported leaders in the mineral-rich Katanga region who opposed Lumumba announced their secession from the country. The United Nations sent in a peacekeeping force that restored order in the Congo. But Katanga leaders, with the complicity of Belgium and the United States, who feared that Lumumba favored the Soviet Union, abducted and murdered him in 1961. Both Belgium and the United States supported the Congo's new leader, General Joseph Mobuto (mo-BOO-to), who became a brutal and oppressive dictator. In 1971, Mobuto, who had given his country a new name, Zaire, also changed his name to Mobuto Sese Seko, "Mobuto the All Powerful."

Angola, Guinea-Bissau, and Mozambique

Portugal, ruled by a fascist dictator, had been reluctant to give up its African colonial empire. Revolts had broken out in its three colonies—Angola, Guinea-Bissau, and Mozambique—in the early 1960s, but the Portuguese launched military campaigns to crush them. Angola's liberation movement was divided into three rival factions based on the country's major ethnic groupings. Marxists led the major liberation movements in Mozambique and Guinea Bissau. The visionary leader of the Guinea-Bissau movement, Amilcar Cabral (AH-mill-CAR kah-BRAHL) (1924–1973), emphasized educating the people to empower them; he was assassinated by Portuguese agents in 1973. In 1974, however, Portugal's war-weary army ended the dictatorship in Portugal. The new democratic, socialist-led government granted the colonies their independence in 1975, but violence, insurgencies, and disorder reigned for years.

Zambia, Malawi, and Zimbabwe

The British colonies of the Rhodesias and Nyasaland in southern Africa, all containing white settlers who bitterly resisted efforts at equality for Africans, were among the last African colonies to gain independence under black majority rule. As African nationalists launched largely nonviolent resistance

> "Whereas peaceful power transfers worked in some colonies, widespread violence preceded or accompanied independence in others."

> 66 New African nations typically experienced political and economic challenges that fostered instability: coups, prolonged civil wars, and recurring famines. 99

campaigns in the colonies, the British granted independence to Zambia (Northern Rhodesia) and Malawi (formerly Nyasaland) in 1963. But the large white settler population in Southern Rhodesia declared independence from Britain in 1965 and installed a racist government that imposed stricter segregation. Africans in Southern Rhodesia took up arms against the white settler government in two rival Marxist-led liberation movements. By 1980, African resistance was so strong that the United States and Britain pressured the white government to allow elections, which were won by Robert Mugabe (moo-GAH-bee) (b. 1924), a former political prisoner who had transformed his guerrilla movement into a party. The country became independent as Zimbabwe.

Political Change and Conflict

A West African scholar called *nation* "a magical word meant to exorcise ethnic quarrels and antagonisms— and as such very precious,"[5] but, as he conceded, the magic usually failed to overcome disunity. New African nations typically experienced political and economic challenges that fostered instability: coups, prolonged civil wars, and recurring famines (see Map 30.3). Several million refugees fled violence, repression, and hunger, while corruption and ethnic divisions made dictatorship more common than democracy. During the 1990s, various countries crumbled into brutal anarchy.

 Interactive Map

Although new African nations typically started as parliamentary democracies, only a few sustained democratic systems. Militaries have often been the only groups that can govern effectively, since they have a shared ideology of leadership, good internal communications, and a tradition of discipline. However, military officers have also ruled with a heavy hand and often looted treasuries. Civilian leaders have often favored one-party states because, they

Map 30.3

Contemporary Africa and the Middle East

Sub-Saharan and North Africa contain more than forty nations. Six sub-Saharan African nations and Algeria in North Africa experienced anticolonial revolutions, and a dozen sub-Saharan nations have been racked by civil wars since independence.

© Cengage Learning

argue, such parties incorporate all ethnic groups. While some of these one-party states, such as in the Congo (Zaire), have been despotisms, others have been relatively democratic. Some nations, such as Nigeria and Ghana, shifted back and forth between authoritarian military dictatorships and ineffective,

corrupt civilian governments. Western-style democracy has had little chance to flower in these artificial, multiethnic countries that typically have a tiny middle class and numerous poor people. And, given the deteriorating economic conditions of the past thirty years, governments have had little money for public investment. Furthermore, many nationalist leaders have lost their credibility after a few years, such as Ghana's Kwame Nkrumah, once Africa's greatest hero, who was overthrown for mismanagement and died in exile.

Africa's Leaders: Visionaries, Pragmatists, and Tyrants

African leaders have been a mixed lot. Some have been highly respected, farsighted visionaries, such as Tanzania's Julius Nyerere (NEE-ya-RARE-y) (g. 1962–1985) and Mozambique's Samora Machel (g. 1975–1986), and pragmatic problem solvers, such as South Africa's first black president, Nelson Mandela. Although not all of their initiatives have succeeded, they have used political office largely to improve society rather than enrich themselves. Others have disappointed or brutalized their people. Some, such as the Congo (Zaire) dictator Mobuto (g. 1965–1997) and the Nigerian military dictator Sani Abacha (g. 1993–1998), have been ruthless crooks, arresting or murdering opponents and plundering public treasuries. During the 1970s in Uganda, then ruled by Idi Amin (EE-dee AH-meen) (1925–2004), a poorly educated general, some 300,000 people suspected of opposing Amin were killed, and thousands more were jailed or fled into exile. Even when their credibility has ended, many leaders have rigged elections or had compliant parliaments declare them presidents for life.

Read about Nelson and Winnie Mandela, the courageous South African freedom fighters and leaders in the struggle against apartheid.

Political instability, conflict, and social unrest have grown as people have struggled for their share of the dwindling pie. The blatant corruption, conspicuous consumption, and smuggling in government and the business sector have increased inequalities and deepened public frustrations. Sub-Saharan Africa has the world's highest rate of income inequality. East Africans chastise the wabenzi ("people who drive a Mercedes Benz"), a privileged urban class of politicians, high bureaucrats, professionals, military officers, and businessmen who manipulate their connections to amass wealth. Political, military, and business elites have often squandered scarce resources on imported luxuries.

On the other hand, in some societies relations, between governments and the governed have improved. New grassroots and other nongovernmental organizations have worked for issues such as human rights and the environment. Ordinary people, especially women, have demanded and sometimes gained greater responsibility for improving their lives. For example, by 2000, some 25,000 local women's groups in Kenya had pushed for improved rights and other issues of interest to women, such as environmental protection. Because few Africans can afford health insurance, in countries such as Senegal, poor people have come together to form small mutual health organizations. Strong support from women voters helped Liberian economist Ellen Johnson-Sirleaf (b. 1939), a Harvard-trained banker and former United Nations official, become the first woman president in Africa in 2005, as Liberia sought to recover from a long civil war and then a corrupt dictatorship.

wabenzi
("people who drive a Mercedes Benz") A privileged urban class in Africa since the mid-twentieth century of politicians, high bureaucrats, professionals, military officers, and businessmen who manipulate their connections to amass wealth.

Endemic Problems

The combination of artificial boundaries, weak national identity, and economic collapse has produced chronic turmoil in several African nations, resulting in what one discouraged African observer called the dark night of bloodshed and death. For example, Liberia and Sierra Leone, once among the more stable countries, disintegrated in the 1990s as ethnic-based rebel groups challenged their country's government for power. In drought-plagued Somalia, when longtime military rule collapsed in 1991, the country divided into regions ruled by feuding, armed Somali clans. As the Somali economy disintegrated, causing thousands to starve to death, the United Nations dispatched a humanitarian mission. But some Americans in the United Nations force were killed, and the United Nations withdrew in 1994, unable to achieve a unified government. While the fighting lessened, Somalia remained a country in name only, controlled by warlords.

Sometimes hatreds have led to genocide, killing directed at eliminating a particular group. This happened in the small, impoverished, and densely populated state of Rwanda, most of whose population belonged to the majority Hutu and minority Tutsi ethnic groups. The German and then the Belgian colonizers had ruled through Tutsi kings. Soon after independence, the Hutu rebelled against the Tutsi-dominated government, slaughtering thousands of Tutsi and forcing others out of the country. In 1994, the extremist Hutu government in Rwanda began a genocide against the remaining Tutsi and moderate

Hutus, murdering more than 500,000 people. Tutsi exiles based in Uganda then invaded Rwanda, forcing the Hutu leadership and its followers into the neighboring Congo. More than 2 million Hutu fled. The new Tutsi-led government continued to face militant Hutu resistance groups based in the Congo, leading to Rwandan military incursions into the Congo.

Nigeria: Hopes and Frustrations

The hopes and frustrations of contemporary Africa are mirrored in Nigeria, which in 2005 was home to some 130 million people, about one-fifth of Africa's total population. Like many African countries, Nigeria contains an extraordinary variety of ethnic groups, languages, religions, and even ecologies. While some 250 ethnic groups live in Nigeria, about two-thirds of the people belong to the Hausa-Fulani, Igbo (Ibo), or Yoruba groups. Nigeria's oil wealth has brought income—80 percent of the nation's total revenues—but has also corrupted politics and increased social inequality.

Nigeria's history has frequently been punctuated by coups, countercoups, riots, political assassinations, and civil war rooted in regional and ethnic rivalries. Between 1967 and 1970, Nigeria endured a bloody civil war to prevent the secession of the Igbo-dominated and oil-rich southeast region. The religious divide between Christians, who dominate the south, and Muslims, who control the north, has also complicated politics. Following a Muslim revival among the Hausa-Fulani, northern states have often imposed strict Islamic law, antagonizing non-Muslims.

The Nigerian oil industry, while creating some prosperity, has also made Nigeria dependent on oil exports and spawned political and economic problems. A few politicians, bureaucrats, and businessmen have monopolized oil profits, fostering corruption, sometimes outright plunder of public wealth, and inequitable wealth distribution. By 2005, the top 20 percent of Nigerians received 56 percent of all the country's wealth, while the bottom 20 percent got only 4.4 percent. Sporadic protests, including sabotage of the oil pipelines, have been met with military force; protest leaders are accused of treason and sometimes executed. Disenchanted Nigerians refer to a "republic of the privileged and rich" and a "mon-

eytocracy." Oil money created high expectations in the 1970s, but the economic boom turned to bust in the 1980s when world oil prices collapsed, increasing economic hardship and social unrest and forcing the nation to take on massive foreign debt to pay its bills. Meanwhile, the debate about whether Nigeria should seek to adopt Western models or attempt to retain its own indigenous traditions has never abated.

The New South Africa

Another large country, South Africa, experienced conflict and inequality for more than three centuries. From World War II to the early 1990s, South Africa remained the last bastion of institutionalized white racism on the continent. The white population, some 15 percent of the total and divided between an Afrikaner majority (descendants of Dutch settlers) and an English minority, ruled the black majority (74 percent) and the Indians (2 percent) and mixed-descent Coloreds (9 percent). Aided by a ruthless police security system, the result was nearly unparalleled cruelty, a chilling juxtaposition of comfort for whites and despair for blacks.

Apartheid: Entrenched White Supremacy

South African white supremacy, in place for several centuries, became more systematic after 1948, when Afrikaner nationalists won the white-only elections and declared full independence from Britain. A top nationalist leader claimed: "We [whites] need [Africans] because they work for us but they can never claim political rights. Not now, nor in the future."[6] Their new policy, apartheid (uh-PAHRT-ate) ("separate development"), set up a police state to enforce racial separation and passed strict segregationist laws that reached into all aspects of peoples' lives. While white families usually lived comfortably in well-furnished apartments or houses, a typical house in Soweto, a dusty African suburb of Johannesburg, was bleak, with the residents using candles or gas lamps for lighting. Only one-quarter of the Soweto houses had running water and perhaps fifteen in one hundred enjoyed electricity.

Apartheid also created what white leaders called tribal homelands, known as bantustans, rural reservations where black Africans were required to live if they were not needed in the modern economy. The system allocated whites 87 percent of the nation's land and nonwhites the other 13 percent. Every year, thousands of Africans were forcibly resettled to the impoverished bantustans, which contained little fertile land and few jobs and services. Infant mortality rates in the bantustans were among the world's highest. Under this system, black families were fractured as men and women were recruited on annual contracts for jobs outside the bantustans.

Natural Resources and Economic Disparity

Rich in strategic minerals such as gold, diamonds, uranium, platinum, and chrome, South Africa became the most industrialized nation on the continent, but the wealth was monopolized by the white minority. By 1994, the ratio of average black to white incomes stood at 1 to 10, the most inequitable income distribution in the world. African unemployment reached 33 percent. Nonetheless, because of the country's mineral wealth and extensive foreign investment, the South African government enjoyed the support of several powerful industrialized countries, including the United States, Britain, and Japan, who feared that unrest or black majority rule might threaten their billions in investments and access to lucrative resources.

Resistance and Emergence of the African National Congress

Despite the repression, Africans resisted and often paid a price for their defiance. South African leaders forged the world's leading police state, with the world's highest rate of execution and brutal treatment of dissidents. Among the victims was Stephen Biko (1946–1977), a former medical student and resistance leader who was beaten to death in police custody. Hundreds of Africans were arrested each day for "pass law" violations and held for days or weeks before being released. Death squads of off-duty policemen sometimes assassinated black leaders, such as Victoria Mxenge (ma-SEN-gee), a lawyer who defended anti-apartheid activists. Defying the government, strikes, work interruptions, and sabotage became common.

The African National Congress (ANC), long a voice for nonviolent resistance, emerged as the major opposition organization. The ANC remained multiracial, with some whites, Coloreds, and Indians serving in its leadership. In 1955, despairing of peaceful protest, a more militant ANC leadership had framed its inclusive vision in the Freedom Charter: "South Africa belongs to all who live in it, black and white."[7] But the ANC was declared illegal, and government repression forced it underground, where it adopted a policy of violent resistance and trained young South Africans in exile how to use weapons. Several of its main leaders, including Nelson Mandela (man-DEL-uh) (b. 1918), spent as many as thirty years in prison for their political activities.

Women played an influential role in the ANC, often, like the men, facing arrest and mistreatment.

Mandela's Victory

Ultimately, moderation and realism in both the ANC and the ruling National Party brought a more just and democratic society. International isolation, economic troubles, the increasing incompatibility between apartheid's restrictions and a need for more highly skilled black workers, and growing black unrest forced the government to relax apartheid and release Mandela from prison. The two parties agreed on a new constitution requiring "one man, one vote." In 1994, white supremacy came to a stunning end in the first all-race elections in South African history, which installed Mandela as president and gave the ANC two-thirds of the seats in Parliament.

The ANC government enjoyed massive goodwill but has also faced daunting challenges in healing a deeply fragmented society while restoring the pride and spirits of African communities destabilized by apartheid. Mandela worked to find the right mix of racial reconciliation and major changes to benefit the disadvantaged black majority. In 1999, Mandela left office, a still-popular figure, and the ANC retained power in free elections. It improved services in black communities, raised black living standards, and created opportunities for Africans, fostering a growing black upper and middle class. Yet challenges linger: crime has rapidly increased, violent protests have broken out, and black unemployment has remained high. South Africa has one of the world's highest rates of HIV/AIDS, with some 5 million South Africans infected. Nonetheless, South Africa has become the model of progress for sub-Saharan Africa, and people everywhere hope that the nation succeeds in healing racial wounds while spreading the benefits of its wealth to all citizens.

LO⁴ Changing African Economies, Societies, and Cultures

In the decades since the 1960s, for many sub-Saharan African nations, achieving economic development and true independence has seemed a desperate struggle. African nations have tried various strategies to generate development to benefit the majority of people, but no strategy has proved effective over the long term. Economic problems have proliferated, but Africans have created new social and cultural forms as they reckon with their political and economic problems.

Economic Change and Under-development

Modern Africa has experienced severe economic problems. Africans have mostly supplied agricultural and mineral resources, such as cocoa and copper, to the global economy, but this has not brought widespread wealth. Only a few countries have enjoyed consistently robust economic growth or substantially raised living standards. Sub-Saharan Africa contained nineteen of the world's twenty poorest countries in 2004. With more than 670 million people (almost 13 percent of the world population) by 2004, this region accounts for only 1 percent of the world's production of goods and services, about the same as one of the smallest European nations, Belgium, with 10 million people. Half of the people live in poverty, earning less than $1 per day, the highest poverty rate in the world. Sub-Saharan Africa has also had the world's highest infant mortality rates and lowest average life expectancies.

Prospects: More People . . . Less Food

The economic doldrums have been linked to other problems. The region's economies have generally grown by 1 to 2 percent per year, but its population increase is the world's highest, more than 3 percent. Since 10 to 15 percent of babies die before their first birthday, parents have had an incentive to bear many children. At current rates, the population will double to 1.3 billion by 2025, but new jobs, classrooms, and food supplies will not keep pace. Only a few nations have enjoyed self-sufficiency in food production; most require food imports from Europe and North America. Women grow the bulk of the food, but the male farmers growing cash crops for export receive most of the government aid. Millions of Africans, perhaps one-third of them children, are chronically malnourished, and as a result often have permanent brain damage. Several million children die each year from hunger-related ailments. Severe drought and the drying up of water sources is a chronic problem in many regions, while less than half of school-age children attend school. Some 25 million girls receive no elementary education.

> "Africans have mostly supplied agricultural and mineral resources, such as cocoa and copper, to the global economy, but this has not brought widespread wealth."

Neo-Colonial Capitalism

To achieve economic development, Africans have sought viable economic strategies. The most common development model has been termed "neocolonial capitalism," because it involved close economic ties to the Western nations and free markets of some sort. The countries following this model favored the cash crops and minerals that had dominated the colonial economy, often at the expense of food production, and welcomed western European and U.S. investment and economic advice. A few countries prospered with this strategy, at least for a time, but the political consequences were often negative. Ivory Coast (or Côte d'Ivoire) and Kenya were among the most hospitable to a Western presence, and in the 1960s and 1970s, both countries enjoyed high rates of growth and rising incomes. Ivory Coast remained a major exporter of coffee and cocoa, while Kenya, with world-famous game parks, lived from tourism and the export of coffee, tea, and minerals. By the mid-1980s, both had per capita incomes about double the African average. But both countries eventually became one-party states that, while stable, grew despotic. Well-placed leaders plundered the economies, and the environment suffered. By the late 1990s, as world prices for coffee and cocoa collapsed, the economies experienced increasing stress, protesters demanded more democracy, the delicate ecologies became dangerously unbalanced, and crime rates soared. By the early 2000s, Ivory Coast was engulfed in civil war, while Kenyans had forced out a dictator and elected a reformist government that has failed to fulfill its promises.

 **African Studies Internet Resources** (*http://www.columbia.edu/cu/lweb/indiv/africa/index.html*). Provides valuable links to relevant websites on contemporary Africa.

The most disastrous example of neocolonial capitalism was the Democratic Republic of the Congo (known as Zaire between 1971 and 1997). A huge country, with 60 million people, Congo enjoys a strategic location in the center of Africa, rich mineral resources, and good land. But it became Africa's biggest failure. Over the years, the United States and Belgium poured billions of investment and aid into the Congo to keep President Mobuto Sese Seko in power. To the

Congolese, however, Mobuto was unforgivingly corrupt, looting the treasury and foreign aid to amass a huge personal fortune—some $4 to $5 billion—while repressing his opponents. As a result, the Congo suffered one of the world's highest infant mortality rates, limited health care, and widespread malnutrition. In 1998, a long-festering rebellion gained strength, forcing Mobuto into exile, where he died. Rebels took over, but they have done little to foster democracy or development. The Congo was soon fragmented in civil war and interethnic fighting, and rebel groups controlled large sections of the sprawling country. Nearly 4 million Congolese died from the fighting and its side effect, the collapse of medical care, between 1998 and 2004, causing a humanitarian crisis.

Reason for Hope: Ghana and Botswana

The most recent showcases for economic success have been Ghana and Botswana. For several decades, after Kwame Nkrumah lost power, Ghana had experienced a roller coaster of corrupt civilian governments interspersed with military regimes. In the 1990s, the leaders gradually strengthened democracy and mixed capitalism with socialism. Ghana became increasingly prosperous: by 2000, it enjoyed one of the continent's highest annual per capita incomes, $1,600. Investment in schools resulted in one of Africa's most educated populations. Beginning as a failure like Ghana, Botswana, when it gained independence in 1966, exported nothing and was one of the world's poorest countries. Gradually, however, using ethnic traditions as a foundation, Botswanans carved out a successful democracy; the economy, health care, education, and protection of resources all steadily improved, despite deadly droughts. By 2000, Botswanans had fostered living standards higher than those of most African and many Middle Eastern, Asian, and Latin American societies, boasting an annual per capita income of more than $3,000, an economy growing by 11 percent per year, and a literacy rate of 70 percent. Unfortunately, the AIDS epidemic, which hit Botswana particularly hard, rapidly undermined economic and health gains.

African Socialisms

To foster development, some African nationalists have pursued revolutionary or reformist strategies.

> " To foster development, some African nationalists have pursued revolutionary or reformist strategies. "

They have concluded that the political and economic institutions inherited from colonialism could not spark economic development, because they transferred wealth and resources to the West. After independence, more wealth still flowed out of Africa than into it, and the disparity has increased every year. The radicals argued that, to empower Africans, it was necessary to reduce the colonial state to ashes and replace it with something entirely new.

Various social revolutionary regimes emerged from the long wars of liberation against entrenched colonial or white minority governments. Some Africans looked toward communist-ruled China or the USSR for inspiration. Marxist revolutionary governments came to power in Angola and Mozambique after the Portuguese left, but they struggled to implement socialism. To counter these governments, the white-ruled South African state sponsored opposition guerrilla movements, aided by a U.S. government wanting to overturn Marxist regimes, that kept these countries in civil war for several decades. During Angola's long civil war, more than 1.5 million people died. The war eventually ended, but Angola, which is blessed with coffee, oil, diamonds, and other minerals but plagued with corruption, still struggled to foster development. The civil war in Mozambique, one of the world's poorest nations, resulted in 1 million deaths and 5 million refugees. Since its war ended in 1992, the pragmatic Marxist leaders introduced free multiparty elections and liberalized the economy, raising the per capita income to $1,200.

One social revolutionary state, Zimbabwe, the former British colony of Southern Rhodesia, at first became Africa's biggest success story. The Marxist-influenced government, led by the liberation hero Robert Mugabe, a schoolteacher turned lawyer, proved pragmatic for more than a decade, respecting democratic processes and human rights, encouraging the white minority to stay, and trying to raise living standards and opportunities for black Zimbabweans. The country became one of the few food-exporting nations on the continent. Zimbabwe eventually faced severe problems, however, including tensions between rival African ethnic groups. Continuing white ownership of the best farmland produced resentment among land-hungry blacks.

During the 1990s, Mugabe, succumbing to the allure of power and wealth, became more dictatorial and used land disputes to divide the nation. As his support among both whites and Africans waned, he rigged elections, harassed or jailed his opponents, and ordered the seizure of white-owned farms. By 2005, commercial agriculture had collapsed, the country was gripped by drought, life expectancy had dropped sharply, and Mugabe's police had demolished the homes and shops of poor blacks who favored the opposition. The nation, once one of Africa's most promising, veered toward catastrophe.

> "Exciting new musical genres have emerged as musicians have sought to make sense of their changing social identities, world-views, and lives."

Cities, Families, and Gender Relations

Modern Africa has seen rapid social change. Since the 1940s, more people have lived in cosmopolitan cities where traditional and modern attitudes meet, mix, and clash. Cities have grown rapidly: between 1965 and 2000, the percentage of sub-Saharan Africans living in urban areas doubled, from 14 to 30 percent, but people concentrate in one or two key cities for each country. Hence, Abidjan in Ivory Coast and Luanda in Angola each contain one-quarter of their country's population. With their modern office towers, theaters, and shopping centers, cities have become the centers for political and economic power as well as for cultural creativity and social change. In fact, cities have grown so fast that services such as buses, water, power, police, schools, and health centers cannot meet the needs of their populations. Such growth is exemplified by Nigeria's largest city, Lagos, which grew from less than 1 million in 1965 to a chaotic megalopolis of some 10 million by 2000.

The family, while remaining the primary social unit, has also changed. The extended family of the villages declined in the cities and was often replaced by the smaller nuclear family. Individualism increasingly challenged village communalism, where marriages were largely arranged by elders; in the cities, young people often arrange their own marriages. Traditionally, village men had an economic incentive to take more than one wife, since women did most of the routine farm work, but with no farming option, urban women have lost economic status, and men no longer need several wives. Men enjoy more educational opportunities than women and hence dominate the job market. Sometimes governments erected barriers against women in the economy: President Mobuto in the Congo stressed an authoritarian male model and discouraged women from seeking paid work, and in the 1980s, Nigeria's military regime blamed market women for high prices, raiding their stalls and beating them.

Nonetheless, gender roles have changed as women have become more independent, and a growing number served in governments and parliaments. Indeed, sub-Saharan Africa ranks ahead of the rest of the developing world in the percentage of women (16 percent) in legislative positions. For example, the Kenyan Grace Ogot (OH-got) (b. 1930) served in parliament while writing short stories in which her heroines confronted traditional values and change. Women have formed groups to work for society's improvement. For instance, the Nigerian Eka Esu-Williams (b. 1950), the daughter of a midwife, earned a Ph.D. in Immunology and pursued an academic career before forming Women Against AIDS in Africa in 1988. Women are usually left with self-employment in low-wage activity, such as the small-scale trade of hawking goods and keeping stalls in city markets, a female profession for centuries; domestic work as maids, cooks, or nannies; or hairdressing.

African Culture and Religious Change

Africans have reconstructed their cultures in creative ways. In the popular arts, especially music and literature, imported ideas are combined with African culture. Urbanization, the growth of mass media, and the mixing of ethnic groups and outside influences have all created a fertile ground for mixed popular music styles that have reflected social, economic, and political realities. Exciting new musical genres have emerged as musicians have sought to make sense of their changing social identities, world-views, and lives. Miriam Makeba (muh-KAY-ba) (b. 1932), the South African jazz and pop singer who was forced by the apartheid government to spend decades in exile, explained, "I live to sing about what I see and know. I don't sing politics, I sing truth."[8] The rise of varied African-based popular music styles has helped Africans adjust to change while affirming their spirit in the face of external influences and internal failures. For instance, the *juju* music of the Nigerian Yoruba reflects Yoruba traditions and values while mixing local and Western instruments, such as electric guitars.

Songs as a Weapon Against Injustice

African popular musicians reach an international audience, performing and selling recordings around the world. Perhaps the greatest African superstar, the Senegalese Youssou N'Dour (YOO-soo en-DOOR) (b. 1959), collaborates with leading Western musicians but remains true to his roots, living in Dakar and following his tolerant Sufi Muslim faith. Some musicians are highly political. The Nigerian Fela Kuti (1938–1997), whose music mixed jazz, soul, rock, and Yoruba traditions, used his songs as a weapon to attack the Nigerian government and its Western sponsors, and faced frequent arrest and beatings for his protests. Like Bob Marley, Fela gained worldwide fame for his use of music to attack injustice and influence politics.

African Literature: An Emerging International Force

As with popular musicians, writers have produced distinctive literatures by combining old traditions with new influences to comment on modern society. African literature has questioned the status quo, asserted African identity, and attempted to influence political change and economic development. Major figures have often written in English or French to better develop an international reputation. For example, the Nigerian Wole Soyinka (WOE-lay shaw-YING-kuh) (b. 1934)—a Yoruba poet, playwright, novelist, and sometime filmmaker who won the 1986 Nobel Prize for literature—mixes Yoruba mysticism with criticisms of Western capitalism, racism, cultural imperialism, and African failures. A former political prisoner, Soyinka has denounced repressive African leaders, including Nigeria's, with as much venom as he attacks Western imperialists, chastising "Nigeria's self-engorgement at the banquet of highway robberies, public executions, public floggings and other institutionalized sadisms, casual cruelties, wanton destruction."[9] The powerful criticism of governments offered by Soyinka and his Nigerian colleague Chinua Achebe has often forced both authors to live in exile.

Writers and artists have also tried to find authentic African perspectives. Negritude is a literary and philosophical movement to forge distinctively African views that first developed in the 1930s. The Senegalese writer and later the first president of his country after independence, Leopold Senghor, was a major negritude voice, attempting to balance

negritude
A twentieth-century literary and philosophical movement to forge distinctively African views.

African Cultural Expression Africans have developed diverse and vibrant popular music, often by mixing Western and local traditions. In Nigeria, juju music, played by bands such as Captain Jidi Oyo and his Yankee System in this 1982 photo, has been popular among the Yoruba people.

the Western stress on rational thought with African approaches to knowledge, such as mysticism and animism, long disdained by Europeans as superstition. One of the best-known writers in Francophone West Africa, Ousmane Sembene (OOS-man sem-BEN-ee) (b. 1923) of Senegal, was influenced more by Marxism than negritude. His writings, often set in the colonial period, show African resistance to Western domination and social inequality. Sympathizing with exploited people, his work also attacks Senegal's privileged elite, including greedy businessmen and government officials.

English-language literature has also flourished in South Africa and East Africa. For example, Kenyan Ngugi Wa Thiongo (en-GOO-gee wah thee-AHN-go) (b. 1938), a former journalist turned university professor who studied in England, has written several novels that explore the relationship between colonialism and social fragmentation, showing Gikuyu society struggling to retain its identity, culture, and traditions while adjusting to the modern world. His 1979 novel, *Petals of Blood*, portrays a Kenya struggling to free itself from neocolonialism but also beset with corruption. His attacks on the privileged local elite allied with Western exploitation earned Ngugi several terms in Kenyan jails and later forced him into exile.

Religion in Contemporary Africa Africans have maintained a triple religious heritage: animism/polytheism, Islam, and Christianity. All of these faiths have many followers, although the older animism has lost influence, and the relations between the traditions are not always easy. With their links to wider worlds, Christianity and Islam are also globalizing influences, spreading Western or Middle Eastern political, social, and economic ideas. Africans often view religions in both theoretical and practical terms, refusing to divorce metaphysical speculation from everyday life. They adopt views that help them survive the changes of modern times, rejecting old ideas and adding new ones as needed. Religion has remained in constant flux.

Christianity became Africa's largest religion, attracting some 250 to 300 million followers by 2000, both the fervent and the nominal in faith. Some countries, such as Congo, South Africa, and Uganda, became largely Christian. Africans are prominent in the world leadership of the Anglican and Catholic churches. Christianity has proven a powerful force for social change. Believers often favor the liberation of women, and mission schools have educated many African leaders, influencing their worldviews. A growing number of independent churches,

some blending African traditions into worship and theology, have no ties to the older Western-based denominations; some African churches have enjoyed spectacular growth, with services that attract thousands of congregants each Sunday. Yet many Africans have viewed Christianity critically. According to a popular nationalist saying: "When the missionaries came the Africans had the land and the Christians had the Bible. They taught us to pray with our eyes closed. When we opened them they had the land and we had the Bible."[10]

More than 200 million black Africans follow Islam. About one-fourth of all sub-Saharan countries have Muslim majorities. Some revivalist and Wahhabi movements have gained influence, especially in northern Nigeria, where some states have imposed Islamic law, sparking deadly clashes with Christian minorities. But most Muslims and Christians remain moderate and inclusive. While politicians use religion as a wedge issue, and Christian-Muslim clashes have occurred in countries such as Ivory Coast, tolerance has more often marked relations among Christians, Muslims, and animists. Ethnicity often divides people more than religion.

Africa in the Global System

African developments have occurred in a global context. During the Cold War, some African countries gained aid from the superpowers, but the rivalry also fostered manipulation. Countries such as Congo and Angola often became pawns in the Cold War, with the superpowers helping to support or remove leaders. But with the Cold War over, the Western world has largely ignored Africa, and the wealth gap between African countries and the Western industrialized nations has grown even wider than during colonial times. Today the gap between the richest Western nations and the poorest African countries is around 400 to 1.

The World Economy Global conditions have often proven counterproductive for Africans. Only when the world economy boomed in the 1950s and 1960s did African economies show steady growth. Since the 1970s, however, as the world economy soured and the world prices for many African exports collapsed, African economic growth rates steadily dropped. Western experts have encouraged a policy known as "structural adjustment," in which international lenders, such as the International Monetary Fund (IMF) and the World Bank, loan nations money on the condition that these nations open their economies to private investment and, to balance national budgets, reduce government spending for health, education, and farmers. The resulting hardship on average people increases unrest and resentment both of governments and of the Western nations that control the IMF and World Bank. This private investment also promotes a shift away from traditional farming to modern agriculture. But modern agriculture, with its reliance on tractors, chemical fertilizers, and new seeds, entails a large environmental and social cost.

By 1998, as a percentage of total output, African countries had the largest foreign debts in the world: $230 billion. At the same time, the world prices for most of Africa's exports, such as coffee, cotton, and tobacco from Tanzania and cocoa from Ghana, have steadily dropped since the 1960s. African farmers cannot compete with highly subsidized Western farmers and the tariff barriers erected in Europe, North America, and Japan against food and fiber imports from Africa. Increasingly desperate, countries such as Guinea-Bissau and Somalia have agreed to allow dangerous toxic waste, such as deadly but unwanted chemicals produced in the West, to be buried on their land in exchange for cash.

Africa's economic problems have had diverse roots. Some resulted from colonialism, which imposed economic policies that caused severe environmental destruction, such as desertification and deforestation, while incorporating the people into the world economy as specialized producers of minerals or cash crops for export rather than food farmers. Hence, Zambia relies on exploiting copper, Uganda coffee, Malawi tobacco, and Nigeria oil (95 percent). Nations have remained vulnerable to drops in world commodity prices for their exports. Since independence, bad policy decisions, poor leadership, corruption, unstable politics, and misguided advice from Western experts have also contributed to the economic crisis. In addition, the rapid spread of HIV/AIDS has ravaged African nations, killing and affecting millions (see Chapter 26). In some nations, one-third of the population has HIV.

The Vision of a New Society

But although falling behind much of Asia and Latin America economically, Africans have had both successes and failures. Using foreign aid and their own resources, they have made rapid strides in literacy, social and medical services, including active birth-control campaigns, and road construction. Some nations, such as South Africa and Uganda, have a feisty free press. Africans have also attempted to work together to resolve problems. The African Union, formed in 2000 with 54 members, has sent peacekeeping troops into violence-torn countries such as Sudan. Many nations have moved toward more democratic systems and private enterprise. However, political leadership has often failed to root out corruption, restructure existing institutions, and foster food production. Millions still live in poverty. Africa suffers a particularly acute "brain drain" as academics, students, and professionals, seeking a better life, move to Europe or North America.

African history is not only an authentic, dynamic saga of indigenous African development but also part of a larger global process. Over the past half-century, Western influence has remained strong, and Africans have not enjoyed complete control of their destiny. The Ghanaian historian Jacob Ajayi (a-JAH-yee) laid out the challenge: "The vision of a new [African] society will need to be developed out of the African historical experience. The African is not yet master of his own fate, but neither is he completely at the mercy of fate."[11]

 Listen to a synopsis of Chapter 30.

CHAPTER 31

South Asia, Southeast Asia, and Global Connections,
Since 1945

Learning Outcomes

After reading this chapter, you should be able to answer the following questions:

LO¹ What factors led to the political division of South Asia?

LO² What have been the major achievements and disappointments of the South Asian nations?

LO³ What were the causes and consequences of the wars in Indochina?

LO⁴ How has decolonization and globalization shaped the new Southeast Asian nations?

66 This music sings the struggle of [humanity]. This music is my life. This is the revolution we have begun. But the revolution is only a means to attain freedom, and freedom is only a means to enrich the happiness and nobility of human life. 99

—Hazil, the Indonesian revolutionary nationalist in Mochtar Lubis's novel *A Road with No End* (1952)[1]

In 1950, a small, idealistic group of leading Indonesian writers published a moving declaration promoting universal human dignity: "We [Indonesians] are the heirs to the culture of the whole world, a culture which is ours to extend and develop in our own way [by] the discarding of old and outmoded values and their replacement by new ones. Our fundamental quest is [helping] humanity."[2] These writers hoped that Indonesia could combine the most humane ideas of East and West to become a beacon to the world, open to all cultures and showing respect for the common people. While delighted with independence, the writers warned against the dangers of a narrow nationalism that devalued other cultures.

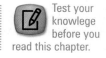

Test your knowlege before you read this chapter.

What do you think?

Both South Asian and Southeast Asian nations faced widespread conflict in their quests for self-governance.

Strongly Disagree						Strongly Agree
1	2	3	4	5	6	7

The writers had been inspired by the irreverent Sumatran poet Chairul Anwar (CHAI-roll ON-war) (1922–1949), who believed the revolution had destroyed the old colonial society and opened up the possibility of building a new, open society. Anwar excited Indonesian writers with his path-breaking poems that stretched the possibilities of the Indonesian language. But he had died when just twenty-seven years old, leaving it to others, among them the liberal Sumatran author Mochtar Lubis (MOKE-tar LOO-bis) (b. 1920), whose work is quoted above, to carry on the campaign. The declaration's noble aspirations and recognition of Indonesia's connection to the wider world reflected a new sense of possibility as walls of colonialism were being knocked down.

But the writers' idealism was soon dashed by the realities of the early post–World War II years. While Southeast Asians longed for human dignity, other, more immediate goals took precedence,

<<**Commuting to Work** Vietnam has largely recovered from its decades of war and has experienced increasing economic growth. These women in Hanoi are commuting to work by bicycle.

including securing independence, building new nations, and addressing economic problems. Despite false starts and conflicts, over the following decades, Indonesians and other nations of South and Southeast Asia sought, and sometimes found, answers to their challenges while increasing their links to global networks.

The societies of South and Southeast Asia, which changed dramatically without destroying tradition, offer striking contrasts with the wider world as well as with each other. Except for East Asia, this is the most densely populated part of the world: more than 1.5 billion people live in the lands stretching eastward from Pakistan and India to Indonesia and the Philippines. It is also a very diverse area, containing a wide array of languages, ethnic groups, religions, world-views, governments, and levels of economic development. This region of contrasts has played an important role in the world for more than four millennia and continues to be one of the corner-stones of the world economy.

LO¹ The Reshaping of South Asia

World War II undermined British colonial control and led to independence for the peoples of South Asia. The British, who were economically drained by the war and realizing that continued control of India would be costly, handed power over to local leaders. The first prime minister of independent India was Jawaharlal Nehru (NAY-roo) (1889–1964), whose idealism about India's independence was tempered by the realities of the challenges ahead. India's long struggle for independence, marked by the nonviolent philosophy of Mohandas Gandhi (1868–1948), had ironically ended with Gandhi assassinated and British India divided into several separate, often hostile countries—India, Pakistan, Bangladesh, and Sri Lanka. Each of the four nations had its achievements and failures, but the

> "As violence flared, thousands of Hindus and Sikhs fled Pakistan for India, and thousands of Muslims fled India for Pakistan."

geographically largest and most populous, India, has been the regional colossus and a major player in world affairs.

Decolonization, Partition, and the Nehru Years

The religious divisions of South Asia undermined regional unity. During World War II, relations between the British and the mainly Hindu leadership of the Indian National Congress ruptured (see Chapter 25). Taking advantage, and fearing domination by the much larger Hindu community in India, the Muslim League pressed its case with the British for a separate Muslim nation, to be called Pakistan. After the war ended, negotiations to bring the Congress and the Muslim League together in a common vision broke down in 1946 amidst widespread rioting and violence; in Calcutta alone, five thousand people died. Subsequently, the Muslim leader, Mohammed Ali Jinnah (1876–1948), announced that if India were not divided, it would be destroyed. In 1947, British negotiators reached an agreement with Congress and Muslim League leaders to create two independent nations, India and a Pakistan formed out of the Muslim majority areas of eastern Bengal and the northwestern provinces along the Indus River.

Religious Violence in India and Pakistan

The two nations emerged in hopefulness. In a speech to his new nation, India, Prime Minister Nehru proclaimed: "Long years ago we made a tryst with destiny, and now the time comes when we shall redeem our pledge. At the stroke of the midnight hour, when the world sleeps, India will awake to life and freedom."³ A similar mood of renewal struck people in Pakistan, but the euphoria in both new nations proved short-lived, as partition sparked hatreds between local members of the majority faith, who felt empowered, and religious minorities, who feared discrimination. As violence flared, thousands of Hindus and Sikhs fled Pakistan for India, and thousands of Muslims fled India for Pakistan. Altogether some 5 million refugees crossed the India–West Pakistan border, and 1 million crossed

Virtual Library: South Asia (http://www.columbia.edu/cu/libraries/indiv/area/sarai/). A major site maintained by Columbia University.

the India–East Pakistan border. About half a million refugees died from the religious violence.

Mohandas Gandhi

The sixty-eight-year-old Mohandas Gandhi labored to stop the killing. Moving into the Muslim quarter of Delhi, he toured refugee camps without escort, read aloud from the scriptures of all religions, including Islam's holiest book, the Quran, and confronted Hindu mobs attacking mosques. Finally, in desperation, and hoping to send a powerful message, Gandhi, who weighed only 113 pounds, began a fast that he said would last until all the violence in the city had stopped or he died. He quickly fell ill, but Gandhi's effort worked, allowing him to break off his fast. After the violence subsided, a substantial Muslim and Sikh minority remained in India and a Hindu and Sikh minority in Pakistan. But partition had been shattering. Furthermore, Gandhi's support for Muslim victims of Hindu violence outraged Hindu extremists, who regarded Gandhi as a traitor. In January 1948, one of them assassinated Gandhi, shocking the world.

India's Firm Foundation

Despite its bloody start, India was built on a solid political foundation. Britain bequeathed the basis for parliamentary democracy, a trained civil service, a good communications system, and an educated elite committed to modernization. India became a republic with a constitution based on the British model, led by a prime minister chosen by the majority party in an elected parliament. However, given its extraordinary diversity, India had difficulty building national unity. To accommodate the many religious minorities, regions, and diverse cultures, India adopted a federal system, with elected state governments, and was officially secular with complete separation of religion and state. Kashmir (CASH-mere), a mountainous Himalayan state on the India–Pakistan border, became a constant source of tension between India and Pakistan, because it had a Muslim majority but a Hindu ruler who opted to join India.

The Vulnerability of Pakistan

The new Pakistan confronted numerous problems. Its two wings were separated by a thousand miles of India. The nation's founding leader, Jinnah,

> 66 Despite its bloody start, India was built on a solid political foundation. 99

died soon after independence, and his successor was assassinated. Before independence, Muslims had been over-represented in the British Indian military, and the army now played a stronger role in Pakistan's politics than in India's. The loss of top civilian leaders, lack of a balanced economic base, massive poverty, and geographic division made Pakistan vulnerable to political instability and military rule.

India's first prime minister, Nehru, a close associate of Gandhi and the son of a respected early Indian nationalist, dominated Indian politics for sixteen years (1948–1964). A gifted speaker and brilliant thinker, Nehru enjoyed widespread popular support. The majority of Indians lived in overcrowded, unhealthy urban slums or dusty villages that lacked electricity and running water, but Nehru promised to address the nation's overwhelming poverty. He believed firmly in democracy, emphasizing

Muslims Leaving India for Pakistan During Partition As India and Pakistan split into two new nations in 1947, millions of Muslims and Hindus fled their homes to escape violence. This photo shows displaced Muslims, carrying a few meager belongings, jamming a train headed from India to Pakistan.

consent rather than coercion. While India lagged behind communist-ruled China in economic development, it developed a system of personal freedom. Believing in peaceful coexistence with neighbors and renouncing military aggression, Nehru helped to found the Non-Aligned Movement of nations, such as Egypt and Indonesia, which were unwilling to commit to either the U.S. or Soviet camps in the Cold War.

Nehru's Pragmatic Leadership

Nehru's policies derived from his complex ideals. Although the British-educated lawyer admired Western politics, literature, and economic dynamism, he also respected India's cultural heritage and moral strength. Raised a Hindu, Nehru was nevertheless a secularist who believed that Congress should represent, and promote justice for, all Indians. Although himself a high-caste brahman, he distrusted the influence of the Hindu priests. Nehru shared Gandhi's opposition to the caste system and fought gender inequalities. In 1955, after years of struggle, Nehru convinced parliament to approve new laws on untouchability and women's rights that provided penalties for discrimination. The lowest-ranking social group, untouchables, acquired special quotas in government services and universities, while Hindu women gained equal legal rights with men, including the right to divorce, property rights, and equal inheritance. But some laws that challenged centuries of tradition were often ignored in rural areas.

Nehru's government built the framework for productive economic change. Nehru introduced a planning system to foster modern technology and mixed capitalism and socialism, private capital and a strong state sector. He left established industries in private hands but set up public ventures to build power plants, dams, and irrigation canals. In the 1960s, the Green Revolution (see Chapter 26) fostered a dramatic rise in food production. Nehru employed five-year plans to make India independent of foreign suppliers for power, steel, basic commodities, and food. By the 1970s, India was one of the world's ten most industrialized nations and nearly self-sufficient in food.

Nehru's Mixed Record

But some of Nehru's policies proved failures. Government control of the private sector through regulations gave bureaucrats great power, fostered corruption, and shackled private enterprise. Nehru failed to cultivate good relations with Pakistan or with China, and in 1962, Chinese troops humiliated Indian forces during a border dispute. Nehru also failed to address unchecked population growth, which rose from 389 million in 1941 to 434 million in 1961. The government built schools and universities but failed to substantially raise literacy rates. Yet, when Nehru died in 1964, millions mourned the end of an idealistic era that had earned India respect in the world. Furthermore, Congress had no leader of comparable stature to follow Nehru.

The Making of Pakistan and Bangladesh

Pakistan faced greater challenges than did India. Jinnah had pledged to make the nation happy and prosperous, but the leaders who followed him had only limited success, in part because of tensions between ethnic groups who shared an Islamic faith but often little else. From the beginning, tensions flared between the nationalistic Bengalis, who dominated the east, and the Punjabis and Sindhis, who dominated the west. The two regions differed in language, culture, and outlook. The factionalized Pakistani parliament proved unworkable, providing an excuse for military leaders to take over the government in 1958. By 1969, dissatisfaction with military dictatorship led to riots, prompting martial law.

At the end of the 1960s, ethnic tensions came to a boil, eventually fracturing Pakistan into two nations, Pakistan and Bangladesh (see Map 31.1). The Bengalis

Interactive Map

in East Pakistan had felt they did not get a fair share of the nation's resources and political power. After the Awami League, a Bengali nationalist party, won a majority of East Pakistan's seats in national elections, in early 1971, Pakistani troops arrested the party leader, Sheikh Mujiber Rahman (shake MOO-jee-bur RAH-mun) (1920–1975). Then, hoping to crush Awami League support, troops opened fire on university dormitories and Hindu homes, causing hundreds of casualties.

> **"** At the end of the 1960s, ethnic tensions came to a boil, eventually fracturing Pakistan into two nations, Pakistan and Bangladesh. **"**

Inspired by Sheikh Mujiber, the Awami League then declared independence. In response, troops from West Pakistan poured into East Pakistan, terrorizing the Bengali population with massacres, arson, and the raping of thousands of women. At least half a million Bengalis died at Pakistani hands, and 10 million desperate, starving Bengali refugees fled to India. World opinion turned against Pakistan. India appealed for world support of East Pakistan, armed the Bengali guerrillas, and, after an ill-advised Pakistani attack on Indian airfields, declared war and sent troops into both West and East Pakistan, rapidly gaining the upper hand. Fearful of India, Pakistan had long cultivated an alliance with China and the United States, both of which supplied it with military aid. American President Richard Nixon ignored the massive killing of Bengalis, and China threatened to intervene on behalf of Pakistan, but Soviet backing of India discouraged such a move. By the end of 1971, Pakistani troops in Bengal had surrendered to Indian forces, and the Awami League, led by Sheikh Mujibur, established a new nation, Bangladesh, in what had been East Pakistan.

Awami League
A Bengali nationalist party that began the move from independence from West Pakistan.

The Indira Gandhi Era

With the sudden death of Nehru's respected successor in 1966, the Congress selected Nehru's daughter, Indira Gandhi (1917–1984), to be the nation's first woman prime minister. She had worked closely with her father while her husband (no relation to Mohandas Gandhi) served in parliament. A shrewd campaigner, Mrs. Gandhi enjoyed a decade and a half in power. When her support waned in the 1967 elections, she responded aggressively with policies to win back the poor. Her status was elevated by India's smashing military victory over archenemy Pakistan. But Mrs. Gandhi's war triumph and mounting domestic problems also fostered her use of increasingly harsh policies. Powerful vested interests ignored her reforms, the economy faltered, and many Indians turned against the Congress.

The Indian Crisis of 1975

In 1975, Gandhi declared a state of emergency, suspending civil rights,

Map 31.1
Modern South Asia
India, predominantly Hindu, is the largest South Asian nation and separates the two densely populated Islamic nations of Bangladesh and Pakistan. Buddhists are the majority in Sri Lanka, just off India's southeast coast. The small kingdoms of Bhutan and Nepal are located in the Himalayan mountain range.

closing state governments, and jailing some ten thousand opposition leaders and dissidents. Her actions were condemned, but some of her policies improved the economy. Meanwhile, her youngest son, Sanjay Gandhi (1946–1980), launched two controversial programs designed to reduce birth rates and clear out urban slums; these proved unsuccessful and were deeply unpopular. In 1977, Indira lifted the emergency and announced general elections. After thirty years in power, the Congress Party, and with it Indira Gandhi, was voted out of office and replaced by an uneasy coalition of diverse parties that included Hindu nationalists. But the coalition government solved few problems, and in 1980 it collapsed.

Sikh Rebellion of Amritsar

Indira Gandhi and the Congress returned to power in the 1980 elections, restoring the Nehru dynasty. But they also faced deep cynicism, growing unemployment, and unrest. In 1980, Sanjay Gandhi died in a plane crash, and Indira Gandhi elevated her eldest son Rajiv (1944–1991), an apolitical airline pilot, as her heir apparent. Mrs. Gandhi's final crisis broke out in the Punjab, India's richest state. The growing political consciousness of the Sikhs, whose religion mixes Hindu and Muslim ideas, had led to a desire for statehood. In 1983, armed Sikh extremists, demanding an independent Sikh homeland, occupied the Golden Temple at Amritsar (uhm-RIT-suhr), the holiest shrine in the Sikh religion, and turned it into a fortress. In 1984, the Indian army stormed the Golden Temple against fierce resistance. When the fighting ended, the temple was reduced to rubble and over one thousand militants and soldiers lay dead.

The End of Nehru's Dynasty

Violence had returned to Indian political life. The destruction of their holiest temple shocked the Sikhs and led to the shooting death of Indira Gandhi by two of her Sikh bodyguards. The assassination in turn generated rioting and attacks on Sikhs. Hindu mobs roamed Delhi, burning Sikh shops and killing Sikhs, often by pouring gasoline over them and setting them ablaze. The dead numbered in the thousands. Rajiv Gandhi, succeeding his mother at only forty years old, proved ineffective. In 1991, while campaigning in the southern city of Madras, he was blown up by a young Sri Lankan woman handing him flowers. Yet despite this tumult, India remained a functioning democracy and a thriving nation.

LO² South Asian Politics and Societies

South Asian societies changed beginning in the 1970s, each forging its own political role in the region. With a little more than 1 billion people by 2005 and 65 percent of the land in the subcontinent, the Republic of India rose to regional dominance. Indian governments began to liberalize the economy, stimulating growth. At the same time, growing Hindu nationalism has challenged the domination of India's Congress Party, threatening its secular vision. Meanwhile, India's neighbors in South Asia have struggled to achieve stability and economic development. Both Pakistan and Sri Lanka have experienced persistent ethnic violence, while India and Pakistan remain on bitter terms. Whatever the political tensions that divide them, however, they also share some life patterns, as ancient customs exist side by side with modern machines and ways of living.

Indian Politics

When India celebrated its fiftieth jubilee of independence in 1997, the nation's president reminded his people that India's challenge was to achieve economic growth with social justice. That goal remains elusive, but Indians can boast that, in politics, their country has maintained one of the few working multiparty democracies outside of the industrialized nation-states, one that fosters lively political debate and forces candidates to appeal to voters.

Democracy's Role in India

India rejected the revolutionary path of China, instead promoting civil liberties and constitutional democracy. To some observers, democracy provides a flexible system for accommodating the differing interests of the diverse population. Others, however, argue that democracy has intensified differences between groups. Certainly, tensions between Hindus and Muslims and between high-caste and low-caste Hindus, manipulated by opportunistic politicians, have complicated political life. There are also differences over how real the effects of democracy are in the presence of powerful economic and political elites. Some say that democracy has become only a safety valve for popular frustration, creating the illusion of mass participation that prevents a frontal attack on caste and class inequalities.

The Congress Party has remained nationally influential for more than five decades but has had to contend with rivals. On the left, several communist parties dominate politics in West Bengal in the northeast and Kerala in the southwest, repeatedly

> "India rejected the revolutionary path of China, instead promoting civil liberties and constitutional democracy."

winning elections by pro-
moting modernization and
support for the poor within
a democratic framework.
On the right, several Hindu
nationalist parties opposed
the secular Congress, but with limited success until
the 1990s. In the southern Indian states, various parties representing regional interests gradually gained
strength, generally dominating state
governments and becoming part of
federal coalitions. These regional parties, often led by stars of the local film
industries, have worked to protect local
languages while preserving English as
a national language. All of India's parties have suffered from corruption.

Since 1989, Indian politics has
become more pluralistic. The Congress
lost several elections to coalitions that
included Hindu nationalists. The major
Hindu nationalist party, the Bharatha
Janata (BJP), gained influence in north
India with a platform of state support
for Hindu issues. The BJP slogan, "One
Nation, One People, One Culture," con-
fronts the Gandhi–Nehru vision of a
tolerant multicultural state. By the
late 1990s, India suffered from rising
political corruption, violent secession-
ist movements in border regions, caste
conflict, religious hostilities, and political fragmentation. In 2002, major Hindu–Muslim
violence broke out again, leaving more than one
thousand people dead and more than 100,000 terrified Muslims, burned out of their cities, huddled in
tent camps.

In 2004, the Congress, led by Rajiv Gandhi's
Italian-born, sari-wearing widow, Sonia Gandhi (b.
1946), a Roman Catholic who met Rajiv when both
were students in England, capitalized on disenchantment among the poor and Muslims and unex-
pectedly defeated the ruling BJP-led coalition. She
formed a new government committed to secularism
and economic growth. A Pakistan-born Sikh economist, Manmohan Singh, became the first non-Hindu
prime minister. A free press monitors Indian politics: in 2005, a television station's investigation of
corruption forced several members of parliament to
resign.

The Indian Economy
in Transition

India has struggled to
resolve problems inher-
ited from colonial times:

> ❝ India has
> struggled to
> resolve problems
> inherited from
> colonial times:
> economic
> backwardness,
> skyrocketing
> population growth,
> and crushing
> poverty. ❞

economic backwardness, skyrocketing population
growth, and crushing poverty. While Nehru's dream
of eradicating these problems has not yet been realized, Indians can boast of many gains, especially its
great success in strengthening its agricultural and
manufacturing production. After 1991, Indian leaders
dismantled the socialist sector of the economy built
by Nehru while sparking economic revival. Reform,
deregulation, and liberalization contributed to an
economic growth rate of 6 to 7 percent
per year by the late 1990s. Several cities, especially Bangalore and Bombay
(Mumbai), became high-tech centers
closely linked to global communications. Hundreds of international corporations, taking advantage of a
growing, educated Indian middle
class, have moved information and
technical service jobs, such as call-in
customer service and computer pro-
gramming, from North America and
Europe to India. India's boom has even
prompted thousands of highly educated Indians living in North America
and Europe to return to India and join
its high-tech sector. Significant progress also has been made in agriculture.
Since 1947, India has doubled food
production, thanks largely to the
Green Revolution of improved seeds
and fertilizers. The nation now grows
enough wheat and rice to feed the
entire population, but persisting inequalities have
prevented equitable distribution.

Population and
Poverty: Ongoing
Problems

Despite the economic
revival, India's economy
has not succeeded in
delivering a better life to
most Indians. More than
half still live below the poverty line, and 40 percent
lack an adequate diet. While China nears universal
literacy, only half of Indians can read and write.
Meanwhile, population growth eats away at the
national resources: every year, 30 million Indians are
born. By 2050, India will have 1.5 billion people, more
than China. Ironically, success in doubling life expectancy contributes to overpopulation, which causes
overcrowded cities, a lack of adequate sanitation, and
insufficient health care. Millions of Indians sleep on
city sidewalks for lack of money and housing. While
affluent Indians increasingly buy fancy imported
cars, many commuters ride on the roofs of jammed
buses and trains.

Jagadeesh/Reuters/Corbis

Global Communications India's call centers provide low-paid English-speaking workers and high-speed telecommunications for customer service help lines around the world. Here, Indian employees are working at a call center in the southern Indian city of Bangalore.

The stark contrasts between the modern and traditional sectors of the economy have produced uneven development and raised questions as to who benefits from the changes. Successive Indian governments have been unable to challenge vested interests such as the powerful landlords. Meanwhile, poor peasants, unable to make a living from their small farms, fall further behind. Poverty fosters growing urban crime and rural banditry, especially in several densely populated northern states. The population below the official poverty line lacks purchasing power to sustain local industry. Economic growth and poverty ravage the environment as cities encroach on farmland and people cut down trees for firewood. The Chipko forest conservation movement, based on traditional and Gandhian principles and led mostly by women, is one of many groups working to protect the environment.

Indian Cities, Gender Patterns, and Cultures

In his will, India's first prime minister, Jawaharlal Nehru, asked that his ashes be scattered in the Ganges River, not because of the river's traditional religious significance to Hindus but because it symbolized to him India's millennia-old culture, ever-changing and yet ever the same. Such a pattern has indeed characterized India's society and culture. Ancient traditions such as caste, gender stereotypes, and family practices have persisted but in modified forms, and Indians make religion both central to their lives and a source of conflict. Indians have also used literature, film, and other cultural forms to examine their society and place in the world.

The Abiding Power of Tradition

The contrast between the villages, where 80 percent of Indians live, and the cities remains stark. The growing urban middle class enjoy recreations and technologies, from golf to video games, that are available to the affluent around the world. Whether they live in the Punjab, Calcutta, or Bangalore, educated urban young people are becoming more cosmopolitan, often listening to the same music and buying the same consumer goods, a homogenization that

> "The contrast between the villages, where 80 percent of Indians live, and the cities remains stark."

conservatives see as a threat to local cultures. Practices that ensure strict divisions between castes, such as avoiding physical contact or sharing food, are harder to maintain in cities than in villages, where caste remains more firmly rooted. At the bottom of the caste system, the untouchables, some 20 percent of India's population, still live difficult lives, even though government assistance and reforms have enabled some low-caste people to enter high-status occupations and positions. The grooves of tradition run deep, particularly in the rural areas, and changes can bring demoralization and disorientation as well as satisfaction.

 Internet Indian History Sourcebook (*http://www.fordham.edu/halsall/india/indiasbook.html*). An invaluable collection of sources and links on India from ancient to modern times.

However, in some regions, especially in cities, families have changed. Modern life has hastened the breakup of traditional extended families; some Indians now live in smaller, nuclear families. New forms of employment, which can cause family members to move to other districts or countries, have undermined family cohesion. A traditional preference for male babies, however, has continued, and today the ability of technology to determine the sex of a fetus has led many Indians who want male children to terminate pregnancies.

Women in Indian Society

Nehru had believed that India could progress only if women played a full part in the nation. Accordingly, new laws banned once-widespread customs such as polygamy, child marriage, and sati. Female literacy has risen, from 1 percent in 1901 to 27 percent in 2000, though it is still only half the male rate. But some changing customs have penalized women. For example, the practice of requiring new brides to provide generous dowries to their in-laws, once restricted to higher castes, has become common in all castes. As a result, especially in rural areas, reports have increased of families banishing, injuring, or killing young brides whose own families failed to supply the promised dowries. Notions of women's rights, common in cities, are less known in villages.

Yet many Indian women have benefited from education, becoming leaders in such fields as journalism, business, trade unions, the arts, and government. An antipatriarchy women's movement, growing for a century, has become more active since the 1970s, suggesting that women's issues will remain on the nation's agenda. Outside the big cities, however, women have remained largely bound by tradition, expected to demonstrate submission, obedience, and absolute dedication to their husbands. By 2004, AIDS grew rapidly as a health problem, a result largely of women being forced into prostitution to serve the sexual needs of increasingly mobile male workers such as long-haul truckers.

Religion, Politics, and Violence

Religion, like society, has changed, becoming intertwined with politics. Although Hindus form a large majority, India's population also includes 120 million Muslims, more than 20 million Sikhs, and nearly 20 million Christians. Religious differences have become politicized. Some upper-caste Hindus, for instance, particularly in the BJP, have used the notion of a Hindu nation to marginalize Muslims and low-caste Hindus. Civil unrest involving violent attacks on Muslims by militant Hindu nationalists has caused political crises. Yet, despite the tensions, Muslims occupy high positions in India's government, business, and the professions and play a key role in cultural expression. India's most famous modern artist, Tyeb Mehta (b. 1925), is a Shi'ite Muslim whose works, much of which address the Hindu–Muslim divide, sell all over the world.

Bollywood

Indians have also eagerly embraced modern cultural forms to express ideas. While Indian-born novelists such as Arundhati Roy (AH-roon-DAH-tee roy) and Salman Rushdie have achieved worldwide fame, a more popular cultural form in contemporary India has been film. India has built the world's largest film industry; it makes about one thousand movies per year, and finds audiences among both Indian emigrants and non-Indians around the world. The Mumbai film industry, known as Bollywood, has become India's largest, churning out films in Hindi. Many films, especially musicals, portray a fantasy world that enables

 Read about Raj Kapoor, Bollywood film star, and the first real superstar of Indian film.

viewers to forget their troubles. Religious divisions are muted in Bollywood, and the leading directors, writers, and stars often come from Muslim backgrounds. Voters in southern India have even favored stars of the local film industry as state leaders.

Islamic Politics and Societies

South Asia's two densely populated Muslim countries, Pakistan and Bangladesh, have struggled to develop economically and to maintain political stability. Both countries are divided between secular and devout Muslims, have alternated between military dictatorships and elected civilian governments, and have generally conservative cultures.

Containing 150 million people, more than 95 percent of them Sunni Muslims, Pakistan has had difficulty transforming its diverse ethnic and tribal groups into a politically stable, unified nation. The most long-lasting civilian leader, Zulkifar Ali Bhutto (zool-KEE-far AH-lee BOO-toe) (r. 1971–1977), a lawyer educated overseas, came to power with great ambitions. Although he came from a wealthy landowning family, he pursued socialist policies that were unpopular with the wealthy. Accusing him of corruption, the army took power and later executed Bhutto. The Soviet occupation of Afghanistan in 1979 and the Pakistan-supported Islamic resistance to the Soviets that followed (see Chapter 30) distracted Pakistanis from their unpopular military regime and brought more U.S. military aid to Pakistan.

Benazir Bhutto

Pakistani politics has remained turbulent. In 1986, Bhutto's daughter, Benazir Bhutto (BEN-ah-ZEER BOO-toe) (1953–2007), a graduate of Britain's Oxford University, put together a movement to challenge the military regime. As unrest increased in 1988, Bhutto became prime minister. She was respected abroad but struggled to govern effectively. Accused of abuse of power, she was dismissed in 1990, returning to power after the 1993 elections. But critical problems persisted, including growing fighting between ethnic factions and attacks by militant Sunnis on the small Shi'a Muslim and Christian minorities. In 1996, she was once again removed. Bhutto was assassinated in 2007 in the midst of one last comeback campaign.

In 1999, the military took over, installing as president Indian-born General Pervez Musharraf (per-VEZ moo-SHAR-uff) (b. 1943), whose family had fled to Pakistan during the partition in 1947. He faced the same challenge as his predecessors: to halt factional violence, punish corruption, collect taxes from the wealthy, restore economic growth, and balance the demands of militant and secular Muslims. Although Musharraf allied with the United States after the 2001 Al Qaeda attacks and the resulting U.S. invasion of Afghanistan, many Pakistanis resent the West, in part because the United States, while seeking Pakistani help in the war on international terrorism, is reluctant to remove high tariff barriers against Pakistani textiles, a major export that accounts for nearly half of all manufacturing jobs. Experts argue that an expansion of this work might relieve the high unemployment rate and hence reduce the appeal of extremist Islam for desperate young men.

Repression of Pakistani Women

Pakistani society and culture have remained conservative. Pakistan's founding leader, Jinnah, a cosmopolitan British-educated lawyer, had favored more rights for women, but national leaders who shared this view were reluctant to challenge the strong opposition to women's rights, especially in rural areas. In 1979, an Islamizing military government pushed through discriminatory laws that made women who were raped guilty of adultery, a serious offense. Women enjoyed far fewer legal rights than men and were more commonly jailed or punished than men for adultery. Women's groups who courageously protested in the streets faced military attacks. By the 1990s, things had changed little: only 10 percent of adult women were employed outside the home, and fewer than 20 percent were literate. The United Nations ranked Pakistan near the bottom of nations in women's equality.

Bangladesh: Political and Social Struggles

Even more so than Pakistan, Bangladesh, overcrowded with 125 million people, has encountered barriers to development. Mostly flat plains, the land is prone to devastating hurricanes, floods, tornados, and famine. The nation's founder, Sheik Mujiber Rahman, had hoped that the nation he envisioned—secular, democratic, and socialist— would rapidly progress, but, after tightening his power, he was assassinated by the military. None of the governments after him, whether military or civilian, has had much success in resolving problems, and all have suffered from corruption. Several leaders have been assassinated.

After 1991, democracy became the main pattern, and the two largest parties have been led by women. The conservative Islamic and pro-capitalist Khaleda Zia (ZEE-uh) (b. 1945), the widow of an assassinated leader, heads one party, while the left-leaning Sheikh Hasina Wajed (shake ha-SEE-nah WAH-jed) (b. 1947), the daughter of the assassinated Sheik Mujibur Rahman, the nation's first prime minister, leads the Awami League. Sheikh Hasina escaped an assassination attempt in 2004. The two women, bitter rivals, have alternated as the nation's prime minister.

Despite political turbulence, however, Bangladesh has had more success than Pakistan. The nation has been a pioneer among developing nations in programs to eliminate poverty and now provides some formal education to 60 percent of its children. The Grameen Bank, which loans small amounts of money, particularly to poor women for starting a village business, has helped millions of people, earning world attention (see Chapter 26). A visionary activist, Fazle Hasan Abed, launched a movement to improve rural life through forming cooperatives. But the nation's per capita income remains $120 per year (35 cents per day), and only 35 percent of adults are literate. Nearly half the population live below the official poverty line. Conflict and instability continue to plague the country.

As in Pakistan, social and cultural issues have divided Bangladesh. Unlike Pakistan, Bangladesh is officially a secular state and has a large Hindu minority (16 percent). Although over the centuries the Bengalis incorporated Hindu and Buddhist influences as well as Sufi mysticism into their version of Islam, making them tolerant of opposing views, militant Muslim political movements seeking an Islamic state gained strength in the 1990s, heightening divisions among Muslims. The militants, allied with Khaleda Zia's party, succeeded in restricting women's rights. Islamic militants also pressured the government to prosecute feminist writers such as the medical doctor turned novelist Taslima Nasreen (b. 1962), who wrote critically of religion, conservative culture, and irrational, blind faith. Muslim militants condemned Nasreen's writing as blasphemy against Islam, a capital offense. Nasreen fled into exile in Europe to escape death threats.

Sri Lanka and Its Conflicts

Sri Lanka, an island nation of 20 million people, shares problems of ethnic conflict and poverty with its South Asian neighbors but, like India, has generally maintained a democracy. In 1948, the leaders of the majority ethnic group, the Sinhalese—some 75 percent of the population and mostly Theravada Buddhists—negotiated independence from Britain and inherited a colonial economy based on rubber and tea plantations. Laws passed by the Sinhalese-dominated government that discriminated against

the language and culture of the major ethnic minority, the Tamils, mostly Hindus, generated fighting between the two groups. A Tamil community had existed in northern Sri Lanka for generations, but many Sri Lankan Tamils descended from immigrants who were recruited from India in the nineteenth century to work on British coffee, tea, and rubber plantations.

In 1959, Sirimavo Bandaranaike (sree-MAH-vo BAN-dar-an-EYE-kee) (1916–2004), the Sinhalese widow of an assassinated leader, led her party to victory and became the world's first woman prime minister. Her enemies derided her as a "kitchen woman," yet she proved to be a strong leader and dominated her nation's politics in the 1960s and 1970s. Although she implemented socialist policies that improved economic and social conditions, Bandaranaike faced resistance from a communist-led rebellion among the poor. Sinhalese-dominated Sri Lankan governments sponsored textile and electronics manufacturing to reduce dependence on cash crop exports. While socialist policies discouraged free enterprise, they fostered the highest literacy rates (85 percent) and, by providing rice and free medical care to the poor, the longest life span (sixty-nine years) in South Asia. These policies benefited all of the nation's ethnic groups.

In 1983, a section of the Tamil minority seeking independence for their region began a rebellion that has kept the island in a constant state of tension. The assassination of top political leaders and communal fighting became common. In 1994, Chandrika Kumaratunga (CHAN-dree-ka koo-MAHR-a-TOON-ga) (b. 1945), the University of Paris–educated daughter of Sirimavo Bandaranaike, led her party to victory and became Sri Lanka's second woman leader. She sought both military victory over the Tamils and political peace but achieved neither, narrowly escaping an assassination attempt in 2000. Nearly 60,000 people, many innocent civilians, have died in twenty years of violence between Tamils and Sinhalese. The violence split the Buddhist clergy between those advocating peace and tolerance and those demanding defeat of the Hindu Tamils, whom they view as a threat to Buddhism. Although national reconciliation has proven elusive, the Sinhalese and moderate Tamils continue to practice democratic politics.

South Asia in the Global System

Since 1945, South Asian nations have grown in geopolitical and economic stature. Although Nehru strode the world stage as a major leader of the nonaligned nations, seeking a middle ground between the United States and the USSR, his successors lacked his international influence. However, in the past decade, India has become a center of advanced technology and one of the most industrialized nations outside of Europe and North America. Every year, Indian universities turn out thousands of talented engineers and computer scientists who have built up homegrown industries and have also helped staff the high-tech silicon valleys of North America and Europe. By the early twenty-first century, experts debated whether India or China might eventually compete for world economic leadership with the United States, whose multidimensional power Indian leaders admired. Some pointed to India's large number of English-speakers, solid financial system, and vibrant democracy as advantages. However, critics argued that to become a world power, India needed to contain social tensions and reduce poverty in the cities and villages.

South Asian technology and ingenuity have led to scientific achievements. In 1975, the Indian government launched into orbit its first satellite, named after Aryabhata (OUR-ya-BAH-ta), a major Indian scientist and mathematician who lived more than fifteen hundred years ago. In 1998, India openly tested its first nuclear bomb, triggering India–Pakistan rivalries and inspiring Pakistan to develop nuclear weapons. Since the late 1990s, the weapons experts of many nations and international organizations have worried about Pakistan's nuclear abilities, since Islamic militants, some with possible links to global terrorist networks, play a key role in local and national politics. In 2004, a top Pakistani nuclear scientist admitted to selling nuclear secrets to other nations.

Global and regional politics have intensified Indian-Pakistani rivalries. After U.S. president George W. Bush, in the wake of the 2001 terrorist attacks on the United States, justified preemptive military attacks against potential threats, some Indians, adapting that justification to their own ends, wondered why India should not preemptively attack Pakistan. But India–Pakistan relations have remained combustible: a coordinated terrorist attack on various sites in Mumbai, India in late 2008 killed or wounded hundreds of Indians. Still, after 2000 Indian and Pakistani leaders have promoted a thaw in relations, visiting each others' countries, co-sponsoring sports competitions, and giving hope that tensions might diminish.

South Asians have also made a distinctive contribution to world politics. Although maintaining traditional social patterns and cultural viewpoints, the four major South Asian nations, all democracies some or most of the time, have been led by women at various times. Hence, while women remain disadvantaged, they have enjoyed more high-level political power than in other nations. The political power of a few women is just part of the great complexity of this region.

LO³ Revolution, War, and Reconstruction in Indochina

From the 1940s through the 1970s, the peoples of the Southeast Asia region that the French called Indochina—Vietnam, Cambodia, and Laos—experienced the most wrenching violence as two powerful Western nations, France and the United States, attempted to roll back revolutionary nationalism. The end of World War II and the rise of the Cold War set the stage for two successive struggles with global implications. During the first struggle, known

CHRONOLOGY

Indochina, 1945–Present

1945	Formation of Viet Minh government in Vietnam
1946–1954	First Indochina War
1953	Independence of Laos, Cambodia
1961–1975	U.S.-Vietnamese War
1963	Assassination of South Vietnam president Ngo Dinh Diem
1964	Gulf of Tonkin incident
1968	Tet Offensive
1970	Overthrow of Prince Sihanouk in Cambodia
1975	Communist victories in Vietnam, Cambodia, Laos
1978	Vietnamese invasion of Cambodia

as the First Indochina War (1946–1954), the French attempted to maintain their colonial control of Vietnam against communist-led opposition, a conflict that eventually ended in French defeat. The second and more destructive war, in which the United States and its Vietnamese allies waged an ultimately unsuccessful fight against communist-led Vietnamese forces, also dragged in the peoples of neighboring Cambodia and Laos. When the turmoil ended, all of the societies involved had to rebuild.

The First Indochina War and Partition

For Vietnam, the first decade after World War II included an anticolonial revolution. In 1945, the Japanese army in southern Vietnam had surrendered to British forces, who moved into the major southern city, Saigon, and then prepared the ground for a French return to power. Meanwhile, the Viet Minh, a communist-led anti-Japanese guerrilla force that, armed and trained partly by the United States during the war, had occupied much of northern and central Vietnam during the Japanese occupation, captured the colonial capital in the north, Hanoi, and in 1945, declared the end of French colonialism. Although it only controlled the northern part of the country, the Viet Minh–led government, headed by Ho Chi Minh, became the first non-French regime in Vietnam in more than eighty years. In his address to a half-million jubilant Vietnamese who gathered in Hanoi's main square, Ho quoted the U.S. Declaration of Independence and added: "It means: All the peoples on earth are equal from birth, all the peoples have a right to live and to be happy and free."[4] In northern Vietnam, the Mandate of Heaven, an ancient concept that gave legitimacy to Vietnamese emperors, had now passed to the Viet Minh. Both French and American observers on the scene noted that the majority of Vietnamese supported the Viet Minh.

Resistance to Vietnamese Independence

However, Vietnamese independence faced formidable roadblocks. The French, desperate to retain their empire in

> "Worried about the spread of communism, the United States shifted from supporting the Viet Minh during World War II to opposing all left-wing nationalists, including Ho and the Viet Minh."

Southeast Asia especially because of its rubber, rice, and tungsten, quickly reoccupied southern Vietnam. Meanwhile, the Republic of China sent its troops to disarm the remaining Japanese soldiers in northern Vietnam. This provocative move made the Vietnamese fear a permanent presence by their traditional enemy, China. The United States, an ally of both France and republican China, was alarmed at Ho Chi Minh's association with the USSR and communism. Worried about the spread of communism, the United States shifted from supporting the Viet Minh during World War II to opposing all left-wing nationalists, including Ho and the Viet Minh.

Vietnam remained tense. The French, refusing to accept Ho's government, had allies among Vietnamese Catholics and pro-Western nationalists. Ho negotiated with the French for recognition of Vietnamese independence in the north. The French did arrange for Chinese troops to withdraw but refused to give up their claims to northern Vietnam. Ho also appealed to the U.S. president, Harry Truman, for U.S. political and economic support for Vietnam's independence but received no answer. In 1946, Ho warned a French diplomat that a war would be unwinnable: "You will kill ten of my men while we will kill one of yours, but you will be the ones who will end up exhausted."[5] When the French ended peaceful negotiations, brutal warfare ensued.

The First Indochina War

During the First Indochina War from 1946 to 1954, the French attempted, with massive U.S. aid, to maintain their colonial grip. Sending in a large military force, the French pushed the Viet Minh out of the northern cities, but brutal French tactics alienated the civilian population. In rural areas, the Viet Minh won peasant support and new recruits by transferring land to poor villagers. As his forces became bogged down in what observers called a "quicksand war," a French general complained that fighting the Viet Minh was "like ridding a dog of its fleas. We can pick them, drown them, and poison them, but they will be back in a few days."[6] After a major military defeat in 1954, when Viet Minh forces overwhelmed a key French base, the French abandoned their efforts and went home.

The peace agreements negotiated at a conference in Geneva, Switzerland, in 1954 divided the country into two Vietnams, displeasing the Vietnamese people. The agreements left the Viet Minh in control of North Vietnam and called for elections in 1956 to determine whether the South Vietnamese wanted to join with the North in a unified country. Ignoring the Geneva agreements, which it had not signed, the United States quickly filled the political vacuum left by the French departure and helped install Ngo Dinh Diem (no dinh dee-EM) (1901–1963), an anticommunist who had been a long-time resident in the United States, as president of South Vietnam. With U.S. support, Diem refused to hold reunification elections. His government and Ho's North Vietnam differed dramatically. Ho's government built a disciplined state that addressed the inequalities of the colonial period. Land reform redistributed land from powerful landlords to poor peasants. However, the government's authoritarian style and socialist policies prompted nearly a million anticommunist North Vietnamese, mostly middle class or members of the Catholic minority, to move to South Vietnam, where President Diem, an ardent Catholic from a wealthy mandarin family, established a government based in Saigon. The United States poured economic and military aid into South Vietnam, but Diem's regime became increasingly unpopular, especially since he opposed land reform.

The Viet Cong

Soon the political dynamics intensified. By the late 1950s, dissidents in South Vietnam, including former Viet Minh soldiers, had formed a communist-led revolutionary movement, the National Liberation Front (NLF), often known as the Viet Cong. Armed by North Vietnam, the insurgency in South Vietnam grew, and the Diem government responded with repression, murdering or imprisoning thousands of suspected rebels. Adding to the anti-Diem mood, Buddhists resented the government's pro-Catholic policies, and nationalists generally viewed Diem as an American puppet. Meanwhile, the NLF spread their influence in rural areas, often assassinating government officials. By the early 1960s, the NLF, now aided by North Vietnamese troops, controlled large sections of South Vietnam, and thousands more American troops, still called military advisers, became more involved in combat. In 1963, U.S. leaders, judging Diem ineffective, sanctioned his overthrow by his own military officers, who killed him. As the situation deteriorated, U.S. concerns about a possible Communist sweep through Southeast Asia provided the rationale for U.S. action. The stage was set for another war.

National Liberation Front (NLF)
Often known as the Viet Cong, a communist-led revolutionary movement in South Vietnam that resisted American intervention in the American-Vietnamese War.

> " Despite their technological superiority, U.S. forces struggled to work with South Vietnamese leaders and find effective strategies to overcome the communists. "

The American-Vietnamese War

By the mid-1960s, the United States had escalated the conflict into a full-scale military commitment (see Map 31.2). U.S. president Lyndon Johnson's (g. 1963–1969) excuse was an alleged North Vietnamese attack on a U.S. ship in the Gulf of Tonkin in 1964, which probably never occurred. Johnson and other U.S. leaders wanted to spread democracy and capitalism, but they had little understanding of the nationalism and defiance that had shaped Vietnam, a country with many historical reasons for mistrusting foreign powers.

 Interactive Map

Soon the war intensified, drawing in a larger U.S. presence and more North Vietnamese forces and expanding the violence across the country. In 1965, Johnson ordered an air war against targets in both South and North Vietnam and a massive intervention of ground troops, peaking at 550,000 Americans by 1968. Meanwhile, Diem was succeeded by a series of military regimes that never achieved credibility with the majority of South Vietnamese. Military supplies and thousands of North Vietnamese troops regularly moved south through the mountains of eastern Laos and Cambodia, along what came to be known as the Ho Chi Minh Trail.

America at a Disadvantage

Despite their technological superiority, U.S. forces struggled to work with South Vietnamese leaders and find effective strategies to overcome the communists. Because the South Vietnamese army, largely conscripts, suffered from high desertion and casualty

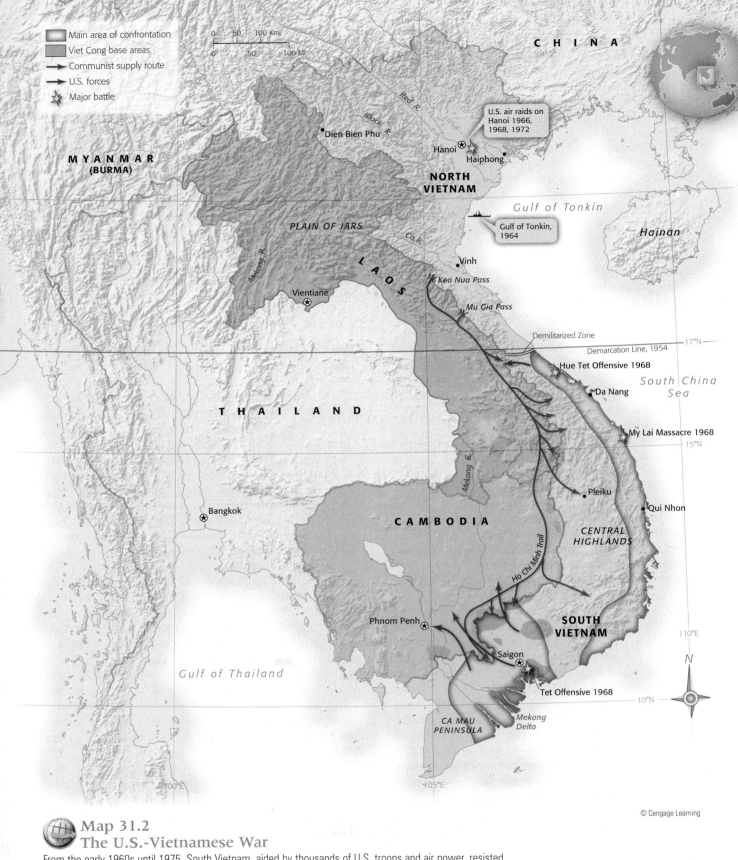

Map 31.2
The U.S.-Vietnamese War

From the early 1960s until 1975, South Vietnam, aided by thousands of U.S. troops and air power, resisted a communist-led insurgency aided by North Vietnam, which sent troops and supplies down the Ho Chi Minh Trail through Laos and Cambodia.

Map legend:
- Main area of confrontation
- Viet Cong base areas
- Communist supply route
- U.S. forces
- Major battle

Labels on map:
CHINA
MYANMAR (BURMA)
Dien Bien Phu
Red R.
Black R.
Hanoi
Haiphong
U.S. air raids on Hanoi 1966, 1968, 1972
NORTH VIETNAM
20°N
Gulf of Tonkin
Gulf of Tonkin, 1964
Hainan
PLAIN OF JARS
Ca R.
Vinh
Mekong R.
LAOS
Vientiane
Keo Nua Pass
Mu Gia Pass
Demilitarized Zone
Demarcation Line, 1954
17°N
Hue Tet Offensive 1968
South China Sea
Da Nang
THAILAND
My Lai Massacre 1968
15°N
Pleiku
Bangkok
CAMBODIA
Qui Nhon
CENTRAL HIGHLANDS
Mekong R.
Ho Chi Minh Trail
Phnom Penh
SOUTH VIETNAM
110°E
Saigon
Gulf of Thailand
Tet Offensive 1968
10°N
N
CA MAU PENINSULA
Mekong Delta
100°E
105°E
© Cengage Learning

rates, Americans did much of the fighting. U.S. strategists viewed Vietnam chiefly in military terms: they measured success by counting the enemy dead and creating free fire zones, areas where civilians were ordered to evacuate so that U.S. forces could attack any people remaining as the enemy. Such policies made it difficult for the United States to win the "hearts and minds" of the South Vietnamese. Vietnam became the most heavily bombed nation in history, as the United States dropped nearly triple the total bomb tonnage used in World War II. The resulting destruction, combined with the use by U.S. forces of chemical defoliants to clear forests and wetlands, caused massive environmental damage. Thanks to the toxic chemicals sprayed on the land and water, Vietnam today has the world's highest rate of birth defects and one of the highest rates of cancer.

South Vietnamese had to choose sides. For procommunist Vietnamese, the American-Vietnamese War was a continuation of the First Indochina War to expel the French and rebuild a damaged society. For poor peasants, inequitable land ownership was the key issue of the war, and the communists gained peasant support by advocating land reform. Other South Vietnamese supported the pro-U.S. government or rejected both sides, repulsed by war's destruction and violence.

....

The Tet Offensive
By 1967, the U.S. military strategy had brought about a military stalemate, but a turning point came in 1968 with the Tet Offensive, in which communist forces attacked the major South Vietnamese cities during the Vietnamese new year. Although the communists suffered high casualties, Tet proved a major setback for the United States and caused Americans to reappraise the conflict. By the late 1960s, a majority of Americans had turned against the commitment to a seemingly endless, costly war with uncertain goals. Even the death of Ho Chi Minh in 1969 did not alter the situation. The United States began a gradual withdrawal of troops and negotiated peace agreements with North Vietnam. In 1973, U.S. ground forces left Vietnam but maintained air support. By 1975, the NLF and North Vietnam had defeated the South Vietnamese forces and reunified the country under communist leadership. As communist forces marched into Saigon, more than 70,000 South Vietnamese who had worked with the United States fled the country, most of them finding asylum in the United States. The devastating war cost the United States 58,000 dead and 519,000 physically disabled. Around 4 million Vietnamese were killed or wounded—10 percent of the total population. By 1975, the fighting had ended, and Vietnam turned to reconstruction.

War and Reconstruction in Indochina

Laos and Cambodia became pawns in the American-Vietnamese War, eventually engulfed in its violence. Anticolonial sentiment had grown in both societies during and after the Japanese occupation of World War II. In 1953, the French granted Laos independence under a conservative, pro-French government dominated by the ethnic Lao majority. At the same time, Cambodia gained its independence from France under the popular Prince Norodom Sihanouk (SEE-uh-nook) (b. 1922), who won the first free election in 1955. The United States began an intervention in Laos in the late 1950s, intensifying an internal conflict between U.S.-backed anti-communist right-wingers, people favoring neutrality between the superpowers, and the Pathet Lao, revolutionary Laotian nationalists allied with North Vietnam. In 1960, right-wing forces advised and equipped by the U.S. Central Intelligence Agency (CIA) seized the Laotian government, controlling the south and the Mekong Valley, while the Pathet Lao gained control in the northern mountains.

....

The Cost of War in Laos
The fighting engulfed the entire nation. The pro-U.S. Laotian regime, bloated with corruption, had an ineffective U.S.-financed army. To overcome this disadvantage, Americans turned to the hill peoples for recruits, including the Hmong, who sought autonomy from the Laotian government. Promising them permanent U.S. support and protection, in 1960, the CIA recruited a secret army of some 45,000 soldiers that attacked North Vietnamese forces along the Ho Chi Minh Trail and fought the Pathet Lao. Ten percent of the Hmong population, some 30,000 people, died during a conflict that was largely unknown to the American public, while thousands of others fled into refugee camps. The war killed some 100,000 Laotians. In 1975, the Pathet Lao took full control of a war-weary Laos. Thousands of anti-communist Laotians fled into Thailand, many later moving to the United States and other Western nations.

Tet Offensive
Communist attacks on major South Vietnamese cities in 1968, a turning point in the American-Vietnamese War.

Pathet Lao
Revolutionary Laotian nationalists allied with North Vietnam during the American-Vietnamese War.

"Like Laos, Cambodia also became part of the Indochina conflict."

Prince Sihanouk and the Khmer Rouge

Like Laos, Cambodia also became part of the Indochina conflict. Its first president, the multitalented Prince Sihanouk, ruled as a benevolent autocrat, diplomatically maintaining Cambodian independence and peace. But during the 1960s, both the Vietnamese communists and the United States violated Cambodian neutrality, and the Khmer Rouge (kmahr roozh) ("Red Khmers"), a communist insurgent group seeking to overthrow the government and led by alienated intellectuals, built a small support base of impoverished peasants. In addition, military officers and big businessmen began to resent Sihanouk's dictatorial rule and desired to share in the U.S. money and arms flowing into neighboring states.

In 1970, Sihanouk was overthrown by U.S.-backed generals and civilians, beginning a tragic era in Cambodian history. With Sihanouk in exile, U.S. and South Vietnamese forces soon invaded eastern Cambodia in search of Vietnamese communist bases, and the resulting instability created an opening for the Khmer Rouge to recruit mass support. The pro-U.S. government lacked legitimacy and became increasingly dependent on U.S. aid for virtually all supplies, and the ineffective Cambodian army suffered from corruption and low morale. Meanwhile, U.S. planes launched an intensive, terrifying air assault through the heart of Cambodia's agricultural area, where most of the population lived. The bombing killed thousands of innocent civilians, and rice production declined by almost half. Amid the destruction, the Khmer Rouge rapidly enlarged its forces, recruiting from among the shell-shocked peasantry. From 1970 through 1975, between 750,000 and 1 million Cambodians, mostly civilians, perished from the conflict between the Khmer Rouge and the U.S.-backed government. In 1975, the Khmer Rouge seized the capital, Phnom Penh.

Reform and Healing in Vietnam and Laos

After years of war and destruction, Vietnam, Laos, and Cambodia began the challenging task of reconstruction. In the largest nation, Vietnam, socialist policies failed to revitalize the economy, and the reunification of North and South Vietnam proved harsh. Between 1978 and 1985, half a million refugees, known as "boat people," risked their lives to escape Vietnam in rickety boats, becoming easy targets for pirates. After spending months or years in crowded refugee camps in Southeast Asia, most of the refugees were resettled in North America, Australia, or France. In the 1980s, the Vietnamese government regrouped and introduced market-oriented reforms similar to those in China favoring private enterprise and foreign investment. These reforms increased productivity, fostered some prosperity in the cities, and ended the refugee flow. Emphasis on education more than doubled the 1945 literacy rates to 85 percent of adults, but the shift from rigid socialism also widened economic inequality, leaving most farmers living just above the poverty line. Politically, Vietnam, like China, remained an authoritarian one-party state, but restrictions on cultural expression loosened. Several former soldiers became pop music stars, and many writers addressed contemporary problems and the war's legacy in fiction.

Gradually, the communists expanded ties to the West and the world economy. In the late 1990s, the United States and Vietnam resumed diplomatic relations, and U.S. president Bill Clinton lifted the U.S. economic embargo. Bustling Saigon, now renamed Ho Chi Minh City, enjoyed especially dynamic growth and prosperity. Consumers in the United States now buy shrimp and underwear imported from Vietnam, while many Americans, including former soldiers and Vietnamese refugees, visit Vietnam.

Like the Vietnamese, Laotians also needed to deal with the divisions and destruction caused by the war. Many Laotians fled into exile, among them 300,000 Hmongs who settled in the United States. Since the 1980s, Laotian leaders have sought warmer relations with neighboring Thailand and China as well as with the United States, but rigid communists still dominate the one-party state. While several cities and districts have vibrant economies, attracting Western tourists, most Laotians remain poor.

Repression Under the Khmer Rouge

Cambodia has faced a far more difficult challenge than Vietnam and Laos, because war was followed by fierce repression. When the communist Khmer Rouge, hardened by years of brutal war, achieved

Honoring Ho Chi Minh These schoolgirls, dressed in traditional clothing and parading before Ho Chi Minh's mausoleum in Hanoi, are part of an annual festival to honor the leading figure of Vietnamese communism.

Vietnam's Intervention in Cambodia

The situation changed in 1978, leading to a new government. The Vietnamese, alarmed at Khmer Rouge territorial claims and the murder of thousands of ethnic Vietnamese in Cambodia, invaded Cambodia, and rapidly pushed the Khmer Rouge to the Thailand border. The Vietnamese invasion liberated the Cambodian people from tyranny and installed a less brutal communist government. But military conflict continued for years as a Khmer Rouge–dominated resistance, subsidized chiefly by China and the United States, controlled some sections of the country. Cambodia proved to be an endless sinkhole of conflict that drained scarce wealth and complicated Vietnam's relations with the West. In the early 1990s, a coalition government was formed under United Nations sponsorship that brought about change. The Khmer Rouge, which refused to take part, splintered and collapsed. While the resulting peace was welcomed by all, the government remained repressive and corrupt. Sihanouk returned from exile to become king but had little power and served largely as a symbol of Cambodia's link to its past. Life for many Cambodians remained grim, but some organized in support of more democracy and social reforms. Nevertheless, the new government has transformed a still-haunted Cambodia into a functioning society, kept afloat largely by Western tourism and aid.

power in 1975, they turned on the urban population with a fury, driving everyone into the rural areas to farm. The Khmer Rouge's radical vision of a propertyless, classless peasant society, combined with their violence against suspected dissenters, led to the flight of thousands of refugees into neighboring countries and what survivors called the "killing fields": the Khmer Rouge executed thousands of victims in death camps and shot or starved many others, indiscriminately. Ultimately, the Khmer Rouge and their brutal leader, Pol Pot (1925–1998), were responsible for the death of 1 to 2 million Cambodians.

LO⁴ New Nations in Southeast Asia

In addition to the Indochinese countries, the post–World War II nationalist thrust for independence produced other new nations in Southeast Asia (see Map 31.3), but the building of states capable of improving the lives of their people had only just begun. Indonesia, the Philippines, Burma, and the other new nations avoided the destructive warfare rocking Indochina

Interactive Map

© Cengage Learning

Map 31.3
Modern Southeast Asia

Indonesia, covering thousands of islands, is the largest, most populous Southeast Asian nation. Southeast Asia also includes four other island nations, five nations on the mainland, and Malaysia, which sprawls from the Malay Peninsula to northern Borneo.

but did have to overcome economic underdevelopment, promote national unity, and deal with opposition to the new ruling groups. The years between 1945 and 1975 were marked by economic progress, Cold War–inspired conflict, and dictatorships; the years following brought even more change and growth. Some nations, including Indonesia, Malaysia, Singapore, and Thailand, have gained reputations as "tigers" because of their economic dynamism. At the same time, governments often have become authoritarian in an effort to ensure social stability.

Indonesia: The Quest for Freedom and Order

Indonesian independence came through struggle. The violent resistance to Dutch colonialism of the late 1940s, known as the Indonesian Revolution, was a bitter conflict in which the Dutch used massive violence to suppress the Indonesian nationalists, who fought back. In a short story about the brutal battle to control the east Javanese city of Surabaya, a nationalist writer noted that the revolutionary soldiers "killed [the Dutch soldiers] with great determination, spirit and hunger."[7] The United States, fearing regional instability, pressured the Dutch to grant independence in 1950.

Sukarno and Indonesian Nationalism

Indonesia still faced the challenge of fostering a unified nation. Given the diversity of islands, peoples, and cultures, Indonesian leaders became obsessed with creating national unity. During the 1950s and early 1960s, Indonesia was led by the charismatic but increasingly authoritarian president Sukarno (soo-KAHR-no) (1902–1970), the son of a Javanese aristocrat and a Balinese mother. A spell-binding orator who was able to rally popular support and bring different factions together, Sukarno worked to unite a huge nation in which villagers on remote islands and cosmopolitan city dwellers on Java knew little about each other. Despite his efforts, however, the multiparty parliamentary system became divisive in the 1950s. Regionalism grew as outer islanders resented domination by the Javanese, who constituted more than half of Indonesia's population and, many outer islanders believed, were favored by Sukarno. Sukarno's poorly implemented economic policies contributed to a severe crisis by the early 1960s and deepened divisions between communist, Islamic, and military forces.

Indonesia's 1965 Military Coup

By 1965, Indonesia had become a country of explosive social and political pressures. After a failed attempt by a small military faction with communist sympathies to seize power, a group of discontented generals arrested Sukarno, took power, and launched a brutal campaign to eliminate all leftists, especially the communists who had gained influence among poor peasants in Java. The resulting bloodbath, led by the army and Muslim groups, killed perhaps half a million Indonesians, including communists and members of the large, unpopular Chinese minority. Most communist leaders were killed or arrested; thousands of leftists were held in remote prison camps for years. Sukarno died in disgrace in 1970.

> **Given the diversity of islands, peoples, and cultures, Indonesian leaders became obsessed with creating national unity.**

Suharto's New Order

Between 1966 and 1998, the government, known as the New Order, headed by general-turned-president Suharto (b. 1921), a Javanese former soldier first in the Dutch colonial and then in the nationalist army, mixed military and civilian leadership to maintain law and order. Suharto used force to repress regional opposition in both East Timor, a small, former Portuguese colony where the mostly Christian population sought independence, and north Sumatra, where the fiercely Islamic Achehnese sought independence. However, although it limited political opposition, the New Order improved Indonesia's economic position and encouraged the rise of an educated urban middle class and vibrant popular culture. Per capita income, life expectancy, and adult literacy increased, aided by an annual economic growth rate of nearly 5 percent by the 1990s, although one-third of the population still earned less than a dollar per day.

> **New Order**
> The Indonesian government headed by President Suharto from 1966 to 1998, which mixed military and civilian leadership.

 East and Southeast Asia: An Annotated Directory of Internet Resources (http:// newton.uor.edu/ Departments&Programs/ AsianStudiesDept/).

Islamic Challenges to Secular Indonesia

Yet, for all the economic productivity, the New Order also started some negative trends. During these years, Indonesia became economically dependent on exporting oil, which represented 80 percent of foreign earnings. When world oil prices declined in the 1980s, Indonesia was forced to accumulate an enormous foreign debt. Adding to the problems, the rapid development of mining, forestry, and cash crop agriculture took a toll on the environment. Furthermore, income disparities between classes and regions widened, while political and business

CHRONOLOGY

Non-Communist Southeast Asia, Since 1945

1945–1950	Indonesian Revolution
1948	Independence of Burma
1963	Formation of Malaysia
1965	Secession of Singapore from Malaysia
1965–1966	Turmoil in Indonesia
1966–1998	New Order in Indonesia
1997	Economic crisis in Southeast Asia

corruption became a major problem. The wealthy frolicked in nightclubs, casinos, and golf courses built across the street from slums or on land appropriated from powerless villages. Suharto, the son of poor peasants, became one of the world's most corrupt leaders, and he and his family acquired more than $15 billion in assets from their business enterprises and from access to public coffers.

Many Indonesians disliked the New Order. For some, Islam provided the chief vehicle for opposition. Some 87 percent of Indonesians are either devout or nominal Muslims, but few have supported militant Islamist movements like those in the Middle East and Pakistan. Suharto discouraged such Islamic radicalism as a threat to national unity in a country that also includes Christians and Hindus. However, devout Muslims have often opposed the government's secular policies and have desired a more Islamic approach to social, cultural, and legal matters, while a progressive, democratic strand of Indonesian Islamic thought has favored liberal reform. Muslim liberals tap into the traditional emphasis on harmony, consensus, and tolerance that was incorporated into Indonesian, especially Javanese, Islam; they thus offer a stark contrast to the more dogmatic Islam common in countries such as Pakistan and Saudi Arabia.

By the 1990s, Indonesian society was suffering from increasing class tensions, insecurities, student protests, and labor unrest, all of which set the stage for dramatic changes. When the economy collapsed, throwing millions out of work and raising prices for essential goods, riots throughout the country resulted to Suharto's resignation in 1998. With the longtime strongman gone, the country fell into turmoil, and protests and ethnic clashes proliferated. Many civilians, particularly among the urban middle class, wanted to strengthen democracy, and in 1999, free elections were held. Later, Megawati Soekarnoputri (MEH-ga-WHA-tee soo-KAR-no-POO-tri), the daughter of Indonesia's first president, Sukarno, became Indonesia's first woman president. Like her father, Megawati followed secular, nationalist policies but also showed little faith in grassroots democracy and resolved few problems. By 2004, popular support for her regime had ebbed, and she was defeated for reelection by a Javanese general.

> "Filipinos have struggled to create a clear national identity out of the diverse mosaic of local languages and regions."

The End of Suharto's New Order

The end of Suharto's New Order, and the disorderly democracy that replaced it, brought unprecedented freedom but also new problems. Removing New Order restrictions allowed long-simmering ethnic hostilities to reemerge, especially in East Timor and Acheh. Terrorist attacks in Indonesia, especially the bombing of popular tourist venues on Bali in 2003 and 2005, added to the growing tensions, raising questions about the long-term viability of Indonesian democracy. Complicating the political problems, in 2004, more than 100,000 Indonesians perished from earthquakes and a deadly tidal wave, or tsunami, that destroyed cities and washed away coastal villages on Sumatra. Efforts to recover from these major setbacks further undermined the economy.

Politics and Society in the Philippines and Malaysia

The Philippines achieved independence from the United States on July 4, 1946, though the two countries remained bound by close political and economic links. The new nation soon faced problems sustaining democracy. A small group of landowners, industrialists, and businessmen who had prospered under U.S. rule manipulated elected governments to preserve their power and to protect U.S. economic interests. Free elections involved so much violence, bribery, and fraud that disillusioned Filipinos spoke of them as decided by "guns, goons, and gold." Furthermore, nationalists often believed that continuing U.S. influence hindered the creation of a truly independent Filipino identity and culture. Filipinos have struggled to create a clear national identity out of the diverse mosaic of local languages and regions.

Political Instability and the Rise of Ferdinand Marcos

Economic inequality and social divisions have fueled conflict. The communist-led Huk Rebellion from 1948 to 1954 capitalized on discontent among the rural poor. Only heavy U.S. assistance to the government suppressed the rebellion. In the 1970s, the communist New Peoples Army (NPA) controlled many rural tenant farmers and urban slum dwellers. Religious differences have also led to conflict. While most Filipinos became Christian in Spanish times, the southern islands have large Muslim populations, some of whom have taken up arms to protest the Christian-dominated government. In 1972, President Ferdinand Marcos (1917–1989) used the restoration of law and order as an excuse to suspend democracy, and from 1972 until 1986, he ruled as a dictator. On Marcos's watch, economic conditions worsened, rural poverty became more widespread, the population grew rapidly, and political opposition was limited by the murder or detention of dissidents, censorship, and rigged elections.

The dictator and his cronies looted the country for their own benefit, amassing billions. In the capital, Manila, a tiny minority lived in palatial homes surrounded by high walls topped with bits of broken glass and barbed wire, while homeless families slept in bushes. The majority of rural families were landless, and child malnutrition increased. To escape poverty, Filipinos often migrated, temporarily or permanently, to other Asian nations, the United States, or the Middle East. Some 10 million Filipinos lived abroad by 2006.

Collapse of the Marcos Regime

The failures of the Marcos years led to massive public protests in 1986 that brought down Marcos and restored democracy. The opposition had rallied around U.S.-educated Corazon Aquino (ah-KEE-no) (b. 1933), a descendant of a Chinese immigrant, whose popular politician husband had been assassinated by Marcos's henchmen. In a spectacular nonviolent revolution under the banner of "people's power," street

People's Power Demonstration in the Philippines In 1986, the simmering opposition to the dictatorial government of Ferdinand Marcos led to massive demonstrations in Manila. Under the banner of "people's power," business people, professionals, housewives, soldiers, students, and cultural figures rallied to topple the regime.

WWW Southeast Asia Guide (*http://www.library.wisc.edu/guides/SEAsia/*). An easy-to-use site on Southeast Asia.

demonstrations involving students, workers, businessmen, housewives, and clergy demanded justice and freedom. Marcos and his family fled into exile in the United States, which had long supported his regime. When thousands of demonstrators broke into the presidential palace, they found that the dictator's wife, Imelda Marcos, a former beauty queen, had acquired thousands of pairs of shoes and vast stores of undergarments, symbolizing the Marcos's corruption and waste. Corazon Aquino became president and reestablished democracy.

Yet the hopes of democracy were dashed as Filipino politics remained turbulent. The government, while open to dissenting voices, continued to be dominated by the wealthiest Filipinos, mostly members of the hundred or so landowning families. Corazon Aquino, herself a member of one of these families, voluntarily left office at the end of her term in 1992. Her successors had rocky presidencies; one of these men, a former film star with a reputation for heavy drinking, gambling, and womanizing, was impeached for corruption and vote-rigging. In 2001, another woman, Gloria Macapagal-Arroyo (b. 1947), a Ph.D. in economics and the daughter of a former president, became president but also faced allegations of corruption. She was reelected in 2005 but faced constant challenges questioning her legitimacy. Two decades after the overthrow of Marcos, the public seems disillusioned with the results. Many Filipinos also resent the continuing close ties to the United States.

Yet post-Marcos governments had successes and failures. Democracy returned, a free press flourished, and the economy improved after 1990, yet much of the economic growth was eaten up by the region's fastest population growth, because Filipinos maintained their preference for large families. And none of the governments successfully addressed poverty or seemed willing to curb the activities of influential companies exploiting marine, mineral, and timber resources. Differences in access to health care, welfare, and related services continued to reflect the great gaps in income between social classes and regions.

> "In Thailand, leaders sought to build a national culture based on Thai cultural values, including reverence for Buddhism and the monarchy, which had little formal power but symbolized the nation."

Diversity and Dictatorship in Thailand and Burma

Thailand and Burma also struggled to create national unity and stability. Although historical rivals, the two countries have shared certain patterns. The majority ethnic groups, the Thais and the Burmans, are both Theravada Buddhists who assert authority over a variety of ethnic minorities, including sizable immigrant trading communities of Chinese and Indians. Both countries also have experienced insurgencies by disaffected ethnic, religious, or political factions. However, while Burma had been a restless British colony since the mid-1800s, Thailand (once known as Siam) was the only major Southeast Asian country to avoid colonization. As a result, Thais have had more control over their government, economy, and culture than other Southeast Asians. Since the 1970s, the contrasts between prosperous Thailand and stagnant Burma have become striking. Both nations have had a long history of military dictatorship, but only the Thais, finding the repressive atmosphere chilling, made a transition to more open government.

Political Turmoil in Post-War Thailand

In Thailand, leaders sought to build a national culture based on Thai cultural values, including reverence for Buddhism and the monarchy, which had little formal power but symbolized the nation. Thai culture promotes respect for those in authority and values social harmony. However, this conservatism has also fostered authoritarian governments and bureaucratic inertia. Ethnic and religious diversity has also posed political problems. Thailand's political history after 1945 was characterized by long periods of military rule, often corrupt and oppressive, followed by short-lived democratically elected or semidemocratic governments. Not until the 1970s would a true mass politics develop in Thailand, as opposition movements challenged the long entrenched military regime. Opposition gained sway in part from Thais' resentment of the United States, which supported the military regime and had military bases and some 50,000 troops in the country. The presence of free-spending American soldiers created a false prosperity while also posing a challenge to Buddhist moralists, who were outraged by the sleazy bars, nightclubs, and brothels that often exploited poor Thai women.

Collapse of Military Rule

In 1973, antigovernment feelings boiled over, and the military regime was overthrown following student-led mass demonstrations that involved several hundred thousand people. The military strongman was forced to flee the country, and the collapse of military rule opened a brief era of political liberalization. For the first time in Thai history, democracy and debate flourished. But right-wing military officers and bureaucrats became alarmed at challenges to their power and privileges, and Thai society became increasingly polarized between liberals and conservatives. Finally, in 1976, bloody clashes between leftist students and right-wing youth gangs led to a military coup and martial law, which resulted in the killing or wounding of hundreds and the arrest of thousands of students and their supporters. The return of military power reestablished order, but the massacres discredited the military.

By the 1980s, Thailand had turned away from military dictatorship and developed a semidemocratic system combining traditions of order and hierarchy, symbolized by the monarchy, with notions of representative, accountable government. While most successful political candidates came from wealthy families, often of Chinese ancestry, the rapidly expanding urban middle class generally supported more democracy. A new constitution adopted in 1997 guaranteed civil liberties and reformed the electoral system, and a lively free press emerged.

Thailand has generally enjoyed high rates of economic growth since the 1970s. Despite a growing manufacturing sector, the export of commodities such as rice, rubber, tin, and timber remains significant. Although the Chinese minority, some 10 percent of the population, controls much of the wealth, Thais enjoy high per capita incomes and standards of public health by Asian standards, yet perhaps one-quarter are very poor, especially in rural areas. The economic "miracle," as some have called it, has, in many respects, been built on the backs of women and children, many from rural districts, who work in urban factories, the service sector, and the sex industry. Problems besides widespread poverty and sexual exploitation also challenge Thais. The economic collapse of 1997 that affected much of Asia also threw many Thais out of work. The rapidly growing, over-crowded capital, Bangkok, is one of the most polluted cities in Asia, and the nation's once-abundant rain forests disappear at a rapid rate, a fact lamented by Thai musicians and poets (see Witness to the Past: A Thai Poet's Plea for Saving the Environment). Health issues have arisen too: the AIDS rate skyrockets. Yet, despite their problems, Thais possess a talent for political compromise, and Buddhism teaches tolerance, respect for nature, and a belief in the worth of the individual. Thais have the basis for a democratic spirit, a more equitable distribution of wealth, and an environmental ethic.

Burmese Independence and Political Chaos

To the west of Thailand, Burma emerged from the Japanese occupation devastated, with whole cities blasted into rubble by Allied bombing. After the war, the British returned to reestablish their colonial control. However, facing a well-armed Burmese nationalist army and weary of conflict, they elected to negotiate independence with the charismatic nationalist leader Aung San (1915–1947). In 1948, the British left Burma, but newly elected Prime Minister Aung San was assassinated by a political rival. He was replaced by his longtime colleague, U Nu (1907–1995), an idealistic Buddhist who also supported democracy. Soon key ethnic minorities, fearful of domination by the majority Burmans, each organized armies and declared their secession from Burma. For the next four decades, the central government rarely controlled more than half the nation's territory as the ethnic armies and communist insurgents fought each other and the Burmese army. To fund themselves, insurgents often relied on the opium trade.

Burma Under Military Rule

In 1962, the army deposed U Nu and seized control. Skeptical of democracy for a fragmented nation, military rulers suspended civil liberties, seized economic control, imposed censorship, and devoted most government revenue to the military. However, by the 1980s, as a result of the military's oppressive control, economic stagnation and political repression had fostered dissent, and various secession movements continued. According to the United Nations, Burma became one of the world's ten poorest nations. Sparked by economic decline and political repression, mass protests in 1988, led by students and Buddhist monks, demanded civil liberties. These protests ended, however, when soldiers killed hundreds and jailed thousands of demonstrators. The regime increased its repression.

Witness to the Past

A Thai Poet's Plea for Saving the Environment

Angkhan Kalayanaphong (AHN-kan KALL-a-YAWN-a-fong), born in 1926, the most popular poet in Thailand for decades, also gained fame as an accomplished graphic artist and painter. His poems often addressed social, Buddhist, and environmental themes. In his long poem, "Bangkok-Thailand," he examines Thailand and its problems in the 1970s and 1980s. The author pulls no punches in condemning Thai society for neglecting its heritage; he skewers politicians, government institutions, big business, and the entertainment industry. In this section, Angkhan pleads for Thais to save the forest environment being destroyed by commercial logging.

Oh, I do not imagine the forest like that
So deep, so beautiful, everything so special.
It pertains to dreams that are beyond truth. . . .
Dense woods in dense forests; slowly
The rays of half a day mix with the night.
Strange atmosphere causing admiration.
Loneliness up to the clouds, stillness and beauty.
Rays of gold play upon, penetrate the tree-tops
rays displayed in stripes, the brightness of the sun.
I stretch out my hand drawing down clouds mixing
them with brandy.
This is supreme happiness. . . .
The lofty trees do not think of reward for the scent of
their blossoms. . . .
Men kill the wood because they venerate money as in
all the world. . . .

The lofty trees contribute much to morals.
They should be infinitely lauded for it.
The trace of the ax kills. Blood runs in streams. . . .
You, trees, give the flattering pollen attended by
scents.
You make the sacrifice again and again.
Do you ever respond angrily?
You have accepted your fate which is contemptuous of
all that is beautiful.
But troublesome are the murderers, the doers of future
sins.
Greedy after money, they are blind to divine work.
Their hearts are black to large extent, instead of being
honest and upright.
They have no breeding, are lawless. . . .
Thailand in particular is in a very bad way.
Because of their [commercial] value parks are 'puri-fied,' i.e., destroyed.
Man's blood is depraved, cursed and base.
His ancestors are swine and dogs. It is madness to say
they are Thai.

Thinking About the Reading

1. What qualities does the poet attribute to the forest?
2. What motives does he attribute to the loggers and businessmen who exploit the forest environment?

Source: Klaus Wenk, *Thai Literature: An Introduction* (Bangkok: White Lotus, 1995), pp. 95–98. Copyright © 1995 Klaus Wenk. Reprinted with permission.

In 1990, Burma, now renamed Myanmar (my-ahn-MAH), allowed elections under international pressure, though with restrictions. Even though most of its leaders were in jail, the opposition quickly organized and won a landslide victory. Aung San Suu Kyi (AWNG sahn soo CHEE) (b. 1945), daughter of the founding president and an eloquent orator, returned from a long exile in England to lead the democratic forces. But the military refused to hand over power, put Aung San Suu Kyi under house arrest, and rounded up hundreds of opposition supporters. Refusing to compromise and becoming a courageous symbol of principled leadership, Aung San Suu Kyi won the Nobel Peace Prize in 1991.

Today the military regime remains in power and still detains opposition leaders, including Aung San Suu Kyi. The generals cleverly manipulate politics while slightly relaxing their grip. Although many Burmese still dream of democracy, others have accommodated themselves to military rule, valuing stability. To expand the economy and thus increase its own revenues, the government began welcoming foreign investment. Western, Japanese, and Southeast Asian corporations invest in Burma, diminishing the willingness of other countries to punish Burma for gross human-rights violations.

Diversity and Prosperity in Malaysia and Singapore

Compared with some of its neighbors, governments proved more stable in Malaya after independence. After World War II, the British sought to dampen political unrest in Malaya as communist-led insurgents kept the colony on edge for a decade. In 1957, with the insurgency crushed, Malaya became independent as a federation of states under a government led by the main Malay party, UMNO (United Malays National Organization). However, the predominantly Chinese city-state of Singapore, a major trading center and military base, remained outside the federation as a British colony. In Malaya, the majority ethnic group, the Malays, nearly all Muslim, dominated politics, but the Chinese, one-third of the population, were granted liberal citizenship rights and maintained strong economic power. British leaders, seeing their colonial role in Singapore as well as in two northern Borneo states they controlled, Sabah and Sarawak, as burdensome, suggested joining them with Malaya in a larger federation, to be called Malaysia. This new, geographically divided Malaysia was formed in 1963.

Ethnic and Political Tension in Malaysia

In the years that followed, Malaysia struggled to create national unity out of deep regional and ethnic divisions. Singapore withdrew from Malaysia in 1965 and became an independent nation. Given the need to reduce political tensions, sustain economic growth, and preserve stability, the leaders of the key ethnic groups in Malaya—Malays, Chinese, and Indians—cooperated through political parties that allied in an UMNO-dominated ruling coalition, but below the surface, ethnic tensions simmered. After 1970, Malay-dominated governments pursued policies designed to reshape Malaysia's society and economy.

Over time, Malaysia and Singapore, both open to the world as they have been for centuries, have achieved exceptional political stability and economic progress. The two nations have shared a similar mix of ethnic groups, and both countries maintain democratic forms, but the ruling parties sometimes arrest or harass opposition leaders. After 1970, Malaysia has remained politically stable by maintaining a limited democracy and holding regular elections in which the ruling, modernizing Malay-led coalition of parties controls the voting and most of the media. The Chinese-dominated ruling party in Singapore has used similar strategies to maintain its hold on power. Because the print and broadcast media are controlled by the government or their allies in both nations, dissidents use the Internet to spread their views on their societies. Both countries have successfully diversified their economies and thus stimulated economic development, and they have also raised living standards and spread the wealth.

Religion and Prosperity in Malaysia

In Malaysia, religion has remained vital, including in politics, which has often divided the Muslim majority from the Christian, Hindu, Buddhist, and animist minorities. Islamic movements with dogmatic, sometimes militant views have gained support among some young Malays who are alienated by a Westernized, materialistic society. These movements, which discourage contact with non-Muslims and encourage women to dress modestly, often alarm secular Malays and non-Muslims. In response, Malay women's rights groups use Islamic arguments to oppose restrictions favored by conservatives. They find some support among the numerous women holding high government positions. Hence, Sisters in Islam, founded in the 1980s by the politically well-connected academic, Zainab Anwar, espouses an Islam supporting freedom, justice, and equality.

Supported by abundant natural resources, economic diversification, and entrepreneurial talent, Malaysia has become a highly successful developing nation, surpassing European nations like Portugal and Hungary in national wealth. High annual growth rates have enabled Malaysia to achieve a relatively high per capita income and to build light industry that employs cheap labor to make shoes, toys, and other consumer goods for export. Many of these workers are women; half of Malaysian women work for wages. The manufacturing sector has continued to grow rapidly, and oil and timber have become valuable export commodities. Malaysia recovered rapidly from the 1997 Asian economic collapse by imposing more government controls on the economy, ignoring Western economic advice.

But economic growth comes at the price of toxic waste problems, severe deforestation, air pollution, and social change. Violence between Chinese and Malays in 1969 resulted in the New Economic Policy;

Kuala Lumpur Dominated by new skyscrapers, including some of the world's tallest buildings, and a spectacular mosque, the Malaysian capital city, Kuala Lumpur, has become a prosperous center for Asian commerce and industry.

aimed at redistributing more wealth to Malays, it has fostered a substantial Malay middle class. Official poverty rates dropped from some 50 percent in 1970 to around 20 percent by 2000. Nevertheless, the gap between rich and poor remains and may have widened. In the bustling capital city, Kuala Lumpur, jammed freeways, glittering malls, and high-rise luxury condominiums contrast with shantytown squatter settlements and countless shabbily dressed street hawkers.

The Example of Singapore

Restricted to a tiny island, Singapore has done even better than Malaysia economically, despite few resources, and has become among the world's most prosperous nations. The predominance of Chinese, the descendants of immigrants during the past two centuries, makes Singapore unique in Southeast Asia. The Singapore government has mixed free-wheeling economic policies with an autocratic lead-

ership that tightly controls the 5 million people and limits dissent. Singapore is run like a giant corporation, efficient and ruthless. People pay a stiff fine if they are caught spitting, littering, or even tossing used chewing gum on the street. Yet it is also one of the healthiest societies, enjoying, for example, the world's lowest rate of infant mortality. Singapore has devoted more of its national budget to education than other nations: everyone studies English in school, and the nation's approach to math education is widely admired. Businesspeople from around the world have flocked to this globalized city, just as they had flocked to the Straits of Melaka's trading states centuries ago.

Southeast Asia in the Global System

After the mid-1970s, a shift of economic direction allowed several Southeast Asians to develop and play a greater role in the world economy. By the 1990s, experts talked about a vibrant Pacific Rim that included the "tiger" nations as well as Japan, China, Taiwan, and South Korea (see Chapter 27). Some forecast a Pacific Century in which these nations would lead the world economically and increase their political strength.

To promote economic growth and political stability, Southeast Asian countries began cooperating as never before. Founded in 1967 by Malaysia, Indonesia, Thailand, Singapore, and the Philippines, ASEAN (Association of Southeast Asian Nations) was a regional economic and political organization aimed at fostering economic exchange among the non-communist Southeast Asian nations. ASEAN's priorities shifted after the end of the wars in Indochina in 1975, and Vietnam, Cambodia, Laos, Burma, and the tiny, oil-rich state of Brunei, on Borneo, became members. ASEAN emerged as the world's fourth largest trading bloc and provided a forum for the various nations to work out their differences and deal with the wider world.

Although Southeast Asians still export the natural resources they did in colonial times, some nations have seen major economic growth through industrialization and exploitation of other resources, including oil, timber, rubber, rice, tin, sugar, and palm oil. With these exports, as well as manufactured goods such as computer chips, clothing, and sports equipment, the region has fostered some of the fastest growing economies in the world. Malaysia, Thailand, Singapore, and, to some extent, Indonesia and Vietnam have become major recipients of foreign investment. Growth did bring challenges: In 1997, most Southeast Asian countries faced a severe economic crisis, part of a broader global collapse. Causes included poorly regulated banking systems, overconfident investments, and government favoritism toward well-placed business interests. By the early 2000s, however, as the crisis eventually bottomed out, several countries began to put their economies back on a rapid growth track.

Southeast Asians have also influenced global politics. Vietnamese communists under Ho Chi Minh, in their ultimately successful fifty-year fight against French colonialism, Japanese occupation, and then U.S. intervention, stimulated a wave of revolutionary efforts, from Nicaragua to Mozambique, to overthrow Western domination. Women have long played an influential role in Southeast Asia, and the political leaders such as Corazon Aquino in the Philippines and Aung San Suu Kyi in Burma have become inspirations to people worldwide. By the early twenty-first century, the Southeast Asian nations were shifting their focus from the United States to China, which they viewed as the rising world power with which they must cooperate for regional stability.

Engagement with the outside world has shaped modern Southeast Asia. Global influences and economic development have increasingly modified lives, especially in the cities. Yet even rural areas have become more connected to wider networks by televisions, outboard motors, motor scooters, and phones. Still, change has often been superficial. For every youngster who joins the fan club for a Western pop star, another identifies with an Islamic, Buddhist, or Christian organization, sometimes a militant one. Many people find themselves perched uneasily between the cooperative village values of the past and the competitive, materialistic modern world.

Listen to a synopsis of Chapter 31.

ASEAN
(Association of Southeast Asian Nations) A regional economic and political organization formed in 1967 to promote cooperation among the non-communist Southeast Asian nations; eventually became a major trading bloc.

Societies • Networks • Transitions

The Contemporary World, Since 1945

The world has changed dramatically since 1945. Some observers have described these years as the most revolutionary age in history. All regions of the world have become part of a global system. The Indonesian thinker Soedjatmoko (so-jat-MOH-ko) described a world of collapsing "national boundaries and horrifying destructive power, expanding technological capacity and instant communication [in which] we live in imperfect intimacy with all our fellow human beings."[1] This interconnected and rapidly changing global society, and the people who shape it, have produced both great good and indescribable horrors.

The contemporary world has become a global unity within a larger diversity. Globalization has fostered or intensified networks of exchange and communication: international trade pacts and electronic fund transfers, jet-speed travel and cell phones. Yet, even as they have become more closely linked, nations have not been able to work together to meet the challenges facing humanity, such as poverty and environmental distress. No clear international consensus has emerged on maintaining strong local cultures in the face of global influences, correcting the widening gap between rich and poor nations, and achieving a better balance between environmental preservation and economic development. Solving these problems requires complex strategies and the joint efforts of many nations.

Globalization and Cultures

Over recent centuries, humans have built a web, or networked society—a global system that today encompasses most of the world's 6.5 billion people. All of these terms imply transnational connections and the institutions that foster them, such as the World Bank, the Internet, and religious missionaries. Around the world, people speak, with fear or enthusiasm, of globalization. Some observers see the trend as dangerous folly, others as a boon, and still others have mixed feelings.

Globalization and Its Impacts

The roots of globalization go deep into the past. During the first millennium of the Common Era, trade networks such as the Silk Road, which linked China and Europe across Central Asia and the Middle East, and the spread of religions such as Buddhism, Christianity, and Islam, connected distant societies. One thousand years ago, an Eastern Hemisphere–wide economy based in Asia and anchored by Chinese and Indian manufacturing and Islamic trade networks represented an early form of globalization. The links between the hemispheres forged after 1492—during which Europeans competed for a share of the growing trade in raw materials—expanded the reach of this economy. In the nineteenth century, the Industrial Revolution and European imperialism extended the connections even further, aided by technological innovations such as steamships and trans-oceanic cables.

 **Globalization Guide** (*http://www.globalisationguide.org*). A useful collection of essays and links.

The integration of commerce and financial services today is more developed than ever before. As the global system has become increasingly linked, societies have become more dependent on each other for everything from consumer goods and entertainments to fuels and technological innovations. For example, all over the world, people consume Chinese textiles, U.S. films, Persian Gulf oil, Indian yoga, and Japanese electronics. Videoconferencing allows business partners in Los Angeles, Berlin, and Hong Kong to confer instantaneously with one another. During the early twenty-first century, the world's most powerful nation, the United States, has become increasingly reliant on Asian nations, especially China, to finance its skyrocketing national debt.

Such interdependence, as well as the reach of political, cultural, and social events across distances, has had an increasing impact in a shrinking world. For instance, in 2005, when Hurricane Katrina devastated the Gulf Coast of the United States, the export of corn from the U.S. Midwest through the port of New Orleans was disrupted. Japan, a major consumer of that corn, then turned to South Africa for supplies, which deprived people in Malawi of South African corn, causing widespread starvation in Malawi. While globalization affects every country to some degree, the great bulk of world trade and financial flow and activity is concentrated in, and has the largest impact on, the peoples of North America, Europe, and a group of Asian nations stretching from Japan to India.

Furthermore, many observers believe that globalization is unmanageable. U.S. journalist Thomas Friedman has noted, "Globalization isn't a choice. It's a reality, and no one is in charge. You keep looking for someone to complain to, to take the heat off your markets. Well guess what, there's no one on the other end of the phone."[2] This powerlessness to affect massive global economic forces has become chillingly evident in the global recession that began in 2008. This impersonal globalization, operating independent of governments, has had major impacts on societies, politics, economies, cultures, and environments. The best way for governments to adapt seems to be by educating their citizens, especially their young people, for a new, more competitive world. Various Asian nations, such as India, Taiwan, and Singapore, have adapted to these changes deftly, pouring money into education, science, and technology. The Western nations that have successfully adjusted to globalization are mainly those, especially in Scandinavia, that have combined open markets with strong societal and environmental protections.

Global forces, symbolized by advertising for foreign-made goods and satellites miles up in the sky relaying information around the world, interact with local cultures. As a result, local traditions and products sometimes get replaced, and imported and local cultures blend. An example of blending comes from France, where, with its large Arab immigrant population, Arab entrepreneurs have prospered by selling fast-food hamburgers and pizza prepared according to Muslim requirements and adapted to Arab taste. People around the world consume global products, from fast food to fashionable footwear to action films, but still enjoy cultural traditions that are distinctly local, such as Thai boxing or sumo wrestling in Japan.

The Globalization Website (*http://www .sociology.emory.edu/ globalization/*). A very useful site with many resources and essays related to globalization.

To flourish in an interconnected world, people have had to become aware of international conditions. In North America, activists seeking to fight inequality or preserve the environment have urged people to think globally but act locally. Acting locally, Brazilian environmental and citizens' groups work to save their rain forests, while environmentally conscious North Americans and Europeans support organizations, businesses, and political leaders committed to improving the global environment. Others argue that people must think and act both globally and locally—to embrace both global and local citizenship. But, despite greatly increased travel and migration, only a small minority of people have become true citizens of the world, comfortable everywhere. Moreover, world government remains a distant prospect at the beginning of the twenty-first century.

Cultural Imperialism: The Globalization of Culture

The inequitable relationship between the dominant West and the developing nations has compelled observers to examine global change. Arising from this effort has been the concept of cultural imperialism, in which the economic and political power of Western nations, especially the United States, enables their cultural products to spread widely. Some African writers have called this pattern a "cultural bomb," arguing that Western products and entertainments destroy local cultures. In this view, the developed countries export popular music, disco dancing, skimpy women's clothing, and sex-drenched films and publications reflecting these countries' own values and experiences. Other societies adopt these products, which modify or suffocate their own traditions. For instance, big-budget Hollywood films attract large audiences, whereas local films, made on small budgets, cannot compete, and the local film industries often die as a result. To survive, local filmmakers adopt the formulas used by successful Hollywood filmmakers: sex and violence. Critics of Western power argue that cultural exchange has been common throughout history, but in the modern world has become largely a one-way street, leading to domination by Western, especially Anglo-American, culture.

Popular culture produced in the United States, entertaining but also challenging to traditional values, has emerged as the closest thing available to a global entertainment. The Monroe Doctrine—the early-nineteenth-century declaration by Congress that the United States would interfere in Latin American political developments—has now become, in the view of certain wags, the "Marilyn Monroe Doctrine," after the famous American actress who, for many non-Americans, symbolized U.S. culture in the 1950s.

Some American icons have become symbols of a new global modernity and capitalism. In 1989, two young East Germans crossed the Berlin Wall and discovered their first McDonald's restaurant. One of them remembered, "It was all so modern, the windows were so amazing. I felt like a lost convict who'd just spent twenty-five years in prison. I was in a state of shock."[3] Not even the Chinese, with one of the world's most admired cuisines, were immune to the appeal of modern U.S. marketing techniques and convenience for harried urbanites, judging from the growing number of McDonald's franchises in Beijing. Yet, Chinese restaurants flourish around the world.

Global Problems and the Culture of Capitalism (*http://faculty.plattsburgh .edu/richard.robbins/ legacy/*). An outstanding site, aimed at undergraduates, with a wealth of resources on many topics.

Still, popular American entertainments often face opposition. Governments, from the Islamic clerics running Iran to the more democratic leaders of India, have attempted to halt or control the influx of what they consider destabilizing, immoral pop culture. In 2005, representatives of many nations, meeting under the auspices of the United Nations cultural organization, agreed that all nations had the right to restrict cultural imports, outraging American political and entertainment leaders.

Forming New World Cultures

Whatever the real scope of cultural imperialism, a new world culture appears to be on the rise. The world is becoming one vast network of relationships as ideas, people, and goods move between its different regions. Mexican and Brazilian soap operas, Indian (Bollywood) films, Nigerian novels, Arab, African, and Caribbean pop music, and Japanese comics and electronic games have been popular all over the globe. And the cultural traffic flow is not one way. In North America, western Europe, and Australia, people take up Indian yoga, Chinese *tai qi,* and other Asian spiritual disciplines; patronize Thai, Indian, Chinese, and Japanese restaurants; enjoy Brazilian and African pop music; learn Latin American dances; and master Asian martial arts. In 1998, the Chinese cellist Yo Yo Ma, born in Paris and later a U.S. resident, founded the Silk Road Ensemble, which brings together Western, East Asian, and Middle Eastern musicians to tour the world playing music that mixes the instruments and traditions of both East and West.

The meeting of global and local cultures fosters hybridization, the blending of two cultures, a process that can be either enriching or impoverishing. Record stores in Western cities set aside some of their display space to sell a hybrid form called "world music," popular music originating largely outside of the West that mixes Western influences with local and other traditions. World music has introduced Western and global audiences to a rich variety of sounds, often rooted in Asian, African, Caribbean, and Latin American traditions. While reshaping music for a global market, world music has also given Asian, African, and Latin American musicians a larger audience. Just like Western pop stars, some world musicians—such as the Brazilian singer-songwriter Caetano Veloso, and the Senegalese Youssou N'Dour, the descendant of griots, who mixes guitars with West African talking drums—perform around the world.

Inequality and Development

Globalization, resulting from interconnections transcending the boundaries of nations, benefits some people but not all equally. The gap between rich and poor nations, and rich and poor people within nations, has grown and remains one of the world's major problems. In 1960, the richest one-fifth of the world's population had a total income thirty times the poorest one-fifth; by 2000, the ratio had more than doubled. The former Soviet leader Mikhail Gorbachev, a keen student of world affairs, has asked: "Will the whole world turn into one big Brazil, into countries with complete inequality and [gated communities] for the rich elite?"[4]

The North-South Gap

With the changes in the global system since World War II, nations on every continent have improved their living standards, lowered poverty rates, and increased their stake in the global economy, which has more than quintupled in size since 1950. The average per capita income in the world grew 2.6 times in the same period, to some $5,000 per year. But the rising tide of the world economy has not lifted all ships, leaving some nations, especially in the southern lands near or below the equator, poor relative to the northern countries. The economies of these nations, known as underdeveloped nations, have stagnated or enjoyed only very modest growth, leaving the majority of their people in poverty. More than 1 billion people live in extreme poverty, with an income of less than $1 per day. The gap between the richest and poorest countries, often known as the North-South gap, has widened steadily (see map). For instance, the difference in average per capita incomes between industrialized and nonindustrialized nations grew from 2 to 1 in 1850 to 10 to 1 in 1950 to 30 to 1 by 2000. Today the industrialized North contains one-quarter of the world's population but accounts for more than three-quarters of its production of goods and services.

 Interactive Map

The growing North-South disparity in consumption is striking. For example, while Americans, 5 percent of the world's population, consume 40 percent of the world's resources, people in a Bolivian valley experience an impoverished material life. According to a study of the valley: "In a man's lifetime, he will buy one suit, one white shirt, perhaps a hat and a pair of rubber boots. The only things which have to be purchased in the market are a small radio-record player, the batteries to run it, plaster religious figures, a bicycle, and some cutlery."[5] Food consumption also differs dramatically. On average, North Americans consume twice as many calories each day as Haitians and Bangladeshis. While overeating contributes to widespread obesity in industrialized nations, one-sixth of the world's people are chronically malnourished, often suffering permanent brain damage because of it, and lack access to clean water. Fifteen million children die each year from hunger-related ailments.

There are also other indicators of difference in wealth. The 10 percent of people who live in the most industrialized nations consume two-thirds of the world's energy. Literacy rates range from a low of 14 percent in Niger, in West Africa, to a high of 99 percent in some twenty wealthy countries. Life expectancy ranges from a high of eighty years in Japan to a low of thirty-seven years in Sierra Leone, in West Africa. More than 60 percent of the world's poorest people are women.

Challenges of Development

Of course, the experiences of the Asian, African, and Latin American nations involve more than the bleak story of poverty and underdevelopment. Life expectancy worldwide has grown by nearly half, and infant mortality has

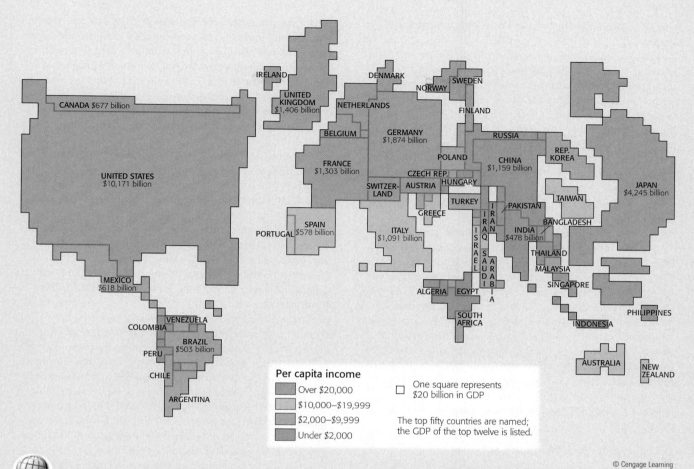

Global Distribution of Wealth

Per capita income

- Over $20,000
- $10,000–$19,999
- $2,000–$9,999
- Under $2,000

One square represents $20 billion in GDP

The top fifty countries are named; the GDP of the top twelve is listed.

CANADA $677 billion

UNITED STATES $10,171 billion

MEXICO $618 billion

VENEZUELA

COLOMBIA

BRAZIL $503 billion

PERU

CHILE

ARGENTINA

IRELAND

UNITED KINGDOM $1,406 billion

DENMARK

NORWAY

SWEDEN

FINLAND

NETHERLANDS

BELGIUM

GERMANY $1,874 billion

RUSSIA

FRANCE $1,303 billion

POLAND

CZECH REP.

SWITZER-LAND

AUSTRIA

HUNGARY

TURKEY

GREECE

SPAIN $578 billion

PORTUGAL

ITALY $1,091 billion

ISRAEL

IRAQ

IRAN

SAUDI ARABIA

PAKISTAN

INDIA $478 billion

BANGLADESH

CHINA $1,159 billion

REP. KOREA

JAPAN $4,245 billion

TAIWAN

THAILAND

MALAYSIA

SINGAPORE

ALGERIA

EGYPT

SOUTH AFRICA

INDONESIA

PHILIPPINES

AUSTRALIA

NEW ZEALAND

© Cengage Learning

The countries of North America, northern Europe, and Japan have the most wealth and the world's highest per capita incomes, averaging more than $20,000 per year. At the other extreme, many people in South America and most people in the poor countries of sub-Saharan Africa, South Asia, and the Middle East earn less than $2,000 per year.

dropped by two-thirds since 1955. Some Asian and Latin American nations have achieved literacy rates comparable to those of some European nations. The number of countries the United Nations considers to have "high human development" grew from sixteen to fifty-five between 1960 and 2004. The rapidly industrializing nations of East and Southeast Asia have led the way: Singapore and South Korea achieved similar world economic rankings with such European nations as Italy, Greece, and Portugal. Several Latin American nations, Caribbean islands, and small oil-rich Persian Gulf states joined the top development category. Many rising nations—such as Malaysia, Thailand, India, and Brazil—formed a growing group of Newly Industrializing Countries (NICs), which have enjoyed high economic growth rates since the 1960s. Malaysia, for example, has dramatically reduced poverty rates, whereas India and Singapore have become centers of high technol-

ogy. Nor is technological innovation restricted to the well educated.

While some countries are on the rise, others struggle to spur economic growth that benefits all of the population. Valiant efforts have failed to substantially raise living standards for everyone. For instance, in much of Latin America, the wealthiest 20 percent have enjoyed huge income increases, whereas the poorest 40 percent have lost income. Capitalism supported by Western investment has helped a few countries, especially those that combine strong governments with social and economic reform, as in South Korea, Malaysia, and Thailand, but reliance on free markets and Western investment has often failed to sustain development. Little of the trickle-down of wealth from the rich to the poor—predicted by Western economists who favor free enterprise—has occurred. Instead, the result has often been trickle-out: the loss of a country's wealth to multinational corporations and international banks.

At the same time, alternatives to capitalism have not necessarily brought improvement. Communist and other social revolutionary countries have experienced severe problems. Some of these countries, such as Fidel Castro's Cuba and Mao Zedong's China, did a good job of delivering education and health care but were unable to create much wealth. Some communist countries, such as Angola and Vietnam, also sometimes faced civil wars and trade embargoes imposed by the West that drained their economies. Because in most cases neither capitalism nor socialism by itself proved the answer, most communist regimes eventually allowed private companies and Western investment while maintaining strong, centralized governments.

Since adopting this model after the end of the Maoist era, China, for example, has generated the world's most rapid economic growth; in recent years, Vietnam has tried to follow the same path. However, economic liberalization that dismantles government services has deprived millions of Chinese and Vietnamese of the free education and health care they enjoyed under socialism, fostering unrest. The formula of mixing capitalism and socialism has worked well in much of East and Southeast Asia. In these regions, a dynamic, largely unfettered private sector has evolved along with planning, land reform, investment in education, and other public policies to benefit the common people.

Envisioning a New World Order

The challenge of development is only a part of a larger contemporary question: how societies, working together, can forge a new, more equitable world order. Even after World War II, decolonization, and the rise of revolutionary states such as China, a few nations, mostly in the West and East Asia, still held disproportionate power and influence. The United States has played the key role and borne the major costs in managing the global system through military alliances (such as NATO), trade pacts (such as GATT), and international organizations (such as the World Bank). However, since the 1960s, observers have argued that fostering widespread economic development also requires addressing the inequalities within the global system and cooperating on international issues. The United Nations has been one major attempt at global cooperation but has had a mixed record.

The current world order contains many problems and the looming reality of limited resources, including water, food, and oil. Conflicts over resources in one nation often spill over into neighboring nations, complicating international relations. The prospect of fostering a more equitable sharing of world resources raises questions about the availability of resources. Experts worry that the world's resources and environment could not support a Western standard of living for all of the world. If every Chinese, Indian, Egyptian, and Peruvian, they argue, consumed the same products and calories as Americans, Swedes, or Japanese, world resources would quickly diminish. For all 6.5 billion people in today's world to live at a western European standard of living would require a 140-fold increase in the consumption of resources and energy. Present oil supplies would run out in one or two decades, assuming the oil could be pumped and refined into petroleum that fast. Furthermore, most of the world's population growth is occurring in the developing nations, putting even more pressure on diminishing resources.

China's recent economic success shows the challenges ahead. By the early twenty-first century, a China rushing toward development had become a huge consumer of the world's industrial, agricultural, and natural resources, energizing global trade but causing shortages elsewhere. For example, world oil prices have soared since 2000 in part because of China's increasing energy appetite as Chinese—1.3 billion people, compared with 300 million Americans—switch from bicycles to cars. If the Chinese consumed as much oil per capita as Americans, their demand would exceed the present world production. China's living standards remain far below those of Japan and South Korea, but should they rise to that level in the next decade or two, China will further stress the supply chain. Assuming China does not experience a revolution, civil war, or economic collapse, experts expect it to have the world's largest economy by 2035 or 2040. As occurred in the industrializing West earlier, rapid Chinese development has also led to environmental degradation, including dangerous air pollution. People in nations such as China and India do not believe that the industrialized Western peoples have any more right to consume the world's resources than they do, and they want their fair share.

Resolving problems of underdevelopment, and the poverty it brings, requires change within individual countries, such as implementing land reform, curbing corruption, and reducing bureaucratic obstacles to enterprise. Many experts have advocated bottom-up development that involves peasants, workers, and women, rather than bureaucratic elites, in decision making. Such decisions would include shaping policies that provide families with adequate economic security, hence reducing the desire among parents for many children to ensure their support in old age. The Grameen Bank in Bangladesh, which loans money to poor women, is an outstanding example of such a bottom-up policy.

International cooperation is hobbled because the leaders of rich and poor nations often disagree on how to address global inequality. For economic and strategic reasons, Western nations want to protect their access to and heavy consumption of resources such as oil and copper and also worry about trade competition from Newly Industrializing Nations. In democratic nations, these leaders have had to answer to voters, who fear compromising their own prosperity. Beginning in the 1970s, various conferences and movements have debated modifying

Protesting Global Warming This demonstration by environmental activists concerned with global warming—a potentially dangerous trend caused by burning fossil fuels such as coal that produces more carbon dioxide—took place in Turkey.

AP/Wide World Photos

the world economic order by, for example, stabilizing world prices for natural resource exports, which chiefly come from developing nations, so that governments could better anticipate annual revenues. Responding to a worldwide campaign to help poor nations, in 2005, the industrialized nations canceled the burdensome debts of the poorest nations. Yet critics wondered whether poor nations with corrupt governments would use increased revenues wisely, while Western nations are often resistant to changes that could threaten their powerful position in the world economy.

Sustainable Environments

The decades since the mid-twentieth century were unusual for the intensity of environmental deterioration and the centrality of human effort in sparking it. The industrialized nations especially had become used to rapid economic growth and were dependent on abundant cheap energy and fresh water, needs that led to unparalleled environmental destruction. By the dawn of the twenty-first century, the challenge of a changing environment became obvious. On every continent, but especially in Eurasia and North America, gas-guzzling vehicles, smoky factories, coal-fired power plants, and large farming operations produce large amounts of carbon dioxide and other

pollutants, contributing to rising average temperatures that scientists call global warming. This climate change, if it continues, may have a catastrophic impact on human life. Problems such as global warming raise the question of whether the natural environment can maintain itself in the long term and support plant, animal, and human life—a pattern known as sustainability.

Societies and Environmental Change

Human activity has altered environments since prehistory, sometimes with catastrophic results. Environmental collapse triggered by agricultural practices or deforestation helped undermine the Mesopotamians, Romans, and Maya, among others. But modern industrial societies and rapidly growing populations encroach on their natural settings even more heavily. Between the 1890s and the 1990s, the world economy grew fourteen times larger, industrial output twenty times, energy use fourteen times, carbon dioxide emissions seventeen times, water use nine times, and marine fish catches thirty-five times. These increases contributed to, among other pressing problems, air and water pollution, disposal of hazardous waste, declining genetic diversity in crops, and a mass extinction of plant and animal species. With their heavy economic production and consumption, people today are borrowing from tomorrow.

The atmosphere faces particular dangers, including a measurable warming. Earth's climate changed little, with only minor fluctuations, between the last Ice Age, which ended 10,000 years ago, and the end of the eighteenth century, when the Industrial Revolution began in Europe, but it has been changing fast over the past two centuries. Since 1985, the world has experienced the highest average annual temperatures on record and unprecedented droughts. Scientists now largely agree that global warming has been increasing, although they debate its causes and dangers. Without major efforts to curb warming, scientists forecast a rise of somewhere between an alarming 2.5 and a catastrophic 10.4 degrees by 2100, which, if it happens, will change human life dramatically.

Scientists speak of a Greenhouse Effect, the overheating of earth from human-made pollutants. The main culprits are gases such as carbon dioxide, chlorofluorocarbons, and methane, which accumulate in the atmosphere and trap heat. The amount of heat-trapping carbon dioxide in the atmosphere increased by one-third between 1900 and 2000, mostly from burning coal and oil. The greenhouse gases come largely from factory smokestacks, coal-fired power plants, and gasoline-powered vehicle exhausts. The United States accounts for some 25 percent of the carbon dioxide and up to 50 percent of the other polluting chemicals. Europe, Russia, Japan, and China produce much of the rest. Some pollutants also destroy the ozone layer, a gaseous region in the upper atmosphere that protects humans from the cancer-causing ultraviolet rays of the sun. Scientists discovered that the ozone depletion rate in the 1990s was twice as fast as was thought a decade earlier.

In the pessimistic scenarios, the consequences of rising temperatures for many of the world's peoples are devastating. Earth gets baked, rich farmland turns to desert, and forests wilt. Fresh water, already scarce, becomes even harder to find as lakes and streams dry up. Rising ocean temperatures damage fisheries and kill most protective coral reefs while also increasing the intensity of hurricanes. Tropical and subtropical nations find agriculture and life generally more difficult. In North America, farming becomes tougher in the southern United States, though more productive in a warming Canada.

Some peoples might face even more daunting challenges. Global warming has reduced the ice covering the Arctic Ocean by half in recent years, while thawing the adjacent land; these developments diminish the habitat for cold-adapted animals, such as polar bears, and threaten the livelihood and settlements of Arctic peoples. At the other end of the world, the West Antarctic ice shelf holds a vast amount of water, and in some places has already begun to melt. If this trend accelerates, it will raise sea levels enough over the next two centuries to cover much low-lying coastal land. This will have disastrous consequences for regions such as the U.S. Gulf Coast and Florida, the Low Countries of northwest Europe, Bangladesh and eastern India, and small island nations already now barely above sea level, including Tonga, Tuvalu, the Bahamas, and the Maldives.

Environmental Issues and Movements

The exploitation of the earth's resources for human benefit, which has accelerated since 1945, has undermined sustainability. While soil, forests, and fisheries are renewable resources if properly managed, mineral resources such as oil and copper cannot be replaced once they are used up. Oil experts disagree as to when all known recoverable oil reserves will become exhausted. Anticipating future resource and energy shortages, experts have for years recommended that industrial nations conserve oil by reducing dependence on it as the main fuel while developing renewable energy resources, such as solar, tidal, and wind power. Some nations have turned toward building more nuclear power plants, which are expensive and potentially dangerous but do less damage to the climate than burning fossil fuels. So far a few developing nations and some European countries have shown the most commitment to conservation and developing renewable energies.

Scientific conclusions about global warming and the need to reduce dependence on oil have often challenged powerful economic interests and upset governments that favor economic growth and worry about economic competition from rival nations. For example, since the 1970s, U.S. presidents and Congress, fearing possible negative effects on U.S. business, have often opposed environmental agreements, such as the Kyoto treaty of 1997, which was an effort, supported by most of the world's nations, to begin reducing greenhouse gases, as well as a European proposal seeking a 15 percent alternative energy use by 2010 (versus 1 percent today). Leaders of a few other powerful nations, including Japan, Russia, Britain, and China, have also been reluctant to cooperate with the world community on environmental issues. In 2005, 150 nations met in Montreal, Canada, and reaffirmed their commitment to the Kyoto treaty. To sustain environmental health, a Canadian statesman has argued, requires a "revolution in [our] thinking as basic as the one introduced by Copernicus who [in the 1500s] first pointed out that the earth was not the center of the universe."[6]

An environmental movement began in the West in the late nineteenth century, eventually sparking similar movements around the world. By the 1970s, organizations such as Greenpeace, Earth First!, and the Rainforest Action Network pressed for a global commitment to stop environmental destruction. In 1992, a UN–sponsored global conference in Rio de Janeiro issued a proclamation urging sustainable development: "Human beings are entitled to a healthy and productive life in harmony with nature."[7] But the realities of modern politics, national rivalries, and fierce economic competition continue to make such a change difficult.

Global Pasts and Futures

The study of history helps us understand today's news and views as they are reported in daily newspapers, broadcast on radio and television, and disseminated online. Historians often describe their work as involving a dialogue between past, present, and future. A few years ago, French scientist René Dubos argued: "The past is not dead history. It is living material out of which makes the present and builds the future."[8] Current global problems have their roots in the patterns of world history. While seeking to understand how the past shaped the present, historians also speculate on how current trends may shape the future.

Understanding the Global Past

World historians offer several ways of understanding the world of yesterday, today, and tomorrow. One view is that contacts and collisions between different societies produce change. Whether through peaceful exchange or warfare or perhaps both, when societies encounter other societies, they are exposed to different customs and ideas. Around two thousand years ago, thanks to advances in transportation and growing economies, increasingly mobile peoples began to encounter others far away, laying the roots for a global system to emerge after 1450. Historians also emphasize continuity, the persistence of social, cultural, political, and religious ideas and patterns, as well as change, the transformations in ways of life, work, and thought. Continuities are common. For example, many Christians, Muslims, Jews, Buddhists, and Hindus still look at the world through the prism of traditional religious values that were forged millennia ago and are still meaningful today. For instance, Islam increased its following from 400 million people in 1960 to 1.3 billion by 2004.

Yet changes, too, are everywhere. Thus most people, among them the devout followers of the old religions, also engage in activities, face challenges, and use forms of transportation and communication that were nonexistent a few generations ago. As a result, missionaries and clerics often use radio, television, and the Internet to spread their message. Another insight offered by global historians is that great transitions, such as the agricultural and industrial revolutions or, more recently, the rise of high technology, can turn history in new directions.

As a result of the spread of Western cultural influences, market economies, economic consumption practices, and individualistic values, some scholars see a growing standardization of the world's societies. Many people welcome this standardization as a sign of progress, whereas others perceive it as a threat to local traditions. Still others consider the claim that societies and cultures are standardizing inaccurate, seeing instead a real increase in differences, especially the growing gap between rich and poor nations. In fact, living standards in the world have not been standardized. While people in the rich countries usually own several expensive electrical appliances, from washing machines to plasma televisions, millions of people in the poor nations do not even have electricity. Still, thanks to contacts between distant societies, the Western value of materialistic indulgence has became common, even if it is often out of reach for the poorest half of the world's people.

The experiences of most societies over the past half century reveal a mix of change and continuity. For example, Western ideas have gained even greater influence in the world since 1945 than they had before. People in different lands have adopted Western ideas of government, such as constitutions and elections, although not necessarily the substance of democracy, along with Western-rooted ideologies and faiths: capitalism, socialism, nationalism, and Christianity. Western pop culture, from rock music to soft drinks and blue jeans, has spread widely, leading to the "Coca-Colazation" of the world stemming from Western economic power, including advertising. Yet influences from the West are usually strongest in large cities and penetrate less deeply into the villages in Africa, Asia, and the Middle East, where traditional ways reflect continuity with the past. As a result, city youth in Malaysia or Tanzania may follow the latest recordings from Western pop stars, but these recordings may be unknown to their rural counterparts. Yet the urban youth may also share with rural youth traditional views about family and faith, and rural youth may, like their city counterparts, own motorcycles, boom boxes, and cell phones that make their lives different from those of their parents.

As a result of the transition to globalizing technology, culture, and commerce, the contacts between societies and their interdependence have vastly increased since 1945. In different ways, nuclear weapons, multinational corporations, earth-circling satellites, World Cup soccer, and cable news networks draw people together, willingly or not. Closer contact, of course, does not necessarily mean friendly relations and a less dangerous world; it can also bring collisions. Guided missiles and planes carrying bombs can reach 10,000 miles from their base. Terrorist plots hatched in Afghanistan by Islamic militants who blame the United States for Middle Eastern problems killed Americans in New York City and Washington, D.C., in 2001. Some of the terrorists involved in planning or carrying out those and other attacks were once secular Muslims who went to Europe or the United States for college and, culturally disoriented and resentful of Western policies, became Islamic militants and then joined a terrorist organization with global reach and access to high technology such as satellite phones, computers, and the Internet.

The same technologies that allow people to instantly access and share information around the world also allows governments to spy on citizens and criminals to use cyberspace for their own purposes. Meanwhile, hackers can live anywhere and disrupt computer operations all over the world. Technology also threatens governments. In 2005, the search engine company, Google, made available a program, Google Earth, that can be freely downloaded and allows a user anywhere to see aerial and satellite photos of any location in the world. Governments from Algeria to India to Russia protested unsuccessfully that this violated their laws and revealed data, such as the layout of military bases, that they did not want available to the general public.

The contacts, changes, and transitions since 1945 have created a global village, a single community of exchange and interaction. In some regions, even remote villages have become part of this global village. By the 1960s, for example, people living in the once-isolated interior of the island of Borneo, divided between Indonesia and Malaysia, could access the outside world through battery-powered transistor radios and cassette players, and also by means of visiting traders, Christian missionaries, and government officials. Borneo's interior people also often left their remote villages to find work at logging camps, oil wells, or plantations as their rain forest environment and small farms rapidly disappeared, destroyed by international timber and mining operations that cut forests and stripped land. As once-remote peoples, like those in the Borneo interior, are brought into the global system, and ethnic minorities are incorporated into nations, they find it harder to maintain their cultures and languages. Half of all languages are in danger of dying out over the next several decades, and less than 1 percent of languages are used on the Internet.

Toward the Future

In 1974, the American economic historian Robert Heilbroner, asking what promise the future holds, doubted the permanence of modern industrial society and even democracy in the face of population explosion, environmental degradation, resource depletion, militarization, and the increasing economic desperation of people in the poorest countries. Heilbroner believed most people are not willing to sacrifice for the good of future generations. Like him, other experts often despair. The world's long history of war, inequality, and exploitation, even when seemingly offset by progress, does not foster optimism. Indeed, some respected experts predict human extinction if people do not adopt more sustainable ways, and scientific studies are more frequently pessimistic than optimistic about the future. One environmental analysis concludes: "Our generation is the first to be faced with decisions that will determine whether the earth our children inherit will be habitable."[9]

Yet, since World War II, humanity has produced many green shoots of hope. Western Europe moved rapidly to political and economic unity, defusing centuries of conflict. Eastern Europeans and Russians overturned dogmatic communist regimes, ending the long Cold War between the superpowers. The Scandinavian nations, one hundred years ago among the poorest European societies,

International Women's Day 2005 Women around the world became more willing to assert their rights. Activists from diverse Indian nongovernmental organizations who were interested in women's rights marched in New Delhi, India's capital, in 2005 to mark International Women's Day.

have virtually eliminated poverty, achieving the world's highest quality of life. Several Asian nations rapidly developed, dramatically improving living standards and national wealth. A century ago desperately poor, China has become not only able to feed and clothe its huge population but also to export industrial products to the world.

Thanks in part to global efforts, black majority rule came to South Africa. More than two dozen nations, including some in Asia, Latin America, and the Caribbean, have elected women presidents or prime ministers, and women, making their voices heard, have increasingly gained more power over their lives in many countries. Despite some notable conflicts, wars have become less common than before. Unlike the Cold War years between 1946 and 1992, when fighting between and within nations was frequent, between 1992 and 2005, the number of wars with more than one thousandbattle deaths per year declined by 80 percent.

Hopeful developments have also resulted from international cooperation. A large majority of nations have signed agreements to ban weapons of mass destruction, punish genocide, and reduce gases contributing to global warming. Drastic reductions in the arms race have diminished the threat of nuclear war. United Nations agencies have improved lives for children and women in many countries and spurred cooperation on environmental issues. Local nongovernmental organizations, often with international connections, have also become active, working for the rights of women, children, workers, and peasants and for a healthier environment. Human rights groups with chapters around the world have worked courageously to promote civil liberties and the release of political prisoners. Encouraged by environmental activists abroad, brave tribal groups in tropical rain forests have resisted the logging and mining destroying their habitats. Not least in its effects, the growing information superhighway now instantly links millions of computers with people, libraries, and other information sources around the world.

A history not only of cruelty and exploitation but also of compassion and sacrifice provides hope in navigating troubled times. Remembering when people behaved magnificently may foster inspiration to answer the challenges. The contemporary age offers ample examples of inspiring people: democracy activists such as Nelson Mandela, Vaclav Havel, Mohandas Gandhi, and Aung San Suu Kyi; social activists such as Wangari Maathai, Dr. Martin Luther King, Jr., Shirin Ebadi, and Mukhtaran Bibi; cultural figures such as Wole Soyinka, Violeta Parra, Simone de Beauvoir, and Cui Jian; and figures who have built links between societies such as Jean Monnet, Bono, and the Dalai Lama. Historians sometimes view the past as a stream with banks. The stream is filled with people killing, bullying, enslaving, and doing other things historians usually record, while on the banks, unnoticed, women and men build homes, raise children, tend farms, settle disputes, pray, sing songs, sculpt statues, trade with their neighbors, and chat with travelers from other lands. Historians often ignore the banks for the stream, but what happens on the banks may be more reassuring.

Some observers, believing that cultural differences will increasingly drive international politics, forecast a clash of civilizations, such as between the Christian West and Islam, which are seen as irreconcilably opposed in world-views. But simplistic formulas miss the complexity of the global order. None of the great religions and the cultures that they shaped are monolithic, the divisions among

United Nations (*http://www .un.org*). The pathway to the websites of the many United Nations agencies, operations, and ongoing projects.

Christians or Muslims, Westerners or Middle Easterners, being as great as their differences with other traditions. No cultures or religions have a monopoly on values such as peace, justice, charity, tolerance, public discussion, and goodwill. In any case, nations generally shape their foreign policies according to their national interests rather than ideology. Wars over resources, such as oil and water, some observers claim, are more likely to occur than wars over cultural differences.

Other observers doubt that, whatever the tensions, any titanic military struggle like the two world wars of the twentieth century is inevitable; they expect that the world will cooperate on major issues and tolerate different concepts of economics, government, God, morality, and society for years to come. Furthermore, thanks to the many available information sources, people can become informed about why past societies, such as the Mesopotamians and Maya, destroyed their environments and collapsed, and how countries blundered into wars or failed to develop cooperative relations with their neighbors that maintained peace. These insights, if acquired, may help people today to avoid repeating the mistakes of the past and construct a better future.

Four centuries ago, the English playwright William Shakespeare wrote that the past is prologue to the present. The study of world history allows us to ask questions about the global future, because we understand the changing patterns of the global past, including the building of societies, their interactions through networks, and the great transitions that reshaped humanity. The contemporary age has been marked by a complex mix of dividing and unifying forces, unique societies differing greatly in standards of living but linked into a global system of exchange. People today cannot yet know with certainty where the path will lead, but they can help build it.

Nineteenth-century British novelist Lewis Carroll (1832–1898) suggested a way of looking at the problem in his novel *Through the Looking Glass*, about Alice in Wonderland. Lost and perplexed in Wonderland, Alice asked the Cheshire Cat: "Would you tell me, please, which way I ought to go from here?" The enigmatic cat pondered the query for a few moments and then replied: "That depends a great deal on where you want to get to."[10] Societies, working together, must chart that course into the future.

Test your understanding of the material covered in Part VI.

Suggested Reading

Baylis, John, et al., eds. *The Globalization of World Politics: An Introduction to International Relations,* 3rd ed. New York: Oxford University Press, 2004. Essays on world politics by British scholars.

Brown, Lester. *Plan B 2.0: Rescuing a Planet Under Stress and a Civilizaion in Trouble.* New York: W.W. Norton, 2006. A survey of the world's environmental and resource challenges and some possible solutions.

Hannerz, Ulf. *Transnational Connections: Culture, People, Places.* New York: Routledge, 1996. Interesting essays on cultures and networks in the age of globalization by a Swedish scholar.

Held, David, ed. *A Globalizing World? Culture, Economics, Politics.* New York: Routledge, 2000. An excellent collection of essays and readings on various aspects of globalization, compiled by British scholars.

Hobsbawm, Eric. *On the Edge of the New Century.* New York: The New Press, 1999. Thoughts on the past, present, and future by a British historian.

Kennedy, Paul. *Preparing for the Twenty-First Century.* New York: Random House, 1993. A study of how population, technology, and the environment shaped the contemporary world and various regions.

Mayor, Federico, and Jerome Bindé. *The World Ahead: Our Future in the Making.* New York: Zed Books, 2001. A comprehensive study, prepared by European scholars for the United Nations, of political, economic, social, cultural, and environmental trends.

Mazrui, Ali. *Cultural Forces in World Politics.* London: Heinemann, 1990. A challenging examination of world-views and patterns by a distinguished African scholar.

Newland, Kathleen, and Kamala Chandrakirana Soedjatmoko, eds. *Transforming Humanity: The Visionary Writings of Soedjatmoko.* West Hartford, CT: Kumarian Press, 1994.

Thoughtful essays on development, violence, religion, and other issues in the contemporary world by an influential Indonesian thinker.

Pieterse, Jan Nederveen, ed. *Global Futures: Shaping Globalization.* London: Zed Books, 2000. Provocative essays on world trends by scholars from around the world.

Sachs, Jeffrey. *The End of Poverty: Economic Possibilities for Our Time.* New York: Penguin, 2005. Controversial but stimulating discussion of global poverty issues.

Seager, Joni. *The Penguin Atlas of Women in the World,* revised and updated. New York: Penguin, 2003. Creative, indispensable examination of women around the world.

Sen, Amartya. *Identity and Violence: The Illusion of Destiny.* New York: W.W. Norton, 2006. Provocative critique by an India-born economist of the clash of civilizations idea.

Smith, Dan, and Ane Braein. *Penguin State of the World Atlas,* 7th ed. New York: Penguin, 2003. The latest edition of an invaluable map based reference providing an overview of world conditions.

State of the World. New York: W.W. Norton. Informative annual surveys of the world's environmental health that are published annually by the Worldwatch Institute in Washington, D.C.

Taylor, Timothy D. *Global Pop: World Music, World Markets.* New York: Routledge, 1997. A fine study of the world music industry and major musicians.

Index

Abacha, Sani, 827

Abbas, Shah, 420

Abbasid caliphate, 417

Abd al-Qadir, 562

Abed, Fazle Hasan, 848

Abidjan (Ivory Coast), 832

Abolition (abolitionists), 497, 681; in Britain, 544, 545; in China, 465; in France, 492; in Latin America, 535; in Siam, 587; in United States, 522, 523, 524, 528

Aborigines, of Australia, 540; land rights of, 793

Abortion. *See also* Birth control; in China, 709, 730; in Europe, 632, 714, 757; in India, 846; in Latin America, 803; in Soviet Union, 765; women's movement and, 672, 757

Absolutism (absolute monarchy): in Russia, 389–390; in England, 392–393; in Europe, 387; in France, 389, 398; Greek revolt against, 505

Acadia (Nova Scotia), 434, 439–440

Accra, Ghana, 664

Achebe, Chinua, 807, 832

Acheh, Sumatra, 457, 478, 482, 857; tsunami in (2004), 858; women rulers in, 459

Adenauer, Konrad, 749

Administration: *See also* Bureaucracy; Russian, 390; Ottoman, 418; Spanish colonial, 432, 433, 436; in English North America, 439, 445; Mughal India, 451; Siamese, 457; Chinese, 464, 465; colonial Africa, 549, 553, 554; Dutch colonial, 461, 582; British, in India, 575; British, in Iraq, 670; U.S. military in Japan, 732

Adriaenz, Job, 372–373*(illus.)*

Afghanistan (Afghans), 700, 811*(map)*; Mughal India and, 450, 451, 454; Safavid Persia and, 421–422, 423; British war with, 575; Russia and, 575, 615; Pashtun tribes in, 575; Soviet occupation of, 696, 717, 764, 767, 784, 819, 847; refugees from, 711; U.S.-led invasion of, 687, 717, 847; Taliban rule of, 784, 819; Pakistan and, 847

Afghan Wars (1839–1880), 575

Africa (Africans), 634. *See also* East Africa; North Africa; Sub-Saharan Africa; West Africa; coastal trade, 403*(map)*; chronology (1482–1750), 404; Portuguese exploration of, 408–410, 430; American foods in, 415, 480; Western colonialism in, 508, 510; European colonies in (1914), 511, 512*(map)*, 547–549 *and map*, 556; European modernism and, 521; migrant workers within, 555; chronology (1912–1936), 660; nationalism in, 664–666, 807; poverty in, 701; desertification in, 710; China and, 725; in European parliaments, 758; decolonization in, 750, 807; rioting, in France, 775; AIDS in, 711, 829, 831, 832, 835; socialism in, 831–832; arts and literature of, 833–834; in global system, 834–835

African Americans (blacks): mulatto children of, 436, 446; in colonial North America, 436, 446, 489; slavery and, 522, 523, 528, 544; racial segregation and, 528, 789; lynching of, 528, 633; railroads and, 529; in World War II, 642; jazz and, 446, 633, 666, 759; music of, 712, 791; civil rights movement and, 788, 789; Obama presidency and, 789

African National Congress (ANC), 552, 665; majority rule and, 829

African nationalism, 664–666, 807

African slavery, 680; in colonial Brazil, 370, 378, 495–496; in colonial North America, 370, 378, 439, 489; maroon societies, 446; in plantation zone, 426, 478, 489; in Portuguese Macao, 469

African slave trade, 475; African societies and, 371, 404; in Americas, 371, 413 *and map*, 414 *and illus.*; in Atlantic System, 413–414 *and map*; British industrialization and, 500; Dutch and, 412; emancipation and, 401; Europeans and, 407–408; middle passage and, 414 *and illus.*; mortality rates in, 444, 445; Portugal and, 409, 410; women in, 481; end of, 544–545; Omani Arabs and, 411, 545

African Union, 835

Afrikaans language, 551

Afrikaners, 551, 666, 828. *See also* South Africa

Afro-Brazilians, 445–446, 495–496; music and dance of, 536, 675

Afro-Caribbeans, 496, 675

Afro-Cubans, 799

Afro-Haitians, 496, 497

Afro-Jamaicans, 497, 805

Agenda for the New Millennium, 706

Age of Revolution: American Revolution, 488, 489–490, 677; in Caribbean and Latin America, 494–497, 498*(map)*, 499; chronology, 488, 495; French Revolution, 485, 490–493, 677; modern revolutions, 488; Napoleonic Era, 493, 494*(map)*

Agriculture. *See also* Cash crops; Farmers and farming; Plantation zone; Eastern European, 379; in France, 389; in North American colonies, 434; in South Africa, 412; in China, 464, 466, 468, 595, 653; in Japan, 471, 472, 610; in Korea, 470, 608; irrigation for, 452, 589, 595, 608, 610; Soviet collectivization of, 629, 630; in Great Depression, 634; Mexican land reform and, 674; peasant-based, 676; in Australia, 680; communal, in China, 721–722; Chinese reform of, 727; Green Revolution in, 704, 709, 782, 840, 844; in New Zealand, 794; in Latin America, 802; in India, 840, 844

Aguinaldo, Emilio, 587, 588

Ahmad Ibn 'Abd Allah, Muhammad, 560–561; tomb of, 543*(illus.)*

544; in Meiji Japan, 611(illus.);
Great Depression and, 633; local
cooperative, 705, 707, 848, 870;
crisis in Southeast Asia, 865
Al-Banna, Hasan, 671
Bantu-speaking peoples: migration
of, 407, 681–682; trading cities
and kingdoms, 406–407; Xhosa,
407, 550, 552, 554; Zulu, 407,
412, 550, 551–552
Bantustans, 828–829
Baptists, 520
Barbados, 434, 444, 496
Barbarians, Westerners as: in China,
596, 597; in Japan, 449(illus.),
607, 608
Barbusse, Henri, 625
Baroque art, 395
Barter economy, 378
Baseball, in Japan, 632
Basel (Switzerland) Zionist
conference (1897), 567
Basho, Matsuo, 473
Basques (ETA), in Spain, 639, 716,
749(illus.), 750
Basra (Iraq), 417
Bastile Day Parade, in Vietnam,
586(illus.)
Bastille, storming of (Paris),
491(illus.)
Batavia (Jakarta), 458(map), 461,
462 and illus., 583, 591, 707
Batista, Fulgencio, 672
Baule people of Ivory Coast, 555
Bay of Pigs invasion (Cuba,
1961), 799
Beatles (musical group), 759,
765, 791
Bedouin tribes of North Africa, 564
Bedreddin, Seyh, 419
Beethoven, Ludwig von, 520
Beijing, 465(illus.), 466, 598, 603,
604; Jesuits in, 469; Forbidden
City, 719, 722(illus.); Nixon in,
725; fast-food restaurants in, 867
Beijing Massacre (1989), 728
Beijing University, 651, 652
Beirut, Lebanon, 562; civil war in, 816
Belgian colonies. See also Belgian
Congo; in 1913, 512(map); in
Africa, 511, 512(map), 554;
independence of, 691(map)
Belgian Congo, 547, 548(map). See
also Congo; rubber plantations
in, 554, 555 and illus.; rival ethic
groups in, 553, 648; forced labor
in, 554–555

Belgium, 678. See also Flanders;
Antwerp, 373, 374, 375(illus.);
Catholicism in, 387, 520;
Habsburgs and, 504;
industrialization in, 502; World
War I in, 622, 623(map); quality
of life in, 694, 830; monarchy in,
748; European Community
and, 753
Belize (British Honduras), 673(map)
Bell, Gertrude, 670
Bellini, Giovanni, 381, 418
Bengal (Bengalis), 451, 455, 479.
See also Bangladesh; British and,
456, 571–572; famine in, 659;
merchants of, 452; Muslims in,
581, 582, 658, 838; nationalism in,
841; opium in, 597
Benin, 371, 405, 415, 416; bronze
artistry of, 406(illus.)
Benz, Karl, 521
Berbers, 422, 562
Bergen-Belsen death camp, 642
Berlin: airlift to (1948), 751;
immigrants in, 758; population
of, 517
Berlin Conference (1884–1885),
547, 549
Berlin Wall, 764; dismantling of,
746–747(illus.), 771, 772
Bernhardt, Sarah, 519
Bernini, Gianlorenzo, 395
Bernstein, Eduard, 508
Berry, Chuck, 759, 791
Beverley, Robert, 440
Bhakti mysticism, in Hinduism,
452–453
Bhangra (Indian folk music), 759
Bharatha Janata (BJP, India),
844, 846
Bhutto, Benazir, 847
Bhutto, Zulkifar Ali, 847
Bibi, Mukhtaran, 716, 875
Bible, the: Luther's translation of,
383; literal interpretation of, 714
Biermann, Wolf, 766
Big business. See also Corporations;
capitalism and, 380, 467;
monopoly and, 503, 529; in United
States, 529, 788; in Japan, 639,
735; in Brazil, 799; in
Cambodia, 854
Biko, Stephen, 829
Bill of Rights (England, 1689),
393, 492
Bill of Rights (United States, 1792),
490, 506, 522

Bin Laden, Osama, 717, 815. See also
Al Qaeda; in Afghanistan, 784,
819, 820
Biological weapons, 699
Birmingham (England), 754;
industrialization in, 500, 502(map)
Birth control, 835. See also
Abortion; Catholics and, 709,
757, 760; contraceptives for,
707, 757; in Europe, 519, 632;
women's movement and, 757;
in Japan, 632, 737; in China,
709, 730; in India, 846
Birthrate, decline in, 709; in Europe,
775; in India, 842; in Japan, 737;
in South Korea, 742; in Soviet
Union, 765
Bishops, 385
Bismarck, Otto von, 505
Bison (buffalo) hunting, 435, 528
Black Death, 479
Black empowerment, 689
Black Hand (Bosnian Serb
group), 621
Black Hole of Calcutta, 571
Black Legend, Spanish colonials and,
437, 439
Black Orpheus (film), 804
Black Robes, 434. See also Jesuit
missionaries
Black Sea region: Ottomans and,
417; Russia and, 390, 423, 481,
557 and map, 615
Blackshirts (Italian fascists), 636
Black Zion movement, 556
Blair, Tony, 775
Blake, William, 517
Blues (music), 446
Boat people (Vietnamese
refugees), 854
Boats, colonial cash crops and,
649(illus.)
Boers (South Africa), 412–413,
550–551, 552(illus.)
Boer War (1899–1902), 550
Bolivar, Simon, 496–497 and illus.,
499, 535, 677, 797
Bolivarian Revolution, in
Venezuela, 797
Bolivia: Spanish conquest of,
432; independence of, 497,
498(map); Indians of, 442, 796;
silver mines in, 442, 476;
regional wars and, 531;
poverty in, 868
Bollywood (Indian) films,
846–847

Bugeaud (French general), 562
Bulgaria (Bulgarians), 773(map); Ottoman control of, 387, 416, 482; Soviet domination of, 766
Bunraku theater (Japan), 473
Burakumin class (Japan), 737
Bureaucracy (bureaucrats): See also Administration; Civil service; in African kingdoms, 405, 406; Ottoman, 419; China, 465, 601; French, 492; Japanese, 610; Chinese, 721; North Korean, 743; Soviet Russia, 629, 762, 763, 767; Mexican, 798; Thai, 860; Indian, 841
Burkina Faso, 707
Burma (Myanmar), 457, 865; literacy in, 476; British colony, 510, 584–585, 650, 660; nationalism in, 650, 660, 664; Indian immigrants in, 660, 860; independence of, 690, 691(map); Japanese control of, 659; political opposition in, 715; military rule in, 861–862
Burmans, 584–585, 660, 861
Bush, George H. W., 700
Bush, George W.: preemptive war doctrine and, 784–785, 786, 849; war on terrorism of, 717, 786, 820
Bush Doctrine, 784–785, 786
Business and businessmen: See also Big business; Corporations; capitalism and, 379, 398, 500; Javanese women, 461; Spanish, 463; imperialism and, 510; British, in Latin America, 534; in British India, 572; European, in Africa, 556; American, in Philippines, 588; Western, in Southeast Asia, 587, 589; Chinese, abroad, 601; Western, in China, 600 and illus., 602; in South Korea, 701; in Japan, 632, 694, 701, 732, 740; Mexican, 798; in Africa, 827
Byzantine Empire, 416

Cable news networks, 714
Cabot, John, 377(map), 430
Cabral, Amilcar, 693, 825
Cahokia, moundbuilders of, 427
Cairo: University of, 404; population growth in, 707; modernization in, 566(illus.), 806–807(illus.)
Cajuns, of Louisiana, 440
Calcutta, India, 455, 680, 707; British trade in, 456, 571, 574(map); Hindu College in, 575

Calendar, 469; Aztec, 425; Western, in East Asia, 604, 612
Calicut (India), 454
California: Spanish in, 432; Chumash of, 437; annexation of, 525, 526(map), 527, 533; gold in, 527; Dust Bowl migrants in, 634
Caliphates: Abbasid, 417; Sokoto, 547
Calles, Plutarcho Elias, 674
Callot, Jacques, 388(illus.)
Calvin, John, 383, 385
Calvinism, 383, 384(map); French Huguenots, 384(map), 387; in Netherlands, 387; Puritans, 385, 392, 439, 490; in United States, 523; in South Africa, 550
Calypso music, 446, 536, 665, 685
Cambodia, 457, 865; as French colony, 586, 660; Buddhism in, 703(illus.); genocide in, 698; refugees from, 711; Khmer Rouge in, 854–855; U.S. war in, 782, 854; Vietnam War and, 851, 852(map); nationalism in, 849, 853
Canada, 484, 536, 678; Norse Vikings in, 427; French exploration of, 434; colonial, 434–435, 439–440; Loyalists in, 490, 538; French-speakers in, 440, 537, 538–539, 791; as British colony, 489, 537; British investment in, 510; United States and, 523, 537–538, 779, 780, 791; immigration to, 538 and illus., 539, 681; self-rule in, 538–539; Japanese immigration restricted in, 683; church decline in, 714; welfare system in, 694–695; same-sex marriage in, 791; quality of life in, 694, 787, 791
Canals: See also Irrigation; Aztec, 432; Suez, 510, 560, 566(illus.), 578, 670, 684, 809; in United States, 523; Panama Canal, 536, 684
Canary Islands, 376
Cannon, 410. See also Artillery; Ottoman, 417; of Safavid Persia, 420; Moroccan, 423; shipboard, 376, 449, 454, 474; Spanish, 476; in French Revolution, 491; Japanese, 607
Canoes, North American explorers and, 429
Canton. See Guangzhou (Canton)
Can vuong (Vietnam), 585–586
Cao Xueqin, 466
Cape Colony, 549–550. See also South Africa

Cape of Good Hope, 407, 408, 412, 549
Cape Town, South Africa, 412, 549, 649
Cape Verde Islands, 408
Capitalism, 474, 678. See also State capitalism; church and, 375; commercial, 379–380, 499; dark side of, 398–399, 520; mercantilism and, 380; Protestantism and, 385, 392; rise of, in Europe, 374–375, 378–380, 393; urbanization and, 395; failure of, in China, 467; Great Depression and, 635, 649–650; industrial, 500, 503, 504, 530; Marxist critique of, 507, 508, 509, 678; colonialism and, 503, 530, 649–650; democracy and, 627, 650, 695, 779, 786, 851; globalization of, 701, 715, 778; in China and Vietnam, 693, 870; in Taiwan, 744; European welfare states and, 755; Russian transition to, 768; Castro on, 799; and socialism in East Asia, 702, 870; in Egypt, 809; and socialism in India, 840; neocolonial, in Africa, 830; Western investment and, 869
Caravel (ship), 376
Cárdenas, Lázaro, 674
Caribbean Community and Common Market, 805
Caribbean region (West Indies), 634, 795(map). See also specific island nation; Native peoples of, 427, 428–430 and map; Spanish exploration of, 370, 428, 429–430; European colonization of, 433, 445, 496; African slavery in, 370, 413(map), 444–445 and illus., 478, 681; monoculture in, 442; sugar plantations in, 444–445 and illus., 478; Haitian Revolution and, 494, 496; end of slave trade in, 544; poverty in, 679; African culture in, 675; decolonization in, 750; democracy in, 794; immigration from, 710, 758; music of, 446, 536, 665, 759, 791; global system and, 805; United States' interventions in, 797, 799
Carib people, 428; voyages of, 429(map)
Carnegie, Andrew, 681
Carnival: in Brazil, 536, 804; in Trinidad, 536
Carolinas: native peoples of, 440; slave rebellion in, 446

Vietnam, 696; in Soviet Union, 761–765; in Vietnam, 850, 853, 854; collapse of, in Soviet bloc, 768–769; in Cambodia, 854–855; in Indonesia, 857

Communist bloc: *See also* Soviet bloc; Second World and, 694; breakup of (1989), 768–769

Communist Manifesto (Marx and Engels), 507, 509

Communist Party, 508; French, 647, 750; Indochinese, 661; Indonesian, 662; North Korean, 743; Western Europe, 750; Yugoslavian, 766; Russian, 769; Eastern Europe, 771–772; Indian, 843–844

Communist Party (China), 652; Long March and, 654*(map)*, 655 *and illus.*; Mao Zedong and, 655, 656, 722 *and illus.*; economic development and, 721, 729–730; dissent and, 727, 728–729

Communist Party (Soviet Union), 625; central planning by, 767; civil war and, 627–628 *and map*; Lenin and, 627; Stalin and, 761; Gorbachev and, 768

Companies: *See also* Corporations; East India Companies; joint-stock, 380, 392; foreign, in China, 600 *and illus.*

Compass, 376

Computers, 787, 849; Internet, 704, 714, 715*(illus.)*, 730–731, 863, 866, 873; in Taiwan, 744

Concentration camps: *See also* Prison camps; in colonial Africa, 550, 814 *and illus.*; World War II, 642, 644; in North Korea, 743

Confederate States of America, 528. *See also* Civil war, in United States

Confederation, Iroquois, 435

Confucianism: Voltaire and, 398; Christianity and, 469; neo-Confucianism, 466, 482; rationalism and, 515; in Vietnam, 661; Chinese nationalism and, 651; in Qing China, 476, 595, 603, 607; and patriarchy, in China, 726; in Japan, 471, 739; in Korea, 470, 608, 614, 741, 743; in Taiwan, 745; cultural heritage of, 740

Congo, 553; as Belgian colony, 547, 548*(map)*, 553, 554–555 *and illus.*, 648; rubber in, 554, 555 *and illus.*, 701; United Nations troops in, 699*(illus.)*; foreign investment in, 830; refugees from, 711; hybrid pop music of, 712; Mobutu in,

825, 827, 830–831; Rwanda and, 828; as Zaire, 824, 825, 826, 830–831

Congo River Basin, 406, 415. *See also* Kongo; Belgium and, 547; exploration of, 546; ivory trade in, 545

Congregation of the Index, 385

Congress of Vienna, 493, 494*(map)*

Congress Party (India), 842. *See also* Indian National Congress; Nehru and, 840, 841

Congress (U.S.), 527, 530, 624; Cuba and, 536; League of Nations and, 625; Prohibition and, 633; Korean War and, 782; Democratic majority in, 789; Senate, 780; environmental agreements and, 872

Conquistadors of Spain, 431–433 *and illus.*

Conscription (military draft), 610, 614; of colonials, in World War I, 625, 648, 664; in Iran, 669; in Russia, 614–615; in Vietnam War, 851

Conservatives: in Latin America, 532; in Manchu China, 593, 595, 601; in Japan, 632; fascism and, 636; free market, in Europe, 756, 774; in Soviet Union, 767; in United States, 788–789; Islamic, in Middle East, 814, 817; Islamic, in Pakistan, 847; in Thailand, 860

Constantinople. *See* Istanbul

Constituent Assembly (France), 492

Constitutional monarchy: in Europe, 392, 393, 493, 499, 748; in Japan, 610; in Thailand, 660

Constitution(s): Swiss, 392; Iroquois, 435; United States, 435, 490, 492, 506, 522; Cherokee, 527; French, 492; Mexican, 534; Cuban, 536; Ottoman, 559, 567; Persian, 561; Philippines, 588; British India, 581, 658, 839; Chinese, 604; Japanese, 610, 732, 734; in Middle East, 671; Turkish, 669; European Union, 774; Bahrain, 808; South Africa, 829; Thai, 861

Consumer goods: in Europe, 379, 510, 753; in India, 845; in China, 727, 729, 730

Consumerism: in Japan, 735; in United States, 868

Containment policy (United States), 696, 699, 780

Contraceptives, 707, 757. *See also* Birth control

Contras (Nicaragua), 716

Conversos (Christian converts), 437

Cook, James, exploration by, 539

Copernicus, Nicolaus, 381, 396

Copper, 672, 870; in Africa, 830; in China, 594; in Zambia, 555, 835

Coptic Christians, 560, 670

Corn. *See* Maize (corn)

Corporations, 530. *See also* Business; foreign, in Latin America, 534–535; foreign, in poor countries, 705; Japanese conglomerates (zaibatsu), 610–611 *and illus.*, 732, 735, 736; multinational, 702–703, 787, 802; American, in Guatemala, 797; in South Korea, 743*(illus.)*

Corruption: in Ottoman Empire, 419; in colonial Latin America, 495; in Persia, 561; in Vietnam, 585; in China, 653, 728; in Russia, 617, 771; in South Korea, 742; in Taiwan, 745; in Europe, 750; in United States, 788–789; in Argentina, 796; in Brazil, 799; drug trade and, 802; in Iran, 813; in Africa, 825, 827, 831; in Nigeria, 807, 828; in Bangladesh, 847; in India, 841, 844; in Indonesia, 858; in Philippines, 860

Cortés, Hernán, 32, 425, 426, 429*(map)*

Cosmopolitanism. *See also* Multiethnicity: on Java, 461, 857; Orientalist, 576; world economy linkage and, 710; in United States, 789; in Africa, 832; in Indian cities, 845

Cossacks (Russian warriors), 423, 681

Costa Rica, 704

Cote D'Ivoire. *See* Ivory Coast (Cote d'Ivoire)

Cotton (cotton industry): African trade, 415; plantations, 441, 478; spinning machines, 397; in China, 397, 464, 466; in colonial North America, 444; in India, 452, 478, 576, 578, 579; in Britain, 499, 501; mechanization in, 501; women workers in, 555; in United States, 522, 523; Egyptian, 559; in colonial Africa, 554, 555

Cotton gins, 464

Council of chiefs: Iroquois, 435; Yoruba women, 405

Council of Europe, 753

Council of State (Iraq), 670

Council of Trent (1545–1563), 385–386, 760

De Gaulle, Charles (France), 644, 749, 757

Delhi, 422; Mughals in, 571, 577

Delors, Jacques, 747

Democracy. *See also* Parliamentary democracy; Protestantism and, 385; representative, 387; in England, 393; Locke and, 398; in North American colonies, 439, 488, 489; in United States, 515, 523, 696; constitutional, 506; village, 506, 553, 554; in Iran, 561; in Africa, 553; World War I and, 625; fascism and, 637; African Americans and, 642; capitalism and, 627, 650, 695, 779, 786, 851; in Chile, 672, 801; in Japan, 632, 732, 734; political stability and, 694; in Thailand, 702, 861; in South Korea, 702, 742; on Taiwan, 702; social, in Western Europe, 750, 755–756; in Indonesia, 702, 858; in Eastern Europe, 771–772 *and illus.*; in Soviet Union, 767; in Latin America, 777, 796; in Middle East, 812; in Philippines, 860; in Africa, 826, 830, 831; in China, 728, 731; in India, 839, 843, 849

Democratic Party (United States), 789

Democratic Progressive Party (Taiwan), 745

Democratic Republic of the Congo, 830. *See also* Congo

Demonstrations. *See* Protests; Student protests

Deng Xiaoping, reforms of, 727, 728, 730

Denmark (Danes), 493. *See also* Scandinavia; Lutheranism in, 388; Sweden and, 393; Norway and, 504; slave trade and, 413, 544; social democracy in, 635; abortion rights in, 757; anti-Muslim movement in, 758, 775; European Community and, 753; in Common Market, 752(*map*)

Depression (late 1800s), 503, 530. *See also* Great Depression

Derrida, Jacques, 760

Dervishes, 419, 482. *See also* Sufi mysticism

Descartes, René, 395, 396, 397, 466

Desertification, 709, 710; in Africa, 479, 835

Deshima, Nagasaki Bay, 472

Despotism: *See also* Authoritarianism; Dictatorship; Tyrants; in Manchu China, 594; in czarist Russia, 630; in Africa, 826, 830–831

Dessalines, Jean Jacques, 496

Developing (poor) nations: American investment in, 779; United States interventions in, 782–783; Arab, 821; population growth in, 705, 870; globalization and, 866, 867; resources from, 871; debt relief for, 712, 871

Development: underdevelopment, 704–707, 830–831, 870; challenges of, 868–870; in Africa, 829–831; envisioning new world order, 870–871; inequality and, 868–871; North-South gap, 868, 869(*map*)

Dewey, George, 587

Diallo, Ayuba Suleiman, 401, 402

Diamond mining, in Africa, 549, 551, 620, 829

Dias, Bartholomeu, 408

Diaspora, trade: Armenian, 421; Indian, 452; in Latin America, 535; Chinese, 600–601

Diaz, Porfirio, 533

Dickens, Charles, 520

Dictatorship: *See also* Authoritarianism; Military dictatorship; in French Revolution, 492, 493; in Latin America (caudillos), 484, 532, 666, 777; in Brazil, 674; in Soviet Union, 629–630, 723 (*See also* Stalin, Joseph); in Turkey, 669; regional tensions and, 700; in South Korea, 742; United States' support for, 783; in Haiti, 797; in Philippines, 859–860; fascist, in Portugal, 825; in Congo (Zaire), 825

Diem, Ngo Dinh, 851

Ding Ling, 653, 656, 723

Dipenegara, Prince (Java), 568–569(*illus.*)

Diplomacy: Chinese and, 470; African queens and, 410; in Siam, 511; gunboat, in China, 602

Direct *vs.* indirect rule: in British India, 577; in colonial Africa, 553; in Southeast Asia, 589

Discrimination: *See also* Racism; in British-ruled India, 578; against homosexuals, 758

Disease: *See also* Medicine (physicians); in Columbian exchange, 435, 479–480; epidemic,

432, 528, 547, 562; in Kongo, 409; Native Americans and, 370, 425, 427, 432, 435, 437, 439, 479, 480(*illus.*), 539; Pacific Islanders and, 431; plague, 464, 479, 562; in European cities, 399, 517; malaria, 412, 434, 511, 547, 711; sanitation and, 521; Australian Aborigines and, 540; cholera, 547, 562, 711; smallpox, 425, 432, 435, 479, 480(*illus.*), 521, 547; vaccines against, 521; syphilis, 435, 480; tuberculosis, 385, 435, 611; weaponized, 699; World Health Organization and, 698; in World War I, 622, 666; global spread of, 711; AIDS/HIV, 711, 729, 829, 831, 832, 835, 846

Diversity. *See* Cultural diversity; Ethnic diversity

Divine kingship, of German Kaiser, 621

Divine right of kings, 389. *See also* Absolutism

Divorce: Henry VIII and, 385; Ottoman, 418; in China, 726; in Japan, 736; in Soviet Union, 764; in Europe, 757; in United States, 791; in Latin America, 803

Dr. Zhivago (Pasternak), 762

Doctors. *See* Medicine (physicians)

Doctors Without Borders, 699, 711

Domesticated animals: *See also specific animals;* Eurasian, in Americas, 435

Dominican religious order, 438

Dominican Republic, 531; United States and, 536, 633, 783

Dominion of Canada, 538–539

Domino theory, 782

Dom Pedro II (Portugal), 499, 532

Don Quixote (Cervantes), 382

Dostoyevsky, Fyodor, 617

Dowlah, Siraja (Bengal), 571, 573(*illus.*)

Drake, Francis, piracy of, 434

Drama (theater): Shakespeare, 382, 383; Japanese kabuki, 473 *and illus.*, 739; Burman, 584–585

Drought: famine and, 707, 827; in Great Depression, 634; in Africa, 710, 830, 832; global warming and, 872

Drug trade. *See also* Opium trade; heroin, 701, 802; marijuana, 791, 805; coca (cocaine), 435, 701, 802; AIDS and, 711; Latin American, 802

Egalitarianism, 453. *See also* Equality and inequality; Native American, 397

Egypt, 485; Ottoman rule of, 416, 417*(map)*; Mamluks in, 559; Muhammad Ali's modernization in, 559, 560*(illus.)*, 564; Napoleon's invasion of, 543–544, 559; British control of, 559–560; women's rights in, 564, 565; terrorists in, 716, 717, 784, 817; Arab nationalism in, 670, 687; Palestinians in, 711; Suez Canal, 510, 560, 566*(illus.)*, 578, 670, 809; conflict with Israel, 811*(map)*, 812; literature of, 819

Egyptian hieroglyphics, 543

Einstein, Albert, 521, 636, 697

Eisenhower, Dwight, 695, 780, 797; atomic weapons and, 697

Elections. *See also* Voting rights; in China, 604; in British-ruled India, 658; in Taiwan, 745; in United States, 789; fraudulent, in Mexico, 798; black majority in Africa, 829; in Burma, 862; in Malaysia, 863

Electoral College (United States), 522

Electric power, 503, 521, 528, 729

Electronics industry, 735, 742, 848, 866. *See also* Computers

Elephants, military use of, 449, 453

El Greco, 381

Elites. *See* Upper class (elites)

Elizabeth I (England), 382, 385, 387; parliament and, 392; speech to her subjects, 386

Elizabeth II (Britain), 692*(illus.)*

El Salvador, 531; Indian massacre in, 672; United States military in, 633, 797; death squads in, 796

E-mail (electronic mail), 714

Emancipation, of serfs, 615

Emancipation Proclamation (1862), 528

Embargo. *See* Economic sanctions (boycott; embargo)

Empire. *See* Imperialism (empires)

Empiricism, 398. *See also* Science

Enclosure policy (England), 398

Encomienda (labor tax), 442

Engels, Friedrich, 507, 509

Engineering, 849; Panama Canal, 536

England. *See* Great Britain (England)

English colonies. *See* British empire

English language: in Siam, 587; in Canada, 537, 538; in India, 575, 578, 704, 844; in Philippines, 588, 678; pidgin, 665; as world language, 714–715, 767; in China, 731; in South and East Africa, 834; in Singapore, 864

Enlightenment, 397–398 *and illus.*, 500, 544, 572; salons of, 398*(illus.)*; Catherine the Great and, 614; China and, 398, 476, 482, 513; North American colonists and, 439, 488, 489, 490; Latin American liberty and, 495, 496; liberalism and, 506, 636; rationalism of, 397, 496, 520, 564, 636, 759; Muslim modernists and, 564; Nietzsche and, 520; Mozart and, 520; fascism and, 636

Entrepreneurs: *See also* Business and businessmen; in Surat, 452; in China, 467, 729; British, 561, 578; globalization and, 867; in Malaysia, 863

Environment, the. *See also* Deforestation; Global warming; Pollution; island fragility, 431; population growth and, 479; early modern world, 479–480; global warming and, 709; resource consumption rates and, 709; destruction of, 715, 801; in Japan, 735–736; Soviet Union and, 763; economic growth and, 845, 866; in India, 710, 845; in Indonesia, 857; in Kenya, 827; globalization and, 709, 867; United States and, 872; Vietnam War, 853; in China, 729, 870; in Western Europe, 750, 867; issues and movements, 872; sustainability of, 871–872

Epidemics: *See also* AIDS/HIV; in Iraq, 562; Native Americans and, 432, 528; in Africa, 547; plague, 464, 479, 562

Equality and inequality, 453. *See also* Income inequality; Native American, 397; in colonial Java, 461–462; in colonial Philippines, 460; Napoleonic era, 493; socialism and, 507, 508; abolition of slavery and, 544; in Latin America, 535; Ottoman reform and, 559; in British India, 572; in Vietnam, 585; in United States, 630; in global economy, 679–680; for women, 726 (*See also* Women's rights); in China, 598, 605, 722, 726, 730; of African Americans, 789; development and, 868–871; new world order, 870; North-South gap, 868

Equiano, Olaudah, 414

Erie Canal (New York state), 523

Eritrea (northeast Africa), 549

Estado Nuovo (Brazil), 674

Estates General (France), 491

Estonia, 761

Esu-Williams, Eka, 832

ETA. *See* Basques in Spain

Ethiopia, 403*(map)*, 549; Christianity in, 407, 412; Italian invasion of, 511, 549, 639, 650; Rastafarians and, 805; refugees from, 711

Ethnic conflict: in colonial Africa, 549, 553, 648, 650, 664, 665; in Dutch Indonesia, 648, 661; nationalism and, 664; in Caribbean, 650; in Yugoslavia, 695, 766; in colonial Southeast Asia, 589, 650; in Europe, 750; in former Soviet Union, 769; in Eastern Europe, 772, 773*(map)*; in Latin America, 796; in Middle East, 816; in Pacific Islands, 794; in Afghanistan, 820; Rwandan genocide and, 827–828; in Pakistan, 841, 843; in Sri Lanka, 843; in Malaysia, 662, 863; in Burma, 860, 861; in Indonesia, 858

Ethnic diversity (minorities): *See also specific ethnic minorities;* in Ottoman Empire, 418, 577–578; in United States, 523, 528, 529, 789–790; in Congo, 677; in New Zealand, 794; World War I and, 621, 625; in Canada, 792; in Malaysia, 865

Ethnocentrism: in China, 464, 598; of Europeans in Africa, 546, 553–554; Western culture and, 598; colonialism and, 648

Eurasia: Chinese economy and, 476; Columbian exchange and, 479–480; growing trade of, 479; gunpowder empires in, 474; Russian expansion in, 511, 512*(map)*, 614–617 *and map*

Eurasians, in Java, 462

Euro (currency), 747, 774

Europe (1450–1750), 371, 373–399; in 1740, 394*(map)*; absolutist and despotic monarchies, 389–390, 391*(map)*; African slave trade and, 408, 413*(map)*; American foods in, 480; arts and philosophy, 395–396; capitalism in, 374–375, 378–380, 398–399; changing states and politics in, 387–395; chronology, 379; cultural and social transformation, 395–399; Enlightenment in, 397–398 *and illus.*; expansion and capitalism

and, 479; in Mughal India, 452; tenant farmers, 374, 460, 576, 578; American, 528, 530; in New Zealand, 541; in Australia, 540; in colonial Africa, 550, 551, 552, 556, 664; kibbutz, in Palestine, 567, 810; in British India, 576, 578, 581; government subsidies for, 705, 835; in United States, 633, 634; Green Revolution and, 704, 782, 840, 844; in Africa, 816, 830, 835; global warming and, 872

Fascism: appeasement of, 639–640; in China, 653; doctrine of, 637; in Europe, 636; in Germany (See Nazi Germany); imperialism and, 637, 639; in Italy, 636, 637; in Japan, 639, 678; rise of, 636–640; in Spain, 639; in Thailand, 661; in Brazil, 672, 674

Fathers: See also Patriarchy; and childcare, in Sweden, 756(illus.); and families, in China, 726

Federalism: in United States, 522; in India, 839

Federal Republic of Germany. See West Germany

Feminine Mystique (Friedan), 790

Feminism (feminists), 685, 716. See also Women's rights; in Europe, 519 and illus., 760; in United States, 524, 790; in Southeast Asia, 591; in Chile, 672; in Japan, 632, 736; in Soviet Union, 765; in China, 604, 653, 725, 730; in Latin America, 803; in Iran, 813–814; in Middle East, 816–817; in Egypt, 671, 816

Fenians (Ireland), 505

Ferdinand (Spain), 428

Fertility rates: See also Birth rates; birth control and, 707; working women and, 709

Festivals: in Philippines, 460; in China, 465(illus.); Carnival, 536, 804; Chinese, in Australia, 793(illus.); American rock music, 788; in Vietnam, 855(illus.)

Feudalism: end of, in Europe, 374, 398; in Japan, 472, 739; in Eastern Europe, 517

Fiji Islands, 794; Christianity on, 540; deforestation of, 539; Indian workers in, 579

Filipinos. See Philippines (Filipinos)

Fillmore, Millard, 608

Film industry (motion pictures), 635, 711; American, 684, 867; Chinese,

728, 731; European, 759; Indian, 712, 844, 846–847; Japanese, 739, 759; Brazilian, 804; cultural imperialism in, 867

Finance: See also Banks and banking; Investment; Indian merchants and, 452; French Revolution and, 491; industrial capitalism and, 500; iuternational, 701 (See also World Bank)

Finland, 393, 504. See also Scandinavia; women's rights in, 519; Russia and, 614, 616(map), 627; independence of, 625

Firearms. See Guns (gunpowder weapons)

First Indochina War (1946–1954), 850–851, 853

First Nations, 430, 792. See also American Indians

First World concept, 694

Fishing (fishermen), 481; Iberian, 376; African, 407; by Native Americans, 429; off Newfoundland, 427, 434; in Pacific islands, 431, 794; Aboriginal Australians, 540; decline in world harvest, 709

Five Guarantees (China), 723

Five-Year Plans: Soviet Union, 629, 630, 762–763; India, 840

Flamethrowers, 621

Flanders (Flemish), 373, 442. See also Belgium; capitalism in, 378; Catholicism in, 387; mapmaking by, 375; painters, 382(illus.)

"Floating world" in Japan, 473 and illus.

Floods (flooding): in China, 598; from hurricanes, 787

Florence, Italy, 381

Florida, 432, 525

Flowers in the Mirror (Li), 593–594

Folk songs (folk music): Burmese, 585; Brazilian, 675, 684; Indian bhangra, 759; in 1960s, 791; Chilean, 804

Folk traditions, African, 446. See also Traditional culture

Food crops. See Cash crops; Crops; specific foods

Food (diet): See also Agriculture; Famine; in Africa, 415; sugar in, 444; from Americas, 374, 415, 516; in Columbian exchange, 480; Hindu-Muslim prohibitions, 577, 867; in Japan, 735; North-South disparity in, 868; globalization and, 867

Football (soccer), 517, 685, 804–805

Footbinding, in China, 466, 593; movement against, 651

Forbidden City (Beijing), 719, 722(illus.)

Forced labor. See also Prison camps; Slavery; Native Americans and, 430, 432, 440(illus.), 442; indentured, 439, 579, 600; in colonial Africa, 554–555, 556, 648; in World War II, 640, 662

Ford, Henry, 529

Ford Motor Company, 529

Foreign debt, 693; in Africa, 835; in Brazil, 799; in Chile, 801; in Indonesia, 857; in Nigeria, 828

Foreign investment: British, 534; American, 779; in Taiwan, 744; economic growth and, 678, 705; in Asia, 701; in Latin America, 534–535, 779, 802–803; in South Africa, 829; in Burma, 863; in Southeast Asia, 854, 865; capitalism and, 869

Foreign policy, China, 723, 725

Foreign policy, United States: Cold War, 695, 797; containment, 696, 699, 780; isolationist (1920s), 633; Muslim terrorism and, 716, 784; unilateralism, 780, 784–785; Canadian opposition to, 791

Forests. See also Deforestation; Brazilian, 799, 867; rainforests, 710, 802, 861, 874, 875; tree-planting campaigns, 710, 845

Fortifications: British, in India, 456; Portuguese, 408, 412, 423, 454

Fossil fuels, pollution from, 707. See also Oil and oil industry; global warming and, 871 and illus., 872

Fourteen Points (Wilson), 624

Fourth World concept, 694

Fox, Vicente, 797

France: See also under French; Bourbon lands, 387, 394(map); centralization in, 375; absolutism in, 389, 398; Thirty Years' War and, 388 and illus.; Huguenots in, 384(map), 387; in War of Spanish Succession, 388, 389; literature of, 383; mercantilism in, 380; slavery in, 408; slave trade and, 413, 447; exploration by, 434; Atlantic trade of, 443(map); rivalry with English, 455–456; Siam and, 458–459, 463; American Revolution and, 490, 491; revolution in, 485, 488, 490–493, 496, 504; Napoleonic Era,

France, *continued*
493–494 *and map*; nationalism in, 504; Jews in, 505; as great power, 487, 510; Greece and, 504, 557; alliances of, 510; industrialization in, 502; modern art in, 521; women's rights in, 519; Mexico and, 533; invasion of Egypt by, 543–544, 559; Crimean War and, 614–615; in World War I, 619, 620, 621, 622, 623*(map)*, 624, 657; Russian civil war and, 627, 628*(map)*; war with China, 597–598, 599*(map)*; Great Depression in, 633–634; Vichy government, 619, 640, 641*(map)*, 642, 662; in World War II, 639, 640, 641*(map)*, 644, 679; Lebanon and, 667, 668*(map)*; Ottoman partition and, 666, 667, 668*(map)*; atomic weapons of, 698, 752*(map)*; Suez crisis and (1956), 809; postwar reconstruction of, 748; protests in (1968), 716; reconciliation with Germany, 749; European Union and, 753, 774; immigrants in, 758, 775, 818, 867; protests in (2005–2006), 775
Francis Xavier, Saint, 385
Franco, Francisco (Spain), 639
Franz Ferdinand, Archduke, assassination of, 621
Frederick II, the Great (Prussia), 393
Free blacks, 446; African colonies of, 545–546; in United States, 523
Freedom, for slaves, 401, 446, 465, 490, 544; in Latin America, 497
Freedom, Locke and, 398
Freedom of religion. *See* Religious freedom
Free expression (speech), 490, 492, 506; in China, 728
Free French forces, in World War II, 641*(map)*, 644
Freetown, Sierra Leone, 545
Free trade (free market). *See also* Capitalism; laissez faire and, 500; "Open Door," in China, 602; British, in China, 596, 680; British, in Egypt, 559; British India, 572; United States and, 522, 523, 633; conservatives and, 756, 774, 798; in Russia, 769; European, 748, 753, 755; in Japan, 732; in Latin America, 534, 798, 799, 801, 802–803; African neocolonialism and, 830; globalization of, 702, 715; development and, 869
Free World concept, 695

French colonies (French Empire), 371, 378, 474, 485, 511, 678; in Canada (New France), 370, 434–435, 439–440, 510; Napoleonic era, 493–494 *and map*, 510; in Africa, 485, 511, 512*(map)*, 548*(map)*, 549, 553, 823; in Caribbean, 433, 445, 496 (*See also* Haiti); in 1913, 512*(map)*; "civilizing mission" of, 513, 554, 585, 679; French Guiana, 496, 673*(map)*, 692; in India, 571, 574*(map)*; Indochina, 586 (*See also* Vietnam, French rule of); Algeria, 562, 823; in Pacific region, 540, 794; in Southeast Asia, 458*(map)*, 584*(map)*; in West Africa, 679; independence of, 691*(map)*, 750, 808, 823
French East India Company, 455
French exploration, in North America, 434
French impressionism, 521, 607
French language, 767; in Canada, 440, 537, 538–539, 791; in Africa, 693, 834; in Louisiana, 440
French Revolution (1789), 485, 490–493, 614; American revolution and, 490, 491, 522, 677; causes of, 491–492; Haitian Revolution and, 496; Jacobins and, 492, 493, 504; legacy of, 492–493; as social revolution, 488
Freud, Sigmund, 636
Friedan, Betty, 790
Friedman, Thomas, 866–867
Frontiers, settling, 680–681
Fugger, Jacob, 379
Fuggers of Augsburg, 379
Fujian, China, 468
Fulani jihad, 546, 547. *See also* Hausa-Fulani
Fulani people, 402
Fundamentalist religions, 714
Fur trade: in Alaska, 539; beaver, in North America, 434; bison massacre and, 528; in Canada, 440, 539; Russian, 469, 539
Fusae, Ichikawa, 685

Gaelic language, 393
Gagaran, Yuri, 762
Galileo Galilei, 396, 482
Galleons (ships), 376, 462–463
Gallipoli, World War I in, 622
Gamelan music (Indonesia), 591, 684
Ganda people of Buganda, 406
Gandhi, Indira, 841–843; assassination of, 843

Gandhi, Mohandas K., 664, 677, 875; caste system and, 659, 840; nonviolent resistance and, 579, 657, 789, 838; on Western civilization, 513; on women, 659–660; assassination of, 838, 839
Gandhi, Rajiv, 843
Gandhi, Sanjay, 842, 843
Gandhi, Sonia, 844
Ganges River (India), 845
Gao of Sudanic Africa, 402
García Márquez, Gabriel, 804
Garibaldi, Giuseppi, 505
Gast, John, 525*(illus.)*
Gatling, Richard, 684
Gatling gun, 547, 684
Gauchos (Argentine cowboys), 681
Gauguin, Paul, 521
Gaza, 810*(illus.)*, 811*(map)*, 812
Gender relations. *See also* Homosexuality; Marriage; Women; Sexuality; Enlightenment and, 398; in Europe, 399; changes in, 481–482; in colonial Africa, 555; Portuguese and, 455; female roles and, 518; in Philippines, 461, 587; in China, 593; in Japan, 473, 612; in colonial Southeast Asia, 590–591; in India, 452, 581, 659–660; in Europe, 632, 757; in United States, 791; in Latin America, 803; in sub-Saharan Africa, 832
General Agreements on Trade and Tariffs, 702
General Song (Neruda), 804
Geneva, Calvinism in, 383, 385
Geneva Agreements (1954), 851
Genoa, Italy, 374
Genocide, 640, 875; Armenian, 558, 666; Nazi Holocaust, 642, 672, 698, 748, 760, 810; in Rwanda, 698, 827–828; Serbian "ethnic cleansing," 698, 772; in Sudan, 816; in Cambodia, 698, 855
Gentile, Giovanni, 637
Gentry: *See also* Landowners; Chinese landlords, 465, 653; in eastern Europe, 517
Geoffrin, Maria-Therese, 397*(illus.)*
George III (Britain), 596
Georgia (Caucasus), 557 *and map*, 615
Georgia (North America), 441; Sea Islands, 446; Cherokees of, 527
German colonies (German Empire), 678; in 1913, 512*(map)*; in Africa, 511, 512*(map)*, 548*(map)*, 549, 556, 624, 625; in Pacific, 540, 584*(map)*, 622, 624, 632; in China,

Government of India Act (Britain, 1858), 577

Goya, Francisco de, 520

Grameen Bank (Bangladesh), 707, 848, 870

Gran Colombia, 498(map)

Grand Canal (China), 464, 466

Grassroots movement: economic development and, 707; in Africa, 827

Great Britain (England), 394(map). See also under British; centralization in, 375; ships of, 376; Calvinism in, 385; mercantilism in, 380; enclosure policy in, 398; homosexuality in, 399; in War of Spanish Succession, 388–389; Ireland and, 392, 393; parliamentary government in, 392–393; Renaissance drama, 382, 383; rural poverty in, 398; skin color in, 415; slave trade and, 413, 447; Atlantic trade of, 423, 442, 443(map); use of sugar in, 444; French rivalry with, 455–456; market economy in, 476; American Revolution and, 489–490; as great power, 487; Greece and, 504, 557; Industial Revolution in, 499–501, 502(map), 503(illus.), 523; industrialization in, 442; Jews in, 504, 505; maritime trade of, 477(map), 510, 523; alliances of, 510, 606, 612; Napoleonic Era and, 493–494 and map; nationalism in, 504; social welfare programs in, 517; textile industry in, 487, 499, 501, 679; nuclear family in, 517; investment, in Latin America, 496, 534; United States and, 523, 526(map); women's rights in, 519 and illus.; China and, 596, 597, 599(map), 603; slavery abolished in, 544; Japan and, 606, 612, 622, 632; Crimean War and, 614–615; in World War I, 620, 621, 622 and illus., 623(map), 624; Ireland and, 504, 505–506, 625, 677, 716; Russian civil war and, 627, 628(map); Great Depression in, 635; in World War II, 640, 641(map), 644, 679; Middle East and, 666, 667, 668(map), 808; Iranian oil and, 697; Zionism and, 671, 672, 810; atomic weapons of, 698; monarchy in, 748; pop music of, 759, 765, 791; postwar reconstruction of,

748; conservative party rule in, 756; European Community and, 753, 794; invasion of Iraq and, 670, 717, 820; boycott of Iran by, 812–813; immigrants in, 758; New Zealand and, 794; Suez crisis (1956) and, 809; South African investment, 829

Great Depression (1930s) 658, 660; causes of, 633; in Europe and Japan, 635–636; failure of capitalism in, 635, 649–650; fascism and, 638, 674; global impact of, 630–631, 633–634; imperialism and, 647–648; in Latin America, 649–650, 666, 672; nationalism and, 690; reforms in United States and, 634–635

Great Exhibition of 1851 (London), 486–487 and illus.

Great Lakes (North America), 434, 538

Great Leap Forward (China), 722–723, 726, 727

Great Migration, of African Americans, 633

Great Northern War (1700–1709), 390

Great Plains (North America): 526, 539; Indians of, 435, 528

Great Salt March (India, 1930), 658

Great Trek (South Africa), 550–551, 552(illus.)

Greco-Roman traditions, Renaissance and, 380, 381

Greece (Greeks), 530, 560; Ottoman control of, 387, 416, 417(map), 504; independence of, 504–505, 506(illus.), 557; Turkey and, 667; in World War I, 620; in World War II, 640; democracy in, 749; in NATO and Common Market, 752(map)

Greek language, 543

Greek Orthodox Church, 389, 418, 504, 520, 558

Greenbelt Movement (Kenya), 710

Greenhouse effect, 521, 729, 872. See also Global warming

Greenland, Viking settlement of, 427

Green Party, in Europe, 750, 774

Greenpeace (organization), 872

Green Revolution, 709; in India, 704, 782, 840, 844; in Mexico and Philippines, 704, 782

Grimke, Angelina, 523, 524

Grimke, Sarah, 523, 524, 528

Gross domestic product, in Europe, 754(map)

Gross National Product (GNP): Soviet Union, 630; United States, 633; Nazi Germany, 638

Guadeloupe Island, 434

Guam: Spanish discovery of, 431; United States and, 531, 692

Guangdong, China, 598, 602

Guangxu (China), 603

Guangzhou (Canton, China), 466, 469, 470, 598; opium trade in, 597; rattan factory in, 600(illus.); Western trade in, 596(illus.)

Guantanamo naval base (Cuba), 536

Guatemala: Indians of, 797; intervention of United States in, 697, 782, 797; poverty in, 797; Protestantism in, 804; refugees from, 711; death squads in, 796, 797

Guernica (Spain), bombing of, 639

Guerrilla warfare: colonialism and, 510; in Africa, 550, 825, 831; in Philippines, 588; in Vietnam, 663, 850; against superpowers, 696; in China, 653, 656; in Algeria, 808; in Bengal, 841

Guianas, 433, 434, 673(map), 692; Afro-Caribbeans in, 496; plantation workers in, 535

Guicciardini, Ludovico, 373

Guilds: capitalism and, 398; European, 378; Japanese, 471; Ottoman, 418

Guinala, 405

Guinea-Bissau, 405, 408, 825, 835; social revolution in, 693

Guinea Coast (West Africa), 405

Gujerat (India), 452

Gulags, 629–630. See also Prison camps, Siberian

Gulf Coast (United States) hurricanes, 787, 866

Gullah language, 446

Gunboat diplomacy, in China, 602

Gun control laws: in Europe, 757; in Japan, 736

Gunpowder empires, 474–475

Guns (gunpowder weapons), 376, 396, 407. See also Weapons and military technology; African trade in, 404, 410, 412, 415; naval gunnery/cannon, 387, 449, 454, 474; Ottoman, 417; in trade with Indians, 441; Moroccan, 423; muskets, 420, 449, 453, 472; of Spanish conquistadors, 425, 432, 433(illus.); European, 450, 476; of Marathas, 454; Japanese, 472, 607; in French Revolution, 491;

456, 478; trade network of, 478–479; women in, 451, 453, 481

Indian immigrants, 649; in Burma, 660, 860; on plantations, 535, 579, 583, 590, 681; on Fiji, 579; in Southeast Asia, 590; merchants, in East Africa, 552; in Britain, 758

Indian National Army, 659

Indian National Congress, 581–582, 657–659, 838

Indian numerical system, 376

Indian Ocean maritime trade: East African cities and, 403(map), 406, 411; European control of, 449–450, 474; Omani Arabs and, 416; Portuguese and, 409, 411, 454–455

India (1945–present): Hindu nationalism, 842, 843, 844, 846; independence of, 690, 691(map), 750, 838; decolonization and partition of, 838–839, 840(illus.); Nehru years in, 838, 839–841; China and, 840, 841, 849; Chipko movement in, 710, 845; Cold War neutrality of, 840, 849; communists in, 696; computer services in, 704; English language in, 704, 715; films and music of, 712, 844, 846–847; Indira Gandhi era, 841–843; migrant workers from, 707; population growth in, 708(map), 709; Pakistan and, 838, 839; atomic weapons of, 698; politics in, 843–844; AIDS in, 711; China and, 840, 841, 849; cities and gender patterns in, 845–846; high technology in, 701, 715, 844, 849, 869; economic growth in, 774(illus.), 869; energy needs of, 822, 870; globalization and, 867; women's rights in, 840, 874(illus.)

Indios in Philippines, 461

Indirect rule. See Direct vs. indirect rule

Individualism: in Africa, 832; capitalism and, 385; Renaissance and, 380; state and, 396, 398; in United States, 490, 523, 530

Indochina. See also Cambodia; Laos; Vietnam; French federation of, 586; revolution, war, and reconstruction in, 849–855; chronology (1945–1978), 849

Indo-Islamic architecture, 453

Indonesia, Dutch rule of, 371, 556, 570, 678, 680; cultivation system in, 582–583; end of, 750; exporting resources from, 649(illus.); government in, 649; Japanese occupation, 642, 643(map); Muslims in, 661–662; nationalism in, 660, 661–662, 663–664, 677, 856; population growth in, 649; rival ethic groups in, 648; revolution in, 856

"Indonesia Accuses" (Sukarno), 663

Indonesia (Indonesians), 700. See also Java; slaves from, 412; coffee in, 447, 679, 680; communism in, 696; democracy in, 702; in Dutch Guiana, 535; East Africa and, 406; feminism in, 591; independence of, 690, 691(map); Islam in, 402, 459, 857, 858; literature of, 837–838; oil in, 815, 857; quest for freedom and order, 856–858; New Order in, 857–858; terrorism in, 717

Indonesian language, 837

Indonesian Nationalist Party, 662

Indulgences, selling of, 383

Industrialization: See also Industrial Revolution; in France, 389; Dutch, 461; in England, 442; in Europe, 447, 556; in Britain, 487; imperialism and, 415–416, 508, 510, 620; in United States, 523, 528–529; attempted, in Latin America, 534; social life and, 517–519; spread of, 680, 703–704; in Japan, 594, 603, 610, 612; in Canada, 791; in Russia, 617, 626; slave trade and, 447; in South Korea, 687, 781; in Soviet Union, 629, 630; in Chile, 672; in Asia, 703, 754; in Taiwan, 744; export-oriented, in Asia, 740; in China, 599, 722, 731, 781; in East Asia, 869; in Argentina, 796; in India, 840, 849; in South Africa, 829; in Southeast Asia, 865, 869; in Turkey, 822

Industrialized nations: See also Western nations; specific countries; China as, 464, 466; social Darwinism and, 513; society and family life in, 517–519; capitalism and, 649; as First World, 694; global economy and, 701; oil embargo (1973) and, 815; obesity in, 868; energy conservation in, 872; pollution in, 871

Industrial Revolution, 499–503; age of machines and, 501; in Britain, 485, 499–501, 502(map), 503(illus.), 523; capitalism and, 499–500; economic growth and, 499–503; imperialism and, 511, 866; roots of, 499–500; second, 503, 703; socialism and, 507, 508; spread of, 501–503; end of slavery and, 544; in Europe, 485, 501–503, 544, 679; third, 703–704; in Egypt, 559

Industry: See also Industrialization; specific industry; Indian, 452; science and, 503; globalization of, 704; Chinese, 722; North Korean, 743; military-industrial complex, 780; in Malaysia, 863

Inequality. See Equality and inequality; Income inequality

Infant mortality: in London, 399; in Africa, 828–829, 830, 831; in Arab countries, 821; drop in, 705, 801; drop in, worldwide, 868–869

Infantry. See Armed forces

Inflation: in Weimar Germany, 631; in Russia, 770; in Brazil, 799

Information sector, 704. See also Communication; Computers; Libraries; Mass media

Information superhighway, 714, 875. See also Internet

Inquisition. See Holy Inquisition

Intellectuals (intellectual life). See also Enlightenment; Philosophy; in early modern Europe, 385, 395; in Netherlands, 392; in colonial North America, 436; in China, 465, 466; nationalism and, 504; American, 523; Islamic modernization, 564–566; Russian Revolution and, 629; Vietnamese, 661; New Culture Movement (China), 651; Chinese, 653, 723, 725, 728; Hindu, in India, 579–580, 658; Korean, 609; Egyptian, 671; Afro-Caribbean, 675; Soviet Union, 762, 765, 767

Interest on loans (usury), 375, 379

Intermarriage: in Africa, 412; in Sri Lanka, 455; in colonial Americas, 424(illus.), 435, 436, 438, 440–441, 481; in colonial Philippines, 460 and illus.; cultural change and, 480; migration and, 480, 481; in Southeast Asia, 590, 591; in Qing China, 594

Internal combustion engine, 503, 521, 528

International banks, 870

International cooperation, 870, 875

International financial institutions, 701

International law, 698, 785

International Monetary Fund (IMF), 645, 702; private investment and, 834–835

International settlements, in China, 598

International trade. *See* World economy

International Women's Day, 874*(illus.)*

Internet, 714, 715*(illus.)*; in China, 730–731; English language on, 704; global system and, 866; religion and, 873; dissident views on, 863

Internment camps, in World War II, 643

Interventions, by United States. *See* Military interventions, United States

Interwar years (1920s), 630, 631–633

Intifada (Palestinian uprising), 812

Inuit (Eskimo), autonomy for, 792 *and map*

Investment: *See also* Foreign investment; capitalism and, 378, 380; colonial, 447; monopoly and, 503, 510; British colonial, 510, 750; in new technology, 499, 500; globalization and, 701; American, 650–651, 777, 791, 797; slave trade and, 447; in Latin America, 650–651, 777, 797, 802, 805; Asian, 805; western, in Africa, 830, 835

Iqbal, Muhammad, 822

Iranian Revolution, 687, 700, 813

Iran (Persia), 678; Safavid, 371, 402, 417*(map)*, 420–422 *and illus.*, 423, 454; challenges and reform in, 561; nationalism in, 697, 812–813; oil in, 670, 692, 697, 811*(map)*, 814; modernization in, 676; Pahlavi dynasty in, 669–670; nuclear weapons and, 698; Shi-ite Islam in, 561, 669; Kurds in, 667, 816; United States' intervention in, 697, 782, 783; Russia and, 775; in "axis of evil," 785; Islamic Revolution in, 687, 700, 813; war with Iraq, 687, 784, 814; female pop singers in, 818; human rights abuse in, 808;

Iraq (Iraqis): 819*(illus.)*; Ottoman division of, 562; art of, 811*(map)*; Shi'ism in, 566, 670, 820; Wahhabism in, 564; British and, 622, 666, 667, 668*(map)*, 670, 820; invasion of Kuwait by, 700, 784;

Kurds in, 667, 670, 784, 814, 816, 820; oil in, 562, 666, 670, 687, 775, 785; Shi'ia-Sunni hostility in, 562, 714, 717, 814, 817; U.S. war in, 687, 714, 717, 775, 785, 786, 820

Ireland (Irish): Catholicism in, 392, 393, 712; potatoes in, 480; Britain and, 392, 393, 504, 505–506, 677, 716; famine in, 505; in Americas, 439, 518*(map)*, 529, 530; independence of, 505–506; emigrants from, 505, 517, 529, 530, 540; quality of life in, 694; European Community and, 753; in Common Market, 752*(map)*; woman president in, 757–758

Irish Republican Army, 505–506

Iron and steel industry: steel swords, 410, 461, 471; African, 446; British, 499, 500, 502*(map)*, 503*(illus.)*; British India, 579; Japanese, 471, 607; in China, 722

Iron curtain, in Europe, 748, 752*(map)*, 761

Iron Rice Bowl (China), 726

Iroquois Indians, 435, 481; alliance with English, 440, 441*(illus.)*

Irrigation, 589, 595, 608, 610; in Mughal India, 452

Isabella (Spain), 428, 430

Isfahan, 420, 475; Afghan sack of, 421

Islamic clerics. *See* Muslim clerics

Islamic empires. *See* India, Mughal Empire in; Ottoman Empire

Islamic law (shar'ia), 404, 558, 571; in Afghanistan, 819, 820; in Nigeria, 828, 834; in Iran, 813; Wahhabism and, 563, 564, 671, 814, 834

Islamic militancy (Islamists), 758–759. *See also* Jihad; in Afghanistan, 696, 700, 764, 784; in Sudan, 700; Al Qaeda, 717, 775, 784, 820; September 11 (2001) attacks and, 775, 784; in Central Asia, 768; in Europe, 775; in Iran, 700, 813; in Middle East, 815, 822; Muslim Brotherhood and, 671, 817; Palestinian, 716–717; terrorism and, 775, 816, 820; in Bangladesh, 848; in Indonesia, 858; in Malaysia, 863; high technology and, 873

Islamic Revolution (Iran), 687, 700, 813

Islamic Union (Indonesia), 662

Islam (Islamic world). *See also* Muslims; Shi'ism; Sufis; Sunni Islam; Christian rivalry with, 376, 455, 457, 875; ideas and technology of, 380, 396; Ottoman, 384*(map)*, 387, 418, 419, 482; in Central Asia, 420, 423, 574, 615, 617; in Middle East, 402, 563–564, 807–808; in Africa, 404, 405*(illus.)*, 406, 411, 546; in Sudan, 546–547; modernism and, 560, 564–566, 581; Napoleon and, 543; in Southeast Asia, 459; spread of, 402, 818*(map)*, 873; revivalism, 563, 581; Wahhabism, 563–564, 581, 671, 815, 834; westernization and, 560, 564, 566; alcohol prohibition in, 562, 818, 820; change and conflict in, 815–816; Red Crescent in, 685; Turkish modernization and, 667, 669; in Europe, 758, 760; in Indonesia, 661–662, 857, 858; reformist, in Iran, 813–814; Zionism and, 670; birth control discouraged in, 709; in West Africa, 546; Western culture and, 560, 564, 566, 822; in China, 731; in Pakistan, 712, 847

Ismail (Egypt), 560

Isma'il (Safavids), 420

Isolationism: Qing China, 595–596; seclusion policy (Japan and Korea), 606, 608; in United States (1920s), 632, 633

Israel: birth of, 810; allied with United States, 699, 717, 810; Arab-Israeli conflicts, 687, 809–812, 811*(map)*, 816; immigration to, 765, 812; nuclear weapons of, 698; Palestinian terrorism and, 716–717; Western support for, 753, 815; Egypt and, 809; music in, 818

Istanbul, 416, 419, 667; Greek independence and, 504; multiethnicity in, 558; trade in, 418, 478; University of, 558

Italian colonies, 512*(map)*, 563; in Africa, 511, 512*(map)*, 548*(map)*, 549; independence of, 691*(map)*, 808

Italy (Italians), 493, 504, 667, 678; artists of, 381, 395; slavery in, 408; China and, 469 (*See also* Polo, Marco); merchants in Africa, 407; unification of, 505; women's rights in, 505; invasion of Ethiopia by, 511, 549, 639, 650; in World War I, 620, 621, 622; fascism in, 636,

Japan, 734, 735; in Sri Lanka, 848; in Malaysia, 863; in Southeast Asia, 865

Manumission, 446. *See also* Freedom for slaves

Maoism, 656, 721–727, 728; *See also* China, People's Republic of; Cultural Revolution, 725–726, 727; Great Leap Forward, 722–723, 726, 727; in North Korea, 743; women and family under, 726

Maori of New Zealand, 541, 794

Mao Zedong, 678, 690, 743, 870. *See also* Maoism; Chiang Kai-shek and, 653, 655; Communist Party and, 722; North Korea and, 723; personality cult of, 722*(illus.)*, 725; quote from, 719; death of, 726

Mapmaking (cartography), 428, 470, 482; in Europe, 375; Ottoman, 396; Polynesian, 539

Maratha confederacy (India), 454, 571, 572

Marconi, Guglielmo, radio and, 521

Marcos, Ferdinand (Philippines), 858–860

Marcos, Imelda, 860

Marijuana, 791, 805

"Marilyn Monroe Doctrine," 867

Maritime expansion: *See also* Exploration (expeditions); of Europe, 476

Maritime trade. *See* Ships and shipping

Market economy, 378, 696. *See also* Capitalism; Free market; in Europe, 476; in China and Vietnam, 693, 854; Russian conversion to, 769

Market Leninism, 728–729

Markets: Antwerp, 373, 375*(illus.)*; African, 405–406; Isfahan bazaar, 420, 421; in Goa, 455*(illus.)*

Market socialism: in China, 727–728, 768; in Hungary, 766, 768, 771; *perestroika,* in Soviet Union, 767–768

Market women: in Africa, 404, 679, 832; colonialism and, 591, 679; in Siam, 457

Marley, Bob, 693, 805, 833; in Zimbabwe, 689

Maronite Christians, 562

Maroons (escaped slaves), 446

Marquesa Islands, 540

Marriage. *See also* Divorce; Intermarriage; Flemish, 382*(illus.)*; Henry VIII and, 385; in Europe, 399, 632; Columbus and, 428; in India, 451; in Japan, 473, 612, 736–737; early modern era, 517–518; in British India, 581; love matches in, 518, 581; polygamy, 451, 459, 554, 591, 832; Indonesian women and, 459; in Egypt, 671; reform of, in China, 726; in Japan, 736; in South Korea, 742; in Europe, 758; homosexuals and, 714, 758, 791; in United States, 791; sexual revolution and, 757; in Middle East, 817; in Latin America, 803; reform of, in India, 846

Marshall, George, 748

Marshall Plan for Europe, 748

Martí, Jose, Cuba and, 534

Martial law: *See also* Military dictatorship; in South Korea, 742

Martin, Emma, 507

Martinique Island, 434

Marx, Karl, 507–508, 509; legacy of, 650, 678; Russian Revolution and, 626

Marxism, 507–508, 630; in Angola, 693, 831; in Vietnam, 661; nationalism and, 648, 650, 676; revolution and, 678; in Latin America, 675, 796; Maoism and, 721; deconstruction and, 760; in Mozambique, 825, 831; in Senegal, 834

Marxism-Leninism, 629, 656

Mary (mother of Jesus), 383, 437, 460

Mary Tudor (England), 385

Massachusetts, 490, 527

Mass culture, spread of, 635, 683, 685–685, 759. *See also* Popular culture

Mass media, 635, 711. *See also* Newspapers; Radio; Television; cultural synthesis and, 712; Internet and, 863; Latin American, 804; Russian control of, 771; in United States, 788, 789, 791

Mass production, 444, 501, 503, 529, 631. *See also* Manufacturing

Mass transit: in Europe, 753; in Japan, 735, 737*(illus.)*

Materialism, capitalism and, 873

Mathematical Principles of Natural Philosophy (Newton), 396

Mathematics: Arab, 376, 381; European, 376, 396, 475; Ottoman, 418; Indian, 376, 679

Matrilineal societies: Native American, 434; in West Africa, 402, 404, 405

Mau Mau Rebellion (Kenya), 814 *and illus.*

Mauritius, 579

Mawlay Hassan, Sultan (Morocco), 562

Maxim, Hiram, 684

Maxim gun, 511, 547, 602*(illus.)*, 684

Maximilian (Mexico), 533

Maya, 427, 430, 435; in Yucatan, 436, 437

May Fourth Movement (China), 652, 653

Mazzini, Giuseppi, 505

Mecca, 563, 564, 666; Hashemites of, 670, 671

Mechanization, 519; of agriculture, 517, 704; Luddite protest against, 501

Media. *See* Mass media

Medicine (physicians), 398, 475. *See also* Disease; Health care; in Kongo, 409; women in, 581, 764; mission hospitals, 554, 561, 598; modern era, 521; in colonial Africa, 547, 554; Ottoman, 418; in Soviet Union, 630, 764; Doctors Without Borders, 699, 711; in China, 726; British National Health, 755

Medina, 564, 666, 671

Mediterranean area, Ottoman control of, 416, 417*(map)*

Mehmed II, Sultan, 418

Mehta, Tyeb, 846

Meiji Japan, 609–614; economic and social reforms, 610–612; government and military in, 609–610; Korea and, 613–614 *and map*; westernization and expansion of, 612–613, 614*(map)*; legacy of, 740

Mekong River (Vietnam), 457, 463

Melaka, 463, 583; Portuguese in, 378, 449, 458*(map)*, 461, 481

Melanesia, 540, 794

Mendes family, 478

Menelik (Ethiopia), 549

Mercantilism, 387, 476; capitalism and, 380, 500; in France, 389; in Spain, 380, 447; in British India, 571; in Japan, 735

Mercator, Gerardus, mapmaking and, 375

Mercenary soldiers: in Europe, 398–399; in Morocco, 423; in Ottoman Empire, 417; American, in Nicaragua, 536; in British India, 572

Merchant marine. *See* Ships and shipping

and, 615; decolonialization and, 690; social revolution and, 693; Taiwanese, 744; North Korean, 743, 744; Soviet buildup, 763, 767; French, in Vietnam, 850; Taliban, in Afghanistan, 820; power of, in Middle East, 808; in Suez crisis (1956), 809; Israeli, 810*(illus.)*, 812; Portuguese, in Africa, 825

Military, United States. *See also* Armed forces, United States; in Mexico, 527, 650; in Philippines, 587; interventions by, 527, 530, 536, 633; in World War I, 624; in Russian civil war, 627, 628*(map)*; Cold War buildup, 695, 697–698, 699; in Saudi Arabia, 717; in South Korea, 742, 743; in Taiwan, 745; in Japan, 732; Korean War and, 741–742 *and map*; interventions by, 695, 751, 781*(map)*, 782–783, 822; worldwide (1945–present), 780, 781*(map)*, 785; in Turkey, 808; in Laos and Cambodia, 782, 854; in Vietnam War, 782, 783*(illus.)*; in Afghanistan, 785; in Iraq, 687, 714, 785; in Panama, 797; in Thailand, 860–861

Military dictatorship (military rule): in Japan, 639; in Latin America, 484, 531, 672, 686, 777; in Thailand, 660–661; in South Korea, 742; in Argentina, 796; in Brazil, 798–799; in Chile, 801, 804; human rights abuses and, 797, 807, 863; in Iraq, 670, 814; in Nigeria, 807; in Africa, 825, 826, 827; in Paksitan, 841; United States' arms sales to, 780, 784; in Burma and Thailand, 860–862; in Indonesia, 857–858

Military draft. *See* Conscription (military draft)

Military-industrial complex, 780

Military technology. *See* Weapons and military technology

Mill, John Stuart, 506

Mindon (Burma), 585

Ming dynasty (China), 463, 464, 466

Mining and minerals. *See also* Gold; Iron and steel industry; *specific metals*; in colonial Bolivia, 442; coal, in Britain, 499, 500, 501, 502*(map)*; in British Malaya, 583; imported, in Japan, 735; in colonial Africa, 554, 555; in South Africa, 551, 665, 829; in Congo, 824

Minorities. *See* Ethnic minorities; *specific minorities*

Mirabai, 453

Missionary impulse, 630, 712. *See also* Catholic missionaries; Christian missionaries

Mississippian culture, 427

Mississippi River, French exploration of, 434

Mitsui conglomerate, 610, 611*(illus.)*

Mixed-descent people: *See also* Mestizos; Mulattos; Eurasians, in Java, 462; in Latin America, 436, 495, 535; Metis, in Canada, 440, 539; in Portuguese communities, 455; coloreds, in South Africa, 550, 828, 829

Mobutu Sese Seko (Zaire), 825, 827; despotism of, 830–831, 832

Moctezuma II (Aztec), 432

Modernization. *See also* Westernization; in Ottoman Empire, 558–559; in Burma, 585; in Egypt, 559, 560*(illus.)*, 566*(illus.)*, 809; Islam and, 560, 564–566, 581; in Japan, 511, 594, 607, 609, 613*(map)*, 676, 677; in Siam, 511, 586–587, 676; in Korea, 614; in Russia, 614, 615*(illus.)*, 626; in Brazil, 674; in China, 601, 603, 652–653, 727–732; in Turkey, 667, 669 *and illus.*, 676; opposition to, in Iran, 669–670; in Taiwan, 745; in Middle East, 817, 822; in Saudi Arabia, 814

Moldavia, 557

Moluccas. *See* Maluku (Moluccas)

Mombasa (East African city), 408, 411

Monarchy. *See* Kingship (emperors; monarchy)

Monasteries and monks, Buddhist, 457, 703*(illus.)*

Monet, Claude, 521

Monetary system. *See also* Currency; American metals in, 452; Bretton Woods, 645, 753; European Union, 774

Mongkut (Siam), 587

Mongolia (Mongols): China and, 463*(map)*, 465, 606; communism in, 695

Mongolian Empire, breakup of, 423

Moniz, Donha Felipa, 428

Monnet, Jean, 753, 875

Monoculture economies, 442, 445. *See also* Cash crops; Plantation zone; in Latin America, 495; in

American South, 528; in colonial Africa, 555; in Southeast Asia, 589

Monomotapa (East Africa), 403*(map)*, 412

Monopoly, 529; big business and, 503, 504

Monopoly trade: Chinese government, 467, 597; Dutch, in Southeast Asia, 461; empire building and, 510; British, in Persia, 561; Indian salt trade, 658

Monotheism, Islam and, 450

Monroe, James, 527

Monroe Doctrine, 527, 867

Montaigne, Michel Eyquem de, 383

Montenegrins, 773*(map)*

Montesque, Baron de, 489, 506

Montreal, 434, 440, 872

Morality: power and, 381; Protestant, 385, 392; Confucian, 595, 601; Indian caste system and, 581; Japanese, 732

Morelos, Jose Maria (Mexico), 497, 499

Morgan, Henry, 434

Morgan, J. P., 529

Morocco, 420, 475, 808; expansion of, 404, 423; Sa'dian dynasty in, 422–423; European colonization of, 562; labor migration from, 758; terrorism in, 717

Moronobu, 473 *and illus.*

Moros, in Philippines, 460

Moscow, 627, 642

Moshoeshoe (Sotho), 550

Mosques: in Africa, 405*(illus.)*; in Ottoman Empire, 418; in China, 728; in Kuala Lumpur, 864*(illus.)*

Mossadeq, Mohammad, 697

Mothers and Grandmothers of the Plaza de Mayo (Argentina), 777–778

Motion pictures. *See* Film industry

Mozambique, 552, 707, 827; slaves from, 412; Portuguese in, 408, 410; as Portuguese colony, 412, 415, 648, 825; European colonialism in, 544, 553; forced labor in, 648; independence of, 691*(map)*; Marxism in, 825; civil war in, 831

Mozart, Wolfgang Amadeus, 520

Mugabe, Robert (Zimbabwe), 825, 831–832

Mughal Empire. *See* India, Mughal Empire in

Muhammad Ali (Egypt), 559, 560*(illus.)*, 564

Religion(s). *See also* Buddhism; Catholicism; Christianity; Gods and goddesses; Hinduism; Islam; Priests; *under* Religious; Enlightenment thinkers and, 398; evolutionary theory and, 521; in Mughal India, 450, 452–453; Shinto, in Japan, 471, 739; African, 446; Marxist critique of, 507–508; Bahai, in Persia, 561; in Soviet Union, 765; global networks, 712–713 *and map*, 714; Hindu polytheism, 450; in China, 712, 728, 731; in Europe, 520, 760; in United States, 788; in Latin America, 803–804; Rastafarianism, 805; African polytheism, 553, 554, 712, 834; and conflict, in Middle East, 816; in India, 845; in Malaysia, 863

Religious freedom, 387, 388; in colonial America, 439, 490; in England, 385, 393

Religious militancy, 700. *See also* Islamic militancy

Religious tolerance: in Ottoman Empire, 418; in Europe, 395, 520; in Mughal India, 451; in Siam, 457; liberalism and, 506; in Africa, 554; in China, 728

Remarque, Erich Maria, 621–622

Rembrandt van Rijn, 395

Remington, Philo, 684

Renaissance: in Europe, 380–382; art and literature, 381–383; philosophy and science of, 380–381; chronology (1350–1615), 381; Confucian, in China, 466; in Siam, 457; in Chile and Caribbean, 675, 801; Southeast Asia, 662

Renoir, Pierre, 521

Reparations, World War I, 624–625, 638

Representative government, 488, 493. *See also* Parliamentary democracy; in Europe, 387, 392–393; in India, 581

Republican era, China, 604, 605, 652–653, 850

Republican party (United States), 633, 709

Republicans (Spain), 639

Republic of China, 720, 725*(map)*, 744. *See also* Taiwan

Resources. *See* Natural resources

Revolts. *See* Rebellions (revolts)

Revolution. *See also* Age of Revolution; Social revolution; scientific, 396–397; in Europe

(1830–1831), 493; Marxism and, 507, 508; Mexican, 533–534, 646–647*(illus.)*, 650; in Philippines, 587, 588, 861–862 *and illus.*; in imperial China, 603–604, 605, 677; in Japan, 609; Russian, 617, 624, 625–627 *and illus.*, 677; nationhood and, 677–678; social, in China, 656, 690, 719, 720; Cultural (China), 725–726, 727; sexual, 757; Soviet backing of, 764; Green (agricultural), 704, 709, 782, 840, 844; Islamic, in Iran, 687, 700, 813; anticolonial, in Africa, 826*(map)*; Cuban, 686, 799–800 *and illus.*; in Dutch-ruled Indonesia, 856; in Philippines

Rhee Syngman (South Korea), 741

Rhodes, Cecil, 513, 549

Rhodesia. *See* Zambia; Zimbabwe

Ricci, Matteo, 469

Rice cultivation, 480; in China, 466; in French Indochina, 585, 679, 850; in India, 452, 844; in Japan, 471; in Korea, 608; in Siam (Thailand), 587; in Southeast Asia, 589

Rich nations, 705. *See also* Industrialized nations; Wealth and wealthy

Riel, Louis, 539

Rifles, 622*(illus.)*, 676, 684; of Africans, 546*(illus.)*; in British India, 577

Rights. *See* Human rights

Rio de Janeiro, 802; shantytowns in, 535, 705*(illus.)*; Carnival in, 535, 804; United Nations conference in, 872

Rivera, Diego, 675

Rizal, Jose, 677

Roads and highways: in India, 452; in United States, 787; in Africa, 835

A Road with No End (Lubis), 837

Roanoke colony (North Carolina), 434

"Roarin' 20s" (1920s, United States), 633

Robber Barons (United States), 529, 530

Robinson, Mary, 757–758

Rockefeller, John D., 529

Rockefeller family, 503

Rock music, 788; in China, 728; punk, 759, 791; in Soviet Union, 765 *and illus.*

Roman Catholicism. *See* Catholic Church

Romania, 416, 505, 557; Hungarians in, 771, 773*(map)*; Soviet domination of, 766; World War I and, 620, 622

Romanticism, 520, 523

Romany (Gypsies), 642

Rome, 387. *See also* Papacy; Renaissance art in, 381

A Room of One's Own (Woolf), 636

Roosevelt, Franklin D.: New Deal of, 634–635; Pearl Harbor attack and, 642; at Yalta meeting, 645

Rosas, Juan Manuel de (Argentina), 532

Rosetta stone, 543

Roy, Arundhati, 846

Roy, Ram Mohan, 576

Royal Dutch Shell, 705

Rubber and rubber plantations, 435, 510, 576, 579, 634, 649; in Brazil, 534, 701; in British Malaya, 583, 589, 590, 620, 681; colonialism and, 589; in Congo, 554, 555 *and illus.*, 701; in French Indochina, 585, 679, 850; Indian workers on, 590; in Liberia, 546; in Malaysia, 700; in Sri Lanka, 573, 700–701, 848; in World War II, 642, 662

Rufisque, Senegal, 481

Ruhr district (Germany), 502

Ruling class. *See* Aristocracy; Upper class (elites)

Rural areas (rural society). *See also* Peasants; Villages; in England, 398; in British India, 575, 578; in United States, 525; African, 664; in Philippines, 460, 858–859; in Japan, 632, 732, 735; social services in, 705; urban pop culture and, 712; Chinese reforms and, 727, 728; in Bangladesh, 848; in India, 846; in Vietnam, 850, 851; in Thailand, 861

Rural-to-urban migration: *See also* Urbanization; in Europe, 517; in South Africa, 551; in China, 729, 730; in Soviet Union, 764; in Latin America, 802; in Iran, 813

Rushdie, Salman, 759, 846

Russian language, 617, 762, 765

Russian Orthodox Church, 389, 617, 765, 771

Russian Revolution (1905), 617

Russian Revolution (1917), 617, 624, 625–627, 677; Bolsheviks and, 626–627 *and illus.*; roots of, 626–627

Russia (Russian Empire), 474, 678. *See also* Soviet Union (USSR); czars

and despotism, 389–390; Central
Asia and, 423, 594; Ottoman
Empire and, 371, 419, 557 *and
map*; Siberia and, 390, 391*(map)*,
423, 463*(map)*, 469, 481, 607,
609, 615; Napoleonic France and,
493, 494*(map)*; Poland-Lithuania
and, 395, 423, 492; alliances of,
510; British India and, 575, 615;
expansion of, 389–390, 391*(map)*,
394*(map)*, 423, 485, 511, 557*(map)*,
594; China and, 423, 463*(map)*,
469, 476; Greece and, 504, 557;
Jews in, 505, 517, 567, 642; Persia
and, 421, 561; sale of Alaska by,
525; Afghanistan and, 575, 615; as
great power, 487; famine in, 517,
626; industrialization in, 617, 626;
Manchuria and, 603, 612; unrest
and revolution in, 624; in World
War I, 620, 621, 622–623 *and map*,
626; civil war in (1918–1921),
627–628 *and map*, 762; peasants
and serfdom in, 379, 517, 626;
nuclear waste explosion in, 709;
post-Soviet, 768–771, 775
Russification policy, 617, 762, 765
Russo-Japanese War (1904–1905),
612, 617
Rwanda, genocide in, 698, 700, 784,
827–828
Ryukyu Islands, Japan and,
644, 732
Ryunosuke, Akutagawa, 632

Sabah, Borneo, 583, 863
Sa'dians (Morocco), 422–423
Safavid Empire (Persia), 371,
402, 420–422, 474; culture,
421; decline of, 421–422, 556;
expansion of, 417*(map)*, 420, 454;
Shi'ite Islam in, 420, 421, 422,
423; trading network, 420–421,
478, 479; women, 421, 422*(illus.)*
Safety net. *See* Social safety net
Sahara Desert, expansion of, 877
Sahel region, desertification
in, 479
Saigon. *See* Ho Chi Minh City
(Saigon)
Saikaku, Ihara, 473
St. Lawrence River, 537
St. Petersburg, 390 *and illus.*, 617;
Bolsheviks in, 627
Sakhalin Island, 612
Sakharov, Andrei, 762
Salaryman, in Japan, 736
Salavarrieta, Policarpa de, 497
Salim, Jawad, 819*(illus.)*

Salons, in Paris, 397*(illus.)*
Salt trade, in India, 658
Salvador da Bahia, 433
Salvation, Protestantism and, 383
Samba (dance), 446, 536, 675
Samoa, 511, 692, 794; Christianity
in, 540
Samory Toure (Mandinka), 549
Samurai (Japanese warriors), 471,
472, 473; Meiji restoration and,
609, 610, 611; weaponry of, 607
Sandanistas (Nicaragua), 796, 803
Sanitation, 521, 579, 649
Sankore, University of, 404
Sankore Mosque (Timbuktu),
405*(illus.)*
San Martin, José de, 496, 497, 535
Santa Anna, Antonio Lopez de,
532–533
Santo Domingo, Hispaniola, 431
Sao Paolo (Brazil) 433, 709, 710
Sarajevo, 621
Sarawak, Borneo, 856*(map)*, 863
Sarte, Jean-Paul, 750; existentialism
and, 759–760
The Satanic Verses (Rushdie), 759
Satellites: Russian, 762;
communications and, 787;
Indian, 849
Sati (widow burning), 451, 453, 846;
ban on, 575, 576, 581
Saud, Abdul Aziz Ibn, 564, 671
Saud, Muhammad Ibn, 563
Saudi Arabia, 668*(map)*; migrant
workers in, 707; oil wealth of,
564, 671, 687, 814–815 *and illus.*;
terrorism in, 717, 784, 815,
817; United States and, 784,
811*(map)*; Wahhabism in,
563–564, 671, 814
Saudi royal family, 668*(map)*, 671,
814, 815
Savannah, colonial era, 479
Savuka (pop music group), 807
Sayyid Sa'id, 545
Scandinavia (Scandinavians). *See
also* Denmark; Finland; Norway;
Sweden; Lutheranism in, 383,
384*(map)*; homosexuality in, 399;
feminism in, 519; in United States,
518*(map)*, 530; socialist economics
in, 635; quality of life in, 694, 874;
monarchy in, 748; social welfare
in, 755–756 *and illus.*; globalization
and, 867
Schiller, Frederich, 520
The Scholars (Wu), 466
Schools and scholars. *See also*
Education; Islamic, 381, 404,

814; Japanese, 476, 607; Chinese,
465, 466, 469; Philippines, 460;
Siamese (Thai), 457, 661; French
public, 520; African American,
528, 789; colonial Africa, 554;
French, in Egypt, 543; Orientalists,
575–576; Ottoman, 418, 558; Arab
nationalist, 567; India, 575, 841;
Javanese, 591; Confucianist, in
Taiwan, 745; Christian missions
and, 554, 561, 598, 651, 834;
Chinese, 593, 598, 603, 651, 722;
African, 831, 834
Schools for girls. *See* Women,
education of
Schuman, Clara, 519
Schuman, Robert, 753
Science. *See also* Astronomy;
Mathematics; European, 381,
395, 396; Locke's empiricism
and, 398; Ottoman, 419; Chinese,
464, 469; physics, 381, 396,
521, 636; in British India, 581,
679; industrialization and, 503,
703–704; Western, in Japan, 608;
global exhange in, 715; Christian
conservatives and, 788; in India,
849; global warming and, 872
Scientific Revolution, in Europe,
396–397
Scotland (Scots): in colonial
America, 439; English and,
392, 393, 504; potatoes in, 480;
Presbyterianism in, 385
Script, Persian, 451. *See also* Writing
Seclusion of women. *See* Women,
seclusion of
Seclusion policy, in Japan and
Korea, 606, 608
Second Continental Congress, 489
Second Industrial Revolution,
503, 504
Second Vatican Council (1962–
1965), 760
Second World concept, 694
Secret police: czarist Russia, 614;
Iranian, 813; Soviet KGB, 629,
630, 762, 765, 767
Secularization (secularism), 398; in
Europe, 379; of European Jews,
505; in Mexico, 533; in Ottoman
Empire, 558–559; Christian
opposition to, 714; in China,
731; in Japan, 739; in Soviet
Union, 765; in India, 839, 840,
844; Islam and, 814, 817; of
Turkey, 669, 817
Security Council (United Nations),
698–699

Slaves (slavery). *See also* African slavery; in colonial Brazil, 433, 445–446; in Dutch South Africa, 550; freedom for, 446 (*See also* Slavery, abolition of); Native Americans as, 438, 440*(illus.)*, 442; revolts by, in Americas, 446; in Siam, 457; in United States, 490, 522, 523, 528; women as, 523

Slave trade, 445. *See also* African slave trade; Atlantic system and, 413–414 *and map*, 446–447; economic impact of, 446–447; end of, 485

Slavophiles, 617

Slavs (Slavic peoples), 621; Nazi Germany and, 642

Slovaks (Slovakia), 621; seceded from Czechs, 771, 773*(map)*

Slovenes (Slovenia), 772, 773*(map)*

Smallpox, 547; Native Americans and, 425, 432, 435, 479, 480*(illus.)*; vaccines against, 521

Smith, Adam, 500

Smith, Jacob, 588

Soccer (football), 517, 685, 804–805

Social Darwinism, 513, 529

Social Democrats, in Europe, 508, 631, 635, 750, 758, 774

Socialism: Marxist thought and, 507–508, 650, 678; fascism and, 637; in Egypt, 809; in Europe, 625, 755; in Russia, 626; in Venezuela, 796–797; in Cuba, 799–800; in Chile, 800–801; in North Vietnam, 851; in Ghana, 823, 831; and capitalism in India, 840; in Africa, 831–832; in Sri Lanka, 848; and capitalism, in Asia, 870

Socialist realism, 630

Socialist Revolutionary Party (Russia), 617

Social revolution: in China, 656, 690, 719, 720; decolonization and, 693; French Revolution as, 488; nationalism and, 690; in Africa, 831

Social safety net (welfare), 687, 695, 738, 750. *See also* Welfare state; in Eastern Europe, 771; Hamas and, 812; in Soviet Union, 764, 769

Social security, in United States, 635

Social structure (social order): feudalism and, 374; in colonial Philippines, 459, 460–461; Indian castes, 450, 452, 453, 576, 581, 659, 840, 846; Latin American, 436, 535; Qing China, 465–466;

colonial Java, 461–462; Korean, 470; socialism and, 507; in colonial Africa, 553–554; Japan, 472, 611–612; in Europe (1920s), 631–632; race and, in United States, 789

Social welfare. *See* Social safety net; Welfare state

Society Islands, 540

Society of Jesus. *See* Jesuit missionaries

Society (social conditions): Ottoman diversity, 418; Native American, 426–427; plantation slavery, 445; Siamese, 457–458; cultural change and, 480–482; Filipino, 459; industrialization and, 499; United States, 523–524; reshaping of, in British India, 577–582; colonialism and, 648; modernization and, 676; Japanese, 607, 736–739; Soviet Union, 764–765; Western Europe, 755–760; Latin America, 803–804; Indian, 845; Indonesia, 858; environmental change and, 871–872

Soedjatmoko, 866

Soekarnoputri, Megawati, 858

Sofala (East African city), 406, 410, 412

Sokoto Caliphate, 547

Soldiers. *See* Armed forces; Infantry; Mercenaries; Military

Solidarity (Poland), 766, 771, 772

Solomon (Hebrew), 407

Solzhenitsyn, Alexander, 762

Somalia, 549, 700, 835; civil war in, 700; United States' intervention in, 784, 811*(map)*; famine in, 827

Somoza Debayle, Anastasio (Nicaragua), 651, 803

Song Empire (China), 467

Songhai Empire, 402, 403*(map)*; Morocco and, 404, 423

Sotho people of South Africa, 550, 551

South, United States: colonial era, 439, 441, 446; plantation slavery in, 522, 523, 528; segregation in, 642

South Africa (South Africans), 866; Portuguese explorers in, 408; Bantu-speakers in, 407, 550, 551–552; Angola and, 693; Asians in, 552; Black Zion movement in, 556; Boer War (1899–1902), 551; Dutch colony in, 371, 392, 412, 415, 549–550; hybrid social group in, 481; Christianity in, 550,

551, 552; European colonialism in, 544, 650, 681; slavery in, 461, 550; musicians from, 665 *and illus.*, 807, 832; nationalism in, 665–666; migrant workers in, 707; white minority rule in, 550–552, 825; in World War I, 622; apartheid in, 828–829, 832; black majority rule in, 687, 829, 874; diamond mining in, 549, 551, 620; Mandela in, 827, 829

South America, 484. *See also* Latin America; European colonies in, 370; African slavery in, 370; in Atlantic economy, 443*(map)*; Spanish exploration of, 428; in 1930, 673*(map)*; political stability in, 686

South Asia, 485. *See also* Bangladesh; India; Pakistan; Sri Lanka; chronology (1450–1750), 454; intermarriage in, 455; new challenges to, 455–456; Portuguese and, 454–455 *and illus.*; British expansion in, 573–574 *and map*; chronology (1744–1906), 570; labor migration from, 710, 711; chronology (1914–1945), 657; reshaping of, 687, 836–843; chronology (1945–1999), 839; Islamic politics and societies in, 402, 847–848; in the global system, 848–849

South Carolina, slave revolt in, 446

Southeast Asia. *See also* Burma; Cambodia; Indonesia; Malaysia; Philippines; Thailand; Vietnam; Buddhist and Islamic societies in, 457–459; China trade and, 464, 468; Dutch in, 392, 458 *and map*; Europeans in, 426; global connections and, 456–459; Japanese in, 471; transitions and trade, 456–457; chronology (1350–1767), 457; European colonies in, 371, 457, 458*(map)*, 485; Islam in, 459; British influence in, 510; Chinese merchants in, 464, 478, 481, 590, 595, 604, 649; American navy in, 527, 588; chronology (1786–1910), 582; colonization of, 582–590, 584*(map)*; natural resources in, 583, 586, 865; social and cultural change in, 590–591; world economy and, 589, 720; Great Depression in, 649; Japanese occupation of, 642, 643*(map)*, 644, 645, 660, 661, 662–664;

United States, 632, 633; in colonial Africa, 556, 664, 665; in Great Depression, 635; in Egypt, 670; Indian nationalism and, 657, 658; global (1960s), 715; in Europe, 774; in Poland, 762; in Iran, 813

Structural adjustment policy, 839

Stuart dynasty (England), 392–393

Student protests: in China, 652, 725; against colonialism, 650; in Egypt, 670; against war (1960s), 715–716; in Japan, 739; in United States (1960s), 788; in Europe (1968), 757; in Mexico (1968), 798; in Thailand and Burma, 861

Submarine warfare: in World War I, 624; German, in World War II, 640; Soviet, 697–698

Sub-Saharan Africa: early modern era, 402–408; end of slave trade and, 544–545; new societies of, 545–546; chronology (1804–1912), 545; colonization of, 544–549, 552–556; Christian missions, 553, 554; colonial governments in, 553; European exploration of, 407, 546; legacy of colonialism, 687; nationalism in, 660; quality of life in, 694; political change and conflict in, 825–828; Islamic resurgence in, 834; chronology (1945–present), 823; nationalism and decolonization in, 822–825; socialism in, 831–832; underdevelopment in, 830–831; cities, families and gender in, 832; cultural expression in, 832–834; religious change in, 834

Suburbanization, in United States, 787, 789

Sudan (Sudanic Africa), 700, 835; trading cities of, 407; slave trade in, 415; Mahdi uprising in, 543(illus.), 560–561; Anglo-Egyptian, 561; Islamic resurgence in, 546–547; cotton in, 555; Egypt and, 671; refugees from, 711; genocide in, 816

Suez Canal, 566(illus.), 578, 684; British and, 510, 560, 670, 809; crisis (1956), 809

Suffrage. See Voting rights (suffrage)

Sufis (Sufi mysticism), 759, 817; in Java, 459; in Morocco, 423; in Mughal India, 452, 453, 476, 482; in Ottoman Empire, 419, 476, 482; Safavids and, 420, 421; in West Africa, 547, 549; Islamic revivalism and, 563; in Bangladesh, 848

Sugar plantations, 441, 589, 634; in Americas, 476, 480, 522; in Atlantic economy, 441, 443(map); on Atlantic islands, 423; in Caribbean, 444, 445 and illus., 496; colonial era, 444, 445 and illus., 496, 675(illus.); in colonial Java, 582, 589, 680; in Cuba, 444, 534, 649–650, 679; in Brazil, 410, 433, 445; in Hawaii, 530–531; slavery on, 444, 445 and illus., 478, 496, 544; in Haiti, 496; indentured labor for, 579; in India, 452, 579; in Latin America, 534, 672; in Philippines, 460, 463; in South Africa, 681; wealth from, 447

Suharto (Indonesia), 857–858

Suicide bombers: in Arab-Israeli conflict, 716–717, 812; in Iraq, 820; in Lebanon, 816

Sukarno (Indonesia), 662, 663, 677; as autocrat, 856–857; military coup and, 857

Sulawesi, 461, 582

Suleiman the Magnificent, Sultan, 416, 417, 418

Sultans and sultanates: Ottoman, 416–417, 418, 419; in Zanzibar, 411; in Brunei, 583, 695, 865

Sumatra: Acheh in, 459, 478, 482, 857, 858; Dutch control of, 461, 582; Islam on, 857

Summer of Love (1967), 788

Sumo wrestling, in Japan, 739, 867

Sunni Islam, 422; Kurds and, 561, 562, 667; in Ottoman Empire, 420; in Pakistan, 658, 847; in Iran, 423, 482, 813; in Iraq, 562, 670, 717, 814; Uzbeks and, 423

Sunni-Shi'ite rivalry, 561, 566, 808, 847; in Iran, 423, 482, 813; in Iraq, 562, 714, 717, 814, 817

Sun Yat-Sen (Sun Zhong Shan), 603–605, 652

Superpowers, in Cold War, 645, 767, 778–784. See also Soviet Union; United States; Africa and, 834; conflict in, 690; Egypt and, 808, 809; interventions by, 697, 808; Korean War, 741–742 and map, 764; nationalism and, 692; nonaligned nations and, 695, 809; nuclear arms race, 697–698; rivalry between, 778; United Nations and, 698–699; United States as sole, 699, 769, 778, 797

Supreme Command of Allied Powers (SCAP), 732, 734

Supreme Court (United States), 526–527, 789, 791

Surat (India), 452, 455, 456

Suriname (Dutch Guiana), 433, 579, 683

Survival of the fittest, 513, 529

Susenyos (Ethiopia), 412

Sustainable environments, 871–872

Swahili trading cities, 406, 408, 410–411

Sweden, 640. See also Scandinavia; Lutheranism in, 388. 393; independence of, 393; wars with Russia, 389, 390, 393; Finland and, 504; women's education in, 519; social democracy in, 635; in European Union, 774; quality of life in, 756 and illus.

Sweet potatoes, 594

Switzerland, 640, 678, 760; Calvinism in, 383, 385; as constitutional confederation, 392; higher education for women in, 519; nationalism in, 504, 520; Red Cross in, 685; independence of, 388, 774; homosexual rights in, 758

Syphilis, 435, 480

Syria (Syrians), 560, 564; Ottoman rule in, 416, 562, 666; immigrants from, 535; Christians in, 562; French control of, 666, 667, 668(map); Arab nationalism in, 567, 667; Palestinians in, 810; conflict with Israel, 811(map), 812, 816

Tagore, Rabindranath, 579–580, 657, 679

Tahiti, 539, 540, 794

Tai Chen, 466

Taino people, 428, 429–430; enslavement of, 430

Taiping Rebellion, 598–599 and map, 603, 613, 677

Taiwan, 687, 733(map); China and, 465, 469, 481, 745; Dutch in, 469, 476; as Japanese colony, 612, 613(map), 632, 744; democracy in, 702; labor migration from, 711; economy of, 720, 734(map), 740, 744, 745; Chiang Kai-shek in, 719, 720, 723, 744; China and, 724(map), 731, 744, 745; United States' aid to, 723, 744; globalization and, 701, 867

Tajiks (Tajikistan), 765

Taj Mahal, 453

The Tale of the Kieu (Nguyen Du), 585

Taliban (Afghanistan), 784
Tamil-speakers, 590; in Sri Lanka, 573, 848
Tanganyika: as German colony, 549, 553, 555; World War I in, 622
Tango (dance), 535
Tanzania, 705, 835; colonial, 824; Nyerere in, 694, 827
Tariffs. *See also* Protectionism; United States, 523, 528; British industry and, 579, 680; in Europe, 753, 835
Tartar states, 389, 423
Taxation, 475; in Ottoman Empire, 419; Spanish, 447; in Mughal India, 451, 454; of Muslim merchants, 457; colonial cash crops and, 460; in China, 466, 651, 656; on Chinese merchants, 467, 468; French Revolution and, 491; in British North America, 489; in colonial Latin America, 496; in colonial Africa, 553, 556, 648; in British India, 576, 578, 579; in British Malaya, 583; in Japan, 610; in Russia, 771; United States' military and, 780, 782, 785; in welfare states, 755; in Chile, 801
Taylor, Harriet, 519
Tayson Rebellion (Vietnam), 585
Tchaikovsky, Pyotr, 617
Tea ceremony, in Japan, 471, 739
Tea trade, 510, 576, 579, 830; taxation on, 489; Chinese, 463, 464, 466; Ceylon (Sri Lanka), 511*(illus.)*, 573, 848
Technology: *See also* High technology; Science; Arab, 376; European, 376, 396–397; Chinese, 376, 464, 475; Ottoman, 419; Western European, 470; British, 475, 510; Industrial Revolution, 501; spread of, 683; innovation and, 703–704, 866
Tecumseh (Shawnee), 538
Tehran, Iran, 561
Telegraph, 559, 561, 610, 683; undersea cables, 511; wireless, 521. *See also* Radio; railroads and, 684
Telephone, 684, 714
Telescopes, 396
Television, 711; cable news networks, 714, 822; Latin American, 804
Tell, William, Swiss nationalism and, 520
The Tempest (Shakespeare), 373, 383

Temples: Aztec, 432; Hindu, 451; Buddhist, in China, 728; Sikh, in Amritsar, 453, 843
Tenant farmers: in Europe, 374; in Philippines, 460; in India, 576, 578
Tenochtitlan, 436; Spanish conquest of, 425, 432
Terrorism: *See also* Al Qaeda; Portuguese, 454; in French Revolution, 492; in Ottoman Empire, 558; racist, in United States, 633; in Russia and Soviet Union, 617, 629–630; in China, 651, 652; Bengali women and, 660; United States and, 686; global networks, 716–717, 784; in North Korea, 744; Basques, in Spain, 716, 749*(illus.)*, 750; George Bush's war on, 717, 786; in Europe, 775; September 11 (2001), 717, 775, 784, 873; in Chile, 801; in Arab-Israeli conflict, 810, 812; in Iran, 813; in Afghanistan, 820; in Bali, 858; in India, 849
Tet Offensive (Vietnam, 1968), 852*(map)*, 853
Texas, annexation of, 525, 526*(map)*, 527, 533
Textiles (textile industry). *See also* Cloth and clothing; Cotton; Silk; European, 374; Chinese, 397, 600; Persian, 421; dyes for, 433; Indian, 452, 454, 456, 463, 478, 680; innovation in, 475; British (English), 487, 499, 501, 679; spinning machines in, 397, 499; steam power for, 501; in New England, 523, 529*(illus.)*, 530; Egyptian, 559; women in, 437, 518–519, 529*(illus.)*, 530, 600, 611; Japanese, 611; Sri Lankan, 848
Thackeray, William, 501
Thailand (Siam), 678. *See also* Siam; independence of, 485; modernization of, 676; nationalism in, 660; AIDS prevention in, 861; Internet cafe in, 715*(illus.)*; military rule of, 860–861; United States and, 783, 860–861; Laos and, 853; Buddhism in, 860, 861; democracy in, 702, 861; economic growth in, 702, 856, 865, 869
Thatcher, Margaret, 756
Theocracy: in Switzerland, 385; of Safavid Persia, 420, 421; Islamic, 563; in Iran, 813
Theology, 383, 395; liberation, 712, 803

Theravada Buddhism, 456; in Burma, 660, 860, 861; in Siam (Thailand), 457, 482, 860, 861; in Sri Lanka, 848
Third Estate (France), 491, 492
Third Industrial Revolution, 703–704
Third World, 694, 695; globalization and, 701–702; local economies in, 705
Thirty Years War (1618–1648), 388 *and illus.*, 392
Three Gorges Dam (China), 729
"Three Principles of the People" (Sun), 604, 605
Through the Looking Glass (Carroll), 875
Thuku, Harry, 664, 677
Tiananmen Square (Beijing), 719, 728
Tibet: British invasion of, 578; Buddhism in, 450, 699; China and, 463*(map)*, 465, 606, 723, 729
Tilak, Bal Gangadhar, 581–582
Timbuktu (Africa), 402, 403*(map)*, 404; Moroccans and, 420; mosque in, 405*(illus.)*
Timor, colonization of, 458*(map)*, 461
Tin mining, 583, 589, 634
Tito, Josip Broz (Yugoslavia), 766, 772
Tlaxcalans, Aztecs and, 432
Tobacco, 429, 435, 447, 522, 583, 703*(illus.)*; in Atlantic economy, 443*(map)*; in China, 480; in Africa, 835; in Europe, 480; prohibition of, 453; slave labor for, 441, 445
Tobacco lords, of Glasgow, 447
Tocqueville, Alexis de, 487, 523
Tokugawa Ieyasu, 471, 472
Tokugawa shogunate (Japan), 371, 475, 676; stability and seclusion, 472–473; culture and society in, 607; defeat of, 609; opening of, 607–608; political crisis in, 608; Qing China compared, 606–607
Tokyo (Edo), 472; bank in, 611*(illus.)*; imperial residence in, 609–610; subways in, 736, 737*(illus.)*; Tokugawa era, 606, 607; population growth in, 709, 736; stock exchange, 700, 739
Tolerance. *See* Religious tolerance
Toleration Act (England), 393
Tolstoy, Leo, 617
Tomatoes, 480
Tonga, 540
Tonghak Rebellion (Korea), 613

United Nations, *continued*
744; World Conference on Women
(1995), 716; peacekeeping by,
699 *and illus.*, 772, 825; Somalia
and, 784, 827; Iraq and, 785, 814;
Israel and, 810; sustainability
conference, 872; Cambodia and,
855; cultural imports and, 867;
global cooperation and, 870, 875
United States, 484. *See also* Armed
forces; Military, United States;
Superpowers, in Cold War; war of
independence, 489–490; Haitian
republic and, 496; voting rights
in, 490, 522; Britain and, 523;
chronology (1750–1914), 522;
rising global power, 521–531;
government and economy, 510,
522–523; Latin America and, 527;
society and culture, 523–524;
war with Mexico (1846–1848),
527; westward expansion of,
522, 525–527 *and map*; abolition
of slavery in, 522, 528, 544; civil
war in, 522, 528, 559; Canada
and, 523, 537–538; capitalism and
empire, 530–531; Hawaii and, 511,
530–531, 540, 677; immigration
and urbanization in, 529–530;
industrialization in, 503, 528–529,
680; war with Spain, 531, 534,
536, 588; Panama Canal and,
536; Arab immigrants in, 562;
colonies of, 530–531; imperialism
of, 536, 651, 677, 697, 781,
805; Philippines and, 485, 513,
587–588; Japan and, 607–608,
639; Cuba and, 531, 534, 536;
in World War I, 620, 623*(map)*,
624; isolationism, in 1920s, 632,
633; economic supremacy of, 679,
695; Great Depression in, 634;
New Deal reform in, 634–635; in
World War II, 640–644 *and maps,*
663, 664, 679, 778; Japanese
immigration restricted, 632, 683;
Mexico and, 650; decolonization
and, 690, 691*(map)*, 692; Latin
America and, 777, 802; loans
to Europe by, 748, 778; popular
culture of, 635, 684, 759, 791,
797, 867; post-war occupation of
Japan, 732; automobile industry
in, 703; as sole superpower, 699,
769, 778, 797; multinational
corporations based in, 702; birth
control in, 709; Nicaragua and,
716; North Korean famine and,
744; global economy and, 701,

729; Korean War and, 741–742
and map, 764; aid to European
recovery, 748; alliance with Japan,
734, 740; Philippines and, 690,
691*(map)*, 858, 860; citizenship
in, 776–777*(illus.)*; Gulf Coast
hurricanes, 787, 866; prosperity,
technology and inequality in,
785, 787; China and, 652–653,
721, 725, 727, 731; Egypt and,
809; Canada and, 779, 780, 791;
national debt of, 633, 731, 781–
782; New Zealand and, 794; Iran
and, 813; Israel and, 699, 717,
810; oil embargo (1973) and, 815;
South African investment, 829;
global system and, 784–785, 870;
Pakistan and, 841; Vietnam and,
850, 851 (*See also* Vietnam War);
Indonesian independence and,
856; cultural imperialism of,
867; in Persian Gulf War (1991),
814; resource consumption in,
868; terrorist attacks in, 775,
849; war in Afghanistan, 775,
819, 820; greenhouse effect
and, 872
United States, economic sanctions
by. *See* Economic sanctions
(boycott; embargo)
Universal human dignity, 837. *See
also* Human rights
Universities and colleges, 755. *See
also* Student protests; in colonial
Latin America, 436, 442; in Islamic
Africa, 404; women in, 519, 790;
in Africa, 554; in Istanbul, 558; in
Lebanon, 562; in Persia, 561; in
India, 575, 578, 841, 849; Islamic,
581; nationalist movements in,
650; in Beijing, 651, 652; in Japan,
736, 739
Untouchables (pariahs), 659,
840, 846
U Nu (Burma), 861
Upper class (elites). *See also*
Aristocracy; conspicuous
consumption of, 378; in Ottoman
Empire, 418, 419; planter class,
444; family size and, 519; Mughal
India, 452; Chinese women, 466,
482; Latin American creole, 436,
437, 496, 497, 499, 531–532, 535;
in United States, 522; in Egypt,
560; Vietnam, 585; Italian fascism
and, 636; Qing China, 468, 601,
607; colonialism and, 678–679;
Soviet Union, 763; African urban,
827, 834; in India, 839, 843

Urbanization. *See also* Cities and
towns; Rural-to-urban migration;
capitalism and, 395; in Europe,
516, 517; in United States, 529–
530; in Southeast Asia, 591; in
Japan, 737; in Africa, 832
Urdu language, 450–451, 577, 658
Uruguay, 438, 497, 498*(map)*, 797;
immigration to, 535
Usury (interest), 375, 379
Uthman dan Fodio, Hausa jihad and,
546–547
Utopian socialism, 507
Utrecht, Treaty of (1714), 388–389
Uzbeks (Uzbekistan): Muslim, 765;
terrorist threat in, 420, 423,
629, 717

Vaccination, against disease, 521
Vaisya (Indian merchant caste), 452
Van Gogh, Vincent, 521, 607
Van Linschoten, Jan Huygen,
455*(illus.)*
Vargas, Getulio (Brazil), 674
Vatican. *See also* Papacy (popes);
Sistine Chapel in, 381; Second
Council (1962–1965), 760
Vega, Garcilaso de la, 438
Veiling of women. *See under* Women,
seclusion of
Veloso, Caetano, 868
Velvet Revolution, in
Czechoslovakia, 771, 772*(illus.)*
Venezuela: Spanish claims to,
430, 432; cattle ranching in,
442; independence of, 496, 497,
498*(map)*; European immigration
to, 535; Colombians in, 711;
oil industry in, 796; Chavez in,
796–797
Venice (Venetians), 387; as art
center, 381; capitalism in, 374;
decline of, 389
Veracruz, Mexico, 432
Verdi, Giuseppe, operas of, 566*(illus.)*
Verdun, Battle of (1916), 622
Vermeer, Jan, 395
Vernacular language, 712
Verrazano, Giovanni da, 430
Versailles palace, 389
Versailles Treaty (1919), 631,
652, 667; Wilson and, 624–625;
German reparations in, 636, 638
Vespucci, Amerigo, 430
Viceroyalties, 436. *See also* Spanish
colonies
Vichy government (France),
641*(map)*, 642, 662; Pétain and,
619, 640

Weapons of mass destruction, 875. *See also* Nuclear weapons; alleged, in Iraq, 717, 785, 786, 820

Weaving, women and, 437. *See also* Textiles (textile industry)

Wei Jingsheng, 728

Weimar Republic (Germany), 636

Welfare state (welfare systems), 508, 694–695; in Europe, 517, 687, 702, 750, 755–756, 774–775, 787; end of, in Eastern Europe, 771; end of, in Russia, 770; Japan as, 736; New Zealand as, 787, 794

Wesley, John, Methodism and, 520

West Africa: Atlantic system and, 441; desertification in, 479; slave trade in, 371, 401, 413–414, 415, 481; Portuguese exploration of, 407; Bondu kingdom in, 401; coastal trade of, 403*(map)*; gold from, 376, 405; cash crop plantations in, 555; early modern states in, 402, 403*(map)*, 404–406; European trade with, 402, 405–406 *and illus.*; music of, 665, 868; new societies in, 545–546; French in, 679; peanuts in, 480; hybrid social groups in, 481; Islam in, 546; World War I and, 648; immigrant labor from, 711, 758; nationalism in, 664; Sufi mysticism in, 547, 549

West Bank, 810*(illus.)*, 811*(map)*, 812

Western Asia, 371, 485, 671; nationalism in, 687; Ottoman rule in, 666, 668*(map)*; tradition *vs.* modernity in, 817

Western colonialism, 569–570, 696, 810. *See also* Western imperialism

Western Europe: *See also* Europe (1450–1750); changes in (1920s), 631; industrialization in, 499; Ottoman Empire and, 419; world economy and, 476

Western Europe (1945–present). *See also* European Union; chronology, 749; from cooperation to community, 751–753 *and map*; European Movement, 748–749; humanitarian groups in; immigration in, 710, 755, 758–759; Marshall Plan for, 748; nationalism and decolonization, 750; NATO and Cold War in, 750–751, 752*(map)*; China and, 727; politics in remaking of, 749–750; revival and unity in, 747–755; revolutions and; social democracy in, 750, 755–756; social

reform and gender relations in, 756–758; societies and cultures, 755–760; thought and religion in, 759–760; unemployment in, 754–755; United States and, 696, 781; welfare states in, 695–696, 755–756

Western Front, World War I, 622 *and illus.*, 623*(map)*

Western Hemisphere. *See* Americas, the (New World)

Western imperialism (Western domination): *See also* Colonialism; Imperialism; in Africa, 485; challenges to, 648–651; global economy and, 676, 677; globalization and, 511, 513; Ho Chi Minh and, 647–648; industrialization and, 508, 509; nationalism and, 580; resurgence of, 508, 509–513; Japan and, 607, 608, 610; China and, 599–600

Westernization (Western culture), 635; in British India, 575, 576, 578; in China, 601, 728, 730; neo-colonialism and, 693; in Russia, 389–390, 617; in Southeast Asia, 662; of Turkey, 667, 669 *and illus.*; in global system, 678, 679; Islam and, 560, 564, 566, 822; in Japan, 473, 612, 632, 739; Derrida's deconstruction of, 760; opposition to, in Iran, 670; in Middle East, 670–671; global culture and, 868

Western nations: *See also* Western Europe; United States; *specific nations*; immigrant labor in, 711; resource consumption of, 678, 709, 870; Russian civil war and, 627, 628*(map)*; investment by, 705, 830; support for Israel, 753, 815; wealth of, 834

Western Samoa, 794

West Germany, 771; economic growth of, 699, 749, 767, 773; European Community and, 753; France and, 749; homosexuality in, 758; in NATO, 752*(map)*; postwar reconstruction of, 748; reunification and, 773; as welfare state, 755; immigrants in, 758

West Indies. *See* Caribbean region

Westphalia, Treaty of (1648), 388

Whale hunting, 539

Wheat, 480; in Canada, 434, 539, 620; government subsidies for, 705; in India, 452, 844

White collar workers, 631, 736

"White man's burden," 513, 588

White Russians, 627, 628*(map)*

White supremacy, in South Africa, 412, 550–551, 552, 657, 665, 828–829. *See also* Racism

Whitman, Walt, 523

Widow burning. *See* Sati (widow burning)

Wilde, Oscar, 519

Wilhelm II, Kaiser (Germany), 621, 624

William and Mary (England), 387, 393

William I, Kaiser (Germany), 505

William of Orange, 387, 393

Wilson, Woodrow, 531; World War I peace and, 625; Fourteen Points of, 624; Russian communism and, 627; Latin America and, 650–651

Windmills, in Caribbean, 445*(illus.)*

"Winner-take-all" economy, 787

Winthrop, John, Puritans and, 490

Witches, torture of, 399

Wollstonecraft, Mary, 492–493, 519

Wolof people of Senegal, 549

Women. *See also* Feminism; Gender; Women, seclusion of; in African politics, 404–405, 410, 411*(illus.)*, 832; as African slave traders, 481; Arawak, 428*(illus.)*, 429; footbinding, in China, 466, 651; and Islam, in Sudanic Africa, 402; in Japan, 472–473, 482; Latin American, 436, 437, 497; in American Revolution, 490; in Mexican Revolution, 533*(illus.)*, 534; in Mughal India, 451, 453, 481; African colonialism and, 555; Native American, 439; Islamic modernization and, 564, 565, 806–807*(illus.)*; as novelists, 636; Ottoman, 418; Persian, 421, 422*(illus.)*; as poets, 453, 482; as prostitutes, 439, 585, 614, 662, 711, 769, 846, 861; sati (widow burning) and, 451, 453, 575, 576, 581; in Siam, 457; as slaves, 523; in Soviet Union, 764; Filipina, 461, 707; sexual harrassment of, 703, 707, 737*(illus.)*, 790; development and, 707; in Japan, 736–737; Argentinian protests, 777–778; protests by, in Poland, 766; Palestinian Muslim, 812

Women, education of: in China, 465–466, 726; in Europe, 519; in Africa, 554; in Indonesia, 591; in Siam, 591; in Russia, 617; reduced fertility and, 709; in Japan, 736; in

Yorktown, Battle of (1781), 490

Yoruba people, 828; Benin and, 405; slave trade and, 415; colonial government and, 549, 553, 554; polytheism of, 554; art of, 676(*illus.*); nationalism and, 664, 822; juju music of, 832, 833(*illus.*)

Young Italy movement, 505

Young Turks, 559

Youth culture: *See also* Popular culture; Student protests; in Europe, 759; in Soviet Union, 765 *and illus.*; in United States, 759

Yuan Shikai, 604, 606

Yucatan, Maya of, 436, 437

Yugoslavia, 625, 644; civil war in, 768, 772, 773(*map*), 784; communism in, 645, 766; "ethnic cleansing" in, 698, 772; ethnic conflict in, 695, 700, 772, 773(*map*); NATO intervention in, 772, 775

Yunus, Muhammad, 707

Zaghlul, Saad, 670

Zaibatsu (Japanese conglomerates), 610, 611(*illus.*), 732, 735

Zaire (Congo), 824, 826. *See also* Congo; Mobutu in, 825, 827, 830–831, 832

Zambezi River, 406, 412

Zambia: as Northern Rhodesia, 549, 555; copper from, 555, 835; independence of, 825

Zanzibar: as British colony, 549; ivory trade in, 411, 545

Zapata, Emiliano, 533–534

Zappa, Frank, 712

Zeng Guofan, 598

Zhang Han, 468

Zheng He, travels of, 426

Zia, Khaleda, 847–848

Zimbabwe, 406; as colonial Southern Rhodesia, 549, 650; Mugabe in, 825, 831–832; nationalism in, 690; white minority rule in, 689

Zionism, 505, 567, 667, 670, 671–672, 812; Arab nationalism and, 671, 810

Zographos, Panagiotis, 506(*illus.*)

Zoroastrians, 561; Parsis, in India, 456

Zulu people, 407, 412, 552; warrior tradition, 550, 551

To help you take your reading outside the covers of WORLD, each new text comes with access to the exciting learning environment of a robust eBook.

Working with Your eBook

You can read WORLD wherever and whenever you're online by paging through the eBook on your computer. But you can do more than just read. Your eBook also contains hundreds of live links to

 Primary source documents

 Interactive maps

 Web links for further investigation

 Interactive quizzes

 Audio resources

 Historical simulation activities

 Profiles of key historical figures

Each link takes you directly to the source or interactive feature. Your eBook also features easy page navigation, bookmarking, highlighting, note taking, a search engine, and a print function.

You can save your WORLD user name and password for future reference here:

User Name: _____ Password: _____

Access your eBook and other online tools by going here:

4ltrpress.cengage.com/world/

Click on the book you are using and enter the Student area of the site. Register using the access code on the card bound into your textbook. Click on the links and have fun exploring!

Add your own favorite websites here:

_____

_____

_____

_____

_____

_____

_____

Key Terms

LO¹ capitalism
An economic system in which property, exchange, and the means of production are privately owned.

bourgeoisie
The urban-based, mostly commercial, middle class that arose with capitalism in the Early Modern Era.

commercial capitalism
The economic system in which most capital was invested in commercial enterprises such as trading companies, including the world's first joint-stock companies.

mercantilism
An economic approach that emerged in Early Modern Europe based on a government policy of building a nation's wealth by expanding its reserves of precious metals.

LO² Reformation
The movement to reform Christianity that was begun by Martin Luther in the sixteenth century.

Protestants
Groups that broke completely with the Roman Catholic Church as the result of the Reformation.

Counter Reformation
A movement to confront Protestantism and crush dissidents within the Catholic Church.

LO³ absolutism
A form of government in which sovereignty is vested in a single person, the king or queen; monarchs in the sixteenth and seventeenth centuries based their authority on the theory of the divine right of kings (i.e., that they had received their authority from God and were responsible only to Him).

LO⁴ baroque
An extravagant and, to many, shocking European artistic movement of the 1600s that encouraged release from restraints of thought and expression.

Scientific Revolution
An era of rapid European advance in knowledge, particularly in mathematics and astronomy, that occurred between 1600 and 1750.

Enlightenment
A philosophical movement based on science and reason that began in Europe in the late seventeenth century and continued through the eighteenth century.

empiricism
An approach that stresses experience and the testing of propositions rather than reason alone in acquiring knowledge.

CHRONOLOGY

1350–1615	Renaissance
1517–1615	Protestant Reformation
1588	Defeat of Spanish armada
1600–1750	Scientific Revolution
1618–1648	Thirty Years' War
1675–1800	Enlightenment
1641–1645	English Civil War
1688–1689	English Glorious Revolution

LO¹ How did exploration, colonization, and capitalism increase Western power and wealth?

- Europe's political decentralization, improved technologies, and increased exploration allowed for the growth of cities and the development of capitalism.

- Motivated by "Gold, God, and Glory," Europeans, led by the Spanish and the Portuguese, set up colonies in the Americas, Africa, and Asia.

- Contesting medieval Christian attitudes, capitalism took hold in western Europe, while eastern European leaders resisted it and instead mandated serfdom.

- Commercial capitalists, assisted by the mercantilist policies of their countries, increased their market power by pooling resources in such organizations as joint-stock companies.

LO² How did the Renaissance and Reformation mark a crucial cultural and intellectual transition?

- Renaissance humanists questioned the authority of the Catholic Church and challenged accepted truths of morality, science, and astronomy. Renaissance artists and writers such as Michelangelo and Shakespeare and Cervantes aimed to represent humanity more realistically.

- Martin Luther criticized the corruption of the Catholic Church and set the Reformation in motion; it was propelled by others like John Calvin, whose ideas were taken up by the Puritans, and King Henry VIII of England, who made England Protestant.

- In the Counter Reformation, the Catholic Church attempted to reassert its dominance, but ultimately it focused on converting non-Europeans.

- Religious conflicts sparked several wars between Catholic and Protestant nations as well as continued conflicts with the Muslim Ottoman Empire.

LO³ What type of governments emerged in Europe in this era?

- Europeans fought a series of wars, some religiously motivated and some not; for example, in the Thirty Years' War, which involved many countries, Catholic France triumphed over the Catholic Habsburgs.

- Absolutist monarchs included Louis XIV of France, who lived in astounding luxury and wielded great power, and Russian czars Ivan the Terrible and Peter the Great.

- Representative governments arose in the Netherlands, where the Dutch instituted a decentralized republican system of government, and in England, where political power became more equally shared between the monarch and Parliament.

- Amidst the ongoing political turmoil in Europe, Austria and Prussia became major powers, Sweden saw its fortunes rise and fall, and Poland and Lithuania came under Russian power.

LO⁴ How did major intellectual, scientific, and social changes help to reshape the West?

- The extravagant baroque style that followed the Renaissance emphasized artistic freedom, while Dutch painters eschewed religious themes for natural ones.

philosophes
The intellectuals who fostered the French Enlightenment.

enclosure
Arising in Early Modern Europe, the pattern in which landlords fenced off common lands once used by the public for grazing livestock and collecting firewood.

- Bacon and Descartes emphasized the role of reason in science and philosophy, respectively, while Thomas Hobbes developed a pessimistic political philosophy.

- Advances in astronomy, particularly those made by Galileo, greatly antagonized Catholic officials, while Isaac Newton discovered fundamental laws of physics.

- Locke and Voltaire were among the prominent thinkers of the Enlightenment, a movement that favored reason over unquestioning faith.

- First in England and then elsewhere in western Europe, rural peasants were impoverished by landowners' greed and served as a ready source of labor for industry. In addition, the economic role of women declined, as, in many cases, did their social standing.

Key Terms

LO¹ Darkest Africa
Those areas of the African continent least known to Europeans but, in European eyes, awaiting to be "opened" to the "light of Western civilization."

LO² racism
A set of beliefs, practices, and institutions based on devaluing groups that are supposedly biologically different.

Boers
Dutch farming settlers in South Africa in the eighteenth century.

trekking
The migrations of Boer settlers in cattle-drawn wagons into the interior of South Africa whenever they wanted to flee government restraints.

Middle Passage
The slave's journey by ship from Africa to the Americas.

Atlantic System
A large network that arose with the trans-Atlantic slave trade; the network spanned western and Central Africa, the east coast and southern region of English North America, the Caribbean Basin, and the northern and eastern coastal zones of South America.

imperialism
The control or domination, direct or indirect, of one state or people over another.

colonialism
Government by one society over another society.

LO³ janissaries
("new troops") Well-armed, highly disciplined, and generally effective elite military corps of infantrymen in the Ottoman Empire.

LO⁴ Cossacks
Tough adventurers and soldiers from southern Russia who were descendants of Russians, Poles, and Lithuanians fleeing serfdom, slavery, or jail.

CHRONOLOGY

1300–1923	Ottoman Empire
1482–1497	Portuguese encounters with East Africa
1507–1543	Rule of Alfonso I in Kongo
1526–1870	Trans-Atlantic slave trade
1501–1736	Safavid Persia
1514–1517	Ottoman Conquest of Syria, Egypt, and Arabia
1520–1566	Suleiman the Magnificent
1591	Destruction of Songhai
1554–1659	Sa'dian Morocco
1652	Dutch settlement of Cape Town
1682–1699	Ottoman wars with Habsburg Austria
1715	Beginning of Russian conquest of Turkestan

LO¹ How did the larger sub-Saharan African societies and states differ from each other in the sixteenth century?

- Songhai, the last great Sudanic kingdom with its trading city Timbuktu, produced many scholars of Islam, and its society was relatively open to contributions from women.

- West African states were extremely varied and included the strict Islamic kingdom of Kanem-Bornu, the Hausa traders, the Yoruba in western Nigeria, and the kingdom of Benin.

- In Bantu-speaking East Africa, coastal city-states such as Kilwa and Malindi grew wealthy from trade; the Shona exported gold and ivory; Buganda traded extensively with East African coastal cities; and Kongo on the Atlantic coast was one of the first African states to be visited by Europeans.

- Enslavement of many peoples was widespread when western Europeans began to obtain African slaves.

LO² What were the consequences of African–European encounters in this era, especially the trans-Atlantic slave trade?

- Early Portuguese relations with Africa included cooperation with the Kongo kingdom, conflict with the Khoikhoi, and failed attempts to trade with East African coastal city-states.

- Under Christian King Alfonso I, Kongo attempted to emulate Portugal, but relations soured as the Portuguese began to enslave large numbers of Kongolese to work on sugar plantations in Africa and Brazil, and eventually the Portuguese conquered both Angola and Kongo, which then became the major source of slaves for the trans-Atlantic slave trade.

- In their ultimately unsuccessful attempt to dominate Indian Ocean trade, the Portuguese established control over the East African coast, but they failed to dominate Africa's gold trade and eventually lost influence.

- Dutch settlers in southern Africa, later called Boers, imposed white supremacy over the lands they seized but lived in close contact with their imported African and Asian slaves.

- Millions of West African slaves were shipped to North America on the horrific journey known as the Middle Passage, because they were the cheapest form of labor available to work the farms and mines. Many slaves died, committed suicide, or mutinied en route.

- The slave trade led to racist views, as many Europeans justified the practice by claiming that Africans were inherently inferior.

- The slave trade destabilized and harmed many African societies, but some prospered by selling neighboring peoples into slavery.

- As a result of the slave trade, European nations established imperial and colonial control over much of Africa, and their impression of Africa shifted from respect to condescension.

LO³ What factors made the Ottoman Empire such a powerful force in the region?

- Under Suleiman the Magnificent, the Ottoman Empire stretched across vast areas of the Middle East, North Africa, and southeastern Europe, and it controlled the overland trade routes between Europe and the Indian Ocean.

- Leaders of the Ottoman Empire were chosen on the basis of merit, not birth, and even Christians served as administrators and soldiers.

- The Ottoman Empire was culturally and religiously diverse and attracted a range of artists and thinkers from across Eurasia, though some believe that state influence on Islam caused it to become more close-minded.

- Though the Ottoman Empire remained strong through much of the seventeenth century, its military discipline, weaponry, and political stability soon began a gradual decline, while European power and influence grew.

LO⁴ How did the Persian and Central Asian experience differ from that of the Ottomans?

- Under the leadership of a charismatic boy named Isma'il, the Safavids, originally from Azerbaijan, conquered Persia and made the Persians convert from Sunni to Shi'a Islam.

- Under the Safavids, Persia was a major exporter of silk and remained a major conduit of trade.

- The Safavid Empire patronized art and literature, and Safavid artists became famous for their miniature painting and their carpet weaving.

- Safavid religious leaders, increasingly relying on their own authority rather than that of the Quran, eventually became more influential as the power of Safavid rulers declined and then collapsed.

- Morocco, the far western outpost of Islam, absorbed many fleeing Iberian Muslims and grew into a powerful state that, under the Sa'dians, eventually defeated the Portuguese.

- With the aid of the Cossacks, Russia engaged in a large territorial expansion to create a land-based empire, coming into conflict with Siberian and Islamic Central Asian peoples, including the Uzbeks in Turkestan.

Key Terms

LO² conquistadors
The leaders of Spanish soldiers engaged in armed conquest in the Americas.

LO³ Columbian Exchange
The transportation of diseases, animals, and plants from one hemisphere to another that resulted from European exploration and conquest between 1492 and 1750.

audiencias
Judicial tribunals with administrative functions that served as subdivisions of viceroyalties in Spanish America.

creoles
People of Iberian ancestry who were born in Latin America.

mestizos
Groups in Latin America that blended white and Indian ancestry.

mulattos
Groups in Latin America that blend African ancestry with white and Indian ancestry.

Black Legend
The Spanish reputation for brutality toward Native Americans, including the repression of native religions, execution of rebels, and forced labor.

Metis
People in Canada of mixed French and Indian descent.

LO⁴ haciendas
Vast ranches in Spanish America.

encomienda
("Entrustment") The Crown's grant to a colonial Spaniard in Latin America of a certain number of Indians from whom he extracted tribute.

monoculture
An economy dependent on the production and export of one chief commodity.

development
Growth in a variety of economic areas that benefits the majority of people; the opposite of monoculture.

plantation zone
A group of societies with economies that relied on enslaved African labor; the plantation zone stretched from Virginia and Kentucky southward through the West Indies and the east coast of Central America to central Brazil and the Pacific coast of Colombia.

CHRONOLOGY

1492	First Columbian voyage
1494	Treaty of Tordesillas
1497	Cabot's landing in North America
1500	Portuguese claim of Brazil
1519–1521	Magellan's circumnavigation of the globe
1521	Spanish conquest of Aztecs
1535	Spanish conquest of Incas
1604	French settlement in Canada
1607	English settlement in Virginia
1627	Colony of New France
1759	English defeat of French in Quebec

LO¹ How did encounters between Europe and the Americas increase in the 1500s?

- In 1500, many American peoples lived by hunting, gathering, and fishing, while others lived in the widespread, often repressive empires created by the Incas and the Aztecs.

- From 1000 on, Norse from Greenland intermittently settled in Newfoundland, and other Europeans may have crossed the Atlantic in search of fish.

- Beginning in 1492, Christopher Columbus's travels and his discovery of Atlantic wind patterns opened up exploration of the Americas. Columbus gradually gave up on the idea that he had discovered an Atlantic route to Asia, which was later discovered by Magellan.

- European nations divided up the Western Hemisphere according to the Treaty of Tordesillas, and as Europeans explored the Americas, some seeking riches and others converts, their diseases and weapons decimated native populations.

- Pacific Island societies, which ranged from the highly stratified Hawaiians to subsistence atoll inhabitants, were generally not visited by Europeans in the 1500s.

LO² How did Europeans conquer and begin settling the American societies?

- The Spanish under Cortés were able to conquer the Aztecs because of their superior weaponry, their alliances with other American peoples, and a smallpox epidemic that ravaged the Aztecs.

- From their base in Mexico, the Spanish pushed north and south, proceeding to rule much of South America with great cruelty.

- The Portuguese fended off attempts by the French and the Dutch to colonize Brazil and enslaved many of its Indians.

- The Spanish, Portuguese, Dutch, French, and English all struggled for colonial control of the Americas, with pirates from each country preying on other countries' ships.

- The English established colonies in what is now the eastern United States, while the French did so in eastern Canada, New Orleans, and the Mississippi River Basin.

- Many North American colonies thrived on fish and fur, while others practiced agriculture, and all eventually pushed native peoples off their lands.

LO³ What were the major consequences of European colonization of the Americas?

- As a result of American colonization, people, diseases, commodities, and many animal and plant species were exchanged between Europe and the Americas in what is called the Columbian Exchange.

- The Spanish exploited the resources of their American colonies and ruled them harshly, inspiring several rebellions and earning the label of the "Black Legend," though other countries sometimes used similar methods.

- In the Spanish American colonies, a recognizable culture developed, more rigidly Catholic than in Europe and featuring American-born Spanish (creoles) and mixed-race peoples (mestizos and mulattos).

- In their attempts to convert Native Americans to Catholicism, the Spanish and Portuguese often trampled on Native American customs and crushed resisters harshly. As English and French colonists vied for authority, Indian tribes were often caught between the warring powers.

LO⁴ What impact did the trans-Atlantic slave trade and emerging Atlantic system have on European and American societies?

- Using Indian labor, Spanish colonists became wealthy at first through ranching and mining gold and silver, but their economies eventually suffered from a lack of diversification.

- Plantations run with African slave labor and focused on producing a single product—sugar in Latin America and the Caribbean, cotton in southeastern North America—also eventually created impoverished societies. Sugar became a fundamental part of the European diet.

- Areas of the Americas with the greatest natural resources ended up being the poorest, while those with the least natural resources, such as the northern English colonies, were forced to develop more broad-based economies and became wealthy and well developed.

- African slaves in the Americas were treated as commodities, and resistance to slavery was rarely successful. But elements of African religion, music, language, and agriculture all found their way into American cultures.

- The slave trade and plantation economies helped spur European capitalism and were extremely profitable to Europeans and North American colonists.

- Spain and Portugal wasted the wealth they derived from their colonies, but the Dutch and the English invested it wisely and, as a result, gained an advantage over other world powers.

Key Terms

LO1 Urdu
A language developed in Mughal India that mixed Hindi, Arabic, and Persian and was written in the Persian script.

Sikhs
("Disciples") Members of an Indian religion founded in the Early Modern Era that adopted elements from both Hinduism and Islam, including mysticism.

LO2 Hispanization
The process by which, over nearly three centuries of Spanish colonial rule beginning in 1565, the Catholic religion and Spanish culture were imposed on the Philippine people.

Moros
The Spanish term for the Muslim peoples of the southern Philippines.

Indios
The Spanish term for Filipinos, who for the most part held the lowest social status.

LO4 ukiyo-e
Colorful Japanese woodblock prints that celebrated the life of the "floating world," the urban entertainment districts of Tokogawa Japan.

bunraku
The puppet theater of Tokugawa Japan.

kabuki
The all-male and racy drama that became the favored entertainment of the urban population in Tokugawa Japan.

haiku
The seventeen-syllable poem that proved an excellent vehicle for discussing the passage of time and the change of seasons in Early Modern Japan.

CHRONOLOGY

1350–1767	Ayuthia
1368–1644	Ming dynasty
1392–1573	Ashikaga Shogunate
1392–1910	Yi dynasty in Korea
1498	Arrival of Vasco da Gama in India
1511	Portuguese conquest of Melaka
1526–1761	Mughal India
1557	Portuguese base at Macao
1556–1605	Reign of Akbar
1565	Spanish conquest of Philippines
1592–1598	Japanese invasions of Korea
1600	Founding of British East India Company
1603	Tokugawa Shogunate founded
1639–1841	Japanese seclusion policy
1640s	Dutch conquests in Ceylon
1644–1912	Qing dynasty
1688	Siamese expulsion of French
1689	Treaty of Nerchinsk

LO1 What were the major achievements and failures of the Mughal Empire?

- The Muslim Mughal Empire attained great riches and, especially under Akbar, maintained an enlightened rule over religiously diverse India, but it began to decline after the fall of Akbar.
- The Indian economy, already strong, expanded greatly as extensive foreign trade brought an influx of silver and enriched entrepreneurs.
- Tensions existed between Indian Muslims and Hindus, though some were able to bridge the gap through mysticism or alternative sects such as the Sikhs.
- The Mughal decline hastened under Aurangzeb, a harsh and corrupt ruler who was particularly resented by non-Muslims. Meanwhile, Portuguese traders gained a significant share of trade with India.
- The Portuguese, Dutch, French, and English all competed for dominance in trade with India, with the English growing increasingly strong by the mid-eighteenth century.

LO2 How did Southeast Asia become more fully integrated into the world economy?

- Increased trade in Southeast Asia led to greater political centralization and increased the influence of major world religions such as Islam and Buddhism. Europeans were attracted by Southeast Asia's riches and resources.
- Theravada Buddhism thrived in Siam, while Islam flourished on the Malay Peninsula, where an orthodox form took hold, and in the Indonesian archipelago, where it blended with local traditions.
- The Spanish conquered the Philippine Islands and eventually succeeded in converting local people to Christianity, though the Filipinos shaped Christianity to their own ends.
- The militaristic Dutch came to dominate Southeast Asia, particularly Java, which they turned into a highly profitable coffee exporter, but whose culture they did not attempt to transform.
- As a result of European colonization, Southeast Asia entered the world economy, though European speculators often focused on making quick money rather than strengthening the region's economy for the long term.

LO³ What factors enabled China to remain one of the world's strongest societies?

- During the Ming dynasty, China maintained its economic power, but it turned increasingly inward and anti-foreign and was ultimately undermined by plague, famine, and pressures from Japan.

- The Qing dynasty was established by foreign Manchus, who assimilated to many Chinese ways, amassed the greatest Eurasian land empire since the Mongols, and added Taiwan to China's holdings.

- Chinese neo-Confucians incorporated elements of Buddhism and Daoism into their thinking and emphasized reason, but over time neo-Confucianism discouraged the growth of new ideas.

- China's economy remained extremely strong but never developed full-scale capitalism or industrialization, perhaps because it lacked an exploitable overseas empire, and perhaps because the government failed to encourage entrepreneurship.

- China had fitful encounters with Europeans, including Portuguese traders who irked Chinese authorities and established a colony at Macao, and missionaries who had little success and were ultimately banned for undermining Chinese traditions. The Russians also sought influence in the area north of China.

LO⁴ How did Korea and Japan change during this era?

- The Chinese helped Korea to rebuff a 1592 Japanese invasion, but as a result Korean culture began to liberalize and shed some customs borrowed from China.

- Ashikaga Japan saw tremendous economic and population growth, but it was undermined by a lengthy civil war, during which Europeans introduced guns and Christianity, upsetting Japan's social order.

- The Tokugawa Shogunate ended Japan's civil war, restored strict order, and expelled Europeans, with the exception of a small group of Dutch traders who were uninterested in missionary work.

- Despite the Tokugawa leaders' attempt to halt change, the Japanese economy grew rapidly, tensions in Japanese society increased, and Japan's culture flourished.

- Tokugawa Japan was quite stable, but its rigidity hampered its growth and made it vulnerable when Western powers returned in the mid-nineteenth century.

19 Modern Transitions: Revolutions, Industries, Ideologies, Empires, 1750–1914
Chapter in Review

Key Terms

LO¹ Age of Revolution
The period from the 1770s through the 1840s when revolutions rocked North America, Europe, the Caribbean, and Latin America.

Jacobins
A radical faction in the French Revolution that believed civil rights had to be set aside in a crisis; the Jacobins executed thousands of French citizens.

LO³ Industrial Revolution
A dramatic transformation in the production and transportation of goods that transformed western Europe from the 1770s to the 1870s.

laissez faire
Restriction of government interference in the marketplace, such as laws regulating business and profits.

Luddites
Anti-industrialization activists in Britain who destroyed machines in a mass protest against the effects of mechanization (see Industrial Revolution).

LO⁴ ideology
A coherent, widely shared system of ideas about the nature of the social, political, and economic realm.

nationalism
A primary loyalty to, and identity with, a nation bound by a common culture, government, and shared territory.

nation-states
Politically centralized countries with defined territorial boundaries.

Zionism
A movement arising in late-nineteenth-century Europe that sought a Jewish homeland.

liberalism
An ideology of the Modern Era, based on Enlightenment ideas, that favored emancipating the individual from all restraints, whether governmental, economic, or religious.

parliamentary democracy
Government by representatives elected by the people.

socialism
An ideology arising in nineteenth-century Europe offering a vision of social equality and the common, or public, ownership of economic institutions such as factories.

proletariat
The industrial working class.

CHRONOLOGY

1770s–1870s	First Industrial Revolution
1775–1783	American Revolution
1776	Adam Smith's *Wealth of Nations*
1776	The American Declaration of Independence
1789–1815	French Revolution
1791–1804	Haitian Revolution
1800	British Act of Union
1804	Crowning of Napoleon as emperor of France
1810–1826	Spanish-American wars of independence
1815	Defeat of Napoleon at Battle of Waterloo; Congress of Vienna
1848	Marx's *The Communist Manifesto*; waves of uprisings across Europe
1859–1870	Unification of Italy
1862–1871	Unification of Germany
1870–1914	Second Industrial Revolution

LO¹ What were the major consequences of the American and French Revolutions?

- Many North American colonists, inspired by Enlightenment thinkers, chafed against British rule and pushed for independence, while other Americans, including many Indians and black slaves, sided with the British.

- After a first failed attempt at confederation, the thirteen American colonies agreed upon a system that balanced federal and state powers, but the American Revolution did little to change the social order and did not extend equal rights to blacks, women, and Indians.

- The French Revolution achieved some of its progressive goals and was an inspiration to some societies, but it led to a period of war and widespread terror.

- In the tumultuous aftermath of the French Revolution, Napoleon Bonaparte seized power, implemented some reforms, and sought to conquer Europe, but his eventual defeat led to the Congress of Vienna, at which many pre-Revolution boundaries were restored. Throughout the first half of the nineteenth century, other revolutions led to gradual progress.

LO² How did the Caribbean and Latin American revolutions compare with those in Europe and North America?

- Spain controlled its American colonies tightly, leaving little room for intellectual freedom or economic mobility, and put down many revolts through the end of the eighteenth century.

- After more than a decade of revolutionary struggle, the Afro-Haitian slaves won their freedom from the French, but they soon fell under the control of an African-born despot.

- Rising dissatisfaction among South Americans, particularly creoles, led to successful independence movements throughout the continent, though the newly free nations had trouble forming democratic governments.

- After Mexico obtained its independence, the coalition that had opposed the Spanish fell apart, while members of the Portuguese royal family who fled to Brazil helped it to obtain its independence peacefully.

LO³ How did industrialization reshape economic and social life?

- The Industrial Revolution began in England and gradually spread throughout western Europe and North America. Industrial capitalism centered on manufacturing, and economic philosophers such as Adam Smith advocated laissez faire, the idea that the market, if left alone, would improve everyone's standard of living and create ever-increasing wealth and progress.

- As technology played an increasingly important role in the economy and in people's lives, with machines constantly evolving and being put to new uses, some people marveled at the technological change while others, such as the Luddites, resisted it.

- The Second Industrial Revolution ushered in an age of specialization and mass production, and it favored monopolistic corporations that could afford enormous investments in new technology.

LO^4 How did nationalism, liberalism, and socialism differ from each other?

- With the rise of nationalism, the inhabitants of a given country came to identify with each other as distinct from, and often better than, the inhabitants of other countries.

- Greece attained nationhood through revolution, Italy through a unification movement, and Germany through collective war against others, while the Poles, the Irish, and the Jews struggled unsuccessfully to form nations.

- Liberalism, which favored maximizing individual liberty, was particularly influential in Britain and the United States of America.

- Socialism aimed to achieve economic equality through common ownership of industry, and its major proponent, Karl Marx, argued that history is driven by class struggle and that capitalism would inevitably give way to a communist society.

- Social Democrats, who rejected Marx's revolutionary ideas and instead favored working to better the lot of workers within a capitalist democracy, managed to greatly improve working conditions by the early 1900s.

LO^5 What factors spurred the Western imperialism of the later 1800s?

- The Industrial Revolution led Great Britian, and later other western nations, to seek new territories for resources and markets. The result was a renewed scramble for colonial domination.

- As the world became connected by economic and political networks, many African, Asian, and Pacific peoples struggled for their independence, but the technological advantage of Western nations often proved insurmountable.

- Westerners rationalized imperialism and colonization as good for the colonized, who were offered the fruits of Western culture in exchange for their independence.

Key Terms

LO¹ feminism
A philosophy that became strong in the twentieth century, promoting political, social, and economic equality for women with men.

romanticism
A philosophical, literary, artistic, and musical movement that questioned the Enlightenment's rationalist values and instead glorified emotions, individual imagination, and heroism.

modernism
A cultural trend that openly broke with romanticism and other traditions by embracing progress and welcoming the future.

LO² Manifest Destiny
Americans' conviction that their country's institutions and culture, regarded as unmatched, gave them a God-given right to take over the land.

sphere of interest
An area in which one great power assumes exclusive responsibility for maintaining peace and attempts to monopolize the area's resources.

LO³ caudillos
Latin American military strongmen who acquired and maintained power through force between the early nineteenth and mid-twentieth centuries.

samba
A Brazilian popular music and dance that arose in the early twentieth century.

calypso
A song style in Trinidad that often featured lyrics addressing daily life and topical subjects.

LO⁴ dominion
A country that has autonomy but owes allegiance to the British crown; developed in the early twentieth century.

CHRONOLOGY

1763	British defeat of French forces in North America
1770s	Cook expeditions to Polynesia, Australia, and New Zealand
1788	First British penal colony in Australia
1803	Louisiana Purchase
1812–1814	U.S.-British War of 1812
1823	Monroe Doctrine
1823–1889	Abolition of slavery
1846–1848	U.S.-Mexican War
1840s–1890	Western colonization of Pacific islands
1859	Publication of Charles Darwin's *On the Origin of the Species*
1861–1865	Civil War, abolition of slavery
1862–1867	French occupation of Mexico
1867	Canadian Confederation
1869	Completion of transcontinental railroad
1875–1884	War between Chile and Peru-Bolivia
1885–1898	Cuban revolt against Spain
1889	Brazilian republic
1896	Women's suffrage in Finland
1898–1902	Spanish-American War
1898	Annexation of Hawaii
1898–1902	Spanish-American War, colonization of Philippines
1901	Platt Amendment to Cuban constitution
1901	Australian Commonwealth
1905	Publication of Albert Einstein's general theory of relativity
1907	New Zealand self-government
1910–1920	Mexican Revolution
1914	Panama Canal

LO¹ How and why did European social, cultural, and intellectual patterns change during this era?

- In Europe, better crops and health care produced higher populations, which led to increasing urbanization, impoverishment, and emigration.

- As Europe became more industrialized and interconnected, the nuclear family and love marriages became increasingly common, while women, who were initially relegated to the home, began to gain legal rights and economic opportunities.

- While some Protestants attempted to stamp out behavior they considered sinful, Europeans as a whole became more secular, and the Catholic Church's influence declined.

- Cultural trends such as romanticism, realism, and modernism emerged, while advances in science and technology led to improved medical care, the theory of evolution, greater understanding of the physical world, and new sources of energy.

LO² How did westward expansion, industrialization, and immigration transform American society?

- Politically, the United States balanced individual liberty with systems designed to check disorder; economically, it balanced protectionist and free-market interests.

- A distinctive American culture developed that celebrated democracy and practicality but also was influenced by the persistence of African slavery.

- Americans gradually expanded west, taking advantage of abundant natural resources, going to war with Mexico, inflicting great suffering on Native Americans, and exerting its influence in Latin America.

- The Civil War killed hundreds of thousands, did tremendous damage to the South's economy, and freed the slaves, though discrimination and segregation continued for at least another century.

- American industry advanced rapidly, producing immense wealth for a small number of tycoons, helping others to prosper, and creating difficult, hazardous work for many.

- Millions of immigrants poured into the United States, seeking opportunity and often finding discrimination, while social movements sought better treatment for workers and greater rights for women.

- In the interests of promoting and protecting American business interests, the U.S. military intervened in the affairs of many foreign countries and territories, most notably in the Spanish-American War, which brought the United States its first formal colonies.

LO³ What political, economic, and social patterns shaped Latin America after independence?

- After gaining independence from Spain, Latin American nations were plagued by instability, undemocratic governments, and socioeconomic inequality along racial lines.

- After a disastrous period as a republic, a brief occupation by the French, and a pro-business dictatorship, a long, violent revolution finally led to political stability in Mexico.

- Latin American economies tended to focus on the export of one or two natural resources, which created instability and made them susceptible to foreign domination.

- The abolition of slavery and the arrival millions of immigrants from Europe, India, Japan, and elsewhere transformed Latin American societies, and new cultural forms emerged from its diverse peoples.

- The United States repeatedly intervened in Latin American affairs, most directly in Cuba, whose diplomatic affairs it dominated for three decades, and Panama, through which it built the Panama Canal.

LO⁴ Why did the foundations for nationhood differ in Canada and Oceania?

- Over time, Canada became increasingly independent of Britain and overcame the challenges of its French and English speakers and threats from the neighboring United States.

- Western nations, starting with Britain and France but later including Russia, the United States, and Germany, colonized the Pacific islands and exploited their natural resources.

- Starting as penal colonies, British settlers in Australia and New Zealand clashed with indigenous peoples but eventually prevailed, establishing the two countries as dominions of the British Empire.

21 Chapter in Review

Key Terms

LO³ direct rule
A method of ruling colonies whereby a largely European colonial administration supervised all activity, even down to the local level, and native chiefs or kings were reduced to symbolic roles.

indirect rule
A method of ruling colonies whereby districts were administered by traditional (native) leaders, who had considerable local power but were subject to European officials.

LO⁴ Young Turks
A modernizing group in Ottoman Turkey that promoted a national identity and that gained power in the early twentieth century.

Bahai
An offshoot of Persian Shi'ism that was founded in 1867; Bahai preached universal peace, the unity of all religions, and service to others.

LO⁵ Islamic revivalism
Arab movements beginning in the eighteenth century that sought to purify Islamic practices by reviving what their supporters considered to be a purer vision of Islamic society.

Wahhabism
A militant Islamic revivalist movement founded in Arabia in the eighteenth century.

kibbutz
A Jewish collective farm in twentieth-century Palestine that stressed the sharing of wealth.

CHRONOLOGY

1794–1925	Qajar dynasty in Persia
1805–1848	Rule of Muhammad Ali in Egypt
1806	British seizure of South Africa from Dutch
1840	French colonization of Algeria
1842	Ending of trans-Atlantic slave trade by most European nations
1859–1869	Building of Suez Canal
1874–1901	British-Ashante wars
1878	Belgian colonization of the Congo
1882	British colonization of Egypt
1884–1885	Berlin Conference on colonialism
1897	First Zionist Conference
1899–1902	Boer War
1908	Discovery of oil in Persia
1911–1912	Colonization of Libya and Morocco

LO¹ How did Western nations obtain colonies in sub-Saharan Africa?

- Opposed by many Europeans on humanitarian and religious grounds and losing its economic usefulness, African slavery was phased out by the end of the nineteenth century.

- With the end of the slave trade, Europeans began to explore Africa's interior and to take advantage of its vast store of natural resources.

- At the same time, tensions increased between purist and moderate West African Muslims, and Uthman dan Fodio, who led the Fulani jihads, established the Sokoto Caliphate, which became a strong presence in the Sudan.

- European nations rapidly colonized Africa by engaging in deceptive negotiations, by threatening and often carrying out acts of violence, and by exploiting existing rivalries among groups of Africans.

- By 1914, all but a small portion of Africa had been divided up among the European powers, which squabbled over control of various territories and sometimes met fierce resistance from Africans, such as the Ashante.

LO² How did white supremacy shape South Africa?

- Dutch settlers of South Africa, called Boers, pursued a policy of white supremacy despite more liberal British policies. South Africa was also shaped by the conquests of Shaka, a Zulu leader.

- The Boers fled inland to escape British control, but when diamonds and gold were discovered in the Boer republics, the British instigated and won the South African War, after which they agreed to enforce white supremacist policies in order to gain Boer cooperation.

- Blacks suffered greatly in white-dominated South Africa, but many resisted through poetry, music, dance, and political organizations such as the African National Congress. Indians and other Asians came to form the middle class in many African societies.

LO³ What were some of the major consequences of colonialism in Africa?

- African colonial governments served the interests of the colonizers, though the colonizers' involvement in local affairs varied between forms of direct and indirect rule.

- Colonizers divided Africa into countries with artificial boundaries, disrupting cultures and exacerbating hostilities among peoples. And while Christian missionary schools provided a small minority of Africans with skills they could use in the white world, they largely ignored and often damaged the native African culture.

- As African economies came to depend on a single commodity desired by Europeans, colonized Africans lost their subsistence skills, were sometimes forced into near slavery, and were often forced to work far from home.

- While some Africans resisted European rule, colonization transformed the continent, did little to materially improve African lives, and prevented Africans from building diversified and strong economies.

LO⁴ What political and economic impact did Europe have on the Middle East?

- After 1750, the Ottoman Empire's power began to wane under pressure from Russia and western Europe and also from the Armenians, who exerted pressure from within the empire for greater autonomy.

- The Ottomans modernized their army, adopted French-style laws, and became increasingly secular, but their decline continued until the empire was broken apart in World War I.

- After Napoleon left Egypt, an Ottoman-appointed governor, Muhammad Ali, attempted an ambitious and somewhat successful program of modernization; ultimately, however, Britain gained control of the Suez Canal and made Egypt a colony.

- Persia, fragmented under the rule of the Qajars, came to be dominated economically by Britain, and interference by both Britain and Russia helped to end a brief period of progressive rule.

- Westerners became increasingly influential in Syria, Lebanon, and Iraq, and successfully colonized Northwest Africa: first Algeria, where settlers established a racist society; then Morocco, which was shared by France and Spain; and finally Tunisia and Libya.

LO⁵ How did Middle Eastern thought and culture respond to the Western challenge?

- One response to European pressure was Islamic revivalism, which was most influential in Arabia, where militant followers of al-Wahhab and Ibn Saud favored theocracy and eventually formed Saudi Arabia.

- Some intellectuals tried to modernize their religion, but modern European ideas such as equality continued to clash with Islamic practices such as slavery and the subjugation of women, and Western nationalism was at odds with the idea of a universal brotherhood under God.

- Some tried to inspire pan-Arab nationalism, but religious divisions and rivalries made this a difficult task.

- Muslims were also challenged by European Zionists, who moved to Palestine despite Ottoman objections, and Palestinian Arabs, setting the stage for future conflict.

Key Terms

LO¹ Marathas

A loosely knit confederacy led by Hindu warriors from west-central India; one of several groups that challenged British domination after the decline of the Mughals.

Black Hole of Calcutta

A crowded jail in India where more than one hundred British prisoners of a hostile Bengali ruler died from suffocation and dehydration in 1757. This event precipitated the beginning of British use of force in India.

sepoys

Mercenary soldiers recruited among the warrior and peasant castes by the British in India.

Westernization

A deliberate attempt to spread Western culture and ideas.

Orientalism

An eighteenth- and nineteenth-century scholarly interest among British officials in India and its history that prompted some to rediscover the Hindu classical age.

LO³ cultivation system

An agricultural policy imposed by the Dutch in Java that forced Javanese farmers to grow sugar on rice land.

plural society

A medley of peoples who mix but do not blend, instead maintaining their own cultures, religions, languages, and customs.

can vuong

("Aid-the-king") Rebel groups who waged guerrilla warfare for fifteen years against the French occupation of Vietnam.

CHRONOLOGY

1757	Battle of Plassey
1788–1802	Tayson rule in Vietnam
1802	British colonization of Sri Lanka
1819	British colony in Singapore
1824–1886	Anglo-Burman Wars
1839–1842	First Anglo-Afghan War
1850	Completion of British India
1857–1858	Indian Rebellion
1858	Introduction of colonial system in India
1858–1884	French conquest of Vietnam
1869	Opening of Suez Canal
1878–1880	Second Anglo-Afghan War
1885	Indian National Congress
1885–1886	Completion of British conquest of Burma
1898–1902	United States conquest of Philippines
1903	British invasion of Tibet
1906	Formation of Indian Muslim League
1908	Dutch defeat of last Balinese kingdom

LO¹ How and why did Britain extend its control throughout India?

- Fragmented after the decline of the Mughals, India was unable to resist encroachment by the Portuguese, Dutch, British, and French.

- In reaction to the Black Hole of Calcutta, the British under Robert Clive took over Bengal and proceeded to plunder its riches; although his successor, Warren Hastings, was more respectful, many governor-generals disregarded Indians' rights.

- Though initially opposed by the French, the British East India Company gradually expanded its control over India by employing local collaborators and playing groups off against each other, and by 1850, Britain controlled all of India.

- The British expanded into Sri Lanka, Nepal, and Afghanistan with varying success, and tried to make Indians more Western by abolishing customs they considered backward.

- By having peasants pay their taxes in cash rather than in crops, the British began to shift India from a barter economy to a money economy, a change that undermined centuries of rural stability.

- Though some Indians supported Westernization, periodic revolts occurred, and in 1857, the sepoys began a large rebellion that led to much bloodshed and eventually Indian defeat.

LO² How did colonialism transform the Indian economy and foster new ideas in India?

- After 1857, the British monarchy ruled India through the British *Raj,* which built palatial buildings, a large railroad system, and an expanded English-language school system, spreading western ideals such as nationalism and sowing the seeds for an Indian revolution against Britain.

- Britain stifled Indian industry by using India as a market for British industrial products, and it turned Indian peasants into tenants who had to grow cash crops for Britain rather than their own food, thus destroying the centuries-old village economy and exacerbating famine and poverty.

- As the Indian population increased, many poor Indians were driven to work all over the world in indentured servitude, while other Indians emigrated to work as laborers, merchants, and moneylenders.

- While some Hindus and Muslims wanted to combine the best in British and Indian culture, others sought to revive more traditional practices. The caste system became more rigid under British rule, and women facing greater restrictions in some cases and expanded opportunity in others.
- As Indian nationalists began to unite in their opposition to the British, the Hindu majority formed the Indian National Congress in 1885, but it was opposed by some aristocrats, who feared losing their privileges, and by Muslims, who formed the All-India Muslim League in 1906.

LO³ How did the Western nations expand their control of Southeast Asia?

- As the Dutch expanded their control over the Indonesian archipelago, they joined together vastly disparate cultures and disrupted the traditional economy, such as by forcing Javanese farmers to grow sugar on rice land and to sell it at unfairly low prices.
- The British expanded control over the Malay Peninsula and Burma, gaining key strategic trading centers while suppressing dissent and local traditions.
- After conquering Vietnam, the French faced fierce resistance from can vuong rebels, but they ultimately conquered the rebels and opened the country to exploitation by French commercial interests.
- Unlike the rest of Southeast Asia, Siam (now Thailand) avoided colonization because of its fortunate geographic location and its far-seeing leaders, who gave in to some Western demands and consolidated popular support.
- After defeating the Spanish in the Philippines and supporting local rebels, the U.S. government turned against the Filipinos and, after a bloody struggle, established a colony geared toward American economic needs.

LO⁴ What were the major political, economic, and social consequences of colonialism in Southeast Asia?

- Colonized Southeast Asian peoples were allowed varying degrees of autonomy, though in general they had very little and were frequently joined into countries with little ethnic or cultural unity.
- Economic life in colonies was reshaped to serve Western nations' needs for raw materials, especially rubber, and for markets for their goods, and in many cases it led to destruction of the natural environment and the impoverishment of native Indonesians.
- Millions of Chinese immigrated to Southeast Asia, where many prospered as merchants and retailers, while a smaller number of Indians came to work in Malayan rubber plantations.
- Economic changes caused by colonization especially affected women's lives, while education and cultural interchange between Westerners and colonized peoples produced new cultural forms, such as kronchong music.

Key Terms

LO¹ extraterritoriality
Freedom from local laws for foreign subjects.

international settlements
Special zones in major Chinese cities set aside for foreigners in the later nineteenth century where no Chinese were allowed; arose as a result of China's defeat in the Opium and Arrow Wars.

LO² gunboat diplomacy
The Western countries' use of superior firepower to impose their will on local populations and governments in the nineteenth century.

LO⁴ Meiji Restoration
A revolution against the Tokugawa shogunate in Japan in 1867–1868, carried out in the name of the Meiji emperor; led to the successful modernization of Japan.

state capitalism
An economic system in which the state takes a leading role in supporting business and industrial enterprises; introduced by the Meiji government in Japan.

zaibatsu
The most powerful Japanese corporations that dominated the national economy beginning during the Meiji regime and maintained an especially close relationship to the government.

LO⁵ Russification
A czarist policy in the nineteenth century that promoted Russian language and culture for non-Russian peoples; created resentment among many Muslims in Central Asia and the Caucasus.

Slavophiles
Nineteenth-century Russians who emphasized Russia's unique culture and rejected Western models.

CHRONOLOGY

1392–1910	Yi Dynasty in Korea
1600–1867	Tokugawa Shogunate in Japan
1762–1796	Reign of Catherine the Great
1800–1870s	Russian conquest of Turkestan and Caucasus
1839–1842	Opium War
1850–1864	Taiping Rebellion
1853	Opening of Japan by Perry
1861	Emancipation of Russian serfs
1867–1868	Meiji Restoration
1894–1895	Sino-Japanese War
1900	Boxer Rebellion
1904–1905	Russo-Japanese War
1905	First Russian Revolution
1910	Japanese colonization of Korea and Taiwan
1911	Chinese Revolution

LO¹ What were the causes and consequences of the Opium War?

- By the nineteenth century, China faced increasing problems as well as pressure from Westerners for greater trade opportunities, but the Qing refused to allow an open trading system, thus creating a severe trade imbalance between the West and the East.

- To solve this imbalance, the British began smuggling opium into China, and when China protested, the British defeated China in the Opium War and forced the Chinese to agree to highly unfavorable terms that allowed the British to trade in China.

- After another war, China was forced to set aside special areas exclusively for Westerners, called international settlements, and to also allow Christian missionaries into the country.

- Economic insecurity, famine, and Western interference eventually led to the Taiping Rebellion, a widespread and devastating revolt that was ultimately put down by the Qing with help from Western powers.

- China's economy was increasingly penetrated and transformed by Western powers, and millions of Chinese emigrated throughout the world, some to be indentured workers and others to go into business.

LO² Why did Chinese efforts at modernization fail?

- By the late 1800s, China's autonomy had been all but eliminated by gunboat diplomacy, under which Western powers ensured the safety of Westerners in China through the use of force. Conservatives and liberals, meanwhile, argued over the degree to which China should reform in the face of the Western challenge.

- After China lost its influence over Korea in the Sino-Japanese War and the Boxer Rebellion failed to rid China of foreigners, liberals moved to modernize and Westernize Chinese education and culture.

- Sun Yat-Sen, born to Chinese peasants but educated in Western schools, formed a secret society devoted to replacing imperial rule with a Western-style republic and set out three principles: nationalism, republicanism, and economic equality.

- A revolution inspired by Sun Yat-Sen succeeded in toppling the Qing dynasty with the assistance of General Yuan Shikai, but Sun's republic was short-lived, as Yuan seized power. Yuan's reign was weakened by Japanese encroachment and the loss of influence over areas such as Mongolia and Tibet, and after his death China entered a period of civil war.

LO³ What factors aided Japan in the quest for modernization?

- Japan was better able than China to deal with foreign pressures because of its compactness and homogeneity, its openness to outside ideas, its balance of power between groups of elites, its strong merchant class, and its sensitivity to foreign threats.

- Late Tokugawa Japanese culture was vigorous and open to Western learning, but internal decay in Japan led to riots, revolts, and subsequent reforms. However, when faced with a choice between war and opening Japan to American trade, the Japanese shogun chose trade, which led to the opening of Japan to the West.

LO⁴ How did the Meiji government transform Japan and Korea?

- After the Meiji Restoration, which overthrew the Tokugawa shogunate, Japanese samurai and other reformers established a regime that was dedicated to making Japan open to and competitive with the rest of the world.

- The Meiji regime modernized Japan by breaking down social distinctions, pursuing industrial and military strength, and establishing a constitutional monarchy.

- In the late 1800s, Meiji leaders worked to balance traditional practices with newly adopted Western ones, and Japan fought successful wars against both China and Russia. Japanese were torn between pride in Meiji successes and regret over traditions they had abandoned.

- Meiji Japan forced Korea to accept unequal trade agreements and, after defeating China in the Sino-Japanese War, turned Korea into a colony and ruled it harshly, brutally suppressing dissent and exploiting its men and women during World War II.

LO⁵ What factors explain the expansion of the Russian Empire?

- The Russian leader Catherine the Great paid lip service to Enlightenment values, but she presided over an era of royal opulence, territorial expansion, and expanded serfdom, and she was followed by the despotic Nicholas I, who led the nation to defeat in the Crimean War.

- Russian expansion brought it control of eastern Siberia, Muslim Central Asia, and the Caucasus states, although some peoples, such as the Chechens, fiercely resisted.

- Russia's economy expanded along with its territory, creating a discontented proletariat, and while many Russian thinkers embraced Western ideals, the Slavophiles argued for the superiority of traditional Russian culture. Some members of the proletariat joined terrorist groups and supported a revolution in 1905, which, while suppressed, led to reforms.

Key Terms

LO2 Bolsheviks
The most radical of Russia's antigovernment groups in the early twentieth century, who embraced a dogmatic form of Marxism.

soviets
Local action councils formed by Russian radicals before the 1917 Russian Revolution that enlisted workers and soldiers to fight the factory owners and military officers.

Marxism-Leninism
The basis for Soviet communism, a mix of socialism (collective ownership of the economy) and Leninism.

New Economic Policy (NEP)
Lenin's pragmatic approach to economic development, which mixed capitalism and socialism.

Stalinism
Joseph Stalin's system of government, which included state ownership of all property, such as lands and businesses, a planned economy, and one-man rule.

gulags
Russian shorthand for harsh forced-labor camps in Siberia.

socialist realism
Literary and artistic works that depicted life from a revolutionary perspective, a style first introduced in Stalin's Russia.

LO3 Great Depression
A collapse of the world economy that lasted in varying degrees of severity through the 1930s.

Dust Bowl
Parts of the U.S. Midwest and Southwest during the 1930s where disappearing topsoil and severe drought threw agriculture badly out of balance.

New Deal
A new U.S. government program of liberal reform within a democratic framework introduced by President Franklin Roosevelt to alleviate suffering caused by the Great Depression.

cubism
An early-twentieth-century form of painting that rejected visual reality and emphasized instead geometric shapes and forms that often suggested movement.

LO4 fascism
A twentieth-century ideology that typically involved extreme nationalism, hatred of ethnic minorities, ruthless repression of opposition groups, violent anticommunism, and authoritarian government.

CHRONOLOGY

1914	Outbreak of conflict
1917	U.S. intervention; Russian Revolution
1918	End of conflict
1919	Versailles Treaty
1921	Irish Free State
1926	Fascist state in Italy
1929–1941	Great Depression
1933	Nazi triumph in Germany
1933–1945	Presidency of Franklin D. Roosevelt
1936–1939	Spanish Civil War
1937	Japanese invasion of China
1938	German takeover of Austria and Czechoslovakia
1939	German invasion of Poland; World War II begins
1940	Tripartite Pact Between Germany, Italy, and Japan
1941	Japanese attack on Pearl Harbor
1944	Bretton Woods Conference
1945	Allied invasion of Germany; atomic bombs dropped on Japan; war's end

LO1 What was the impact of World War I on the Western world?

- The early 1900s in Europe were marked by great affluence and stability, expanding markets, and shared notions of culture, justice, and human rights, but imperial tensions and secret alliances sowed the seeds of conflict.

- Sparked by the assassination of Austrian archduke Franz Ferdinand in Sarajevo, the war soon involved Austro-Hungary, Germany, Britain, France, and the Ottoman Empire, all of which employed unprecedented military technology that caused millions of deaths.

- In 1917, Russia left the war and Germany seemed on the verge of victory when the United States entered the fighting, in part because of economic ties with France and Britain and in part because of outrage over German submarine attacks on U.S. ships.

- The United States helped the French and British win the war, but U.S. president Woodrow Wilson could not prevent the French from dictating punishing settlement terms for Germany.

- The horrors of World War I led to the radicalization of many Europeans; a growth of antiwar sentiment; the breakup of the Ottoman Empire and Germany; the breakup of much of the Russian and Austro-Hungarian Empires, which were carved into new countries; and the world dominance of the United States.

LO2 How did communism prevail in Russia and transform that country?

- In March 1917, a spontaneous revolution overthrew the czar, but its urban liberal leaders could not satisfy the people's demand for reform and an end to the war, so radical soviets, including the Bolsheviks—a group of Marxist revolutionaries led by Vladimir Lenin—seized power, after which they removed Russia from the war.

- Lenin and the Bolsheviks soon faced the Russian Civil War, launched by the White Russians, who included defenders of the aristocracy and were funded and armed by Western nations that were disturbed by the Bolshevik revolution. The Bolsheviks prevailed, establishing Marxism-Leninism in the USSR, a brand of socialism achieved through ruthless one-party rule that failed to achieve a true connection between the masses and the government.

- Lenin's successor, Joseph Stalin, sent millions to forced-labor camps called gulags and imposed state ownership of all property and a planned economy, which led to decreased harvests and widespread misery. Rapid industrialization made the USSR the second largest world economy by 1932, but at the cost of many lives and limitations of human rights.

LO⁵ Holocaust
The Nazis' deliberate murder of
Jews and Romany (Gypsies), one of the worst
genocides in world history.

LO³ How did the Great Depression reshape world politics and economies?

- After the war, Germany experienced rapid inflation because of its postwar debt, Europe lost economic ground to the United States and Japan, and women entered the workforce and the political sphere.

- Many Japanese benefited from postwar economic growth, while Japan played a larger role in world affairs and clashed with the United States over its treatment of Japanese immigrants and Japanese ambitions in Asia.

- American fear of communism led to the "Red Scare" and a more conservative, isolationist phase in American politics, while the split widened between the poor, who suffered under government policies, and the affluent, who enjoyed the "Roaring 20s."

- Among the factors contributing to the Great Depression were trade protectionism, risky investment practices, and the uneven distribution of income. With millions of Americans jobless, homeless, and hungry, President Franklin Delano Roosevelt instituted the New Deal, greatly expanding the federal government's role.

- The Great Depression hit Europe and Japan even harder than the United States, rendering Germany unable to pay its heavy debts and causing Japan to become more authoritarian and expansionist, while Scandinavian nations emerged in better condition by combining socialism and democracy. Western artists, writers, and intellectuals responded to the challenges of modernity in new and innovative ways.

LO⁴ What were the main ideas and impacts of fascism?

- A new ideology, fascism, that developed in Italy and Germany out of economic collapse, stressed extreme nationalism, an authoritarian state, and hatred of minorities and leftists.

- Suffering from the Depression, resentful of post–World War I reparations, and fearful of socialism, many Germans supported Adolph Hitler's Nazi Party, which blamed problems on minorities such as the Jews and revived the economy through a military buildup.

- Japan became increasingly nationalistic and imperialistic, blamed its problems on foreigners, took over most of eastern China, and signed a pact with Germany and Italy.

- Tensions rose as Italy invaded Ethiopia, fascists took over Spain, and Germany took over Austria and Czechoslovakia; France and Britain declared war after Germany signed a nonaggression pact with the Soviet Union and invaded Poland.

LO⁵ What were the costs and consequences of World War II?

- Germany rapidly took over most of Europe and used it as a source of raw materials, but the British withstood extended bombing, and Germany wasted valuable resources on an ultimately unsuccessful invasion of the Soviet Union.

- Nazi Germany deliberately killed 6 million Jews and a half million Gypsies in death camps, along with millions of others; historians are divided on how much the German people knew about the death camps and how responsible they were for them.

- After Japan attacked Pearl Harbor, the United States entered the war in both Asia and Europe, and many women and blacks found work in professions that had until then been closed to them, while Japanese Americans were put in internment camps.

- After the United States entered the war, the Allies slowly began to win the war in Europe, and in the spring of 1945, with U.S. forces advancing from the west and the Soviets from the east, Hitler committed suicide and Germany surrendered. After Japan refused to agree to a total surrender despite serious setbacks, the United States dropped atomic bombs on Hiroshima and Nagasaki, killing, injuring, and sickening scores of thousands.

- More than 50 million military personnel and civilians were killed in World War II, but in its aftermath, Germany, Italy, and Japan were aided rather than punished, and the United States and Soviet Union emerged as the world's dominant powers.

Imperialism and Nationalism in Asia, Africa, and Latin America, 1914–1945

Chapter in Review

Key Terms

LO2 **warlords**
Local political leaders with their own armies.

New Culture Movement
A movement of Chinese intellectuals started in 1915 that sought to wash away the discredited past and sprout a literary revival.

May Fourth Movement
A radical nationalist resurgence in China in 1919 that opposed imperialism and the ineffective, warlord-controlled Chinese government.

Jiangxi Soviet
A revolutionary base, established in 1927 in south-central China, where Mao Zedong organized a guerrilla force to fight the Guomindang.

Long March
An epic journey, full of hardship, in which Mao Zedong's Red Army fought their way 6,000 miles on foot and horseback through eleven Chinese provinces in the mid-1930s to establish a safe base of operation.

people's war
An unconventional struggle that combined military action and political recruitment, formulated by Mao Zedong in China.

Maoism
An ideology promoted by Mao Zedong that mixed ideas from Chinese tradition with Marxist-Leninist ideas from the Soviet Union.

LO3 **nonviolent resistance**
Noncooperation with unjust laws and peaceful confrontation with illegitimate authority, pursued by Mohandas Gandhi in India.

LO4 **Viet Minh**
The Vietnamese Independence League, a coalition of anti-French groups established by Ho Chi Minh in 1941 that waged war against both the French and the Japanese.

lingua franca
A language widely used as a common tongue among diverse groups with different languages.

highlife
An urban-based West African musical style mixing Christian hymns, West Indian calypso, and African dance rhythms.

pidgin English
The form of broken English that developed in Africa during the colonial era.

CHRONOLOGY

1909–1933	U.S. military force in Nicaragua
1912	Formation of ANC in South Africa
1916	Arab revolt against the Turks
1916–1927	Warlord Era in China
1917	Balfour Declaration
1919	Amritsar massacre
1920–1922	Nationalist unrest in Kenya
1921–1979	Pahlavi dynasty in Iran
1922	Formation of Turkish republic by Ataturk
1926–1927	Communist uprising in Indonesia
1928–1937	Republic of China
1930	Indochinese Communist Party; Ghandi's Great Salt March; Independence for Iraq
1930–1931	Military governments throughout Latin America
1930–1945	Estado Novo in Brazil
1934	Fulgencio Batista Cuban dictator
1934–1940	Cardenas presidency in Mexico
1935	Government of India Act; Discovery of oil in Saudi Arabia
1935–1936	Conquest of Ethiopia by Italy; Chinese Communist Long March
1936	British–Egypt alliance
1936–1939	Civil war in Palestine
1941–1945	Japanese occupation of Southeast Asia
1942	Gandhi's Quit India campaign

LO1 What circumstances fostered nationalism in Asia, Africa, and Latin America?

- World War I affected colonies in Asia, Africa, and the Caribbean as thousands of colonial subjects were forced to fight and die for France, Germany, and Britain, and promises of democratic reforms and veterans' benefits were not carried out.

- Colonial governments imposed heavy taxes and hard labor on the colonial peoples, a state of affairs that was defended by the Western idea that the colonial peoples could not yet govern themselves.

- When western capitalism disrupted traditional rural life in many colonies and caused further anguish during the Great Depression, many frustrated colonial subjects turned to nationalism and Marxism as alternatives.

- Despite local opposition, Western nations expanded their colonial reach between 1900 and 1945: Italy brutally conquered Ethiopia; France and Britain took over former Ottoman colonies; and the United States continued to meddle in Central America.

LO2 How and why did the Communist movement grow in China?

- After the end of the imperial system, rival warlords controlled China during a period of civil war, and intellectuals formed the New Culture Movement, which called for a modernized China that fostered individualism and equality.

- Japan's aggressive demands after World War I enraged the Chinese, and some were attracted to communism, but Sun Yat-sen's successor, the pro-business Chiang Kai-shek, allied the nationalist movement with the United States.

- Chiang Kai-shek's Republic of China launched a modernization program, but it was hampered by a split with the communists, persistent rural poverty, and the Japanese seizure of Manchuria.

- Mao Zedong organized peasants into a communist revolutionary army and then led them on the punishing Long March in search of safety from Chiang Kai-shek's far stronger army, which might have triumphed had it not been diverted by a 1937 Japanese invasion.

- The Chinese people lost faith in Chiang's government as it squeezed them for taxes to support a failing war against Japan, while Mao's communists instilled hope through guerrilla warfare and a promise of equality and progress through shared sacrifice.

LO³ What were the main contributions of Mohandas Gandhi to the Indian struggle?

- In the aftermath of World War I, in which tens of thousands of their people died, Indians were angry that Britain denied them greater autonomy and imposed higher taxes to pay for the war, and resentment peaked with the massacre of hundreds of peaceful protesters at Amritsar.

- Mohandas Gandhi, the foremost Indian nationalist leader, promoted nonviolent resistance to British rule, including strikes, boycotts, and refusal to pay taxes, and won a massive popular following for the Indian National Congress.

- Although even his Indian supporters considered some of Gandhi's ideas naive and utopian, campaigns such as the Great Salt March were highly effective in winning concessions from the British.

- Feeling threatened by the predominantly Hindu National Congress, the Muslim League, led by Jinnah, argued that Indian Muslims should have a country of their own, which they called Pakistan. The Muslim League grew increasingly powerful, and eventually, after World War II, both Pakistan and India gained independence from Britain.

- Leaders of the untouchables, the lowest Hindu caste, pushed for and obtained greater opportunities, and women were given the right to vote and allowed somewhat more freedom.

LO⁴ How did nationalism differ in Southeast Asia and sub-Saharan Africa?

- Southeast Asian nationalism was strong in places such as Burma, which experienced harsh colonial rule, and even emerged as a rallying cry in Siam (Thailand), which was never colonized but where a military coup of middle-class background overthrew the royal government.

- Vietnamese resistance to French rule became more radical under the terrorist Vietnamese Nationalist Party, which the French harshly repressed, and the Viet Minh, a coalition led by the communist Ho Chi Minh. In the Dutch East Indies, a variety of groups representing Muslims, women, and communists worked toward independence, and of these the Indonesian Nationalist Party, which incorporated both Islam and Marxism, was most influential.

- Southeast Asians suffered greatly under Japanese occupation, but Japanese control of Southeast Asia during World War II also showed that Westerners could be defeated and primed the colonized peoples to resist recolonization by Westerners after the war was over.

- Although African nationalist movements were hampered by the existence of rival ethnic groups within artificial colonies, anger over the poor treatment of Africans who had fought in World War I inspired many, especially in cities, to work for independence.

LO⁵ What factors promoted change in the Middle East and Latin America?

- In the post–World War I breakup of the Ottoman Empire, Iraq, Syria, and Lebanon sought freedom but were instead colonized by Britain and France. Turkey revived under the leadership of Ataturk, who modernized the country and minimized the role of Islam.

- Reza Khan, the British-supported shah of Persia, attempted to modernize his country as Ataturk had Turkey, though with less success, while Britain, in reaction to violent opposition, granted Egypt and Iraq increasing independence.

- Arab leaders debated how to balance modernization with Islam; the most puritanical form of Islam, Wahhabism, came to dominate Saudi Arabia; and the return of Jews to Palestine caused great tensions with the Arabs who had lived there for centuries.

- Vulnerable Latin American economies were greatly damaged during the Great Depression, which led to instability and the rise of military dictators in many countries.

- Impoverished and frustrated after a long revolution, many Mexicans were pleased by the rule of Lazaro Cardenas, who gave land to agricultural cooperatives, nationalized industries, and supported women's rights, but who was followed by less progressive leaders.

- Latin American and Caribbean artists, musicians, and writers produced art that expressed their unique cultural perspectives.

Key Terms

LO¹ First World
A later-twentieth-century term for the industrialized democracies of western Europe, North America, Australia–New Zealand, and Japan.

Second World
A later-twentieth-century term for the Communist nations, led by the USSR and China.

Third World
A later-twentieth-century term for the societies in Asia, Africa, Latin America, and the Caribbean, which were shaped by mass poverty and a legacy of colonization or neocolonialism.

Fourth World
A later-twentieth-century term for the poorest societies, with very small economies and few exploitable resources.

LO² Cold War
A conflict lasting from 1946 to 1989 in which the United States and the USSR competed for allies and engaged in occasional warfare against their rivals' allies rather than against each other directly.

guerrilla warfare
An unconventional military strategy of avoiding full-scale direct confrontations in favor of small-scale skirmishes.

nuclear weapons
Explosive devices that owe their destructive power to the energy released by either splitting or fusing atoms.

LO³ globalization
A pattern in which economic, political, and cultural processes reach beyond nation-state boundaries.

multinational corporations
Giant business enterprises that operate all over the world; multinationals have gained a leading role in the global marketplace.

Third Industrial Revolution
The creation since 1945 of unprecedented scientific knowledge of new technologies more powerful than any invented before.

Green Revolution
A later-twentieth-century term for increased agricultural output through the use of new high-yield seeds and mechanized farming.

desertification
The transformation of once-productive land into useless desert.

CHRONOLOGY

1945	Formation of the United Nations
1950–1953	Korean War
1946–1975	Decolonization in Asia, Africa, and Caribbean
1959–1975	U.S.–Vietnam War
1946–1989	Cold War
1968	Widespread political protests
1962	Cuban Missile Crisis
1989–1991	Dismantling of Soviet bloc and Soviet Union
2001	Al Qaeda attack on United States

LO¹ How did decolonization change the global system?

• Between 1946 and 1975, most Western colonies achieved independence, though the United States continued to oppose communist anticolonial movements, and the Soviet Union's vast colonial empire endured until 1989.

• Western nations maintained a great deal of influence over many of their former colonies, which led some intellectuals to call for "decolonizing the mind."

• Revolutionary regimes, often inspired by Marxism, came to power in several Asian, African, and Latin American nations, though they met with mixed economic success.

• The division of the world's nations into First, Second, and Third Worlds grew blurry as some Third World nations developed First-World-level economies and the Soviet Union collapsed. Democratic countries tended to be more stable and offer more support to their citizens.

LO² What roles did the Cold War and superpower rivalry play in world politics?

• During the Cold War, the United States and the USSR struggled for world control, with the United States generally favoring democracy and capitalism, and the USSR supporting emerging communist regimes and movements.

• Though the United States and the USSR never fought directly, they were involved in dozens of wars and military interventions in other countries, such as Vietnam and Afghanistan.

• The United States and the USSR participated in a massive arms race, spending trillions of dollars on nuclear weapons, which led to widespread fear of mass destruction.

• The United Nations was formed with the goal of promoting world peace and human rights and to facilitate an international justice system.

• When the Soviet Union collapsed, the United States was the sole superpower, but religious extremism and ethnic and nationalist conflicts have ensured continuing conflict.

LO³ What were some of the main consequences of a globalizing world economy?

• Globalization has boosted world economies and has reaped great rewards for countries such as the United States and China, but it has not always benefited the lives of poor people and has also led to continued foreign domination of some groups and nations by others.

• The World Bank and the International Monetary Fund have lent money to developing nations but sometimes dictate economic policies to borrowers, while multinational corporations have become so large that they exert great influence over governments.

• Industrialization has spread throughout Asia and Latin America; the Third Industrial Revolution has created powerful new technologies; the Green Revolution has allowed for increased agricultural production; and the service and information industries have grown rapidly; but some globalization practices have produced hardships.

LO4 global village
global village
A later-twentieth-century term for an interconnected world community in which all people, regardless of their nationality, share a common fate.

terrorism
Small-scale but violent attacks aimed at undermining a government or demoralizing a population.

- Despite worldwide economic growth, some countries remain underdeveloped and the gap between the wealthy and poor is striking; however, the developing world has made great improvements in infant mortality and adult literacy.

- Women have faced great problems in the modern economy as they have been drastically underpaid for their contributions, but grassroots programs such as the Grameen Bank have offered some increased economic opportunity.

- Over the past fifty years, the world population has exploded in developing countries, while fertility rates have dropped and populations have grown older in Europe, North America, and Japan.

- Industrialization and population growth have led to increased pollution and deforestation, which have led to massive extinction of plant and animal species and global warming.

LO4 How did growing networks linking societies influence social, political, and economic life?

- In the new global village, millions of people have immigrated to foreign countries seeking greater economic opportunity or an escape from insufferable conditions at home.

- Modern medicine has eliminated many diseases, but cholera and malaria are still a serious problem, and AIDS has seriously affected Africa, India, and areas of Southeast Asia.

- Western consumer culture has spread around the world, while musical forms from different cultures have mingled, and performers have expressed political and often controversial views.

- The world's major religious traditions have remained numerically strong, and some have worked to adapt to the modern world; many Muslims and Christians have grown more fundamentalist.

- Worldwide communication was facilitated by technologies such as radio, television, and the Internet, making a vast array of information available, despite efforts by some governments to limit its availability.

- Increased global communication led to political movements that transcended conventional borders, such as Amnesty International, the 1968 youth protests, and the women's movement.

- Terrorism, which had been used throughout the twentieth century by marginalized groups, became more deadly, culminating in the radical Muslim group Al Qaeda's 2001 attack on the United States.

Key Terms

LO¹ Pacific Rim
The economically dynamic Asian countries on the western edge of the Pacific Basin: China, Japan, South Korea, Taiwan, and several Southeast Asian nations.

Pacific Century
The possible shift of global economic power from Europe and North America to the Pacific Rim in the twenty-first century.

communes
Large agricultural units introduced by Mao Zedong that combined many families and villages into a common system for pooling resources and labor.

Great Leap Forward
Mao Zedong's ambitious attempt in the later 1950s to industrialize China rapidly and end poverty through collective efforts.

Great Proletarian Cultural Revolution
A radical movement in China between 1966 and 1976 that represented Mao Zedong's attempt to implant his vision, destroy his enemies, crush the stifling bureaucracy, and renew the revolution's vigor.

Red Guards
Young workers and students who were the major supporters of the Great Proletarian Cultural Revolution in Mao's China.

Iron Rice Bowl
A model of social equality in Mao's China in which the people, especially in the villages, shared resources and the peasants enjoyed status and dignity.

LO² market socialism
A Chinese economic program used between 1978 and 1989 that mixed free enterprise, economic liberalization, and state controls and that produced economic dynamism in China.

market Leninism
A policy followed after the Beijing Massacre in 1989, whereby the Chinese Communist state asserted more power over society while also fostering an even stronger market orientation in the economy than had existed under market socialism.

LO³ Japan, Inc.
The cooperative relationship between government and big business that has existed in Japan after 1945.

salaryman
A Japanese urban middle-class male business employee who commits his energies and soul to the company, accepts assignments without complaint, and takes few vacations.

CHRONOLOGY

1945–1949	Chinese civil war
1946–1952	U.S. occupation of Japan
1949	Chinese communist triumph
1950–1953	Korean War
1960	Sino–Soviet split
1960s–1989	Rapid economic growth
1966–1976	Great Proletarian Cultural Revolution
1978	Four modernizations policy
1997	Asian financial collapse

LO¹ How did Maoism transform Chinese society?

- After Japan was defeated in World War II, Chinese communists and nationalists fought a civil war in which Mao Zedong's communists triumphed over Chiang Kaishek's nationalists.

- To develop its economy, China first employed Stalinism, which featured central planning dominated by a bureaucratic elite, and then shifted to Maoism, which emphasized mass mobilization of the people, but under Maoism millions starved to death and many suffered under political repression.

- China reasserted itself as a world power, reclaiming Tibet, becoming involved in the Korean War, ultimately splitting with the USSR, and reestablishing formal relations with the United States in the 1970s.

- Frustrated with China's development, Mao led a decade-long cultural revolution that caused great economic problems and brought misery to many. He also reshaped Chinese society, improving literacy rates and health care, expanding the rights of women, and encouraging the people to produce their own literature and art.

- While Mao restored China as a world power and brought many out of poverty, after his death in 1976 many Chinese wanted to join the modern world and global economy.

LO² What factors explain the dramatic rise of Chinese economic power in the world since 1978?

- Under Deng Xiaoping, China opened up to Western economic ideas and investment, as well as to political, religious, and cultural currents that had been suppressed under Mao.

- Although many supported Deng's reforms, they led to increasing corruption, a growing gap between rich and poor, and, in 1989, a violent suppression of prodemocracy dissidents in the Beijing Massacre.

- Under market Leninism, the Chinese state increased political and social control while privatizing the economy, which grew briskly, though there was stagnation in many rural areas and environmental damage in others.

- The growth of China's economy has improved access to consumer goods and Western culture, but has also led to increased crime and drug use, and an effort to limit population has led to the killing of female babies.

- China has enjoyed a great recovery and return to world prominence in recent decades, though it still has uncertain relations with Taiwan and Japan, and its living standard remains much lower than many other countries.

LO³ How did Japan rise from the ashes of defeat in World War II to become a global economic powerhouse?

- After World War II, a U.S.-led occupation of Japan (SCAP) worked to rebuild Japan's economy while demilitarizing the country and encouraging the return of democracy, much of which was successful.

- The Liberal Democratic Party dominated Japanese politics for decades, and the constitutional statute preventing military development freed up resources to help fuel

LO⁴ Little Dragons

South Korea, Taiwan, Singapore, and Hong Kong, which were strongly influenced by Chinese culture and built rapidly growing, industrializing economies in the twentieth century.

the economy. The economy has grown at a phenomenal rate, though it has caused environmental problems and great personal sacrifices on the part of workers.

- Japan's cities have become increasingly congested, men are expected to devote all of their energy to work, women struggle for equality, and students face the pressure of an arduous education system.

- Japanese have managed to blend their traditions with modern and foreign influences and have maintained a high degree of social order despite low participation in organized religion.

- In the early 2000s, Japan's economy began to recover from a decade-long downturn, while in world politics, Japan has played an important role, though it has been hesitant to assert its power too forcefully.

LO⁴ What policies led to the rise of the "Little Dragon" nations and their dynamic economies?

- After World War II, communist North Korea, assisted by the USSR and China, fought a war with South Korea, assisted by a U.S.-dominated United Nations force, that caused thousands of deaths and devastation and ended with the same border that existed at the start of the war.

- South Korean governments have grown more tolerant of internal dissent and more open to relations with former enemies, such as communist North Korea and China, though their primary emphasis has been on economic growth.

- After the Korean War, North Korea recovered with support from the USSR and China and was ruled as a repressive communist dictatorship with a centrally planned economy, whose shortcomings led to widespread food shortages in the 1990s.

- With the communists ruling mainland China, nationalists took over Taiwan, which they ruled as a police state and turned into an economic powerhouse, but relations with mainland China have continued to be tense.

- China and the "Little Dragons" (Taiwan, South Korea, Singapore, and Hong Kong) grew rapidly in the late twentieth century, leading to predictions of increased Asian influence in the future.

Key Terms

LO¹ Marshall Plan
A recovery program proposed for western Europe by the United States that aimed to prevent communist expansion and to spread liberal economic principles.

Greens
A twentieth-century political movement in western Europe that rejected militarism and heavy industry and favored environmental protection over economic growth.

British Commonwealth of Nations
A forum, established by Britain in 1931, for discussing issues of mutual interest with its former colonies.

Truman Doctrine
A policy formed in 1947 that asserted that the United States was the leader of the free world and was charged with protecting countries like Greece and Turkey from communism.

NATO
(North Atlantic Treaty Organization) A military alliance, formed in 1949, that linked nine western European countries with the United States and Canada.

Soviet bloc
In the twentieth century, the Soviet Union and the communist states allied with it.

Warsaw Pact
A defense alliance formed in 1955 that linked the communist-ruled eastern European countries with the USSR.

ostpolitik
("Eastern politics") A West German policy, promoted by Chancellor Willy Brandt, that sought a reconciliation between West and East Germany and an expanded dialogue with the USSR.

LO² welfare states
Government systems that offer their citizens a range of state-subsidized health, education, and social service benefits; adopted by western European nations after World War II.

bhangra
A popular music that emerged in Britain from a blending of traditional folk songs brought by Indian immigrants with Caribbean reggae and Anglo-American styles, such as rock, hip hop, and disco.

existentialism
A European intellectual approach contending that truth is not absolute but constructed by people according to their society's beliefs.

postmodernism
A European intellectual approach contending that truth is not absolute but constructed by people according to their society's beliefs.

CHRONOLOGY

1945–1948	Formation of communist governments
1946–1989	Cold War
1949	Formation of NATO
1955	Warsaw Pact
1957	European Common Market
1979–1989	Soviet war in Afghanistan
1989	End of communist governments
1991	Maastricht Treaty; breakup of Soviet Union
2004	Expansion of European Union into Eastern Europe

LO¹ What factors fostered the movement toward unity in western Europe?

- World War II devastated western Europe's population, infrastructure, and economy, but it enjoyed a remarkable period of rebirth, aided by extensive U.S. funding. New patterns in European politics included right-wing Christian Democrat parties, leftist social democrats, and the emergence of the Greens.

- A wave of decolonization followed World War II, though former colonizing nations usually maintained economic ties with their former holdings.

- The Cold War shaped European politics, with eastern Europe allied with the USSR and western Europe allied with the United States, but over time some European leaders advocated dialogue with the USSR.

- European countries joined together in the European Community, which became the world's largest free-trade zone and led to increased prosperity; however, the 1970s brought hard times, and European unity sometimes threatened to give way.

LO² How did the rise of welfare states transform western European societies?

- Western European governments have generally instituted the welfare state, a mix of capitalism and socialism in which citizens pay high taxes in exchange for an extensive safety net.

- In 1968, a wave of radical protest swept Europe, and over the decades European society was liberalized by the sexual revolution.

- The large numbers of immigrants who came to western Europe reshaped the cultures of many regions, while rock and later punk music became extremely popular among European youth.

- Philosophies such as existentialism, which urged people to control their own lives, and postmodernism, which claimed that complete objectivity is impossible, became popular in postwar Europe.

- Organized religion became less influential in postwar Europe, while tensions among branches of Christianity faded, Roman Catholicism liberalized, and Muslims became a significant portion of the European population.

LO³ What factors contributed to political crises in the Soviet Union and eastern Europe?

- Under Stalin, the USSR ruthlessly suppressed dissent; under Khrushchev, it moderated somewhat and focused on economic and technological development; under Brezhnev, it became more repressive again.

- Although the Soviet economy grew under communism, it suffered from lack of innovation, inept planning, and an overemphasis on the military, and it created a privileged class of Communist Party and military insiders.

- U.S.–USSR relations were strained by the Cuban Missile Crisis, the Berlin Wall, and Soviet support for communist Cuba and North Vietnam, but the USSR's foreign interventions were usually motivated by its national interest rather than a desire to spread communism.

- In exchange for limited freedom, Soviet citizens were offered extensive social services, but many non-Russians in Central Asia and the Baltics resented Russian cultural domination, while Soviet youth turned to rock music to express their rebellion.

- Much of eastern Europe was effectively colonized by the USSR, though Yugoslavia pursued an independent communist course, and citizens of Poland, Hungary, and Czechoslovakia mounted challenges to Soviet rule.

- With the USSR losing ground, Soviet leader Mikhail Gorbachev introduced reforms designed to democratize the USSR, to liberalize its economy, and to allow eastern European countries greater self-determination.

LO⁴ How did the demise of the communist system contribute to a new Europe?

- The collapsing Soviet bloc and Soviet decay created problems for Gorbachev, and he was replaced by Boris Yeltsin, who allowed independence for all the non-Russian Soviet republics, and pursued a rapid shift to capitalism.

- However, as a result of this "shock therapy," a small group of former Communist Party officials became extremely wealthy, while most Russians suffered economically. Yeltsin was replaced by the more authoritarian Vladimir Putin, who brought back some stability.

- With the fall of the USSR, formerly communist eastern Europe became more democratic, though many countries struggled economically and others suffered political upheaval, especially Yugoslavia, which experienced violent civil war and "ethnic cleansing."

- German reunification, celebrated at first, yielded mixed results, while the European Union grew to include twenty-five nations by 2004 but faced questions over whether to admit non-Christian nations and over what form its constitution should take.

- European nations struggled to navigate the evolving world economy, to deal with Islamic terrorism, and to work out relations with each other and with the United States.

Key Terms

LO^1 **domino theory**
A theory that envisioned countries falling one by one to communism and that became a mainstay of U.S. policy during the Cold War.

multilateralism
In the twentieth and twenty-first centuries, a foreign policy in which the United States sought a common front and a coordination of foreign policies with allies in western Europe, Japan, and Canada, avoiding activities that might enflame world opinion against the United States.

unilateralism
In the twentieth and twenty-first centuries, a foreign policy in which the United States acted alone in its own perceived national interest even if key allies disapproved.

containment
The main U.S. strategy aimed at preventing communists from gaining power, and the USSR from getting political influence, in other nations during the Cold War.

Mutually Assured Destruction
A policy, known as MAD, in which the United States and the USSR used the fear of nuclear weapons to deter each other during the Cold War.

preemptive war
A U.S. doctrine, triggered by the 2001 terrorist attacks, that sanctioned unilateral military action against potential threats.

LO^3 **Castroism**
Innovative socialist policies introduced by Fidel Castro to stimulate economic development in Cuba while tightly controlling its population.

LO^4 **neoliberalism**
An economic model encouraged by the United States in the developing world that promoted free markets, privatization, and Western investment.

liberation theology
A Latin American movement that developed in the 1960s in Latin America to make Catholicism more relevant to contemporary society and to address the plight of the poor.

New Song
A Latin American musical movement based chiefly on local folk music and closely tied to progressive politics and protest; became popular in the 1960s and 1970s, especially in Chile.

CHRONOLOGY

1946–1989	Cold War
1950–1953	Korean War
1959	Cuban Revolution
1962–1990	Decolonization of Pacific islands
1963–1975	U.S. war in Vietnam
1964–1985	Military government in Brazil
1973	End of "white Australia" policy
1973–1989	Military government in Chile
1994	Formation of NAFTA
2001	Al Qaeda terrorist attacks in United States
2008	Barack Obama elected U.S. President

LO^1 How did the Cold War shape U.S. foreign policies?

- For several decades after World War II, the United States enjoyed a period of economic growth and helped western Europe and Japan to recover, while later aid to developing nations was not administered as effectively.

- During the Cold War, McCarthyism targeted U.S. citizens for supposed communist sympathies; U.S. presidents aimed to contain the spread of communism through unilateral action; and defense spending became a key factor in the U.S. economy.

- On the basis of the domino theory, which argued that if communism was not stopped it would take over the world, the United States fought communists in Korea and Vietnam, but neither war achieved U.S. goals, and the Vietnam War severely crippled the U.S. economy.

- During the Cold War, the United States opposed communist movements and noncommunist leftist movements in several countries, sometimes helping to replace them with brutal military dictatorships.

- In response to the terrorist attacks of September 11, 2001, U.S. president George W. Bush proclaimed a policy of preemptive war and led the country to war in Afghanistan and then in Iraq. The war in Iraq had little public and global support.

LO^2 How and why are the societies of the United States, Canada, and Australia similar to and different from each other?

- On average, U.S. residents are among the wealthiest in the world, yet in recent decades, many industrial jobs have been moved overseas, and the gap between rich and poor has grown wider.

- In the 1950s, political conservatism dominated the United States; in the 1960s, liberalism was prominent; and since the 1970s, conservatism has been generally dominant, though the country is sharply divided politically.

- After 1945, more Americans lived in suburbs, African Americans gained legal rights through the civil rights movement, immigrants made America more diverse, women increasingly entered the workforce, and homosexuals became more visible but still struggled for equal rights.

- American culture became popular around the world, particularly music such as rock, which energized youth in the 1950s and 1960s, and rap, which emerged in African American communities in the 1980s.

- While Canada's culture and economy are strongly influenced by the United States, in many ways Canada resembles western Europe, with a strong social safety net and a more liberal attitude on social issues.

- Australia and New Zealand have maintained their traditional ties with Britain but have also traded increasingly with their Southeast Asian neighbors, while many Pacific islands have gained independence but still face challenges such as rising sea levels, poverty, and ethnic conflict.

Rastafarianism
A religion from Jamaica that arose in 1930 and that mixed Christian, African, and local influences; Rastafarianism attracted urban slum dwellers and the rural poor by preaching a return of black people to Africa.

reggae
A popular music style that began in Jamaica in the 1960s and that blended North American rhythm and blues with Afro-Jamaican traditions; reggae is marked by a distinctive beat maintained by the bass guitar.

LO³ Why have democracy and economic development proven to be difficult goals in Latin America?

- In Latin America, right-wing and left-wing movements competed for power; right-wing movements were dominant from the 1950s through the 1980s, and moderates and leftists such as Venezuela's Hugo Chavez gained more power in the 1990s.

- Many Latin Americans resented U.S. interference in their economies and support for the overthrow of leftist governments, while others welcomed the U.S. example of democracy and free trade.

- The Mexican Revolution led to decades of single-party rule that failed to significantly help the poor, and a reformist president elected in 2000 also failed to improve their lot.

- Under a brutal U.S.-supported military dictatorship, Brazil enjoyed a period of impressive growth but then experienced extreme inflation and increasing gaps between rich and poor; democracy returned in the mid-1980s, and the economy recovered in the late 1990s.

- Under Castro, communist Cuba attempted to control its people but also provided social services; however, the withdrawal of aid from the USSR in 1991 and the U.S. embargo have left its economy struggling.

- Alarmed by the popularity of a democratically elected leftist government in Chile, the United States supported a 1973 coup there as well as the brutal military dictatorship that resulted, which was replaced by a democratic government in 1989.

LO⁴ How have Latin American and Caribbean cultures been dynamic?

- Latin American economies have been marked by overdependence on natural resources, extreme inequality of income, export agriculture, and failed experiments with free trade.

- Although men continue to dominate Latin American society, more women have made progress, while liberation theology—a Catholic movement addressing the plight of the poor—and Protestantism gained a following.

- Latin American culture has flourished, with writers employing magic realism to explore their region's experience, others airing political views through poetry and music, and many preferring to use local traditions and forms rather than foreign ones.

- In the Caribbean, the Jamaican religion of Rastafarianism promoted redistribution of wealth and a closely related musical form, reggae, that frequently included calls for social justice.

- Latin American and Caribbean nations forged closer relations, signed several trade pacts, and shared an uneasy economic relationship with the United States, while Asian nations also became important competitors with and investors in their economies.

30
The Middle East, Sub-Saharan Africa, and New Conflicts in the Contemporary World, Since 1945
Chapter in Review

Key Terms

LO¹ Intifada
("Uprising") A resistance begun in 1987 by Palestinians against the Israeli occupation of Gaza and the West Bank.

Ba'ath
A political party in the Middle East that favored socialism and Arab nationalism and strongly opposed Israel.

OPEC
(Organization of Petroleum Exporting Countries) A cartel formed in 1960 to give producers more power over the price of oil and leverage with the consuming nations.

LO² Islamists
Antimodern, usually puritanical Islamic militants who seek an Islamic state.

rai
("opinion") A twentieth-century pop music of Algeria based on local Bedouin chants, Spanish flamenco, French café songs, Egyptian pop, and other influences and featuring improvised lyrics that often deal with forbidden themes of sex and alcohol.

mujahidin
("holy warriors") Conservative Islamic rebels who rebelled against the pro-Soviet regime in Afghanistan in the 1970s and 1980s.

Taliban
("students") A group of Pashtun religious students who organized a military force in the 1980s to fight what they considered to be immorality and corruption and to impose order in Afghanistan.

LO³ pan-Africanism
The dream, originating in the early twentieth century, that all Africans would cooperate to eventually form some sort of united states of the continent.

Mau Mau Rebellion
An eight-year uprising in the 1950s by the Gikuyu people in Kenya against British rule.

wabenzi
("people who drive a Mercedes Benz") A privileged urban class in Africa since the mid-twentieth century of politicians, high bureaucrats, professionals, military officers, and businessmen who manipulate their connections to amass wealth.

apartheid
("separate development") A South African policy to set up a police state to enforce racial separation; lasted from 1948 to 1994.

bantustans
Rural reservations in South Africa where black Africans under apartheid were required to live if they were not needed in the modern economy.

CHRONOLOGY

1948	Formation of Israel
1948	Apartheid in South Africa
1954–1962	Algerian Revolution
1957–1965	African decolonization
1967	Arab–Israeli Six-Day War
1973	OPEC oil embargo
1975	Independence for Portuguese colonies
1979	Islamic revolution in Iran
1994	Black majority rule in South Africa
2003	United States invasion of Iraq

LO¹ How have Arab–Israeli tensions and oil shaped contemporary Middle Eastern politics?

- After World War II, nationalist governments replaced many colonial regimes in the Middle East, but the region has failed to develop many working multiparty democracies.

- Egyptian leader General Gamal Abdul Nasser threw off British influence, seized control of the Suez Canal, and pursued socialist policies, but neither he nor his pro-American successors brought prosperity to Egypt.

- Traumatized by the Holocaust, many Jews moved to Palestine after World War II and established the state of Israel, which led to a war between Jews and Arabs, a mass exodus of Palestinians into refugee camps, and enduring tensions.

- After the 1967 Arab-Israeli War, Israel occupied lands with a large Arab population and severely limited their freedom, while Palestinians became increasingly militant in their opposition.

- After nationalists overthrew the Iranian shah, the United States helped return him to power; he ruled ruthlessly until 1979, when he was overthrown by Islamic fundamentalists.

- From 1958 on, Iraq was ruled by ruthless military dictatorships dominated by the Sunni minority, and in 1979, Saddam Hussein came to power, launched a costly war against Iran, and then was attacked by the United States after invading Kuwait.

- Saudi Arabia grew extremely wealthy from oil sales, but many citizens have remained poor, and conservative religious leaders and their followers have criticized the Saudi royal family and its ties with the United States.

LO² What roles has Islam played in the contemporary Middle East?

- For several decades, Lebanon was divided among a variety of warring factions supported by foreign governments; in the Sudan, Arab Muslims fought with African Christians and launched a genocide against African Muslims; and the Kurds came into conflict with the governments of several Middle Eastern countries.

- Although some Middle Eastern women have attained greater freedom and adopted Western dress, many remain in the home, subject to male authority.

- Middle Eastern societies have been divided between Islamists and secular Muslims, and popular musicians and writers have raised the ire of religious conservatives.

- In Afghanistan, U.S.-supported Islamic rebels and Soviet-assisted communists fought for a decade until the Soviets withdrew, after which the Taliban took over much of the country and allowed terrorist groups such as Al Qaeda to base themselves there.

- After Al Qaeda's September 2001 attack on the United States, a U.S.-led invasion overthrew the Taliban and set up a weak pro-Western government; in 2003, the United States invaded Iraq, generating massive looting and persistent, violent opposition, even by Iraqis who hated Saddam Hussein.

- Middle Eastern societies have been torn between those who promote modernization and those who champion tradition, while the region has remained strategically important to outside powers.

LO³ What were the main political consequences of decolonization in sub-Saharan Africa?

- European colonial rulers had played rival ethnic groups in Africa against each other, but after World War II, Ghana became the first colony to achieve independence.

- Most British colonies attained independence through peaceful means, but Kenya's transition was long and violent, as was that of the Belgian Congo, Angola, Guinea-Bissau, Mozambique, and Zimbabwe.

- After independence, many African nations were ruled by military dictatorships or corrupt civilians; many nationalist leaders lost favor over time; the gap between rich and poor widened; and some nations experienced ongoing violence, disorder, and genocide.

- Nigeria, home to rival ethnic and religious groups, has experienced civil war, coups, and corrupt military rule, and while its oil reserves have brought wealth to the elite, they have hardly benefited the poor.

- Under apartheid, a white minority in South Africa viciously suppressed the black majority, but the African National Congress, led by Nelson Mandela, ultimately won control of the government in 1994.

LO⁴ What new economic, social, and cultural patterns have emerged in Africa?

- African countries have struggled economically, with many being forced to import food and others, like the Congo, to enter into neocolonial relationships with Western powers, but Ghana and Botswana have managed to significantly improve their economies.

- Marxist revolutionary governments, which appealed to many Africans who wanted to erase the colonial legacy, came to power in Angola and Mozambique, both of which then entered into long civil wars, as well as in Zimbabwe.

- African cities have grown rapidly and often lack necessary services, individualism has grown more common, and women have lost some of the economic value they had in agricultural villages, though some have become successful professionals.

- African musicians, writers, and artists have drawn on local traditions as well as influences from the West to create original forms and works that criticize both Western encroachment and homegrown corruption.

- While animism has grown less influential in Africa, Christianity is the most popular religion but has been seen by some as connected to Western imperialism, while Islam is followed by 200 million Africans.

- The economic gap between Africa and the industrialized West continues to grow, and Western attempts to help Africa through the IMF and the World Bank often include requirements that harm the environment and the poor.

Chapter in Review

Key Terms

LO¹ Awami League
A Bengali nationalist party that began the move from independence from West Pakistan.

LO² Bharatha Janata (BJP)
The major Hindu nationalist party in India.

Bollywood
The Mumbai film industry in India.

LO³ National Liberation Front (NLF)
Often known as the Viet Cong, a communist-led revolutionary movement in South Vietnam that resisted American intervention in the American-Vietnamese War.

Tet Offensive
Communist attacks on major South Vietnamese cities in 1968, a turning point in the American-Vietnamese War.

Pathet Lao
Revolutionary Laotian nationalists allied with North Vietnam during the American-Vietnamese War.

Khmer Rouge
("Red Khmers") A communist insurgent group that sought to overthrow the government in Cambodia during the 1960s through the mid-1990s.

LO⁴ New Order
The Indonesian government headed by President Suharto from 1966 to 1998, which mixed military and civilian leadership.

ASEAN
(Association of Southeast Asian Nations) A regional economic and political organization formed in 1967 to promote cooperation among the non-communist Southeast Asian nations; eventually became a major trading bloc.

CHRONOLOGY

1945–1950	Indonesian Revolution
1946–1954	First Indochina War
1947	Independence for India and Pakistan
1948–1964	Nehru era in India
1948	Independence of Burma
1963–1975	U.S.-Vietnamese War
1966–1998	New Order in Indonesia
1971	Formation of Bangladesh
1975	Communist victories in Vietnam, Cambodia, Laos
1984	Assassination of Indira Ghandi
1997	Asian economic crisis

LO¹ What factors led to the political division of South Asia?

- After World War II, when majority Muslim Pakistan broke off from majority Hindu India, religious violence and a dispute over the territory of Kashmir set the stage for continued tension between the two countries.

- Nehru attempted to expand the rights of women and, through a mix of capitalism and socialism, vastly increased India's industrial and agricultural output, but the population expanded at a dangerously rapid rate, and not all policies were successful.

- East and West Pakistan were divided along ethnic lines, and a military crackdown on a Bengali nationalist party led to a bloody civil war in which India intervened on behalf of East Pakistan, which then became a separate country, Bangladesh.

- Nehru's daughter, Indira Gandhi, was prime minister for more than a decade, but she treated her opposition harshly and was assassinated in the midst of clashes between Hindus and Sikhs; her son and successor, Rajiv Gandhi, was also assassinated.

LO² What have been the major achievements and disappointments of the South Asian nations?

- India's multiparty democracy has endured despite religious and caste tensions, and the Congress Party has been consistently influential, though communist parties and Hindu nationalists also have large followings.

- Despite great advances in agricultural and industrial production, India still suffers from extensive poverty, and its rapidly growing population is likely to perpetuate this problem.

- While caste distinctions have remained strong in villages, they have broken down somewhat in cities; women have advanced in education and opportunity, though they are still less educated than men; and religion continues to be a source of tension.

- Pakistan has alternated between civilian and military governments and has been slow to grant women equal rights, while Bangladesh has battled poverty and has generally accepted religious minorities, though militant Muslim groups have gained influence in recent years.

- Since it became independent, Sri Lanka has been a democracy; it elected the world's first woman prime minister, and it has nurtured a well-educated, healthy population, but since 1983 the minority Tamils have fought for independence.

- India has produced talented engineers and computer scientists and made advances in technology, although its nuclear arms race with Pakistan has raised the worry of nuclear weapons being in the hands of Islamic terrorists.

- Though women's rights are not universal in South Asia, more South Asian women have achieved positions of great power than in other areas of the world.

LO³ What were the causes and consequences of the wars in Indochina?

- After World War II, Ho Chi Minh's communist Viet Minh took partial control of Vietnam and declared independence, but the U.S.-supported French fought back in the First Indochina War, which ended in Viet Minh victory.

- Instead of allowing an election to determine the future of South Vietnam, the United States installed Diem as president, but he was opposed by the communist National Liberation Front.

- Using a questionable attack as a pretext, the United States went to war to rid Vietnam of communism, but could not triumph over the communists, who gained control of Vietnam two years after the United States pulled out its ground forces.

- In Laos, the United States recruited Hmong hill people to fight the Pathet Lao revolutionaries, who took control of the country in 1975, while in Cambodia, the United States bombed areas occupied by North Vietnamese and supported a weak, dependent government, which was overthrown in 1975 by the Khmer Rouge.

- Vietnam struggled after the war, but in the 1980s, it opened up its economy, and by the 1990s, it had reestablished ties with the rest of the world, including the United States.

- Many Laotians fled into exile, while Cambodia endured vicious repression under the Khmer Rouge, who continued to wreak havoc even after a Vietnamese invasion pushed them out of power.

LO⁴ How has decolonization and globalization shaped the new Southeast Asian nations?

- After a hard-won independence from the Dutch, Indonesia struggled to attain unity under Sukarno, but a group of generals removed Sukarno from power.

- Under Suharto, the Indonesian New Order government repressed regional opposition and improved the economy, but Suharto was corrupt and forced to resign in 1997.

- After attaining independence, the Philippines remained strongly influenced by the United States and struggled with economic inequality and a Muslim insurgency. Under Marcos, the Philippines was divided between the very rich and the poor; eventually he was forced out, and the governments that followed were more democratic but still dominated by the wealthy.

- Thailand alternated between long periods of military rule and short periods of democratic or semidemocratic rule. Since the 1980s, its semidemocratic system has enjoyed economic growth.

- Burma endured decades of factional fighting and, since 1962, brutal military domination. In recent years, its corrupt regime has failed to take advantage of ample natural resources and has stifled its opposition.

- Malaysia has taken advantage of abundant natural resources to become highly successful, while Singapore, with fewer resources, thrives through a combination of economic freedom and political restriction.

- With their rapidly growing economies, the Southeast Asian "tigers" have inspired developing nations around the world, and while most of the region has modernized, tradition thrives in them as well.